ADMINISTRATIVE LAW IN VENEZUELA
3d Edition

Allan R. BREWER-CARÍAS

Profesor emérito de la Universidad Central de Venezuela
Past Fellow, Trinity College, Cambridge UK.
Simón Bolívar Professor, University of Cambridge, UK (1985-1986).
Professeur Associé, Université de Paris II (1989-1990)
Adjunct Professor of Law, Columbia University, New York, (2006-2008).
Vice President, International Academy of Comparative Law (1982-2010)

ADMINISTRATIVE LAW IN VENEZUELA

Third Edition

Colección Cursos y Manuales

Editorial Jurídica Venezolana International

Caracas / New York

2021

http://www.allanbrewercarias.com
Email: allan@brewercarias.com

ISBN: 978-980-365-199-2
First Edition, 2013
Second Edition, 2015
Third Edition, 2021
Editorial Jurídica Venezolana International

Originally edited by: Editorial Jurídica Venezolana
Avda. Francisco Solano López, Torre Oasis, P.B., Local 4, Sabana Grande, Apartado 17.598 – Caracas, 1015, Venezuela
Teléfono 762.25.53, 762.38.42. Fax. 763.5239
http://www.editorialjuridicavenezolana.com.ve
Email fejv@cantv.net

Printed by: Lightning Source, an INGRAM Content company
for Editorial Jurídica Venezolana International Inc.
Panamá, República de Panamá.
Email: ejvinternational@gmail.com

Layout, composition and assembly
by: Mirna Pinto, in font: Times New Roman, 10,5
Interlining exact 11, Mark 19 x 12.5

CONTENTS

PART THREE

PRINCIPLES OF ADMINISTRATIVE LAW RELATED TO ADMINISTRATIVE ACTION: ADMINISTRATIVE PROCEDURE, AND ADMINISTRATIVE ACTS

PART FOUR

PRINCIPLES OF ADMINISTRATIVE LAW RELATED TO PUBLIC CONTRACTAS, PUBLIC INTEREST CONTRACTS AND ADMINISTRATIVE CONTRACTS

PART FIVE

PRINCIPLES OF ADMINISTRATIVE LAW RELATED TO ECONOMIC FREEDOM AND PROPERTY RIGHTS

PART SIX

PRINCIPLES OF ADMINISTRATIVE LAW RELATED TO ENVIRONMENT PROTECTION AND TO THE MINING AND OIL INDUSTRIES

PART SEVEN

SOME PRINCIPLES OF ADMINISTRATIVE LAW ON THE PROMOTION AND PROTECTION OF INVESTMENTS

PART EIGHT

SOME PRINCIPLES OF ADMINISTRATIVE LAW REGARDING THE STATUS OF INDIVIDUALS AND CITIZENS

PART NINE

JUDICIAL REVIEW OF ADMINISTRATIVE ACTION AND THE PROBLEM OF THE LACK OF INDEPENDENCE OF THE JUDICIARY

AUTHOR'S NOTE

Administrative Law has been a subject on which, since 1963, as an Administrative Law Professor and as a researcher at the *Public Law Institute* of the Central University of Venezuela of Caracas (1960-1987), I have been working, writing and publishing, being my first article published in 1960 referred to matters of administrative procedure, and my first book published in Caracas in 1964, referred to "The Fundamental Institutions of Administrative Law and the Venezuelan Jurisprudence" (*Las Instituciones Fundamentales del Derecho Administrativo y la Jurisprudencia Venezolana*, Universidad Central de Venezuela, Caracas 1964). In 2013, I recollected all my published works and writtings on the matter in my "Administrative Law Treaty" (*Tratado de Derecho Administrativo)*, published by Editorial Civitas, Thomson Reuters, Madrid 2013 in six volumes, and more that sixthousands pages).

Allmost all such books and articles treating matters of Administrative Law and of Constitutional Law, were published in Spanish; some of them were published in French, like the books on "Public Enterprises in Comparative Law" (*Les entreprises publiques en droit compare*, Paris 1968; and on "Administrative Procedure in Comparative Law" (*La procedure administrative non contentiesuse en droit compare*, Economica, Paris 1992). All those works were latter recollected, with others in English and French, in my book: "Works on Comparative Public Law" (*Études de droit public comparé*, Bruillant, Burxelles 1990).

I began to work in English in 1985-1986, when I wrote the Course of Lectures that I gave as Simon Bolivar Professor at the LLM Program of the Law Faculty of the University of Cambridge, on "Judicial review in Comparative Law," which was published in my book on *Judicial Review in Comparative Law,* Cambridge University Press, Cambridge 1989.

Twenty years latter I reassumed my work in English, after fixing my permanent residence in New York in 2005, when I wrote as Adjunct Professor of Law the Lectures, I gave at Columbia Law School of the University of Columbia in New York, in the Seminar I gave on "Constitutional Protection of Human Rights in Latin America," which was published in my book on *Constitutional Protection of Humans Rights in Latin America*, Cambridge University Press, New York, 2009.

In parallel, due to my work in New York, in addition to my work and research that resulted in books and articles published in Spanish, I also focused my work on mater of Constitutional Law, resulting in the publishing of the following books: *Dismantling Democracy. The Chávez Authoritarian Experiment*, Cambridge University Press, New York 2010; *Constitutional Courts as Positive Legislators*,

Cambridge University Press, New York 2011; *Constitutional Law. Venezuela*, Wolters Kluwer, Netherland 2012; *Authoritarian Government v. the Rule of Law. Lectures and Essays (1999-2014) on the Venezuelan Authoritarian Regime Established in Contempt of the Constitution*, Fundación de Derecho Público, Editorial Jurídica Venezolana, Caracas / New York 2014; *Judicial Review. Comparative Constitucional Law Essays, Lectures and Courses (1985-2011),* Fundación de Derecho Público, Editorial Jurídica Venezolana, Caracas / New York 2014; and *The Collapse of the Rule of Law and the Struggle for Democracy in Venezuela. Lectures And Essays (2015-2020),* Colección Anales, Cátedra Mezerhane sobre democracia, Estado de Derecho y Derechos Humanos, Miami Dade College, 2020, 618 pp.

In parallel to such academic work, during these past years, as a lawyer and legal expert on matters of Public Lae and Comparative Law, as a member of the Law Firm *Baumeister & Brewer* of Caracas, I have been asked by various Law Firms in the United States and Europe to write and give Legal Opinions on matters related to the Venezuelan Constitutional and Administrative Law system, that were submitted to International Arbitral Tribunals or National Courts, in cases in which the courts had to decide based on the principles and the legal provisions of Venezuela Public Law, as the applicable law. In such Opinions, over the years, I have covered almost all the general principles and trends of Venexuelan Administrative Law.

That work is precisely the origin of this book, in which I have systematized and organized all that written material that I had finished, complemented with other academic works that I have also written for academic purposes, also related to administrative law, in order to give a general overview on the general principles on the matter.

On the other hand, this book is a general confirmation of the unfortunate lack of contemporary written English publications on Latin American Law, and in particular, on Latin American Administrative Law, and of course, specifically, on the Venezuelan legal system; as well as a confirmation of the current absence of the academic interest on matters of Latin American Law, in contrast to the one that existed many decades ago in some Universities in the United States. Such interest has almost completely disappeared, and Latin American matters are in general only studied from the historical or political point of view.

In any case, the only purpose of this book is to contribute to fill the gap and provide to those English-speaking academics and practicing lawyers with interest in the legal system of Latin America, and specifically of Venezuela, an English text that could be useful for their research.

A *First edition* of this book was published in 2013, and a *Second* one in 2015, including among other aspects, many changes introduced in the Venezuelan legal system on matters of public law, particularly because of the consolidation of an Authoritarian State that had developed in the country. In this *Third edition*, in order to update the book, I have included new written materials on legal issues that I have finished since the last edition.

New York, January 2021

INTRODUCTION

The Venezuelan legal system follows the general pattern and trends of the Romano-Germanic civil law traditions[1] that have influenced the development of the law in continental Europe and Latin America, among other parts of the world.

As in all Latin American countries, Venezuela's private law began to be codified in the nineteenth century under the influence of the European Codes, and particularly the French Civil Code, and has developed according to contemporary civil law tradition trends. For instance, the main legal provisions regarding obligations contained in the 1942 Civil Code were directly inspired by the "Franco Italian Project on Obligations," and the basic regime on commercial law was influenced by the Italian Code. On matters of public law, the influence of France and Italy has also been determinant in the shaping of the Venezuelan procedural and criminal law. On matters of administrative law, the Venezuelan legal system and principles are inspired by the French system of administrative law. Consequently, the Venezuelan legal framework follows the general trends of the civil law traditions, being the general principles of law applied in Venezuela like those applied and used for interpretation in all the continental European and Latin American countries.

Regarding the general principles of administrative law and procedure,[2] that is, the legal regime governing administrative action and the legal standards applied to Public Administration, it can be said that they follow the same general rules and principles developed during the past century in continental Europe, in particular, in Germany, France, Italy and Spain; principles that have been adopted in all Latin American countries, including Venezuela.[3]

This book is devoted, precisely, to study the main principles of administrative law in Venezuela, for which it is divided in Eight Parts: *Part One*, refers to the general trends of the Organization of the Venezuelan State; *Part two*, refers to the General Principles of Administrative Law and of Public Administration; *Part three*: refers to

---

1 See Mary Ann Glendon, Michael W. Gordon and Paolo G. Carozza, *Comparative Legal Traditions*, West Group, St. Paul, Minn. 1999, p. 13 ff.

2 See Allan R. Brewer-Carías, *Derecho Administrativo*, 2 Vols., Universidad Externado de Colombia, Bogotá 2005; "Panorama general del derecho administrativo en Venezuela (2004)," in Santiago González-Varas Ibáñez (Coordinator), in *El Derecho Administrativo Iberoamericano*, N° 9, Ministerio de Administraciones Públicas (INAP)-Instituto de Investigación Urbana y Territorial, Granada, España 2005, pp. 745-791.

3 See the recent publication of Víctor Hernández Mendible (Coordinator), *Desafíos del Derecho Administrativo Contemporáneo. Conmemoración International del Centenario de la Cátedra de Derecho Administrativo en Venezuela*, 2 Vols., Ediciones Paredes, Caracas 2010, p. 1473.

Principles of Administrative Law related to Administrative Action: Administrative Procedure and Administrative Acts; *Part Four*: refers to the Principles of Administrative Law related to Pubic Contracts, Public Interest Contracts, and Administrative Contracts; *Part Five*: refers to Principles of Administrative Law related to Economic Freedoms; *Part Six:* refers to the Principles of Administrative Law related to Environmental Protection and to the Mining and Oil Industries; *Part Seven:* refers to some Principles of Administrative Law related to the Promotion and Protection of Investments; *Part Eight*: refers to some Administrative Law Principles regarding the Status of Individuals and Citizens; and *Part Nine*: refers to the General Principles regarding Judicial Review of Administrative Action.

Being Administrative Law a branch of law related to the State and to the legal principles that are to be applied to the legal relations that are commonly established between the organs and entities of Public Administration and the citizen, its content is inevitably conditioned by the political system and the political regime existing in the particular country.[4] During the past twenty years, the democratic system of Venezuela has been progressively dismantled,[5] and the country has being progressively subjected to an authoritarian system of government[6] that has consolidated its grip in all the institution in contempt of the Constitution, affecting the rule of law,[7] which of course is the cornerstone of Administrative Law.

That is why, many of the principles of Administrative Law in Venezuela, explained in this book, on which so many public law professors and academics have worked for so many years, currently in many cases are just principles that unfortunately in many cases lack of means for its enforcement in the country, particularly because the subjection of the Judiciary to the Executive. [8]

In any case the general bibliography on the subject in the country is the following:

BASIC GENERAL BIBLIOGRAPHY:

J.M. HERNÁNDEZ RON, *Tratado elemental de derecho administrativo,* Edit. Las Novedades, Caracas, 1942.

---

4 See Allan R. Brewer-Carías, "Los condicionantes políticos de la Administración Pública," en *Libro homenaje a la Academia de Ciencias Políticas y Sociales en su Centenario*, Academia de Ciencias Políticas y Sociales, Caracas 2015.

5 See Allan R. Brewer-Carías, *Dismantling Democracy. The Chávez Authoritarian Experiment*, Cambridge University Press, New York 2010, 418 pp.; and *The Collapse of the Rule of Law and the Struggle for Democracy in Venezuela. Lectures And Essays (2015-2020),* Colección Anales, Cátedra Mezerhane sobre democracia, Estado de Derecho y Derechos Humanos, Miami Dade College, 2020, 618 pp.

6 See Allan R. Brewer-Carías, *Estado Totalitario y Desprecio a la Ley. La desconstitucionalización, desjuridificación, desjudicialización y desdemocratización de Venezuela*, Fundación de Derecho Público, Editorial Jurídica Venezolana, 2014, 532 pp.

7 See Allan R. Brewer-Carías, *Authoritarian Government v. The Rule of Law. Lectures and Essays (1999-2014) on the Venezuelan Authoritarian Regime Established in Contempt of the Constitution*, Fundación de Derecho Público, Editorial Jurídica Venezolana, Caracas 2014, 986 pp.

8 See Allan R. Brewer-Carías, "The Government of Judges and Democracy. The Tragic Situation of the Venezuelan Judiciary," in *Venezuela. Some Current Legal Issues 2014, Venezuelan National Reports to the 19th International Congress of Comparative Law, International Academy of Comparative Law, Vienna, 20-26 July 2014*, Academia de Ciencias Políticas y Sociales, Caracas 2014, pp. 13-42.

TOMÁS POLANCO, *Derecho administrativo especial,* Universidad Central de Venezuela, Caracas, 1958.

CÉSAR TINOCO R., *Nociones de derecho administrativo y Administración Pública,* Edit. Arte, Caracas, 1958.

ANTONIO MOLES CAUBET, *Lecciones de derecho administrativo* (1960), Edit. Mohingo, Caracas, 1975.

ELOY LARES MARTÍNEZ, *Manual de Derecho Administrativo* (1964), 12ª ed., Universidad Central de Venezuela, Caracas, 2001.

ALLAN R. BREWER-CARÍAS, *Las instituciones fundamentales del derecho administrativo y la jurisprudencia venezolana,* Universidad Central de Venezuela, Caracas, 1964.

ALLAN R. BREWER-CARÍAS, *Derecho administrativo,* t. I, Universidad Central de Venezuela, Caracas, 1975.

ARMANDO RODRÍGUEZ GARCÍA y GUSTAVO URDANETA TROCONIS, *Derecho administrativo I,* guía de estudio, Caracas, Universidad Central de Venezuela, 1982; íd., *Derecho administrativo II,* Universidad Nacional Abierta, Caracas, 1983.

JOSÉ PEÑA SOLÍS, *Lineamientos del derecho administrativo,* v. I: "La organización administrativa venezolana", v. II, "El derecho administrativo y sus fuentes", Universidad Central de Venezuela, Caracas, 1997

JOSÉ PEÑA SOLÍS, *Manual de derecho administrativo, Manual de Derecho Administrativo - Adaptado a la Constitución de 1999 - Vol. I,* Tribunal Supremo de Justicia, Caracas, 2000.

JOSÉ PEÑA SOLÍS, *Manual de Derecho Administrativo* - Adaptado a la Constitución de 1999 y a la Ley Orgánica de la Administración Pública de 2001- Vol. II, Tribunal Supremo de Justicia, Caracas, 2001.

JOSÉ PEÑA SOLÍS, *Manual de Derecho Administrativo* La actividad de la Administración Pública: de Policía Administrativa de Servicio Público, de Fomento y de Gestión Económica, - Vol. III. Tribunal Supremo de Justicia, Caracas, 2003, 696 pp.

ANTONIO IZQUIERDO TORRES, *Derecho administrativo especial.* Caracas, 1997.

GALSUINDA VEDA PARRA MANZANO, *Manual de derecho administrativo,* Vadell Hermanos, Valencia, 2005.

ALLAN R. BREWER-CARÍAS, *Derecho administrativo,* t. I: Principios del derecho Público, Administración Pública, Personalidad Jurídica, t. II: Organización Administrativa, Bogotá, Universidad Externado de Colombia, 2005.

JOSÉ ARAUJO JUÁREZ, *Derecho Administrativo* Parte General, Ediciones Paredes, Caracas, 2007.

JOSÉ ARAUJO JUÁREZ, *Derecho Administrativo General.* Procedimiento y Recurso Administrativo, Ediciones Paredes, Caracas, 2010.

ALLAN R. BREWER-CARÍAS, *Tratado de Derecho administrativo,* 6 vols., Editorial Civitas, Thomson Aranzadi, Madrid 2013.

PART ONE

GENERAL PRINCIPLES OF ADMINISTRATIVE LAW RELATED TO THE ORGANIZATION OF THE STATE

I. THE SOURCES OF ADMINISTRATIVE LAW

1. The written and unwritten sources of Administrative Law

Being the Venezuelan legal system part of the Civil or Roman Law family of law, the sources of Administrative Law are basically those included in the formal written sources of law, that is, in the Constitution; in the statutes issued by the National Assembly; in the decree laws issued by the National Executive when legislation is delegated upon it by the National Assembly; in the other acts or Resolutions of the same National Assembly issued with the same rank as of the statutes; and in the Regulations and in the other administrative normative acts (with general effects) issued by the National Executive, as well as by the other competent administrative authorities.

Regarding the Constitution, in Venezuela, in particular after the enactment of the 1999 Constitution, it can be said that the basic principles and rules of administrative law have been constitutionalized,[1] being the text of the Constitution the most important source of such principles.

Subjected to the provisions of the Constitution, the main source of administrative law are the statutes enacted by the National Assembly (Art. 202 Constitution) or issued through decree laws by the National Executive according to specific legislative delegation by means of enabling laws (Articles 203. 236.8, Constitution). Among the most important Law the following can be mentioned: Organic Law on Public Administration, Public Officials Statute, Organic Law on Administrativa Procedure, Public Contracting Law, Organic Law of the Promotion of Private Investments through Concessions, Organic Law on the Financial Management of the

1 See Allan R. Brewer-Carías, "Algunos aspectos de proceso de constitucionalización del derecho administrativo en la Constitución de 1999," in *Los requisitos y vicios de los actos administrativos. V Jornadas Internacionales de Derecho Administrativo Allan Randolph Brewer-Carías,* Caracas 1996, Fundación Estudios de Derecho Administrativo (FUNEDA), Caracas 2000, pp. 23-37.

Public Sector, Public Assets Law, Law against Corruption, General Audit Office Organic Law, Organic law on the Contentious Administrative Jurisdiction. [2]

Other acts with the same rank as of the statutes are the acts of government, like the executive decrees declaring the states of emergency (Articles 236,7, 337, Constitution), as well as the resolutions issued by the National Assembly according to its attribution, which have the same rank of statutes.

The third written source of administrative law are the Resolutions issued by the National Executive (article 236.10, Constitution) and all the other administrative acts with general effects (normative character), issued by administrative authorities.

In addition, according to article 4 of the Civil Code, another source of administrative law has historically been the "general principles of law,"[3] being established in such provision that "when there is no precise provision in a Statute, the provisions regulating similar cases or analogous matters must be taken into consideration, and if doubt persist, the general principles of law must be applied."[4]

These principles, which have had particular importance on matters of administrative law before the general laws were enacted, mean that administrative action is not only subjected to "the Law" as a formal written source, but to all other written and unwritten sources of law, that traditionally have formed in Venezuela the block of legality. Within it, the most important ones have been the said "general principles of administrative law," many of which eventually were progressively incorporated as positive law in many statutes, as has been the case, for instance, of the Organic Law on Public Administration, the Organic Law on Administrative Procedure, and the Organic Law on Public Contracts.

2. The judicial precedents and the binding constitutional interpretations issued by the Constitutional Chamber of the Supreme Tribunal

In Venezuela, as in many other countries that follow the Civil or Roman Law system, the court decisions are not direct sources of law, not having any general application the *stare decisis* principle that for instance exists in North American Law. Such principle in fact, particularly on constitutional matters, has always been

---

2 See the text of all these laws Allan R. Brewer-Carías, *Código de Derecho Administrativo*, Editorial Jurídica venezolana, Caracas 2013.

3 In all the Administrative Law Manuals and Treatises, in absence of specific provisions included in statutes or regulations, the general principles of law have been traditionally considered as the most important source of administrative law applicable to administrative action. See for instance, Eloy Lares Martínez, *Manual de Derecho Administrativo*, XIV Edición, Caracas 2013, pp. 143 ss.

4 *"Article 4. Cuando no hubiere disposición precisa de la Ley, se tendrán en consideración las disposiciones que regulan casos semejantes o materias análogas; y, si hubiere todavía dudas, se aplicarán los principios generales del derecho."* Based precisely on such provision of article 4 of the Civil Code, Lares Martínez argues, that "In administrative law, in the absence of written provision, the general principles of law are applicable as legal (juridical) principles in which the positive legal order has its basis." See Eloy Lares Martínez, *Manual de Derecho Administrativo*, XIV Edición, Caracas 2013, pp. 144

considered "peculiar to the common law systems of law and alien to the Roman law systems."[5]

As explained by M. Cappelletti and J.C. Adams:

> "Under the Anglo-American doctrine of *stare decisis*, a decision by the highest court in any jurisdiction is binding on all lower courts in the same jurisdiction, and thus as soon as the court has declared a law unconstitutional, no other court can apply it . . . stare decisis, however, is not normally part of the Roman law systems, and thus in these systems, the courts are not generally bound even by the decisions of the highest court."[6]

Mauro Cappelletti later developed the argument in his book *Judicial Review in the contemporary world*, when he wrote:

> "Since the principle of *stare decisis* is foreign to civil law judges, a system which allowed each judge to decide on the constitutionality of statues could result in a law being disregarded as unconstitutional by some judges, while being held constitutional and applied by others. Furthermore, the same judicial organ, which had one day disregarded a given law, might uphold it the next day, having changed its mind about the law's constitutional legitimacy."[7]

Therefore, as I argued many years ago in my book *Judicial Review in Comparative Law* (1989), in the:

> "Venezuelan procedural system, the *stare decisis* doctrine has no application at all, the judges being sovereign in their decisions, only submitted to the constitution and the law. Therefore, decisions regarding the inapplicability of a law considered unconstitutional in a specific case do not have binding effects, neither regarding the same judge who may change his legal opinion in other cases, nor regarding other judges or courts."[8]

The exception is when the Constitutional Chamber of the Supreme Trbunal of Justice, as Constitutional Jurisdiction, annuls a statute or other State act of general *erga omnes* effects, in which case the decision is universally binding.

Consequently, besidesuch cases, Supreme Tribunal decisions (including those issued by the Constitutional Chamber) are not a source of law, except if the Constitutional Chamber establishes and explicitly declares an *interpretation of a constitutional rule or principle as having "binding character" pursuant Article 335 of the Venezuelan Constitution.*

Otherwise, the decisions of the Supreme Tribunal carry no more weight than the interpretations of legal scholars and other branches of government. And that is why the Constitutional Chamber, since 2000, has been conscious about the two possible sorts of constitutional interpretations that it can issue: those considered

---

5 As I expressed in 1989 in my book: Allan R. Brewer-Carías, *Judicial Review in Comparative Law,* Editorial Jurídica Venezolana, 2014, p. 198. Available at: http://allanbrewer carias.com/wp-con-tent/uploads/2014/02/JUDICIAL-REVIEW.-9789803652128-txt-PORTADA-Y-TEXTO-PAG-WEB. pdf

6 *See Id.* (quoting Mauro Cappelletti and J.C. Adams, "*Judicial Review of Legislation: European Antecedents and Adaptations,*" *Harvard Law Review, 1966,* No 79 pp. 1207, 1215.

7 *See Id.* (quoting Mauro Cappelletti, *Judicial Review in the Contemporary World,* 1971, p. 58).

8 *See Id.* at 374.

binding and those that are not binding; establishing on judgment N° 1347 of November 11, 2000 (Case: *On the Scope of the Recourse of Constitutional Interpretation*), the following criteria on the subject:

> "the interpretations of this Constitutional Chamber, in general, or those issued by way of an interpretative recourse, will be understood as binding with respect to the core of the case studied, all in a sense of minimum limit, and not of border untranslatable by a jurisprudence of values originating from the Chamber itself, the other Chambers or all the courts of instance. [...].
>
> The statements that, without referring to the central nucleus of the debate object of the decision, affect a collateral issue relevant to it, normally linked to the legal reasoning outlined to settle the solution to the case, will not logically be binding, nor in this nor in any other sense." [9]

This explains why the Constitutional Chamber has been emphatic in affirming repeatedly since 2001, that "it is clear that in our legal order, except the doctrine of constitutional interpretation established by this Chamber, *the jurisprudence is not a direct source of law*."[10]

Thus, it can be affirmed, that the Constitution does not confer a "binding" character on any phrase, argument, or reasoning stated within the Constitutional Chamber decisions. On the contrary, an interpretation is "binding" pursuant to Article 335 of the Constitution only when the Constitutional Chamber expressly states *in the text of a decision that it is establishing a "binding interpretation"* (rule of explicitness) with general effects, requiring the need for its publication in the *Official Gazette* (rule of publicity).

Ever since 2000, a few months after the current Constitution was ratified, I expressed my opinion that a binding interpretation must be "an *express* interpretation" established by invoking Article 335 of the Constitution.[11] I reaffirmed this criterion a few years later in 2004 when I wrote that the Constitutional Chamber must invoke Article 335 to "establish the interpretation of the [constitutional] norm," which "must be *expressly* pointed out"[12] in the sense of expressing, in one way or another, that a binding interpretation under Article 335 is being established.

As I wrote in 2009 in relation to this *very* matter:

---

9 See in *Revista de Derecho Público*, No. 84, Editorial Jurídica Venezolana, Caracas 2000, p. 269. Available at: http://allanbrewercarias.com/wp-content/uploads/2007/08/2000-REVISTA-84.pdf

10 *See* Supreme Tribunal of Justice, Decision No. 31, Jan. 30, 2009, ,Case Alejandro Humberto Sosa vs. Decisión Sala de Casación Civil del Tribunal Supremo de Justicia, in *Revista de Derecho Público,* No 117, Editorial Jurídica Venezolana, Caracas 2009, p. 135 (citing Supreme Tribunal Decision No. 856 of June 1, 2001). Available at: http://allanbrewercarias.com/wp-content/uploads/2010/07/2009-REVISTA-117.pdf

11 *See* Allan R. Brewer-Carías, *El Sistema de justicia constitucional en la Constitución de 1999,* Editorial Jurídica Venezolana, Caracas 2000, pp. 86, 87 . Avalable at: http://allanbrewer cariasnetContent/449725d9-f1cb-474b-8ab2-41efb849fea5/Content/II,%201,%2090.%20EL%20 SISTEMA%20DE%20JUSTICIA%20CONSTITUCIONAL%20DEFINITIVO.pdf

12 See Allan R. Brewer-Carías, *La Constitución de 1999. Derecho Constitucional Venezolana,* Tomo II, Editorial Jurídica Venezolana, 2004, p. 999.

"Article 335 of the Constitution, […] sets forth that 'the interpretations' that are established by the Constitutional Chamber 'concerning the content or scope of the constitutional norms are binding,' which require the Chamber to determine exactly and precisely in its generally extensive judgments, what is exactly the part of them that contains the binding interpretation; an operation that cannot be in any case left up to the reader of the rulings. In other words, the 'binding' nature of a constitutional interpretation on the content or scope of the constitutional regulations that is made in a Constitutional Chamber judgment, cannot fall on any phrase or interpretative reasoning it contains. On the contrary, the judgment must expressly be derived from the interpretation of the Chamber 'on the content or scope of the constitutional regulations and constitutional principles,' which is the part that has [such character], that does not extend to any argument or sentence used in the judgment for the normative interpretation."[13]

Addressing the same matter in a 2019 book, I wrote:

"The [Constitutional] Chamber, in its judgment interpreting a constitutional norm must expressly indicate specifically that it is establishing the 'binding' doctrine. That is, not all interpretation or usage of provisions made by the Constitutional Chamber can or should be considered as a "binding interpretation" of the Constitution; and in the judgment in which the Constitutional Chamber effectively makes a binding interpretation of a constitutional norm or principle, it must necessarily make reference to the application of article 335 of the Constitution [See for instance, Rafael Laguna Navas, "El recurso extraordinario de revisión y el carácter vinculante de las sentencias de la Sala Constitucional del Tribunal Supremo de Justicia," in *Congreso Internacional de Derecho Administrativo en Homenaje al profesor Luis Henrique Farías Mata*, Vol. II, 2006, pp. 91-101. That is, as I have expressed since 2000, "the reasoning or the 'motivating' part of the decisions cannot be considered as binding, but only the interpretation made, specifically, of the content or scope of a specific rule of the Constitution" [See Allan R. Brewer-Carías, *El sistema de justicia constitucional en la Constitución de 1999,* Editorial Jurídica Venezolana, Caracas 2000, p 87]. In other terms, "what can be binding in a decision, can only be its "resolutive" part [the Holding], in which the Constitutional Chamber determines the interpretation of a norm, and this must be expressly stated." See Allan R. Brewer-Carías, *La Justicia constitucional. Procesos y procedimientos constitucionales*, Editorial Porrúa, México 2007, p. 415.[14]

Along the same lines, Ramón Escovar León has written that a binding interpretation is always related to the *thema decidendum* of the decision and not "to the *dictum* that refers to marginal, peripheral, circumstantial or superabundant

---

13 *See* Allan R. Brewer-Carías, "La potestad la Jurisdicción Constitucional de interpretar la Constitución con efectos vinculantes" in Jhonny Tupayachi Sotomayor (Coord.), *El Precedente Constitucional Vinculante en el Perú (Análisis, Comentarios y Doctrina Comparada),* Editorial Adrus, Lima 2009, pp. 791-819; available at: http://allanbrewercarias.com/wp-content/uploads /2011/02/638.II-4-648-LA-INTERPRETACI%C3%93N-VINCULANTE-DE-LA-CONSTITUCI %C3%93N-_Venezuela_.-Lima-2009.doc.pdf (pdf. p. 10).

14 *See* Allan R. Brewer-Carías, *Sobre las Nociones de Contratos Administrativos, Contratos de Interés Público, Servicio Público, Interés Público y Orden Público, y su Manipulación Legislativa y Jurisprudencial,* Editorial Jurídica Venezolana, Caracas 2019, pp. 150-151. Available at: http://allanbrewercarias.com/wp-content/uploads/2019/02/9789803654450-txt.pdf

motivations, which are not binding with *erga omnes* effects, since the latter are only persuasive."[15] In other words of the same author: "The binding nature of the constitutional decision focuses on what constitutes the *core* of the motivation and cannot be extended to the marginal or peripheral sectors of motivation,"[16] and thus "the constitutional precedent refers to the motivation that supports the *thema decidendum*. Marginal or peripheral motivations are not part of the precedent."[17]

Likewise, Hernando Díaz Candia, has written that "the binding interpretation established by the Constitutional Chamber can only refer to the legal principles derived from the main *thema decidemdum*," that is, the "holding,"[18] and cannot refer "to simple assertions made by the Chamber or incidental questions, even referring to the content or scope of constitutional norms and principles.[19] [...] The '*dictum*' or '*dicta*' in the decisions of the Constitutional Chamber *should not be binding*, since with respect to them the Chamber does not properly exercise its jurisdictional function, and the legal analysis exercised is usually less thorough."[20]

Along the same lines, in one of its first decisions interpreting the 1999 Constitution, the Constitutional Chamber explained that:

> "when ruling on a recourse for interpretation of the Constitution, this Chamber will specify, if applicable, the core of the constitutional precepts, values or principles, in response to reasonable doubts regarding its meaning and scope, originating in an alleged antinomy or obscurity in the terms whose intelligence is pertinent to clarify in order to satisfy the need for legal certainty. It consists primarily of a mere statement, with binding effects, on the minimum core of the norm studied, its purpose or extension, which would affect the features or properties that are predicated of the terms that form the precept and the set of objects or dimensions of reality covered by it, when they are doubtful or obscure."[21]

---

15 See Ramón Escovar León, "Límites a la interpretación constitucional," in *Revista de Derecho Público*, No. 157-158, Editorial Jurídica Venezolana, Caracas 2019, pp. 46-47. Available at: http://allanbrewercarias.com/wp-content/uploads/2020/04/REVISTA-157-158-PRIMER-SEMESTRE-2019-pag.-web.pdf

16 *Idem*, p. 54

17 *Idem*, p. 59

18 See Hernando Diaz Candia, "El principio *Stare Decisis* y el concepto de precedente vinculante a efectos del artículo 335 de la Constitución de la República Bolivariana de Venezuela de 1999," in *Revista de Derecho Constitucional*. Edit. Sherwood, N° 8, Caracas, 2003, pp. 228

19 *Idem*, pp. 219, 227

20 *Idem*, p. 228

21*See* Supreme Tribunal of Justice, Decision No. 1415, Nov. 22, 2000, p. 7. See *also* Allan R. Brewer-Carías, "La potestad la Jurisdicción Constitucional de interpretar la Constitución con efectos vinculantes," in Jhonny Tupayachi Sotomayor (Coord.), *El Precedente Constitucional Vinc"ulante en el Perú (Análisis, Comentarios y Doctrina Comparada)*, Editorial Adrus, 2009, pp. pp. 791-819; available at: http://allanbrewercarias.com/wp-content/uploads/2011/02/638.II-4-648-LA-INTERPRETACI%C3%93N-VINCULANTE-DE-LA-CONSTITUCI%C3%93N-_Venezuela_.-Lima-2009.doc.pdf, (pdf. p. 10); Ramón Escovar León, "Límites a la interpretación constitucional," in *Revista de Derecho Público*, No. 157-158, Editorial Jurídica Venezolana, Caracas 2019, pp. 48, 55, 60; Available at: http://allanbrewercarias.com/wp-content/uploads /2020/04/REVISTA-157-158-PRIMER-SEMESTRE-2019-pag.-web.pdf; Hernando Diaz Candia, "El principio Stare Decisis y el concepto de precedente vinculante a efectos del artículo 335 de la

This means that the Constitutional Chamber in its decisions can make two distinct types of constitutional interpretation — (1) "binding interpretation" pursuant to Article 335 of the Constitution (referred to as *jurisdatio*), and (2) non-binding interpretation that applies only to the particular facts at issue in a given case before the court (referred to as *jurisdictio*). As the Constitutional Chamber explained in its decision N° 276 of April 24, 2014 (Case: *Gerardo Sanchez Chacón*) (mentioning its previous decision N° 1309 of July 19, 2001, Case: *Hermann Escarrá*), whereas she decided to "interpret the notion and scope of its own interpretative powers":

> "[the Constitution] sets forth two sorts of constitutional interpretations, that is, the individualized interpretation that is contained in the ruling as individualized norm, and the general or abstract interpretation established in article 335, which is a true jurisdatio, in the sense that it declares erga omnes and *pro futuro* (*ex nunc*), the content and scope of the constitutional principles and norms whose interpretation is requested through the corresponding extraordinary action. This jurisdatio is different to the functions of concentrated control of constitutionality of laws, because such monophyletic function is, as Kelsen said, a true negative legislation that decrees the invalidity of the provisions that contradict the Constitution, besides [that] the mentioned general and abstract interpretation does not refer to sub constitutional provisions but to the constitutional system itself. The straight sense of article 335 of the Constitution of the Bolivarian Republic of Venezuela made possible the extraordinary action of interpretation, since otherwise, such provision would be redundant to what is established in article 334 ejusdem, which can only lead to individualized norms, as are, even, the Constitutional Chamber rulings on matters of amparo [constitutional protection]. The difference between both sorts of interpretation is patent and produces decisive juridical consequences in the exercise of the constitutional jurisdiction by this Chamber. These consequences are referred to the different effects of the jurisdictio and of the jurisdatio, and this is because the efficiency of an individualized norm is limited to the case decided, while the general norm produced by the abstract interpretation has erga omnes value and constitutes a real jurisdatio, a quasi-authentic and para-constituent interpretation, which expresses the declared constitutional content of the fundamental text."[22]

Consequently, as already mentioned, Article 335 of the Constitution does not confer a "binding" character on any phrase, argument, or reasoning in Constitutional Chamber decisions. On the contrary, an interpretation is binding pursuant to Article 335 only when the Constitutional Chamber expressly states in the body of a decision that it is establishing a "binding interpretation."

Nonetheless, despite the aforementioned decisions of the Constitutional Chamber, some authors, such as Eduardo Meier García, were still troubled by the lack of any formal provisions in the Organic Law of the Supreme Tribunal to prevent the arbitrariness that can escort the power to interpret constitutional

---

Constitución de la República Bolivariana de Venezuela de 1999," *Revista de Derecho Constitucional,* No. 8, Editorial Sherwood, Caracas 2003, pp. 219, 228.

22 Available at: https://vlexvenezuela.com/vid/gerardo-sanchez-chacon-593352510

provisions and principles with binding effect.[23] Meier García argued that the Constitutional Chamber's power of constitutional interpretation needed to be subject to a process of "procedural self-restraint" to ensure "congruence, proportionality, and reasonability;"[24] or, as the Constitutional Chamber itself put it, to guarantee "the principle of exercising power under the law, an essential element of the rule of law and of the democratic system, according to which autocracy and arbitrariness are execrated." "Said principles," wrote the Chamber in one of its early decisions on the matter in 2000, "while fundamental to the rule of law, require the distribution of functions among various organs and their actions with reference to pre-established norms, either as a way of interdicting arbitrariness or as mechanisms of efficiency in the fulfillment of the tasks of the State."[25]

In decision N° 276 of April 24, 2014, the Constitutional Chamber recognized that, based on these principles:

> "The Constitutional Chamber has been always very careful in not usurping with her interpretation, attributions of the other Chambers (for instance, the recourse of interpretation of legal text); and to avoid that this action is intended to substitute pre-existing procedural resources; or an attempt is made to surreptitiously obtain quasi-jurisdictional results that go beyond the clarifying purpose of this type of action, that is, that what is proposed rather seeks to resolve a specific conflict between individuals or between these and public bodies, or between the latter among themselves; or that there is a veiled intention to obtain a prior opinion on the unconstitutionality of a law."[26]

In the exercise of judicial self-restraint, and bearing in mind the difference between individualized interpretations of a constitutional provision limited to the case being decided (*jurisdictio*) and abstract interpretations of a constitutional principle or provision producing a "general norm" (*jurisdatio*) with *erga omnes* applicability and effects, the Constitutional Chamber in her decisions, has developed at least two very important procedural rules for identifying which of its interpretations are intended to be binding pursuant to Article 355 of the Constitution: (i) that the binding character of the interpretation is *expressly stated in the body of the decision* (known as the "rule of explicitness"); and (ii) that the decision includes an *order for its publication* in the *Official Gazette* of the Republic (known as the "rule of publication").

Ruben J. Laguna N. describes these two rules as "complementary conditions," writing that "to be binding, in addition, [the Constitutional Chamber decisions] must fulfill certain complementary conditions: 1. That the binding character of the decision be expressly signaled;" and "2. The need for the decision to be published in

---

23 To which I have referred as "an example of a case of the pathology of judicial review." See Allan R. Brewer-Carías, *Constitutional Courts as Positive Legislators. A Comparative Law Study*, Cambridge University Press 2011, pp. 37-40.

24 See Enrique Meier García, "Luces y sombras del precedente constitucional en Venezuela," in Edgar Carpio Marcos and Pedro P. Grández Castro (Coord.), *Estudios al precedente constitucional*, Edit. Palestra,Lima 2007, pp. 204, 211.

25 See Decision of the Constitutional Chamber No. 1415 del 22 de noviembre de 2000. Available at: https://vlexvenezuela.com/vid/freddy-h-rangel-rojas-283525775

26 Supreme Tribunal of Justice Decision No. 276.

the *Official Gazette*."[27] Jesús María Casal has also explained that when a binding interpretation is established pursuant to Article 335 of the Constitution, in general, "the Constitutional Chamber has *expressly* established the binding nature of the *ratio decidendi*, and has ordered the publication of the corresponding judgement in the *Official Gazette*."[28] Likewise, as I have already pointed out, I have also explained that when the Constitutional Chamber issues a binding interpretation, this must be "expressly pointed out." [29]

This "rule of explicitness" has been followed by the Constitutional Chamber from the outset of its interpretation of the 1999 Constitution. Whenever the Constitutional Chamber has adopted or established a binding interpretation of the content or scope of a constitutional principle or provision, it has *explicitly declared the binding character of the interpretation in the text of the decision*, and in some cases in subsequent decisions. Consequently, an interpretation can be considered binding only when the decision itself explicitly establishes its binding character.

The following cases are illustrative:

Decision N° 1 of January 20, 2000 (Case: *Emery Mata Millán*), explicitly establishing the binding character of an interpretation regarding procedural rules for amparo proceedings. [30]

Decision N° 2 of January 20, 2000 (Case: *Domingo G. Ramírez M.*), explicitly establishing the binding character of an interpretation regarding jurisdictional rules for amparo proceedings against High Officials. [31]

Decision N° 1555 of December 8, 2000 (Case: *Yoslena Chanchamire B. v. Instituto Universitario Politécnico Santiago Mariño*), explicitly establishing the binding character of an interpretation regarding rules of judicial procedure and jurisdiction for amparo proceedings. [32]

---

27 See Ruben J. Laguna Navas, *La Sala Constitucional del Tribunal Supremo de Justicia: su rol como máxima y última intérprete de la Constitución*, Universidad Central de Venezuela, Serie Trabajos de Grado No 7. Caracas, 2005 (Chapter V: The abstract decisions of the Constitutional Chamber. Its binding character), p. 233. See the quotation in Francis Marval, "La jurisprudencia vinculante de la Sala Constitucional y el principio *iura novit curia*," in *Magistra*, Año 2, No. 1, Caracas 2008, pp. 179, 183.

28 See Jesús M. Casal H., "Cosa juzgada y efecto vinculante en la justicia constitucional," in *Revista de venezolana Derecho Constitucional* No 8, July-December, 2003, Caracas p. 193, 215, 219.

29 See Allan R. Brewer-Carías, "Los efectos de las sentencias constitucionales en Venezuela, ," in *Anuario Internacional sobre Justicia Constitucional*, No. 22, Centro de Estudios Políticos y Constitucionales, 2008, pp. 19, 64. Available at: http://allanbrewercarias.com/wp-content/uploads/2009/02/Brewer.-Efectos-de-las-sentencias-constitucionales.-2008-Anuario-DC.pdf.

30 See in *Revista de Derecho Público*, No. 81, Editorial Jurídica Venezolana, Caracas 2000, p. 230. Available at: http://allanbrewercarias.com/wp-content/uploads/2007/08/2000-REVISTA-81.pdf

31 Id., p. 238.

32 See in *Revista de Derecho Público*, No. 84, Editorial Jurídica Venezolana, Caracas 2000, p. 311. Available at: http://allanbrewercarias.com/wp-content/uploads/2007/08/2000-REVISTA-84.pdf

Decision N° 1013 of June 12, 2001 (Case: *Elías Santana, Queremos Elegir*), explicitly establishing the binding doctrine of an interpretation regarding Articles 57 and 58 of the Constitution. [33]

Decision N° 833 of March 5, 2001 (Case: I*nstituto Autónomo Policía Municipal de Chacao vs. Corte Primera de lo Contencioso Administrativo*), explicitly establishing the binding character of an interpretation of Article 334 of the Constitution regarding the two methods of judicial review that exist in Venezuela: the concentrated judicial review method attributed to the Constitutional Chamber and the diffuse judicial review powers attributed to all courts. [34]

Decision N° 2553 of November 23, 2001, (Case: *Impugnación de la Ordenanza de Impuestos*), explicitly establishing the binding effect for all courts of an interpretation regarding Constitutional Jurisdiction and Contentious Administrative Jurisdiction with respect to matter of judicial review. [35]

Decision N° 488 of April 6, 2001 (Article 35 of the Organic Amparo Law), explicitly establishing the binding character of an interpretation regarding appellate rules for amparo proceedings. [36]

Decision N° 332 of March 14, 2001 (Article 28 of the Constitution), explicitly establishing binding interpretation the one made regarding such provisions in order to assume the exclusive power to decide on matters of action of habeas data. [37]

Decision N° 1126 of August 3, 2012 (Case: *Constitutional review of a judicial ruling*), expressly said that it interpreted with binding character the scope of civil extra-contractual liability of Airlines. [38]

Regarding the "rule of publicity," the Constitutional Chamber generally requires publication of its binding interpretation decisions in the *Official Gazette* of the Republic, ordering such publication in the body of the decision itself. The following are examples:

Decision N° 1318 of August 2, 2001 (Case: *Nicolás J. Alcalá R.*), ordering that "the Labor Courts, when they hear from now on situations such as the one raised in this case, must abide by the doctrine contained in this ruling for the

---

33 See in *Revista de Derecho Público*, No. 85-88, Editorial Jurídica Venezolana, Caracas 2001, p. 117. Available at: http://allanbrewercarias.com/wp-content/uploads/2007/08/2001-REVISTA-85-86-87-88.pdf

34 Id. p. 369. See on the two methods of judicial review in Venezuela: Allan R. Brewer-Carías, "Judicial Review in Venezuela," in *Duquesne Law Review*, Vol 45, No. 3, Spring 2007, pp. 439-465. Available at: http://allanbrewercarias.net/Content/449725d9-f1cb-474b-8ab2-41efb849fea8/Content/II,%204,%20502.%20Judicial%20Review%20in%20Venezuela.%202006%20Duquesne%20Nov.%202006%20Revised%20version.pdf

35 See in *Revista de Derecho Público*, No. 85-88, Editorial Jurídica Venezolana, Caracas 2001, p. 387. Available at: http://allanbrewercarias.com/wp-content/uploads/2007/08/2001-REVISTA-85-86-87-88.pdf

36 Id. p. 472.

37 Id. p. 492.

38 See in *Revista de Derecho Público*, No. 131, Editorial Jurídica Venezolana, Caracas 2012, p. 203 ff. Availale at: http://allanbrewercarias.com/wp-content/uploads/2014/07/9789803653521-txt.pdf

effective administration of justice, therefore, this ruling will have *ex tunc* effects as of its publication, since the interpretations established by the Constitutional Chamber on the content or scope of the constitutional norms and principles are binding for the other Chambers of the Supreme Court of Justice and other courts of the Republic."[39]

Decision N° 2817 of November 18, 2002 (Case: *Impugnación de varias disposiciones de la Ley Orgánica del Poder Electoral*), stating that the Constitutional Chamber "interpreted, with binding character the application of article 214 of the Constitution, so that order is given for the publication of this decision in the Official Gazette of the Republic."[40]

Decision N° 1682 of July 2005 (Interpretation of Article 77 of the Constitution), interpreting Article 77 of the Constitution on matters relating to marriage and stating that "due to its binding character, according to article 335 of the Constitution, [the Chamber] orders the publication of this ruling in the Official Gazette of the Republic."[41]

Decision N° 650 of May 23, 2012 (Case: *Irwin Oscar Fernández Arrieche Revisión de sentencia*), interpreting the Constitution with respect to the applicability of Article 104 of the Labor Organic Law, explicitly declaring the binding character of the interpretation, and ordering the publication of the ruling in the Official Gazette of the Republic. [42]

Decision N° 1005 of July 26, 2013 (Case: *Ninfa Denis Gavidia*, Constitutional review of judicial decision), interpreting the term to issue judicial decisions, explicitly declaring the binding character of the interpretation for all Venezuelan courts, and ordering the publication of the ruling in the Official Gazette of the Republic.[43]

Decision N° 1063 of August 5, 2014 (Applicability of Article 425 of the Labor Organic Law), explicitly establishing binding criteria for all Venezuelan courts regarding access to justice in labor judicial procedures according to Articles 26 and 257 of the Constitution and ordering the publication of the ruling in the Official Gazette of the Republic.[44]

---

39 See in *Revista de Derecho Público*, No. 85-88, Editorial Jurídica Venezolana, Caracas 2001, p. 265. Available at: http://allanbrewercarias.com/wp-content/uploads/2007/08/2001-REVISTA-85-86-87-88.pdf

40 See in *Revista de Derecho Público*, No. 89-92, Editorial Jurídica Venezolana, Caracas 2002, p. 492. Available at: http://allanbrewercarias.com/wp-content/uploads/2007/08/2002-REVISTA-89-90-91-92.pdf

41 Id. p. 124

42 See in *Revista de Derecho Público*, No. 130, Editorial Jurídica Venezolana, Caracas 2012, p. 475 ff. Available at: http://allanbrewercarias.com/wp-content/uploads/2013/05/9789803653514-txt.pdf

43 See in *Revista de Derecho Público*, No. 135, Editorial Jurídica Venezolana, Caracas 2013, p. 89 ff. Available at: http://allanbrewercarias.com/wp-content/uploads/2017/01/9789803653095-txt.pdf

44 See in *Revista de Derecho Público*, No. 139, Editorial Jurídica Venezolana, Caracas 2014, p. 86. Avalable at: http://allanbrewercarias.com/wp-content/uploads/2017/01/9789803653132-txt.pdf

Decision N° 97 of May 14, 2019 (Case: Organic Law on Children and Adolescents), interpreting Article 76 of the Constitution, explicitly establishing the binding character of the interpretation, with ex tunc and *ex nunc* effects, and ordering the publication of the ruling in the Official Gazette of the Republic. [45]

In some cases, even when establishing binding interpretations of statutes, the Chamber always has ordered the publication of its decision, as occurred, for instance, in the following cases:

Decision N° 1573 of July 12, 2005 (Case: *Carbonell Thielsen, C.A.*), establishing a binding interpretation regarding the quantum for filing cassation appeals (*recurso de casación*) and ordering publication of the ruling in the Official Gazette of the Republic due to the binding character of the ruling for all Venezuelan courts. [46]

Decision N° 1379 of October 29, 2009 (Case: *Gerardo Gil Peña y otro*), deciding not to apply Article 177 of the Organic Law on Labor Procedure, explicitly declaring that the interpretation is binding on all Venezuelan courts, and ordering the publication of the ruling in the Official Gazette of the Republic.[47]

On the other hand, as aforementioned, even within a decision in which the Constitutional Chamber issues a binding interpretation, it is limited to the *thema decidendum* of the decision and not "to the *dictum* that refers to marginal, peripheral, circumstantial or superabundant motivations, which *are not binding with erga omnes effects*, since the latter are only persuasive."[48]

---

45 See in *Revista de Derecho Público*, No. 157-158, Editorial Jurídica Venezolana, Caracas 2019, p. 324. Available at: http://allanbrewercarias.com/wp-content/uploads/2020/04/REVISTA-157-158-PRIMER-SEMESTRE-2019-pag.-web.pdf

46 See in *Revista de Derecho Público*, No. 103, Editorial Jurídica Venezolana, Caracas 2005, p. 117. Available a: HTTP://ALLANBREWERCARIAS.COM/WP-CONTENT/UPLOADS/2007/08/ 2005-REVISTA-103.PDF

47 See in *Revista de Derecho Público*, No. 120, Editorial Jurídica Venezolana, Caracas 2009, p. 107 ff. Available at: http://allanbrewercarias.com/wp-content/uploads/2012/08/2009-REVISTA-120.pdf

48 *See* Escovar León, Ramón Escovar León, "Límites a la interpretación constitucional," in *Revista de Derecho Público*, No. 157-158, Editorial Jurídica Venezolana, Caracas 2019, p. 48; Available at: http://allanbrewercarias.com/wp-content/uploads/2020/04/REVISTA-157-158-PRIMER-SEMESTRE-2019-pag.-web.pdf ; *see also* Diaz Candia, "El principio Stare Decisis y el concepto de precedente vinculante a efectos del artículo 335 de la Constitución de la República Bolivariana de Venezuela de 1999," in *Revista de Derecho Constitucional,* No. 8, Editorial Sherwood, Caracas 2003,pp. 220-221, 227-229 ("the binding interpretation established by the Constitutional Chamber can only refer to the legal principles derived from the main *thema decidemdum,*" and cannot refer "to simple assertions made by the Chamber or incidental questions, even referring to the content or scope of constitutional norms and principles").

II. SOME ASPECTS OF THE FEDERAL SYSTEM OF THE STATE

1. The formal "Decentralized Federal State

Principles of administrative law in Venezuela are conditioned by the specific form of the organization of the State. According to Article 4 of the 1999 Constitution,[49] the Republic is formally defined "as a decentralized Federal State under the terms set out in the Constitution" governed by the principles of "territorial integrity, solidarity, concurrence and co-responsibility." Nonetheless, "the terms set out in the Constitution," are without a doubt centralizing, and Venezuela continues to be a contradictory "Centralized Federation."[50]

Article 136 of the 1999 Constitution states that "public power is distributed among the municipal, state and national entities," establishing a Federation with three levels of political governments and autonomy. Each one with its Public Administration: *a national level* exercised by the Republic (federal level); the *States level*, exercised by the 23 States and a Capital District; and the *municipal level,* exercised by the 338 existing Municipalities. On each of these three levels, the Constitution requires "democratic, participatory, elected, decentralized, alternating, responsible, plural and with revocable mandates" governments (Article 6). Regarding the Capital District, it has substituted the former Federal District which was established in 1863, with the elimination of traditional federal interventions that existed regarding the authorities of the latter.

The organization of the political institutions in each of the territorial level is formally guided by the principle of the organic separation of powers, but with different scope. On the *national level*, with a presidential system of government, the national public power is separated among five branches of government, including: the "Legislative, Executive, Judicial, Citizen and Electoral" (Article 136). Thus, the 1999 Constitution has surpassed the classic tripartite division of power by adding to the traditional Legislative, Executive and Judicial branches, the Citizen branch, which includes the Public Prosecutor Office, the General Comptrollership Office, and the People's Rights Defender Office, as well as an Electoral branch of government controlled by the National Electoral Council.

The new Citizen and Electoral branches, as well as the Judiciary, are reserved only to the national or federal level of government. Therefore, Venezuela does not have a Judiciary at the State level. In fact, since 1945, the Judicial branch has been reserved to the national level of government, basically due to the national character of all major legislation and Codes (Civil, Commercial, Criminal, Labor and Procedural Codes). Consequently, since Courts are national (federal), there is no room for State Constitution regulations on these matters. Regarding judicial review, the Constitutional Chamber of the Supreme Tribunal of Justice is the constitutional

---

49 See *Official Gazette* N° 5.453 of Mars 24, 2000. See in general on the 1999 Constitution, Allan R. Brewer-Carías, *La Constitución de 1999. Derecho Constitucional Venezolano*, 2 Vols., Editorial Jurídica Venezolana, Caracas 2004.

50 See Allan R. Brewer-Carías, *Federalismo y Municipalismo en la Constitución de 1999,* Universidad Católica del Táchira-Editorial Jurídica Venezolana, Caracas, 2001; "Centralized Federalism in Venezuela", in *Duquesne Law Review*, Volume 43, Number 4, Summer 2005. Duquesne University, Pittsburgh, Pennsylvania, 2005, pp. 629-643.

organ with power to review and annul with *erga omnes* effects (Article 336) all laws (national, state and municipal) including state constitutions when contrary to the national Constitution, so there are no state courts or judicial organization.

Pertaining to the Legislative branch, it must be noted that the Constitution of 1999 established a one-chamber National Assembly, thus ending the country's federalist tradition of bicameralism by eliminating the Senate. As a result, Venezuela has also become a rare federal state without a federal chamber or Senate where the States, through its representatives, can be equal in the sense of equal vote. In the National Assembly there are no representatives of the States, and its members are global representatives of the Citizens and of all the States collectively. Theoretically, these global representatives are not subject to mandates, or instructions, but only subject to the "dictates of their conscience" (Article 201). This has effectively eliminated all vestiges of territorial representation.

Regarding the States branch of government, the 1999 Constitution established that each State has a Governor who must be elected by a universal, direct and secret vote (Article 160). Each State must also have a Legislative Council comprised of representatives elected according to the principle of proportional representation (Article 162). According to the Constitution, it is the responsibility of each states' Legislative Council to enact their own Constitution in order "to organize their branches of government" along the guidelines of the national Constitution, which in principle guarantees the autonomy of the States (Article 159).

Consequently, each State has constitutional power to enact its own sub-national constitution in order to organize the state's Legislative and Executive branches of government, and to regulate the state's own organ for audit control. But in spite of these regulations on the organization and functioning of the State branches of government, the scope of States' powers has also been seriously limited by the 1999 Constitution, particularly due to the fact that for the first time in federal history, the Constitution refers to a national legislation for the establishment of the general regulation on this matter.

In effect, and in relation to the States' Legislative branch of government, the 1999 Constitution states that the organization and functioning of the States' Legislative Councils must be regulated by a *national statute* (Article 162), a manifestation of centralism never envisioned, according to which the national Legislative power has the power to enact legislation in order to determine the organization and functioning of all of the State legislatures.

According to this power, the National Assembly has sanctioned an Organic Law for the State Legislative Councils (2001)[51] in which detailed regulations are established regarding their organization and functioning, and in addition, even without constitutional authorization, regarding the statutes and attributions of the Legislative Council members, as well as regarding the general rules for the exercise of the legislative functions, or the law enacting procedure itself. With this national regulation, the effective contents of the State Constitutions regarding their Legislative branch have been voided and are limited to repeat what is established in the said national organic law or statute.

51 *Official Gazette* N° 37.282 of September 13, 2001.

Additionally, the possibility of organizing the Executive branch of government of each state was also limited by the 1999 Constitution, which has established the basic rules concerning the Governors as head of the executive branch. The Constitution has additional regulations referring to the public administration (national, states and municipal), public employees (civil service), and the administrative procedures and public contracts in all of the three levels of government. All of these rules have also been developed in two national Organic Laws on Public Administration[52] and on Civil Service.[53] Therefore, state constitutions have also been voided of real content in these matters, have limited scope, and their norms tend to just repeat what has been established in the national organic laws or statutes.

Finally, regarding other states organs, in 2001, the National Assembly also sanctioned a Law on the appointment of the States' Controller,[54] which limits the powers of the State Legislative Councils on the matter without constitutional authorization. In addition, the national intervention regarding the various state Constitutions and their respective regulations in relation to their own state organizations, has been completed by the Constitutional Chamber of the Supreme Tribunal of Justice. Specifically, the Constitutional Chamber of the Supreme Tribunal of Justice's rulings after the enactment of the 1999 Constitution included the annulment of the Articles of three state constitutions creating an Office of the Peoples' Defender, on the grounds that Citizens rights is a matter reserved to the national (federal) level of government.[55]

As mentioned, the National Constitution establishes three levels of territorial autonomy and regulates the distribution of state powers, directly regulating the local or municipal government in an extensive manner. Therefore, the states' constitutions and legislations can regulate municipal or local government only according to what is established in the national Constitution, and in the National Organic Law on Municipal Power,[56] which leaves very little room for the state regulation.

Thus, without any possibility for the state legislatures to regulate anything related to civil, economic, social, cultural, environmental or political rights; and with the limited powers to regulate their own branches of government, as well as other state organizations including the General Comptroller and Peoples' Defender, very little scope has been left for the contents of sub-national constitutions.

2. The constitutional system of distribution of powers within the national, state and municipal levels of government

Federalism is based on an effective distribution of powers within the various levels of government, and in Venezuela, between the national, states and municipal

52 *Official Gazette* N° 6.147 Extra of November 17, 2014.

53 *Official Gazette* N° 37.522 of September 6, 2002.

54 *Official Gazette* N° 37.304 of October 16, 2001.

55 See decisions N° 1182 of October 11, 2000, N° 1395 of August 7, 2001 and N° 111 of February 12, 2004 (States of Mérida, Aragua and Lara), in *Revista de Derecho Público*, N° 84, Editorial Jurídica Venezolana, Caracas, 2000, pp. 177 ff; and in *Revista de Derecho Público* N° 85-88, Editorial Jurídica Venezuela, Caracas, 2001.

56 *Official Gazette* N° 6.015 Extra. of December 28,2010.

levels. Accordingly, the National Constitution enumerates the competencies attributed in an exclusive way to the national (Article 156), state (Article 154), and municipal (Article 178) levels of government, but in fact, under these regulations, these exclusive matters are almost all reserved to the national level of government, an important portion attributed to the municipalities, and very few of the exclusive matters are attributed to the States.[57]

According to Article 156, the National Power has exclusive competencies in the following matters: international relations; security and defense, nationality and alien status; national police; economic regulations; mining and oil industries; national policies and regulations on education, health, the environment, land use, transportation, industrial, and agricultural production; post, and telecommunications; and legislation concerning constitutional rights; civil law, commercial law, criminal law, the penal system, procedural law and private international law; electoral law; expropriations for the sake of public or social interests; public credit; intellectual, artistic, and industrial property; cultural and archeological treasures; agriculture; immigration and colonization; indigenous people and the territories occupied by them; labor and social security and welfare; veterinary and sanitary hygiene; notaries and public registers; banks and insurances; lotteries, horse racing, and bets in general; and the organization and functioning of the organs of the central authority and the other organs and institutions of the State. The administration of justice, as mentioned, also falls within the exclusive jurisdiction of the national government (Article 156.31).

Article 156,32 of the Constitution also specifies that the national level of government also has legislative attributions on all matter of "national competence", which explicitly attributes to the National Assembly power to legislate regarding the following matters: armed forces and civil protection; monetary policies; the coordination and harmonization of the different taxation authorities; the definition of principles, parameters, and restrictions, and in particular the types of tributes or rates of the taxes of the states and municipalities; as well as the creation of special funds that assure the inter-territorial solidarity; foreign commerce and customs; mining and natural energy resources like hydrocarbon, fallow and waste land; and the conservation, development and exploitation of the woods, grounds, waters, and other natural resources of the country; standards of measurement and quality control; the establishment, coordination, and unification of technical norms and

---

57 See Gustavo J. Linares Benzo, "El sistema venezolano de repartición de competencias", in *El Derecho Público a comienzos del siglo XXI. Estudios homenaje al Profesor Allan R. Brewer-Carías,* Tomo I, Instituto de Derecho Público, UCV, Civitas Ediciones, Madrid, 2003, pp. 702-713; Manuel Rachadell, "La distribución del poder tributario entre los diversos niveles del Poder Público según la Constitución de 1999", in *Revista de Derecho Administrativo,* N° 8 (enero-abril). Editorial Sherwood, Caracas, 2000, pp. 179-205; and Allan R. Brewer Carías, "Consideraciones sobre el régimen de distribución de Competencias del Poder Público en la Constitución de 1999", in *Estudios de Derecho Administrativo: Libro Homenaje a la Universidad Central de Venezuela,* Volumen I. Imprenta Nacional, Caracas, 2001, pp. 107-138, and "La distribución territorial de competencias en la Federación venezolana", in *Revista de Estudios de la Administración Local, Homenaje a Sebastián Martín Retortillo,* N° 291, enero-abril 2003, Instituto Nacional de Administración Pública, Madrid, 2003, pp. 163-200; and "Consideraciones sobre el régimen constitucional de la organización y funcionamiento de los Poderes Públicos", in *Revista Derecho y Sociedad de la Universidad Monteávila,* N° 2 (abril), Caracas, 2001, pp. 135-150.

procedures for construction, architecture, and urbanism, as well as the legislation on urbanism; public health, housing, food safety, environment, water, tourism, and the territorial organization; navigation and air transport, ground transport, maritime and inland waterway transport; post and telecommunication services and radio frequencies; public utilities such as electricity, potable water, and gas. Furthermore, the Constitution attributes to the national power the powers to conclude, approve, and ratify international treaties (Article 154); and legislate on antitrust and the abuse of market power (Articles 113 and 114).

Regarding local governments, Article 178 assigns the municipalities power to govern and administrate the matters attributed to it in the Constitution and the national laws with respect to local life, and within them, the ones related to urban land use, historic monuments, social housing, local tourism, public space for recreation, construction, urban roads and transport, public entertainment, local environmental protection and hygiene, advertising regulations, urban utilities, electricity, water supply, garbage collection and disposal, basic health and education services, municipal police, funerals services, child care and other community matters. Only the matters related to local public events and funerals can be regarded as exclusive powers of the municipalities, and the rest are concurrent with the national government. Nonetheless, these maters can always be regulated by national legislation, as the municipal autonomy is essentially limited (Article 168).

Regarding state competencies, the National Constitution fails to enumerate substantive matters within exclusive state jurisdiction, and only assigns as matters corresponding to them, generally in a concurrent way, the municipal organizations, the non-metallic mineral exploitation, the police, the state roads, the administration of national roads, and the commercial airports and ports (Article 164). Nonetheless, for instance, in the Constitution, the possibility for the state legislature to regulate its own local government is also very limited, being subjected to what is established in the national Organic Municipal Law.

According to the Constitution, State Legislative Councils can enact legislation on matters that are in the States' scope of powers (Article 162). However, these powers are referred to concurrent matters, and according to the National Constitution their exercise depends on the previous enactment of national statutes and regulations (framework laws). As a result, the legislative powers of the States are also very limited, and in any event, the resulting states legislation on concurrent matters must always adhere to the principles of "interdependence, coordination, cooperation, co-responsibility and subsidiary" (Article 165).

On the other hand, regarding residual competencies, the principle of favoring the states as in all federations, although being a constitutional tradition in Venezuela, in the 1999 Constitution has also been limited by expressly assigning the national level of government a parallel and prevalent residual taxation power in matters not expressly attributed to the states or municipalities (Article 156.12). Furthermore, Article 156,33 provides for the jurisdiction of the national power "in all other matters that correspond to it due to their nature or kind," establishing an implicit powers clause in favor of the federal government[58] that has been strengthened by the

58 See. Carlos Ayala Corao, "Naturaleza y Alcance de la Descentralización Estadal", in Allan R. Brewer-Carías *et al.*, *Leyes y reglamentos para la Descentralización Política de la Federación* 94 (Caracas 1990), referring to the *Exposición de Motivos* of the 1961 Constitution.

Constitutional Chamber jurisprudence.[59] In summary, the general residual power allocated to the states is a rather theoretical one, and in practice, in case of doubt, the presumption in favor of federal powers will virtually always prevail.

Another aspect that must be mentioned regarding the distribution of competencies between the national and states level is the provision in the 1999 Constitution, following the same provision of the 1961 Constitution, allowing the possibility of decentralizing competencies via their transfer from the national level to the states.[60] This process was regulated in the 1989 Law on Delimitation, Transfer and Decentralization Competencies between public entities,[61] and even though important efforts for decentralization were made between 1990 and 1994 in order to revert the centralizing tendencies,[62] the process, unfortunately was later abandoned. Since 2003, the transfers of competencies that were made, including health services, started the reversion process, which has been completed in 2008,[63] in particular with the reform of the aforementioned 1989 Decentralization Law, sanctioned by the National Assembly on Mars 17, 2009, reverting to the national level the "exclusive" competence of the States for the management and making use of national highways, bridges and commercial ports located in the States, established in article 164,10 of the Constitution.[64]

3. The End of the Federation and the parallel State organization: The Constitutional State and the Communal State

The result of all this process has been that the Federation in Venezuela has almost disappeared,[65] as a result of a continuous process of voiding the States and Municipalities of the country of almost all their competencies and powers, first, by

59 See decision of the Constitutional Chamber of the Supreme Tribunal of 15 April, 2008, in Revista de Derecho Público, N° 114, Caracas 2008.

60 See José Peña Solís, "Aproximación al proceso de descentralización delineado en la Constitución de 1999", in *Estudios de Derecho Público: Libro Homenaje a Humberto J. La Roche Rincón,* Volumen II. Tribunal Supremo de Justicia, Caracas, 2001, pp. 217-282.

61 The Law was originally sanctioned in 1998. See in *Official Gazette* N° 4153 Extra of December 28, 1989.

62 See Allan R. Brewer-Carías *et al., Leyes y reglamentos para la Descentralización Política de la Federación,* Editorial Jurídica Venezolana, Caracas 1990; *Informe sobre la descentralización en Venezuela 1993. Informe del Ministro de Estado para la Descentralización,* Caracas 1994.

63 See Decree N° 6.543, on the renationalization of the Health Care services in Miranda State, *Official Gazette* N° 39.072 of December 3, 2008.

64 *Official Gazette* N° 39.140 of Mars 17, 2009. For the purpose of this reform, the Constitutional Chamber previously issued decision N° 565 of April 15, 2008 "interpreting" the Constitution, changing the character of such "exclusive" competency into a "concurrent" one. See in http://www.tsj.gov.ve/decisiones/scon/Abril/565-150408-07-1108.htm. See Allan R. Brewer-Carías, "La Sala Constitucional como poder constituyente: la modificación de la forma federal del estado y del sistema constitucional de división territorial del poder público, in *Revista de Derecho Público*, N° 114, (April-June 2008), Editorial Jurídica Venezolana, Caracas 2008, pp. 247-262.

65 See Allan R. Brewer-Carías, and Jan Kleinheisterkamp, "Venezuela: The End of federalism?," in Daniel Halberstam and Mathias Reimann (Editors), *Federalism and Legal Unification: A Comparative Empirical Investigation of Twenty Systems*, Springer, London 2014, pp. 523-543.

centralizing them at the national level; and second, by transferring them to new organizations located outside the organization of the Constitutional State, which conform what has been called the "Communal State" or the "Popular Power State."

This new "State" organization, after being rejected by the people in a referendum held in December 2007, was nonetheless imposed violating the Constitution and the popular will, by means of ordinary legislation in 2010, when the National Assembly sanctioned the Organic Laws on the Popular Power; the Communes; the Communal Economic System; the Public and Communal Planning; the Social Comptrollership; [66] and also sanctioned the reform of the Organic Law of Municipal Public Power and the Public Policy Planning and Coordination of the State Councils, and of the Local Council Public Planning Laws.[67] Finally, in 2012 a Law on the States and Municipalities Power and Competencies Transfer System to Popular Power Organizations was also approved, [68] in order to implement the voiding of the competencies of the organs of the Constitutional State, which was reformed in 2012 and 2014 by the Law on the Communitarian Management of Competencies, Services and other Attributions. [69]

This "Communal State" has been established in parallel to the Constitutional Federal State (the Decentralized Federal Democratic and Social of Law and Justice provided in the Constitution of 1999) established for the exercise of the "Popular Power" not through elected representatives in universal, direct and secret elections, but by means of Citizens Assemblies, controlled by the Central Government.

---

66 See *Official Gazette* N° 6.011 Extra. of Dec. 21, 2010. See on these Laws the comments in Allan R. Brewer-Carías, Claudia Nikken, Luis A. Herrera Orellana, J. M. Alvarado Andrade, José Ignacio Hernández, Adriana Vigilanza, *Leyes Orgánicas sobre el Poder Popular y el Estado Comunal (Los Consejos Comunales, las Comunas, la Sociedad Socialista y el Sistema Económico Comunal)*, Editorial Jurídica Venezolana, Caracas 2011.

67 See *Official Gazette* N° 6.015 Extra. of Dec. 28, 2010.

68 See *Official Gazette* N° 39954 of June 28, 2012. See on this Decree Law the comments of José Luis Villegas Moreno, "Hacia la instauración del Estado Comunal en Venezuela: Comentario al Decreto Ley Orgánica de la Gestión Comunitaria de Competencia, Servicios y otras Atribuciones, en el contexto del Primer Plan Socialista-Proyecto Nacional Simón Bolívar 2007-2013, in *Revista de Derecho Público*, N° 130 (Estudios sobre los decretos leyes 2010-2011), Editorial Jurídica Venezolana, Caracas 2012, pp. 129-138; Juan Cristóbal Carmona Borjas, "Decreto con rango, valor y fuerza de Ley Orgánica para la Gestión Comunitaria de Competencias, Servicios y otras Atribuciones, *Idem*, pp.139-146; Celilia Sosa G,. "El carácter orgánico de un Decreto con fuerza de Ley (no habilitado) para la gestión comunitaria que arrasa lentamente con los Poderes estadales y municipales de la Constitución," *Idem*, pp. 147-157; José Ignacio Hernández, "Reflexiones sobre el nuevo régimen para la Gestión Comunitaria de Competencias, Servicios y otras Atribuciones," *Idem*, pp. 157-164; Alfredo Romero Mendoza, "Comentarios sobre el Decreto con rango, valor y fuerza de Ley Orgánica para la Gestión Comunitaria de Competencias, Servicios y otras Atribuciones," *Idem*, pp. 167-176; and Enrique J. Sánchez falcón, "El Decreto con Rango, Valor y Fuerza de Ley Orgánica para la Gestión Comunitaria de Competencias, Servicios y otras Atribuciones o la negación del federalismo cooperativo y descentralizado," *Idem*, pp. 177-184.

69 See *Official Gazette* N° 40.540 of Nov. 13, 2014. See the previous reform in *Official Gazette* N° 39954 of June, 28, 2012

In this way the Constitutional State has been progressively "deconstitutionalized,"[70] originating a bizarre public parallel organization, with two States and two ways of exercising sovereignty, one, the Constitutional State governed by the Constitution and the other, the Communal or Socialist State, governed by unconstitutional organic laws, bur arranged in such a way that the latter has the means in order to strangling the former, surrounding it in order to destroy it. For such purpose the already mentioned Law on the Communitarian Management of Competencies, Services and other attributions was enacted in order to regulate the process of transfer of powers, competencies and resources, from the National Power and the political entities (States and Municipalities) to the popular organizations (Social Property Communal Enterprises) controlled by the Central Government. The purpose of this Law is precisely the voiding of powers and competencies of the Constitutional Federal State in the benefit of the Communal State.

III. SOME GENERAL COMMENTS ON THE VARIOUS NATIONAL STATE ACTS AND THEIR CLASSIFICATION

According to the 1999 Constitution, National State acts in Venezuelan Public Law are the following: (i) acts issued by the National Assembly (Legislative Power), which are the "laws" (statutes) (art. 202) and the Parliamentary Resolutions (without the form of statute) (art. 187); (ii) the acts of the National Executive (Executive Power) which are the decree laws (Art. 236.8), the acts of government (e.g. 236.7); (iii) the acts of Public Administration, which are the Regulations (Art. 236.10) and the administrative acts (Art. 259,9); (iv) the acts or decisions issued by the courts (*sentencias*) (Art. 253); and (v) the administrative acts and Regulations issued by the other branches of government, that is, the Administrative organs of the Judicial Power (*Dirección Ejecutiva de la Magistratura*) (Art. 267), and organs of the Citizen Power (Art. 273) and of the Electoral Power (Art. 292), which are administrative acts.

All these State acts, apart from the *decisions* issued by the courts, can be classified following two different criteria, referred to their content, and to their addressees.

According to their content, the distinction is made based on the normative or non-normative character of the State act, that is, between those acts that contains norms (general provisions), which are to be incorporated in the legal order; and those that contain decisions that are not of normative character. In 1964, I referred to this distinction pointing out that the normative acts "produce *general, impersonal and objective effects*;" and that the non-normative acts "produce *particular, individual*

70 See Allan R. Brewer-Carías, "The Process of "Deconstitutionalization" of the Venezuelan Constitutional State, as the Most Important Current Constitutional Issue in Venezuela," *Duquesne Law Review*, Volume 51, Number 2, Spring 2013, Pittsburgh 2013, pp. 349-386; "The 'Bolivarian Revolution' in Venezuela and the regime's comptempt of Constitucional law,", en Uwe Kischel und Christian Kirchner (Coord.), *Ideologie und Weltanschauung im Recht*, Gesellschaft für Rechtsvergleichtung e.V., Rechtsvergleichung und Rechtsvereinheitlichung, Mohr Siebeck, Tübingen 2012, pp. 121-148.

and subjective effects."[71] I ratified this approach in 1979, referring to the classification of administrative acts according to its effects, expressing that they:

> "can be classified in a different way: a distinction can be made between the acts of "general effects," that is, of normative content, which consequently creates, declares, modifies or extinguishes general legal situations; and the acts of particular effects that are those of non-normative content, that is, which creates, declares, modifies and extinguishes particular legal situations." [72]

This distinction is only based on the normative or non-normative content of the act, and not in its addressees, which means that an act of normative content (like a statute or a Regulation) can be addressed to an undetermined number of persons, and also to a particular number of persons. In both cases it has normative content, but it can be either of general applicability or of particular applicability.

That means that, according to their addressees or recipients, there is a second distinction of State acts based on their recipients, that can be established between those that are directed to an undetermined and undeterminable number of persons; and those directed to a determined and determinable number of persons to which they are directed. In 1963, Eloy Lares Martínez referred to this distinction pointing out that the former "are those addressed to indeterminate persons," while the latter "are those that refers to one or few persons, but all of them determined."[73] I also referred to this distinction in 1979 highlighting the existence of acts "directed to an undetermined number of persons" and acts "directed to a determined or determinable group of persons." [74]

---

71 Regarding this distinction, and referring to administrative acts, I have used the "general administrative acts and individual administrative acts." See Allan R. Brewer-Carías, *Las instituciones fundamentales del derecho administrativo y la jurisprudencia venezolana*, Universidad Central de Venezuela, Caracas 1964, reproduced in the collective book: José Ignacio Hernández (Coordinator), *Libro Homenaje a Las instituciones fundamentales del derecho administrativo y la jurisprudencia venezolana del profesor Allan R. Brewer-carías en el cincuenta aniversario de su publicación 1964-2014*, Editorial Jurídica venezolana, Caracas 2015, p. 547.

72 See Allan R. Brewer-Carías, "El recurso contencioso-administrativo contra los actos de efectos particulares," in *El Control jurisdiccional de los Poderes Públicos en Venezuela*, Instituto de Derecho Público, Facultad de Ciencias Jurídicas y Políticas, Universidad Central de Venezuela, Caracas 1979, pp. 169-194. The text was also published in Allan R. Brewer-Carías, *Jurisprudencia de la Corte Suprema 1930-1974 y Estudios de derecho administrativo, Tomo v: La Jurisdicción contencioso-administrativa, Vol. 1. Los órganos y el recurso de anulación,* Instituto de Derecho Público, Universidad Central de Venezuela, Caracas 1978, pp. 58-59. In such Article I followed what I had expressed one year before in my book: Allan R. Brewer-Carías, *El control de la constitucionalidad de los actos estatales*, Editorial Jurídica Venezolana, Caracas 1977, p. 8. See also, Allan R. Brewer-Carías, "Sobre la importancia para el derecho administrativo de la noción de acto administrativo y de sus efectos," in *Los efectos y la ejecución de los actos administrativos. Terceras Jornadas Internacionales de Derecho Administrativo Allan Randolph Brewer-Carías*, Fundacion Estudios de Derecho Administrativo, Caracas 1997, p. 37

73 Regarding this distinction, Lares Martínez used the following expressions: "general acts or of general effects" and "individual acts that is, acts of particular effects." See Eloy Lares Martínez, *Manual de Derecho Administrativo* (1963), Universidad Central de Venezuela, XIV Edition, Caracas 2013, pp. 188-189.

74 See Allan R. Brewer-Carías, "El recurso contencioso-administrativo contra los actos de efectos particulares" en *El Control jurisdiccional de los Poderes Públicos en Venezuela*, Instituto de Derecho Público, Facultad de Ciencias Jurídicas y Políticas, Universidad Central de Venezuela, Caracas 1979, pp. 172 ss.

The distinction in this latter case, is constructed regarding the addressees of the act, not on their content that can be normative or non-normative, being the *acts of general applicability* addressed to everybody, in the sense of an indeterminate and indeterminable number of persons or subjects, without distinction, having therefore, in general, *erga omnes* effects; and, on the contrary, being the *acts of particular applicability* those that *that are not of general applicability,* that are addressed to one person or entity, or a group of persons or entities, which are identified or can be determinate.

Both distinctions have been used in the Constitution and in many legal texts, although in a mixed way, in order to determine, for example, the standing to sue for judicial review of State acts, using the expressions "*general acts*" (Arts. 259; 266.5) or "*acts of general effects,*" including in such expressions both, normative acts and acts that are of general applicability; and in the expressions "*individual acts*" (Arts. 259; 266.5) or "*acts of particular effects,*" including in such expressions both, non-normative acts and acts that are of particular applicability.

This is the sense followed, for instance, in the Organic Law of the Supreme Court of Justice of 1976, the Organic Law of the Supreme Tribunal of Justice of 2010 and the Organic Law of the Administrative Contentious Jurisdiction of 2010.

In effect, regarding the Organic Law of the Supreme Court of Justice of 1976, articles 42.4 and 112 referring to the State acts that were subjected to judicial review by such Supreme Court, and to the standing to sue, stated as follows:

> "Article 42.4. It is the power of the Court as the highest Tribunal of the Republic: 4. To declare the total or partial nullity of *regulations* and all other *acts of general effects* of the National Executive Power, contrary to the Constitution."[75]

> "Article 112. Any natural of juridical person plainly capable, affected on his rights and interests by a law, regulation, ordinance or other act of general effects issued by any of the national, states or municipal deliberative bodies or by the National Executive Power, can request before the Court its nullity because unconstitutionality or illegality, except the cases indicated in the Transitory Provisions."[76]

According to the two distinctions made regarding acts of State, this expression used by this Law referring to "acts of general effects" comprise acts of normative content and also acts of general applicability. Consequently, acts of non-normative content or that are not of general applicability could not be challenged through a popular action before the Supreme Court.

---

75 "*Artículo 42.4. Es de la competencia de la Corte como más alto Tribunal de la República: 4. Declarar la nulidad total o parcial de los reglamentos y demás* actos de efectos generales *del Poder Ejecutivo Nacional, que colidan con la Constitución.*"

76 "*Artículo 112. Toda persona natural o jurídica plenamente capaz, que sea afectada en sus derechos o intereses por ley, reglamento, ordenanza u otro* acto de efectos generales *emanado de alguno de los cuerpos deliberantes nacionales, estadales o municipales o del Poder Ejecutivo Nacional, puede demandar la nulidad del mismo, ante la Corte, por razones de inconstitucionalidad o de ilegalidad, salvo lo previsto en las Disposiciones Transitorias de esta Ley.*"

Regarding specifically to administrative acts, the provision of article 26 of the Organic Law of the Supreme Tribunal of Justice of 2010, states as follows:

> "Article 26. It is the power of the Politico Administrative Chamber of the Supreme Tribunal of Justice [to decide on]: 5. The nullity suits against administrative acts of general and particular effects issued by the President of the Republic, the Executive Vice President of the republic, the Ministers, as well as by the highest authorities of the other organs with constitutional rank, when the competence is not assigned to other organ of the Administrative Contentious Jurisdiction due to the content."[77]

The same can be say regarding the article 9.1 of the Organic Law on the Administrative Contentious Jurisdiction of 2010, which states that:

> "Article 9. The organs of the Administrative Contentious Jurisdiction have the power to decide about: 1. Challenge filed against *administrative acts of general and particular effects* when contrary to the rule of law, even due to power deviation."[78]

In this two Laws regarding judicial review of administrative acts, the expression "*acts of general and particular effects,*" when referred to administrative acts, comprise all acts of normative and non-normative content as well as acts of general applicability and of particular applicability. All can be challenged before the Judicial review of Administrative actions courts.

Regarding the two mentioned distinction of acts of State, between normative and non-normative acts, and acts of general applicability and of particular applicability, also for the purpose of establishing rules for judicial review, the jurisprudence of the Supreme Court has also applied it, although in a mixed way, including whiting the *general acts*, altogether those that are of normative content and those that are of general applicability.

For instance, in decision of 14 March of 1960, the former Federal Court stated that the *acts of general effects* generally challenged for judicial review through the *actio popularis* are those "that because having normative and general content, applies *erga omnes*, and therefore its enforcement affects and interest everybody without distinction."[79]

---

77 "*Artículo 26. Es de la competencia de la Sala Político Administrativa del Tribunal Supremo de Justicia: 5. Las demandas de nulidad contra los* actos administrativos de efectos generales o particulares *dictados por el Presidente de la República, el Vicepresidente* Ejecutivo de la República, los Ministros o Ministras, así como por las *máximas autoridades de los demás organismos de rango constitucional, cuyo conocimiento no estuviere atribuido a otro órgano de la Jurisdicción Administrativa en razón de* la materia." See *Official Gazette* No. 39483 of August 9, 2010.

78 "*Artículo 9. Los órganos de la Jurisdicción Contencioso Administrativa serán competentes para conocer de: 1. Las impugnaciones que se interpongan contra los* actos administrativos de efectos generales o particulares *contrarios a derecho, incluso por desviación de poder.*" See *Official Gazette*, 39451 of June 22, 2010

79 See in *Official Gazette* No. 26.222 of April 1, 1960. See the abstract in Allan R. Brewer-Carías, *Jurisprudencia de la Corte Suprema 1930-1974 y Estudios de derecho administrativo, Tomo v: La Jurisdicción contencioso-administrativa, Vol. 1. Los órganos y el recurso de anulación,* Instituto de derecho Público, Universidad Central de Venezuela, Caracas 1978, pp. 292-293

Later, in a decision of 24 April 1980 (Case *Fiscal General de la República*), the Supreme Court of Justice followed the same criteria in order to distinguish between acts of general effects and acts of particular effects, arguing as follows:

> "in the case, it has been filed an action of nullity established in article 112, Title V, Chapter II, Second Section of the Supreme Court of Justice. This action is admissible against acts like the one challenged of the General Prosecutor of the Republic Attorney that, because being of normative character, its effects are general, that is, affects all the citizens, and due to that, they have a special procedure to be challenged before the courts, being the most highlighted characteristics the imprescriptible character of the action of nullity (art. 134 LOTSJ) and the generic quality of any citizen to file the popular action."[80].

Also, the First Court of the Administrative Contentious Jurisdiction in a decision of June 1, 1982 on the matter, argued as follows:

> "The Organic Law of the Supreme Court of Justice only distinguishes regarding the recourse of nullity base on illegality, between those directed to challenge the acts of general effects and those directed to challenge the acts of particular effects, being necessary determine, according to such text, to which category refers the current case.
>
> The prevalent Venezuelan doctrine, when interpreting the mentioned provisions, considers that the acts of general effects are only those of normative content. The acts of particular effects are those that in contrary sense lack such content, even when directed to a group of subjects. Brewer Carías distinguishes in this second category between general acts of particular effects the are those directed to a specific group of determined or determinable persons and the individual acts of particular effects directed to a specific legal subject (*El Control Jurisdiccional de los Poderes Públicos en Venezuela*, UCV., pp. 172 y ss). Other opinion considers that acts of general effects in an analogous notion to the one of general acts, that is, the one that creates, modify or extinguishes subjective situations or declares legal certitude regarding an undetermined collectivity of persons. The act of particular effects, or particular act, produce the same effects but regarding one or more determined or determinable persons (See the opinion of the Fiscal General de la República expressed in the file N° 79–573 of this Court, pp. 212 ff.). From the aforementioned it is evident that the character of the act of general effects implies for the doctrine whether the normative character contained in it or the character undetermined of its addressees."[81]

That means, according to this conclusion of the First Court on Contentious Administrative Jurisdiction, that the expression used in the legislation when referred to "acts of general effects" follows the two distinctions made on acts of State, comprising not only the acts of normative character or content, but also the acts of general applicability.

On the other hand, these two classifications of State acts were incorporated in the Organic Law on Administrative Procedures enacted in 1981,[82] regarding the

---

80 See the abstract in Allan R Brewer-Carías, *Tratado de derecho Administrativo. Derecho Público en Iberoamérica. Tomo III. Los actos administrativos y los contratos administrativos.* Editorial Civitas Thomson Reuters, Madrid 2013, pp. 470-472

81 See in *Revista de Derecho Público*, No. 11, Editorial Jurídica Venezolana, Caracas 1982, p. 129.

82 See in *Official Gazette* No. 2818 of July 1, 1981.

classification of the administrative acts according to its effects made through the two approaches already mentioned: first, the normative or non-normative content of the acts; and second, the addressees of the acts.

As I expressed in 1992 when commenting such Organic Law on the classifications of specifically administrative acts:

> "The classification of administrative acts according to their effects is made by the Law under two angles. First, according to the normative or non-normative content of the acts and second, according to the recipients of the acts.
>
> First, according to the normative or non-normative character of administrative acts, these are classified in acts of general effects and acts of particular effects. It can be said, thus, that the Organic Law on Administrative Procedures follows this first way to classify the administrative acts according to their effects, in the sense that it classifies the administrative acts in normative acts (of general effects) and non-normative acts (of particular effects). This is the classification that according to the Organic Law of the Supreme Court of Justice, allows to distinguish the administrative acts of general effects from the administrative acts of particular effects. The former ones [the administrative acts of general effects], are those of normative content, that is, that creates norms that integrate the Legal order; instead, the latter ones, the administrative acts of particular effects, are those that contains a non-normative decision, whether to be applied to one or multiple individuals. It can be said that the Organic Law on Administrative Procedures identifies the administrative acts of general effects, with those that qualified in article 13 as "acts or provisions of general character;" and the administrative acts of particular effects, with those that the same provision qualifies as administrative acts of "particular character." In this provision, when it is established that an administrative act of particular character cannot infringe what is established in an "administrative provision of general character," what is pointing out is that an act of particular effects (on non-normative content) cannot infringe a normative act or an act of general effect, adopting in article 13, the principle of non-singular derogation of regulations or of administrative acts of general effects.
>
> Consequently, it can be said that in article 13 of the Organic Law has the key for the classification of administrative acts according to its content or effects in normative or non-normative acts, identifying the acts of general effects, that is, of general content or character with the normative acts; and consequently, the acts of particular effects or particular content or character those that do not have normative content. [...]
>
> Additionally, in relation to the classification of the acts according to their effects, the Organic Law of Administrative Procedures also allows to classify them according to their effects, in relation to the recipients of the acts.
>
> Thus, it can be said that the Organic Law adopts the classification of the administrative acts according to their recipients, by distinguishing general administrative acts from individual administrative acts. General administrative acts are those aimed at a plurality of individuals, whether formed by an undetermined number of persons or by a determined number of persons; in contrast, individual administrative acts are those aimed at a single individual."[83]

---

83 See Allan R. Brewer-Carías, *El derecho administrativo y la Ley Orgánica de Procedimientos Administrativos. Principios del Procedimiento Administrativo*, Editorial Jurídica Venezolana, Caracas 2002, pp. 143-144.

Based on the aforementioned legal, doctrinal and jurisprudential construction regarding the classification of State acts in Venezuelan law, it can be said that in general, Laws, Decree Law and Executive Regulations, having normative content, they can be also considered in general as of general applicability, that is, directed to an undetermined and undeterminable number of persons, no matter is they are general or special laws or regulations. One such case of those normative acts of general applicability, is for instance, the *Organic Law on Hydrocarbons* of 2001, which regulated all what is related to the exploration, exploitation, refining, industrialization, transport, storage, commercialization and conservation of hydrocarbons, as well as the refined products and the works to be required by such activities (art. 1), which is directed to be applied to an undetermined and undeterminable number of people. [84]

But that doesn't mean that all normative acts are always of general applicability. Normative acts can also be of particular applicability, in spite of containing norms, when they are nonetheless only applied to a determined or determinable group of persons or corporations. This is the case, for instance, of another act in the same Oil sector, the Decree Law No. 5.200 of February 26, 2007, containing the *Law on Migration to Mixed Enterprises of the Association Agreements of the Orinoco Oil Belt as well as the Agreements for the Exploration at Risk and under Shared Profits,* [85] which although being an act of normative content, it was not of general applicability, that is, according to its title and content, it was not a Law issued to be applied to an undetermined and undetermined number of persons, but on the contrary, to be applied to a group of persons or corporations and to specific contracts. Such Decree Law 5.200, in effect, was issued to be applied to the then "*existing associations*" between Petróleos de Venezuela S. A. affiliates, and the private sector operating in the Orinoco Belt, and to the so-called "Exploration at Risk and Profit-Sharing Agreements" according to the Congress authorization adopted in 1995, [86] imposing for them to "be adjusted to the legal framework governing the national oil industry by becoming mixed companies pursuant to the provisions set forth in the Organic Hydrocarbons Law" (art. 1)

Decree Law 5.200, therefore, was only and specifically addressed to a reduced number of juridical persons and contracts, the Association Agreements, and their Parties, that where in existence at the time of the issuing of the Decree Law (February 2007), ordering them to adjust to the legal framework that was established in the 2001 Organic Hydrocarbons Law, and to become mixed companies pursuant to the provisions set forth in such Organic Law. Consequently, Decree Law No 5.200, as it is expressed in the same article 1st, was exclusively addressed to be apply, beside the public enterprises involved in the process like *Petróleos de Venezuela, S.A.* (PDVSA) and *Corporación Venezolana de Petróleo, S.A.*, to the following legal entities: *First*, the enterprises: *Petrozuata, S.A., Sincrudos de Oriente, S.A., Sincor, S.A., Petrolera Cerro Negro S.A. and Petrolera Hamaca, C.A.*, that were Association or Strategic Agreements developing activities in the Orinoco Belt; *second*, the Association

84 See in *Official Gazette* No. 37.323 of November 13, 2001

85 See in *Official Gazette* No. 38.623 de 16-2-2007.

86 Venezuelan Congress, "Resolution Approving the Execution of Association Agreements for Exploration at Risk of New Areas and the Production of Hydrocarbons under the Shared Profits System in Eight of the Areas Determined by the Ministry of Energy and Mines," *Official Gazette*, No. 35,988 of June 26, 1996.

Agreements of *Golfo de Paria Oeste, Golfo de Paria Este* and *La Ceiba*, as well as the companies or consortia incorporated in their execution, that were developing activities under the modality of Exploration at Risk and Profit Sharing; *third*, *Orifuels Sinovensa, S.A.*, and *forth*: to all the affiliates of such companies that conduct business activities in the Orinoco Belt, and throughout the production chain.

Specifically, the purpose of the Decree Law was to order the abovementioned companies to compulsory transfer all the activities that they were developing up to that date, "to the new mixed companies" that the decree ordered to be constituted. Consequently, through the Decree Law 5.200 with such particular effects, the National Executive not only decided to unilaterally terminate specific Agreements entered into by the State with foreign enterprises, but to order the entities enumerated in the text of the Decree Law to transfer its activities to new mixed companies that were to be established, in which the *Corporación Venezolana de Petróleo, S.A.* or another affiliate of Petróleos de Venezuela, S.A. (PDVSA), was to have a minimum 60% share of the equity (Art. 2).

In addition, in its article 4, the Decree Law gave the enumerated *private sector companies that had been part of the extinguished Orinoco Belt Association Agreements* and the so-called Exploration at Risk and Profit-Sharing Agreements, a term of four (4) month that started on the date the Decree Law was published (February 26, 2007), and that finalized on June 26, 2007, to "agree on the terms and conditions of their *possible participation* in the new Mixed Companies." If no agreement was reached "*on the incorporation and operation of the Mixed Companies," then the Decree Law established that the Republic, through* Petróleos de Venezuela, S.A. or any of its affiliates, was to *directly take over the activities* exercised by the associations to ensure their continuity, by reason of their character of public use and social interest (Art. 5); which effectively occur.

Other provision of the Decree Law that could be highlighted, also of particular effects, that is, exclusively directed to the enumerated Orinoco Belt associations and of the so-called Exploration at Risk and Profit-Sharing Agreements, is the one included in Article 7, which provided that the infrastructure, transportation services and improvements of the affected Associations agreements, were to be "freely used" according to the guidelines that were to be issued by the Ministry for Energy and Petroleum.

Consequently, Decree Law 5.200, was an act of State that *was not of general applicability*, in the sense that it was not addressed to an indeterminate and undeterminable universe of persons, but on the contrary to the aforementioned ones.

Finally, and specifically regarding the concept of "law" in the Venezuelan constitutional system, it must be pointed out that according to article 202 of the Constitution, it is not constructed by its normative content or their general applicability, but rather by the way they are approved and enacted. As mentioned by Eloy Lares Martínez:

> "the definition of law [set forth in article 202 of the Constitution] has been evidently made from the purely formal point of view. According to our constitutional order law is any act sanctioned by the National Assembly according to the procedure established in the Fundamental Charter in order to sanction laws. [...] It is not thus, the general or individual content what characterizes the legislative act, but the organ that enact it and the procedure followed for its conception.

Consequently, in our country laws are all the decisions issued by the National Assembly according to the aforementioned procedure, no matter which its content could be.

It has to be recognized that the majority of laws have a general and abstract content, that is, they contain impersonal and objective legal rules; and only some of them have a non-normative, particular and specific content, as the ones that authorize the National Executive to negotiate a loan [...]

There is no problem in determine if a legislative provision has or not general character, being enough for such purpose to establish if it is or not applicable to an undetermined group of persons [...]

It is then possible to affirm with certainty that in our positive law the sign of generality is not of the essence of the [concept of] law, but indeed, of its nature. That is, the acts sanctioned by the National Assembly have commonly normative character; only exceptionally they are decisions on particular and specific cases."[87]

Since 1964 I have also expressed my coincident opinion regarding the formal definition of Law in the Venezuelan constitutional system, without any reference to its content or recipients,[88] following the doctrine established by the Supreme Court of Justice, in decision of March 15, 1962, as follows:

"Article 162 of the Constitution [equivalent to article 203 of the 1999 Constitution] defines law as the acts sanctioned by the Legislative Chambers acting as co-legislative bodies."

According to this criterion which is also expressed in previous Constitutions, the Venezuelan constitutional trend has separated, in this point, from the doctrine that add other conditions like the generality and abstract character, in order to determine the concept of law. The Constitution has only adopted that simple but very precise way to characterize such concept, which means that the mere circumstance of a provision to be sanctioned by the Legislative Chambers as co-legislators is enough for a law to be configured in our legal order. This clear and precise concept of what the Constitution considers as Law, do not admit and could not admit interpretations contrary to its text, and much less the inclusion of other requirement or conditions that, if is possible to be attributed or be accepted in legislations of other countries where the concept of law respond to other doctrinal criteria, there are in no way according to what the Venezuela Constitution has strictly established."89

The aforementioned 1962 decision of the Supreme Court of Justice was issued in a constitutional process for judicial review of the Law approving a contract entered into between the Republic and the Banco de Venezuela, which was at that time a

87 See Eloy Lares Martínez, *Manual de Derecho Administrativo* (1963), Universidad Central de Venezuela, XIV Edition, Caracas 2013, pp. 94-95

88 See Allan R. Brewer-Carías, *Las instituciones fundamentales del derecho administrativo y la jurisprudencia venezolana*, Universidad Central de Venezuela, Caracas 1964, reproduced in the collective book: José Ignacio Hernández (Coordinator), *Libro Homenaje a Las instituciones fundamentales del derecho administrativo y la jurisprudencia venezolana del profesor Allan R. Brewer-carías en el cincuenta aniversario de su publicación 1964-2014*, Editorial Jurídica venezolana, Caracas 2015, pp. 456-458.

89 See the abstract of the decisión of the Supreme Court of Justice of March 15, 1962, in Allan R. Brewer-Carías, Allan R. Brewer-Carías, *Jurisprudencia de la Corte Suprema 1930-1974 y Estudios de derecho administrativo, Tomo I. Ordenamiento Constitucional y funcional del Estado,* Instituto de derecho Público, Universidad Central de Venezuela, Caracas 1975, pp. 210-211.

private bank to perform services to the National Treasury. Due to the lack of general effects and general applicability of the challenged Law, the discussion resulting from the question of the normative or non-normative character of the law was completely rejected by the Court, concluding that "in order to qualify a legal provision as a law, it is enough only to determine if it is or not an act sanctioned by the Chambers as co-legislator bodies," ratifying, as it had decided in numerous other previous cases that not only laws with general and abstract content are considered as "law" according to the Constitution, but also other laws sanctioned by the Legislative Chambers lacking "general application and abstract content."[90]

All acts of State, whichever could be their content (normative or non-normative content) or their addressees (undetermined or determined number of persons), all are subjected to judicial review, by the Constitutional Jurisdiction (Constitutional Chamber of the Supreme Tribunal of Justice) in the case of the statutes, decree laws, acts of government or Parliamentary acts without the form of statute, or by the Contentious Administrative Jurisdiction, is the case of Regulations and administrative acts. Judicial acts (sentencias) of the courts are subject to judicial review through the ordinary or extraordinary judicial recourses (appeals, cassation).

90 Idem.

PART TWO

GENERAL PRINCIPLES OF ADMINISTRATIVE LAW AND OF PUBLIC ADMINISTRATION

I. BASIS OF ADMINISTRATIVE LAW AND PROCEDURE

1. The Principle of Legality and the Rule of Law

The most important principles of Venezuelan public law are the principles of supremacy of the Constitution and of legality. The 1999 Constitution,[1] in effect, expressly set forth that "[t]he Constitution is the supreme norm and the foundation of the legal order," to which all persons and public entities are subjected (Articles 7 and 131).[2] Only on matters of human rights is the principle of supremacy of the Constitution conditioned, because the same constitutional text gives prevalence to the provisions of international treaties on human rights over the internal legal system, if they contain a more favorable provision for their enjoyment and exercise (Article 23).

The supremacy of the Constitution is also confirmed through the declaration in the 1999 Constitution of the State as being a Democratic and Social Rule of Law State (*Estado Democrático y Social de Derecho*) following the model already adopted in the 1961 Constitution.[3] This implies that all the activities of all public entities must be subjected to the Constitution, statutes, regulations and all other applicable provisions adopted by the competent authorities; that is the principle of legality regarding administrative activities of the State implies the obligation of all Public Administration organs and entities to act subject to the law.[4] In this regard, Article 137 of the Constitution declares that "the Constitution and the law define the

---

1 See *Official Gazette* N° 5.453 of Mars 24, 2000. See in general on the 1999 Constitution, Allan R. Brewer-Carías, *La Constitución de 1999. Derecho Constitucional Venezolano*, 2 Vols., Editorial Jurídica Venezolana, Caracas 2004.

2 I was the drafter of this provision in the 1999 National Constituent Assembly. See Allan R. Brewer-Carías, *Debate Constituyente, (Aportes a la Asamblea Nacional Constituyente)*, Vol. II, (Septiembre 9-Octubre 17, 1999), Fundación de Derecho Público-Editorial Jurídica Venezolana, Caracas 1999, p. 24.

3 See in general, Allan R. Brewer-Carías, *Cambio político y reforma del Estado en Venezuela. Contribución al estudio del Estado democrático y social de derecho*, Editorial Tecnos, Madrid 1975.

4 See Antonio Moles Caubet, "El principio de legalidad y sus implicaciones" in *Revista de la Facultad de Ciencias Jurídicas y Políticas*, N° 82, Universidad Central de Venezuela, Caracas 1991, pp. 49-115; Allan R. Brewer-Carías, *Principios Fundamentales del Derecho Público (Constitucional y Administrativo)*, Editorial Jurídica Venezolana, Caracas 2005, p. 33.

attributions of the organs of the State, to which they must conform;" and Article 141 of the same Constitution referring to the principles governing Public Administration establishes that it must act "fully subject to the statutes and the law" (*con sometimiento pleno a la ley y al derecho*). Consequently, all the activities of the State and in particular of the organs and entities of Public Administration must be performed according to what is provided in the law, and within the limits it establishes. In addition, Article 4 of the Organic Law of Public Administration (OLPA)[5] expressly repeats the principle of legality regarding Public Administration by stating that:

> "Public Administration is organized and acts in conformity with the principle of legality, so the assignment, distribution and exercise of its attributions is subject to the Constitution, the statutes and administrative acts of general effects previously enacted in a formal way according to the law as a guaranty and protection of public freedoms established in the protagonist democratic and participative regime."

The consequence of these principles of constitutional supremacy and of legality is the provision in the Constitution of a whole system for the judicial control (judicial review) of State acts, on the one side, through a complete system of judicial review of a mixed character, combining the diffuse (Article 334) and the concentrated methods of judicial review, the latter attributed to the Constitutional Chamber of the Supreme Tribunal (Article 336) (*Jurisdicción Constitucional);*[6] and on the other, through a complete system of judicial review of administrative action (*Jurisdicción Contencioso Administrativa*) (Articles 259 and 297).[7]

2. Powers of State Organs

One of the most important consequences of the principle of legality is that the powers and competencies assigned to all public entities and State organs must always be expressly provided in a statute, following the principle of territorial distribution of State Powers between the National State, the states of the federation

---

5 See *Official Gazette* N° 6.147 Extra. of November 17, 2014. See on the Organic Law on Public Administration, Allan R. Brewer-Carías, Rafael Chavero Gazdik and Jesús María Alvarado Andrade, *Ley Orgánica de la Administración Pública,* Editorial Jurídica Venezolana, Caracas 2009, p. 17.

6 See Allan R. Brewer-Carías, *Instituciones Políticas y Constitucionales,* Vol. VI: *La justicia constitucional,* Universidad Católica del Táchira-Editorial Jurídica Venezolana, Caracas-San Cristóbal 1996; *El sistema de justicia constitucional en la Constitución de 1999 (Comentarios sobre su desarrollo jurisprudencial y su explicación, a veces errada, en la Exposición de Motivos)*, Editorial Jurídica Venezolana, Caracas 2000; *La Justicia Constitucional. Procesos y procedimientos constitucionales*, Universidad Nacional Autónoma de México, México 2007; Allan R. Brewer-Carías and Víctor Hernández Mendible, *Ley Orgánica del Tribunal Supremo de Justicia,* Editorial Jurídica Venezolana, Caracas 2010.

7 See Allan R. Brewer-Carías, *Instituciones Políticas y Constitucionales,* Vol. VII: *La justicia contencioso administrativa,* Universidad Católica del Táchira-Editorial Jurídica Venezolana, Caracas-San Cristóbal 1996; Allan R. Brewer-Carías and Víctor Hernández Mendible, *Ley Orgánica de la Jurisdicción Contencioso Administrativa*, Editorial Jurídica Venezolana, Caracas 2010, p. 9 ff.

and the municipalities, as a result of the federal form of government (Article 136).[8] In this matter, Venezuela is one of the countries that since the beginning of the nineteenth century adopted the federal form of government,[9] nonetheless giving progressively origin to a "centralized federation."[10] But notwithstanding this centralized tendency in the organization of the State, the legal consequence of the vertical distribution of Powers in a federal framework is the existence of three levels of Public Administration: National Public Administration, State Public Administration and Municipal Public Administration.[11] All three levels of Public Administration are subjected to the general principles established in the Constitution regarding central public administration organization (Articles 236 and 20), and decentralized public administration (Articles 142 and 300); administrative action (Article 141); civil service (Articles 145 to 149) and their liability (Article 139); assets of the State (Articles 12, 181 and 304); access to public information (Article 143); public contracts (Articles 150 and 151); State liability (*responsabilidad patrimonial del Estado*) (Article 140); and control of administrative management (Articles 62, 66, 287 and 315).

As mentioned, one of the consequences of the principle of legality particularly regarding Public Administration is that in order to protect public liberties in a democratic State, the organs and entities of Public Administration must always be authorized in an express way through a statute (competency)[12] and when enacting administrative acts that could affect in any way the rights and interests of the individuals (Article 4 of OLPA), it must have a specific legal basis or cause.[13]

In other words, all public officials can only act when a specific statute gives him express attributions, and that is why in Venezuela it is compulsory for public officials, to always formally and legally justify their actions being obliges, as it is set forth in article 9 and 18.5 of the Organic Law on Administrative Procedure, being

8 See my proposal in Allan R. Brewer-Carías, *Debate Constituyente (Aportes a la Asamblea Nacional Constituyente)*, Vol. II, September 9-October 17, 1999, Fundación de Derecho Público, Caracas 1999, pp. 161-164.

9 See Allan R. Brewer-Carías, *Instituciones Políticas y Constitucionales,* Vol. II: *El Poder Público: Nacional, Estadal y Municipal*, Universidad Católica del Táchira-Editorial Jurídica Venezolana, Caracas-San Cristóbal 1996, p. 111 ff.

10 See in general, on the federation, Allan R. Brewer-Carías, "La descentralización política en la Constitución de 1999: Federalismo y Municipalismo (una reforma insuficiente y regresiva)," in *Boletín de la Academia de Ciencias Políticas y Sociales*, N° 138, Year LXVIII, January-December 2001, Caracas 2002, pp. 313-359.

11 See in general, Allan R. Brewer-Carías, "Consideraciones sobre el régimen de distribución de competencias del Poder Público en la Constitución de 1999," in Fernando Parra Aranguren and Armando Rodríguez García (Eds.), *Estudios de Derecho Administrativo. Libro Homenaje a la Universidad Central de Venezuela*, Vol. II, Tribunal Supremo de Justicia, Caracas 2001, pp. 107-136; Allan R. Brewer-Carías, "Consideraciones sobre el régimen constitucional de la organización y funcionamiento de los Poderes Públicos," in *Revista Derecho y Sociedad de la Universidad Monteávila*, N° 2 (April), Caracas 2001, pp. 135-150.

12 See Allan R. Brewer-Carías, *Principios del Régimen Jurídico de la Organización Administrativa*, Editorial Jurídica Venezolana, Caracas 1991, p. 47 ff.

13 See Organic Law on Administrative Procedures, *Official Gazette* N° 2.818 Extra. July 1, 1981. See Allan R. Brewer-Carías, *El Derecho Administrativo y la Ley Orgánica de Procedimientos Administrativos. Principios del Procedimiento Administrativo*, Editorial Jurídica Venezolana, Caracas 2009, pp. 169-175.

obligated to always make reference to the express provisions in the Law (statute), which constitute the legal foundation (base legal) of their actions.

Consequently, the actions of public officials accomplished without any legal attribution, according to article 26 of the Organic Law on Public Administration as well as to article 19.1 of the Organic Law on Administrative Procedures, must be considered null and void because such public official has acted with "manifest lack of attributions" (*incompetencia manifiesta*). The importance of the Organic Law on Public Administration provision is that it adds that the action taken by a public official manifestly without attribution, "are to be considered inexistent."

3. Principles governing administrative actions: *Bona fide* and legitimate expectation.

Administrative acts, even when issued exercising discretionary powers, according to Article 12 of the Organic Law on Administrative Procedures (OLAP),[14] must always be issued according to their factual basis; must always correspond to the purposes of the legal provision authorizing the action; must always maintain the due proportionality (which implies the principles of reasonability, logic, coherence, equality, impartiality, bona fides, and legitimate expectation); and must always fulfill all the conditions and formalities established for their validity and efficacy.[15] All these principles are complemented in Article 1 of the Organic Law on Public Administration that provides that the activity of Public Administration will be based on the principles of economy, celerity, simplicity, accountability, efficacy, proportionality, opportunity, objectivity, impartiality, participation, accessibility, uniformity, modernity, honesty, transparence, bona fide, formal parallelism, responsibility, subjection to the law, and suppression of non-essential formalities.

In particular, and deriving from the principle of bona fides, the principle of legitimate confidence or legitimate expectation (*confianza legítima*) has been recognized as one that governs administrative action, implying that when the Administration, through its action and relations with an individual, has created legitimate expectations, it must then respect such expectations.[16]

The legitimate confidence or legitimate expectation principle is connected with legal safety that governs State action, protecting the relations between state and individuals, and adjusting itself more harmoniously than other principles (such as

---

14 See Organic Law on Administrative Procedures in *Official Gazette* Nº 2.818 Extra. of July 1, 1981. See on this Law, Allan R. Brewer-Carías et al., *Ley Orgánica de Procedimientos Administrativos*, Editorial Jurídica Venezolana, 12th Ed., Caracas 2001.

15 See Allan R. Brewer-Carías, *El Derecho Administrativo y la Ley Orgánica de Procedimientos Administrativos. Principios del Procedimiento Administrativo*, Editorial Jurídica Venezolana, Caracas 2002, pp. 176-178.

16 In general, on the principle of legitimate confidence see Caterina Balasso Tejera, "El principio de protección de la confianza legítima y su aplicabilidad respecto de los ámbitos de actuación del poder público," in *El Derecho Público a los 100 números de la Revista de Derecho Público 1980-2005*, Editorial Jurídica Venezolana, Caracas 2006, pp. 745 ff.

bona fide, for instance) and informing its activity to bestow the functioning password to the society at large.[17]

About such principle the Political-Administrative Chamber of the Supreme Tribunal of Justice has stated that reiterative actions of Public Administration create legal expectations for individuals that have to be weighted by the judge, since administrative criteria, although susceptible to change from time to time, can create such expectations.[18] When setting its criteria, the Political-Administrative Chamber based the conclusion on Article 11 of the Organic Law on Administrative Procedures, stating that such provision:

> "...is nothing more than the application of the principle of non-retroactivity of general provisions to situations created prior to their pronouncement. The provision also states that change of criteria is not a cause for review of final administrative acts. Article 11, briefly analyzed, is considered one of the most relevant examples of Venezuelan law of the legitimate confidence principle, based on which, reiterated actions of one subject in respect of another, in this case, the Public Administration, create legal expectations that have to be appreciated by the judges and, precisely, administrative criteria, although mutable, are capable of creating such expectations...."[19]

Consequently, if the Public Administration acts in such a way as to go against the logical deduction of its previous actions, there is a violation of the legitimate confidence principle, since "when referring to the conduct that generates the expectation the same encompasses not only actions, but also omissions and negative manifestations or voluntary omissions...."[20]

The basis of this principle lays, as the Electoral Chamber of the Supreme Tribunal of Justice has stated, in the confidence that the behavior of the Public Administration causes in the citizen, behavior that must follow the legal framework and be oriented to the protection of the general interest.[21]

In sum, the principle of protection of the legitimate confidence or legitimate expectation governs the relationship between the citizens and the State, and accordingly, the latter must recognize the legitimate nature of the expectations based in its previous reiterative behavior, as well as respect such expectations, being banned from changing them irrationally, abruptly, suddenly and without warning as for the effects that such changes could cause.

In any event, it must be pointed out that such principle of legitimate expectations must be based on legitimate and legal administrative acts or actions,

---

17 See Federico A. Castillo Blanco, *La protección de confianza en el Derecho Administrativo*, Marcial Pons Editores, Madrid 1998, pp. 273-274.

18 See Decision N° 514 of the Political-Administrative Chamber of the Supreme Tribunal of Justice of April 3, 2001 (Case of *The Coca-Cola Company v. Ministerio de la Producción y el Comercio*), in *Revista de Derecho Público*, N° 85-88, Editorial Jurídica Venezolana, Caracas 2001, pp. 231-232.

19 *Idem.*

20 See Hildegard Rondón de Sansó, *El Principio de Confianza Legítima o Expectativa Plausible en el Derecho Venezolano*, Caracas 2002, p. 3.

21 See Decision N° 98 of the Electoral Chamber of the Supreme Tribunal of Justice of August 1, 2001 (Case of *Asociación Civil "Club Campestre Paracotos"*), in *Revista de Derecho Público*, N° 85-88, Editorial Jurídica Venezolana, Caracas 2001, pp. 232-238.

and cannot be construed on the basis of illegal actions of the Administration. As argued by Hildegard Rondon de Sansó, legitimate expectations cannot be based on "a *promise that does not comply with the rules, or even, is contrary to the rules*."[22] That is, the principle applies only when the expectation is "legitimate" in the sense of being subject to "all the requirements of the legal order"[23] and "not contrary to an express rule."[24] As the same author also wrote regarding the subjective element of the expectation: "The legitimacy of the claim could not be a decisive factor because it could lead to a plausible expectation or confidence when deriving from a fact that has not evidence of legality. For instance, it could happen that a matter considered illegal is going to be placed in the field of legality,"[25] which is obviously unacceptable. This is why the same author, emphasizes that "it is necessary for the *expectation to be established in accordance with the legal order*, in a way that there is no provision that could be opposed to the satisfaction of the claim."[26] For this same reason, Caterina Balasso, has expressed that a legitimate expectation must be "justified"–that is, the act on which the expectation is based "*must be subject to the legal order* and oriented toward the protection of the general interest."[27]

Therefore, no "legitimate expectation" could possibly arise from the execution of an illegal act, as was for instace decided by the Political-Administrative Chamber of the Supreme Tribunal, in 2007, in the case *Repro Sportny vs. Universidad Central de Venezuela* (UCV),[28] originated in a suit whereas a plaintiff (personal firm Repro Sportny) requested the court to condemn defendant (the Central University) to pay an amount of money for sporting garments that he had allegedly made for the University, which had been effectively made and delivered, and even used by students. The University alleged that the contract was not properly concluded, and that the process of selection of the private contracting party established in the Biding Law and rules of the University had been violated because lacking the required authorization issued by the University Council.[29] The situation was, then, that if it was true that an initial offer for the making of the uniforms was approved, and the garment were effectively made and delivered and they were effectively used by the students, the process of selection of the private contracting party did not follow the provisions of the Biding regime.

In studying the violation of the provisions of the Biding regime, particularly the absence of the prior authorization by the University Council, the Political Administrative Chamber arrived to the conclusion that such illegality provoked "the

---

22 See Hildegard Rondón de Sansó, "Visión General del Principio de Expectativa Plausible," en *Boletín de la Academia de Ciencias Políticas Y Sociales, 2003, No* 141, p. 300.

23 *Id.* p 301.

24 *Id.* p 328.

25 *Id.* 349.

26 *Id.* p. 341

27 See Caterina Balasso Tejera, "El Principio de Protección de la Confianza Legítima y su *Aplicabilidad* Respecto de los Ámbitos de Actuación del Poder Público," in *Revista De Derecho Público* No. 145-146, Editorial Jurídica venezolana, Caracas 2006, p. 100

28 *See* decision of the Supreme Tribunal of Justice of July 3, 2007 at 20,

29 *Id.* p.20-25

non-existence of the manifestation of the will by the University in order to be liable." [30]

Nonetheless, due to the fact that the initial offer submitted by the plaintiff was approved by the University, and that the sporting garments were made, delivered and effectively used by the students, the Political Administrative Chamber, based on the general principle of liability originated in cases of "enrichment without cause" established in article 1.184 of the Civil Code, decided partially in favor of the claim filed by the plaintiff, making reference to the principle of legitimate expectation as an expression of the "specific principle of good faith regarding administrative activity, for the purpose of giving private parties guaranties of certainty in their legal administrative relation." Consequently, considering that when the plaintiff made the garments there was "an appearance of legality" in the contracting process, and that the plaintiff effectively made the garments and deliver them to the University whose students used them, the Chamber concluded considering that in the case, the University was liable:

> "as a result of the benefit obtained on the occasion of the use of the aforementioned assets, for which reason it corresponds to said Institution to compensate the impoverishment produced in the estate of the personal firm Repro Sportny" [31]

As a matter of fact, due to the illegality affecting the contract in its formation (absence of consent for lack of the expression of the will of the University due to the absence of the University Council´s prior authorization), the Chamber expressed decided in its ruling that the:

> "Universidad Central de Venezuela is compelled to compensate only to the extent of its enrichment, compensation that cannot be greater than the impoverishment suffered by the personal firm Repro Sportny. Therefore, agreeing to the payment of default interest or monetary correction as the plaintiff intends would constitute a contravention of the provisions of article 1,184 of the Civil Code previously transcribed and, also, would entail a new alteration in the equity balance of the parties, reason for which the Chamber declares this request inadmissible."' [32]

It is then clear that in this ruling the Political Administrative Chamber did not accept any principle of legitimate expectation based on violations of public order, referring to the matter only to establish the liability for enrichment without cause. As per the illegality committed by the University, the Chamber exhorted the University to conform its future actions on matter of contracts, to the procedures established in the Law and its regulations.

In any case, the idea that the principle of legitimate expectation can be based upon an illegality has been expressly rejected by the same Political Administrative Chamber of the Supreme Tribunal, in many other cases. For instance, in its decision of November 20, 2019 in the *Propatrimonio* case, the Chamber ruled that "legitimate expectations or plausible expectations are not principles or values that can be invoked or predicated in a situation of illegality or outside the law, since this would imply reinforcing and perpetuating conducts contrary to law instead of

30 *Id.* p.20-25

31 *Id* p. 22-25

32 *Id.* p. 24.

contributing to the consolidation of legal security and stability of the legal system Venezuelan[,] [and thus] the plaintiff cannot claim to enjoy the principle of legitimate expectations or to have a plausible expectation born from illegitimate action "[33]

Previously, in its decision of March 24, 2015 in the *Cámara Venezolana de la Construcción et al* case, the Chamber ruled that "the legitimate confidence or plausible expectation are not principles or values that can be invoked or predicated in a situation of illegality or outside the law."[34] Likewise, in its decision of May 5, 2010 in the *Seguros Carabobo* case, the Chamber ruled that "a justified expectation could not exist based on an interpretation that does not conform to what is prescribed in the Law."[35]

In her 2019 book on the principle of legitimate expectations, Professor Karla Velazco Silva refers to the *Cámara Venezolana de la Construcción et al* and *Seguros Carabobo* decisions, concluding that they "make it clear that the principle of legitimate confidence [expectations] cannot be invoked when it was born from an illegal action that damages the legal sphere of the community."[36]

More recent, the same *Political* Administrative Chamber of the Supreme Tribunal in a decision issued on November 20, 2019 (case*: Propatrimonio*), has been more precise on the matter by ruling that:

> "legitimate expectations or plausible expectations are not principles or values that can be invoked or predicated in a situation of illegality or outside the law, since this would imply reinforcing and perpetuating conducts contrary to law instead of contributing to the *consolidation* of legal security and stability of the legal system Venezuelan. Ergo, the plaintiff cannot claim to enjoy the principle of legitimate expectations or to have a plausible expectation born from illegitimate action […]."[37]

4. Discretionary powers and their limits

On the other hand, regarding discretionary power, it can be exercised only when the law gives the public officer freedom to choose between different possibilities or measures, pursuant to an evaluation of the opportunity and convenience of the action to be adopted.[38] So in the cases of administrative discretionary actions, the law is

---

33 *See* decision of the Political-Administrative Chamber of the Supreme Tribunal of November 20, 2019, p.35.

34 *See* decision of the Political Administrative Chamber of the Supreme Tribunal of March 24, 2015 (case *Cámara Venezolana de la Construcción et al*), p. 20; available at: http://histori-co.tsj.gob.ve/decisiones/spa/marzo/175768-00292-25315-2015-2009-1056.html

35 *See* decision of the Political Administrative Chamber of the Supreme Tribunal of May 5, 2010 (case *Seguros Carabobo*), p. 27,

36 *See* Karla Velazco Silva, *La confianza legítima ante actuaciones de funcionarios de hecho,* Universidad del Zulia, 2019, p. 66

37 See decision of the Political Administrative Chamber of the Supreme Tribunal, of November 20, 2019.

38 See Allan R. Brewer-Carías, "Los límites a la actividad discrecional de las autoridades administrativas," in *Ponencias Venezolanas al VII Congreso Internacional de Derecho Comparado* (*Uppsala, agosto 1966*), Instituto de Derecho Privado, Law School, Universidad

what gives the Public Administration the possibility to evaluate the opportunity or convenience of its action, in harmony with the public interest, so it has been defined as "the freedom to choose between different alternatives all of them fair."[39] The discretionary actions must be distinguished from the application of what has been called the "undetermined legal concepts" in which public officials can only determine the sense of the corresponding provision containing the concept, which only allows for one correct and just solution, which is no other than the one derived according to its spirit, reason and purpose.[40] In any case, all discretionary action, when duly authorized by statute, has limits expressly established by Article 12 of the Organic Law on Administrative Procedures,[41] which states:

> "When a statutory or regulatory provision leaves a measure to be adopted according to the judgment of the competent authority, the said measure must maintain due proportionality, be adjusted to the factual basis of the act, and be conformed to the purposes (but) of the provision, and it must also be issued following the procedure and formalities needed to support its validity and efficacy."

In effect, according to Venezuelan Administrative Law, administrative discretional activities can only exists when a statute expressly gives the Administration the power to evaluate the timing and convenience of its actions, which occurs when a statute gives a public officer the power –not the duty –to act following his evaluation of the given circumstances.[42] As was affirmed by the former federal Court of Venezuela in a judgment dated July 17, 1953:

Central de Venezuela, Caracas 1966, pp. 255-279, and in *Revista de la Facultad de Derecho*, N° 2, Universidad Católica Andrés Bello, Caracas 1966, pp. 9-35.

39 See Decision N° 100 of the Political-Administrative Chamber of the Supreme Court of Justice of May 19, 1983, in *Revista de Derecho Público,* N° 34, Editorial Jurídica Venezolana, Caracas 1988, p. 69, as well as Rulling of the Political-Administrative Chamber of the Supreme Court of Justice dated August 1st, 1991, in Caterina Balasso Tejera, *Jurisprudencia sobre los Actos Administrativos (1980-1993)*, Editorial Jurídica Venezolana, Caracas, 1998, pp. 209 ff.

40 See *Idem*, Decision N° 100 of the Political-Administrative Chamber of the Supreme Court of Justice of May 19, 1983, in *Revista de Derecho Público,* N° 34, Editorial Jurídica Venezolana, Caracas 1988, p. 69.

41 See Organic Law on Administrative Procedures in *Official Gazette* N° 2.818 Extra. of July 1, 1981; Allan R. Brewer-Carías et al., *Ley Orgánica de Procedimientos Administrativos*, Editorial Jurídica Venezolana, 12th Ed., Caracas 2001, pp. 175 and ss.; Allan R. Brewer-Carías, *El Derecho Administrativo y la Ley Orgánica de Procedimientos Administrativos,* Editorial Jurídica Venezolana, Caracas 1982, pp. 45-48.

42 See on discretionary power and its limits, Allan R. Brewer-Carías, *Las Instituciones Fundamentales del Derecho Administrativo y la Jurisprudencia Venezolana,* Caracas 1964, p. 52 ss.; *Fundamentos de la Administración Pública,* Vol. I, Caracas 1980, pp. 203-222; "Los límites al poder discrecional de las autoridades administrativas" in *Ponencias Venezolanas al Vil Congreso Internacional de Derecho Comparado,* Caracas 1966, pp. 255-278, and in *Revista de la Facultad de Derecho,* Universidad Católica Andrés Bello, N° 2, Caracas 966, pp. 9-35; "Sobre los límites al ejercicio del poder discrecional," in Carlos E. Delpiazzo (Coordinador), *Estudios Jurídicos en Homenaje al Prof. Mariano Brito*, Fundación de Cultura Universitaria, Montevideo 2008, pp. 609-629; "Algunos aspectos del control judicial de la discrecionalidad," in Jaime Rodríguez Arana Muñoz et al. (Eds.), *Derecho Administrativo Iberoamericano (Discrecionalidad, Justicia Administrativa y Entes Reguladores), Congreso Iberoamericano de Derecho Administrativo,* Vol. II, Congrex SA, Panamá 2009, pp. 475-512.

"...discretionary acts exist when the Administration is not subject to the accomplishment of special provisions regarding the opportunity to act, this not meaning that it could act without being subject to any rule, because administrative authorities must always observe the provisions regarding the formalities of administrative acts. On the contrary, regulated acts (*actos reglados*) are those compulsory acts that the public official is compelled to issue strictly subject to the law."[43]

In another pronouncement the same Court stated that:

"...in the regulated administrative acts, the law establishes if the administrative authority must act, which is it and how it must act, determining the conditions of the administrative conduct in a way not leaving margin to elect the procedure; instead, in discretionary administrative acts, bearing in mind the needs of Public Administration, the administrative authority, in many cases, will appreciate past facts or future consequences, and for such purpose, will have certain freedom of appreciation, this not meaning that it could act arbitrarily."[44]

From the aforementioned, what basically results in Venezuelan administrative law is that discretionary powers need to be expressly provided in a specific statute. Consequently, as was established by the former Federal and Cassation Court in 1938, "[N]ever, in any case, can a public officer exercise discretionary powers, unless a statute in a direct and categorical way gives it such power."[45] And as aforementioned, even if a statute gives a public officer the power to decide matters in a discretionary way, according to Article 12 of the Organic Law of Administrative Procedures, it must act maintaining due proportionality, adjusting itself to the facts and to the purposes of the provision, and following the formalities, and the requirements needed for the validity and efficacy of the action. That is, discretionary actions when authorized by the law, can never be arbitrary or unjust actions ("*la discrecionalidad no implica arbitrariedad ni injusticia*"),[46] and must always conform to the principle of rationality (a discretionary decision can never be irrational or illogical); the principle of justice or equity (a discretionary decision can never be unjust, inequitable, evil); the principle of equality (a discretional decision cannot be discriminatory); the principle of proportionality (a discretionary decision cannot be disproportionate, and needs to be in conformity with the facts and the decision); and the principle of good faith (a discretionary decision cannot be misleading)."[47]

---

43 See Decision of the former Federal Court of July 17, 1953, in *Gaceta Forense*, 2d Stage, Nº 1, Caracas 1953, p. 151.

44 See Decision of the former Federal Court of November 26, 1959, in *Gaceta Forense*, 2d Stage, Nº 26, Caracas 1959, p. 125.

45 See Decision of the former Federal and Cassation Court in Federal Chamber of August 11, 1949, *Gaceta Forense*, 1ª etapa (2d Ed.), Year I, Nº 2, Caracas 1949, p. 140, in Allan R. Brewer-Carías, *Jurisprudencia de la Corte Suprema de 1930-1974 y Estudios de Derecho Administrativo,* Vol. I, Caracas 1975, p. 615.

46 *Gaceta Forense,* Nº 11, Caracas 1956, pp. 27-30; See Allan R. Brewer-Carías, *Jurisprudencia de la Corte Suprema de 1930-1974 y Estudios de Derecho Administrativo,* Vol. I, Caracas 1975, pp. 611-612.

47 See Allan R. Brewer-Carías, "Los límites del poder discrecional de las autoridades administrativas," *loc. cit.*, pp. 27-33. See the comments in Gustavo Urdaneta Troconis, "Notas sobre la distinción entre actos reglados y discrecionales y el control jurisdiccional sobre estos," in

5. Due process and administrative procedure

On the other hand, one of the main elements necessary in order to secure the respect of the rule of law by administrative action, is to compel administrative acts to be issued following the administrative procedure established by the law, which is set forth, not only to secure the efficacy of administrative actions, but to secure also individual rights before Public Administration. Administrative procedure is governed, as provided in Article 141 of the Constitution by "the principles of honesty, participation, celerity, efficacy, efficiency, transparency, accountability and liability in the exercise of public functions and with full subjection to the statute and the law;" and as indicated in Article 10 of the Organic Law on Public Administration by the principles of economy, celerity, simplicity, objectivity, impartiality, honesty, transparency and good faith.

In particular, in all cases in which an act of Public Administration can affect rights or interests of individuals, in order to be issued, the Administration is obliged to follow an administrative procedure in which the due process rules and rights must be respected, and in particular, the right to defense must be guaranteed. This right to defense is part of the general due process clause found in Article 49 of the Constitution that is a guarantee not only before the courts but also regarding administrative actions, and is further completed, as mentioned, by the provision that declares administrative acts enacted in complete and absolute absence of any administrative procedure, as affected with absolute nullity, as seen in Article 19.4 of Organic Law on Administrative Procedures.

The consequence of this constitutional principle, for instance, in an administrative procedure for reviewing an administrative act for its revocation, is that the previous hearing of the interested parties is a condition for the validity of the resulting revocation, inasmuch as it guarantees the fundamental right of the individual involved to defend himself and be heard. That is to say, the right to due process applies to all administrative action, and the Administration has always had a duty to initiate an administrative proceeding prior to issuing an act or measure that could affect rights or interests of an individual or corporation, so the latter is granted an opportunity to present his defense. The Political-Administrative Chamber of the Supreme Court of Justice, even prior to the 1999 Constitution, held in repeated rulings as follows:

> "Article 68 [equivalent to 49 of the Constitution of 1999] of our Constitution establishes that the right to a defense is an inalienable right in all stages and degrees of the proceeding, which has been interpreted by repeated rulings of this High Tribunal in its broadest form, extending to and including the right to be heard, to present allegations, to deny opposing arguments, to promote and present pertinent proofs, 'both in the proceeding constituting the administrative act as well as in administrative appeals allowed by Law to purge and cleanse

---

Tendencias de la Jurisprudencia venezolana en materia contencioso administrativa, Caracas 1986, pp. 395-399; Gabriel Ruan Santos, *El principio de legalidad, la discrecionalidad y las medidas administrativas*, Fundación de Estudios de Derecho Administrativo, FUNEDA, Caracas 1998.

such proceeding' (see ruling of the Political-Administrative Chamber of the Supreme Court of Justice dated May 8, 1991, '*Ganadería El Cantón*')."

In this context, the Administration has the duty to inform the interested parties of the opening of a proceeding –and especially so if it is a proceeding that could result in sanctions or encumbrances– so that before the final act is issued, the parties can have access to the file and therefore make the pertinent allegations and present appropriate evidence. This was established by the Political-Administrative Chamber in, among other decisions, the ruling dated Nov. 17, 1983, that provided: 'The right to a defense must be considered not just as the opportunity for the citizen who is sued or the assumed violator to make his allegations heard, but as the right to demand that the Government, before any sanctions are levied, complies with such acts and proceedings that allow him to know specifically the facts with which he is charged, the legal provisions applicable thereto, allow him to make, in a timely manner, the allegations discharging the same and to hear evidence in his favor. This perspective of the right to a defense is comparable to that which in other States has been called as the principle of due process.'"[48]

In a ruling by the First Contentious Administrative Court dated May 15, 1996, it reads as follows:

"[I]t must be affirmed that the right to a defense is inherent to any proceeding (either jurisdictional or administrative) where an individual is being judged. The rulings in this sense have been repeated, providing that the Administration must grant individuals whose subjective rights or legitimate interests may be harmed, a procedural opportunity to state their allegations and present the proofs that they deem pertinent; and the purpose of this duty on the part of the administrative bodies is to guarantee the individual's right to a defense, which is applicable not just to the judicial sphere, but also extends – as we have already stated – to the administrative sphere. Consequently, any administrative act whose effects are to extinguish, modify or vary any subjective right or qualified interest of individual parties, or those which levy sanctions or charges, must have a previous proceeding in order to be valid and effective, thereby allowing, even in an informal way, the exercise of the fundamental right to a defense which is held by all citizens as a civil right contained in the Constitution."[49]

These principles, as mentioned, have been restated by the provision of Article 49 of the 1999 Constitution, where the constitutional guaranty of due process of law and to self-defense was set as inviolable not only in all judicial processes but also in all administrative procedures; a guaranty that cannot be surpassed even by the Legislator itself.[50]

---

48 See Decision of the Political-Administrative Chamber of the Supreme Tribunal of Justice of October 8, 1996, in *Revista de Derecho Público*, Nos. 67-68, Editorial Jurídica Venezolana, Caracas 1996, p. 171.

49 See *Revista de Derecho Público*, Nos. 65-66, Editorial Jurídica Venezolana, Caracas 1996, p. 156.

50 For this reason, it has been because of the prevalence of the right to a defense that the Constitutional Chamber, following Constitutional doctrine established by the former Supreme

The Political and Administrative Chamber of the Supreme Tribunal of Justice set criteria on the interpretation and scope of Article 49 of the 1999 Constitution, stating:

"[I]t is a complex right encompassing a group of guaranties that are expressed in a diversity of rights for the defendant, among which, the right to access justice, the right to be heard, the right to have an articulated proceeding, the right to the legal appeals, the right to a competent, independent and impartial Court, the right to obtain a resolution duly founded in law, the right to a process without groundless delays; the right to compulsory compliance with rulings, among others that the jurisprudence has been building. All these rights originate in the interpretation of the eight paragraphs of Article 49 of the Constitution. Such Article provides that due process of law is a right that applies to all actions either by the judiciary or the administration, provision that has its foundation in the principle of equality before the Law, since due process means that both parties to the administrative or judiciary act, must have equal opportunities both in the defense of their respective rights as in the production of those proofs to demonstrate them. In the same sense, the right to defense provided generally as a principle in Article 49 of the Constitution, adapted and accepted by repeated rulings in administrative matters, has been provided also multiple times in the Organic Law on Administrative Procedures, which, in various provisions, sets its sense and expressions. In this way there are other connected rights like the right to be heard, the right to be part of the proceeding, the right to be served, to access the file, to submit allegations and proofs and to be informed of the appeals and recourses available to exercise a proper defense."[51]

Similarly, the Constitutional Chamber, in its ruling N° 321 dated February 22, 2002 (Case of *Papeles Nacionales Flamingo, C.A. v. Dirección de Hacienda del Municipio Guácara del Estado Carabobo*), indicated that any restrictions on the right to a defense, being a fundamental right, only come from the Constitution itself; and if the Legislator broadens the sphere of those restrictions, then they become illegitimate:

"It must be noted that both Article 68 of the repealed Constitution as well as 49.1 of the current Constitution authorize the law to regulate the right to a defense, which regulation is found in the procedural code. This does not in any way mean that the scope of this right is available to the legislator, as this is clearly defined in the provisions noted; on the contrary, it implies a mandate to the legislative body to provide the adoption of mechanisms to assure the exercise of the right of defense by those who are charged, not just in the jurisdictional courts, but also in the governmental sphere, under the terms stated

Court, has no longer applied, for example, standards that allow the principle of *solve et repete* as a condition to have access to contentious-administrative courts, as it considers these to be unconstitutional. See Decision N° 321 of the Constitutional Chamber of the Supreme Tribunal of Justice of February 22, 2002 (Case of *Papeles Nacionales Flamingo, C.A. v. Dirección de Hacienda del Municipio Guácara del Estado Carabobo*), in *Revista de Derecho Público*, N° 89-92, Editorial Jurídica Venezolana, Caracas 2002.

51 See Decision N° 2742 of the Political-Administrative Chamber of the Supreme Tribunal of Justice of November 20, 2001, available at http://www.tsj.gov.ve/decisiones/spa/Noviembre/02742-201101-15649.htm.

in our Constitution. As such, any limits on the right to a defense, as a fundamental right, come from the text of the Constitution, and if the Legislator extends or broadens the sphere of those limitations, then they become illegitimate; that is, the legal framework for restrictions of the exercise of a defense does not justify these limitations, but rather the degree to which they obey the Constitutional mandate."[52]

The right to a defense is therefore an absolute Constitutional right, stated by the Constitution as "uninfringeable" in all stages and degrees of the cause, both in judicial as well as in administrative proceedings, and it is a right held by every person, without distinction of any kind, individual or legal entity, and therefore cannot be subject to any exceptions or limitations.[53] This right "is a fundamental right protected by our Constitution, and as such cannot be suspended in the sphere of the rule of law, as it is one of the bases over which such concept is raised."[54]

Furthermore, the Constitutional Chamber of the Supreme Tribunal of Justice, after the 1999 Constitution became effective, has also insisted on the absolute and inviolable nature of the right to a defense. It is the case, for instance, of decision N° 97 dated March 15, 2000 (*Agropecuaria Los Tres Rebeldes, C.A. v. Juzgado de Primera Instancia en lo Civil, Mercantil, Tránsito, Trabajo, Agrario, Penal, de Salvaguarda del Patrimonio Público de la Circunscripción Judicial del Estado Barinas*), in which the Chamber ruled:

> "Due process is the process that gathers all the indispensable guarantees that allow for effective judicial protection. This is the notion alluded to in Article 49 of the Constitution, when it declares that due process shall apply to all judicial and administrative actions.
>
> However, the Constitutional provision does not establish a specific type of process, but rather the need, regardless of the procedural venue selected for the defense of those rights or legitimate interests, for the procedural laws to guarantee the right of the defendant to a defense and the possibility for effective judicial protection."[55]

---

52 See Decision N° 321 of the Constitutional Chamber of the Supreme Tribunal of Justice of February 22, 2002 (Case of *Papeles Nacionales Flamingo, C.A. v. Dirección de Hacienda del Municipio Guácara del Estado Carabobo*), in *Revista de Derecho Público*, Nos. 89-92, Editorial Jurídica Venezolana, Caracas 2002.

53 The First Contentious-Administrative Court spoke to this in its Decision of August 15, 1997 (Case of *Telecomunicaciones Movilnet, C.A. v. Comisión Nacional de Telecomunicaciones (CONATEL)*), as follows: "The levying of sanctions, prohibitive measures or in general any kind of limitation or restriction on the subjective sphere of those administered without the opportunity to exercise their right to a defense, is inconceivable." See *Revista de Derecho Público,* N° 71-72, Caracas 1997, pp. 154-163.

54 So established by the Political-Administrative Chamber of the former Supreme Court in its Sentence N° 572 of August 18, 1997 (Case of *Aerolíneas Venezolanas, S.A. (AVENSA) v. the Republic (Ministry of Transport and Communications)*), in *Revista de Derecho Público,* Nos. 71-72, Caracas 1997, p. 158 ss.

55 See Decision N° 97 of the Constitutional Chamber of the Supreme Tribunal of Justice of March 15, 200, available at http://www.tsj.gov.ve/decisiones/scon/Marzo/97-150300-00-0118.htm.

From this existence of due process rules derives the possibility for the parties to use the means or recourses provided in the legal framework to defend their rights and interests. Consequently, any failure to respect the rules of procedure which leads to the inability of the parties to use the mechanisms that guarantee their right to be heard results in a state of defenselessness and a violation of the right to due process and the right of the parties to a defense.

In administrative law, as a consequence of the general principle of due process, within the main principles governing administrative procedures and the resulting administrative acts, is the principle of *audire alteram parte*, according to which no administrative act that may affect interests or rights of individuals can be ever issued in any way whatsoever without a previous hearing of the interested parties, allowing them to exercise their rights to be heard, to allege and produce proofs of its assertions. The right to be heard even on administrative procedures has a constitutional basis (Article 49.1) and has been imposed to be respected in all administrative procedures by precedents of the Supreme Tribunal. The Political Administrative Chamber of the Supreme Tribunal since 1985 has held on the subject as follows:

> "The right to be heard must be considered not only as the opportunity given to the individual who has presumably committed an infraction in order for its allegation to be heard, but as the right to request from the State to comply, before imposing a sanction, with a set of acts and procedures directed to allow the individual to know with precision the facts that are incriminated as well as the legal applicable provisions, to promptly allow him to allege in his defense and to present proofs in his favor. In this perspective, the right to be heard is equivalent to what is called in other Rule of Law States, as due process of law."[56]

To ensure such right to be heard, the Organic Law on Administrative Procedures provides for a series of correlated rights such as: to be served of any procedure that could affect subjective rights or legitimate, personal or direct interests of an individual (Article 48); to be heard and to have the opportunity to become a party at any moment in an administrative procedure (Article 23); to have access to the administrative files, and to inspect it and copy it (Article 59); to file proofs and to submit files (Articles 48 and 58); for the administrative act to formally have its motivation (Article 9); to be personally served of any act that could affect the rights and legitimate, personal and direct interests of the individual (Article 73); and to be informed of the legal means in order to exercise the right to appeal the act (Articles 73 and 77).

6. The meaning of the legal declarations of some activities as of Public Usefulness and Social Interest

In Venezuela, is very common to find in statutes express declaration considering certain activities or in general, the matters regulated in the law, as of public usefulness of social interest. It is the case, as an example, of Article 4 of the 2001

---

56 See Decision of Political-Administrative Chamber of the Supreme Court of Justice, Decision of November 17, 1983, in *Revista de Derecho Público*, N° 16, Caracas 1983, p. 151.

Organic Hydrocarbons Law in which it is declared that all activities involving industrial and commercial activities for hydrocarbons referred to therein, as well as all works that are necessary to achieving these, are considered "for the public usefulness and of social interest". In the same sense, the same declaration is made in Article 4 of the Organic Gaseous Hydrocarbons Law[57], which states that activities referred to in the law on gaseous hydrocarbons "are declared as of public usefulness", as are any works required to operate them.

This expression of public usefulness (*utilidad pública*) is referred to activities that are just considered of "general benefit" or of "public usefulness," being completely different to the notion of "public utility" in English, ("*servicio público*" in Spanish), which refers to activities reserved to the State accomplished for the satisfaction of essential collective needs. Therefore, "*utilidad pública*" (public usefulness)" cannot be translated as "public utility" (*servicio público*"). The distinction is so clear, that it is established in an express way in the same Organic Hydrocarbon Law: "*utilidad publica*" as public usefulness is used in article 4, and "*servicio público*" as "public utility" is used in article 60 of the Law, each one with their own different meaning.

In Venezuelan law, this declaration that specific activities are "in the public usefulness or social interest" is grounded in and motivated by the traditional constitutional provision that regulates guarantees of property rights, providing that the expropriation of private property can only be made for "reason of public usefulness and social interest" (Art. 115, Constitution of 1999). [58] This has also traditionally been required by the Expropriation Law for reasons of public usefulness or social interest (Art. 7.1 and Art. 13),[59] that has to be declared in a statute, as a prior condition for the expropriation to go forward. As a consequence, in order for a decree ordering the expropriation of private assets to be issued, it is always necessary for a specific prior legislative declaration to be issued that the activity concretely serving as the grounds for the expropriation, is considered to be of public usefulness or of social interest, which in general is made through special statutes, which implies that no further later declaration of "social interest or public usefulness" is needed in order to begin the expropriation procedure.[60] That is why

57 See the *Official Gazette* No. 36.793 of 23-09-1999

58 Article 115 of the Constitution: "The right of property is guaranteed. Every person has the right to the use, enjoyment, usufruct and disposal of his or her goods. Property shall be subject to such contributions, restrictions and obligations as may be established by law in the service of the public or general interest. *Only for reasons of public usefulness or social interest* by final judgment, with timely payment of fair compensation, the expropriation of any kind of property may be declared."

59 See the Expropriation Law for reasons of Public Usefulness or Social Interest, in *Official Gazette* No. 37.475 of 01-07-2002. See the comments on this law in Allan R. Brewer-Carías, "Introducción General al régimen de la expropiación, in Allan R. Brewer-Carías, Gustavo Linares Benzo, Dolores Aguerrevere Valero y Caterina Balasso Tejera, *Ley de Expropiación por Causa de Utilidad Pública o Interés Social*, Colección Textos Legislativos, N° 26, 1st Ed., Editorial Jurídica Venezolana, Caracas 2002, pp. 7-100.

60 For example, regarding more recent laws, even though many have already been repealed or amended, we highlight the following: in Law for the Defence of Persons in Accessing Goods and Services, Decree-Law No. 6.092 of 27-May-2008, all assets required for producing, manufacturing, importing, storing, transporting, distributing, and selling food, goods, and services that have been declared essential have been declared to be in the public and social interest, in *Official Gazette* No. 5889 of 31-July-2008; in the Law on Integrated Agricultural Health (Decree

many statutes contains similar declarations regarding the public usefulness and social interest of the matters regulated, as is the case of the statutes dealing with water resources, Forestry, Land Use, Transports, consumer protection health, housing, food production

Therefore, when an activity is declared to be in the public interest or as public usefulness in a specific law, the only goal of this is to facilitate expropriation procedures, and it does not imply a general *publicatio* of the matter regulated in the statute or that everything that must be done regarding the activity is necessarily reserved to the State. That is, this declaration alone cannot transform the entire legal regime governing an activity and make it subject only to public law, or change the nature of contracts that are signed for activities regulated under the specific law, which do not become administrative contracts by virtue of such a declaration.

That is, for instance, a contract to be a "administrative contract," as was clarified in a historical ruling handed down in the *Acción Comercial* case in 1983, by the former Supreme Court in the Political Administrative Chamber, it thas to be identified by its object, which must always intend to achieve "the satisfaction of specific needs" "that are in the *general or collective interest*." For a public contract to be qualified as a "administrative contract" is therefore not enough that its object matter could be declared as being an activity that of public usefulness or of public interest, but rather, as has been set forth in jurisprudence, its object must be a specific activity directed to *satisfies collective interests*, that is, activities accomplished *in the interest of the entire community*, for which the Administrative Authorities calls on "the cooperation of the individual in satisfying" the aforementioned collective needs.[61] It is therefore incorrect to consider, consequently, that a public contract is an "administrative contract" when it is referred to an activity just declared of "public usefulness" ("*utilidad pública*").

Law N° 6.129 de 03-June-2008), all goods and services involved in integrated agricultural health were declared to be in the national and public interest. This means that where there are security reasons, goods and services involved with integrated agricultural health may be seized without the need for any other formality, in whole or in part, when they are required for works or activities related to integrated agricultural health. In the Law for the National Housing Institute (INAVI) (Decree Law N° 6.267 de 30-07-2008), housing to be directly or indirectly built by the Instituto Nacional de la Vivienda (INAVI) is declared to be in the public interest, (*Gaceta Oficial* N° 5.890 Extraordinaria de 31-July-2008. And in the Organic Law on Agri-food Security and Sovereignty (Decree Law NO. 6.071 de 14-May-2008), all assets ensuring the accessibility and opportune availability of food as well as all related infrastructure is declared to be in the public interest. (*Official Gazette* N° 5.889 of 31-07-2008).

61 See the references to the ruling of the Political Administrative Chamber on 11 July 1983, in the same Chamber's sentence, No. 178 on 11 August 1983, in *Revista de Derecho Público* (Public Law Review), No. 16, Editorial Jurídica Venezolana, Caracas 1983, pp. 162- 163. Also see the citation of the aforementioned sentence in Allan R. Brewer-Carías, *Contratos Administrativos. Contratos Públicos. Contratos del Estado*, Editorial Jurídica Venezolana, Caracas 2013, pp. 194-195. In any case, the concepts of "public usefulness" and "public service", furthermore, in the oil industry, cannot under any circumstances have the same meaning when the legislative body has expressly made a clear distinction on this in specific provisions both in the Organic Hydrocarbons Law (Arts. 4, 5) and the Organic Gaseous Hydrocarbons Law (Arts. 4 and 60)

II. GENERAL PRINCIPLES RELATED TO THE EXECUTIVE BRANCH OF GOVERNMENT

1. General principles related to the National Executive

Article 226 of the Constitution provides that the President of the Republic is both the Chief of State, and the Chief of the National Executive branch, and in which capacity he directs the government. It is elected through direct, secret and universal suffrage, by relative majority of votes (Article 228), for a term of six (6) years. For the first time since the XIX century, after forbidding presidential elections, the 1999 Constitution provided that the President could be reelected for the consecutive term, although only once (Article 230). This limit was eliminated through a constitutional amendment approved by referendum on February 14th 2009.

One of the innovations in the Constitution of 1999 was the creation of the office of the Executive Vice President, which is a non-elected organ directly tied to the office of the President, which has the power to freely appoint or dismiss him. The Executive Vice President must meet the same qualifications for office as the President, and must have no blood or marriage relation with the President. The Executive Vice President is thus an immediate collaborator of the President in his capacity as Chief Executive (Article 238). Consequently, its creation in the Constitution does not alter the nature of the presidential system of government[62]. Its main attributions are the following (Article 239): to collaborate with the President in the direction of Government action; to coordinate National Public Administration according to the President's instructions; to propose to the President the appointment and dismissal of Ministers; to preside over the Council of Ministers, with prior authorization of the President (Article 242); to coordinate the relations of the National Executive with the National Assembly; and to fill the temporal absences of the President (Article 234).

As mentioned, the Executive Vice President is appointed and dismissed by the President of the Republic. Nonetheless, according to Article 240 of the Constitution, a motion to censure the Vice President, arising from a vote of at least three-fifths (3/5) of the members of the National Assembly, will result in his removal from office. In such a case the Executive Vice President may not occupy that office or that of a Minister for the remainder of the President's term in office. On the other hand, three (3) removals of Executive Vice Presidents due to legislative motion to censure approved during the same constitutional term of the Legislature, authorizes the President of the Republic to dissolve the National Assembly. This is the only occasion in which the President is entitled to dissolve the National Assembly, being difficult to conceive the situation, unless the Assembly itself provoked its own dissolution by voting to approve a third motion to censure. In such case, the Executive Decree dissolving the Assembly implies the need to convene new elections for the National Assembly that must take place within sixty (60) days of its dissolution. In no case can the Assembly be dissolved during the last year of its constitutional term.

---

62 See Carlos Ayala Corao, *El Régimen Presidencial en América Latina y los planteamientos para su Reforma,* Caracas, 1992.

The Ministers' offices are also directly linked to the President of the Republic, being directly under his control. The Ministers, sitting together with the President and the Executive Vice President, constitute the Council of Ministers (Article 242). The Ministers are usually the head of the Ministries, which are the most important executive organs of the Government. They are freely appointed and dismissed by the President (Article 236.3). Nonetheless, Article 246 of the Constitution establishes the possibility for the National Assembly to approve motions to censure the Minister, and when the motion arises from a vote of not less than three-fifth (3/5) of the members present in the National Assembly, the decision will result in the Minister's removal. The Minister may not then occupy any other office of Minister or of Executive Vice President for the remainder of the Presidential term.

The number, organization and functions of the Ministries are establish by the President of the Republic, by Executive Decree (Article 236.20) according to the general provisions established in the Organic Law of Public Administration.[63] In accordance with Article 243 of the Constitution, the President of the Republic may also name Ministers of State, who, in addition to forming part of the Council of Ministers and without a Ministerial Office, assist the President and Vice President in certain functions.

The Ministers have the right to speak before the National Assembly (Article 211); and they can take part in its debates, although without vote (Article 245). On the other hand, the National Assembly can convoke the Ministers to its sessions, having the Assembly the right to question them. The Ministers, as well as any public official, are also obliged to appear before the Assembly and to give them all the information and documents it requires for its legislative and control functions (Article 223). The National Assembly has the power to declare political responsibility of the Ministers and can ask the Citizen Branch to prosecute them. As already mentioned, the Assembly can also approve motions of censure of the Ministers (Article 246). Finally, the Ministers must deliver before the National Assembly, within the first 60 days of each year, a motivated sufficient memoir referring to their activities in the previous year (Article 224).

As indicated, when sitting together with the President and the Executive Vice President, the Ministers constitute the Council of Ministers (Article 242). According to Article 236 of the Constitution, the President of the Republic, sitting in Ministers' Council, is required to exercise a set of functions designated in sections 7, 8, 9, 10, 12, 13, 14, 18, 20, 21, 22 of that Article, as well as those imposed by statutes. Within these attributions that the President must always exercise in Council of Ministers are the following: declaration of states of exception and the suspension of constitutional guaranties; issuing of decrees laws according to the legislative delegation made by the National Assembly; convening of the National Assembly to extraordinary sessions; issuing of regulations to statutes; approval of the National Plan for Development; the fixation of the number and organization of the Ministries; ordering the dissolution of the National Assembly, and convening referendums. The Council of Ministers is presided over by the President of the Republic, although the President may authorize the Executive Vice President to preside when unable to

63 *Official Gazette* N° 6.147 Extra. of November 17, 2014. See for instance decree of Ministerial Organization N° 6.732 of June 2, 2009 in *Official Gazette* N° 39.202 of June 17, 2009.

attend. In all events, decisions of the Ministers' Council must always be ratified by the President.

The Attorney General of the Republic is also an Executive organ of the Government and is required to attend the Council of Ministers but only with the right to speak, without the vote (Article 250). It is defined in the Constitution as an organ of the National Executive Branch that assists, defends, and represents the interests of the Republic in judicial and non-judicial matters (Article 247). In particular, the Constitution requires the advice of the Attorney General with respect to the approval of contracts of national public interest to be signed by the executive (Article 247).

One of the innovations of the Constitution of 1999 was the creation of the Council of State as a superior advisory organ of the Government and of the National Public Administration (Article 251). The Council of State is formally charged with making policy recommendations regarding matters of national interest that the President of the Republic recognizes as being of special importance, requiring the Council's point of view. The Council of State's specific functions and attributes have been established in the Organic Law of the Council of State.[64] Regarding the constitutional provisions, the Executive Vice President must preside over the Council of State, which must be integrated, in addition, by five (5) individuals named by the President of the Republic, a representative designated by the National Assembly, a representative designated by the Supreme Tribunal of Justice, and a Governor collectively designated by the chief executives of the States (Article 252). In practice, during the first decade of the 1999 Constitution, the Council of State has not been integrated and has not functioned.

Another innovation in the 1999 Constitution was the creation of the Federal Council of Government in charge of planning and coordinating the policies and actions for the process of decentralization and transfer of competencies from the national level of government to the States and Municipalities. This Council is presided over by the Executive Vice President, and integrated by the Ministers, the States Governors, one mayor from each State and by representatives of the organized society. An Inter territorial Compensatory Fond established in the Constitution depends on this Council (Article 185), in order to finance the public investments to promote the equitable development of the regions, the cooperation and complementation of development policies and initiatives of the public territorial entities.[65] In 2012, the Federal Council of Government has been regulated by

---

64 Decree Law N° 8.791 of January 31, 2012, in *Official Gazette* N° 39.865 of February 15, 2012.

65 See Manuel Rachadell, "El Consejo Federal de Gobierno y el Fondo de Compensación", in *Revista de derecho del Tribunal Supremo de Justicia,* N° 7, Caracas, 2002, pp. 417 a 457; Emilio Spósito Contreras, "Reflexiones sobre el Consejo Federal de Gobierno como máxima instancia de Participación administrativa", in *Temas de derecho administrativo, Libro Homenaje a Gonzalo Pérez Luciani,* Vol. II, Tribunal Supremo de Justicia, Colección Libros Homenaje, N° 7, Caracas, 2002, pp. 827 a 863; and José V. Haro, "Aproximación a la noción del Consejo Federal de Gobierno prrevisto en la Constitución de 1999", in *Revista de Derecho Constitucional,* N° 7 (enero-junio), Editorial Sherwood, Caracas, 2003, pp. 161-166.

Organic Law in a very centralistic shape, controlled by the Federal Executive, and not as an effective intergovernmental body.[66]

Finally, Article 323 of the Constitution has also created the Council of Nation's Defense, presided over by the President of the Republic, as the country's highest authority for defense planning, advice, and consultation regarding all public entities (Public Powers) on all matters related to the defense and security of the Nation's sovereignty, territorial integrity, and strategic thinking. [67]

2. Administrative functions of the National Executive

The President of the Republic is at the same time the Head of the State and the Head of Government and of Public Administration, and as such, directs the Government actions (Article 226). Thus, two are the basic functions of the National Executive, political and administrative, being subjected in both cases to the control of the National Assembly.

A. The President of the Republic as Head of Public Administration

According to Article 236.11 of the Constitution, the President is the head of the Public Administration, which he administers. In all his acts in these matters the Ministers must always countersign the corresponding executive acts. In particular, the President is empowered in Article 236.20 of the Constitution to determine the numbers, competencies and organization of the Ministries and other organs of Public Administration. In all these administrative matters the National Assembly also exercises its control over Public Administration (Article 187.3), being competent to discuss and approve the national budget and all public debt statutes (Articles 187, 6; 314; 317).

In his position of Head of Public Administration, Article 236 of the Constitution assigns the President with the following attributions: to appoint and dismiss the Executive Vice President and the Ministers (Article 236,3); to appoint, after parliamentary approval, the Attorney General of the Republic as well as the ambassadors and head of permanent diplomatic missions (Article 236,15; Article 187,14); and in general, to appoint all other public officials when attributed in the Constitution by statutes (Article 236,16).

On matters of public contracts, the same Article 236 of the Constitution assigns the President of the Republic in Council of Ministers, the power to negotiate public national debt (Article 236,12); and to sign national interest contracts according to the Constitution (Article 236,14). For the signing of these contracts, the National Assembly must approve them only when it is expressly required by a statute (Article 150), except in cases of contracts to be signed with foreign States of official foreign entities, or enterprises not domiciled in the country, in which cases the parliamentary approval is necessary (Article 187.9). Also, a parliamentary authorization is required in cases of public contracts selling public immoveable property (Article 187.12).

---

66 *Official Gazette* N° 5.963 of February 22, 2010.

67 See the Organic Law of the Nation's Security, in *Official Gazette* N° 6.156 of November 19, 2014.

B. The formulation of the National Development Plan

Article 236.18 of the Constitution assigns the President of the Republic in Council of Ministers the attribution to formulate the national Development Plan and direct its execution. The National Assembly must approve the general guidelines of the economic and social development plan, which the National Executive must file before the Assembly within the first trimester of the first year of the constitutional term (Article 236.18).[68]

3. The regulatory powers of the Executive branches

A. National, states and municipal regulations

An essential part of the administrative functions is the power assigned to the Executive branch of government to enact regulations in order to develop and facilitate the application of statutes. Consequently, in each of the three levels of government: The President of the Republic in the national level (Article 156,10); the Governors in the states level, and the Mayors in the municipal level, have the power to issue regulations referring to the respective national, states or municipal laws.

In addition, the other branches of government have been empowered in the Constitution to issue regulations in order to develop specific statutes, like the National Electoral Council regarding the Electoral Laws (Article 293.1). In other cases, it is in specific statutes that the regulatory powers have been established, like the case of the Comptroller General of the Republic regarding his fiscal control functions according to the Organic Law on the General Comptroller of the Republic (Article 13.1). Regulatory power has also been assigned to the Ministers by the Organic Law on Public Administration,[69] and to specific independent administrative or regulatory authorities by the corresponding statute creating them, like the Superintendence of Banks and Financial Institutions, Superintendence of Insurance, Superintendence on Free Competition protection, Stock Exchange control Commission. Also, the Supreme Tribunal of Justice has regulatory powers regarding the organization and functioning of the Judiciary (Article 267, Constitution).

B. Limits to the Executive Regulatory Powers

In all cases, the principal limit to the regulatory powers are those established in Article 156,10 of the Constitution when assigning it to the President of the Republic in the sense that they must always be exercised, regarding statutes, "without altering its spirit, purpose and reason." The consequence of this principle is that regulations are always administrative acts, although of general content, and consequently always subjected to the statutes whose contents always prevail over the regulations. Nonetheless, it is possible for administrative organs to issue "autonomous regulations", in the sense of regulations that are not intended to specifically develop a particular statute and are generally referred to organizational matters. In these cases, the limit is always its sub legal character, and that their validity ceases if the matters are later regulated in a statute passed by the National Assembly.

---

68 See the the Organic Law on Public and Popular Planing, in *Official Gazette* N° 6.148 of November 17, 2014.

69 *Official Gazette* N° 6.148 Extra. Of November 17, 2014.

Regulations, as all administrative acts, are subjected to judicial review by the Judicial Review of Administrative Action Courts (Article 259).

4. Liabilities

The President of the Republic is responsible for his acts and for the accomplishment of his duties. He is specifically obliged to seek for the guaranty of the Citizens' rights and liberties, as well as for the independence, integrity, sovereignty of the territory and the defense of the Republic (Article 232). The declaration of states of exception does not modify the liability principles regarding the President, or the Executive Vice President and the Ministers (Article 232).

On the other hand, the Executive Vice President and the Ministers are also individually (civil, criminal and administrative liability) responsible for their actions (Article 241, 244). They are also politically responsible before the President of the Republic, as head of Government, and before the National Assembly that can censure them.

According to Article 242 of the Constitution, the Executive Vice President and all the Ministers that have concurred in a decision of the Council of Ministers are jointly liable for their decisions. Only those that have formally expressed a dissenting or negative vote are excluded from this liability. The President of the Republic is, of course, also subject to joint liability for the Council's decisions, when he presides over it.

III. GENERAL PRINCIPLES RELATED TO PUBLIC ADMINISTRATION

1. The Constitutional principles related to Public Administration and administrative activities

A. General Principles

The 1999 Constitution includes in the title referred to as the "Public Power", a specific section related to "Public Administration,"[70] whose provisions have been developed by the Organic Law on Public Administration of 2001, reformed in 2008 and in 2014.[71] These provisions are applicable to all the organs and entities of all national branches of government exercising administrative functions, and not only of the Executive branch, and also to the national, states and municipal public

70 See Antonieta Garrido de Cárdenas, "La Administración Pública Nacional y su organización administrativa en la Constitución de 1999", in *Estudios de Derecho Administrativo: Libro Homenaje a la Universidad Central de Venezuela,* Volumen I, Imprenta Nacional, Caracas, 2001, pp. 427-471.

71 See *Official Gazette*. N° 5.890 Extra. of July 31, 2008, and *Official Gazette*. N° 6.148 Extra. of November 17, 2014 See the comments on the Law in Allan R. Brewer-Carías *et al*, *Ley Orgánica de la Administración Pública*, Caracas, 2002; Gustavo Briceño Vivas, "Principios constitucionales que rigen la Administración en la nueva Ley Orgánica de la Administración Pública", in *Temas de derecho administrativo, Libro Homenaje a Gonzalo Pérez Luciani,* Vol. I, Tribunal Supremo de Justicia, Colección Libros Homenaje, N° 7, Caracas, 2002, pp. 351 a 372.

administrations.[72] The Constitution sets forth a series of principles related to Public Administration, and within them, those that are common to all of the organs of the branches of government: principle of legality, principle of liability of the State and of its officials, and principle of finality.

The *first* principle related to Public Administration and to all State organs is the principle of legality enunciated in Article 137 of the Constitution when establishing that "The Constitution and the law would define the attributions of the organs exercising Public Power, to which they must subject all the activities they perform." This provision imposes the necessary submission of Public Administration to the law, being the consequence of it, that all administrative activities contrary to it can be reviewed by the Constitutional Jurisdiction (Article 334) and by the Administrative Jurisdiction (Article 259), whose courts have the power to annul illegal acts). The principle of legality is also declared in the Constitution as one of the foundations of Public Administration, defined as the "complete subjection to the law" (Article 141), being one of the basic missions of the organs of the Citizen Power, to assure "the complete subjection of the administrative activities of the State to the law" (Article 274).

The *second* general principle of Public Administration is the principle of State liability, incorporated in an express way in the 1999 Constitution (Article 140), setting forth that "The State is liable for the damages suffered by individuals in their goods and rights, provided that the injury be imputable to the functioning of Public Administration," being possible to comprise in the expression "functioning of Public Administration", its normal or abnormal functioning.[73] Although doubts can result from the wording of the Article regarding the liability of the State caused by legislative actions that nonetheless are derived from the general principles of public law,[74] regarding the liability caused by judicial acts, it is clarified by the express

---

72 See Allan R. Brewer-Carías, *Principios del Régimen Jurídico de la Organización Administrativa Venezolana*, Caracas 1994, pp. 11 y 53.

73 See Jesús Caballero Ortiz, "Consideraciones fundamentales sobre la responsabilidad administrativa en Francia y en España y su recepción en la Constitución venezolana de 1999", in *Estudios de Derecho Público: Libro Homenaje a Humberto J. La Roche Rincón,* Volumen II. Tribunal Supremo de Justicia, Caracas, 2001, pp. 255-271; Luis A. Ortiz-Álvarez, "La responsabilidad patrimonial del Estado y de los funcionarios públicos en la Constitución de 1999", in *Estudios de Derecho Administrativo: Libro Homenaje a la Universidad Central de Venezuela,* Volumen II. Imprenta Nacional, Caracas, 2001, pp. 149-208, and in *Revista de Derecho Constitucional*, N° 1 (septiembre-diciembre), Editorial Sherwood, Caracas, 1999, pp. 267-312; María E. Soto, "Régimen constitucional de la responsabilidad extracontractual de la Administración Pública", in *Revista Lex Nova del Colegio de Abogados del Estado Zulia,* N° 239, Maracaibo, 2001, pp. 49-72; Ana C. Núñez Machado, "La nueva Constitución y la responsabilidad patrimonial del Estado", in *Comentarios a la Constitución de la República Bolivariana de Venezuela",* Vadell Hermanos Editores, Caracas, 2000, pp. 35-64; and "Reflexiones sobre la interpretación constitucional y el artículo 140 de la Constitución sobre responsabilidad patrimonial del Estado", in *Revista de Derecho Administrativo,* N° 15 (mayo-diciembre), Editorial Sherwood, Caracas, 2002, pp. 207-222.

74 See Carlos A. Urdaneta Sandoval, "El Estado venezolano y el fundamento de su responsabilidad patrimonial extracontractual por el ejercicio de la función legislativa a la luz de la Constitución de 1999", in *Revista de Derecho Constitucional*, N° 5 (julio-diciembre), Editorial Sherwood, Caracas, 2001, pp. 247-301.

provisions of Articles 49.8 and 255 of the Constitution, in which it is established, in addition, the State liability caused because of "judicial errors or delay."[75]

The *third* general constitutional principle regarding Public Administration is the principle of liability of public officials in the exercise of public functions established in Article 139 of the Constitution, based on the "abuse or deviation of powers or the violation of the Constitution or of the law'. In addition, Article 25 of the Constitution, following a long constitutional tradition, expressly establishes the specific civil, criminal and administrative liability of any public officials when issuing or executing acts violating human rights guaranties in the Constitution and the statutes, not being acceptable any excuse due to superior orders.

The *fourth* principle of Public Administration incorporated in the 1999 Constitution is the principle of finality or purpose (Article 141), emphasizing that "Public Administration is at the service of Citizens," and as an organ of the State, it must also "guaranty the inalienable, indivisible and interdependent enjoyment and exercise of human rights to all persons, according to the principle of progressiveness and without discrimination."

And *fifth,* Article 141 of the Constitution also enumerates in an express way the general principles concerning administrative activities, providing that all activities of Public Administration are founded in the principles of "honesty, participation, celerity, efficacy, efficiency, transparency, accountability and liability in the exercise of public functions, with complete subjection to the law."

All these principles have been developed in the Organic Law on Public Administration (Article 12), adding to them, the principles of economy, simplicity, objectivity, impartiality, good faith and confidence (Article 12), and in the Administrative Procedure Organic Law.[76]

B. Constitutional provisions related to the Organization of Public Administration: Centralized and decentralized Public Administration

The Constitution establishes the basic principles for the organization of Public Administration, distinguishing between the Central Public Administration and the Decentralized Public Administration.

Regarding Central Public Administration, it is conformed in each of the three levels of government, according to the federal form of the State by the Executive organs of the State: at the national level, the President of the Republic is the head of National Public Administration; at the States level, the Governors of the States are the head of their States Public Administrations (Article 160); and at the municipal level, the Mayors are the Heads of the Municipal Public Administrations (Article 174).

Regarding the Central National Public Administration, as aforementioned, it is basically organized around the Ministries, being the President of the Republic the

---

75 See Abdón Sánchez Noguera, "La responsabilidad del Estado por el ejercicio de la función jurisdiccional en la Constitución venezolana de 1999", in *Revista Tachirense de Derecho,* N° 12 (enero-diciembre). Universidad Católica del Táchira, San Cristóbal, 2000, pp. 55-74.

76 *Official Gazette* N° 2818 Extra. Of July 1, 1981. See Allan R. Brewer-Carías *et al., Ley Orgánica de Procedimientos Administrativos*, Editorial Jurídica Venezolana, 12 edición, Caracas 2001, pp. 175 y ss.

competent organ, following the general principles established in the Organic Law on Public Administration, to determine their number, attributions and organization as well as of the other entities of Central Public Administration (Article 236.20).[77]

Regarding the National Decentralized Public Administration, the Constitution basically refers to the creation of autonomous institutions (public corporations), which is a power reserved to statutes (Article 142), and such institutions are always subjected to State control. Other forms of administrative functional decentralization, like State-own enterprises or public foundations, are regulated in the Organic Law on Public Administration, except for *Petróleos de Venezuela S.A.*, the State own oil company, which is regulated in Article 302 of the Constitution as a nationalized entity, and in the 2001 Hydrocarbon Law.

Regarding independent Regulatory Administrations, they are all regulated by statutes (Banking Superintendence, Insurance Superintendence, Free competition Superintendence, Stock Exchange Commission), except for the Central Bank that is also regulated as an autonomous entity in the Constitution (Article 320).

C. Constitutional principles regarding administrative information

Finally, Article 143 of the Constitution is also innovative regarding Citizens Rights to be informed and to have access to administrative information. In the first place, it provides for the right of Citizens to be promptly and truly informed by Public Administration regarding the situation of the procedures in which they have direct interest, and to know about the definitive resolutions therein adopted, to be notified of administrative acts and to be informed on the courses of the administrative procedure.

The constitutional Article also establishes for the individual right everybody has to have access to administrative archives and registries, without prejudice of the acceptable limits imposed in a democratic society related to the national or foreign security, to criminal investigation, to the intimacy of private life, all according to the statutes regulating the matter of secret or confidential documents classification. The same Article provides for the principle of prohibition of any previous censorship referring to public officials regarding the information they could give referring to matters under their responsibility.[78]

---

77 See Daniel Leza Betz, "La organización y funcionamiento de la administración pública nacional y las nuevas competencias normativas del Presidente de la República previstas en la Constitución de 1999. Al traste con la reserva legal formal ordinaria en el Derecho Constitucional venezolano", in *Revista de Derecho Público,* N° 82 (abril-junio), Editorial Jurídica Venezolana, Caracas, 2000, pp. 18-55.

78 See Orlando Cárdenas Perdomo, "El derecho de acceso a los archivos y registros administrativos en la Constitución de 1999", in *Estudios de Derecho Administrativo: Libro Homenaje a la Universidad Central de Venezuela,* Volumen I. Imprenta Nacional, Caracas, 2001, pp. 177-217; Manuel Rodríguez Costa, "Derecho de acceso a los archivos y registros de la Administración Pública", in *El Derecho Público a comienzos del siglo XXI. Estudios homenaje al Profesor Allan R. Brewer-Carías,* Tomo II, Instituto de Derecho Público, UCV, Civitas Ediciones, Madrid 2003, pp. 1483-1505; Javier T. Sánchez Rodríguez, "La libertad de acceso a la información en materia del medio ambiente", in *Revista de derecho del Tribunal Supremo de Justicia,* N° 7, Caracas, 2002, pp. 459 a 495.

D. Constitutional principles regarding civil service

In the 1999 Constitution, also in an innovative way, the general principles of the organization of civil service are established (Article 144 ff.), which have been developed by the Statute on the Civil Service.[79] In the first place, Article 145 establishes the general principle that all public officials are at the State service, and that they cannot serve any political group, providing also that their appointment and dismissal cannot be determined by political affiliation or orientation. Unfortunately, this constitutional principle has not been respected, due to the authoritarian government that has developed during the last decade (1999-2010) in the country, characterized by political discrimination in Public Administration regarding those citizens that signed petitions for presidential repeal referendums in 2003-2004), the absence of pluralism, and the interrelation between the official party and Public Administration)

In the second place, the Constitution distinguishes between two sorts of public officials: those following career position and those in positions of free appointment and dismissals (Article 146), establishing in an express way that all career positions in the Public Administration must always be filed through public competition (*concurso público*), based on honesty, competence and efficiency considerations. Also, the promotions must be subjected to scientific methods based on a merit system, and the transfer, suspension and dismissals must be decided according to their performance. Unfortunately, due to the strict political control of all the bureaucracy, neither of these constitutional provisions factually is in force.

In the third place, the Constitution also establishes the general principle of discipline in public spending regarding the provisions of public official positions, in the sense that being paid as provided in the budget law (Article 147). The scale of remunerations for public officials must be established by statute, and the National Assembly has been empowered to establish limits to municipal, states and national public officers (Article 229)[80]. The regime for pensions and retirements are also attributed in the Constitution to be established by the National Assembly.[81]

In addition, other constitutional provisions are established regarding public officers. For instance, the principle of incompatibility to occupy more than one remunerated position (Article 148), except in cases of academic, transitory, assistant, or teaching positions. In any case of acceptance of a new position, it implies the renunciation of the first, except in cases of deputies, up to the definitive replacement of the principal. In addition, the Constitution provides that public officer cannot benefit from more than one pension (Article 148).

---

79 *Official Gazette* N° 37.522 of September 6, 2002. See Jesús Caballero Ortíz, "Bases constitucionales del derecho de la función pública", in *Revista de Derecho Constitucional,* N° 5, julio-diciembre-2001, Editorial Sherwood, Caracas, 2002, pp. 21 a 46; Antonio de Pedro Fernández, "Algunas consideraciones sobre la función pública en la Constitución de la República Bolivariana de Venezuela", in *Estudios de Derecho Administrativo: Libro Homenaje a la Universidad Central de Venezuela,* Volumen I, Imprenta Nacional, Caracas, 2001, pp. 307-342.

80 Organic Law fixing the remuneration of High States and Municipal public servants, *Official Gazette* N° 37.412 of Nars 26,2002.

81 Law on the Retrat and Pension Regime rearding National, States and Municipal Public Administration employees, *Official Gazette* Extra N° 6.156 of November 19, 2014.

The Constitution also establishes the prohibition for public officers to sign contracts with the Municipalities, the States, the Republic and with any other public law or state-owned entity (Article 145).

2. Principles related to the of the Organization of Public Administration

Under the Constitution of Venezuela of 1999, the Venezuelan Government is organized according to the principle of the separation of powers, dividing the National Public Power (*Poder Público Nacional*), in the sense of public *potestas* (article 136 of the Constitution), into five Branches of Government: *Legislative, Executive, Judiciary, Citizen, and Electoral* (article 136). All the organs and entities of the State exercise one or the other public *potestas* and are organized according to the provisions of the Constitution and of its corresponding statutes.

Those Branches correspond respectively to the following organs: National Legislative Assembly (*National Legislative Power*, articles 186-224), the President of the Republic and the other bodies of the National Executive Power (*National Executive Power*, articles 225-252), the Supreme Tribunal of the Republic and other courts (*Judicial Power*, articles 253-272), the General Prosecutor of the Republic, the General Comptroller of the Republic, and the People's Defender (*Citizen Power*, articles 273-291), and the National Electoral Council and other electoral bodies (*Electoral Power*, articles 292-298).[82] Each of these bodies has its own functions, and must cooperate with each other in the realization of the purposes of the Government (articles 3 and 136).

All the organs and entities of the Venezuelan State are necessarily integrated into one of the five aforementioned Branches of Government; that is, there are no organs or entities of the State that could be considered to be outside the scope of the five Branches of Government. Therefore, there is no possibility in the Venezuelan Constitution to find an organ or an entity of the State located outside those five Branches of Government.

In particular, regarding the National Executive Power, it is exercised by all the organs and entities that comprise the National Public Administration (Articles 141-143), which are integrated into two general organizations: on the one hand, *Central Public Administration*, comprised of the organs that are directly dependent on the President and the Ministers of the Executive that act through the public officers determined by the law (Art. 225), which conforms the Central government; and on the other hand, other entities or instrumentalities of the State established in the Constitution, identified as "decentralized entities," characterized by the fact that they have a separate legal personality from that of the State (the Republic). These decentralized entities, are referred to in various articles of the Constitution; and, in particular, with the form of *persons of public law*, in Articles 142, 189 related to the autonomous institutes (*institutos autónomos*); and in Articles 318 referring to the Central Bank of Venezuela; and with the form of *persons of private law*, in Article

82 See in relation to the Organization of the Government in Venezuela, Allan R. Brewer-Carías, *La Constitución de 1999: Estado democrático y social de derecho.* Colección Tratado de Derecho Constitucional, Tomo VII, Fundación de Derecho Público, Editorial Jurídica Venezolana, Caracas 2014 pp. 503-504 Available at: http://allanbrewercarias.com/wp-content/uploads/2014/07/BREWER-TRATADO-DE-DC-TOMO-VII-9789803652548-txt.pdf

300, referred to state owned enterprises (business) or the foundations or association of the State (social)); and in Articles 184.4 and 301 which also refers to State owned enterprises or public enterprises

All these entities conform the *Decentralized Public Administration*, comprised of all the entities created by law (persons of public law) or incorporated according to the provisions of the Civil or Commercial Code (persons of private law), that as already mentioned have their own personality (separated from that of the Republic), and the autonomy as provided by law. All of the decentralized entities with *public law personality* are created by statutes, like the public institutions (*institutos autónomos*) (public corporations) (article 142), and like the Central Bank of Venezuela which in addition is referred to in Article 318 of the Constitution; and the decentralized entities with *private law personality* are always incorporated according to the private law provisions, generally established in the Commercial Code and the Civil Code, such as State owned enterprises, State foundations, and State associations (articles 300), some of which are also referred to in the Constitution as is the case of *Petróleos de Venezuela S.A.* (Article 303).[83]

In all these cases, all those entities classified as decentralized entities are expressly described in the Constitution as "State's persons of public law or of private law" (article 145, 322), or State legal persons (Articles 180, 190) or as legal persons of the public sector (Articles 289.3; 289.4); all of them being, regardless from their legal form, legal basis or statute, always subjected to the control of the State, according to what, in each case, is established by statute (Article 142).[84] This control is regulated in general, in the Organic Law on Public Administration[85] for the autonomous institutes, state owned enterprises, State associations or State foundations, or in a special statute, as is the case in particular of the Central Bank of Venezuela, which is a decentralized entity of the National Public Administration, historically configured with personality of public law, that notwithstanding its autonomy, is only subjected to the control of the State as specifically provided in the Central Bank of Venezuela Law.[86]

Regarding the aforementioned Organic Law on Public Administration, its article 15 provides for "Public Administration" to be integrated by "organs," "entities" *(entes),* and "missions" (*misiones*).

---

83 See Allan R. Brewer-Carías, "Sobre las personas jurídicas en la Constitución de 1999," in *Derecho Público Contemporáneo. Libro Homenaje a Jesús Leopoldo Sánchez*, Estudios del Instituto de Derecho Público, Universidad Central de Venezuela, enero-abril 2003, Volumen 1, pp. 7-10. Available at: http://allanbrewercarias.com/wp-content/uploads/2007/08/473.-440.-SOBRE-LAS-PERSONAS-JUR%C3%8DDICAS-EN-LA-CONSTITUCION-DE-1999.pdf

84 See in relation to the legal persons in the organization of the State: Allan R. Brewer-Carías, *Tratado de Derecho Administrativo. Derecho Público Iberoamericano, Tomo I: El derecho Administrativo y sus principios fundamentales*, Tomo I, Editorial Civitas, Madrid 2013, pp.336-339; 793; 835-843. Available at: http://allanbrewercarias.com/wp-content/uploads/2013/07/BREWER-TRATADO-DE-DA-TOMO-I-9789803652067-txt-1.pdf

85 Decree Law N° 1.424, in *Official Gazette* N° 6.147 Extra. of November 17, 2014. See on the previous 2008 Law: Allan R. Brewer-Carías, Rafael Chavero Gazdik and Jesús María Alvarado Andrade, *Ley Orgánica de la Administración Pública, Decreto ley N° 4317 de 15-07-2008*, (Coordinador y Editor), Editorial Jurídica Venezolana, Caracas 2009.

86 See Decree-Law No 2197 of December 30, 2015, in Official Gazette No. 6211 Extra of December 30, 2015

The *organs* are administrative units of the Republic, of the States, of the Metropolitan Districts and of the municipalities when being assigned functions whose exercise can produce legal effects regarding third parties, or when their acts have regulatory character (obligatory force). These organs, in principle, conforms the Central Administration within each of the three territorial levels of government: national, states and municipal.

The *entities* are all those "functionally decentralized administrative organizations" established as separate legal persons, with their own and different legal personhood (*personalidad juridica*),[87] in general subject to control, evaluation and follow up of their actions by the commanding organs (*órganos rectores*), the organs of attachment and by the Central Planning Commission.".

The "missions" are organizations created to take care of urgent and fundamental needs of the people. They were regulated in the 2008 reform of the Organic Law on Public Administration (art. 131) in order to formalize the informal development of administrative organizations that in a very disorderly way were created between 2002 and 2008 to develop social programs, without any previous studies or planning, mainly established with legal personality borrowed from private law (*fundaciones*).[88] In 2014 the "missions" were regulated by a special statute, the Organic Law on Missions, Great Missions and Micro-Missions, which defined them as social "public policies" rather that organs or entities, than can take the shape or forms of the later.[89]

According to article 19 of the same Organic Law, the activity of the organs and entities of National Public Administration "shall pursue the effective accomplishment of the objectives and goals established in the norms, plans and management compromises, under the orientation of the policies and strategies established by the President of the republic, the Central Planning Commission ..." In addition, according to article 46 of the Law, the President of the Republic, as Head of the State and of the National Executive, directs the government and Public Administration action, with the immediate collaboration of the Vice President of the Republic. Regarding the Ministers, according to article 77.13 they are the organs that "exercise the command of the public policies developed by the functionally decentralized entities attached to their offices" (par. 13), as well as "to represent the shares owns by the Republic in the State-owned enterprises assigned to them, as well as the shareholders control" (par. 14).

---

87 In order to understand the organization of Public Administration in the Venezuelan federal State according to the Organic Law, the notion of "person" and "*personalidad*" (legal status of a person) are fundamental, in the sense that the condition of having *personalidad* (statute of being a legal person) is the one that allows any entity to act in the legal world of inter relations, and to have rights and duties, and be subject to liability; that is, to sue and to be sued in its own name, to contract in its own name and to hold property in its own name. The notion of *personalidad* thus is fundamental in Roman law systems, in any of their branch of law (Article 19, Civil Code), and, in particular, in Administrative Law.

88 See Allan R. Brewer-Carías, "El sentido de la reforma de la Ley Orgánica de la Administración Pública," in *Revista de Derecho Público. Estudios sobre los decretos leyes 2008*, Nº 115, (julio-septiembre 2008), Editorial Jurídica Venezolana, Caracas 2008, pp. 155-162.

89 *Official Gazette* Nº 6.154 Extra. of November 19, 2014.

3. Principles related to the decentralized organization in the Public Administration

In this context, in order to understand the organization of Public Administration in the Venezuelan federal State according to the Organic Law, the notion of "person" and *"personalidad"* (legal status of a person) are fundamental, in the sense that the condition of having *personalidad* (statute of being a legal person) is the one that allows any entity to act in the legal world of inter relations, and to have rights and duties and be subject to liability; that is, to sue and to be sued in its own name, to contract in its own name and to hold property in its own name. The notion *of personalidad* thus is fundamental in Roman law systems, in any of their branch of law (Article 19, Civil Code), and, in particular, in Administrative Law.[90]

In this latter branch of law, in particular, regarding the various units that conform the Venezuelan "State" or the public sector, as it is establish in one of the aforementioned Statutes referred to the public sector (Organic Law on Financial Administration of the Public Sector),[91] it is possible to distinguish two sort of legal persons integrated in the public sector: On the one hand, the legal persons that are established as the result of the political organization of the country, that is, as political subdivisions of the State, as is the case of a federal State. In it, the territorial distribution of the State power (political decentralization), necessarily implies the creation of various legal persons with different territorial jurisdictional scope. On the other hand, there are the legal persons established also as a consequence of a decentralization process, but only of administrative nature, by means of the creation of separate entities or legal persons generally outside the hierarchy of Public Administration in order to help the Government to accomplish its activities.

In this sense, within the first decentralization process, the political one, in Venezuela, being a Federal State (Bolivarian Republic of Venezuela), is essential to distinguish the following legal persons derived from the political subdivision of the country: the Republic, the States, the Metropolitan Districts and the Municipalities They are all public law "territorial or political legal persons", established as consequence of the adopted vertical or territorial system of distribution of State power (political decentralization). As legal persons, they have their own scope of action or competencies, and their own administrative components and units for the development of their activities. All are considered to be "the Venezuelan State", but in the internal point of view, they are different persons. For instance, in matters of hydrocarbon and oil activities, the attributions of the Venezuelan State on such matters are exclusively attributed to its national political person (the Republic) (article 156.16 of the Constitution).

---

90 Véase Allan R. Brewer-Carías, "Sobre las personas jurídicas en la Constitución de 1999" en *Derecho Público Contemporáneo. Libro Homenaje a Jesús Leopoldo Sánchez*, Estudios del Instituto de Derecho Público, Universidad Central de Venezuela, enero-abril 2003, Volumen 1, pp. 48-54; "El régimen de las personas jurídicas estatales político-territoriales en la Constitución de 1999" en *El Derecho constitucional y público en Venezuela. Homenaje a Gustavo Planchart Manrique*, Tomo I, Universidad Católica Andrés Bello, de Tinoco, Travieso, Planchart & Núñez, Abogados, Caracas 2003, pp. 99-121; "La distinción entre las personas jurídicas y las personas privadas y el sentido de la problemática actual de la clasificación de los sujetos de derecho" en *Revista Argentina de Derecho Administrativo*, N° 17, Buenos Aires 1977, pp. 15-29.

91 See in *Official Gazette* N° 39.465, July 14, 2010

Each of the legal persons that conform the political subdivision of the State, that is, the Republic, the States and the Municipalities, according to the Public Administration Organic Law, have "organs", that are the ones whose functions, when exercised, can produce legal effects regarding third parties, or whose acts have obligatory force. These organs of these public law territorial legal persons are the ones that can be considered as part of Public Administration pursuant the terms of article 15 of the Organic Law. In the case of the Republic, for instance, within the organs, the most important ones are the Ministries. For instance, in the environmental field, the most important organ of the Republic and its National Public Administration organization was the Ministry of Environment, in the mining field, is the Ministry for Basic Industries and Mining, and in the hydrocarbon and oil field, is the Ministry of Energy and Oil.

According to the provisions of the Public Administration Organic Law, therefore, in no case, the decentralized entities or commercial companies established as State-own enterprises, as separate legal persons regarding Central Administration can therefore be considered as "organs" of Public Administration as they are regulated in article 15 of its Organic Law.

As I explained in 2015 that in Venezuela, the Constitution establishes the basic principles for the organization of Public Administration, distinguishing between the Central Public Administration and the Decentralized Public Administration, as follows:

> "Regarding Central Public Administration, it is composed of each of the three levels of government, according to the federal form of the State by the Executive organs of the State: at the national level, the President of the Republic is the head of National Public Administration; at the States level, the Governors of the States are the head of their States Public Administrations (Article 160); and at the municipal level, the Mayors are the Heads of the Municipal Public Administrations (Article 174).
>
> Regarding the Central National Public Administration, as aforementioned, it is basically organized around the Ministries, being the President of the Republic the competent organ, following the general principles established in the Organic Law on Public Administration, to determine their number, attributions and organization as well as of the other entities of Central Public Administration (Article 236.20).
>
> Regarding the National Decentralized Public Administration, the Constitution basically refers to the creation of autonomous institutions (public corporations), which is a power reserved to statutes (Article 142), as such institutions are always subjected to State control. Other forms of administrative functional decentralization, like State-own enterprises or public foundations [State's private law persons], are regulated in the Organic Law on Public Administration, except for *Petróleos de Venezuela S.A.*, the State-owned oil company, which is regulated in Article 302 of the Constitution as a nationalized entity, and in the 2001 Hydrocarbon Law.
>
> Regarding independent Regulatory Administrations, they are all regulated by statutes (Banking Superintendence, Insurance Superintendence, Free Competition Superintendence, Stock Exchange Commission), except for the Central Bank of

Venezuela that is also regulated as an autonomous entity in the Constitution (Article 320)."[92]

As mentioned, the universe of the National Public Administration has been mainly regulated by the Public Administration Organic Law,[93] declaring that it consists of "organs, entities and missions" (art. 15): the *first*, comprises the "Central Level of National Public Administration" (articles 44 ff.), including among other organs the Ministries (articles 61 ff.); the *second*, comprises the Decentralized Public Administration (articles 92 ff.), integrated, as stated in article 29, by entities with public law and private law personality;[94] that is, in addition to those decentralized entities created and regulated by special laws such as the Central Bank of Venezuela and the public corporations (*institutos públicos*) (articles 96 ff.); the decentralized entities incorporated according to the Civil or Commercial Law, like the state-owned enterprises (articles 103 ff.), the State's Foundations (articles 109 ff.) and the State Civil Associations (articles 116 ff.); and the *third* are the so called "Missions" (article 132).

Consequently, all those entities are considered as part of the public sector according to article 5 of the Financial Management of Public Sector Organic Law, which includes in addition to the public corporations (*institutos autonomous*), the National Universities, the National Academies, the State Associations, the State Foundations, and all the State legal persons of public law (which includes the Central Bank of Venezuela), the state-owned enterprises and their direct subsidiaries.[95]

---

92 See Allan R. Brewer-Carías, *Administrative Law in Venezuela*, Editorial Jurídica Venezolana, Second Edition, 2015, p. 52. Available at: Available at: http://allanbrewercarias.com/wp-content/uploads/2013/08/9789803651992-txt.pdf

93 See *Official Gazette* N° 6.147 Extra. of November 17, 2014. Available at: http://www.conatel.gob.ve/wp-content/uploads/2015/02/Ley-Org%C3%A1nica-de-Administraci%C3%B3n-P%C3%BAblica.pdf

94 Article 29: The functional decentralized entities are of two types: Decentralized entities with private law form, which are conformed by legal persons incorporated according to the provisions of private law [...]. 2. Decentralized entities with public law form, which are conformed by those legal persons created and rued by public law provisions and which can have been attributed to exercise public powers."

95 Article 5.8. The commercial societies in which the Republic and the other persons aforementioned in this article have a share equal or more to 50% of its capital. Also subjected to the law, are the companies totally owned by the State, that through holding shares of other companies, have the function of coordinating the entrepreneurial management of a sector of the national economy. 9. The commercial societies in which the persons referred to in the previous numeral, have a participation equal to or more than 50% of its outstanding capital." See *Official Gazette* No 6.210 Extra of December 30, 2015. Available at: http://www.bod.com.ve/media/97487/GACETA-OFICIAL-EXTRAORDINARIA-6210.pdf.. The State owned enterprises were defined by the Constitutional Chamber of the Supreme Tribunal (in a 2002 decision) as "State legal persons with the form of commercial companies, subjected to a mixed legal regime, of public and private law, although preponderantly of private law, due to its form, but not exclusively, because their close relation with the State, imposes their subjection to mandatory public law provisions sanctioned in order to secure the best organization, functioning and execution of control by the Public Administration, by its organs or by those that contribute to attain their objectives. See decision N° 464 of March 18, 2002 (Case: *Interpretación del Decreto de la Asamblea Nacional Constituyente de fecha 30 de enero de 2000, mediante el cual se suspende por 3 días la negociación de la Convención Colectiva del Trabajo)*, in *Revista de Derecho Público,* N° 89-92,

New, regarding the "entities" as part of Public Administration, according to the same article 15 of the Organic Law, they are all those legal persons created as a consequence of the process of functional administrative decentralization, as separate and different legal persons regarding the legal persons derived from the political subdivision of the country, that is, from the Republic, the States, of the Metropolitan Districts and of the Municipalities.

Such separate legal persons, particularly referring to the economic activities, can have a public law form when the person is created directly by statute, as is the case of the *institutos autónomos* or *institutos públicos* (Government Corporations) or of a private law form, like the one attributed to the commercial companies or public enterprises *(compañía or sociedad anónima)* according to the Commercial Code regulations.

The basic characteristic for all these "entities" in order to be considered as part of the Public Administration is that they must be created by the already mentioned territorial legal political persons (Republic, States. Municipalities) as integrating the public sector, as a consequence of a process of administrative decentralization, or by an "entity" already created by them. The imbrications between central Public Administration (organs) and decentralized Public Administration (entities), is such, that according to article 38, "Public Administration can temporally assign the accomplishment of material or technical activities of its attributions to their respective functionally decentralized entities ..."

Article 29 of the Public Administration Organic Law, establishes the general framework of all these functional decentralized "entities" basically referring to the National Level of government (National Public Administration) that can be created by the organs of the State, that can be of two sorts, with "public law form" or "private law form," as follows:[96]

1. Functional decentralized entities with public law statute comprising those legal persons created and subjected to public law statutes and that can also be attributed the exercise of public powers.

2. Functional decentralized entities with private law statute comprising those legal persons established and subjected to private law statutes, which can or not adopt the entrepreneurial form in accordance with the purpose seeking with its creation and bearing in mind if their fundamental income comes from their own activities or from public funds.

In the first place, the "entities" of Public Administration established as functional decentralized entities with "public law form," are those separate legal persons created and ruled by public law provisions and that could have attributed the exercise of public powers." The classical public law form of functional decentralization is the *instituto autónomo* or *instituto público* (Government Corporation) that must be created by statute (article 98), in order to accomplish specific State activities including entrepreneurial ones.

Editorial Jurídica Venezolana, pp. 218 ff. Available at: http://allanbrewercarias.com/wp-content/uploads/2007/08/2002-REVISTA-89-90-91-92.pdf

96 The distinction can also be found in article 7 of the already mentioned Organic Law of the Financial Administration of the Public Sector.

In the second place, the functionally decentralized entities created with "private law form," that conforms the legal persons established according to private law provisions, that can adopt or not the entrepreneurial form in accordance to the goals and objectives that originated their incorporation, and bearing in mind if the origin of their resources come form their own activity or from public funds. The classical private law form of functional decentralization are the State own enterprises (*empresas del Estado*), that must be created with the authorization of the President of the Republic (article 104), and in which the Republic or any other decentralized entity owns more than the 50% of its shares (article 103). This are functional decentralized "entities" created by the organs of the State which are subject to private law statutes, are those with entrepreneurial purposes in the sense that their principal activity is the production of goods or services directed to be sold and whose income or resources basically derive from such activity. Their legal personality is acquired through the incorporation of the company in the Public Commercial Registry (Article 104).

4. Principles related to State-own enterprises as part of Public Administration

A. Definition and creation

The legal persons named in the Public Administration Organic Law, as "State own enterprises" *(empresas del Estado),* are all those commercial companies in which the Republic, the States, the Municipalities, or any other functional decentralized entities provided in such Organic Law like the Government Corporations *(institutos autónomos),* and other State-own enterprises, on their own or together, have more than the 50% of the shares of the stock of the company (article 103).[97]

Therefore, regarding "public enterprises,"[98] only those incorporated as first and second tier subsidiaries are "State own enterprises" in the terms of the Public Administration Organic Law. This implies that none of its provisions are applicable

97With this legal definition, all the erratic effort to define "State-own enterprises" for the purpose of determining the jurisdiction of the Judicial Review of Administrative Action Courts *(contencioso administrativo),* where overcome. See decisión of the Constitucional Chamber of the Supreme Tribunal N° 2724 of December 18,2001 (Case: *Impugnación del artículo 2o ordinal 9o de la Ley del estatuto Sobre el Régimen de Jubilaciones y Pensiones de los Funcionarios o Empleados de la Administración Pública Nacional, de los Estados y de los Municipios).* See also, the decision of the Civil Cassation Chamber of the Supreme Tribunal of April 25, 2003 (Case: *Leonardo Segundo Cenci E. vs. Gobernación del Estado Táchira),* in *Revista de Derecho Público,* N° 93-96, Editorial Jurídica Venezolana, Caracas 2003, pp. 473 ff.

98The expression "public enterprises" is an economic concept referred to all sort of organizations (organs or entities) of the State that develop commercial activities; a concept different to "State-own enterprises" used in the strict sense of the Organic Law on Public Administration, referred only to the first and second tier State own companies or subsidiaries. See in general, regarding public enterprises: Allan R. Brewer-Carías, *Les entreprises publiques en droit comparé*, Paris 1978; *Las empresas públicas en el derecho comparado*, Universidad Central de Venezuela, Caracas 1967; E*l régimen jurídico de las empresas públicas en Venezuela*, Ediciones del Centro Latinoamericano de Administración para el Desarrollo, Caracas 1980; and Jesús Caballero Ortíz, *Las Empresas Públicas en el Derecho Venezolano*, Editorial Jurídica Venezolana, Caracas 1982

to third tier commercial companies, even if considered as "public enterprises," and eventually part of the public sector.

The Public Administration Organic Law also expressly authorizes the Republic, the States, the Municipalities, and the other decentralized entities, to create commercial companies with just one shareholder (art. 106). In such cases of state-owned enterprises with one shareholder, the decision to create it, if adopted by the Republic, the States or the Municipalities it must be respectively issue by the President of the Republic in Council of Ministers, the Governor or the Mayor, through a Decree or resolution (art. 104).

This possibility to establish commercial companies with only one single shareholder[99] is regulated in article 106 of the Organic Law as a formal exception to the partnership contractual basis generally required in all commercial companies according to the Commercial Code. Previous to this provision now applicable to all State-own enterprises, only the case of *Petróleos de Venezuela S.A.* (PDVSA) could be distinguished as a commercial company incorporated with only one shareholder, in such case, the Republic, according to the provisions of the 1975 Nationalization Law.[100] Later, due to the decision to transform two Government Corporations *(institutos autónomos)* acting in the Oil Industry, the *Instituto Venezolano de Petroquímica* and the *Corporación Venezolana del Petróleo,* to be commercial companies, the respective Statutes provided for the incorporation of the commercial companies *Intevep* S.A. and *Corpoven* S.A., as subsidiaries of *Petróleos de Venezuela S.A.*, with this holding company as the only shareholder.

According to the regulations of the Public Administration Organic Law, the State own enterprises acquires their juridical legal personality statute *(personalidad)* by registering their incorporation document and their by-laws in the Commercial Registrar of its domicile, which must also register the *Official Gazette* where has been published the decree or resolution authorizing its incorporation act (Art. 104). All these documents must also be published in the *Official Gazette* of the Republic or in the gazettes of the States or Municipalities (art. 105). Being private law legal persons, the State-own enterprises are subjected to the "ordinary legislation", particularly, that established in the Commercial Code, except regarding what it is established in the Public Administration Organic Law (article 108). Nonetheless, being public enterprises, the State own enterprises are also subjected to the applicable statutes referred to the whole public sector.

B. Representation

Being the state-owned enterprises, commercial companies constituted according to private law commercial provisions, its activities, as commercial enterprise, must always be subjected to their own by-laws. Consequently, their representation to act as a company can only be exercised according to what is determined in those by-laws, particularly for entering into contracts with third parties. The common trend

99 See Allan R. Brewer-Carías, *Las empresas públicas en el derecho comparado,* Universidad Central de Venezuela, Caracas, 1967, pp. 115 ff.

100 See Allan R. Brewer-Carías, "Aspectos organizativos de la industria petrolera nacionalizada", en *Archivo de Derecho Público y Ciencias de la Administración, Régimen Jurídico de las nacionalizaciones en Venezuela,* Caracas, Vol. III, 1972-1979, Tomo I, Instituto de Derecho Público, Universidad Central de Venezuela, Caracas, 1981, pp. 407 ff.

on these matters, inserted in those by-laws, is that, in general, contracts to be signed by the public company must be approved by the Board of Directors and signed by its President. The Board of Directors could also expressly authorize other persons to act as the representatives of the company.

Referring to national public enterprises, therefore and according to the Constitution, the Organic Law on Public Administration and the Organic Law on Administrative Procedure, the respective Minister to which the public enterprises are assigned or attached cannot act on their behalf. As all public officials, they can only act when specific attributions are given to him through statutes in order to accomplish specific activities. The Ministers of the National Executive are organ of the President of the Republic, and therefore, members of the National Executive, and as such they have no express attribution to act as a representative of the public enterprises attached to them, and could not sign contracts representing those company.

On the other hand, also referring to the representation of public enterprises, the Attorney General of the Republic cannot act representing such entities. The Attorney General is the representative of the Republic, having as his principal function, according to the Constitution and the Organic Law of the Attorney General's Office to assist, represent and defend before the courts of justice or *extrajudicially* the assets, rights and interest of the Republic (arts. 1, 14). Regarding the Republic's decentralized entities, like the state-own enterprises, he has just the attribution to give legal advice to them when expressly asked by the competent public official of the national Executive exercising administrative control upon them, that is the respective Minister of attachment (art. 21), and also the attribution to participate (*intervenir*) in judicial processes in which the decentralized entities are party (art. 76).

That is, regarding legal advice, the Attorney General is empowered to give his legal advice to public enterprises regarding their activities, when requested through the Minister to which they are attached (article 21of the Organic Law of the General Attorney's Office).

Regarding the participation (*intervención*) in judicial processes in which a public enterprise is a party, the Attorney General has the express attribution to participate when he considers that the patrimonial rights or interest *of the Republic* can be affected (article 76). For such purpose, the Organic Law compels the courts to notify to the Attorney General regarding any judicial action involving public enterprises (art. 5).

But none of the aforementioned attributions of the Attorney General gives him any quality whatsoever to judicially or extrajudicially "represent" the public enterprises, nor to approve or not approve contracts signed by them, nor to authorized or not authorized them, or to act in a judicial process in the name or representing the public enterprises.

C. Attachment to a Ministry and control of *adscripción*

The most important provisions of the Public Administration Organic Law in relation to national State-own enterprises, beside the aforementioned provisions regarding their incorporation and the required level of subsidiary (first and second) in order to be considered as such, are those set forth for the purpose of assuring the control regarding their activities by organs of Public Administration.

This Organic Law, in this regard, establishes a system of what is called *"control de adscripción"* (attachment control), which is provided in particular to be applied in the relationship between Public Administration organs and administrative decentralized entities (separate legal persons), in order to distinguish it from the hierarchical control that corresponds to the relationship between the organs of Public Administration of one of the political subdivisions of the State.

The "adscription" control only exists when the administrative relationship is established between different legal persons, for instance among the Republic and a Government Corporation (*instituto autónomo*) or a state-own enterprise. That is why, all "entities" considered part of the National Public Administration have to be attached to a Ministry or organ of "adscription" (articles 118, 119), which have the following attributions listed in article 120: to define the policy to be developed by the company, for which purpose it can formulate the necessary general directives; to permanently exercise the coordination, supervision and control functions; to continuously evaluate the accomplishment and results of its management and promptly inform the President of the Republic; to inform quarterly the national organ of planning regarding the executions of the plans by the enterprise; and to propose the President of the Republic, the needed reforms, in order to modify or eliminate the ascribed State-own enterprise.

In the case of national state-own enterprises subjected to the Public Administration Organic Law, the adscription (attachment) control established in it, is called "shareholding control" because it is the one that is exercised by means of the public official (organs of Public Administration) representing the shares of the Republic in the Shareholders meetings of the State-own enterprise. That means that the Ministers, in relation to the companies that are attached to their Ministries, have basically the power to represent the shares of the Republic in the company, as it is expressly stated in article 78.14 of the Organic Law on Public Administration, exercising the shareholding control regarding the activities of the company; but such representation of the shares of the Republic in the public enterprises, for instance, does not authorize the Ministers to represent the company before third parties or to act on behalf or representing the attached enterprises, nor to sign on their behalf contracts with third parties "representing" the company.

In the Public Administration Organic Law this control is only set forth expressly regarding first tier State-own enterprises subsidiaries, like the case of PDVSA subjected to the shareholding control exercise by the Ministry of Energy and Oil. Nonetheless, according to the 2001 Hydrocarbons Law,[101] the national Oil companies are governed in addition to the provisions of the Law and its Regulations, by the provisions enacted by the National Executive through the Ministry of Energy and Oil (article 29); which according to article 30 of the same Law is in charge of inspecting and controlling the public Oil enterprises and its subsidiaries, being authorized to enact general rules and policies applicable to these matters.

In order to the adscription control be exercise in the national level of the State (Republic) by the organs of national Public Administration, the Organic Law assigns

101 See in *Official Gazette* Nº 38.493 of August 4, 2006

to the President of the Republic the duty to issue a Decree establishing the adscription of Government Corporations, State-own enterprises, State foundations or State civil associations to the corresponding organs of Central Public Administration, particularly, to the Ministries. According to article 117 of such Decree, the President is also empowered to vary the adscription according the changes in the organization of the *Ministerios* (Ministries); to change the share ownership from one to other Public Administration organ, or transfer it to a decentralized entity; to merge State-own enterprises and transform foundations or administrative services in State-own enterprises.

The Decree of Adscription of entities to the Ministries of Public Administration, was initially issued in 2001[102], and for instance, regarding the then Ministry of Energy and Mines, the only State-own enterprise ascribed to it was PDVSA (art. 10), because it is the only State-own enterprise in the oil industry whose shares are owned by the Republic. The subsidiaries of PDVSA were not ascribed to the Ministry, as none of the second and their tier subsidiaries companies established in the oil industry have never been ascribed to it.

The adscription of public entities to the Ministries was later establish in the Decree on the Organization and Functioning of the national Public Administration of 2009,[103] in which again, for example, PDVSA was the only oil State-own enterprise directly own by the Republic and ascribed to the Ministry of the Popular Power of Energy and Oil (Transitory Disposition Twentieth). None of the subsidiaries of PDVSA or their subsidiaries are ascribed to the Ministry, and therefore according to the Organic Law on Public Administration are not subjected to the direct control or supervision by the Government. Nonetheless, as mentioned, according to the Organic Law on Hydrocarbons, all the State-own enterprises that conform the oil sector are subject to the inspection and control of the Ministry of Energy and Petroleum, and to the rules and policies it enacts (articles 29, 30).

Consequently, the subsidiaries of PDVSA, as all second tiers of level public enterprises, even being subjected to the Organic Law for other purposes, are not and have never been ascribed to any Ministry. Such adscription control is reserved to first level State-own enterprises, and therefore it is not and has not been exercised regarding second and third level subsidiaries public enterprises.

In relation to the first level State-own enterprises, that is, those in which the Republic is the shareholder, as is the case, for example, of *Petróleos de Venezuela S.A.* (PDVSA), article 118 of the Public Administration Organic Law, assign the Ministry of Energy and Oil, with the general power to define the policy to be developed by the company, for which purpose it can formulate the necessary general directives; to permanently exercise the coordination, supervision and control functions; to continuously evaluate the accomplishment and results of its management and promptly inform the President of the Republic; to inform quarterly the national organ of planning regarding the executions of the plans by the enterprise; and to propose the President of the Republic, the needed reforms, in order to modify or eliminate the ascribed State-own enterprise. None of these

102 See *Official Gazette* N° 5.556 Extra, of November 13, 2001

103 See Decree N° 6.670 of April 22, 2009 in *Official Gazette,* N° 39.163, of April 22, 2004.

powers or attributions can be directly exercise neither regarding the subsidiaries of the PDVSA nor regarding the subsidiaries of the subsidiaries of PDVSA.

In addition, according to article 120 of the Public Administration Organic Law, the Ministry of attachment must determine the management index applicable for the evaluation of the institutional accomplishments of the ascribed State-own enterprises, which as mentioned, are those in which the ownership of the shares corresponds to the Republic. For such purpose, the Organic Law prescribes the need for the ascribed State-own enterprises to sign a management agreement *(compromiso de gestión),* for which a detailed content of them is enumerated in article 132 ff. of the Organic Law. Those State-own enterprises must also send an annually to the Ministry of Adscription a report with the accounts of its management (article 122).

Regarding the second-tier subsidiaries public enterprises that are not subjected to the adscription control system established in the Organic Law, the only provision of the Public Administration Organic Law indirectly applicable to them, is establish in article 124, imposing the first level State-own enterprises (like PDVSA) the obligation to inform the Ministry of Adscription, any shareholding participation that they could reach in other enterprises, and on its economic results.

From what has been previously said, is possible to conclude that the provisions of the Public Administration Organic Law, regarding national public enterprises, are only applicable to the first and second tier subsidiaries establish as commercial companies by the organs of Public Administration and by other entities, which are the ones considered as State-own enterprises in such Law. Regarding these first and second tier public enterprises, the Constitutional Chamber of the Supreme Tribunal, in a decision of 2002, referred to them after identifying the legal nature of PDVSA and its subsidiaries, considering them as "State legal persons with the form of commercial companies, subjected to a mixed legal regime, of public and private law, although preponderantly of private law, due to its form, but not exclusively, because their close relation with the State, impose they subjection to obligatory public law provisions sanctioned in order to assure the best organization, functioning and execution control by the Public Administration, by its organs or by those that contribute to attain their objectives".[104]

Therefore, for example, the enterprises subsidiaries of one of the subsidiaries of PDVSA, and therefore a third level subsidiary public enterprise of PDVSA S.A., even considered as a "public enterprise" integrated in the national public sector of Venezuela, it cannot formally be considered a "State own enterprise" in the terms of the Public Administration Organic Law, and are not subjected to the provisions of the say Organic Law, which define State-own enterprises only up to the second *level* subsidiaries, and establish a control system regarding the State-own enterprises that is only applicable to the first level subsidiaries.

---

104 See decision N° 464 of March 18, 2002 (Case: *Interpretación del Decreto de la Asamblea Nacional Constituyente de fecha 30 de enero de 2000, mediante el cual se suspende por 3 días la negociación de la Convención Colectiva del Trabajo),* in *Revista de Derecho Público,* N° 89-92, Editorial Jurídica Venezolana, pp. 218 y ss. See in general, Isabel Boscán de Ruesta, "Consideraciones sobre la naturaleza jurídica de Petróleos de Venezuela, S.A.," in *Revista de Derecho Público,* N° 9, Editorial Jurídica Venezolana, Caracas, 1982, pp. 55-60.

5. Principles related to Petróleos de Venezuela S.A (PDVSA) as a State-owned enterprise

Petróleos de Venezuela S.A. (PDVSA) has been since 1975, without doubts, the most important public enterprise in Venezuelan legal system, and the only directly regulated in the 1999 Constitution.[105]

A. The creation of PDVSA

This public enterprise was created in 1975 as a state-owned enterprise established by the Republic, in application of the Organic Law of the nationalization of the Oil Industry (*Ley que Reserva al Estado la Industria y el Comercio de los Hidrocarburos*).[106] It was created as an instrumentality of the Venezuelan State, in order to manage, as a Holding, the Venezuelan Oil Industry once such Law began to be enforced. The company was created as a commercial company in order to manage the Industry with autonomy from the Government, but without excluding diverse mechanism of control, with the economic purpose of generating profits, without political interference, and only contributing economically to the State through income tax laws.

Initially PDVSA, as was expressly stated in the *Report for the nationalization of the Oil Industry* discussed in the Venezuelan Congress in 1975, drafted by the Presidential Commission on the Oil Reversion of 1974, was conceived for the task of assuming the management of the Oil Industry, once nationalized, as "an

---

105 See on the legal regime of Petróleos de Venezuela S.A.: Allan R. Brewer-Carías and Enrique Viloria, *El holding público*, Editorial Jurídica Venezolana, Caracas 1986; Allan R. Brewer-Carías and Enrique Viloria, *Sumario de las Nacionalizaciones (Hierro y Petróleo)*, Ediciones Conjuntas, Editorial Jurídica Venezolana-Universidad Católica del Táchira, Caracas-San Cristóbal, 1985; Allan R. Brewer-Carías, "El carácter de Petróleos de Venezuela S.A. como instrumento del Estado en la Industria Petrolera" en *Revista de Derecho Público*, N° 23, Editorial Jurídica Venezolana, Caracas, julio-septiembre 1985, pp. 77-86; "Aspectos organizativos de la industria petrolera nacionalizada en Venezuela" en *Archivo de Derecho Público y Ciencias de la Administración*, Vol. III, 1972-1979, Tomo 1, Instituto de Derecho Público, Facultad de Ciencias Jurídicas y Políticas, Universidad Central de Venezuela, Caracas 1981, pp. 407-491; Consideraciones sobre el régimen jurídico-administrativo de Petróleos de Venezuela S.A." en *Revista de Hacienda*, N° 67, Año XV, Ministerio de Hacienda, Caracas 1977, pp. 79-99; "El proceso jurídico-organizativo de la industria petrolera nacionalizada en Venezuela" en *Revista de la Facultad de Ciencias Jurídicas y Políticas*, N° 58, Universidad Central de Venezuela, Caracas 1976, pp. 53-88, and in "El proceso jurídico-organizativo de la industria petrolera nacionalizada en Venezuela" en Marcos Kaplan (Coordinador), *Petróleo y Desarrollo en México y Venezuela*, Universidad Nacional Autónoma de México, México 1981, pp. 333-432.

106 See in *Official Gazette* N° 1.769, August 29, 1975. See our works regarding Petróleos de Venezuela: Allan R. Brewer-Carías, "Consideraciones sobre el Régimen Jurídico-Administrativo de Petróleos de Venezuela, S.A.", en *Revista de Hacienda* N° 67, Caracas 1977, p. 79-99; "Aspectos organizativos de la Industria Petrolera Nacionalizada en Venezuela", in Instituto de Derecho Público, en *Archivo de Derecho Público y Ciencias de la Administración*, 1972-1979, Vol. III, Tomo I, Caracas 1981, p. 407-491; y en Marcos Kaplan (Coordinador), *Petróleo y Desarrollo en México y Venezuela*, UNAM, México 1981, p. 333 a 432; Allan R. Brewer-Carías, "El proceso Jurídico Organizativo de la Industria petrolera Nacionalizada en Venezuela", en *Revista de la Facultad de Ciencias Jurídicas y Políticas* N° 58, Caracas 1976, p. 53-88; Allan R. Brewer-Carías, "El carácter de Petróleos de Venezuela, S.A. como instrumento del Estado en la industria petrolera", *Revista de Derecho Público*, N° 23 (julio-septiembre), Editorial Jurídica Venezolana, Caracas 1985, pp. 77-87.

independent entity different to the [Central] Public Administration, subject to the directives inserted by the State as expressed in the Nation Plan." The Report insisted in affirming that the intention was to "keep the Oil Administration out of bureaucratic rules and practices conceived for public bodies and not for modern and complex entities devoted to large-scale production for large and frequent transactions." In fact, the Oil Management Organization to be created was conceived as a "vertically integrated organization, multi-company and directed by a Holding exclusive and sole property of the State," with companies that were to be "capable of acting with full efficiency in the commercial field," acting with "self-sufficiency and capacity for the renewal of its management cadres."[107]

It was in accordance with these recommendations that on August 29, 1975, Congress enacted the *Organic Law Reserving to the State the Industry and Commerce of Hydrocarbons,*[108] whereas to continue with the performance of the reserved activities (developed up to that moment by foreign private companies), Article 5 provided that "the State" was to perform them "directly by the National Executive or through entities of its own property" (art. 15). The Legislator theoretically assigned to the Executive, the decision to directly take care of the nationalized industry or through entities of the decentralized administration. Despite this apparent liberty, the Law established the guidelines for the Executive to take care of the nationalized industry through decentralized entities, that is to create them "with the legal form it considers convenient, the enterprises it deems necessary to perform regular and efficiently" the reserved activities (art. 6). The provision also authorized the National Executive to "assign one of the enterprises the functions of coordination, supervision and control of the activities of the others, assigning the ownership of the shares of any of such enterprises." According to Article 7 of the same Organic Law, such enterprises "will be governed by the Organic Law and its Regulations, by its own by-laws, by the disposition enacted by the National Executive and by the ordinary law that could be applied." That is, the state-owned enterprises were to be governed preponderantly by private law, although not exclusively because being a state-owned enterprise, they were also subject to public law.[109]

---

107 See the references to the *Report*, in Allan R. Brewer-Carías, "Consideraciones sobre el régimen jurídico-administrativo de Petróleos de Venezuela S.A.," in *Revista de Hacienda*, No. 67, Año XV, Ministerio de hacienda, caracas, 1977, p. 80. Available at: http://allanbrewercarias.net/Content/449725d9-f1cb-474b-8ab2-41efb849fea8/Content/II.4.107.%20CONSID.REG.JUR.ADMIN.PETROLEOS%20VZLA%201977.pdf

108 See *Official Gazette* No. 1769 Aug. 29, 1975.

109 See Allan R. Brewer-Carías, "Consideraciones sobre el régimen jurídico-administrativo de Petróleos de Venezuela S.A.," in *Revista de Hacienda*, No. 67, Año XV, Ministerio de hacienda, caracas, 1977, pp. 83-84. Available at: http://allanbrewercarias.net/Content/449725d9-f1cb-474b-8ab2-41efb849fea8/Content/II.4.107.%20CONSID.REG.JUR.ADMIN.PETROLEOS%20VZLA%201977.pdf. In this regard, the Constitutional Chamber of the Supreme Tribunal in its decision No. 464 of March 3, 2002, has define the state owned enterprises like PDVSA, as "state persons with the legal form of private law," which implies, as a consequence, that "the legal regime applicable to them is a mixed regime, both of public law as well as private law, even when it is predominantly private law, due to its form, but not exclusively, since their intimate relationship with the State, subjects them to the mandatory rules of public law dictated for the best organization, operation and control of execution of the Public Administration, by the organs that

Accordingly, the day after the enactment of such *Nationalization Organic Law*, the President of the Republic issue Decree No. 1123 of August 30, 1975[110] creating as "a state-owned enterprise, with the form of commercial corporation (*Sociedad anónima*), that will fulfill and execute the policy dictated by the National Executive, through the Ministry of Mines and Hydrocarbons on matters of hydrocarbons" (Art. 12). [111] The enterprise was created with a stock represented in shares exclusively owned by the Republic, as sole shareholder, and the by-laws were inscribed in the Commercial Registrar on September 15, 1975.[112]

As a consequence, as I expressed in 1985, there is no doubt that the:

> "intention of the Legislature was to organize the Nationalized Oil Administration, through state-owned enterprises (entities or State persons), with the form of commercial corporations and therefore with a mixed regime of public law and private Law."[113]

Therefore, as I also wrote in 1985:

> "PDVSA is a State-own enterprise, wholly owned by it and responding to the policies that it dictates, and as such, is integrated within the general organization of the State Administration, as a decentralized administration entity, but with the form of a commercial corporation, that is, of a person of private law."[114]

---

are integrated to it or contribute to the achievement of its tasks." (Case: *Interpretación del Decreto de la Asamblea Nacional Constituyente de fecha 30 de enero de 2000, mediante el cual se suspende por 3 días la negociación de la Convención Colectiva del Trabajo),* in *Revista de Derecho Público,* N° 89-92, Editorial Jurídica Venezolana, Caracas 2000, pp. 218, 219. Available at: http://allanbrewercarias.com/wp-content/uploads/2007/08/2002-REVISTA-89-90-91-92.pdf.

110 See See Decree N° 1.123, August 30, 1975 *Official Gazette* N° 1.770 Extra, August 30, 1975. See Allan R. Brewer-Carías, "Consideraciones sobre el régimen jurídico-administrativo de Petróleos de Venezuela S.A.," in *Revista de Hacienda*, No. 67, Año XV, Ministerio de hacienda, caracas, 1977, pp. 83-84. Available at: http://allanbrewercarias.net/Content/449725d9-f1cb-474b-8ab2-41efb849fea8/Content/II.4.107.%20CONSID.REG.JUR.ADMIN.PETROLEOS%20VZLA %201977.pdf.

111 That is why the Constitutional Chamber of the Supreme Tribunal has explained that PDVSA and its subsidiaries are state owned enterprises with private law form. See decision No. 464 of March 3, 2002 (Case: *Interpretación del Decreto de la Asamblea Nacional Constituyente de fecha 30 de enero de 2000, mediante el cual se suspende por 3 días la negociación de la Convención Colectiva del Trabajo),* in *Revista de Derecho Público,* N° 89-92, Editorial Jurídica Venezolana, Caracas 2000, pp. 218, 219. Available at: http://allanbrewercarias.com/wp-content/uploads/2007/08/2002-REVISTA-89-90-91-92.pdf

112 N° 23, Tomo 99-A, Publisher in *Municipal Gazette, Federal District Federal*, N° 413, September 25, 1975

113 *See* Allan R. Brewer-Carías, "*El* carácter de Petróleos de Venezuela, S.A. como instrumento del Estado en la industria petrolera," in *Revista de Derecho Público*, N° 23, Julio-Septiembre 1985, Editorial Jurídica Venezolana, Caracas 1985, pp. 77, 80. Available at: http://allanbrewercarias.com/wp-content/uploads/2007/08/rdpub_1985_23.pdf.

114 *Idem.* at 81. Therefore, pursuant with the Venezuelan Constitution and relevant statutes, PDVSA and its subsidiaries, as was also affirmed in decision No. 464 of March 3, 2002 (Case: *Interpretación del Decreto de la Asamblea Nacional Constituyente de fecha 30 de enero de 2000, mediante el cual se suspende por 3 días la negociación de la Convención Colectiva del Trabajo),* of the Constitutional Chamber of the Supreme Tribunal, are part of the National Public Administration, observing that: "although [PDVSA] is a company incorporated and organized in the form of a public limited company, it is beyond doubt, and reaffirmed as such by the

As it has been mentioned, in Venezuela, Public Administration is comprised of the "Central Public Administration" and the "Decentralized Public Administration." According to the Venezuelan Constitution (Article 242) and the Organic Law on Public Administration (Articles 59-61), the National Central Public Administration directed by the National Executive, consists of the organs of the government itself, such as the various Ministries.[115] The National Decentralized Public Administration, on the other hand, consists of entities such as public corporations and state-owned commercial enterprises like PDVSA and its subsidiaries, which are not part of the government itself, being nonetheless attached to the corresponding government Ministry.[116] That is why, the Constitutional Chamber of the Supreme Tribunal with regard to the legal regime applicable to PDVSA and its subsidiaries, has explained that it "allows them to be clearly differentiated, not only from the centralized Public Administration and autonomous institutes, but also from other state owned enterprises."[117]

In any case, as all state-owned enterprises, PDVSA and its subsidiaries are subject to rules of public law. For instance, in addition to the provisions of the Organic Law on Public Administration, to the provisions of the Public Contracting Law (Article 3)[118] and the Organic Law of the General Audit Office (Article 9).[119] As a decentralized entity of the National Public Administration is of course subject to all the general regulations and principles related to the functioning of Public Administration included in the Organic Law (in particular, Title II. Principles and basis of the functioning and organization of Public Administration: articles 3-28, 33-43), as well as in other laws referred to the organs and entities of the Public Administration, like the Organic Law of Administrative Procedure; the Organic Law on Public Assets (Article 4);[120] and the Financial Management of the Public Sector Organic Law (article 6).[121]

Constitution of the Bolivarian Republic of Venezuela, that it is framed within the general structure of the National Public Administration . . ." [Case: Interpretation of the Decree of the National Constituent Assembly dated January 30, 2000, by which the negotiation of the Collective Labour Convention is suspended for 3 days], See in *Revista de Derecho Público,* N° 89-92, Editorial Jurídica Venezolana, pp. 219. Available at: http://allanbrewercarias.com/wp-content/uploads/2007/08/2002-REVISTA-89-90-91-92.pdf

115 *See* Articles 160, 174, 236.20 of the Constitution; *see also* Allan R. Brewer-Carías, *Administrative Law in Venezuela*, Editorial Jurídica Venezolana, Second Edition, 2015, p. 52; available at: http://allanbrewercarias.com/wp-content/uploads/2013/08/9789803651992-txt.pdf.

116 *See* Articles 142; 300.

117 See Constitutional Chamber of the Supreme Tribunal decision No. 464 of March 3, 2002 (Case: *Interpretación del Decreto de la Asamblea Nacional Constituyente de fecha 30 de enero de 2000, mediante el cual se suspende por 3 días la negociación de la Convención Colectiva del Trabajo),* in *Revista de Derecho Público,* N° 89-92, Editorial Jurídica Venezolana, Caracas 2000, pp. 218, 219. Available at: http://allanbrewercarias.com/wp-content/uploads/2007/08/2002-REVISTA-89-90-91-92.pdf

118 *See Official Gazette* N° 6.154 Extra., November 19, 2014. Available at: http://www.mindefensa.gob.ve/COMISION/wp-content/uploads/2017/03/LCP.pdf.

119 *See Official Gazette* N° 37.347, December 17, 2001. Available at: http://www.oas.org/juridico/spanish/mesicic3_ven_anexo23.pdf

120 See *Official Gazette* N° 39.952 of June 26, 2012.

121 Article 5. See *Official Gazette* No. 6210 Extra., December, 2015, available at: http://historico.tsj.gob.ve/gaceta_ext/diciembre/30122015/E-30122015-4475.pdf#page=1

State owned enterprises are also part of the "Public Sector" as defined in Article 5 of the Financial Management of Public Sector Organic Law, which specifically encompasses:

> "8. Commercial companies in which the Republic or other persons referred to in this Article have a shareholding equal to or greater than fifty per cent of the share capital. This also includes the wholly state-owned companies, whose role, through the holding of shares of other companies, is to coordinate the public business management of a sector of the national economy [...]"[122]

In addition and following the sense of the provisions of the 1975 Nationalization Law, PDVSA was constitutionalized in Article 303 of the 1999 Constitution, which directly assigs it what it already had, "the management of the oil industry." According to the article 2 of its by-laws, PDVSA, in fact, was established since 1975 to fulfill its corporate purpose implementing the national policy on matters of hydrocarbons; that is, to generate profits as an economic enterprise in such sector. Such was the "national policy to be implemented."[123] Therefore, it is not correct to say that "PDVSA was created by presidential decree not to generate profits but as a national company to implement national policy on hydrocarbons" as was affirmed in the United States District Court D. Delaware, (*Crystallex International Corporation v. Bolivarian Republic of Venezuela* of 9 August 2028), accepting the statement made of Crystallex (p. 402). On the contrary under the Nationalization Law and to the decree of creation, PDVSA was to generate profit and *that* was the "national policy to be implemented."

Despite of the public law provisions regulating PDVSA, the fact is that PDVSA, according to the aforementioned, was incorporated as a private commercial law company, registered in the Commercial Registrar following the rules of the Commercial Code, and providing in its by-laws that the members of the Board of Directors of the company, although appointed by the President of the Republic, were to perform their activities in a full time character (article 20), not having the status of public officials, and thus, being regulated by Labor Law.

This implied that no Minister, members of the National Executive or any other public officer could be appointed as member of the Board of Directors of PDVSA. On the contrary, the Minister of Energy and Petroleum was only to be a member of the Shareholders Meeting of the company (article 7 and 11), not having any direct involvement in the management of the company, and much less any control on the day-to-day operations of the company. In particular, article 29 of the original By-Laws of PDVSA setted forth the following:

> "*Clausc Twenty-nine*. The Ministers of the Executive, the members of the Supreme Tribunal of Justice, the Attorney General of the Republic and the Governors of the States, and the Federal District may not be members of the Company's Board of Directors during the exercise of their positions. Nor can be members of the Board of Directors of the company, persons related to the

122 *See Official Gazette* No 6.210 Extra., December 30, 2015. Available at: http://www.bod.com.ve/media/97487/GACETA-OFICIAL-EXTRAORDINARIA-6210.pdf.

123 *See* for instance the By-Laws of PDVSA, reformed by Decree No. 2184, *Gaceta Oficial No. 37.588* (Dec. 10, 2002).

President of the Republic or the Minister of Energy and Mines in fourth degree of consanguinity or second of affinity."[124]

Based on all those provisions, Petróleos de Venezuela, S.A., is and has been a public and State own enterprise, wholly owned by the Republic of Venezuela (national artificial territorial person), which responds to the policies dictated by the National Executive, and is part of the Public Administration organization, as an entity or State-own enterprise, although with the legal form of a commercial company, that is, private law person. It is the only State own company that is directly and expressly regulated in the 1999 Constitution, in which it is set forth that the State shall remain the only shareholder of the company (art. 303).

The consequence of these provisions is that according to the Venezuelan Commercial Code, Petróleos de Venezuela S.A. (PDVSA), as a commercial company ("*compañía anónima* or *sociedad anónima*"), is basically subjected to its provisions, and in addition, to all other commercial law rules and practices applicable, and in particular, to what is established in its own by-laws which were adopted at the partnership incorporation, expressly establishing that it is governed "by the rules established in the by-laws" ("*regida por las bases establecidas en este documento*"). In addition to the provisions of the Commercial Code and to the provisions of its own by-laws, it can also be subjected in some extend to some administrative law statutes applicable to entities that are integrated in the national public sector.

The company PDVSA, in this regard, can be considered in some aspects and by some Statutes as a "public enterprise" (*empresa pública*), and in other, as a "State-own enterprise" ("*empresa del Estado*") which is another important concept of Venezuelan administrative law, which is applicable to certain public enterprises that are formally considered as "entities" that form part of the Public Administration organization. That is, according to the Public Administration Organic Law, Public Administration is integrated by "organs" or "entities", and within the later, the "State-own enterprises" which are only the first and second tier public enterprises subsidiaries of the Republic.

It is necessary to study both concepts: "public enterprise" and "State-own enterprise" in Venezuelan administrative law and its legal effects regarding the company, which frequently are incorrectly included without distinction in the single English expression "State-own enterprise".

B. PDVSA as public enterprise subjected to some statues referred to the National Public Sector

As aforementioned, the expressions "public enterprise" and "State-own enterprise" are different in Venezuelan Administrative Law and cannot be confounded, which can occur, particularly when the expression "State-owned enterprises" is used in English comprehending both Spanish expressions, *empresas públicas* (public enterprises) and *empresas del Estado* (State-own enterprises). In Spanish and in Venezuelan Administrative Law these expressions have different meaning: The former, "public enterprise," basically has an economic connotation

124 See for instance the By-Laws of PDVSA dated 2002, modified by Decree N° 2.184 of December 10, 2002, in *Gaceta Oficial* N° 37.588 of December 10, 2002.

referring to units or organizations that are part of the public sector, and the latter, "State-own enterprise", has more a formal or organic connotation regarding the Public Administration organization. Accordingly, is possible to say that all "State-own enterprises" can be considered as "public enterprises", but not all "public enterprises" can be considered as "State-own enterprises".

The subject of public enterprises was the object of a comparative law study that I completed in 1966,[125] being the main conclusion that the expression "public enterprise" is a generic term given to all the economic organizations of the "public sector" accomplishing commercial or industrial activities, independently of the legal form used for structuring them and their relation with the Public Administration, whether being a unit hierarchically inserted within the organs of Public Administration (as used to be, for instance, the Post Offices); an *établisment public*, *instituto autónomo*, Public Corporations or Government Corporation (like for instance the classic case of the Tennessee Valley Authority); or a commercial company established by entities of the State subjected to the commercial law rules and practices. All these varied organizations can be considered "public enterprises," just because their industrial and commercial purposes, that is, their economic activities allow to comprehend them within the "public sector", independently of their being considered or not as instruments or instrumentality of the State or of the degree of autonomy they could have in their management.

In Venezuela, this expression "public enterprise" has had this broad sense of entrepreneurial organization established within the "public sector" for the accomplishment of commercial and industrial activities.[126] Being part of the public sector, they are in principle subjected to the provisions of many Statutes that have been sanctioned to regulate, in general, the "public sector," each one establishing the scope of its application, particularly regarding the level of creation of commercial companies, that is, the degree of the subsidiary of the companies, whether second tier or third tier subsidiary. That is, not all Statutes concerning the public sector are applicable to all public enterprises in the same way.

It is the case, for instance, of the Organic Law of Financial Administration of the Public Sector,[127] sanctioned with the purpose of regulating the "financial administration, the internal control system of the public sector, and the aspects referred to the macro economic coordination" (article 1). For such purpose, this Law enumerates in an express way which are the legal persons, units or entities of the public sector that are subject to its provisions, for which purpose article 5 identifies the following: "1. The Republic; 2. The States; 3. The Metropolitan District of

---

125 See Allan R. Brewer-Carías, "Le régime des activités industrielles et commerciales des pouvoirs publics en droit compare" in *Rapports Généraux au VIIe Congrès International de Droit Comparé, Acta Instituti Upsaliensis Jurisprudentiae Comparativae*, Stockholm 1966, pp. 484-565. The Report was latter published as a book: *Les entreprises publiques en droit compare,* by the Faculté internationale pour l'enseignement du droit comparé, Paris, 1968. An Spanish version was also published as: *Las Empresas Públicas en el Derecho Comparado (Estudio sobre el régimen de las actividades industriales y comerciales del Estado)*, by Universidad Central de Venezuela, Caracas 1967 (pp. 200).

126 See Allan R. Brewer-Carías, *El regimen jurídico de las empresas públicas en Venezuela*, published by the Latin American Center for Development Administration (CLAD), Caracas 1980.

127 See *Official Gazette* N° 6.154 of November 19, 2014

Caracas; 4. The Districts; 5. The Municipalities; 6. The *institutos autónomos* (Government Corporations); 7. The public law legal persons; 8. The commercial companies in which the Republic, or the other legal persons referred to in this article have a shareholder participation equal or more that the 50% of the stock (capital social) of the company. In addition, the companies totally owned by the State with the function to coordinate public entrepreneurial management of specific sectors of the national economy by means of its possession of shares in other companies, are also comprised; 9. The commercial companies in which the artificial persons referred to in the previous paragraph, have a shareholder participation equal or more that the 50% of the stock (capital social). 10. The foundations, civil associations and other institutions established or directed by any of the artificial persons referred to in this article, when all the budget resources or contributions made by one or few artificial persons referred in this article, represents the 50% or more of their budget.

Regarding state-own enterprises, that is, commercial companies created by the organizations of the public sector, the general conclusion from what is set forth in paragraphs 8 and 9 of article 5 of this Organic Law, is that all commercial companies created by the enumerated public legal persons, owning shares equal or more that the 50% the stock of the company (first level commercial companies), as well as the commercial companies established by the latter (second tier commercial companies) also owning shares equal or more that the 50% the stock of the company, are considered as integrating the public sector and are subjected to the regulations of the Organic Law. This means that PDVSA as a state-own enterprise is subjected to the Organic Law of Financial Administration of the Public Sector, particularly in matters of budget, public debt, public accounting system, and internal control system.

In effect, regarding the budget of the public enterprises subjected to the Organic Law, although not being part of the National Budget, it must follow the provisions established for its elaboration (article 62 ff.); be analyzed by the National Budget Office (art. 63); be approved by the President of the Republic in Council of Ministers (art. 63) who must publish a synthesis of its content in the Official Gazette (article 64); and be incorporated in the Public Sector Consolidated Budget that the Executive must submit to the National Assembly for its information (articles 75 ff.). Being this Organic Law applicable to public enterprises, these provisions are applicable to commercial companies considered as public enterprises, such as PDVSA

In matters of public debt, the limits established in this Organic Law regarding state-own enterprises, are also applicable to PDVSA as a commercial company, as are those referred for instance to the parliamentary authorization needed for such purpose (article 79). But in this regard of public debt, all the state-own enterprises established according to the Nationalization Organic Law of the Hydrocarbon Industry are excluded from the provisions of the Organic Law of Financial Administration of the Public Sector (article 101.4).

In matters of the Public Accounting System establish in this Organic Law (articles 121 ff.) regarding the public sector, also PDVSA as an enterprise subjected to the Organic Law, is obliged to submit to the National Accounting Office the required financial statements and other accounting information, when requested (article 128).

Finally, regarding the Internal Control System, the National Superintendence for Internal Audit is empowered to direct the internal audit in the organizations that form the Central Public Administration and the entities of the decentralized administration enumerated in the aforementioned article 5 of this Organic Law. This also imply that those provisions are applicable to commercial companies, considered as public enterprises, such as PDVSA

Other important Statute referred to the whole public sector is the General Comptroller's Office Organic Law,[128] which has a more general scope of application regarding state-own enterprises. In principle, when enumerating the entities subjected to its provisions, regarding commercial companies, the Law includes "the societies of any nature in which the legal persons referred in the provision (Republic, States, Municipalities, Government Corporations, and other public law artificial persons) participate in its stock (capital social), as well as those established with the participation of these" (article 9,10). If it is true that this provision, in principle, could also signify the exclusion from the applicability of the provisions of the statute, of the third tier subsidiary commercial companies considered as state-own enterprises; the doubts are resolved in other provision of the Statute, which include in its scope, all legal persons which "in any way enter in contract, business or operations" with other entities subjected to the statute, "or receive resources, funds, subsidies, transfers, fiscal incentives or intervene in any way in the administration, handling or custody of public funds" (art. 9,12). In this respect, and contrary to the other statutes aforementioned, the provisions of the Organic Law of the General Comptroller's Office can be considered as applicable to third tier subsidiaries commercial companies considered as public enterprises.

Similar regulations are established in the Anti-Corruption Law,[129] which is then applicable to commercial companies considered as state-own enterprises, as is the case of PDVSA.

From what has been previously said, PDVSA, is then a commercial company, created by the State as a public enterprise integrated in the national public sector of Venezuela, subject to all the Statutes that have been sanctioned in order to regulate the main general aspects of the functioning of the whole public sector.

C. PDVSA as a State-own enterprise subject to the Public Administration Organic Law

But being considered as a state-own enterprise, as aforementioned, PDVSA is also considered as an entity of Public Administration, in the sense of such term is established and defined, regarding the organization of Public Administration, in the Public Administration Organic Law. [130] As it was declared by the Constitutional Chamber of the Supreme Tribunal in decision No. 464 of March 3, 2002, specifically regarding Petróleos de Venezuela S.A. as an entity that notwithstanding its private law form is integrated in the National Public Administration:

> "although Petróleos de Venezuela S.A. is a company incorporated and organized in the form of a public limited company, it is beyond doubt, and

128 See *Official Gazette* N° 37.347 of December 17, 2001

129 See *Official Gazette* N° 6.155 Extra. of November 19, 2014.

130 See in *Official Gazette* N° 6.147 Extra of November 17, 2014.

reaffirmed as such by the Constitution of the Bolivarian Republic of Venezuela, that it is framed within the general structure of the National Public Administration....”[131]

In effect, as aforementioned, according to article 15 of this Organic Law, the universe of “Public Administration” is integrated by “organs” and by “entities” (*entes*) and “Missions,” being the “entities”, all those organizations functionally decentralized established as separate legal persons, that is, with different *personalidad* as of the Republic, of the States, of the Metropolitan Districts and of the Municipalities.

In Administrative Law, in particular, regarding the various units that conform the Venezuelan “State” or the public sector, as it is establish in Organic Law on Financial Administration of the Public Sector, it is possible to distinguish two sort of legal persons integrated in the public sector: On the one hand, the legal persons that are established as the result of the political organization of the country, that is, as political subdivisions of the State, as is the case of a federal State. In it, the territorial distribution of the State power (political decentralization), necessarily implies the creation of various legal persons with different territorial jurisdictional scope. On the other hand, there are the legal persons established also as a consequence of a decentralization process, but only of administrative nature, by means of the creation of separate entities or legal persons generally outside the hierarchy of Public Administration in order to help the Government to accomplish its activities.

In this sense, within the political and constitutional decentralization process, in Venezuela, being a Federal State (Bolivarian Republic of Venezuela), is essential to distinguish the following legal persons derived from the political subdivision of the country: the Republic, the States, the Metropolitan Districts and the Municipalities They are all public law “territorial or political legal persons”, established as consequence of the adopted vertical or territorial system of distribution of State power (political decentralization). As legal persons, they have their own scope of action or competencies, and their own administrative components and units for the development of their activities. All are considered to be “the Venezuelan State”, but in the internal point of view, they are different persons. For instance, in matters of hydrocarbon and oil activities, the competency of the Venezuelan State on such matters are exclusively attributed to its the national political person (the Republic) (article 156.16 of the Constitution).

Each of the legal persons that conform the political subdivision of the State, that is, the Republic, the States and the Municipalities, according to the Public Administration Organic Law, have “organs”, that are the ones whose functions, when exercised, can produce legal effects regarding third parties, or whose acts have obligatory force. These organs of these public law territorial legal persons are the ones that can be considered as part of Public Administration pursuant the terms of article 15 of the Organic Law. In the case of the Republic, for instance, within the

---

131 Idem. p. 219. The Supreme Tribunal explains that PDVSA and its subsidiaries are state owned enterprises with private law form. *Idem*, pp. 218, 219. Regarding PDVSA being part of the National Public Administration, see Allan R. Brewer-Carías, “El carácter de Petróleos de Venezuela, S.A. como instrumento del Estado en la industria petrolera,” in *Revista de Derecho Público*, N° 23, Julio-Septiembre 1985, Editorial Jurídica Venezolana, Caracas 1985, pp. 77-86. Available at: http://allanbrewercarias.com/wp-content/ uploads/2007/08/rdpub_1985_23.pdf

organs", the most important ones are the Ministries. In the hydrocarbon and oil field, the most important organ of the Republic and its National Public Administration organization is the Ministry of Energy and Oil.

According to the provisions of the Public Administration Organic Law, therefore, in no case, the commercial companies established as state-own enterprises as separate legal persons can therefore be considered as "organs" of Public Administration as they are regulated in article 15 of its Organic Law.

Regarding the other components of Public Administration, that is, the "entities", as mentioned before, according to the same article 15 of the Organic Law, they are all those legal persons created as a consequence of the process of functional administrative decentralization, as separate and different legal persons regarding the legal persons derived from the political subdivision of the country, that is, from the Republic, the States, of the Metropolitan Districts and of the Municipalities.

Such separate legal persons, particularly referring to the economic activities, can have a public law form when the person is created directly by statute, as is the case of the *institutos autónomos* or *institutos públicos* (Government Corporations), or of a private law form (state-own enterprise), like the one attributed to the commercial companies (*compañía or sociedad anónima*) according to the Commercial Code regulations.

The basic characteristic for all these "entities" in order to be considered as part of the Public Administration, is that they must be created by the already mentioned territorial legal political persons (Republic, States, Municipalities) as integrating the public sector, as a consequence of a process of administrative decentralization, or by an "entity" already created by them.

Article 29 of the Public Administration Organic Law, establishes the general framework of all these functional decentralized "entities" that can be created by the organs of the State that can be of two sorts:

1. Functional decentralized entities as private law persons comprising those legal persons established and subjected to private law statutes, which are of two types:

a. Functional decentralized entities without entrepreneurial purposes, which are those decentralized entities that do not develop activities directed to the production of goods or services to be sold, and whose income and resources are basically provided by the budget of the Republic, the States, the metropolitan District and the Municipalities.

b. Functional decentralized entities with entrepreneurial purposes, which are those whose principal activity is the production of goods or services directed to be sold and whose income or resources basically derive from such activity.

2. Functional decentralized entities as public law persons, comprising those legal persons created and subjected to public law statutes and regulations, with entrepreneurial or non-entrepreneurial goals, which can also be attributed the exercise of public powers.

This same distinction can be found in article 6 of the already mentioned Organic Law of the Financial Administration of the Public Sector.[132]

Within the first type of functional decentralized "entities" created by the organs of the State which are subject to private law statutes, are those with entrepreneurial purposes in the sense that their principal activity is the production of goods or services directed to be sold and whose income or resources basically derive from such activity.

This artificial persons are the ones expressly regulated in this Public Administration Organic Law with the name of "State-own enterprises" (*empresas del Estado*), where they are defined as the commercial companies in which the Republic, the States, the Metropolitan Districts, the Municipalities, or any other functional decentralized entities provided in such Organic Law like the Government Corporations (*institutos autónomos* or *institutos públicos*), and other State-own enterprises, on their own or together, have more than the 50% of the shares of the stock of the company (article 100). Therefore, regarding public enterprises, only those incorporated as first and second tier subsidiaries are "State-own enterprises" in the terms of the Public Administration Organic Law. This implies that all its provisions are applicable to PDVSA, as a State-own enterprise.

The Public Administration Organic Law also expressly authorizes the Republic, the States, the Municipalities, the Metropolitan Districts, the Municipalities and the entities referred to in the Statute, to create limited commercial companies with just one shareholder (art. 106). In such cases, if the decision is adopted by the Republic, the States or the Municipalities it must be respectively issue by the President of the Republic in Ministers Council, the Governor or the Mayor, by mean of a Decree or resolution (art. 104).

This possibility to establish commercial companies with only one single shareholder[133] is regulated in article 106 of the Organic Law as a formal exception to the partnership contractual basis generally required in all commercial companies according to the Commercial Code. Previous to this provision now applicable to all State-own enterprises, only the case of Petróleos de Venezuela S.A. (PDVSA) could be distinguished as a commercial company incorporated with only one shareholder, in such case, the Republic[134]. Later, due to the decision to transform two Government Corporations (*institutos autónomos*) acting in the Oil Industry, the *Instituto Venezolano de Petroquímica* and the *Corporación Venezolana del Petróleo*, to be commercial companies, the respective Statutes provided for the incorporation of the commercial companies Intevep S.A. and Corpoven S.A., as subsidiaries of Petróleos de Venezuela S.A., with this holding company as the only shareholder.

---

132 See in *Official Gazette* N° 6.154 Extra. of November 19, 2014

133 See Allan R. Brewer-Carías, *Las empresas públicas en el derecho comparado,* Universidad Central de Venezuela, Caracas, 1967, pp. 115 y ss.

134 See Allan R. Brewer-Carías, "Aspectos organizativos de la industria petrolera nacionalizada", en *Archivo de Derecho Público y Ciencias de la Administración, Régimen Jurídico de las nacionalizaciones en Venezuela,* Caracas, Vol. III, 1972-1979, Tomo I, Instituto de Derecho Público, Universidad Central de Venezuela, Caracas, 1981, pp. 407 y ss.

According to the regulations of the Public Administration Organic Law, the State-own enterprises acquires their juridical legal person statute (*personalidad*) by registering their incorporation document and their by-laws in the Commercial Registrar of its domicile, which must also register the *Official Gazette* where has been published the decree or resolution authorizing its incorporation act (Art. 104). All these documents must also be published in the Official Gazette of the Republic or in the gazettes of the States or Municipalities (art. 105).

Being legal person of private law, the State-own enterprises are subjected to the "ordinary legislation", particularly, that established in the Commercial Code, except regarding what it is established in the Public Administration Organic Law (article 108). Nonetheless, being public enterprises, the State-own enterprises are also subjected to the applicable statutes referred to the public sector, as mentioned before.

The most important provisions of the Public Administration Organic Law in relation to state-own enterprises, beside the aforementioned provisions regarding their incorporation and the required level of subsidiary (first and second) in order to be considered as such, are those set forth for the purpose of assuring the control regarding their activities by organs of Public Administration. This Organic Law, in this regard, establishes a system of what is called "*control de adscripción*" (adscription control) (art. 119 ff.), which is provided in particular to be applied in the relationship between Public Administration organs and administrative decentralized entities (separate legal persons), in order to distinguish it from the hierarchical control that corresponds to the relationship between the organs of Public Administration of one of the political subdivisions of the State. The "adscription" control only exists when the administrative relationship is established between different legal persons, for instance, among the Republic and a Government Corporation of a State-own enterprise.

In the case of national State-own enterprises subjected to the Public Administration Organic Law, the adscription control established also implies shareholding control, which is also exercised by means of the public official representing the shares of the organs of Public Administration in the Shareholders meetings of the State-own enterprise. In the Organic Law this control is only set forth expressly regarding first tier State-own enterprises subsidiaries, like the case of PDVSA subjected to the shareholding control exercise by the Ministry of Energy and Oil.

In order to the adscription control be exercise in the national level of the State (Republic) by the organs of national Public Administration, the Organic Law assigns to the President of the Republic the duty to issue a Decree establishing the adscription of Government Corporations, State-own enterprises, State foundations or State civil associations to the corresponding organs of Central Public Administration, particularly, to the Ministries. According to article 117 of such Decree, the President is also empowered to vary the adscription according to the changes in the organization of the *Ministerios* (Ministries); to change the share ownership from one to other Public Administration organ, or transfer it to a decentralized entity; to merge State-own enterprises and transform foundations or administrative services in State-own enterprises.

The Decree of Adscription of entities to the Ministries of Public Administration of 2001[135], and regarding the then Ministry of Energy and Mines, the only State-own enterprise ascribed to it was Petróleos de Venezuela S.A. (art. 10), because it is the only State-own enterprise in the oil industry whose shares are owned by the Republic. The adscription of public entities to the Ministries was leter established in the Decree on the Organization and Functioning of the National Public Administration of 2009,[136] in which Petróleos de Venezuela S.A. again was the only oil public enterprise owned by the Republic and ascribed to the Ministry of the Popular Power of Energy and Oil (Transitory Disposition Fifteenth). Additionally, the Mixed Oil Companies are also ascribed to the Ministry, but none of the subsidiaries of PDVSA or its subsidiaries are ascribed to it.

In relation to first level State-own enterprises, that is, those in which the Republic is the shareholder, as is the case of Petróleos de Venezuela S.A. (PDVSA), is that article 120 of the Public Administration Organic Law that assigns the Ministry of Energy and Oil with the general power to define the policy to be developed by the company, for which purpose it can formulate the necessary general directives; to permanently exercise the coordination, supervision and control functions; to continuously evaluate the accomplishment and results of its management and promptly inform the President of the Republic; to inform quarterly the national organ of planning regarding the executions of the plans by the enterprise; and to propose the President of the Republic, the needed reforms, in order to modify or eliminate the ascribed State-own enterprises.

In addition, according to article 121 of the Public Administration Organic Law, the Ministry of adscription must determine the management index applicable for the evaluation of the institutional accomplishments of the ascribed State-own enterprises, which as mentioned, are those in which the ownership of the shares corresponds to the Republic. For such purpose, the Organic Law prescribes the need for the ascribed State-own enterprises to sign a management agreement (*compromiso de gestión*), for which a detailed content of them is enumerated in article 134 ff. of the Organic Law. Those State-own enterprises must also send an annually to the Ministry of Adscription a report with the accounts of its management (article 123).

Finally, the Public Administration Organic Law in article 124 imposes the State-own enterprise, an obligation to inform the Ministry of Adscription, any shareholding participation that they could reach in other enterprises, and on its economic results.

Regarding PDVSA, the Constitutional Chamber of the Supreme Tribunal, in a decision of 2002, after identifying the legal nature of PDVSA, considering it as a "State legal persons with the form of commercial company, subjected to a mixed legal regime, of public and private law, although preponderantly of private law, due to its form, but not exclusively, because their close relation with the State, impose they subjection to obligatory public law provisions sanctioned in order to assure the

135 See *Official Gazette* Nº 5.556 Extra. del 13 de noviembre de 2001.

136 See *Official Gazette* Nº 39.163 of April 22, 2009

best organization, functioning and execution control by the Public Administration, by its organs or by those that contribute to attain their objectives".[137]

Therefore, PDVSA as a public enterprise integrated in the national public sector of Venezuela, is considered a State-own enterprise in the terms of the Public Administration Organic Law, and it is subjected to the provisions of the say Organic Law, which establish a control system regarding those decentralized entities.

In addition, article 7 of the Oil Industry Nationalization Law establishes that the enterprises created according to its provisions, that is, PDVSA and its subsidiaries, "will be subjected to this Law, to its regulations, to their by-laws, *to the disposition issued by the National Executive* and to the applicable *derecho común*" (general legislation). In the Decree N° 1.123 of August 30, 1975, of creation of PDVSA, modified in 1979, it was stated that, considering that PDVSA had the task of "continue and develop the oil industry reserved to the State," such task must be accomplished in compliance with the policy established on matters of hydrocarbons by the National Executive, through the Minister of Energy and Mines, (art. 2).

In the same sense, in the PDVSA by-laws reformed in 1979,[138] it was also expressly established that "the enterprise will be subjected to the Organic Law that reserves the State the Industry and Commerce of Hydrocarbons, to its regulations, to its by-laws, to the disposition issued by the National Executive and to the applicable *derecho común"* (Third Clause).

D. The institutional framework of the process of erasing the effective separation between the Government and PDVSA (2002-2019)

The effective separateness status of PDVSA regarding the Central Public Administration that existed when PDVSA was created, and that was carefully preserved by all democratic governments for more than 25 years, was the key factor contributing to the development of PDVSA as a commercial company, managed independently from any political control or interferences, which acted for the purpose of generating profits as the State entity managing the oil industry, only economically contributing to the State through the income taxation system

This was the status of PDVSA until 2002, when unfortunately, all this separateness began to be changed after the then President Hugo Chavez on July 2002 decided to appoint Rafael Ramírez as Minister of Energy and Mines, in order to assure the political intervention of PDVSA,[139] for the creation of what was later so-called the "new PDVSA," completely controlled by the Government, at the service of the "Venezuelan revolution,"[140] provoking its complete politization.

---

137 See la sentencia N° 464 de 18-03-2002 (Caso: *Interpretación del Decreto de la Asamblea Nacional Constituyente de fecha 30 de enero de 2000, mediante el cual se suspende por 180 días la negociación de la Convención Colectiva del Trabajo),* en *Revista de Derecho Público,* N° 89-92, Editorial Jurídica Venezolana, pp. 218 y ss. Véase en general, Isabel Boscán de Ruesta, "Consideraciones sobre la naturaleza jurídica de Petróleos de Venezuela, S.A., *Revista de Derecho Público,* N° 9, Editorial Jurídica Venezolana, Caracas, 1982, pp. 55-60.

138 See Decree N° 250 of August 23, 1979, in *Official Gazette* N° 31.810, of August 30, 1979

139 See *Official* Gazette No. 37.486, July 17, 2002, pp. 32.628 and 324.629

140 See "La nueva PDVSA es la institución de la revolución Venezolana," November 2006, available at:

Accordingly, from being the successful business it used to be, managed separately from the government, which in 1994 was ranked the second largest oil enterprise in the world,[141] and the biggest enterprise in any field in Latin America,[142] PDVSA was progressively transformed into a direct and controlled sort of *de facto* agency of the Government, particularly for undertaking its social policies, abandoning in a complete way its business-minded former character; taking the Government a complete control of the enterprise, annihilating its technical autonomy,"[143] and consequently, clearing "the way for politicization in the national oil industry."[144] Chávez, himself, expressed his goal in a message before the National Assembly, about how important was for his political purposes the need to "take such hill that was PDVSA," confessing that for such purpose he expressly provoked the crisis of the industry,[145] initially by firing not only the top executive of PDVSA but in just a few hours 23.000 of its employees, among them, 12.371 professionals, technicians and supervisors.[146]

The consequence was that PDVSA progressively and excessively began to be controlled by the Government, a process under which, the Government began to use

---

http://www.pdvsa.com/index.php?option=com_content&view=article&id=1845:3184&catid=10&Itemid=589&lang=es

141 See "Pdvsa, Segunda petrolera más grande del mundo. La empresa estatal Petróleos de Venezuela (PDVSA) es la segunda corporación petrolera más importante del mundo, según la última clasificación de la publicación especializada *Petroleum Inteligence Weekly* (PIW),"in EFE, *El Tiempo*, Bogotá, 12 diciembre 1994, available at: https://www.eltiempo.com/archivo/documento/MAM-263571

142 See José Toro Hardy, "Sobre la tragedia de la industria petrolera," forward to the book: Allan R. Brewer-Carías, *Crónica de una destrucción. Concesión, Nacionalización, Apertura, Constitucionalización, Desnacionalización, Estatización, Entrega y degradación de la Industria petrolera*, Universidad Monteávila, Editorial Jurídica Venezolana, Caracas 2018, p. 20. Available at: http://allanbrewercarias.com/wp-content/uploads/2018/06/9789803654276-txt-Cr%C3%B3nica-destrucci%C3%B3n-ARBC-PAGINA-WEB.pdf

143 See José Ignacio Hernández, "La apertura petrolera o el primer intento por desmontar el pensamiento estatista petrolero en Venezuela," forward to the book: Allan R. Brewer-Carías, *Crónica de una destrucción. Concesión, Nacionalización, Apertura,* Constitucionalización, *Desnacionalización, Estatización, Entrega y degradación de la Industria petrolera*, Universidad Monteávila, Editorial Jurídica Venezolana, Caracas 2018, p. 52. Available at: http://allanbrewercarias.com/wp-content/uploads/2018/06/9789803654276-txt-Cr%C3%B3nica-destrucci%C3 % B3n-ARBC-PAGINA-WEB.pdf

144 See the reference in Henry Jiménez Guanipa, "La destrucción y la ruina de Venezuela. ¿cómo legamos a este punto?, forward to the book: Allan R. Brewer-Carías, *Crónica de una destrucción. Concesión, Nacionalización, Apertura, Constitucionalización, Desnacionalización,* Estatización, *Entrega y degradación de la Industria petrolera*, Universidad Monteávila, Editorial Jurídica Venezolana, Caracas 2018, p. 68. Available at: http://allanbrewercarias.com/wp-content/uploads/2018/06/9789803654276-txt-Cr%C3%B3nica-destrucci%C3%B3n-ARBC-PAGINA-WEB.pdf

145 *Idem*

146 See the reference in Eddie A. Ramírez, "Años de desatino (2002-2018)," forward to the book: Allan R. Brewer-Carías, *Crónica de una destrucción. Concesión, Nacionalización, Apertura,* Constitucionalización, *Desnacionalización, Estatización, Entrega y degradación de la Industria petrolera*, Universidad Monteávila, Editorial Jurídica Venezolana, Caracas 2018, p. 37. Available at: http://allanbrewercarias.com/wp-content/uploads/2018/06/9789803654276-txt-Cr%C3%B3nica-destrucci%C3%B3n-ARBC-PAGINA-WEB.pdf

PDVSA's assets as its own; ignored the separate status of the company by reforming its by-laws and appointing a minister of the National Executive as President of its Board; deprived PDVSA of its independence, assuring a close political control similar to an organ of the Central Public Administration; subjected the company to obtain approvals for ordinary business decisions from the Executive; and diverted the activities of the company from the oil sector, to execute governmental social policies, acting directly on behalf of the Executive. As Eddie Ramirez explained: "Until 2002 PDVSA and its subsidiaries were efficiently managed as a business," and since then it "went from being a company that was in the hydrocarbons business, to being a company whose mission is social, which has activities related to hydrocarbons." [147]

For such purpose, as aforementioned, since 2004 a symbiosis was established during the government of Chávez, continuing during the government of Nicolás Maduro, formally enduring until 2018, according to which, the Minister of Petroleum, member of the National Executive Cabinet was always, simultaneously, the President of the Board of Directors of PDVSA, *de facto* transforming the enterprise into one depending to the Central government.

For such purpose, Chávez previously reformed the by-laws of PDVSA in May 2001, creating a "Council of Shareholders" to "advise the National Executive" -that is- the Ministry of Energy and Mines, "in the formulation and monitoring of compliance with the guidelines and policies that, through the Ministry of Energy and Mines, must establish or agree in accordance with the Second Clause of this Articles of the By-Laws" (article 38, 39), allowing the Minister to intervene in the functioning of the company.[148]

Two years later, in November 2004, President Chávez achieved his goals of intervening directly in the management of PDVSA, by appointing his Minister of Energy and Mines, Rafael Ramírez, simultaneously as President of PDVSA,[149] ignoring the prohibition established in the by-laws of the company for Ministers to be members of the Board of the company (clause 29). The open violation of the By-Laws of PDVSA with this appointment provoked a new *ex post facto* reform of the By-Laws of the company, in order precisely to allow the Minister of Petroleum to be appointed in the Board as President of the company.[150]

A new amendment to the By-Laws was passed through Executive Decree on 2008[151], whereby it was expressly stated that, in achieving her purpose, PDVSA was to follow the guidelines and policies of the National Executive established -or made in accordance with applicable laws-, "through the Ministry of Popular Power of Energy and Petroleum" (Second Clause as modified). Furthermore, an addition was made to allow the President of the Republic to authorize either the President of

147 *Idem*, pp. 38, 41.

148 See Decree N° 1.313 of May 29th, 2001 in *Official Gazette* No. 37.236, July 10, 2001, pp. 318.941

149 See *Official* Gazette No. 38.082, December 12, 2004, p. 336.308

150 See amendment to the Twenty Ninth Clause on Decree N° 3.299 dated December 7th, 2004, in *Official* Gazette No. 38.081, December 7th, 2004, pp. 336.271

151 See Decree N° 6.234 of July 15th, 2008 in *Official Gazette* No. 38.988, August 6th, 2008, pp. 363.187

PDVSA or any of the members of the Board of Directors, to be directors or political organizations while in office; an activity otherwise –and until such amendment- expressly forbidden (Thirtieth Clause, as amended).[152]

The By-Laws of PDVSA were reformed again in 2011, now in order to allow, in addition of the Minister of Energy and Mines who was at the same time President of the company, the appointment two additional Ministries in the Board of PDVSA, the Minister of Finances and Planning, Jorge Giordani, and the Minister of Foreign Relations, Nicolás Maduro. For such purpose, with this reform, the aforementioned clause 29 of the Bylaws was abrogated.[153] Therefore, since 2011, three members of the National Executive Cabinet were acting members of the Board of Directors of PDVSA. In addition, the Deputy Minister of Energy and Mines (Bernard Mommer) was also member of the Board of Directors of PVDSA

After the election of Nicolas Maduro as President of Venezuela in April 2013, Rafael Ramírez continued to be President of PDVSA, and on April 22, 2013, was simultaneously ratified as Minister of Petroleum and Mining in the new government,[154] positions that he held until September 2014. This means that during ten continuous years, Rafael Ramírez, the Minister of Petroleum in Venezuela, was at the same time the President of PDVSA, and responsible for the dismantling of the original independence and autonomy that the oil company had since its creation in 1975.[155]

Such practice of having the Minister of Petroleum being at the same time the President of PDVSA involved in the day-today operations of the company, continued after Ramirez, so on September 2014, the then President Maduro appointed Eulogio Del Pino (who was President of Corporación Venezolana del Petróleo, an affiliate of PDVSA, and also a former member of the Board of Directors of PDVSA) as President of PDVSA,[156] and in August 2015, he appointed him simultaneously to be Minister of Petroleum and Mining.[157]

This symbiosis was briefly interrupted only for a few months, when on August 24, 2017, Euliogo Del Pino was reappointed as Minister of Petroleum,[158] but Nelson Martínez was appointed President of PDVSA.[159] Both held such positions until

152 See comments about this amendment on https://www.analitica.com/economia/desde-pdvsa-hasta-psuvsa/

153 See Decree No 8.238, in *Official Gazette* 39681, May 25, 2011

154 See Official *Gazette* No. 40151, April 22, 2013, p. 400.835

155 See in general on this process: Allan R. Brewer-Carías, *Crónica de una destrucción. Concesión, Nacionalización, Apertura, Constitucionalización, Desnacionalización, Estatización, Entrega y degradación de la Industria petrolera*, Universidad Monteávila, Editorial Jurídica Venezolana, Caracas 2018. Available at: http://allanbrewercarias.com/wp-content/uploads/ 2018/ 06/9789803654276-txt-Cr%C3%B3nica-destrucci%C3%B3n-ARBC-PAGINA-WEB.pdf

156 See Official *Gazette* No. 40.488, September 2nd, 2014, p. 414.654

157 See Official *Gazette* No. 40.727, August 19, 2015, p. 422.884. Asdrubal Chavez, also former member of the Board of Directors, was briefly appointed as Minister of Petroleum and Mining prior to Eulogio Del Pino, see *Official Gazette* No. 40.488, September 2nd, 2014, p. 414.652

158 See Decree No. 3.042 of August 24, 2017 in *Official Gazette* No. 41.221, August 24, 2017, p. 437.327

159 See Decree No. 3.043 of *Official Gazette* No. 41.22, August 24, 2017, p. 437.328

November 4, 2017, when they were detained under criminal corruption charges.[160] Martinez died while in detention in December 2018.[161]

Their substitution took place on November 26, 2017, when Manuel Quevedo, a general of the National Guard, was appointed by Maduro simultaneously as Minister of Petroleum[162] and as President of PDVSA,[163] positions that he kept into Maduro's usurpation of the Presidency, until 27 April 2020.[164] On that date, Nicolás Maduro appointed Asdrúbal José Chávez Jiménez as Interim President of PDVSA.[165]

E. The "transitory" rules for the management of the Oil Industry (2018)

It must also be mentioned that in January 2018, the National Constituent Assembly installed in Venezuela in 2017, against the provisions of the Constitution, [166] issued a " Constitutional Law" (a notion that doesn't exist in Venezuelan Constitutional Law) in order to fight against the "economic war for the rationality and uniformity in the acquisition of assets, services and public works,"[167] providing for the possibility of by-passing all the provisions of the Public Contracting Law regarding the bidding processes for the selection of the contracting parities in public contracts, in particular those entered into by the "State entities with entrepreneurial purposes" (art. 19), and empowering the President of the Republic to establish such special regimes through Executive decrees.

In execution of such provision of the " Constitutional Law," on April 12, 2018, the National Executive (President in Council of Ministers), issued Decree No 3.368 of April 12 2018 (containing within itself other Decree No. 44 issued in the framework of the Economic Emergency and State of Exception established in Decree N° 3.239 of January 9, 2018), establishing a "special and transitory regime for the administrative and operational management of the national oil industry," with force until December 31, 2018, extendable for one year (art. 12, "Constitutional law"), in order to "contribute to the increase of the productive capabilities of *Petróleos de Venezuela S.A.*, PDVSA" (Article 1).

---

160 See the information in https://www.lapatilla.com/2017/11/30/saab-confirma-detencion-de-eulogio-del-pino-y-nelson-martinez/;https://www.noticiascandela.informe25.com/2017/12/en-detalles-la-detencion-de-del-pino.html

161 See the information in: https://elpais.com/internacional/2018/12/13/america/ 15447219 65258574.html; https://www.elnacional.com/venezuela/politica/reuters-fallecio-nelson-martinez-presidente-pdvsa_263171/

162 See Decree No. 3.177, November 26th, 201 in *Official Gazette* No. 6.343 Extra., November 26, 2017.

163 See Decree No. 3.178 dated November 26th, 2017. *Official Gazette* No. 6.343 *Extra,* November 26, 2017.

164 See Official *Gazette* No. 6.531 *Extra,* April 27th, 2020.

165 See Decree No. 4.191 Dated November 27, 2020. *Official Gazette* No. 6.531 *Extra* of April 27th, 2020.

166 See Allan R. Brewer-Carías, *La inconstitucional convocatoria de una Asamblea Nacional Constituyente en mayo de 2017. Un nuevo fraude a la Constitución y a la voluntad popular*, Colección Textos Legislativos, No. 56, Editorial Jurídica Venezolana, Caracas 2017

167 See *Oficial Gazete* N° 41.318 of January 11, 2018.

For such purpose, the Decree assigned to the Minister of Petroleum, "in addition to its attributions of control established in the legal order" (Hydrocarbon Organic Law and in Organic Law on Public Administration), the "most broad powers of organization, management and administration over the public enterprises in the oil industry of the public sector, specially, PDVSA, and its subsidiaries enterprises."

As a consequence of such general provisions, through Article 3 of the Decree, the President assigned to the Minister of Petroleum, extensive attributions of all sort on matters of public contracting, including, specifically, the possibility to create, suppress and modify the public enterprises of the oil public sector, "including *Petróleos de Venezuela S.A.* and its subsidiaries enterprises" (art. 3.1), as well as to "create, suppress, modify or centralize the direction administration and management organs of such enterprises" (art. 3.2). Those reforms of the public enterprises, according to the Decree, must be reflected in modifications of the corresponding By-Laws of the enterprises (art. 3).

The provision regarding the elimination of PDVSA can be considered unconstitutional, due to the fact that it is a public enterprise directly regulated in article 303 of the Constitution as the holding of the oil industry which can only be modify through organic law – Article 302, Constitution-). And regarding the subsidiary's enterprises, all those created by Executive decree, cannot be modify except by another Executive decree, and not by resolution of the Minister of Petroleum.

In addition, the main provisions of the Decree in order to reorganize the oil industry were devoted to eliminating all the procedures seeking transparency in the public contracting processes of selection of the private contracting party, mainly through bidding processes, establishing instead only two modalities of contracting: the "price consulting" procedure (article 4), and the "direct contracting" or award (art. 5).

F. The reinstatement of PDVSA as an instrumentality of the State managed separately from the Government, beginning in 2019

In 2019, the aforementioned situation of PDVSA completely subjected to the Government began to be changed when the National Assembly of Venezuela decided to assume the transition process towards democracy, after the office of the Presidency of the Republic was usurped - since January 2019- by an officer (Nicolás Maduro) whose "reelection" in May 2018 was even rejected and declared non-existent by the same National Assembly, and in general by much of the international community. The National Assembly, in effect, on January 15, 2019, issued a "*Resolution on the declaration of the usurpation of the Presidency of the Republic by Nicolás Maduro Moros and the restoration of the validity of the Constitution,*"[168] providing for "the declaration of the usurpation of the Presidency of the Republic by Nicolas Maduro Moros and the restoration of the validity of the Constitution," or "*of the constitutional order pursuant to articles 5, 187, 233, 333, and 350 of the Constitution.*"

As a consequence of such Resolution, the National Assembly, exercising its legislative power according to article 187.1 of the Constitution, and based on its articles 7 and 333,[169] enacted the *Statute that governs the transition to democracy in*

168 Text available at https://www.infobae.com/america/venezuela/2019/01/15/la-asamblea-nacional-de-venezuela-declaro-a-maduro-usurpador-del-presidencia/ .

169 Text available at http://www.asambleanacional.gob.ve/documentos_archivos/estatuto-que -rige-la-transicion-a-la-democraciapara-restablecer-la-vigencia-de-la-constitucionde-la-republica-

order *to reinstate the Constitution of the Bolivarian Republic of Venezuela* (*Transition Statute)* on February 5th, 2019, which is a law (statute) aimed at "establishing the regulatory framework governing the democratic transition in the Republic" (article 1). According to the provisions of the Constitution, and as it is regulated in such *Statute*, the President of the National Assembly, Juan Guaidó Márquez, assumed the functions of President in charge of the Presidency of the Republic, or Interim President. As such, and pursuant to the provisions of the *Transition Statute,* the Interim President, constitutionally and legally appointed the members of the *Ad-hoc Board of Directors of Petróleos de Venezuela S.A.*, with all legal effects, in order, not only to assure the safeguard of the assets of the company abroad, but to guaranty the functioning of PDVSA as a separate entity from the Government, with the required autonomy for the accomplishment of its economic and business purposes.

Such *Transition Statute,* formally enacted by the National Assembly as a "normative act" adopted "in direct and immediate implementation of Article 333 of the Constitution of the Bolivarian Republic of Venezuela," is "of mandatory compliance for all public authorities and officials, as well as for individuals" (article 4).

Pursuant to articles 15 and 34 of such *Transition Statute,* after being authorized by the National Assembly, the Interim President of the Republic, appointed an *Ad-Hoc Management Board of Directors of PDVSA* and of its affiliates, to assume the management and administration of the company abroad, and to take the necessary measures for the control and protection of their assets abroad. The *Transition Statute* was precise in providing that "the *functional autonomy of those enterprises* and, in particular, of PDVSA" was to be ensured. For that purpose, Article 34.3 provided, in particular referring to *PDV Holding, Inc,* which is the subsidiary of PDVSA in the United States, that the "*autonomous management* of the commercial sector" of such enterprise and its subsidiaries "will meet commercial efficiency criteria, keeping safe the control and accountability mechanisms exercised by the National Assembly within the framework of its powers, and the other applicable control mechanisms," reaffirming that:

> "*PDV Holding, Inc.* and its affiliates *shall have no relationship with those who currently usurp the Presidency of the Republic*. While such a situation of

---

bolivariana-de-venezuela-282.pdf. Also available at https://www.prensa.com/mundo/estatuto-que-rige-la-transicion-a-la-democraciapara-restablecer-la-vigencia-de-la-constitucionde-la-republica-bolivariana-de-venezuela-282_LPRFIL20190205_0001.pdf. See comments to said Statute and its constitutional basis in Allan R. Brewer-Carias, Allan Brewer-Carías, "Some Constitutional and Legal Challenges posed by the process of transition towards democracy decreed by the National Assembly of Venezuela, since January 2019,"17 July 2019, pp 239-241. Available at: http://allanbrewercarias.com/wp-content/uploads/2019/07/1232.-Brewer.-Constitutional-challenges.-Process-Transcition-towards-Democracy.-FIA.-17-July-2019-1.pdf. See also Allan R. Brewer-Carias, *La transición a la democracia en Venezuela. Bases constitucionales y obstáculos usurpadores*, Iniciativa Democrática España y las Américas, Editorial Jurídica Venezolana, Caracas / Miami 2019, pp. 242-251. Available at: http://allanbrewercarias.com/wp-content/uploads/2019/06/193.-Brewer.-bis-5.-TRANSICI%C3%93N-A-LA-DEMOCRACIA-EN-VLA.-BASES-CONSTITUC.-1-6-2019-para-pag-web-1.pdf

usurpation persists, *PDV* Holding, *Inc*. and its subsidiaries will not make any financial payments or contributions to PDVSA."[170]

Based on these provisions, in practice, it can be affirmed that beginning in February 2019 there has been a clear corporate separation between the Republic and PDVSA, as managed by the *Ad-Hoc Board*[171] which has been able to act as an instrumentality of the Republic, with the needed autonomy for the accomplishment of its economic functions, within the rule of separateness from the Government, not being no longer appropriate to pretend to pierce the corporate veil and consider it in the USA as a *alter ego* of the Republic, as it was decided by the United States District Court, D. Delaware in the case *Crystallex International Corporation v. Bolivarian Republic of Venezuela* (C.A. No. 17-mc-151-LPS) of August, 9, 2018.[172] That could have been thr diyustion before 2019, regarding the PDVSA controlled by the Maduro regime, but cannot apply to the PDVSA managed by the *Ad-Hoc Management Board* appointed by Guaidó in order to protect the assets of PDVSA and its subsidiaries abroad, specifically in the United States.

As was expressly recognized by the United States District Court for the *Southern* District of Texas Houston Division, in its judgement issued on May 20, 2020 (Case: *Impact Fluid Solutions LP; aka Impact Fluid Solutions LLC vs Bariven S.A.*) (Civil Action No. 4:19-CV-00652):

> "the National Assembly has barred those appointed [on the Board of Directors of the subsidiaries of PDVSA] by former-President Maduro from exercising any power over PDVSA or its affiliates. Under article six of the Resolution:
>
> 'As long as the usurpation of the Presidency of the Republic exists and in accordance with the Statute that Governs the Transition to Democracy to Restore the Validity of the Constitution of the Bolivarian Republic of Venezuela, all rights and powers which correspond to the Shareholders Meeting, the Board of Directors and the Presidency of Petróleos de Venezuela, S.A. (PDVSA) and its affiliates incorporated in Venezuela, existing or appointed after January 10, 2019 as well as those rights and powers of the Ministry responsible for hydrocarbons and, in general any other ministry, body or entity that may act on the Republic's name or behalf at the Shareholders' Meeting of Petróleos de Venezuela, S.A. (PDVSA) and its subsidiaries incorporated in Venezuela are hereby suspended.'
>
> [...] In doing so, the National Assembly *stripped all management power from the previous regime and vested it in the Ad-Hoc Management Board*. Therefore, any actions taken by the board of directors appointed by Maduro to

---

170 Reference is here made to the *usurped* PDVSA, that is, the one whose´s Board of Directors has been appointed by the usurping government of Nicolás Maduro Moros.

171 Conversely, this refers to PDVSA as directed by the *Ad-Hoc Management Board of Directors* appointed by Juan Guaido, as authorized by the National Assembly under the *Transition Statute*.

172 Available at: https://www.italaw.com/sites/default/files/case-documents/italaw10190.pdf

PDVSA are null and void, including its appointment of GST for legal representation here." (p. 11). [173]

The decisions adopted by the National Assembly within the Transition towards democracy process, according to the provisions of the *Transition Statute*, as well as the decisions issued by the Interim President of the country, Juan Guaidó, were recognized worldwide by more than 50 States, including the United States of America. Nonetheless, the Constitutional Chamber of the Supreme Tribunal of Venezuela, which was completely lacking any sort of autonomy and independence required by any court of justice in a rule of law state -being, on the contrary, since 2000 completely controlled by the Government -, purported to annul the *Transition Statute*, the decisions of the National Assembly and of the Interim President. This was done through a series of unconstitutional decisions, adopted *ex-officio*, which of course are constitutionally and legally forbidden in Venezuela, violating all the most elemental rules of due process and the right to defense guaranteed in article 49 of the Constitution. Therefore, those decisions must be considered null and void pursuant to article 25 of the same Constitution, not having any effect.[174] Additionally, those decisions, not being issued by an independent court of justice, following a proceeding developed *"according to the course of a civilized jurisprudence,"* are judicial rulings that no court of justice can recognize as a comity, as has been decided by the US Supreme Court since 1895.

As a consequence of the decisions adopted since February 2019 by both the National Assembly and the Interim President within the framework of the *Transition Statute Toward Democracy*, and taking into account the United States District Court D. Delaware judgement issued on August 9, 2018 in the case *Crystallex International Corporation v. Bolivarian Republic of Venezuela* (C.A. No. 17-mc-151-LPS);[175] it can be said that the state-own Venezuelan enterprise Petróleos de Venezuela S.A. PDVSA, represented by the *Ad-Hoc management Board of Petróleos de Venezoela S.A*. PDVSA appointed by the Interim President of Venezuela, Juan Guaidó, authorized by the National Assembly, through Decree of February 8, 2019 amended by Decree No. 3 of April 10, 2019,[176] has been a company that has functioned separately from the Maduro's regime (who nonetheless could exercises "*de facto* control" over the company in Venezuela), and also – and more relevant – from the legitimate Government of Venezuela recognized by the United States leaded by Juan Guaidó as Interim President of the Country, who exercise the "*de jure control*" over

173 Available at: https://www.courtlistener.com/recap/gov.uscourts.txsd.1640090/gov.us courts.txsd.1640090.55.0.pdf

174 See Allan R. Brewer-Carías, "The Unconstitutional *Ex Officio* Judicial Review Rulings Issued by the Constitutional Chamber of the Supreme Tribunal of Venezuela Annulling all the 2019 National Assembly Decisions Sanctioned within the framework of the 2019 Transition Regime Towards Democracy and for the Restoration of the enforcement of the Constitution," in the book: *VII Congreso de Derecho Procesal Constitucional 2021*, Universidad Monteávila, Caracas 2021.

175 333 Federal Supplement, 3d Series, pp. 380-426. Available at: https://www.italaw.com /sites/default/files/case-documents/italaw10190.pdf

176 See *Legislative Gazette* N° 6, dated April 10, 2019. Available at: http://www. asambleanacional.gob.ve/gacetas

the company, particularly abroad.[177] This means that currently, PDVSA[178] cannot be considered a company over which the Venezuelan Government exercises "extensively control" in its day-to day with a relationship of principal and agent, as was considered by the United States District Court D. Delaware in the aforementioned decision, as well as by the United States Court of Appeals, Third Circuit in its decision of April 15, 2019, *Case Crystallex International Corporation v. Bolivarian Republic of Venezuela Petróleos de Venezuela S.A.* (Nos. 18-2797 & 18-3124, No. 18-2889),[179] referring to PDVSA prior to February 2019. This is why, since February 2019, PDVSA, managed by the *Ad-Hoc Management Board* cannot be considered as an *alter ego* of the Republic of Venezuela.

Consequently, since February 2019 PDVSA has been managed by the *Ad-Hoc management Board of Petróleos de Venezuela S.A* appointed by Interim President Juan Guaidó, with the authorization of the National Assembly elected in 2015; and has acted as a government instrumentality according to the rules set forth when she was created pursuant to the provisions of the *Organic Law Reserving to the State the Industry and Commerce of Hydrocarbons,* 29 of August 29, 1975.[180] This means that since 2019, it has been a company managed by its board of directors appointed by the government consistent with what is established in the Law, as a separate juridical body from the Government and its Central Administration, with the power to hold and sell property and to sue and be sued, being responsible for its own finances, and being run as a distinct economic entity, not subjected to the same budgetary requirements as the National Executive, and not having the members of its board of directors nor the rest of the personnel the status of public employees.

6. Principles related to the Central Bank of Venezuela as a decentralized entity of the Public Administration of the Venezuelan State

The Central Bank of Venezuela is described in the Constitution of 1999, as a *legal person of public law* (Article 318), that is a "decentralized entity" of the Venezuelan State, following the tradition initiated when it was created by Law in 1939, even originally with the legal form of an "anonymous company" (commercial society). Such regulation was clarified by the former Federal and Cassation Court in

177 I am using the distinction made by the United States District Court for the Southern District of Texas on May 20, 2020, case *Impact Fluid Solutions LP; aka Impact Fluid Solutions LLC (Plaintiffs), VS. BARIVEN S.A.,* et al.: "De jure control refers to the control that arises as a matter of right. On the other hand, de facto control refers to control that arises as a matter of fact, without respect to whether a right to such control exists." The Court in his decision stated that "it appears the Maduro regime still may possess de facto control over Defendants (Bariven S.A., a subsidiary of PDVSA), but adding that "To begin, the Court finds that Special Attorney General Hernández and the Ad-Hoc Management Board of PDVSA clearly possess de jure control over the Defendants,"

178 Again, I am referring here to PDVSA as directed by the *Ad-Hoc Management Board of Directors* appointed by Juan Guaido, duly authorized by the National Assembly under the *Transition Statute*

179 932 Federal Reporter 3d. Series, pp. 126-152. Available at: https://www.leagle.com/decision/infco20190729051

180 See Official *Gazette* No. 1769, Aug. 29, 1975.

a decision of December 20, 1940, in which it stated that despite its legal form as a private law company, the Bank "was not a private institute," but a *public entity.*[181]

In any case, the terminological confusion regarding the qualification of the Central Bank with anonymous society form, but as a *public law person*, and thus as a *decentralized entity of the State*, was definitively clarified in the reform of the Central Bank Law of 1974, in which it was not only described as a "*legal public person* with form of an anonymous company" (Art. 1), but any possibility of private ownership of its capital stock was completely eliminated, as it was completely nationalized. That is why, after the enactment of the new 1999 Constitution, in another reform of the Law in 2002, the Central Bank was definitively described as a *legal person of public law*, following the provision incorporated in the 1999 Constitution (Article 318), as had been the case since 1974.

The matter of the characterization of the Central Bank of Venezuela as a decentralized entity of the Venezuelan State, and as part of the National Public Administration, which has been always accepted,[182] had also been the object of multiple decisions issued by the Supreme Court.

First, the Decision issued by the President of the Politico-Administrative Chamber of the Supreme Court of Justice of December 2, 1980, in which was declared that:

> "the Central Bank of Venezuela, as the first monetary and credit authority of the country, is *one of the fundamental cells of the decentralized public administration*, and as such, its decisions have the character of administrative acts, which can be challenged on grounds of nullity before the organs of the contentious administrative jurisdiction." [183]

---

181 See M. R. Egaña, *Documentos relacionados con la creación del Banco Central de Venezuela,* Caracas, 1980, Tomo III, pp. 183-188

182 See: Allan R. Brewer-Carías, "Introducción general al régimen jurídico de la Administración Pública," in Allan R. Brewer-Carías, Rafael Chavero Gazdik, Jesús María Alvarado Andrade, *Ley Orgánica de la Administracion Pública*, Editorial Jurídica Venezolana, Caracas 2008, p. 68; Allan R. Brewer-Carías, *Derecho Administrativo*, Universidad Externado de Colombia, Tomo I, Bogotá 2005, p. 390, 398-400, 433-434; Allan R. Brewer-Carías, *Principios del régimen jurídico de la Organización Administrativa*, Editorial Jurídica Venezolana, Caracas 1991. Available at: http://allanbrewercarias.net/Content/449725d9-f1cb-474b-8ab2-41efb849 fea5/Content/II.1.62% 20PRIN.REG.JUR.ORG.ADM.%201991.pdf . (Text reproduced in Allan R. Brewer-Carías, *Tratado de Derecho Administrativo. Derecho Público Iberoaericaco,* Vol. II, Editorial Civitas, Editorial Jurídica Venezolana, 2013, pp. 353-356, 367. Available at: http://allanbrewercarias. com/wp-content/uploads/2013/07/BREWER-TRATADO-DE-DA-TOMO-II-9789803652074-txt-1.pdf . See also, about the Central Bank of Venezuela, as part of the Decentralized National Public Administration, in *Informe sobre la Reforma de la Administración Pública Nacional,* Comisión de Administración Pública, Presidencia de la República, Caracas, 1972, Tomo I, pp. 298, 300, 310, 311, and 611-624.

183 See the quotation of this Decision of the President of the Political Administrative Chamber of the Supreme Court of Justice (Case Henry Pereira Gorrín) in the text of the Decision of the Chamber in the same Case of February 19, 1981, in *Gaceta Forense*, Tercera Etapa, Año 1981, enero-marzo, Vol I, pp. 129, No. 111, p. 276.; and in the text of the decision of the same Chamber of July 18, 1985 (Case *Leopoldo Díaz Bruzual*), in *Gaceta Forense*, Tercera Etapa, Año 1985, Julio Septiembre, Vol I, No. 129, pp. 151-152. Also quoted in *Revista de Derecho Público*, No 24, octubre-diciembre 1985, Editorial Jurídica Venezolana, Caracas 1985 p. 103. Available at: http://allanbrewercarias.com/wp-content/uploads/2007/08/rdpub_1985_24.pdf

Second, the Decision of the Politico-Administrative Chamber of the Supreme Court of Justice of February 19, 1981 in which the Supreme Court declared that the Central Bank of Venezuela "constitutes an associative public corporation (*establecimiento público asociativo*) that forms part of the *decentralized administration.*"[184]

Third, the Decision of the Politico-Administrative Chamber of the Supreme Court of Justice of July, 18 1985, in which the Supreme Court qualified the Central Bank of Venezuela, as a "*public entity*, part of the *decentralized administration*," with the character of being a "*public legal person*." [185]

Fourth, the Decision of the Politico-Administrative Chamber of the Supreme Court of Justice of November 30, 1994 in which the Supreme Court qualified the Central Bank of Venezuela, as an associative public corporation" (*establecimiento público asociativo*), created by law, which is part of the Decentralized Administration, and is subjected to a mixed legal regime, configurated by public law and private law provisions.[186]

Fifth the Decision of the Constitutional Chamber of the Supreme Tribunal of Justice No. 259 of March 31, 2016 *(Case: Review of the constitutionality of the Central Bank Law at the request of the President of the Republic, N. Maduro*), in which the Chamber declared that the Central Bank of Venezuela:

> "is a *legal person of public law* with autonomy for the formulation and exercise of the policies of its competency," [being] "*an organ that is part of the National Public Administration with functional autonomy, integrated within the structure of the State.*"[187]

Finally, in the doctrine related to the organization of the Venezuelan State, and in *particular* to its National Public Administration, centralized or decentralized, the Central Bank of Venezuela has always been considered within the decentralized entities of the National Public Administration; [188] which has been also confirmed in

184 See the text of the Decision (Case *Henry Pereira Gorrín vs. Central Bank of Venezuela*) in *Gaceta Forense*, Tercera Etapa, Año 1981, enero-marzo, Volumen I, pp. 129, No. 111, p. 276. See quotation in *Revista de Derecho Público*, No 5, enero-marzo 1981, Editorial Jurídica Venezolana, Caracas 1981 p. 125. Available at: http://allanbrewercarias.com/wp-content/uploads/2007/08/rdpub_1980_5-1.pdf Quoted also in *Revista de Derecho Público* No 24, octubre-diciembre 1985, Editorial Jurídica Venezolana, Caracas 1985 p. 103. Available at: http://allanbrewercarias.com/wp-content/uploads/2007/08/rdpub_1985_24.pdf.

185 See the text of the Decision of July 18, 1985 (Case: Leopoldo Díaz Bruzual), in *Gaceta Forense*, Tercera Etapa, Año 1985, julio-septiembre, Vol I, No. 129, p. 152.

186 See an extract of the decision (Case: *Seguros Saint Paul de Venezuela*) in *Revista de Derecho Mercantil*, Año VI, No. 160-17, Caracas 1994, p. 265.

187 This decision No. 259 of March 31, 2016 is extensively quoted in the text of the decision of the Constitutional Chamber No 618 of July 20, 2016.

188 See: Allan R. Brewer-Carías, *Principios del régimen jurídico de la Organización Administrativa*, Editorial Jurídica Venezolana, Caracas 1991 pp. 117-120; 134-135. Available at: http://allanbrewercarias.net/Content/449725d9-f1cb-474b-8ab2-41efb849fea5/Content/II.1.62%20PRINC.REG.JUR.ORG.ADM.%201991.pdf); Allan R. Brewer-Carías, *Derecho Administrativo*, Universidad Externado de Colombia, Tomo I, Bogotá 2005, p. 390, 398-400, 433-434; Allan R. Brewer-Carías, "Introducción general al régimen jurídico de la Administración Pública," in Allan R. Brewer-Carías, Rafael Chavero Gazdik, Jesús María Alvarado Andrade, *Ley Orgánica de la Administración Pública*, Editorial Jurídica Venezolana,

official reports, including the 1972 "*Report on the reform of National Public Administration,*" issued by the Public Administration Presidential Commission, in which is clearly stated that the Central Bank of Venezuela was an "associative public corporation" (due to its form as anonymous society) (*establecimiento público asociativo*), that was part of the Decentralized National Public Administration.[189] That is why, for instance, Giuseppe Rosito Arbia, expressed in 1993 that the Central Bank of Venezuela is a "State's legal person of public law, part of the functional decentralized public administration, and specifically of the national decentralized public administration;[190] and Claudia Nikken, without any doubt, qualifies the Central Bank of Venezuela as a "decentralized entity" that is part of the "decentralized public administration."[191]

When considering this matter of the Central Bank of Venezuela as a decentralized entity of the Venezuelan State, part of the National Public Administration, in any case is important to bear in mind the general scope of the Organization of the State in Venezuela, and of its Public Administration.

In effect, together with all the other organs and entities of the National Executive (President, Ministers) and of the Public Administration, exercises the Executive Power, although without subordination to other organs of the National Executive (President, Ministers. Notwithstanding that the appointment of the President and Directors of the Central Bank of Venezuela according to the Central Bank Law is the responsibility of the President of the Republic as head of the National Executive, the Bank exercises its powers with autonomy (article 318 of the Constitution), not subject to the directives or instructions or control by the National Executive, and is only under control, as provided in article 319 of the Constitution, by the Audit General Office, by the Superintendence of Banks and by the National Assembly.

Consequently, the Central Bank of Venezuela, without doubt is one of the decentralized entities of the National Public Administration within the organization of the Venezuelan State, being considered as an "autonomous constitutional organ with its own legal personality."[192] As such decentralized entity, the Bank, is subject,

---

Caracas 2008, p. 68. More recently on the character of the Central Bank of Venezuela: Allan R. Brewer-Carías, "Sobre el Banco Central de Venezuela, como ente descentralizado de la Administración Pública del Estado, con personalidad jurídica de derecho público directamente prevista en la Constitución. New York, 9 de mayo 2019; available at: http://allanbrewer carias.com/wp-content/uploads/2019/05/196.-Brewer.-Sobre-el-BCV-y-representacion-del-procu-rador-especial-2019..pdf

189 See *Informe sobre la Reforma de la Administración Pública Nacional,* Comisión de Administración Pública, Presidencia de la República, Caracas, 1972, Tomo I, pp. 298, 300, 310, 311, and 611-624.

190 See Giuseppe Rosito Arbia, "Consideraciones sobre la naturaleza jurídica del Banco Central de Venezuela," in *Revista de la Facultad de Derecho de la Universidad Católica Andrés Bello* / Universidad Católica Andrés Bello, Facultad de Derecho.-- Caracas, No 46 (junio) (1993), pp. 373-377; 388-390;395,, 407

191 See Claudia Nikken, "Naturaleza jurídica del Banco Central de Venezuela," in *Revista de Derecho Público,* No. 63-64, julio-diciembre 1995, Editorial Jurídica Venezolana, Caracas 1995, pp. 517-519. Available at: http://allanbrewercarias.com/wp-content/uploads/2017/01/1995-RE-VISTA-63-64.pdf

192 See Maria Amparo Grau, "La organización de los Poderes Públicos en la Constitución del 9: Desarrollo y situación actual," in the book: *El derecho público a los 100 números de la Revista*

for instance, to the Public Contracting Law (Article 3),[193] to the Organic Law on Public Assets (Article 4),[194] and to the Organic Law of the General Audit Office (Article 9);[195] and of course to many of the provisions of the Organic Law of Public Administration.

In effect, the basic statute enacted in Venezuela to regulate all the organs and entities of Public Administration is the Organic Law on Public Administration, which establishes the general legal regime applicable to all of them, with some exceptions, like the case of the Central Bank of Venezuela, which due to its autonomy established in the Constitution, is not subjected to the general regime of *control* established in the Organic law for other decentralized entities.

But apart from being exempt from that regimen of administrative control by the organs of the National Executive, the Central Bank of Venezuela, as a decentralized entity of the National Public Administration is of course subjected to all the general regulations and principles related to the functioning of Public Administration included in the Organic Law (in particular Title II. Principles and basis of the functioning and organization of Public Administration: articles 3-28, 33-43), as well as in the Organic Law of Administrative Procedure; the Public Contracting Law (Article 3);[196] the Organic Law on Public Assets (Article 4);[197] the Organic Law of the General Audit Office (Article 9);[198] and the Financial Management of the Public Sector Organic Law (article 6).[199]

That is, although it is a decentralized entity in terms of article 15 of the Organic Law on Public Administration, the provisions of the Organic Law referring to the Central Administration (Title III: article 44-91), and to the "Functional Decentralization" (Title IV: articles 92-131) are not applicable to the Central Bank of Venezuela, due to its character as a decentralized entity with autonomy under the Constitution, subject to the provisions of its own specific Law (Central Bank of Venezuela Law). This alone is the meaning of the expression used in Decision No. 259 of March 31, 2016 of the Constitutional Chamber of the Supreme Tribunal when affirming that the Central Bank of Venezuela "does not form part of either the Central Administration or the functionally Decentralized Administration" (of course as provided in the Organic Law of Public Administration). And this is obvious in light of the fact that the Organic Law on Public Administration enumerates those

---

de Deecho Público 1980-2005, Editorial Jurídica Venezolana, Caracas 2005, p. 331. Available at: http://allanbrewercarias.com/wp-content/uploads/2007/08/EL-DERECHO-P%C3%9ABLICO-A-LOS-100-N%C2%B0-DE-LA-RDP-1980-2005-MAYO-20061.pdf

193 See *Official Gazette* N° 6.154 Extra. of November 19, 2014. Available at: http://www.mindefensa.gob.ve/COMISION/wp-content/uploads/2017/03/LCP.pdf

194 See *Official Gazette* N° 39.952 of June 26, 2012.

195 See *Official Gazette* N° 37.347 of December 17, 2001. Available at: http://www.oas.org/juridico/spanish/mesicic3_ven_anexo23.pdf

196 See *Official Gazette* N° 6.154 Extra. of November 19, 2014. Available at: http://www.mindefensa.gob.ve/COMISION/wp-content/uploads/2017/03/LCP.pdf

197 See *Official Gazette* N° 39.952 of June 26, 2012.

198 See *Official Gazette* N° 37.347 of December 17, 2001. Available at: http://www.oas.org/juridico/spanish/mesicic3_ven_anexo23.pdf

199 Article 5. See *Official Gazette* No. 6210 Extra of December, 2015, available at: http://historico.tsj.gob.ve/gaceta_ext/diciembre/30122015/E-30122015-4475.pdf#page=1

"functional decentralized entities" that are subject to its provisions and administrative control by Ministers of the National Executive in a precise way: *public institutes* (articles 98-10)1; *state own enterprises* (articles 102-109); *State foundations* (articles 110-114); and *State Civil Associations* (articles 116-117); providing for all of them the means for their administrative control by the organs of the Central Administration (articles 118-131). This list would not have been necessary if all decentralized entities were subject to all provisions of the Organic Law. The Central Bank of Venezuela is not within that enumeration, because it is not a *public institution, nor a state-owned enterprise, nor a State Foundation nor a State Association.* It is a unique decentralized entity part of the National Public Administration, which due to its autonomy, is subject to its own Law and means of control, thus not being enumerated in the Organic Law on Public Administration.

Decision No 259 of March 31, 2016 acknowledges this, affirming that the Central Bank of Venezuela is:

> "a legal person of public law with autonomy for the formulation and exercise of the policies of its competence. In this sense it is a body that belongs to the *National Public Administration with functional autonomy, integrated into the structure of the State,* which in an autonomous, exclusive and excluding manner exercises monetary competence, with its own legal regime [...] It is a unique entity and the relationship established between the National Executive and the Central Bank of Venezuela is a relationship of general and special coordination and not of subordination."

In conclusion, the Central Bank of Venezuela is a decentralized entity of the National Public Administration. It is not one of the decentralized entities *enumerated in the Organic Law on PublicAdministration.* This means that the Central Bank of Venezuela is a decentralized entity of the National Public Administration, although not subject to the provisions of the Organic Law on Public Administration on matters of administrative control by the National Executive, but to its own Law.

That is why, the Central Bank of Venezuela is not listed in Decree No. 2.378 of July 12, 2016 on the General Organization of National Public Administration. And this is obvious. This Decree, as all the previous Decrees of that sort, identifying the decentralized entities as attached, for the purpose of administrative control, to the corresponding organs of the Central Administration (Ministries), was issued according to the provision of article 119 of the Organic Law on Public Administration, which provides that:

> "Article 119: Every functional decentralized entity *must be attached to a determined organ or entity of Public Administration, for the purpose of the exercise of the corresponding control.*"[200]

Consequently, article 121 of the same Organic Law imposes the obligation for the Central organs of Public Administration to publish in the *Official Gazette:* "the list of the decentralized entities *attached or subjected to control*, with the indication of

200 Artículo 119. Todo ente descentralizado funcionalmente se adscribirá a un determinado órgano o ente de la Administración Pública, a los efectos del ejercicio del control correspondiente

the amount of capital, if they are a *State-owned enterprise*, or the confirmation of assets if they are a *public institute*, *autonomous institute*, or a *State foundation*."

Consequently, although the Central Bank of Venezuela is without doubt a decentralized entity of the National Public Administration, due to its specific autonomy (initially established in the Law creating it and now provided in the Constitution), it is not and cannot be subjected to attachment to any other organ of Central Administration for the purposes of control. That is why it is not listed in the aforementioned Decree.

Regarding the aforementioned decision of the Constitutional Chamber No. 259 of March 31, 2016, the Chamber did not affirm that the Central Bank was not a decentralized entity; on the contrary, the text of the decision is clear affirming that the Central Bank of Venezuela "belongs to the *National Public Administration with functional autonomy, integrated in the structure of the State,"* which is another way of saying that it is a decentralized entity of the Venezuelan State.

Other decision that must be mentioned is decision No. 618 of July 20, 2016 of the Constitutional Chamber of the Supreme Tribunal, which was issued in a case involving interpretation of articles 150, 187.9, 236.14 and 247 of the Constitution in the context of "national public interest contracts" (case *Brigitte Acosta Isasis*, "*Interpretación Constitucional de los artículos 150, 187.9, 236.14 y 247 de la Constitución)*.[201] After quoting the aforementioned Decision No. 259 of March 31, 2016, the Supreme Tribunal concluded that "the Central Bank of Venezuela is a legal person of public law, of constitutional rank, with autonomy in the exercise of the policies of its competency," adding the phrase that it "is not part of the *Central Administration* nor of the *Functionally Decentralized Administration*" although affirming that it is part of the so called "*Administration with functional autonomy*." What is clear is that the Chamber did not rule that the Central Bank of Venezuela was not a decentralized entity of the State; it just affirmed that it was not part of the "functional decentralized entities" included in the list in the Organic Law on Public Administration (*public institutions, state-owned enterprises, State foundations and State Associations*).

It must be mentioned that the subject matter of the decision was not the character of the Central Bank. The case concerned the scope of the need for parliamentary authorization over public interest contracts (specifically, a public debt contract between the Central Bank and the *Fondo Latinoamericano de Reservas* created in an international convention*)*, for which purpose the Constitutional Chamber considered the legal nature of the Central Bank of Venezuela to decide that the specific contract at issue was not subject to parliamentary control by the National Assembly. This decision was issued after the Government lost its absolute political control of the National Assembly (that it had exercised since 2005) in the parliamentary elections of December 2015, in order to prevent the newly elected National Assembly from exercising its constitutionally mandated control over public interest contracts entered into by decentralized entities.

What is definitive is that the Constitutional Chamber in its Decision No. 618 of July 20, 2016, did not declare and did not rule, in any way whatsoever, that the

201 See in http://historico.tsj.gob.ve/decisiones/scon/julio/189144-618-20716-2016-16-0683.HTML

Central Bank of Venezuela was not a "*decentralized entity*" of the Venezuelan State; a phrase that is not even used in the text of the decision. Such a conclusion would have been in contradiction with the Constitution and with the previously mentioned Decision No. 259 of March 31, 2016 issued when reviewing the constitutionality of the Central Bank Law. It would also have been in contradiction of the already mentioned long jurisprudential tradition that goes back to 1940,

In summary, under Venezuelan law, as with all other public corporations (public institutes, autonomous institutes) with legal personality of public law, the Central Bank is without doubt a decentralized entity of the Venezuelan State, and part of Public Administration. It is not part of the "Central and Decentralized Public Administration" as it is described in the Organic Law on Public Administration. That is why the Central Bank of Venezuela is not subject to those provisions of the Organic Law relating in particular to the functions of the organs of the Central Administration to control the "Functional Decentralized" entities (public institutes, State owned enterprises, State foundations, state civil associations or societies); but it is subject to the other provisions of the Organic Law that establish principles applicable to all the organs and entities of Public Administration. The "Functional Decentralized Public Administration" entities listed in the Organic Law of Public Administration are not all of the entities that are "decentralized entities" in a wider sense, the latter including the Central Bank. In other words, the Public Administration Organic Law[202] contains a partial list of the "decentralized entities," described as forming the "Functional Decentralized Public Administration" (Articles 98-131). This enumeration did not include all decentralized entities.

202 See *Official Gazette* N° 6.147 Extra of November 17, 2014. Available at: http://historico.tsj.gob.ve/gaceta_ext/noviembre/17112014/E-17112014-4128.pdf#page=1

PART THREE

PRINCIPLES OF ADMINISTRATIVE LAW RELATED TO ADMINISTRATIVE ACTION: ADMINISTRATIVE PROCEDURE, AND ADMINISTRATIVE ACTS

I. GENERAL PRINCIPLES REGARDING ADMINISTRATIVE PROCEDURE

Ten years after Argentina passed its Law of Administrative Procedures (Law N° 19.549 of 1972), Venezuela sanctioned its Organic Law of Administrative Procedures that went into effect on January 1, 1982,[1] after a vaunted process of preparation that included ideas and proposals that had been gathered and discussed since the beginning of the 1960s.[2] This Organic Law is with doubts, the most important Law enacted in the field of administrative law in Venezuela, where its Administration had never been subject to a body of law that so broadly and precisely regulated the central aspects of the relations between the Public Administration and the citizens, making this the most important general regulation of substantive activities in Public Administration.

This Law differed from previous regulations dealing only with the internal organization of Public Administration. Now, on the contrary, the Administrative Procedure Law establishes the legal framework of the relations between the Public Administration and the citizens, providing on the one hand for the Public Administration to have a set of powers, prerogatives and obligations in order to provide for the general interest, and on the other, for individual citizens to have a

---

1 See in *Official Gazette* N° 2.818 Extra. Of July 1, 1981. See on the Organic Law n Admnistrative Preocedures the comments in: Allan R. Brewer-Carías et al., *Ley Orgánica de Procedimientos Administrativos,* Editorial Jurídica Venezolana, Caracas, 1982. See Allan R. Brewer-Carías, "Régimen general del procedimiento administrativo en la Ley Orgánica de Procedimientos Administrativos de Venezuela de 1981," in Héctor M. Pozo Gowland, David A. Halperin, Oscar Aguilar Valdez, Fernando Juan Lima, Armando Canosa (Coord.), *Procedimiento Administrativo. Tomo II. Aspectos Generales del Procedimiento Administrativo. El Procedimiento Administrativo en el Derecho Comparado,* Ed. La Ley, Buenos Aires 2012.

2 The first draft of the Law was elaborated in 1961-1962 at the Public Administration Commission (drafted by Tomás Polanco Alcantara); followed by a draft prepared for the Ministry of Justice in 1965 (drafted by Sebastián Martín-Retortillo, Francisco Rubio Llorente and Allan R. Brewer-Carías); which was re-written again in 1972 (drafted by Allan R. Brewer-Carías) for the same Public Administration Commission. See *Informe sobre la Reforma de la Administración Pública Nacional,* Comisión de Administración Pública, Caracas, 1972, Vol. 2, pp. 391-406.

series of rights and obligations in their relations with the Administration that allows them to control its subjection to the law.

1. Initial Impact of the Law

The 1981 Organic Law of Administrative Procedures, as previously noted, brought a profound legal transformation within the Public Administration, seeking to replace informality by formality regarding the activities of the Administration; and to replace the lack of rights available to the citizens by a series of rights upon which they could lean when dealing with the Administration.

A. Formality vs. Informality

Prior to the Organic Law of Administrative Procedures, it can be said that the Venezuelan Public Administration was characterized by complete informality. In contrast with the unilateral acts ruled by private law that are subjected to greater formality under the terms of the Civil Code, particularly in cases in which they are not the result of a confrontation of wills (e.g., mortgage, donations); unilateral action by the Public Administration (administrative acts), was not subjected to specific formalities for its enactment, having case law admitted procedural discretion and informality as a principle. In view of this situation, this Organic Law revamped it and began to require formalism as a principle of administrative procedure, seen both in the requirement for certain formalities in the production of administrative acts (procedures, processes) as well as in their forms. The Law also erected formalism as a duty of public servants who are required to follow a process (Article 3), conduct it (Article 54) or take charge of carrying out proceedings (Article 53), to prove allegations of fact for administrative acts (Article 69) and to decide on matters and appeals within determined periods of time (Articles 2, 5, 41, 60, 62, 67, 89). On the other hand, the Organic Law for the first time also established specific forms for unilateral administrative acts (Article 18), thereby positivizing the general principles established by the jurisprudence of the Supreme Court.

The Law, on the other hand, established the principles in order to overcome the traditional administrative secrecy which had existed as a rule with regards to the interested parties. As a result of this secrecy, the citizens affected directly by them had no awareness not only that sometimes a proceeding had been filed against them, but also of the content of the documents and acts based on which the Administration could decide the proceeding, and which could potentially result in a violation of their rights and interests. This eternal administrative confidentiality was sought to be finally terminated as a result of the Administration's obligation to notify the interested parties whose rights or interests could be affected by the administrative proceeding (Articles 48, 68). These rights now include the right to be heard, to submit evidence and allegations (Articles 48, 58) and to have free and previous access to the Administration file (Article 59) which must be just one single piece or folder (Articles 31, 51). Before the law was enacted, the right to be heard and the right to review the Administration file was not guaranteed; rather, the rule was administrative secret and reservation of the Administration's files.

On the other hand, and secondly, formalism led to the specific regulation of aspects that had not previously been regulated, such as those relating to advisory organs of the Administration. The Organic Law in effect established at least three fundamental principles that relate to an advisory organs: first, the principle of the non-binding nature of consultations and decisions entered prior to the issuance of an administrative act (Article 56), except those that are expressly established by law; second, the principle of the non-binding nature of consultations, opinions and resolutions (Article 57), except as expressly established by law; and third, the principle that the proceeding cannot be suspended when there are no said decisions or consultations (Article 56), except when expressly established by law. In this way the basic principles relating to an advisory organ were regulated, which before had not been precisely set-in law.

Thirdly and finally, another sign of the formalism imposed by the Organic Law on the Administration are standards that relate to the publication and notification of administrative acts, for purposes of making them effective. Other aspects of the Organic Law set the condition that there must be notice to the interested party for the administrative act to start tits effects (Article 73), which could not be replaced in principle by publication of the administrative act in the *Official Gazette* of the Republic, or the Gazette of the corresponding territorial entity. The Law in this way prescribed which acts must be published in the *Official Gazette,* in particular normative acts, (Article 72); and in terms of the formalities regarding notice (Article 75), it regulated the cases where notices could not be served for publication in the *Official Gazette,* but in a newspaper of general circulation (Article 76). Regulations on notifications and publication of administrative acts definitely transformed a previously informal situation.

B. Rights vs. an Absence of Rights

The second aspect of the legal transformation that was caused by the Organic Law of Administrative Procedures and that radically changed the previous situation was the creation of a set of rights and guarantees that are available to the citizens, which had not existed before. In this regard and as previously noted, the Organic Law established a balance between the rights of the citizens and the powers of the Administration, regulating as a fundamental right, the right to defense before the Administration, following the principles established in the Constitution. This right imply a series of derivative rights, as are: the right to be notified of all proceedings that could affect the interested party on its subjective rights or its legitimate, personal and direct interests (Article 48); the right to be heard and to take part in an administrative proceeding, at any time (Article 23); the right to have access to the Administration file, to examine it and to make copies (Article 59); the right to present evidence and to make allegations (Articles 48, 58); the right for the administrative act to formally state the reasons behind it (motivation) (Article 9); the right to receive personal notice of all administrative acts that could affect the individual's legitimate, personal and direct rights and interests (Article 73); and to be informed of the legal means of defense against the act (Articles 73, 77). These rights had not been expressly recognized before the enactment of the 1981 Organic Law, and although jurisprudence had aimlessly established some of these as general principles of law, as a whole they were more frequently trampled than respected by the Administration.

In any event, from the legal point of view, the Organic Law did not just trigger a legal revolution in administrative actions and practice, but also had a noticeable effect on the development of the theory of administrative law. This Organic Law can in effect still be considered as the most important law in Venezuelan administrative law, not just because it set in writing many general principles of administrative law that had been established by jurisprudence, but because the successive interpretation and application of its standards has resulted in a progressive enrichment of this branch of law, which previously lacked a basic body of law on which it could base its dogma.[3]

C. Administrative transformations

However, the legal revolution brought on by the new Organic Law was followed by an administrative revolution in the practice of the Public Administration, establishing a series of requirements in terms of administrative rationalization. In effect, if the legal image of the Public Administration prior to the Law was marked by informality, the practice of administrative actions was marked by absolute discretion that governed the proceeding and its forms. In view of this situation, the Law set down the required systemization of all documents (Article 32), unification of the case files (Article 31), the establishment of administrative procedures and

---

3 See on this impact, Allan R. Brewer Carías, *El Derecho Administrativo y la Ley Orgánica de Procedimientos Administrativos,* Editorial Jurídica Venezolana, Caracas, 1985. See in addition, in general on the Venezuelan Law: Allan R. Brewer-Carías, "Comentarios a la Ley Orgánica de Procedimientos Administrativos", en *Revista de Derecho Público,* N° 7, Caracas 1981, pp. 115-117; José Araujo Juares, *Derecho Administrativo Formal,* Vadell Hermanos Editores, 3era Edición, Caracas, 1998; José Araujo Juares, *Principios Generales del Derecho Procesal Administrativo,* Vadell Hermanos Editores, Caracas, 1998; Luis Beltrán Guerra, *El Acto Administrativo. La Teoría del Procedimiento Administrativo*, Caracas 1977; Antonio De Pedro Fernández, *El procedimiento administrativo en Venezuela*, Editorial M&H C.A., Caracas, 1994; Luis H. Farías Mata, *Procedimientos Administrativos*, Materiales de Estudio. Escuela de Estudios Políticos y Administrativos Universidad Central de Venezuela (mimeografiado), 1978; Agustín Gordillo, "Algunos aspectos del procedimiento administrativo en Venezuela", in *Revista de Derecho Público* N° 9, pp. 29-39; Víctor R. Hernández-Mendible, *Procedimiento Administrativo. Proceso Administrativo y Justicia Constitucional,* Vadell Hermanos Editores, Caracas-Valencia, 1997, Eloy Lares Martínez "Los Procedimientos Administrativos" in *Libro Homenaje a la Memoria de Joaquín Sánchez Covisa*, Caracas 1975, pp. 481-492; Henrique Meier E., *El Procedimiento Administrativo Ordinario,* Editorial Jurídica Alva, S.R.L., Caracas, 1992; Antonio Moles Caubet, "Vicisitudes del Procedimiento Administrativo en Venezuela", in *Revista Internacional de Ciencias Administrativas*, Bruselas, 1972, pp. 270-276; José Rodríguez Ramos, "Breves notas sobre la Ley Orgánica de Procedimientos Administrativos", en *Revista del Colegio de Abogados del Estado Lara*, diciembre 1981, pp. 105-115; Hildegard Rondón de Sansó, "El Procedimiento Administrativo en el Derecho Comparado", in *Libro Homenaje a la Memoria de Joaquín Sánchez Covisa*, Caracas 1975, pp. 577-620; Hildegard Rondón de Sansó, "Análisis crítico de la Ley Orgánica de Procedimientos Administrativos", in *Revista del Consejo de la Judicatura*, N° 22, Caracas 1981, pp. 15-35; Hildegard Rondón de Sansó, *Procedimiento Administrativo,* Editorial Jurídica Venezolana, 2da. Edición, Caracas, 1983; Gabriel Ruan Santos, "La Administración y la Ley Orgánica de Procedimientos Administrativos", in *Revista de Derecho Público,* N° 18, 1984, pp. 57-83. See the collective books on the Law: *El Procedimiento Administrativo*, Vol IV of the *Archivo de Derecho Público y Ciencias de la Administración*, Instituto de Derecho Público, Caracas, 1982; in particular the articles of Antonio Moles Caubet, "Introducción al Procedimiento Administrativo" and of Luis Henrique Farías Mata, "El Proceso de elaboración de la Ley Orgánica de Procedimientos Administrativos"; *Contencioso Administrativo, I Jornadas Internacionales de Derecho Administrativo,* FUNEDA, Caracas, 1995, in particular the article of Sandra Morelli, "El procedimiento administrativo y el proceso contencioso administrativo"; *La relación jurídico administrativa y el procedimiento administrativo, IV Jornadas Internacionales de Derecho Administrativo,* FUNEDA, Caracas, 1998.

systems to improve administrative efficacy (Article 32), document registry (Article 44) and a broad system of downward-moving information (Article 33) in order to open the Administration to individuals.

In this sense the Organic Law had the objective of providing an "open window" where the public would be informed on what should or should not be done in proceedings and get all applicable requirements, forms and timing, and, as a result, these proceedings would no longer be the exclusive right of some obscure official who dominated proceedings from behind their impenetrable 'reception office,' sometimes in corrupt combination with external handlers or intermediaries, so these proceedings would now be open, public and available to all. But this change has not been easy as this transformation touches on and affects spheres and areas of power, areas that are sometimes more powerful than the highest official: the rights of the bearer or receiver of the document, or the person holding the power to reject and dispose, tyrannically, of the rights and interests of those administered.

2. General Content of the Organic Law of Administrative Procedures and its Sphere of Application

A. General content of the Law

In general terms, this Organic Law regulated four fundamental aspects of the Public Administration and its relations with the citizens. On the one hand it regulated an entire legal system or set of legal situations on the part of both the Public Administration as well as individuals. In this aspect the Law, on the one hand, specified a series of administrative powers and established a series of duties and obligations on the part of the public servant; on the other hand, it regulated and established a series of rights held by the individual citizen regarding the Administration, even as it placed precise obligations on the form of their relations with the Administration. This was the first area regulated by the Law: the legal situations of individuals and those of the Public Administration.

Secondly, it regulated the administrative act; that is, the specific decision resulting from the actions of the Public Administration in terms of the legal effects of the decisions adopted by it, in certain situations. The Law regulated precisely the requirements of the act, making it subject to certain conditions in order to be valid and regarding the legality of the actions of the Administration. The Law likewise regulates the effects of the acts: their review, both on its own and by appeal; as well as the form in which the administrative decisions are issued, establishing not just an expedited decision but also creating the innovation that administrative silence is a tacit negative administrative decision. Consequently, and pursuant to the Law, administrative silence was no longer a form of avoiding making a decision or resolution on a matter so that it simply vanished as time passed, but rather became a form of a tacit decision, basically denying the request, petition or the appeal filed. Establishing silence as a tacit decision opened new routes to individual citizens for protection or appeal, when their requests had not been decided within the periods set. This also led to a change in the mentality of the public servant, who many times simply remained silent or did not act, basically abstaining from making any decision on a matter and thereby maintaining the status quo. This silence, however, began to have effects with the enactment of the Law, as the decision is considered as having been made simply by the lapse of time in the periods provided by the Law. The request is considered as having been denied at the conclusion of that period, and that denial gives the individual the possibility of appealing that denial, either before a superior level in the hierarchy, or through the Courts. It also makes the public servant responsible for his omission and failure to act, and if this behavior is repeatedly, he incurs an administrative liability.

In addition to regulating administrative legal situations and administrative acts, the Law thirdly regulated administrative procedure, that is, the complete set of processes, requirements and formalities that must be completed by the Administration and in relations between the Administration and individuals in order to cause administrative decisions, i.e., administrative acts.

Finally and in the fourth place the Law regulated the processes for review of administrative acts within the Administration itself; that is, the system of recourses requesting a reconsideration or review and the hierarchy that allows the individual to formally make a claim against the Administration, not as a favor but as a matter of law, against administrative acts; and which requires the Administration to decide on these recourses within a determined period of time, and failure to do so is considered a tacit denial of the recourse.

With regards to the sphere of application of the Organic Law of Administrative Procedures,[4] this refers both to the organizational sphere of application, i.e., the determination of what organs and entities it applies to; as well as the substantive sphere of application, i.e., to what proceedings it applies, or if it applies to all the proceedings that are performed by the bodies that fall under their regulation.

B. Organizational sphere

The organizational sphere of application of the Organic Law is clearly defined in Article 1st that states that the National Public Administration and the Decentralized Public Administration, consisting of the form set forth in their respective Organic Laws, shall adapt their activities to the prescriptions set by the Law. The article in this way distinguishes two organic sets: on the one hand the *Central National Public Administration*, and on the other hand of the *Decentralized Public Administration,*[5] both of which form part of the *National Public Administration* and are regulated in the Organic Law on Public Administration Act of 2008.[6]

a. The (National) Central Public Administration

Article 44 of the Organic Law on Public Administration distinguishes three types of *superior bodies* in the organization of the Central Level of the National Public

4 See Allan R. Brewer-Carías, "Ámbito de la aplicación de la Ley Orgánica de Procedimientos Administrativos", in *Revista de Control Fiscal*, N° 104, Caracas, 1982

5 See on the Public Administration, in general Allan R. Brewer-Carías, *Fundamentos de la Administración Pública*, Tomo I, Caracas, 2da. Edición, 1984; Allan R. Brewer-Carías, *Principios del Régimen Jurídico de la Organización Administrativa Venezolana,* Editorial Jurídica Venezolana, Caracas, 1994

6 Organic Law on Public Administration, *Official Gazette* N° 6.147 Extra. Of November 17, 2014. See Allan R. Brewer-Carías et al., *Ley Orgánica de la Administración Pública*, Editorial Jurídica Venezolana, Caracas 2009.

Administration:[7] the superior directive bodies, the superior bodies for coordination and control centralized planning, and superior consultation bodies that are exercised by the Executive Branch under the terms of Article 225 of the Constitution. The Law enumerates the following as *superior directive bodies* of the Central Level of the Public Administration: The President of the Republic, the Executive Vice President, the Council of Ministers, the Ministers, the Deputy Ministers, and regional authorities. The *Superior body that coordinates and controls centralized planning* is the Central Planning Commission. As for *superior consultation bodies* at the Central Level of the National Public Administration, Article 44 of the Law lists the following: The Office of the Attorney General of the Republic, the State Council, the National Council of Defense, the sectorial boards (former sectorial cabinets) and the ministerial boards (formerly ministerial cabinets) which also exercise Executive Power (Article 225 C). Consequently, not all of the Central Administration is regulated in the Law; so, the superior coordination and control and the consultative bodies are regulated under their own laws.

b. The Decentralized Administration

However, the Organic Law also applies to the Decentralized Public Administration,[8] which for the purpose of the Law is composed by the public entities with public law personality, that can only be created by law (art. 145, Constitution of 1999) in order to transfer them Public Power, consequently being empowered to enact administrative acts. The Decentralized Public Administration, as aforementioned, and according to the provisions of the Organic Law of Public Administration of 2008 (Arts. 29 and 32 LOAP) is composed by entities created by the territorial entities of the State (Republic, States, Municipalities), assigning them public law personality, like the public corporations (*institutos autónomos* or *institutos públicos*) or private law personality like a commercial company (*state own enterprises*).[9] The former are created by statute, through which public powers can be transferred; the latter are created by means of incorporation of the company as a commercial entity in the Commercial Registry.[10] Consequently, being the private law entities created by the State subjected to private law, and without being empowered to exercise Public Power in order for example to enact administrative acts, the Organic Law on Administrative Procedure is not applicable to them. The

7 See on the Cenral Administration: Allan R. Brewer-Carías, "Principios Generales de la Organización de la Administración Central, con particular referencia a la Administración Ministerial", in *Revista de Derecho Público*, N° 2, Caracas 1980, pp. 5-22

8 See on the decentralized administration: Allan R. Brewer-Carías, *Fundamentos de la Administración Pública*, Tomo I, 2da Edición, Caracas, 1984, pp. 223-248; Jesús Caballero Ortíz, "La Administración Descentralizada Funcionalmente" in *Revista de Derecho Público*, N° 8, Caracas 1981, pp. 5-25; Jesús Caballero Ortíz, "La Administración Descentralizada. Coordinación y control", in *Revista de Control Fiscal*, N° 18, Caracas 1985; Juan Garrido Rovira, *Temas sobre la Administración Descentralizada en Venezuela,* Editorial Jurídica Venezolana, Caracas, 1984.

9 On the legal persons See: Allan R. Brewer-Carías, "La distinción entre las personas jurídicas y las personas privadas y el sentido de la problemática actual de la clasificación de los sujetos de derecho" in *Revista Argentina de Derecho Administrativo*, N° 17, Buenos Aires 1977, pp. 15-29.

10 On the public enterprises, See Allan R. Brewer-Carías, *El régimen jurídico de las empresas públicas en Venezuela*, Ediciones del Centro Latinoamericano de Administración para el Desarrollo, Caracas 1980.

Organic Law in reality applies only to decentralized entities having public law personality as the already mentioned Public Corporations.

It must also be noted that regarding public law entities, that not all the activities that they perform are subjected to the Organic Law. In particular, despite their public personality, they also perform activities that are entirely rule by provisions of private law, civil or commercial, in which neither authorities nor public powers are exercised. That is, the legal relations that fall within the regulations of private law, civil and mercantile, would not be governed by the standards of the Organic Law. Conversely, regarding these public law entities, the Organic Law will only apply to the procedures that lead to the issuance of administrative acts, giving rise to legal relations between the entity and the citizen, governed by administrative law.

c. The Public Administration of other Public Powers

Article 1 of the Organic Law of Administrative Procedure establishes, in addition, that the States and Municipal Administrations, the Office of the Comptroller General of the Republic and the Office of the Public Prosecutor, will also adapt their activities to the provisions of the Law, whenever applicable. Here, unfortunately, the Law mixes institutions that should not be mixed; on the one hand it mentions territorial political institutions, such as States and Municipalities, that are politically autonomous in the federal form of the State; and immediately lists national organs such as the Office of the Comptroller and that of the Public Prosecutor, established in the Constitution as being integrated in one separate branch of government, the Citizens Power that also comprises the People's Defender Office. In addition, the Constitution has created a fifth Branch of Government, which is Electoral one, integrated by the National Electoral Council. All these organs of the State, and not only the two named in the Organic Law of 1982 (the Office of the Attorney General and that of the Comptroller General of the Republic) have traditionally being considered as constitutional entities with functional autonomy, not being part of the Central or Decentralized Administration, because they are not dependent on any of the three classic State Powers, whose function being to control other entities. As previously noted, beginning in 1999 those bodies, form part of the division of Public Power (as branches of Government).

Nonetheless, although nor being strictly part of the Executive Public Administration, the sense of the provisions of the Organic Law is that the activities and actions of such organs of the Citizens Branch of Government (Office of the Attorney General of the Republic, Office of the Comptroller General of the Republic, Ombudsman's Office), as well as of the Electoral Power (National Electoral Council) and even the Judicial Branch (the Executive Office for the Courts, Art. 267), are subjected to those provisions, for instance, when issuing administrative acts, for instance, when they appoint public officials or impose sanctions to individuals or to public officials.

d. State and Municipal Administrations

The Organic Law in its Article 1st also states that it governs a third group of bodies: The State and Municipal Administrations;[11] and that these must adapt their

11 See on the States and municipal administrations, Allan R. Brewer-Carías, "La Administración Pública Regional. Los Estados y los Municipios", *Jornadas para un mejor conocimiento de la Administración Pública,* Fundación Procuraduría General de la República,

activities to the Law wherever this may be applicable. This basically deals with political-territorial entities with territorial political autonomy deriving from the federal form of the State. Consequently, according to the Constitution, the Law should not be applied directly to States and Municipalities, as it is the Constitution that establishes which national laws can be directly applied to those entities according to the general standards relating to the Public Branch that will govern the entire Public Administration (national, state and municipal) under the terms of Articles 141 and following.

These constitutional precepts established nothing regarding the possibility of a national law concerning administrative procedures that could be applied to States and Municipalities. Therefore, in principle, the States would have to dictate their own regulatory standards to govern administrative procedure, as some States had done in the past, and which the Municipalities would have to do through Municipal Ordinances. As for the rest, application of the Organic Law is based on the general principles of administrative law regarding, for example, respect for the right to be heard, the right to a defense, the right to provide evidence and the right to have access to the administrative file, all principles that if not positively established had in any case been guaranteed to individuals by jurisprudence.

C. Substantive sphere

In addition to the Law's organizational sphere of application with the specifications noted above that arise from Article 1, a substantive sphere of application can also be determined in the sense of determining if all procedures carried out within those bodies must comply its regulations; or there are procedures regulated by special laws that are not subjected to the general provisions of the Organic Law.

a. Special procedures and their preferential application over general procedure

The Organic Law in its Article 47 specifies that "Administrative procedures contained in Special Laws shall be applied with preference over the ordinary procedure provided in this Chapter, *in matters that constitute a special case.*"[12] This provision is included in the Chapter of the Law that refers to *Ordinary Procedure*, which means that provisions of special laws would not apply to those matters regulated in the other chapters on summary procedure (II); procedure when the statute of limitations has run (III); publication and notice of administrative resolutions (IV); and execution of administrative acts (V). That is, the matters that constitute a special case in the procedures provided in special laws will have preferred application only with respect to the standards of ordinary procedure established for the formation of administrative act (Chapter I of Title III) and not

---

Caracas 1987, pp. 59-70 y 78-88; *Federalismo y Municipalismo en la Constitución de 1999 (Alcance de una reforma insuficiente y regresiva)*, Caracas 2001; Alfredo Arismendi, "Organización Político-Administrativa de los Estados en Venezuela", en *Estudios sobre la Constitución. Libro Homenaje a Rafael Caldera*, Caracas 1979, Tomo I, pp. 351-382; Alfredo Arismendi, "Régimen constitucional y administrativo de los Estados y Municipios en Venezuela", en *Libro Homenaje al Profesor Antonio Moles Caubet*, Caracas 1981, Tomo I, pp. 293-312.

12 See Hildegard Rondón de Sansó, "Problemas fundamentales que plantea la Ley Orgánica de Procedimientos Administrativos en las materias en la cuales rigen procedimiento especiales (con particular referencia a la Ley de Propiedad Industrial)", in *Revista de Derecho Público*, N° 10, Caracas 1982, pp. 119-128.

with respect to other standards of administrative procedure that are regulated in Chapters II to V of Title III, which in any event govern, even over the standards provided in special laws. This must be noted with respect to the regulation established by the Organic Law in Title IV, regarding the review of administrative resolutions and especially with respect to administrative recourses.

b. The exclusion of procedures governing security and defense of the State

On the other hand, the substantive sphere of application of the Organic Law expressly excludes some procedures as those indicated in Article 106, "concerning the security and defense of the State." This expression, however, requires the need to apply a strict definition of such matters, because otherwise, with a broad definition, almost everything done by the State would be excluded from application of the Law. In effect, an analysis of Articles 322 and following of the Constitution of 1999 and of the provisions of the Organic Security and Defense Law of 1976 in effect can lead to the conclusion that very few State/s activities escape the interest and area of security and defense. This covers not just the military field and problems of internal security of the State and the police, but the broad concept of security and defense covered by the Organic Security and Defense Law, which include, among other things, matters of economic and social development of the country. As a result, this expression of "security and defense of the State" must be interpreted as referring, on the one hand, with regard to the aspects that are of interest to the defense, in the sense of procedures linked to the military area and to the Ministry of the Defense; and with regard to State security, in the sense of procedures linked to internal security and to the police.

3. Consolidation of the Principle of Administrative Legality

One of the most important aspects of the Organic Law on Administrative procedure is that through its regulation, the consolidation and amplification of the obligation of the Administration to submit to the legality expressly defined in Article 141, has now an express legal provision of positive law. That article establishes that the Public Administration shall adapt its activities to the prescriptions set by law, using the imperative of "to adapt," which derives into various rights of the individual regarding the Administration, as a concrete sign of the Rule of Law in our country. The Law, in effect, indirectly defines and specifies the principle of legality[13] through the establishment in Article 1 of *an obligation* for

13 On the principle of legality, See: Allan R. Brewer-Carías, "El principio de la legalidad en la Ley Orgánica de Procedimientos Administrativos", in *Revista del Consejo de la Judicatura*, N° 22, Caracas 1981, pp. 5-14; and "Los principios de legalidad y eficacia en las leyes de procedimiento administrativo en América Latina", in *La relación jurídico administrativa y el procedimiento administrativo, V Jornadas Internacionales de Derecho Administrativo*. FUNEDA, Caracas 1998, pp. 21-90; Ana Elvira Araujo García "El Principio de legalidad y Estado de Derecho", in *Los requisitos y los vicios de los actos administrativos, V Jornadas Internacionales de Derecho Administrativo*, FUNEDA, Caracas 2000, pp. 39-59; Eloy Lares Martínez, "El principio de la legalidad aplicado a la Administración" in *Boletín de la Academia de Ciencias Políticas y Sociales,* N° 35, Caracas 1967, pp. 45-92; Enrique Meier E., "El principio de la legalidad administrativa y la Administración Pública, in *Revista de Derecho Público* N° 5, Caracas 1981, pp. 45-56; Antonio Moles Caubet, *El principio de la legalidad y sus implicaciones*, Caracas 1974; Gabriel Ruán Santos, *El Principio de Legalidad, la Discrecionalidad y las Medidas Administrativas.* FUNEDA, Caracas, 1998.

all bodies that are subject to its provisions to adapt their activity to the prescription of the Law and, in a broad sense, o legality. This is also established in Article 141 of the Constitution, which provides for the "full submission to the Law and law," as a principle of the Public Administration.

On the other hand, when the Constitution refers to the organs of the Contentious Administrative Jurisdiction (Article 259), it requires that the Administration adapt to law and therefore not just to the Law as a formal written source, but to all other written and unwritten sources of law, that have traditionally in Venezuela formed the block of legality and within it, the most important ones have been the general principles of administrative law, many of which are now incorporated as positive law in the Organic Law.

A. The sublegal nature of administrative activity

The Law first specifies the sublegal nature of administrative activity and actions; that is, administrative actions as part of State activities must be carried out within and subject to the law, under the law, and therefore cannot invade jurisdictions that are constitutionally reserved to the Legislator.[14] That "legal reserved area" of the legislator has traditionally been considered as defined in the Constitution with respect to at least three fundamental aspects: the creation of taxes and contributions; the establishment of crimes and sanctions, and the regulation or limitation of Constitutional rights and guarantees; all matters that the Administration is not allow to regulate. That is, the Administration cannot create trough regulations any taxes or establish contributions (Article 317 of the Constitution); nor can it create sanctions or administrative faults (Article 19 ordinal number 6 of the Constitution); nor can it limit or restrict Constitutional rights. These are matters that are reserved to the legislator.

Even though it could be said that Article 10 of the Organic Law is apparently redundant in view of the formulation of these principles that are based on the Constitution, in reality this is not the case. This provision in effect establishes that no administrative act can create sanctions or modify those that may have been established in the Laws; create taxes or other contributions of public law, except within the limits determined by Law. This provision, on the one hand corroborates the sublegal nature of the administrative activity, although on the other hand it leaves open the possibility for the Administration to regulate these matters "within the limits determined by Law." This is an express reflection of the legislative practice applied by the Legislator, to leave the establishment of some aspects of sanctions or aspects of taxes through regulations by the executive branch. However, apart from this possibility, the importance of the standard lies in the precision of how the administrative acts and of course the Regulations cannot create sanctions or modify those that may have been established in the Laws.

B. The hierarchy of administrative acts

In addition to consolidating the sublegal nature of the Administration actions and the administrative act and therefore its submission to the Law, the Organic Law of Administrative Procedures in consolidating the principle of legality, establishes

---

14 See Allan R. Brewer-Carías, *Principios fundamentales del derecho público*, Editorial Jurídica venezolana, caracas 2005, pp. 32 ff.

another enormously important principle that refers to the express establishment of a hierarchy of administrative acts. Article 13 of the Law is also of great importance in consolidating that legality, as it establishes that no administrative act can violate another that is established in by a superior hierarchy body in the administrative organization. As a result, and in accordance with this standard, the administrative act is not just necessarily subject to the Law and to executive regulations; it must also be subject to other administrative acts that are issued higher in the hierarchy. That is, acts issued by officials that are lower in the hierarchy cannot violate acts that have been established at higher levels. This expressly confirm the principle of hierarchy in the administrative organization, in the sense that administrative act cannot violate the terms of an act issued by a higher level of the hierarchy because being a violation of the principle of legality, and that action would be controllable through the courts.

According to these, it is clear that a Presidential Decree prevails over Ministerial Resolutions because it is issued by the President of the Republic; and Ministerial Resolutions prevail over the other acts, that is orders, rulings and decisions that are dictated by lower bodies in the hierarchy; and in these, the hierarchy of the acts is determined by the hierarchy of the official issuing them. The legal definition of the Decrees, Ministerial Resolutions, and other administrative acts is established in the Organic Law in its Articles 15, 16 and 17.

C. Singular Non-revocability of the Regulations

Article 13 of the Law, in addition to establishing the principle of hierarchy and that acts from the lower levels of the hierarchy as subject to those of a higher hierarchy, sets out another principle, is the prohibition of which singular revocation of the Regulations. The principle implies that administrative acts with general effects cannot be revoked or violated by administrative acts with individual effects. The Law then goes beyond this and establishes that individual administrative acts cannot violate the terms of a general administrative provision, "even when these are dictated by an authority of equal or superior rank to the one who dictated the general provisions."

Consequently, a general administrative act, like a Regulation, cannot be modified or revoked by an administrative act with individual effects, even when it is dictated by a higher body. As a result, if a Regulatory Resolution is issued by a Minister, that official not only cannot modify or revoke that general resolution with a resolution issued with individual effects, but neither can the President of the Republic violate that general provision with an act with individual effects. In this way, if the Minister wishes to deviate from a general act to decide on a specific case, he cannot do so without first modifying the general act; that is, the Resolution must first be reformed and after that, the act with individual effects can be dictated. The same thing occurs with respect to acts of a higher-level body: if there is a Ministerial Resolution with general effects, the President of the Republic cannot modify that general ministerial act with a Decree with individual effects; he would have to first issue a general or regulatory act, to later issue his act with individual effects, but first revoking the general act or Resolution that he wished to modify.

D. The value of precedence and the inability for administrative acts to be retroactive

On the other hand, the Organic Law in its Article 11 also regulated a series of principles that govern administrative activity as part of the consolidation of the principle of legality, principles that refer to the possibility that the Administration could modify its interpretative criteria in its actions against individuals. The Law in that article determines the value of administrative precedence, and indirectly establishes another principle, which is the inability to make administrative acts retroactive. This article, as a general principle, in effect indicates that criteria established by the different bodies of the Public Administration can be modified; that is, the Administration is not subject to its precedents, and therefore can adopt new interpretations in new situations. However, this possibility for the Administration to modify its criteria is also restricted: first the new interpretation cannot be applied to previous situations. Therefore, once an administrative act has been issued at a determined point according to one interpretation, any later change to that interpretation cannot affect the previous situation and act. Therefore, the new act issued according to the new interpretation, has no retroactive effect.

This could be considered to be a principle that derives from the interpretation of the constitutional principle that Laws cannot be retroactive (Art. 24 of the Constitution), now provided in the Organic Law as the principle of non-retroactivity of administrative acts, in which an exception is also established in the sense that the new interpretation can still apply to previous situations when this is more favorable to the subjects. This is also in line with the provisions of Article 24 of the Constitution, according to which criminal laws can be retroactive when they are more favorable to a defendant. In any event, this possibility of modifying administrative criteria and the restriction on the applicability of new criteria to previous situations is expressly provided in Article 11 of the Law. According to this, the Administration's modification of criteria does not give the right to appeal final acts decided according to the previous criteria. In short: The Administration can vary its criteria; however, the new criteria cannot be applied to previous situations and therefore cannot have retroactive effects on administrative acts. However, the new criteria applied do not give the right to an individual to request the modification of a final act that affected him in the past. That is, if the criteria have been changed, then the Administration cannot be compelled to modify acts issued by it pursuant to the previous criteria. There is no alleged right of an individual, after the variation in the criteria, to apply that new criteria to preceding acts. This, in addition to the principle that the administrative act cannot be retroactive, implies the establishment of the principle that administrative acts are irrevocable. That is, they are not freely revocable inasmuch as the individual in this case has no right to request that the Administration freely modify its acts.

E. Subjection to Administrative Res Judicata

Another aspect that was consolidated in the Law related to the principle of legality is the recognition of the value of *res judicata* referred to final administrative acts, meaning that the Administration, as a matter of principle, cannot be freely revoked them, being obligated to submit to its own acts when they create or declare rights in favor of individuals. The Organic Law turned into positive law such principle of the irrevocability of administrative acts,[15] by establishing in its Article 82, in contrary sense, the power to revoke them only when they *do not create or declare* rights or legitimate, personal and direct interests for an individual. In such cases, the administrative act can be revoked at any time, in whole or in part, by the same authority that dictated them or by a higher hierarchical level. By reversing the interpretation, the other principle arises in the sense that administrative acts that create or declare law cannot be revoked.

This principle is confirmed in the Organic Law as it sanctions any administrative act that revokes a previous one that creates or declares individual rights, with absolute nullity. Article 19, ordinal number 2 expressly establishes that administrative acts that give final resolution to a case that was previously decided by another administrative act and that created individual rights, are absolutely null. Consequently, principles relating to the revocation of administrative acts that were previously established by jurisprudence were in this way legally established, so that (i) if the administrative act did not create rights in favor of individuals it is freely revocable by the Administration; (ii) if the act creates or declares rights in favor of individuals, it is irrevocable; and (iii) if the Administration revokes it, then that act of revocation is considered absolute nullity.

With regard to the administrative acts that are considered absolutely null, they cannot have any effect and can be reviewed at any time without restriction, according to the provisions of Article 83; that is, the Administration can *recognize* the absolute nullity of acts issued by it at any time, on their own or upon petition. Of course, the absolute nullity, which is one of the central chapters of the Law, is reduced in the law to five causes specifically and expressly established in Article 19: 1. When the nullity is expressly determined in a legal or constitutional provision; 2. When the act resolves a case on which final resolution was previously entered and creates individual rights, unless expressly allowed by Law. 3. When the content of the act is illegal or impossible to be executed; 4. When the administrative act is issued by a manifestly incompetent authority; or 5. When the administrative act is issued with total and absolute absence of the legally established procedure. As a result, in principle and except in those logical and reasonable cases that are causes for absolute nullity, the other irregularities or imperfections are causes for annulment and therefore, relative nullity.

F. Limits to discretionary power

Lastly, as part of the consolidation of the principle of legality, the Organic Law for Administrative Procedures in its Article 12 expressly establishes the limits to the discretionary power of the Administration.[16] Discretionary power is without doubt,

---

15 See Allan R. Brewer-Carías, "Comentarios sobre la revocación de los actos administrativos," in *Revista de Derecho Público*, N° 4, Editorial Jurídica Venezolana, Caracas, octubre-diciembre 1980, pp. 27-30

16 See on the discfetionary powers and its limits: Allan R. Brewer-Carías, "Los límites al poder discrecional de las autoridades administrativas" in *Ponencias Venezolanas al VII Congreso Internacional de Derecho Comparado*, Caracas 1966, pp. 255-278 and in *Revista de la Facultad de Derecho,* UCAB, N° 2, Caracas 1966, pp. 9-35; Juan Carlos Balzán "Los límites a la discrecionalidad, la arbitrariedad y la razonabilidad de la Administración", in *Los requisitos y los vicios de los actos administrativos, V Jornadas Internacionales de Derecho Administrativo*, FUNEDA, Caracas 2000, pp. 61-101; J. M. Hernández Ron, "La potestad discrecional y la teoría

essential for the development of administrative activity. Consequently, it can be said that there would be no real and effective possibility for the Administration to act in the area of economic and social life if it did not have the legal freedom that would allow it to appreciate the opportunity and convenience of certain actions, and after judging that opportunity and convenience, to adopt determined decisions. However, just as discretionary power is essential for the Administration it is also the first source of administrative arbitrariness. For this reason, discretion cannot be become arbitrariness. Unfortunately, however, the boundaries of that restriction have frequently been overstepped, and many times discretional acts, ultimately becomes arbitrary acts. For that reason, discretion requires boundaries; and those after being determined by jurisprudence, have now become positive law in the Organic Law. Article 12 of the Law in effect expressly regulates the limits to discretion by establishing that when a legal or regulatory provision leaves any measure or order to the opinion or judgment of the competent administrative authority, said measure or act adopted, must remain in proportion and appropriate to the allegation of fact and the purposes of the provision authorizing the action, and also comply with the processes, requirements and formalities necessary for it to be valid and effective. This Article 12 holds, by establishing these principles, open the real possibilities of controlling administrative action.

a. Proportionality

On the one hand, it establishes that the discretionary act must maintain due proportionality, which is one of the limits that is traditionally placed by jurisprudence on the administrator authority on discretion. The discretionary act cannot be disproportionate, because a lack of proportion is arbitrariness. If a provision establishes, for example, that a sanction applicable to the violation of a standard can be between two extremes, maximum and minimum, according to the seriousness of the fault in the opinion of the administrative authority within its free appreciation of the situation, then the Administration cannot act arbitrarily and apply disproportionate measures. The decision made by it must be proportionate to the allegation of fact. Of course, proportionality as a restriction of discretionally actions governs not just the application of sanctions, but in general with respect to all discretionary measures adopted by the Administration.

b. Adaptation to the situation of fact

The Organic Law in the same Article 12 likewise establishes, as an added limit to discretion that the administrative act must be consistent with the factual; situation that constitute the cause or motive for its adoption. That is, the act must be reasonable, fair and equitable with respect to its causes. This means, first, that administrative acts must have a cause or a reason, identified precisely in the situation of fact that originates it. Consequently, the cause is an essential element of the act; there can be no administrative act without a cause and without an allegation of fact. Secondly, the decision must be consistent with the allegation of fact; and for this to be true, that allegation of fact must have been proven, and the Administration

---

de la autolimitación de los poderes", in *Revista del Colegio de Abogados del Distrito Federal*, Nos. 30-31, Caracas 1942, pp. 5-9; J. M. Hernández Ron, "La potestad administrativa discrecional", in *Revista del Colegio de Abogados del Distrito Federal*, Nos. 35-36, Caracas 1943, pp. 7-11; Gabriel Ruán Santos, *El Principio de Legalidad, la Discrecionalidad y las Medidas Administrativas*, FUNEDA, Caracas, 1998.

is required to prove it. The act therefore cannot be based simply on the arbitrary appreciation of a public servant. For example, it is not sufficient to indicate that a factory contaminates to have it shut down. If the official believes that an industrial installation is a polluter, then it must prove that it pollutes and the effects of those pollutants must be indicated in the case file.

According to this, the burden of proof in administrative actions falls on the Administration, as a very important general principle. However, in addition to proving the facts or cause of the act, the Administration must adequately qualify the allegations of fact. If, using the same example, the smoke expelled by the factory is not toxic, even though the smoke is issued into the atmosphere, this is not sufficient to say that it is a polluter and the factory is to be closed. It can be the reason for ordering the use of additional filters, for example, but it cannot be the reason to take just any measure. As a result, it is not sufficient to just prove the allegations of fact; those allegations of fact must also be correctly qualified. These elements constitute an area I n which very frequently defective administrative acts are issued, because imperfection in the cause, in proving the facts, in qualifying the facts and even in the very existence of the allegation of fact. The entire false supposition (*falso supuesto*) of procedural law finds here its fundamental base in the area of administrate law. That is, acts cannot be based on false suppositions, but rather must be based on allegations that have been tested, proven and correctly qualified. On the other hand, the Administration cannot distort the facts, which is also not an infrequent thing; rather it must rationally deal with the technically proven facts. This also opens an entire series of limits deriving from rationalization, justice, and equitable treatment of the procedures.

c. The purpose sought with the administrative action

Article 12 of the Organic Law also requires that the discretionary act be consistent with the purposes established in the provision that authorizes its issuance by the official. This means that the purpose of the administrative acts must always be consistent with the purpose provided for the action in the law, meaning that the public official by issuing them cannot deviate from those purposes, and seek purposes other than those provided in the law. Inconsistency with the purpose provided in the law leads to the known vice of misuse of power (*desviación de poder*) which is expressly described in Article 259 of the Constitution.

d. Formality

Another limit to the discretionary action, according to the last part of Article 12, is that it must comply with the procedures, requirements and formalities necessary for the administrative act to be valid and effective.

e. Equality

In addition, no matter how discretionary they may be act, it cannot violate or threaten the principle of equality, which is a principle set by the Constitution (Art. 21). Therefore, if a specific measure was applied to an allegation of fact, then an equal measure must be applied to an individual when there is an equal allegation of fact. Consequently, the Administration is not free to sanction individuals as they please, according to their isolated appreciation of each case; rather they must respect the principle of equality, of impartiality, in cases of legal situations of individuals, finding the basis for impartiality in Article 30 of the Law, and finding the sanction in the principle that proceedings must not be distorted to prejudice individuals, as set forth in Article 3 of the Law in connection with Article 100.

4. Requirements for Rationalization in Administrative Actions

The third aspect relating to the scope of the Organic Law, in addition to its sphere of application and consolidation of the principle of legality, is the demands for administrative rationalization established in benefit of both the Administration as well as the private individual. This has been complemented by the provisions of the Simplification of Administrative Processes Law which was enacted in 1999 and amended in 2008 and 2014.[17] These requirements for administrative rationalization are presented in four distinct aspects: in administrative rationalization, in descending information, in the processing treatment and in the administrative organization.

A. Administrative rationalization

First of all, the Organic Law provides principles designed to achieve administrative rationalization of administrative action by providing for instance in Article 32, the need for the establishment of uniform documents and administrative files, requiring that these must be uniform so that each series or type must have the same characteristics. This represents an enormous administrative effort that is required to uniform administrative documents and files throughout the country and related to the different administrative bodies. What does appear evident is that each body cannot by itself begin to create uniform documents and files.

B. Descending information

In addition to the rules for administrative rationalization there are others that are also linked to the Administration's rationale, such as those relating to the establishment of a system of descending administrative information, particularly based on the citizen's right to administrative information, established in the Constitution of 1999 (Art. 143).[18] In this regard, the Organic Law in its Article 33 establishes the obligation of the Administration to inform individuals. For this purpose, Regulations and instructions referring to structures, functions, communications and hierarchies of the different dependencies must be prepared and published in the *Official Gazette.* Likewise, all public service offices must give information using the most appropriate media, on the purposes, jurisdiction and functioning of their different bodies and services. For such purpose, a partial Regulation of the Organic Law was even issued on public information services and

---

17 Organic Law on the Simplification of Administrative actions, *Official Gazette* N° 6.149 Extra. of November 18, 2014.

18 See in general, Allan R. Brewer-Carías, "Consideraciones sobre la actividad interna de la administración y sus formalidades", in *Revista de Derecho Público*, N° 21, Caracas 1985, pp. 39-43; Allan R. Brewer-Carías, "El derecho administrativo y la participación de los administrados en las tareas administrativas", in *Revista de Derecho Público*, N° 22, Caracas 1985, pp. 5-32; Andrés Álvarez Iragorry, "El derecho de acceso al expediente administrativo (artículo 59 de la Ley Orgánica de Procedimientos Administrativos. Problemas que plantea: Particular referencia a su influencia a la Ley Orgánica de la Administración Central", in *Revista de la Fundación Procuraduría General de la República,* Caracas 1991, pp. 183-240; Alberto Blanco Uribe, "El derecho a la información y el acceso a los documentos administrativos", in *Revista de Derecho Público*, N° 48, Caracas 1991, pp. 47-50.

on the delivery and receipt of document.[19] However, the Law imposes not just the obligation on the Administration to provide information to the public on the purposes, jurisdiction and functioning of the different bodies, it establishes a right of the citizen to be informed of what each body does. This individual right has sought to change the traditional system of insecurity which sometimes placed the individual in the position of following a procedure through a system of trial and error, finding in each process that they lacked a requirement, that appears in the next action, making the procedure interminable and basically denying them their right. The Administrative Simplification Law of 1999 amended in 2008, in this sense is a notable advance that must be noted.

C. Handling under the procedure

a. *The file unity*

The Organic Law also presents demands for rationality in handling the administrative procedure, and in particular establishes the principle of the file unity. Article 31 in effect establishes that all matters must be brought together in a single file which must be kept together as well as with the respective decision, regardless of the different Ministries and Institutes that may intervene. This does not deal with simply the custom that is normally set by auxiliary officials with good judgment to place the documents that more or less refer to the same matter in a single folder; rather it deals with a rationalization task deriving from a legal requirement to have a file unity, so that there is a unified decision. This requirement for the file unity is ratified in Article 51 of the Organic Law, which requires that an administrative file must be opened when a petition or application is filed, to hold all the documents, reports or documents related to the matter. The file unity is extremely important, as the Administration cannot, as often happened, carry two or more files on one matter, with one of them containing the documents that it considers may be seen by the individual, and hiding others that may favor the petition of the interested party. The file unity is what guarantees that right of the citizens to have access to that file and to defend themselves, which is regulated in Article 59 of the Organic Law, and is what makes said right sensible and effective.

b. *Filed document registry*

On the other hand, in this same area of a rational handling of the proceeding, the Law requires the creation of registries of documents filed with the Administration, for which purpose a partial Regulation of the Organic Law was issued regarding the delivery and receipt of documents.[20] Article 44 of the Law requires that all public bodies keep a registry of documents filed, making note of all the documents, petitions and recourses filed by citizens, as well as communications that may be addressed to other authorities, and refers the organization and functioning of the registry to a Regulation. This Registry is enormously important, as it changes the traditional system used by public bodies for the receipt of correspondence, a system that was occasionally managed by officials without appropriate qualifications and whose function is limited to simply placing a "received" stamp. According to the Law, the registry must be the responsibility of an official, and a professional at that, because according to Article 46 of the text of the Law not only should the receipt of

19 *Official Gazette* N° 36.199 of May 6, 1997

20 See *Official Gazette* N° 36.199 of May 6, 1997

everything presented be noted, indicating the corresponding registry number, but also the official must advise the person filing the document of any omissions that there may be in his petition or request, so that these can be cured by the individuals. After advising the interested party of the omissions and irregularities noted, the receptionist cannot refuse receipt of the application.

On the other hand, the number and order of receipt has another consequence, and is the need for the Administration to respect this order of petitions in resolving the proceedings deriving from them. Article 34 of the Law expressly indicates that all matters must be handled strictly in the order in which they were filed. Consequently, the Registry will indicate the order for resolution of the problems; and only for reasons of public interest and through a founded decision that must be held in the file, can the Head of the Office modify the order. The organization and functioning of the document receipt registry, according to the requirements of Article 44 of the Law, should be established in a regulation, for which purpose a Regulation of the Document Presentation Registry was established in Decree N° 1364 of 30-12-1981.[21]

c. Production of serial documents

Other provisions of the Organic Law related to the matter of administrative rationality in terms of procedure, refers to serial decisions in cases where this is justified by the matters processed. In this regard, Article 35 authorizes the Administration to use expeditious procedures, or means of a serial production of actions that can be repeated, but always respecting the legal rights of the individuals. This same serial production of actions respecting individual rights is repeated in Article 36 in cases of issuing certificates adopted in series or according pre-established forms, making it extremely difficult to note the existence of any cause for denial.

d. Filing documents by mail

Another standard with repercussions on managing the procedure refers to the possibility of considering documents that have been filed in the appropriate time when periods of time are established for filing, if the documents are sent to the competent body of the Administration, by mail. According to Article 43 the Ministry of Transportation and Communications must issue a regulation for processing these documents, and of course, once again, the reception of correspondence from executive offices must comply with its methods of action, so that it can be determined when one of the documents received by mail is a document that should go to a file or comply with a determined process. Of course, in more recent times, new provisions for reception of some documents by means of electronic filing have been adopted in some Public Administration Offices according to the Organic Law on Public Administrative of 2008 (art. 11).

D. Determination of jurisdictions in the structure of the hierarchy

Lastly, as part of these requirements for administrative rationality, the Organic Law requires that the areas of jurisdiction among the different organs of an administrative body be precisely determined, as well as the functions of the different officials in the hierarchy, in order to determine responsibilities. We noted above that

21 See *Official Gazette* N° 32.385 of January 4, 1982

the Law is a text that seeks a balance between the administrative powers and individual rights, tilting towards the latter. It establishes many rights of the citizens, which correlate to the responsibilities of the officials for omission, delay or distortion of the proceedings. To apply the sanctions provided in Article 100 and following of the Law, it is necessary to first determine the responsibility, which also requires a rationalization of the administrative organization. For such purpose, the Law establishes a system of responsibilities and sanctions, making it possible to precisely determine who is responsible. To do this, delegations must be inscribed accurately so that any delegation of authority toward inferior officials must states exactly what is the area delegated to know who is responsible, the Minister or for instance the General Director. In cases of delegations of signature, if it this is a lower level, it shall specify exactly the delegation signing, to know the scope of the area of shared responsibility. Greater importance must be given to the Internal Regulations of each of the Ministries, as it is there where the official's responsibility is determined, particularly, what corresponds to each office, each unit, each section, each department, and in fact the extent of the responsibility of each official. Failure to specify those responsibilities leads to the risk of making accountable those who are not and allowing those who are really responsible from not taking responsibility.

5. Some General Principles of Administrative Procedure in the Organic Law

According to Article 141 of the Constitution, Public Administration is founded on "the principles of honesty, participation, swiftness, efficacy, efficiency, transparency, accountability and responsibility in the exercise of public functions, fully subject to the rule of law." These principles are repeated in Article 10 of the Organic Law on Public Administration of 2008 as it specifies that the Public Administration will be developed based on "the principles of economy, promptitude, simplicity, accountability, efficacy, proportionality, timeliness, objectivity, impartiality, participation, honesty, accessibility, uniformity, modernity, transparency, good faith, parallelism of forms and responsibility, with subjection to the Law and laws, and eliminating formalities that are not essential." In addition, the Administrative Processes Simplification Law lists in its Article 5 the following principles, according to which the simplification plans shall be prepared: "Presumption of good faith on the part of the citizen; simple, transparent, prompt and effective actions by the Public Administration; Public Administration activities at the service of the citizens; and de-concentration of the decision-making process by directive bodies." And with regard to the Organic Law on Administrative Procedure, Article 30 lists the principles of administrative procedure as "principles of economy, efficacy, promptness and impartiality."[22]

---

22 Véase en general, Allan R. Brewer-Carias, *Principios del procedimiento administrativo*, Prólogo de Eduardo García de Enterría, Editorial Civitas, Madrid 1990; "Principios del Procedimiento Administrativo en España y América Latina," en *200 Años del Colegio de Abogados, Libro Homenaje*, Tomo I, Colegio de Abogados del Distrito Federal, Avila Arte/Impresores, Caracas 1990, pp. 255 -435; *Les principes de la procédure administrative non contentieuse. Études de Droit Comparé (France, Espagne, Amérique Latine)*, Prólogo de Frank Moderne, Editorial Economica, París 1992; también publicado en *Etudes de droit public comparé*, Académie International de Droit Comparé, Ed. Bruylant, Bruxelles 2001, pp. 161-274; y

A. The principle of impartiality

The general principles that govern administrative procedures in effect include the principle of impartiality, which derives from the principle of equality and non-discrimination of citizens. According to this principle, the Administration, in the course of the proceeding and when issuing its decision, must not take part or incline the balance or illegally benefit one party to the detriment of another. It must make its decision according only to the legal applicable provisions and based on the general interest motivating it. This principle, regulated in Article 30 of the Organic Law on Administrative Procedure, requires the Administration to treat all individuals equally without discrimination of any kind, and further requires the Administration to remain impartial and to take no position on the matter at hand. This therefore has two results according to the Law. First, is the obligation established in Article 34 to respect the order of filing when deciding the matters presented according to the registration number assigned according to Article 47; then pursuant to Article 34 the matters are to be resolved strictly following that same order in which they were filed. The Head of the Office can modify the order only by resolution expressly stating the reasons of public interest, with a note made in the file of those reasons.

B. The principle of economy

Another general principle of administrative procedure provided in the Organic Law on Administrative Procedure is the principle of procedural economy, meaning basically that the procedures must generally be considered as established to resolve, not to delay, matters. For such purpose, the Organic Law on Administrative Procedure is imbued with the principle of procedural economy; that is, with the need to make prompt administrative decisions and shortening time periods. Consequently, if the Law sets down certain forms, then it is to adequately show the will of the Administration, i.e., for entry of an order, not to delay the decisions.

C. The principle of promptness

Linked to the principle of officially and also expressly formulated in the Organic Law on Administrative Procedure is the principle of promptness, which implies that if the procedure is a matter of the Administration, that is if the Administration is responsible for the procedure, then the consequential procedure established to defend the rights of individuals is that it must be carried out as prompt as possible. This involves provisions regarding *ex officio* actions, regulation of periods and terms. and the entire system for simplifying processes.

D. The principle of simplicity and individual rights

Article 12 of the Organic Law on Public Administration provides that the simplification of administrative processes as well as the suppression of those that are unnecessary will be a permanent task of the organs and entities of Public Administration, all in accordance with the principles and standards established in the corresponding law. That Law is the Organic Administrative Processes

---

Principios del Procedimiento en América Latina, Universidad del Rosario, Editorial Legis, Bogotá 2003; Allan R. Brewer-Carías, "Principios del Procedimiento Administrativo. Hacia un estándar continental," en Christian Steiner (Ed), *Procedimiento y Justicia Administrativa en América Latina,* Konrad Adenauer Stiftung, F. Konrad Adenauer, México 2009, pp. 163-199.

Simplification Act of 2008, which applies to "organs and entities" of the National, State and Municipal Public Administration (Art. 2), specifically develops, in detail, this principle of simplification in order to rationalize processes carried out by individuals before the Public Administration; to improve their efficiency, pertinence and use, in order to make them prompt and more functional; to reduce operating costs; to achieve national budget savings; to cover fiscal insufficiencies and to improve relations between the Public Administration and the citizens. In any event, since the Public Administration is at the service of the citizens and in general individuals, Article 6 of the Organic Law on Public Administration requires that these activities must be organized and carried out in a way that will allow the people:

> "1. To resolve their matters, to be assisted with the formal drafting of administrative documents, and to receive information of interest to them by any written, oral, telephone, electronic or computer media;
>
> 2. To file claims on the functioning of the Public Administration;
>
> 3. To easily access up-to-date information on the organization of the organs and entities of Public Administration, as well as informative guidelines on administrative procedures, services and benefits offered by them."

Article 22 of the same Organic Law on Public Administration likewise provides a principle that the Public Administration organization must provide institutional simplicity and a transparent organizational structure, assignment of jurisdictions, administrative assignments and inter-institutional relations. The organizational structure must also provide understanding, access, closeness and individual participation that will allow them to resolve their problems, receive assistance and receive information through any means.

E. The principle of good faith

The principle of good faith is established in two-way form necessary in the relations between the Administration and the citizen: first of all, as a presumption benefiting the citizen in the Administrative Processes Simplification Act (Art. 5, "The presumption of the citizen's good faith") which implies, for example, that "the statement of the interested parties in all actions made by the Public Administration shall be understood as true, except when proven otherwise" (Art. 23); and secondly, that the Administration itself shall act in accordance with the principle of good faith, all as specified in Article 10 of the Organic Law on Public Administration.

F. The principle of general information (Internet)

The Organic Law on Public Administration, to comply with the principles established therein, provides in Article 11, that the organs and entities of the Public Administration shall use new technologies developed by science such as electronic or informatics media, in its organization, functioning and relations with individuals. In this sense and by express provision of the Organic Law, each body and entity of the Public Administration must establish and maintain a webpage that contains, among other things, the information considered relevant, information corresponding to its mission, organization, procedures, governing standards, services provided, documents of interest for the individuals, location of its offices and contact information (Art. 11).

G. The principle of publicity of general acts

All regulations, resolutions and administrative acts with a general scope issued by the organs and entities of the Public Administration shall, without exception, be published in the *Official Gazette* of the Republic or, as applicable, in the official publication medium of the States or of the corresponding Municipality, as provided in article 12 of the Organic Law on Public Administration. The provision includes the general principle of the beginning of the efficacy of administrative acts with general effects (normative effects) or general in nature (applicable to various individuals), subject to publication in the *Official Gazette*. In addition, Article 13 of the same Organic Law, however, when referring to the regulations and to administrative acts of a general nature, also mentions "resolutions," which according to the Organic Administrative Procedures Law (Art. 16) are the administrative acts that are issued by the Ministries of the National Executive Branch, and therefore, whether with general effects or general in nature, must be published in the *Official Gazette*. Acts issued by States, Metropolitan Districts and Municipalities, that are normative acts or general in nature must also be published in the corresponding "official publication" of the respective entities.

H. The principle of being subject to plans, goals and objectives and to centralized planning

Organs and entities of the Public Administration shall in their functioning respect the policies, strategies, goals and objectives that are established in the respective strategic plans, management commitments and guidelines set down according to centralized planning (Art. 18 Organic Law on Public Administration). This shall likewise include monitoring activities, as well as the evaluation and control of institutional performance and the results achieved. The activity of administrative technical support and logistics units in particular shall adapt to the substantive administrative units of the organs and entities of the Public Administration (Art. 19).

I. The principle of efficacy

The activity of the organs and entities of Public Administration shall pursue an effective compliance with the objectives and goals set in the corresponding provisions authorizing the action, the plans and management commitments, under the guidelines of the policies and strategies established by the President of the Republic, the Central Planning Commission, the governor and the mayor, as the case may be (Art. 19 Organic Law on Public Administration). In any event, the functioning of the organs and entities of the Public Administration shall include monitoring activities as well as the evaluation and control of institutional performance and the results achieved (Art. 18).

J. The principle of adapting the financial means to the purposes

The allocation of resources to the Public Administration organs and entities and all organizational forms that use public resources shall strictly respect the requirements of the organization and functioning to achieve their goals and objectives, with a rational use of human, material and budgetary resources (Art. 20 Organic Law on Public Administration). Public Administration organs and entities shall likewise ensure that their administrative support units do not consume a percentage of the Budget destined to the corresponding sector that is greater than is strictly necessary. In this regard, those exercising the organizational authority of the Public

Administration organs and entities, with a prior economic study and based on the most effective indices according to the corresponding sector, shall determine the minimum percentages of cost allowed in administrative support units (Art. 20). On the other hand, according to Article 21 of the same Organic Law on Public Administration, the organizational structure and dimension of the Public Administration organs and entities must be proportional and consistent with the purposes and objectives assigned to them. The organizational forms adopted by the Public Administration must be sufficient to comply with the goals and objectives and must favor the rational use of public resources. As an exception and if the services of professional specialists are required for temporary and transitory activities, Public Administration organs and entities can include advisers whose remuneration shall be established by contract based on professional fees or other forms set in accordance with the law (Art. 21).

K. The principle of privatization and communal management

When the activities of Public Administration organs and entities exercising public powers allowed them by their nature, because being more economic and efficient, to perform them through the management of Communal Councils and other forms of community or private sector organization, said activities can be transferred to these organs or private institutions. In such cases, the Public Administration must reserve the oversight, evaluation and control of performance and results of the management transferred (Art. 20 Organic Law on Public Administration).

L. The principle of coordination and cooperation

Pursuant to Article 23 of the Organic Law on Public Administration, the activities of Public Administration organs and entities must be carried out in coordination and in line with the purposes and objectives of the State, based on guidelines issued according to centralized planning. According to Article 136 of the Constitution, entities and bodies of Public Administration must cooperate with each other and with other branches of the Public Powers in carrying out the purposes of the State (Art. 24, Organic Law on Public Administration).

N. The principle of institutional loyalty

According to Article 25 of the Organic Law on Public Administration, the organs and entities of the Public Administration shall act and relate with one another in accordance with the principle of institutional loyalty; consequently, they shall:

"1. Respect the legitimate exercise of their respective jurisdictions.

2. In exercising their powers, weigh all of the public interests involved.

3. Facilitate the information requested on the activity carried out in exercising their powers.

4. Cooperate and actively assist as they may be required within the sphere of their jurisdictions".

6. General Approach

From all the aforementioned provisions, it is obvious that the Organic Law of Administrative Procedures of 1982 constituted in Venezuela the starting point for the development of contemporary administrative law, completely changing the traditional relationship between the Administration and its subjects. Until then, those relations had tilted in favor of the Administration. Almost all the powers, authorities and rights had been held in the hands of the Administration, with very few duties and obligations to the individual, and what the subjects normally found before the Administration were situations of duty, of submission, of subordination, with no real rights or mechanisms to enforce his rights. As a result, we hold that according to tradition, the balance had been in favor of the Administration. The Law changed the balance, and from the time that it was enacted there was no longer a situation of administrative powers and a lack of individual rights. Rather, the Law clearly establishes a balance between the powers of the Administration and the rights of the individual, which are guaranteed. This on the other hand is the essence of the principle of legality and legal regulations that govern the Administration: the balance that must exist between powers and administrative prerogatives and the rights of individuals. By completely changing the balance between those two extremes and establishing equilibrium, the Law necessarily proposed a change of attitude in the form and method of action of the Administration. The Administration could no longer act as the overbearing and arrogant body that granted favors or largesse to the individual who in turn had no right or any way to claim them, and who was crushed and on occasion censured by the Administration. This without doubt changed, and with it a need arose to change attitudes and minds. The administered was no longer an individual with no defense against the Administration, but now in legal relations with it, armed with many legal rights and many judicial mechanisms to guarantee those rights and to control any attitude that could lead to diminishing those rights. Therefore, the Organic Law caused a phenomenal impact on the functioning of the Public Administration, similar to an administrative revolution, seeking to transform regulatory dispersion and disorder related to administrative activity, to convert it into a positivized procedural formalism in which the subjects began to fit within a situation that is covered with rights and guarantees.

II. GENERAL PRINCIPLES REGARDING THE RIGHT TO PETITION AND THE ISSUING OF ADMINISTRATIVE ACTS

As aforementioned, administrative procedures are established and regulated in statutes in order to instruct the Public Administration in the passing of administrative acts. Consequently, once initiated an administrative procedure at the initiative of the same Administration, or at the request of individual or private entity exercising their right to petition, the Administration is obliged to follow the procedure and to conclude it, by issuing the corresponding pronouncement. That is why Article 2 of the Venezuelan Organic Law on Administrative Procedures[23] sets forth that all administrative authorities "must resolve the petitions filed before them,

---

23 See in *Official Gazette* N° 2.818 Extra. July 1, 1981. See Allan R. Brewer-Carías et al., *Ley Orgánica de Procedimientos Administrativos*, Editorial Jurídica Venezolana, 12th Ed., Caracas 2001; Allan R. Brewer-Carías, *El Derecho Administrativo y la Ley Orgánica de Procedimientos Administrativos. Principios del Procedimiento Administrativo*, Editorial Jurídica Venezolana, Caracas 2002.

and in due case, express the motives not to resolve" (Article 2). That is, a decision or administrative act, in any event, must be issued.

In order to secure the accomplishment of this duty by the Administration, it has been a common trend in contemporary administrative law legislation and jurisprudence, to give some effects to the absence of a Public Administration pronouncement, namely, to the administrative silence, as a protection of the petitioner's rights, giving to the inaction of the Administration's specific legal effects, whether negative or positive.[24] The general trend on this matter in comparative law, for instance, can be considered as summarized in the provisions of the Law on Administrative Procedure of Peru, which establishes that in administrative procedures subject to positive administrative silence, the petitions are considered as automatically approved in the terms they were filed, once the term established for the decision to be taken in the procedure has elapsed without the petitioner receiving notification of the decision (Article 188.1). In these cases, administrative silence has for all purposes the character of a resolution that brings the procedure to an end, without prejudice of the possibility of the presumed act to be declared null and void (Article 188.2). In cases of administrative procedures subject to the formula of negative administrative silence, it has the purpose of granting the petitioner the possibility of challenging the presumed negative decision by means of the corresponding administrative or judicial means (Article 188.3). Nonetheless, in these cases and in spite of the negative administrative silence effect, the Administration continues with the obligation to decide, until the matter has been submitted to judicial or administrative review by means of the corresponding recourses (Article 188.4). In general terms, these general trends are followed in Venezuela.

1. The right to petition and the effects of administrative silence as its guarantee.

Pursuant to Article 51 of the 1999 Constitution, everyone has the right to make petitions or representations before any authority or public official concerning matters within their jurisdiction, and to obtain a timely and adequate response; adding that whoever violates this right shall be punished in accordance with the law, including the possibility of dismissal from office.[25] This right to petition has been developed by Article 9 of the Organic Law of Public Administration[26] and Article 2

24 See Allan R. Brewer-Carías, *Principios del Procedimiento Administrativo en América Latina*, Lexis, Bogotá 2003, pp. 171-176.

25 See Allan Brewer Carías, *La Constitución de 1999. Derecho Constitucional Venezolano, Tomo I, Editorial Jurídica Venezolana,* Caracas 2004, pp. 565.

26 *Official Gazette* N° 6.147 Extra. of November 17, 2014. Article 9: "Public Officials have the obligation of receiving and taking care, without exception, of petitions or requests filed by persons, through any written, oral, telephone, electronic of informatics mean; as well as of timely and adequately responding them, independently of the right that they have in order to file the corresponding administrative and judicial recourses, according to the law. In any case in which a public official abstain from receiving petitions of requests from persons, or do not adequately and timely respond to them, shall be sanctioned in conformity with the law."

of Organic Law on Administrative Procedures,[27] and also in an indirect way in Article 32 of the Organic Law on the Administrative Contentious Jurisdiction.[28] The latter provisions are meant to secure the people's right to file petitions before administrative authorities, and to obtain a prompt and due response, while the public officers are in charge of making a determination and giving a response, that is, they are "compelled to come to a decision on the matters submitted to them on the terms established,"[29] and incur liability when they do not accomplish it.

Among the specific legal remedies provided for the protection of this civil right to obtain a prompt and adequate response to petitions filed before administrative authorities, particularly in cases of absence of such response in the legally set term, as aforementioned, the most effective one has been to legally assign specific effects to the absence of the expected pronouncement, that is, to the silence of the Administration. This has been called in administrative procedural law the *administrative silence* principle which has been included in various statutes, either assigning negative (negative administrative silence) or positive (positive administrative silence) effects to the administrative abstention.[30]

The right to have a due and prompt response to petitions would not be really secured by punishing the public officers that violate it, since eventually what the petitioner needs to know is what the determination of the Public Administration in charge would be, when considering the petition. Thus, the security provided by law has been to assign to the public officer's silence a specific effect, being legally understood that once the term for the Administration to issue its determination accrues, without the expected pronouncement being issued, a tacit administrative act is due to exist, either with positive or negative effects, according to the specific case,[31] providing the petitioner with a determination on the matter under

---

27 *Official Gazette* N° 2.818 Extra. of July 1, 1981, Article 2: "Every interested person, directly or through representative, Could file request or petitions before any organ, entity or authority. The latter must resolve the requests or petitions received, or declare, if is the case, the motives in order not to respond."

28 Article 32.1: "The legal term for the nullity action shall expire: In case of administrative acts of specific effects, 180 continuous days alter its notification to the interested person, or when the Administration has not resolved the corresponding administrative recourse in the term of 90 workable days from the date of its filing. The illegality of an administrative act can always be opened as an exception, unless a special provision is provided." See Organic Law of the Administrative Contentious Jurisdiction, *Official Gazette* N° 39.451 of June 22, 2010.

29 See Allan R. Brewer-Carías, *El Derecho Administrativo y la Ley Orgánica de Procedimientos Administrativos. Principios del Procedimiento Administrativo*, Editorial Jurídica Venezolana, Caracas, 2002, p. 93. See also José Martínez Lema, "El derecho de petición, el silencio administrativo y la acción de abstención o negativa a través de la jurisprudencia de la Corte Primera de lo Contencioso Administrativo," in *Revista de Derecho Público*, N° 45, Editorial Jurídica Venezolana, Caracas 1991, p. 186.

30 See Armando Rodríguez García, "El silencio administrativo como garantía de los administrados y los actos administrativos tácitos o presuntos" in Allan R. Brewer-Carías, *IV Jornadas Internacionales de Derecho Administrativo*, FUNEDA, Caracas 1998, p. 205.

31 See on the regime of administrative silence in comparative law, Allan R. Brewer-Carías, *Principios del Procedimiento Administrativo*, Civitas, Madrid 1990, pp. 159-169.

consideration, either in an affirmative way, granting what was asked, or in a negative way, rejecting the petition:[32]

> "The mechanism of the administrative silence is justified to palliate, although partially, the absence of response and the legal uncertainty that such an omission implies, beyond being just a security of the right to petition and the possibility to file the subsequent appeals. Notwithstanding, the silence does not fully satisfy such right to petition and to obtain a prompt and proper answer, but only succeeds as a temporary remedy from the lack of an express pronouncement.
>
> In such way, as the Constitutional Chamber set in ruling dated April 6, 2004 (case: *Ana Beatriz Madrid*):
>
> '...the administrative silence is, we insist, a security of the constitutional right of due process, since it prevents the petitioner from having his subsequent defense means –administrative and judicial–obstructed when facing the formal passiveness of the Administration, but does not secure the fundamental right to petition, since the implied pronouncement does not comply, altogether, with the requirements of a prompt and proper answer in the terms the precedents of this Chamber that have been previously referred to, and thus the Administration retains the duty to expressly make a decision even if the administrative silence has operated and thus, as well, this Chamber has deemed in previous occasions that, by the absence of a prompt and express answer is possible to seek an injunction for the protection of the fundamental right to petition.'"[33]

The tacit administrative act produced as a consequence of administrative silence, is to be considered as a real administrative act, in the same sense as has been expressed in the Spanish Law 30/1992, dated November 26, 1992 on the Legal Regime of Public Administrations and the Common Administrative Procedure, reformed in 1999 (Law 4/1999), whose Article 43.5 sets forth that "Administrative acts produced by means of administrative silence can be used before the Administration and against any natural or artificial, public or private person" and Article 43.3 of the same Law that states, "The effects of administrative silence must be considered to all purposes as an administrative act that puts the procedure to an end." In such cases, as Eduardo García de Enterría and Tomás-Ramón Fernández mention, particularly regarding its positive effects, "...administrative silence is a presumed authentic administrative act, in all equivalent to the express act, so once the term to make a decision provided by a legal provision has elapsed, the 'subsequent resolution after the issuing of the act can only be adopted if it is confirmatory of the same'."[34]

---

32 See Humberto Romero-Muci, "El efecto positivo del silencio administrativo en el Derecho Urbanístico venezolano," in Allan R. Brewer-Carías et al., *Ley Orgánica de Ordenación Urbanística*, Editorial Jurídica Venezolana, Caracas 1988, p. 141.

33 See in Daniela Maggi Urosa and José Ignacio Hernández, "Vicisitudes del Silencio Administrativo y los efectos negativos en la Legislación venezolana," in *Temas de Derecho Administrativo, Libro Homenaje a Josefina Calcaño de Temeltas*, FUNEDA, Caracas 2010, p. 731.

34 See Eduardo García de Enterría and Tomás-Ramón Fernández, *Curso de Derecho Administrativo*, Vol. I, Décima Tercera Edición, Thomson Civitas, Madrid 2006, p. 607.

2. The general rule regarding administrative silence as negative silence in the Organic Law of Administrative Procedures

The general rule established in the Organic Law on Administrative Procedures follows the principle of *negative* administrative silence, in the sense that if the Administration does not make a decision and responds to petitioner within the legally established term to do so, it is understood that it has decided to reject the petition, namely it has made a negative determination regarding the claim made. This rule is expressly provided by Article 4 of the Organic Law on Administrative Procedures, as follows[35]:

> "Article 4. When an entity of the Administration does not make a decision on a matter or recourse within the corresponding terms, it is understood that it has made a decision in a negative way, and the interested party may file the subsequent immediate appeal, except when an express provision establishes the contrary. This provision does not exempt the administrative entities, and their officials, from the liabilities that could result because of their omission or delay."
>
> Single Paragraph: The reiterative negligence by the officers responsible for resolving the matters or appeals that results in them to be deemed as being decided in a negative way as established in this provision, will cause written warnings according to the *Estatuto del Funcionario Público* (Civil Service Law), without prejudice to the fines that can be applied to them pursuant to article 100 of this Law."

Two general rules follow from this provision: First, the understanding that the Administration has adopted a decision in a negative sense with regard to what has been petitioned; and second, the interested party can exercise his right to defense through the subsequent appeal against such presumed decision of rejection. As I had written many years ago, this is the consequence of the rule imposed by the provision upon the Administration, implying that as a consequence of the exhaustion of the term established for the decision to be taken, if no decision is issued, it must be presumed that a tacit administrative act exists rejecting the petition or the recourse that has been filed.[36]

---

35 See on the presumption inserted in Article 4 of the Organic on Administrative Procedures, Allan R. Brewer-Carías, *El Derecho Administrativo y la Ley Orgánica de Procedimientos Administrativos. Principios del Procedimiento Administrativo*, *loc. cit.*, pp. 225-227. See also Armando Rodríguez García, "El silencio administrativo como garantía de los administrados y los actos administrativos tácitos o presuntos," in Allan Brewer-Carías, *IV Jornadas Internacionales de Derecho Administrativo*, FUNEDA, Caracas 1998, pp. 207-208; Juan de Stefano, "El silencio administrativo," in *Revista de la Facultad de Ciencias Jurídicas y Políticas de la Universidad Central de Venezuela*, Nº 70, Caracas 1988, p. 81; José Antonio Muci Borjas, "El recurso jerárquico por motivos de mérito y la figura del silencio administrativo (Estudio comparativo con el derecho venezolano)," in *Revista de Derecho Público*, Nº 30, Caracas April-June 1987, pp. 11 ff.

36 See Allan R. Brewer-Carías, *El Derecho Administrativo y la Ley Orgánica de Procedimientos Administrativos. Principios del procedimiento administrativo*, *loc. cit.*, pp. 97-101.

In addition, and as a consequence of this legal presumption, the interested party can file the corresponding administrative or judicial review appeals against the tacit administrative act that is presumed to exist rejecting the interested party's petition.[37] Consequently, as I have affirmed in other work, "regarding the defenselessness in which the citizens are when no prompt decision is adopted by the Administration regarding their petitions and recourses, the only sense that the provision of administrative silence in the Organic Law has by presuming that a decision rejecting the corresponding request or recourse, is no other than to establish a benefit for them, precisely in order to overcome such defenselessness. Consequently, the provision of Article 4 of the Organic Law on Administrative Procedures has been set in support of the petitioners and not of the Administration."[38]

This implies, on the other hand, that challenging the implied administrative act resulting from the administrative silence is a right of the petitioner, and never a burden. The petitioner is free to either challenge the tacit act resulting from the administrative silence or to wait for the Administration to issue an express determination.[39] On the other hand, the administrative silence can never be understood as a firm administrative act with respect to the existence of an expiration term for challenging it.[40] The aforementioned has been highlighted in judgment N° 767 of the Political-Administrative Chamber of the Supreme Tribunal of Justice dated June 3, 2009, reaffirming principles that the Tribunal established since the 1980's.[41]

---

37 *Idem* p. 97. See also María Amparo Grau, "Comentario jurisprudencial sobre el trata-miento del silencio administrativo y la procedencia del la acción de amparo contra éste," in *Revista de Derecho Público*, N° 47, Caracas July-September 1991, p. 197.

38 Allan R. Brewer-Carías, "El sentido del silencio administrativo negativo en la Ley Orgánica de Procedimientos Administrativos," in *Revista de Derecho Público*, N° 8, Caracas October-December 1981, p. 28. See also Luis A. Ortiz-Álvarez, *El silencio administrativo en el derecho venezolano*, Editorial Sherwood, Caracas 2000, pp. 13-14 and 18-41.

39 See José Araujo-Juárez, *Derecho Administrativo. Parte General*, Ediciones Paredes, Caracas 2008, p. 982.

40 See Allan R. Brewer-Carías, "El sentido del silencio administrativo negativo en la Ley Orgánica de Procedimientos Administrativos," in *Revista de Derecho Público*, N° 8, Caracas October-December 1981, pp. 29-30.

41 The decision, which basically referred to Article 20.21 of the former 2004 Organic Law of the Supreme Tribunal of Justice (equivalent to Article 32 of the current Organic Law on the Administrative Contentious Jurisdiction, *Official Gazette* N° 39.451 of June 22, 2010), stated: "Specifically the Chamber in decision N° 827 of July 17, 2008, ratified the opinion issued in decision of June 22, 1982 (Case of *Ford Motors de Venezuela*, in which the scope of the administrative silence established in the then in force Article 134 of the Organic Law of the Supreme Court of Justice, equivalent to paragraph 20 of Article 21 of the Organic Law of the Supreme Tribunal of Justice, was interpreted. In that decision, which is one more time ratified, the Chamber concluded as follows: *'1° That the provision included in the first part of Article 134 of the Organic Law of the Supreme Court of Justice (today paragraph 20 of Article 21 of the Organic Law of the Supreme Tribunal of Justice) establishes a legal guaranty which signifies a benefit for the individuals. 2° That as such guaranty, it must be interpreted in an extended and non restrictive sense, because on the contrary, instead of being favorable to the individual, as it was established, what could result is in encouraging arbitrariness and reinforcing privileges of the Administration. 3° That such guaranty consists in allowing, in the absence of an express administrative act finishing the administrative procedure, access to judicial review. 4° That the exhaustion of the term for the administrative silence, without the interested party filing the judicial review recourse,*

3. The provisions granting administrative positive effects to administrative silence

In many countries, contrary to the general rule established in Venezuela regarding the effects of the abstention of the Public Administration from ruling on petitions, the principle of positive silence is adopted as the general rule. This principle of the positive administrative silence has also been adopted in Venezuela but only when expressly established in a statute, as an exception to the general rule set forth in by the Organic Law on Administrative Procedures we have already referred to.

In Spain, for instance, the general principle is to give positive effects to administrative silence, as is provided by Article 43.2 of the Law 30/1992, of November 26, 1992 on the Legal Regime of Public Administration and Common Administrative Procedure (modified by 4/1999, of January 13, 1999) that establishes that "in any sort of petition, the interested parties can assume by virtue of administrative silence, that their requests have been granted, except when the contrary is established in any provision with legal rank or in a provision of Communitarian [European] Law." There is only one exception to this general rule: The Legislator has excluded from the positive effects the silence regarding petitions whose favorable acceptance would result in transferring to the petitioner or third parties' rights regarding public domain or public service, in which case the principle of negative silence applies (Article 43).

In those cases where positive effects are given to administrative silence, the law recognizes that for all purposes the result is that "an administrative act bringing to an end the administrative procedure exists" clarifying –nonetheless- that the presumed act, when contrary to the legal order, as a matter of law (*de pleno derecho*) is to be deemed null and void when lacking the essential conditions set forth for the acquisition of rights (Article 62.1.f). Thus, in cases of positive silence the existence of a tacit administrative act granting the petition is presumed, being normally applied in cases of authorizations and permits. In regard to this matter, Eduardo García de Enterría and Tomás Ramón Fernández have pointed out that

---

does not mean that he will lose the possibility to file the recourse against the act that could eventually be issued. 5° That the silence is not in itself an act, but the abstention of decision, and consequently it cannot be understood that it converts itself into a firm act because the simple exhaustion of the term to impugn it. 6° That the silence does not excuse the Administration from its duty to issue an express decision, duly motivated. 7° That the petitioner is the one that must decide the opportunity to file a recourse before the judicial review of administrative action jurisdiction, within the term established in Article 134 (today, part 20 of Article 21), or later, when the Administration decides the administrative recourse. 8° That when the Administration expressly decides the administrative recourse, after the terms established in Article 134 (today part 20 of Article 21) have been exhausted, the petitioner can file the judicial review against such particular act. 9° That from the moment in which an express decision of the administrative recourse is notified to the interested party, the general term of six months established to file the corresponding judicial review recourse begins.; and 10° That if an express administrative decision is never issued, the interested party would not be able to file the judicial review of administrative action recourse after the terms established in Article 134 of the LOCSJ (today part 20 of Article 21 of the LOTSJ) are exhausted." See Decision N° 827 of the Political-Administrative Chamber of the Supreme Tribunal of July 17, 2008 (Case of *Roque's Air & Sea C.A.*), available at http://www.tsj.gov.ve/decisiones/spa/Julio/00827-17708-2008-2006-1505.html.

"since the beginning, as administrative silence mainly referred to authorizations and approvals, the silence has been deemed as a real administrative act, equivalent to the express authorization or approval it substitutes; and the precedents have assumed, also from the beginning, that once [the act] has been produced, it is not possible for the Administration to decide in an express way in contrary sense to the presumed granting of the authorization or approval."[42]

The principle of positive administrative silence has also been established as the general applicable one in statutes in Chile (Article 64 of the Law 1980 on Administrative Procedure), Peru (Article 33 of the Law on Administrative Procedure), and Ecuador (Article 28 of the State Modernization Law). In other countries the principle of positive effects of administrative silence is specifically established in all administrative procedures referring to authorizations, as is the case in Costa Rica (Article 330, General Law on Public Administration).

In other counties like Colombia (Article 41 of the Contentious Administrative Code), Argentina (Article 10 of the National Law on Administrative Procedure), and Venezuela, also regarding authorizations,[43] the positive effects of administrative silence have been provided through special statutes. This is the case in Venezuela in the statutes providing for Land Use and Planning and for extension of concessions granted for mining activities[44] and in the Regulation of the Organic Law of Science, Technology and Information as well as the Technical Rules that discipline independent media producers.

As mentioned, in the case of the principle of positive silence, it has been generally established by statutes regarding authorizations that individuals must obtain from the Public Administration in order to develop a lawful activity,[45] and regarding which the Supreme Tribunal of Justice in Politico Administrative Chamber has said that:

"Administrative silence with positive effects has been established in order to give speediness and flexibility to control (*policía*) activity on matters related to the Administration and constitutes a guaranty for the individual, not only of a procedural administrative character, but of allowing the effective possibility to

---

42 See Eduardo García de Enterría and Tomás R. Fernández, *Curso de Derecho Administrativo,* Vol. I, 6th Ed., Editorial Civitas, Madrid 1993, pp. 572-573.

43 See, for instance, a remote antecedent in the case of the 1979 Law on Quality Control and Technical Norms, in Allan R. Brewer-Carías, "Comentarios a la Ley sobre normas técnicas y control de calidad de 30 de diciembre de 1979," in *Revista de Derecho Público*, N° 1, Editorial Jurídica Venezolana, Caracas 1980, p. 78.

44 See Luis A. Ortiz-Álvarez, *El silencio administrativo en el derecho venezolano*, Editorial Sherwood, Caracas 2000, pp. 41-73; Daniela Maggi Urosa and José Ignacio Hernández, "Vicisitudes del Silencio Administrativo y los efectos negativos en la Legislación venezolana," in *Temas de Derecho Administrativo, Libro Homenaje a Josefina Calcaño de Temeltas*, FUNEDA, Caracas 2010, p. 731.

45 See Humberto Romero-Muci, "El efecto positivo del silencio administrativo en el Derecho Urbanístico venezolano," *loc. cit.*, p. 147.

perform activities that must be inspected by the Administration, provided that a legal text exists for such purpose."[46]

The traditional provision in this regard has been established in the Organic Law on Land Use Planning (OLLUP), which also applies to certain approvals related to mining activities, where the result of the administrative silence regarding petitions for authorizations and approvals is the presumption of a real administrative act granting it.[47] Pursuant to Articles 49 and 55 of the Organic Law on Land Use Planning Law, the administrative silence and the resulting tacit administrative act is understood to be produced once the term of sixty (60) days that the Administration has to make a decision on matters of authorizations and approvals, has elapsed. In such cases, in addition, the Administration is compelled to issue "proof or evidence" of said authorization or approval when requested to do so, in order to certify that the term provided by the Law has elapsed without a pronouncement being issued.[48] This was the principle applied for many years, for instance, on matters of urban land use and planning pursuant to Article 85 of the Organic Law on Urban Land Use Planning,[49] whereas in cases of silence of the Public Administration, the requested urban development authorizations were tacitly granted.[50]

The general characteristic of the application of the principle of positive effects to administrative silence according to these statutes is that once the administrative act is understood as existing and granting the petition, it creates rights for the petitioner that subsequently cannot be ignored or revoked by the Administration, the only exception being to consider such tacit administrative act as null and void (affected of absolute nullity) according to Article 19 of the Organic Law on Administrative Procedures.

---

46 See Decision N° 1414 of the Political-Administrative Chamber of the Supreme Tribunal of Justice of June 1, 2006, available at http://www.tsj.gov.ve/decisiones/spa/Junio/01414-010606-2003-1547.htm.

47 See Margarita Escudero León, "El requisito procesal del acto previo a la luz de la jurisprudencia venezolana," in *Revista de Derecho Público*, N° 57-58, January-June, 1994, pp. 479-481.

48 See Allan R. Brewer-Carías, "Introducción al régimen jurídico de la ordenación del territorio," in *Ley Orgánica de la Ordenación del Territorio*, Editorial Jurídica Venezolana, Caracas, 1984, pp. 64-68. See also Humberto Romero-Muci, "El efecto positivo del silencio administrativo en el Derecho Urbanístico venezolano," *loc. cit.*, pp. 152-157; Román J. Duque Corredor, "La Ley Orgánica para la Ordenación del Territorio y el Urbanismo Municipal," in *Revista de Derecho Público*, N° 18, April-June 1984, p. 107.

49 Organic Law on Urban Land Use Planning, *Official Gazette* N° 33.868 de 16 de diciembre de 1987.

50 See Allan R. Brewer-Carías, "Comentarios a la Ley Orgánica de Ordenación Urbanística: el control urbanístico previo y la nueva técnica autorizatoria," in *Revista de Derecho Público*, N° 32, Caracas October-December 1987, pp. 53-54. See also Humberto Romero-Muci, "El efecto positivo del silencio administrativo en el Derecho Urbanístico venezolano," in Allan R. Brewer-Carías et al., *Ley Orgánica de Ordenación Urbanística*, Editorial Jurídica Venezolana, Caracas 1988, pp. 158 ff.; Juan Domingo Alfonzo Paradisi, "Aplicabilidad del silencio administrativo positivo en la Ley Orgánica de Ordenación Urbanística," in Fernando Parra Aranguren (Ed.), *Temas de Derecho Administrativo. Libro Homenaje a Gonzalo Pérez Luciani*, Vol. I, Tribunal Supremo de Justicia, Caracas 2002, pp. 61 ff.

If the petitioner has complied with all the formal and substantive conditions legally set for his petition,[51] once the term granted to the Administration to make a decision on the petition goes by, the authorization requested is deemed granted, and a tacit administrative act declaring rights for its holder is presumed to exist that cannot be revoked or repealed by the Administration. That is to say, when the principle of positive administrative silence is applied, the Administration is prevented from issuing another decision in a different sense, which means that once the positive silence has produced its effects, the Administration cannot make an express decision rejecting the petition. On the contrary, such a decision would be null and void pursuant to Article 19 of the Organic Law on Administrative Procedures.

4. Positive administrative silence effects regarding administrative procedures for the extension of Mining Concessions

As aforementioned, the 1999 Mines Law is another special statute that has granted a positive effect to administrative silence on matters of petitions for an extension of mining concessions. As we have already mentioned, this statute has provided for the application of both negative and positive effects in cases of administrative silence. Regarding the principle of *negative* silence effects and in spite of the general rule provided by the Organic Law on Administrative Procedures, it expressly provides in two cases that once the term given to the Administration to make a decision is exhausted, it must be understood that the petition has been rejected. This is the case of Article 30, regarding petitions for authorizations concerning negotiations on the concessions, where the Statute provides that once the term established for the pronouncement to be issued (45 days) elapses, without an express determination, the absence of response is equivalent to a tacit administrative act of rejection of the request.

Another case refers to the admission of petitions for mining concessions. Pursuant to Article 41, once such a petition has been formally filed and the conditions established in the Law have been met, the Ministry must expressly admit or reject the petition and start the substantiation of the corresponding procedure, which must be notified to the interested party no later than forty (40) continuous days after the date of its filing (with a possible extension of ten (10) additional working days). If the petitioner is not notified of either an admission or rejection of his request, the petition "would be considered as rejected by operation of law (*de pleno derecho*)," meaning that the silence of the Administration stands for a rejection of the petition.

Contrasting with these two cases of *negative* effects of administrative silence, when regulating petitions for an extension of mining concessions already granted,

---

51 The tacit administrative act containing an authorization, because the application of the principle of administrative silence, cannot be contrary to the provisions of the Law. Otherwise, as ruled by the Political-Administrative Chamber of the Supreme Tribunal of Justice in Decision N° 1217 of July 11, 2007, the tacit administrative act according to Articles 82 and 83 of the Organic Law on Administrative Procedures, can be considered null and void, and as not granted, adding that "[t]he authorization granted by virtue of positive silence, could not be contrary to the law, not having administrative silence any derogatory effects regarding statutes." See Decision N° 1217 of the Political-Administrative Chamber of the Supreme Tribunal of Justice of July 11, 2007 (Case of *Inversiones y Cantera Santa Rita, C.A. v. Ministerio del Poder Popular para el Ambiente*), in *Revista de Derecho Público*, N° 111, Editorial Jurídica Venezolana, Caracas 2007, p. 208.

the Mines Law, after establishing the obligation of the Ministry to decide such petitions within the same term of six (6) months in which the petition is due to be filled, adopted the principle of *positive* administrative silence, assigning to the silence positive effects. Article 25 of the Law expressly sets forth that if there is no notice of a determination answering a petition requesting an extension of a concession, "it is understood that the extension is granted." Thus, the administrative silence produces a tacit administrative act granting the requested extension, which has the same general effects of non-revocability that all administrative acts have. Namely, once the extension is granted through the tacit administrative act, the Administration cannot issue another subsequent act in contrary sense, purporting to have decided the petition denying the extension. On the contrary, if such decision is made, as any other repealing the effects of the tacit administrative act, it would be considered null and void pursuant to Article 19 of the Organic Law on Administrative Procedures.

III. GENERAL PRINCIPLES REGARDING ADMINISTRATIVE ACTS

1. General Principles regarding Administrative Acts

Administrative Acts are one of the results of administrative procedures, being in the Organic Law on Administrative Procedures,[52] the main legal provisions regulating their formation, enactment and effects. Such Law was adopted in 1982 following the contemporary trends on the matter, which have been complemented with the provisions of the aforementioned the Organic Law on Public Administration, and those of the Law on Administrative Simplification Procedures of 1999.[53] The Organic Law on Administrative Procedures was mostly inspired in the 1958 Spanish Law on Administrative Procedure and, as in almost all Latin American countries,[54] contains a detailed regulation on administrative acts and their formal and substantive conditions of validity and efficacy; the process of their formation and enactment; the need to be formally and sufficiently motivated; and based on relevant facts that ought to be accredited and proved by the Administration, as well as correctly qualified by the Administration, without distorting them; the principle of irrevocability that governs their effects when

52 Sec in *Official Gazette* N° 2.818 Extra. of July 1, 1981. See Allan R. Brewer-Carías et al., *Ley Orgánica de Procedimientos Administrativos*, Editorial Jurídica Venezolana, 12th Ed., Caracas 2001; Allan R. Brewer-Carías, *El Derecho Administrativo y la Ley Orgánica de Procedimientos Administrativos. Principios del Procedimiento Administrativo*, Editorial Jurídica Venezolana, Caracas 2002.

53 See Law on Administrative Simplification Procedures, *Official Gazette* N° 6.149 Extra. of November 18, 2014. See in Allan R. Brewer-Carías et al., *Ley Orgánica de Procedimiento Administrativos, loc. cit.*, p. 199 ff.

54 See Allan R. Brewer-Carías, *Principios del Procedimiento Administrativo*, Editorial Civitas, Madrid 1990; Allan R. Brewer-Carías, *Principios del procedimiento Administrativo en América Latina*, Universidad del Rosario, Editorial Legis, Bogotá 2003; "Principios del Procedimiento Administrativo. Hacia un estándar continental," in Christian Steiner (Ed.), *Procedimiento y Justicia Administrativa en América Latina*, Konrad Adenauer Stiftung, n F. Konrad Adenauer, México 2009, pp. 163-199.

declaring or creating rights in favor of individuals; the vices affecting them, and their review at administrative level by means of administrative appeal.[55]

The most important classifications of administrative acts are based on their content and on to their addressees. The first classification distinguishes between administrative acts of normative (also called of general effects) and administrative acts of non-normative content (also called of particular effects).

The second classification distinguishes between administrative acts of general applicability and administrative acts of specific or particular applicability; being he acts of general applicability those that are addressed to an undetermined and undeterminable group of persons (like the Regulations that can be issued by Executive Decree or through Ministerial resolution); and the administrative acts of particular applicability those addressed to one or to a determinable group of people or institutions.[56]

Both normative acts and acts of general applicability can be included in the broad expression of general acts included in Article 259 of the Constitution.

In addition, according to their effects, administrative acts can be classified depending on their substantive contents, between those that contain a declaration, an ablation (*ablatorios*), a concession or an authorization.[57] Accordingly, declarative administrative acts are those that grant certitude to specific acts or facts, giving legal qualifications to facts, persons or legal relations. Within these acts are the registry acts, containing declarations of certainty or knowledge, and the certifications, through which the Administration certifies specific acts or facts accomplished by others. The ablation administrative acts are those through which the Administration deprives persons of some of their legal rights or interests, like those that deprive property rights (expropriations, confiscation) or the right to use property (requisitions); or deprive freedom (arrests, detentions); or those that impose obligations to give (fines) or to do (demolitions, for example). Administrative acts of concessions are, contrary to the ablation acts, those that amplify the subjective legal scope of individuals, so through them, a right is assigned to it as addressee, which it does not previously have. Generally, these acts are bilateral in nature, in the sense that they contain obligations that the concessionaire must accomplish. Finally, the Administrative acts of authorization are those allowing a person to exercise a pre-existent right he had, having the purpose of removing the existing legal obstacles preventing such exercise. This is the case of the administrative licenses, permits and authorizations, so common in contemporary administrative law, widely used by all Administrations according to the degree of intervention in private activities.

On the other hand, administrative acts can be classified according to the way in which the Administration expresses its will. The normal way to do it is in a formal express way, normally in writing, through a document that in some cases must even

---

55 See Allan R. Brewer-Carías, *El derecho administrativo y la Ley Orgánica de Procedimientos Administrativos*, Editorial Jurídica Venezolana, Caracas 1982, p. 133 ff.

56 See Allan R. Brewer-Carías, *El control de la constitucionalidad de los actos estatales*, Editorial Jurídica Venezolana, Caracas 1977, p. 7 ff.

57 See, for example, Massimo Severo Giannini, *Diritto Amministrativo*, Giuffre, Milano 1970, Vol. II, p. 825 ff.

be published in the *Official Gazette*. But in other cases, the administrative act can be a tacit one, when a particular statute grants in an express way, specific effect to the administrative silence, or to the absence of express decision of the Administration in the legally prescribed term. Once the prescribed term elapses, the statutes can give to it positive effects, in the sense that it must be considered that what has been asked or petitioned has been granted; or negative effects, that is, to consider that once the term to decide has elapsed without a decision expressly adopted, the statute provides that the petition must be considered as rejected. This is generally established regarding petitions for authorizations.

In addition, as administrative acts are normally due to be expressed in writing (oral administrative acts are exceptional, like some police orders, for instance), being materialized in a signed Letter or a document, such texts, once signed by the competent public official, can also be considered as "public documents" in the terms of Article 1.357 of the Civil Code, provided that the public official signing them has the power to give public certainty (*fe pública*) to the facts or acts that he himself executes, or that he declares to have seen or to have heard, which normally occurs with the administrative acts of registry, or of certification; for instance, the Acts written to testify to some actions or facts, which on the other hand in such cases are the only means in order to prove the specific acts or facts. Regarding these administrative acts, the presumption of certitude that they have imposes on the Administration and the individuals the duty to sustain their content, unless it is proven that the declaration of the public official has been false or in error.

On the other hand, in particular, regarding the effects in time of administrative acts of specific effects, regarding their sustainability permanence in time or their irrevocability (firmness), the general principle set forth by the Organic Law on Administrative Procedures is that any administrative act of specific effects declaring or creating rights or interests in favor of individuals cannot be reviewed and revoked by the Administration, being the principle of revocation established only for administrative acts that do not create or declare rights (Article 82). The consequence of this principle of irrevocability of administrative acts that have created or declared rights or interests in favor of individuals is so firmly established by the Organic Law on Administrative Procedures that its Article 19.2 provides for the absolute nullity of administrative acts that decide on cases that have been previously decided in a definite way, creating individual rights, that is, that revoke previous administrative acts that have created rights or interests in favor of individuals. The consequence of an act affected of the sanction of absolute nullity, is that they are null and void pursuant to Article 83 of the same the Organic Law on Administrative Procedures, and cannot produce any legal effect, allowing the Administration to recognize at any moment such absolute nullity.

On matters of administrative procedure, the Organic Law on Administrative Procedures provides for its duration, allowing the possibility of controlling the omissions or delays; the effects of administrative silence, whether originating from positive or negative tacit administrative acts; the regulation of the different formal steps to be accomplished before the administrative act is enacted, safeguarding due process (access to administrative files, burden of proof, notices, appeals); the vices affecting administrative acts as null and void (manifest lack of attributions, absolute and total absence of a procedure, vices on the object, violation of the Constitution);

and the means in order to execute administrative acts even in compulsory way, basically through fines.[58]

2. The "administrative res judicata" effects of administrative acts

Administrative acts produce effects and are binding on the Public Administration upon due notice or publication thereof. If they create or declare subjective rights or interests in favor of individuals, and are final –namely, are not legally challengeable– they have the effects of administrative *res judicata* and cannot be revoked by the Administration, to the point that pursuant to Article 19.2 of the Organic Law on Administrative Procedures, administrative acts are null and void "when they make a resolution on a case previously resolved as final that created individual rights."

Administrative acts are final when the periods legally provided for administrative or judicial challenge have elapsed and said acts have not been challenged.[59] Thus, there is no administrative *res judicata* if an administrative act can still be challenged, since if there is still time to challenge it, an individual can bring out cause and the Administration can revoke the act. It is only after the periods provided for challenging a given act have elapsed that such an act is final, since it cannot be revoked and "causes *res judicata*," provided it is not affected by any vice that would bring them to be absolute null and void.

Hence, pursuant to the aforementioned, for an administrative act to be final when it creates individual rights, and become administrative *res judicata*, namely, not being challengeable or revocable, the following conditions have to be met:

First, the administrative act ought to be specific –as opposed to general– since general administrative acts are essentially revisable and revocable. For general administrative acts (regulations), the Civil Code principle providing that laws are reversed by other laws applies (Article 7), so regulations are reversed by other regulations, without limitation. Hence a regulation, or a general administrative act, is never *final*.

Second, the administrative act must create or declare individual rights. If, in contrast, the act does not create or declare individual rights, it would never have the effect of *res judicata* and could always be reviewed and revoked by the Administration. As Article 82 of the Organic Law on Administrative Procedures provides:

> "Administrative acts that do not create subjective rights or legitimate and direct individual interests can be revoked at any time, in whole or in part, by the same authority who issued them, or by their respective hierarchal superior."

---

58 See in general the jurisprudence about administrative acts in Caterina Balasso, *Jurisprudencia sobre los Actos Administrativos (1980-1993)*, Editorial Jurídica Venezolana, Caracas 1998.

59 See Allan R. Brewer-Carías, "Las condiciones de recurribilidad de los actos administrativos en la vía contencioso administrativa," in *Perspectivas del Derecho Público en la segunda mitad del Siglo XX, Homenaje al Profesor Enrique Sayagués Lazo*, Vol. V, Instituto de Estudios de Administración Local, Madrid 1969, pp. 743-769, and in *Revista del Ministerio de Justicia*, N° 54, Year XIV, Caracas January-December 1966, pp. 83-112.

Third, the act ought to be final, namely, its lawfulness cannot be directly challenged either at the administrative or judicial level. The individual must be prohibited from bringing a challenge against it. It is from the moment that the act is final that it becomes administrative *res judicata* and non-revocable. If a challenge can still be brought against an administrative act, it is not possible to say there is *res judicata*; because if there is still time to bring a challenge, someone could do it and the act could be reviewed and revoked. It is only after the time legally given to challenge an act has elapsed that the act is final, cannot be reversed, and becomes *res judicata*.

Fourth, the act must be valid and effective, capable of creating or declaring individual rights, so that if the act is affected by absolute nullity, it is not capable of creating or declaring rights, being essentially revocable (Article 83 of the Organic Law on Administrative Procedures). That is to say, only acts that are legally valid and are not affected by vices that cause them to be absolutely null and void can be final, because if a given act has a vice of such magnitude, under Article 83 of the Organic Law on Administrative Procedures, the Administration can, at any time, either by request or by its own initiative, revoke it recognizing it to be null and void. That explains why *res judicata* only exists as for valid acts and, in any case, with respect of acts that are not affected by absolute nullity vices.

Like I have already said on other occasions:

> "[A] consequence of the non-retroactivity of administrative acts principle is the general principle that the rights or subjective situations acquired or born from individual administrative acts cannot be later removed by other administrative acts. This is the general principle of intangibility of the situations born from individual acts, or of the irrevocability of administrative acts creating individual rights; a principle that has received legal receipt in administrative procedure acts throughout Latin America."[60]

In this sense, following the decision of the Political-Administrative Chamber of the Supreme Court issued on July 26, 1984, (Case: *Despachos Los Teques*), it results that:

> "... in first place, the final character (*firmeza*) of administrative acts is always traduced in the need of a finalist essence for the legal framework, both for the efficiency of the act and the legal protection of individuals; and in second place, that the Administration can and ought to declare the absolute nullity, by its own initiative, at any time, of those acts that are against the law and are affected of absolute nullity; without prejudice that it can also do so regarding those acts with relative nullity vices that have not created vested rights."[61]

---

60 See Allan R. Brewer-Carías, *Principios del Procedimiento Administrativo*, Editorial Civitas, Madrid, 1990, p. 122.

61 See *Revista de Derecho Público*, N° 19, Editorial Jurídica Venezolana, Caracas 1984, pp. 130-132. See also Allan R. Brewer-Carías and Luis Ortiz-Álvarez, *Las Grandes Decisiones de la Jurisprudencia Contencioso Administrativa (1961-1996)*, Editorial Jurídica Venezolana, Caracas 1994, pp. 610-616; Caterina Balasso Tejera, *Jurisprudencia sobre los Actos Administrativos (1980-1993)*, Colección Jurisprudencia N° 7, Editorial Jurídica Venezolana, Caracas 1998, p. 853 ff.

The consequence of the inclusion of these principles of *res judicata* in the Organic Law on Administrative Procedures, entailing the irrevocability of administrative acts creating individual rights, is that pursuant to its Article 19.2, those acts that resolve a situation previously decided by a final act that created individual rights, namely, those acts that revoke an irrevocable act, are absolutely null and void.

These principles have been integrated into the precedents of the Supreme Court. In fact, in Judgment N° 154, pronounced on May 14, 1985 (Case of *Freddy Rojas Perez v. Unellez*), the Political-Administrative Chamber stated that:

> "One of such relevant exceptions concerns, precisely, to the case at hand. In fact, the administrative doctrine maintains, unanimously, that the Administration cannot go back on its steps and reverse its own acts when those have created some individual rights and that is because such reversal of acts creating individual rights would struggle with the intangibility of legal individual situations.
>
> The irrevocability of acts declaring rights means –as Royo Villanova teaches– that the Administration, afterwards, cannot make another decision that contradicts the legal situation created by the first. Therefore, a pronouncement, even illegal, if not challenged in proper time and manner by the individuals or the own Administration, is final and not only cannot be revoked or reversed through an appeal, but cannot be so by another pronouncement issued by the Administration's initiative. "Such an act holds what has been called as formal and material force." (Antonio Royo Villanova: *Elementos de Derecho Administrativo*, Librería Santarín, 1948, p. 119-121).
>
> Likewise, the German administrative lawyer Fritz Fleiner, for whom the principles *quieta non movere* and good faith are valid also for administrative authorities, said. "Sure enough –states– the possibility of having a pronouncement reversing the one that favors him, is a permanent threat for an individual. Consequently, the lawmaker had to think seriously on restraining the ability to reverse a pronouncement, taking into account those cases in which legal safety so required. So, then, the lawmaker has secured mostly the immutability of those pronouncements that create rights and duties" (Fritz Fleiner, *Instituciones de Derecho Administrativo*, Editorial labor, Barcelona. p. 161. Similar opinion can be found in: Gascón y Marín, *Derecho Administrativo*, Edit. Bermejo, 1947, pp. 42-43; Jesús González Pérez, *Derecho Procesal Administrativo*, Instituto de Estudios Políticos, Madrid, 1960, pp. 858-862; and in domestic doctrine: Brewer-Carías, *Las Instituciones Fundamentales del Derecho Administrativo y la Jurisprudencia Venezolana*, Publicaciones de la Facultad de Derecho, U.C.V. 1964, p. 142)."[62]

In another judgment, N° 1.033 dated May 11, 2000, the same Political-Administrative Chamber of the Supreme Tribunal stated that:

62 See *Revista de Derecho Público*, N° 23, Editorial Jurídica Venezolana, Caracas, 1985, pp. 143-148. See also Caterina Balasso Tejera, *Jurisprudencia sobre los Actos Administrativos (1980-1993)*, Colección Jurisprudencia N° 7, Editorial Jurídica Venezolana, Caracas 1998, p. 813 and ss.

"... administrative acts declaring individual rights, once final, because of elapsing of the terms for their challenge, become irrevocable even in those cases that they are affected by a vice that makes them subject to be annulled. Not so if they are absolutely null and void.

In this sense Margarita Beladiez Rojo, in her book *Validez y Eficacia de los Actos Administrativos*, Editorial Marcial Pons, Madrid, 1994, asserting that the ideas of order and stability are in themselves incompatible, she considers convenient that a moment comes when situations that have been created, and for which some time has elapsed, consolidate and cannot be erased from the world of the Law, since otherwise the trust of citizens would be betrayed in a legal order that shows as certain and final situations that can be changed.

So, in her words it is obvious that to allow indefinitely the possibility to declare acts unlawful, when these have created individual rights entails depriving the beneficiaries of the trust in certainty of situations declared by the Administration which, without doubt, encompasses an attack to the principle of legal safety and res judicata in the terms stated. Thus, as a way to harmonize the interest in keeping the effects produced by administrative acts with the interest in the lawfulness of administrative acts, the power to challenge them through proper appeals that allow the right to lawfulness to be effective has been restricted in timing, and once the terms for doing so have elapsed without anyone challenging the unlawful act, then the rest of the interested parties in the conservation of the act will have acquired the right for it to be preserved."[63]

The aforementioned principles, of course, condition the generally admitted Administration's review powers, which can only be exercised on individual administrative acts in those cases provided for by law and that, satisfy legally established conditions.

3. The presumption of validity of administrative acts

As a matter of principle, once they began to produce effects, administrative acts enjoy of a presumption of validity and legitimacy,[64] which allows the Administration to enforce them. Such presumption exists until the administrative act is annulled whether by the competent contentious administrative court or by the same Administration. The competence of the contentious administrative courts to annul administrative acts is established in article 259 of the Constitution and article 9.1 of

63 See Decision N° 01033 of the Political-Administrative Chamber of the Supreme Tribunal of Justice of May 11, 2000 (Case of *Aldo Ferro García v. la marca comercial KISS*), available at http://www.tsj.gov.ve/decisiones/spa/Mayo/01033-110500-13168.htm.

64 See for instance what is stated by Carlos García Soto, in "Auto tutela administrativa y tutela cautelar," in *Derecho y Sociedad. Revista de Estudiantes de Derecho de la Universidad Monteavila*, Universidad Monteávila, Facultad de Ciencias Jurídicas y Políticas, Editorial Altolitho, No. 6, abril 2005, Caracas, p. 277. Available at: http://www.ulpiano.org.ve/revistas/bases/artic/texto/DERYSO/6/deryso_2005_6_271-292.pdf.. See a summary of the different concepts on the matter by Gonzalo Pérez Luciani, in "La llamada 'presunción de legitimidad' de los actos administrativos," in *Revista de Derecho*, No. 1, Tribunal Supremo de Justicia, Caracas, 2000, pp 113-154, This author highlights the concept that the presumption is not absolute, and cannot be alleged in cases of manifest vices of the administrative acts, p.118.

the Organic Law on the Contentious Administrative Jurisdiction of 2010; and the competence of the Administration to annul administrative acts is established in article 83 of the Organic Law on Administrative Procedure of 1982.

Before the enactment of the Organic Law on Administrative Procedure, it was possible to sustain that only the judicial authority could annul administrative acts and therefore a presumption of legality and legitimacy existed until an act was declared null by a court of justice;[65] but after the enactment of such Organic Law on Administrative Procedure in 1982, it is just incorrect to claim that only the courts can annul administrative acts.[66]

In particular, according to article 83 of the Organic Law on Administrative Procedure, as explained further on, the Administration can annul its own administrative acts when they are null and void according to article 19 of the same Organic Law, that is, when such nullity is expressly determined by a constitutional or legal provision (such as article 25 of the Constitution that states that acts that violate fundamental rights are null and void, or article 138 that states that acts enacted by an usurped authority are null and void); when the administrative act deals with a matter that has been previously decided creating rights for individuals; when the content of the act is impossible or illegal to comply with; and when the administrative acts have been issued by authorities manifestly without competency (attributions), or in total and absolute absence of the procedure legally prescribed. In such cases, according to article 83 of the Organic Law, the Administration is empowered to annul the administrative act, without any restriction.

On the other hand, as I argued many years ago when commenting on a decision of the former Politico Administrative Chamber of the Supreme Court of Justice dated

65 See for instance the criteria of the former Federal and Cassation Court expressed in 1938: "No act can be considered null, even when it is affected of the most grave vice, without a court declaring it as such." See decision of April 4, 1938, *Memoria* de la Corte Federal y de Casación, 1939, pp. 490-491. See extract in Allan R. Brewer-Carías, *Jurisprudencia de la Corte Suprema 1930-1974 y estudios de derecho administrativo, Tomo III: La actividad administrativa. Vol 1. Reglamentos, procedimientos y actos administrativos,* Ediciones del Instituto de Derecho Público, Facultad de Derecho, Universidad Central de Venezuela, Caracas 1976, p. 349. Nonetheless, even before the enactment of the Organic Law on Administrative Procedure, in the opinion of the Attorney General Office expressed in 1964, the presumption of legitimacy of all administrative acts "can be reversed through the exercise of the corresponding recourse, by the competent *administrative or judicial* authority to review the act. The act, due to this presumption is considered valid, produces all its effects and can be compulsory enforced as long as it is not revoked or annulled." See Dictamen Nº 4636 de 22 de septiembre de 1964, Sección de Asesoría del Estado. See the extract in Allan R. Brewer-Carías, "Aspectos de la ejecutividad y de la ejecutoriedad de los actos administrativos fiscales y la aplicación del principio solve et repete," in *Revista del Ministerio de Justicia*, No 53, año XIV, Caracas, abril-diciembre 1965, pp. 67-86., at pp. 71-72.

66 On the contrary, as I have expressed in many works, "an administrative act, once it is effective, can be enforced immediately and produce effects as long as it is not revoked or annulled, that is, as long as it is not formally extinguished by the Administration or by a Court." See Allan R. Brewer-Carías, *Tratado de Derecho Administrativo*, Tomo III, Editorial Jurídica Venezolana, Caracas 2013, p. 509. Available at: http://allanbrewercarias.com/wp-content/uploads/ 2013/07/ BREWER-TRATADO-DE-DA-TOMO-III-9789803652081-txt-1.pdf See in the same sense, what is stated by José Araujo Juárez, in *Derecho Administrativo*, Ediciones Paredes, Caracas 2013, p. 494.

21 November 1989 (*case Arnaldo Lovera*), when administrative acts are null and void in an absolute way according to article 19 of the Organic Law on Administrative Procedure, such acts do not benefit from any presumption of validity, and that is why they can be revoked and declared null and void by the Administration at any time. [67] That is why more recently I have also expressed that "an administrative act vitiated of absolute nullity cannot be presumed legitimate, and the Administration cannot order its compliance."[68] In the words of the former Politico Administrative Chamber of the Supreme Tribunal of Justice in its decision of August 13, 1991, in such cases of absolute nullity ,"the presumption of legitimacy that produces the administrative act cannot prevail against the logic." [69] And that is why, the same Chamber of the Supreme Tribunal in its decision of April 6, 1993 (Case: *Eduardo Contramaestre*) ruled on this matter as follows:

> "the absolute nullity is the gravest consequence derived from the vices of the administrative act and means that the act cannot produce effect in any way whatsoever, due to the fact that the act null of absolute nullity has to be considered as never enacted; consequently, it could not and cannot produce effects." [70]

Also, in the words of Tomás Ramón Fernández, an administrative act which is null "cannot produce effects and its author cannot impose it." What its author has

> "is an obligation to declare it null and void from the moment in which he realizes by himself or is warned by an interested party of the existence of a nullity cause, due to the fact that it is not allowed to anybody, due to the most elemental requirements of justice, to obtain benefits from his own clumsiness (*allegans propriam turpitudinem non auditur*)."[71]

---

67 In such comment on Decision of the Politico Administrative Chamber of the Supreme Court, of 9 November 1989 (Case *Arnaldo Lovera*) I affirmed that "the presumption of legitimacy of administrative acts does not exist when the acts are vitiated of absolute nullity, in which case they could not be enforced." See in Allan R. Brewer-Carías, "Consideraciones sobre la ejecución de los actos administrativos (a propósito de los actos administrativos que ordenan el desalojo de viviendas), en *Revista de Derecho Público*, No. 41, enero-marzo 1990, Editorial Jurídica Venezolana, Caracas 190, p. 165. Available at: http://allanbrewercarias.com/wp-content/ uploads /2007/08/rdpub_1990_41.pdf More recently I have repeated that opinion: *Tratado de Derecho Administrativo*, Tomo IV, Editorial Jurídica Venezolana, Caracas 2013, p. 289. Available at: http://allanbrewercarias.com/wp-content/uploads/2013/07/BREWER-TRATADO-DE-DA-TOMO -IV-9789803652098-txt-2.pdf

68 See Allan R. Brewer-Carías, "Presentation to the Second Edition, "On some principles of the invalidity of administrative acts in Latin American legislation," in the book of Tomás Ramón Fernández, *La nulidad de los actos administrativos*, Ediciones Olejnik, Santiago, Buenos Aires, Madrid 2019, p. 29.

69 See in *Revista de Derecho Público*, No. 47, Editorial Jurídica Venezolana, Caracas 1991, p. 111. Available at: http://allanbrewercarias.com/wp-content/uploads/2007/08/rdpub_1991_ 47. pdf

70 See in *Revista de Derecho Público*, No. 55-56, Editorial Jurídica Venezolana, Caracas 1993, p. 198. Available at: http://allanbrewercarias.com/wp-content/uploads/2007/08/rdpub _1993 _55-56-1.pdf. See comments in José Araujo Juárez, *Derecho Administrativo General*, Ediciones Paredes, Caracas 2011, p. 174.

71 See Tomás Ramón Fernández, *La nulidad de los actos administrativos*, Ediciones Olejnik, Santiago, Buenos Aires, Madrid 2019, p. 53.

In this same sense, Carlos Luis Carrillo after affirming that in cases of administrative acts that are null and void the Administration has "the obligation" to annul them, has said that the inclusion of article 19 in the Organic Law on Administrative Procedure "implies that such an act [null and void] could never produce expectations of rights, personal, direct and legitimate interests and much less subjective rights for its addressee, because as we have said, nobody could claim to be the beneficiary of effects emanating from a will expressed upon a basis that is null and against the law." [72] As Eloy Lares Martínez expressed: "In this case, the principle of auto-control of the Administration upon its own acts is not limited by vested rights of individuals, because no rights whatsoever can be based on administrative acts vitiated of absolute nullity."[73] In addition, Gustavo Linares Benzo, in the same sense, said: "Absolute nullity is referred to as an intrinsic vice of the act, to its constitutive elements. Thus, the act vitiated never produces effects, from the beginning. Due to the general character of the vice, absolute nullity can be alleged against anybody, *erga omnes*." [74]

4. Public Administrations auto control powers regarding administrative acts, its limits and the revocation of administrative acts

In fact, as a consequence of the legality principle –under which actions of the Administration must comply with the Law– the power of self-review of the Administration is recognized in administrative law, which implies the power of the Public Administration not just to review and correct any errors it may have made in any of its administrative acts, but also –in principle– to revoke them when they are deemed illegal or contrary to the general interest. As the Political and Administrative Chamber has stated in the aforementioned decision N° 1033 dated May 11, 2000:

> "Among the most important manifestations of self-tutelage of the Administration is, precisely, the power to revoke, which is no more than the ability to review and correct its administrative actions, and consequently, the power to extinguish administrative acts by administrative action."[75]

---

72 See Carlos Luis Carrillo Artilez, "La imbricación de la noción y contenido de la potestad de autotutel de la Administración en Venezuela," p. 26. Published in: *Derecho Administrativo Iberoamericano*, Ediciones paredes, Caracas 2007. Available at: http://www.carrilloartiles.com/wp-content/uploads/PotestadAutotutelaAdministracion.pdf In the same sense see what is stated by Henrique Meier García, *Teoría de las Nulidades en el derecho administrativo*, Editorial Jurídica Alba, Caracas 1991, p. 77.

73 See Eloy Lares Martínez, *Manual de Derecho Administrativo*, XIV Edición, Caracas, 2013, p. 246.

74 See Gustavo Linares Benzo, "Notas sobre los actos administrativos," in the book: *El derecho público a los 100 números de la Revista de Deecho Público 1980-2005*, Editorial Jurídica Venezolana, Caracas 2005, p. 783. Available at: http://allanbrewercarias.com/wp-content/uploads /2007/08/EL-DERECHO-P%C3%9ABLICO-A-LOS-100-N%C2%B0-DE-LA-RDP-1980-2005-MAYO-20061.pdf

75 *Idem*, available at http://www.tsj.gov.ve/decisiones/spa/Ma-yo/01033-110500-13168.htm, also cited in Pronouncement N° 0072 by the same Political-Administrative Chamber of the Supreme Tribunal of Justice on January 22, 2009, File N° 1995-11643, available at http://www .tsj.gov.ve/deci-siones/spa/Enero/00072-22109-2009-1995-11643.html.

Thus, as a warranty arising from the duty the Administration has to further the general interest and the Law, this self-tutelage power implies that an unlawful pronouncement or a decision that is against the general interest could be –in principle– reviewed and revoked by the same administrative authority who adopted it. It can even be said that the most important outcome of the legality principle according to which administrative action ought to follow the Law, is the administrative ability to self-review and self-correct the mistakes it may have made.

However, since such power arises from what I have previously explained on the *res judicata* principle, that self-reviewing power is conditioned first by the intensity or seriousness of the alleged illegality as well as by the contents of the administrative act, specifically, whether it has created individual rights.[76]

Considering what has been said, as well as the provisions of the Organic Law on Administrative Procedures, this self-tutelage power has been widely treated by the judicial precedents, pointing out the intensity or seriousness of the illegality as a cause for its exercise. In this sense, the Political and Administrative Chamber of the former Supreme Court, in the aforementioned judgment pronounced on July 26, 1984 (*Despacho Los Teques, C.A* case) set forth the following criteria on the matter:

> "For many years the pronouncements of this Court have recognized the existence of the so-called power of self-tutelage of the Public Administration, pursuant to which the competent bodies comprising it can and must revoke, ex officio and at any time, those acts which are contrary to the law and which are subject to absolute nullity; without prejudice to the fact that this is also applicable to acts issued by them which are subject to relative nullity and which have not led to the acquisition of any rights. This power has been recognized as an attribute that is inherent to the Administration and not a "mere consequence" of the jurisdictional power, as noted in the judgment of this Court dated Nov. 2nd, 1967, where it was stated that 'the power of the administrative authority to act in this sense is part of the principle of self-tutelage of the Public Administration, which bestows it the power to revoke and amend administrative acts that in its opinion affect the merit or legality of cases heard by it [...].'"[77]

Later, in Judgment N° 154 of the same Political and Administrative Chamber dated May 14, 1985 (Case of *Freddy Martin Rojas Perez v. Unellez*), it stated the following:

> "The matter of the revocation powers of the Public Administration, its limitations and scope, has been studied abundantly by both domestic and international doctrine, and has been analyzed several times in the jurisdiction of this Supreme Tribunal. Both recognize, as a general principle the extinction of administrative acts, that the Administration has the ability to deprive

---

76 See in general, Allan R. Brewer-Carías, "Comentarios sobre la revocación de los actos administrativos," in *Revista de Derecho Público*, N° 4, Editorial Jurídica Venezolana, Caracas 1980, pp. 27-30.

77 See *Revista de Derecho Público*, N° 19, Editorial Jurídica Venezolana, Caracas 1984, pp. 130-132. See also Allan R. Brewer-Carías and Luis Ortíz-Álvarez, *Las Grandes Decisiones de la Jurisprudencia Contencioso Administrativa (1961-1996),* Editorial Jurídica Venezolana, Caracas 1994, pp. 610-616; Caterina Balasso Tejera, *Jurisprudencia sobre los Actos Administrativos (1980-1993), loc. cit.*, p. 853 ff.

administrative acts of their validity, either by its own initiative or by individual request of an interested party, and they point out, as the cause of such ability, reasons of legality when the act is affected by a vice that prevents it from been valid and lawful, and reasons of opportunity in the case of regulatory acts, since it is logical and convenient that the Administration is entitled to accommodate its actions to the changes and mutations of reality, taking in a given moment, those measures that it deems more appropriate for the general interest."[78]

In 2000, the Political and Administrative Chamber of the Supreme Tribunal also said about this subject the following:

"Among the more important manifestations of the self-review power of the Administration lies, precisely, in the revoking power, that is nothing more than the ability to review and correct its administrative actions and, as a way of consequence, the ability to extinguish its own acts by way of administrative action.

This power is regulated, in first place, in Article 82 of the Organic Law on Administrative Procedures, in the sense that administrative acts can be revoked at any time, in whole or in part, either by the same authority who adopted them or its hierarchal superior, if and when they do not create individual rights or legitimate, personal and direct interests, for a given person. In the latter cases the Law sanctioned with absolute nullity those acts resolving situations previously decided in a definitive way creating individual rights, unless expressly authorized by law.

However, if such express authorization does not exist, the general principle is that if an act creating individual rights is revoked, the revoking act is absolutely null and void; which implies the possibility of the Administration of recognizing –and of the individuals to request– at any point in time, for it to formally declare such nullity." [79]

More recently, in its decision of December 4, 2002, the Political-Administrative Chamber of the Supreme Tribunal of Justice provided that:

"...the power of self-tutelage as a means to protect public interest and the principle of legality that governs administrative activity, includes both the possibility to review the factual and legal foundations of the administrative acts through a petition for administrative recourse, as well as ex officio at the initiative of the Administration itself.

---

78 See *Revista de Derecho Público*, Nº 23, Editorial Jurídica Venezolana, Caracas, pp. 143-148. See also Allan R. Brewer-Carías and Luis Ortiz-Álvarez, *Las Grandes Decisiones de la Jurisprudencia Contencioso Administrativa*, Editorial Jurídica Venezolana, Caracas 1996, pp. 617-619; Decision Nº 01033 of the Political-Administrative Chamber of the Supreme Tribunal of Justice of May 11, 2000 (Case of *Aldo Ferro García v. la marca comercial Kiss*), available at http://www.tsj.gov.ve/decisiones/spa/Mayo/01033-110500-13168.htm.

79 See Decision Nº 01033 of the Political-Administrative Chamber of the Supreme Tribunal of Justice of May 11, 2000 (Case of *Aldo Ferro García v. la marca comercial KISS*), available at http://www.tsj.gov.ve/deci-siones/spa/Mayo/01033-110500-13168.htm.

This last possibility is provided in Chapter I of Title IV of the Organic Law of Administrative Procedures, 'Ex Officio Review,' which establishes the form and the scope of the power of the Administration for the ex officio review of its acts.

Thus, pursuant to the law, the power to conduct ex officio reviews in turn includes several specific powers, recognized both by doctrine as well as by the country's jurisprudence, to wit: the power to validate, the power to rectify, the power to revoke and the power to annul, as provided in Articles 81 to 84 of the Organic Administrative Procedures Act – each of them with special requirements and different scopes.

The purpose of the first two is to preserve administrative acts that are affected by slight irregularities that do not make them subject to absolute nullity, and that can be cured, allowing the administrative act to stand and with it the completion of the public purpose for which it was issued as an act of this nature.

The purpose of the last two, which deal with the declaration of either the relative or absolute nullity of the act, with no need for the assistance of the courts, is to protect the principle of legality that governs all administrative activities.

Now then, these two powers, to revoke and to annul, are differentiated by the conditions for their application. The power to revoke is used in some cases for reason of merit or opportunity when required by the public interest, as well as in cases of acts that are affected by relative nullity, if they have not created subjective rights or personal, legitimate and direct interests for an individual; while the power to annul does not distinguish between acts that create rights and those that do not grant a personal right or interest, inasmuch as these apply only in cases of acts that are subject to absolute nullity.

This being the case, the Administration, when reviewing an act that generated rights or interests for any individual, must analyze and determine the irregularity with the greatest care possible, because any declaration annulling an act that is not subject to absolute nullity would be tantamount to sacrificing the stability of the legal situation created or recognized by the act, and therefore the principle of legal security –essential and necessary for any legal order– in exchange for a flaw that does not represent a major problem.

As such, the stability of administrative acts and the principle of legal security that are part of the legal order, could be waived only in the face of grave threat to another principle that is not less important, the principle of legality, which would be affected by the permanence of a seriously flawed act" (underlining and bold print added).[80]

In yet another more recent decision, N° 72 dated January 22, 2009, the same Chamber of the Supreme Tribunal has ratified such principles, stating what follows:

80 See Decision N° 01388 of the Political-Administrative Chamber of the Supreme Tribunal of Justice of December 4, 2002 (Case of *Iván Darío Badell v. Fiscal General de la República*), available at http://www.tsj.gov.ve/decisiones/spa/Diciembre/01388-041202-0516.htm.

> "Like this Chamber has stated in judgment N° 01033 dated May 11, 2000, among the more important manifestations of the self-review power of the Administration lies, precisely, in the revoking power, that is nothing more than the ability to review and correct its administrative actions and, as a way of consequence, the ability to extinguish its own administrative acts at administrative level.
>
> This power is regulated, in first place, in article 82 of Organic Law on Administrative Procedures, in the sense that administrative acts can be revoked at any time, in whole or in part, either by the same authority who adopted them or its hierarchal superior, if and when they do not create individual rights or legitimate, personal and direct interests, for a given person. In the latter cases the Law absolutely prohibited the possibility for the Administration to revoke such acts creating individual rights, unless expressly authorized by law. For such reason article 19, 2 of Organic Law on Administrative Procedures sanctioned with absolute nullity those acts deciding situations previously resolved as final and that have created individual rights in favor of individuals.
>
> On the other hand, the power to revoke is provided for by article 83 ejusdem, which authorizes the Administration, at any given time and either by its own initiative or through individual petition, to recognize absolute nullity of acts previously issued. The Law provides that those acts creating individual rights cannot be revoked, but an act that is affected be vices of absolute nullity –at an administrative level– is not susceptible of creating rights.
>
> Notwithstanding, although article 83 of Organic Law on Administrative Procedures provides for the possibility to review previously issued administrative acts at any given time, either by its own initiative or through individual petition, such review power must be exercised if and when some of the vices resulting in absolute nullity provided for by article 19 of Organic Law on Administrative Procedures, occurs." [81]

The scope of the power of self-tutelage varies, as it has been already said, principally pursuant to two criteria: the first, related to the intensity or seriousness of the illegality and the second, related to the content of the act, and in particular whether it has created individual rights. Consequently, like it results from the judgment cited above, regarding the different situations where the administrative power of self-tutelage may be exercised, this is allowed for reasons of merit as well as legality, and in this last case the difference between flaws that would cause absolute nullity and those that would cause relative nullity must be established, as well as whether or not there are any vested rights as proclaimed by or deriving from the administrative act.

---

81 See Decision N° 72 by the same Political-Administrative Chamber of the Supreme Tribunal of Justice of January 22, 2009 (Case of *Aldo Ferro García*), available at http://www.tsj.gov.ve/deci-siones/spa/Enero/00072-22109-2009-1995-11643.html.

5. Principles related to Public Administration revocation powers regarding administrative acts

A. The revocation of administrative acts due to reasons of merit

Article 82 of the Organic Law on Administrative Procedures provides for a broad power of the Administration to revoke administrative acts, both for merit reasons and legality, at any point in time, as long as they have not created individual rights. Conversely, when an administrative act creates individual rights, the same the Organic Law on Administrative Procedures is categorical in prohibiting their revocation. Such administrative acts cannot be revoked by the Administration for reasons of merit.

It has so been held by the Political and Administrative Chamber of the Supreme Tribunal of Justice in its Decision N° 01033 dated May 11, 2000, when it stated:

> "The Administration's power to revoke is limited to acts that do not create or declare rights in favor of individuals: as acts that do create or declare rights, once final, cannot be revoked for reasons of merit to the detriment of those in favor of which were granted by the Administration."[82]

The same Chamber of the Supreme Tribunal of Justice, in its judgment N° 01388 dated Dec. 4, 2002, has held:

> "[T]he powers to revoke is used in some cases for reasons of merit or opportunity when it is required for reasons of public interest, and also in cases of acts which are subject to relative nullity, if they have not created subjective rights or personal, legitimate and direct interests for an individual." [83]

In my comments on the Organic Law on Administrative Procedures published shortly after its enactment in 1992, I stated that:

> "If the act does not create rights in favor of individuals, it is essentially revocable; the Administration can revoke it at any time, for any reason, as established in Article 82 of the Law (of Administrative Procedures). However, if it is a permanent act that creates legitimate interests and rights in favor of individuals, the act cannot be revoked by the Administration, pursuant to Article 19.2 of the Law. Still, this principle has some mitigation [in the sense that]: The Administration cannot revoke it for reasons of opportunity and convenience, i.e., for reasons of merit, at any time…."[84]

On his part, Eloy Lares Martínez on the same subject held that:

> "Individual administrative acts that grant rights and which are judicially regular are intangible, except under express provisions of the Law. Therefore, in

---

82 See Decision N° 01033 of the Political-Administrative Chamber of the Supreme Tribunal of Justice of May 11, 2000 (Case of *Aldo Ferro Garcia v. la marca comercial KISS*), available at http://www.tsj.gov.ve/deci-siones/spa/Mayo/01033-110500-13168.htm.

83 See Decision N° 01388 of the Political-Administrative Chamber of the Supreme Tribunal of Justice of December 4, 2002 (Case of *Iván Darío Badell v. Fiscal General de la República*), available at http://www.tsj.gov.ve/decisiones/spa/Diciembre/01388-041202-0516.htm.

84 See Allan R. Brewer Carías, *El Derecho Administrativo y la Ley Orgánica de Procedimientos Administrativos*, Editorial Jurídica Venezolana, Caracas 1997, p. 223.

the case of a regular administrative act which creates or gives rights to certain parties, the Administration has no discretionary power to revoke it for reasons of merit, or opportunity, unless that power is expressly granted to it in the text of the law, in which case it can be exercised only subject to the procedural norms and forms provided in the legal text."[85]

The fundamental doctrine on the revocation of administrative acts and its limits can be found in the judgment of the Political and Administrative Chamber entered on May 14, 1985, (Case of *Freddy Martín Rojas Pérez v. UNELLEZ*) where, after interpreting the provisions of the Organic Law on Administrative Procedures, set the following principles:

1. It recognizes, as a general principle, the power of self-tutelage of the Public Administration, according to which the bodies comprising the Administration can revoke acts that they previously produced (Article 82).

2. It specifies that such revocation, ex officio or upon petition, is allowable at any time when its acts are affected by absolute nullity (Article 83).

3. It clearly and categorically states the flaws, in detail, which could cause the absolute nullity of the administrative act (Article 19).

4. It determines that, outside of the specific flaws indicated for absolutely nullity, all other irregularities which may be present in the administrative act affect only its relative nullity (Article 20).

5. It establishes that acts affected by causes for relative nullity can also be revoked at any time by the Administration (Article 82).

6. It exempts from the possibility of revocation, administrative acts that are subject to relative nullity from which individual rights or legitimate, personal and direct interests arise (Article 82).

7. It clarifies that administrative acts that are affected by vices of relative nullity –namely, that can be annulled–if they create rights in favor of individuals and are final (as the periods of time allowed for executive action or jurisdictional appeal have lapsed), cannot be revoked by the Administration and if they are indeed revoked, then the act of revocation is affected of absolute nullity (Articles 11, 19.2 and 82)."[86]

B. Principles regarding compensation in cases of revocation of non-revocable administrative acts

The consequence of the aforementioned principles is that if the Public Administration, for reasons of public order or interest, notwithstanding the

85 See Eloy Lares Martínez, *Manual de Derecho Administrativo,* Universidad Central de Venezuela, Caracas 1983, p. 216.

86 See *Gaceta Forense*, N° 128, Vol. I, Caracas 1985, pp. 299-318. See also Allan R. Brewer-Carías and Luis Ortiz-Álvarez, *Las Grandes Decisiones de la Jurisprudencia Contencioso Administrativa*, Editorial Jurídica Venezolana, Caracas 1996, pp. 617-619; See Decision N° 01033 of the Political-Administrative Chamber of the Supreme Tribunal of Justice of May 11, 2000 (Case of Aldo Ferro García v. la marca comercial KISS), available at http://www.tsj.gov.ve/decisiones/spa/Mayo/01033-110500-13168.htm.

prohibition to do so, revokes administrative acts creating individual rights, against *res judicata*, that would be the same as to expropriate the rights created by the act and would give rise to the obligation to pay just compensation for the damages caused to the interested individuals.

Therefore, even though the regulation in the Organic Law on Administrative Procedures is extreme, in the sense that it establishes an absolute prohibition against revoking those acts that create individual rights, punishing such revocation with absolute nullity, if the Administration nevertheless revokes for reasons of public order or public interest, it would have to pay compensation and damages caused by the revocation. Moreover, this is the general trend in Latin American legislation, where revocation of administrative acts creating individual rights is admitted as an exception, when accompanied by compensatory payment. It is so provided, for instance, in the Administrative Procedure Acts of Argentina, (Art. 18), Peru (Art. 205) and Costa Rica (Art. 155), the latter going even further stating that if the revocation act does not recognize and calculate the total amount to be paid, then it would be absolutely null and void (Art. 155.1). In Honduras, the Administrative Procedure Act expressly provides that revocation of an administrative act only results in payment of compensation when it is so provided by law (Art. 123).[87]

In Venezuela, also, according to the general principle of absolute nullity affecting the administrative acts revoking others that had created or declared individual rights (Art. 19.2 of the Organic Law on Administrative Procedures), the only way in which such nullity would not occur would be if the former encompassed compensation for the extinction of the right and, evidently, with the proper reasoning related to public interest.

Thus, even when acts create individual rights they can be revoked by the Administration upon payment of compensation, because the Administration's power to make public interest prevail over private interest cannot be stopped. Likewise, the Administration can expropriate any kind of goods or rights if public interest so dictates, this can also by applied by analogy in these cases. The purpose of the legal provisions in Venezuela is to protect private individuals against arbitrary behavior of the Administration in revoking without proper motivation its acts, but this cannot be interpreted in the sense as to impair the Administration's power to revoke administrative acts even if they have created individual rights, substituting the individual right created by the revoked acts, by the right to be compensated for the lost suffered with the revocation.

Spanish doctrine (García de Enterría and Fernandez) holds the same criteria regarding the revocation of acts that create individual rights for mere considerations of merit, stating as follows:

> "An act declaring individual rights in favor of an administered party that shows no flaws in its issuing, cannot be revoked ex officio by the Administration, under the pretext that the act has at a given time become untimely or inconvenient."[88]

---

87 See Allan R. Brewer-Carías, *Principios del Procedimiento Administrativo en América Latina*, Universidad del Rosario, Bogotá 2003, pp. XXXVIII-XLII.

88 See Eduardo García de Enterría and Tomás-Ramón Fernández, *Curso de Derecho Administrativo*, Vol. I, 6th Ed., Editorial Civitas, Madrid 1993, p. 637.

However, authors cited above hold that such principle might be too rigid, and therefore propose:

> "a balanced solution that would guarantee both the public interest as well as that of individuals would be to allow revocation simply for reasons of timeliness or convenience, conditioned nonetheless on the recognition and payment of adequate compensation caused by the loss of the rights bestowed by the act revoked."[89]

Nevertheless, they point out that to be viable such solution requires a provision allowing revocation for merit reasons, which in any event shall recognize the rights of the affected individuals to receive compensation, pursuant to the principle of administrative responsibility for individual sacrifice or the loss of equality in the presence of public burdens.[90]

In conclusion, only administrative acts of general effects and individual administrative acts that do not create or declare subjective rights in favor of an individual are revocable for reasons of merit or convenience. Exceptionally, the Administration can revoke administrative acts that create rights, for reasons of merit or timeliness, only when expressly authorized by a provision of law, in which case the individual with the right shall be paid the corresponding compensation.

This has been expressly admitted by the Political-Administrative Chamber of the Supreme Tribunal of Justice in its pronouncement dated May 11, 2005, where it held that:

> "...the power to declare nullity is provided by Article 83 ejusdem, when authorizing the Administration, at any time, ex officio or upon petition, to recognize the absolute nullity of acts dictated by it. The Law provides for the irrevocability of administrative acts creating individual rights in favor of individuals, but an act which is absolutely null –in administrative level– cannot create rights.
>
> The fundamental consequence of this principle is that the revocation or suspension of effects of an administrative act creating or declaring individual rights in a way not authorized by the legal order, gives such individuals the right to be compensated for harm and damages caused by the revocation or suspension of the effects of the act."[91]

C. Principles on the revocation of administrative acts due to reasons of illegality

When an administrative act infringes the legal order but does not create individual rights, then it can be revoked at any time, regardless of the seriousness of the flaw that affects its validity. On the contrary, as stated above, administrative acts that are final and generate subjective rights or legitimate interests, can be revoked only if the

89 *Idem* p. 637.

90 *Idem*.

91 See Decision N° 01033 of the Political-Administrative Chamber of the Supreme Tribunal of Justice of May 11, 2000 (Case of *Aldo Ferro García v. la marca comercial KISS*), available at http://www.tsj.gov.ve/decisiones/spa/Mayo/01033-110500-13168.htm.

illegality that affects them also makes it subject to absolute nullity.[92] And if the irregularity incurred by the Administration is a cause only for annulment (relative nullity) of the act, then when it becomes final, revocation cannot take place, because it would harm the rights of the individuals.

Thus, administrative acts that are final and create individual rights can only be revoked if they are flawed by a cause of absolute nullity, upon compliance with the formalities of due process. As for the rest, the general principles of self-tutelage pursuant to the Articles 81 to 83 of the Organic Law on Administrative Procedures that regulate the power of the Administration to review, amend and revoke its acts, apply:

First, administrative acts that do not create individual rights can be revoked at any time, in whole or in part, by the same authority issuing them or by the respective superior authority (Article 82). It is irrelevant whether the act is affected by any ground for relative or absolute nullity, and the Public Administration can exercise its power of self-tutelage to correct, validate or revoke it, because there is no direct effect on any individual rights or interests.

Second, as for acts that create individual rights, the power of self-tutelage is restricted, precisely to protect those subjective rights or legitimate interests already created; in those cases, the Public Administration would be able to revoke only administrative acts that are subject to absolute nullity (Article 83).

The Political-Administrative Chamber of the Supreme Tribunal of Justice has discussed the matter in judgment dated May 11, 2000, stating:

> "Although Article 83 of the Organic Law on Administrative Procedures provides the possibility to review any time by petition or its own initiative, administrative acts, such power must be exercised if and only if some of the flaws of absolute nullity pursuant to Article 19 of the Organic Law on Administrative Procedures are detected." [93]

And such Political-Administrative Chamber further concluded, in the same judgment that:

> "... in the first place, the stability of administrative acts is always traduced in a finalist essence to the legal framework, both for the validity of the act and legal safety of the individuals, and in the second place, the Administration can and must, at any time, declare null and void such acts that are contrary to law when affected by absolutely nullity; without prejudice that it may also do so with such acts that are relatively null but did not create individual rights."[94]

---

92 See, in general, on the nullity of administrative acts, Allan R. Brewer-Carías, "Comentarios sobre las nulidades de los actos administrativos," in *Revista de Derecho Público*, N° 1, Caracas 1980, pp. 45-50. The jurisprudence on the matter can be consulted in Allan R. Brewer-Carías, *Jurisprudencia de la Corte Suprema de Justicia 1930-1974 y Estudios de Derecho Administrativo*, Vol. III, Caracas 1976, p. 348 ff.; Caterina Balasso Tejera, *Jurisprudencia sobre los Actos Administrativos*, Caracas 2003, pp. 796-800.

93 See Decision N° 01033 of the Political-Administrative Chamber of the Supreme Tribunal of Justice of May 11, 2000 of May 11, 2000 (Case of *Aldo Ferro García v. la marca comercial KISS*), available at http://www.tsj.gov.ve/decisiones/spa/Mayo/01033-110500-13168.htm.

94 *Idem.*

D. The absolute nullity vices of administrative acts

It results from the aforementioned that the distinction among flaws of absolute or relative nullity is essential to understanding the limitations of the Administration's self-review powers. Like the Political-Administrative Chamber of the former Supreme Court of Justice use to point out (in the leading and already cited pronouncement dated July 26, 1984 (Case: *Despacho Los Teques*):

> "Long before the Organic Law on Administrative Procedures was sanctioned, the precedents of this Court had taken on the doctrinal thesis that distinguishes the cases of absolute or radical nullity from the cases of relative nullity or annulment, in relation to those situations of unlawfulness of administrative acts. In that sense we can mention a judgment of the former Federal and Cassation Court, in Federal Chamber, dated Dec-11-1935, in which the tribunal clearly assumed such distinction and ... indicated that '...radical nullity or the inexistence of an act does not disappear with time, nor by any act of confirming, ratifying or willful completion, since inexistence amounts to nothing, not being, and over that there is no human possibility to create anything....' (*omissis*)
>
> This jurisprudential situation was reflected in the administrative law doctrine. Thus, we find that two qualified Venezuelan scholars of this discipline, as are Eloy Lares Martínez and Allan Brewer Carías, revealed with amplitude the difference among both situations and their legal consequences, in their works published prior to the passing of the cited Organic Law."[95]

Now, in Venezuela, the principle is that absolute nullity of administrative acts only occurs in the events expressly listed by Article 19 of the Organic Law on Administrative Procedures. In all other situations the acts are only considered subject to annulment (Article 20). Those flaws of absolute nullity are described as the more serious consequences of flawed administrative acts, and prevent these acts from having any effects of any kind, as the act, deemed absolutely null, cannot be understood as ever issued. Consequently, doctrine speaks in these situations about flaws of public order, and sometimes qualifies administrative acts that absolutely null and void as non-existent.

In any event, since administrative acts that are absolutely null and void cannot validly create individual rights, Article 83 of the Organic Law on Administrative Procedures provides that "[t]he Administration can, at any time, ex officio or upon petition, recognize the absolute nullity of the acts issued by her." Therefore, administrative acts affected by a flaw of absolute nullity can be revoked at any time, even when their purpose was to create rights within the legal sphere of an individual, since such right is not considered to be validly acquired as it arises from an administrative act that is affected by one of the serious flaws for absolute nullity.

---

95 See *Revista de Derecho Público*, N° 19, Editorial Jurídica Venezolana, Caracas 1984, pp. 130-132. See also Allan R. Brewer-Carías and Luis Ortiz-Álvarez, *Las Grandes Decisiones de la Jurisprudencia Contencioso Administrativa (1961-1996)*, Editorial Jurídica Venezolana, Caracas 1994, pp. 610-616; Caterina Balasso Tejera, *Jurisprudencia sobre los Actos Administrativos (1980-1993), loc. cit.*, p. 853 ff.

E. Absolute nullity cases in the Organic Law on Administrative Procedures

Following the trend of other Latin American administrative procure laws,[96] Venezuela's the Organic Law on Administrative Procedures also assumed the system of *numerus clausus* listing the set of circumstances under which administrative acts are to be considered absolutely null and void. Article 19 of the Law provides that "Acts by the Administration are absolutely null" in the following situations:

1. When it is so expressly determined by a constitutional or legal provision;

2. When they resolve a situation previously decided as final that created individual rights, except as expressly authorized by law.

3. When implementation of its content is illegal or impossible; and

4. When the authorities issuing the act were manifestly incompetent, or when acting in the complete and absolute absence of established legal procedure.

Pursuant to such provision, then, absolute nullity accrues only in the circumstances listed, namely: In the *first place*, an act would be flawed with absolute nullity *when it so expressly provided by a constitutional* or legal provision (Article 19.1). As such, in the first situation listed, either the Constitution or a Statute must expressly and specifically provide that the consequence of the violation of a given provision is absolute nullity, as it happens for example, when acts violate constitutional rights and guarantees or when acts are dictated by a party usurping public authority or functions. In such situations, Articles 25 and 138 of the Constitution expressly provide that acts that violate or infringe constitutional rights or guarantees or that are dictated usurping public authority or functions, or issued as a result of the direct or indirect threat of force, are all null and void. This nullity prescribed in constitutional provisions is doubtless an absolute nullity, and the acts so affected are therefore without legal effect. Special laws, on the other hand, have similar provisions whereby they prescribe that certain acts contrary to them are null and void. This is the case, for instance, of the Organic Law on Land Use Planning, when providing that "authorizations for land use given in violation of the plans are null" (Article 66). The nullity established in these cases would also be an absolute nullity.

In the *second place*, another situation of absolute nullity, pursuant to Article 19.2 of the Organic Law on Administrative Procedures, is when a given administrative act violates administrative *res judicata*. As the provision states: "if and when they resolve a previous case that was decided as final and that created individual rights, unless expressly authorized by Law. As such, the act revoking a previous final administrative act that created or declared individual rights is absolutely null, except when that revocation is expressly authorized by law.

The *third* situation of absolute nullity provided for by Article 19.3 of the Law, is a flaw in the content, when completion or implementation of the content of a given administrative act is impossible or illegal.

---

96 See Allan R. Brewer-Carías, *Principios del Procedimiento Administrativo en América Latina*, Ed. Lexis, Bogotá 2003, pp. 246-251.

And in the *fourth place,* Article 19.4 provides for the flaw of manifest incompetence, with respect to which the former Supreme Court of Justice, in a pronouncement issued on October 19, 1989, stated that it encompassed three situations, namely, "the so-called usurpation of authority, usurpation of public functions, and exceeding one's powers,"[97] stating the following criteria:

> "Usurpation of authority occurs when a resolution is dictated by somebody who has not been invested with absolutely any powers of public office. This flaw is sanctioned by absolute nullity of the resolution, pursuant to Article 119 of the National Constitution.
>
> Usurpation of public functions includes the situation when a determined administrative body with public powers exercises public powers that are attributed to a different Branch of the Government.
>
> Finally exceeding one's authority basically consists of the performance by an administrative authority of an action for which it has no express legal jurisdiction.
>
> All resolutions dictated by an incompetent authority are flawed. However, the flaw of incompetence attached thereto does not necessarily cause the absolute nullity of the resolution, as pursuant to the terms of Ordinal N° 4 of Article 19, the incompetence must be manifest. Therefore, if the incompetence is 'manifest,' namely notorious and obvious, so that without an excessive interpretative effort it is possible to realize that another entity is the one authorized to issue it, or when it can be determined that the entity issuing the resolution was not authorized to do so, then that resolution would be absolutely null (Ordinal N° 4, Article 19 of the Organic Administrative Procedures Act). If the incompetence is not manifest, then it would be subject to relative nullity (Article 20, ejusdem).
>
> In summary, it can be said that usurpation of authority determines the absolute nullity of the resolution, pursuant to the terms of Article 119 of the National Constitution; however, usurpation of public functions and exceeding one's powers do not always cause absolute nullity of the issued act, since that will depend on the notoriety or obviousness of the impersonation of the action."[98].

In the *fifth place*, we have the flaw of complete and absolute absence of the legally prescribed procedure (Art. 19.4 of the same the Organic Law on Administrative Procedures).

Only these five circumstances cited lead to absolute nullity and no other flaw of administrative acts can result in absolute nullity, and therefore, to the possibility of

---

97 See Allan R. Brewer-Carías, "Consideraciones sobre la ilegalidad de los actos administrativos en el derecho venezolano," in *Revista de Administración Pública*, Instituto de Estudios Políticos, N° 43, Madrid 1964, pp. 427-456, and in *Revista del Colegio de Abogados del Distrito Federal*, N° 127-128, Caracas January-December 1964, pp. 19-61.

98 See Decision of the Political-Administrative Chamber of October 19, 1989, in *Revista de Derecho Público*, N° 40, Caracas 1989, pp. 85-86, and in Caterina Balasso Tejera, *Jurisprudencia sobre Actos Administrativos*, *op cit.*, p. 656.

the act so flawed in being revoked. As the Political and Administrative Chamber of the Supreme Tribunal has stated:

> "The revocation powers of the administration are limited to those acts that do not create or declare rights in favor of individuals, since when the acts are final and create or declare individual rights, they cannot be revoked by the administration to their prejudice for reasons of merit or illegality and, exceptionally the Administration can declare their nullity but only for reasons of illegality, which is, if the act is flawed by absolute nullity, regardless if the individual benefited by it (by mistake) believes his rights have been infringed."[99]

F. The absolute nullity vice of administrative acts due to violation of administrative *res* judicata principle

As noted, before, pursuant to Article 19.2 of the Organic Law on Administrative Procedures, an administrative act is null and void when it violates administrative *res judicata*, namely, "when it resolves on a case previously decided as final that created individual rights, unless otherwise expressly authorized by law."

Therefore, the administrative act that revokes a previous final act that created or declared rights in favor of individual parties is absolutely null and void. As the Supreme Court of Justice has recognized when referring to the power of administrative self-tutelage, although this is regulated by Article 82 of the Organic Law on Administrative Procedures in the sense that administrative acts can be revoked at any time, in whole or in part, either by the same authority that issued the act or its superior, if and only if it does not create subjective rights or legitimate personal and direct interests for an individual, such Law:

> "... prohibited, in absolute terms, the possibility for the Administration to revoke administrative acts that created rights in favor of individuals, unless expressly authorized otherwise by law. For this reason, ordinal 2 of Article 19 of the cited Law [OLAP] punished as absolutely null those acts that resolved situations that had previously been decided as final, and that created rights in favor of individuals, unless otherwise expressly authorized by Law.
>
> Now, if there is no such express authorization, then the governing principle will be the general principle that if an act creating subjective rights for an individual is revoked, that act of revocation will be flawed by absolute nullity, which would imply the possibility of the Administration recognizing, and of the interested parties requesting, at any time, that the act be declared as null."[100]

---

99 See Decision N° 01033 of the Political-Administrative Chamber of the Supreme Tribunal of Justice of May 11, 2000 (Case of *Aldo Ferro García v. la marca comercial KISS*), available at http://www.tsj.gov.ve/decisiones/spa/Mayo/01033-110500-13168.htm.

100 See Decision N° 01033 of the Political-Administrative Chamber of the Supreme Tribunal of Justice of May 11, 2000 (Case of *Aldo Ferro García v. la marca comercial KISS*), available at http://www.tsj.gov.ve/decisiones/spa/Mayo/01033-110500-13168.htm.

G. The revocation of administrative acts due to non-compliance of obligations regarding their execution

Pursuant to the provisions of the Law, the power to revoke can be exercised by the Public Administration as a mechanism to impose sanctions when there is a failure by the party benefitting from the act, to comply with the obligations deriving from it.

This is particularly relevant in cases where there are administrative acts whose execution involves obligations to do or to give, on the part of the individual person or entity to which the act is directed. Those duties must be expressly set in the administrative act at hand, or in the statute or regulation that governs the issuance of the act. In any event, the precedents of the contentious administrative courts have recognized the validity of revocation of administrative acts for failure to comply with an obligation deriving from said acts, if and when all formalities of due process have been met. The Political-Administrative Chamber of the Supreme Court referred to this in its ruling dated July 13, 2005, stating:

> "...the criteria of this Chamber, according to which the right to defense must be granted to the holder of a public service concession, through the initiation of an administrative proceeding, when there is an attempt to revoke that concession for reasons of serious breach or failure; notwithstanding, this decision also shows that the collective interest that causes this type of contracting is preeminent over the individual interest of the Administration's co-contractor."[101]

In these cases where the revoking act is issued as a penalty for the failure to comply with some duties, the need for a previous administrative procedure is equally a required condition for the validity of the revoking act. Failure to comply is a factual situation that must be presumably alleged as the fault of the individual, who has to be granted throughout the procedure his right to be heard and to be presumed innocent, with all the guarantees secured by Article 49 of the Constitution, allowing him to defend himself as he deems appropriate to protect his rights and interests.

In the cases, for instance, provided in Article 98 of the Mining Law referring to the powers of the Administration to declare the termination (*caducidad*) of mining concessions, although not being a classical revocation of administrative acts due to the bilateral character of concessions, being analogous in its effect to the revocation of administrative acts due to non-compliance of obligations regarding their execution, it is also necessary, as aforementioned, to guarantee the due process rights of the concessionaire by means of an administrative procedure, and to assure the strict application by the Administration all the principles governing administrative actions.

6. The revocation of administrative acts and due process principles on administrative procedure

In any event, when there are indeed reasons to believe that an individual administrative act could be revoked by the Public Administration though the exercise of its powers, it must initiate and follow due course of an administrative

---

101 See Decision N° 4911 of the Political-Administrative Chamber of the Supreme Tribunal of Justice of July 13, 2005 (Case of *Juan Serva Cammarano*), available at http://www.tsj.gov.ve/decisiones/spa/Julio/04911-130705-2000-1115.htm.

procedure, where those benefitting from the administrative act whose validity is questioned and revocation proposed, can fully exercise his right to be heard and to a defense.

Administrative acts that revoke a previously issued administrative act even if the Administration considers it as null and void, is a decision that affects the subjective rights and interests of those that benefited from such administrative act, and therefore prior to such revocation an administrative proceeding must be followed in order to guarantee the right to a defense of such interested parties.

The jurisprudence in this matter has been uniform in demanding that cases regarding the revocation of administrative acts due to illegality must always have a previous administrative proceeding whereby the right of the interested parties to defend themselves is preserved. Only in cases of revocation of administrative acts and, in particular, mining concessions, due strictly to reasons of merit, i.e., for reasons of general interest, in which the interested party has the right to receive compensation, an administrative proceeding has been considered not to be mandatory due to the discretionary powers of the Administration in these matters. As such, for example, in cases of anticipated termination of concessions pursuant to Article 46(d) of the Organic Law on the Promotion of Private Investment through Concessions, since what has to be established is "...the early extinction of the concession by the Public Administration, for reasons of public interest...," the Political-Administrative Chamber in decision Nº 1.447 of August 8, 2007 has stated that this "is and must be the result of an administrative act, duly founded (as expressly required by Article 53 of the abovementioned Organic Law on the Promotion of Private Investment through Concessions)." Therefore, their control corresponds exclusively to the contentious administrative jurisdiction, adding that:

> "...in cases such as these where self-tutelage rules apply, in principle there is no obligation to open an administrative proceeding (to guarantee the rights of the individual involved) (sic). Given the degree of discretion allowed in this type of administrative decision (act) which must be sufficiently founded on fair appraisal and balance that the Administration must make between a 'primary interest' (represented by the general interest) and some 'secondary interests' (represented by public or private interests), that sometimes must be set aside for reasons of convenience, in favor of the primary interest. That is, the question of discretion basically imposes the value to be given to the public interest facing other interests (heterogeneous), which are also protected by the legal order. This mechanism in itself constitutes the guarantee offered by the Administration to its citizens in these cases, and it is for this reason that in the absence of a previous administrative proceeding, these acts are controlled and the rights of the individuals involved guaranteed by the courts. It is precisely this control of the contentious administrative jurisdiction and the due proportionality and conformity to the public interest that the Administration must respect, that guarantees for the citizens, the limit and equilibrium that the Constitution

establishes regarding the exercise of Public Power and that of rights and guarantees of individuals."[102]

The same criteria have been held by the Political-Administrative Chamber in all administrative decisions regarding mining concessions, when it has applied the principle of discretion, for example, to consider that they have expired (*caducado*), indicating that this occurs when the decision is adopted:

> "...based on a fair appraisal and balance between a primary interest –general interest– and a secondary interest –public or private–, which in some cases and for reasons of convenience must be set aside in favor of that primary interest. Therefore, the Chamber notes that in cases such as the one at hand, the Administration is not required to open an administrative proceeding for purposes of declaring the expiration of mining concessions due to the principle of discretion governing its actions, that must always be directed towards satisfying the general interest in achieving the common good as the first and overriding purpose of the social state of law and justice, provided in Article 2 of the Constitution."[103]

In any event and except in those cases of revocation founded on reasons of merit, where the right of the act's beneficiary is guaranteed through his right to compensation,[104] or in cases where the law grants a discretionary power to the Administration to make a decision, all other cases for revocation of an administrative act must be the result of a corresponding administrative proceeding, which implies that if this is not done, the act of revocation would be flawed for absolute nullity under the terms of Article 19.4 of the Organic Law on Administrative Procedures.

As the contentious administrative jurisprudence has affirmed even prior to the 1999 Constitution, due process, as described above,[105] constitutes an inviolable right in all degrees and stages of the proceeding, regardless of its nature, and expressly with regard to administrative proceedings.

---

102 See Decision N° 1447 of the Political-Administrative Chamber of the Supreme Tribunal of August 8, 2007, available at http://www.tsj.gov.ve/decisiones/spa/Agosto/01447-8807-2007-2004-0779.html.

103 See Decision N° 847 of the Political-Administrative Chamber of the Supreme Tribunal of Justice of July 17, 2008 (Case of *Minas San Miguel C.A.*), available at http://www.tsj.gov.ve/decisiones/spa/Julio/00847-17708-2008-2005-3529.html. The same criteria was applied in Decision N° 395 of the same Chamber of the Supreme Tribunal of Justice of March 25, 2009 (Case of *Unión Consolidada San Antonio*), available at http://www.tsj.gov.ve/deci-siones/spa/Marzo/00395-25309-2009-2005-5526.html.

104 Article 53 of the Organic Private Investment Promotion Act under the Plan of Concessions (*Official Gazette* N° 5.394 of October 25, 1999), by consecrating the power of the Administration to cancel the concession early for reasons of public interest, recognizes the right of the concession holder to receive comprehensive compensation.

105 See Decision N° 207 and 208 of the Political-Administrative Chamber of the Supreme Court of Justice of October 8, 1996, and of the First Contentious Administrative Court of May 15, 1996, in *Revista de Derecho Público*, N° 67-68, Editorial Jurídica Venezolana, Caracas 1996, p. 171, and in *Revista de Derecho Público*, N° 65-66, Editorial Jurídica Venezolana, Caracas 1996, p. 156.

IV. GENERAL PRINCIPLES REGARDING ACCESS TO ADMINISTRATIVE INFORMATION

On his first day in office (February 21, 2009), President Obama said, referring to the Government, that "For a long time now, there has been too much secrecy in this city," expressing that on the contrary, "Transparency and rule of law will be the touchstones of this presidency." He then ordered that: "Starting today every agency and department should know that this administration stands on the side not of those who seek to withhold information, but those who seek to make it known."[106] For such purposes that same day he issued two presidential Memoranda, one on the "Freedom of Information Act," and the other on "Transparency and Open Government."

Quoting Justice Louis Brandeis who referred to the "sunlight" as "the best of disinfectants," Obama ordered the Freedom of Information Act to be administered with a clear presumption "in favor of disclosure", in the sense that "in the face of doubt, openness prevails," so in general, "The Government should not keep information confidential." In the second Memorandum, the President affirmed that his "Administration is committed to creating an unprecedented level of openness in Government" considering that "openness will strengthen our democracy and promote efficiency and effectiveness in Government," adding that: "*Government should be transparent*. Transparency promotes accountability and provides information for citizens about what their Government is doing."[107]

This whole concept of transparency in Government responds to the political idea of the "the crystal house" image (*la maison de verre*), that after so many years of opacity began to be developed, associated with the symbolism of the visible and accessible, in contrast to what is closed, mysterious, inaccessible or inexplicable; being transparency related to the sense of tranquility and serenity that results from what can be dominated or rationalized, in contrast to the anguish and perturbation caused by what is mysterious or unknown.[108]

This concept of transparency has been one of the key elements that in the evolution of Public Administration has helped the transformation of the traditional Bureaucratic State into the current Democratic Administrative State of our times, more devoted to citizens than to the King or to the bureaucracy. That Bureaucratic State was the one characterized by Max Weber as an organization seeking "to increase the professional knowledge superiority of public officials precisely by means of secret and of the secrecy of their intentions." That is why, he said, bureaucratic governments, because of their tendency, are always "governments that excludes publicity."[109]

---

106 See speech at the swearing-in ceremony for Senior Officials of the Executive Office, February 21, 2009. See the report of Sheryl Gay Stolberg "On First Day, Obama Quickly Sets a New Tone", *The New York Times*, February 22, 2009, p. A1.

107 January 21, 2009. Presidencial Memoranda, in www.whitehouse.gov.

108 Jaime Rodríguez-Arana, "La transparencia en la Administración Pública," in *Revista Vasca de Administración Pública*, N° 42, Oñati 1995, p. 452.

109 Max Weber, *Economía y Sociedad*, Vol. II, Fondo de Cultura Económica, México 1969, p. 744.

On the contrary, in the contemporary world, openness and transparency are the rules, and that is why any governmental expression in this sense, as the one announced last month must always be welcomed, even in a country like the U.S., with a long tradition in these matters. As we all know, the U.S. was one of the first countries to approve legislation on transparency and access to public information in 1966, in the Freedom of Information Act. Before that year, since 1951 there existed in Finland a statute on access to public information ,[110] being the common trend of both legislative acts, that their enactment was due to legislative initiative provoked by legislative activism regarding the Executive to impose transparency policies, and in both cases, the legislation was promoted by the opposition parties.[111] Now, after more than forty years of application of such legislation, the same policy of transparency is defined again in the U.S. but at the initiative of the same Executive; a situation that contrast with the policy in Venezuela, where on the contrary, Public Administration during the past years (1999-2010) has been covering itself with an "iron roof."[112]

In contrast, for instance, in Mexico, in 2002, a Federal Law on Transparency and Access to Public Governmental Information[113] was sanctioned at the initiative of NGO's (Oaxaca Group, for instance) and based on a Draft submitted to the Congress by the Executive[114] (Fox Government), and most important, with the big difference that in this case, the legislation was devoted to guaranty the enforcement of a constitutional right incorporated in the Mexican Constitution in 1977 through an amendment establishing the citizens' right to information.

The Mexican Constitution, in effect, in contrast with the U. S. Constitution where no fundamental right to have access to public information can be found, article 6 provides for the citizen's right to information that the "the State shall guaranty" (article 6). It was then based on this constitutional right and regarding public information, although 15 years later, that the Federal Law was approved having among its purposes to contribute to the democratization of Mexican Society and to

110 In 1766, a statute was passed in Sweden on the same subject of access to information.

111 Regarding the FIOA, its origin drives from the creation during the fifties of both Senate and Representative Commissions in order to resolve the lack of effective access to information according to the provisions of the 1946 Administrative Procedure Act whose provisions, although being very important at the time, were described by Representative John E. Moss, as part of the "bureaucratic theory" that allowed each public entity to decide the type of information considered convenient to reach the public (See Pierre-Francois Divier, "Etats-Unis L'Administration Transparente: L'accés des citoyens américains aux documents officiels," in *Revue du Droit Public et de la Science Politique en France et a l'étranger*, n° 1, Librairie Générale de Droit et de Jurisprudence, Paris 1975, p. 64 ; Miguel Revenga Sánches, *El imperio de la política. Seguridad nacional y secreto de Estado en el sistema constitucional norteamericano*, Ariel, Madrid 1995, p. 153). FOIA was later reformed in 1974 and 1976 in order to make it more effective. In the same years, after the *Watergate* and the *Pentagon Papers* scandals, two new statutes were sanctioned: the *Federal Privacy Act* and the *Federal Government in the Sunshine Act*. See James Michael, "Freedom of information in the United States," in *Public access to government-held information* (Norman Marsh Editor), Steven & Son LTD, London, 1987.

112 See for instante decision of the Constitutional Chamber of the Supreme Tribunal N° 745 of July 15, 2010 (Case *Asociación Civil Espacio Público*), available at Véase en http://www.tsj.gov.ve/decisio-nes/scon/Julio/745-15710-2010-09-1003.html.

113 Some articles of the Law were reformed in 2006.

114 By the *Ministro de Gobernación* Santiago Creel, of the Fox Administration.

guaranty the effective enforcement of the rule of law; to guaranty the right of everybody to have access to information; to seek for the transparency of public service through the diffusion of public information; to reinforce the possibility for public accountability; and to protect personal data on public registries (article 6).

In addition, and in order to broaden the scope of its protection, the Federal Law expressly provided that the right to have access to public information was to be interpreted not only in conformity with the Constitution, but also with the provisions of the Universal Declaration of Human Rights; the International Covenant on Civil and Political Rights; the American Convention on Human Rights; the Convention on the elimination of any kind of discrimination against women, and the other international instruments ratified by México (article 6); and in addition, to the interpretation given to those instruments by the specialized international institutions, referring to the Inter American Commission on Human Rights and to the Inter American Court on Human Rights.[115]

With this legislation a transparency and openness policy began to be implemented in Mexico in order to resolve the never-ending conflict between "secrecy" and "openness" that all Public Administrations have experienced. A conflict that has existed not only in the cases of atavistic secrecy situations that for so many years have been the rule, and not the exception, in many of the Latin American Public Administrations, but also, in cases of circumstantial secrecies situations that have developed for instance, as a consequence of the Post War spy syndrome that marked the Cold War era, or of the Post 9/11 War against Terror.[116]

In order to impose transparency and to guaranty the right to have access to public information, the 2002 Mexican Federal Transparency Law also defined the presumption in favor of publicity, providing that the interpretation of its provisions

---

115 This very important declaration of subjection to international rules and principles, inherent to a democratic government, contrasts with the situation in other countries like Venezuela (2013), where unfortunately, the Supreme Tribunal of Justice not only has ruled that on matter of freedom of expression the Recommendations of the Inter American Commission are not obligatory in the country, but that the decisions themselves of the Inter American Court on Human Rights are non enforceable in the country. This was decided last December 2008, regarding the decision of the Inter-American Court of Human Rights, on August 5th, 2008, issued in the *Apitz Barbera y otros ("Corte Primera de lo Contencioso Administrativo") vs. Venezuela* Case, in which the Court ruled that the Venezuelan State had violated the judicial guaranties of various dismissed judges established in the American Convention of Human Rights, condemning the State to pay them due compensation, to reinstate them to a similar position in the Judiciary, and to publish part of the decision in Venezuelan newspapers (See decision on Excepción Preliminar, Fondo, Reparaciones y Costas, Serie C Nº 182, in www.corteidh.or.cr). Nonetheless, on December 12, 2008, the Constitutional Chamber of the Supreme Tribunal of Venezuela issued the decision Nº 1939, (Expediente: 08-1572), Case: *Abogados Gustavo Álvarez Arias y otros*, declaring that the aforementioned Inter American Court on Human Rights decision of August 5, 2008, was non enforceable (*inejecutable*) in Venezuela, asking the Executive to denounce the American Convention of Human Rights, and accusing the Inter American Court of having usurped powers of the Supreme Tribunal.

116 That is why the new Memoranda of President Obama have been considered as the reversal of the post 9/11 policy that makes it easier for the government agencies to deny requests for records under the Freedom of Information Act. See the report of Sheryl Gay Stolberg "On First Day, Obama Quickly Sets a New Tone", *The New York Times*, February 22, 2009, p. A1.

must be done in favor of the "principle of greatest publicity" in public entities, that is, contrary to secrecy.

But as has always happened with these legislations, the sole declarations of principles they contain do not resolve the conflict between secrecy and openness, particularly because of the broad sort of exceptions also established in the statutes, directly declaring some information as confidential, and leaving in the hands of the Head of Public Administration Offices (article 16) the power to declare other information as "reserved." In all these cases, the information remains out of the reach of citizens, and regarding it, no right to access of information can then effectively exist.

The problem in the Mexican Law does not refer to the information that its Article 18 considers as "confidential," referring to the one filed by individuals before Public Administration with their petition, and to their personal data contained in registers that require their consent in order to be released or distributed.[117] The problem exists regarding the power that the statute assigns to the head officials of all public entities to classify certain information as reserved for a period of 12 years (article 15),[118] regarding information whose diffusion could compromise national security, public security or national defense; that could affect the direction of international negotiations or relations; that could harm the financial, economic or monetary stability of the country; that could place personal life, security and health in danger; and that could seriously affect law enforcement activities, crime prevention, justice, tax collection, migration control, and procedural strategies in judicial or administrative proceedings before its final resolution (article 15).

It is true that the Law expressly excludes from this broad scope of reserved information those that are related to grave violations of human rights and crimes against humanity (article 14), but undoubtedly, the broad wording used in the enumeration for the classification of information as reserved could lead to contradict the same openness purposes of the Law.

Anyway, in order to avoid this distortion and to control the possible deviations of its application, the Law has created a Federal Institute of Access to Public Information in charge of eventually deciding on the rejection of petitions filed seeking access to information, and for the protection of personal data existing in public entities archives (article 34). The Law, in order to guaranty the right to petition for information, has also established a precise term of 20 days for the official response to be issued; and most importantly, has provided for the presumption of an "affirmative response" ("positive silence") by considering the petition as granted once the term for response has elapsed without express decision. In this regard, the Transparency Law has changed in this field the general rule established in the 1994 Federal Law on Administrative Procedures that in a contrary sense established the general presumption of "negative response" in the absence of a timely answer to petitions, considering in such cases, as its denial (article 17).

Regarding the problem of the exemptions to the right to information and to the right to have access to information, it can be considered as aggravated in the Law,

117 Regarding personal information contained in public registries, it is not considered as confidential.

118 In the U.S. FIAO, the term is of 25 years.

because in addition to all those cases in which the authorities can classify certain information as reserved, the text of the Law has also directly classified other information as such, without the need for any further authority declaration. This refers to information that has already been declared in a previous statute as confidential, like the commercial, industrial, fiscal, banking or trust secrets. Also, it refers to preliminary investigation's files; to the files of judicial or administrative procedures not yet definitively decided; to public official liability procedures not yet definitively decided; and to opinions, suggestions or points of view given by public officials in all deliberative procedures until a definitive decision is adopted. All these exceptions, unfortunately, are an open door to more secrecy (article 14).

But in any case, the sanctioning of a statute like the 2002 Federal Law on Transparency and access to governmental public information and its enforcement, for anybody that has been involved in Latin American Public Administration reform processes, more than a reform, it can be considered as the beginning of an administrative revolution that although will need many years in order to produce definitive results, has already produced an important sense of openness in Public Administration in Mexico, which can even be perceived in news media reports in a way never before imagined.

The result of this process has also been the approval in 2007 of a new constitutional amendment regarding the same article 6 of the Constitution in order to add to the initial declaration of the right to information that the State must guaranty, also with constitutional rank the following principles that all public entities and agencies must follow for such purposes. In the first place, the aforementioned presumption of publicity, that is, the principle that all information in possession of any authority or public entity is to be considered public, being the exception to the rule, its temporal declaration as reserved based on public interest motives. That is why, in the interpretation of the constitutional right, the 2002 Federal Law provides for the principle that "greatest publicity must always prevail." This is also the same presumption in favor of disclosure defined in President Obama's Memorandum of January 21, 2009, so in case of doubt, openness must prevail; but with the great difference that in México, it is now a provision of the Constitution, as an entrenched right of the people, and not just an Executive policy expressed regarding the application of a statute that can be changed by other governments, as has happened in the past.

The other principles included in the 2007 Mexican constitutional reform amendment, already developed in the Federal Law, are the express provision of everybody's right to have information related to private life and personal data duly protected; and the right to have cost-free access to public information, to personal data and to its rectification. For such purpose, legislation must provide for the adequate means in order to guaranty access to information and also, simple and prompt review procedures before impartial, autonomous and specialized entities.

The 2002 Mexican legislation was not the first statute on these matters in Latin America. In Colombia, in 1985, the Law N° 57 on publicity of official and administrative documents was sanctioned and in January of 2002, before the Mexican Law, in Panama was sanctioned the Law N° 6 on provisions for transparency in public management and on habeas data action. Beside these cases, the fact is that in all the other laws passed in Latin America in the past six years, the

Mexican Federal Law has had a definitive influence in their drafting when referring to transparency and to the right of access to public information.[119] It has been the case of the statutes approved Peru in 2003 (Law N° 27806 on Transparency and access to public information); in Ecuador in 2004 (Organic Law on Transparency and access to public information), and the same year in Dominican Republic (General Law N° 200-04 on the Free access to public information); in Honduras in 2006 (Law of Transparency and access to public information); in Nicaragua in 2007 (Law N° 621-2007 of access to information); and in Chile (Law on Transparency and access to information), in Guatemala (Law on access to public information), and in Uruguay (Law N° 18381 on access to public information and on the *amparo informativo*), the same year 2008.

All these Laws in order to promote transparency of administrative functions in all public entities establish the right of access to information as a fundamental right of all persons; expressly presume that all information produced by public entities is to be considered public, except regarding confidential documents or those declared as reserved; almost all establish the affirmative response presumption in the absence of express answer to petition on information; they oblige public entities to publicize the information concerning their organization or functioning. Nonetheless, in many of these laws, and departing from the Mexican precedent, specific provisions are established for the judicial protection of the right to have access to information, also setting forth for the so-called habeas data action, which is a sort of *amparo informativo* as it is called in the Uruguayan Law.

In effect, even though Mexico is the country of birth of the amparo action, in this matter of the right to have access to information, the Mexican regime in general term when compared with the other Latin American provisions, failed to guaranty in the Constitution and in the Law the habeas data action, that is, the specific judicial mean designed to guaranty the protection of the information rights without the need to previously exhaust any administrative review recourses. This specific habeas data action, originally established for the protection of personal data and progressively extended for the protection of the right to have access to public information, has been established in the Constitutions of Argentina, Brazil, Ecuador, Paraguay, Peru and Venezuela, in addition to the other judicial means for the protection of human rights like the amparo and the habeas corpus actions. In other countries such recourse has been established by statute (Panamá, Uruguay).

On this matter of judicial protection, the Federal Law in Mexico has only established the possibility to have access to the Judiciary (article 59) in order to challenge the definitive decisions of the Federal Institute of Access to Public Information through a judicial review of administrative action procedure or through an amparo suit; when those decisions are adopted resolving revision administrative recourses filed before it against the final decisions of the corresponding administrative entities denying information (article 49). That is, following the U.S. trend, the possibility to have access to judicial protection of the right to have access to public information in Mexico, is subjected to the previous exhaustion of administrative recourses and decisions, *first,* within the corresponding Public

119 The Federal law also had a significant importance in the drafting of the States' legislation.

Administration that has the information and denies it, and *second,* before the Federal Institute of Access to Public Information.

This is an important pattern of the Mexican system that contrast with other Latin American legislation, where the access to judicial protection of the right to have access to public information is immediate and direct, without the need to previously exhaust any administrative recourses before Public Administration of Independent Agencies.

It is the case, for instance, of the 2002 Law on Transparency and Access to information of Panamá, promulgated before the Mexican Law, in which the action of habeas data was established in order to guaranty the right of every person to have access to public information as established in the law, in the cases in which the public official responsible for the registry, the archive or the data bank containing the requested information or personal data, denies the information or provides it in an insufficient or inexact way (article 17). In such cases, a habeas data action can be filed before the same Superior Courts competent to decide in general on matters of amparo actions, when the action refers to public officials that are responsible of municipal or provincial registries or archives. In case of public officials with jurisdiction over more than two provinces or in the whole Republic, the competent court to decide the habeas data action is the Supreme Court of Justice (article 18).

This habeas data action must be decided in a procedure governed by the same rules of the action of amparo, without formalities and without the need of attorney's assistance.

In this same sense, the last of the Latin American Laws referred to the right to have access to public information, which is the Uruguayan 2008 Law, also has provided for a special judicial "action of access to information" (*amparo informativo*) that everybody has in order to have his right to have access to information fully guaranteed. This action can be filed by any interested person of his representatives (article 24) against any public official obliged by the Law, when he denies giving the requested information or the information is not released in the terms established in the Law. The competent courts to decide the action are in general the First Instance courts with jurisdiction in civil matters or in contentious administrative matters (article 23), and the procedure to be applied is established in the same Law in a very expeditious way (article 25) and without judicial procedural incidents (article 30), providing for a public hearing that must take place within the following three days under the direction of the court, in which the parties must argue their claims and file the corresponding proofs. The final decision must be issued within the next twenty-four hours (article 26). In any case, the courts have broad powers to adopt the needed provisional measures in order to protect the right or freedom claimed to have been violated (article 27). The final judicial decision must determine what is needed to be done in order to guaranty the right to have access to public information, within a term that most not exceed more than 15 days (Article 28). These decisions are subjected to appeal and to a second instance review (articles 29).

In the case of Ecuador, where also a Law Organic Law on Transparency and access to public information was passed in 2004, since 1997, the Constitutional Judicial Review Law, in addition to the habeas corpus and amparo actions for the protection of human right, has established the action of habeas data, specifically in order to guaranty any person the right to have access to information related to the claimant or his properties, and to know the use and purpose of the data (article 34). The habeas data recourse that can be filed before any court or tribunal (article 37) has the purpose of seeking from the corresponding entity to give the information in a complete, clear and certain way; to obtain the rectification or suppression of information and to avoid its disclosure to third parties; and to obtain copies and verification of the correction or suppression of information (article 35). Nonetheless, the habeas data action will not proceed when professional secrecy could be affected; when justice can be obstructed; and in cases of reserved documents because national security reasons (article 36). The procedure in the habeas data recourse also imposes the need for the court to convene for a public hearing that must take place in a term of 8 days, and the final decision must be adopted in the following two days (article 38). The defendant must give the information within the next eight days, with an explanation of it (article 39), and the decision is subjected to appeal before the Constitutional Tribunal (article 42). But in addition to this habeas data action, in Ecuador, the 2004 Organic Law on Transparency and access to public information specifically provides for a "recourse for access to information," established without prejudice of the amparo action in order to judicially guaranty the right to have access to public information (article 22). This recourse can be filed by anybody whose request for any kind of information established in the Law has been tacitly or expressly denied, whether by the express rejection of the request, of when receiving incomplete, altered or false information, including cases in which the rejection of information is based in the reserved or confidential character of the requested information. The recourse can be directly filed before any first instance court or tribunal of the domicile of the public official having the information, and the court within the following 24 hours must also convene for a public hearing on the matter. The final decision must be issued in no more than two days after the hearing, even if the public official that has the requested information do not show up to the hearing. The requested information must be given to the court within the following eight days, and in case of reserved or confidential information that fact must be proved. When the court finds that this qualification is correct it must confirm the denial of the information requested. In contrary case the court must order the authority to release the information in 24 hours, and this decision can by appealed before the Constitutional Tribunal when the public official sustains the confidentiality or reserved character of the information. In this case, the Ecuadorian Law also assigns the competent courts broad powers to adopt preliminary measures in cases in which the information could be at risk of occultation, disappearance or destruction.

In Peru, the matter of the protection of the right to have access to information is not established in the 2003 Law N° 27806 on Transparency and access to public information, but in the 2004 General Code on Constitutional Procedure, in which in addition to the actions of amparo and of habeas corpus, the process of habeas data has been also provided. This constitutional process has been established in particular for the protection of the constitutional rights to have access to information and for the personal of familiar intimacy to be protected (article 2, 5 and 6), and in particular, in order to guaranty the access to all information gathered by public entities whatever could be its form of expression, and to know, update, include, suppress or rectify information or data referred to the claimant gathered in any form in public or private institutions giving services of access to third parties. This right includes the possibility to ask for the suppression of to impede the rendering of sensible or private character information that could affect constitutional rights (article 61). The habeas data action can only be filed once the interested person has made the request before the corresponding authority and the same has been rejected, or when filed the request, the authority has not given a response in a term of 10 days or 2 days according to the claimed right (article 62). The corresponding court have the power to request from the defendant all the information it deem necessary (article 63), and the procedure to be applicable is the same established in the Code for the action of amparo, except regarding the need for an attorney that in this case is facultative (article 65).

In addition, the habeas data recourse has been established only for the protection of personal data guarantying the right to have access to official records or data bank that contain it and the rights to rectify or correct such information, in the 1988 Constitution of Brazil, which was the first Latin American country to have constitutionalized this recourse (Article 5, LXXII); in the Constitution of Argentina (1994 Reform) (article 43); and in the 1992 Constitution of Paraguay (article 135). It is also the case of Venezuela where the 1999 Constitution provides for the action of habeas data, in order to guaranty the peoples' right to have access to the information and data concerning themselves contained in official or private registries or data banks, as well as to know about the use made of that information and about its purpose, and to petition before the competent court for its updating, rectification or destruction in cases of erroneous records or when it unlawfully affects the petitioner's rights (Article 28). The same provision of the Constitution, guaranties the right of everybody to have access to documents of any nature containing information of interest to communities or group of persons. The foregoing is established without prejudice to the confidentiality of sources from which information is received by journalists, or to secrecy in other professions as may be determined by law. Nonetheless, the lack of legislative developments regarding this habeas data action within the authoritarian government that has developed in the country during that past decade (1999-2009) have reduced the scope of this action; having the Constitutional Chamber of the Supreme Tribunal reserved for itself the decisions of the cases.

On the other hand, it must also be mentioned that the important step taken in Mexico in 1977 to guaranty the right to information and to have access to it in the text of the Constitution (article 6), has been followed only by some Latin American countries. This is the case of the 1988 Brazilian Constitution, which contains a declaration regarding the guaranty of "the right of everybody to have access to information" (article 5, XIV). In Colombia, the 1991 Constitution of Colombia only provides for the right to have access to public documents as a right of the opposition political parties (article 112), and in Peru, the Constitution of 2000 establishes the right of everybody to request form public entities without expressing any particular motive, the information needed, and to received it in the term established by law. Only information referred to privacy and those expressly established by law because of security reasons, are excluded; and the information services cannot render information that could affect personal or family intimacy (article 2, 5 and 6). In the case of the 1999 Venezuelan Constitution, the citizens' rights to be informed and to have access to administrative information is also expressed (articles 28 and 147). The Constitution, in effect, establishes the right of all citizens to be promptly and truly informed by Public Administration regarding the situation of the procedures in which they have direct interest, and to know about the definitive resolutions therein adopted; to be notified of administrative acts and to be informed on the course of the procedure (Article 147). In addition, the same constitutional provision also establishes the individual right of everybody to have access to administrative archives and registries, only subject to "acceptable limits imposed in a democratic society related to the national or foreign security, to criminal investigation, to the intimacy of private life, all according to the statutes regulating the matter of secret or confidential documents classification." The same article prohibits any previous censorship referring to public officials regarding the information they could give referring to matters under their responsibility.

Nonetheless, the most important aspects on this matter are that constitutional declarations of rights to transparency and to have access to public information, and its guaranty by means of statutes like all those that are in force in Latin America, although being a very important step towards the democratization of Public Administration, are not enough in order to guaranty its enforceability.

Other elements are indispensable for such purpose, like for instance, the need for a real configuration of a professional, stable and effective Civil Service that could adopt the principle of transparency as one of it owns values. A system of public servants that is subjected to political changes and at the mercy of the changes of governments, or to the political parties' will, or to the will of a Head of State, is completely incompatible with the principle of public presumption of information and of free access, particularly because, on the contrary, secrecy is the principle that can guaranty their survival.

On the other hand, in order to really guaranty the right to information, the previous existence of such information is also indispensable, in the sense that it must be previously gathered in good and safe organized public registries and archives. A Public Administration without memory regarding its own information, a situation that exists in many of our countries where no culture of preserving information exists or in which a deliberate policy of destruction of historic documents prevail, citizens cannot have a real guaranty to have access to information or to be informed, except regarding what the public official in charge wants to inform or can inform.

Another element is indispensable in order to guaranty the right to have access to public information, and it is the existence of a free press that can diffuse the cases of lack of transparency and that could claim for openness. In this regard, for instance, the progress made since the sixties in the U. S. in these matters, in addition to the Legislative activism, can undoubtedly be credited to the effective guaranty of the freedom of expression and of a free press that have helped and encouraged it. But of course, the media's right to inform is only one aspect of the matter, being the most important one the right of citizens to be informed, and not only what and when the press or other media wants to inform.

Without liberty of expression and freedom of press, no guaranty of the citizen's right to be informed and to have access to public information can be guaranteed,[120]

120 That is why, in the same way I considered that it was important to stress the significance of the first Executive decision adopted last month by President Obama on his first day in office, proclaiming the policy of Transparency and Openness in Government, it was also important to

and in fact no possibility exists for ordinary citizen to be inform about when for instance, the lack of transparency marks some governmental actions.

For instance, I began this notes by praising the announcements of President Obama in his Inauguration (February 2009) on matters of transparency and openness in Government which was informed to ordinary citizens through the press, but one month later, it was also possible for ordinary citizens to be aware of perhaps some retrocession in that policy, also informed by the press, like the state-secret argument made by a lawyer of the Justice Department before a U.S. Court of Appeal, in a very criticized case where serious allegations of torture had been made regarding the extraordinary rendition program designed by the previous Administration.[121] That is why, eventually, no possibility to claim for transparency could be really achieved without a free press; and free press can only exist in democracies. That is why transparency and openness in Government are democratic policies, designed to strengthen the democratization of Public Administration, that are incompatible with authoritarian governments.

---

register the reaction of some reporters assailing the new Government that same day of lack of transparency, only because media photographers were not allowed to witness the second oath given the President that same day by the Chief Justice of the Supreme Court, a fact that, nonetheless, everybody was duly informed through an official photograph. The importance aspect resulting from that situation is that the right of everybody to be informed and to have access to public information cannot just be mistaken with the right of every news media to be present in any public act. The right to be informed is one thing and the right to search for information and to inform is another.

121 See John Schwartz, "Obama Backs Off A Reversal On Secrets," in *The New York Times*, February 10, 2009, pp. A12 and A16, and the Editorial on "Continuity of the Wrong Kind," in *The New York Times*, February 11, 2009, p. A30.

PART FOUR

PRINCIPLES OF ADMINISTRATIVE LAW RELATED TO PUBLIC CONTRACTS, PUBLIC INTEREST CONTRACTS AND ADMINISTRATIVE CONTRACTS

I. THE CONSTITUTIONAL REGIME OF PUBLIC CONTRACTS

1. Public interest contracts

The 1999 Constitution, in its Section Fourth of Chapter I "Fundamental regulations" of Title IV "Public Power," regulates the "Public Interest Contracts"[1] (Arts. 150-151) identifying as such, those entered into by public entities or bodies, that is, entities which in general terms are part of the public sector or of the "State." Consequently, being public interest contracts those entered by national, states or municipalities entities, they are classified in the Constitution as "national public interest contracts," "states public interest contracts" or "municipal public interest contracts" (Article 150).

The Constitution has completed the process of constitutionalization of the public contracts' regime,[2] also regulating some "inter administrative public contracts," that is, those signed between public entities. This is the case of the inter-governmental contracts entered by the Republic and the States or between the States, or entered by the States and the Municipalities, particularly as consequence of the process of

---

1 See among many other works regarding the tradicional notion of "national public interest contracts:" Eloy Lares Martínez, "Contratos de interés nacional," in *Libro Homenaje al Profesor Antonio Moles Caubet,* Tomo I, Caracas, UCV, 1981, p. 117; *José Melich Orsini,* "La Noción de contrato de interés público," in *Revista de Derecho Público n° 7, Caracas, 1981, p. 61;* Allan R. Brewer-Carías, "Los contratos de interés público nacional y su aprobación legislativa" *in Revista de Derecho Público,* N° 11, Caracas, 1982, pp. 40-54; *Gonzalo Pérez Luciani,* "Contratos de interés nacional, contratos de interés público y contratos de empréstito público," *in Libro Homenaje al Doctor Eloy Lares Martínez, Tomo I, Caracas, 1984, p. 103; and* Jesús Caballero Ortiz, "Los contratos administrativos, los contratos de interés público y los contratos de interés nacional en la Constitución de 1999," *in Estudios de Derecho Administrativo: Libro Homenaje a la Universidad Central de Venezuela,* Volumen I, Imprenta Nacional, Caracas, 2001, pp. 139-154.

2 See Allan R. Brewer-Carías, "Algunos aspectos del proceso de constitucionalización del Derecho administrativo en Venezuela", in *V Jornadas internacionales de Derecho Administrativo Allan Randolph Brewer Carías, Los requisitos y vicios de los actos administrativos,* (FUNEDA), Caracas 2000, pp 21 a 37.

transfer of competencies derived from the decentralization process (Article 170).[3] The 1999 Constitution provides, in this regards, for contracts to be entered between the States and the Municipalities, for the transfer of services and competencies to them (Article 165); and for contracts that can be signed by the Municipalities (*mancomunidades*) in order to develop activities together (Article 170). The Constitution also has provisions regarding contracts signed between the States and the Municipalities with the organized community for the transfer of services to them (Article 184).

The Constitution also establishes some prohibitions regarding public contracts, for instance, on territorial matters, due to the constitutional principle that "the national territory could never be ceded, trespassed, leased or in any way sold, even temporally or partially to Foreign States or international law entities" (Article 13). Consequently, no public contract can be entered for such purpose, being the only constitutional exception on this regard referred to the land needed for foreign embassies (Article 13).

These contractual prohibitions also refer to all the cases of public domain declared in the Constitution, regarding which the State cannot sign any contracts that could signify the loss of such character. It occurs with the subsoil, mines and hydrocarbons (Article 12); with the maritime coast (Article 12); with all waters (Article 304); with war weapons (Article 324); and with the shares of Petróleos de Venezuela S.A., the State own oil company (Article 303), all considered in the constitution as public domain. Nonetheless, regarding natural resources and their exploitation, the Constitution establishes the possibility for the State to subscribe temporal concession contracts with private parties (Article 113), with the express prohibition to sign for mines concessions for indefinite term (Article 156,16). Regarding immoveable property of public entities, some of those lands have also a constitutional prohibition to be sold, as is the case of national land located on islands (Article 13) and municipal lands in urban areas that can only be sold for urban development (Article 181).

The same restriction regarding public contracts exists in all the cases in which the State has reserved by statute some services, exploitations or industries for national interest motives (Article 302), as is the case of the oil industry, the iron mining industry, and the natural gas industry all nationalized since 1975,[4] and the cement, and steel industries nationalized in 2008.[5] This implies, for instance, regarding the oil industry, that since the sanctioning of the 2001 Organic Law on Hydrocarbons,[6] the only way in which the private companies can participate in the exploitation of

---

3 Organic Law on Decentralization, Delimitation and Transfer of attributions among public entities. *Official Gazette* N° 39 140 del 17 de marzo de 2009.

4 Organic Law reserving the State the Industry and Commerce of Hydrocarbon, *Official Gazette* N° 35.754 de 17-07-75. See *Régimen jurídico de las Nacionalizaciones en Venezuela, Homenaje del Instituto de Derecho Público al Profesor Antonio Moles Caubet*, Archivo de Derecho Público y Ciencias de la Administración, Vol. VIII (1972-1979), Instituto de Derecho Público, Universidad Central de Venezuela, Caracas, 1981.

5 See in Antonio Canova González, Luis Alfonso Herrera Orellana, and Karina Anzola Spadaro, *¿Expropiaciones o vías de hecho? (La degradación continuada del derecho fundamental de propiedad en la Venezuela actual*," Funeda, Universidad Católica Andrés Bello, Caracas 2009.

6 See the last reform in *Official Gazette* N° 38.493 de 4-8-2006.

the oil industry is through their participation in mixed public enterprises, with state own majority of shares).

Other prohibitions established in the Constitution and applicable to all public contracts (national, state or municipal) are referred to the private party in the contracts, in the sense that public officials or public servants (national, state or municipal) cannot enter into contracts with public (national, state or municipal) entities (Art. 145); and representatives/members (*Diputados*) of the National Assembly (National Legislative Branch) cannot be owners, managers or directors of corporations which enter into contracts with public entities (Art. 190).

2. Public contracts and public interest contracts

The provisions in the Constitution referred to public interest contracts were conceived in the sense of "public contracts", that is, the same nation equivalent to the Spanish *Contratos p0úblicos*[7], *Contratos del Estado*[8], or *Contratos de la Administración*[9]; to the English *Public Contract*[10]; to the French *Contrats de l'administration*[11]; to the Italian *Contratti della pubblica ammistrazione*[12]; or to the Portuguese, *Contratos de Administração Pública*[13]; all of them identified, in general, because one of the parties in the contractual relationship is the State, the Public Administration, or a public entity, and because, in general, they have a public interest purpose. This was the intention of the proposal made in the National Constituent Assembly during the discussions of the 1999 Constitution.[14]

Since the Venezuelan State is organized as a Federation (Art. 4, Constitution) with three levels of autonomous governments (National –federal–, States and Municipal) (Art. 136, Constitution), the intention behind the regulation of the classification of public interest contracts under Article 150 of the Constitution, as "national public interest contracts," "state public interest contracts" and "municipal public interest contracts" was to refer to the contracts entered into, respectively, by national public entities, state public entities or municipal public entities[15]. Consequently, the

7 Sabino Álvarez Guendín, *Los contratos públicos*, Madrid, 1934.

8 Jorge Enrique Romero Pérez, *Los contratos del Estado*, San José Costa Rica, 1993.

9 Alvaro Pérez Vives, *De los contratos de la Administración*, Bogotá, 1984.

10 Marco D'Alberti, *I "Public contracts" nell'esperienza Britanica*, Napoli, 1984.

11 André de Laubadère, *Traité Théorique et Pratique des Contrats Administratifs*, 3 vols., Paris, 1956.

12 Francesco di Renzo, *I contratti della pubblica amministrazione*, Milano, 1969; Francesco Paolo Pugliese, I *contratti delle amministrazioni federali negli Stati Uniti d'America*, Padova, 1974.

13 Juarez de Oloiveira, *Licitações e Contratos de Administração Pública*, Sao Paulo 1993.

14 See Allan R. Brewer-Carías, *Debate Constituyente (Aportes a la Asamblea Nacional Constituyente)*, Tomo II, Caracas, 1999, pp. 173 ff.

15 See in general: Jesús Caballero Ortiz, *"Los contratos administrativos, los contratos de interés público y los contratos de interés nacional en la Constitución de 1999"*, in *Estudios de Derecho Administrativo: Libro Homenaje a la Universidad Central de Venezuela*, Volumen I, Imprenta Nacional, Caracas, 2001, pp. 139-154; Jesús Caballero Ortíz, *"Deben subsistir los contratos administrativos en una futura legislación?"*, in *El Derecho Público a comienzos del siglo XXI: Estudios homenaje al Profesor Allan R. Brewer-Carías,* Tomo II, Instituto de Derecho Público, UCV, Civitas Ediciones, Madrid, 2003, pp. 1765-1777; Allan R. Brewer-Carías, *"Los*

intention of the regulation was to consider as national public interest contracts, those concerning the national level of government (different to the state and municipal level of government), because they are entered into by a national public entity, that is to say, a national government agency (the Republic) or a national public corporation or a national public enterprise; that is Centralized or Decentralized National Public Administration.

3. Obligatory clauses in all public contracts and their exceptions

A. The jurisdiction immunity clause

Following the trends of the 1961 Constitution, the 1999 Constitution has also established in its norms, a series of contractual clauses that must be expressly or tacitly incorporated into all public contracts, such as the Sovereign immunity jurisdiction clause and the "*Calvo*" clause regarding international claims, or into some of them, such as the environmental protection clause.

Article 151 of the Constitution establishes that in all public interest contracts (national, state and municipal), if it were not unsuitable according to their nature, a clause must be considered as incorporated even if not expressly provided, according to which all doubts and controversies that could arise from such contracts and that could not be amicably resolved by the contracting parties, must be decided by the competent courts of the Republic according to its laws.[16]

It is the principle of the State relative sovereign immunity, which expressly established the exception to the jurisdiction immunity regarding contracts in which, because of its nature, such clause would be improper (Art. 151, Constitution)[17]. Consequently, in contracts with commercial purposes, for example (*ius gestionis*), the Venezuelan State can accept to submit contractual controversies to be resolved by arbitration and even subjected to foreign law.[18] Due to this exception, it can be

contratos de interés público nacional y su aprobación legislativa" in *Revista de Derecho Público,* N° 11, Caracas, 1982, pp. 40-54; Allan R. Brewer-Carías, *Contratos Administrativos,* Caracas, 1992, pp. 28-36; Allan R. Brewer-Carías, *Debate Constituyente, Aportes a la Asamblea Nacional Constituyente,* Tomo II, Caracas, 1999, p. 173; Alfonso Rivas Quintero, *Derecho Constitucional,* Paredes Editores, Valencia-Venezuela, 2002, pp. 287 ff.; Hildegard Rondón de Sansó, *Análisis de la Constitución venezolana de 1999,* Editorial Ex Libris, Caracas, 2001, pp. 123 ff; y Ricardo Combellas, *Derecho Constitucional: Una introducción al estudio de la Constitución de la República Bolivariana de Venezuela,* Mc Graw Hill, Caracas, 2001, pp. 115 ff.

16 See in general, Beatrice Sansó de Ramírez, *"La inmunidad de jurisdicción en el Artículo 151 de la Constitución de 1999",* in *Libro Homenaje a Enrique Tejera París, Temas sobre la Constitución de 1999,* Centro de Investigaciones Jurídicas (CEIN), Caracas, 2001, pp. 333-368; Allan R. Brewer-Carías, "Comentarios sobre la doctrina del acto de gobierno, del acto político, del acto de Estado y de las cuestiones políticas como motivo de inmunidad jurisdiccional de los Estados en sus Tribunales nacionales", in *Revista de Derecho Público*, N° 26, Editorial Jurídica Venezolana, Caracas, abril-junio 1986, pp. 65-68.

17 I was the proponent of this article during the discussions of the new Constitution in the National Constituent Assembly of 1999, following what was established in the previous 1961 Constitution, containing the exception regarding the Sovereign State immunity. See Allan R. Brewer-Carías, *Debate Constituyente, Aportes a la Asamblea Nacional Constituyente*, Tomo I, Caracas, 1999, pp. 209 ff.

18 See Allan R. Brewer-Carías, "Algunos comentarios a la Ley de Promoción y Protección de Inversiones: contratos públicos y jurisdicción" in *Arbitraje comercial interno e internacional.*

considered that the Venezuelan legal order has abandoned the absolute State sovereign immunity system and has followed the principle of relative State sovereign immunity, allowing the possibility for the State and other public entities, as a consequence of the execution of certain public interest contracts, to be subject to a foreign jurisdiction or to arbitration; and to establish a foreign law as the Law Applicable to a contract.[19]

Of course, no universal formula can be given in order to determine the "nature" of the contracts for the establishment of the exception to the State sovereign immunity principle. It has been accepted in international law that the consideration of the nature of the contract for that purpose cannot be based on the sole fact that the State or a public entity is a party to it, or that they are using their sovereignty or State powers, or in consideration of the contract being a public interest contract. Consequently, the nature of the contract in order to allow the possibility of subjecting the resolution of the contractual controversies or disputes to a foreign jurisdiction or to arbitration, or to adopting a foreign law as the applicable law to the contract, is based on the consideration of its being of a commercial nature, particularly regarding contracts in which the other party is a foreign corporation. The Supreme Court decision of August 17, 1999 (*Apertura Petrolera* Case) has also admitted other considerations different to the commercial nature of the contract, in relation to their economic importance, evaluated by the Public Administration and the National Assembly, in order to establish arbitration.

B. The "Calvo" Clause

The second obligatory clause that the Constitution imposed regarding all public interest contracts, also in Article 151, is the so-called "*Calvo* Clause", which implies that in all public interest contracts, a provision must be considered tacitly incorporated according to which, in no case can the execution of such contracts originate foreign claims"[20]. The origin of this clause is to be found in the 1893 Constitution as a consequence of the international diplomatic claims the European countries initiated by force against Venezuela as a consequence of contracts signed by the country and foreign citizens; being its conception the work of Carlos Calvo in his book *Tratado de Derecho Internacional*, initially edited in 1868, after studying the Franco-British intervention in Rio de la Plata and the French intervention in Mexico.[21] This Calvo clause also helps the adoption of the so called *Drago Doctrine* conceived in 1902 by the then Argentinean Minister of Foreign Relations, Luis María Drago, who regarding the threats of using force made by Germany, Great

---

Reflexiones teóricas y experiencias prácticas, Academia de Ciencias Políticas y Sociales, Caracas 2005, pp. 279-288; «El arbitraje y los contratos de interés nacional" in *Seminario sobre la Ley de Arbitraje Comercial*, Biblioteca de la Academia de Ciencias Políticas y Sociales, Serie Eventos, N° 13, Caracas 1999, pp. 169-204.

19 See Allan R. Brewer-Carías, *Contratos Administrativos, cit.*, pp. 130 a 137.

20 See Allan R. Brewer-Carías, *Contratos Administrativos, cit.*, pp. 137 y ss.; See Allan R. Brewer-Carías, "Algunos aspectos de la inmunidad jurisdiccional de los Estados y la cuestión de los actos de Estado (*act of state*) en la jurisprudencia norteamericana" in *Revista de Derecho Público*, N° 24, Editorial Jurídica Venezolana, Caracas, octubre-diciembre 1985, pp. 29-42

21 See Carlos Calvo, *Tratado de Derecho Internacional,* Vol. I, paragraph 205, *cit.,* by L.A. Podestá Costa, *Derecho Internacional Público,* Vol. I, Buenos Aires, 1955, pp. 445-446.

Britain and Italy against Venezuela, formulated its thesis condemning the compulsory collection of public debts by the States.[22]

Consequently, according to the Calvo Clause, no Foreign States' diplomatic claims can be made against the Venezuelan State, when the Foreign States acts on behalf of foreign citizens of corporations, based on the consideration that all foreign persons in Venezuela must be treated in the same equal conditions as Venezuelans, excluding all possibility of considering the controversies between the parties in a public contract, when the counter-party of the Venezuelan public entity is a foreign citizen or corporation, such as an international controversy[23].

C. The temporal clause in concessions

The third obligatory clause for public contracts established in the Constitution is the temporary clause that must be established in all contracts for the exploitation of natural resources owned by the Nation or for rendering public services or utilities (*servicios públicos*). Article 113 of the Constitution sets forth that those public contracts must always have a limited time for their execution and, additionally, they must always have clauses with adequate benefits for the public entity according to the public interest. Article 156,10 of the Constitution also prohibits the awarding of mining concessions for an indefinite period.

D. The environmental protection clause

Article 129 of the Constitution also imposes the obligation for National Public Administration to include an environment protection clause in any national public contract whose execution could affect natural resources,[24] providing for the obligation of the private party to the contract to preserve the ecological equilibrium, to allow the access and transfer of environmental protection technology, and to restore the environment to its natural state if altered. It must be noted that the Constitution, refers to contracts that may affect natural resources entered into by the "Republic;" consequently, *stricto senso*, the constitutional obligation to incorporate this clause only refers to the National State.

---

22 See Victorino Jiménez y Núñez, *La Doctrina Drago y la Política Internacional,* Madrid, 1927.

23 The origin of the clause, which explains its name "Calvo", was the argument contained in his book, *Tratado de Derecho Internacional* edited initially in 1868, in which the author mentioned the Anglo-French intervention in Rio de la Plata and the French intervention in Mexico, expressing that they were based merely on the pretext of protecting private commercial interests, and that according to international public law, the armed intervention of European States in the States of the New World, could not be accepted. This "Calvo" clause has also influenced in the conception of the " Drago Doctrine", formulated in 1902 by the then Foreign Relations Minister of Argentina, Luis Maria Drago, as a reaction against armed actions by Germany, Great Britain and Italy against Venezuela in order to collect by force public debts owed to the Europeans. See Victorino Jiménez y Núñez, *La Doctrina Drago y la Política Internacional,* Madrid, 1927.

24 See Alberto Blanco-Uribe Quintero, "La tutela ambiental como derecho-deber del Constituyente. Base constitucional y principios rectores del derecho ambiental", in *Revista de Derecho Constitucional,* N° 6 (enero-diciembre), Editorial Sherwood, Caracas, 2002, pp. 31-64.

4. Principles related to the State's contractual liabilities

In parallel to the provision of the general regime of State liability (Article 140), the 1999 Constitution also establishes the general basis and conditions for the contractual liability of the State, providing that it will only recognize as contracted obligations those entered by legitimate organs of the State; a constitutional provision that had its origin in the XIX century when the State was sued because of damages caused in civil wars by rebels who claimed to be acting as the legitimate government.

In any case, the legitimacy for contracting obligations is related to the competency of the respective public officer to sign the contract, for which purpose the Constitution assigns, for instance, the President of the Republic power to enter into national public contracts (Article 236,14) and to negotiate national public debt (Article 236,12); powers that of course are not exclusive, because such attributions can and are assigned to the corresponding Ministries as its direct organs (Article 242). On the other hand, the Constitution imposes some budget restrictions in the execution of contracts by providing that no spending can be made if not established in the budget's annual statute (Article 314).

II. THE NOTION OF NATIONAL PUBLIC INTEREST CONTRACTS ACCORDING TO THE CONSTITUTION

1. The approval and authorization by the National Assembly of national public interest contracts

Article 150 of the 1999 Venezuelan Constitution provides for the approval of "public interest contracts" by the National Assembly, as follows:

> "Article 150. The execution of national public interest contracts shall require the approval of the National Assembly in those cases in which such requirement is determined by law.
>
> No municipal, state or national public interest contract shall be executed with foreign States or official entities, or with companies not domiciled in Venezuela, or shall be transferred to any of them without the approval of the National Assembly.
>
> In public interest contracts, the law may demand certain nationality and domicile conditions, or conditions of other nature, or require special guarantees."

The same provision, specifically referring to the authorization of national public interest contracts is repeated by Article 187.9 of the same Constitution, as follows:

> "Article 187. It is the role of the National Assembly to: [...] 9. Authorize the National Executive to enter into contracts of national interest, in the cases established by law. Authorize contracts of municipal, state and national public interest, with States or official foreign entities or with companies not domiciled in Venezuela."

The same expression "national public interest contracts" is also used in articles 151,[25] 236.14,[26] and 247[27] of the Constitution.

On the other hand, in addition to the provision of article 150 of the Constitution, it must be mentioned that specifically related to national public interest contracts of public debt, article 312 of the Constitution establishes the principle that "public debt operations will require, for their validity, a special law that authorizes them, except for the exceptions established by the organic law." The National Assembly has stablished the need for parliamentary authorization regarding these public debt contracts, through the Financial Management of the Public Sector Organic Law, in which it has provided for some exceptions, as is the case, for instance, of the Central Bank of Venezuela and the state-owned enterprises of the Oil sector (art. 101).

Articles 150 and 151 of the Venezuelan Constitution have the main purpose of establishing, first, the scope of the powers of the National Assembly to control the Government and Pubic Administration on matters of "public interest contracts;" and second, certain limits regarding the clauses that can be included in such contracts; being the notion "public interest contracts" used in a broad sense, comprising all public contracts entered into by public organs and entities at the three territorial levels of the State.

As the Venezuelan State is organized as a federal one (Art. 4,) there are three levels of autonomous governments (National, State, and Municipal) (Art. 136), being possible for the organs and entities in each of such levels to enter into public contracts, which under Article 150 of the Constitution are classified in three sub categories: *national* public interest contracts, *state* public interest contracts and *municipal* public interest contracts; depending on whether they are entered into, respectively, by an organ of the Central Public Administration of each of the territorial entities of the State (Republic, States, Municipalities) or by a decentralized entity (autonomous institutions, state-owned enterprises) of the Public Administration of the said three territorial levels of the State.

Notwithstanding the inclusion of all the aforementioned provisions in the Constitution of 1999, in its text no express definition of the concept of public interest contracts was included, establishing only a "generic" concept of " public interest contracts" and its "species": "national public interest contracts," "state public interest contracts" and "municipal public interest contracts," that is, public contracts that are entered into by the public entities that conform to the Public Administration in the three levels of government.

---

25 "Article 151. In the *public interest contracts*, unless inapplicable by reason of the nature of such contracts, a clause shall be deemed included even if not expressed, whereby any doubts and controversies which may arise concerning such contracts and which cannot be resolved amicably by the contracting parties, shall be decided by the competent courts of the Republic in accordance with its laws, and shall not on any grounds or for any reason give rise to foreign claims."

26 "Article 236. The following are powers and duties of the President of the Republic: [...] 14. To enter into contracts *of the national interest,* subject to this Constitution and applicable laws."

27 "Article 247. The Office of the General Attorney of the Republic advises, defends and represents in and out of court the property interests of the Republic, and must be consulted for purposes of approval of *contracts of national public interest*."

Specifically, regarding the national level of government, the intention of the provisions included in said Articles 150 and 151 of the Constitution, was to comprise in the notion of "national public interest contracts," not only those entered by the Republic through any of her national government agency or organs, but also by any other national public decentralized entity like a public corporation or a state-owned enterprise. In other words, the Public Administration in Venezuela is not only the Central Administrations in the three levels of government (Republic, States and Municipalities), but it encompasses all the universe of public entities that constitutes the public sector in each level of government, including state-owned enterprises.

It is important to remind that at the national level of government, according to the principles established for its organization in the Public Administration Organic Law,[28] is constituted not only by the Central Public Administration, that is, the organs of the National Executive like the Ministries, but also by the Decentralized Public Administration, composed of the Public Corporations created by statute and the state-owned enterprises, incorporated according to commercial law provisions.

The Organic Law, in effect, when identifying Public Administration declares that it consists of "organs, entities and missions" (art. 15): the first (organs), comprises the "Central Level of the National Public Administration" (articles 44 ff.), including among other organs the Ministries (articles 61 ff.); the second (entities), comprises the Decentralized Public Administration (articles 92 ff.), integrated by public corporations (*institutos públicos*) (articles 96 ff.), state-owned enterprises (articles 103 ff.), State's Foundations (articles 109 ff.) and State Civil Associations (articles 116 ff.); and the third are the so called "Missions" (article 132.).[29] Consequently, all those entities are considered as part of the public sector according to article 5 of the Financial Management of Public Sector Organic Law, which included within the state-owned enterprises:

> "8. Commercial companies in which the Republic or other persons referred to in this Article have a shareholding equal to or greater than fifty per cent of the share capital. In addition, wholly state-owned companies, whose role, through the holding of shares of other companies, is to coordinate the public business management of a sector of the national economy [...] 9. Commercial companies in which the persons referred to in the preceding numeral have a shareholding equal to more than fifty per cent of the share capital."[30]

Those state-owned enterprises, as part of the Public Administration, are also subject, for instance, to the Public Contracting Law (Article 3),[31] and to the Organic

---

28 See *Official Gazette* N° 6.147 Extra of November 17, 2014. Available at: http://historico.tsj.gob.ve/gaceta_ext/noviembre/17112014/E-17112014-4128.pdf#page=1

29 See *Official Gazette* N° 6.147 Extra of November 17, 2014. Available at: http://www.conatel.gob.ve/wp-content/uploads/2015/02/Ley-Org%C3%A1nica-de-Administraci%C3%B3n-P%C3%BAblica.pdf

30 See *Official Gazette* No 6.210 Extra of December 30, 2015. Available at: http://www.bod.com.ve/media/97487/GACETA-OFICIAL-EXTRAORDINARIA-6210.pdf.

31 See *Official Gazette* N° 6.154 Extra. of November 19, 2014. Available at: http://www.mindefensa.gob.ve/COMISION/wp-content/uploads/2017/03/LCP.pdf

Law of the General Audit Office (Article 9),[32] and are included in what is defined by Article 15 of the Public Administration Organic Law as "entities;" that is, according to the Constitutional Chamber of the Supreme Tribunal (in a decision No. 464 of March 3, 2002):

> "State legal persons with the form of commercial companies, subjected to a mixed legal regime, of public and private law, although predominantly of private law, due to its form, but not exclusively, because their close relation with the State subjects them to the mandatory rules of public law in order to secure the best organization, functioning and execution of control by the Public Administration, by its organs or by those that contribute to attain their objectives."[33]

As a result of all these provisions, the National Public Administration encompasses not only the Central Public Administration composed of the organs of the Government (of the Republic), but also the decentralized organs of the State that comprise the Decentralized Public Administration, which include the state-owned enterprises, that is, the commercial instrumentalities of the national government.

The current text of Article 150 of the Constitution regarding national public interest contracts was included in 1999 in the debates at the National Constituent Assembly,[34] among other reasons, for the purpose of changing the sense of the provision of the former Article 126 of the 1961 Constitution.[35] During four decades, the text of this article had provoked endless discussions on the interpretation of the notion of "public interests contracts," and about when they were or were not related to the "normal conduct of the public administration," to determine if they were or were not to be submitted to the approval or authorization of Congress.[36]

---

32 See *Official Gazette* N° 37.347 of December 17, 2001. Available at: http://www.oas.org/juridico/spanish/mesicic3_ven_anexo23.pdf

33 See decision N° 464 of March 18, 2002 (Case: *Interpretación del Decreto de la Asamblea Nacional Constituyente de fecha 30 de enero de 2000, mediante el cual se suspende por 3 días la negociación de la Convención Colectiva del Trabajo),* in *Revista de Derecho Público,* N° 89-92, Editorial Jurídica Venezolana, pp. 219.. Available at: http://allanbrewercarias.com/wp-content/uploads/2007/08/2002-REVISTA-89-90-91-92.pdf

34 As a Independent member of the National Constituent Assembly of 1999, I proposed to include this provision of article 150 in the Constitution, following in part what was previously established in the 1961 Constitution, changing the regulation regarding the National Assembly intervention on matters of public contracts. See the proposal in "Régimen General del Poder Público y las competencias del Poder Público Nacional" in Allan R. Brewer-Carías, *Debate* Constituyente (Aportes a la Asamblea Nacional Constituyente), Tomo II (9 septiembre–17 octubre 1999), Fundación de Derecho Público, Editorial Jurídica Venezolana, Caracas 1999, pp. 175-177. Available at: http://allanbrewercarias.net/Content/449725d9-f1cb-474b-8ab2-41efb849fea5/ Content/II,%201,%2086.%20APORTES%20AL%20DEBATE%20CONSTITUYENTE%20TOMO%20II.pdf. See also Allan R. Brewer-Carías, *Debate Constituyente (Aportes a la Asamblea Nacional Constituyente, 8 agosto-8 septiembre 1999),* Fundación de Derecho Público, Editorial Jurídica Venezolana, Tomo I, Caracas 1999, pp. 212, 231, 232.

35 Such article 126 provided the following: "Article 126. Without the approval of *Congress*, no *contract of national interest* may be entered into, except as necessary for the normal conduct of the Public Administration or as permitted by law."

36 See among many other works regarding the discussions on the traditional notion of "national public interest contracts": Eloy Lares Martínez, "Contratos de interés nacional," in *Libro Homenaje al Profesor Antonio Moles Caubet,* Tomo I, Caracas, UCV, 1981, p. 117; *José Melich*

In sum, the 1999 Constitution, apart the provision of its article 312 related to public debt contracts to be authorized by special statutes, distinguished two basic regimes related to the intervention of the legislative branch on matters of "public interest contracts":

First, ratifies the principle that public interest contracts, when entered into by public entities with "States or official foreign entities or with companies not domiciled in Venezuela" have always to be previously authorized by the National Assembly. Consequence, for a foreign company to enter into a public interest contract with a public entity in Venezuela, it has to be domiciled in Venezuela.

Second, establishes the rule that the submission of public national interest contracts to the approval or authorization of the National Assembly is necessary only when a statute so expressly provided, granting the Assembly the power to establish in said statute the exceptions to its own regulations.

Consequently, based on all those provisions of the Constitution and of the Organic Law on Public Administration, regarding the notion of national public interest contracts, it comprises all public interest contracts entered into by the Republic and by all the entities of it Decentralized Administration. There is no basis to argue that only the Republic can be a party into a "national public interest contract;" a criterion that on the other hand, in practical terms would turn meaningless such constitutional notion and the basis for parliamentary control due to the fact that the overwhelming majority of national public interest contracts are entered into not by the Republic (for example signed by the President of the Republic, Article. 236.14, which are almost inexistent), but by national decentralized entities of the Public Administration, that is, national public corporations or national state-owned enterprises.

2. The notion of public national interest contracts includes not only those in which the Republic is a party but also those in which national decentralized entities are parties

Such notion of public national interest contracts including those entered into by decentralized entities of National Public Administration, has been the one I have maintained since 1982 when I expressed in a Legal Opinion I gave to the Senate of Venezuela, that "national interest contracts are those entered into by national political and administrative entities (Republic, autonomous institutions and other public corporations and national state-owned enterprises)."[37] I ratified and summarized that same criterium in 2005, expressing the following:

Orsini, "La Noción de contrato de interés público," in *Revista de Derecho Público n° 7, Caracas, 1981, p. 61;* Allan R. Brewer-Carías, "Los contratos de interés público nacional y su aprobación legislativa" *in Revista de Derecho Público,* N° 11, Caracas, 1982, pp. 40-54; *Gonzalo Pérez Luciani,* "Contratos de interés nacional, contratos de interés público y contratos de empréstito público," *in Libro Homenaje al Doctor Eloy Lares Martínez, Tomo I, Caracas, 1984, p. 103; and* Jesús Caballero Ortiz, "Los contratos administrativos, los contratos de interés público y los contratos de interés nacional en la Constitución de 1999," *in Estudios de Derecho Administrativo: Libro Homenaje a la Universidad Central de Venezuela,* Volumen I, Imprenta Nacional, Caracas, 2001, pp. 139-154..

37 *See* the text of the Opinion I gave to the Senate in 1982, considering contracts entered into by state own enterprises like PDVSA, as "national public interest contracts," in Allan R. Brewer-

"Contracts of the State or public contracts are all those in which one of the parties is a state legal person,[38] that means, that it is integrated in the organization of the State, whether a politico-territorial legal person (Republic, States, Municipalities), or public law persons (vg. autonomous institutes) or private law persons of the State (vg. commercial companies or state-owned enterprises).

These contracts in my opinion, have been qualified in the Constitution as public interest contracts (national, states or municipal) and in some statutes, and some of them have been qualified as administrative contracts.

In fact, in the 1999 Constitution, as supreme law and principal source of law, on matters of contracts of the State, in Section Four of Chapter I of Title IV on the "Public Power," it is provided for the "public interest contracts," a notion that in articles 150 and 151 was adopted to identify contracts entered into by public entities, that is, legal State persons, or those that integrate the public sector and that in general comprise the notion of "State." The notion can be equivalent to [public contracts] tending to identify contracts in which one of the parties in the contractual relationship is the State, the Public Administration, or a public entity, which in general, have a public interest purpose. This was the intention of the proposal I made39 regarding such provision before the National Constituent Assembly during the drafting of the 1999 Constitution.

Since the Venezuelan State is organized as a Federation (Art. 4, Constitution) with three levels of autonomous governments (National –federal–, States and Municipal) (Art. 136, Constitution), the intention behind the regulation of the classification of public interest contracts under Article 150 of the Constitution, as "national public interest contracts", "state public interest contracts" and "municipal public interest contracts" is to refer to the contracts entered into, respectively, by national public entities, state public entities or municipal public entities[40]. Consequently, the intention of the regulation was to consider as

---

Carías, "Los contratos de interés nacional y su aprobación legislativa," in *Estudios de Derecho Público (Labor en el Senado* 1982), Tomo I, Ediciones del Congreso de la República, Caracas 1984, pp. 186-189. Avalable at: http://allanbrewercarias.net/Content/449725d9-f1cb-474b-8ab2-41efb849fea5/Content/II.1.49.pdf. See also Allan R. Brewer-Carías, "La aprobación Legislativa de los contratos de interés nacional y el contrato PDVSA-Veba Oel," in *Estudios de Derecho Público (Labor en el Senado 1983), Tomo II,* Ediciones del Congreso de la República, Caracas 1984, pp. 5-82. Available at: http://allanbrewercarias.net/Content/449725d9-f1cb-474b-8ab2-41efb849fea5/Content/II.1.44.pdf

38 On the regulation of legal persons in the Constitution see:, Allan R. Brewer-Carías, "Sobre las personas jurídicas en la Constitución de 1999" en *Derecho Público Contemporáneo: Libro Homenaje a Jesús Leopoldo Sánchez*, Estudios del Instituto de Derecho Público, Universidad Central de Venezuela, enero-abril 2003, Volumen 1, pp. 48-54. Available at: http://allanbrewer carias.com/wp-content/uploads/2007/08/473.-440.-SOBRE-LAS-PERSONAS-JUR%C3%8DDI CAS-EN-LA-CONSTITUCION-DE-1999.pdf.

39 See Allan R. Brewer-Carías, *Debate Constituyente (Aportes a la Asamblea Nacional Constituyente)*, Tomo II, Caracas, 1999, pp. 173 ff. Available at: http://allanbrewercarias.net/Content/449725d9-f1cb-474b-8ab2-41efb849fea5/Content/II,%201,%2086.%20APORTES%20AL%20DEBATE %20CONSTITUYENTE%20TOMO%20II.pdf.

40 See in general: Jesús Caballero Ortiz, *"Los contratos administrativos, los contratos de interés público y los contratos de interés nacional en la Constitución de 1999,"* in *Estudios de*

national public interest contracts, those concerning the national level of government (different to the state and municipal level of government), because it was entered into by a national public entity, that is to say, a national government agency (the Republic) or a national public corporation or a national state-owned enterprise."[41]

In summary, public interest contracts "are those contracts entered into by public entities, that is, legal State persons, or those that integrate the public sector, which in general comprise the notion of 'State;'" being "the intention of the constitutional provision to consider national public interest contracts, those concerning the national level of government (different to the State and municipal level of government), because they were entered into by national public entities, that is, the Republic or national autonomous institutions or national state owned enterprises."[42]

And this has been, with the only exception of Eloy Lares Martínez,[43] the general opinion of the overwhelming majority of Venezuelan public law scholars, all of which agree that national public national interest contracts include, not only those entered into by the Republic, but also contracts entered into by national public corporations and national state-owned enterprises whereas national interest is involved.

For instance, Luis Henrique Farías Mata, was always emphatic considering that national public interest contracts include contracts entered into by decentralized public entities of the *National Public Administration*, arguing that:

> "the Constitution does not establish distinctions regarding the organ that enters into the contract: if it is a contract of national interest, regardless of

Derecho Administrativo: Libro Homenaje a la Universidad Central de Venezuela, Volumen I, Imprenta Nacional, Caracas, 2001, pp. 139-154.

41 See Allan R. Brewer-Carías, "Nuevas consideraciones sobre el régimen de los contratos del Estado en Venezuela,", en *Los Contratos administrativos. Contratos del Estado. VIII Jornadas* Internacionales *de Derecho Administrativo Allan Randolph Brewer-Carías*, Fundación Estudios de Derecho Administrativo, Tomo II, Caracas 2006, pp. 449-450. Availble at: http://allanbrewer carias.net/Content/449725d9-f1cb-474b-8ab2-41efb849fec1/Content/VIII% 20 JORNADAS%20-INTERNACIONALES%20DE%20DA%20ARBC%20FINAL.pdf.

42 See *See* Allan R. Brewer-Carías, "Nuevas consideraciones sobre el régimen de los contratos del Estado en Venezuela," en *VIII Jornadas Internacionales de Derecho Administrativo Allan Randolph Brewer-Carías, Los Contratos administrativos. Contratos del Estado.* Fundación Estudios de Derecho Administrativo, Tomo II, Caracas 2006, pp. 449. Availble at: http://allan brewercarias.net/Content/449725d9-f1cb-474b-8ab2-41efb849fec1/Content/VIII%20JORNA-DAS%20INTERNACIONALES%20DE%20DA%20ARBC%20FINAL.pdf. See also *See* Allan R. Brewer-Carías, *Debate Constituyente (Aportes a la Asamblea Nacional Constituyente)*, Tomo II, Caracas, 1999, pp. 173 ff. Available at: http://allanbrewercarias.net/Content/449725d9-f1cb-474b-8ab2-41efb849fea5/Content/II,%201,%2086.%20APORTES%20AL%20DEBATE%20 CONSTI-TUYENTE%20TOMO%20II.pdf..

43 Eloy Lares Martínez, after affirming that "national interest contracts are administrative contracts *entered* into *by the National Public Administration,*" nonetheless wrote in a restrictive way that only the Republic could be a party to national public interest contracts *See*. Eloy Lares Martínez, "Contratos de Interés Nacional, " in *Libro Homenaje al Profesor Antonio Moles Caubet*, Vol I, Caracas 1981, pp. 117, 137.

which organ of the Venezuelan Public Administration appears in it as a party, it must, in all cases, meet the requirements set forth therein."[44]

That is why, Margot Y. Huen Rivas considers that one of the characteristics of public interest contracts is "at least a *public entity* is one of the parties;" [45] and Isabel Boscán de Ruesta when referring to *national* public interest contracts in particular, agrees that such contracts "are those entered into by the National Public Administration." [46] Also Luis Britto García has stated his opinion in this sense, stating that "administrative contracts or public interest contracts, are ones in which the *[Public] Administration*, acting as such, that is pursuing purposes of public policy which it is in charge of comply, enter into a contract whose object tend to fulfill a purpose of public interest."[47]

This same general approach was followed by José Melich Orsini when he affirmed that "what typifies a 'contract of public interest' is that it is a great contract entered into by the *national Public Administration*,"[48] without mentioning any specific public entity within the centralized or decentralized Public Administration at the national level.

On the other hand, José Araujo Juárez in particular regarding state-owned enterprises has said that they "can enter into contracts that can be qualified as public interest contracts, and thus, subject to the parliamentary regime control established in the Constitution."[49] In the same regard, Román José Duque Corredor has considered that state-owned enterprises, as entities within the Public Administration, can enter into public interest contracts."[50]

---

44 See Luis Henrique Farías Mata, "La Teoría del Contrato Administrativo en la Doctrina, Legislación y Jurisprudencia Venezolanas," *in Libro Homenaje al Profesor Antonio Moles Caubet*, Vol II, Caracas 1981, pp. 935, 974.

45 *See* Margot Y. Huen Rivas, "El arbitraje internacional en los contratos administrativos," in *VIII Jornadas Internacionales de Derecho Administrativo Allan R. Brewer-Carías, Contratos del Estado,* Fundación Estudios de Derecho Administrativo, Caracas 2005, Vol. I, p. 404. Available at: http://allanbrewercarias.net/Content/449725d9-f1cb-474b-8ab2-41efb849fec1/Content/VIII%20JORNADAS%20INTERNACIONALES%20DE%20DA%20ARBC%20FINAL.pdf.

46 *See* Isabel Boscán de Ruesta, "La Inmunidad de Jurisdicción en los Contratos de Interés Público," in *Revista de Derecho Público*, No. 14, Editorial Jurídica Venezolana, Caracas, 1983, p. 38.

47 *See* Luis Britto García, "Régimen Constitucional de los Contratos de Interés Público," *in Revista de Control Fiscal y Tecnificación Administrativa*, No. 50, 1968, pp. 89-90; quoted in Juan Carlos *Balzán* Perez, "El arbitraje en los contratos de interés público a la luz de la cláusula de inmunidad de jurisdicción prevista en el artículo 151 de la constitución de 1999," in VIII *Jornadas Internacionales de Derecho* Administrativo *Allan R. Brewer-Carías, Contratos del Estado,* Fundación Estudios de Derecho Administrativo, Caracas 2005, Vol. II, p. 308. Available at: http://allanbrewercarias.net/Content/449725d9-f1cb-474b-8ab2-41efb849fec1/Content/VIII%20 JORNADAS%20INTERNACIONALES%20DE%20DA%20ARBC%20FINAL.pdf.

48 *See* José Melich Orsini, "La Noción de Contrato de Interés Público," in *Revista de Derecho Público* No. 7, Editorial Jurídica Venezolana, Caracas, 1981, pp. 62.

49 *See* José Araujo Juárez, "Régimen general de derecho público relativo a las empresas del Estado," in *Nacionalización, Libertad de Empresa y Asociaciones Mixtas, Caracas 2008, pp.* 191, 229. Professor Araujo Juárez also expressed his same opinion in his book: *Derecho Administrativo General*, Vol. II, Ediciones Paredes, Caracas 2011, pp. 263-264.

50 *See* Román J. Duque Corredor, "*Opinión sobre la inconstitucionalidad del Bono PDVSA 2020,*" April 19, 2020, p. 4. See the information on this Opinion in: https://presidenciave.

Also, since 1982 Jesús Caballero Ortíz has stated that national public interest contracts include not only contracts to which the Republic is a party, but also contracts entered into by decentralized entities of the Public Administration, specifically referring to "public enterprises, public law persons" (autonomous institutions or public corporations).[51] It is true that when analyzing the "Calvo clause" in national public contracts, Caballero mentioned that the Republic cannot be considered a "private party" to the contract;[52] but from such statement it is not possible to deduct that a national public interest contract must have the Republic as a party. A careful reading of what Caballero wrote in 2001 reveals that in no part of his public interest contracts´ analysis does he address which specific organs or entities can or cannot enter into such contracts. He simply analyzed public interest contracts from a substantive point of view with respect to the regime of authorization and/or approval of such contracts by the National Assembly, and in no way whatsoever restricted the concept of national public interest contracts to contracts entered into by the Republic.

In the same general way, in 2004 Rafael Badell expressly acknowledged that contracts of public interest can be entered into by entities of the decentralized Public Administration "if they affect directly the interest of the Republic as territorial entity, or of the States or Municipalities,"[53] and thus further stated that "contracts signed by public companies may be considered as national public interest contracts, when the national interests that correspond to the Republic are directly affected."[54] In support of this proposition, Badell cited the decision on the case *EDECLA* (*Lucía Antillano*) of 2003[55] whereas the Constitutional Chamber of the Supreme Tribunal *expressly acknowledged that contracts entered into by a public corporation were national public interest contracts*.

---

com/regiones/jurista-roman-j-duque-corredor-respalda-la-inconstitucionalidad-de-los-bonos-pdvsa-2020/. See the text in: https://www.acienpol.org.ve/wp-content/uploads/2020/04/Nulidad-de-la-Bonos-2020-de-PDVSA.pdf.

51 *See* Jesús Caballero Ortiz, *Las empresas públicas en el derecho venezolano*, Editorial Jurídica Venezolana, Caracas 1982, pp. 333-334. See also Jesús Caballero Ortíz, *Institutos autónomos*, Editorial Jurídica Venezolana, Caracas, 1995, pp. 206-207

52 See Jesús Caballero Ortiz, "Los Contratos Administrativos, los Contratos de Interés Público y los Contratos de Interés Nacional en la Constitución de 1999," en *Estudios de Derecho Administrativo, Libro Homenaje a la Universidad Central de Venezuela,* Tomo I, Caracas 2001, p. 154

53 Rafael Badell Madrid, "Sobre la Inmunidad de Jurisdicción y la Procedencia de Cláusulas Arbitrales en los Contratos de Interés Público Nacional," *in Congreso Internacional de Derecho Administrativo Homenaje al Prof. Luis Henrique Farías Mata*, Margarita 2006, Tomo II, pp. 159-160.

54 Rafael Badell also opined in other of his works, in the same sense that public interest contracts are not only those entered into by the Republic, the States, and the Municipalities, but also those entered into by the "functional decentralized administration" if they affect the interest of the territorial entities, and, in particular, those "entered into by state-owned enterprises, when they affect in a direct way the national interest assigned to the Republic." *See* Rafael Badell Madrid, "Contratos de interés público nacional" *in Revista de Derecho Administrativo*, No. 19, Editorial Sherwood, Caracas 2005, pp. 7, 9. Available at: https://www.badellgrau.com/?pag=7¬i=132,

55 Supreme Tribunal of Justice, Constitutional Chamber, Decision No Supreme Tribunal's decision No. 953 of April 29, 2003, pp. 11-12. The text of the decision is available at: https://vlexvenezuela.com/vid/lucia-antillano-283457047.

In a lecture given in 2018, Rafael Badell was emphatic in affirming that national public interest contracts are "contracts entered into by the State, through its territorial entities (Republic, States or Municipalities), and even its functionally decentralized administration (state companies, autonomous institutes, civil associations, foundations),"[56] and that "public interest contracts include those concluded by the public administration, centralized as well as territorially or functionally decentralized; which means that this category includes those contracts of public interest that have been entered into by autonomous institutes, *state-owned companies*, foundations, and other state entities of public or private law."[57]

More recently, the same author, in an article written precisely on the matter of "public interest contracts," has expressed in a very clear manner that:

> "Public interest contracts are those contracts: (i) carried out by the State, through its territorial entities, Republic, States or Municipalities, and even its functionally decentralized administration, State companies, autonomous institutes, civil associations and foundations; [...]
>
> "[...] the 1999 Constitution standardized the name of this type of contracts by referring to "contracts of public interest" in its articles 150 and 151, discriminating that this type of contract may be national, state and municipal in nature and, therefore, those contracts made not only by the President of the Republic, representing the Republic, but also by the functionally and territorially decentralized administration may be included in this category of contracts." [...]
>
> "[...] we consider that public interest contracts include those concluded by both the centralized public administration and the territorially or functionally decentralized one; which means that this category of contracts encompasses those contracts of public interest that have been agreed upon by autonomous institutes, state companies, foundations, and other state entities of public or private law [...][58]

3. The notion of national public interest contracts has not been the object of any binding judicial interpretation reducing them only to those entered into by the Republic, and excluding the decentralized national entities as being parties thereto

The aforementioned notion of "national public interest contract" derived from articles 150, 151, 189.9 and 247 of the Constitution, comprising contracts entered into by the Republic, national autonomous institutions and national state-owned enterprises, has not being changed in any way through any binding judicial constitutional interpretation.

---

56 See Rafael Badell Madrid, "Contratos de interés público," text of the Lecture given at the III Academic Conference on Public Contracting, Institute of Legal Studies, Bar of Carabobo State, Valencia-Carabobo, June 29, 2018, pp. 3, 4. Available at: www.badellgrau.com.

57 *Idem*, p. 5.

58 See Rafael Badell Madrid, "Contratos de interés público," in *Revista de Derecho Público*, No. 159-160, Julio-diciembre 2019, Editorial Jurídica Venezolana, Caracas 2020, p. 11, 12, 13. Also published in published in Badell & Grau Law Firm Portal, http://www.badellgrau.com/, available at: http://www.badellgrau.com/?pag=205&ct=2592

That is, no "binding interpretation" on the notion of national public interest contract included in such articles of the Constitution has been issued by the Constitutional Chamber of the Supreme Tribunal pursuant article 335 of the Constitution, or by any other Venezuelan court, establishing that national public interest contracts must have only the Republic as a party, excluding decentralized national entities of public administration.

The Constitutional Chamber has indeed, in some decisions, referred only to public contracts entered into by the Republic, but without establishing any binding restrictive interpretation excluding from the notion other national public interest contracts entered into by decentralized entities. To the contrary, the former Supreme Court of Justice, and the Constitutional and Political-Administrative Chambers of the current Supreme Tribunal have issued multiple decisions accepting that contracts entered into by autonomous institutions (public corporations) and state-owned enterprises, which are part of the decentralized National Public Administration, are national public interest contracts.

This traditional judicial doctrine in the country was reflected, for instance, in the important decision issued by the former Supreme Court of Justice on August 17, 1999, when the 1999 Constitution was being drafted, in the case involving national public contracts (*Association Agreements*) for oil exploitation entered into by state owned enterprises in the so-called *Apertura Petrolera* policy (Case: *Simón Muñoz Armas et al. Challenging Clauses of the Congress Resolution of July 4, 1995*), which the Court in addition considered "administrative contracts." They were entered into by decentralized entities of the oil industry, which were subsidiaries of Petróleos de Venezuela S.A. PDVSA, having been expressly qualified as "national public interest contracts" based on the provision of the 1961 Constitution that on the matter had similar wording as the 1999 Constitution.[59] That is why Eugenio Hernández Bretón affirmed, commenting such decision, that the "Association Agreements" entered into by PDVSA and its subsidiaries are all "contracts of public interest."[60]

---

59 See. Allan R. Brewer-Carías, *El Caso de la Apertura Petrolera (Documentos del caso 1996-1999)*, 2001, pp. 318-319. Available at: http://allanbrewercarias.com/wp-content/ uploads/2007/09/57.-I-2-22.-APERTURA-PETROLERA.-DOCUMENTOS-DEL-JUICIO.pdf The decisión can also be consulted in Allan R. Brewer-Carías, *Crónica de una destrucción. Concesión, Nacionalización, Apertura, Constitucionalización, Desnacionalización, Estatización, Entrega y Degradación de la Industria Petrolera,* Apendix, Colección Centro de Estudios de Regulación Económica-Universidad Monteávila, N° 3, Universidad Monteávila, Editorial Jurídica Venezolana, Caracas, 2018.

60 *See* Margot Y. Huen Rivas, "El arbitraje internacional en los contratos administrativos," in *VIII Jornadas Internacionales de Derecho Administrativo Allan R. Brewer-Carías, Contratos del Estado,* Fundación Estudios de Derecho Administrativo, Caracas 2005, Vol. I, p. 404. Available at: http://allanbrewercarias.net/Content/449725d9-f1cb-474b-8ab2-41efb849fec1/ Content/ VIII% 20JORNADAS%20INTERNACIONALES%20DE%20DA%20ARBC%20FINAL.pdf (quoting Eugenio Hernández Bretón, "El Controversial Artículo 127," *in Revista Gerente,* 1999. I also considered the contracts entered into by PDVSA as "national public interest contracts" when expressing my opinion before the Venezuelan Senate in 1982. *See* Allan R. Brewer-Carías, "Los contratos de interés nacional y su aprobación legislativa," in *Estudios de Derecho Público (Labor en el Senado* 1982), Tomo I, Ediciones del Congreso de la República, Caracas 1984, pp. 183-193. Avalable at: http://allanbrewercarias.net/Content/449725d9-f1cb-474b-8ab2-41efb849fea5/ Content /II.1.49.pdf.

In that same regard, the Political-Administrative Chamber of the Supreme Tribunal after the enactment of the 1999 Constitution, issued multiple decisions relating to national public interest contracts, generally accepting that such contracts can be entered into by decentralized entities of the National Public Administration such as *Diques y* Astilleros *de Nacionales S.A. (DIANCA*), a national state-owned enterprise (Decision N° 847 of July 16, 2013);[61] *Corporación Venezolana de Guayana (CVG)*, a national autonomous institution created by law (Decision N° 1690 of December 7, 2011);[62] and *Compañía Anónima Venezolana de Televisión (VTV),* also a national state-owned enterprise (Decision N° 855 of April 5, 2006 - Case *VTV v. Eletronica Industriale*).[63]

The conclusions of these straight forward decisions issued by the Political Administrative Chamber of the Supreme Tribunal, nonetheless, have been tarnished by the confusing text of some decisions issued by the Constitutional Chamber of the Supreme Tribunal, particularly after the parliamentary elections of December 2015, [64] period in which the Constitutional Chamber began to consistently attempted to neutralize, undermine, and, in some instances, usurp the National Assembly's powers,[65] especially in relation to its political and administrative control over the Public Administration and the Government.

---

61 Supreme Tribunal of Justice, Political-Administrative Chamber, Decision No. 847 Case: *Diques y Astilleros Nacionales (DIANCA),* Jul. 16, 2013.

62 Supreme Tribunal of Justice, Political-Administrative Chamber, Decision No. 1690 Case: *Minera Las Cristinas (MINCA)* Dec. 7, 2011, p. 43. In this 2011 decision, the Political-Administrative Chamber of the Supreme Tribunal also referred to its previous decision No. 832 of July 14, 2004, in which it also recognized that mining concessions, in that case also entered into by autonomous institutes (public corporations) like the *Corporación Venezolana de Guayana* and the same *Mineras Las Cristinas S.A.* were "national public interest contracts," pp. 41, 72

63 Supreme Tribunal of Justice, Political-Administrative Chamber, Decision No. 855, Case: *Compañía Anónima Venezolana de Televisión (VTV),* Apr. 5, 2006, p.78.

64 See the comments on all the decisions issued by the Constitutional Chamber after 2015, in Carlos M. Ayala Corao y Rafael J. Chavero Gazdik, *El libro negro del TSJ de Venezuela: Del secuestro de la democracia y la usurpación de la soberanía popular a la ruptura del orden constitucional (2015-2017)*, Editorial Jurídica Venezolana, Caracas 2017, 394 pp.; *Memorial de agravios 2016 del Poder Judicial. Una recopilación de más de 100 sentencias del TSJ,* 155 pp., research by ONGs: Acceso a la Justicia, Transparencia Venezuela, Sinergia, espacio público, Provea, IPSS, Invesp. Available at: https://www.scribd.com/-document/336888955/Memorial-de-Agravios-del-Poder-Judicial-una-recopi-lacion-de-mas-de-100-sentencias-del-TSJ; and José Vicente Haro, "Las 111 decisiones inconstitucionales del TSJ ilegítimo desde el 6D-2015 contra la Asamblea Nacional, los partidos políticos, la soberanía popular y los DDHH," en *Buscando el Norte*, 10 de julio de 2017. Available at: http://josevicenteharo-garcia.blogspot.com/2016/10/las-33-decisiones-del-tsj.html; Ramón Guillermo Aveledo (Coodrinador), *Contra la representación popular. Sentencias inconstitucionales del TSJ de Venezuela*, Instituto de Estudios Parlamentarios Fermín Toro Universidad Católica Andrés Bello, Caracas 2019, pp 1-4. Available at http://www.fermintoro.net/portal/wp-content/uploads/2019/07/CONTRA-EL-PODER-LEGISLATIVO-WEB.pdf..

65 *See* Allan R. Brewer-Carías, "El desconocimiento judicial de los poderes de control político de la Asamblea Nacional," en *Revista de Derecho Público,* No. 145-146, (enero-junio 2016), Editorial Jurídica Venezolana, Caracas 2016, pp. 348-368, available at: http://allanbrewer carias.com/wp-content/uploads/2017/01/9789803653699-txt.pdf . See also my comments regarding all the decisions issued by the Constitutional Chamber since 2016, in:in Allan R. Brewer-Carías, *Dictadura judicial y perversión del Estado de derecho. La Sala Constitucional y la*

It was in this political and constitutional context that the Constitutional Chamber specifically issued two decisions, quoting a previous one issued in 2002 (Decision N° 2241), whereas she referred to the matter of national public interest contracts, not for the purpose of interpreting such notion, but only to resolve other questions; namely, (i) the character (binding or not) of the opinions given by the Attorney General under article 247 of the Constitution for the approval of national public interest contracts ruling that a national interest contract of public debt (Notes), to be entered into by a decentralized entity of Public Administration, in particular by the *Banco de Desarrollo Agropecuario* (*Bandagro*) which, according to the said provision of the Constitution, being a national public interest contract needed to be submitted before the Attorney General Office to obtain its legal opinion (No. 1460 of July, 2007); and, (ii) the nature of the Central Bank of Venezuela as a decentralized special entity of the State and of a contract to be entered into by such entity with a foreign international entity in the framework of an international agreement, to exclude it from parliamentary authorization (No. 618 July 20, 2016).

If it is true that none of these decisions established any sort of binding interpretation on the scope and content of article 150 of the Constitution regarding the notion of national public interest contract, their content have created confusions, due to the quotations made in their text of the already mentioned decision of the Constitutional Chamber issued in 2002 (Decision N° 2241), which was mainly related to a specific aspect of national *public debt contracts* entered into by the National Executive. The decision annulled an article of the Organic Law of Financial Management of the Public Sector, because it could allow for public debt contracts of the Republic to be entered into by National Executive with foreign companies not domiciled in the country, without the required parliamentary authorization; decision that in no way established according to Article 335 of the Constitution, any binding interpretation of the notion of national public interest contract.

A. Decision N° 2241 Of September 24, 2002 (Case: *Andrés Velazquez et al.*) annulling Article 80 of the Financial Administration of the Public Sector Organic Law

In the first of the aforementioned decisions, issued in 2002 by the Constitutional Chamber of the Supreme Tribunal (N° 2241 of September 24, 2002 *Andrés Velazquez et al.* case), which was subsequently quoted in the other two decisions of 2007 and 2016, the *thema decidendum* was the declaration of unconstitutionality and subsequent annulment of a provision of the Organic Law of Financial Management of the Public Sector, not having the Chamber established in it, under article 335 of

---

destrucción de la democracia en Venezuela, Colección Estudios Políticos, No. 13, Editorial Jurídica Venezolana International, Segunda edición ampliada. New York-Caracas, 2016, pp. 1-8; Available at http://allanbrewercarias.com/wp-content/uploads/2016/06/Brewer.-libro.-DICTADU-RA-JUDICIAL-Y-PERVERSI%C3%93N-DEL-ESTADO-DE-DERECHO-2a-edici%C3%B3n-2016-ISBN-9789803653422.pdf; Allan R. Brewer-Carías, *La consolidación de la tiranía judicial. El Juez Constitucional controlado por el Poder Ejecutivo, asumiendo el poder absoluto*, Colección Estudios Políticos, No. 15, Editorial Jurídica Venezolana International, Caracas / New York, 2017, pp. 1-8; available at: http://allanbrewercarias.com/wp-content/uploads/2017/06-/ALLAN-BREWER-CARIAS-LA-CONSOLIDACI%C3%93N-DE-LA-TIRAN%C3%8DA-JUDICIAL-EN-VZLA-JUNIO-2017-FINAL.pdf

the same Constitution, any binding interpretation of article 150 or any other provision of the Constitution, or on the notion of public interest contracts.

In the case, the Constitutional Chamber was deciding a constitutional judicial review action brought by several citizens (*Andrés Velázquez* and others) against Article 80 of the Organic Law on Financial Administration of the Public Sector,[66] which provided, in relevant part, that "once the annual indebtedness law was sanctioned, the National Executive will proceed to enter into contracts of public debt in the best attainable conditions possible and must inform periodically to the National Assembly."[67] The plaintiffs argued that, as written, this provision seemed to allow the National Executive to enter into public debt contracts of national interest with foreign states, official foreign entities, and companies not domiciled in Venezuela in violation of Article 150 of the Venezuelan Constitution, that is, without National Assembly authorization.[68]

The *issue* of the case was –thus- the unconstitutionality of Article 80 of the Organic Law. Agreeing with the plaintiffs that the relevant provision was unconstitutional, the Constitutional Chamber declared it null and void.[69] This partial annulment of Article 80 of the Organic Law (which was the *thema decidendum* of the case) is the only part that could be considered binding in the sense of having general *erga omnes* effects, along with it the reaffirmation that, in the case of national public interest contracts entered into with official foreign entities or foreign companies not domiciled in Venezuela, the prior National Assembly authorization is "inescapable."[70]

Bearing this context in mind, it cannot be deduced, from this decision, that the term "contracts of national public interest" in the 1999 Constitution only encompasses contracts concluded by the Republic through the competent bodies of the National Executive. The Constitutional Chamber did not rule in any way whatsoever that only the Republic can be a party to such contracts and that decentralized entities within the National Public Administration, such as public corporations and state-owned enterprises, cannot enter into national public interest contracts.

In this case the Constitutional Chamber noted that national public interest contracts "is a contracting species which *includes* '[…] contracts concluded by the Republic through the competent organs of the National Executive' (par. 100) implying that the National Executive is but one entity that may enter into such contracts, not the *only* entity.

The reason the Constitutional Chamber focused in this decision on national public interest contracts entered into by the National Executive, is that *those were the only* contracts *expressly mentioned in the challenged provision of Article 80 of the*

66 Supreme Tribunal of Justice, Decision No. 2241 Case: *Andrés Velásquez y otros, nulidad parcial artículo 80 de la Ley Orgánica de Administración Financiera del sector Público,* Sept. 24, 2002. Available at: https://vlexvenezuela.com/vid/andres-velasquez-elias-mata-enrique-283459075

67 *Id* p. 11-12.

68 *Id.* p 3.

69 *Id.* p 19.

70 *Id..*

Organic Law. As Román J. Duque Corredor has likewise observed, the "decision emphasizes public interest contracts of the Republic" because it was issued "in reference to the nullity of article 80 of the Financial Management of the Public Sector Organic Law, which governs the public debt operations of the Republic." That is, the Constitutional Chamber's analysis:

> "was centered on public interest contracts of the Republic, concluding that article 80 was contrary to the constitutional obligation of the National Executive to request the National Assembly's authorization to enter into contracts of national public interest, in the framework of public debt operations, when such contracts are entered into with States, foreign official entities or foreign companies not domiciled in Venezuela."[71]

In the words of Duque Corredor, the interpretation of the decision that a national state own enterprise, "is not subject to article 150 of the Constitution, because such provision only applies to the Republic and not to the state-owned enterprises like PDVSA" is no more than a "manipulation of the interpretation of the decision," which "does not establish that state-owned enterprises are excluded from article 150 of the Constitution."[72] The decision "equates the Republic to the National Executive, but does not do so with the intention of excluding the decentralized entities like state owned-enterprises from complying with article 150."[73]

In any event, proof that the Constitutional Chamber did not intend to limit the concept of national public interest contracts to comprise only those entered into by the Republic, came just months later in the decision N° 953 of April 29, 2003 (*EDELCA* case), whereas the Constitutional Chamber expressly recognized that contracts entered into by a national state-owned enterprise, *C.V.G Electrificación del Caroní, C.A. (Edelca)*, with two foreign corporations, *Centrais Elétricas Brasileiras S/A (Eletrobras)* and *Centrais Elétricas Do Norte Do Brasil S/A (Eletronorte),* were national public interest contracts, holding as follows:

> "Regarding the legal figure concluded, which is based on the international commitments signed by the National Executive, it is noteworthy that although it is the product of the aforementioned acts of government, it turns out to be a stipulation of a contractual nature, which constitutes a public interest contract, since a high interest of the Republic has been committed in the framework of its international relations with the Federative Republic of Brazil for the supply of electricity. Regarding this, the agreement concluded is subsumed within the limits defined by this Chamber, on public interest contracts."[74]

This decision of the Constitutional Chamber issued only seven months later, makes it impossible to deduct from decision N° 2241 any interpretation tending to

---

71 *See* Román J. Duque Corredor, "*Opinión sobre la inconstitucionalidad del Bono PDVSA 2020*," April 19, 2020, pp. 2, 3. See the information on this Opinion in: https://presidencia ve.com/regiones/jurista-roman-j-duque-corredor-respalda-la-inconstitucionalidad-de-los-bonos-pdvsa-2020/. See the text in: https://www.acienpol.org.ve/wp-content/uploads/2020/04/Nulidad-de-la-Bonos-2020-de-PDVSA.pdf

72 *Id.* Pp. 2, 3.

73 *Id.*

74 Supreme Tribunal of Justice, Decision No. 953, April. 29, 2003, pp. 11–12. The text of the decision is available at: https://vlexvenezuela.com/vid/lucia-antillano-283457047.

exclude from the concept of national public interest contracts, those entered into by decentralized entities of the State, with foreign corporations not domiciled in Venezuela.

In any case, I have been particularly critical of decision N° 2241, not because the annulment of the challenged provision of Article 80 of the Financial Administration of the Public Sector Organic Law, but because with it, perhaps inadvertently, the Chamber created the opportunity to spread confusion and politically motivated arguments by not mentioning, when discussing national public interest contracts, contracts entered into by decentralized entities within the National Public Administration.[75]

The Chamber, in effect, when referring to the notion of "public interest contracts" contained in Articles 150, 151 and 187.9 of the Constitution, only mentioned those entered into by the Republic, the States and the Municipalities where the national, state or municipal public interest is involved. The Chamber said that the notion of public interest contracts derived from the:

> "generic-species relation that exists between the concept of public interest and the notions of national, state and municipal public interest, considering that the determinant element would be the participation of the Republic, the States and the Municipalities."[76]

This originated the confusion leading to the opinion of considering that public contracts entered into by a national public corporation or a national state-owned enterprise could not be considered "national public interest contracts" under such Articles of the Constitution, which would be absurd and contrary to the intention of the Constitution.

That is why, referring to this particular point of such decision of the Constitutional Chamber, in 2011 I expressed that:

---

75 See Allan R.Brewer-Carías, "La Mutación de la Noción de Contratos de Interés Público Nacional Hecha Por la Sala Constitucional, para Cercenarle a la Asamblea Nacional sus Poderes de Control Político en Relación con la Actividad Contractual de la Administración Pública y sus Consecuencias," in *Revista de Derecho Público, No* 151–152, Editorial Jurídica Venezolana, Caracas 2017, pp. 371, 379.). In 2005, I said that this decision could lead to the misimpression that a contract entered into by PDVSA was not a national public interest contract, and that such assertion "has no sense. Nonetheless, without doubt, it is a national public contract entered into by a State public entity, in particular, a state-owned enterprise or a State private law person." *See* Allan R. Brewer-Carías, "*Nuevas consideraciones sobre el régimen jurídico de los contratos del estado en Venezuela,*" *in VIII Jornadas Internacionales de Derecho Administrativo Allan R. Brewer-Carías*, Tomo II, Fundación Estudios de Derecho Administrativo, Caracas 2006, pp. 449, 451. Availble at: http://allanbrewercarias.net/Content/449725d9-f1cb-474b-8ab2-41efb849fec1 /Content/VIII%20JORNADAS%20INTERNACIONALES%20DE%20DA%20ARBC%20FINAL .pdf, I have expressed this opinion since 1982, when, as a Senator for the Federal District, I prepared a memorandum to the President of the Venezuelan Senate on the notion of public national interest contracts and their legislative approval. Letter from Allan R. Brewer-Carias to Godofredo Gonzalez, President of the Venezuelan Senate, (Aug. 11, 1982), pp. 2, 6, 7. Available at: http://allanbrewercarias.com/wp-content/uploads/2020/04/Brewer-Car%C3%ADas.-Opini%C3 %B3n-al-Senado.-Contratos-de-inter%C3%A9s-publico-nacional.-11-Agosto-1982.pdf

76 The main argument of the Constitutional Chamber of the Supreme *Court* of Justice of September, 2, 2002, referred to the need for previous parliamentary authorization of all public debt and public interest contracts entered into by the Republic, the States and the Municipalities.

"On the contrary, in my view, contracts entered into by, for instance, national public corporation and State-own enterprises, according to article 150 of the Constitution have to be considered as 'national public interest contracts.' The contrary has no sense, and according to the Supreme Tribunal doctrine could lead one to consider that, for instance, a contract entered by *Petróleos de Venezuela S.A. (PDVSA)* could not be considered as a national public interest contract, which, I insist, has no sense at all. Nonetheless, and in spite of this erroneous doctrine, without doubt, that contract is a public interest contract, that is, a national public interest contract entered into by a State public entity in particular, a State-own enterprise or State legal person of private law." [77]

I have ratified these conclusions on this matter again in 2015, expressing that with this 2002 decision, an incorrect conclusion could be deducted in the sense that the Supreme Tribunal had restricted:

"in an unjustified way the notion of 'public interest contracts' expressed by Articles 150, 151 and 187.9 of the Constitution, referring only to those entered into by the "Republic, the States and the Municipalities" where the national, state or municipal public interest is involved. Under this Supreme Court analysis (which was addressed only to public debt contracts), public interest contracts entered into by a national public corporation or by national state-owned enterprises could be considered not to be "national public interest contracts" pursuant to Article 150 of the Constitution."[78]

This of course is incorrect, and even considering that the Chamber deliberately made the restrictive interpretation, it would be with no general effect, because in any case, the Constitutional Chamber in such decision of 2002 did not rule as *thema decidendum* on the matter of interpreting those constitutional provisions, being the decision adopted only related to another matter, specifically, to the partial nullity of article 80 of the Financial Management of the Public Sector Organic Law.

As I wrote in 2017, "regrettably and without any need to resolve the *thema decidendum*, which was the nullity of the last paragraph of article 80 of the Organic Law on Financial Administration of the public sector, [the Chamber]" began what could be interpreted as an "inconvenient process of reduction over the notion of contracts of national interest." To counteract this possible argument, I clarified that:

"the determinant [factor] in the Constitution in order to identify public interest contracts is not the participation of the Republic, of the States or of the Municipalities, but the determinant [factor] is the participation of state persons of public or private law in the three territorial levels, and that in addition to the

---

77 See in Allan R. Brewer-Carías, "Sobre los contratos del Estado en Venezuela," en *Revista* Mexicana *Statum Rei Romanae de Derecho Administrativo,* No. 6, Homenaje al Dr. José Luis Meilán Gil, Facultad de Derecho y Criminología de la Universidad Autónoma de Nuevo León, Monterrey, Enero-Junio 2011, pp. 207-252. http://allanbrewercarias.com/wp-content/uploads/2011/08/684.-677-SOBRE-LOS-CONTRATOS-DEL-ESTADO-EN-VENEZUELA.-Revista-Mexicana-Dcho-Administ-2010.-_IX-FIDA.-Mendo.pdf

78 See in Allan R. Brewer-Carías, *Administrative Law in Venezuela*, Editorial Jurídica Venezolana, 2015, p. 133. Available at: http://allanbrewercarias.com/wp-content/uploads/2013/08/9789803651992-txt.pdf

Republic, States and Municipalities, are for instance, the autonomous institutions or the state-owned enterprises at the three territorial levels."[79]

As I also wrote in 2011, referring to the possible "doctrine" in contrary sense that someone might try to deduce from the decision No. 2241:

"On the contrary, in my opinion, the contracts entered into for example, by national public corporations and state-owned enterprises, have to be considered as 'national public interest contracts' according to article 150 of the Constitution. The contrary has no sense and could lead to consider that according to the doctrine of the Supreme Tribunal, for instance, a contract entered into by Petróleos de Venezuela (PDVSA) could not be considered as a national public interest contract, which I insist, has no sense at all." Nevertheless, and in spite of this erroneous doctrine, without doubt, such contract is a national public contract entered into by a state public entity, in particular, a state-owned enterprise or state person of private law."[80]

In any case, I must point out that in none of my multiple works commenting decision N° 2241, I have ever accepted -much less affirmed or argued- that it contained a binding decision issued by the Constitutional Chamber pursuant to article 335 of the Constitution on any mater, and certainly *not* regarding the notion of national public interest contracts. That is why I must here clarify that although in a "footnote" to a study of mine published in 2005,[81] in which I referred critically to that decision, after mentioning the "restrictive" nature of the approach or interpretation made on the matter by the Chamber the qualifier "binding" was added, it was no more than an unfortunate and inadvertent material error, which appeared of course without any argumentation - as there could not be any -, since this not only was not -and is not- true, but did not respond to my own opinion held since 2000, about when and how the Constitutional Chamber of the Supreme Tribunal establishes "binding" interpretations in the terms of article 335 of the Constitution.[82]

---

79 Allan R. Brewer-Carías, "Nuevas consideraciones sobre el régimen jurídico de los contratos del Estado en Venezuela", in *VIII Jornadas Internacionales de Derecho Administrativo Allan Randolph Brewer-Carías. Contratos Administrativos. Contratos del Estado,* Fundación de Estudios de Derecho Administrativo FUNEDA, Caracas, 2006, Vol II, p. 379. Availble at: http://allanbrewercarias.net/Content/449725d9-f1cb-474b-8ab2-41efb849fec1/Content/VIII%20 JORNADAS%20INTERNACIONALES%20DE%20DA%20ARBC%20FINAL.pdf

80 *See* Allan R. Brewer-Carías, "Sobre los contratos del Estado en Venezuela," in *Revista Mexicana Statum Rei Romanae de Derecho Administrativo,* No. 6, Homenaje al Dr. José Luis Meilán Gil, Facultad de Derecho y Criminología de la Universidad Autónoma de Nuevo León, Monterrey, Enero-Junio 2011, (pp. 207-252), p. 4 of pdf; available at: http://allanbrewercarias.com/wp-content/uploads/2011/08/684.-677-SOBRE-LOS-CONTRATOS-DEL-ESTADO-EN-VENEZUELA.-Revista-Mexicana-Dcho-Administ-2010.-_IX-FIDA.-Mendo.pdf

81 Allan R. Brewer-Carías, "Nuevas consideraciones sobre el régimen jurídico de los contratos del Estado en Venezuela", in *VIII Jornadas Internacionales de Derecho Administrativo Allan Randolph Brewer-Carías. Contratos Administrativos. Contratos del Estado,* Fundación de Estudios de Derecho Administrativo FUNEDA, Caracas, 2006, Vol II, p. 541. Availble at: http://allanbrewercarias.net/Content/449725d9-f1cb-474b-8ab2-41efb849fec1/Content/VIII%20 JORNADAS%20INTERNACIONALES%20DE%20DA%20ARBC%20FINAL.pdf

82 As it is argued in the First part of this book. See also Allan R. Brewer-Carias, *El sistema de justicia constitucional en la Constitución de 1999,* Editorial Jurídica Venezolana, Caracas 2000, pp. 84-87

A condition that does not exist in the case of decision No. 2241 of September 24, 2002.[83]

Unfortunately, the material error included in the aforementioned footnote[84] was reproduced *verbatium* in other publications made later, whereas the text of the 2005 study was literally "republished," especially abroad,[85] as well as it appeared reproduced, in the same inadvertent way, in one of my books published in 2019.[86]

In the latter case, the nature of such material error that meant the inadvertently addition of the qualifier "binding" included in the aforementioned "footnote," was evident, since in the same text of the said book, I not only criticized the ruling, but I referred extensively to the issue of when the Constitutional Chamber establishes binding interpretations,[87] which was not the case of decision N° 2241 of September 24, 2002, whereas the Constitutional Chamber, as I have said, did not establish any

---

83 That is why, when criticizing extensively such decision in my book *Sobre las nociones de contratos administrativos, contratos de interés público, servicio público, interés público y orden público, y su manipulación legislativa y* jurisprudencial, Caracas 2019, pp. 230-238, I did not, in any way, refer to it as establishing any "binding" interpretation In the same sense, previously, in my other works in which since 2013 I studied and analyzed the *Andrés Velazuez* decision, I never used, argued or elaborated about it containing any "binding" interpretation, which it do not have. See the first edition of this book: Allan R. Brewer-Carías, *Administrative Law in Venezuela*, Editorial Jurídica Venezolana, 2013, p. 119; and in Allan R. Brewer-Carías, "La mutación de la noción de contratos de interés público nacional hecha por la Sala Constitucional, para cercenarle a la Asamblea Nacional sus poderes de control político en relación con la actividad contractual de la administración pública y sus consecuencias," in *Revista de Derecho Público,* No. 151-152, (julio-diciembre 2017), Editorial Jurídica Venezolana, Caracas 2017, pp. 376-377. Available at: http://allanbrewercarias.com/wp-content/uploads/2019/01/RDP-151-152-PARA-LA-WEB-9789803654412-txt.pdf.

84 I cannot but regret the evident failure in the proof reading of the original manuscript of the study, which I wrote during the month of October 2005, coinciding with the eventful weeks of the beginning of my now long exile in New York. The study was prepared during those days to be presented at the *VIII International Conference on Administrative Law Allan R. Brewer-Carías,* held in Caracas a few weeks later, at the beginning of November 2005, and which obviously I could not attend.

85 The text of the 2005 study (with the footnote) was reproduced literally (*verbatium*) later and for various academic purposes over the following years (along with the wrong mention in the foot note), in various Journals and Collective Works, among others: in *Revista Mexicana Statum Rei Romanae de Derecho Administrativo,* No. 6, Homenaje al Dr. José Luis Meilán Gil, Facultad de Derecho y Criminología de la Universidad Autónoma de Nuevo León, Monterrey, Enero-Junio 2011, pp. 207-252; in the collective book directed by Juan Carlos Cassagne (Director), *Tratado General de los Contratos Públicos*, Ed La Ley, Buenos Aires 2013, Vol. II, pp. 8-66; in my *Tratado de Derecho Administrativo. Derecho Público en Iberoamérica. Tomo III. Los actos administrativos y los contratos administrativos*, Editorial Civitas Thomson Reuters, Madrid 2013; Fundación de Derecho Público, Editorial Jurídica Venezolana, Caracas 2013, pp. 833, 893, 878; in in the first edition of my book *Contratos Administrativos, Contratos Públicos, Contratos del Estado*, Colección Estudios Jurídicos, No. 100, Editorial Jurídica Venezolana, Caracas 2013, pp. 316, 370, 388, in which the paper was also reproduced.

86 See Allan R. Brewer-Carías, *Sobre las nociones de contratos administrativos, contratos de interés público, servicio público, interés público y orden público, y su manipulación legislativa y jurisprudencial*, Caracas 2019, pp. 86 y 119.

87 In the book I elaborated extensively on the issue of when is it that a ruling of the Constitutional Chamber can be considered to contain a "binding interpretation." See Idem, pp. 147-157.

binding interpretation of article 150 of the Constitution or on the notion of national public interest contracts.[88]

Any reader more or less knowledgeable with my work could have noticed that it was an inadvertent material error, the existence of which, however, I myself did not realize until the first months of 2020, on the occasion of a judicial process in New York in which I argued as Legal Expert that such decision N° 2441 does not contain -as in fact it does not contain- any binding interpretation regarding the notion of public interest contracts or regarding the content or scope of Article 150 of the Constitution. On that occasion, the material error was brought to my attention although for the purpose, without reason, to argue that I was supposedly contradicting myself.[89] There was no contradiction, since I never before or after argued that such decision had such a character, which it does not have according to my own criteria about when the Constitutional Chamber establishes those binding interpretations based on article 335 of the Constitution, as it has been explained in the First part of this book.

In any case, in relation to this same matter, Rafael Badell Madrid has been emphatic in arguing, when analyzing the same ruling N° 2241 of September 24, 2002, that, when issuing it, the Constitutional Chamber expressly indicated that its examination was to determine whether "the National Executive when carrying out public credit operations may enter into contracts that may be included in the notion of contracts of national public interest...," therefore:

> "It was not subject to the consideration of the Constitutional Chamber, in the aforementioned action for annulment based on unconstitutionality, to elucidate the scope of Article 150 of the Constitution, or to determine whether legal persons of the functional public administration can sign contracts of public interest. The *subjudice* case referred to contracts of the Republic and hence the

---

88 That s why, in none of the critical analyzes that I began to write about such decision from 2013 (see, for instance, the Second Edition of this book: Allan R. Brewer-Carías, *Administrative Law in Venezuela*, Editorial Jurídica Venezolana, 2013, p. 119; and Allan R. Brewer-Carías, "La mutación de la noción de contratos de interés público nacional hecha por la Sala Constitucional, para cercenarle a la Asamblea Nacional sus poderes de control político en relación con la actividad contractual de la administración pública y sus consecuencias," en *Revista de Derecho Público,* No. 151-152, (julio-diciembre 2017), Editorial Jurídica Venezolana, Caracas 2017, pp. 376-377), I made no mention referred to said ruling having established any binding interpretation of the notion of public interest contracts. Precisely for this reason, I did not use this expression in any way when, in any of my critical analysis of the same decision No. 2441

89 See the Legal Opinions I filed as a Legal Expert Witness before the *United States District Court, Southern District of New York*, en el juicio *Petróleos de Venezuela S.A , PDVSA Petróleo S.A and PDV Holding, Inc., against Mufo Union Bank, N.A., and Glas Americas LLC;* the text of which are public and are available with the dcuments of the process in: https://www. courtlistener.com/recap/gov.uscourts.nysd.525475/gov.uscourts.nysd.525475.119.2.pdf; y en https://www.courtlistener.com/recap/gov.uscourts.nysd.525475/gov.uscourts.nysd. 525475.162.0.pdf. In any case, I am grateful that the aforementioned material error has been brought to my attention in the course of said process, as this has given me the opportunity to explain here the evident and inadvertent material error, and in any case, to ratify the criterion that I have always had in the sense that decision No. 2241 of September 24, 2002 does not contain any binding interpretation on anything, and much less on article 150 of the Constitution and the notion of contracts of national public interest.

ruling was limited to the consideration of public interest contracts to be signed by the Republic.

On the other hand, the scope of the nullity action of unconstitutionality set forth in article 336.1 of the Constitution, specifically seeks the declaration of nullity or validity of the challenged provision with *erga omnes* effects. In this case, the nullity was decided with effect *ex nunc*. It was not an action for the interpretation of the constitutional provisions that regulates public interest contracts, in which case the tribunal could have provided in the decisive part of the ruling the binding nature of the interpretation, as permitted by article 335 of the Constitution.

In this case, the ruling was limited to annul the provision, due to the fact that no provision establishes an exception or reference to the mandatory control of the National Assembly over the conclusion by the National Executive of contracts of national public interest within the framework of public credit transactions, but instead a general authorization through the annual indebtedness law and subsequent information.

Thus, in view of the matter under discussion, the content of the reasons of the ruling, the nature of the action decided and the text of the decisive part, it can be stated that the Andrés Velásquez, Elías Mata and others judgment established criteria, which have been reiterated in subsequent rulings by the highest court, as will be developed below, but in no case can be understood as a binding criterion for the exclusion of functionally decentralized administration entities as possible subjects [parties] of public interest contracts, therefore subject to parliamentary authorization. This explains that, in subsequent rulings, even reiterating statements made in the Andrés Velásquez, Elías Mata and others case, the highest court has admitted, expressly or implicitly, as will be seen below, that a functionally decentralized entity can sign contracts that are considered of interest public, if the other quantitative characteristics mentioned are met, in which case, the application of the constitutional regime of parliamentary authorization would be pertinent."[90]

Indeed, as I argued in the aforementioned 2019 book when commenting on the right of contractors to terminate contracts in advance in accordance with the contractual clauses and specifically referring to decision of Constitutional Chamber N° 1658 of June 16 of 2003 (*Fanny Lucena Olabarrieta* -Review of judgment case-), and N° 167 of March 4, 2005 (*IMEL CA*, -Review of judgment - Case),[91] the reading of said judgments was enough to verify that the Chamber, when issuing them, did not exercise any interpreting powers under Article 335 of the Constitution, which is not mentioned in them, not having established any binding doctrine in those cases on the interpretation of the Article 138 of the Constitution.

The same must be said, as also argued by Rafael Badell in the aforementioned quotation, regarding decision N° 2241 of September 24, 2002 whereas nothing was

90 See Rafael Badell Madrid, "Contratos de interés público," en *Revista de Derecho Público*, No. 159-160, Editorial Jurídica Venezolana, Segundo semestre de 2019, p. 15.

91 See Allan R. Brewer-Carías, *Sobre las nociones de contratos administrativos, contratos de interés público,* servicio *público, interés público y orden público, y su manipulación legislativa y* jurisprudencial, Caracas 2019, pp. 126 ss.

expressed about it being "binding" nor was Article 335 of the Constitution cited when issuing it. As I have said and explained, the "binding" nature of a constitutional interpretation on the content or scope of a constitutional provision that is made in a ruling by the Constitutional Chamber, must be expressly indicated in the text of the ruling, and must refer to the *thema decidendum* or core of what is resolved. It is not possible to consider binding any phrase or interpretive reasoning that a giving ruling may contain. In other words, from the text of the decision itself, the interpretation of the Chamber "on the content or scope of the constitutional norms and constitutional principles" must be expressly stated, which is the part that would have such a binding character, not extending to any arguments or phrases contained in the decision for the normative interpretation." [92] Therefore, as I have mentioned before, the Chamber, in its interpretation of a constitutional norm, must expressly and specifically indicate that it is establishing the a "binding" doctrine and, in addition, it must refer to Article 335 of the Constitution. [93]

This is, as I have said, the criterium I have expressed and maintained since 2000, having indicated that "the reasoning or explanation of motives of the ruling cannot be considered as binding, but only the interpretation that is made, specifically, of the content or scope of a specific norm of the Constitution."[94] In other terms, "what can be binding on a ruling can only be the decisive part, whereas the Constitutional Chamber fixes the interpretation of a norm, and this must be expressly indicated."[95]

That is why, in the case of decision N° 2241 of September 24, 2002, the only binding ruling it contains is the *erga omnes* annulment of article 80 of the Organic Law of Financial Administration of the Public Sector, and nothing else.

B. Decision N° 1460 of July, 2007 (Case: *Attorney General of the Republic, interpretation of Article 247 of the Constitution.*)

The reasonings about national public interest contracts expressed in decision N° 2241 of 2002 were copied a few years later, in decision N° 1460 of July 12, 2007 (Case *Attorney General of* the *Republic, Interpretation of article 247 of the Constitution),*[96] of the same Constitutional Chamber of the Supreme Tribunal, when a request to determine whether the legal opinions given by the Attorney General of the Republic were binding for the Administration, was filed. In this case, the Chamber, again, without any relation to the *thema decidendum* (which was the binding character or not of the Attorney General´s opinion) quoted the prior non-

---

92 See Allan R. Brewer-Carías, "La potestad la jurisdicción constitucional de interpretar la constitución con efectos vinculantes," in Jhonny Tupayachi Sotomayor (Coordinador), *El Precedente Constitucional Vinculante en el Perú (Análisis, Comentarios y Doctrina Comparada)*, Editorial ADRUS, Lima, setiembre del 2009, pp. 791-819..

93 See, for instance, Rafael Laguna Navas, "El recurso extraordinario de revisión y el carácter vinculante de las sentencias de la sala Constitucional del Tribunal Supremo de Justicia," en *Congreso Internacional de Derecho Administrativo en Homenaje al profesor Luis Henrique Farías Mata*, Vol. II, 2006, pp. 91-101.

94 See *Allan* R. Brewer-Carías, *El sistema de justicia constitucional en la Constitución de 1999*, Editorial Jurídica venezolana, Caracas 2000, p 87..

95 See Allan R. Brewer-Carías, *La Justicia constitucional. Procesos y procedimientos constitucionales,* Editorial Porrúa, México 2007, p. 415.

96 Supreme Tribunal of Justice, Constitutional Chamber, Decision No. 1460 Case: *Interpretación consltas del Procurador General de la República*, Jul. 12, 2007.

binding *Andrés Velásquez'* decision, eventually deciding that such Opinions of the Attorney General were of a non-binding character.

In the ruling the Chamber made no reasoning on the public entities that can be a party to national public interest contracts, and in particular, there is not a single word expressing that national public interest contracts are *only* those entered into by the Republic, or that the decentralized entities of the Public Administration cannot be a party to those contracts.

On the contrary, the ruling of the case specifically refers to a contract *entered* into by a decentralized entity of the National Administration (autonomous institution), the *Banco de Desarrollo Agropecuario*, accepting that *public debt contracts entered into by decentralized entities of the National Public Administration are national public interest* contracts. It was for such purpose that the Chamber in its arguments, transcribed parts of the *Andrés Velázquez* decision related to the matter of national public interest contracts.

As Rafael Badell pointed out, in this case, the Constitutional Chamber reiterated the discussion in *Andrés Velázquez et al.* on the nature and characteristics of public *interest* contracts and then declared that public credit transactions carried out by *Bandagro*, an entity within the decentralized Public Administration, are public national interest contracts. In this sense, the Constitutional Chamber recognized that the decentralized Public Administration can enter into contracts of public interest, in that case through public credit operations, and that:

> "for the corresponding issuance of the administrative act, in support of the formation of the will of the organ of the active administration consultation with the Office of the Attorney General of the Republic is constitutionally required, in accordance with Article 247 of the Constitution and Article 11 of the Organic Law of the Office of the Attorney General of the Republic."[97]

In fact, as already mentioned, the case involved the interpretation of Article 247 of the Venezuelan Constitution which requires the opinion of the Attorney General only regarding the character of such opinions for the approval of national public interest contracts. Specifically, the Constitutional Chamber was asked to clarify whether an Attorney General's opinion issued pursuant to Article 247 is binding on the Public Administration entity seeking to determine that the opinion is merely consultative.[98] That was the *thema decidendum* of the case. There were no abstract requests for interpretation of any constitutional provision, but rather a specific request for interpretation regarding the nature of Attorney General opinions with respect to specific public debt contracts (promissory notes) of the *Banco de Desarrollo Agropecuario (Bandagro)*, which is a public corporation within the decentralized National Public Administration.[99] The Constitutional Chamber ruled in this non-binding decision that the Attorney General opinions, while required by Article 247 of the Constitution, were merely consultative in nature;[100] and did not

---

97 *See* Contratos de interés público," text of the Lecture given at the III Academic Conference on Public Contracting, Institute of Legal Studies, Bar of Carabobo State, Valencia-Carabobo, June 29, 2018, p. 6. Available at: www.badellgrau.com.

98 *Id.* at 18.

99 Supreme Tribunal of Justice Decision 1460, *pp.* 19, 21.

100 *Id.* at 19, 22, 23.

address, in any way, the notion of what entities may enter into a national public interest contract, much less the supposed requirement of the Republic itself be a party.

Thus, not only did the Constitutional Chamber not affirm in its ruling N° 1460 of July 12, 2007 that public interest contracts are only those where the Republic is a party, but, to the contrary, the Chamber expressly accepted in this decision that "public debt contracts" (promissory notes) issued by a public corporation as a decentralized entity of the National Public Administration (and not the Republic) had to be submitted to the General Attorney for approval in accordance with Article 247 of the Constitution, which applies only to "national public interest contracts."[101]

C. Decision N° 618 of July 20, 2016 (Case: *Brigitte Acosta Isasis*, Interpretation of Articles 150, 187.9, 236.14, and 247 of the Constitution.)

Also a few years after the *Andrés Velazquez* decision, the Constitutional Chamber issued decision No. 618 of July 20, 2016 (*Brigitte Acosta Isasis,* Interpretation *of articles* 150, 187.9, 236.14, and 247 *of the Constitution*),[102] for the purpose of determining whether a specific contract to be entered into by the Central Bank of Venezuela (in the framework of an international agreement), which is also a decentralized entity of the State although with unique character, had or not to be submitted to legislative authorization.

The decision was issued only a few months after the opposition won control of the National Assembly in December 2015, when the Constitutional Chamber was already vigorously acting in collusion with the National Executive, to neutralize, undermine, and, in some instances, usurp the National Assembly's powers, especially in relation to its political and administrative control over the National Public Administration.[103] Thus, in such case, it can be considered that in fact, the Supreme Tribunal was acting not really as a court of justice, but rather as an agent of the Executive. In other words, as an agent of authoritarianism to neutralize the democratically elected National Assembly, which was internationally recognized since January 2019 (including by the United States) as the only legitimate, democratically elected body of the Republic. The actions of the Supreme Tribunal

---

101 *Id.* at 18, 21, 22.

102 http://historico.tsj.gob.ve/decisiones/scon/julio/189144-618-20716-2016-16-0683.HTML

103 See the comments on the Constitutional Chamber decisions in:Carlos M. Ayala Corao y Rafael J. Chavero Gazdik, *El libro negro del TSJ de Venezuela: Del secuestro de la democracia y la usurpación de la soberanía popular a la ruptura del orden constitucional (2015-2017)*, Editorial Jurídica Venezolana, Caracas 2017, 394 pp.; *Memorial de agravios 2016 del Poder Judicial. Una recopilación de más de 100 sentencias del TSJ,* 155 pp., research by ONGs: Acceso a la Justicia, Transparencia Venezuela, Sinergia, espacio público, Provea, IPSS, Invesp. Available at: https://www.scribd.com/-document/336888955/Memorial-de-Agravios-del-Poder-Judicial-una-recopi-lacion-de-mas-de-100-sentencias-del-TSJ; and José Vicente Haro, "Las 111 decisiones inconstitucionales del TSJ ilegítimo desde el 6D-2015 contra la Asamblea Nacional, los partidos políticos, la soberanía popular y los DDHH," en *Buscando el Norte*, 10 de julio de 2017. Available at: http://josevicenteharo-garcia.blogspot.com/2016/10/las-33-decisiones-del-tsj.html; Ramón Guillermo Aveledo (Coodrinador), *Contra la representación popular. Sentencias inconstitucionales del TSJ de Venezuela*, Instituto de Estudios Parlamentarios Fermín Toro Universidad Católica Andrés Bello, Caracas 2019. Available at http://www.fermintoro.net /portal/wp-content/uploads/2019/07/CONTRA-EL-PODER-LEGISLATIVO-WEB.pdf

can only be understood in light of its lack of independence and autonomy, which is the product of almost two decades of political subjugation.[104]

Specifically, ruling N° 618 of the Constitutional Chamber in the *Brigitte Acosta Isasis* case was issued without any respect for due process, without giving any notice to the National Assembly and without hearing arguments from any interested parties. [105] The decision was issued, as highlighted by Román José Duque Corredor:

> "in the framework of a permanent coup d'Etat against the National Assembly" […] "with the sole purpose of obstructing the National Assembly's controls."[106]

The decision, as mentioned, had the only purpose of supposedly "interpret" a few Articles of the Venezuelan Constitution with the sole purpose of establish if a contract to be entered into by the Central Bank of Venezuela (a decentralized entity of the State) was a national public interest contract.[107] The Chamber concluded, in order to prevent the newly elected National Assembly from exercising control over public interest contracts entered into by the Central Bank of Venezuela, in blatant disregard of the Constitution, that such entity was not a decentralized entity of Public Administration.[108]

---

104 *See* Allan R. Brewer-Carías, *Dictadura judicial y perversión del Estado de derecho. La Sala Constitucional y la destrucción de la democracia en Venezuela*, Colección Estudios Políticos, No. 13, Editorial Jurídica Venezolana International, Segunda edición ampliada. New York-Caracas, 2016, pp. 1-8; Available at http://allanbrewercarias.com/wp-content/uploads/2016/06/Brewer.-libro.-DICTADURA-JUDICIAL-Y-PERVERSI%C3%93N-DEL-ESTADO-DE-DERECHO-2a-edici%C3%B3n-2016-ISBN-9789803653422.pdf; Allan R. Brewer-Carías, *La consolidación de la tiranía judicial. El Juez Constitucional controlado por el Poder Ejecutivo, asumiendo el poder absoluto*, Colección Estudios Políticos, No. 15, Editorial Jurídica Venezolana International, Caracas / New York, 2017.

105 The Chamber employed a "process for constitutional interpretation" which consists only of consultation with its own past decisions, purporting to rule as a "mere law matter" and denying interested parties (such as the National Assembly) any opportunity to be heard. This procedure has been criticized as violating the most elemental rules of due process. *See* Allan R. Brewer-Carías, *La patología de la justicia constitucional*, Editorial Jurídica Venezolana, Caracas 2014, p. 177. Available at: http://allanbrewercarias.com/wp-content/uploads/2014/11/9789803652739-txt.pdf; and Luis Alfonso Herrera Orellana, "El 'recurso' de interpretación de la Constitución: reflexiones críticas de la argumentación jurídica y la teoría del discurso," in *Revista de Derecho Público*, No. 113, 2008, Editorial Jurídica Venezolana, Caracas 2008, pp. 26-27. Available at: http://allanbrewercarias.com/wp-content/uploads/2008/12/2008-REVISTA-113.pdf.

106 *See* Román J. Duque Corredor, "*Opinión sobre la inconstitucionalidad del Bono PDVSA 2020*," April 19, 2020, p. 4. See the information on this Opinion in: https://presidenciave.com /regiones/jurista-roman-j-duque-corredor-respalda-la-inconstitucionalidad-de-los-bonos-pdvsa-2020/. See the text in: https://www.acienpol.org.ve/wp-content/uploads/2020/04/Nulidad-de-la-Bonos-2020-de-PDVSA.pdf.

107 *See* El Tribunal Supremo de Justicia Sala Constitucional [], No. 618, Jul. 20, 2016, available at: in http://historico.tsj.gob.ve/decisiones/scon/julio/189144-618-20716-2016-16-0683.HTML.

108 See my criticism of this decision in Allan R. Brewer-Carías, "La mutación de la noción de contratos de interés público nacional hecha por la Sala Constitucional, para cercenarle a la Asamblea Nacional sus poderes de control político en relación con la actividad contractual de la administración pública y sus consecuencias," in *Revista de Derecho Público,* No. 151-152, (julio-diciembre 2017), Editorial Jurídica Venezolana, Caracas 2017, pp. 383-384. Available at:

In fact, the *thema decidendum* or "the central point of the request for constitutional interpretation filed," as quoted by the same decision, was:

> "none other than to clarify if the potential loan contract to be entered into by the Central Bank of Venezuela with the *Fondo Latinoamericano de Reservas* (FLAR) could be considered as a national public interest contract and therefore subject to the authorization of the National Assembly and in need of the legal opinion of the Attorney General."[109]

The Constitutional Chamber's entire ruling was that:

> "the potential loan contract to be entered into by the Central Bank of Venezuela with the *Fondo Latinoamericano de Reservas* (FLAR), is carried out in execution of an International Agreement signed and ratified by the Bolivarian Republic of Venezuela (Law of Approval of the Agreement for the establishment of the *Fondo Latinoamericano de Reservas*, published in the Official Gazette of the Republic of Venezuela No. 34172 of March 61989) and consequently, must not be considered as a public national interest contract, and therefore, is not subject to the authorization of the National Assembly, nor does it require of the opinion of the Republic's Attorney General's Office, as advisor organ of the National Executive, as expressly provided in article 247 of the Constitution."[110]

The decision did not rule in general terms regarding the notion of national public interest contracts, nor that only the Republic could enter into national public interest contracts and did not exclude from the notion of public interest contracts those entered into by decentralized entities.[111] Otherwise it would have simply ruled that the specific contract was not a national public interest contract because the Republic was not a party.

In fact, the Constitutional Chamber spends numerous pages in this decision analyzing the "unique nature" and functions of the Central Bank of Venezuela and his relations to the different powers and branches of government, concluding (among other things) that it is:

> "a legal person of Public Law, of constitutional rank, endowed with autonomy for the exercise of the policies of its competence, which is not part of either the Central Administration or the functionally decentralized Administration, but, according to the provisions of the Constitution of the Bolivarian Republic of Venezuela that regulate it and that have been developed by the Special Law that governs it, is part of the so-called Administration with

---

http://allanbrewercarias.com/wp-content/uploads/2019/01/RDP-151-152-PARA-LA-WEB-9789803654412-txt.pdf

109 Supreme Tribunal of Justice, Decision No. 618 Case: Brigitte Acosta Isasis, Jul. 20, 2016, p. 18.

110 *Id.* p. 33.

111 This is why, when discussing the *Brigitte Acosta Isasis* decision, Professor Rafael Badell Madrid referred to the criteria discussed in *Andrés Velázquez* that could "seem to exclude decentralized public administration from entering into public interest contracts" as "overruled criteria." *See* Rafael Badell Madrid, "Contratos de interés público," in *Revista de Derecho Público*, No. 159-160, Julio-diciembre 2019, Editorial Jurídica Venezolana, Caracas 2020, p. 7. Also published in published in Badell & Grau Law Firm Portal, http://www.badellgrau.com/, available at: http://www.badellgrau.com/?pag=205&ct=25927.

functional autonomy, which constitutes an element essential for the fulfillment of the purposes assigned by law; therefore, it requires a special arrangement and organization, proper and different from the common one applicable to other public or private entities."[112]

It was "based on these factual and legal arguments" regarding the "unique nature" of the Central Bank, including that supposedly it is not part of either the centralized or the decentralized Public Administration, that the Constitutional Chamber ruled as it did, on the "central point of the request for constitutional interpretation,"[113] to determine if such contract was or was not subjected to parliamentary authorization. The decision, of course, did touch on the question of whether contracts entered into by entities such as state-owned enterprises, which are indisputably part of the decentralized Public Administration, can qualify as national public interest contracts.

That is, it was in the context of the aforementioned specific request, and not in an abstract way, that the Constitutional Chamber ruled that the specific contract to be entered into by the Central Bank was not a national public interest contract requiring National Assembly authorization. In other words, as already mentioned, this ruling was not an abstract interpretation of general effect regarding the concept of national public interest contracts.

The Constitutional Chamber, on the other hand, after quoting a prior decision holding that the Central Bank "*belong[s] to the National Public Administration, with functional autonomy*" and is "integrated within the structure of the State" (No. 259 of March 31, 2016), a concept that reflects the very notion of decentralized administration, declared in a contradictory way that the Central Bank was *not* part of the Central or Decentralized National Public Administration.[114] This declaration was made with the main purpose of excluding the specific contract to be entered into with a foreign entity (*Fondo Latinoamericano de Reservas*) from the need to have the prior National Assembly authorization, arguing in addition that such entity was created by an international treaty that had already being approved by law of the same National Assembly. The Constitutional Chamber, although excluding the contract, for such specific purpose, from the category of national public interest

---

112 Supreme Tribunal of Justice Decision No. 618, pp. 29-30.

113 *Id.* at 18.

114 On the contrary, the Central Bank of Venezuela is and has been always considered part of the decentralized entities of the National Public Administration. *See*: Allan R. Brewer-Carías, "Introducción general al régimen jurídico de la Administración Pública," in Allan R. Brewer-Carías, Rafael Chavero Gazdik, Jesús María Alvarado Andrade, *Ley Orgánica de la Administracion Pública*, Editorial Jurídica Venezolana, Caracas 2009, p. 68; Allan R. Brewer-Carías, *Derecho Administrativo*, Universidad Externado de Colombia, Tomo I, Bogotá 2005, p. 390, 398-400, 433-434. Allan R. Brewer-Carías, *Principios del régimen jurídico de la Organización Administrativa*, Editorial Jurídica Venezolana, Caracas 1991 (Text reproduced in Allan R. Brewer-Carías, *Tratado de Derecho Administrativo*, Vol. II, Editorial Civitas, Editorial Jurídica Venezolana, 2013, pp. 353-356, 367. Available at: http://allanbrewercarias.com/wp-content/uploads/2013/07/BREWER-TRATADO-DE-DA-TOMO-II-9789803652074-txt-1.pdf.
See also, about the Central Bank of Venezuela, as part of the Decestralized National Public Administration, in *Informe sobre la Reforma de la Administración Pública Nacional,* Comisión de Administración Pública, Presidencia de la República, Caracas, 1972, Tomo I, pp. 298, 300, 310, 311, and 611, 613-615

contracts, it did not conclude, however, that only contracts entered into by the Republic are subject to article 150 of the Constitution, or that contracts entered into by entities that *are* part of the decentralized Public Administration, are not subject to such provision. On the contrary, this ruling could be interpreted as implying that such other entities can enter into public national interest contracts.

That is, according to the interpretation adopted by the Constitutional Chamber of the Supreme Tribunal regarding the provisions of articles 150 and 187.9 of the Constitution, when referring to the Central Bank of Venezuela as supposedly not being part of Public Administration, there is no doubt that in the case of national public interest contracts signed for instance by State owned enterprises, which are part of the National Public Administration, when entered into with foreign States, foreign official entities, or enterprises not domiciled in Venezuela, are national public interest contracts that must be authorized by the National Assembly.

As Román José Duque Corredor has argued, the Constitutional Chamber's statement that "the Public Administration is the one that can enter into contracts of national public interest" was made "with the purpose of pointing out that the Central Bank of Venezuela is not the National Public Administration, and thus, it is not subject to the mentioned article 150." That is why, in the words of Duque Corredor, it is possible to deduct from this decision that:

> "entities that are part of the Administration with functional autonomy, are exempt from the requirement of authorization or approval of public interest contracts; and that, on the contrary, the legal persons with public law or private law form created by the holders of the organizational power of Central Administration are not [exempted], because such persons are part of the National Decentralized Public Administration, of which the commercial companies of the State are part."[115]

I criticized this decision in my above-referenced 2017 article, pointing out that it was issued as part of a "judicial activism restrictive of the functions of the National Assembly" and with the specific purpose of "securing the exclusion of parliamentary control on specific loan contracts to be entered into by the Central Bank."[116] Given this purpose, it was convenient for the government to try to reduce

---

115 See Román J. Duque Corredor, "*Opinión sobre la inconstitucionalidad del Bono PDVSA 2020*," April 19, 2020, p. 4. See the information on this Opinion in: https://presidenciave.com/regiones/jurista-roman-j-duque-corredor-respalda-la-inconstitucionalidad-de-los-bonos-pdvsa-2020/. See the text in: https://www.acienpol.org.ve/wp-content/uploads/2020/04/Nulidad-de-la-Bonos-2020-de-PDVSA.pdf.

116 See Allan Brewer-Carías, Allan R. Brewer-Carías, "La mutación de la noción de contratos de interés público nacional hecha por la Sala Constitucional, para cercenarle a la Asamblea Nacional sus poderes de control político en relación con la actividad contractual de la administración pública y sus consecuencias," in *Revista de Derecho Público,* No. 151-152, (julio-diciembre 2017), Editorial Jurídica Venezolana, Caracas 2017, p. 383. Available at: http://allanbrewercarias.com/wp-content/uploads/2019/01/RDP-151-152-PARA-LA-WEB-9789 803654412-txt.pdf. That is why, on April 28, 2020, the National Assembly issued a resolution "ratifying that none of the decisions issued by the Constitutional Chamber of the Supreme Court of Justice since December 23, 2015 can be considered a valid and effective ruling, much less binding in the terms of article 335 of the Constitution, as they are the result of the illegitimate composition of the Supreme Tribunal of Justice and, furthermore, are part of the political decisions aimed at dismantling the constitutional order in Venezuela" (First Article). This resolution was based in

the scope of national public interest contracts to only those entered into by the territorial public law entities, excluding contracts entered into by entities like the Central Bank of Venezuela, which I considered "continues to be contrary to what is established in the Constitution."[117] Thus, as I wrote in my 2017 article, the Constitutional Chamber purported to "void of content" the concept of national public interest contracts,[118] completely seeking to distort a concept "so fundamental and important to administrative law."[119] In fact, the real purpose of the ruling was to sustain that because the Central Bank had a special status under the Constitution, it was not a decentralized entity of the State,[120] and as having constitutional autonomy regarding the National Executive power, it was not being subjected to National Assembly control pursuant to Article 150.[121]

Fortunately for the principles of administrative law in Venezuela, this decision, as well as the *Andrés Velazquez* decision, did not establish any "binding interpretation" under Article 335 of the Constitution, and thus the ruling applies only to *the specific loan* agreement *entered into by the Central Bank of Venezuela and the Fondo Latinoamericano de Reservas*. From a ruling so specific and limited in scope it is impossible and erroneous to conclude that the Constitutional Chamber established any general interpretation, much less any "binding interpretation," regarding any matter.

---

part on the fact that in those decisions "the Supreme Tribunal has contributed to disown the powers of the National Assembly" (Recital 4). *See* Asamblea Nacional, *Acuerdo de rechazo a la decisión de la ilegítima sala constitucional número 59 de 22 de Abril de 2020 Y de ratificación de la usurpación de la procuraduría General de la república por Reinaldo Muñoz Pedroza* (Apr. 28, 2020)).

117 See Allan R. Brewer-Carías, "La mutación de la noción de contratos de interés público nacional hecha por la Sala Constitucional, para cercenarle a la Asamblea Nacional sus poderes de control político en relación con la actividad contractual de la administración pública y sus consecuencias," in *Revista de Derecho Público,* No. 151-152, (julio-diciembre 2017), Editorial Jurídica Venezolana, Caracas 2017, p. 383. Available at: http://allanbrewercarias.com/wp-content/uploads/2019/01/RDP-151-152-PARA-LA-WEB-9789803654412-txt.pdf

118 *Id.* at 388.

119 *Id.* at 389.

120 As I mentioned when criticizing the Constitutional Chamber decision, it was issued "with the specific purpose of assuring the exclusion of the parliamentary control regarding specific credit contracts entered into by the Central Bank of Venezuela." For such purpose "it was necessary to reduce the scope of the public interest contracts to only those entered into by the territorial public law persons (Republic, States, Municipalities), excluding from the notion the contracts entered into by decentralized entities, like state owned enterprises, which in my opinion continued to be contrary to what is established in the Constitution." *See* in Allan R. Brewer-Carías, "La mutación de la noción de contratos de interés público nacional hecha por la Sala Constitucional, para cercenarle a la Asamblea Nacional sus poderes de control político en relación con la actividad contractual de la administración pública y sus consecuencias," in *Revista de Derecho Público,* No. 151-152, (julio-diciembre 2017), Editorial Jurídica Venezolana, Caracas 2017, pp. 383. Available at: http://allanbrewercarias.com/wp-content/uploads/2019/01/RDP-151-152-PARA-LA-WEB-9789803654412-txt.pdf.

121 It must be pointed out that *Petróleos de Venezuela S.A.* is also referred to in article 303 of the Constitution but, in a different way from the Central Bank of Venezuela, only for the purpose of providing that the State will retain all its shares, but not those of the "subsidiaries, strategic joint ventures, companies, and any other venture that is or has been established as a consequence of the business development of *Petróleos de Venezuela, S.A.*".

In conclusion, from the analysis made of the aforementioned decisions: N° 2241 of September 24, 2002 (Case: *Andrés Velásquez et al.*); N° 1460 of July 12, 2007 (Case: *Attorney General of the Republic II*); and/or N° 618 of July 20, 2016 (Case: *Brigitte Acosta Isasis*), issued by the Constitutional Chamber of the Supreme Tribunal on matters related to public interest contracts, it derives that they have not established any binding interpretation regarding when a public contract can be considered as a national public interest contract. That is, they have not established any binding interpretation pursuant to article 335 of the Constitution considering that only the Republic can be a party to national public interest contracts, and that contracts entered into by national decentralized entities are not national public interest contracts requiring prior parliamentary authorization according to article 150 of the Constitution. Thus, these decisions have no *binding* character under Venezuelan law with respect to the concept of national public interest contracts.

4. The principal consequence for a contract to be considered a national public interest contract: the parliamentary approval or authorization as a matter of public order

The whole discussion regarding the notion of national public interest contracts according to the Constitution, refers to one of the most important consequences of such notion, which is that under its article 150 they are subject to control by the National Assembly in two ways: first, they must be approved by the National Assembly when a law provides for such approval; and second, they must be authorized by the same National Assembly when entered into with a Foreign State, a foreign official entity or a foreign company not domiciled in Venezuela.

A. The prior parliamentary approval or authorization regarding national public interest contracts when a statute so provides

The first provision by article 150 of the Constitution requiring the approval or authorization of national public interest contracts by the National Assembly is when such parliamentary control is expressly provided by a specific statute, that is, "those cases in which such requirement is determined by law."

This means that under this first provision of Article 150 of the 1999 Constitution, and regarding the national public interest contracts, they only require such approval when a statute so expressly determines.

It is pursuant to this constitutional provision that many statutes have provided for the National Assembly's control over national public interest contracts. It is the case, for instance, of article 33 of the Hydrocarbon Organic Law on national public interest contracts of association for the "establishment of joint ventures and the conditions governing the realization of primary [hydrocarbon] activities," establishing that they are subjected to "the prior approval of the National Assembly."[122]

Examples of such national public interest contracts related to the oil industry and regulated by the Hydrocarbon Organic Law are all those that have been entered into by *Petróleos de Venezuela S.A* and its subsidiaries, like for instance *Corporación*

---

122 See *Official Gazette* No. 38.493 of August 4, 2006. Available at: http://historico.tsj.gob.ve/gaceta/agosto/040806/040806-38493-12.html.

Venezolana del Petróleo, with private corporations to establish mixed companies for the purpose of developing the oil exploitation and extraction. All those contracts, signed by *Petróleos de Venezuela S.A.* and by its subsidiaries before 2016 as national state-owned enterprises, were all authorized by the National Assembly.[123]

The parliamentary control over the oil industry has been so formal and exacting – particularly when the Government has had political control of the National Assembly – that even for an amendment of just one of the terms and conditions of those public interest contracts already approved for the incorporation of mixed companies, related to the special benefits for the Mixed enterprises to be given to the Republic, the National Assembly´s intervention was sought.[124]

The prior authorization of the National Assembly, according to articles 150 and 312 of the Constitution, has also been traditionally required in Venezuela for national public interest contracts of public debt. The relevant regulation was formerly provided in the old Law on Public Debt[125] and during the past twenty years in the Financial Management of the Public Sector Organic Law.[126] The latter according to the provision of article 312 of the Constitution, provides a complete regulation requiring parliamentary intervention and control by the National

---

123 It was the case, for example, of the approval by the National Assembly, through Resolution dated March 31, 2006 of the "Terms and conditions for the incorporation and functioning of Mixed Companies, as well as the model of the corresponding public contract to be signed between *Corporación Venezolana del Petróleo* and private corporations which between 1992 and 1997 had entered into Operational contracts. See *Official Gazette* No. 38.410, March 31, 2006, available at: http://historico.tsj.gob.ve/gaceta/marzo/310306/310306-38410-33.html. Based on this legislative authorization given by the National Assembly according to article 150 of the Constitution and article 33 of the Hydrocarbon Organic Law, the same National Assembly, subsequently approved, at the request of the National Executive the following Resolutions: 1) Resolution of May 5, 2006, establishing the terms and conditions for *Corporación Venezolana del Petróleo* to enter into national public interest contracts for the incorporation and functioning of the following Mixed enterprises: Baripetrol, S.A.; Boquerón, S.A.; Lagopetrol, S.A.; Petroboscan, S.A.; Petrocabimas, S.A.; Petrocuragua, S.A.; Petroguárico, S.A.; Petroindependiente, S.A.; Petrolera Kaki, S.A.; Petronado, S.A.; Petroperljá, S.A.; Petroquiriquire S.A,;. Petroregional Del Lago. S.A.; Petrorltupano, S.A.; Petrovbn-Bras, S.A.; Petrowarao, S.A.; Y, Petrowayu, S.A. (See *Official Gazette* No. 38.430 May 5, 2006; available at: http://historico.tsj.gob.ve /gaceta/ mayo/050506/050506-38430-39.html). 2) Resolution dated July 6, 2016, establishing the terms and conditions for *Corporación Venezolana del Petróleo* to enter into national public interest contracts for the incorporation and functioning of the following Mixed enterprises: Petrocumarbbo, S.A.; Petrodelta, S.A.; Petrokariña. S.A., Previously Known As Petromiranda. S.A.; Petrorjnoco, S.A.; Petrolera Mata, S.A. (See *Official Gazette* No. 38.473 July 6, 2006; available at: http://historico.tsj.gob.ve/gaceta/julio/060706/060706-38473-10.html). And 3) Resolution dated September 25, 2006, establishing the terms and conditions for *Corporación Venezolana del Petróleo* to enter into a national public interest contracts for the incorporation and functioning of the Mixed enterprise: Petrolera Sino-Venezolana, S.A., previously known as PETROCARACOL, S.A. (See *Official Gazette* No. 38.529 September 25, 2006; available at: http://historico.tsj.gob.ve/gaceta/septiembre/250906/250906-38529-26.html).

124 See *Official Gazette* No. 39273 September 28, 2009 (http://historico.tsj.gob.ve/gaceta/ septiembre/2892009/2892009.pdf#page=1).

125 See Luis Casado Hidalgo, *Notas para un estudio sobre el régimen legal del crédito público en Venezuela*, Caracas 1976, pp. 23, 42.

126 See *Official Gazette* No.6210 Extra of December 30, 2015. Available at: http://historico.tsj.gob.ve/gaceta_ext/diciembre/30122015/E-30122015-4475.pdf#page=1.

Assembly in public debt contracts, specifically providing for such purpose, among other acts, for the sanction of a Special Annual Indebtedness Law establishing a maximum amount for public debt transactions during the year (art. 82); and some prohibitions like the one set forth in article 105 providing that "No public debt operation could be contracted with a guaranty or privilege in national, state or municipal assets or income."

The Financial Management of the Public Sector Organic Law, on these matters of public debt, also as it is authorized in article 312 of the Constitution, provides for some exceptions, expressly excluding some public decentralized entities from the application of the whole Title III of the Law regarding the system of public debt (Articles 76-107). In that sense, article 101 of the Law excludes from its provisions the Central Bank of Venezuela and the "commercial companies created or that would be created in accordance with the Organic Hydrocarbons Law and those created or that would be created in accordance with Article 10 of Decree Law No. 580 of November 26, 1974, by means of which the Industry of the exportation of iron minerals is reserved to the state." This exemption covers among others, the state-owned enterprises of the Oil sector, only of course regarding public debt contracts related to their normal commercial activities when entered into with corporations domiciled in the country of Venezuela; not covering public debt operations entered with foreign corporations not domiciled in Venezuela.

In fact, such exception established in the Financial Management of the Public Sector Organic Law, as was even ruled by the Constitutional Chamber of the Supreme Tribunal in its decision No. 2241 of September 24, 2002,[127] cannot be extended to national public interest contracts when they are entered into by public entities with foreign States, foreign official entities or companies not domiciled in Venezuela. As the Constitutional Chamber has considered, such national public interest contracts with foreign counterparties are always subject to the constitutional requirement of prior legislative authorization, notwithstanding any other statutory exception that may apply. In fact, because of this, the Constitutional Chamber partially annulled article 80 of the Financial Management of the Public Sector Organic Law, considering that it:

> "directly and manifestly oppos[ed] Article 150, first paragraph and 187 numeral 9, second part of the Constitution, by not enshrining the constitutional obligation of the National Executive to require the authorization of the National Assembly for the conclusion of contracts of national public interest, in the context of public credit transactions, where such contracts are concluded with States, foreign official entities or companies not domiciled in Venezuela." [128]

Thus, although the Constitutional Chamber in the decision was not asked to decide the scope of the public entities that fall within the national public administration (and that are thus capable of entering into national public interest contracts), it ruled that when national public interest contracts are entered into with foreign counterparties (States, foreign official entities or companies not domiciled in

127 Available at http://historico.tsj.gob.ve/decisiones/scon/septiembre/2241-240902-00-2874 %20.HTM

128 *Idem.*

Venezuela), the Constitutional control provided by National Assembly authorization in Articles 150 and 187.9 is "inescapable":

> "the Organic Law on the Financial Management of the Public Sector can only authorize the National Executive to enter into public credit transactions by simply approving the Public Sector Indebtedness Law for the respective Fiscal Year, without the need for the control enshrined in Articles 150 and 187 numeral 9, of the Constitution of the Bolivarian Republic of Venezuela, where such operations consist of, for example, the issuance or placement of securities or the holding of contracts of national public interest with companies domiciled in Venezuela, but not where such transactions involve the conclusion of national public interest contracts with foreign states or entities or companies not domiciled in Venezuela, as in such cases, the application of the system of prior control or authorization for procurement by the National Assembly is inescapable." [129]

It follows that any national public interest contract for instance of public debt entered into by for instance a state-owned enterprise, as a decentralized entity, part of the National Public Administration, with corporations not domiciled in Venezuela, in order to be valid, it ought to have been previously authorized by the National Assembly. Signed without such parliamentary authorization, the contract must be considered invalid, illegal (unconstitutional), and thus, null and void *ab initio*, and non-enforceable.

B. The prior parliamentary authorization regarding national public interest contracts entered into with foreign States, foreign entities or foreign companies not domiciled in Venezuela

The second provision of article 150 of the Constitution establishes the requirement of the prior authorization by the National Assembly regarding all public interest contracts, when entered into with a Foreign State, a foreign official entity or a foreign company not domiciled in Venezuela.

On this provision, one of the ICSID Arbitral Tribunal in an award issued on November 18 2014, in the ICSID No. ARB/10/19: *Flughafen Zürich A.G. and Gestión e Ingeniería Idc S.A) v. República Bolivariana de Venezuela*, [130] in which the Veneuelan State as Defendant argued that the public interest contract considered in the case was null and void because it lacked of legislative authorization, the Tribunal, regarding contracts entered into with foreign companies expressed that in the "writing of article 150 of the Venezuelan Constitution there was a "clear terminological distinction," in the sense that:

> "205. This provision requires legislative authorization for the signing of State contracts with "foreign official entities and with companies non domiciled in Venezuela." Notice that the provision refers to "foreign official entities" and to "companies not domiciled -not to "foreign companies"-. The terminological precision cannot be casual:

---

129 *Idem.*

130 Available at: https://www.italaw.com/sites/default/files/case-documents/italaw4069.pdf

- In the case of "foreign official entities," the authorization is perceptive, even if the official foreign entity would not have a branch in Venezuela;

- In the case of "companies not domiciled," the creation of a Branch and its subsequent domiciliation excluded the need for the parliamentary intervention.

206. There are reasons of legislative policy that could justify this different treatment: to contract with a foreign official entity could affect sovereignty conditions; instead, contracting with a foreign company that has followed the conditions of registry and transparency required by the Venezuelan Commercial Registry, and has a representative in the territory of Venezuela, can be equated with the contracting with a Venezuelan company – that do not require parliamentary authorization."

The ICSID Tribunal in its award also referred to the legal provisions according to Venezuelan Law related to the procedure for a foreign company to be domiciled in Venezuela. It ruled as follows:

"200. ¿What must be understood for "companies non domiciled in Venezuela? The Commercial Code.

201. The Commercial Code contains an express provision regarding foreign companies and the establishment of Branches in Venezuela. In its article 354 III it allows foreign companies to establish branches in the country, as long as they register in the Commercial Registrar: "the company contract and the other documents needed for the incorporation of the company, according to the laws of its nationality and a copy due legalized of the provisions of such laws."

202. The following article requests that the foreign companies have in Venezuela a representative vested with full faculties.

203. In Exchange for the fulfillment of those requirements, the Commercial Code grants them the privilege of retaining its nationality of origin, but be considered companies "domiciled" in Venezuela:

"Companies also incorporated abroad that only had branches in the Republic, or exploitations that do not constitute their main purpose, retain their nationality but will be considered domiciled in Venezuela.

204. Article 354 of the Commerce Code thus establishes that a foreign company, by registering a branch in the Commercial Registry, maintains its foreign nationality but acquires domicile in Venezuela. The precept clearly distinguishes between:

- "foreign companies" – those incorporated out of Venezuela,

- "national companies" – those incorporated according to Venezuelan Law and have Venezuelan nationality,

- "companies domiciled in Venezuela" – the national companies and also the companies incorporated outside Venezuela, but that have met the requirements to register a branch in Venezuela."[131]

131 Available at: https://www.italaw.com/sites/default/files/case-documents/italaw4069.pdf

Consequently, all public interest contracts entered into with foreign companies not domiciled in Venezuela must be authorized by the National Assembly.

In this regard, for instance, and referring specifically to a public debt contract entered into by a state owned enterprise, Juan Cristóbal Carmona Borjas affirmed that according to Article 150 of the Constitution, when entered into with sovereign States, official foreign entities, or *companies not domiciled in Venezuela*, the contracts must always be approved by the National Assembly,[132] expressing that if it is true that "according to article 101.3 of the Organic Law of Financial Management of Public Sector, public debt contracts entered into by state-owned enterprises of the hydrocarbon sector, are exempted of the need to be previously authorized by the National Assembly:[133]

> "according to articles 150, 187.9 and 312 of the Constitution, the legal regime applicable to national public interest contracts is different "when they are concluded with States or official foreign entities, or with companies not domiciled in Venezuela. The difference seems to be that in these cases, there is no room for the exception of the law referred to in the heading of the article, in other words, this type of contract will always require the authorization of the National Assembly."[134]

Carmona went further, affirming that according to Article 150, "when the contract is of national interest but it is also [entered into with] a sovereign State, an official foreign entity or with a company not domiciled in Venezuela, the approval of the National Assembly will always be required."[135] Quoting a decision of the Supreme Tribunal, he affirmed that such authorization must be given prior to the signing of the contract "so that the contract to be entered into can be recognized as valid in accordance with the Constitution."[136]

Also specifically referring to public debt contracts entered into by public enterprises of the oil sector with corporations domiciled abroad, Román José Duque Corredor has opined, that they "have all the elements to be considered as national public interest contracts," because they are entered into by a state-owned corporation. [137] In the same sense, Rafael Badell Madrid, has also specifically referred to public interest public debt contracts entered into by state owned enterprises, considering that they are "national public interest contracts that have to be subject to the procedure of review and authorization by the National Assembly, pursuant to Article 150 of the Constitution, and to acquisition of the prior opinion of

132 *See* Juan Cristóbal Carmona Borjas, *Derecho y Finanzas. Hidrocarburos y Minerales.* Volumen II: *Actividad Petrolera y Finanzas Públicas en Venezuela*, Caracas 2016.

133 *Id.*

134 *Id.* at 429.

135 *Id.* at 431.

136 *Id.* at. 432.

137 *See Román* J. Duque Corredor, "*Opinión sobre la inconstitucionalidad del Bono PDVSA 2020*," April 19, 2020, p. 1. See the information on this Opinion in: https://presidenciave.com/regiones/jurista-roman-j-duque-corredor-*respalda*-la-inconstitucionalidad-de-los-bonos-pdvsa-2020/. See the text in: https://www.acienpol.org.ve/wp-content/ uploads/2020 /04/Nulidad-de-la-Bonos-2020-de-PDVSA.pdf..

the Office of the Attorney General of the Republic, as required by Article 247 of the Constitution."[138]

As already mentioned, Articles 150 and 187.9 of the Venezuelan Constitution require the control of the National Assembly over "public interest contracts," in two cases: first, in the case of *national public interest contracts*, when a law [statute] establishes that such contracts must be approved or authorized by the National Assembly; and second, in the case of *municipal, state or national public interest* contracts, every time they are going to be concluded with foreign States or official entities, or with companies not domiciled in Venezuela, or be transferred to any of them, in which case the Constitution requires the prior authorization of the National Assembly.

The second circumstance is independent of the first. In other words, if a national public interest contract is to be entered into with foreign States or official foreign entities, or with companies not domiciled in Venezuela, the National Assembly´s prior authorization is required even if is not established on any statute. In Venezuela, it is a very simple legal formality to domicile a foreign company, being enough to file a petition before the Commercial Registrar according to articles 354 and 355 of the Commercial Code.

Consequently, if the foreign company is not domiciled in the country, as it was ruled by the Constitutional Chamber of the Supreme Tribunal of Venezuela in decision N° 2241 of September 24, 2002 (*Andres Velázquez et al*, case), whereas article 80 of the Organic Law on Financial Administration of the Public Sector was annulled, "the application of the system of prior control or authorization for procurement by the National Assembly is *inescapable*."[139]

Thus, as I have recently written:

> "aside from the cases of the National Assembly approval of national public interest contracts when established by a statute, the Constitution also imposes that in any case the 'national, state and municipal public interest contract' to be entered into with 'foreign States, foreign official entities or companies not domiciled in Venezuela,' or when they are to be transferred to them, they must be submitted to the 'approval [authorization] of the National Assembly,' without the need, in such cases, that a statute provides for it."[140]

---

138 *Id.* at 19

139 In decision No. 2241 of September 24, 2002, the Constitutional Chamber of the Supreme Tribunal partially annulled article 80 of the Financial Management of the Public Sector Organic Law because this article did "not enshrin[e] the constitutional obligation of the National Executive to require the authorization of the National Assembly for the conclusion of contracts of national public interest, in the context of public credit transactions, when such contracts are *concluded* with States, foreign official entities or companies not domiciled in Venezuela." *See* Tribunal Supremo de Justicia, Sala Constitucional, decision No. 2241 Case: *Andrés Velásquez y otros, nulidad parcial artículo 80 de la Ley Orgánica de Administración Financiera del sector Público*). Available at http://historico.tsj.gob.ve/decisiones/scon/septiembre/2241-240902-00-2874%20.HTM.

140 *See* Allan R. Brewer-Carías, "La mutación de la noción de contratos de interés público nacional hecha por la Sala *Constitucional*, para cercenarle a la Asamblea Nacional sus poderes de control político en relación con la actividad contractual de la administración pública y sus consecuencias," in *Revista de Derecho Público,* No. 151-152, (julio-diciembre 2017), Editorial

C. Some consequences resulting from the lack of the required legislative authorization: the nullity of the contract.

In the first circumstance under Article 150 –approval/authorization required by statute– the requirement is for approval *after* the contract has been executed as a condition for the contract to become effective. However, as the Supreme Tribunal has held in accordance with scholarly opinion, in the second circumstance –contracts with foreign/non-domiciled counterparties– *prior* authorization is required as a condition of valid consent and contract formation.[141]

If the authorization of the National Assembly is not obtained when constitutionally required, there can be no valid consent and thus no contract can be formed. Accordingly, a public interest contract executed without the required National Assembly authorization is invalid and null and void *ab initio*.[142] Such a contract is illegal in the sense that it was signed in violation of the Venezuelan Constitution. Not only is such a contract entirely unenforceable, but it cannot be subsequently validated because it never came into existence in the first place due to a lack of valid consent.

As it was decided by the Political Administrative Chamber of the Supreme Tribunal in 2007, when ruling a case related to a public contract supposedly entered into by a public University (*Universidad Central de Venezuela*) with a private contracting party, without obtaining the prior authorization given by the University Council as provided in the University bidding regulations: such illegality provoked "the *non-existence of the manifestation of the will* by the University in order to be liable." In that case, due to the illegality affecting the contract in its formation (absence of consent for lack of the expression of the will of the University due to the

---

Jurídica Venezolana, Caracas 2017, pp. 376-377. Available at: http://allanbrewercarias.com/wp-content/uploads/2019/01/RDP-151-152-PARA-LA-WEB-978980365412-txt.pdf

141 In *decision* No. 2241 of September 24, 2002, the Constitutional Chamber of the Supreme Tribunal held that "by virtue of the expression 'no contract in the municipal, state or national public interest may be [executed] ...' contained in the first of those constitutional provisions (Article 150), it must be concluded that this second control mechanism consists of *an authorization that must be granted prior to the conclusion of the contract* of national, state, or municipal public interest, in order for the contract to be entered into to be recognized as valid in accordance with the Constitution." In support of its decision, the Constitutional Chamber quoted Professor Jesús Caballero Ortíz, who explained as follows in 2001: "If the contract cannot be [executed], it obviously concerns an authorization of a *conditio juris* for its validity, and as the very text of the rule confirms that it is a prior act, then, we insist, the contract [cannot be concluded]. So, the provision in Article 187, numeral 9 is then the one that must prevail and appears correctly drafted: it is for the National Assembly to authorize the National Executive to [execute] contracts of national interest and to authorize contracts of municipal, state and national public interest with foreign official entities or with companies not domiciled in Venezuela." *See* Jesús Caballero Ortíz, "Los contratos administrativos, los contratos de interés público y los contratos de interés nacional en la Constitución de 1999," en *Libro Homenaje a la Universidad Central de Venezuela, Caracas*, TSJ, 2001, p. 147; *see also* Rafael Badell Madrid, "Contratos de interés público nacional," in *Revista de Derecho Administrativo*, No. 19, Caracas 2004, p. 1964, p. 61, available at: https://www.badellgrau.com/?pag=7¬i=132..

142 *See* Allan R. Brewer-Carías, "La formación de la voluntad de la Administración Pública Nacional en los contratos *administrativos*," in *Revista de la Facultad de Derecho*, N° 28, Universidad Central de Venezuela, Caracas 1964, pp. 81-82. Available at: http://allanbrewercarias.net/Content/449725d9-f1cb-474b-8ab2-41efb849fea8/Content/II.4.13.pdf.

absence of the University Council´s prior authorization), the Chamber, due to the fat that the private contracting party provided the University with goods requested, constructed its decision ruling that the Universidad Central de Venezuela in the case, was due "to compensate *only to the extent of its enrichment, compensation that cannot be greater than the impoverishment* suffered" by the private contracting party. Therefore, the Chamber rejected the claim for payment of default interest or monetary correction, considering that it would constitute a contravention of the provisions of article 1,184 of the Civil Code that set forth for the liability in cases of enrichment without cause.143

The *ab initio* nullity of actions of Public Administration for which a prior authorization is required, and was not obtained, was established by the Office of the Venezuelan Attorney General since 1959, when it expressed that:

> "there is unanimity in the administrative doctrine regarding that the 'authorizations' that according to the Constitution or the statutes, public officials or agents of Public Administration require in order to adopt or issue certain legal acts, *are a constitutive element and necessary for the 'consent;' consequently, the omission of the authorization does not vitiate the consent, but prevents it, impeding its legitimate manifestation; and as consent is an essential element of the existence of the act, once it has been omitted, also the act, legally speaking, is inexistent.*"[144]

In the same regard, professor Eloy Lares Martínez has explained that:

> "When the Constitution or a Law requires an authorization for entering into a contract, such authorization is *necessary* for the validity of the contract. The authorization is a presupposition of legitimacy. If the contract is entered into without the authorization required by the Constitution or the law, it will be the product of a will that could not be expressed. Thus, the lack of authorization

---

143 See decision of the Political Administrative Chamber of the Supreme Tribunal, No. 1171 of July 3, 2007 *(Case: Universidad Central de Venezuela, UCV)*.

144 *See Informe de la Procuraduría de la Nación al Congreso Nacional 1959*, Caracas, 1960, pp. 624-625. *See also* "La formación de la voluntad de la Administración Pública Nacional en los contratos administrativos" in *Revista de la Facultad de Derecho*, N° 28, Universidad Central de Venezuela, Caracas 1964, pp. 81-82. Available at: http://allanbrewercarias.net/Content/449725d9-f1cb-474b-8ab2-41efb849fea8/Content/II.4.13.pdf. That is why, for instance, the National Assembly through its Resolution of September 25, 2018, regarding the public national interest contracts entered into by state-owned enterprises in the oil sector with private companies without the authorization of the National Assembly, declared the following: *"First*: To request the National Executive Power, and in particular the Minister of the Popular Power of Oil, to inform the National Assembly on the services contracts with private enterprises in which they have been allowed to perform primary activities related to hydrocarbon deposit, in order for the Plenary of the Assembly to discuss and approve such contracts according to what is established in the Constitution and in the Hydrocarbon Organic Law. *Second*: To declare null all the services contracts referred to exploration, exploitation, recollection, transport and initial storage of hydrocarbon deposit, in which private companies intervene that have not been approved by the National Assembly." Text available at: http://www.asambleanacional.gob.ve/actos/_acuerdo-en-rechazo-a-los-contratos-de-servicios-suscritos-por-pdvsa-que-permiten-que-empresas-privadas-actuen-en-actividades-primarias-de-hidrocarburos

influences in the regularity of the formation of the act. That is why it is a condition of validity."[145]

D. The rules regarding the formation of the contracts, including the parliamentary authorization are matters of public order

One important legal issue referred to these matters related to the formation of the national public interest contracts, and particularly, those related to the expression of the will of the public contracting party, in order to express consent, including the prior authorization by the Legislative body, is that they are matters of public order, and as such, governed by Venezuelan public law. This means that according to Venezuelan law, public contracting parties, in national interest contracts are not free to select the law of another jurisdiction to govern the formation and validity of the contracts they enter into.

That is, the relative sovereign immunity clause regulated in Article 151 of the Constitution, which allows public contracts of a commercial nature to provide that doubts and controversies that may arise on such contracts when they cannot be resolved amicably by the contracting parties can be resolved by foreign jurisdictions and according to foreign law, refers only to doubts and controversies arising from *the conduct or performance* of the contracts. It does *not* permit a public contracting party to select foreign law to govern the validity of the execution of the contract itself. In accordance with Article 151 of the Venezuelan Constitution, such validity is a matter of public order regulated and subject *only* by/to Venezuelan law.

In fact, according to the express provision of article 151 of the Constitution, among the contractual clauses all public interest contracts must contain – except when considered inappropriate pursuant to the nature of the object of the contracts -, are those related to the relative foreign sovereign immunity clause of the State and to international claims related to public contracts (known as a *Calvo* clause),[146] being both of these clauses applied to contracts entered into by the Republic, the States, and the Municipalities, as well as by all public decentralized entities of the State such as public corporations and state-owned enterprises.[147] Such provision sets forth:

"In public interest contracts, unless inappropriate according with the nature of such contracts, a clause shall be deemed included even if not expressed,

---

145 *See* Eloy Lares Martínez, *Manual de Derecho Administrativo*, 10 Edit., Caracas 1996, p. 302.

146 Allan R. Brewer-Carías, *Administrative Law in Venezuela*, Editorial Jurídica Venezolana, Second edición 2015, p. 369-*370*, available at: http://allanbrewercarias.com/wp-content/uploads/2013/08/9789803651992-txt.pdf.

147 As I wrote in 1992, seven years before the 1999 Constitution was approved, according to the 1961 Constitution, *then* in force: "The notion of "contracts of public interest" was fixed in the same Constitution (Article 126) as comprising "contracts of national, states and municipal public interest." That is, contracts of public interest not only entered by the Republic, but also by the States and by the Municipalities, as well as by public national, states and municipal entities (public corporations and state-owned enterprises. *See* Allan R. Brewer-Carías, *Contratos Administrativos,* Editorial Jurídica Venezolana, Caracas 1992 (reedición 1997), pp. 28-30.), reproduce in *Tratado de Derecho Administrativo,* Tomo III, Editorial Jurídica Venezolana ed., Caracas 2013, pp. 635-641. Available at: http://allanbrewercarias.com/wp-content/uploads/2013/07/BREWER-TRATADO-DE-DA-TOMO-III-9789803652081-txt-1.pdf

whereby any doubts and controversies which may arise concerning such contracts and which cannot be resolved amicably by the contracting parties, shall be decided by the competent courts of the Republic, in accordance with its laws, and shall not, on any grounds, or for any reason, give rise to foreign claims."

Regarding the relative sovereign immunity jurisdiction clause, Article 151 of the Constitution establishes, as an exception, the possibility for the parties in a public interest contract to choose, when *appropriate according with the nature* of the public interest contract, for it to be governed by foreign law, as well as to submit to a foreign jurisdiction the solution of doubts and controversies that may arise concerning the performance of such contracts and that cannot be resolved amicably by the contracting parties. This can occur, for instance, regarding public interest contract of commercial nature, [148] like public debt contracts, or like the contracts entered into for the exploitation of the Oil industry as was the case of the joint ventures of the *Apertura Petrolera* during the nineties, and of the contracts for mixed companies regulated in the 2001 Organic Hydrocarbon Law, providing for arbitration. [149]

The important point to highlight regarding the exception is that it applies only to doubts and controversies arising from the *conduct or performance of the contract;*[150] therefore it does not apply to matters that arise prior to the conclusion of the contract, for instance regarding the formation of the contract in relation to the expression of the will of the public contracting party; which are matters related *to the validity of the contract.*[151] This distinction, of course, is not expressly mentioned in the text of Article 151of the Constitution, because it is not specific to such provision. Rather, the distinction is inherent in one of the most basic foundations of Venezuelan law (indeed, of all private, public, and private international law)—that parties cannot contractually exempt themselves from laws governing the public order.

---

148 *See* Allan R. Brewer-Carías, "Comentarios sobre la doctrina del acto de gobierno, del acto político, del acto de Estado y de las *cuestiones* políticas como motivo de inmunidad jurisdiccional de los Estados en sus Tribunales nacionales", in *Revista de Derecho Público*, N° 26, Editorial Jurídica Venezolana, Caracas, abril-junio 1986, pp. 65-68, available at: http://allanbrewer carias.com/wp-content/uploads/2007/08/rdpub_1986_26.pdf

149 As I mentioned in 1992, regarding public debt contracts, they can be subjected "in their performance that occur abroad" to a foreign law and jurisdiction. *See* Allan R. Brewer-Carías, Contratos Administrativos *Contratos Administrativos, Editorial* Jurídica Venezolana, Caracas 1992 (reedición 1997), pp. 136–37.

150 The Organic Hydrocarbons Law of 2001, *Gaceta Oficial* No. *37.323*, (Nov. 13, 2001). reformed in 2006 expressly *recognized* the possibility to submit to arbitration the solution of disputes resulting from activities in the hydrocarbon sector when mixed companies were constituted with private investors.

151 As for instance has been observed by Haydee Barrios de Acosta, when the parties select a foreign law to be applied to the contract, it is in order to be applied to the "contractual obligations," or as pointed out by the former Supreme *Court* of Justice in a decision of April 27, 1971, that the author quotes, the intention of the legislator is to allow "the parties to "determine the *law applicable to the performance of the contracts*." *See* Haydee Acosta de Barrios, "La interpretación del contrato por el juez en el derecho interno y en el derecho internacional privado," in *Libro Homenaje a José Melich Orsini*, Universidad Central de Venezuela, 1982, p. 171.

This is particularly true with respect to the public contracting party's power of consent, which is a matter of public order. That is to say, the freedom of the parties, including public entities such as state owned enterprises incorporated according to Commercial Law, to choose the applicable law to a contract, extends only to what has been called the "personal and property matters of the parties" and cannot affect the "imperative provisions and general clauses tending to protect consent," the "imperative provisions of public nature" or "public order,"[152] or, in the case of public contracts, the imperative provisions of public law governing the powers (competence) of the public contracting party to enter into contracts and the process of formation of the contract or the expression of consent by the public contracting party.[153]

This means that only Venezuelan law, not foreign law, must govern the conditions of validity of national public interest contracts subject to National Assembly authorization. Article 1141 of the Civil Code, which is applicable to all contracts, including those entered into by public entities, establishes the general principles regarding the validity of contracts as follows:

> "Article 1141. The conditions required for the existence of the contract are: 1. Consent of the parties; 2. Object that may be a matter of contract; and 3. Lawful cause."[154]

The first condition of validity set forth in this provision, that the parties must mutually consent, which is a condition for the validity of any contract, provides, not only that the parties must express a deliberate approval for the proposed clauses to be included in an agreement, but also that they must have the legal capacity, power, or competency to give such consent in accordance with the law governing their actions.

In the case of contracts entered into by Venezuelan public entities, such legal competency is a matter of public order governed by Venezuelan public law, including the Venezuelan Constitution. Thus, as I explained in 1992, "apart from the clauses themselves of the agreement (which have force of law between the parties), and the complementary Civil Code provisions, all public contracts are subject in one

---

152 *See* Nuria Bouza Vidal, "Aspectos actuales de la autonomía de la voluntad en la elección de la jurisdicción y de la ley aplicable a los contratos internacionales," paragraph 4, p. 4; paragraph 7, p. 6: available in: file:///C:/Users/Allan%20Brewer-Carias/Downloads/slidex.tips_aspectos-actuales-de-la-autonomia-de-la-voluntad-en-la-eleccion-de-la-jurisdiccion-y-de-la-ley-aplicable-a-los-contratos-internacionales%20(1).pdf

153 That is why, for instance, Roberto Ruiz Díaz Labrano observes that the parties to a contract can submit "their contractual *relations*" or "their contractual obligations," which have "*inter partes* effects," to a foreign law, but always "with the limitations resulting from imperative or public order provisions to which the applicability of the foreign law is subjected." *See* Roberto Ruiz Díaz Labrao, "El principio de la autonomía de la voluntad y las relaciones contractuales," in *Libro Homenaje al profesor Eugenio Hernández Bretón*, Academia de Ciencias Políticas y Sociales, Editorial Jurídica Venezolana, Caracas 2019, Tomo I, pp. 735-740

154 Artículo 1.141.- Las condiciones requeridas para la existencia del contrato son: 1° Consentimiento de las partes; 2° *Objeto* que pueda ser materia de contrato; y 3° Causa lícita

way or another to public (administrative) law regulations, at least when referring to the competency or attributions of the public entity to sign them."[155]

The competency of a public contracting party to enter into a public contract must always be justified and must be exercised within applicable legal constraints.[156] As I observed in 1964:

> "The public contracting party needs to have legal competency, by the subject matter of the contract, the territory, the timing, the hierarchy, and the legal powers conferred on to it in order to enter into the contract. It is because of such principle that the Constitution says that the State shall not recognize obligations other than those entered into by legitimate bodies of the Public Power, in accordance with the law."[157]

A public entity seeking to enter into a public contract must have the express competency to do so and must comply, among other things, with all mandatory conditions of validity required prior to entering into the contract, such as the prior National Assembly authorization required by the Constitution for public interest contracts to be entered into with foreign states, foreign entities, or corporations not domiciled in Venezuela.[158] These conditions and requirements, having the character of public order, cannot be relinquished in any way (much less in the contract itself) by the public contracting party.[159]

---

155 *See* Allan R. Brewer-Carías, *Tratado de Derecho Administrativo*, Vol. III, Editorial Civitas, Editorial Jurídica Venezolana, 2013, p. 846. Available at: http://allanbrewercarias.com /wp-content/uploads/2013/07/BREWER-TRATADO-DE-DA-TOMO-III-9789803652081-txt-1.pdf *See* in Allan R. Brewer-Carías, *Administrative Law in Venezuela, Editorial* Jurídica Venezolana, 2015, p. 144, available at: http://allanbrewercarias.com/wp-content/uploads/2013/08/ 9789803651992-txt.pdf.

156 *See* Allan R. Brewer-Carías, *Derecho Administrativo*, Universidad Externado de Colombia, Tomo II, Bogotá 2005, p. 62 (Text *reproduced* in Allan R. Brewer-Carías, *Tratado de Derecho Administrativo*, Vol. II, Editorial Civitas, Editorial Jurídica Venezolana, 2013, pp. 431, available at: http://allanbrewercarias.com/wp-content/uploads/2013/07/BREWER-TRATADO-DE-DA-TOMO-II-9789803652074-txt-1.pdf.

157 Artículo 232, of the 1961Constitución (Currently: Article 312 of the 1999 Constitution). *See* Allan R. Brewer-Carías, *Instituciones Fundamentales del Derecho Administrativo y la Jurisprudencia venezolana,* , Caracas 1964, p. 166; available at: http://allanbrewercarias.net/ Content/449725d9-f1cb-474b-8ab2-41efb849fea5/Content/II.1.1%20(TESIS)%201964.pdf

158 I addressed this matter many years ago in a 1964 article entitled "The formation of the will of the Public Administration in administrative contracts." *See* Allan R. Brewer-Carías, "La formación de la voluntad de la Administración *Pública* Nacional en los contratos administrativos," in *Revista de la Facultad de Derecho*, Universidad Central de Venezuela, No, 28, Caracas 1964, pp. 79-82. Available at: http://allanbrewercarias.net/Content/449725d9-f1cb-474b-8ab2-41efb 849 fea8/Content/II.4.13.pdf..

159 As Joaquín Sánchez-Covisa explains: "By establishing a standard of public policy, the State determines the "duty to be" mandatory and imperative and is required at that time by the legal awareness of the group. As a result, those rules cannot be waived or relaxed by contracts between private parties. In this sense the duty to faithfulness between spouses, compensation for professional accidents or the payment of taxes cannot be relaxed by the will of the private parties. These are provisions of public policy, and therefore represent the idea of what is the purpose in that legal community of our days." *See* Joaquín Sánchez-Covisa, *La vigencia temporal de la Ley en el ordenamiento jurídico venezolano*, Academia de Ciencias Políticas y Sociales, Caracas 2007, p. 179. In this same sense, Francisco López Herrera, quoting Henri De Page (*Traité Élementaire*

That is, in Venezuela, as in elsewhere, the general exception to the freedom of the parties in contracts, are the public order (*orden público*) provisions, which, as expressed in Article 6 of the Venezuelan Civil Code, "cannot be renounced or relaxed by private agreements." Being an exception, this concept of public order, must be interpreted strictly, and in the Venezuelan legal system refers to legal provisions relating to the legal order that is general and essential for the existence of the community itself and thus cannot be relaxed according to the wishes of the parties.[160]

In this regard, the Public Administration Organic Law expressly establishes that the legal provisions regulating the competency or powers of public entities comprising the Public Administration are provisions governing public order,[161] and therefore, must be governed by Venezuelan law. For instance, Article 26 of the Organic Law of the Public Administration provides that:

> "*All powers attributed to Public Administration organs and entities shall be mandatory and binding and exercised under the conditions, limits and procedures established; they shall be not subject to waiver, nor delegated, nor extended and cannot be relaxed by any contract*, except for the cases that are expressly set forth in the laws and other regulatory acts.
>
> Any *activity carried out by an organ or entity that is manifestly incompetent, or usurped by those without public authority, is null and void and its effects shall be non-existent*. Those who undertake such acts shall be liable under the law, without the claim that they followed higher orders serving as any form of excuse."[162]

---

de Droit Civil Belge, Bruilant, Bruxelles, 1941-1949, Vol. I, p. 102), stated that "public policy laws and provisions are those that refers to the essential interest of the State or that affect the Collectivity, or that fix in private law the legal fundamental basis on which is based the economic and moral order of a determined society. In order to determine the public policy provision, it is needed to analyse in each case, the spirit of the Institution and to examine what and why it has relation with essential demands of the Collectivity or the fundamental basis of private law." *See* Francisco López Herrera, *La nulidad de los contratos en la legislación civil de Venezuela*, Caracas 1952, p. 96.).

160 For instance in Decision No 276 of the Cassation Chamber of the Supreme Tribunal of 31 May 2002, based on the opinion of *the* Italian author Emilio Betti, ruled that "the concept of public order represents a notion that crystallizes all those rules of public interest that demand unconditional observance, and that cannot be repealed by means of a private agreement. The indication of these characteristic signs of the concept of public order, that is, the need for the unconditional observance of its rules, which the parties cannot renounce, makes it possible to discover with reasonable margin of confidence, when somebody is or is not in a case of a violation of a rule of public order." Available at http://historico.tsj.gob.ve/decisiones/scc/mayo/RC-0276-310502-00959.HTM.

161 I wrote in 2005 that "the statutes that provides for the attributions or competencies are those called of public policy, which *implies* that the cannot be relaxed or abrogated by agreements between parties (article 6 C.C.) nor by virtue of the will of the public official that is called to exercise the competency." *See* Allan R. Brewer-Carías, *Derecho Administrativo*, Universidad Externado de Colombia, Tomo II, Bogotá 2005, p. 102 (Text reproduced in Allan R. Brewer-Carías, *Tratado de Derecho Administrativo*, Vol. II, Editorial Civitas, Editorial Jurídica Venezolana, 2013, pp. 432, available at. http://allanbrewercarias.com/wp-content/uploads/2013/07/BREWER-TRATADO-DE-DA-TOMO-II-9789803652074-txt-1.pdf

162 *See Gaceta Oficial No. 6.147*, Nov. 17, 2014

Thus, even in cases where the exception to the relative sovereign immunity clause is applied and the public contracting party agrees to accept the application of foreign law for the resolution of doubts and controversies arising from the performance or conduct of the contract, public entities are nonetheless *always required to comply with all of the conditions of validity of public interest contracts established in Venezuelan* public *law, as it is not possible for those conditions of validity to be waived or governed in any way whatsoever by any foreign law*. This includes the requirement that the National Assembly authorize public interest contracts to be entered into with a foreign State, a foreign entity, or a corporation not domiciled in Venezuela, which must be fulfilled before the contract can be executed, as a condition for the legal expression of the will of the public contracting party (consent).

Consequently, even though when in a national public interest contract, according to the exception established in article 151 of the Constitution, the parties establish that it is to be governed by the laws of a foreign State, the consent and validity of such contracts regarding the public contracting parties, as decentralized public entities of the National Public Administration, being mattes of public policy can only be governed by Venezuelan law.

5. Some Conclusions

The provisions of Articles 150 and 151 of the Constitution, when subjecting "national public interest contracts" to the control (approval or authorization) of the National Assembly, is applicable to all public contracts entered into by the Republic through any of her national government agency or organs, as well as by all the national public decentralized entity like national public corporations and national state-owned enterprises.

That has been the opinion I have expressed on the matter since 198 and was the intention for the inclusion of such provisions in the text of the Constitution during the discussions for its drafting in the 1999 National Constituent Assembly. This has also been the opinion of the overwhelming majority of Venezuelan public law scholars, all of which agree that national public national interest contracts include, not only those entered into by the Republic, but also contracts entered into by national decentralized entities. This has also been the criteria that has been followed by the former Supreme Court of Justice, and by the current Supreme Tribunal of Justice through decisions issued by its Constitutional Chamber and Political Administrative Chamber.

This notion of "national public interest contract," which is also included in articles 189.9 and 247 of the Constitution, comprising contracts entered into by the Republic, national autonomous institutions and national state-owned enterprises has not being changed in any way through any binding judicial constitutional interpretation. That is, the Constitutional Chamber of the Supreme Tribunal pursuant article 335 of the Constitution, or any other Venezuelan court, have established that national public interest contracts must have only the Republic as a party, excluding decentralized national entities of public administration.

In particular, the Constitutional Chamber of the Supreme Tribunal in its decision N° 2241 of September 24, 2002 (*Andrés Velazquez et al.* case), when annulling article 80 of the Organic Law of Financial Management of the Public Sector, although it referred to national public interest contracts entered into by the National Executive, which were the only regulated in the annulled legal provision, did not rule in any way applying article 335 of the Constitution, establishing any binding decision in order to reduce the notion of national public interest contracts to be applied only to those entered into by the Republic; or to exclude from such notions contracts entered into by decentralized entities of national Public Administration. Evident proof that the Constitutional Chamber did not intend to limit the concept of national public interest contracts to comprise only those entered into by the Republic, is that a few months later in its decision N° 953 of April 29, 2003 (*EDELCA* case), the Constitutional Chamber expressly qualified contracts entered by a national state-owned enterprise as national public interest contract.

The Constitutional Chamber, in two subsequent decisions, referred in a marginal way to the notion of national public interest contracts quoting some paragraphs of decision N° 2241 of 2002, but not for the purpose of interpret such notion as established in the Constitution, but only to resolve other questions, namely, the character (binding or not) of the opinions that the Attorney General has to give under article 247 of the Constitution for the approval of national public interest contracts (No. 1460 of July, 2007*)*; and, the nature of the Central Bank of Venezuela in order to exclude from parliamentary authorization a contract to be entered into by such decentralized entity of the State with an international entity created in an International agreement that had already been approved by the National Assembly (No. 618 July 20, 2016).

In none of such decisions the Constitutional Chamber affirmed that public interest contracts are only those where the Republic is a party. To the contrary, in decision No. 1460 of July, 2007 the Chamber expressly accepted that "public debt contracts" (promissory notes) issued by a national public corporation as decentralized entity of the National Public Administration were national public interest contracts; and in decision N° 618 of July 20, 2016, what the Chamber decided was that as only the Public Administration can enter into national public interest contracts, not being the Central Bank of Venezuela part of the Central or Decentralized National Public Administration, a specific contract to be entered by it and an international organization was not to be subjected to parliamentary authorization according to article 150 of the Constitution.

As aforementioned, the Constitutional Chamber in none of those decisions issued any binding interpretation on the sense and scope of the notion of national public interest contracts established in articles 150 and 151 of the Constitution, and did not determine, pursuant to article 335 of the same text, that only contracts entered into by the Republic can be considered national public interest contracts. The Chamber did not rule in an express way in such sense, not having even use the word "binding" or mentioned such provision of article 335 of the Constitution in the decisions. In addition, the Chamber did not order to publish the decisions in the *Official Gazette,* as it generally occur when a binging interpretation is established; and if the publication was ordered regarding decision No. 2241 of September 20, 2002, it was by imposition of the Organic Law of the Supreme Tribunal, because it annulled a provision of a statute.

In any case, the consequence of a contracts entered into by decentralized entities of National Public Administration to be considered as national public interest contracts, is that they are subjected to parliamentary control according to articles 150 and 151 of the Constitution, an in particular, the prior authorization of the National Assembly when they are going to be entered with Foreign States, foreign entities or foreign companies not domiciled in Venezuela.

I such cases, the prior parliamentary authorization is a condition of validity of the contract, as integral part of the process of formation of the will of the public contracting party. As such, and as a matter of public order, it can only be regulated by national law, not being possible for a public contracting party to renounce to the applicability of national law to the conditions of validity of the contract and to agree to subject to foreign law the process of formation of the will of the public entity. The possible agreement that the public contracting parties can include in national public interest contracts regarding toe applicability of foreign law, only refers to the matters related to the performance of the contract, and can never refer to matter of public order, as are the conditions of validity of contracts.

III. THE NOTION OF "ADMINISTRATIVE CONTRACT"

1. Legal provisions regarding administrative contracts

As previously explained, the only public contracts regulated by the Constitution are the "public interest contracts", characterized by the sole fact that one of its parties must always be a public entity (The Republic, the States or the Municipalities, according to the restrictive Supreme Court interpretation). No consideration whatsoever is made in the Constitution regarding other aspects of the contracts or to their purpose in order to be considered public interest contracts. Therefore, regarding contracts, the only distinction established in the Constitution refers to the level of government where the public entity which is a party to the contract is located: at the national, state or municipal level, which give rise to the distinction between national public interest contracts, state public interest contracts or municipal public interest contracts. No reference is made in the Constitution to so-called "administrative contracts", a concept that was formerly used in only a few legal provisions and developed by Supreme Courts decisions' doctrine (*jurisprudencia*) and by the legal doctrine.

Nonetheless, it is a fact that some "public contracts" (those in which a public entity is a party) have been traditionally qualified as "administrative contracts" following the administrative law terminology initially adopted in France for jurisdictional purposes, notion which has been adopted by almost all civil law countries. According to this terminology, administrative contracts have been distinguished from another supposed category of "private law contracts of Public Administration", based in the legal regime applicable to them: public or private law. This distinction, anyway, has been abandoned because in contemporary world the existence of a public contract only submitted to civil or commercial law (and not to public law) is impossible.[163]

But in Venezuela up to 2008, no general regulations referring to "public contacts" or to "administrative contracts" exists; and in fact, only two statutes used to use the expression "administrative contract:" [164] the Organic Law of the Supreme Tribunal of Justice,[165] and the Forestry, Soil and Water Law[166] when it qualified as such, the forestry products' exploitation contracts (Article 65).

Regarding the 2004 Organic Law on the Supreme Tribunal of Justice[167] which, followed the trends of the previous Laws regulating the former Supreme Court of Justice, established a procedural norm attributing jurisdiction to resolve all controversies related to "administrative contracts" entered by the Republic, the States or the Municipalities, to the Political Administrative Chamber of the Supreme Tribunal of Justice (Art. 5, 25). This competency was related to the Judicial Review of Administrative Action Jurisdiction (*Jurisdicción contencioso administrativa*) (Art. 259, Constitution). Based on this provision, a wide and equivocal case law doctrine was elaborated, trying to identify, among public contracts or public interest contracts, some which can be considered "administrative contracts", in order to

163 See Allan R. Brewer-Carías, "La evolución del concepto de contrato administrativo" in *El Derecho Administrativo en América Latina, Curso Internacional,* Colegio Mayor de Nuestra Señora del Rosario, Bogotá 1978, pp. 143-167; in *Jurisprudencia Argentina*, N° 5.076, Buenos Aires, 13-12-1978, pp. 1-12; in *Libro Homenaje al Profesor Antonio Moles Caubet*, Tomo I, Facultad de Ciencias Jurídicas y Políticas, Universidad Central de Venezuela, Caracas, 1981, pp. 41-69; and in Allan R. Brewer-Carías, *Estudios de Derecho Administrativo,* Bogotá, 1986, pp. 61-90; «Evoluçao do conceito do contrato administrativo» in *Revista de Direito Publico* N° 51-52, Sao Paulo, July-December 1979, pp. 5-19. See also, Allan R. Brewer-Carías, *Contratos Administrativos*, Colección Estudios Jurídicos, N° 44, Editorial Jurídica Venezolana, Caracas, 1992.

164 See Jesús Caballero Ortíz, "*Deben subsistir los contratos administrativos en una futura legislación?",* in *El Derecho Público a comienzos del siglo XXI. Estudios homenaje al Profesor Allan R. Brewer-Carías,* Tomo II, Instituto de Derecho Público, UCV, Civitas Ediciones, Madrid, 2003, pp. 1773. Apart from these two statutes, as indicated by Rafael Badell Madrid, "we know of no other statutes in our legal order which expressly refer to or define 'administrative contracts'", adding that "Notwithstanding, there are other statutes which regulate contracts that evidently are 'administrative contracts'", citing only as examples, statutes referring to public services or utility concessions, publicly owned natural resources' exploitations and fiscal reserved activities' concessions (the Organic Law of Municipal Powers; Auction Law; the Organic Law for the Promotion of Private Investments by means of Concessions; the Telecommunications Law; the Electricity Services Law; the Mining Law; and Law of Income from Matches. See Rafael Badell Madrid, *Régimen Jurídico del Contrato Administrativo*, Caracas 2001, pp. 49-51.

165 Articles 5, 25; *Official Gazette* N° 37.942, May 20, 2004. See Allan R. Brewer-Carías, *Ley Orgánica del Tribunal Supremo de Justicia,* Editorial Jurídica Venezolana, Caracas, 2000. Regarding the previous statute see Allan R. Brewer-Carías and Josefina Calcaño de Temeltas, *Ley Orgánica de la Corte Suprema de Justicia*, Editorial Jurídica Venezolana, Caracas 1989.

166 Article 65; *Official Gazette*, N° 1.004 *Extra.* January 26, 1966. See Allan R. Brewer-Carías, *Derecho y Administración de las Aguas y otros Recursos Naturales Renovables*, Caracas 1976, pp. 112 ff.

167 *Official Gazette,* N° 37.942 of May 2° 2004.

attract the jurisdiction of the Political Administrative Chamber of the Supreme Court[168]. This provision was eliminated in the 2010 reform of such Law.

Secondly, the other statute that used to employ the expression "administrative contract" was the Forestry, Soil and Water Law when qualifying as such, the forestry products' exploitation contracts (Article 65). Such provision was also eliminated in the 2008 reform of the Law. Apart from these two statutes, as indicated by Rafael Badell Madrid, "we know of no other statutes in our legal order which expressly refer to or define 'administrative contracts'", adding that "Notwithstanding, there are other statutes which regulate contracts that evidently are 'administrative contracts'", citing only as examples, statutes referring to public services or utility concessions, publicly owned natural resources' exploitations and fiscal reserved activities' concessions (the Organic Law of Municipal Powers; Auction Law; the Organic Law for the Promotion of Private Investments by means of Concessions; the Telecommunications Law; the Electricity Services Law; the Mining Law; and Law of Income from Matches)[169].

Beside the aforementioned two laws, with respect to public contracts, that is to say, those contracts entered into by public entities, including administrative contracts, before 2008, no general normative statute existed governing those contracts, as has been the case, for instance, of the Law on Public Administrations Contracts of Spain[170] or the Law of State Contracts of Colombia.[171] Before 2008, the statute referred in general to public contracts was the Bidding Law (*Ley de Licitaciones*) enacted in 1990.[172] This Law was substituted by the Public Contracts Law (*Ley de contrataciones públicas*) of 2008,[173] reformed in 2014, [174] in which the

168 See Allan R. Brewer-Carías and Luis Ortiz Álvarez, *Las grandes decisiones de la Jurisprudencia Contencioso-Administrativa 1961-1996*, Caracas, 1999, pp. 174 y ss.

169 Rafael Badell Madrid, *Régimen Jurídico del Contrato Administrativo*, Caracas 2001, pp. 50-51

170 See *Comentarios a la Ley de Contratos de las Administraciones Públicas*, Ed, Civitas, Madrid, 1996.

171 Jorge Vélez García and Allan R. Brewer-Carías, *Contratación Estatal, Derecho Administrativo y Constitución*, Bogotá, 1995; Rafael Badell Madrid, *Régimen Jurídico del Contrato Administrativo*, Caracas 2001, pp. 30-31.

172 See Allan R. Brewer-Carías, "El régimen de selección de contratistas en la Administración Pública y la Ley de Licitaciones" en *Revista de Derecho Público*, N° 42, Editorial Jurídica Venezolana, Caracas, abril-junio 1990, pp. 5-25

173 The Law was originally published in *Official Gazette* N° 5.877 of March 14, 2008. A reform of the Law was published in *Official Gazette* N° 39.165 of April 24, 2009. On this Law see Allan R. Brewer-Carías, "Los contratos del Estado y la Ley de Contrataciones Públicas. Ámbito de aplicación," in Allan R. Brewer-Carías, Víctor Hernández Mendible, Miguel Mónaco, Aurilivi Linares Martínez, José Ignacio Hernández G., Carlos García Soto, Mauricio Subero Mujica, Alejandro Canónico Sarabia, Gustavo Linares Benzo, Manuel Rojas Pérez, Luis Alfonso herrera Orellana y Víctor Raúl Díaz Chirino *Ley de Contrataciones Públicas*, Editorial Jurídica Venezolana, Colección Textos legislativos N° 44 (2ª Edición Actualizada y aumentada), Caracas 2009, pp. 9-47. See in addition, Allan R. Brewer-Carías, "Sobre los Contratos del Estado en Venezuela," en *Derecho Administrativo Iberoamericano (Contratos Administrativos, Servicios públicos, Acto administrativo y procedimiento administrativo, Derecho administrativo ambiental, Limitaciones a la libertad), IV Congreso Internacional de Derecho Administrativo*, Mendoza, Argentina, 2010, pp. 837-866.; and in *Revista Mexicana Statum Rei Romanae de Derecho*

expression "administrative contracts" is not used, which applies to all contracts for the acquisition of goods, the rendering of services, and the execution of works (art. 1), entered not only by offices and entities of the Central and Decentralized National, State and Municipal levels of government (art. 3.1), but also by the state own enterprises where the latter could have shares in a proportion of 50% or more (art. 3.4), as well as those other state own enterprises where the latter also could have more than the 50% of their shares (art. 3.4).

2. Case-Law doctrine regarding "administrative contracts"

The notion of administrative contracts therefore, was been a creation of the judicial doctrine set forth by the former Supreme Court of Justice, developed by the legal doctrine, in order to identify the public contracts whose conflicts were to be resolved exclusively by the Supreme Court and not by the lower courts of the Judicial review of administrative action Jurisdiction (*Jurisdicción contencioso-administrativa*).

The notion evolved from a traditional and strict sense once, to a broader sense definition, according to which "administrative contracts" result to be almost equivalent to any "public contracts". In this regard, for instance in decision N° 357 of April, 14th 2004, the Politico-Administrative Chamber of the Supreme Tribunal of Justice stated:

> "The legal doctrine and the "*jurisprudencia*" [judicial doctrine] of this Chamber had indicated the following as essential characteristics of administrative contracts: a) That one of the Parties be a public entity; b) That the purpose of the contract be related to a public usefulness or a public service; c) and as a consequence of the later, it must be understood the presence in such contracts of certain and exorbitant Public Administration prerogatives, even though they are not expressly inserted in the their text."[175]

According to this broad definition, eventually, any public contract can be considered an administrative contract; being the consequence of a public contract to be considered an administrative contract, the existence in an explicit or implicit way, of exorbitant clauses that allow Public Administration to unilaterally decide on contractual matters; therefore being the qualification of a contract as an administrative one, because of the possibility of the use of these extraordinary powers by the Public entity, an *ex post facto* matter.

On the other hand, up to May 2004, the justification to distinguish administrative contracts among public contracts, has been a judicial one, due to the already mentioned monopoly the Politico-Administrative Chamber of the Supreme Tribunal use to have regarding the resolution of conflicts referring to administrative contracts.

Administrativo, N° 6, Homenaje al Dr. José Luis Meilán Gil, Facultad de Derecho y Criminología de la Universidad Autónoma de Nuevo León, Monterrey, Enero-Junio 2011, pp. 207-252.

174 *Official Gazette* N° 6.154 Extra. of November 19, 2014.

175 Case: *Empresa Constructora Irpresent vs. Alcaldía San Carlos de Austria del Estado Cojedes.*

This monopoly disappeared since the May 2004 Organic Law on the Supreme Tribunal of Justice[176], corresponding now to all courts of the said Judicial review of administrative action Jurisdiction to resolve matters regarding all claims against public entities, including those arising from all sort of public contracts, including administrative contracts, which in fact, has provoked the loss of the interest of the distinction.

In any event, judicial decision's doctrine as well as the general legal doctrine, had identify among public contracts those traditionally called "administrative contracts", because of the obvious public interest involved in their execution. Among them, for instance, always have been considered as administrative contracts, contracts with the purpose of rendering a public service in the sense of public utility (*servicio público*) such as the public transportation concessions; and also, the concessions for the exploitation of natural resources, like the mining concessions; the concessions for water supply to urban areas; the contracts of operation of public services facilities, like a port of public use; the contracts for the execution of public works; the contracts of public debts, or the contracts for the supplying of goods for the regular functioning of Public Administration.

In this sense, for instance, the Supreme Court of Justice in decision of August 8, 1999 (Case: *Apertura Petrolera*), considered as "administrative contracts" those entered between State own enterprises of the nationalized Oil Industry and private companies for the establishment of Association Agreements for the exploitation of oil in the Orinoco Belt, because of the evident public purpose of those contract. [177] On the other hand, these qualifications were used in order to justify the possible exercise of some extraordinary powers by the public entity which is a party to the contract, in order to achieve and safeguard the public interest involved. Nonetheless, the practical effect of the Supreme Tribunal judicial doctrine is that these so-called extraordinary clauses ("*cláusulas exhorbitantes*"), can be justify and can be found in all sort of public contracts, particularly when the Public Party decides to act accordingly by its application; therefore, considering the contract as an administrative contract. That is why the Supreme Tribunal judicial doctrine has considered that such exorbitant clauses are "inherent" to all administrative contracts. For that purpose, in any event, they have to be regulated in particular statutes referring to specific public contracts or in the text of the contracts' clauses.

---

176 *Official Gazette*, N° 37942, 19-05-2004. See Allan R. Brewer-Carías, *Ley Orgánica del Tribunal Supremo de Justicia*, Caracas 2004, pp. 210 ff.

177 See the Supreme Court Decision of August 17, 1999 rejecting the challenging of the constitutionality of the initial parliamentary act authorizing the Framework of Conditions for the "Association Agreements for the Exploration at Risk of New Areas and the Production of Hydrocarbons under the Shared-Profit Scheme" *("Convenios de Asociación para la exploración a riesgo de nuevas áreas y la producción de hidrocarburos bajo el esquema de ganancias compartidas")* (also known as Shared-Risk-and Profit Exploration Agreements) dated July 4, 1995, in Allan R. Brewer-Carías (Compilator), *Documentos del juicio de la Apertura Petrolera (1996-1999),* Caracas 2004, in www.allanbrewercarias.com (Biblioteca Virtual, I.2. Documentos, N° 22, 2004), pp. 280-328. I acted as counsel for PDVSA in this proceeding, defending the constitutionality of the parliamentary authorization.

3. Legal doctrine regarding administrative contracts

I have, as well as all administrative law professors and researchers, extensively written on the subject of administrative contracts.[178] One of the first Venezuelan contemporary studies on the subject was written as a Chapter ("The Theory of Administrative Contracts") in my Doctoral Thesis *Las Instituciones Fundamentales del Derecho Administrativo y la Jurisprudencia Venezolana*, Caracas 1964, pp. 155-223. In said Thesis, written in France between 1962 and 1963 while following administrative law courses in the Law Faculty of the University of Paris, doubtless influenced by the French Administrative Law doctrine, the definition then adopted in order to identify administrative contracts was the "purpose of public service" sought through the contract.[179] Later I even questioned the same notion of "administrative contracts," [180] and continued to study the subject from the more general approach of "public contracts." [181]

---

178 See: Allan R. Brewer-Carías, «Los contratos de la administración en la jurisprudencia venezolana» in *Revista de la Facultad de Derecho*, N° 26, Universidad Central de Venezuela, Caracas, 1963, pp. 127-154; «La formación de la voluntad de la Administración Pública Nacional en los contratos administrativos» in *Revista de la Facultad de Derecho*, N° 28, Universidad Central de Venezuela, Caracas, 1964, pp. 61-112; «La formación de la voluntad de la Administración Pública Nacional en la contratación administrativa», (with references to Uruguayan law by Horacio Casinelli Muñoz) in *Revista de Derecho, Jurisprudencia y Administración*, Tomo 62, N° 2-3, Montevideo 1965, pp. 25-56; «Los contratos de la Administración en la doctrina de la Consultoría Jurídica» in *Revista del Ministerio de Justicia*, N° 48, Año XIII, Caracas, enero-marzo 1964, pp. 27-75; «Los contratos de la Administración en la doctrina de la Procuraduría General de la República» in *Revista de la Facultad de Derecho*, N° 30, Universidad Central de Venezuela, Caracas, December 1964, pp. 173-232; «Los contratos de la administración en la doctrina de la Procuraduría General de la República II» in *Revista de la Facultad de Derecho*, N° 31, Universidad Central de Venezuela, Caracas, June 1965, pp. 269-299; «La facultad de la Administración de modificar unilateralmente los contratos administrativos» en *Libro-Homenaje a la Memoria de Roberto Goldschmidt*, Facultad de Derecho, Universidad Central de Venezuela, Caracas, 1967, pp. 755-778; «La facultad de la Administración de modificar unilateralmente los contratos administrativos (con especial referencia a los contratos de obra pública en el derecho venezolano)» in *Revista de Derecho Español y Americano*, Instituto de Cultura Hispánica, N° 19, Year XIII, Madrid, January-March 1968, pp. 101-117; «Algunas reflexiones sobre el equilibrio financiero en los contratos administrativos y la aplicabilidad en Venezuela de la concepción amplia de la Teoría del Hecho del Príncipe», in *Revista Control Fiscal y Tecnificación Administrativa*, Year XIII, N° 65, Contraloría General de la República, Caracas, 1972, pp. 86-93; «La autorización legislativa» en *Procedimientos Parlamentarios para la aprobación de Contratos de interés nacional*, Imprenta del Congreso de la República, Caracas, 1973, pp. 77-92; «Consideraciones sobre los efectos de la ruptura de la ecuación económica de un contrato administrativo por una ley declarada nula por inconstitucional» en *Cuadernos de Derecho Público*, Facultad de Derecho, Universidad de Los Andes, N° 2, Mérida 1976, pp. 5-26; Allan R. Brewer-Carías, *Jurisprudencia de la Corte Suprema 1930-1974 y Estudios de Derecho Administrativo,* Tomo III: *La Actividad Administrativa.* Vol. 2. *Recursos y Contratos Administrativos***,** Ediciones del Instituto de Derecho Público, Facultad de Derecho, Universidad Central de Venezuela, Caracas, 1977, 587 pp

179 Allan R. Brewer-Carías, *Las Instituciones Fundamentales del Derecho Administrativo y la Jurisprudencia venezolana*, Caracas, 1964, p. 162.

180 Allan R. Brewer-Carías, See Allan R. Brewer-Carías, «La evolución del concepto de contrato administrativo» in *El Derecho Administrativo en América Latina, Curso Internacional,* Colegio Mayor de Nuestra Señora del Rosario, Bogotá 1978, pp. 143-167; in *Jurisprudencia Argentina*, N° 5.076, Buenos Aires, 13-12-1978, pp. 1-12; in *Libro Homenaje al Profesor Antonio*

Now, regarding the original idea of the "purpose of public service" in the sense of management of public interests by the Public Administration,[182] which justified the administrative law regime applicable to those administrative contracts and the jurisdiction of the Political Administrative Chamber of the then Supreme Court of Justice regarding the controversies that could arise from their execution;[183] which were not applicable to private law contracts entered into by the Public Administration. The definition was based on the analysis of the Supreme Court decisions adopted in the forties and fifties, particularly referring to administrative contracts, in which the Public Administration was using its public powers or prerogatives, because of the public interest purposes of the contract or because it

---

Moles Caubet, Tomo I, Facultad de Ciencias Jurídicas y Políticas, Universidad Central de Venezuela, Caracas, 1981, pp. 41-69; and in Allan R. Brewer-Carías, *Estudios de Derecho Administrativo,* Bogotá, 1986, pp. 61-90; «Evoluçao do conceito do contrato administrativo» in *Revista de Direito Publico* Nos. 51-52, Sao Paulo, July-December 1979, pp. 5-19; «Algunas consideraciones sobre las cláusulas de variación de precios en los contratos administrativos» in *Boletín de la Academia de Ciencias Políticas y Sociales*, N° 81, Caracas, July-September 1980, pp. 251-262; «Los contratos de interés nacional y su aprobación legislativa» in *Revista de Derecho Público*, N° 11, Editorial Jurídica Venezolana, Caracas, July-September 1982, pp. 40-54; «Los contratos de interés nacional y su aprobación legislativa», Allan R. Brewer-Carías, *Estudios de Derecho Público,* Tomo I, *(Labor en el Senado 1982),* Ediciones del Congreso de la República, Caracas, 1983, pp. 183-193; «La aprobación legislativa de los contratos de interés nacional y el contrato Pdvsa-Veba Oil», in Allan R. Brewer-Carías, *Estudios de Derecho Público,* Tomo II, *(Labor en el Senado),* Ediciones del Congreso de la República, Caracas, 1985 pp. 65-82; «La evolución del concepto de contrato administrativo», Allan R. Brewer-Carías, *Estudios de Derecho Administrativo*, Ediciones Rosaristas, Colegio Nuestra Señora del Rosario, Bogotá, 1986 pp. 61-90; «Las cláusulas obligatorias y los principios especiales en la contratación administrativa», Allan R. Brewer-Carías, *Estudios de Derecho Administrativo*, Ediciones Rosaristas, Colegio Nuestra Señora del Rosario, Bogotá 1986 pp. 91-124; «Principios especiales y estipulaciones obligatorias en la contratación administrativa» in *El Derecho Administrativo en Latinoamérica*, Vol. II, Ediciones Rosaristas, Colegio Mayor Nuestra Señora del Rosario, Bogotá 1986, pp. 345-378; «Las cláusulas obligatorias y los principios especiales en la contratación administrativa» in Allan R. Brewer-Carías, *Estudios de Derecho Administrativo*, Bogotá, 1986, pp. 91-124; «Consideraciones sobre los derechos del contratista en los contratos de obra pública: el derecho al precio y a su pago en la forma convenida» in *Revista de Derecho Público*, N° 28, Editorial Jurídica Venezolana, Caracas, October-December 1986, pp. 35-46; «El régimen de selección de contratistas en la Administración Pública y la Ley de Licitaciones» in *Revista de Derecho Público*, N° 42, Editorial Jurídica Venezolana, Caracas, April-June 1990, pp. 5-25; Allan R. Brewer-Carías, *Contratos Administrativos*, Colección Estudios Jurídicos, N° 44, Editorial Jurídica Venezolana, Caracas, 1992, 302 pp.;.

181 See Allan R. Brewer-Carías, «Algunos comentarios al régimen de la contratación estatal en Colombia» in *Revista de Derecho Público,* N° 59-60, Editorial Jurídica Venezolana, Caracas, July-December 1994, pp. 75-80; and in *Estudios Jurídicos en Memoria de Alberto Ramón Real*, Instituto de Derecho Administrativo, Facultad de Derecho, Universidad de la República, Montevideo, 1996, pp. 455-461; «El Derecho Administrativo y el derecho de la contratación estatal en Colombia y en el panorama jurídico contemporáneo», in Allan R. Brewer-Carías and Jorge Vélez García, *Contratación Estatal, Derecho Administrativo y Constitución*, Pontificia Universidad Javeriana, Quaestiones Juridicae N° 6, Bogotá, 1995, pp. 7-37; «El arbitraje y los contratos de interés nacional» in *Seminario sobre la Ley de Arbitraje Comercial*, Biblioteca de la Academia de Ciencias Políticas y Sociales, Serie Eventos, N° 13, Caracas, 1999, pp. 169-204..

182 Allan R. Brewer-Carías *Las Instituciones Fundamentales del Derecho Administrativo y la Jurisprudencia venezolana*, Caracas, 1964, p. 114.

183 *Idem,* p. 158.

was entered into with *servicio público* criterion.[184] The definition of "*servicio público*" at that time was a broad definition, not particularly and exclusively related with public services or utilities[185]. Even though the definition of administrative contracts was therefore extremely wide in the sense that any public contract could be considered an administrative contract, the examples given to identify them allowed a more precise picture of them: public work contracts, public debt contracts, supply contracts for the Public Administration, public transportation contracts and public utilities contracts or concessions.[186]

One of the main characteristics of administrative law is its mutability and adaptability to the transformation of the State and public activities. That is why the concept of administrative contract with the close equation: "public interest or public service purpose/administrative law regime/judicial review of administrative action jurisdiction" had been questioned by doctrine in Venezuela and elsewhere. That is why, Rafael Badell Madrid talks about the "contradictory and confused criterion" used regarding administrative contracts[187], and Rafael Gómez Ferrer Morant, in his study "*La mutabilidad de la figura de los contratos administrativos,*" he refers to "the difficulty of constructing once and for all the institution of administrative contracts" pointing out that its "evolution hasn't finished yet."[188]

Two decades after publishing my Doctoral Thesis, in a work published written in 1981 named "*La evolución del concepto de contrato administrativo,*"[189] and later developed in my book *Contratos Administrativos*, Caracas 1992, I questioned the concept of administrative contracts when solely based on the dichotomy "administrative contracts administrative law regime/private law contracts entered by Public Administration-private law regime", qualifying it as absolutely inadmissible.[190] Apart from the clauses themselves of the agreement (which have force of law between the parties), and the complementary Civil Code provisions, all public contracts are subject in one way or another to public (administrative) law regulations, at least when referring to the competency or attributions of the public entity to sign them, or to the selection of the correspondent private party (auction procedure), or to their execution, so there are no public contracts subject only to private law as opposed to administrative contracts subject to administrative law.[191]

184 See as an example, Federal and Cassation Court, December 5, 1944, Federal Court decision of December, 3 1959 and Political Administrative Chamber decisions of December 12, 1961 and August 13, 1964, in Allan R. Brewer-Carías, *Jurisprudencia de la Corte Suprema 1930-1974 y Estudios de Derecho Administrativo*, Tomo III, vol. 2, Caracas, 1977, pp. 727-733.

185 See Rafael Badell Madrid, *Régimen Jurídico del Contrato Administrativo*, Caracas 2001, pp. 37-47.

186 Allan R. Brewer-Carías, *Las Instituciones Fundamentales del Derecho Administrativo y la Jurisprudencia venezolana*, Caracas, 1964, p. 162.

187 See Rafael Badell Madrid, *Régimen Jurídico del Contrato Administrativo*, Caracas, 2001, p. 32.

188 See in *El Derecho Público a comienzos del Siglo XXI. Estudios en homenaje al Profesor Allan R. Brewer-Carías*, Madrid, 2003, p. 1749-1764.

189 See in *Libro Homenaje al Profesor Antonio Moles Caubet*, Tomo I, Caracas, 1982, pp. 41-69.

190 Allan R. Brewer-Carías, *Contratos Administrativos*, Caracas, 1992, p. 13.

191 Allan R. Brewer-Carías, *Contratos Administrativos, cit.*, pp. 14, 42, 43, 52, 53, 55, 71, 72.

Instead, I have sustained that "the notion of administrative contracts can only be accepted for identifying one sort of public contract (Public Administration contract) which, because of the public entity purpose being sought through the contract, is subject to a preponderant public law regime, but not for the purpose of discriminating between a contract with a public law regime and other public contracts supposedly subject to a private law regime. The preponderance of one regime or the other is what is important now."[192]

I have insisted on the subject, and in another essay on "*La interaplicación del derecho público y del derecho privado a la Administración Pública y el proceso de huída y recuperación del derecho administrativo*", I explained that "Public Administration's activities are subject both to public and private law, in a degree of preponderance which varies according to its purpose and nature"; and that "all public contracts are always subject both to public and private law.[193]

The most recent critical approach in Venezuela regarding the notion of administrative contracts is the work of Jesús Caballero Ortíz, "*Deben subsistir los contratos administrativos en una futura legislación*?[194] in which he has pointed out, in similar terms used by Rafael Badell Madrid ("contradictory and confused criterion")[195], the very vague and imprecise criterion used for its identification. This situation has led some distinguished administrative law Professors to consider the notion of administrative contracts as useless and with no effects.[196]

Of course, in spite of the imprecision of some decisions of the former Political Administrative Chamber of the Supreme Court of Justice, some public contracts can be considered and have always been considered to be administrative contracts. This is the case of public utility concessions, such as public transportation, gas, electricity, water, garbage recollection, telephone; and of public works contracts[197]. In these contracts, due to the public interest involved, the public entity Party in the contract is considered to have the above-mentioned extraordinary power regarding the contract. But regarding other public contracts, where public interest is not so obvious, the notion of administrative contract, in the end, can be considered as an *ex post facto* notion[198], in the sense that any public contract subscribed by the Republic,

192 *Idem*, p. 14.

193 See in *Las Formas de la Actividad Administrativa. II Jornadas Internacionales de Derecho Administrativo "Allan Randolph Brewer-Carías"*, Fundación de Estudios de Derecho Administrativo, Caracas, 1996, pp. 58-60.

194 Published in *El Derecho Público a comienzos del Siglo XXI: Estudios en homenaje al Profesor Allan R. Brewer-Carías*, Madrid, 2003, p. 1765-1778.

195 See Rafael Badell Madrid, *Régimen Jurídico del Contrato Administrativo*, Caracas, 2001, p. 32.

196 See Gonzalo Pérez Luciani, "Los contratos administrativos en Venezuela", in Allan R. Brewer-Carías (Director), *Derecho Público en Venezuela y Colombia: Archivo de derecho Público y Ciencias de la Administración*, Caracas, 1986, p. 253.

197 Allan R. Brewer-Carías, *Contratos Administrativos*, *op. cit.*, p. 46; Rafael Badell Madrid, *Régimen Jurídico del Contrato Administrativo*, Caracas, 2001, pp. 50-51.

198 See "La interaplicación del derecho público y del derecho privado a la Administración Pública y el proceso de huída y recuperación del derecho administrativo" in *Las Formas de la Actividad Administrativa: II Jornadas Internacionales de Derecho Administrativo Allan Randolph Brewer-Carías*, Fundación de Estudios de Derecho Administrativo, Caracas, 1996, pp. 59.

the States or the Municipalities can become an administrative contract, if the public entity which is a Party to the contract uses some extraordinary public law powers regarding its performance and execution and the Political Administrative Chamber of the Supreme Tribunal of Justice decides to consider the public contract as an administrative contract, simply to confirm its jurisdiction to resolve the controversies which derived from their execution.

As has been said, the French origin of the distinction between administrative contracts and private law contracts executed by the Public Administration has resulted in the distribution of judicial competencies between the judicial review of administrative action jurisdictions and ordinary judiciary jurisdiction[199]; a distinction that was followed in all written law Latin countries, like Venezuela. The French notion of "*service public*" was also used in our countries, and that is why it was used four decades ago[200]. The very well-known crisis of the "*service public*" notion also brought about the already mentioned crisis of the notion of administrative contracts, which cannot now be defined because of their "public service" purpose or mission, due to the risk of there not existing any substantive criteria to identify such purpose or mission, or simply because they are identified with all public contracts, or public interest contracts. If such is the case, then the notion of administrative contract is useless, except for the Political-Administrative Chamber of the Supreme Tribunal of Justice when deciding to assume jurisdiction regarding certain contracts subscribed by the Republic, the States or the Municipalities[201]. And even in those cases, the Supreme Court also has used the strict criteria of "public service", in order to justify the existence in an administrative contract of certain extraordinary clauses containing public prerogatives[202].

IV. THE APPLICABLE LAW TO ADMINISTRATIVE CONTRACTS

1. Administrative Law regime

All public contracts are subject in one way or another to the Venezuelan administrative law rules contained in the general statute on public contracts like the *Ley de Contrataciones Públicas*, in which are regulated, for instance, the general rules of competencies of public entities to enter a contract or the administrative procedure rules (*licitación*) in order to choose the private party in all public contracts. They are also subjected to other statutes, for instance, those devoted to regulate some specific sort of contracts like the public works concessions or the public services concessions, regulated in the Law for Promotion and Protection of Investments through Concessions[203]; or to regulate a specific public activity like

199 Allan R. Brewer-Carías, *Contratos Administrativos*, *op. cit.*, p. 39.

200 *Idem*, p. 40, 51.

201 *Idem*, p. 55.

202 See, for instance, the Political-Administrative Chamber of the Supreme Court of Justice decision of August 11, 1983, in *Revista de Derecho Público*, EJV, Nº 20, Caracas, 1984, pp. 163-164; and in Allan R. Brewer-Carías, *Contratos Administrativos*, *op. cit.*, pp. 161-163.

203 *Official Gazette*, Nº 5.394 Extra. 25-10-1999.

public transporting, mining exploitation oil industry strategic associations. But as previously indicated, no general statute has yet been sanctioned establishing the general rules referring *all* public contracts or all "administrative contracts."[204]

In any event, all public contracts, are also subjected to private (civil) law regulations. This implies that as a matter of principle and as it happens in any contract, the contractual relations derived from any public contracts, including "administrative contracts" are also basically regulated in the text of the contractual clauses, the Civil Code being only of complementary application.

Therefore, all contracts, including public contracts, can regulate the parties' relationships in a different way as of the general rules referring to contracts established in the Civil Code; the only limit being that parties' agreements cannot modify or alter "statutes, the application of which is concerned with public order or good customs" (Art. 6, Civil Code). This expression "public order", of course, should not be confused with the expressions "public purpose", "general interest" or "public usefulness."

Thus, as a matter of principle, in all public contracts, the main regulation regarding contractual relations is contained in the contracts clauses that must be elaborated according to the applicable public law regulations (statutes) concerning the concrete activity to which the contract is related, being the general regulations of the Civil Code or the Commercial Code of complimentary character to what is regulated in the contract clauses.

2. The general principles of private law applicable to public contracts

In all contracts, being or not considered as public or administrative contracts, the clauses entered by the parties have the force of law between them (Art. 1159, Civil Code). Therefore, the Public and the Private parties in a public contract are always subjected to the contract's provisions as drafted by them, which the parties can only modify by mutual agreement.[205] And even considering a public contract to be "administrative contracts", such qualification does not alter the contractual relationship set forth by the Parties in order to regulate their rights and duties and to protect their economic rights.

Therefore, in order to determine the general legal regime applicable to public contracts, the discussions regarding their consideration or not as an "administrative contract", have no importance whatsoever. Whether or not they are "administrative contract" or whether or not the Public entity party in the contracts has or not the possible use of extraordinary public powers, the execution and performance of the contract is above all governed by the particular contract's clauses, which in general terms must be presumed valid and elaborated pursuant to applicable law to the contract. Additionally, in the contractual clauses of many public contracts, it is common to find declarations from the Public party certifying the conformity of the contractual clauses, with the applicable law.

---

204 See Rafael Badell Madrid, *Régimen Jurídico del Contrato Administrativo*, Caracas 2001, p. 47. Badell states that the Venezuelan legal order lacks a regulatory instrument which uniformly defines administrative contracts, such as exists in other countries where there are statutes which regulate the matter in an orderly manner (e.g.: Spain, Uruguay, Brazil), p. 47, note 40.

205 Eloy Maduro Luyando, *Curso de Obligaciones. Derecho Civil III*, Caracas, 1975, p. 626.

These contract clauses, in principle, cannot be modified unilaterally by the Parties, even by the Public party, particularly regarding the economic clauses of the contract, or the protective economic clauses established on behalf of the Private party rights; except through just compensation[206]. That is why it has been considered that even in administrative contracts the economic clauses are "intangible and immutable."[207]

According to the Venezuelan legal system, as mentioned before, the contractual relationship between the Parties is basically regulated by the terms set forth in the clauses of the contract itself, being the Civil Code only applicable in a complementary (*supletoria*) way, in the sense that it is applicable only in those matters not expressly regulated by the Parties themselves.

Therefore, in principle, the Parties are free to establish without legal restriction or intervention the contents and conditions of the contracts, which they can draft according to their own particular interests, without being subject to the rules set forth in the Civil Code, whether related to each type of contract it regulates or to the specific rules concerning each contract. Consequently, in contractual matters, the principle is that the private law statutory provisions are complementary to the will of the parties and only complement the absence or insufficiency of the parties' provisions.

That is why, according to Article 1270 of the Civil Code, obligations contained in the contracts must be complied precisely as they have been undertaken; and according to Article 1160 of the same Code, contracts shall be performed in good faith and the Parties are obliged not only "to comply with what is expressly stated", but all the consequences resulting from them, pursuant to equity, use or the law.

Consequently, according to Venezuelan law, the contractual relationship between the parties is established in the contract, and the basic legal limit to the parties' will, according to Article 6 of the Civil Code, is that through contracts the Parties cannot alter provisions of statutes on which the "public order and good customs" are involved. Regarding public contracts matters, those provisions are generally established in public law statutes. This concept of "public order" in the Venezuelan legal system refers to situations where the application of a status *concerns the general and indispensable legal order for the existence of the community*, which cannot be bequeathed; and it does not apply in cases that only concern the parties in a contractual controversy. For instance, as a matter of general principle, public order provisions in public law are those establishing competencies or attributions to the public entities, including the Judiciary, and those concerning the taxation powers of public entities. In private law, for instance, all the provisions referring to the status of persons (for instance: *patria potestas*, divorce, adoption) are norms in which public order and good customs are involved.[208]

But in many cases, it is the lawmaker itself that has expressly declared in a particular statute its provisions as having "public order" character, in the sense that its norms cannot be modified through contracts. That is the case for instance, of the

---

206 Allan R. Brewer-Carías, *Contratos Administrativos*, Caracas, 1992, pp. 211 ff.

207 Eloy Lares Martínez, *Manual de Derecho Administrativo*, Caracas, 1983, p. 335; Allan R. Brewer-Carías, *Contratos Administrativos*, *cit.*, p. 191

208 Allan R. Brewer-Carías, *Contratos Administrativos*, Caracas, 1992, pp. 265-268.

2014 Just Prices Organic Law[209], where Article 2 sets forth that its provisions are of public order and may not be renounced by the parties. In other cases, the "public order" character of a statute or of a regulation is an implicit notion derived from public law principles: for instance, constitutional or legal regulations referring to obligatory clauses that must be incorporated expressly or tacitly in all public contracts[210]; constitutional regulations referring to civil rights or liberties; legal regulations referring to the obligatory exercise of its competencies by public entities, including power of taxation.[211]

Regarding this last area of statute regulations that cannot be negotiated trough contracts, what is to be considered as of "public policy" character is the State power of taxation, that is to say, the obligatory exercise by the State of the power to impose taxes to individuals, and the competencies of public entities to obligatory collect taxes.

Nevertheless, according to 1999 the Investments Promotion and Protection Law[212], no longer in force, the Republic of Venezuela was authorized to enter with private parties in "contracts of legal stability" in order to assure to an investment during the term of the contract, the stability of some economic conditions, and trough which it could be guaranteed to an investment, among other rights, "the stability of the national taxes regimes in force at the moment of entering to the contract" (art. 17,1). Thus, this statute authorized the Republic, for instance, to not to approve new taxes which could be applicable to certain investments, when protected by such "contracts of legal stability"; in which case, such contracts required parliamentary authorization (Art 17, *Unico)*. The 1999 Investment Law, nonetheless, was repeal in 2014 by a new Law on Foreign Investments, in which such provision was eliminated. [213]

But if the matter is referred to the exercise of attributions of public bodies which are not obligatory or compulsory and do not affect the power of taxation, but rather, according to express regulations in a statute, of facultative character subjected to the appreciation of the Administration, then in those cases the exercise of such facultative attributions can be regulated in public contracts by mean of an agreement between the interested parties.

On the other hand, the classical approach regarding contracts entered by public entities has always been their classification as "administrative contract," basically

---

209 *Official Gazette*, N° 40.340, January 23, 2014.

210 See Allan R. Brewer-Carías, "Las cláusulas obligatorias y los principios especiales en la contratación administrativa", in Allan R. Brewer-Carías, *Estudios de Derecho Administrativo*, Ediciones Rosaristas, Colegio Nuestra Señora del Rosario, Bogotá 1986 pp. 91-124; «Principios especiales y estipulaciones obligatorias en la contratación administrativa» in *El Derecho Administrativo en Latinoamérica*, Vol. II, Ediciones Rosaristas, Colegio Mayor Nuestra Señora del Rosario, Bogotá 1986, pp. 345-378.

211 Allan R. Brewer-Carías, «Las transacciones fiscales y la indisponibilidad de la potestad y competencia tributarias» en *Revista de Derecho Tributario*, N° 18, Caracas, mayo-junio 1967, pp. 1-36; also Publisher in Allan R. Brewer-Carías, *Jurisprudencia de la Corte Suprema 1930-1974 y Estudios de Derecho Administrativo, Tomo I: El Ordenamiento Constitucional y Funcional del Estado*, Caracas 1975, pp. 43-78.

212 *Official Gazette* N° 5.390 Extra. October 22, 1999

213 *Official Gazette* N° 6.152 Noviembre 18, 2014

because the extraordinary powers supposedly held by the Administration regarding an administrative contract (*cláusulas exorbitantes del derecho común*), without taking into consideration that those powers in fact always exist and are inherent to the State's power to intervene in favor of public interest, independently of the contract clauses. That is why the Supreme Court of Justice's decision of August 17, 1999 (*Apertura Petrolera* Case) has ruled that these extraordinary powers not found in private law contracts "do not define (administrative contracts) as such, because they are a consequence and not an element for its determination"; adding that the fact of a contract having or not such clauses "is no more than a consequence of the necessary and obligatory protection of the general interest".

On the other hand, even if a law of public order is enacted, having immediate effects on public contracts, it cannot affect the economic clauses of the contract, and if so, the private party to the contract have the right to be compensated for the prejudices produced by the law and the loss of his rights produced by the law. As Joaquín Sánchez Covisa pointed out:

> "When the new law affects a property economic interest, the specific harmed interest may be in contradiction with the public interest, which the law that arbitrarily harms the individual legal situation tends to further. In this case the right to demand the validity of the general norm before the arbitrary norm is transformed into the right to obtain compensation.
>
> This happens, for example, when a new law modifies the economic content of a contract executed between the State and a private party (This is not the case when the law modifies the general content of the contracts through a general and objective norm). If the law responds to a collective interest, and in such virtue harms the individual legal situation of the private party, the latter will not be able to oppose to its validity, but will have the right to receive compensation. This compensation will reestablish the economic equilibrium between the parties and will deprive the law of its original defect, since in this manner, it would not modify the contractual economic content.
>
> A special case of the transformation of the right in an individual legal situation into the right to compensation is expropriation, which is expressly regulated and guaranteed in numeral 2 of article 32 of the National Constitution. In fact, when a law particularly affects the individual legal situation of the owner of a property and there are reasons of public or social utility that justify the deprivation of property, the vested right of the owner to have his individual legal situation respected is transformed into the right to receive compensation. The fact that this is the most common case of a modification of an individual legal situation by virtue of the will of the State, explains why it is expressly established in the Constitution and special legal texts. We understand, however, that, even if that express regulation of expropriation did not exist, the same general doctrine would be applicable."[214]

---

214 Joaquín Sánchez-Covisa, *La Vigencia Temporal de la Ley en el Ordenamiento Jurídico Venezolano*, (Thesis, Caracas 1943), Reprinted, Academia de Ciencias Políticas y Sociales, Caracas 2007, pp. 237-238.

3. The Public Contracting Law and its provisions of "public policy" (*public order*)

As aforementioned, according to the Venezuelan legal system, the relations between the parties in all contracts, whether public contracts or private contracts, are in principle governed by the will of the parties as established in their own clauses, which constitute the "law between them" (Art. 1159 Civil Code). In all other matters not explicitly regulated by the parties in the contracts, the regulations of the Civil Code and the other laws that are applicable to the object of the contract or the parties to the contract, in a supplementary way.

This means that as a matter of principle, in the Venezuela legal system, the parties have complete freedom to establish the content of their contractual obligations and relations in the clauses that they deem appropriate for their particular interests as contracting parties. On matters of contractual freedom this is the consequence that derives from the economic freedom guarantee in the Constitution (art. 112). Consequently, the provisions referred to contracts in the Civil Code and in the other statutes or regulations that could have relation with the object of the contract, as a matter of principle are of supplementary character, in the sense that their content could only be applied when those matters are not explicitly regulated by the parties in the clauses of the contract, or when the clauses of the contracts are insufficient.

The general exception to the autonomy of will of the parties in their contractual relations, is when a provision of a statue is considered to be of public policy (*orden público*) character, in which case, according to the Civil Code (article 6), it is directly applicable to contracts and cannot be modified by agreements between the parties. Regarding these provisions of public policy, the first aspect that must be bear in mind, is that in order to be of mandatory application incapable of modification by contract, the provisions have to be incorporated in statutes. The aforementioned article 6 of the Venezuelan Civil Code expresses this principle, stating that:

> Article 6 Civil Code: "Laws in which public policy or good morals are involved cannot be renounced or relaxed by private agreements."

The expression "laws" in such provision, according to the Constitution, is referred to "statutes," in the sense of laws sanctioned by the "the National Assembly acting as legislative body" (article 202), because according to the Constitution (art. 112) only through statutes is that restrictions or limitations can be imposed upon economic freedom. Those limits can also be established, exceptionally, through decrees with rank and force of laws enacted as delegate legislation by the President of the Republic, when expressly authorized by the National Assembly by means of an enabling law ("*ley habilitante*") (articles 202; 236.8).

The provisions of public policy once enacted through statutes, on the other hand, not only cannot be modified by the parties to contracts, but if they enter into force after the signing of a contract, are also applicable to it, subject to any admissible right of the contracting party to be compensated for the effects on its acquired rights and the disturbance of the contract's economic balance.

This concept of public policy, therefore, as an exception to the autonomy of will of the parties, must be interpreted strictly and refers, in the Venezuelan legal system, to situations in which the application of a legal provision *relates to the legal order that is general and essential for the existence of the community itself*, which cannot be relaxed at the wishes of the parties, a concept which of course does not apply to matters which only concern the parties in a contractual relationship or dispute. Therefore, a provision of public policy is not any legal provision, but only those which make up the basic structure of society, such as for example those which limits or restricts the exercise of constitutional freedoms and guarantees, or those that establishes *faculties or attributions of the State's entities and bodies, those which concern, for example, the tax powers of public entities, or those which refer to the inalienability of the State's assets, such as those which belong to the public*, none of which may be relaxed by agreements between private parties.[215] Specifically in the field of private law, for example, which was where the concept originated, provisions that are regarded as being public policy are all those which relate to the status of persons (for example, *custody of children*, divorce, adoption), in which it is felt that public order and good practices are at stake.[216]

As Joaquín Sánchez-Covisa explains:

> "The provisions of public policy are standards that at any given time embody the objective concept of justice that rules in a human community. By establishing a standard of public policy, the State determines the "duty to be" mandatory and imperative and is required at that time by the legal awareness of the group. As a result, those rules cannot be waived or relaxed by contracts between private parties. In this sense the duty to faithfulness between spouses, compensation for professional accidents or the payment of taxes cannot be relaxed by the will of the private parties. These are provisions of public policy, and therefore represent the idea of what is the purpose in that legal community of our days."[217]

---

215 For instance in Decision No 276 of the Cassation Chamber of the Supreme Tribunal of 31 May 2007 deems that a regulation of public policy is not any kind of regulation, but those of *constitutional public order* regarding the guarantee of due process and the right to defence which are those that logically are considered in the decision as public policy, and regarding those therein, it is stated: "the concept of public policy represents a notion that *crystallises all regulations of public order which require unconditional observance*, and that may not be waived due to private provision. The indication of these characteristic signs of the concept of public policy, which is to say, the need for unconditional observance of their regulations, and the corresponding unavailability of the details, allows knowing with a reasonable amount of certainty, whether or not is a case of breach of a regulation of public policy" (See http://historico.tsj.gob.ve/decisiones/scc/mayo/RC-0276-310502-00959.HTM).

216 See Allan R. Brewer-Carías, *Contratos Administrativos. Contratos Públicos*, Editorial Jurídica Venezolana, Caracas 2013, pp. 316-323.

217 See Joaquín Sánchez-Covisa, *La vigencia temporal de la Ley en el ordenamiento jurídico venezolano*, Academia de Ciencias Políticas y Sociales, Caracas 2007, p.179. In this same sense, Francisco López Herrera, quoting Henri Lepge (*Traité Élementaire de Droit Civil Belge*, Bruilant, Bruxelles, 1941-1949, Vol. I, o. 101), "stated that "public policy laws and provisions are those that refers to the essential interest of the State or that affect the Collectivity, or that fix in private law the legal fundamental basis on which is based the economic and moral order of a determined society. In order to determine the public policy provision, it is needed to analyse in each case, the spirit of the Institution and to examine what and why it has relation with essential demands of the Collectivity or the fundamental basis of private law." See Francisco Lópes Herrera, *La nulidad de los contratos en la legislación civil de Venezuela*, Caracas 1952, p. 96.

According to this definition, Sánchez-Covisa argued that the "effectiveness of a standard of public policy means that a new objective concept of justice is an imperious demand of the group in a determined sector of social life, that is, it is a defined concept of the group interest that governs the mattes affected by the standard in question."[218]

Within these provisions of public policy are mentioned, for instance, those "regulating the length of the working day, the transport tariff, or the participation of the employee in the profits of the enterprise," [219] being thus the "nature of the provision" the only aspect that allow to qualify a provision as of "public policy," and consequently of obligatory application.[220] That is why the Organic Law on Labour declares in general that all its provisions are of public policy.

On matters of public law, as mentioned, in addition to the provisions restricting or limiting the exercise of constitutional rights and freedoms, are in general of public policy all the provisions included in statutes attributing public powers or attributions to the bodies or entities of Public Administration, as it is provided for example, in Article 26 of the Organic Law of the Public Administration, setting forth that:

> "Article 26. All powers attributed to Public Administration bodies and entities shall be mandatory and binding and exercised under the conditions, limits and procedures established; they shall be not subject to waiver, nor delegated, nor extended and cannot be relaxed by any contract, except for the cases that are expressly set forth in laws and other normative acts."

Therefore, the parties to the contracts are obliged to identify the provisions of public policy that may be established in the texts of the laws that may be applicable to the contractual relationship, and that cannot be affected by contract clauses, being absolutely exceptional that all the provisions of a Law to be expressly and globally declared as public policy. One of such exception is for instance, in addition to the Organic Law on Labour, the 2014 Fair Prices Law[221] in which article 2 establishes that "The provisions of this law are of public policy and cannot be waived by the parties;" and the 2009 Organic Law that reserves to the State goods and services connected to primary Hydrocarbon activities, whose article 7 established that "The provisions of this Law are of public policy and shall apply with preference to any other legal provisions in effect for said matters."[222]

In the case of public contracts, the Public Contracting Law as the body of law applicable to public contracts for the purpose of acquiring goods, providing services and performing works (Art. 1) executed by public entities that are listed therein (Art. 3), do not contain any similar general declaration that all its provisions are of public policy. Nonetheless, that does not exclude that some of its provisions are to be considered as of public policy character, such as for instance, those that regulate the processes of selecting the private contracting party and awarding the contracts ("processes of selection of contractors", "open tender", "closed tender", "direct

218 *Idem,* p. 180.

219 *Idem,* p. 185.

220 *Idem,* p. 206.

221 *Official Gazette*, N° 40,340 of 23-01-2014

222 *Official Gazette* N° 39,173 of May, 7 2009

contracting", "electronic hiring" arts. 84-122), that are always mandatory.[223] Also, are to be considered as provisions of public policy in the Public Contracting Law, all those that for instance, assigns to Public Administration bodies and entities specific powers, faculties or attributions that are considered mandatory and binding and must be exercised under the conditions, limits and procedures established in the Law. Those attributions assigned to public organs and entities cannot be relaxed by any contract, as is the case, for example, of the mandatory character for the organs of Public Administration to apply the provisions related to those processes of awarding the contracts or selecting the private contracting party, or those referring to powers attributed to the public entities or bodies, which are always mandatory.

The Public Contracting Law, as a whole, therefore, is not a law of public policy, nor does it so declare in its articles. In addition, if it is true that Article 1 of that Law declares that that "the processes referred to in this Law" are mandatory, that does not mean that all of its provisions are "mandatory." That expression is only a ratification that the provisions of the Law that refers to the processes of awarding the contract or selecting the contractor are mandatory, an aspect that always have been as of public policy, being the core of such statute.

In effect, since the enactment of the Tender Law (*Ley de Licitaciones*) in 1990, which was replaced by the Public Contracting Law published in 2008, the purpose of the Legislator was to regulate the processes for selecting contractors for the award of public contracts; so, the new Law basically continued to regulate these processes, almost exclusively. That is why after the enactment of the Public Contracting Law in 2008, I said that:

> "despite its name, the Law neither regulates all state contracts, nor the public contracting activities in general of public entities or Public Administrations (national, state and municipal). In reality it continues, with some changes, to be a law with a specific scope, basically destined to regulate the process for selecting contractors (tenders) and regarding certain (not all) public contracts. Therefore, the only preceding Law that is expressly repealed by this new Law is the old Public Tender Law, which basically continues to be a body of law destined to regulate the system used to select contractors (Art. 36 to 92) in certain public contracts."[224]

The reform of the Law of 2014, as expressed in its Explanation of motives,[225] was based on the concern expressed in its preamble regarding the persistence of "some significant deficiencies in the processes," and on the purpose of reinforcing the processes for awarding contracts and selecting contractors according to the provisions of the Law. The introduction of the last phrase of Article 1 in the text of

---

223 See Carlos García Soto, "Posición de la Administración en su actividad contractual. El caso de la Ley de Contrataciones Públicas y su reglamento," in Allan R. Brewer-Carías et al., *Ley de Contrataciones Públicas*, Editorial Jurídica Venezolana, Caracas 2012, pp. 198ff.; and José Ignacio Hernández, "El contrato administrativo en la Ley de Contrataciones Públicas venezolana," in Allan R. Brewer-Carías, et al., *Ley de Contrataciones Públicas*, Editorial Jurídica venezolana, Caracas 2012, pp. 184-186.

224 See Allan R. Brewer-Carías, "Ámbito de aplicación de la Ley de Contrataciones Públicas," in Allan R. Brewer-Carías *et al.*, *Ley de Contrataciones Públicas*, Editorial Jurídica Venezolana, Caracas 2008, pp. 11-12.

225 See *Official Gazette* Extra No. 6154 of November 19, 2014.

the reform of the Law in 2014, was intended to ratify the "mandatory" nature of the "processes referred to in this law" which are none other than those established for awarding the contracts and select contractors (open tender, closed tender, direct contracting, electronic contracting). These contractor selection processes, and not all of the articles and provisions of the statute, are the ones that the legislator felt it imperative to ratify to be mandatory and binding for all public entities a body, as provisions of public policy.

As mentioned, those processes were established since the enactment of the *Ley de Licitaciones* (Public Tender Law) of 1990, later incorporated in the Public Contracting Law beginning in 2008, in an equally binding way. Therefore, the reform of 2014, with the addition of the mentioned last phrase in article 1, actually did not change anything, but rather ratified the character of the contractor selection processes as mandatory and binding for the Public Administration in all public contracts.

In addition to the "processes of awarding contracts or selection of contractors" ("*procesos de selección de contratistas*" (formerly tendering "*licitación*") regulated in the Law that are of public policy character, the Public Contracting Law also has explicit regulation of other powers assigned to the public contracting party in relation to all the public contracts regulated in the statute, that can also be considered as on public policy character, like the obligation of the Public Administration body or entity to supervise and inspect the execution of the services that are the object of the contract (Art. 112; art. 136 Law 2014); and the powers to unilaterally modify the conditions of the execution of the object of the contract (Art. 106, 107; arts. 130, 131 Law 2014); to sanction breaches by the contractor (Art. 139); and to unilaterally terminate the contract (Art. 127; arts. 152ff. Law 2014).[226]

Beside these provisions of the Public Contracting Law that are considered as of public policy, in general terms, the other provisions of the statute are only of supplementary character, that is, they apply to public contracts only if the parties have not provided for it in the clauses of the contract.

One example of these sort of provisions that have a supplementary character is, for example, article 141 of the 2014 Public Contracting Law on matters of form of payments, when providing that the public contracting party "*shall proceed to pay* the obligations stipulated in the contract, *complying with the following*: 1. Verification of the compliance in relation to the supply of the good or service, or the carrying out of the work, or part of said work; 2. Receipt and review of the invoices submitted by the contractor; 3. Conformity by the supervisor or inspecting engineer of compliance with the established conditions; and 4. Payment authorization by the competent persons."[227]

---

226 See Carlos García Soto, "Posición de la Administración en su actividad contractual. El caso de la ley de Contrataciones Públicas y su reglamento," in Allan R. Brewer-Carías et al., *Ley de Contataciones Públicas*, Editorial Jurídica Venezolana, Caracas 2012, pp. 198ff.; and José Ignacio Hernández, "El contrato administrativo en la Ley de Contrataciones Públicas venezolana," en Allan R. Brewer-Carías, et al., *Ley de Contrataciones Públicas*, Editorial Jurídica venezolana, Caracas 2012, pp. 184-186.

227 *"Article 141. Conditions for payments.* The contracting party shall proceed to pay all obligations stipulated in the contract, complying with the following: 1. Verification of compliance in relation to the supply of goods, provision of services, carrying out of works or part of said

This Article, as it is written, does not provide for anything extraordinary regarding the compliance of contracts, public or private, and only provides normal and common sense requirements for payments, to be complied with by public entities and in general, by any party payer in a contract, in the sense of confirming the performance of the service, receive and review the invoices and instruct that payment should be made by the authorized person in the public entity, but it does not impose any specific timing for such verifications. In this latter aspect, therefore, the provision cannot be considered as of public policy character.

This timing can be established in the contracts within the clauses establishing the way of payments. According to article 6.5 of the Public Contracting Law (2010), the parties are the ones to determine the way of payments in the clauses of the contracts, according to its nature, purpose and object of each contract. This provision specifically defines the "contract" as: "The legal instrument that governs the carrying out of the work, the supply of a service or the allotment of goods, including the orders and service orders that at least must contain the following conditions: price, amount, method of payment (*forma de pago*), *time and way of delivery* and the specifications contained in the Specification document, if applicable" (Art. 6.5). Consequently, according to the text of the Law, the parties are free to elect any desired way of payment including timing, according to such provision of the same Public Contracting Law.

On this matters the same Public Contracting Law even admits in its article 128,[228] the possibility to perform advance payments ("*anticipos*") up to half of the total amount of the contract entered into by the Public entity, even before the contract commences to be performed. Hence, if Article 141 of the Public Contracting Law were a provision of public policy on matters of timing for the verification of the conditions set forth in it, the legislator would not have allowed the possibility to perform advance payments because in such cases advance payments are performed even before the beginning of the execution of the object of the contract. This imply that the verifications of the requirements established in Article 141 of the Law, can be made after payment, according to the nature of the contract, if agreed by the parties in cases like advances payments, providing of course for the adequate guarantees for recovery or reimbursement of amounts due, if needed, a matter regarding which the provision of article 141 did not provide anything in its supplementary regulation referred only to the requirements of payments.

---

works ./ 2. Receipt and review of invoices submitted by the contractor. / 3. Approval by the supervisor or inspecting engineer of compliance with the established.conditions. / 4. Payment authorization by the competent persons."

228 *Article 128.- Contractual Advance*. Advances may be granted in agreements subscribed, the payment of which shall not be an essential condition for the commencement of the supply of the good or the service, unless such prior payment is established in the agreement./ An advance cannot exceed fifty percent (50%) of the price of the agreement. Payment of the advance shall be subject to the financial availability of the principal. / In the event that the contractor were to fail to present an advance bond, they must commence performance of the agreement in accordance with the agreed specifications and timetable, which shall form an integral part of the agreement. Upon presenting an advance bond and its acceptance by the principal, the contractor shall be paid the amount of the relevant advance within a term not to exceed fifteen calendar days, taken as of the date of presentation of the petition for payment. / The advance granted must be progressively amortized with each payment made and in the same percentage as it was granted.

In any case, being the provision of public policy according to article 6 of the Civil Code, a matter reserved to laws, the consequence is that it can only be provided in a statute issued by the Legislative organ of the State exercising legislative powers; thus, no other act of State of rank inferior to the laws can contain provisions that can be considered as of public policy. The matter is one of statutory reserve (*reserva legal*), and therefore, in the Venezuelan legal system, a Regulation (*Reglamento*), which is the normative State act enacted by the President of the Republic according to article 236.10 of the Constitution in order to develop the provisions of statutes, cannot contain provisions that can be considered as of public policy.

That is why, in particular on matters of public contracts, the Regulation of the Public Contracting Law, enacted by the President of the Republic by means of Decree No. 6708 of 19 May 2009[229], does not and cannot contain any provision considered as of public policy. The provisions of that Regulation are not mandatory but only of a supplementary character, and they can only be considered as of public policy, by extension, only if they are developing a public policy provision of the law. Except these cases, the only other way in which the content of the Public Contracting Law Regulation could have been considered as of public policy would have been if the Law had expressly established for the mandatory application of the Regulation content to public contracts, which is not the case.

For example, on matters of mutual responsibility in the execution of contracts, in the absence of legal provisions for such purpose of public policy character in the text of the Public Contracting Law, only if the parties do not provide specific clauses for such purpose, then for instance, articles 169 and 170 Public Contracting Law Regulation[230] could be invoked and applied as provisions of supplementary character. But if for example, the parties have agreed and provided in the text of the contract for the contractual regime regarding their mutual responsibilities, such contractual clause is the one to be applied on such matters, because articles 169 and 170 of the PCL Regulation are not mandatory and cannot constitute public policy provisions.

229 *Official Gazette* No. 39181 of 19 May 2009.

230 Article 169. "*Responsibility for proper execution of the construction work.* The Contractor shall be solely responsible for the proper execution of the construction work. 1. If it is found that any part of the construction work has been executed in a defective manner, the Contractor shall repair it and reconstruct it at its expense. 2. If the Contractor refuses it and does not correct the defects in a timely manner, the contracting body or entity may do it with its own items or with those of the Contractor. 3. The cost of any work necessary to be done in the manner indicated above plus the applicable damages, shall be deducted from what the contracting body or entity owes to the Contractor for any reason arising from the contract including the use of materials and equipment. The provisions above do not affect the right applicable to the contracting body or entity to unilaterally rescind the contract and to make use of the other guarantees, remedies, withholding and actions granted to it by the contract and laws."

Article 170. "*Liability for damage in the execution of the construction work.* The Contractor shall be liable for any damages which occur during the execution of the work, either due to errors, omissions or negligence of the Contractor or of the personnel for which it is responsible or caused with the equipment and machinery it uses. Therefore, it shall maintain strict monitoring of the facilities and operations, taking the precautions necessary to prevent damage caused to the construction work or to third parties. In addition, it shall protect the property and goods of the Republic as well as those of individuals, and the environment generally."

Therefore, articles 169 and 170 of the PCL Regulation could not override a contractual provision for the mutual responsibilities of the parties in a different manner.

4. The possibility to choose a Foreign Law and a Foreign Jurisdiction to Govern the Performance of National Public Interest Contracts

The relative sovereign immunity clause established in article 151 of the Constitution, allows public interests contracts of commercial nature to provide that the doubts and controversies that may arise on such contracts can be resolved by foreign jurisdictions and according to foreign law, is only referred to the doubts and controversies arising from the conduct or performance of the contracts, and of course, it does not permit a public contracting party to select a foreign law to govern the validity of the contract itself. Such validity is a matter of public order and can only be regulated by Venezuelan law.

In effect, as already mentioned, among the obligatory contractual clauses that, according to the Constitution all public interest contracts must contain, are the ones related to the relative foreign sovereign immunity clause of the State and to international claims related to public contracts (known as a *Calvo* clause). These clauses are referred to in its article 151, which provides that:

> "Article 151. In public interest contracts, unless inapplicable by reason of the nature of such contracts, a clause shall be deemed included even if not expressed, whereby any doubts and controversies which may arise concerning such contracts and which cannot be resolved amicably by the contracting parties, shall be decided by the competent courts of the Republic, in accordance with its laws, and shall not, on any grounds, or for any reason, give rise to foreign claims."

Regarding this provision, imposing that the doubts and controversies that may arise on such public interest contracts and that could not be resolved amicably by the contracting parties, shall be decided by the competent courts of the Republic, in accordance with Venezuelan law, ono exception was established in the sense it is possible for the public contracting parties in such public interest contracts, according to their nature (for instance, in cases of public interest contracts with commercial nature - *ius gestionis*), to include in the text of the public interest contract an express clause accepting that the resolution of the doubts and controversies that may arise on such contract may be decided by a foreign court or by arbitral tribunals, and also, to allow that for such purpose the decision be adopted applying a foreign law and not Venezuelan Law.[231]

Consequently, due to this exception, on matter of public interest contracts the Venezuelan legal order abandoned the absolute State sovereign immunity system and currently follows the principle of relative State sovereign immunity, allowing the

231 See Allan R. Brewer-Carías, "Comentarios sobre la doctrina del acto de gobierno, del acto político, del acto de Estado y de las cuestiones políticas como motivo de inmunidad jurisdiccional de los Estados en sus Tribunales nacionales", in *Revista de Derecho Público*, N° 26, Editorial Jurídica Venezolana, Caracas, abril-junio 1986, pp. 65-68, available at: http://allanbrewer carias.com/wp-content/uploads/2007/08/rdpub_1986_26.pdf

possibility for the State and other public entities, as a consequence of the execution of public interest contracts of commercial nature, for instance, to be subject to a foreign jurisdiction or to arbitration; and to establish a foreign law as the law applicable to a contract, for the resolution of doubts and controversies arising from the conduct or performance of the contract.[232] In such cases of doubts and disputes or controversies that may arise as a consequence of the performance of the contract, if the law that has been chosen to be applied is a foreign law, such law is the one that governs the performance of the contract.

That is, according to the Constitution, such doubts and disputes or controversies that may arise regarding the contracts that the public contracting party can agree to submit to resolution by a foreign or an arbitral tribunal applying foreign law, are only disputes or controversies that may arise as a consequence of the *conduct or performance* of the contact already signed, not regarding contractual matters that must be addressed before the signing of the contract.[233]

This means, of course, that in such cases, such foreign law cannot govern for instance the conditions of validity of the contract, which must be complied or fulfilled before the contract could be entered into, which for the public contracting party are regulated in provisions of Venezuelan law. In effect, for instance, article 1141 of the Civil Code (inspired by the Napoleon Code), which is applicable to all contracts, including those entered into by public entities, establishes the general principles regarding the validity of contracts as follows:

> "Article 1141. The conditions required for the existence of the contract are: 1st Consent of the parties; 2nd Object that may be a matter of contract; and 3rd Lawful cause."[234]

---

232 See Allan R. Brewer-Carías, *Contratos Administrativos,* Editorial Jurídica Venezolana, Caracas 1992 (reedición 1997), pp. 130 a 137 (Text reproduced in Allan R. Brewer-Carías, *Tratado de Derecho Administrativo*, Vol. III, Editorial Civitas, Editorial Jurídica Venezolana, 2013, pp. 708-714, available at: http://allanbrewercarias.com/wp-content/uploads/2013/07/ BREWER-TRATADO-DE-DA-TOMO-III-9789803652081-txt-1.pdf. It was based on this provision of article 151 of the Constitution, that many statutes provided for the relative sovereign immunity jurisdiction clause, like for instance, was the case of the Decree Law N° 1.510 of November 2, 2001, through which was issued the Organic Hydrocarbons Law (*Ley Orgánica de Hidrocarburos, Official Gazette* N° 37.323 of November 13, 2001. The Law was reformed in 2006, in which it was provided that contracts establishing mixed companies for the exploitation of hydrocarbons, "shall be deemed incorporated", even if "they do not expressly appear," a clause establishing that "the questions and disputes of any nature that may arise in connection with the conduct of activities and that cannot be resolved amicably by the parties, *including arbitration* ...." will be resolved by the courts (Article 34.3.b). This provision expressly recognized in the Law the possibility to submit to arbitration the solution of disputes resulting from activities in the hydrocarbon sector when mixed companies were constituted with private investors.

233 As for instance has been observed by Haydee Barrios de Acosta, when the parties select a foreign law to be applied to the contract, it is in order to be applied to the "contractual obligations," or as pointed out by the former Supreme Court of Justice in a decision of April 27, 1971, that the author quotes, the intention of the legislator is to allow "the parties to "determine the *law applicable to the performance of the contracts*." See Haydee Acosta de Barrios, "La interpretación del contrato por el juez en el derecho interno y en el derecho internacional privado," in *Libro Homenaje a José Melich Orsini*, Universidad Central de Venezuela, 1982, p. 171.

234 *Artículo 1.141.- Las condiciones requeridas para la existencia del contrato son: 1° Consentimiento de las partes; 2° Objeto que pueda ser materia de contrato; y 3° Causa lícita.*

The first condition of validity set forth in this provision, is that the consent given by the parties, or mutual assent, which is a condition for the validity of any contract in all legal systems, implies not only that the parties must express a deliberate approval for the proposed clauses to be included in an agreement, but for such purpose, above all, they need to have the legal capacity or the legal power or competency to give such consent, according to the provisions of the law that governs their actions.

In the case of contracts entered into by Venezuelan public entities, as a matter of principle, the expression of consent by it, can only exist when the public entity and its representative have the legal competency or power to give the required consent, and have fulfilled all the mandatory constitutional and legal requirements to be able to enter into the contract, such legal competency being a matter of public order, governed by Venezuelan public law.

That is, as I explained in 1992, "apart from the clauses themselves of the agreement (which have force of law between the parties), and the complementary Civil Code provisions, all public contracts are subject in one way or another to public (administrative) law regulations, at least when referring to the competency or attributions of the public entity to sign them,"[235]

Such competency of the public contracting party in order to enter into a public contract, in no case can be presumed, and always must be expressly provided in a statute, which means that the competency to contract must always be justified and must be exercised within the limits set forth in the corresponding statute.[236] As I observed in 1992:

> "The public contracting party needs to have legal competency, by the subject matter of the contract, the territory, the timing, the hierarchy, and the legal powers attributed to it in order to enter into a contract. It is because of such principle that the Constitution says that the State could not recognize obligations other than those entered into by legitimate organs of the branches of government, according to what is provided in the laws." [237]

And precisely, in order to express the will of Public Administration for the purpose of entering into public contracts, the public entity must have the express competency

---

235 See Allan R. Brewer-Carías, *Contratos Administrativos*, Editorial Jurídica Venezolana, Caracas 1992 (reedición 1997), pp. 14, 42, 43, 52, 53, 55, 71, 72. (Text reproduced in Allan R. Brewer-Carías, *Tratado de Derecho Administrativo*, Vol. III, Editorial Civitas, Editorial Jurídica Venezolana, 2013, pp. 621 ff. Available at: http://allanbrewercarias.com/wp-content/uploads /2013/07/BREWER-TRATADO-DE-DA-TOMO-III-9789803652081-txt-1.pdf See in Allan R. Brewer-Carías, *Administrative Law in Venezuela*, Editorial Jurídica Venezolana, 2015, p. 144, available at: http://allanbrewercarias.com/wp-content/uploads/2013/08/9789803651992-txt.pdf.

236 See Allan R. Brewer-Carías, *Derecho Administrativo*, Universidad Externado de Colombia, Tomo II, Bogotá 2005, p. 62 (Text reproduced in Allan R. Brewer-Carías, *Tratado de Derecho Administrativo*, Vol. II, Editorial Civitas, Editorial Jurídica Venezolana, 2013, pp. 431, available at: http://allanbrewercarias.com/wp-content/uploads/2013/07/BREWER-TRATADO-DE-DA-TOMO-II-9789803652074-txt-1.pdf.

237 Artículo 232, of the 1961Constitución. See Allan R. Brewer-Carías, *Contratos Administrativos*, Editorial Jurídica Venezolana, Caracas 1992 (reedición 1997), pp 104 ff. (Text reproduced in Allan R. Brewer-Carías, *Tratado de Derecho Administrativo*, Vol. III, Editorial Civitas, Editorial Jurídica Venezolana, 2013, p. 658. Available at: http://allanbrewer carias.com/wp-content/uploads/2013/07/BREWER-TRATADO-DE-DA-TOMO-III-978980 365 2081-txt-1.pdf

to do so, and must comply with all the conditions and requirements for such will to be legally expressed and formed, complying, among other things, with all the mandatory conditions of validity required prior to entering into the contracts, like for instance, the prior legislative authorization set forth in the Constitution for public interest contracts when entered into with foreign states, foreign entities, or corporations not domiciled in Venezuela;[238] conditions and requirements that having the character of public order, cannot be relinquished in any way by the public contracting party.[239]

In fact, as already mentioned, the general exception to the autonomy of will of the parties in their contractual relations in Venezuela, is when a provision of a statute is considered to be in the nature of public order (*orden público*), in which case, according to the Civil Code (article 6), it is directly applicable to contracts and cannot be modified by agreements between the parties. Regarding these provisions of public order, the first aspect that must be borne in mind, is that they are of mandatory application and incapable of being modified by contract.

In the text of article 6 of the Civil Code ("Laws in which public order or good morals are involved cannot be renounced or relaxed by private agreements"), the expression "laws" according to the Constitution is referred to "statutes," in the sense of laws sanctioned by the "the National Assembly in legislative session" (article 202), because under the Constitution (art. 112), restrictions or limitations upon economic freedom can only be imposed through statutes.

Therefore, as already mentioned, this concept of public order, as an exception to the autonomy of will of the parties, must be interpreted strictly, and in the Venezuelan legal system refers to legal provisions relating to the legal order that is general and essential for the existence of the community itself, which cannot be relaxed at the wishes of the parties; a concept that of course does not apply to matters which only concern private parties in a contractual relationship or dispute. Therefore, a provision

---

238 This is a matter that I studied many years ago, in 1964, in an article titled "The formation of the will of the Public Administration in administrative contracts." See Allan R. Brewer-Carías, "La formación de la voluntad de la Administración Pública Nacional en los contratos administrativos," in *Revista de la Facultad de Derecho*, Universidad Central de Venezuela, No, 28, Caracas 1964, pp. 61-112. Available at: http://allanbrewercarias.net/Content/449725d9-f1cb-474b-8ab2-41efb849fea8/Content/II.4.13.pdf.

239 As Joaquín Sánchez-Covisa explains: "By establishing a standard of public policy, the State determines the "duty to be" mandatory and imperative and is required at that time by the legal awareness of the group. As a result, those rules cannot be waived or relaxed by contracts between private parties. In this sense the duty to faithfulness between spouses, compensation for professional accidents or the payment of taxes cannot be relaxed by the will of the private parties. These are provisions of public policy, and therefore represent the idea of what is the purpose in that legal community of our days." See Joaquín Sánchez-Covisa, *La vigencia temporal de la Ley en el ordenamiento jurídico venezolano*, Academia de Ciencias Políticas y Sociales, Caracas 2007, p.179. In this same sense, Francisco López Herrera, quoting Henri Lepge (*Traité Élementaire de Droit Civil Belge*, Bruilant, Bruxelles, 1941-1949, Vol. I, o. 101), "stated that "public policy laws and provisions are those that refers to the essential interest of the State or that affect the Collectivity, or that fix in private law the legal fundamental basis on which is based the economic and moral order of a determined society. In order to determine the public policy provision, it is needed to analyse in each case, the spirit of the Institution and to examine what and why it has relation with essential demands of the Collectivity or the fundamental basis of private law." See Francisco López Herrera, *La nulidad de los contratos en la legislación civil de Venezuela*, Caracas 1952, p. 96.

of public order is not any ordinary legal provision, but only those which make up the basic structure of society and the State, such as, for instance, those establishing competencies or attributions of the State's entities and organs, like the legislative, executive and judicial branches, that cannot be relaxed by agreements between parties to a contract.[240]

This means that regarding public interest contracts, even in cases in which the exception to the relative sovereign immunity clause is applied, and the public contracting party agrees to accept the application of a foreign law for the resolution of doubts and controversies that arise from the performance or conduct of the contract, the public entity entering into the contract is nonetheless always required to comply with all the conditions of validity of public interest contracts established in Venezuelan public law, as it is not possible for those conditions of validity, in any way whatsoever, to be governed by any foreign law.

In other words, when the parties in a public interest contract agree according to article 151 of the Constitution to subject the resolution of doubts and controversies arising from such contracts to foreign law, those doubts or controversies are only those derived from the performance and conduct of the contract once signed by the parties, which means that such foreign law cannot govern the conditions of validity of the contract, such as the requirements for the consent to be given by the public contracting party (like parliamentary authorization), which must be fulfilled before the contract can be entered into. Those requirements and conditions can only be regulated by Venezuelan law, in particular, by all the provisions of public law establishing the competencies of public organs and entities, as it is, for instance, the constitutional attribution and duty of the National Assembly to authorize public interest contracts when entered into with a foreign State, a foreign entity or a corporation not domiciled in Venezuela; or the legal competence of the organ and public official to sign the contract on behalf of the public entity; which are all provisions concerning public order.

V. SO-CALLED "*CLÁUSULAS EXORBITANTES DEL DERECHO COMÚN*"

1. The principles in administrative law

The traditional consequence of a substantive character, of a contract being considered to be an administrative contact, refers to the possible use by the public entity which is Party to the public contract, of extraordinary public powers. These powers are called in legal doctrine and in the courts decision's doctrine, as "*cláusulas exorbitantes de derecho común*", that is to say, extraordinary powers that

240 For instance in Decision No 276 of the Cassation Chamber of the Supreme Tribunal of 31 May 2002, based on the opinion of the Italian author Emilio Betti, ruled that "the concept of public order represents a notion that crystallizes all those rules of public interest that demand unconditional observance, and that cannot be repealed by means of a private agreement. The indication of these characteristic signs of the concept of public order, that is, the need for the unconditional observance of its rules, which the parties cannot renounce, makes it possible to discover with reasonable margin of confidence, when somebody is or is not in a case of a violation of a rule of public order." Available at http://historico.tsj.gob.ve/decisiones/scc/mayo/RC-0276-310502-00959.HTM.

correspond to public entities in order to preserve public interest, which are not to be found in private law contracts.

As mentioned, these public powers or prerogatives have been considered inherent to Public Administration, not being necessary to expressly incorporate them in the contract, because they are considered implicit clauses,[241] derived from the applicable legislation. Because of the public interest involved in the contract, these clauses are the public entity's powers to direct and control its execution; to sanction the breach of the contract by the private party; to unilaterally modify the clauses of the contract; and to unilaterally decide the termination of the contract,[242] as those powers are provided in the laws. That is, those powers in general do not result from the clauses of the public contracts themselves, but from the general superior legal position of Public Administration regarding individuals, as the guarantor of public interest, and according to the applicable legislation. That is why the former Political Administrative Chamber of the Supreme Court of Justice had consistently decided that those clauses do not need to be in the text of the contract, and are considered to be tacitly in all public contracts, regardless of their nature and purpose,[243] as they are provided, for instance in the Organic Law for the Promotion of Private Investments by means of Concessions.[244]

These public powers or prerogatives, consequently although not being necessary to be in the text of the contract, [245] must be established in a law, because as all public competencies to be exercised by public organs or entities, they must always have a legal basis. This was stressed by the Politico Administrative Chamber of the Supreme Tribunal in decision N° 384 of 21 April 2004, when ruling that "the Powers attributed by law to Public Administration, even if they are not incorporated in the text of the contract, must be considered inserted in its text of the contract,"[246] which imply that they must be attributed in a statute. As it has been said by José Ignacio Hernández", "if the exorbitant clauses are in fact extraordinary powers, their source cannot be linked to the object of the contract, but rather to a statute provision. Is the Law –and not the contract– the one that legitimize the Administration to use of such powers. Consequently, its exercise could not be subjected to the object of the contract, that is, to its "administrative" character." Hernandez added that if there

241 Allan R. Brewer-Carías, *Contratos Administrativos, op. cit.*, pp. 43,47, 164.

242 See Allan R. Brewer-Carías, *Contratos administrativos*, Caracas, 1992, pp. 164-185.

243 See in particular the Politico-Administrative Chamber of the former Supreme Court of Justice decision of June 14, 1983 (Case: *Acción Comercial, S.A.)* in Allan R. Brewer-Carías and Luis Ortíz-Alvarez, *Las Grandes Decisiones de la Jurisprudencia Contencioso Administrativa (1961-1996),* Editorial Jurídica Venezolana, Caracas 1994. Cf. Allan R. Brewer-Carías, Allan R., "La Evolución del Concepto de Contrato Administrativo", *in Libro Homenaje a Antonio Moles Caubet*, Universidad Central de Venezuela, Caracas, 1981, Tomo I, p. 63. In the same sense, see decision of the former Supreme Court of August 17, 1999 in Allan R. Brewer-Carías (Comp.), *Documentos del Juicio de la Apertura Petrolera (1996-1999),* Caracas 2004, available at www.allanbrewercarias.com (Biblioteca Virtual, I.2. Documentos, N° 22, 2004), pp. 280-328

244 *Official Gazette,* N° 5.394 Extra, October, 25 1999.

245 See Allan R. Brewer-Carías, *Contratos Administrativos, op. cit.*, pp. 43, 47, 164.

246 See Caso *David Goncalves Carrasqueño vs. Alcaldía del Municipio Miranda del Estado* Zulia disponible en http://www.tsj.gov.ve/decisiones/spa/Abril/00384-210404-2003-0654.htm

is no statute providing for them, "these powers can only be exercised when they are expressly established in the text of the contract."[247]

These clauses in administrative contracts are for instance, the powers that the Administration has in order to direct and control the execution or accomplishment of the contract; in order to sanction the breaches of the private party to the contract; in order to unilaterally modify the clauses of the contract; or to unilaterally decide the revocation of the contract.[248] These powers, as mentioned, due to the principle of legal attribution of competencies, must be bases on a legal text, as is the case of the Law for the promotion of Private Investment through concessions of 1999,[249] in which it is expressly provided the power of the Administration to inspect and control the concession (Art. 37); to unilaterally interpret it (Art. 38); to unilaterally modify its clauses (Art. 39); to sanction some breaches by the private party (Art. 43); to unilaterally rescind the contract in cases of grave breaches to the obligations of the concessionaire (Art. 46, c); and to rescue the concession before its term, by motives of public utility or interest (Art. 53). These powers or prerogatives of the Administration, of course, could also be expressly provided in the clauses of the contract, which in general occur in those traditionally qualify as "administrative contracts," like the public works contracts, or the public services concessions, from which practice precisely derive the provisions of the aforementioned Law on Concessions. That is why, for example, regarding public works contracts, the old regulation containing the General Conditions of those contracts[250] also expressly established the public entity party powers in those contracts to supervise and control the work's execution.[251]

The extraordinary powers or prerogatives of the Public entity regarding public contracts, and particularly, "administrative contracts," as mentioned, can also be expressly regulated in the contract clauses regarding, for instance, the inspection and audit rights of the Public party and the termination clauses by such Public party.

The use of extraordinary powers by the public entity as Party to a public contract, thus, must comply with what is established in the contract which has force of law between the parties; and if the extraordinary powers are not expressly regulated in the contract clauses, but are considered implicit Public Administration legal general powers, then the public entity must always act by issuing formal administrative decisions, or "administrative acts,"[252] through a formal administrative procedure with all the formalities established in administrative law regulations, namely the

247 See José Ignacio Hernández, "El contrato administrativo en la Ley de Contrataciones Públicas venezolana," en Allan R. Brewer-Carías, et al., *Ley de Contrataciones Públicas*, Editorial Jurídica venezolana, Caracas 2008, pp. 234-235.

248 See Carlos García Soto, "Posición de la Administración en su actividad contractual. El caso de la Ley de Contrataciones Públicas," in Allan R. Brewer-Carías et al., *Ley de Contrataciones Públicas*, Editorial Jurídica Venezolana, Caracas 2008, p. 184; Allan R. Brewer-Carías, *Contratos administrativos, op. cit.*, pp. 164-185.

249 *Official Gazette,* N° 5.394 Extr. de 21-10-1999.

250 Decree N° 1417, July 31 1996, *Official Gazette* N° 5.096 July 31, 1996.

251 Allan R. Brewer-Carías, *Contratos Administrativos, op. cit.*, p. 165.

252 Allan R. Brewer-Carías, *Contratos Administrativos, op. cit.*, p. 47.

Organic Law of Administrative Procedure.[253] This statute is applicable to Public Administration entities and public enterprises when issuing administrative acts (Art. 1), according to its article 1st, and to the provisions of the Organic Law of Public Administration (Article, 1st).[254] Consequently, the extraordinary powers that can be exercised by the Public party in administrative contracts must always be manifested by means of a formal administrative decision (administrative act), issued following an administrative procedure, in which the Public party must guarantee the due process and the Private party rights to be heard and to self-defense.[255]

In effect, for instance, if the use of extraordinary powers regarding a public contract, affects economic contractual rights of the Private party, or its general legal statute, such as the modification of the contract, the sanctioning of the Private party, the intervention of the contract, the substitution of the Private party or the anticipated termination of the contract, then the Public entity except otherwise establish in the text of the contract, must follow an administrative procedure in order to guarantee the due process ante the Private party right to self-defense, and the result of the procedure must end in an administrative act, duly motivated.

This has been reiterated by the Supreme Tribunal of Justice in recent decisions. For instance, in a decision of the Politico-Administrative Chamber N° 568 , dated June 20, 2000 (Case: *Aerolink Internacional, S.A. vs. Instituto Autónomo Aeropuerto Internacional de Maiquetía*), the Court stated that the act by means of which the Administration terminate an administrative contract is an administrative act that must be precede by a procedure guaranteeing the right to self-defense and to due process of the concessionary, even if such procedure is expedite, like the summary procedure regulated in the Administrative Procedure Organic Law. In this respect, the Court stated that in case of the Private party breach of an administrative contract, the Public party:

> "...has the power to unilaterally rescind the contract, but has to guarantee the subjective rights of the concessionaries, in the sense that the act deciding to rescind [the concession]) being an administrative act, it must be preceded of an [administrative] procedure in which the right to self-defense and due process would have been guaranteed, even is the procedure be an expedite one, as is the case of the summary procedure regulated in the Administrative Procedure Organic Law.
>
> In this context, the [Politico-Administrative] Chamber, as interpreter of the fundamental norms embodied in the Constitution, observes that in the actual circumstances of the country, where the need for investments exists in order to reactivate the productive framework and where the citizens expects to have

253 *Official Gazette*, N° 2.818 Extra July 1st, 1981. See Allan R. Brewer-Carías et al, Ley *Orgánica de Procedimientos Administrativos*, Caracas, 1987, pp. 19 ff.

254 See Allan R. Brewer-Carías, *El Derecho Administrativo y la Ley Orgánica de Administración Pública*, Caracas 1982, pp. 27 ff.; Allan R. Brewer-Carías, *Principios del procedimiento Administrativo en América Latina*, Bogotá 2003, p. 11.

255 Allan R. Brewer-Carías, *Les principes de la procédure administrative non contentieuse Étude de droit comparé: France, Espagne, Amérique Latine, Economica*, Paris 1992, pp. 139 ff.; Allan R. Brewer-Carías, *Principios del procedimiento Administrativo en América Latina*, Bogotá 2003, p. 261 ff.

public services as a result of the contributions, charges and taxes they pay; on the one hand, the continuity and correct supply of public utilities must be guaranteed, and, in the other hand, the investment made by the concessionaries must also be guaranteed by means of the respect of their right to self-defense and due process when the Administration tend to unilaterally decide to rescind this type of contracts."[256]

The same principle has been explained by the same Politico-Administrative Chamber of the Supreme Tribunal of Justice, in its decision N° 1836 of August, 8th 2001, deciding the challenging of a municipal administrative act that terminated a concession contract for the exploitation of a gravel pit, whereby the Court declared "on the judicial doctrine (*jurisprudencia*) that has been wielded in relation to these causes for extinguishing concessions", noting the following:

> "The jurisprudence of this Political-Administrative Chamber has been repeating the authority had by the Administration to unilaterally rescind a contract (concession) in those cases of breach by the co-contractor (concessionaire) pursuant to Article 46, c) of the Organic Law on the Promotion of Private Investment under the Concessions Régime, published in Official Gazette N° 5.394, Extraordinary, of October 25, 1999, case in which, as the jurisprudencia of this Chamber affirms, there exists the need for a prior procedure that guarantees the right to defense and due process.
>
> That is why in many of these cases this Maximum Tribunal has provided as follows:
>
> […] The plaintiff claims that, notwithstanding the fact that the administration has proven the facts that gave rise to the breach of the referred clauses, it shall give the latter the chance to explain or allege its legal reasons and pertinent evidence to demonstrate that there was no such breach, that is, that there should be initiated an administrative procedure that will guarantee the exercise of its right to defense enshrined in Articles 68 and 69 of the magna Carta […]
>
> […] In this respect the Chamber observes that, if the claim made by the defense lawyer of the plaintiff – regarding the absence of procedure prior to the unilateral action by which the Ministry of the Environment and Natural Resources agreed to the resolution of the administrative contract entered into with the plaintiff on January 25, 1984, the latter's right to defense had been undermined, in such a way that, in this particular case, the Maximum Tribunal, admits the cautionary protection and shall, based on sufficient means of proof, obtain presumption of the alleged breach. And as has been the criterion of the Chamber since the decision initiated on 10-07-91, the impugned action itself may constitute the proof required for admitting the cautionary protection…". (Sent. of the SPA-CSJ of February 10, 1994, case: *Industria Maderera del Caparo*, C.A.)"[257]

---

256 See in *Revista de Derecho Público*, N° 82, Editorial Jurídica Venezolana, Caracas 2002, p. 439

257 Caso: *David Montiel y otro vs. Cámara Municipal del Municipio Almirante Padilla del Estado Zulia*, en *Revista de Derecho Público*, N° 85-88, Caracas 2001, pp. 249 y ss.

Consequently, pursuant to the doctrine of the Supreme Tribunal, in case of unilateral termination of an administrative contract for breach of contractor's obligations, the Administration shall open an administrative procedure and guarantee due process and right to defense on the Private party, and eventually has to issue an administrative act, formally motivated that could be the object of judicial control. A similar requirement is compulsory in order to adopt any other unilateral decision which affects the economic rights of the Private party or the protective economic clauses of the contracts.

In no case it could be stated that the general need to preserve the due process of law clause could be contrary to general interests; and if some extraordinary circumstances could arise, imposing the need to decide that public interests must prevail upon particular interests, they must be constitutionally formalized by means of a formal declaration of a state of exception according to article 337 of the Constitution and to the Organic Law of States of Exception[258]. According to such norms, the guarantee of the exercise of some fundamental rights could be legally restricted, but in such cases a Presidential Decree is needed in order to regulate the restriction (art. 339). In absence of a decree declaring the State of Emergency, the constitutional rights to self-defense and to due process of a private Party in a public contract can never be considered incompatible with the public interest. According to article 49 of the Constitution, the constitutional guaranty of a due process of law and to self-defense "is inviolable" in all judicial and administrative procedures, and cannot even be surpassed by the Legislator itself.[259]

The Constitutional Chamber has clearly stipulated in decision N° 321 of February 22, 2002 (Case: *Papeles Nacionales Flamingo, C.A. vs. Dirección de Hacienda del Municipio Guacara del Estado Carabobo)* that limitations to the right to self-defense, as a fundamental right, must always derive from the text of the Constitution and if the Legislator regulations broadens the scope of such limitations, the latter become illegitimate, pointing out the following:

> "It shall be observed that both Article 68 of the repealed Constitution and 49.1 of the one currently in force, enable the law to regulate the right to defense, regulation that is attended by the corresponding regulation. This by no means intends to mean that the content of such right is available to the legislator, since such right is clearly defined in the mentioned provisions; on the contrary, it implies a mandate for the legislative body to ensure the enshrinement of mechanisms that guarantee the exercise of defense by those on trial, not only in the jurisdictional sense, but in that of governance too, under the terms provided in the Magna Carta. In this manner, limitations to the right to defense as a fundamental right, derive by themselves from the constitutional text, and if the Legislator broadens the scope of such limitations, the latter become illegitimate; in other words, the mere legal provision restricting the exercise of the right to

258 *Official Gazette* N° 37261 de 15-08-2001

259 Because of the prevalence of the right so self defense, the Constitucional Chamber of the Supreme Tribunal, following the judicial doctrine set forth by the previous Courts, has declared the unconstitutionality of the *solve et repete* condition to bring judicial review actions before the Administrative Action Judicial Review jurisdiction. See decision N° 321 February 22, 2002 (Case: *Papeles Nacionales Flamingo, C.A. vs. Dirección de Hacienda del Municipio Guácara del Estado Carabobo*, in *Revista de Derecho Público*, N° 89-92, Editorial Jurídica Venezolana, Caracas 2002.

defense does not justify them, but only in a manner that they follow the abovementioned constitutional mandate."[260]

Therefore, the right to defense is an absolute constitutional right, "inviolable" in every state and level of the cause, says the Constitution, both in legal and administrative procedures, corresponding to any person, with no distinction whatsoever, whether an individual or a company, since it admits no exceptions nor limitations[261]. Such right "is a fundamental right that our Constitution protects and is such that it cannot be suspended within the rule of law, since it represents one of the bases of such concept"[262].

Additionally, after the enactment of the 1999 Constitution, the Constitutional Chamber of the Supreme Tribunal of Justice insisted on the absolute and inviolable character of the right to defense. So, for example, in decision N° 97 of March 15, 2000 (Case: *Agropecuaria Los Tres Rebeldes, C.A. vs. Court of First Instance in Matters Civil, Commercial, Transit, Labor, Agrarian, Criminal, and Safeguarding of Public Patrimony of the Judicial Circuit of Barinas State*), the Chamber stated:

> "Due process is that process which contains the guarantees that are indispensable for the existence of an effective judicial control. This is the concept to which Article 49 of the Constitution refers when it expresses that due process shall be applied to all judicial and administrative proceedings.
>
> But the constitutional ruling does not establish a determined type of process, but rather that whatever the procedural process chosen for the defense of legitimate rights or interests, the procedural laws shall guarantee the existence of a procedure that ensures the party's right to defense and the possibility of an effective judicial control.
>
> From the existence of due process comes the possibility that the parties can make use of the means or recourses provided in the regulations to defend its rights and interests. Therefore, in any case in which from the inobservance of procedural rules comes the impossibility for the parties to make use of the mechanisms that guarantee their right to be heard at trial, a situation of lack of defense and violation of the parties' guarantee of due process and guarantee of defense, shall be produced."[263]

Additionally, the use of extraordinary public prerogatives by the public entity Party regarding administrative contracts (*cláusulas exorbitantes*), as aforementioned, can only be exercised subject to what is established in the particular statute in which

260 See in *Revista de Derecho Público,* N° 89-92, Editorial Jurídica Venezolana, Caracas, 2002.

261 For this reason, for example, the First Court in Contentious-Administrative Matters, in its Sentence of 15-08-97 (Case: *Telecomunicaciones Movilnet, C.A. vs. Comisión Nacional de Telecomunicaciones (CONATEL)* stated: "it is inconceivable in a State of Law, to impose sanctions, prohibitive measures or, in general, any type of limitation or restriction to the subjective sphere of those administrated, without them having any chance to exercise their due defense". See *Revista de Derecho Público,* N° 71-72, Caracas, 1997, pp. 154-163.

262 As established by the Political-Administrative Chamber of the previous Supreme Court of Justice in Sentence N° 572 of 18-8-97. (Case: *Aerolíneas Venezolanas, S.A. (AVENSA) vs. República (Ministerio de Transporte y Comunicaciones)*.

263 See *Revista de Derecho Público,* N° 82, EJV, Caracas, 2000.

those prerogatives are regulated. The general principle regarding Public Administration of the expressed legal attribution of competencies[264] is applicable in this respect, in the sense that all public entities need the expressed attribution of competencies through statutes, in order to be exercised. This principle applies regarding the public entity powers for controlling the execution of administrative contracts, the extension of which must be legally established. Also, in the case of the powers to impose sanctions on a private party in administrative contracts, it must be noted that according to Venezuelan administrative law, any sanction to be imposed by a public entity must be expressly and previously regulated in a statute. In other words, criminal or administrative sanctions are a matter reserved to the statute's regulations, and cannot be imposed if the concrete crime or offence, and its corresponding sanction, is not expressly set forth in a statute. Thus, public entities cannot apply sanctions which are not set forth in advance in the contract's clauses or in a statute[265], as is constitutionally guaranteed in the due process principle regulated by Article 49,6 of the Constitution. In general terms, the sanctions that can be imposed by the public entity Party in case of breach of contractual obligations ("*cláusula penal*")[266] should be contained in the clauses of an administrative contract; and if the contract's clauses do not regulate those sanctions, the public entity cannot impose them, except when set forth in a statute.

But of course, when referring to the possible use of public prerogatives or powers by the public entity in relation to a public or administrative contract, in no way these can be contrary to the contract provisions. As has been said, according to Article 1159 of the Civil Code which is applicable to all contracts (private law contracts and public contracts), the clauses of the contracts have force of law between the Parties, and in spite of a contract being considered or not as an administrative contract, its clauses are binding for the Parties. The possible use of extraordinary powers by the public entity Party, even when those powers are not established in the text of the contract, can in no event imply to ignore the contract's clauses.

On the other hand, the use of public prerogatives not regulated in contractual provisions, such as the unilateral modification of the contract, can never affect its economic and protective clauses, and if it has affected or diminished the contractual rights of the Private party, this always implies the need for compensation. That is to say, if the Public entity which is a party to a public or administrative contract, by using its extraordinary powers or prerogatives affects the contractual rights of the Private party, particularly affecting the protective and economic clauses of the contract, then the public entity is obliged to indemnify the private party for the damages and losses the decision has caused. Consequently, any modification of the clauses of the contract which affects the contractual rights of the Private party must be compensated[267]; and any damages caused by an administrative decision tending to unilaterally modify or terminate the contract when not following the contract provisions, must also be compensated.[268]

264 See Allan R. Brewer-Carías, *Principios del Régimen Jurídico de la Organización Administrativa Venezolana*, Caracas, 1991, 47 ff.

265 Allan R. Brewer-Carías, *Contratos Administrativos, op. cit.*, pp. 165-166.

266 Allan R. Brewer-Carías, *Contratos Administrativos, op. cit.*, p. 241.

267 Allan R. Brewer-Carías, *Contratos Administrativos, op. cit.*, p. 160.

268 *Idem,* p. 160, 161, 184, 218.

In particular, if the public entity which is a Party to an administrative contract affects the contractual rights of the private Party by using extraordinary public prerogatives, particularly the protective and economic clauses of the contract, then the public entity is obliged to indemnify the private party for the damages and losses the decision has caused. That is to say, the use of public prerogatives when not following the contractual provisions can never affect the economic and protective clauses of the contract, and if it has affected or diminished the contractual rights of the other party, this always implies the need for compensation. In particular, for instance, any modification of the clauses of the contract which affects the contractual rights of the private party must be compensated[269]; and any damages caused by an administrative decision tending to unilaterally terminate the contract when not following the contract provisions, must also be compensated[270]. In this case, the just compensation results from the expropriation of the contractual rights, and the procedure must follow the regulations of Article 115 of the Constitution and of the Expropriation Law.[271]

2.The "Exorbitant Clauses" as legal provisions of "public policy" in the Public Contracting Law

Among the provisions of public policy incorporated in the Public Contracting Law are those that regulate the so-called exorbitant clauses of common law for all public contracts, that is, extraordinary powers that are held by public entities in order to preserve public interest, and that could not be found in private contracts. As decided by the former Supreme Court in its ruling of August 17, 1999 (Case Oil and Gas Opening), these extraordinary powers do not define the administrative contract as such, as they are a consequence and not the condition for its determination. In addition to which the fact that a contract has or does not have such clauses is only the consequence of the necessary and mandatory protection of the general interest,[272] as expressly provided by the law. That is, "exorbitant clauses" only exist when they have been regulated by a law, and therefore being provided in a law, that implies that they do not need to be expressed in the text of the contract.

In effect and as stated by the Plenary Chamber of the former Supreme Court in the ruling referred to above regarding administrative contracts, "these exorbitant clauses are implicit provisions of the administrative contract, that set forth prerogatives in favor of the Public Administration, justified by the collective interest involved in that negotiation, whose proportion is so great that they are unacceptable in a common contract relationship," adding that these are "provisions that an individual would not accept to include in a contract with another individual, because this

269 Allan R. Brewer-Carías, *Contratos Administrativos, op. cit.*, p. 160.

270 *Idem*, p. 160, 161, 184, 218.

271 *Official Gazette* N° 37.475 July 1, 2002. See Allan R. Brewere-Carías et al., *Ley de Expropiación por causa de utilidad pública y social*, Caracas 2002, pp. 25 ff.

272 See the text of the decision of the Plenary Court of 17 August 1999 en Allan R. Brewer-Carías (Comp.), *Documentos del Juicio de la Apertura Petrolera (1996-1999),* Caracas 2004, available at www.allanbrewercarias.com (Biblioteca Virtual, I.2. Documents, No. 22, 2004), pp. 280-328.

specifically reveals or materializes the administrative powers in a legal transaction."[273]

These public powers or prerogatives must always have a legal source, as no public jurisdiction can ever be exercised by a public entity without a law granting it that power, and that is why they have been considered as inherent or implicit in administrative contracts, because being in the text of a statute, they do not need to be repeated or incorporated in the contract clauses.[274] This was admitted, for example, by the Political Administrative Chamber of the Supreme Court in Ruling No. 384 of April 21, 2004, when it noted that "powers granted by law to the Public Administration, including when they are not expressly included in the text of the contract, must be considered as inserted therein,"[275] however with the important observations that as indicated by the Chamber, said powers must be "granted by law."

According to Jose Ignacio Hernandez, "If exorbitant clauses in reality are extracurricular powers, then their source cannot be anchored in the purpose of the contract but rather in reality, in the Law. It is the Law - and not the contract - that legitimizes the Administration to deploy those powers, consequently their do not depend on the purpose of the contract, that is in its administrative nature." As for the rest, Hernandez adds, "These powers can be exercised only when they have been expressly included in the text of the contract."[276] From here we see the uselessness of attempting to use the concept of "administrative contract" to attempt to justify the existence of exorbitant clauses, when in any event their origin must be found in provisions of law. It is for this reason that we have stated that the difference between administrative contracts and private contracts of the Administration for purposes of attempting to justify the existence of exorbitant clauses is, in reality, "useless, as the extraordinary powers (exorbitant clauses) established in the laws, can always be exercised by the contracting Administration, independently of the purpose of the contract and the content of its clauses, when so required by public interest", precisely as these are expressly provided in a Law.[277]

These exorbitant clauses in "administrative contracts" have traditionally been identified, for example, with the powers that the contracting Administration has to direct and control the execution of the contract; to sanction breaches by its counterparty to the contract; to unilaterally modify the services that are the object of

---

273 *Idem.*

274 See Allan R. Brewer-Carías, *Contratos Administrativos. Contratos Públicos. Contratos del Estado*, Editorial Jurídica Venezolana, Caracas 2013, pp. 93, 97, 197.

275 See Case *David Goncalves Carrasqueño vs. Office of the Municipality of Miranda, State of* Zulia available at http://www.tsj.gov.ve/decisiones/spa/Abril/00384-210404-2003-0654.htm)

276 See José Ignacio Hernández, "El contrato administrativo en la Ley de Contrataciones Públicas venezolana," en Allan R. Brewer-Carías, et al., *Ley de Contrataciones Públicas*, Editorial Jurídica venezolana, Caracas 2012, pp. 184-185.

277 See Allan R. Brewer-Carías, "Sobre los Contratos del Estado en Venezuela," in *Revista Mexicana Statum Rei Romanea de derecho Administrativo,* No. 6, Universidad Nacional Autónoma de México, Monterrey 2011, pp. 207-252; transcribed in the book Allan R. Brewer-Carías, *Contratos Administrativos. Contratos Públicos. Contratos del Estado* Editorial Jurídica Venezolana, Caracas 2013, pp. 327, 339. See Allan R. Brewer-Carías, *Administrative Law in Venezuela*, EJV International, 2015, p. 156.

the contract; or to terminate the contract unilaterally.[278] These powers, if they are not contained in the clauses of the contract, under the principle of the attribution of public faculties only by means of the law, must always be regulated in some legal text, as for examples is the case with the 1999 Law on the Promotion of Private Investment under the Concessions regime,[279] where there is explicit regulation of the powers of the contracting Administration to inspect and control (Art. 37); to interpret unilaterally (Art. 38); to modify unilaterally (Art. 39); to order sanctions for breaches by the concessionaire (Art. 43); to terminate the contract unilaterally on the grounds of serious non-fulfilment of the concessionaire's obligations (Art. 46.c); and to cancel the concession early in the public interest or for public benefit (Art. 53).

It is for instance the case of the power of the public contracting party to modify the public contract, which according to article 130 of the Law, refers to the clauses related to the "supply of goods", the "service to be supply" or the "perform of the works," that is, those referred to the object of the contract, and not to other clauses. In other words, the powers to modify the contracts, are only referred to the clauses relating to the conditions of execution of the contract, for example, a modification that tries to change the scope of the service provisions or the conditions of its performance.[280] What is more, this is a criterion that I have maintained since 1964, when I explained that what the jurisprudence of the old Federal Court recognized from the outset was the Administration's "right to unilaterally modify administrative contracts, changing the scope of the service provisions to be carried out by the co-contracting party", in other words, only regarding the clauses relating to the object or service provision of the contract.[281]

---

278 See Carlos García Soto, "Posición de la Administración en su actividad contractual. El caso de la Ley de Contrataciones Públicas," en Allan R. Brewer-Carías et al., *Ley de Contrataciones Públicas*, Editorial Jurídica Venezolana, Caracas 2012, pp. 201ff.; Allan R. Brewer-Carías, *Contratos administrativos. Contratos Públicos. Contratos del Estado*, Editorial Jurídica Venezolana, Caracas 2013, pp. 196-216.

279 *Official Gazette,* No. 5,394 Extr. of 21-10-1999.

280 See regarding this what I actually expounded in the book that has been incorrectly quoted: Allan R. Brewer-Carías, *Contratos Administrativos*, Editorial Jurídica Venezolana, Caracas 1992, the text of which was reproduced in the book: Allan R. Brewer-Carías, *Contratos Administrativos. Contratos Públicos. Contratos del Estado*, Editorial Jurídica Venezolana, Caracas 2013, pp. 201, 202.

281 See Allan R. Brewer-Carías, *Las Instituciones Fundamentales del Derecho Administrativo y la Jurisprudencia venezolana*, Caracas, 1964, pp. 11, 15. where we quote in support the ruling of the old Federal Court of 12–11–54, and of the old Federal Court and of the Federal and Cassation Court of 9–3–39 in *Memoria* of 1940, volume I, p. 346), and of 5–12–45, *Actions* of 1945, p. 304. 162. The relevant text on State contracts in the above-mentioned book was reproduced in the book: Allan R. Brewer-Carías, *Contratos Administrativos. Contratos Públicos. Contratos del Estado*, Editorial Jurídica Venezolana, Caracas 2013, pp 11-13 On the subject of French law, in that work I also made reference to J. Dufan, "Le pouvoir de modification unilatérale de l'Administration et les contrats de concession de service public," in *Actualité Juridique*, N° 7, 1955; A. De Laubadère, « Du pouvoir de l'Administration d'imposer unilatéralement des changements aux dispositions du contrat administratif », in *Revue de droit public (RDP)*, 1954, p. 36. The possibility of unilateral modification of Administrative Contracts in 1964, we said, was also specifically established in the Draft Organic Law of Public Finance of 1963, in which it was proposed, in its article 24, that the "National Executive Branch, when it thus suits the interests of the Republic and without the need to obtain the consent of the co-contracting party, may *introduce*

Some years later, in 1968, I expanded further on the subject of unilateral modification of "administrative contracts", particularly public works contracts,[282] agreeing with Eloy Lares Martínez that the "basis of this power of unilateral modification is rooted in the demands of the general interest of the community,"[283] and was expressed by the old Federal Court to the effect that "when dealing with public works contracts, such as a port, a highway, the Administration may, in order to greater satisfy collective needs, modify to a greater or lesser extent the amounts of work to be carried out by the contractor."[284] In other words, a power of modification that is only conceivable in relation to the clauses that relate to the service provisions that are the object of the contract.

For this reason in particular, in relation to unilateral modifications that are accepted in administrative contracts, particularly those involving public works, I said at that time that they could only refer "to the modalities of execution, to the actual object of the contract (increase or reduction in the volume of work)" leading to "qualitative or quantitative modifications to the work," as was indicated at the time by the Attorney-General of the Republic, "although in public works contracts generally speaking a certain quantity of work is contracted, this does not prevent the carrying out, during the execution of the works by the contractor, of extra works that were not quantitatively or qualitatively envisaged in the original contract" (1966) This power, in any case, as I have been saying for years, was explicitly established in the General Conditions for Contracting for the execution of works decreed by Decree No. 1.821 of August 1991, Article 32) which began by saying that "The Contracting Entity may, before or after the work begins to be carried out, introduce into it any changes or modifications that it regards as appropriate, and the guarantors must be notified of this." This text, which should have been incorporated into these Conditions in the text of the works contracts, was the remote ancestor of article 130 of the 2014 Public Contracting Law, which begins similarly stating that: "The contracting party may, before or after the beginning of the supply of the goods, the provision of the services or the carrying out of the work, introduce any modifications that deem necessary, of which the contractor must be notified in writing."

Therefore, I concluded in the 1968 study on unilateral modification of public works contracts, that "the Administration may, first of all, introduce modifications into the ways in which the work is carried out, since these modifications would

---

alterations into the object of the contract; but, if such alterations lead to any direct injury to the co-contracting party, the latter shall have the right to fair and reasonable compensation". The relevant text from this book was also reproduced in the book: Allan R. Brewer-Carías, *Contratos Administrativos. Contratos Públicos. Contratos del Estado*, Editorial Jurídica Venezolana, Caracas 2013, pp. 41.

282 *See* Allan R. Brewer–Carías, "La facultad de la Administración de modificar unilateralmente los contratos administrativos con especial referencia a los contratos de obras públicas en el Derecho venezolano," en *Revista de Derecho Español y Americano*, No. 19, Madrid, 1968, p. 1–17. The text of this work was included in the book *Contratos Administrativos,* Editorial Jurídica Venezolana, Caracas 1992, the text of which was reproduced in the book: Allan R. Brewer-Carías, *Contratos Administrativos. Contratos Públicos. Contratos del Estado*, Editorial Jurídica Venezolana, Caracas 2013, pp. 204-213.

283 *Cf.* Eloy Lares Martínez, *Manual de Derecho Administrativo*, *cit.*, p. 215.

284 *See* Decision of 5 December 1944, in *Memoria 1945*, volume I, p. 285.

always bear some relation to the works that are the object of the contract. On the other hand, the Administration may impose the execution of additional works if these are supplementary to the work that is the object of the contract, with this nature, in other words, it may impose the carrying out of works that have not been envisaged, but not ones that are totally separate from the work that has been contracted."[285] It was therefore made quite clear that the modifications to "administrative contracts" that the contracting Administration could introduce could only affect the object of the contract, in other words, the specific service provision, the scope of the service to be provided, the execution of the public work, or the exploitation of the asset in the public domain, specifically, without to think even in so-called administrative contracts that the Administration could unilaterally modify other clauses in the contract that do not concern its object, which has never been accepted in the theory of administrative law.

In any case, of course, on this subject of unilateral alterations of administrative contracts, the basic consequence is that if the exercise of the power of unilateral alteration leads to injury to the rights of the contractor as a result of the unilateral modification, the latter must be compensated. For that reason, the old Federal and Cassation Court did not only from the outset recognize fully the power of the Administration to unilaterally modify the object or the service provision of administrative contracts in the light of the public interest, but it also explicitly acknowledged that when these "changes or corrections are of such a magnitude that they change the nature or change substantially the work or service that has been contracted, the contractor's right to request extensions and compensations and even the termination of the contract is recognized."[286]

Based on all these principles that have been established in Venezuela during the past decades, the power of unilateral modification that the public contracting party has, based on article 130 of the Public Contracting Law, could never affect contractual clauses other than those that relate to the object of the contract. In other words, never could it affect for instance contractual clauses regarding the form of payment that was agreed legally and freely by the parties, which could only be modified by agreement between the parties.

3. The right of the parties to include in their contracts, contractual clauses for its unilateral termination

Notwithstanding the power of the public contracting party to unilaterally terminate public contracts, and the provisions on this matter in the Public Contracting Law, in the text of the public contracts, the parties can also agree for the possibility of the private contracting party to also unilaterally terminate the contract. In such clauses it can be granted, for instance, to the private contracting party the right to terminate

---

285 *V.* Allan R. Brewer-Carías, "La facultad de la Administración de modificar unilateralmente los contratos administrativos con especial referencia a los contratos de obras públicas en el Derecho venezolano," en *Revista de Derecho Español y Americano*, No. 19, Madrid, 1968, p. 1-17. A work included in the book Allan R. Brewer-Carías, *Contratos Administrativos,* Editorial Jurídica Venezolana, Caracas 1992, whose text was reproduced in the book: Allan R. Brewer-Carías, *Contratos Administrativos. Contratos Públicos. Contratos del Estado*, Editorial Jurídica Venezolana, Caracas 2013, pp. 201-214.

286 See Decision of December 5, 1944, in *Record 1945*, volume I, p. 285

the contract, without judicial intervention, when the public contracting party beached some specific contractual duties. In those cases, the clause can be understood as the will of the parties included in the contract, and being the law between the parties, it could not be ignored by the public contracting party.

The inclusion of a termination clause of this sort in public contracts does not affect any provision of public policy. Nonetheless, discussions on the matter have arisen due to two decisions issued by the Constitutional Chamber of the Supreme Tribunal of Justice, specifically, decisions No. 1658 of 16 June 2003 (Case of *Fanny Lucena Olabarrieta-Review of Sentence-*),[287] and No. 167 of 4 March 2005 (*IMEL C.A., Review of sentence*).[288] These decisions which were adopted in two judicial review processes on matters of constitutionality regarding two lower courts decisions, according to the attribution of the Chamber set forth in article 336.10 of the Constitution, from which it was deducted that a supposed "binding doctrine" was established considering that contract clauses for unilateral termination in any sort of contracts were unconstitutional and void.

Nonetheless, the fact is that in any of the two decisions a "binding doctrine" on the interpretation of any constitutional provision was established, in the sense of considering null and void such contractual clauses, so no constitutional interpretation has been made on the matter.

The principle that "the interpretations established by the Constitutional Chamber on the content or scope of constitutional provisions are binding for other Chambers of the Supreme Court and other Courts of the Republic," is established in Article 335 of the Constitution, which implies, that for a "binding doctrine" to be established by the Constitutional Chamber, the corresponding decision of the Chamber must necessarily interpret a specific constitutional provision, based on the above mentioned Article 335 of the Constitution. As was specified by the Constitutional Chamber of the Supreme Tribunal in its own decision No. 727 of 8 April 2003:

> "within a decision of the Constitutional Chamber, what is binding is the interpretation on the content and scope of Constitutional provisions, as noted in decision No. 291 of 3 May 2000, on the following terms: "... this Chamber must specify that its binding criteria are referred to the interpretation on the content and scope of constitutional provisions, and not on a legal qualification of facts, not related to constitutional norms."[289]

In this sense no constitutional doctrine can be binding unless the Constitutional Chamber of the Supreme Court has effectively interpreted a provision of the Constitution, based on Article 335 of the Constitution. As I noted many years ago, the "binding character" of a constitutional interpretation on the scope or content of Constitutional norms made in a judgement by the Constitutional Chamber, cannot be referred to any phrase or reasoning contained therein, but only to the express interpretation that the Chamber makes "on the content or scope of the constitutional provision and constitutional principles", which is the binding part of the judgement,

---

287 See http://www.tsj.gov.ve/decisiones/scon/Junio/1658-160603-03-0609.htm

288 See http://www.tsj.gov.ve/decisiones/scon/Marzo/167-040305-04-1518.htm

289 See *Revista de Derecho Público*, N° 93-96, Editorial Jurídica Venezolana, Caracas, 2003, p. 143.

which does not extend to any other argument or phrase used therein for the constitutional interpretation."[290]

Moreover, the Constitutional Chamber must specifically and expressly indicate, in its judgement that when deciding it is actually interpreting a constitutional provision, and that doing that, it is setting the "binding" doctrine.[291] Consequently, not any interpretation or application of articles of the Constitution by the Constitutional Chamber is or can be considered as a "binding interpretation" of the Constitution; and that is why the judgement of the Constitutional Chamber that effectively contains a binding interpretation of a constitutional provision or principle, necessarily must mention Article 335 of the Constitution as being applied.[292] As I have noted since 2000, "reasoning or the 'reasoned' part of decision cannot be considered as binding, but only the interpretation made specifically on the content or scope of a specific Constitutional provision."[293] In other words, what may be considered binding in a decision is the part in which the Chamber resolves, that is the part in which the Constitutional Chamber sets the interpretation of a norm, and this must be expressly noted."[294]

Finally, it must be pointed out that these binding doctrine of constitutional interpretation of a specific provision of the Constitution, are in general issued by the Constitutional Chamber when deciding proceedings regarding judicial review of statutes or when deciding constitutional interpretation recourses, having such decisions in general *erga omes* effects. That is why the Constitutional Chamber decisions in such cases, must be published in the *Official Gazette of the Republic*; which was not the case of the above-mentioned decision.

In effect, regarding the Constitutional Chamber decisions cited above, No. 1658/2003 and No. 167/2005, it can be noted, *firstly,* that they were issued applying Article 335 of the Constitution, which regulates the subject of binding constitutional interpretations,[295] and which is not even mentioned in the judgement; and *secondly,*

---

290 See Allan R. Brewer-Carías, "The power of the Constitutional jurisdiction to interpret with binding effects," in Jhonny Tupayachi Sotomayor (Coordinator), *The binding Nature of Constitutional Precedent (Analysis, Comments and Compared Doctrine)* , Editorial ADRUS, Lima, September 2009, pp. 791-819.

291 See for example the sentence of Constitutional Court for Supreme Court No. 285 of 4 March 2004 which interpreted Constitutional Article 304 "as binding" , in *Revista de Derecho Público*, N° 97-98, Editorial Jurídica Venezolana, Caracas, 2004, pp.278-279, y en http://www.tsj.gov.ve/decisiones/scon/marzo/285-040304-01-2306%20.htm . Likewise see Sentence No. 794 of the Constitutional Court of 27 May 2011 which ordered that "the binding nature on all Courts of the Republic, including for other courts of the Supreme Court of Justice [...] does not apply due to the diffuse control of Constitutionality set in Article 213 of the Law for Banking Sector Institutions. See: Petition for certiori for criminal proceedings for bank crimes. See http://www.tsj.gov.ve:80/decisiones/scon/mayo/11-0439-27511-2011-794.html .

292 See for example Rafael Laguna Navas "The extraordinary appeal for review and binding nature of sentences of the Constitutional Court of the Supreme court" in *International Congress on Administrative Law in Honour of Professor Luis Henrique Farias Mata*, Vol. II, 2006, pp.91-101.

293 See Allan R. Brewer-Carías, *The system of Constitutional Law in the Constitution of 1999*, Editorial Jurídica venezolana, Caracas 2000, p 87.

294 See Allan R. Brewer-Carías, *La Justicia constitucional. Constitutional processes and proceedings,* Editorial Porrúa, México 2007, p. 415.

295 Article 335.

that the Chamber made no reference of any kind to any constitutional provision that could be considered as interpreted. The only constitutional provision mentioned in the first decision (No. 1658/2003), was Article 138 of the Constitution which provides that "all usurped authority is ineffective and its acts are null", only for the purpose of considering that in the case decided, individuals cannot *restrict the constitutional rights and guarantees* of other individuals, without judicial intervention; a decision that in in Venezuela, by the way, has only *at casu et inter partes* effects.

In the decision, in fact, no "constitutional interpretation" of any sort was made by the Constitutional Chamber according to Article 335 of the Constitution, regarding Article 138; which was only applied in order to decide that a Condominium Board could not by its own decision turn off the tap for the supply of water to one apartment in a building, a matter that must be decided only with judicial intervention. From that decision, it cannot be deducted that the Constitutional Chamber has denied the validity of contract clauses providing for unilateral termination, and has not considered that unilateral termination of a contract in accordance with its clauses could be null under the terms of Art. 138 of the Constitution.

It is enough to read the text of both decisions (No. 1658/2003 and No. 167/2005) to observe that when issuing them, the Constitutional Chamber, *first*, did not apply in any way Article 335 of the Constitution, which was not even mentioned therein; *second*, that Article 138 of the Constitution was not "interpreted" in any way, and that no binding doctrine of any kind was set on the interpretation of such provision; *third*, that in decision No. 1658/2003, the Chamber only decided that according to article 138 of the Constitution, a Condominium Board can be considered that is usurping the powers of the judiciary when it decides to shut the supply of water to one apartment in a building, considering that this is a matter that must be decided only with judicial intervention; *fourth*, that in decision No. 167/2005, the Constitutional Chamber only "decided" that it "did not share" the decision of a lower court to consider possible and valid the establishment of contract clause for termination without judicial intervention, considering that such criteria was "contrary and therefore completely ignores the binding interpretation set by Article 138 of the Constitution in decision No. 1658/2003," but ignoring, at the same time, that the latter judgement did not establish "any binding interpretation" of a constitutional provision; and *fifth,* that neither judgement affirmed that the clauses for unilateral termination of contracts implies the usurping of jurisdictional function.

As mentioned, in decision No. 1658/2003 which was cited in decision 167/2005, what was affirmed was only that when individuals exercise their powers "limiting the constitutional rights and guarantees of others" they are considered to usurp the jurisdictional function, but that was referred to actions taken by a Condominium Board on a residential building, to shut the supply of water to an apartment, which was considered essential for the right to quality of life of one of the condominium owners, which could not be unilaterally denied.

In effect, in the specific case of decision No. 1658 of 16 June 2003 (*Fanny Lucena Olabarrieta -Review of sentence-* case), issued by the Constitutional Chamber it was the result of a constitutional review petition of a judicial decision issued by a lower court (Superior Civil, Mercantile and Traffic Court of Caracas), in which, as aforementioned, the Constitutional Chamber did not make any interpretation of Constitutional provisions, nor did it set any binding interpretation of a provision of the Constitution.

In that case, the Constitutional Chamber simply reviewed a judgement from a lower court, considering that the restriction or limits of constitutional rights and guarantees can only be declared by the courts of justice, and any decision adopted by a single individual setting justice by itself, harming the *constitutional rights and guarantees* of another party, constitutes a seizing (usurping) of authority under the terms of Article 138 of the Constitution. In that case the Court made no "interpretation" of that article, which was not necessary to be "interpreted," and therefore offered no binding doctrine of any kind.

In fact, the lower court decision reviewed in that case was the dismissal of a petition for an injunction filed by Ms. Lucena against the Condominium Board of a residential building, in a case that was not referred to contract matters or to termination clauses included in contracts. The conflict that caused the petition for an injunction arose from the decision of the Condominium Board to unilaterally *suspend water service* to the home of Ms. Lucena, as provided in the Condominium Regulation, because failure to pay the homeowners maintenance quota for the condominium. The petitioner alleged that the decision of the Condominium Board violated her right "to obtain public water service, and thereby assure the health of herself and her family," and that Condominium Board had "taken justice into its own hands". That allegation was based, as summarized by the Constitutional Chamber, on the argument that the Law on the matter of apartment ownership "which establishes a legal mechanism for collection of past due condominium homeowners quotas" and "that the decision adopted by the Board imply taking justice into its own hands and lead to the violation of the guarantee established in Article 253 of the Constitution, that provides that the State has the exclusive monopoly through the bodies of the Judicial Branch, to hear matters determined by the law."

After studying the arguments, the Constitutional Chamber proceeded to review the judgement issued by the lower court, considering that the jurisdictional function is called to "resolve on conflicts between individuals," and therefore must be exercised by "an impartial and specialized body" that can "arbitrate with authority a conflict of interests between subjects," a function that has been assigned to the State "since remote times". That power to dispense justice, according to the Court, "is a public function entrusted to a body of the State for the purpose of administering justice in specific cases" and "is not conceived so that individuals can substitute" in that duty, and arbitrarily and without law, proceed to resolve their conflicts." The Court considered that it is "a function of the Public Power" that corresponds to the bodies of the Judicial Branch established in the Constitution.

The Constitutional Chamber, in light of the above, concluded that:

> "When an individual, in case of conflict of interests, decides to act restricting rights or freedoms and imposing its criteria, by adopting a determined position that limits the rights of others, [that conduct] constitutes an appropriation of State's functions in order to replace the State to obtain recognition of his rights without pursuing the corresponding legal proceeding; [action] that is illegitimate and contrary to the law, and should be considered as non-existent, according to

what is established in Article 138 of the Constitution, which provides that: "All usurped authority is ineffective and its acts are null".

The Court also considered that the actions of the Condominium Board in the case at hand, *violated "a fundamental element for all human beings, for life, as water is a vital and fundamental liquid to assure the quality of life of a citizen*, the use of which the State must protect, according to the provisions of Article 55 of the Constitution". The Court concluded that the challenged conduct "is not only subject to censure because it arbitrarily and reprehensibly assumes a right that it does not have, but also basically because it violates the rights and guarantees provided in the Constitution," and that *also violates the right of any citizens to live* (article 43), to a *physical, mental and moral health* (article 46), *to health* (article 83), *to a home* (article 82), *to an atmosphere free of contamination* (article 127) and to *property* (article 115).

As a result of the above, the Constitutional Chamber proceeded to review the lower court judgement and to annul it, without establishing any binding doctrine of constitutional interpretation derived from the application in the case of article 138 of the Constitution. In these cases of proceeding of judicial review of lower courts judgements, the general principle is that the Constitutional Chamber decision has only *at casu et inter partes*, i.e., to the parties intervening in the specific case at hand.[296] That is why the decision was not published in the *Official Gazette of the Republic*.[297]

In addition, the Chamber decision did not consider or argue anything on matters of termination of contracts or regarding contract clauses for termination. That was not part of the *thema decidendum*; being the only matter debated the terms of a Condominium homeownership Regulation regarding the powers of a Condominium Board to possibly order the water supply to suspended to one of the homeowners; an action that was considered to limit its basic rights, and therefore could not be decided without judicial intervention.

Consequently, it can be said that decision No. 1658/2003 of the Constitutional Chamber of the Supreme Tribunal did no establish any binding interpretation on constitutional provisions, and specifically it did not rule that contract termination clauses can be considered null and void.

---

296 For the effectiveness of sentences handed down by the Constitutional Court see Allan R. Brewer-Carias, "The effects of Constitutional sentences in Venezuela", *Anuario Internacional sobre Justicia Constitucional*, No. 22, Centro de Estudios Políticos y Constitucionales, Madrid 2008, pp. 19-66.

297 On the contrary, in cases where the Constitutional Court adopts a decision with binding effects *erga omnes*, in addition to the requirement that this must be expressly declared, it must also be published in the *Official Gazette*. For example, we find the recent sentence of 8-12-2011 of the Constitutional Court in which the Court "no longer applies by diffuse Constitutional control of Articles 471-a and 472 of the Venezuelan Criminal Code in the cases where there is a conflict between individuals arising from agricultural activities" [...]. That sentence declares that the application *of the ordinary agrarian proceeding* established in Chapter VI of the Lands and Agrarian Development Act *is binding* on cases where there is a conflict between individuals arising from agrarian activities", and "orders the publication of the entire decision in the Judicial Gazette and in the Official Gazette for the Bolivarian Republic of Venezuela." File Nº 11-0829. See http://www.tsj.gov.ve/informacion/notasdeprensa/notasdeprensa.asp?codigo=9054

The only constitutional principle derived from the Chamber decision, in a conflict originated from the shutting of the water supply to a residence, is that such decision, because affecting or limiting constitutional fundamental rights of individuals, cannot be adopted by other individuals, corresponding exclusively to the judicial authorities. Therefore, a Condominium Board cannot order the water supply to be shut to a tenant for lack of payment, because it limits the most elemental rights of an individual, a matter that can only be decided by a court of justice.

With respect to the other decision issued by the Constitutional Chamber, No. 167/2005, this too was issued in a judicial review proceeding of a lower court decision at the request of a party, according to Article 336.10 of the Constitution. In the case, the reviewed decision was one issued by a lower court (Superior Civil, Mercantile, Traffic and Agrarian Court (Accidental) for the State of Bolivar), in a case in which a party (home construction company: IMEL C.A.) filed a complaint against a non-profit organization, in regard to a contract for the construction of homes, which was terminated by the former, according to the termination clause included in the contract.

The plaintiff requesting the review before the Constitutional Chamber, alleged that in its opinion, although the specific contract contained an express termination clause, the acceptance by the lower court of the right of one of the parties in the case to terminate the contract and "take justice in its own hands" "without judicial intervention", implied a process that "was completely lacking due process."

In fact, the contract in that case contained a clause for its unilateral termination, which the lower court considered to be valid as it was a product of free will of the parties, finding that nothing prevented "one or both parties, each individually, from reserving in the contract the power to end or amend it by their own will".

The Constitutional Chamber in decision No. 167/2005 when reviewing the lower court judgement observed that it found that "in our legal system, a contract can validly establish the possibility for one of the parties to decide to end the contract relationship, with no need for judicial intervention." This criterion of the lower court, which is perfectly compatible with the Venezuelan Constitutional system, however, was not "shared" by the Constitutional Chamber in its review of the lower court decision, arguing in a decision with only effects between the parties to the contract and in an erroneously way, that the "criteria" of the lower court:

> "is contrary and completely ignores the binding interpretation of Article 138 of the Constitution of the Bolivarian Republic of Venezuela, set down in Judgement No. 1658/2003 of 16 June, in Fanny Lucena Olabarrieta."

This is an obvious and clearly error, because as aforementioned, such prior decision of the Chamber did not establish any binding interpretation of any constitutional provision according to article 335 of the Constitution, and particularly of Article 138 of the Constitution referring to matters of contractual termination clauses.[298] In such decision, the Constitutional Chamber only applied such provision

298 The Constitutional Court, perhaps aware of its error, in its sentence made the exception that "only in administrative contracts, in which general interest prevails over that of the individual, is a unilateral termination of the contract possible and valid, as this "is the product of the exercise of administrative powers, no contract powers" (See s.S.C. No. 568/2000 of 20 June, *Aerolink*

in a specific case referred to the restrictions of fundamental constitutional rights imposed by an individual against other.

Nevertheless, as a consequence of the erroneous application of a "criterion" that actually was not established, the Constitutional Chamber proceeded to review the lower court decision, annulling it, but again, without establishing any binding doctrine that could have derived from any interpretation of a constitutional provision. In any case, the decision, even though erroneous, also had only *at casu et inter partes*, the reason why the decision was not ordered to be published in the *Official Gazette of the Republic.*

The conclusion on the matter, in relation to the two decisions cited from the Constitutional Chamber, is that no binding doctrine of any kind has been established in Venezuela that could consider as null and void express termination clauses in contracts, that can be freely included by the parties. On the other hand, this absence of any such binding interpretation, has been confirmed by subsequent decisions issued be the same Supreme Tribunal of Justice, through the Civil Cassation Chamber, finding these termination clauses to be valid.

It was the case, as an example, of decision No. 460 of 5 October 2011 (case: *Transporte Doroca C.A. vs. Cargill de Venezuela S.R.L, Petition for Cassation*)[299], issued by the Civil Cassation Chamber, regarding a case in which was debated the decision of one of the parties to a contract to unilaterally terminate the contract, with prior notice to the other party, and with no need for judicial intervention, as provided in the contract clause and due to the breach of the other party of its contractual duties.

After debating the value of email communications between the parties under the Data Message and Electronic Signatures Act, which had allegedly been violated (cassation by violation of law), the Cassation Chamber dismissed the recourse filed, finding that the messages sent in that case were truthful, and therefore concluding that the petitioner company had breached clauses of the contract; from which it resulted, as the Cassation Chamber found:

> "that Petitioner, under Clause Seven of the contract entered by the parties, unilaterally terminated that contract in advance, which was perfectly authorized to do given that it was so agreed by the parties, in the event that the contractor should breach the rules of transportation and carrying of merchandise."

From all of the above, we can therefore conclude that, in Venezuela, contracts – private contracts or public contracts - can provide for the possibility of a unilateral termination without the intervention of the judicial branch.

International S.A.; 1097/2001 of 22 June: *Jorge Alois Heigl et al*)." See http://www.tsj.gov.ve/decisiones/scon/Junio/1658-160603-03-0609.htm

299 See http://www.tsj.gov.ve/decisiones/scc/Octubre/RC.000460-51011-2011-11-237.html

VI. THE ECONOMIC EQUILIBRIUM IN PUBLIC CONTRACT AND THE RIGHT OF THE PRIVATE CONTRACTING PARTY TO BE COMPENSATED BY THE PUBLIC CONTRACTING PARTY WHEN SUCH EQUILIBRIUM IS AFFECTED BY ACTS OF STATE

1. The role of General Principles of Law in Administrative Law

The principle of submission of the organs of Public Administration to the rule of Law is expressed in general terms in articles 137, 141 and 259 of the Constitution when establishing: first, that the organs of the State must act subjected to the attributions defined in the Constitution and in the statutes (*ley*); second, that Public Administration must exercise its administrative function acting with full subjection to the law (*ley*) and to the rule of Law (*derecho*); and third that administrative acts, general or individual, can be annulled by the contentious administrative courts when contrary to the rule of Law (*derecho*).

These provisions mean that all administrative action not only must be subjected to "the Law" as a formal written source, but to all other written and unwritten sources of law, that have traditionally in Venezuela formed the block of legality. Within it, the most important ones have been the general principles of administrative law,"[300] many of which have progressively been incorporated as positive law in many statutes, as has been the case, for instance, of the Organic Law on Public Administration, the Organic Law on Administrative Procedure, and the Organic law on Public Contracts.

However, before all these statutes were sanctioned and even after their sanctioning, in the absence of specific provisions expressly established in the text of the laws (statutes) in order to regulated specific actions of the organs of Public Administration, it has been generally admitted that the most important source of law that must be apply in such cases are the "general principles of law,"[301] following the general principle of law established in article 4 of the Civil Code, according to which "when there are no precise provision in a Statute, the provisions regulating similar cases or analogous matters must be taken into consideration, and if doubt persist, the general principles of law must be applied."[302]

---

300 See Allan R. Brewer-Carías, *Administrative Law in Venezuela*, (Second edition), Editorial Jurídica Venezolana, EJV International Editions, 2013, p. 86

301 In all the Administrative Law Manuals and Treatises, in absence of specific provisions included in statutes or regulations, the general principles of law have been traditionally considered as the most important source of administrative law applicable to administrative action. See for instance, Eloy Lares Martínez, *Manual de Derecho Administrativo*, XIV Edición, Caracas 2013, pp. 143 ss.

302 *"Article 4. Cuando no hubiere disposición precisa de la Ley, se tendrán en consideración las disposiciones que regulan casos semejantes o materias análogas; y, si hubiere todavía dudas, se aplicarán los principios generales del derecho."* Based precisely on such provision of article 4 of the Civil Code, Lares Martínez argues, that "In administrative law, in the absence of written provision, the general principles of law are applicable as legal (juridical) principles in which the positive legal order has its basis." See Eloy Lares Martínez, *Manual de Derecho Administrativo*, XIV Edición, Caracas 2013, pp. 144

And this has been precisely the case on matters of administrative law, which in comparative law and in particular, in Venezuela, in absence of a codification of its rules, has been historically constructed mainly based on the elaboration of such general principles of law, in the sense of principles in which the whole legal order is based. Those principles have been constructed by the commentators and authors that have written on the matter, and in a recurrent feedback process, through the judicial application of such principles by the contentious administrative courts.[303]

This was the case, for instance, in the absence of a General Law on Public Administration for all the principles referred to the organization of Public Administration,[304] many of which were latter incorporated in the Organic Law on Public Administration of 2001;[305] it was also the case, in the absence of a General Law on Administrative Procedure, for all the principles that governed the issuing of administrative acts,[306] many of which were latter incorporated in the Organic Law on Administrative Procedure of 1982;[307] and it was also the case, in the absence of a General Law on Public or Administrative Contracts, for all the principles that governed public contracting,[308] many of which have been incorporated in the Public Contracting Law of 2010.[309]

One of such general principles of public (constitutional and administrative) law, as has been mentioned, is the principle of the vertical or territorial distribution of

---

303 See for instance: Allan R. Brewer-Carías, *Las instituciones fundamentales del derecho administrativo y la jurisprudencia venezolana*, Universidad Central de Venezuela, Caracas 1964; *Principios fundamentales del derecho público (Constitucional y Administrativo)*, Cuadernos de la Cátedra Allan R. Brewer-Carías de Derecho Administrativo Universidad Católica Andrés Bello, Editorial Jurídica Venezolana. Caracas, agosto 2005.

304 Allan R. Brewer-Carías, *Principios del régimen jurídico de la organización administrativa venezolana*, Colección Estudios Jurídicos, N° 49, Editorial Jurídica Venezolana, Caracas 1991.

305 See Ley Orgánica de la Administración Pública, *Gaceta Oficial*, Extra. N° 6.147 of November 17, 2014. See the comments in Allan R. Brewer-Carías (editor) and Rafael Chavero Gazdik y Jesús María Alvarado Andrade, *Ley Orgánica de la Administración Pública, Decreto Ley No. 4317 de 15-07-2008,* Colección Textos Legislativos N° 24, 4ª edición actualizada, Editorial Jurídica Venezolana. Caracas 2009,

306 Allan R. Brewer-Carías, *Principios del procedimiento administrativo* (Prólogo de Eduardo García de Entería), Editorial Civitas, Madrid 1990, *El derecho administrativo y la Ley Orgánica de Procedimientos Administrativos. Principios del procedimiento administrativo,* Editorial Jurídica Venezolana, 6ª edición ampliada, Caracas 2002.

307 See Ley Orgánica de Procedimientos Administrativos, *Gaceta Oficial* N° 2.818 Extra. of July, 1st, 1981 See the comments in Allan R. Brewer-Carías (editor), and Hildegard Rondón de Sansó y Gustavo Urdaneta, *Ley Orgánica de Procedimientos Administrativos,* Colección Textos Legislativos, N° 1, Editorial Jurídica Venezolana, Caracas 198.

308 Allan R. Brewer-Carías, *Contratos administrativos*, Colección Estudios Jurídicos, N° 44, Editorial Jurídica Venezolana, Caracas 1992; *Contratos Administrativos, Contratos públicos, Contratos del Estado,* Colección Estudios Jurídicos, No. 100, Editorial Jurídica Venezolana, Caracas 2013.

309 See Ley de Contrataciones Públicas, *Gaceta Oficial* N° 6.154 Extra. of November 19, 2014. See the comments in Allan R. Brewer-Carías (editor) and Víctor Hernández Mendible, Miguel Mónaco, Aurilivi Linares Martínez, José Ignacio Hernández G., Carlos García Soto, Mauricio Subero Mujica, Alejandro Canónico Sarabia, César A. Esteves Alvarado, Gustavo Linares Benzo, Manuel Rojas Pérez, Luis Alfonso Herrera Orellana y Víctor Raúl Díaz Chirino, *Ley de Contrataciones Públicas*, Editorial Jurídica Venezolana, Colección Textos legislativos No. 44, 3ª edición actualizada y aumentada, Caracas 2012,

Public Power (*Poder Público*), in which the whole organization of the State organization has its basis, as a Federal State,[310] imposing the existence of three levels of Government whose organs exercise the National Power, the States Power and the Municipal Power, each with constitutional autonomy.

For such purpose, Article 136 of the Constitution provides that, "The Public Power is distributed between the Municipal Power, the States power and the National Power" and that "each of the branches of Public Power has its own functions, but the organs to which its exercise correspond will collaborate among each other in the realization of the State's goals."

This principle imply hat in Venezuela the State is organized in three territorial levels of Government exercising Public Power (*Poderes Públicos*): the national level (the Republic, often called the "Venezuelan State" exercising the National Power); the state level (the states of the Federation, exercising the State's Power), and the municipal level (the municipalities as local governments, exercising the Municipal Power).

Each of the three levels of Government Power has its own Public Administration (National Public Administration, State Public Administration, and Municipal Public Administration), comprising not only organs of central administration but also by decentralized entities with separate legal personality, like State owned enterprises (which can be national public enterprises, states public enterprises or municipal public enterprises).

Having each level of Government its own respective functions, its exercise through Acts of State or administrative acts in each level, can of course affect the actions or activities developed in other of the levels of Government, and among them, such acts can affect the public or administrative contracts that have been entered into in another level of Government.[311]

In order to resolve such conflicts that can resort between the three levels of Governments established according to the principle the vertical distribution or Public Power, originated in Acts of State issued by a level of Government that can affect public contracts entered into by another level of Government, another general principle of administrative law has been developed, known as the principle of *fait du prince*, (*hecho del príncipe, factum principis*), an expression referred to an "obstacle to the performance of the promised activity" in a public contract entered by other branch of Government "that arises from a legislative act or from an administrative authority, for example,"[312] issued by another level or branch of Government.

---

310 See on the "principle of the vertical distribution of the Public Power: The federal form of government," (*el principio de la distribución vertical del Poder Público: la forma federal del Estado*), as a fundamental principle of public law in Venezuela, in Allan R. Brewer-Carías, *Los principios fundamentales del derecho público (constitucional y administrativo),* Editorial Jurídica Venezolana, Caracas 2005, pp. 45 ff.

311 For the purpose of this study, we are using the expression "administrative contracts" as equivalent to "public contracts." See Allan R. Brewer-Carías, *Contratos Administrativos, Contratos públicos, Contratos del Estado,* Colección Estudios Jurídicos, No. 100, Editorial Jurídica Venezolana, Caracas 2013

312 See, José Mélich-Orsini, *Doctrina General del Contrato*, Academia de Ciencias Políticas y Sociales, Serie Estudios N° 61, Caracas 2006, p. 504, fn. 83

The principle, that is common on matters of contracts in all branches of law, has been developed in administrative law on matters of public contracts, as mentioned, related to the effects that can have the Acts of State issued by the different levels of government in the accomplishment by the parties of their obligations in public contracts when also entered into by other level of Government.[313] In that sense, the principle has been applied in order to resolve two main situations: *first*, to determine when an Act of State affecting the economic equilibrium of public contract, originates the right for the private contracting party to the reestablishment of such equilibrium by means of receiving compensation from the public contracting party; and second, to determine when an act of State affecting a public contract, can be considered, particularly for the public contracting party as a non-imputable and extraneous cause that can excuse or justify the non-compliance of its contractual obligations.

In both cases, the principle of *fait du prince*, derived from the principle of the vertical or territorial distribution of Public Power, has been developed by administrative authors and by court decisions.

2. The Principle of *Fait du Prince* applied in Administrative Contracts.

In effect, as mentioned, the principle of *fait du prince* o *hecho del príncipe* (act of State, act of Prince) in administrative law and on matters of public contracts has two specific and different purposes when related to Acts of State.

On the one hand, it is a general principle specifically developed in administrative law referred to the situation of the *private contracting party* into a public contract when an Act of State affects the economic equilibrium of the contract, in which case it is considered that the private contracting party has the right to the reestablishment of such equilibrium by means of receiving compensation from the public contracting party for the damaged caused, when the Act of State in issued by an authority of the same level of Government (*Poder Público*) than that of the public contracting party.

On the other hand, it is also a general principle specifically developed in administrative law, in this case referred to the situation of the *public contracting party* into a public contract when an Act of State prevents such party to comply with its contractual obligations, in which case in has been considered that only if such Act of State has been issued by a different level of Government (*Poder Público*) than that of the public contracting party, it can be considered as a non-imputable and extraneous cause justify or excuse for the non-compliance of its contractual obligations according to the general rules of Force Majeure established in private law on matters of contracts.

That is, in the *first approach*, in order to consider an Act of State as a source for the private contracting party to claim compensation for the rupture of the economic equilibrium of a public contract, the principle is that it must refer to Acts of State issued within the same level of Government (*Poder Público*) in which is located the public contracting party, giving right to the private contracting party to its reestablishment by means of receiving compensation from the public contracting party.

---

313 See for instance: Allan R. Brewer-Carías, "Algunas reflexiones sobre el equilibrio financiero en los contratos administrativos y la aplicabilidad en Venezuela de la concepción amplia de la teoría del Hecho del Príncipe," in *Revista Control Fiscal y Tecnificación Administrativa*, Año XIII, N° 65, Contraloría General de la República, Caracas, 1972, pp. 86-93.

In these cases, when considering the *fait du prince* as a source for the private contracting party to request compensation from the public contracting party for the rupture of the economic equilibrium of the public contract, the act of State must then be issued by an organ of the State located at the same level of government, whether national, states or municipal, in which the public contracting party is located.[314] In these cases, it is understood that being located (the public contracting party and the entity issuing the Act of State) in the same level of Government; the later must be seen as a unity and the public contracting party must bear the economic consequences of the Act of State over the public contract. Consequently, if the act of State is issued in another level of Government (national government, for instance, regarding a municipal contract; or municipal government, for instance, regarding a national contract) the principle of act of State as a source for compensation for the private contracting party against the public contracting party does not apply.

This approach to the *fait du prince* principle derives from the principle adopted in Venezuelan administrative law according to which private contracting parties to public contract have an inherent right that is common to all "administrative contracts," to their financial or economic equilibrium, that is, to the *immutability* of its economic equation by the State, when the mutations can cause prejudices to the private party.[315] This has been the doctrine established by the Supreme Court since the 40's of last century when arguing that in matter of public contracts, one of the applicable rules is "the implicit obligation of the State to not to alter such equilibrium" to the point that if by any act of the State organs such equation is broken, the public contacting party "has the obligation to compensate the concessionary (the private party) for all the damages caused."[316] The Supreme Court has considered this obligation of the State to maintain the economic equilibrium of public contracts "so rational" that it exists "even in case of legal reforms, in spite of the power of the State to enact them;"[317] considering that "the compensation in these cases, as in the cases of expropriation, is what is according to justice and equity."[318]

---

314 See Allan R. Brewer-Carías, *Las Instituciones fundamentales del Derecho Administrativo y la Jurisprudencia Venezolana,* Caracas *1964,* p. 209; Allan R. Brewer- Carías, "Consideraciones sobre los efectos de la ruptura de la ecuación económica de un contrato administrativo por una ley declarada nula por inconstitucionalidad," in *Cuadernos de Derecho Público,* Universidad de los Andes, Mérida, 1976, pp. 5–26; and in *Contratos Administrativos*, Editorial Jurídica Venezolana, Caracas 1992, pp. 221-222.

315 See the former *Corte Federal* decision of November 12, 1954, *Gaceta Forense* N° 6, Caracas 1954, pp. 204-206. See excerpt of this decision in Allan R. Brewer-Carías, *Jurisprudencia de la Corte Suprema 1930-1974 y estudios de derecho administrativo, Tomo III: La actividad administrativa.* vol. 2. *Recursos y contratos administrativos*, Ediciones del Instituto de Derecho Público, Facultad de Derecho, Universidad Central de Venezuela, Caracas 1977, p. 804. See Allan R. Brewer-Carías, *Contratos Administrativos*, Editorial Jurídica Venezolana, Caracas 1992, pp. 202 ff.

316 See decision of March 9, 1940, of the former *Corte Federal y de Casación*, in *Memoria*, Tomo I, pp. 342, 350, 351.

317 *Idem.*

318 See the former *Corte Federal* decision of November 12, 1954, *Gaceta Forense* N° 6, Caracas 1954, pp. 204-206. See excerpt of this decision in Allan R. Brewer-Carías, *Jurisprudencia de la Corte Suprema 1930-1974 y estudios de derecho administrativo,* Tomo III: *La actividad administrativa.* Vol. 2. *Recursos y contratos administrativos*, Ediciones del Instituto de Derecho Público, Facultad de Derecho, Universidad Central de Venezuela, Caracas 1977, p. 804. See Allan

In the *second approach*, according to the general law on contracts also applied to public contracts, in order to consider an act of State as an excuse for the non-compliance of a contractual obligation, a distinction must be made depending of the party alleging the excuse. If it is the private contracting party that allege the excuse, any act of State issued in any level of Government can be alleged to be a non-imputable and extraneous cause to the private contracting party, a situation that the party alleging the excuse must prove;[319] but if it is the public contracting party that is alleging the excuse, the principle is that only acts of State emanating from a different level of Government (*Poder Público*) can be considered extraneous and non-imputable to the public contracting party. That is to say, if the act of State emanates from a public entity located in the same level of government in which the public contracting party is located (same *Poder Público*), it cannot be considered as an extraneous and non-imputable cause to it. For example, for a national state-owned enterprise that is a public contracting party to a public contract, the acts of State adopted by an entity of the national Government (Legislative or Executive), as a matter of principle cannot be considered extraneous to such public contracting party. In this case it is also understood that being the public contracting party and the entity issuing the Act of State located at the same level of Government; the later must be seen as a unity and the public contracting party cannot excuse its non-compliance of contractual obligations based on such act of State.

In any case, in this second case, it is also for the party that alleges the non-imputable, non-attributable cause as an excuse for non-compliance of its obligations under the contract, to prove that the Act of State is effectively extraneous to it.

Summarizing, for a party to a contract, such cause or event of *force majeure* following the provision of 1.271 of the Civil Code, must be a fact strange to the party, that is, it must not be produced or procured by the party obliged to perform an obligation or, of course, by its related entities. Additionally, the fact must not be imputable to such party or, of course, to his related entities; the fact must be considered beyond the reasonable control of the party or, of course, of his related entities; and the fact must be unforeseeable for the contracting parties and for its entities. If it is true that those conditions can be invoked by a public contracting party when the act of State affecting the contract is issued by an organ of a different level of government (a municipal authority, for instance, regarding Legislative of Executive national acts affecting a municipal public contract), as a matter of principle it cannot be invoked when the act of State affecting the public contract is issued by an organ of the same level of Government (a national public enterprise, for instance, regarding Legislative of Executive national acts affecting a national public contract) in which is located the public contracting party .

In other words, referring to acts of State, for a private contacting party to a public contract, in principle they can be considered as a cause of force majeure, being for

R. Brewer-Carías, *Contratos Administrativos*, Editorial Jurídica Venezolana, Caracas 1992, pp. 205.

319 As it is regulated in article 1.271 of the Civil Code, "the debtor or the party obliged to fulfill an obligation "will be condemned to pay damages and prejudices, because non-compliance of the obligation or because delay in it, except if he proves that the non-fulfillment or the delay to fulfill comes from an strange cause non attributable (non-imputable), even if no bad faith have existed from his part."

such party, a cause strange, not attributable (non-imputable) and unforeseeable, and who had no mean in order to prevent its occurrence. In that sense, the private contracting party to the contract could invoke acts of State in order to justify any non-compliance of its contractual obligations.

But regarding the public contracting party to a public contract, in principle, an act of State can only be considered as a strange non-imputable act, when issued by an entity belonging to a different level of government (*pouvoir public, poder público*) to the one where the public contracting party is located. For instance, in a federal State, a national act of State regarding a contract entered by a Municipality, could be an event of *force majeur*. But if the public contracting party is located in the same level of government that the one of the organs that adopts the act of State, such act in principle cannot be considered as an excuse for non-performance of its obligations. It is the case, as mentioned, for instance, of an act of State issued by the national level of Government affecting a public national interest contract entered by a national state-owned enterprise that in integrated into the organization of the national Public Administration. In this case, the act of State, as a matter of principle, could only be considered as an event of *force majeure* for the private contracting party to the contract, but not for the national public entity, that is, the public contracting party, for which it cannot consider it as a "strange and non-imputable fact."

This means that although in the general law applicable to contracts, particularly those entered into by private parties, a *fait du prince* may (depending on the circumstances) excuse the non-performance of an obligation; in public contracts a *fait du prince* cannot serve as an excuse for the non-performance of obligations by a the public contracting party, when the *fait du prince* is an act of State issued at the same territorial level of Governmental Power (national, state, or municipal) to which the contracting public entity belongs.

That is, when the authority from which the *fait du prince* emanates and the public contracting party belong to the same territorial level of Government (same *Poder Público*), the act of State cannot be considered extraneous to the contracting public entity. Otherwise, it would be very easy for the State to relieve its own entities of contractual liability simply by adopting measures that prohibit or otherwise make it impossible for those entities to perform their obligations.

3. The *hecho del príncipe* as a mean for the reestablishment of the economic equilibrium of "Administrative Contracts" when altered by the public contracting party or by another authority of the same level of Government.

The first approach to the doctrine of *fait du prince* on matters of public contracts, which is specifically related to administrative law principles, as already mentioned, is the one derived from the doctrine of the "implicit obligation of the State to not to alter the economic equilibrium" of public contracts, also constructed by French administrative law.

It was defined in Venezuela in the well-known decision of the former Federal and Cassation Court through of March 9, 1940 (Case: *La Guayra Port),* when it began to construct de theory of "administrative contracts" in Venezuela.[320]

In such decision it was established as a general principle of administrative law, that all administrative contracts "contain in its clauses the guaranties given by the State to the concessionary, containing certain financial economic equilibrium for its companies, which allows them to risk its capital investment."[321] This contractual equilibrium is the relation established by the parties when entering in an administrative contract, between the contractual rights of each of them and the amount of burden and obligation they have according to its clauses.[322] This implies according to the Supreme Court decisions, that in all administrative contracts it exists "an implicit contractual obligation for the public contracting party (State) to not to alter such equilibrium,"[323] which must be maintained even "in the case of legal reforms," so even "having the State the power to reform its legislation, it is recognized the obligation for the State to compensate in such case the concessionaire, according to the extent of the damages or the new charges resulting from the reform."[324]

The consequence of the principle of the economic or financial equilibrium of administrative contracts is that in any case of rupture of such equilibrium by means of any governmental or administrative decision adopted by the same level of government of the State, the public contracting party to the contract must compensate the private contracting party. This was clearly established by the former Supreme Court of Justice in a decision dated March 15, 1962 (Case: *Banco de Venezuela contract with the Republic Approval Law)* in which the Court stated:

> "In all public contracts it exists expressly or tacitly, a right of the private contracting party to a certain contractual financial equilibrium; so that if it is true that the private interests must yield in the presence of the general interest of

---

320 See the text in Allan R. Brewer-Carías, *Jurisprudencia de la Corte Suprema 1030-1977 y Estudios de Derecho Administrativo*, Tomo III, vol 2 (*Recursos y contratos administrativos*), Caracas 1977, pp. 772 ff. Also in *Memoria 1940*, pp. 342 ff.

321 *Idem.*

322 See Allan R. Brewer-Carías, *Contratos Administrativos,* Editorial Jurídica Venezulana, Caracas 1992, p. 203

323 That is why Gustavo Linares Benzo argues that the basic distinction between private contracts and administrative contracts, precisely lies in the principle of the economic equilibrium of administrative contracts, which he considers is part of the "essence of administrative contracts." See Gustavo Linares Benzo, "El equilibrio del contrato administrativo en la Ley de Contrataciones Públicas," in Allan R. Brewer-Carías *et al.*, *Ley de Contrataciones Públicas*, Editorial Jurídica Venezolana, Caracas 20102, pp. 368, 369. See also on the direct applicability of the theory of the economic equilibrium of administrative contracts and on the expansive application to contracts, independently of specific regulation that could be inserted in the text of the contracts, the comments of Henrique Iribarren Monteverde, "El equilibrio económico en los contratos administrativos y la teoría de la imprevisión," in *Los Contratos Administrativos. Contratos del Estado, VIII Jornadas Internacionales de Derecho Administrativo: Allan Randolph Brewer-Carías*, Fundación Estudios de Derecho Administrativos, Caracas 2005, Tomo I, pp. 136 ss.

324 See in Allan R. Brewer-Carías, *Jurisprudencia de la Corte Suprema 1030-1977 y Estudios de Derecho Administrativo*, Tomo III, vol 2 (*Recursos y contratos administrativos*), Caracas 1977, pp. 772-783. See also Federal Court decision of August 8, 1959, in *Gaceta Forense* N° 25, Caracas 1959, pp. 202-205.

the community, and because of that, the Administration has, between certain limits, the power to unilaterally modify administrative contracts and even to unilaterally terminate the contracts; these prerogatives of the Administration have their counterpart, which is the private contracting party right to be compensated in all cases in which the modification impose upon him new obligations breaching the financial equilibrium of the contract, or in which the anticipated termination of the contract is not the consequence of the breach of its contractual obligations Thus, the economic (patrimonial) aspect of administrative contracts impose the same respect than property rights, in the sense that property cannot be affected without compensation. That is why the contractual relations cannot be broken without the hearing of the parties which voluntary created those relations."[325]

In the same trend of guarantying the right of the private contracting party to the economic equilibrium of administrative contract, the same former Supreme Court of Justice of Venezuela, in decision of June 14, 1983 (Case: *Acción Comercial, S.A*) specifically referred to the right of the private contracting party to be indemnified by the public contracting party in situation when *fait du prince* alters the economic equilibrium, stating the follow:

> "When collective interest requirements so require, the Administration uses the concept of administrative contract in order to ensure the private party's collaboration in the satisfaction of certain general interest needs. The presence of the Administration –given certain conditions– in the agreement marks it, inevitably, with characteristics different from those of the regular contracting activity, in order to ensure in this manner that the Administration, depository of the general or collective interest, can agree without sacrificing it [the general or collective interest] in benefit of private interests of individuals, however important –individually considered– they may seem. The private contracting parties are in turn protected in this type of agreement, as a result of the intangibility of the economic equation of the contract, by virtue of which a harm to their property resulting from the breach by the Administration of the agreed clauses (rescission for supervening motives: "*hecho del príncipe*," unforeseeable circumstances, force majeure) is compensated with the corresponding reparation to the private party for those damages and prejudices that it may have suffered."[326]

---

325 See the text in Allan R. Brewer-Carías, *Jurisprudencia de la Corte Suprema 1030-1977 y Estudios de Derecho Administrativo*, Tomo III, vol 2 (*Recursos y contratos administrativos*), Caracas 1977, pp. 803 ff. See also in *Official Gazette* N° 760 Extra. March 22, 1962, pp. 11-12.

326 See fomer *Corte Suprema de Justicia, Sala Político Administrativa*, Decision of June 14, 1983 (Case: *Acción Comercial, S.A*) in *Gaceta Forense* No. 121, Vol. I, 1983, pp. 40-72. See the comments on this decisión in Henrique Iribarren Monteverde, "El equilibrio económico en los contratos administrativos y la teoría de la imprevisión," in *Los Contratos Administrativos. Contratos del Estado, VIII Jornadas Internacionales de Derecho Administrativo: Allan Randolph Brewer-Carías*, Fundación Estudios de Derecho Administrativos, Caracas 2005, Tomo I, pp. 132 ss. See also, fomer *Corte Suprema de Justicia, Sala Político Administrativa*, Decision of August 11, 1983 (Case: *Cervecería de Oriente, C.A*) in *Gaceta Forense* No. 121, Vol. I., 1983, pp. 253-264; and fomer *Corte Suprema de Justicia, Sala Político Administrativa*, Decision of April 1, 1986 (Case: *Hotel Isla de Coche*). Excerpts of these decisions are published in Allan R. Brewer-Carías

Consequently, if it is true that in public contracts it is recognized a general power of the public contracting party, between certain limits and when it is required by public interests, to introduce modifications to the contract,[327] or to unilaterally terminate the contract,[328] it is also true that in all cases in which such decision affects the financial equilibrium of the contract by affecting the economic and protective clauses of the contract, the private contracting party have the right to be compensated in all that is needed in order to reestablish the equilibrium.[329]

This was the criteria followed by the former Federal Court on decision of 12 de November de 1954, in which when referring to the powers of the public contracting party in administrative contracts to unilaterally rescind or modify them, it explained:

> "The extended flexibility the characterized the administrative contracts regarding *the powers* of the Administration to administratively rescind them or in order to introduce modifications on it when public interest so imposes, do not exempt in an absolute way, to indemnify the contacting party, when for it, without his fault, prejudices have derived from the termination, or from the nature of the modifications made, a substantial alteration of the contract has been produced, and also, a sensible change in the economic equation of the contract. The compensation in such cases, as happens in an expropriation because of public usefulness, is according to justice and equity."[330]

These important principles were subsequently incorporated in the statutes sanctioned in Venezuela regarding administrative contracts. It was the case of the Organic Law on the promotion of private investment through Concessions of 1999[331] (repealed in 2014), in which text, regarding the power granted to the public contracting party to modify the characteristics of the public works or of the public services in the concessions, its article 39 specifically provided that "in such circumstances the Public

---

and Luis Ortíz Alvarez, *Las Grandes Decisiones de la Jurisprudencia Contencioso Administrativa (1961-1996),* Caracas, Editorial Jurídica Venezolana, 1996, pp. 177, 178, 181 y 185.

327 See Allan R. Brewer-Carías, "La facultad de la Administración de modificar unilateralmente los contratos administrativos" in *Libro-Homenaje a la Memoria de Roberto Goldschmidt*, Facultad de Derecho, Universidad Central de Venezuela, Caracas, 1967, pp. 755-778; "La facultad de la Administración de modificar unilateralmente los contratos administrativos (con especial referencia a los contratos de obra pública en el derecho venezolano) *in Revista de Derecho Español y Americano, Instituto de Cultura Hispánica,* N° 19, Year XIII, Madrid, January-March 1968, pp. 101-117.

328 See Allan R. Brewer-Carías, *Las Instituciones Fundamentales del Derecho Administrativo y la Jurisprudencia Venezolana,* Caracas, 1964, p. 209. Text included in my book: *Contratos Administrativos, Contratos Públicos, Contratos del Estado*, Editorial Jurídica Venezolana, Caracas 2013, pp. 44, 47.

329 See Allan R. Brewer-Carías, "Algunas reflexiones sobre el equilibrio financiero en los contratos administrativos y la aplicabilidad en Venezuela de la concepción amplia de la "teoría del Hecho del Príncipe, in *Revista Control Fiscal y Tecnificación Administrativa*, Year XIII, N° 65, Contraloría General de la República, Caracas, 1972, pp. 86-93; "Consideraciones sobre los efectos de la ruptura de la ecuación económica de un contrato administrativo por una ley declarada nula por inconstitucional" in *Cuadernos de Derecho Público*, Facultad de Derecho, Universidad de Los Andes, N° 2, Mérida 1976, pp. 5-26;

330 See in *Official Gazette* N° 6, 2a etapa, Vol. I, p. 204.

331 Ley Orgánica sobre promoción de la inversión privada bajo el régimen de concesiones, *Official Gazette* N.° 5.394 Extra. October 25, 1999.

contracting party must compensate the concessionaire in case of damages, agreeing with him the corresponding factors of the "economic regime of the concession." The same Law also established that in cases of early termination of the concession by unilateral act of the public contracting party based on motives of public usefulness or social interests, the concessionaire must receive an "integral compensation" (*indemización integral*) including "the retribution that it would not be able to receive be for the remaining time that was fixed for the concession" (article 53).[332]

The same principles was incorporated in the last reform of the Public Contracting Law sanctioned in 2014, referring to contracts for public work, contracts for supply of service contracts, and contracts for the acquisition of goods.[333] According to its provisions, on matters of modifications introduced by the public contracting party in the extend of the works or services to be provided by the private contracting party, the public contracting party would pay the due amounts resulting from the modifications that have been decided (art. 130). Also, the Law expressly establishes that in case of early termination of the contract, for motives not imputable to the private contracting party, the public contracting party must pay just compensation (Article 153).[334]

Consequently, following the doctrine established by the Supreme Tribunal on these matters, as well as the sense of the legal provisions enacted regarding specific public contracts, like concessions of public work or public services, in relation to "administrative contracts," always being one of the parties to the contract a public entity that can use extraordinary powers which can affect contractual rights, any unilateral decision of the public contracting party producing the modification, extinction or elimination of any contractual right, can also be considered as an expropriation of such contractual rights, which can only be accomplished by means of just compensation according to Article 115 of the Constitution.[335] Consequently, any take-over of contractual rights in administrative contracts by the unilateral action of the public contracting party or of another organ of the same level of government, without following the contractual clauses (mutual agreement between the parties), and without following the expropriation procedure set forth in the Constitution, must be considered as a confiscation, which is prohibited in the Constitution.

But the principle of the economic equilibrium of the administrative contract, and the right of the private contracting party to be compensated when such equilibrium is

---

332 On the right of the private contracting party to be compensate when the Administration uses these unilateral powers of modification or early termination of the contract see: Carmelo de Grazia Suárez, "Derechos y prerogativas de la Administración Pública en la ejecución de los contratos administrativos (especia referencia a los contratos de concesión), in *Los Contratos Administrativos. Contratos del Estado, VIII Jornadas Internacionales de Derecho Administrativo: Allan Randolph Brewer-Carías*, Fundación Estudios de Derecho Administrativos, Caracas 2005, Tomo I, pp. 33, 44.

333 See *Official Gazette*, N° 6.154 Extra. of November 19, 2014.

334 These provisions are considered as the legal basis, in Venezuela, for the theory of the financial equilibrium of administrative contracts. See Gustavo Linares Benzo, "El equilibrio financiero del contrato administrativo en la Ley de Contrataciones Públicas," in Allan R. Brewer-Carías *et al.*, *Ley de Contrataciones Públicas*, Editorial Jurídica Venezolana, Caracas 2012, p. 373.

335 The expropriation procedure is regulated in the Law of Expropriation for causes of Public usefulness and social interest, *Official Gazette* N° 37.475 July 1, 2002. See Allan R. Brewer-Carías et al., *Ley de Expropiación por causa de utilidad pública y social*, Caracas 2002, pp. 25 ff.

altered, not only applies when the alterations are produced by the same public contracting party, but when the economic equilibrium of the contract or its economic clauses are affected by acts or actions of other public authorities of the same level of government (same *poder público*). In such case, the private contracting party to the public contracts, also have the right to be integrally compensated for instance by the national public contracting party because of the rupture of the economic equilibrium of the contract caused by acts of State adopted by any other national public organ or entity action. In this sense, the *fait du prince* doctrine in public contracts, as a source for compensation for the private contracting party for the rupture of the economic equilibrium of the contract, only applies (i) to acts of State from the national level of Government regarding national public interest contracts; (ii) to acts of State from the states level of government for states public interest contracts; and (iii) to acts of State of the municipal level of government for contracts of municipal public interest.

In particular, regarding a national public or administrative contract, that is to say, a public national interest contract, the *fait du prince* doctrine applies when the act of State affecting the economic equilibrium of the contract emanates from the national State, for instance, the National Executive, its Central Public Administration, or the National Assembly, or any of the public entities that conforms the decentralized national Public Administration, such as the *institutos autónomos* and the State owned enterprises. In any of such cases, the national acts of State that affects a national administrative contract, modifying its economic equilibrium, give the private contracting party the right to be compensated by the public contracting party.

As I expressed many years ago referring to national administrative contracts:

> "Venezuelan administrative law principles have always recognized the right of the private party to a public contract to be compensated when the financial equilibrium of the contract has been altered as a consequence not only of actions adopted by the public entity that is a party to the agreement, but also by acts adopted by different State entities, and particularly, as a consequence of a statute (a law) sanctioned by the legislative body."[336]

I also sustained the same opinion in other work, referring to national administrative contracts, by expressing that:

> "The private contracting party has the right, inherent to all administrative contracts, to the maintenance of the equilibrium of the contract, and thus, to the immutability of the economic equation of the contract, when the mutation causes prejudices, whether because the modification is made by an act of the same Public Administration; because the modification is made by the unilateral rescission without the fault of the private contracting party, or because of modifications on the economic equation arisen from facts extraneous to the will of the contracting parties, economic natural facts or acts of [national] public

---

336 See Allan R. Brewer-Carías, *Las Instituciones fundamentales del Derecho Administrativo y la Jurisprudencia Venezolana,* Caracas *1964,* p. 209; Allan R. Brewer-Carías, "Consideraciones sobre los efectos de la ruptura de la ecuación económica de un contrato administrativo por una ley declarada nula por inconstitucionalidad," in *Cuadernos de Derecho Público,* Universidad de los Andes, Mérida, 1976, pp. 5-26; and in *Contratos Administrativos*, Editorial Jurídica Venezolana, Caracas 1992, p. 221. See Allan R. Brewer-Crías, *Contratos Administrativos*, Editorial Jurídica Venezolana, Caracas 1992, p. 222.

authorities different to the contracting party. Now, and this is the essential effect of the economic equilibrium of the contract, and of the right to its immutability: the private contracting party has the right to be compensated by the Administration, when a rupture of the equilibrium is produced."[337]

In these cases, in which the alteration of the economic equilibrium of an administrative contract is caused by acts of State that are issued by authorities different to the Public contracting party, but at the same level of government (national, for instance), administrative law doctrine and case law applying the principle of *fait du prince* (*hecho del príncipe*) recognized the right of the affected private contracting party to be integrally compensated by the public contracting party to the contract, when the equilibrium of the contract is affected by such acts of State of the same level of government.

This principle, according to the doctrine of the Attorney General of the Republic,

> "mean that in any administrative contract, expressly or tacitly it exists a right of the private party to a certain economic-financial equilibrium of the contract; the prerogative of the Administration based on the general interest, to unilaterally modify within certain limits the administrative contracts being executed, having its counterweight in the right of the private party to be compensated, provided that the introduced modification imposes it new obligation that breaches the financial equilibrium of the contract."

The principle, according to the same Attorney General:

> "defined in this way finds its practical expression in two theories constructed by the French jurisprudence: the one of the fait du prince (*hecho del príncipe*) and the other of unforeseen (*imprevisión*)." According to the theory of the hecho del príncipe, when the public power (the prince) makes costlier, by its own fact, the conditions of execution of the contract, it can be obliged to compensate the private contracting party (Rivero, Jean, *Droit Administratif*, Dalloz, 1965, p. 112)"[338]

According to this Attorney General doctrine, referring to the expression of "by its own fact," the sense is that "in order for the aforementioned theory to function, the impairment of the economic position of the private party must result from a measure *attributed to* the State, that is, attributed to its will or fault."[339] That is why, according

---

337 See Allan R. Brewer-Carías, "Algunas reflexiones sobre el equilibrio financiero en los contratos administrativos y la aplicabilidad en Venezuela de la concepción amplia de la Teoría del hecho del príncipe," in *Revista Control Fiscal y Tecnificación Administrativa*, Year XII, N° 65, Caracas, 1972, pp. 86-93; and *Contratos Administrativos*, Editorial Jurídica Venezolana, Caracas 1992, p. 206

338 See *Doctrina de la Procuraduría General de la República 1966*, Caracas 1967, pp. 75-76. See the text in Allan R. Brewer-Carías, *Contratos Administrativos*, Editorial Jurídica Venezolana, Caracas 1992, p. 206.

339 *Doctrina de la Procuraduría General de la República 1966, cit*., p. 76. See the comments on the Attorney General's opinión, Henrique Iribarren Monteverde, "El equilibrio económico en los contratos administrativos y la teoría de la imprevisión," in *Los Contratos Administrativos. Contratos del Estado, VIII Jornadas Internacionales de Derecho Administrativo: Allan Randolph Brewer-Carías*, Fundación Estudios de Derecho Administrativos, Caracas 2005, Tomo I, pp. 132 ss.

to the same Attorney General doctrine, "the right to integral compensation is justified in the doctrine and in the jurisprudence in cases of *measures taken by legislative or administrative organs, but not by the effect of decisions from organs exercising the jurisdictional function.*"[340] Consequently, only judicial decisions are excluded for the application of the public law theory of the *hecho del príncipe* regarding administrative contracts, in the sense that if the decision adopted by the State affecting the economic equilibrium of a public contract is a judicial one, the private contracting party to the contract cannot claim integral compensation from the public contracting party, having in such case the judicial decision a similar effect that in private law in the sense that it released the public contracting party from performing its obligation, and from any liability or responsibility for non-performance.[341]

In this same sense, Eloy Lares Martínez, whose opinion was quoted in the aforementioned opinion of the Attorney General, referring to national administrative contracts, affirmed that:

> "in a broad sense, the expression "*hecho del príncipe*" comprises any intervention of the public powers that makes costlier the conditions within which the private party must accomplish the obligations it has assumed. It can consist in measures of general or particular scope or in material operations, and arising from the Legislative Power or the Executive, from the same public person signing the contract or from a different public person,"[342]

adding that

---

340 Idem. p. 77. This author has opined, however, that when the judicial decision affecting the economic equilibrium of the administrative contract is a judicial review decision of the Supreme Court annulling on grounds of unconstitutionality, the right of the private party to the contract subsists in application of the *hecho del príncipe* theory in broad sense, and the State is liable due to its legislative action. See e.g., Allan R. Brewer-Carías, *Contratos Administrativos*, Editorial Jurídica Venezolana, Caracas 1992, pp. 222-229

341 As mentioned before, this is the case of the decision taken by the former *Corte Suprema de Justicia, Sala Político Administrativa,* decision No. 2337, of April 27, 2005, Case *Banco Provincial, S.A.I.C.A., SACA vs. Banco Central de Venezuela,* in which the contract in cause was one entered by a private bank, Banco Provincial and a public entity, the *Banco Central de Venezuela,* in which case it was a criminal court judicial decision the one that prevented the Central Bank of performing its contractual obligations. In such case, the Politico Administrative Chamber considered that in the case, the judicial decision was a *fait du prince*, regarding the non-compliance of the obligations contained in a contract regarding the delivery of financial bonds by the Central Bank to the private bank. Nonetheless, I have sustained that when the judicial decision affecting the economic equilibrium of the administrative contract is a *judicial review* decision of the Constitutional Jurisdiction annulling a statute based on unconstitutionality motives, the right of the private contracting party subsists in application of the broad sense of the *hecho del príncipe* theory, and the State liability derived from its legislative action. See Allan R. Brewer-Carías, *Contratos Administrativos*, Editorial Jurídica Venezolana, Caracas 1992, p. 222-229; "Algunas reflexiones sobre el equilibrio financiero en los contratos administrativos y la aplicabilidad en Venezuela de la concepción amplia de la Teoría del hecho del príncipe," in *Revista Control Fiscal y Tecnificación Administrativa,* Year XII, N° 65, Caracas, 1972, pp. 86-93; and "Consideraciones sobre los efectos de la ruptura de la ecuación económica de un contrato administrativo por una ley declarada nula por inconstitucionalidad," in *Cuadernos de Derecho Público,* Universidad de los Andes, Mérida, 1976, pp. 5 - 26.

342 See Eloy Lares Martínez, *Manual de Derecho Administrativo*, 10a. Edition, Caracas 1996, p. 341.

"it is not necessary, in order to invoke the theory of the *hecho del príncipe*, that the intervention originates from the same authority that has signed the contract, it can emanate from other organ of the same public person [*poder público*]. In this sense, for instance, the repercussions that regarding the execution of a contract of national interest signed by a minister, can have the new laws enacted by Congress, the decrees emanated from the national Executive or the resolutions issued by a Minister different to the one signing the contract, implies that the private party can ask the payment of an integral compensation that such measures could cause, because all the aforementioned authorities are organs of the same public person: the Venezuelan State. Accordingly, the theory of the *hecho del príncipe* do not apply in cases of the repercussions that could have in a [municipal administrative] contract regarding a Municipality, the statutes enacted by the Congress or the decrees of the national Executive, because in this last case the measures are not produced by the same contracting public person – the Municipality-, but by a public person different, that is the Republic of Venezuela."[343]

This opinion of Lares Martínez was based on the aforementioned distribution of State Powers in the Venezuelan State organization established in article 136 of the Constitution, between three territorial levels of government: national ("Venezuelan State"); the States level and the Municipal level of government; being the public interest contracts that are signed in each of these level of government, respectively according to article 150 of the Constitution: *national* public interest contracts; *states* public interest contracts and *municipal* public interest contracts.

In accordance to such distribution of State Powers, and according to the opinion of Lares Martínez, the State acts or actions that can give rise to the application of the theory of the *hecho del príncipe* regarding an administrative contract, giving rise to the right to be compensate by the private contracting party, must be adopted in the same level of government, that is, in the national level regarding national public interest contracts; in the State level, regarding States public interest contracts; and in the Municipal level, regarding the municipal public interest contracts.

Consequently, the theory of the *hecho del príncipe* regarding for instance national administrative contracts undoubtedly applies when the act of State affecting the economic equilibrium of the contract emanates from an organ of the national level of government (national State).[344] In the same sense, Rafael Badell, refers to the different

---

343 Idem.

344 According to article 15 of the Public Administration Organic Law (last reform by Decree Law No. 1.424 of November 17, 2014 published in *Official Gazette* N° 6.147 of November 17, 2014), the National Public Administration is integrated by "organs, entities and missions." The "organs" are "the administrative units of the Republic to which are attributed functions that have legal effects, or whose actions have regulatory character;" and the "entities" are "any functionally decentralized administrative organization with own personality, subject to control, evaluation and follow up of their actions by the commanding organs (*órganos rectores*) of attachment and by the Central Planning Commission." According to article 19 of the same Organic Law, "the activity of the organs and entities of [national] Public Administration shall pursue the effective accomplishment of the objectives and goals established in the norms, plans and management compromises, under the orientation of the policies and strategies established by the President of the republic, the Central Planning Commission ..." In addition, according to article 46 of the Law, the President of the Republic, as Head of the State and of the National Executive, directs the

"legal level" when arguing on the different territorial level of governments and the applicability of the theory of the *hecho del príncipe*:

> "Nonetheless, we recognize that the administrative contract can be affected or harmed by a disposition adopted by an authority belonging to a different legal order. A contract signed by the Republic can be affected by a decision adopted by a municipal; authority. In such cases, when the contract results affected or harmed by a fact or an act strange to the National authority that signed it, the theory of *imprevisión* is applicable, being subjected to it the harming act of the contract."[345]

In this sense, Lares Martínez and Badell followed the trend of the public law theory of the *fait du prince* doctrine established in France regarding the notion of contracting authority, referred also to three different levels of governments: the (national) State, the Departments, and the Municipal authorities (*Pouvoir publics; collectivités territoriales*). That is why, in the French terminology, in order for the theory of the *fait du prince* to be applicable, one of the conditions in the "*inmutability du fait dommageable a la collectivité contratante*."[346] This was explained in a broad sense by André de Laubadère, saying that:

> "*Il suffit, pour que le fait du prince puisse être invoqué, que l'intervention émane d'un organe de la persone publique qui a conclu le contract. Ainsi les autorités* de *l'Etat sont 'étrangères' aux contracts conclus par les départments, les comunes, les établissment publics; mais dans le cadre de l'Etat les répercusions sur un contract signé par un ministre de mesures prises par un autre ministre rentrent dans la théorie de fait du prince, et même celles des*

---

government and Public Administration action, with the immediate collaboration of the Vice President of the Republic." Regarding the Ministers, according to article 77.,13 they are the organs that "exercise the command of the public policies developed by the functionally decentralized entities attached to their offices" (article 77.13), as well as "to represent the shares owns by the Republic in the State owned enterprises assigned to them, as well as the shareholders control" (article 77.14). Regarding the "entities" of the national Public Administration they can be of two types: "1. Functionally Decentralized entities with private law form, integrated by the legal persons established according to private law provisions, that can adopt or not the entrepreneurial form in accordance to the goals and objectives that originated their incorporation, and bearing in mind if the origin of their resources come form their own activity or from public funds." The classical private law form of functional decentralization are the State own enterprises (*empresas del Estado*), that must be created with the authorization of the President of the Republic (article 104), and in which the Republic or any other decentralized entity owns more than the 50% of its shares (article 103). 2. "Functional Decentralized entities with public law form, integrated by those legal persons created and ruled by public law provisions and that could have attributed the exercise of public powers." The classical public law form of functional decentralization are the *institutos autónomo* s that must be created by statute (article 96). The imbrications between central Public Administration (organs) and decentralized Public Administration (entities) is such that according to article 38, "Public Administration can temporally assign the accomplishment of material or technical activities of its attributions to their respective functionally decentralized entities ..."

345 See Rafael Badell Madrid, *Régimen Jurídico de los Contratos Administrativos*, Caracas, 2001, pp. 151-152

346 See André de Laubadère, *Traité théorique et pratique des contracts administraifs* Tome III, LGDJ, Paris 1956, par. 920, p. 32; André de Laubadère, Franck Moderne and Pierre Delvolvé, *Traité théorique et pratique des contracts administraifs* Tome second, LGDJ Paris, 1984, p. 523.

mesures prises par le législateur sur les contracts conclus par le organs exécutifs de l'Etat."[347]

In this same general sense, as aforementioned, the "contracting authorities" in administrative contracts in the Venezuelan legal system are the ones that are located in each of the three constitutional levels of government (public power distribution): national (the Republic), States and municipal (Municipalities), which according to the Constitution, as already mentioned originates three sorts of public interest contracts: national public interest contracts, states public interest contracts and municipal public interest contracts; three sorts of Public Administrations organization: national, States and municipal, with their organs and entities as three sorts of administrative authorities: national, states and municipal.

In this same sense, Rafael Badell is of the opinion that the State responsibility because of the *hecho del príncipe*, following what has been said by Miguel Marienhoff of Argentina,

> "can result from the fact or the act of any organ of the State with the only limits that it must appertain to the same legal order, that is national, states or municipal. In effect, the measure can be originated in any public authority that corresponds to the same legal order or that appertain to the authority that signed the contract. We think that no legal principle opposes; moreover, the basis of the theory of the hecho del príncipe do not make or allow any distinction between the facts and acts emanating from the same public authority that intervened in the signing of the contract or from other state authority. Thus, referring to a contract signed by the Republic or any of its functional decentralized entities, the affecting measure can emanate from any organ related to the same, that is the Republic; and the same can be said regarding the different organs that exists in the States and Municipal Powers."[348]

In the Latin American administrative law doctrine, in effect, Miguel Marienhoff of Argentina follows this same approach to the *fait du prince* in the same broad sense applied in Venezuela, both countries having the federal form of government. He has sustained that for the *hecho del príncipe* to be produced, the harming resolution or disposition regarding the rights of the private party to an administrative contract:

> "can proceed from any public authority, providing that it corresponds to the same legal order to which the authority signing the contract appertains. No principle of law opposes to it; moreover, the constitutional "principles" that supports what has been called the "theory of the hecho del príncipe (in which case, when occurs, the obligation to compensate the Private party rises), do not

347 See André de Laubadère, *Idem,* par. 920, pp. 34-35. The same criteria can be found in the edition of the same book by André de Laubadère, Franck Moderne and Pierre Delvolvé, Tome second, LGDJ Paris, 1984, par. 1302, pp 525-526 in which the authors add that: "*les messures prises par le législateur et qui affectent les contracts conclus par l'État relevant aussi du fait du prince puisque le parlement est un organe de l 'État au meme titre que les autorités exécutives: pour provenir d'organs differents, les mesures en cause émament toujours de la meme personne publique,*" p. 526.

348 See Rafael Badell Madrid, *Régimen Jurídico de los Contratos Administrativos*, Caracas, Fundación Procuraduría General de la República, 1991, pp.68 y 69. In the 2001 edition of this book, the same doctrine is followed although with a wording variation: p. 151.

make or allow any distinction between facts and acts arising from the same public authority that is a party to the contract or from other State authority. Thus, being a contract signed by the Nation, the harming measure can proceed from any organ or part forming it or depending from it; the same applies to the contracts entered into by the provinces.... From it, the so called hecho del príncipe can proceed from any public authority appertaining to the national or provincial State, whichever be the legal political sphere where the contract was signed. There is no reason to limit and to reduce such act or fact to the "same" administrative authority with whom the contract was signed." [...] Thus, it has no importance that the disturbing measure of the economic-financial equilibrium or equation of the contact proceeds or not from the same authority that signed the contract. Such measure, in any case, will be attributed to the "State," whichever is the organ or the part of it from which the harming measure proceeds. ... Within the "national" order or the "provincial" order, what is decided by the corresponding Public Administration authorities –being these centralized or decentralized- must be considered as decided by the Nation or by the corresponding province, being applied the theory of the "hecho del príncipe" even if the harming act does not proceed from the same authority that signed the contract."[349]

Also, Sayagués Laso of Uruguay followed the same approach in the sense that for the application of the theory of the *hecho del príncipe* "it is the same that the act proceeds from the same contracting public person or from a different public person, because the rules in both cases must be the same."[350]

As mentioned, I have followed similar criterion in the sense that the rupture of the economic equation or the financial equilibrium of an national administrative contract, and the right of the private contracting party to the contract to be compensated can be produced by "any legal act (*acto jurídico*) of a [national] public authority different to the contracting Administration" and particularly an act of the Legislative Power.[351] In the same sense, Lares Martínez, always referring to national administrative contracts, said that:

---

349 See Miguel Marienhoff, *Tratado de Derecho Administrativo,* Tome III-A, Abeledo-Perrot, Buenos Aires, pp. 485-488; and also in "Contratos administrativos", in *Primer Congreso Internacional y IV Jornadas Nacionales de Derecho Administrativo, 1977, p. 117*. See also in Rafael Badell, *Régimen Jurídico de los Contratos Administrativos*, Caracas, Fundación Procuraduría General de la República, 1991, p.68. As it has been said by Gabriela Andrea Stortoni, referring to Marienhoff's approach: "the act can come from any administration, that is, the same authority of the contract or other in the same legal sphere." See Gabriela Andrea Stortoni, "El hecho del príncipe y su impacto en los contratos administrativos", in *Contratos Administrativos, Jornadas organizadas por la Universidad Austral Facultad de Derecho*, Editorial Ciencias de la Administración, Buenos Aires , p 312. In the same sense, Raúl Enrique Granadillo Ocampo, *Distribución de los riesgos en la contratación administrativa*, Astrea, Buenos Aires 1990, p. 110.

350 See, Enrique Sayagues Laso, *Tratado de derecho Administrativo*, Tomo II, Montevideo 1959, p. 69-71. See the quotation in Carlos Delpiazzo, *Contratación Administrativa*, Universidad de Montevideo, Montevideo 1999, p. 224.

351 See Allan R. Brewer-Carías, "Consideraciones sobre los efectos de la ruptura de la ecuación económica de un contrato administrativo por una ley declarada nula por inconstitucional" en *Cuadernos de Derecho Público*, Facultad de Derecho, Universidad de Los Andes, Nº 2, Mérida 1976, pp. 5-26.

"Certain dispositions of general character, legislatives or regulatory, can have the effects of modify the clauses of contracts entered by the Administration, or to paralyze the execution of some of them or to early terminate its execution. In such cases the jurisprudence of the French Council d'Etat has decided that in these cases the Administration must pay the private contracting party an integral compensation for the prejudices that such general measures cause to it. The exception refers to the case in which, being a statute, the exclusion of the payment of a compensation has been provided."[352]

As a consequence of all the aforementioned, the principle of the *fait du prince* is the basis for the right of the private contracting party to seek for compensation from the public contracting party when the act of State is issued by entities from the same level of government of the public contracting party.

Other matter is the principle of fait du prince, as an event of *force majerur* hat can excuse the non-compliance of contractual obligations, ad that follows specific rules on matters of public contracts.

VII. THE *FAIT DU PRINCE* AS A DEFENSE TO JUSTIFY THE NON-COMPLIANCE CONTRACTUAL OBLIGATIONS (EVENT OF FORCE MAJEUR) IN PUBLIC CONTRACTS

In effect, the second approach to the *fait du prince* doctrine is the one constructed according to the general law of contracts, but also applicable to public contracts, referred to the acts of State that can be considered as a force majeure and that can excuse the non-compliance of contractual obligations.

In effect, according to the Venezuelan Civil Code, liability for breach of contract – private contracts of public contracts – may be excused when the breach of the obligation is the result of a non-imputable/non-attributable extraneous cause (*causa extraña no imputable*), considered as a *force majeure* event. As set forth in Articles 1271 and 1272 of the Civil Code:

"Article 1271: The debtor shall be ordered to pay damages, both for the non-performance of the obligation as well as for the delay in the performance thereof, unless he proves that the non-performance or delay arises from an external cause not attributable to him, even though there has been no bad faith on his part."

"Article 1272: A debtor shall not be obligated to pay damages when, as the result of an act of God or force majeure event, he has failed to give or do what he was obligated to give or do, or if he has performed an act that was prohibited."

According to these provisions, fait *du prince,* when referred to contracts, as an event of *force majeur* must always be a non-imputable, extraneous cause that

352 See Eloy Lares Martínez, *Manual de Derecho Administrativo*, Universidad Central de Venezuela, Caracas, 1996, p. 343.

prevent the compliance with contractual obligations.[353] For such purpose, Eloy Maduro Luyando and Emilio Pitter pointed out that:

> "The fait du prince meets all the requirements of the non-imputable extraneous cause: absolute impossibility of performance due to general or specific provisions of the law of mandatory compliance, irresistible because there is no possibility of avoiding its effects."[354]

That is why, *fait du prince* has been defined by Venezuelan courts as prohibitive or mandatory measures of the State, for instance, "any intervention of the Public Powers [...] arising from the *Legislative Power or the Executive*,"[355] issued for a general public interest, which creates an unavoidable obstacle and makes performance of a contract absolutely impossible.[356]

In the same sense, as already mentioned, José Mélich Orsini: "*hecho del príncipe*" (*factum principis*) is referred to as the obstacle to the performance of the promised activity that arises from a legislative act or from an administrative authority, for example."[357] Also Eloy Maduro Luyando and Emilio Pittier Sucre noted that:

> "The *hecho del príncipe* includes all the prohibitive or mandatory provisions enacted by the State for reasons of general public interest that must necessarily be accepted by the parties and cause a supervening non-performance of the obligation [....] The hecho del príncipe meets all the requirements of the non-

---

353 See, decision of the *Corte Superior Primera en lo Civil y Comercial de la Circunscripción Judicial del Distrito Federal y Estado Miranda* (Case *F. Jawhari v. La Seguridad, C.A.*), May 12. 1975, in which it was stated that "The breach of obligations can be caused by the spontaneous or voluntary conduct of the defendant, or else to what the doctrine calls a non-imputable external cause, a term that includes the figures of act of God, *force majeure*, victim's act or victim's fault, third party act, and the act of the prince." See in *Jurisprudencia Venezolana, Ramírez y Garay*, Vol. XLD11, Caracas 1975, No. 174-75, pp. 74-81. In the same sense, in the decision of the *Sala Civil y Laboral de la Corte Suprema de Justicia* (*Niemtschik Cadenas Ingenieros S.A. v. Empresas González*, case), November 23, 1988 it was ruled that "Non-imputable extraneous cause includes various scenarios: 1) act of God; 2) *force majeure*; 3) act of a third party; 4) act of the prince (the State); 5) act of the plaintiff; 6) loss of the object of the contract; and 7) fault of the victim.) , in *Jurisprudencia Venezolana. Ramírez y Garay*, No. 929-88, Caracas 1988, pp. 409-410.

354 See Eloy Maduro Luyando and Emilio Pittier Sucre, *Curso de Obligaciones*, Derecho Civil III, Tomo I, Universidad Católica Andrés Bello (2007) pp. 222-223. The former Sala Político Administrativa de la Corte Suprema de Justicia in its leading case decision of June 14, 1983 (Case: *Acción Comercial, S.A*) dealing with administrative contracts, regarding a State decision to terminate a public contract referred to "supervening motives: '*hecho del príncipe*,' unforeseeable circumstances, *force majeure.*" In *Gaceta Forense* N° 121, Vol. I, 1983, pp. 40-72. See also Sala Político Administrativa de la Corte Suprema de Justicia, Decision N° 1090, May 11, 2000 (Case: *Trino Juvenal Pérez Solano v. Alcalde del Municipio Guanipa del Estado Anzoategui*), Exp. 0121, in http://historico.tsj.gob.ve/decisiones/spa/mayo/01090-110500-0121.HTM.

355 See Eloy Lares Martínez, *Manual de Derecho Administrativo*, 10ma. Edición, Facultad de Ciencias Jurídicas y Políticas, Universidad Central de Venezuela, Caracas 1996, p. 341.

356 See, *Banco Provincial, S.A. v. Banco Central de Venezuela* case, Decision No. 2337 of the former *Corte Suprema de Justicia, Sala Político Administrativa*, April 27, 2005 in http://historico.tsj.gob.ve/decisiones/spa/abril/02337-270405-1995-12084.HTM.

357 "*Hecho del Príncipe*" (*factum principis*) is referred to as the obstacle to the performance of the promised activity that arises from a legislative act or from an administrative authority, for example." See, José Mélich-Orsini, *Doctrina General del Contrato*, Academia de Ciencias Políticas y Sociales, Serie Estudios N° 61, Caracas 2006, p. 504, fn. 83

imputable external cause: absolute impossibility of performance due to general or specific provisions of the law of mandatory compliance, irresistible because there is no possibility of avoiding its effects."[358]

The same concept was followed by Rafael Bernad Mainar when referring to the "Decree of the prince":

"It refers to all prohibitive or mandatory provisions taken by the State in consideration of the general public interest which; due to its mandatory character, should be complied with and preclude the performance of the obligations existing before the enactment of such rules. In current times, the Decree of the prince relates to the provisions of the executive power, ratified by the legislative power, which has the power to enact and issue the laws."[359]

In any case, the ability of a party to invoke *fait du prince* to excuse liability for breach of a civil obligation is only available when the party invoking the defense can show that the government act that occurs after the parties have entered into the contract, satisfies all of the requirements of a non-imputable extraneous cause (*causa extraña no imputable*),[360] in particular, that the act; must be unavoidable, unforeseeable, and irresistible; that occurs in the total absence of fault of the defendant; and that it renders performance absolutely impossible.[361]

In the same sense as was decided by the Cassation Chamber of the Supreme Court in the *Niemtschik Cadenas Ingenieros S.A. v. Empresas González* case

"For the non-imputable cause to be operative, the doctrine highlights various conditions, that is: 1) When this cause produces the absolute impossibility of performing the obligation. This condition must not be theoretical, but rather formal or practical; 2) That the absolute impossibility must be supervening, that is, that it occurs after the obligation is assumed; 3) That the non-imputable external cause be unforeseeable; 5) That it be inevitable, that is, it cannot be overcome; and 5) The total absence of negligence or willful misconduct by the debtor."[362]

Consequently, if it is true that for the private contracting party in principle, all acts of State or *fait du prince* can be considered a non-imputable extraneous cause, the same cannot be said regarding the public contracting party, and never if the public contracting party has procured the relevant act, in which case, the elements of force majeur are not satisfied, and the defense is simply not available.[363]

---

358 See Eloy Maduro Luyando and Emilio Pittier Sucre, *Curso de Obligaciones, op. cit*. pp. 222-223.

359 See Rafael Bernad Mainar, *Derecho Civil Patrimonial, Obligaciones*, Tomo I, Universidad Central de Venezuela, Facultad de Ciencias Jurídicas y Políticas, Caracas 2006, p. 172.

360 See Eloy Maduro Luyando and Emilio Pittier Sucre, *Curso de Obligaciones, op. cit.*, pp. 217, 223.

361 *Idem*, pp. 217-223;

362 See *Niemtschik Cadenas Ingenieros S.A. v. Empresas González*, case, former *Corte Suprema de Justicia, Sala Político Administrativa*, November 23, 1988, in *Jurisprudencia Venezolana. Ramírez y Garay*, No. 929-88, Caracas 1988, pp. 409-410.

363 Under Articles 1271 and 1272 of the Civil Code "if the defendant invokes the act of a third party, it is necessary that he has not provoked such act." See José Mélich-Orsini, *Doctrina General del Contrato*, 5ta. Edición (Caracas, 2009) p. 519

On this matters, one of the main conditions of these elements of the defense, is that *fait du prince* must occur in the total absence of any fault by the public contracting party alleging it, that is, the alleged *fait du prince* must be beyond the sphere of, and "deprived of any connection" with, the activity of the public contracting party.[364] And, the breach must be involuntary, that is, resulting from an act that is independent of the public contracting party's will.[365] Otherwise that act must be attributable to such party.[366]

On the other hand, the irresistibility of the act of State being a *force majeur* event, refers to the insurmountable nature of the impediment which forces the defendant to breach. As José Mélich-Orsini explained:

> "Irresistibility refers to the insuperable character of the event. Once the obstacle appears, even if it could be considered unexpected due to its sudden occurrence, it is necessary that the defendant has not been able to overcome it with the best-armed will of resistance. The defendant has the obligation to employ that "supreme effort" to fulfil that which was promised." [367]

Accordingly, party to a contract cannot invoke the defense of *fait du prince* unless he has employed "all licit means available" to comply with what was promised.[368]

Additionally, any *causa extraña no imputable* (among them *fait du prince*), as already mentioned, must occur prior to the contractual breach in order to constitute an irresistible force capable of preventing ordinary performance.

Finally, under Article 506 of the Civil Procedure Code and Article 1354 of the Civil Code, the burden of proof for establishing the *fait du prince* defense is always on the party who raises it.[369]

---

364 "The event from which the impossibility [to comply] derives must be exterior to the activity of the debtor and deprived of any connection with such activity." See José Mélich-Orsini, *Doctrina General del Contrato*, Academia de Ciencias Políticas y Sociales, Serie Estudios N° 61, Caracas 2006, p. 511.

365 "In this regard, it is observed that the doctrine has recognized the existence of two gorups or classifications which are: so-called voluntary or culpable breaches and those defined as involuntary breaches that consist of the failure to perform the obligation as a result of obstacles or causes subsequent to the beginning of the relationship that are independent of the will of the defendant and, therefore, are not imputable to him or her." See *Banco Provincial, S.A. v. Banco Central de Venezuela*, Decision No. 2337 of the *Tribunal Supremo de Justicia, Sala Político Administrativa*, April 27, 2005 in http://historico.tsj.gob.ve/decisiones/spa/abril/02337-270405-1995-12084.HTM, p. 24

366 *Idem*, p. 24.

367 See José Mélich-Orsini, *Doctrina General del Contrato*, Academia de Ciencias Políticas y Sociales, Serie Estudios N° 61, Caracas 2006, p. 509.

368 *Idem* p. 510

369 Article 1354 *Civil Code*: "Whoever requests the fulfillment of an obligation must prove it, and whoever asserts that he or she has been discharged from that obligation must prove the payment or the event that has caused the extinction of that obligation." Article 506 *Civil Procedure Code*: "The parties have the burden of proving their respective assertions of fact. Whoever requests the fulfillment of an obligation must prove it, and whoever asserts that he or she has been discharged from that obligation must, for his or her part, prove the payment or act that extinguishes the obligation. Notorious facts need not be proven." As has been said by Maduro & Pittier, "The defendant has the burden of proving the existence of the non-imputable extraneous cause to rebut the presumption of culpable breach established in [Article 1271]."

All these conditions are of special importance on matters of public contracts, particularly when *fait du prince* is alleged, not by the private contracting party, but by the public contracting party, for instance a state-owned enterprise, in order to excuse the compliance of its contractual obligations.

In this regard, for instance, at the national level of government, due to the organic link that characterized the relationship between National Central Administration and national decentralized administrative entities, including national public corporations and national public enterprises, which are always subjected to the control of the Ministries, it is very exceptional that an act of the national State in whose adoption has intervened the Minister, for instance, when the act of State has been adopted by the President with all the Ministers, in Council of Ministers, could not be considered as being issued in the *total absence of any fault* on the part of such public contracting party, or that it could be considered beyond the sphere of the national public contracting party, or could be issued without "any connection" with the activity of the public contracting party. The Ministry controlling the national public enterprise, according to the legislation regulating the functioning of Public Administration, is obligated to be involved in the adoption of acts of State issued for instance in decisions involving the Council of Ministers, and in such cases, it will be hardly to consider such acts as extraneous to the public enterprises subjected to the control of the Minster.

Consequently, as a matter of principle, an act of national government cannot be considered as an excuse for a national public contracting party to a national public contract, when such act of government is issued by an authority at the same level of government. This, in principle, can only occur when the public contracting party is located in a different level of government (*Poder Público*) from the entity that issues the act of State. In other words, on matters of public contracts, it can be said that as a matter of principle, an act of State alleged by a private contracting party to be *fait du prince* in order to prevent the compliance of its contractual obligations, could only be one issued by an organ from a different level of government regarding the public contracting party.

For instance, in a federal State like the Venezuelan State, regarding for instance municipal public contract, the typical *fait du prince* that can be considered as an excuse for noncompliance for the public municipal contracting party, could be a national legislative or national executive act of State. Conversely, an act of State issued by the legislative or executive organs of the national level of Government, in principle cannot be considered extraneous to a national public contracting party, like a public national enterprise (national state-owned entity), in order to be alleged as an excuse for noncomplying its obligations in a public national contract.

The matter has been resolved in this same sense, and according to the same general principles of law, in other countries. For instance, in France, these principles were applied in the 1970 decision issued by the French *Cour de Cassation,* in the *Air France case,* in which Air France, a national mixed public enterprise (*enterprise publique d'économie mixte*), argued that a decision of its supervising government authority (*autorité de tutelle*) constituted *fait du prince* that prevented Air France from performing its contractual labor obligations with its employees.[370]

In that case, the Court decided that public enterprises such as Air France, even being a mixed public enterprises, could not invoke the decisions of its *autorité de tutelle* as an extraneous, unforeseeable, and insurmountable intervention of a third person (“*fait imprévisible et insurmountable d'un tier qui lui serait étranger*”) as an excuse for the non-performance of its obligations.[371] The *avocat général* Robert Mallottée, arguing in the case, noted that such public enterprise must be considered “in its structure and management closely dependent from the State” in a way that constitutes “a real emanation of the public power,” adding that “in fact, Air France is the State.”

The same a*vocat Général* Mellottée, whose arguments were accepted by the Court, characterized the doctrine of *fait du prince* as a sub-set of *force majeure*, or an external act, that has three important features: (i) it is unavoidable, (ii) it is unforeseeable, and (iii) it presents an obstacle that is insurmountable. In his arguments, he recalled Articles 1147 and 1148 of the French Civil Code (equivalents to Articles 1271 and 1272 of the Venezuelan Civil Code), which provide for exemption from liability of a defendant due to an external act not attributable to the defendant,[372] and examined whether the delays in payment and the harm suffered by the Air France employees were truly attributable to an “external” cause.[373]

In light of Air France's argument that it could not honor its obligations due to the intervention of an external act of the State or *fait du prince*, the *Avocat Général* examined the structure of Air France and emphasized the following points: that Air France was a public enterprise, constituted under a statute; that nearly 70% of its capital was derived from the State; that its board of directors consisted of 16 members, of which at least 8 were government officials or nominated by the State; that the appointment of its Chair or President had be approved by the State; that its financial management was to a certain extent controlled by the State; and that the remuneration provided to its employees was subject to prior approval of the State.[374]

370 French Cour de Cassation (Labor Chamber), Decision N° 69-40253, April 15, 1970; see also Conclusions by General Counsel Robert Mellotée on the French Cour de Cassation (Labor Chamber) Decision N° 69-40253, April 15, 1970, *Recueil Dalloz*, Jurisprudence, Paris 1971, pp. 107-110.

371 “The subsequent irregular intervention of this authority in an attempt, as such, to hinder the performance of the obligations stipulated in such a manner cannot be opposed by the debtor subject to such regulation as an unforeseeable and insurmountable act of a third party external to it.”. See Air France Decision, *Idem.*, p. 2

372 French Civil Code, Article 1147: “A debtor shall be ordered to pay damages, if there is occasion, either by reason of the non-performance of the obligation, or by reason of delay in performing, whenever he does not prove that the non-performance comes from an external cause which may not be ascribed to him, although there is no bad faith on his part”; and Article 1148: “There is no occasion for any damages where a debtor was prevented from transferring or from doing that to which he was bound, or did what was forbidden to him, by reason of force majeure or of a fortuitous event.”

373 Air France Mellottée Conclusions, *Recueil Dalloz*, Jurisprudence, Paris 1971, p. 107.

374 *Idem*, p. 109.

The *Avocat Général* concluded that as a national public enterprise, Air France closely depended on the national State (same *Pouvoir Public*) both in terms of its structure as well as its management.[375] On this basis he reasoned as follows:

> "This being the case, it is extremely shocking that Air France the private entity is taking refuge behind Air France the public entity in order to excuse itself from fulfilling its contractual obligations and to evade the consequences of a delay inherent in the operation of its articles of association [by-laws]. If the contention [of Air France] were admitted, it would become much too easy for enterprises *à statut* to exonerate themselves from their obligations. It would then be sufficient for them to provoke withdrawal of authorization and subsequently invoke the fait du prince. Legal relations would be without stability or security. In fact, in relation to third parties, the enterprise *à statut* and the State form one and the same legal entity; the intervention of the public authority, which is organically linked to the normal functioning of the company, does not constitute an extraneous cause that can be invoked against third persons and contracting parties."[376]

The *Avocat Général* also found that Air France had not taken or even attempted to take any action to challenge the decisions of the *autorité de tutelle*, but only stood by passively, so it could not say that the measure was irresistible.[377] The *Avocat Général* concluded that the *fait du prince* defense was unavailable to Air France, and the *Cour de Cassation* agreed.

These same principles and approach are applicable in the Venezuelan legal system of administrative law, which as is well known, as all the Latin American countries, has followed very closely the principles of French administrative Law.

These principles, on the other hand, can be found in comparative law, applied in many other countries. For instance, Karl Heinz Böckstiegel, after reviewing several international cases in which, like in the *Air France*, case, a state-controlled company sought to invoke an act of its own national Government to excuse a breach of contract, developed a set of "Guidelines" to determine whether the defense of *fait du*

---

375 *Idem*, p. 109.

376 "[…] *il est extrêmement choquant qu'Air France, organisme de droit privé, se retranche derrière Air France, organisme de droit public, pour se soustraire à l'exécution de ses obligations contractuelles et pour échapper aux conséquences d'un retard inhérent au fonctionnement de son statut. Si sa thèse était admise, il deviendrait par trop facile aux entreprises à statut de s'exonérer de leurs obligations. Il leur suffirait de provoquer un retrait d'autorisation et d'invoquer ensuite le fait du prince. Il n'y aurait plus aucun équilibre n'aucune sécurité dans les rapports juridiques. En réalité, à l'égard des tiers, l'entreprise à statut et l'Etat ne représentent qu'un seule entité juridique, et l'intervention de la puissance publique, qui est liée organiquement au fonctionnement normal de l'entreprise, ne constitue pas une cause étrangère opposable aux tiers et aux contractants.* […]"] *Idem*. p. 109.

377 «*Qu'a donc fait, ou simplement tente, Air France pour lever l'obstacle? Apparemment rien, puisqu'elle s'est borne à observer une attitude passive. […]Air France, qui demeurait liée par des engagements contractuels, avait le devoir de faire tout ce qui était en son pouvoir pour assurer le respect de ses engagements.*». *Idem*, pp. 109-110.

prince is available in a given case,[378] reflecting general principles of administrative law that can be also applied in Venezuelan law.

According to the Böckstiegel "Guidelines," although the principle of legal separation between the State and its state-owned enterprises is recognized, the principle is that *fait du prince* is not available to a state-owned enterprise in all situations.[379] Otherwise, the State could always provide a *force majeure* excuse for its State-owned enterprise every time it considers that the fulfillment of a contract becomes no longer advantageous.[380]

Consequently, in order to identify if an act of State can be alleged by a public enterprise as public contracting party to a public contract as an event of *force majeur*, the "Guidelines" provided for the application of some useful basic principles:

First, if the contract itself stipulates that the state-owned enterprise is obligated to indemnify the private contracting party in the event of government action, as some public contracts establishes, then the *fact of prince* defense is unavailable as a defense to a claim for such compensation.[381]

Second, *fact of prince* cannot be considered an excuse for the state-owned enterprise's own breach of the contract when the state-owned enterprise has formally applied or informally asked for the act that allegedly prevented performance.[382]

Third, due to the presumption that a State will not have its executive or legislative organs act to the detriment of its own state-own enterprises, a statute issued for a specific case or specific contracts or entities should in principle not be considered as *force majeure*.[383]

Forth, the public contracting party has the burden to prove that, for instance, a statute was sanctioned by general considerations not connected with a particular contract or a sort of contracts.[384] In this regard, a general statute cannot serve as an excuse if the private contracting party supplies at least *prima facie* evidence that it was issued in the interest of the State for the public contracting party (state-owned enterprise) not to fulfill its contractual obligations.[385]

One of the main elements, for instance, to reject the possibility for a public contracting party to a national public contract, to allege *fait du prince* regarding for instance acts of State issued by the National Executive or the Legislative, as argued before, is the very tight link that exists between the national public enterprise and the Ministry of the Executive in charge of controlling such public enterprise. This relationship makes very unprovable that due to the permanent

378 See Karl-Heinz Böckstiegel, *Arbitration and State Enterprises: A Survey on the National and International State of Law and Practice*, International Chamber of Commerce, Kluwer Law and Taxation Publishers, 1984, pp. 46-48.

379 Böckstiegel Guidelines, *op. cit.* p. 47.

380 *Idem.*

381 *Idem*, p. 46.

382 *Idem.*

383 *Idem.*pp. 47-48.

384 *Idem*, p. 47.

385 *Idem*, p. 48.

administrative relation that exists between the controlling Ministry and the controlled national public enterprise, the later could allege that it did not know about the actions of the Ministry regarding acts of State that could affect the contract, particularly being the Ministries the key organs in the functioning of Public Administration; in charge of drafting Executive and Legislation decrees in their corresponding sectors.

One very important case in Venezuela that can illustrate this matter of a *fait du prince* alleged to be an excuse for non-compliance for public enterprises, as public contracting parties in public contracts, was the issuance of the Decree Law 5200 of February 26, 2007 (*Ley de Migración a Empresas Mixtas de los Convenios de Asociación de la Faja Petrolífera del Orinoco, así como de los Convenios de Exploración a Riesgo y Ganancias Compartidas*)[386] specifically sanctioned by the National Executive through delegate legislation, for the purpose of terminating a group of "administrative contracts" named as "Association Agreements" for the exploitation of the Orinoco Belt as well of those Exploration at Risk and Profit-Sharing Agreements, which were entered by state owned enterprises affiliated to Petróleos de Venezuela S.A. (PDVSA), the holding of the nationalized oil industry, according to the *Apertura Petrolera* policy defined in the 1990's.

In such case, according to the aforementioned principles of administrative law referred to the principle of *fait du prince*, the Oil national public enterprises (PDVSA and its affiliates) as the public contracting parties in such Agreements, as a matter of principle, could not rely on such Decree Law 5.200, as an act of the national Government, to excuse for instance the breach of their own obligations under the Associations Agreements, by claiming that such act was a *fait du prince* extraneous to them.

In Venezuela, in spite of the fact that public enterprises have separate legal identity from the National Government, in this example of the case of the national Oil public enterprises, they have a very close and strict organic links with the national Government, which even exceed those found in the aforementioned *Air France* case, not being available for the Oil industry enterprises, the defense of *fait du prince* for noncompliance of its contractual obligations based on the issuance of Decree Law 5200.

On the contrary, applying the *Air France* doctrine to this example of the Decree Law No. 5.200 through which the National Executive resolved the early termination of the Association Agreements, the public contracting party of the agreements, that is the subsidiaries of PDVSA, could not argue that such Decree Law, as an act of the

386 *Official Gazette*, No. 38.623 of February 16, 2007. See regarding this process: Allan R. Brewer-Carías, "The 'Statization' of the Pre 2001 Primary Hydrocarbons Joint Venbture Exploitations: Their Unilateral termination and the Assets'Confiscation of Some of the Former Private parties" in Oil, Gas & Energy Law Intelligence, www.gasandoil.com/ogel/ ISSN: 1875-418X, Issue Vol 6, Issue 2, (OGEL/TDM Special Issue on Venezuela: The battle of Contract Sanctity vs. Resource Sovereignty, ed. By Elizabeth Eljuri), April 2008; and "La estatización de los convenios de asociación que permitían la participación del capital privado en las actividades primarias de hidrocarburos sucritos antes de 2002, mediante su terminación anticipada y unilateral y la confiscación de los bienes afectos a los mismos," in Víctor Hernández Mendible (Coordinador), *Nacionalización, Libertad de Empresa y Asociaciones Mixtas*, Editorial Jurídica Venezolana, Caracas 2008, pp. 123-188e

National Executive issue, without doubt, as is the rule, at the proposal and participation of the Minister of Energy, who at the time was at the same time the President of PDVSA, could be something extraneous to PDVSA and its affiliates. In such case, using the same expressions of the French *Cassation Court* decision, PDVSA and its affiliates could be considered part of the State (it could be said: "PDVSA is the State,") and as a public enterprises in charge of executing the State oil policy, together with the State, they "form one and the same legal entity," so "the intervention of the public authority [the National Executive], which is organically linked to the normal functioning of the company, does not constitute an extraneous cause that can be invoked against third persons and contracting parties."

The defense of *fait du prince,* in this example of Decree Law 5200, could also be considered as unavailable from the perspective of the aforementioned Böckstiegel "Guidelines," because in the case of the Association Agreements, the subsidiaries of PDVSA that were the public contracting parties to them, not only were all national public enterprises,[387] whose contractual obligations were guaranteed by PDVSA, but were "third tier" subsidiaries of the National State, and "second tier" subsidiaries of PDVSA, and all together with PDVSA, were part of the "national public sector,"[388] subject to the shareholder control by PDVSA and through it, to the *contrôle de tutelle* (political and administrative control) by the National Executive.

On the other hand, the Supreme Court of Justice has held that PDVSA and its subsidiaries are entities integrated in the national Public Administration, notwithstanding their private law forms (*compañías anónimas*), observing that:

> "although Petróleos de Venezuela S.A. is a company incorporated and organized as *sociedad anónima*, it is beyond doubt, and so is reaffirmed by the Constitution of the Bolivarian Republic of Venezuela, that the same is part of the general structure of the National Public Administration." [389]

For purposes of evaluating the availability of the *fait du prince* defense in this example, the "organic link" that arose between the national Government and the normal functioning of the public enterprise, as was applied in the aforementioned *Air France* case decision, [390] can be found in the relationship of ownership and control between the Central government and PDVSA and its affiliates. In this case, a similar if

387 These public enterprises were established pursuant to Congressional authorizations, as required by the 1975 Nationalization Law.

388 According to the Organic Law on the Financial Public Administration (last reform December 2015), the national public sector comprises companies directly owned by the State and the second- and third tier subsidiaries. *Decree with Rank and Force of Law Amending the Organic Law on Financial Administration of the Public Sector, Decree N° 2.174*, published December 30, 2015, Article 5.

389 See Supreme Tribunal of Justice, Constitutional Chamber, Decision N° 464 of March 18, 2002 (Case: *Interpretación del Decreto de la Asamblea Nacional Constituyente de fecha 30 de enero de 2000, mediante el cual se suspende por 180 días la negociación de la Convención Colectiva del Trabajo)* in *Revista de Derecho Público*, N° 89-92, January – December 2002, Editorial Jurídica Venezolana (Caracas, 2004), pp. 219-220. Regarding PDVSA as part of the National Public Administration, see Allan R. Brewer-Carías "El carácter de Petróleos de Venezuela, S.A. como instrumento del Estado en la industria petrolera" in *Revista de Derecho Público*, N° 23 (July-September), Editorial Jurídica Venezolana, Caracas 1985, pp. 77-86).

390 Air France Mellotée Conclusions, *Recueil Dalloz*, Jurisprudence, Paris 1971, p. 109.

not closer structural relationship exists, considering that PDVSA's by-laws are themselves an act of Presidential authority, stating that the "National Executive Power, through the Ministry of Energy and Mines," will set policies, guidelines, and other provisions for PDVSA.[391] All capital stock of PDVSA is provided by the "Republic of Venezuela,"[392] and all the shares of PDVSA, according to article 303 of the Constitution, are and must remain owned by the Republic. The by-laws also provide that the "Ministry of Energy and Mines and other Ministries that may be appointed from time to time by the President of the Republic shall exercise the representation of the Republic in the Shareholders' Meeting, which shall be presided over by the Ministry of Energy and Mines."[393] The Minister of Energy and Mines in addition before and after the issuance of the Decree 5.200 of 2007 served as President of PDVSA, who was appointed after the By-Laws were specially amended in 2004 to allow this dual role.[394] Officials of the Ministry of Energy and Mines served on PDVSA's Board of Directors,[395] and all the high officers of the Ministry were paid by PDVSA, being the Minister, acting as President, empowered to determine the remuneration of PDVSA employees.[396]

On the other hand, regarding specifically the issuance of Decree Law 5.200 terminating the Associations Agreements, the Ministry of Energy, who was at the same time President of PDVSA, according to the Organic Law on Public Administration, in that case was the public official in charge of drafting and proposing the text of Decree Law 5.200 to the President of the Republic, and subsequently submitting it for its approval in Council of Ministers.

In Venezuela, the Ministries, according to the Organic Law on Public Administration,[397] are the State organs of the National Executive responsible for the creation, adoption, monitoring and evaluating of policies, strategies, general plans, programs and projects within the scope of their areas of competence and over which they exercise authority" (Article 60), and as such, are in charge of controlling the national public enterprises acting within their area of competence in each sector. As such, they are the ones in charge of proposing, for instance, to the President and the Council of Ministers, the decisions to be adopted in each sector.

In Venezuela, according to article 225 of the 1999 Constitution, the National Executive is integrated not only by the President but together with the Ministers, to the point that without the active participation of the Ministers, the President of the Republic cannot decide any matter with general effects whatsoever. This means that as a matter of Law, in Venezuela, according to article 236 *in fine* of the Constitution, all the acts and decisions of the President with general effects can only be issued with the close and active participation of the Ministers; and all the decisions of the President

391 See *Partial Amendment of Decree N° 2184 of 10 December 2002, Containing the Bylaws of Petróleos de Venezuela, S.A., Official Gazette* N° 38,081, December 7, 2004, Article 2; *Reprint of Decree* N° *3264 Appointing Rafael Ramírez as President of PDVSA* (issued on November 22, 2004), *Official Gazette 38,081*, December 7, 2004,

392 PDVSA Bylaws, Article 4.

393 PDVSA Bylaws, Article 11.

394 *Idem,* Article 29.

395 *Idem.*

396 *Idem,* Article 34(7).

397 See *Official Gazette* No. 6147 Extra. of Novembre 17, 2014.

(all Decrees, for instance), in order *to be valid*, must be signed by the Minister of the sector, or by all the Minister if approved in Council of Ministers. The only constitutional exception to this rule is the act of appointment or dismissal of Ministers, and the acts adopted as Commander in Chief, which are the only acts that the President can adopt by his own and issue with his only signature.

According to these Constitucional and legal provisions, it is then necessary to conclude that the Ministers are always involved in the issuance of Decrees by the National Executive, having always a preponderant participation and responsibility in its preparation and issuance.

This role, is expressly established in article 65 of the same Organic Law of Public Administration, in which it is stated that the Ministers are the ones in charge of conducting, adopting, following-up and evaluating all the decisions on the matters attributed to them, regarding which they have complete authority. And in particular, on matters of the initiative of the National Executive in order to propose legislation or issue delegate legislation, is provided in article 86 of the same Organic Law establishing that the Ministers are the ones called to begin the process, to draft the project, to present it to the President and to the Council of Ministers, to follow up the decision adopted and perform the necessary studies, and to present again the draft legislation before the Council of Ministers, for its approval if it is a Decree Law; or for sending it, with the explanation of motives, to the National Assembly in case of ordinary legislation for its sanctioning.

All these rules were also incorporated in the Internal Regulation of the Council of Minister,[398] establishing that for all other decisions to be adopted in by the President and all its Ministers, the same legal procedure must be followed, providing that the Ministers are the one having the initiative to bring the matters to the attention of the President (agenda or *punto de cuenta*); to request for the matter, once approved by the President, to be included in the Agenda of the Council of Ministers; to explain and brief all the other Ministers about the proposed decision; and to defend the draft decision in the Council of Ministers.

Consequently, as a matter of law, according to the Constitution, the Organic Law on Public Administration and the Regulations referred to its functioning, regarding the national acts of State issued for example by the National Executive that could have impact in national public contracts, the Minister of the corresponding sector is the main responsible for the definition of the national policy and for the issuance of such acts; and being the Ministers in charge of exercising the *control de tutela* over public enterprises, that decision inevitably could not be considered as an act of State of *fait du prince* extraneous, not attributable or non-imputable to the public enterprise as public contracting party.

This, *mutatis mutandis* draws a similar situation as the one resolved in the *Air France* case by the French *Cour de Cassation* in 1970, establishing the principle that the acts of the government issued by the authority of *tutelle* or in charge of controlling a public enterprise, cannot be considered extraneous to such enterprise particularly when it exists an organic link between both, the authority of control and the controlled entity.

398 See Decree No. 6478 of 21 October 2008, issued by the President of the Republic, in. *Official Gazette* No. 39.044 of October 23 2008.

Consequently, according to such principles, when a tight organic link exists between a Ministry acting as *authorité de tutelle* and the controlled public enterprises, the acts issued by the controlling authority, or in which it has a preponderant participation, as a matter of principle cannot be considered as *fait du prince* that could be extraneous to the controlled public enterprise, which cannot invoke it as an excuse to not comply with its contractual obligations.

In the same line of general principles of administrative law that can be applied on these matters are the already mentioned guidelines described by Karl Heinz Böckstiegel in relation to the principle of *fait du prince* when alleged as an excuse by a public enterprise in order to justify non-compliance.[399] According to the Guidelines, the defense of *fait du prince* is not available (i) when the public enterprise has applied for or informally asked for the act of State to be issued; or (ii) when the act of State is not a general law but a statute referred only to an specific contract or a group of contracts; or (iii) when the public enterprise has interest in the enacting of the act (economic interest). In any of these cases, the excuse of "compliance with law" derived from an act of state, is not available for the public enterprises as fait *du prince*.

Regarding the aforementioned 2007 case of the Decree Law 5200 that terminated the Association Agreements in the Oil sector, according to the provisions of the statutes regulating the functioning of Public Administration, all those three situations enumerated by Böckstiegel existed regarding PDVSA and the government (the public enterprise through his President acting at the same time as Minister applied and asked for the act of State to be issued; the Decree Law was not a general law but a statute referred only to a group of contracts; and the public enterprise has interest in the enacting of the act); being then inevitably to conclude in such example, that PDVSA and its subsidiaries, acting through the President of PDVSA who was at the same time Minister of Energy and Oil in charge of conducting the energy and Oil policy of the country, were involved in the conception and in procuring the sanctioning of Decree Law 5200, which therefore could not be considered as an extraneous non imputable act of State regarding PDVSA and its affiliates.

In other words, in that case, it is not possible to consider that for PDVSA and its affiliates Decree Law 5.200 was a "non-imputable external cause" when they were state-controlled entities (PDVSA subsidiaries) and when the President of PDVSA was at the same time the Minister who conducted the Oil policy of the National Government, and who therefore was in charge of drafting, proposing and seeking for the approval of Decree-Law 5200, and then, as President of PDVSA, helped carry on its implementation. In these circumstances, it cannot be said that Decree 5.200 occurred in the total absence of the fault of PDVSA and its affiliates, or without any connection with their activities or will. For the same reasons, Decree Law 5.200 cannot be considered for PDVSA and its subsidiaries an event of *force majeure* that could have been beyond the reasonable control of" PDVSA and its subsidiaries, or "unforeseen by" PDVSA and its subsidiaries, or that, if foreseeable could not be avoided in whole or in part by the exercise of due diligence by PDVSA and its

399 See Karl-Heinz Böckstiegel, *Arbitration and State Enterprises: A Survey on the National and International State of Law and Practice*, International Chamber of Commerce, Kluwer Law and Taxation Publishers, 1984, pp. 46-48.

subsidiaries. On the contrary, for PDVSA (and its subsidiaries), the Decree Law N° 5.200, being its President at that time one of the Ministers that approved and signed it, and specifically the Minister of Energy and Oil who was in charge of directing the national State's actions and policies in the field, such Executive act could not be considered beyond its reasonable control, or unforeseen by PDVSA and its subsidiaries or that could not be avoided in whole or in part by the exercise of due diligence by PDVSA and its subsidiaries.

In conclusion, it can be said that on matters of public contracts, as in all contracts, in principle, *fait du prince* can be invoked by the contracting parties as an event of *force majeur* in order to excuse the noncompliance of contractual obligations. Nonetheless, when the contracting party alleging the defense is a public contracting party, as a matter of principle, the defense in no case can serve as an excuse for the non-performance of obligations of the public contracting party, when the act of State is an act adopted by an entity of the same territorial level of Governmental Power (*poderes públicos, puovoir publics, collectivités territoriales*) (national, state, or municipal) to which the contracting public entity belongs.[400]

In such case, for instance, referring to the national level of government, an act of State issued by the National Executive cannot be considered extraneous to the national public enterprise as the public contracting party. Otherwise, as aforementioned, it would be too easy for the State to relieve its entities of contractual liability simply by adopting measures that prohibit or otherwise make it impossible for those entities to perform their contractual obligations.

The *fait du prince* defense in such cases is unavailable, except when it is proven by the public contracting party that the act of State was unavoidable, unforeseeable, and irresistible for the public contracting party, completely extraneous, not attributable or non-imputable to it, and issued in the total absence of fault or knowledge by the public contracting party.

---

400 This doctrine does not apply to judicial decisions. See *Doctrina de la Procuraduría General de la República 1966*, Caracas 1967, p. 77.

PART FIVE

PRINCIPLES OF ADMINISTRATIVE LAW RELATED TO ECONOMIC FREEDOM AND PROPERTY RIGHTS

I. CONSTITUTIONAL PRINCIPLES RELATED TO ECONOMIC FREEDOM AND PROPERTY RIGHTS

The 1999 Constitution, also following the general trend of the 1961 Constitution,[1] in addition to the political and social constitutions, contains an economic constitution in which are established the principles governing the economy, including the respective roles played by private initiative and the State in this field. According to these provisions, since the beginning of the oil exploitation, and particularly during the second half of the 20th century, the economic system that has been developed in Venezuela is one of mixed economy or of "social market economy,"[2] which combines economic freedom, private initiative and a free market economic model (as opposed to the model of a state directed economy), and the possibility of State intervention in the economy in order to uphold principles of social justice. This has been possible, particularly because of the special position of the State as owner of the subsoil and of the oil industry which since 1975 was nationalized.[3] This has made the State the most powerful economic entity in the nation, leading it to intervene in the country's economic activity in important ways.

---

1 See Allan R. Brewer-Carías, "Reflexiones sobre la Constitución Económica," in *Estudios sobre la Constitución Española. Homenaje al Profesor Eduardo García de Enterría,* Madrid 1991, pp. 3839-3853.

2 See Henrique Meier, "La Constitución económica," in *Revista de Derecho Corporativo*, Vol. 1, N° 1. Caracas, 2001, pp. 9-74; Ana C. Nuñez Machado, "Los principios económicos de la Constitución de 1999," in *Revista de Derecho Constitucional,* N° 6 (enero-diciembre), Editorial Sherwood, Caracas, 2002, pp. 129-140; Claudia Briceño Aranguren y Ana C. Núñez Machado, "Aspectos económicos de la nueva Constitución," in *Comentarios a la Constitución de la República Bolivariana de Venezuela*, Vadell Hermanos, Editores, Caracas, 2000, pp. 177 y ss.; Jesús Ollarves Irazábal, "La vigencia constitucional de los Derechos Ecónomicos y Sociales en Venezuela," in *Libro Homenaje a Enrique Tejera París, Temas sobre la Constitución de 1999,* Centro de Investigaciones Jurídicas (CEIN), Caracas, 2001, pp. 159 a 192.

3 See Organic Law that reserves to the State the Industry and Commerce of Hydrocarbons, *Official Gazette* Extra, N° 1.769 of August 29, 1975. See Allan R. Brewer-Carías, "Introducción al Régimen Jurídico de las Nacionalizaciones en Venezuela", in *Archivo de Derecho Público y Ciencias de la Administración*, Vol. III, 1972-1979, Tomo I, Instituto de Derecho Público,

1. Constitutional Principles of the Economic System

It is precisely within this context that Article 299 of the 1999 Constitution sets forth that the social-economic regime of the Republic shall be based on the principles of social justice, democratization, efficiency, free competition, protection of the environment, productivity and solidarity, with a view to ensuring overall human development and a dignified and useful existence for the community. For these purposes, this very Article of the Constitution expressly sets forth that the State must, "jointly with private initiative", promote "the harmonious development of the national economy for the purpose of generating sources of employment, a high national level of added value, in order to elevate the standard of living of the population and strengthen the nation's economic sovereignty, guaranteeing legal certainty, solidity, dynamism, sustainability, permanence, and economic growth with equity, in order to guarantee a just distribution of wealth by means of strategic democratic, participative and open planning."

The economic system is therefore based upon economic freedom, private initiative and free competition, although in combination with the participation of the State as a promoter of economic development, a regulator of economic activity, and a planner, together with civil society. As the Constitutional Chamber of the Supreme Tribunal of Justice stated in its decision N° 117 of 6 February 2001[4] this is "a socioeconomic system that is in between a free market (in which the State acts as a simple programmer (*programador*) for an economy that is dependent upon the supply and demand of goods and services) and an interventionist economy (in which the State actively intervenes as the 'primary entrepreneur')". The Constitution promotes, "joint economic activity between the State and private initiative in the pursuit of, and in order to concretely realize the supreme values consecrated in the Constitution", and in order to pursue "the equilibrium of all the forces of the market, and, joint activity between the State and private initiative". In accord with this system, the Courts ruled, the Constitution "advocates a series of superior normative values with respect to the economic regimen, consecrating free enterprise within the framework of a market economy and, fundamentally, within the framework of the Social State under the Rule of Law (the *Welfare State*, the State of Well-being or the Social Democratic State). This is a social State that is opposed to authoritarianism."[5] Nonetheless, in practice, particularly during the past decade (1999-2009), this framework has been changed, due to the authoritarian government that has been developed, inclining the balance toward the State participation in the economy,

---

Facultad de Ciencias Jurídicas y Políticas, Universidad Central de Venezuela, Caracas 1981, pp. 23-44.

4 See in *Revista de Derecho Público,* N° 85-88, Editorial Jurídica Venezolana, Caracas, 2001, pp. 212-218.

5 The values that are alluded to, according to the doctrine of the Constitutional Chamber, "are developed through the concept of free enterprise" (*libertad de empresa*) which encompasses both the notion of a subjective right "to dedicate oneself to the economic activity of one's choice", and a principle of economic regulation according to which the will of the business (*voluntad de la empresa*) to make its own decisions is manifest. The State fulfills its role of intervention in this context. Intervention can be direct (through businesses) or indirect (as an entity regulating the market)". *Idem.*

through a process of progressively "*statization*" of the economy, reducing economic freedom and increasing the dependency of the country on oil exploitation.[6]

A. Private Economic rights

a. *Right to exercise economic activities*

Title III of the 1999 Constitution on constitutional rights and guarantees also contains a declaration of the economic rights (Chapter VII, Articles 112-118), including, economic freedom, and the right to private property.

Regarding economic freedom, Article 112 of the Constitution declares the right of all persons to develop the economic activity of his choice, without other limits than those established by statute for reasons of human development, security, sanitation, environment protection and others of social interest. In any case, the State must promote private initiative, guaranteeing the creation of wealth and it's just distribution, as well as the production of goods and services in order to satisfy the needs of the population, freedom to work, and the free enterprise, commerce and industry, without prejudice to the power of the State to promulgate measures to plan, rationalize and regulate the economy and promote the overall development of the country.

In 2007, by means of the Constitutional Reform Draft that was rejected by referendum held on December that same year, the President of the Republic proposed to eliminate this constitutional provision guarantying economic freedom, substituting it with one only defining as a matter of state policy, the obligation to promote, "the development of a Productive Economic Model, that is intermediate, diversified and independent … founded upon the humanistic values of cooperation and the preponderance of common interests over individual ones, guaranteeing the meeting of the people's social and material needs, the greatest possible political and social stability, and the greatest possible sum of happiness". The proposal added that the State, in the same way, "shall promote and develop different forms of businesses and economic units from social property, both directly or communally, as well as indirectly or through the state," According to this norm, additionally, the state was to promote, "economic units of social production and/or distribution, that may be mixed properties held between the State, the private sector, and the communal power, so as to create the best conditions for the collective and cooperative construction of a Socialist Economy".

b. *Property Rights*

Regarding the right to property, Article 115 of the Constitution, although following the orientation of the previous 1961 Constitution,[7] in the sense of guarantying the right to property, did not establish private property as having a "social function" to be accomplished, as did the 1961 Constitution. Nonetheless, it provides that property shall be subject to such contributions, restrictions and obligations as may be established by law in the service of the public or general

---

6 As reported by Simón Romero in "Chávez Reopens Oil Bids to West as Prices Plunge," published in The New York Times on January 12, 2009, p. 1, in 2009 Venezuela "reliant on oil for about 93 percent of its export revenue in 2008, up from 69 percent in 1998."

7 See Allan R. Brewer-Carías "El derecho de propiedad y libertad económica. Evolución y situación actual en Venezuela," in *Estudios sobre la Constitución. Libro Homenaje a Rafael Caldera,* Tomo II, Caracas 1979, pp. 1139-1246.

interest. On the other hand, Article 115 defines the attributes of the right to property that traditionally were only enumerated in the Civil Code (Article 545), that is, the right to use, the enjoyment, and the disposition of property are now in the Constitution.

This constitutional regime regarding property rights was proposed to be radically changed in the 2007 rejected Constitutional Reforms, in which the President of the Republic sought to eliminate private property as a constitutionally protected right, and substituting the right's conception by a recognition of private property only referred to "assets for use and consumption or as means of production," altogether with other forms of properties, and in particular, public property. The proposed reform regarding Article 115 of the Constitution tended to recognize and guaranty "different forms of property" instead of guaranteeing the right to private property, enumerating them as follows: public property, as the one that belongs to State entities; social property, as the one that belongs to the people jointly and to future generations; collective property, as the one pertaining to social groups or persons, exploited for their common benefit, use, or enjoyment, that may be of social or private origin;" mixed property, as the one constituted between the public sector, the social sector, the collective sector and the private sector, in different combinations, for the exploitation of resources or the execution of activities, subject always to the absolute economic and social sovereignty of the nation; and private property, as the one owned by 'natural or legal persons, only regarding assets for use or consumption, or as means of production legitimately acquired."

Regarding expropriation, Article 115 of the Constitution establishes that it can be decreed regarding any kind of property only for reasons of public benefit or social interest, by means of a judicial process and payment of just compensation.[8] Consequently, the Constitution prohibits confiscation (expropriation without compensation), except in cases permitted by the Constitution itself, regarding property of persons responsible for crimes committed against public property, or who have illicitly enriched themselves exercising public offices. Confiscations may also take place regarding property deriving from business, financial or any other activities connected with illicit trafficking of psychotropic or narcotic substances (Article 116 y 271).

Article 307 of the Constitution declares the regimen of large private real estate holdings (*latifundio)* to be contrary to social interests, charging the legislator to tax idle lands, and establish the necessary measures to transform them into productive economic units, as well as to recover arable land. The same constitutional provision entitles peasants to own land, constitutionalizing the obligation of the State to protect and promote associative and private forms of property in order to guarantee agricultural production, and oversee sustainable arrangements on arable lands to guaranty its food-producing potential. In exceptional cases, the same Article requires that the legislature must establish federal tax revenue to provide funds for financing, research, technical assistance, transfer of technology and other activities aimed to raise productivity and competitiveness of the agricultural sector.

8 See, José L. Villegas Moreno, "El derecho de propiedad en la Constitución de 1999", in *Estudios de Derecho Administrativo: Libro Homenaje a la Universidad Central de Venezuela,* Volumen II. Imprenta Nacional, Caracas, 2001, pp. 565-582.

2. Limits to private economic activities

Article 113 of the Constitution prohibits monopolies. Consequently, any act, activity, conductor agreement of private individuals which is intended to establish a monopoly or which leads by reason of its actual effects to the existence of a monopoly, regardless of the intentions of the persons involved, and whatever the form it actually takes, is declared contrary to the fundamental principles of this Constitution. Also contrary to such principles is the abuse of a position of dominance which a private individual, a group of individuals or a business enterprise or group of enterprises acquires or has acquired in a given market of goods or services, regardless of what factors caused such position of dominance; or the case of a concentration of demand. In all of the cases indicated, the State shall be required to adopt such measures as may be necessary to prevent the harmful and restrictive effects of monopoly, abuse of a position of dominance and a concentration of demand, with the purpose of protecting consumers and producers and ensuring the existence of genuine competitive conditions in the economy.

In the case of the exploitation of natural resources which are the property of the Nation or in the case of public services rendering by private entities, on an exclusive basis or otherwise, the State shall grant concessions for a certain period, in all cases ensuring the existence of adequate compensation regarding public interest (Article 113).

3. State participation in the Economy regime

A. State promotion of economic activities

The Constitution also regulates various forms of State economic intervention that have developed in Venezuela in the last decades.[9] In this regard, the Constitution regulates the State as a promoter, that is, without substituting private initiatives, to foster and order the economy in order to ensure the development of private initiative. In this regard, Article 112 sets forth that in any case, the State must promote private initiative, guaranteeing the creation of wealth and it's just distribution, as well as the production of goods and services in order to satisfy the needs of the population, freedom to work, and the free enterprise, commerce and industry, without prejudice to the power of the State to promulgate measures to plan, rationalize and regulate the economy and promote the overall development of the country.

---

9 I have written extensively on the issue of State intervention in economic freedom and property. See *generally* Allan R. Brewer-Carías, "El derecho de propiedad y la libertad económica. Evolución y situación actual en Venezuela" in *Estudios sobre la Constitución. Libro Homenaje a Rafael Caldera*, Tomo II, Facultad de Ciencias Jurídicas y Políticas, Universidad Central de Venezuela, Caracas 1979, pp. 1,139-1,246; "La evolución y situación actual del régimen del derecho de propiedad en Venezuela" in *Estudios de Derecho Económico*, Vol. III, Universidad Nacional Autónoma de México, México 1979, pp. 7-64; "Aspectos del derecho público interno aplicable a las empresas de producción internacional" in *Regulación Jurídica de las Empresas Multinacionales y Transnacionales*, Colegio Universitario Francisco de Miranda, Caracas 1979, pp. 133-166; "La intervención del Estado en la actividad mercantil" in *Jornadas de Derecho Mercantil*, Facultad de Derecho, Universidad Católica Andrés Bello, Caracas 1978, pp. 529-560; *Evolución del Régimen Legal de la Economía 1939-1779*, Valencia 1980.

In this same regard, Article 299 sets forth that the State, jointly with private initiative, shall promote the harmonious development of the national economy, to the end of generating sources of employment, a high rate of domestic added value, raising the standard of living of the population and strengthening the economic sovereignty of the country; and guaranteeing the reliability of the law, as well as the solid, dynamic, sustainable, continuing and equitable growth of the economy, to ensure a just distribution of wealth through participatory democratic strategic planning with open consultation.

Specifically, regarding the agricultural activities, Article 305 of the Constitution establishes that the State shall promote sustainable agriculture as the strategic basis for overall rural development, and consequently shall guarantee the population a secure food supply, defined as the sufficient and stable availability of food within the national sphere and timely and uninterrupted access to the same for consumers. A secure food supply must be achieved by developing and prioritizing internal agricultural and livestock production, understood as production deriving from the activities of agriculture, livestock, fishing and aquaculture. Food production is in the national interest and is fundamental to the economic and social development of the Nation. To this end, the State shall promulgate such financial, commercial, technological transfer, land tenancy, infrastructure, manpower training and other measures as may be necessary to achieve strategic levels of self-sufficiency. In addition, it shall promote actions in the national and international economic context to compensate for the disadvantages inherent to agricultural activity. The State shall protect the settlement and communities of no-industrialized fishermen, as well as their fishing banks in continental waters and those close to the coastline, as defined by law.

Regarding rural development, Article 306 imposes on the State the duty to promote conditions for overall rural development, for the purpose of generating employment and ensuring the rural population an adequate level of well-being, as well as their inclusion in national development. It shall likewise promote agricultural activity and optimum land use by providing infrastructure projects, supplies, loans, training services and technical assistance.

Regarding industrial activities, the Constitution (Article 308) imposes on the State the role to protect and promote small and medium-sized manufacturers, cooperatives, savings funds, family-owned businesses, small businesses and any other form of community association for purposes of work, savings and consumption, under an arrangement of collective ownership, to strength the country's economic development, based on the initiative of the people. Training, technical assistance and appropriate financing shall be guaranteed. On the other hand, Article 309 provides that typical Venezuelan crafts and folk industries shall enjoy the special protection of the State, in order to preserve their authenticity, and they shall receive credit facilities to promote production and marketing.

On commercial matters, Article 301 reserves to the State the use of trade policy to protect the economic activities of public and private Venezuelan enterprises. In this regard, more advantageous status than those established for Venezuelan nationals shall not be granted to foreign persons, enterprises or entities. Foreign investment is subject to the same conditions as domestic investment.

Finally, Article 310 of the Constitution declares tourism as an economic activity of national interest, and of high priority in the country's strategy of diversification and sustainable development. As part of the foundation of the socioeconomic regime contemplated by the Constitution, the State shall promulgate measures to guarantee the development of tourism and shall create and strengthen a national tourist industry.

B. State Economic planning

Regarding economic planning, Article 112 empowers the State to promulgate measures to plan, rationalize and regulate the economy and promote the overall development of the country. The President of the Republic must formulate the National Plan of Development and, once approved by the National Assembly, direct its execution (Article 187,8; 236,18).

C. State direct assumption of economic activities

No provisions are established in the Constitution in order for the State to promote highly qualified or heavy industries, and what is established is for the State the possibility to reserve for its own exploitation, through an organic law and by reasons of national convenience, the petroleum industry (already nationalized since 1975) and other industries, operations and goods and services which are in the public interest and of a strategic nature. The State shall promote the domestic manufacture of raw materials deriving from the exploitation of nonrenewable natural resources, with a view to assimilating, creating and inventing technologies, generating employment and economic growth and creating wealth and wellbeing for the people (Article 302).

As aforementioned, based on a similar constitutional provision establishing the power of the State to reserve for its own exploitation services or resources (Article 97, 1961 Constitution), the oil industry was nationalized in 1975, being managed by a state-own enterprise, *Petróleos de Venezuela S.A.*, regarding which, Article 303 of the 1999 Constitution set forth that for economic and political sovereignty and national strategy reasons, the State shall retain all shares of such public enterprise, but with the exception of its subsidiaries, strategic joint ventures, enterprises and any other venture established or to be established as a consequence of the carrying on of the business of *Petróleos de Venezuela, S.A*. This last possibility has been considered as a loosening of the strict nationalization process carried out through the 1975 Organic Law that reserves to the State the Industry and Commercialization of Hydrocarbons.[10] In this regard, the 2000 Organic Law on Hydrocarbons allowed the establishment of mixed companies for the exploitation of primary hydrocarbons

---

10 See Allan R. Brewer-Carías, "El régimen de participación del capital privado en las industrias petrolera y minera: Desnacionalización y regulación a partir de la Constitución de 1999", in *VII Jornadas Internacionales de Derecho Administrativo Allan R. Brewer-Carías, El Principio de Legalidad y el Ordenamiento Jurídico-Administrativo de la Libertad Económica,* Caracas noviembre 2004. Fundación de Estudios de Derecho Administrativo FUNEDA, Caracas Noviembre, 2004 pp. 15-58.

activities, although with the State as majority shareholder,[11] which has been implemented in 2006-2007.[12]

On the other hand, regarding public enterprises in general, Article 300 of the Constitution refers to the statutes to determine the conditions for the creation of functionally decentralized entities to carry out social or entrepreneurial activities, with a view to ensuring the reasonable economic and social productivity of the public resources invested in such activities.

4. Means through which the State assumes economic sectors and takes private property

The State intervenes in the economic process trough different means: Nationalization, Reservation, Expropriation and Confiscation.[13]

A. Nationalization

In the Venezuelan legal system, the term "nationalization" is not used in the 1999 Constitution or defined in any law. Accordingly, this term has no fixed meaning and can and has been used in different senses. In my own work, I have used the term "nationalization" to refer to the institution of public law that combines the reserve of an economic activity to the State with the acquisition, normally through expropriation, of private assets used in such activities. I first explained this institution in 1974, when I wrote that "an authentic nationalization of an economic sector results when the measure of reservation and the expropriation technique are

11 Organic Law on Hydrocarbons, *Official Gazette* N° 38.493 de 4-8-2006.

12 See Allan R. Brewer-Carías, "The 'Statization' of the Pre 2001 Primary Hydrocarbons Joint Venbture Exploitations: Their Unilateral termination and the Assets'Confiscation of Some of the Former Private parties" in Oil, Gas & Energy Law Intelligence, www.gasandoil.com/ogel/ ISSN: 1875-418X, Issue Vol 6, Issue 2, (OGEL/TDM Special Issue on Venezuela: The battle of Contract Sanctity vs. Resource Sovereignty, ed. By Elizabeth Eljuri), April 2008; and "La estatización de los convenios de asociación que permitían la participación del capital privado en las actividades primarias de hidrocarburos sucritos antes de 2002, mediante su terminación anticipada y unilateral y la confiscación de los bienes afectos a los mismos", in Víctor Hernández Mendible (Coordinador), *Nacionalización, Libertad de Empresa y Asociaciones Mixtas*, Editorial Jurídica Venezolana, Caracas 2008, pp. 123-188.

13 See in Allan R. Brewer-Carías, "Adquisición de la propiedad privada por parte del Estado en el Derecho Venezolano" in *Revista de Control Fiscal,* N° 94, Contraloría General de la República, Caracas 1979, pp. 61-84; reproduced in Allan R. Brewer-Carías, *Jurisprudencia de la Corte Suprema 1930-1974 y Estudios de Derecho Administrativo, Vol. VI: La Propiedad y la Expropiación por causa de Utilidad Pública e Interés Social*, Ediciones del Instituto de Derecho Público, Facultad de Derecho, Universidad Central de Venezuela, Caracas 1979, pp. 17-45. I have written extensively making a distinction between "reserve to the State," "expropriation" and "nationalization." See *El Régimen Jurídico de las Nacionalizaciones en Venezuela, Archivo De Derecho Público Y Ciencias De La Administración*, Tomo III, 2 Vols. (Homenaje del Instituto de Derecho Público al Profesor Antonio Moles Caubet), Instituto de Derecho Público, Facultad de Ciencias Jurídicas y Políticas, Universidad Central de Venezuela, Caracas, March 1981. My article "Introducción al régimen jurídico de las nacionalizaciones en Venezuela" is the Introduction to that book. *Id.*, Vol. 1, pp. 23-43. My detailed analysis of the nationalization process of the oil industry is in my article "Aspectos organizativos de la Industria Petrolera Nacionalizada en Venezuela." *Id.*, Vol. 1, pp. 407-491.

adopted in conjunction. The latter [expropriation] is the mechanism to make the reservation effective."[14]

The Venezuelan oil industry and commerce were nationalized in 1975 by means of the 1975 Organic Law Reserving to the State the Industry and Commerce of Hydrocarbons (1975 Organic Nationalization Law). Such law was issued in application of Article 97 of the 1961 Constitution (equivalent to Article 302 of the 1999 Constitution). The nationalization was implemented by means of the same 1975 Organic Nationalization Law, which (i) reserved the activity to the State, (ii) terminated the then existing concessions for the exploration and exploitation of oil in the country that were assigned to foreign enterprises, and (iii) provided a procedure for the expropriation of private assets engaged in the activity, including the payment of compensation. This was similar to the process followed in previous and recent cases of nationalization.

In effect, in addition to the 1975 reservation of the oil industry, the following can be mentioned:

- The 1971 reservation of the natural gas industry through the Law reserving to the State the industry of natural gas (*Ley que Reserva al Estado la Industria del Gas Natural*), in *Official Gazette* N° 29.594 of August 26, 1971.

- The 1974 reservation of the iron mineral exploitation industry through Decree-Law N° 580 of November 26, 1974 (*Decreto Ley que Reserva al Estado la Industria de la Explotación del Mineral de Hierro*), in *Official Gazette* N° 30.577 of December 16, 1974.

- The 2008 reservation of the industry of transformation of iron mineral. *See* Decree (Organic) Law N° 6.058 of April 30, 2008 in *Official Gazette* N° 38.928 of May 12, 2008 (reserving for the State the steel transformation industry in the Guayana region (Article 1); ordering the private enterprise (SIDOR C.A.) that developed activities in the sector, to transform into a mixed company with the State as majority shareholder (Article 2); declaring the activities performed by SIDOR C.A. of public utility and social interest (Article 3); and ordering the National Executive to expropriate the shares of those private participants that could not reach an agreement to sell said shares to the State, establishing provisions regarding a measure of compensation (Article 8).

- The 2008 reservation of the cement industry. *See* Decree (Organic) Law N° 6.091 of May 27, 2008 in *Official Gazette* N° 5.886 (Extraordinary) of June 18, 2008 (reserving for the State the industry for the fabrication of Cement (Article 1); ordering the transformation of the private enterprises that developed activities in the sector to transform into mixed companies with the State as majority shareholder (Article 2); declaring the industry of public utility and social interest (Article 3) and ordering the National Executive to expropriate the shares of those private shareholders that could not reach an agreement for the sale of said shares to the

14"*Una auténtica nacionalización de un sector económico se produce cuando se dan conjuntamente, la medida de reserva con la técnica expropriatoria. Esta última es el mecanismo para hacer efectiva la reserva.*"] See Allan R. Brewer-Carías, "Comentarios en torno a la nacionalización petrolera" in *Revista Resumen,* N° 55, Vol. V, Caracas, 1974. p. 22. (English translation). See also, Román J. Duque Corredor, *El Derecho de la Nacionalización Petrolera*, Colección Monografías Jurídicas N° 10, Editorial Jurídica Venezolana, p. 22.

State, establishing provisions regarding a measure of compensation (Article 8). The 2009 reservation of assets and services connected to the primary hydrocarbon activities. *See* 2009 Organic Law that Reserves to the State the Assets and Services Related to Primary Hydrocarbon Activities (*Ley Orgánica que Reserva al Estado Bienes y Servicios Conexos a las Actividades Primarias de Hidrocarburos*) in *Official Gazette* N° 39.173 of May 7, 2009 (reserving for the State, due to its strategic character, assets and services related to the performance of primary hydrocarbon activities provided for in the Organic Hydrocarbon Law (Articles 1, 2); ordering the take of control over such assets and services by Petróleos de Venezuela S.A. or the designated affiliate as of the date of publication of the Law (Article 4); declaring such works, assets and services as a public service and of public utility and social interest (Article 5); authorizing the National Executive to order the expropriation of shares and assets of the enterprises performing these services; establishing provisions regarding a measure of compensation (Article 6); and declaring the law as a law of public order (Article 7).

According to the provisions of the *Ley que Reserva al Estado la Industria y el Comercio de los Hidrocarburos,*[15] the State (the Republic) was to develop the "reserved activities, directly by the National Executive or by means of entities of his ownership" (art. 15), the Legislator leaving theoretically to the decision of the Executive to directly take care of the nationalized industry or through entities of the decentralized administration. In spite of this apparent liberty, the Law established the guidelines for the Executive to take care of the nationalized industry through decentralized entities, by establishing in article 6, that "the National Executive will organize the administration and management of the reserved activities", as follows:

> "1 It will create enterprises with the legal form it considers convenient in order to regularly and efficiently develop such activities, being allowed to assign them one or more of such activities, to modify its object, merger or associate them, extinguish, liquidate or render its stock to one or other of those same enterprises. Those enterprises will be State ownership, notwithstanding the provision of second paragraph, and in case of being incorporated as commercial companies, will have one sole shareholder".
>
> "2. To attribute to one of the enterprises the function to coordinate, supervise and control the activities of the others, being allowed to assignee them the ownership of the shares of any of the others"

15 See in *Official Gazette* N° 1.769, August 29, 1975. See our works regarding Petróleos de Venezuela: Allan R, Brewer-Carías, "Consideraciones sobre el Régimen Jurídico-Administrativo de Petróleos de Venezuela, S.A." en *Revista de Hacienda* N° 67, Caracas 1977, p. 79-99; "Aspectos organizativos de la Industria Petrolera Nacionalizada en Venezuela", en Instituto de Derecho Público, en *Archivo de Derecho Público y Ciencias de la Administración,* 1972-1979, Vol. III, Tomo I, Caracas 1981, p. 407-491; y en Marcos Kaplan (Coordinador), *Petróleo y Desarrollo en México y Venezuela,* UNAM, México 1981, p. 333 a 432; Allan R. Brewer-Carías, "El proceso Jurídico Organizativo de la Industria petrolera Nacionalizada en Venezuela", en *Revista de la Facultad de Ciencias Jurídicas y Políticas* N° 58, Caracas 1976, p. 53-88; Allan R, Brewer-Carías, "El carácter de Petróleos de Venezuela, S.A. como instrumento del Estado en la industria petrolera", *Revista de Derecho Público,* N° 23 (julio-septiembre), Editorial Jurídica Venezolana, Caracas í 985, pp. 77-87.

"6. In order to speed and facilitate the nationalization process of the Oil Industry, the national Executive will incorporate or provide for the incorporation of the enterprises it deems convenient, in order to once extinguished the concessions, will be owned by the enterprises referred to in the second paragraph".

According to this Nationalization Law, the following day of its publication, the President of the Republic, decreed the creation of Petróleos de Venezuela, S.A.[16], as a "State-own enterprise, with the legal form of a *Sociedad Anónima,* in charge of accomplishing and executing the policy that in the matter be dictated by the Ministry of Mines and Hydrocarbons, regarding the assigned activities" dictating its by-laws (articles 1,2*)*. The enterprise was created with a stock represented in shares exclusively owned by the Republic, as sole shareholder, and the by-laws were inscribed in the Commercial Registrar on September 15, 1975.[17]

Therefore, Petróleos de Venezuela, S.A., is and has been a public and State-own enterprise, wholly owned by the Republic of Venezuela (national artificial territorial person), which responds to the policies dictated by the National Executive, and is part of the Public Administration organization, as an entity or State-own enterprise, although with the legal form of a commercial company, that is, private law person.

Regarding the subsidiaries of PDVSA, the intention of the Nationalization Law was also clear in the sense that they were also to be incorporated as commercial companies *(sociedades anónimas),* with their shares wholly owned by PDVSA as the holding company. The initial fourteen subsidiaries of PDVSA that were established as commercial companies owned by PDVSA, latter were merged into four main enterprises (Lagoven, Maraven, Meneven y Corpoven) incorporated in the same manner, as well as it was done with the other subsidiaries later established: Pequiven, Intevep and Bariven. All these enterprises were successively reorganized, particularly in 1997, 1998 and 2002, so that currently, the subsidiaries of PDVSA, that is, the second-tier subsidiary enterprises are PDVSA Petróleos, Palmaren, Bitor, PDVSA Trading, PDVSA Gas.

All these enterprises, as mentioned, are State-own enterprises in terms of the Public Administration Organic Law, subjected to its regulations, and to the control system established in it. In addition, article 7 of the former 1975 Nationalization Law, and articles 29 and 30 of the 2001 Hydrocarbon Law, establishes that the enterprises created according to its provisions, that is, PDVSA and its subsidiaries, "will be subjected to this Law, to its regulations, to their by-laws, to the disposition issued by the National Executive and to the applicable *derecho común"* (common law).

That is why, in the PDVSA by-laws reformed in 1979[18], it was also expressly established that "the enterprise will be subjected to the Organic Law that reserves the State the Industry and Commerce of Hydrocarbons, to its regulations, to its by-laws, to the disposition issued by the National Executive and to the applicable *derecho común"* (Third Clause).

---

16 See Decree N° 3,123. August 30, 1975 *Official Gazette* N° 1.770 *Extra,* August 30 1975.

17 N° 23. Tomo 99-A, Publisher in *Gaceta Municipal del Distrito Federal*, N° 413, September 25, 1975.

18 See Decree N° 250 August 23, 1979 *Official Gazette* N° 31.810, August 30, 1979.

In the case of Decree-Law N° 5.200 an of the Law on Effects of the Migration Process they did not decided any "nationalization," of "reservation" of economic activities to the State because none of those legal instruments reserved any activity to the State, particularly because the oil industry in Venezuela had been reserved to the State since 1975. Decree-Law 5.200 expropriated without compensation rights and assets of private participants in the association's agreements and the Law on Effects of the Migration Process ratified such expropriation without compensation.[19]

B. Reservation

Decree-Law N° 5.200 was not a reservation of the oil sector to the State. Decree-Law N° 5.200 could not have had that effect because the reservation of the oil activities to the State had taken place more than thirty years earlier. The 1975 Organic Nationalization Law reserved the industry and commerce of hydrocarbons (including primary activities of the oil industry) to the State and provided for the expropriation of related assets of private participants in the industry.[20] That reservation was maintained in the 1999 Constitution[21] and the 2001 Organic Hydrocarbons Law.[22]

Nor did Decree-Law N° 5.200 "implement" a reservation because reservations require no implementation. By their terms, reservations have the effect of reserving a particular activity. No further legislative action is required. A reservation may or may not be accompanied by an expropriation of private assets engaged in the now-reserved activity. If it is so accompanied, the expropriation requires the payment of compensation.

---

19 As the expropriation was without compensation, strictly speaking it was a confiscation, which is prohibited by the 1999 Constitution. That is why elsewhere I have called this a process of "statization." See e.g., Allan R. Brewer-Carías, "The 'Statization of the Pre 2001 Primary Hydrocarbons Joint Venture Exploitations: Their Unilateral termination and the Assets' Confiscation of Some of the Former Private Parties" in OGEL and TDM, Vol. 5, Issue 2, *Special Issue on Venezuela: The battle of Contract Sanctity vs. Resource Sovereignty*, ed. By Elizabeth Eljuri, April 2008.) *Available at* www.gasandoil.com/ogel/ ISSN: 1875-418X.

20 *Official Gazette (Extraordinary)* N° 1.769 of August 29, 1975. The 1975 Organic Nationalization Law reserved to the State all matters "related to the exploration of the national territory in search for petroleum, asphalt and any other hydrocarbons; to the exploitation of reservoirs thereof, the manufacturing or upgrading, transportation by special means and storage; internal and external trade of the exploited and upgraded substances, and the works required for their handling [...]" (1975 Organic Nationalization Law, Article 1 (English translation)) Article 5 ordered that these activities be exercised directly by the National Executive or entities owned by it, and authorized private participation through operating agreements or association agreements in certain circumstances. .

21 1999 Constitution, Article 302. ("The State reserves for itself, by means of the corresponding organic law and for reasons of national convenience, the oil activity and other industries, exploitations, services and assets of public interest and strategic character [...])

22 2001 Organic Law of Hydrocarbons in *Official Gazette* N° 37.323 of November 13, 2001, Article 9 (The activities relating to the exploration in search of hydrocarbon reservoirs encompassed in this Decree-Law, to their extraction in natural state, to their initial production, transport and storage, are denominated as primary activities for purposes of this Decree-Law. In accordance with what is provided in article 302 of the Constitution of the Bolivarian Republic of Venezuela, the primary activities indicated, as well as those relating to works required by their management, remain reserved to the State in the terms established in this Decree-Law)

C. Expropriation and Confiscation

As provided in Article 115 of the Constitution, expropriation is the compulsory acquisition of any privately-owned assets, rights, or property by the State, through a specific procedure and with the payment of just compensation, regardless of whether the interests in question are taken individually or as part of a more broadly applicable measure.[23]

An expropriation can be accomplished through an act of general effects like a special statute, as was the case, for instance, with the expropriations effected in the 1970's in connection with the reservation to the State of the iron industry and of the oil industry, and recently in connection with the steel and cement industries. In those cases, the statutes implementing the nationalization declared the reservation and also ordered the expropriation of the interests of the former concessionaries providing for specific rules of procedure.

The 2002 Expropriation Law[24] establishes the general procedure for expropriation and contemplates the possibility of an expropriation decree applying to more than one asset of more than one individual or entity.[25] While this law regulates a procedure for expropriation, Article 4 contemplates that other procedures may be provided by special laws.[26] This possibility includes special laws that expropriate multiple assets of multiple subjects.

Moreover, the Supreme Court of Justice has held that "the institution of expropriation applies not only when the State resorts to it, through the organisms authorized to do so, in compliance with the Law that governs it, but also within its conceptual amplitude, its principles are applied by extension to all the cases of

---

23 The 2002 Expropriation Law (*Official Gazette* N° 37.475 of July 1, 2002) defines expropriation (for the purposes of the law) as: "Article 2 [...] an institution of Public Law, by which the State acts for the benefit of a cause of public utility or social interest, with the purpose of obtaining the compulsory transfer of the right to property or any other right of private parties [*particulares*] to its [the State's] patrimony, through a final judicial decision [*sentencia firme*] and timely payment of just compensation."

24 *Official Gazette* N° 37.475 of July 1, 2002. See text and comments on this law in Allan R. Brewer-Carías, "Introducción General al Régimen de la Expropiación" in Allan R. Brewer-Carías, Gustavo Linares Benzo, Dolores Aguerrevere Valero y Caterina Balasso Tejera, *Ley De Expropiación por Causa de Utilidad Pública o Interés Social*, Colección Textos Legislativos N° 26, 1ª Ed., EJV, Caracas 2002, pp. 7-100. The 2002 Expropriation law replaced the 1947 Law on Expropriation without altering its fundamental rules. *Official Gazette* N° 22.458 of November 6, 1947. For general comments on this law, see *generally* Allan R. Brewer-Carías, Enrique Pérez Olivares, Tomás Polanco e Hildegard Rondón de Sansó, "Expropriation in Venezuela" in A. Lowenfeld (ed.), *Expropriation in the America A. Comparative Legal Study*, New York, 1971, pp. 199-240. For the text of the 1947 law and administrative doctrine and judicial case law regarding expropriation, up to 1965 *see generally* Allan R. Brewer-Carías, *La Expropiación por Causa de Utilidad Pública o Interés Social (Jurisprudencia, Doctrina, Administrativa, Legislación),* Colección de Publicaciones del Instituto de Derecho Público, Vol. 2, Facultad de Derecho, Universidad Central de Venezuela, Caracas, 1966, pp. 416 ff. For case law on the subject up to 1975, see *generally* Allan R. Brewer-Carías, *Jurisprudencia de la Corte Suprema 1930-1974 y Estudios de Derecho Administrativo,* Tomo VI: *La Propiedad y la Expropiación por Causa de Utilidad Pública e Interés Social*, Ediciones del Instituto de Derecho Público, Facultad de Derecho, Universidad Central de Venezuela, Caracas 1979, pp. 690 ff.

25 2002 Expropriation Law, Articles 5 and 6.

26 2002 Expropriation Law, Article 4.

deprivation of private property, or of patrimonial diminution, for reasons of public utility or public interest."[27]

All property, rights, and assets may be subject to lawful expropriation and are protected from unlawful expropriation under Venezuelan law. This follows from Article 115 of the Constitution, which provides the constitutional guaranty of the right to property and refers to the conditions for the expropriation of "any type of assets,"[28] and is also reflected in Article 2 of the 2002 Expropriation Law which refers to the compulsory transfer of the "right to property or any other right of private parties."[29] One of the important changes introduced in the 1999 Constitution and in the 2002 Expropriation Law was precisely to clarify that expropriation, as a compulsory means for the State to acquire assets, can refer not only to "the right to property" (*derecho de propiedad*) but also to "any other right" of private parties (*algún otro derecho de los particulares*) (Article 2), or to "assets of any nature" (*bienes de cualquier naturaleza*) (Article 7).[30] Accordingly, expropriation is related to the constitutional guaranty of the right to property, any other rights or assets of any nature, which cannot be compulsorily taken by the State except through a judicial procedure (juridical guaranty) and by means of just compensation (patrimonial or economic guaranty). Expropriation without compensation is "confiscation" and is unconstitutional except in limited circumstances.[31]

---

27 See Supreme Court of Justice, Politico-Administrative Chamber, Decision of October 3, 1990 (Case: Inmobiliaria Cumboto, C.A.) in *Jurisprudencia Ramírez & Garay*, CXIV, Caracas 1990, pp. 551-552.

28 1999 Constitution, Article 115 ("The right to property is guaranteed [...] Only by reason of public utility [*utilidad pública*] or social interest, by means of a final judicial decision [*sentencia firme*] and with the prompt payment of just compensation, may the expropriation of any type of assets be declared." (English translation (emphasis added).) This guaranty has been established in all the prior Constitutions and is also incorporated in Article 547 of the Civil Code. Venezuelan Civil Code, Article 547 ("Nobody can be obliged to assign his property, or to allow others to use it, except by cause of public or social utility, through a contradictory judicial process and prior compensation. Rules related to expropriation for reason of public or social utility shall be determined by special laws.")

29 2002 Expropriation Law, Article 2.

30 2002 Expropriation Law, Article 7. Eduardo García de Enterría and Tomás Ramón Fernández have said that "The legal regime of expropriation constitutes an ample power of sacrifice in favor of the Administration: every patrimonial juridical situation of any nature (*in rem*, *in personam*, public, private) may be in principle (as long as the requirements of execution and cause that we will refer to later are complied with) sacrificed by the Administration Eduardo García de Enterría and Tomás Ramón Fernández, *Curso de Derecho Administrativo*. Tomo II, Segunda Edición, Editorial Civitas, Madrid 1993, pp. 228-230.

31 Any taking of private property, rights or assets by the State, that is, any extinction of private individual rights by the State without following the expropriation procedures and requirements or the other means that the State has to acquire property (requisition, seizure, reversion, authorized confiscation) is considered a "confiscation" in the Venezuelan system, which is prohibited in the Constitution. Confiscation has been traditionally prohibited in Venezuela, and it is only allowed as a sanction as a consequence of a criminal conviction (Article 116). Román Duque Corredor states that "[t]he deprivation of property of those that hold it as owners, even if there is public utility, but without complying with these procedural and patrimonial guarantees to occupy private assets, may not be qualified as expropriations, but as arbitrary or *de-facto* expropriations, that if in addition, there is no recognition of the owners' right to receive an indemnification for the value of the occupied assets and for the damages caused by the occupation, they constitute a confiscation that

Any "limitations," "contributions, restrictions and obligations" on property, rights, or assets become an expropriation of such interests when they deprive the owner of the essence of his asset or where such regulations annihilate the property, right, or asset in question. For example, based on Articles 115 and 116 of the Constitution, the Constitutional Chamber of the Supreme Tribunal has stated that "such limits must be established on the basis of a legal text, as long as said restrictions do not constitute an absolute or irrational impairment of such property right. That is, impeding the patrimonial capacity of the individuals in such way that it eventually extinguishes it."[32] Moreover, the Supreme Court has explained that:

> "*Article 99* of the Constitution establishes the guaranty of the right to property. [...] the limitation imposed on that right cannot represent an impairment that implies an absorption of its attributions to the extent that it eliminates it. [...] This is, the right to property may be limited, restricted with respect to most of its content, attributions and scope, but this cannot exceed the limit –it is emphasized– by virtue of which such right is left completely empty, there is a central core of that right that is not susceptible of being impaired by the legislator, since if this were so, we would find *ourselves* before another legal institution (for example expropriation)."[33]

And with regards to the prohibition of confiscation, the Court has explained that:

> *"[...] the prohibition of confiscation is related to the principle of reasonability that must guide the adjustment between the actions of the State and the impact on the legal sphere of those subject to the law, for which care must be taken that the activity does not formally or substantially reach the confiscation of the assets of the person, which occurs with the total dispossession of the assets or their equivalent."*[34]

---

implies the violation of the constitutional guaranty of the right to property. See Román Duque Corredor, *Procesos sobre la Propiedad y la Posesión*, Caracas 2009, pp. 451-452.

32 Supreme Tribunal of Justice, Constitutional Chamber, Decision N° 3003 of October 14, 2005 (Exp. 04-2538)

33 See Supreme Court of Justice, Decision of April 29, 1997 in *Revista de Derecho Público,* N° 69-70, Editorial Jurídica Venezolana, Caracas 1997, pp. 391-392 (English translation).] See also, Decision of March 9, 1978 (quoted in Decision N° 108 of February 8, 1996) in *Revista de Derecho Público* N° 65-66, Editorial Jurídica Venezolana, Caracas 1996, p. 439 ("[...] article 99 of the Constitution sets forth limits and restrictions to the right to property but does not extinguish it. The extinction of such right, only proceeds through the means of expropriation or exceptionally through confiscation (articles 101 and 250 of the Constitution)."

34 Supreme Tribunal of Justice, Constitutional Chamber, Decision N° 2152 of November 14, 2007 in *Revista de Derecho Público* N° 112, Editorial Jurídica Venezolana, Caracas 2007, pp. 519 ff (English translation).]

II. PRINCIPLES OF THE EXPROPRIATION PROCEDURE

1. The constitutional guarantee of the right to property

As aforementioned, according to Article 115 of the Venezuelan Constitution, as well as Article 1 of the 2002 Expropriation Law[35], expropriation is an "extraordinary means to acquire property" for the State, "subject by the legislator to the compliance of specific formalities,"[36] in order to ensure the compulsory transfer of private property -or of any other private right- to a public entity by means of a judicial decision and the prompt payment of just compensation.

Therefore, essentially the provision on expropriation is a constitutional guarantee of the right to property that, as stated by the Venezuelan Supreme Court in 1965, "is developed through a special procedure, being its *essential purpose to achieve the transfer of property of the expropriated good*" from private hands to the State by means of the payment of just compensation.[37] That is why the Supreme Court has stated that "any *expropriation supposes just compensation*;" being the function of the expropriation court "limited to declaring the need for the State to acquire the whole or part of the property or any other right; to establish the value of the expropriated good, and assure its payment to the expropriated party."[38]

The 2002 Expropriation Law applies to all expropriations in Venezuela, except where a specific law or Treaty overrides some or all of its provisions, being its purpose to protect private property rights by requiring a detailed procedure for the State to take possession of the expropriated assets, which are not to be transferred to the State until compensation is paid.

For such purpose, the expropriation procedure involving the participation of all Branches of Government has five parts:

First, through a statute issued by the National Assembly, specific activities or assets have to be declared to be considered of public purpose or social interest (*utilidad pública o interés social*) (Articles 7.1 and 13). Also, article 14 of the

---

35 *Official Gazette* N° 37.475 of July 1, 2002. See text and comments on this law in Allan R. Brewer-Carías, "Introducción General al Régimen de la Expropiación" in Allan R. Brewer-Carías, Gustavo Linares Benzo, Dolores Aguerrevere Valero y Caterina Balasso Tejera, *Ley De Expropiación por Causa de Utilidad Pública o Interés Social*, Colección Textos Legislativos N° 26, 1ª Ed., EJV, Caracas 2002, pp. 7-100.

36 See decision of the Federal and Cassation Court, of October 29, 1948, in *Compilación Legislativa 1948-1949*, Anuario 1948, p, 789. See also in Allan R. Brewer-Carías, *Jurisprudencia de la Corte Suprema 1930-1974 y Estudios de Derecho Administrativo, Volume VI, La Propiedad y la Expropiación por causa de utilidad pública e interés social*, Ediciones del Instituto de Derecho Público, Facultad de Derecho, Universidad Central de Venezuela, Caracas 1979, pp. 394-395) (*Jurisprudencia de la Corte Suprema...*).

37 See decision of the Politico Administrative Chamber of the Supreme Court of Justice of February 24, 1965, in *Official Gazette* N° 27676 of 24 February 1965, p. 205.971, Also in *Jurisprudencia de la Corte Suprema..., cit,* pp. 348 – 350.

38 See decision Politico Administrative Chamber, Supreme Court of Justice, of June10, 1968, in *Gaceta Forense* N° 60, 1968, pp. 173-174 (p. 374). In the same sense see decision Politico Administrative Chamber, Supreme Court of Justice, of April 29, 1969, in *Gaceta Forense* N° 64, 1969, pp. 133-134. See also in *Jurisprudencia de la Corte Suprema..., cit.,* pp. 374 and. 427.

Expropriation Law contains a general declaration of public purpose or social interest regarding a wide list of activities or assets.

Second, once the Executive Power considers that a specific good must be expropriated in order to accomplish some of the said activities, it must issue and publish in the *Official Gazette* a decree declaring the need to acquire specific assets (*i.e.*, land) to develop those precise activities previously declared of public interest or social purpose (Article 7.2). This Decree has the main purpose of identifying the good or asset to be expropriated. It can also contain the available information regarding the owner, but any specification on such matter is not binding regarding the final determination of the expropriated party."

Third, the Expropriating Entity must commence an amicable settlement procedure conducted under Venezuelan administrative law in order to acquire the affected property. For such purpose, the Expropriating Entity must publish a newspaper Notice convening all those who consider themselves as having property or possession rights over the expropriated asset, or in general, who claim to have any sort of right over the affected assets (Article 22).

Fourth, if no amicable agreement is reached, the Expropriating Entity must commence a judicial expropriation process, in which, again, the expropriation court must summon all those presumptive owners, possessors, leasers, creditors and in general, all those having any right over the expropriated assets (Article 26). The procedure has the purpose for the court to declare the need of the State to acquire the property or any other right determining those with real property to be compensated (Article 34), as well as the terms, conditions and compensation for the expropriation (Articles 34-44), and provide for its payment (Article 45).

Fifth, during the judicial procedure, the Expropriating Entity may request the court, in urgent cases, to authorize the previous or "anticipatory occupation" of the expropriated assets before concluding the judicial process, through a specific procedure that requires for the court to assure the evaluation of the expropriating assets through a Commission with the participation of the expropriated party, and the payment of the compensation in an indirect way by depositing the amount before the expropriation court. Only in this way can the court allow the expropriating entity to take possession of the expropriated assets, only after posting the value of those assets with the court (Article 56). It is at the sole discretion of the expropriated party to decide to accept such amount deposit in the court as the definitive compensation for the expropriation.

Finally, even in cases of anticipatory occupation, only after payment of the just compensation ordered by the court, the Expropriating Entity may take definitive possession of the expropriated property (Article 45). It is only with the payment of the compensation to the expropriated party, that the transfer of the ownership of the expropriated assets from private hands to the State is materialized and effective (Article 46). Up to that moment, even if the assets have been previously occupied, they remain on the property of their owners.

According to these provisions, the most significant guarantee of private property rights established in the Constitution and according to the expropriation procedure provided in the Expropriation Law, is that the State may not occupy or take over private property before the expropriated assets have been valued by the Evaluation Commission and the State has paid just compensation in cash directly to the expropriated party, on indirectly by the expropriating entity as a deposit of the amount established in the anticipatory occupation procedure in the court.

In any case, as the expropriated party remains owner of the assets until the compensation is paid, during the judicial expropriation process, the Expropriation Law expressly authorizes the possibility for the owner of the affected assets to freely sell the affected assets, providing that any transfers of ownership of those affected assets, by any mean, will not suspend the judicial process. In such cases, the new owner will substitute the previous owner in all his rights and obligations (Article 10), being the compensation to be paid to the expropriated party the guaranty to his rights.

2. The judicial process of expropriation

A. Parties Which May Participate in Expropriation Procedure

After initiated the judicial procedure for the expropriation of private assets, Article 26 of the Expropriation Law mandates that the court publish an order summoning parties with an interest in the property being expropriated to participate in the judicial expropriation proceeding. Interested parties include the "alleged owners, holders, tenants, creditors and, in general, anyone who *might have any rights over the asset* concerned." This includes third parties, even those unknown at the time of the summons, which allegedly possess rights regarding the object of the expropriation.[39]

Consequently, in order for a third party to participate in the judicial expropriation proceeding, it must file before the court "proof of his right regarding the object of the expropriation, a requirement without which he cannot file any claim."[40] This documentary proof of a claim, if needed, might first need to be obtained from the courts of ordinary civil jurisdiction; in such cases, only after presenting its case and obtaining such proof from the general civil courts may a third party present a claim

39 This concept makes the most sense with respect to real property, which is the basis upon which the Expropriation Law was originally drafted. See decision of the Politico-Administrative Chamber, Supreme Court of Justice, June 10, 1963, in *Gaceta Forense* N° 40, 1963, pp. 340-343. See also in *Jurisprudencia de la Corte Suprema..., cit.*, pp. 422, 423. The Court has decided that parties in the expropriation procedure are those mentioned in the request of expropriation, as well as all those that attend the procedure, alleging rights with regard to the expropriated assets.In a particular expropriation procedure, the Supreme Court argued that "as it is established that in the present case the parties were only the expropriating entity (*Compañía Anónima Centro Simón Bolívar C.A.*) and the company Nelson SA that is the expropriated person, the Municipality of the Federal District does not have standing in order to demand the nullity and reposition of the procedure of expropriation." See decision of the Politico-Administrative Chamber, Supreme Court of Justice, of March 12, 1970, in *Gaceta Forense* N° 67, 1970, pp. 253-254 Also see in *Jurisprudencia de la Corte Suprema..., cit.*, p. 389.

40 See decision of the Politico-Administrative Chamber, Supreme Court of Justice, June 10, 1963, in *Gaceta Forense* N° 40, 1963, pp. 340-348. See also in *Jurisprudencia de la Corte Suprema..., cit.* p. 422.

in the judicial expropriation proceeding.[41] The court considering the expropriation claim must then examine the claim and, if applicable, admit it.[42]

B. Matters Excluded from the Jurisdiction of the Expropriating Court

The Supreme Court of Justice has emphasized that the scope of the jurisdiction of the expropriation courts is limited. The expropriating court "can only decide on matters related to the expropriation in itself, without being able to decide in the expropriation proceeding questions that are ruled by general or specific provisions of the jurisdiction of the first instance courts.[43] Under the Expropriation Law, expropriated parties may only oppose the expropriation on two grounds:[44] (a) illegality (violation of law), or (b) requesting total, rather than partial, expropriation where partial expropriation would make the expropriated land useless or improper for the use to which it is devoted (Article 30).[45]

Apart from addressing these claims, the expropriating court has no jurisdiction to decide any other controversies among individuals, or between a third party and the expropriated party, even when they are related to the expropriated assets.[46]

---

41 See decision of the Politico-Administrative Chamber, Supreme Court of Justice, April 29, 1969, in *Gaceta Forense* N° 64, 1969, pp. 133-134. See also in *Jurisprudencia de la Corte Suprem..., cit.* p. 428)

42 See decision of the Politico-Administrative Chamber, Supreme Court of Justice, April 26, 1965, *Official Gazette* N° 27.738.17 May 1965, p. 206.468. See also in *Jurisprudencia de la Corte Suprema..., cit.*, p. 426; adn decision of the Federal and Cassation Court, of February 28, 1935, in *Memoria 1936*, pp. 172-175. See also in *Jurisprudencia de la Corte Suprema..., cit.*, pp. 396-397:

43 See decision of the Federal and Cassation Court, Federal Chamber, of February 1, 1947, in *Memoria 1947*, pp. 122-124. See also in *Jurisprudencia de la Corte Suprema..., cit.*, p. 544.

44 It is not within the expropriation court's competence to determine who is the owner or has a right regarding the expropriated property. See decision of the Politico-Administrative Chamber, Supreme Court of Justice, March 30, 1960, in *Gaceta Forense* N° 27, 1968, p. 168. See also in *Jurisprudencia de la Corte Suprema..., cit.*, pp. 420- 421.

45 As was very clearly decided by the Supreme Court, according to the special provisions that are applicable to expropriation proceedings, in addition to decisions on the need to expropriate determined assets, on their evaluation and on the payment of compensation, "the expropriation courts can only decide the opposition to the expropriation claim based on violation of the law, or on the fact that the expropriation must be total, because the partial expropriation makes the land useless or makes it improper for its given use; the expropriation courts are not able to decide other claims filed by interested persons related with property rights [...] regarding the assets being expropriated." See decision of the Politico-Administrative Chamber, Supreme Court of Justice, of April 24, 1963, in *Gaceta Forense* N° 40, 1963, p. 153. See also in *Jurisprudencia de la Corte Suprema..., cit*, p. 421. Consequently, the Supreme Court jurisprudence since 1947 has held that one must not mix the opposition to the claim for expropriation, which can only be brought by parties claiming rights to the expropriated assets, "with the ordinary procedural means that such persons have in order to obtain the judicial declaration of their rights or credits and their payment. The first is part of the expropriation proceeding, the second are to be decided between the expropriated party and its creditors, without intervention of the expropriating entity that has only to deposit the price over which claims can be filed, without interruption of the expropriating proceeding." See decision of the Federal and Cassation Court, Federal Chamber, February 1, 1946, in *Memoria* 1947, pp. 122-124. See also in *Jurisprudencia de la Corte Suprema, cit.*, p. 544.

46 For instance, the Supreme Court has ruled that privilege creditors as mortgage creditors cannot pretend that "the exceptional judicial competence on expropriation matters could reach the point to decide, in the same process, on the existence, liquidity, and maturity of the respective credits, on which matters decisions from the courts of first instance must be taken." See decision

Consequently, even in such cases the expropriating court may not rule on rights or controversies related to the expropriated property because to do so would represent an improper invasion of the jurisdiction of other courts.[47] As pointed out by the Supreme Court, allowing individuals to use this expropriation procedure to resolve judicial claims involving the parties to a judicial expropriation proceeding (as opposed to the expropriated assets), instead of seeking resolution through general civil courts, would "pervert" the expropriation, an institution that is founded on the subordination of individual interests to the collective interest.[48]

According to the Supreme Court: "The Law does not prevent the filing of actions on property matters regarding the assets or land that has been expropriated, but those actions must be filed before ordinary courts ... without interrupting the expropriation proceeding of affecting its effects."[49] That is, any matter regarding property rights and ancillary matters related to the expropriated assets must be resolved and decided by the ordinary civil courts that are the only courts with jurisdiction to examine claims relating to property[50] and the only courts competent to rule on those property rights.[51]

As a result, judicial expropriation proceedings are not the exclusive, or even appropriate, forum for resolution of such conflicts or rights. Any claim that a third party may have against the "expropriated party" with respect to the expropriated assets must first be filed before the ordinary commercial or civil courts, not the judicial proceedings initiated under Article 22 of the Expropriation Law.[52] Only

---

of the Federal and Cassation Court, Federal Chamber, February 1, 1947, *Memoria 1947,* pp. 122-124. See also in *Jurisprudencia de la Corte Suprema...*, p. 544.

47 In other words, as pointed out by the Supreme Court, "it is not allowed for the expropriating court to decide on matters different to those established in the Law," for which there exist different procedures and tribunals. See decision of the Politico-Administrative Chamber, Supreme Court of Justice, April 26, 1965, in *Official Gazette* N° 27.738.17 May 1965, p. 206.468. See also in *Jurisprudencia de la Corte Suprema..., cit.,* pp. 425-426. See also decisions of the Politico-Administrative Chamber, Supreme Court of Justice, of December 12, 1963, *Official Gazette* N° 905 Extra. 4 May 1963, pp. 26-27. See also in *Jurisprudencia de la Corte Suprema..., cit.,* p. 425; of February 1, 1967, in *Gaceta Forense* N° 55, 1968, pp. 55-56; of January 23, 1969, in *Gaceta Forense* N° 63, 1969, p. 56; of June 11, 1969, in *Gaceta Forense* N° 64, 1969, pp. 299; and of April 24, 1973, in *Official Gazette* N° 16135 Extra, 26 September 1973, p. 33. See also these decisions in *Jurisprudencia de la Corte Suprema..., cit.,* pp. 426, 427, 428, 429.

48 See decision of the Politico-Administrative Chamber, Supreme Court of Justice, of June 16, 1963, in *Gaceta Forense* N° 40, 1963, pp. 340-343. See also in *Jurisprudencia de la Corte Suprema... cit,* pp. 424.

49 Decision of the Politico-Administrative Chamber, Supreme Court of Justice, 30 March 1960, in *Gaceta Forense* N° 27, 1968, pp. 168. See also in *Jurisprudencia de la Corte Suprema..., cit.,* p. 421

50 See decision of the Politico-Administrative Chamber, Supreme Court of Justice, of June 10, 1968, in *Gaceta Forense* N° 60, 1968, pp. 173-174. See also in *Jurisprudencia de la Corte Suprema..., cit.,* p. 374

51 See decision of the Politico-Administrative Chamber, Supreme Court of Justice, June 10, 1963, in *Gaceta Forense* N° 40, 1963, pp. 340-348. See also in *Jurisprudencia de la Corte Suprema..., cit.,* p. 422.

52 Decision of the Politico-Administrative Chamber, Supreme Court of Justice, June 16, 1963, in *Gaceta Forense* N° 40, 1963, pp. 340-343. See also in *Jurisprudencia de la Corte Suprema..., cit.,* p. 424.

after their rights have been definitively proven in the civil ordinary courts, which have exclusive competence over such claims,[53] may third parties seek compensation only regarding the amount due to the expropriated party to be paid in the judicial expropriation proceedings (Article 11, Expropriation Law).

2. Limitations on Third Party Participation in Expropriation Proceedings and the Exclusion of any "*Tercería*" Claim

The aforementioned has a direct procedural consequence for judicial expropriation proceedings, limiting any third-party intervention to those individuals which can claim rights regarding the expropriated assets. Such parties must provide proof of these rights, obtained, if necessary, through judgments of the ordinary civil courts, before they may enforce their sole right in the expropriation proceeding: to be paid for these recognized rights with part of the amount to be paid to the expropriated party as compensation for the expropriated assets, once the amount is entrusted with the court.

The Supreme Court has declared that the expropriation court cannot rule on third party property rights or other rights because: (*a*) those third parties are participating in the procedure only as a result of the judge's public summons (*edicto*); (*b*) as such, those third parties have argued problems regarding assets that are the object of the expropriation procedure; (*c*) addressing such claims is outside the scope of the expropriation proceeding, which is a special action and should not be mixed in with ordinary civil matters; and (*d*) third parties can only claim their rights (as a preferred creditor) regarding the expropriated assets on the amount to be paid as compensation to the expropriated party. This compensation is entrusted with the court (Article 45, Expropriation Law) to guarantee their rights.[54]

The Supreme Court has acknowledged that the expropriation procedure established in the Expropriation Law characterized by its celerity, does not allow any claim on "*demanda en tercería.*"[55] As a matter of principle, therefore, it is not procedurally proper for a party to file an action against the expropriated party in an expropriation proceeding, including a "*demanda en tercería.*" As stated by the Supreme Court, any other procedure would mean inserting a procedural institution for the resolution of private interests into the public law structure of the expropriation procedure.[56]

---

53 Decision of the Politico-Administrative Chamber, Supreme Court of Justice, June `6, 1963, in *Gaceta Forense* N° 40, 1963, pp. 340-343. See also in *Jurisprudencia de la Corte Suprema..., cit.,* p. 423.

54 Decision of the Politico-Administrative Chamber, Supreme Court of Justice, of December 3, 1969, in *Official Gazette* N° 1447, December 15, 1969, p. 6. See also in *Jurisprudencia de la Corte Suprema..., cit.,* p. 429). See *also* Expropriation Law, Article 45

55 See decision of the Politico-Administrative Chamber, Supreme Court of Justice, January 21, 1963, in *Gaceta Forense* N° 39, 1963, p. 31. See also in *Jurisprudencia de la Corte Suprema..., cit.,* p. 431.

56 See Decision of the Federal and Cassation Court, Federal Chamber, of February 1, 1946, in *Memoria 1947* pp, 122-124 (p. 545). Similarly: Decision of the Federal and Cassation Court, February 1, 1947, *Actuaciones 1948*, p. 124. See also in *Jurisprudencia de la Corte Suprema..., cit.,* p. 556.

3. The Anticipatory Occupation of the Expropriated Assets

A. The Legal Provisions concerning the "Anticipatory Occupation"

As previously mentioned, pursuant to the Expropriation Law, the Expropriating Entity may only take possession of the expropriated assets before the conclusion of the expropriation procedure and paying the definitive due compensation, in urgent cases, through an "anticipatory occupation" procedure that must be followed before the competent court. Even then, it may only take possession after indirectly paying the compensation to the expropriated party by posting the value of the assets to be expropriated with the court (Article 56) – such value to be determined by the Evaluation Commission in the context of a judicial proceeding.

To facilitate public purposed and the prompt execution of public policy motivating the expropriation, when a transfer of private property is considered *indispensable and urgent*, and no amicable agreement has been reached with the owner, the Expropriation Law provides that the State may request the anticipatory occupation of the expropriated assets (*ocupación previa*) through a judicial expropriation proceeding.[57] Such an anticipatory occupation that can only occur within a judicial expropriation procedure, requires two preconditions: (i) "the valuation of the expropriated asset by an Evaluation Commission; and [(ii)] the entrusting in the court of an amount equivalent to such just valuation."[58]

In particular, the procedure applicable to an "anticipatory occupation" are set forth in Article 56 of the Expropriation Law,[59] according to which, such anticipatory occupation is only available where: (i) the public purpose or social interest justifying the expropriation is among those included in Article 14 of the Expropriation Law; (ii) the Executive authority performing the expropriation has qualified it as "urgent," that is "pressing," or "compelling"[60]; (iii) the Evaluation Commission established in Article 19 has, at the request of the Expropriating Entity, evaluated the assets and established the amount of the compensation; (iv) the anticipatory occupation has been requested before the expropriation court by the expropriating entity, after the expropriation claim has been filed; (v) the expropriating entity has deposited the amount of the compensation, as determined by the Evaluation Commission, with the expropriation court; (vi) the expropriation court has previously notified the

57 The anticipatory occupation regime (*ocupación previa*) was established "by the legislator as a system of procedural guaranties in order to safeguard the interests or rights that could be affected by such measure. See decision of the Politico-Administrative Chamber, Supreme Court of Justice, of May 12, 1969, in *Gaceta Forense* N° 64, 1969, pp. 157-159 (See also in *Jurisprudencia de la Corte Suprema..., cit.*, p. 366.

58 Decision of the Politico-Administrative Chamber, Supreme Court of Justice, of May 12, 1969, in *Gaceta Forense* N° 64, 1969, pp. 162-164. See also in *Jurisprudencia de la Corte Suprema..., cit.*, p. 362.

59 See decision of the Politico-Administrative Chamber, Supreme Court of Justice, of February 1, 1962, in *Gaceta Forense* N° 35, 1963, pp. 70-72. See also in *Jurisprudencia de la Corte Suprema..., cit.*, pp. 358-359

60 "[...] urgency that is, precisely, what justifies and explains the anticipated occupation procedure." See decision of the Politico-Administrative Chamber, Supreme Court of Justice, of February 15, 1968, in *Gaceta Forense* N° 59, 1968, p. 113. See also in *Jurisprudencia de la Corte Suprema..., cit.*, p. 373.

expropriated party of the amount posted in court according to Article 27, which, if no opposition is made, can be accepted by the expropriated party; and (vi) after such notification, the expropriation court formally decrees or authorizes the anticipatory occupation of the expropriated assets.

In cases of anticipatory occupation, the amount of compensation determined by the Evaluation Commission and deposited with the court is an indirect payment that can be accepted by the expropriated party. And while the amount of compensation made for such purpose cannot be challenged by any of the parties, the expropriated party can always accept the amount deposited for the anticipatory occupation as the just compensation amount for the expropriation of its assets On the other hand, if the amount deposit is not accepted as the payment of the compensation, instead, it is assessed as an "advanced deposit of the probable amount"[61] to be determined at the end of the judicial procedure, in order to permit the anticipatory occupation under urgent circumstances, while, at the same time, providing some assurance to the expropriated party for the payment of just compensation. As explained by the Supreme Court, if the amount is not accepted by the expropriated party, it is "a guarantee for the expropriated party and not the definitive just valuation of the assets."[62] Finally, if the expropriation eventually is not materialized by any reason and the occupied assets are given back to the expropriated party, the amount of the compensation deposit in the court, will serve as a guarantee for damages caused by the occupation.

The consequence of the aforementioned is that the final expropriation of private property by the State always requires the prior direct or indirect payment of just compensation in cash. The Supreme Court has emphasized the constitutional guarantee of private property rights: "The Constitution requires that expropriation cannot be made without previous payment of the corresponding compensation, combining in that way the public interest with the right to property."[63] Consequently, as the same Supreme Court has affirmed: "The payment of the compensation being, from the legal point of view, the fact that determines the transfer of the property, it is when such compensation takes place that the expropriation is perfected." The Court also clarified that the judicial decision in the expropriation proceeding is merely declarative – compensation is the essential prerequisite for expropriation.[64]

61 Decision of the Politico-Administrative Chamber, Supreme Court of Justice, of November 21, 1961, in *Gaceta Forense* N° 34, 1961, pp. 101-102. See also in *Jurisprudencia de la Corte Suprema..., cit.,* p. 360).

62 See decision of the Politico-Administrative Chamber, Supreme Court of Justice, January 30, 1968, in *Gaceta Forense* N° 59, 1968, p. 71. See also in *Jurisprudencia de la Corte Suprema..., cit.,* p. 373. In the same sense: Decision of the Politico-Administrative Chamber, Supreme Court of Justice, of February 15, 1968, in *Gaceta Forense* N° 59, 1968, p. 113. See also in *Jurisprudencia de la Corte Suprema..., cit.,* p. 373.

63 Decision of the Federal and Cassation Court, Federal Chamber, of April 12, 1950, in *Gaceta Forense* N° 4, 1950, pp. 135-136. See also in *Jurisprudencia de la Corte Suprema..., cit.,* p. 542)

64 "The judicial decision issued in the expropriation proceeding is no more than declarative, being the expropriation only materialized when the essential condition of 'previous compensation' imposed in the constitutional provision on the matter is fulfilled." See decision of the Federal and Cassation Court, Federal Chamber, of May 9, 1949, in *Gaceta Forense* N° 2, 1949, pp. 27-28. See also in *Jurisprudencia de la Corte Suprema..., cit.,* p. 550.

B. The unconstitutionality application in expropriation procedures, of statutes authorizing "administrative occupation" of private property in administrative procedures, in order to avoid complying with the provisions of the Expropriation Law

Since 2008, a series of new statues has been passed establishing "special" provisions for the administrative occupation of assets in administrative procedures developed in order to persecute legal infractions, which have been illegally applied in order to occupy expropriated goods and assets used or produced in specific industries or enterprises, but without initiating a judicial expropriating procedure and without guaranteeing for such occupations the previous deposit of the compensation in a court of justice as required in the Expropriation Law (Article 56). One of such statues was the Law for the Defense of Persons regarding the Access to Goods and Services (*Law for the Defense of Persons*),[65] recently substituted by the Organic Law on Just Prices (2014). [66]

These statutes have the specific purpose of assuring the defense, protection and safeguard of individual and collective rights to have access to goods and services generally related to the satisfaction of primary needs, and mainly related to the rights to life and to health (Article 1). For this reason, according to Article 3 of the Law, the following activities are subject to its provisions: (i) agreements with suppliers of goods and services related to the letting of goods, service contracts and any other business of economic interest; and (ii) a monopoly, speculation, boycott or other act that affects food or goods that have been declared as required for the satisfaction of primary needs,[67] by any person in the distribution, production and consumption chain.[68]

With regard to these activities, Article 6 of the Law declares of public purpose and social interest all the goods necessary to accomplish activities of production, manufacture, import, gathering, transport, distribution and trade of goods and services that are regulated in the statute, that is, those goods and services related to the satisfaction of primary needs, and mainly related to the rights to life and to health. In addition, the Law grants power to the Administration to open administrative procedure in order to assure the compliance of the Law, allowing the Administration to apply specific administrative measures such as the occupation of private property in cases of urgency in order to assure the access of the population to the protected goods (art. 111, 112).

The Law for the Defense of Persons, also set forth in Article 6 (article 7 of the Organic Law on Just Prices), for the possibility of the State to expropriate the assets of persons that have committed some of the conduct sanctioned in the Law (speculation, boycott, cornering), in a procedure that must be initiated in parallel to the administrative procedure for the purpose of applying the corresponding sanctions.

---

65 Decree N° 8,133, published in *Official Gazette* N° 39,644 on 29 March 2011; *Ley para la Defensa de las Personas en el Acceso a los Bienes y Servicios* (Law for the Defense of Persons regarding the Access to Goods and Services).

66 Decree N° 1.467, published in *Official Gazette* N° 6.156 Extra. Of November 19, 2014; *Ley Orgánica de Precios Justos* (Organic Law on Just Prices).

67 Article 5, Law for the Defense of Persons, Article 5.

68 Article 3, Law for the Defense of Persons, Article 3

Both procedures, the administrative one for assuring the sanctioning of illegal conducts, and the judicial expropriation one to assure the expropriation of the certain assets, have different purposes and cannot be mixed up. Nonetheless, in an illegal way, in many cases the Administration has apply for the occupation of expropriated assets, the provisions of the Law for the Defense of Persons, in a way contrary to the private property rights guaranteed under the Constitution and the Expropriation Law. Through this irregular action, the State has "occupied and assumed the temporary operation or seizure of the assets," pending the expropriation proceeding, through the immediate possession, operation, administration and use of the industry, building, installations, transport, distribution and services by the expropriating entity, provided in the Law for the Defense of Persons (arts. 6, 112.2), which can only be applied "in order to guarantee the provision of goods and services to the population (*colectividad*)" and not just for expropriation purposes

That is, Article 111 of the Law for the Defense of Persons provided that provisional measures of occupation are available only in situations of danger or harm to the individual, or where collective interests in access to goods and services are at stake, especially those goods and services that are "*inherent to the rights to life, to health and to dwelling.*"[69] The Law in addition, provided that compensation for expropriations pursuant to Article 6 may be reduced in order to pay fines and damages owed to the State by the expropriated party, [70] which can be considered contrary to article 115 of the Constitution

On the other hand, the attempt to apply this law to expropriate any assets that have no relation with the goods and assets regulated in the Law, which are those directed to satisfy basic necessities of the population or collectivity, is also unlawful and unconstitutional because it contradicts the Constitutional guarantee to private property.[71]

5. The Unconstitutional Judicial Occupation of expropriated assets by means of civil procedures precautionary measures

Being established the specific procedure for the anticipatory occupation of the expropriated assets in the Expropriation Law, guarantying the payment of the just compensation to the expropriated party by means of it deposit in the expropriation court, it can be considered unlawful if in request for expropriation the expropriating party request the expropriation court to authorize the occupation of the expropriated assets by means of a "precautionary provisional measure" of occupation (*medida cautelar de ocupación)* (injunction to occupy), issued according to Article 589 of the Civil Procedural Code, without the previous payment or deposit of the compensation.

The procedure described in Articles 585-589 of the Civil Procedural Code, contrary to what is required by the applicable Expropriation Law does not require the entity seeking the judicial occupation of certain assets, to previously deposit the

69 Article 111, Law for the Defense of Persons,

70 Article 6, for the Defense of Persons.

71 See *also* Antonio Canova González, Luis Alfonso Herrera Orellana, Karina Anzola Spadano, *¿Expropiaciones o vías de hecho? (La derogación continuada del derecho fundamental de propiedad en la Venezuela actual),* Funeda, Caracas, 2009, p. 107

amount of the compensation. To grant such judicial measure, allowing the expropriating entity to take possession of the expropriated asset, without imposing the prior obligation to pay compensation for the expropriation in cash, is contrary to Article 115 of the Constitution and to the provisions of the Expropriation Law. In particular, it would violate article 56 of the Expropriation Law concerning the anticipatory occupation of the expropriated assets during the judicial procedure, which is only possible after the payment or deposit of compensation.

The use of this procedure by the expropriating entity and the expropriation court, to assure the occupation of the expropriated assets by-passing the obligation established in the Expropriation Law to deposit the compensation, prior to the occupation, in the amount determined by the Evaluation Commission would be contempt of law.

In effects, regardless of whether lower Venezuelan courts have applied Articles 585-589 of the Civil Procedural Code to issue preliminary injunctions for the occupation of expropriated assets, the Supreme Court has always considered that in the event of an expropriation, the procedure set out in the Expropriation Law must be applied, which is different from the provisions of the civil procedure statutes. In a decision of October 2, 1986, the former Supreme Court ruled that: "The development and regulation of the constitutional provision on expropriation, has its expression in the Expropriation Law, to which provisions the expropriating entity must adapt when applying such constitutional provision."[72] And in another decision of October 1995, the former Supreme Court affirmed that being the fundamental purpose of the expropriation procedure to guarantee the payment of just compensation to the owner of the expropriated asset, the procedure provided in the Expropriation Law for such purpose "differs from the ordinary civil procedure, having as one of its fundamental purposes to guaranty the owner of the expropriated assets to be paid the just compensation for the loss of the possession of his assets".[73]

This special nature of the expropriation procedure explains that other legal provisions, including those established in the Organic Law of the Supreme Tribunal are not applicable in the general context of the expropriation procedure when they differ or contradict those provided in the Expropriation Law. As it was decided by the First Court on Contentious Administrative matters in a decision of Mars 27, 2003:

> "The *special* nature of expropriation means that other statutes, including procedural provisions of the Supreme Court of Justice statute, are not applicable in the context of expropriation to the extent that they differ from or contradict the Expropriation Law:" [74]

72 Decision of the Politico-Administrative Chamber, Supreme Court of Justice, October 2, 1986, ratified in decision N° 1902 of December 21, 1999 in *Revista de Derecho Público*, N° 77-80, Editorial Jurídica Venezolana, Caracas 1999, pp. 438.

73 See decisión of the Político Administrative Chamber of the Supreme Court of Justice of October 11, in *Revista de Derecho Público*, N° 63-64, Editorial Jurídica Venezolana, Caracas 1995, p. 489.

74 See in *Revista de Derecho Público*, N° 93-96, Editorial Jurídica Venezolana, Caracas 2003, p. 363.

Consequently, according to article 66 of the Expropriation Law being the anticipatory occupation of the expropriated assets expressly regulated in article 56 of the Law, the general procedural provisions of the Civil Procedural Code regarding preliminary injunctions (Articles 585-589) cannot be applied for such purpose by the expropriation court. As has been stated by the First Court on Administrative Contentious Proceedings, if the prior payment of the estimated amount of compensation has not been made, granting such anticipatory occupation would violate Article 56 of the Expropriation Law. [75]

That is why that the Supreme Court, even considering that the anticipatory occupation of expropriated assets as a right that the expropriating entity can request to the expropriation court, has considered that such right:

> "is subordinated to the compliance of the conditions established in the law, such as the previous evaluation, the judicial inspection and the posting of the amount of the evaluated compensation, in order to commence the public or social purpose work that under the premise of 'urgency,' must be accomplished." [76]

III. ADMINISTRATIVE LAW PRINCIPLES RELATED TO PUBLIC SERVICES (PUBLIC UTILITIES)

1. Problems related to the notion of "*servicio público*" (public service or utility)

The Spanish expression "*servicio público*" can be literally translated into English as "public service" in the sense of public utility, and not in the sense as referred to any public activity. In effect, in Anglo-American administrative law doctrine, the expression "public service" has, according to the *Black's Law Dictionary*[77], a particular legal meaning that refers to "public utility"[78], an expression that encompasses services rendered to the general public by public entities or by public utility corporations.

---

75 See in *Revista de Derecho Público*, N° 63-64, Editorial Jurídica Venezolana, Caracas 1995, p. 491.

76 Decision No. 6127 of the Politico-Administrative Chamber, Supreme Tribunal of Justice, November 9, 2005, in *Revista de Derecho Público*, N° 104, Editorial Jurídica Venezolana, Caracas 2005, p. 135

77 In *Black's Law Dictionary,* the term "public service" is applied to activities or entities "which specially serve the needs of the general public or conduce to the comfort and convenience of an entire community, such as railroads, gas, water and electric light companies; and companies furnishing public transportation. If the public service is rendered by a privately owned corporation, it must have "an appropriate franchise from the state to provide for the necessity or convenience of the general public, incapable of being furnished by private competitive business, and dependent for its exercise on eminent domain or government agency", West Publishing, St. Paul, Minn., 1991, p. 858.

78 See Peter L Strauss et al., *Administrative Law. Cases and Comments*, University Casebooks Series, New York, 1995, pp. 339 ff. *Cf.* José Peña Solís, *Manual de Derecho Administrativo*, Vol. 3, Caracas 2003, p. 381.

Thus, both in English and in Spanish legal terms, not all public interest activities can be considered to be public services or utilities (*servicio público*), but only those which consist in rendering public interest services to satisfy the needs of the general public or for the comfort and convenience of an entire community, such as railroads, gas, electricity, water, transportation and telephone. Thus, it is wrong to identify "*servicio público*" (public service or utility) with any sort of general interest activities; an approach that made the concept useless.

Nevertheless, the notion of "*servicio público*" (public service or utility), equivalent to the French expression "service public", in continental and Latin American administrative law has been one of the most used and abused concepts of this particular branch of law, to the point that in some cases it has served to identify any activity of public entities, throwing it into a state of permanent conceptual crisis[79].

It is necessary to correctly identify this concept and distinguish it from other public interest activities. According to Venezuelan constitutional and administrative law, and similarly to the equivalent English concept of "public service utility" already mentioned, a public service is above all and always an activity whereby a public entity (or a corporation by means of a concession) regularly renders a commodity or service of public consequence, such as electricity, gas, water, transportation or telephone to the general public or to an entire community. (In Spanish this activity would be identified by the word "*prestación*"[80], through which a public entity directly satisfies general public needs by rendering services to the entire community or the general public). Consequently, the main characteristic of a public service (*servicio público*) is that it always consists in rendering a commodity or a service to the general public, i.e., that it seeks to satisfy public needs, on a continuous and regular base, and which the State or public entities must assume because they have a constitutional or legal obligation to perform it. That is why private persons are not free to engage in those activities, and can only assume them through a concession, a permit, an authorization, a franchise or a registration of the State[81].

This definition of "*servicio público*" (public service or utility) implies the following[82]. First, that it is always an activity that consists in providing or giving a commodity to the general public, whether a service of public consequence or in

---

79 See among the most recent essays on the matter: Jaime Orlando Santofimio, "*Los servicios públicos: vicisitudes y fundamentos de un tema jurídico inconcluso e impreciso*" in *El derecho Público a comienzos del Siglo XXI: Estudios en Homenaje al Profesor Allan R. Brewer-Carías*, Ed. Civitas, Madrid, 2003, pp. 1882-1956; José Ignacio Hernández G., "*Un ensayo sobre el concepto de servicio público en el derecho venezolano*" *Revista de Derecho Público*, N° 89-92, EJV, Caracas, 2002, pp. 47-75.

80 See, for instance, Allan R. Brewer-Carías, "*Comentarios sobre la noción de servicio público como actividad prestacional del Estado y sus consecuencias*" in *Revista de Derecho Público*, N° 6, EJV, Caracas, 1981, pp. 65-71. See also the most recent work of José "Ramón Parada, "*Los servicios públicos en España*", in *El derecho Público a comienzos del Siglo XXI: Estudios en Homenaje al Profesor Allan R. Brewer-Carías*, Madrid, 2003, pp. 1845-1869.

81 See Allan R. Brewer-Carías", *"El régimen constitucional de los servicios públicos", VI Jornadas Internacionales de Derecho Administrativo "Allan R. Brewer-Carías",* Fundación de Estudios de Derecho Administrativo, Tomo I, Caracas, March 5-8, 2002.

82 *Idem.*

benefit of the general public. That is why the concept always refers to utilities such as gas, electricity, water, transport, telephone; and it is always regulated by statutes.

Second, it is a service that the public entities must perform in compliance with a constitutional or legal obligation, hence the necessary existence of a statute that regulates it, and the mentioned doctrine that defends the need for a statute which expressly qualifies an activity as a public service in order that it be considered as such. Thus, not all kinds of services rendered by public entities can be considered to be public services or utilities (*servicios públicos*), but only those engaged in compliance with an obligation established in the Constitution or in a statute. That is why a public service cannot be freely rendered by a private corporation unless the latter has a permit, an authorization or a concession.

Third, since it is an activity which consists in supplying commodities to the general public as a result of a State's obligation, according to the "alter" (*alteridad*) principle that prevails in the relationship: right/obligation, the general public and the user in particular can claim a constitutional or legal right to receive the service, and this can even be claimed judicially[83].

Fourth, when an activity is constitutionally or legally declared a "*servicio público*" (public service or utility), the activity cannot be freely carried out by private persons, but it is subject to some kind of State intervention or restriction. When a "*servicio público*" (public service or utility) is constitutionally or legally declared, the economic freedom of enterprise is thus limited, although in various degrees. The declaration that an activity is a public utility can exclude any possibility for private parties to perform or render the commodity, as for instance happened decades ago with the postal services, which in many countries were reserved to the State; or the services can be performed by private persons through a concession or a permit given by public entities, as happens in general with all public utilities; or they can be performed in a concurrent way by the State and the private sector, without major limitations, as happens, for instance, with the health or educational services[84].

In Venezuela, Article 302 of the Constitution establishes the possibility for the State to reserve for itself, through an Organic Law and based on reasons of national convenience, certain industries, exploitations, goods and "services" of public interest. In such cases, a State monopoly can be established regarding not only certain activities (industries, exploitations) but in particular services. However, with regard to public services or utilities, their legal declaration as a "public service" does not necessarily imply an automatic reservation of the activity for the State, moreover, depending on the degree of State intervention or involvement, they can also be granted to be rendered by private persons through concessions, pursuant to Article 113 of the Constitution; or they can be accomplished by a private party concurrently. Nevertheless, a statute that expressly regulates the activity as a public service or utility is always necessary.

---

83 That is why article 259 of the 1999 Constitution assigns the Judicial Review of Administrative Actions Jurisdiction (*Jurisdicción contencioso-administrativa*) competency to resolve claims related to the performance of public services.

84 See Allan R. Brewer-Carías, *"Comentarios sobre la noción de servicio público como actividad prestacional del Estado y sus consecuencias"* in *Revista de Derecho Público*, N° 6, EJV, Caracas, 1981, pp. 68 ff.

2. The concept of public services or utilities (*servicios públicos*) under the Venezuelan Constitution

As with many administrative law concepts, the notion of "*servicio público*" (public service or utility) has been constitutionalized in Venezuela[85], and the Constitution itself has set forth regulations referring to activities considered to be a "*servicio público*" in the sense of public service or utility. Reference can be made to the following articles of the Constitution[86]:

A. Article 84, which regulates the citizen's right to health care, establishing the "public health service". Also, Article 83 establishes the State's obligation to ensure the "access of persons to the services", and Article 86 refers to "the medical attendance services". Additionally, Article 156,24 assigns powers regarding "national health services" to the national level of government.

B. When regulating the citizen's right to social security, Article 86 of the Constitution declared it to be a non-profit "*servicio público*".

C. When regulating the citizen's right to education, Article 102 set forth that "education is a "*servicio público*". Additionally, Article 103 establishes the State's obligation to maintain "sufficient and well-provided services to ensure the access, continuation and termination of the educational service". Moreover, Article 156,24 assigned competency regarding "the national services of education" to the national level of government.

D. Article 108 of the Constitution, when regulating the media in order to ensure its contribution to the citizen's enlightenment, states that the State will guarantee "*servicios públicos*" of "radio, television and informatics libraries, in order to allow global access to information".

E. Article 156,29 and Article 178 of the Constitution refer to "domiciled public utilities" as municipal "*servicios públicos*" and in particular, to the public utilities of electricity, water, gas and sewerage.

F. Article 164,8 refers to State "*servicios públicos*".

G. Article 196,6 regulates the possibility, in a case of urgency and when the National Assembly is not in session, of conferring power on the President of the Republic, through decree-laws, to establish, modify or suppress "*servicios públicos*". The declaration, therefore, is reserved to the National Assembly and only in a case of urgency and when the Assembly is not in session, can the Executive branch declare an activity to be a "*servicio público*".

H. Article 259 assigns competency to the Judicial Review of Administrative Action Jurisdiction, in order to resolve claims originated in the performance of "*servicios públicos*".

---

85 Allan R. Brewer-Carías, *"Algunos aspectos del proceso de constitucionalización del derecho administrativo en la Constitución de 1999,* in *Los Requisitos y vicios de los actos administrativos, V Jornadas Internacionales de Derecho Administrativo Allan Randolph Brewer-Carías*, FUNEDA, Caracas, 2000, pp. 23-37.

86 See Allan R. Brewer-Carías, *La Constitución de 1999: Derecho Constitucional Venezolano,* Tomo I, Caracas 2004, pp. 303 ff.

I. Article 281,2 assigns competency to the People's Defender to seek for the correct functioning of the "*servicios públicos*".

Additionally, the Constitution expressly regulates "*servicio público*" activities as an obligation of the State in any of the three levels of government (National, States, Municipal), as follows: integral birth control services (Art. 76); information services (Art. 110); identification services (Art. 156,5); postal and telecommunication services (Art. 156,28); police services (Art. 164,6; 178,7); public passenger transportation services (Art. 178,2); garbage collection services (Art, 178,4); public defense service (Art. 268).

According to all the constitutional regulations related to the notion of "*servicio público*" (public service or utility), it can be understood that these activities are accomplished by public entities (or by private persons by means, for instance, of a concession or a permit) in compliance with a constitutional or legal obligation to render certain commodities or services to the general public. Thus, not all activities of public interest can be considered a "*servicio público.*"

For instance, the same distinction between general public interest activities and public service or utility activities is also established in the Organic Hydrocarbons Law, where, among all the activities related to the oil industry considered in general as public interest activities, the only activities expressly qualified as public services or utilities (*servicio público*) are those referring to the internal commercialization of "hydrocarbon derivatives" determined by the Ministry of Energy and Mines, consisting in the supply, storage, transport, distribution, and selling of "hydrocarbons derivatives" dedicated to internal collective consumption (Arts. 59, 60). Thus, the storage, transport, distribution and sale of crude oil is not regulated by Article 60 of the LOH, and is not considered to be a public service or utility (*servicio público*).

IV. ECONOMIC ADMINISTRATIVE LAW: FROM PRIVATIZATION OF PUBLIC ASSETS TO STATE APPROPRIATION OF PRIVATE PROPERTY

1. Privatization Legislation and Process during the 1990's

A. Legal Regulations

In 1995, in order to proceed with the privatization of public sector goods or services, a *Privatization Law* was enacted[87] being its purpose to regulate the process emerging from the policy of privatizing public sector goods or services " through restructuring of entities for purposes of their privatization, including modification of regulatory frameworks, transfer of shares from the public sector to the private sector, concession of public services and utilities, and any other mechanism that makes it possible to achieve the policy's objectives, as well as different contracts or acts of any kind which imply participation by private parties." (Article 1).

87 See *Official Gazette* N° 4.927 Extra. of June 30, 1995

The Privatization Law defined the public sector in article 2, as including 1. The Republic; 2. The autonomous public agencies and other public entities in which the Republic participated; 3. Companies or associations in which the Republic and other public entities held fifty per cent (50%) or more of the capital stock; and companies or associations totally owned by the public sector whose function, through ownership of shares in other companies or associations, was to coordinate the public management of a sector of the national economy, were also included, with the exception of those engaged in the extraction of bauxite, petroleum, and iron ore (The article refers to CVG and PDVSA); 4. Companies or associations in which the persons indicated in the preceding part held fifty per cent (50%) or more of the capital stock; and 5. Foundations created or directed by any of the public entities mentioned in this article, or those whose actions could give rise to financial commitments for said entities.[88]

Article 30 of the *Privatization Law* stipulated that its provisions prevailed over any other legal instrument, agreement, or contract on operations, procedures, forms of action, and spheres of authority in relation to privatization. The *Privatization Law* also expressly provided (in article 28) that any violation of its provisions, or the application of procedures intended to evade them, made such acts or transactions absolutely null and void.

B. The Privatization Policy (1990's)

Pursuant to the provisions of article 6 of the *Privatization Law*, the privatization policy had the following purpose: 1. Free competition and development of the enterprises' competitive capabilities; 2. Democratization and expansion of the ownership of capital production goods and stock ownership; 3. Stimulus for the creation of new forms of business, cooperative, community, co-management or self-management organization; and 4. Modernization of activities or services, transfer of technology, and provision of equipment, goods, or resources that will have a favorable impact on the efficiency of production and administration.

The President of the Republic in Council of Ministers was responsible for approving the privatization policy drawn up by the Venezuelan Investment Fund. The Congress of the Republic, through the Chairmen of both Chambers, was to be informed thereof within the fifteen (15) days following its approval, with an indication of the goods and services the government hopes to privatize under that policy, pursuant to article 10 of the Law.

Pursuant to article 10 of the Privatization Law, each privatization process was to begin with its approval, in the form Decree duly motivated issued by the President of the Republic in Council of Minister. Said Decree was to be published in the *Official Gazette* within the three (3) consecutive days following its approval. The Venezuelan Investment Fund was also to request the authorization stipulated in article 10 of the Privatization Law to privatize properties or companies belonging to decentralized public entities with their own patrimony, different from the Republic.

---

88 The Privatization Law expressly repealed those provisions of the *Organic Law Regulating Alienations of Public Sector Properties Not Part of the Basic Industries* (*Official Gazette* Nº 33632 of January 7, 1987) that are inconsistent with the *Privatization Law*'s provisions and had to do with the transfer to the private sector of the properties now included in the privatization policy formulated by the State pursuant to the *Privatization Law* (Art. 29).

Within the ten (10) consecutive days following that publication, the Venezuelan Investment Fund was to request the Senate and Chamber of Deputies Permanent Finance Committees (or if the Congress is not in session, it's Delegate Committee) for authorization to carry out the privatization process in question. Said authorization was to be granted in joint session within the fifteen (15) consecutive days after formal receipt of the application in ordinary session, but the two Committees could jointly decide to extend that time limit for a period not exceeding thirty (30) days when justified by the complexity of the issue. The Committees was to inform the Venezuelan Investment Fund of the date on which they formally received the application and of any extension of the time limit, before the original fifteen (15) day deadline runs out. In any event, upon the expiration of the fifteen (15) day period in the absence of an extension, or upon the expiration of said extension, if any, in the absence of a decision, the privatization process in question was deemed to have been authorized. Once this authorization had been granted or the time limit had run out in the absence of a response, the National Executive was to publish the decision to go ahead with the privatization process in the *Official Gazette*.

Pursuant to article 11 of the Privatization Law, the partial or total alienation of shares in basic or strategic industries (regardless of the size of the State's holdings therein) had to be approved in advance by the Congress of the Republic.

Pursuant to article 9 of the *Privatization Law*, the National Executive, acting through the Venezuelan Investment Fund, was responsible for carrying out the privatization policy. To that end, the property, company, or activity in question were to be transferred to the Venezuelan Investment Fund in the most convenient fashion. In no case could properties transferred to the Venezuelan Investment Fund be used to secure credits and loans destined for other purposes.

Pursuant to the *Privatization Law's*, article 24, the executives of a company awaiting privatization were obligated to take all measures necessary to preserve the goods and other assets comprising that company's patrimony, and to safeguard their value on reasonable terms. Default upon that obligation constituted damage to the Public Patrimony, and was subject to penalty under the *Public Patrimony Protection Law* of 1982.[89]

The privatization transactions carried out under the Law's authority were subjected to subsequent supervision and control by the Office of the Comptroller General of the Republic, as well as to the requirements stipulated in the regulations of the Law. In any event, said transactions were exempted from the prior authorization required by article 150.2 of the Constitution, and from the need for prior authorization by the Office of the Comptroller General of the Republic office stipulated in article 24 of the *Organic Law National Public Finance Law*[90] in respect of alienations of national properties.

C. The Procedure for the Privatization Process

Pursuant to article 3 of the *Privatization Law*, all alienations of shares or equity allotments in public enterprises carried out under the Law's authority were to be

89 *Official Gazette* N° 3777 of Dec. 23, 1982.

90 *Official Gazette* N° 1660 Extra. of June 21, 1974

made through public competitive bidding. Article 13 of the Law added that the procedure chosen for each privatization were to be public and were to ensure the same opportunities and treatment for all participants therein. But article 3 of the Law provided that the capital market mechanisms, in any of their alternative forms, could be used for the alienations of shares in companies in which the public sector held less than fifty per cent (50%) of the capital stock. The authorization stipulated in article 10 of the Law was always required.

The same article 3 of the Privatization Law provided that the base price for the competitive bidding must in all cases be determined by at least two (2) appraisals performed by different entities, one of which was a physical appraisal of the assets and the other an appraisal under the concept of a "functioning enterprise"; if the company was inactive, there must have been at least two (2) appraisals of public assets by different firms of recognized technical competence.

Pursuant to article 8 of the Privatization Law , the National Executive could impose special conditions on entities in charge of public service or production activities to be privatized, which could refer to the prices or rates for their goods or services; specific investment requirements and obligations; special capital contributions; incorporation of goods, equipment, and new technologies within specified time limits; or application of certain practices intended to preserve the public interest such as democratization of capital or the establishment of restrictions; or conditions for the sale or transfer of the shares or equity allotments of entities which have already been privatized or are in process of privatization.

Pursuant to article 25 of the Law, persons who were declare bankrupt or had been judicially convicted and not rehabilitated, or who were currently under final sentence for crimes against public property or patrimony, could not participate in privatization processes; neither could corporate entities in whose administration or equity structure there were individuals in the circumstances indicated above, except when they held no more than five per cent (5%) of the capital stock.

The Law also excluded from participation in privatization processes all persons that according to article 124 of the *Constitution* could not contract with public entities (art. 25). But employees were exempted from this rule, according to article 13 of the Law, which regulated the pre-emptive right to which they were entitled. In addition, article 25 exempted transactions reached through the Capital Market from the prohibition stipulated by that article, when the privatization was performed in that way.

Article 13 of the *Privatization Law* provided for pre-emptive rights for several classes of persons. The active employees and retired former employees of the entity or service to be privatized could purchase shares or equity allotments under the same conditions as other purchasers. The percentage of shares to be reserved for the employees and pensioners was to be indicated in the publication required by article 10 of the Law; it could not be lower than ten per cent (10%) nor higher than twenty per cent (20%), the exact figure reflecting the intention the employees expressed within a period not to exceed ninety (90) days. The percentage of capital reserved was to be determined in each case before the publication was made. This allocation was mandatory and was subject to the conditions to be negotiated in each case, including the term during which the employees were to exercise their pre-emptive right. Said conditions could stipulate interest rates, time limits, and forms of payment, among others, but was to be equal for the employees and pensioners and was to be made public. Upon the expiration of the ninety (90) days, time limit, in the absence of an agreement with the employees and pensioners for acquisition of the shares to which they are entitled under these provisions, they were to lost that pre-emptive right.

If the employees and pensioners choose to acquire a higher percentage than allocated to them in the notice, they could purchase the excess under the same conditions as were applicable to the rest of the bidders. The employees to which this article referred were those who appeared on a list which was to be filed with the Labor Ministry by the entity to be privatized within the thirty (30) days following publication of the decision to go ahead with the privatization process in the *Official Gazette*. To facilitate the exercise of the employees' pre-emptive right, article 16 of the Privatization Law required the Venezuelan Investment Fund to inform the employees on the entity's financial and legal condition, the privatization mechanism to be applied, and any other conditions or information relating to the process. In every case, the information required by this article was to be furnished in the same form as to other interested parties. The employees could form any kind of association to exercise their pre-emptive right. But the shares or equity allotments were to be owned by the employees individually, and they could not be transferred among living persons in any way as long as the special conditions for their acquisition remained in force. Nevertheless, if the purchaser was another employee or any of the forms of association chosen by the employees to channel their participation in the privatization, the special conditions originally granted were to be remained in force (Art. 15).

Article 21 of the *Privatization Law* provided that the purchaser of each privatized entity was to pay off its pending debts to the Republic or other public or private entities, directly to the Republic or other creditor, in the proportion corresponding to said purchaser's holding of equity in the entity, at the time the privatization transaction was closed.

The Venezuelan Investment Fund was to inform the Senate and Chamber of Deputies Permanent Finance Committees of the expenses incurred in the privatization processes carried out under the Law within the ten (10) consecutive days from the completion of each such process (Art. 21).

D. Regulations on the Use of Funds Proceeding from Privatization

Article 12 of the *Privatization Law* provided that the net funds resulting from the privatization of goods or enterprises belonging to decentralized public legal entities with equity distinct from that of the Republic, were to be invested in: a) Amortization of principal and repurchase of their debts, or of the debts of any other enterprise in which said entities held equity stakes; b) Restructuring of other enterprises in which they held equity stakes; c) Their own assets or those of any of the enterprises in which they held equity stakes.

Pursuant to article 18 of the *Privatization Law*, the net funds resulting from the privatization of goods, enterprises, or services owned by the Republic could be used only for payment of principal on the public foreign debt (with the exception stipulated in the 1995 *Budget Law*).

Accordingly, article 19 of the Law created a separate account in the National Treasury, in the name of the Republic, into which the funds raised from privatizations of goods or services owned by the Republic were to be deposited, along with all earnings, profits, or rents produced thereby; said funds could only be used for the purposes indicated above. This account was to be managed by the Venezuelan Investment Fund in accordance with Finance Ministry instructions and the provisions of the *Organic National Law on Public Finance* and the *Privatization Law*.

Pursuant to article 20 of the Law, the net funds resulting from the privatization of goods or services belonging to the Republic, as well as their earnings, profits and rents, could only be appropriated annually, previous Congressional approval. For that purpose, the annual *Budget Law* drawn up by the Executive must include the amount of such funds actually raised in the preceding fiscal periods which the government intended to invest in the corresponding fiscal year.

Article 20 provided, however, that the net funds resulting from the privatization of goods, companies or services owned by the Republic could be used in the same fiscal year in which they were raised through the procedure regarding additional credit before Congress. In any event, said funds could only be assigned for the purposes indicated above (Art. 18).

Article 21 of the Privatization Law defined the concept of net funds resulting from privatization for purposes of its regulations, as the income and its earnings, profits, and rents, minus the commissions stipulated in the contracts signed by the Venezuelan Investment Fund with the companies to be privatized, the expenses applicable to each such process including those devoted to retraining of personnel and those expenses to safeguard the company's equity values, and payment of pending debts with the Republic or other public entities, in the proportion equivalent to the stake that the Republic continued to hold in each privatized enterprise.

E. Labor Consequences of Privatization

Pursuant to article 27 of the Law, the privatization of any State entity, company, or institute could not impair the employees' rights in their labor relationship. Accordingly, article 27 stipulated that the collective labor contracts, labor-related practices and customs, and entitlements acquired by the employees could not be made any less favorable unless they were replaced by other benefits which, in the aggregate, exceed or at least equal in breadth the rights enjoyed as of the date immediately previous to that of the privatization.

Pursuant to article 17 of the Law, the employees who lose their jobs in connection with a privatization must be given retraining to prepare them for a return to work, preferably in companies of sectors related to their original employment, or in other areas or economic activities. During the course of the retraining activity, which cannot exceed 180 consecutive days, employees who collect Unemployment Insurance payments may only receive retraining bonus payments in an amount which restores 75% of their last basic salary, provided they participate in said programs. The Venezuelan Investment Fund must take responsibility for the personnel retraining programs, either directly or through persons with whom it reaches agreements to that end.

F. Regimen of Prohibitions on Public Entities

Before a privatization was ordered, article 24 of the Law prohibits public agencies from engaging in promotional activities of any kind relating to the entities to be privatized without the favorable opinion of the President of the Republic Council of Ministers; and the Congress was to be informed of said opinion. The company's operating activities were not to be included in said opinion.

Pursuant to article 22 of the Privatization Law, public entities were not to be engaged in transactions leading to the conversion of the public debt to investment in the course of implementing the privatization policy. Neither they could grant guarantees, bonds, loans, or securities of any kind, or financing of any other nature, nor they could make donations, except –in the latter two cases– when necessary for the employees of an entity in process of privatization, to be able to exercise their pre-emptive rights.

Article 23 of the Law also prohibits public entities from investing new funds in entities in process of privatization in which they still hold equity stakes, with the exception of the contributions inherent to their status as shareholders, the expenses required to complete the restructuring processes leading to privatization, or the expenses associated with the privatization of the entity in question.

When the President of the Republic in Council of Ministers determined that it is necessary to preserve the public sector's percentage of equity holding in the privatized entity, the decision to make the required capital contributions was to be supported in every case by the favorable opinion of the Venezuelan Investment Fund. The Congress was to be informed of this decision within the ten (10) consecutive days from the date of the approval in Council of Ministers.

Article 7 of the *Privatization Law* make the Venezuelan Investment Fund responsible for preventing the concentration of the goods, shares, and public utility concessions which were or have been privatized in the hands of companies or groups of companies which had the same interests or which may be engaged in monopolistic or oligopolistic behavior, committing manipulations which might prevent, restrict, falsify, or limit the enjoyment of economic freedom and free competition. Violation of these provisions made the competitive bidding or capital market placement process absolutely null and void.

G. Privatization Process of the Corporación Venezolana de Guayana (CVG) during the 1990's

Pursuant to article 10 of the *Privatization Law*, the Venezuelan Investment Fund, as the agency responsible for carrying out the privatization policy in Venezuela during the 1990's, requested the Council of Ministers approval to begin the privatization of the following enterprises owned by the Corporación Venezolana de Guayana (CVG): C.V.G. Aluminio del Caroní, S.A. (CVG Alcasa); C.V.G. Venezolana de Ferrosilicio, C.A. (CVG Fesilven); C.V.G. Siderúrgica del Orinoco, C.A. (CVG Sidor); C.V.G. Carbones del Orinoco, C.A. (CVG Carbonorca); C.V.G. Industria Venezolana de Aluminio, C.A. (Venalum); C.V.G.Bauxilum. The council of Ministers approved the beginning of the privatization process for those enterprises on November 23, 1994, through Decree N° 448.[91] Subsequently, and

91 *Official Gazette* N° 35.605 of December 8, 1994.

pursuant to article 10 of the *Privatization Law*, the Venezuelan Investment Fund requested the Permanent Finance Commission of the Senate and Chamber of Deputies to give their authorization for the beginning of the privatization process of the enterprises named above. On March 15, 1995, the said commissions authorized the beginning of the process of privatization of the companies to be privatized under the guidance of the Corporación Venezolana de Guayana.

The Corporación Venezolana de Guayana and the Venezuelan Investment Fund signed a trust contract on May 12, 1995, whereby the Venezuelan Corporation for Guayana transferred its shareholdings in Alcasa, Venalum, Bauxilum, and Carbonorca to the Venezuelan Investment Fund in trust.

The trust contract allowed the Venezuelan Investment Fund to proceed to privatize the aluminum companies in the Corporación Venezolana de Guayana system through the total or partial sale of the shares transferred to the Fund in trust. The contract also provided that the privatization process was to be carried out on the basis of coordinated action between the Venezuelan Investment Fund and the Corporación Venezolana de Guayana (this fact was been widely ignored). Pursuant to the trust contract, and to facilitate coordination of the privatization process, the Venezuelan Investment Fund and the Venezuelan Corporation for Guayana appointed an Aluminum Sector Privatization Technical Committee, comprised of four members chosen by agreement between both two agencies. The Aluminum Sector Privatization Technical Committee was responsible for examining the available options for privatization of the aluminum companies, drawing up the contracting terms for retaining the consultants needed in the privatization process (investment banking, auditing, accounting, legal audits, legal counsel, etc.), and generally coordinating the process through which the aluminum companies was going to be privatized.

2. State appropriation, nationalization, expropriation, and confiscation of private assets at the beginning of the XXI Century

In contrast with previous privatization policies, a general trend of the economic policy of the authoritarian government that has taken shape in Venezuela, following the framework established in the 1999 Constitution, has been the progressive appropriation by the state of private industries and services; a public policy that has been fueled during the past decade because of the state's uncontrolled expenditure of outstanding fiscal revenues derived from increased oil prices in the nationalized oil industry.

This process of state appropriation of the economy began at the beginning of XXI century through the consensual acquisition of industries and services by means of private law contracts and agreements, as was the case with the main electricity (*Electricidad de Caracas C.A.*) and telephone (*C.A. Teléfonos de Venezuela*) companies. It also occurred through public law instruments allowed for in the Constitution, like the nationalization of economic sectors, which always implies expropriation of private assets. But, in many cases, the forced appropriation of private assets occurred through unconstitutional confiscations.[92]

92 See, in general, Antonio Canova González, Luis Alfonso Herrera Orellana, and Karina Anzola Spadaro, *¿Expropiaciones o vías de hecho? (La degradación continuada del derecho*

A. The Compulsory Acquisition of Private Assets

In the Venezuelan legal system, the term *nationalization* refers to the public law institution through which the state, by means of a statute, reserves for itself an economic sector or activity, followed by the acquisition, normally through expropriation, of the private assets used in that sector or activity. The institution of nationalization was established in the 1961 Constitution (Article 97) and was first applied in the 1970's, through processes in which always was combined a legislative decision to reserve to the state the economic sector or activity and the administrative process of expropriation of the needed private assets, in order to make the reservation effective."[93]

In effect, Article 97 of the 1961 Constitution established the possibility of the state, through organic law and based on motives of national convenience or interest, reserving for itself some industries and services. That article was initially used to nationalize the natural gas industry in 1971 and the iron mineral exploitation industry in 1974.[94]

The oil industry and commerce were nationalized in 1975 by means of the 1975 Organic Law Reserving to the State the Industry and Commerce of Hydrocarbons,[95] which reserved that activity to the state; terminated foreign enterprises' existing concessions for the exploration and exploitation of oil; and established a procedure to expropriate private assets used for that activity, including payment to private industry participants.

The state's reservation institution was maintained in Article 302 of the 1999 Constitution, which establishes that "the State reserves for itself, by means of the corresponding organic law and for reasons of national convenience, the oil activity and other industries, exploitations, services and assets of public interest and strategic character". Regarding the reservation of the oil industry to the state, which, as mentioned, was decided in 1975, was ratified in the 2001 Organic Hydrocarbons Law, providing in Article 9 that:

---

fundamental de propiedad en la Venezuela actual," Funeda, Universidad Católica Andrés Bello, Caracas 2009.

93 See Allan R. Brewer-Carías, "Introducción al Régimen Jurídico de las Nacionalizaciones en Venezuela", in *Archivo de Derecho Público y Ciencias de la Administración*, III (1972-1979), Instituto de Derecho Público, Universidad Central de Venezuela, Caracas 1981, 2:23-44.

94 *Ley que Reserva al Estado la Industria del Gas Natural*, in *Official Gazette* N° 29.594, Aug. 26, 1971; Decree Law N° 580, Nov. 26, 1974 (*Decreto Ley que Reserva al Estado la Industria de la Explotación del Mineral de Hierro*), in *Official Gazette* N° 30.577, Dec. 16, 1974.

95 *Official Gazette*, Extra. N° 1.769, Aug. 29, 1975. The 1975 Organic Nationalization Law reserved to the state all matters "related to the exploration of the national territory in search for petroleum, asphalt and any other hydrocarbons; to the exploitation of reservoirs thereof, the manufacturing or upgrading, transportation by special means and storage; internal and external trade of the exploited and upgraded substances, and the works required for their handling" (Article 1). Article 5 ordered that the activities be exercised directly by the national executive or entities owned by it and it authorized private participation through operating agreements or association agreements in certain circumstances. See Allan R. Brewer-Carías, "Comentarios en torno a la nacionalización petrolera," in *Revista Resumen* 5, Caracas 1974, 22; Román J. Duque Corredor, *El derecho de la nacionalización petrolera*, Editorial Jurídica Venezolana, Caracas 1975, 22.

> "activities relating to the exploration in search of hydrocarbon reservoirs encompassed in this Decree-Law, to their extraction in natural state, to their initial production, transport and storage, are denominated as primary activities for purposes of this Decree-Law. In accordance with what is provided in Article 302 of the Constitution of the Bolivarian Republic of Venezuela, the primary activities indicated, as well as those relating to works required by their management, remain reserved to the State in the terms established in this Decree-Law."[96]

Other constitutional mean for compulsory acquisition of private rights and property is expropriation, defined in Article 115 of the Constitution as the compulsory acquisition by the state of any privately owned assets, rights, or property through a specific procedure (due process) and with payment of just compensation; which applies regardless of whether the economic sector or activity affected has been or not reserved to the state, and of whether the decision is taken regarding a specific private asset or assets affected to an economic activity. According to the constitutional provision, the 2002 Expropriation Law defines expropriation in Article 2 as:

> an institution of Public Law, by which the State acts for the benefit of a cause of public utility or social interest, with the purpose of obtaining the compulsory transfer of the right to property or any other right of private individuals to its [the state's] patrimony, through a final judicial decision and timely payment of just compensation.[97]

Expropriation can be made through an act of general effects, like a special statute. This was the case, for instance, with the 1970 expropriations in connection with the iron and oil industries. In those cases, the statutes implementing nationalization declared the reservation and ordered expropriation of the interests of the former concessionaries following specific rules of procedure.

The 2002 Expropriation Law establishes the general procedure for expropriation and contemplates the possibility of an expropriation decree applying to more than one asset of more than one individual or entity (Articles 5 and 6). The Expropriation Law also contemplates that through special laws it is possible to provide for other procedures and rules to be applied to specific expropriation cases, including expropriation of multiple assets of multiple subjects (Article 4).

The former Supreme Court of Justice held that "the institution of expropriation applies not only when the State resorts to it, through the organisms authorized to do so, in compliance with the Law that governs it, but also within its conceptual amplitude, its principles are applied by extension to all the cases of deprivation of private property, or of patrimonial diminution, for reasons of public utility or public interest."[98]

---

96 2001 Organic Law of Hydrocarbons in *Official Gazette* N° 37.323, Nov. 13, 2001.

97 *Official Gazette* N° 37.475, July 1, 2002. See the comments to this Law in Allan R. Brewer-Carías et al., *Ley de Expropiación por causa de utilidad pública o social*, Editorial Jurídica Venezolana, Caracas 2002, 7-100.

98 See Supreme Court of Justice, Politico-Administrative Chamber, Decision of Oct. 3, 1990 (Case: *Inmobiliaria Cumboto, C.A.*), in *Jurisprudencia Ramírez & Garay* 114, Caracas 1990, 551-52.

Consequently, in Venezuela, all property, rights, and assets are subject to lawful expropriation and protected from unlawful expropriation, being an important change introduced in the 1999 Constitution and the 2002 Expropriation Law the clarification that expropriation, as the compulsory acquisition of assets by the state, can refer to the right to property (*derecho de propiedad*) and to any other right of private parties (*algún otro derecho de los particulares*) (Article 2) or assets of any nature (*bienes de cualquier naturaleza*) (Article 7). Accordingly, expropriation is conceived in Article 115 of the Constitution as a constitutional guarantee of the right to property, any other rights or assets of any nature, which cannot be taken by the state except through a judicial procedure (juridical guarantee) and with just compensation (patrimonial or economic guarantee). The consequence of these provisions is that any appropriation of private rights by the state without compensation is a confiscation, and it is unconstitutional except as a criminal sanction imposed by judges in cases of corruption or drug trafficking (Article 116). That is, any taking of private property, rights, or assets by the state, or any termination of private individual rights by the state without following expropriation procedures or other means for acquiring property (e.g., requisition, seizure, reversion, criminal sanction) is considered confiscation, which is prohibited in the Constitution.

Consequently, any limitations, contributions, restrictions, or obligations imposed on property, rights, or assets implying deprivation of the essence of the right or asset or when such regulations annihilate the property, right, or asset in question, must be considered as an expropriation. As it was ruled by the Constitutional Chamber of the Supreme Tribunal with respect to Articles 115 and 116 of the Constitution, the limits that can be established regarding private rights and property "must be established on the basis of a legal text, as long as said restrictions do not constitute an absolute or irrational impairment of such property right. That is, impeding the patrimonial capacity of the individuals in such a way that it eventually extinguishes it."[99] In the same sense, the former Supreme Court explained:

> "Article 99 of the Constitution establishes the guarantee of the right to property.... [T]he limitation imposed on that right cannot represent an impairment that implies absorption of its attributions to the extent that it eliminates it.... This is, the right to property may be limited, restricted with respect to most of its content, attributions and scope, but this cannot exceed the limit – it is emphasized – by virtue of which such right is left completely empty, there is a central core of that right that is not susceptible of being impaired by the legislator, since if this were so, we would find ourselves before another legal institution (for example, expropriation)."[100]

With regard to the prohibition on confiscation, the Court also explained:

> "The prohibition of confiscation is related to the principle of reasonability that must guide the adjustment between the actions of the State and the impact on the legal sphere of those subject to the law, for which care must be taken that

99 Supreme Tribunal of Justice, Constitutional Chamber, Decision N° 3003 of Oct. 14, 2005 (Exp. 04-2538).

100 See Supreme Court of Justice, Decision of Apr. 29, 1997, in *Revista de Derecho Público* 69–70, Editorial Jurídica Venezolana, Caracas 1997, 391-92.

the activity does not formally or substantially reach the confiscation of the assets of the person, which occurs with the total dispossession of the assets or their equivalent."[101]

The aforementioned, in general terms, the constitutional and legal framework established in Venezuela in order for the state to acquire private assets and rights, whether or not the state has reserved for itself an economic sector or activity, except in cases of confiscation imposed as a criminal judicial sanction, always implies the right of the affected individual or enterprise to be compensated. Nonetheless, during the past decade and as a state unconstitutional policy, in numerous cases the state has appropriated private rights and assets without compensation.

B. The 2006-2007 State Appropriation of Private Enterprises in the Nationalized Oil Industry

The 1975 Nationalization Organic Law, notwithstanding the decision it contained to reserve the oil industry to the state, provided for private enterprises to participate in primary hydrocarbons activities (Article 5) in two ways: operating agreements and association agreements, including exploration-at-risk and profit-sharing agreements.[102] Consequently, according to the state policy named "oil opening" (*Apertura petrolera*) defined during the 1990's through Congress resolutions (*Acuerdos*),[103] the state-owned oil nationalized enterprises entered into agreements with private foreign and national enterprises. Consequently, pursuant to such public policy, private oil companies did in fact participate in primary hydrocarbon activities in Venezuela through Operating Agreements, Association Agreements for the Exploration at Shared-Risk-and-Profit, and Association Agreements for the development of the Orinoco Oil Belt (*Faja Petrolífera del Orinoco*).

Although the 2001 Organic Hydrocarbons Law changed the legal framework for the participation of private enterprises in the oil industry, reshaping such participation to only mixed companies –thus repealing the 1975 Nationalization Organic Law– in light of the non-retroactive nature of laws (Article 24 of the 1999 Constitution), the association agreements signed in the 1990's and also those signed in 2001,[104] remained as valid compromise executed by the state that continued to be in force.

---

101 Supreme Tribunal of Justice, Constitutional Chamber, Decision N° 2152 of Nov. 14, 2007, in *Revista de Derecho Público* 112 (*Estudios sobre la reforma constitucional*), Editorial Jurídica Venezolana, Caracas 2007, 519ff.

102 Regarding the interpretation of Article 5 of the 1975 Organic Nationalization Law and the participation of private companies in the oil industry activities, see Isabel Boscán de Ruesta et al., *La Apertura Petrolera, I Jornadas de Derecho de Oriente*, Fundación Estudios de Derecho administrativo, Caracas 1997.

103 On these legislative decisions, see Allan R. Brewer-Carías, "El régimen nacional de los hidrocarburos aplicable al proceso de la apertura petrolera en el marco de la reserva al Estado de la Industria Petrolera," in *La apertura petrolera, I Jornadas de Derecho de Oriente*, Fundación de Estudios de Derecho Administrativo FUNEDA, Caracas 1997, 2-3.

104 Still in 2001, after the sanctioning of the new Hydrocarbons Law (*Official Gazette* N° 37.323 Nov. 13, 2001), the "Oil Opening" policy was applied by the government according to Article 5 of the 1975 Organic Nationalization Law. For such purpose, legislative authorization was sought for the signing of an association agreement with the China National Oil and Gas Exploration and Development Corporation, a subsidiary of China National Petroleum Corporation, for the production of bitumen and the design, construction, and operation of a unit for production

Starting in 2006, Venezuela initiated a state appropriation policy of the oil industry through the gradual elimination or reduction, by law, of private capital in oil industry activities. This was not a process of nationalization, which, as aforementioned, in Venezuela combines the decision to reserve to the state certain activities followed by expropriation (with compensation) of the affected assets. The oil industry and commerce, as aforementioned, was nationalized in 1975, so in the process developed in 2006–7, based on the 2001 Hydrocarbon Law, no reserve of activities to the state was decided because the reserve of the oil industry to the state already existed. The new policy produced what was the termination of the agreements entered with private companies but without compensation.[105]

This elimination or sharp reduction of private capital in the industry was achieved through three legislative instruments. First, the Law Regulating Private Participation in Primary Activities, of April 18, 2006, declared the early and unilateral termination of existing operating agreements,[106] considering that they have denaturalized the oil industry "as a result of the so-called Oil Opening, to a point where it violated the higher interests of the State and the basic elements of sovereignty" (Article 1). Hence, Article 2 of that law declared that the content of the operating agreements that arose as a result of the oil "opening" was "incompatible with the rules set forth in the oil nationalization regime." Moreover, "they will be extinguished and the execution of their precepts will no longer be possible as of the publication of this Law in the *Official Gazette*" (Article 2). The termination constitutes an expropriation of rights, even if done through legislative act.[107] Article 3 of the Decree Law ratified the principle set forth in the 2001 Hydrocarbons Organic Law, whereby private capital could participate in primary hydrocarbons activities only by incorporating as mixed companies, which was exactly what had been proposed in the draft constitutional reforms that were rejected in a 2007

---

and emulsification of natural bitumen for the elaboration of *orimulsión* (BITOR Agreement). The agreement was authorized by the National Assembly on Dec. 17, 2001 (*Official Gazette* N° 37.347 of Dec. 17, 2001), just days before the entry into force of the new 2001 Hydrocarbons Organic Law (Jan. 1, 2002). The approval of the BITOR Agreement was possible because when enacting the 2001 Organic Hydrocarbons Law thorugh a Decree Law, the National Executive included a provision postponing its entry into force until Jan. 1, 2002, that is, after the BITOR agreement was already authorized and signed. See the comments in Allan R. Brewer-Carías, "La estatización de los convenios de asociación que permitían la participación del capital privado en las actividades primarias de hidrocarburos suscritos antes de 2002, mediante su terminación anticipada y unilateral y la confiscación de los bienes afectos a los mismos," in *Nacionalización, Libertad de Empresa y Asociaciones Mixtas*, coord.. Víctor Hernández Mendible, Editorial Jurídica Venezolana, Caracas 2008, pp. 123-88.

105 On the concept of nationalization in Venezuela, see Allan R. Brewer-Carías, "Introducción al régimen jurídico de las nacionalizaciones en Venezuela," in *Archivo de derecho público y ciencias de la administración*, Instituto de Derecho Público, Facultad de Ciencias Jurídicas y Políticas, Universidad Central de Venezuela, Caracas 1981, 1:23-44.

106 *Official Gazette* N° 38.419, Apr. 18, 2006.

107 See Allan R. Brewer-Carías, "Algunas reflexiones sobre el equilibrio financiero en los contratos administrativos y la aplicabilidad en Venezuela de la concepción amplia de la Teoría del Hecho del Príncipe," in *Revista Control Fiscal y Tecnificación Administrativa* 13, Contraloría General de la República, Caracas 1972, 86-93.

referendum.[108] To such end, the National Assembly adopted in March 2006 the Accord Approving the Terms and Conditions for the Creation and Operation of Mixed Companies.[109]

Second, Decree-Law N° 5200 Concerning the Migration of the Association Agreements of the Orinoco Belt and of the Exploration-at-Risk and Profit-Sharing Agreements into Mixed Companies, of February 2007, started the early and unilateral termination of the existing association agreements entered into between 1993 and 2001, establishing their compulsory transformation (migration) into new mixed companies with a minimum of 50% state equity participation (2001 Organic Hydrocarbon Law, Articles 22 and 27–32). The law required that if the private investors in associations did opt for a mixed company arrangement, they could only be shareholders of those companies with maximum equity participation of 40%. The state shareholder Corporación Venezolana de Petróleo, S.A., or an affiliate of PDVSA would have a 60% maximum equity share (Article 2). For those companies that could not reach an agreement with the state to transform the joint ventures into mixed enterprises, the Decree Law 5200 if it is true that the decree law could be considered as the beginning of an expropriation process of the contractual rights, that implied the right of the private partners to de Association Agreements to be fairly compensated for the damages caused by the execution of such decree law, the fact was that it configured a confiscation of the private assets, which is prohibited in the Constitution,

On the other hand, the legislative decision to begin the unilaterally and prematurely end of the association contracts implied the need to ensure the state's immediate assumption of actual industrial operations of each association agreement, and Article 4 of the law set a period of four months from the date the law was published (February 26, 2007) –that is, until June 26, 2007– for the private parties to "agree on the terms and conditions of their possible participation in the new mixed companies" with the ministry of Energy and Mines; term that could be extended for two extra months "to submit the aforementioned terms and conditions to the National Assembly for the corresponding authorization, pursuant to the Organic Hydrocarbons Law." Once the four months had elapsed, "without having reached an agreement on the incorporation and operation of the mixed companies," then the Republic, through Petróleos de Venezuela, S.A., or its affiliates, was to directly take over the activities exercised by the associations to ensure their continuity, by reason of their character of public use and social interest (Article 5), as it occurred in many cases. Nonetheless, the law mentioned nothing about indemnifying the private companies that did not agree to continue as mixed companies; so, what could have been a process of expropriation, resulted in a confiscation affecting public contracts and their rights and obligations.

Regarding these two laws, by beginning the process of termination of existing public contracts, it can be said that according to the Constitution, they could have been interpreted as the initiation of an expropriation process of the contractual rights of private companies, made directly by statute without following the general

---

108 See Allan R. Brewer-Carías, *La Reforma Constitucional de 2007 (Comentarios al proyecto inconstitucionalmente sancionado por la Asamblea Nacional el 2 de Noviembre de 2007)*, Editorial Jurídica Venezolana, Caracas 2007, 129 ff.

109 *Official Gazette*, N° 38.410, Mar. 31, 2006.

procedure set forth in the 2001 Expropriations Law. Pursuant to Article 115 of the Constitution, those two laws generated inalienable rights for the contracting companies to be fairly compensated for damages (expropriation of contractual rights) arising from the takeover of assets derived from public contracts they validly entered into with the state. Nonetheless, as mentioned, the decree law was mute regarding the compensation due to the private parties to the Association Agreements.

Third, the Law on the Effects of the Migration Process to Mixed Companies of the Orinoco Belt Association Agreements and the Exploration-at-Risk and Profit-Sharing Exploration Agreements, of October 2007,[110] finished by "confiscating" the interests, shares, participation, and rights of companies that had participated in such agreements and associations but had not complied with the requirement to migrate to mixed companies. That is, according to this law, what might have been initially an expropriation became, by unilateral and early termination of contracts, a confiscation of rights – in this case, the rights of those companies that did not reach an agreement with the state to continue operating as mixed companies.

In effect, according to this Law on the Effects of the Migration Process, the associations referred to in the Law of the Migration "were extinguished" as of the publication date of such Law or of the "decree that ordered the transfer of the right to exercise primary activities to the mixed companies incorporated pursuant to such Law" in the *Official Gazette* (Article 1).

Decree Law N° 5200 made no mention of the rights to compensation of the private companies that had not agreed to continue as partners of the new mixed companies. However, instead of proceeding to do this in the Law on the Effects of the Migration Process, the state definitively confiscated such rights by declaring the agreements "extinguished" in the dates established in the said Law on the Effects, of October 5, 2007. The result of such laws was then, that the public contracting parties to the Association Agreements failed to comply with the contractual obligations that were in effect before the Laws were enacted.

For purposes of executing such confiscation, Article 2 of the Law on the Effects of the Migration Process expressly provided that "the interests, shares and participations" in the associations referred to in Article 1 of the migration law, in the companies incorporated to develop the corresponding projects, and in "the assets used to conduct the activities of such associations, including property rights, contractual and other rights", which, until June 26, 2007 (pursuant to the term established in Article 4 of the migration law), "belonged to the private sector companies with whom agreement was not reached for migrating to a mixed company, are hereby transferred, based on the principle of reversion, without the need for any additional action or instrument, to the new mixed companies incorporated as a result of the migration of the respective associations, except for the provisions of Article 2 herein." This provision, according to the Venezuelan constitutional regime constitutes a confiscation of such assets, which Article 116 of the Constitution prohibits.

In other words, the state, by law, ordered the forced transfer of privately-owned assets to newly incorporated mixed companies without compensation or due

110 *Official Gazette* N° 38.785, Oct. 8, 2007.

process; constituting an unconstitutional confiscation. In these cases, in no way could the takeover be justified by the principle of reversion, which is essentially associated with the figure of administrative concessions, which do not exist in hydrocarbons matters, and is applicable only when the corresponding contract arrives to its term, once assets are duly amortized.[111]

C. The 2008-2009 Nationalization and State Appropriation

a. *The Nationalization of the Iron and Steel Industry (2008)*

On April 30, 2008, in Decree Law N° 6,058[112] issued by the national executive according to the legislative delegation contained in the 2007 enabling law,[113] the iron and steel exploitation and transformation industry located in the Guayana region was nationalized. The motives for nationalization were strategic, as Guayana has the highest iron mineral reserves of the country, and those reserves have been nationalized since 1975[114] (Article 1). As a direct consequence of the reservation to the state of this industry, and to complete the nationalization process by means of expropriation, all business activities of the company SIDOR, C.A., and those of any of its subsidiaries and affiliates were declared of "public utility and social interest" (Article 3).

Therefore, the iron and steel industry were reserved to the state as a consequence of the order to transform SIDOR, C.A., its subsidiaries, and it affiliates to state-owned companies, with state shareholder participation of at least 60%, according to Article 100 of the Organic Law of Public Administration (Article 3).

With regard to the managerial transformation, Article 4 of the decree law establishes that the republic, through the Popular Power Ministry for Basic and Mining Industries or any of its decentralized organizations, would be the legal stockowner of the percentage belonging to the public sector in the newly created state-owned companies. To ensure the proper transfer of all activities resulting from this transformation, and in accordance with Article 5 of the law, the Popular Power Ministry for Basic and Mining Industries or any of its decentralized organizations, within seven days of publication of the law, was to establish a transitional commission for each company that would be incorporated in SIDOR's executive board. For nationalized private companies, Article 5 mandated that they fully cooperate with the nationalization process to guarantee a successful and safe transition, which ended on June 30, 2008. Article 10 of the law exempted from any direct or indirect tax contribution all business agreements, title transfers, and negotiations, as well as any operation that could result in economic gains, needed to transfer the private companies to state-owned companies.

111 As has been said by Eduardo García de Enterría and Tomás R. Fernández, the reversion has lost "its old character of being an essential element of every concession and comes to be regarded as an accidental element of the business, that is, it is admissible only in the case of an express accord, like one more piece, when conceived in this way, of the economic formula that all concessions consist in," in their *Curso de derecho administrativo*, 13th ed., Thomson-Civitas, Madrid 2006, 1:763.

112 *Official Gazette* N° 38.928, May 12, 2008.

113 *Official Gazette* N° 38.617, Feb. 1, 2007.

114 Decree Law N° 580, Nov. 26, 1974 (*Decreto Ley que Reserva al Estado la Industria de la Explotación del Mineral de Hierro*), in *Official Gazette* N° 30.577, Dec. 16, 1974.

To ensure the transfer of property and compensation to private companies being nationalized, Article 6 provided for sixty continuous days, beginning on the publication date of the organic decree law –that is, until August 12, 2008– to agree on the terms and conditions of their possible participation in the state-owned companies. A technical committee with state and private representation was formed in order to determine a fair value to base the appropriate compensation owned to the nationalized companies (Article 7). On March 25, 2009, it was announced that the state and the Argentine enterprise *Techint*, which previously held majority ownership of SIDOR shares, reached an agreement to fix compensation and establish a schedule for payment.

The decree law established that if no agreement for the transformation of the private companies into state-owned companies had been reached by August 12, 2008, as in fact occurred, then the republic, through the Popular Power Ministry for Basic and Mining Industries or any of its decentralized organizations, would assume total control and management of the private companies to ensure the continuous operation of the nationalized industry. Articles 9 and 11 provided that all layoffs were to be frozen from the time of the publication of the organic law until the transformation process was over, and that all employees of the iron and steel industry would be covered under their respective collective contracts.

Additionally, in case no agreement was reached for transformation, Article 8 provided an expropriation clause for the shares of such companies based on the Expropriation Law. However, Article 8 also provided that to estimate the "compensation or fair value" of the assets being expropriated, no lost profit or indirect damages would be taken into account.

b. The Nationalization of the Cement Industry (2008)

Following the same trend used to nationalize the iron and steel industry, on May 27, 2008, in Decree Law N° 6091, as part of the 2007 enabling law, the cement industry was nationalized. The motive for nationalization was strategic (Article 1), and as a direct consequence of the reservation to the state of this industry, and to complete the nationalization process by means of expropriation, the activities developed by the main existing cement companies[115] –as well as any of their subsidiaries and affiliates– were declared of public utility and social interest (Article 3).

Therefore, the cement industry was reserved to the state and transformed, in accordance with Article 100 of the Organic Law of Public Administration, into state-owned companies, with state shareholder participation of at least 60% (Article 3).

Regarding the managerial transformation, Article 4 of the decree law established that the Republic, through the Popular Power Ministry for Basic and Mining Industries or any of its decentralized organizations, would be the legal stockowner of the percentage belonging to the public sector in the newly created state-owned companies. To ensure the proper transfer of all activities resulting from the transformation, and in accordance with Article 5 of the law, the Popular Power Ministry for Basic and Mining Industries or any of its decentralized organizations, within seven days of publishing the law would establish a transitional commission for each company to be incorporated into the executive board of the nationalized

115 Cemex Venezuela, S.A.C.A.; Holcim Venezuela, C.A.; and C.A. Fábrica Nacional de Cementos, S.A.C.A. (Grupo Lafarge de Venezuela).

companies. In fact, no such committee was established, and public officials occupied the enterprises. In any case, Article 5 mandated that private shareholders fully cooperate with nationalization to guarantee a successful and safe transition, to be completed by December 31, 2008 (Article 6). Article 10 of the law exempted from any direct or indirect tax contribution, all business agreements, title transfers, and negotiations needed to conclude the transformation and any operation that could result in economic gains.

Because the takeover of the cement industry was formally a nationalization, to ensure the transfer of property and the compensation due to the private companies being nationalized, Article 6 of the decree law gave them sixty continuous days, beginning on the publication date of the organic decree law –that is, until September 18, 2008– to agree on terms and conditions of possible participation in the new state-owned companies. A technical committee with the participation of state and private representation was formed to determine the fair value to base the appropriate compensation owned to the nationalized companies (Article 7).

The government signed a memorandum of understanding with two of the shareholders of the nationalized enterprises (Holcim and Lafarge), in which they agreed on the compensation price and payment conditions. The agreements were not effective, and at least one of the enterprises initiated international arbitration. The third enterprise (Cemex) did not reach an agreement with the state and submitted to international arbitration. In that latter case, however, the state signed an agreement for technical assistance with the company, with limited duration, that allowed the nationalized industry to continue operations but with the systems of the private company.

In this case of the cement industry, in similar terms to the provisions regarding the nationalization of the iron and steel industry, the decree law established that if no agreement for the transformation was reached by December 31, 2008, as in fact occurred, then the Republic, through the Popular Power Ministry for Basic and Mining Industries or any of its decentralized organizations, would assume total control and management of the private companies to ensure continuous operations of the nationalized industry.

c. *The State Appropriation of Assets and Services Related to Primary Hydrocarbon Activities (2009)*

In May 2009, the National Assembly, also on the basis of strategy, sanctioned the organic law reserving for the state the assets and services related to the primary activities of the oil industry[116] established in the Hydrocarbon Law (Article 1), which were formerly conducted by Petróleos de Venezuela, S.A. (PDVSA) and its subsidiaries, and later assumed by private companies, being activities essential to the industry (Article 2). The consequence of the nationalization was according to Article 1 of the law, that activities were to be "directly executed by the Republic, by Petróleos de Venezuela, S.A. (PDVSA), or any of its designed subsidiaries, or by mixed companies under Petróleos de Venezuela, S.A. (PDVSA) control".

Article 7 of the law assigned "public order" character to its provisions, meaning that provisions "shall have preference over any other legal dispositions related to the matter." However, Article 5 established that all the aforementioned assets and

116 See *Official Gazette* N° 39.173, May 7, 2009.

services provided or required were to be considered "public services and of public and social interest." Such assets and services are enumerated in Article 2 of the law as follows: water, steam, or gas injections aimed to increase the oilfield's energy and improve the recovery factor; gas compression; and all goods and services connected to activities in the Lago de Maracaibo (boats for personnel transport, divers, and maintenance); cargo ships (including diesel, industrial waters, and any other supplies), crane ships, tug boats, buoys, padding and filling cranes, pipe and wire lines, ship maintenance, workshops, docks, floating docks, and ports of any nature.

To carry out the state appropriation, Article 3 of the Law empowered the Popular Power Ministry for Energy and Oil to define by unilateral administrative acts (resolutions) the assets and services listed in the provisions of Articles 1 and 2. In the case that such resolutions are issued, according to Article 3 of the organic law, all previous contracts and agreements regarding the reserved activities and signed between private companies and state-owned companies will be considered *ipso jure* extinguished by virtue of the law. The law recognized the contracts, for the purpose of their early termination, as "administrative contracts" (Article 3).

The reservation to the state of the assets and services related to primary hydrocarbon activities –different from previous nationalization processes– provided that as of the date of the law's publication (May 7, 2009), "Petróleos de Venezuela, S.A., (PDVSA) or any of its subsidiaries will take possession of any assets and control of all operations related to the reserved activities," which effectively occurred. That is, according to the law, an "expedite mechanism" was provided according to the needs of the oil industry, "allowing Petróleos de Venezuela, S.A. (PDVSA) or any of its subsidiaries, to take over assets and control the operations of related the reserved activities, as a previous step to complete the expropriation process".

To that effect, the law authorized the Popular Power Ministry for Energy and Oil to take all available measures to ensure the continuous operation of the reserved activities, with authorization to ask for support from any state organ or entity. In this case, the National Guard was chosen to achieve this goal. Additionally, the law compelled all actors in the process to fully and peacefully collaborate in the transfer of operations, facilities, documents, and property affected by the law provisions; otherwise, they could be subject to administrative or criminal sanctions (Article 4).

To ensure the transfer to the state of all assets and services, Article 8 provided that any permits, certifications, authorizations, and valid registries belonging to the private operating companies, or pertaining to any of the reserved activities, would *ipso jure* be transferred to Petróleos de Venezuela or a designated subsidiary.

Additionally, to facilitate the transfer, Article 9 establishes that any act, business, or agreement related to the transfer of assets and operations enshrined under the organic law would be exempt from any national taxes.

Also, Article 10 of the organic law, as part of the transfer process, gives power to the Popular Power Ministry for Energy and Oil to make any decisions regarding the transfer of all working personnel from the "*statisized*" companies to Petróleos de Venezuela or any of its subsidiaries. The state appropriation and immediate takeover of all goods, services, and assets obligated the state to fairly compensate shareholders of the private companies that the state took over. Nonetheless, for such purpose, the law only referred to the expropriation process as a mere possibility, providing that the state could (*podrá*) decree total or partial expropriation of all shares and assets belonging to any company doing business or conducting any of the reserved, in accordance with the Expropriation Law. In such cases, Petróleos de Venezuela, S.A., or any of its subsidiaries would be the expropriating entity (Article 6).

In the case of the state appropriation of the oil industry assets and services, the law established restricted criteria regarding the just and fair compensation provided for in Article 115 of the Constitution. To estimate the fair value of the assets being expropriated, Article 6 provided that in no case could lost profits or indirect damages be taken into account and that valuation would be based on "book value less all wages, payroll and environmental passives determined by the proper authorities." Article 6 adds that the time to effectively take possession would be taken into account to establish fair value. Additionally, payments could be through cash, bonds, or obligations issued by public entities (Article 6).

In any event, the day after the publication of the organic law, on May 8, 2009, the Popular Power Ministry for Energy and Oil passed Resolution N° 051,[117] listing all services, sectors, goods, and companies "affected by the takeover measures" (Article 1), and instructing Petróleos de Venezuela, S.A., or any of its subsidiaries, "to take control over operations and immediate possession of the mentioned facilities, documents, capital assets and equipment" (Article 2).

To ensure immediate takeover, the law provided that to register all information related to all affected goods, services, and assets, within the following fifteen days an inventory must be made to be signed by Petróleos de Venezuela, S.A., or any of its subsidiaries and the private companies, or be made through a judicial inspection or notarized act (Article 2). In that same resolution, the Popular Power Ministry for Energy and Oil reserved to itself the right to apply any necessary measures to guarantee the continuous operation of the affected business, as well as the right to identify other assets, services, companies, or sectors that follow under the provisions of the organic law (Article 3).

A few days later, on May 13, 2009,[118] the Popular Power Ministry for Energy and Oil passed Resolution N° 54, naming an additional list of companies conducting business and in possession of essential capital assets (gas compression) connected with primary hydrocarbon activities in accordance with the Hydrocarbon Organic Law, the list being considered as a declarative not compelling one (Article 1).

The fact of all the provisions and actions was the immediate takeover of all the assets and services unilaterally enumerated by the state, without any compensation paid or expropriation process initiated. It simply was another confiscation of private property, prohibited in the Constitution.

d. The Reservation to the State of Petrochemical Activities (2009)

On June 2009, the Law for the Development of the Petrochemical Activities was sanctioned,[119] reserving to the state the basic and intermediate petrochemical industry, as well as the works, assets, and installations required for its accomplishment (Article 5). "Basic petrochemical" includes the industrial processes

---

117 See *Official Gazette* N° 39.174, May 8, 2009.

118 See *Official Gazette* N° 39.177, May 13, 2009.

119 See *Official Gazette* N° 39.203, June 18, 2009.

related to physical transformation of the basic components of hydrocarbons, understood as products obtained from hydrocarbons with a very specific chemical formula (Article 4.2). "Intermediate petrochemical" includes industrial processes related to the chemical or physical transformation obtained from the basic petrochemical (Article 4.3).

The reservation to the state of petrochemical activities means that only the state, enterprises it exclusively owns, or mixed enterprises it controls can undertake such activities. Mixed enterprises are subject to prior authorization from the National Assembly, once informed by the Ministry of Energy and Oil about the specific circumstances and conditions in each case (Article 5).

The same law declared that because of economic and political sovereignty and for reasons of national strategy, the state shall remain as the owner of all shares of *Petroquímica de Venezuela*, S.A., or of any other entity that in its substitution could be established to manage the petrochemical industry (Article 6).

D. The State appropriations of Rural Land and Alimentary Industries

Since the enactment of the Land and Farming Law,[120] not only the possibility for the state to occupy and expropriate private land was extended, leading to the massive appropriation of private land by the state, without compensation, but also the possibility for the state to take over rural land simply ignoring its condition of private own property supported in the due registered titles, imposing in many cases to the owner, without legal support, the impossible burden to proof a property tradition for almost two hundred years.[121]

On the other hand, sine 2007, a massive process of expropriation, in many cases without due compensation, and of forced occupation of assets and industries by public authorities, with the support of the national guard, have taken place, based on "strategic" or "alimentary sovereignty" motives.

In the latter case, the process has been based on the provisions of the Organic Law on Farming and Alimentary Security and Sovereignty,[122] which assigns expropriation powers to the executive without the need of a previous declaration of a specific public interest or public utility, and allowing the State to occupy private industries without compensation.[123] Also, the Law for the defense of persons in their

120 See Ley de Tierras y Desarrollo Agrario in *Official Gazette* N° 5.771 Extra. of May 18, 2005.

121 See Antonio Canova González, Luis Alfonso Herrera Orellana and "Karina Anzola Spadaro, *¿Expropiaciones o Vías de hecho? (La degradación continuada del derecho fundamental de propiedad en la Venezuela actual)*, FUNEDA, Caracas 2009, 115 ff. See also Allan R. Brewer-Carías, "El régimen de las tierras baldías y la adquisición del derecho de propiedad privada sobre tierras rurales en Venezuela," in *Estudios de derecho administrativo* 2005-2007, Editorial Jurídica Venezolana, Caracas 2007, 327-74.

122 See Ley Orgánica de soberanía y seguridad alimentaria, *Official Gazette* N° 5.889, Extra., July 31, 2008. See the comments in José Ignacio Hernández G., "Planificación y soberanía alimentaria," in *Revista de Derecho Público (Estudios sobre los Decretos Leyes)* 115, Editorial Jurídica Venezolana, Caracas 2008, 389-394.

123 See Carlos García Soto, "Notas sobre la expansión del ámbito de la declaratoria de utilidad pública o interés social en la expropiación," in *Revista de Derecho Público*, N° 115 (Estudios sobre los Decretos Leyes), Editorial Jurídica Venezolana, Caracas 2008, 149-151; Antonio Canova González, Luis Alfonso Herrera Orellana and Karina Anzola Spadaro, *¿Expropiaciones o Vías de*

access to goods and services [124] has allowed indiscriminate occupations of private property and industries, supporting its takeover by public authorities, in many cases *sine die* and without compensation. [125]

3. The "denationalization" process decreed in sececy ignoring the rule of law in 2020 establishing a "New Economic Policy"

A. Undermining the legal system in order to apply, in secrecy, a "New" Economic Policy of Destatization, Denationalization and Privatization of thee Economy in order to obtain "Additional Income"

The National Constituent Assembly, which was unconstitutionally and fraudulently called and elected in 2017,[126] in October 8th, 2020 approved without much debate[127] an *Anti-blockade Law for the national development and the guaranty of human rights,* so called "Constitutional Law" (a concept that does not exist in the Venezuelan constitutional system, in which the sole body competent for enacting laws is the National Assembly),[128] which was drafted on the basis of a proposal[129] that was submitted by Nicolás Maduro a week before, on October 1, 2020.[130]

---

hecho? (La degradación continuada del derecho fundamental de propiedad en la Venezuela actual), FUNEDA, Caracas 2009, 143 ff.

124 See Decreto Ley N° 6.092 para la defensa de las personas en el acceso a los bienes y servicios, *Official Gazette* N° 5.889 Extra. of July 31, 2008,

125 See Juan Domingo Alfonzo Paradisi, "Comentarios en cuanto a los procedimientos administrativos establecidos en el decreto N° 6.092 con rango valor y fuerza de Ley para la defensa de las personas en el acceso a los bienes y servicios," in *Revista de Derecho Público* 115, *(Estudios sobre los Decretos Leyes)*, Editorial Jurídica Venezolana, Caracas 2008, 246 ff.; Karina Anzola Spadaro, "El carácter autónomo de las 'medidas preventivas' contempladas en el artículo 111 del Decreto Ley para la defensa de las personas en el acceso a los bienes y servicios," in id., 271-79; Antonio Canova González, Luis Alfonso Herrera Orellana and Karina Anzola Spadaro, *¿Expropiaciones o Vías de hecho? (La degradación continuada del derecho fundamental de propiedad en la Venezuela actual)*, FUNEDA, Caracas 2009, 163 ff.

126 See on this matter, Allan R. Brewer-Carías y Carlos García Soto (Coordinators), *Estudios sobre la la Asamblea Nacional Constituyente y su inconstitucional convocatoria en 2017* Colección Estudios Jurídicos N° 119, Editorial Jurídica Venezolana, Caracas 2017

127 See on this matter the report by Sebastiana Barráez, "La Ley Antibloqueo dividió al chavismo: legisladores de su propia asamblea denuncian que viola la Constitución de Venezuela;" available at: *Infobae*, October 12, 2020, available at: https://www.infobae.com/ america/ venezuela/2020/10/12/la-ley-antibloqueo-dividio-al-chavismo-legisladores-de-su-propia-asamblea-denuncian-que-que-viola-la-constitucion/

128 See on this matter, Allan R. Brewer-Carías, *Usurpación Constituyente 1999, 2017. La historia se repite: una vez como farsa y la otra como tragedia*, Colección Estudios Jurídicos, No. 121, Editorial Jurídica Venezolana International, 2018.

129 See the text of the document in "Presidente Maduro presentó ante la ANC proyecto de Ley Antibloqueo," available at: *Aporrea*, 30/09/2020; available at: https://www.lapatilla.com /2020/09 /30 /este-es-la-ley-antibloqueo-presentada-ante-la-constituyente-cubana-documento/

130 See our comments on the proposal in Allan R. Brewer-Carías, "La Ley Antibloqueo: una monstruosidad jurídica para desaplicar, en secreto, la totalidad del ordenamiento jurídico," New York, October 4, 2020; available at: https://bloqueconstitucional.com/efectos-del-informe-de-la-mision-internacional-independiente-sobre-violaciones-a-los-derechos-humanos-en-venezuela-en-relacion-con-el-estado-de-derecho-y-las-elecciones/ Also see on this bill of law, the critique by: Ramón Peña, "El Anti-bloqueo: la panacea," in *The World News,* October 4, 2020; available at:

This "Constitutional Law,"[131] as it is expressed in its provisions, has the basic purpose of obtaining "additional income" (art. 18), through the implementation of a "change" in the economic policy in order to destatisize, denationalize and indiscriminately and secretly privatize the economy, and of new public financial negotiations, in order to supposedly take care of the need of the country; but all of it, subverting the entire legal system.[132] The "Constitutional Law," although did not expressly provide that it prevailed *in toto* over the Constitution (which nonetheless was proposed by the Bill of Law submitted by N. Maduro), it can be wielded to achieve an approximate effect, for it declares its articles to be of "preferential

---

https://theworldnews.net/ve-news/el-anti-bloqueo-la-panacea-por-ramon-pena; Luis Brito García, "Proyecto Ley Antiboqueo," in *News Ultimasnoticias*, October 3, 2020; available at: https://theworldnews.net/ve-news/proyecto-de-ley-antibloqueo-luis-brito-garcia; https://primicias24.com/opinion/294724/luis-britto-garcia-proyecto-de-ley-antibloqueo/ ; and https://ultimasnoticias.com.ve/noticias/especial/proyecto-de-ley-antibloqueo-luis-brito-garcia/; Juan Manuel Raffalli "Proyecto de Ley Antibloqueo crea cuarto oscuro que impide conocer documentos y procesos," in: *Lapatilla.com*, October 1, 2020, available at https://www.lapatilla.com/2020/10/01/juan-manuel-raffalli-proyecto-de-ley-antibloqueo-crea-cuarto-oscuro-que-impide-conocer-documentos-y-procesos/

131 See in en *Gaceta Oficial* No.6.583 Extra. of October 12, 2020. See the comemets regarding the Law, in: Alejandro González Valenzuela, "Ley Antibloqueo: Hacia el deslinde definitivo con la Constitución y el Estado de derecho," in *Bloque Constitucional*, October 12, 2020, available at: https://bloqueconstitucional.com/ley-antibloqueo-hacia-el-deslinde-definitivo-con-la-constitucion-y-el-estado-de-derecho/ ; José Guerra, "Ley Antibloqueo es un golpe de Estado," in Enrique Meléndez, *La Razón*, Octubre 2020; available at: https://www.larazon.net/2020/10/jose-guerra-ley-antibloqueo-es-un-golpe-de-estado/; and *Acceso a la Justicia*, "Ley Antibloqueo de la írrita Constituyente en seis preguntas, en *Acceso a la Justicia*, 16 de octubre de 2020, disponible en: https://www.accesoalajusticia.org/ley-antibloqueo-de-la-irrita-constituyente-en-seis-preguntas/

132 The opinion of Alejandro González Valenzuela is that the "Anti-Blockade Law" reinforces a "constitutional exception regime" by assigning to the Executive Branch of the Government "extraordinary power such as: (i) the de-regulation of economic sectors and activities (by disapplying legal, and eventually, constitutional rules); (ii) holding and closing legal acts and deals; modifying the system for the organization, ownership, management and operation of public and mixed companies in Venezuela and abroad; the administration of assets and liabilities through transactions available in national and international markets; all the above without observing the regime that reserves economic activities instituted by Article 303 of the Constitution; (iii) the implementation of exceptional contracting mechanisms; (iv) the association with illegitimate capitals under illegal conditions, that are also harmful for Venezuela; (v) using a totalitarian repressive apparatus against whoever oppose the "enforcement thereof." See Alejandro González Valenzuela, "Ley Antibloqueo: Hacia el deslinde definitivo con la Constitución y el Estado de derecho," in *Bloque Constitucional*, October 12, 2020; available at https://bloqueconstitucional.com/ley-antibloqueo-hacia-el-deslinde-definitivo-con-la-constitucion-y-el-estado-de-derecho/. In similar sense, José Ignacio Hernández has summarized the purpose of the Law by pointing out that its purpose is to: " Dispose of State assets and manage the Venezuelan economy without parliamentary control, "for which purpose," articles "19, 24, 27 and 29 allow Maduro (i) to carry out public expenditures; (ii) Contract debt operations and, in general, renegotiation operations; (iii) Enter into public interest contracts; and (iv) Reorganize State-owned companies to transfer their assets to private investors, even with respect to assets that have not been formally acquired, as they are affected by "occupation" measures. Anticipating the wave of litigation that these measures could unleash, the "Law" creates a special service for the exercise of legal actions abroad (Article 36)." See José Ignacio Hernández, "La Ley Constitucional Antibloqueo" y el avance de la economía criminal," en *La Gran Aldea*, Octubre 15, 2020; available at: https://lagranaldea.com/2020/10/15/la-ley-constitucional-antibloqueo-y-el-avance-de-la-economia-criminal-en-venezuela/

application" over all laws, of "public order and general interest," and of mandatory enforcement by all territorial levels of the government and by all persons (Art. 2).

This rupture of the legal system can be noted specifically in the following aspects:

First, in the conception of the "Constitutional Law" as a *regulatory framework of a supra-legal rank*, that is, above all, for organic and ordinary laws of the Republic, regarding which the "Constitutional Law" is declared to be of preferential application (First Transitory Provision), which is equivalent to stating what was proposed in the original bill of the Law: that all "rules that collided with the provisions thereof were now suspended" (Second Transitory Provision of the Bill of Law submitted by N. Maduro). In any event, the approved Law achieves similar purpose by setting forth that its provisions prevail over organic and ordinary laws.

Second, in granting a *unlimited power for the Executive Branch of the Government to "disapply" rules having a legal rank in specific cases,* as it deems necessary in order to attain the purposes of the Law (Art. 19), that is, giving it the power to decide in specific cases that an organic law or any other law *does not apply,* which undoubtedly implies establishing an *unlimited legislative delegation in favor of the Executive Branch, to exercise the power to legislate* in order to make up for the absence of rules or the legislative vacuum resulting from to the executive decision to "*disapply*" the rules of the legal order.

Third, it also grants the same *unlimited power for the Executive Branch to "disapply" in specific cases, that is, singularly, regulations and other rules of a sub-legal rank* that are deemed to be counterproductive for achieving the purposes of the Law (Art. 19), infringing the general principle of singular non-modifiability or non-derogability of the regulations that is guaranteed by Article 13 of the Organic Law on Administrative Procedure.

Fourth, the establishment of a *broad power to sign "international treaties, agreements and conventions*, bilateral or multilateral, favoring the integration of free peoples" that should be based on "pre-existing obligations of the Republic" (Art. 10), seeking with this to obviate the necessary approval of said instruments by a law enacted by the National Assembly, as required in the Constitution (Art. 154).

And fifth, the formal and express establishment of a *system of total lack of transparency*, by providing not only to disapply the laws on bids and public contracts (Arts. 21 and 28), but also that all the "procedures, formalities and records made on the occasion of implementing any of the measures" set forth in the Law that "imply disapplying *rules* of a legal or sub-legal rank" shall be *secret and reserved"* (Art. 42).

The foregoing is equivalent to a total undermining of the legal system of the State, which is entirely incompatible with the most elementary principles of the rule of law, materialized in the "regulation" or formal establishment of the "disapplying" of laws, in secrecy, by the Executive Branch._[133] Although qualified as a "*special and*

133 As expressed by the Venezuelan Episcopal Conference, "The so-called" anti-blockade law ", approved by the illegitimate National Constituent Assembly, is one more expression of the government's will to lead our country down paths other than legality, and thus squander the national resources that belong to all, with the aggravating factor, that now it tries to be done in a hidden and totally discretionary way." See, Conferencia Episcopal Venezolana, "Sobre la Dramática situación social, económica, moral y política que vive nuestro país," 15 de octubre de 2020, disponible en:

temporary regulatory framework that provides the *legal tools* for the Venezuelan Public Power" to achieve the purpose set in the Law, in fact it is an "exceptional regime with a vocation of permanence,"[134] to achieve what appears to be a radical change in the economic policy toward a destatization, denationalization and privatization of the economy, for the purpose of "counteracting, mitigating and reducing in an effective, urgent and necessary manner the harmful effects caused by the imposition against the Republic and its people," of what it characterizes as:

> "unilateral coercive measures and other restrictive or punitive measures originating from or issued by another State or group of States, or by actions or omissions arising therefrom, by international organizations and other foreign public or private entities."

According to such "Constitutional Law," those "coercive measures" would affect the human rights of the Venezuelan people, imply attacks against International Law and, as a whole, are crimes against humanity" (Art. 1); which affirmations clash and ignore the crimes against humanity perpetrated and denounced in the "*Detailed Conclusions of the Independent International Fact-Finding Mission on the Bolivarian Republic of Venezuela (443 pp.),*[135] submitted barely a few weeks before, on September 15, 2020, to the United Nations Human Rights Council, in compliance with the Council's Resolution 42/25 of September 27, 2019, and which characterized several of the crimes perpetrated by government officials in Venezuela against human rights, as crimes against humanity.

On the other hand, all this regulatory framework, in the end, has been established for the purpose of obtaining public "new incomes" through the definition of a "new" economic policy of destatization, denationalization and privatization , and new ways of financing, all implemented in secrecy, with the excuse to attain objectives that are not new, for they are contained in the Constitution of 1999 (Arts. 112 - 118, and 399 - 321), and are simply repeated in the Law. This can be deducted from the enunciates of its various articles stating, for example, on the "harmonic development of the national economy geared toward generating sources of employment, high value added, raising the standard of living of the population and strengthening the country's economic sovereignty" (Art. 3.2); the "unalienable right to full sovereignty over all its wealth and natural resources" (Art. 3.3); the protection of "third-party rights, including other States, investors and other individuals or legal entities that deal with the Republic" (Art. 5.3); "guaranteeing the people's full enjoyment of their human rights, the timely access to goods, services, food,

---

https://conferenciaepiscopalvenezolana.com/downloads/exhortacion-pastoral-sobre-la-dramatica-situacion-social-economica-moral-y-politica-que-vive-nuestro-pais

134 Véase Bloque Constitucional Venezolano, "Sobre la pretendida Ley Antibloqueo," en *Bloque Constitucional*, 16 de ocurre de 2020,; available at: http://digaloahidigital.com/noticias/el-bloque-constitucional-de-venezuela-la-opini%C3%B3n-p%C3%BAblica-nacional-e-internacional-sobre-la

135 Report of September 15, 2020, available at: https://www.ohchr.org/Documents/ HRBodies/HRCouncil/FFMV/A_HRC_45_CRP.11_SP.pdf See the comments on this Report in Allan R. Brewer-Carías, "Efectos del Informe de la Misión Internacional Independiente sobre violaciones a los derechos humanos en Venezuela en relación con el Estado de derecho y en las elecciones,' 1 de octubre de 2020, disponible en http://allanbrewercarias.com/wp-content/uploads/2020/10/1261.-Brewer.-efectos-del-informe-de-la-mision-internacional-independiente-en-el-estado-de-derecho-y-en-las-elecciones.pdf

medicines and other products that are essential for life" (Art. 6); the development of "compensatory systems for the workers' salary or true income" (Art. 18.1); funding the "social protection system" (Art. 18.2); "recovering the capacity to provide quality public services" (Art. 18.3); "driving the national productive capacity, especially of the strategic industries, and the selective substitution of imports" (Art. 18.4); the "recovery, maintenance and expansion of public infrastructure"(Art. 18.5); "encouraging and promoting the development of science, technology and innovation" (Art. 18.6); "gradually restoring the value of social benefits, accrued termination benefits and savings obtained by the country's workers" (Art. 22); and the "implementation of national public policies regarding food, health, social security, provision of basic services and other essential economic goods" (Art. 23).

All this is provided in the Constitution, wherefore, if the purpose were to attain those goals, it would suffice for the government to have clearly and transparently defined a *change* in the orientation of the economic policy toward the abandonment of the statization and nationalizing policy that the government has been promoting pursuant to the guidelines of the so-called "21st Century Socialism," which have only brought economic stagnation, misery and poverty to the country. The opening and privatization of the economy that is now purported to be done in secrecy, could also have been effected, -as we noted when studying the first "economic emergency" decrees issued and extended as of 2016-, using the extraordinary and unconstitutional powers that the Executive Branch assigned to itself, beyond all constitutional limits, pursuant to which practically any decision could have been made.[136] However, all the unconstitutionality in these decrees was of no use.

Instead, with the "Constitutional Law," the path taken by the Constituent National Assembly at the request of the Executive Branch, for effecting that "change" of economic policy in order to obtain "new incomes," was to set up a "regulatory" framework, in order to *regulate a situation of disapplying the law*, that is, of all organic and ordinary laws and regulations deemed necessary and, in this regard, enabling all the measures, without limitations, that the Executive Branch deemed convenient.[137] For such purpose the Law has created a new term ("to disapply") in the field of principles related to the temporary force of the law, implying an unlimited legislative delegation for the Executive Branch itself, enabling it to fill the regulatory "void" resulting from "disapplying" the rules.

Furthermore, as stated above, the "Constitutional Law" adds that the express provision of the entire system of prevalence of its provisions over all other organic

---

136 See Decree No. 6214 of January 14, 2020, *Gaceta Oficial* Extra. N. 6219 of March 11, 2016. Allan R. Brewer-Carías, "La usurpación definitiva de la función de legislar por el Ejecutivo Nacional y la suspensión de los remanentes poderes de control de la Asamblea con motivo de la declaratoria del estado de excepción y emergencia económica," in *Revista de Derecho Público,* No. 145-146, (January-June 2016), Editorial Jurídica Venezolana, Caracas 2016, pp. 444-468.

137 As expressed by José Ignacio Hernandez, all this is not new, "it is about the renewal of Maduro's goal of managing the economy at his discretion, thus facilitating arrangements that strengthen his kleptocracy and his alliances with organized crime. That objective, as we will see, began to be forged after the triumph of the opposition in the parliamentary elections of December 2015." See José Ignacio Hernández, "La "Ley Constitucional Antibloqueo" y el avance de la economía criminal en Venezuela," in *La Gran Aldea*, Octubre 15, de 2020; available at: https://lagranaldea.com/2020/10/15/la-ley-constitucional-antibloqueo-y-el-avance-de-la-economia-criminal-en-venezuela/

and ordinary laws, and the disapplying of laws and regulations in specific cases, with the consequential delegation of the legislative power to the Executive Branch, shall be performed within the express frame of a total lack of transparency, that is, within a secrecy and confidential framework, by declaring now that the economic policy is a matter pertaining to the security of the Nation (Arts. 37, 42).

B. The Fundamental Purpose of the Law: Generating "Additional Income" through Privatization of the Economy by means of any kind of Contracts or Negotiations made in Secrecy

The aim of the "Constitutional Law," as aforementioned, is to generate "new incomes," by "changing" in the economic policy to be accomplished outside the law and in full secrecy by the State, based on the destatization, denationalization and privatization of the economy and on engaging in new financial negotiations for "counteracting, mitigating and reducing in an effective, urgent and necessary manner," as stated in its Article 1, "the harmful effects caused by the imposition against the Republic and its people, of unilateral coercive measures and other restrictive or punitive measures."

Nonetheless, such "new income" are not to be spent within the budgetary discipline channel and according to the regime referred to public income in the Constitution, but to be used beside such provisions, for which purpose article 18 of the same "Constitutional Law" provides that it:

> "would be registered separately among the availabilities of the national treasury and would be used to satisfy the economic, social and cultural rights of the Venezuelan people, as well as for the recovery of its quality of life and generating opportunities by fostering their capacities and potentialities."

The consequence is that the measures for obtaining such additional income would be adopted outside the legal system, secretly, providing separate accounting, which overtly is contrary to the provisions of the Constitution regarding the system of public income and budgetary discipline (Arts. 311 – 315).

Among the mechanisms for obtaining "additional income," in addition to the policy of destatization, denationalization and privatization, the "Constitutional Law" provides for a set of *measures for public financing*, establishing that the Executive Branch may "create and implement *large scale* financial mechanisms" (Art. 22), as well as "create or authorize *any form of* new financing mechanisms or sources") Art. 23); adding in Article 32 that "for the purpose of protecting the transactions involving financial assets of the Republic and its entities, the Executive Branch may authorize *the creation and implementation of any financial mechanism* that enables mitigating the effects of the unilateral coercive measures, restrictions and other threats that give rise to this "Constitutional Law," including the use of cryptoassets and instruments based on blockchain technology."

On the other hand, for the obtainment of additional income, and for implementing the policy of destatization, denationalization and privatization of the economy, and of the financing negotiations mentioned, the "Constitutional Law" regulated a *total flexibilization of the public contracting system,* providing, in the first place, the "disapplying" of the legal rules that call for authorizations or approvals of national interest contracts by the National Assembly (Art.21), and, second, that the Executive Branch may "design and implement exceptional mechanisms for contracting, purchasing and paying for goods and services, preferably produced locally, destined for: 1) the satisfaction of the fundamental rights to life, health and food; 2) the generation of income, obtainment of foreign currency and the international mobilization thereof; 3) the normal management of the entities that are subject to the unilateral measures, restrictions and other threats that give rise to this Constitutional Law, and 4) selective import substitution." (Art. 28)

All this implies, without doubt, the general "disapplying" of the provisions of the Law on Public Contracting, the Law on Concessions and all laws governing this matter.

C. The regulations set for implementing the "New" Economic Policy of Destatization, Denationalization and Privatization of the Economy

The "Constitutional Law," in order to guarantee the "additional resources" referred to above, defines throughout its text the "new" economic policy that is sought, and which means a total reversal of the statization policy applied in the last 20 years, which now consists in the destatization, denationalization and privatization of the economy.[138]

Tis result from the following provisions:

a. The provisions pertaining to the generalized policy for destatization or denationalization

The "Constitutional Law," in order to "increase the flow of foreign currency toward the economy and the profitability of assets," provides that the Executive Branch may "develop and implement operations for the *management of liabilities*, as well as for the *management of assets*, through the transactions available in national and international markets, *without impairment to the provisions of the Constitution* (Art. 27), which implies the possibility of disposing of assets with the sole limitation of the provisions in the Constitution; a redundant reference, but this refers to the provisions of Article 303 thereof (as expressly set forth in the Bill of Law), which demands that the shares of PDVSA remain in the hands of the State.

Furthermore, the "Constitutional Law" expressly authorizes the Executive Branch to *"lift trade restrictions on certain categories of subjects in activities that are strategic for the national economy*" (Art. 31) "whenever this is necessary in order to protect the country's core productive sectors and the actors who engage therein."

---

138 As noted by Pedro Luis Echeverría, the "Anti-Blockade Law" has been "Conceived by the regime in order not to admit the destruction it has caused to the national economy, avoid international sanctions against it, illegally benefit the groups that are loyal to the regime, unlawfully get hold of the property and assets of the Nation, eliminate legal or sub-legal rules that prevent the regime from carrying out certain actions and implement measures that facilitate their predatory efforts to sell out the country. It therefore purports to replace numerous provisions contemplated in the National Constitution by an absurdity full of ambiguities, secrecy, uncertainty, surreptitious sell-out of the assets of the Republic to whomever the regime may handpick, in addition to doing so without informing the public or complying with the comptrollership tasks that the legitimate National Assembly must perform. This new dirty trick by the government tries to hide from the country the current incapacity of the Venezuelan economy to generate and supply to the people the bolivars and foreign currency required to satisfy their needs." See Pedro Luis Echeverría, "Ley Antobloqueo / La nueva trampa de Maduro," en *Ideas de Babel.com*, October 12, 2020, available: https://www.ideasdebabel.com/?p=101616

For the purpose of implementing the denationalization policy that is implicit in its provisions, when providing that the Executive Branch has the power to "disapply" all the organic laws and ordinary laws, that implies that the "Constitutional Law" is empowering the Executive Brach of Government to disapply the organic laws that established the nationalization or reserved certain economic activities to the State, among which, basically those related to the industry and trade of hydrocarbons (the 2001 Organic Law on Hydrocarbons and the 2008 Organic Law for the Reorganization of the Domestic Liquid Fuels Market); the petrochemical industry (2009 Law reserving petrochemical activities to the State); the services related to the oil industry (2009 Organic Law that reserves to the State the assets and services related to the oil industry); the iron industry (1974 Organic Law that reserves to the State the industry of exploitation of iron, and the 2008 Organic Law on the nationalization of the industry of iron and steel); the cement industry (2007 Organic Law that reserves to the State the industry of cement); and the activities related to the exploitation of gold (2011 Organic Law on the nationalization of gold mining and trade).

All the foregoing regulations aim specifically at the possibility of the total denationalization of the oil industry and the trade of oil by-products – among which, gasoline-, with the sole and exclusive limitation referred to above, that the shares of Petróleos de Venezuela S.A. (PDVSA), the oil industry's holding company, according to Article 303 of the Constitution must remain the property of the State (this was expressly set forth in Articles 22, 24 and 25 of the Bill of Law). This is inferred now from the equivalent text of Articles 24, 26 and 27 of the "Constitutional Law," which regulates, among its purposes, the privatization of the economy, "without impairment to the provisions of the Constitution." The clarification is obviously not necessary, because no State act or law can violate the Constitution.

In any case, the result of the provisions of the Law is that all the State-owned companies, subsdiaries or affiliates of PDVSA could be fully or partially privatized, without limitation, secretly.

This would even do away with the concept of mixed company or State shareholding participation in more than fifty percent of its capital, as regulated in the Organic Law on Hydrocarbons, which could be "disapplied" in all the "specific cases" that the Executive Branch deems necessary, and all of PDVSA's subsidiaries could become the property of private capitals, without limitation, given the prevalence of the "Constitutional Law" and the executive power to secretly disapply laws.

b. Provisions regarding the privatization of public companies

The implementation of the policy of destatization and denationalization of the economy naturally involves a process of *privatization of public companies,* to which end the "Constitutional Law" authorizes the Executive Branch to "*carry out into all formalities or negotiations that may be necessary* without impairment to the provisions of the Constitution" (that is, without affecting the State's full ownership of PDVSA's shares), in order to protect and "prevent or reverse actions or threats of freezing, seizing or losing control of the assets, liabilities and patrimonial interests of the Republic or its entities as a result of the application of unilateral coercive measures, restrictions and other threats." (Art. 24).

With regard to the privatization of public companies, the "Constitutional Law" set provisions for the total reorganization of the public entrepreneurial sector, authorizing the Executive Branch, pursuant to the abovementioned policy for destatization and denationalization, to "modify the mechanisms for the organization, management, administration and operation of public or mixed companies, both in the national territory and abroad, without impairment to the provisions of the Constitution" (Art. 26). The Law further authorized the Executive Branch to:

> "proceed to organize and reorganize the decentralized state own enterprises, in the country or abroad, seeking their modernization and adjustment to the mechanisms used in international practices, according to the purpose and objectives of the given entity, improving their operation, commercial and financial relations, or the investment made by the Venezuelan State. The organization or reorganization must, above all, guarantee the safeguarding of the patrimony of the Republic and its entities." (Art. 25).

But a privatization, as State policy, can only be accomplished it the most rigorous transparency;[139] on the contrary, what we can witness is the secret distribution of State assets among specific allies of the regime.[140]

c. Provisions regarding the participation, promotion and protection of national and international capital in the economy

The destatization and denationalization policy, by providing for the privatization of public companies, obviously contemplates the need to regulate measures to ensure the participation of national and international private capital in the economy, for which purpose the "Constitutional Law" set forth several express provisions.

It the first place, the "Constitutional Law" defined *measures for alliances with the private sector with respect to companies that were expropriated (expropriated, confiscated, occupied) by the State*, providing the following in its Article 30:

> "the assets that are under Venezuela State's management as a consequence of *any administrative or judicial measure restricting the elements of property* [i.e. use, enjoyment and disposition], that may be required for their urgent

139 As Asdrúbal Oliveros expressed it, "the regime could begin an asset transfer process that could focus on the metal sectors, mixed oil companies, especially for gasoline production, and hotels;" considering that "privatization is necessary in Venezuela, but a privatization in the context of the rule of law, with guarantees for both the State and for citizens and the investor. With transparency, open, carried out through a bidding transparent process and an evaluation of what is being done. Unfortunately, none of this exists because it is extremely opaque." See the report: "Asdrúbal Oliveros: Ley antibloqueo formaliza prácticas ocultas que el chavismo realiza desde hace años," en *El Nacional,* October 14, 2020; available at: https://www.elnacional.com/economia/asdrubal-oliveros-ley-antibloqueo-formaliza-practicas-ocultas-que-el-chavismo-realiza-desde-hace-anos/

140 That is why, José Ignacio Hernández has expressed about the policy established in the law, that it is rather about government measures to "please its economic and political allies, further promoting the *criminalization of the Venezuelan economy."* In other words, "this policy cannot be seen as a kind of "economic opening" towards "capitalism", since its objective is not to expand free enterprise, but rather to distribute strategic assets among Maduro's allies, as in 2016 Citgo was distributed among the 2020 Bond holders and Rosneft." See José Ignacio Hernández, "La Ley Constitucional Antibloqueo" y el avance de la economía criminal," en *La Gran Aldea*, Octubre 15, 2020, disponible en: https://lagranaldea.com/2020/10/15/la-ley-constitucional-antibloqueo-y-el-avance-de-la-economia-criminal-en-venezuela/ .

incorporation to a productive process, could be the object of *alliances with entities of the private sector*, including small and medium industries, or with the organized People's Power, in order to maximize the production of goods and services for satisfying the fundamental needs of the Venezuelan people and achieve the best efficiency for the companies of the public sector."

This implies the possibility for the Executive Branch to privatize all companies and industries that were expropriated or confiscated through administrative and judicial measures during the last 20 years, by means of alliances, as was expressly provided in the Bill of Law proposed by Nicolás Maduro.

In the second place, to ensure the destatization of the economy through the privatization of public companies, the "Constitutional Law" issued *measures for promoting the participation of private capital in the national economy*, providing as an objective thereof, "the attraction of foreign investment, especially at a large scale (Art. 20), and assigning to the Executive Branch of the Government the power to "authorize and implement measures that encourage and favor the *integral or partial participation, management and operation of the national and international private sector* in the development of the national economy." (Art. 29).

In the third place, and in line with the previous measures, the "Constitutional Law" defined *measures for the protection of private investments*, authorizing the Executive Branch to agree "with its partners and investments, during the term contractually agreed upon, *on clauses for the protection of their investments [...] for the purpose of generating trust and stability* (Art. 34). In this regard, under the "Constitutional Law" there could be signed, for example, "legal stability agreements," established in the Law for the Promotion and Protection of Investments of 1999 (now abrogated), which could never be signed because they were deemed to be contrary to the national interest. [141]

Within the specific frame of the *protection of foreign investments*, Article 34 of the "Constitutional Law" further expressly allows "clauses" for the "settlement of disputes," among which there is without doubt the concept of *arbitration*, and particularly, international arbitration, a legal figure that was also very vilified in the last 20 years as contrary to the national interests. It should be noted that the "Constitutional Law" did not include the exhaustion of internal resources in order to

---

141 As the Vice President of the Republic announced to the Diplomatic Corps: "It is expected to use "exceptional" mechanisms to attract additional income. To do this, alliances with private companies and investors of different kinds are established. [...] This law will protect foreign economic investments, "under new forms of association, of society, and there will also be special forms of information protection, to protect those who come to invest in Venezuela." See the report: "Delcy Rodríguez vende la ley antibloqueo como protección a inversiones extranjeras," en *Tal Cual*, 13 de octubre de 2020, disponible en: https://talcualdigital.com/delcy-rodriguez-vende-la-ley-antibloqueo-como-proteccion-a-inversiones-extranjeras/. With that presentation, as explained by Rodrigo Cabezas, former Finance Minister, "it became clear" that "the anti-blockade law is aimed at the international economic sector" [...] "The heart of the proposed law is the oil business and the possible privatizations of national companies and mixed, the privatization of assets such as ports, airports, mines (...) They want to scrape the assets of the Republic without any control." See the report: "Exministro chavista: Quieren 'raspar' los bienes de la República con la ley antibloqueo," en *Tal Cual*, 14 de octubre de 2020, disponible en: https://talcualdigital.com/rodrigo-cabezas-quieren-raspar-los-bienes-de-la-republica-sin-ningun-control/

be able to resort to arbitration, which was contained in the Bill of Law that was submitted to the National Constituent Assembly.

Finally, specifically with regard to fostering private initiative, the Law regulated what it called the "social initiative," providing that the Executive Branch must create and implement "programs that allow and guarantee investments by professionals, technicians, scientists, academicians, entrepreneurs and workers' groups or organizations in the public and private sectors and by the organized people's power, in projects or alliances in strategic sectors." Art. 33)

D. The implementation of the New Economic Policy and of public financing by means of the Executive "Disapplying" of legal rules

In the "Constitutional Law," as already mentioned, for the purpose of executing the "new" economic policy and the financial aforementioned transactions, the provision that must be more highlighted, is the First Transitory Provision (which is by no means "transitory"), according to which:

> "The provisions of this Constitutional Law shall apply *on a preferential basis over the rules of a legal and sub-legal rank, including with regard to the organic and special laws that govern the matter, even in the system arising from the Decree granting the State of Exception and Economic Emergency* throughout the National territory [...]."

The practical effect of the provision is that it can be deemed that *there are no pre-established legal rules* for adopting the measures that the Executive Branch may adopt in enforcing the economic policy –or the change thereof- purported in the Law, because if those contemplated in the current laws differ from the provision of the "Constitutional Law," they shall be in a sort of "suspended" or "inapplicable" status from the moment the Law was published (as expressly set forth in the original Project);[142] that is, a situation of the lack of applicable law, that is purported to be replaced by the authorization granted to the Executive Branch to decree the "disapplying" thereof in "specific cases" and therefore legislate to fill in the legislative void for the purpose of implementing the "economic policy" set forth in the Law.

Precisely for this purpose, the implementation of the general disruption of the legal order that is "decreed" in the Law, with the declaration of the general prevalence thereof, is detailed in its Articles 19 through 21, wherein the Executive Branch is authorized to proceed to "*disapply* rules of a legal or sub-legal rank," when dealing with the implementation of the measures for economic and productive equilibrium" (Art. 21); furthermore, said Branch is specifically authorized to

---

142 The *Bloque Constitucional Venezolano* regarding this Second Transitory Provision of the Law, has indicated that: "it leaves no doubt about the illegitimate purpose of this normative, by pointing out that all the norms that collide with that pseudo law are suspended, in practice promoting a constitutional disruption to create a new economic order (exceptional), starting from a "blank page", which amounts to a true legal aberration, because a "constitutional blank page", to be filled with the only unlimited will of the power holders, is the most unequivocal expression of arbitrariness, of the absence of the rule of law, which will generate greater vulnerability and unpredictability for Venezuelans." See Bloque Constitucional Venezolano, "Sobre la pretendida Ley Antibloqueo,"16 de Octubre 16, 2020, disponible en http://digaloahidigital.com/noticias/el-bloque-constitucional-de-venezuela-la-opini%C3%B3n-p%C3%BAblica-nacional-e-internacional-sobre-la .

"disapply" laws of a legal or sub-legal rank, for specific cases," "when this is necessary in order to overcome the obstacles and offset the damage caused by the unilateral coercive measures and other restrictive or punitive measures to the administrative activity, or whenever this contributes to the protection of the heritage of the patrimony of the Venezuelan State in the face of any act of deprivation or immobilization, or to mitigate the effects of the unilateral coercive measures and other restrictive or punitive measures that affect the flow of foreign currency" (Art. 19), and when the "enforcement thereof is impossible or counterproductive as a result of the effects of a given unilateral coercive measure or other restrictive or punitive measure" (Art. 19).

It can be said that, as of the coming into effect of this "Constitutional Law," the previous existing legal uncertainty has been formalized in an express legal text, but now extends to the effects of the laws and regulations related to the matters governed by said Law, the enforcement of which can be "suspended" by the Executive Branch.

The realm of arbitrariness implied by this absolute executive power to decide when a law or regulations are to be applied or not, which obviously can only give rise to absolutely null and void acts, is only slightly limited by requiring that a "technical report" –obviously not legal at all- be prepared in each case, in order to clearly determine "the provisions being disapplied and the grounds therefor" (Art. 42); that some prior opinions be obtained from certain agencies (Art. 35), and that the suspension be:

> "indispensable for the adequate macro-economic management, the protection and promotion of the national economy, the stability of the local productive and financial systems, the attraction of foreign investments, especially on a large scale, or the procurement of resources to guarantee the basic rights of the Venezuelan people and the official social protection system." (Art. 20).

In any event, the Law established a general limit for exercising this unique and novel power to "disapply" laws, by expressly providing that "in no case will it be possible to disapply rules related to the exercise of human rights" (Art. 21); to do otherwise would be the total negation of the Constitution.

The other limit established is that rules "pertaining to the division of Public Powers" cannot be "disapplied" (Art. 21), but adding that this so long as it "*does not pertain to the power to approve or authorize*," which means that if a law requires the necessary approval by the National Assembly for certain acts or contracts, such rule may notwithstanding be suspended, as has occurred within the frame of the decrees for economic emergency when Nicolás Maduro authorized himself from the onset to sign contracts of national interest without the authorization or approval of the National Assembly,[143] which has been happening since 2016, under the status of

143 See Allan R. Brewer-Carías, "El control político de la Asamblea Nacional respecto de los decretos de excepción y su desconocimiento judicial y Ejecutivo con ocasión de la emergencia económica decretada en enero de 2016, en *VI Congreso de Derecho Procesal Constitucional y IV de Derecho Administrativo, Homenaje al Prof. Carlos Ayala Corao, 10 y 11 noviembre 2016*, FUNEDA, Caracas 2017. pp. 291-336.

judicial contempt in which the Constitutional Chamber has unconstitutionally placed the National Assembly.[144]

Consequently, for example, pursuant to this "Constitutional Law," the Executive Branch could "disapply" the provisions of the Organic Law on Hydrocarbons that require the National Assembly's authorization to incorporate mixed enterprises in the hydrocarbons sector, which would evidently be unconstitutional, because laws can only be abrogated by other laws, and their enforcement or application cannot be "suspended" by an executive decision.

In any event, it should be noted that the authorization given to the Executive Branch in the unconstitutional "Constitutional Law" to "disapply" organic laws and laws, in no case implies the possibility for it to also "disapply" the Constitution, particularly, the provision in its Article 151 that requires that all cases of national public interest contracts intended to be entered into with foreign states, foreign official entities or foreign companies not domiciled in the country must be previously authorized by the National Assembly (Art. 151). Of course, it would be totally inadmissible and unlawful that the Commercial Registry be deemed "secret" and conceal the information about foreign companies that might be domiciled in the country, in order to circumvent this constitutional requirement for parliamentary control.

E. Secrecy as a rule for implementing the "Constitutional Law" and, particularly, with regard to disapplying legal rules

The framework of legal uncertainty that is expressly "regulated" in the "Constitutional Law," based on the power granted to the Executive Branch of Government to disapply all kinds of rules as it may deem indispensable for enforcing the economic measures in order to implement the purposes of the Law, is complemented in an aberrant and astonishing manner by providing that such "disapplying" of rules must necessarily be effected in a concealed frame of secrecy and confidentiality,[145] behind the backs and not known by the citizens.[146]

---

144 See Allan R. Brewer-Carías, "La paralización de la Asamblea Nacional: la suspensión de sus sesiones y la amenaza del enjuiciar a los diputados por "desacato," en *Revista de Derecho Público*, No. 147-148, (julio-diciembre 2016), Editorial Jurídica Venezolana, Caracas 2016, pp. 322-325

145 As it has been recognized by the Vice President of the Republic: "The Law provides for mechanisms of confidentiality in the information, confidentiality in the identity in question, in the development of the activity, there is a system with a technological platform that will allow the protection of these investments." See in en Agencia Efe, "Delcy Rodríguez: No revelaremos la procedencia de las inversiones extranjeras o nacionales," en *Noticiero Digital ND*, October 18, 2020, available at: https://www.noticierodigital.com/2020/10/delcy-rodriguez-no-revelaremos-la-procedencia-de-las-inversiones-extranjeras-o-nacionales/ See also in: EFE, "El régimen dice que Venezuela recibirá inversiones sin revelar su procedencia de fondos," in *El Nacional*, October 18, 2020, available at in: https://www.elnacional.com/venezuela/el-regimen-dice-que-venezuela-recibira-inversiones-sin-revelar-su-procedencia-de-fondos/

146 In this regard, Jesús Rangel Rachadell has stated that "it was said that the law was intended to "shield us," and the first shield is that it is forbidden to inquire about the economic transactions related to this law, because it precludes access to the information. [...] It conceals who acquires State property, how much they pay, terms and conditions, guaranties, exceptions from liability, bids or direct awards, the formalities and records, the applicable jurisdiction (country where the obligations may be enforced), causes for nullity, methods of interpretation [...]

It is elementary that in order for any law or rule to have legal effects vis-à-vis the citizens, the same must be published. However, according to the provisions of this "Constitutional Law," the disapplying of laws and regulations that it authorizes in order to implement the change to an economic policy of destatization, denationalization and privatization, which also affects all the citizens, is declared a matter pertaining to the "security of the Nation" and considered a secret activity of the State. This place the citizens in the absurd situation of not knowing or being able to know –because this is forbidden, it is secret- what rule is applied or not, or what transaction has been made, and under the Organic Law of National Security they may even be subject to imprisonment if they purport to "disclose" the secret (Art. 55).

And it is within this framework that the regime purports the absurdity of implementing measures to "attract" investors, who primarily demand "legal certainty" in any part of the world; that is, unless the purpose of the law is to consider investors that only move in the shadows.

The clearest evidence of this juridical aberration is found in Article 43 of the Law, which provides that:

> "*the procedures, formalities and records made on the occasion of implementing any of the measures set forth*" [...in] this Constitutional Law that "*imply disapplying rules of a legal or sub-legal rank*" are declared to be *secret and reserved* [...].

If this were not enough, based on that general provision of reserve and secrecy, Article 37 establishes what it refers to as a "transitory system for the classification of documents having confidential and secret contents for the purpose of protecting and guaranteeing the efficacy of the decisions made by the Venezuelan Public Power to protect the State against coercive unilateral measures, punitive measures and other threats." –which system is not at all transitory, for it lasts, as stated in Article 43 "up to 90 days after the unilateral coercive measures and other restrictive or punitive measures that have propitiated the situation have ceased."

Article 39 of the "Constitutional Law" further insists on the confidentiality and secrecy, when authorizing the "highest authorities of the bodies and entities of the central and decentralized National Public Administration" to consider "by reasons of national interest and convenience," "as reserved, confidential or of limited disclosure any record, document, information, fact or circumstance, that they become aware of in the performance of their duties, by application of the Constitutional Law," which should be done "by means of a duly *justified* formality, for a given term and with the ultimate purpose of guaranteeing the effectiveness of the measures designed to counteract the adverse effects of the unilateral coercive measures, punitive measures or other threats imposed." The latter, obviously, is of no use because the motivation of state actions is set to allow control of their legitimacy, legality and proportionality; however, since they are secret, it is useless to require their rationale.

What is an outrage is that we citizens remain without knowledge about the disapplying of legal or sub-legal rules in order for the State to negotiate unchecked." See Jesús Rangel Rachadell, "Todo será secreto," in *El Nacional*, October 13, 2020, available at: https://www.elnacional.com/opinion/todo-sera-secreto/

The consequence of the confidentiality statement is that said documentation, characterized as secret, confidential and reserved, "shall be filed in separate case files or records, using mechanisms that guarantee its safety," visibly placing in their "cover the relevant warning, stating the restriction to their access and disclosure and the liabilities incurred by officials or persons who may infringe the respective system" (Art. 40)

There is another consequence arising from this regulation expressing the lack of transparency and this is, as stated in Article 41 of the Law, the establishment of a prohibition to "access documentation that has been characterized as confidential or reserved," which implies that no "simple or certified copies may be issued thereof."

This prohibition to access the documents, generally set forth in Article 41 and specifically developed in Articles 37 et seq., evidently is entirely incompatible with and contradicts the text of Article 38, which provides as a right of the people "to have access to administrative files and records, whatever their form of expression or type of material support that contain them, [...] so as not to affect the effectiveness of the measures for counteracting the effects of the unilateral measures, punitive measures or other threats, nor the operation of public services, nor the satisfaction of the people's needs due to the interruption of the administrative processes set up for such purposes."

If everything is confidential, secret and has restricted access, which, of course, violates the Constitution, it is not possible to guarantee any right of access thereto.

Finally, the provisions in the Law about the subsequent "control" by the Office of the Comptroller General of the Republic (Art. 13), a body that, as is well known, has no autonomy, even appear to be innocuous, because in order for the Comptroller's office to have access to the secret documents, it must "coordinate" the manner of exercising its control with the Executive Branch (Art. 43), which in itself is a negation of control.

The "Constitutional Law" also reaches the absurdity of subjecting the judicial bodies that need the information labeled as confidential, in open violation of the autonomy and independence due to judges, to "formalize" their requests before the Office of the Attorney General of the Republic, who has the last word (Art. 44).

F. Final Considerations

It can be deemed that the "Constitutional Law" approved by the fraudulent and unconstitutional National Constituent Assembly, convened and elected unconstitutionally in 2017, which –even if it had been lawfully elected- would in no event have legislative powers, is of no legal value because it is contrary to the Constitution, being only an act of force against the legal system of the rule of law.[147]

147 For this reason, the National Assembly, by means of Agreement dated October 13, 2020, when "reiterating that the fraudulent National Constituent Assembly is legally non-extant and its decisions are ineffective," agreed to "disavow all parts of the so-called "Anti-blockade law for national development and guaranty of human rights," and, consequently, consider it non-extant and ineffective." See "Acuerdo en desconocimiento de la irrita Ley Antibloqueo dictada de manera inconstitucional por la fraudulenta Asamblea Nacional Constituyente," available at: https://asambleanacional-media.s3.amazonaws.com/documentos/acto/acuerdo-en-desconocimiento-de-la-irrita-ley-antibloqueo-dictada-de-manera-inconstitucional-por-la-fraudulenta-asamblea-nacional-constituyente-20201013204743.pdf

Moreover, it delegated practically unlimited legislative powers to the Executive Branch to fill in the voids arising from the disapplying of laws, which ultimately purports to change the economic policy in a covert, opaque, secret and not at all transparent manner, by destatizing, denationalizing and privatizing the economy by promoting and protecting the participation of national and international private capital in the economy. But it only protects the participation of those who operate in darkness and opacity, being this the outcome of a framework of total legal uncertainty and secrecy that could only lead to the indiscriminate transfer of the State's assets to national and foreign individuals, handpicked at the regime's discretion, absent any guaranty of control or budgetary discipline.[148]

Within this frame of legal uncertainty and executive disapplying of laws in secrecy and with no transparence, it is a total fallacy to expect to effectively attract and incorporate national and international private investments in Venezuelan productive centers, particularly in the oil sector, compatibles with the national interests;[149] with the serious threat that those who finally will be able to take part in the indiscriminate and secret share-out of the remains of the economy in order to deliberately conceal their implications, could not be the best in order to guarantee the rights and interests of the Venezuelan people.[150]

For those interested in history and in similar laws and policies sanctioned and enforced in other countries, one can say that this "Anti-blockade Law," *by itself*, poses the serious risk of ending up giving rise altogether to situations like those that, derived, *on the one hand*, from the Law to Remedy the Distress of People and the

---

148 As Gustavo Rossen pointed out when commenting the "Law: "What can happen in a poorly managed, impoverished, indebted country, dislocated by a statist model? Many things can happen, some predictable, others surprising. Inventing, for example, a law that appeals to anti-blockade but is, in truth, anti-transparency, anti-accountability, anti-control. A law for the country's auction, which justifies or authorizes the sale to the highest bidder of the nation's assets, a "monumental operation of national plunder to launder foreign capital and those of drug cartels" as stated in a statement from a group of Venezuelan political leaders. A law that also blocks information and enshrines secrecy and complicity. Finally, a law that with the offer to save the present ends up seriously compromising the security of the new generations." Véase Gustavo Rossen, "La nueva oligarquía," en *El Nacional*, 19 de octubre de 2020, disponible en: https://www.elnacional.com/opinion/la-nueva-oligarquia/

149 See the review: "Ley antibloqueo faculta a Maduro privatizar participación de PDVSA en empresas mixtas," in *Petroguí@*, October 4, 2020, available at: http://www.petroguia.com/pet/noticias/petr%C3%B3leo/ley-antibloqueo-faculta-maduro-privatizar-participaci%C3%B3n-de-pdvsa-en-empresas. See also in: "Ministro Tareck El Aissami: Ley Antibloqueo fortalecerá la industria petrolera nacional," 1 de octubre de 2020, Available at: https://www.vtv.gob.ve/el-aissami-ley-antibloqueo-fortalecera-industria-petrolera/ ; and in: "Ley Antibloqueo': Maduro busca más poder legal en Venezuela para sellar nuevos negocios petroleros," October 1, 2020, available at: https://albertonews.com/nacionales/ley-antibloqueo-maduro-busca-mas-poder-legal-en-venezuela-para-sellar-nuevos-negocios-petroleros/

150 See, for example, the opinión of several political leaders in the document "Acta de remate de la República," in the report, "Líderes políticos alertan: régimen de Maduro pretende rematar Venezuela. En un documento público, María Corina Machado, Antonio Ledezma, Diego Arria, Humberto Calderón Berti, Asdrúbal Aguiar, Enrique Aristeguieta Gramcko y Carlos Ortega se dirigen a los venezolanos y a la comunidad internacional para denunciar de las maniobras para liquidar y blanquear los activos de la nación en un acto de traición a la patria," in *El Nacional*, October 11, 2020, available at: https://www.elnacional.com/venezuela/lideres-politicos-alertan-regimen-de-maduro-pretende-rematar-venezuela/. Also available at: https://www.el-carabobeno.com/ documento-publico-maduro-se-propone-rematar-en-secreto-bienes-de-la-nacion/

Reich, approved as an "enabling law" by the German Parliament on March 23, 1933, which delegated to Chancellor Adolf Hitler all the legislative powers (for example, Article 1 provided that: "In addition to the procedure prescribed by the constitution, laws of the Reich may also be enacted by the government of the Reich"; and Article 4, that "Treaties of the Reich with foreign states, which relate to matters of Reich legislation, shall for the duration of the validity of these laws not require the consent of the legislative authorities," which law was the fundamental legal basis for the final collapse of the Weimar Republic and the consolidation of Nazi Germany; [151] and, *on the other hand*, those resulting from the *giant program for the privatization of public companies of the former Soviet Union* carried out between 1991 and 1999 under the government of the first Russian President, Boris Yeltsin, which allowed for the most important and oldest public companies to end up, in the midst of great corruption and crimes, in the hands of the so-called "Oligarchs," that is, the "nouveau riche" who were close to the regime.[152]

We hope that none of this happens in Venezuela, and much less what Karl Marx wrote in 1851, that "history occurs twice: first as a tragedy and then as a farce."[153]

V. SOME PRINCIPLES RELATED TO THE PROMOTION AND PROTECTION OF FREE COMPETITION

1. Some general principles in comparative law

In 1973, Chile enacted legislation on Antitrust and Free Competition matters, initially contained in Decree-Law N° 211 of 1973, which after various reforms was officially compiled (*texto refundido*) in 2004, particularly after the reforms introduced by Law N° 19.911 of 1994. Consequently, in the matter of promotion and defense of free competition, Chile can be considered one of the pioneer countries in Latin America in this sort of legislation. It was after such earlier regulations, that almost all Latin American countries, following the European Union and United States regulatory trends, have adopted free competition laws.

---

151 See on this matter, among others, William Sheridan Allen, *The Nazi seizure of power*. Echo Point Books & Media, 2010; and the review published in *Rea Silva*, "La muerte de la democracia en Alemania. Una democracia liberal no muere de un día para otro. Para acabar con el marco legal de un estado de derecho es necesario una serie de actores capaces de minar su legitimidad y estabilidad mediante todo tipo de tácticas políticas," available at https://reasilvia.com/2017/09/la-muerte-la-democracia-alemania/

152 See on this matter, among others, Chrystia Freeland, *Sale of the Century: Russia's Wild Ride From Communism to Capitalism*, Crown Business, 2000; David Hoffman, *The Oligarchs: Wealth and Power in New Russia*, Public Affairs, 2002; and the review by Jeffrey Hay, in *Facts and details*, "Russian Privatization and Oligarchs. Privatization Of Russian Industry," 2016, available at http://factsanddetails.com/russia/Economics_Business_Agriculture/sub9_7b/entry-5169.html

153 Karl Marx's famous phrase with which he began his study about "The Eighteenth Brumaire of Luis Bonaparte," published in *Die Revolution*, New York, 1852, said: "Hegel remarks somewhere that all great world-historic facts and personages appear, so to speak twice. He forgot to add: the first time as tragedy, the second time as farce." See Karl Marx, *El 18 Brumario de Luis Bonaparte*, available at: https://www.marxists.org/archive/marx/works/1852/18th-brumaire/ch01.htm

The Antitrust and Free Competition regulations in Venezuela where established in the "*Ley para promover y proteger el ejercicio de la libre competencia*" (Law for the Protection and Promotion of Free Competition) ("Pro-Competencia Law),[154] in order to promote and protect the exercise of free competition and the efficiency that benefits the producers and consumers, and to prohibit monopolistic and oligopolistic practices and other means that could impede, restrict, falsify, or limit the enjoyment of economic freedom (Article 1). For the purposes of the Pro-Competencia Law, Free competition is understood to be a situation characterized by the existence of adequate conditions which allow any economic agent, be it a supplier or buyer, to freely enter and exit the market, and those that are in the market not to have the possibility either individually or through concerted action to impose any conditions on the exchange mechanism (Article 3).

All of these laws seek to promote and protect the exercise of free competition, establishing rules in order to allow all economic agents to freely enter and exit the market, and to prevent such agent, once they have entered the market, either individually or through concerted action, from imposing any conditions on the exchange mechanism. These laws also establish provisions in order to correct, to prohibit and to repress attempts against free competition in economic activities. A complete listing of conduct that violates principles of free competition can be found in article 3 of the Decree-Law 211.

In comparative law, and particularly in civil law countries (as opposed to common law countries), the regime contained in these laws regulating economic activities in order to promote and protect free competition, has always been part of public law (as opposed to private, civil or commercial law), and particularly, has been considered part of administrative law. Any general book on Administrative Law or on Economic Public Law, lays out this relationship. [155]

The reason for the legal regime of free competition being part of administrative law lays in the fact that the main purpose of the regime is, on the one hand, to limit economic activities of individuals and enterprises in order to assure free competition; and on the other hand, to entrust certain public entities with powers to control and correct economic activities and economic distortions, as well as to prevent economic activities that would violate principles of free competition.

It is this application of the laws that explains why, in all administrative law regimes, the main legal relations deriving from their provisions describe relations, not between individuals or enterprises, but between the State (which promotes and defends free competition and sanctions antitrust conducts) and individuals and

---

154 *Official Gazette* N° 34880 of January 13, 1992. In 2014 this Law was substituted by the Law Antimonopoly. See in *Official Gazette*, N° 40.549 of November 26, 2014.

155 For instance, see José Eugenio Soriano, *Derecho Público de la Competencia (Public Law on Competition),* Madrid, 1998; José Ignacio Hernández González, *Derecho Administrativo y Regulación Económica (Administrative Law and Economic Regulation)*, Caracas 2006, pp. 214 ff; *Estudios de Derecho Público Económico, Libro Homenaje al Prof. Dr. Sebastián Martín-Retortillo (Studies of Public Economic Law, Tribute Book to Profesor Dr. Sebastián Martín-Retortillo)*, Madrid 2003, pp. 719 ff; Gaspar Ariño Ortiz, *Principios de Derecho Público Económico (Principles of Public Economic Law)*, Bogotá, 2003, pp. 184 ff. José Bermejo Vera, *Derecho Administrativo. Parte Especial (Administrative Law, Special Part)*, Madrid, 2005, pp. 801 ff.

enterprises that are the subjects of such sanctions (or that can, in specific situations, benefit from the restrictive or repressive State activities regarding others).

The entities of the State created by these laws on free competition in order to apply their regulations, in order to promote and defend free competition, and to adopt policies and actions in order to enforce the legal prohibitions and to repress attempts against free competition in economic activities by applying the respective sanctions, can be either independent public administration entities or special tribunals created for such purpose.

That is why, in comparative administrative law, two models can be distinguished regarding the organization of the authority called to apply and enforce the free competition laws: First, the creation of entities that are part of public administration, as independent or autonomous agencies; and second, the creation of special courts or tribunals empowered to apply the law.

The first model of public administration entities, as independent or autonomous agencies, has its origin in the framework used for the Federal Trade Commission in the U.S., conceived as an independent regulatory agency that although established outside the Executive Branch, is not part of the Judiciary and is subject to "administrative law," defined by Peter Strauss as: "the body of requirements resting upon administrative agencies that affect private interests by making rules, adjudicating cases, investigating, threatening, prosecuting, publicizing, and advising."[156]

As mentioned, this first model is the one that was followed in Venezuela, being the Superintendence for the Promotion and Protection of Free Competition a public administration entity with operational autonomy, attached to the Ministry of Industry and Commerce (Article 19). Therefore, the "Superintendence" was part of the Executive Branch of Government (Public Administration) and its activities were subjected to administrative law, and the procedure developed before it is an administrative procedure.[157]

Therefore, in the Latin American countries following this model of independent administrative agencies, once the respective decisions are issued by the agency, which are administrative acts, they are subject to judicial review by special courts, integrating the special jurisdiction called "*contencioso administrativo*" (judicial review of administrative action courts), established following the initial French pattern, for the purpose of adjudicating on the validity of the said administrative acts and to annul them when contrary to law. In this sense, for instance, the decisions of the Venezuelan Superintendence are challenged before the First Court on *Contencioso Administrativo*.

The same model of independent regulatory administrations or agencies empowered to apply and enforce the free competition law, is the one followed in

156 Peter Strauss, *Administrative Law*, Keyed to the Strauss casebook, Tenth Edition, Thompson, 2004, pp.1, 3.

157 See Allan R. Brewer-Carías, "Introducción General al Régimen para Promover y Proteger el Ejercicio de la Libre Competencia (General Introduction to the Regime to Promote and Protect the Exercise of Free Competition)", in Allan R. Brewer-Carías *et al.*, *Ley para Promover y Proteger el Ejercicio de la Libre Competencia (Law to Promote and Protect the Exercise of Free Competition),* Caracas 1996, pp. 7-99.

Spain and Argentina, even though such entitles are called "tribunals." In Spain, the *Ley 16/1989 de Defensa de la Competencia* (*Law 16/1989 of Defense of Free Competition)* created the *Tribunal de Defensa de la Competencia* (Tribunal for the Defense of Free Competition) that in spite of its name, was created as an "autonomous organ" (*organismo autónomo*) of the General Public Administration of the State. This "tribunal" was eliminated by the new *Ley 15/2007 de Defensa de la Competencia (Law 15/2007 of Defense of Free Competition)*, and was substituted by another independent administrative agency, named the National Commission of Competition (*Comisión Nacional de la Competencia*). According to this Law, the agency is now organized as an independent public administrative entity subject to the Law on the General Administration of the State, and attached to the Ministry of Economy and Finance (article 19).

This is the same situation in Argentina, where the Ley 25.156 of 1999 of Defense of Competition also created a *Tribunal de Defensa de la Competencia* (Tribunal for the Defense of Competition), as an autonomous public administrative entity *(ente autárquico*) within the Ministry of Economy, Public Works and Services of the Nation, whose members are appointed by the Executive Power (articles 17, 19).

The second model used in order to organize the state agencies in charge of applying the competition laws, is the creation of special courts or tribunals outside the civil or commercial judiciary organization, as is the case in Chile. In the original *Decreto Ley Nº 211 (Decree-Law 211)*, of 1973 which established legal provisions for the defense of free competition (called *Ley Antimonopolio*), the entity in charge of applying the law at the national level in fact was a special hybrid entity named the "Regulatory Commission," with an autonomous status and composed of one member of the Supreme Court, two public officials of the Executive (Ministries of Economy and Finance) and two University Deans. This entity was later eliminated and substituted by the Tribunal for the Defense of Free Competition (*Tribunal de Defensa de la Libre Competencia*) created by the *Ley 19.911 de Creación del Tribunal de Defensa de la Competencia (Law 19.911 of Creation of the Tribunal for the Defense of Free Competition)*.

According to the rewritten 2004 text of the Decree-Law 211, the Free Competition Defense Tribunal (article 2) was created as "a special and independent jurisdictional body subjected to the managerial, correctional and economic supervision of the Supreme Court whose functions are to prevent, correct and punish attempts against free competition" (article 5). Nonetheless, its members are appointed by the President of the Republic and the Council of the Central bank (article 6).

This Tribunal is, without doubts, an "*órgano jurisdiccional,*" as it is named in article 5 of the Decree Law Nº 211, and falls under the sense of the Spanish expression in article 2 of the Inter-American Convention of Letters Rogatory. It has been created by statute, as a special court that has jurisdiction over specific matters, as referred to in article 16 of the same Convention. Accordingly, the promotion and defense of free competition and the application of the law establishing its regime are "*materias objeto de jurisdicción especial*" in the sense of that Spanish expression in article 16 of the Convention.

In any case, whether organized as an independent administrative regulatory agency as integral part of public administration, or as special tribunal, the main consequence of the matters attributed to it regarding the promotion and protection of free competition as being part of administrative law, is that in both cases the petitions and requests filed before those agencies or tribunals, the proceedings before them, and the decisions adopted, are not "proceedings in civil or commercial matters" in the sense of that expression used in article 2 of the Inter American Convention of Letters Rogatory. The proceedings in civil and commercial matters are essentially contentious ones, always confronting a plaintiff against a defendant.

In effect, civil matters are those concerning civil law as the "law of civil or private rights, as opposed to criminal or administrative law,"[158] considering "private right" as those "personal rights, as opposed to rights of the public or the state", and personal rights as those "that form part of a person's legal status or personal condition."[159] These matters are uniformly regulated in Latin American countries in the Civil Codes that in some cases have been complemented by special legislation, for instance regarding family matters (adoption). On the other hand, commercial matters are those concerning commercial law, as the "substantive law dealing with the sale and distribution of goods, the financing of credit transaction on the security of the goods sold, and negotiable instruments."[160] These matters are uniformly regulated in all Latin American countries in the Commercial Codes, and in the U.S. by the Uniform Commercial Code. Similarly, Spanish legal dictionaries define "commercial" law (also known as mercantile law) as the area of private law that regulates relations between merchants and ensures compliance with commercial contracts by both merchants and non-merchants.[161] In its purest sense, commercial law, or "law merchant" in civil law countries is primarily defined as referring to the relations between merchants, while contractual obligations between non-merchants generally fall within the realm of civil law.[162]

Consequently, the matters related to the legislation passed for the purpose of promoting and protecting the exercise of free competition, establishing rules in order to allow all economic agents to freely enter and exit the market, and once being in it, to prevent them of imposing either individually or through concerted action, any conditions on the exchange mechanism, cannot be considered "civil" or "commercial" legislation. These laws are part of administrative law, issued to restrict and prohibit certain conduct in order to guarantee free competition by entrusting public entities, administrative agencies or tribunals the power to control and correct economic activities, repress violations of free competition and impose sanctions. That is, the main feature of these laws is the legal relation established between the state when promoting and defending free competition and repressing and sanctioning anti-trust conduct, and the individuals or enterprises that are subject

158 See *Black's Law Dictionary*, Eighth Edition -Bryan A. Garner, Editor in Chief-, Thomson-West, 2004, p. 263.

159 *Idem*, p. 1.348.

160 *Idem*, p. 285.

161 See E. Caffarena de Jiles, *Diccionario de Jurisprudencia Chilena (Chilean Jurisprudence Dictionary)*, 1959, p. 325; M Ossorio y Florit and G. Cabanellas de las Cuevas, *Diccionario de Derecho (Law Dictionary)*, Vol. I, 2007, p. 260) See E. Caffarena de Jiles, *Diccionario de Jurisprudencia Chilena (Chilean Jurisprudence Dictionary)*, 1959, p. 325; M Ossorio y Florit and G. Cabanellas de las Cuevas, *Diccionario de Derecho (Law Dictionary)*, Vol. I, 2007, p. 260.

162 See *Idem*, pp. 241, 417; and R. Moreno Rodríguez, *Diccionario Jurídico (Juridical Dictionary)*, 1998, p. 237.

to restrictions, prohibitions or sanctions, or those that obtain benefit from the sanctions imposed upon others.

2. Principles of the regime in Venezuela established in the 1990's

In Venezuela, the Antitrust and Free Competition legal regime was first established in 1992 in the aforementioned *Pro-Competencia* Law (*Ley para promover y proteger el ejercicio de la libre competencia*)," [163] in which the *Pro-Competencia* Superintendence for the Promotion and Protection of Free Competition was created, as the institution in charge of monitoring and controlling the practices that could impede or restrict free competition and to determine the violations of Free Competition an Antitrust regulations. Such *Pro-Competencia* Law was substituted in 2014 by the Antimonopoly Law, changing the sense and scope of the statute from one devoted to protect free competition to another designed to limit free competition and to persecute monopoly.[164]

In it, the *Pro Competencia* Superintendence was transformed into an Antimonopoly Superintendence, as a deconcentrated organ on the Public Administration (Article 19), being the Superintendent appointed by the President of the Republic (Article 21).

The Law has now the purpose of protecting, promoting and regulate the exercise of the just economic competition in order to guarantee the democratization of the productive economic activities with social equality in order to strength the national sovereignty and encourage the endogen and sustainable development in order to satisfy the social needs and construct a just, free, solidary and co-responsible society, by means of prohibiting and sanction monopolistic, oligopoly, abuse of dominant position and any other anticompetitive or fraudulent conducts and practices (art. 1),

Nonetheless, when subjecting to its provisions all the persons developing economic activities in Venezuela, the Law excludes the public economic sector, stating that are not subjected to its provisions, the basis organizations of popular power regulated by the Organic Law on the Communal Economic System of 2010; the public or mixt enterprises of strategic character, and the public enterprises for public utilities (*servicios públicos*) (art. 3).

The Antimonopoly Superintendence, as the organ in charge of the application and enforcement of the Law, is an organ that is part of the Executive Branch of Government (Public Administration) not being a judicial body. Its decisions are administrative acts and not judicial decisions, and the public officials that are appointed to work on it, are public servants and not judges. Therefore, they are not necessarily lawyers, and mostly they are professionals with economic studies background.

---

163 *Official Gazette* N° 34.880 of January 13, 1992. See in general on this Law, Allan R. Brewer-Carías, Gustavo Linares Benzo, Luis Ortiz y Faustino Flamarique, *Ley para promover y proteger el ejercicio de la libre competencia,* Colección Textos Legislativos, N° 14, Editorial Jurídica Venezolana, Caracas 1996.

164 Decree N° 1.415 published in *Official Gazette* N° 6.151 of 18 November 2014; *Ley Antimonopolio* (Law Antimonopoly).

According to Article 28 of the Antimonopoly Law, the Antimonopoly Superintendence is the only entity in Venezuela which among other powers and duties, has the followings: To conduct the investigations necessary to verify the existence of anticompetitive practices, and prepare case files concerning such practices; to determine the existence or nonexistence of prohibited practices or conduct, act to proscribe them, and impose the sanctions and fines provided in the Law; to adopt the necessary preventive measures, at its own initiative or at the request of a interested party, to avoid the detrimental effects of the prohibited practices; to authorize practices or conducts in exceptional cases established in the Law (art. 18); to propose to the Executive Branch the regulations necessary for the application of the Law; to issue its internal regulations and rules necessary for its operation; and to issue opinions on matters within its attributions when so requested by the judicial or administrative authorities. Therefore, the Antimonopoly Superintendence has no power whatsoever to grant any compensation judgment.

It must be noted that the Antimonopoly Superintendence is also empowered to create and maintain its own Register and archives of documents. Therefore, all the papers and files of documents produced in the administrative procedures developed before the Antimonopoly Superintendence are held in its own Archives. The originals of all those documents remains in those Archives, and copies and certified copies of all documents must be requested before the Antimonopoly Superintendence, according to the Organic Administrative Procedure Law which applies to all Public Administration organs.

Therefore, no judicial organ, court or tribunal has general power in Venezuela to determine the violations of the Antimonopoly Law, being a matter exclusively assigned to the Executive Branch trough the Antimonopoly Superintendence. Being an Institution that is part of Public Administration, the Antimonopoly Superintendence has no authority to order compensation for damages caused to any interested party as a consequence of the prohibited practices. This is an exclusive power of civil courts, but only after the Antimonopoly Superintendence has decided the case.

That is why Article 57 of the Law establishes as a general principle that *only* when a decision on Antimonopoly matters taken by the Pro-Competencia Superintendence is final, then the affected persons by the prohibited practices may turn to the competent courts to seek compensation for damages that occurred as a consequence of the Antimonopoly conducts determined by the Antimonopoly Superintendence. *Only* as an exception and *in the specific case of unfair competition practices* established in Article 16 of the Antimonopoly Law, persons affected may turn directly to competent civil courts without the need to exhaust the administrative procedure established in the Antimonopoly Law. However, if the affected persons decide to initiate the respective administrative proceeding established in the Antimonopoly Law, then they may not demand judicial redress for any damages they may have suffered as a consequence of the prohibited practices but *only* until after the decision of the Antimonopoly Superintendence becomes final.

According to Article 17 of the Antimonopoly Law, those unfair competition practices that allows a direct actions for compensation before courts, are those commercial practices which tend to eliminate competitors through unfair methods of competition; especially in the following cases: 1° Misleading or false advertising directed to impede or limit free competition; 2° The promoting of products and services based on false declarations with regards to the disadvantages or risks of any other competitors' product or service; and 3° Commercial bribery, the violation of industrial secrets and products simulation.

In addition to the unfair practices, Article 16 of the Antimonopoly Law prohibits in a general way all unfair, misleading and fraudulent practices in the production, distribution and commercialization of goods, as contrary to the economic democratization, because being able to displace persons subjected to the Law accomplishing the same economic activity, in their prejudice, or of the citizens exercising their right to have prompt and just access to goods and services. The Law also prohibits all facts, acts or unfair practices, in any way, when such conduct tends to prevent, restrict, mislead or distort the economic competition, are against economic efficiency, the general welfare and the rights of consumers or users and of the producers (art. 16).

According to the Antimonopoly Law, because its violations must be investigated and determined by the Antimonopoly Superintendence, this Agency can initiate the administrative procedure to determine the violations of the Antimonopoly a Law, whether *ex officio* or by means of a request or denunciation of illegal conduct or practices that can be brought before the Antimonopoly Superintendence by any interested party (article 32). In these cases it is to the Antimonopoly Superintendence to determine if the denounced facts or conducts merit or not to initiate the administrative procedure according to the law (art. 34) There is no provision for a private action under the Law that can be brought by any injured party before the Antimonopoly Superintendence, but only the right to request the initiation of an administrative procedure or to denounce certain facts, practices or conducts considered contrary to the Antimonopoly regulations.

Article 41 of the Antimonopoly Law establishes that the rules that apply to the procedure developed before the Antimonopoly Superintendence are the general rules established in the Organic Law of Administrative Procedure, which applies in all Public Administration entities or bodies. This general Organic Law of Administrative Procedure is the one that establishes that all the relevant facts to the cases brought before any Public Administration organ, including the Antimonopoly Superintendence, can be determined by all means for proof regulated in the Civil and in the Criminal Procedural Codes (Article 58). These Codes contains the general rules that govern all judicial civil and criminal cases, and are only applicable in an alternative way to administrative procedures based in the direct indication already mentioned in the text of the Organic Law on Administrative Procedure.

The administrative acts adopted by the Antimonopoly Superintendence in resolving the administrative procedures cannot be appealed within the Executive Branch of government. Those decisions can only be reviewed by the Administrative Contentious Jurisdiction courts, which have the competence to judicial review the administrative actions, by means of recourses seeking annulment, that can be exercised against administrative acts based on allegations of illegality or unconstitutionality of the decisions contained in them (art. 56).

That is why, Article 55 of the Antimonopoly Law states that the decisions adopted by the Antimonopoly Superintendence exhaust the administrative route, and the only remedy that can be filled against the administrative act within a period of forty-five

(45) calendar days, is the annulment recourse that must be exercised in conformity with the Contentious Administrative Jurisdiction Law of 2010. This recourse, in the case of the Antimonopoly Superintendence acts, must be filled by an interested party before the First Court on Contentious Administrative matters, whose decisions are subject to appeal before the so call Political-Administrative Chamber of the Supreme Tribunal. The procedure that develops before these two judicial instances courts is a judicial procedure for judicial review of administrative acts, in particular, based on arguments of illegality or unconstitutionality of the challenged administrative act or decision. If such action for judicial review against an administrative act is filed, the final decision is the one taken by the of second instance, in this case, the Political-Administrative Chamber of the Supreme Tribunal of Justice.

When a judicial review of administrative action process is initiated in this special jurisdiction courts, the first decision the judge must adopt, *ex-officio* or at the request of the interested party, is the request from the Antimonopoly Superintendence, to send to the Court the Administrative files, that is to say, all the documents and papers filed within the administrative procedure developed for the production of the particular administrative challenged act.

According to the relevant Venezuelan statutes on these matters, the following conclusions can be drowned, from the administrative procedure point of view:

A. The Antimonopoly Superintendence is part of the Executive Branch of Government (Public Administration) not being a judicial body. Therefore, they are not necessarily lawyers, but mostly they are professionals with economic studies background. As an administrative body, Antimonopoly Superintendence is empowered to create and maintain its own Register and archives of documents.

B. The Antimonopoly Superintendence is the only entity in Venezuela with power to determine the violations of the Antimonopoly Law and has no authority to order compensation for damages caused to any interested party as a consequence of the prohibited practices.

C. The administrative procedure before the Antimonopoly Superintendence can be initiated *ex officio* or by means of a request or denunciation of illegal conducts or practices. There is no provision for a private action under the Law that can be brought by any injured party before the Antimonopoly Superintendence. The rules that apply to the administrative procedure are the general rules established in the Organic Law on Administrative Procedure, and only in an alternative way in matters of proof the Civil and in the Criminal Procedural Codes rules applies.

D. The administrative acts adopted by the Antimonopoly Superintendence cannot be appealed within the Executive Branch of government. Those decisions can only be subject to judicial review of administrative action before the Contentious Administrative Jurisdiction courts, by means of recourses seeking annulment based on allegations of illegality or unconstitutionality of the challenged decisions.

In the case of the Antimonopoly Superintendence acts, these recourses must be filled by an interested party before the First Court on Contentious Administrative matters, whose decisions are subject to appeal before the so call Political-Administrative Chamber of the Supreme Tribunal of Justice. If such action for judicial review is filed, the final decision is the one taken in second instance by the

Political-Administrative Chamber of the Supreme Tribunal. When a judicial review of administrative action process is initiated in the special jurisdiction, all the documents and papers filed within the administrative procedure must be sent to the court.

VI. LEGAL REGIME OF THE INTERVENTION AND LIQUIDATION PROCESSES OF BANKS AND FINANCIAL INSTITUTIONS IN VENEZUELA

1. The Legal Framework of the Banking Sector

During the past years, the Banking sector in Venezuela has been regulated by two Statutes: *First*, the "General Law on Banks and other Financial Institutions" (*Ley General de Bancos y otras Instituciones Financieras*) sanctioned by the National Executive through Decree Law N° 1526 of November 2001,[165] which was subsequently reformed by the same National Executive through Decree Law N° 6287 of December 2009,[166] and later by the National Assembly through a statute sanctioned in August 2010;[167] and *second*, the "Law of Institutions of the Banking Sector" (*Ley de Instituciones del Sector Bancario)* sanctioned by the National Assembly in December 2010, [168] which was later reformed by the National Executive through Decree Law N° 8079 of March 2011 ("2011 Banking Sector Law"),[169] and in again, in 2014 by Decree Law 1.402 of November 2014. [170]

Despite of all these reforms, and as well of the change of name of the statute regulating the Banking Sector (*Ley de Instituciones del Sector Bancario* instead of *Ley General de Bancos y otras Instituciones Financieras*), it can be said that on matters of the regulatory regime regarding the Banking Sector, and specifically, regarding the means and extension of the control exercised by the State on banks and financial institutions, of the powers of intervention of such institutions by the State, and of the powers of liquidation of the intervened institutions; the legal regime has remained basically unchanged, and the fundamental functions attributed to the State and its controlling agencies are basically the same.

2. The Regulatory Agencies of the Banking Sector: Sudeban and Fogade, and their Commercial Activities when Operating Banking Institutions in Cases of Intervention and of Liquidation

In all successive statutes and Decree Laws regulating the Banking sector, two agencies have been given regulatory, supervisory and controlling powers on banks and financial institutions: On one hand, the *Superintendencia de las Instituciones del Sector Bancario* (Superintendence of Institutions of the Banking Sector)

165 See *Official Gazette* N° 5555 Extra of November 13, 2001

166 See *Official Gazette* N° 5947 Extra of December 23, 2009

167 See *Official Gazette* N° 39491 of August 19, 2010

168 See *Official Gazette* N° 6015 Extra. of December 28, 2010

169 See *Official Gazette* N° 39627 of March 2, 2011

170 See *Official Gazette* N° 6.154 Extra. of November 19, 2014

(SUDEBAN) with regulatory and intervention powers regarding banks and financial institutions; and on the other hand, the *Fondo de Protección Social de los Depósitos Bancarios* (Fund for Social Protection of Bank Deposits) (FOGADE), with powers to liquidate the intervened institutions, once the matter has been decided by SUDEBAN.

Moreover, pursuant to the provisions of the Banking Sector Law both agencies, SUDEBAN and FOGADE, as instrumentalities of the Venezuelan State, have not only strict regulatory powers regarding the Banking Sector, but also attributions to intervene and to liquidate banks and financial institutions, for which purpose they have and must engage in commercial activities, when operating the intervened institutions, and when liquidating their assets.

Regarding SUDEBAN, in fact, in addition to the regulatory mission of inspecting, supervising, overseeing and sanctioning banks and other financial institutions, it is essential to add the power of intervention of banks and financial institutions, through which SUDEBAN engages in activities similar to those carried out by a private player. In this matters of intervention, the power to decide the intervention of a financial institution when adopted by SUDEBAN, can be considered as part of its regulatory mission with a sovereign objective, but the process of managing or operating the bank or institution once it has been intervened, particularly in cases of "open door" interventions, implies the ineludible task for SUDEBAN of engaging itself in commercial or banking activities, similar to those that private persons ordinarily perform, and that are not normally in the realm of governments.

That is, the operation and management of banks or financial institutions that have been the object of an intervention by SUDEBAN, essentially are of a "commercial attribute" and not merely "essentially governmental responsibilities." That is why article 251 of the 2014 Banking Sector Law expressly imposes to SUDEBAN the duty to "guarantee that the intervened bank or financial institution preserves its *commercial operation* in order to adequate its activities to the instructions given by SUDEBAN and overcome the situation in which is immersed."

Furthermore, regarding the banks and financial institutions that have been intervened, SUDEBAN effectively "operates" them. That is why, the Second Court on Administrative Contentious matters has said that once the intervention of a bank has been decided, this not only means the exercise of powers of control on the banking sector by SUDEBAN, but also the need for SUDEBAN to guarantee "the adequate performance of the banking activity in a banking institution,"[171] which means the need to operate the institution with commercial purposes. On the other hand, if it is true that through the intervention of banks and financial institutions, SUDEBAN does not acquire the "ownership" of the intervened institution, the owners or shareholders of the bank are in fact deprived of its possession and administration, so in practical terms SUDEBAN acts as its "owner" or "shareholder" assuming its management.

As it has been said by the Second Court on Administrative Contentious matters in decision of April 5, 2011 (Case *PERFOALCA y otros vs. SUDEBAN*), the

171 Decision of the Second Court of Administrative Contentious matters of April 14, 2011 (Case: *Banco Capital v. SUDEBAN* Exp. N° AP42-N-2001-024434) available at http://jca.tsj.gov.ve/decisio-nes/2011/abril/1478-14-AP42-N-2001-024434-2011-0612.html

intervention "implies an (extraordinary) interference in [private] activities, implying that the owners or shareholders of an institution are temporarily deprived of its possession and administration".[172]

The same can be said regarding FOGADE, when the decision to liquidate a bank has been taken by SUDEBAN. In the process of liquidation, FOGADE, begins the loan portfolio collection and can proceed to sale real estate or assets in accordance with the liquidation process, in which cases, FOGADE undoubtedly engages in commercial activities. Such activities are similar to those that any given person ordinarily performs, and that are not typically in the realm of governments. That is, the process of loan portfolio collection and real estate sale of banks or financial institutions that have been subject to intervention by SUDEBAN, implies that FOGADE, effectively "operates" the intervened institution in the liquidation process, in order precisely to dissolve it, and such activities indeed have "commercial attribute" not being "essentially governmental responsibilities."

3. The State Decision to Intervene and Liquidate Banks and Financial Institutions, and its Implications.

Article 239 of the 2014 Law on the Banking Sector, expressly regulates the cases of "intervention, rehabilitation or liquidation of the institutions of the Banking Sector as well as the intervention and liquidation of related corporations qualified as such by SUDEBAN, assigning competencies for such purposes to SUDEBAN and FOGADE.

Pursuant to the Law, SUDEBAN and FOGADE, as public entities or State instrumentalities, are the ones in charge of deciding and implementing in the name of the State interventions, rehabilitations and liquidations.[173] In fact, SUDEBAN is

---

172 See Decision of the First Court on Administrative Contentious pronounced on 2011on File N° AW41-X-2011-000004. Case: Nelson Mezerhane and Gilda Pabón v. SUDEBAN (liquidation of Banco Federal) available at http://jca.tsj.gov.ve/decisiones/2011/mayo/1477-9-AW41-X-2011-000004-2011-0518.html; and Decision of the First Court on Administrative Contentious matters pronounced on 2011on File N° AW41-X-2011-000006. Case: Nelson Mezerhane v. SUDEBAN (liquidation of CANEY I, related company, Banco Federal) available at http://jca.tsj.gov.ve/decisiones/2011/ju-nio/1477-9-AW41-X-2011-000006-2011-0675.html

173 According to the decision of the Second Court on Administrative Contentious these are "instruments that the State has in order to control the financial system". See Decision N° 2010-1151 of the Second Court of Administrative Contentious matters dated August 9, 2010. Case: *Gilda Pabon, Nelson Mezerhane, Anibal Latuff, Rogelio Trujillo, Mashud Mezerhane and Enrique Urdaneta v. SUDEBAN*, available at http://jca.tsj.gov.ve/decisio-nes/2010/agosto/1478-9-AW42-X-2010-000008-2010-1151.html . "These are the instruments that the State has in order to control the financial systems." See. Decision of the First Court on Administrative Contentious pronounced on 2011 on File N° AW41-X-2011-000004. Case: *Nelson Mezerhane and Gilda Pabón v. SUDEBAN* (liquidation of Banco Federal) available at http://jca.tsj.gov.ve/decisiones/2011/mayo/1477-9-AW41-X-2011-000004-2011-0518.html ; and Decision of the First Court on Administrative Contentious matters pronounced on 2012 on File N° AW41-X-2010-000016. Case: *SINDICATO AVILA v. SUDEBAN (intervention of a related company, Banco federal*) available at http://jca.tsj.gov.ve/decisiones/2012/febrero/1477-10-AW41-X-2010-000016-2012-0096.html; and Decision of the Second Court on Administrative Contentious matters pronounced on July 6, 2011on File N° AP42-N-2010-000626. Case: *Nelson Mezerhane v. SUDEBAN* (intervention of Seguros Federal, related company, Banco Federal) available at http://jca.tsj.gov.ve/decisiones/2011/julio/1478-6-AP42-N-2010-000626-2011-1032.html.

the State instrumentality in charge of and responsible for not only to the decision making regarding a bank's intervention, but also to operate the intervened bank, with banking commercial purposes, primarily in order to rehabilitate it. In the case of FOGADE, once SUDEBAN has decided that the intervened bank must be liquidated, this is the State instrumentality in charge of and responsible for such liquidation process, being compelled to operate it in order to liquidate it.

Moreover, in order to accomplish their duties, the Law empowers both, SUDEBAN and FOGADE, to appoint managers, managing boards or coordinators who are to carry out in their name and following their instructions, the intervention and liquidation process. Those appointed auditors or liquidators act as delegates of SUDEBAN and FOGADE respectively, and have not, in any way whatsoever, any complete autonomy in the exercise of their functions regarding SUDEBAN and FOGADE. It is through them that SUDEBAN and FOGADE exercise control and manage the banks or institutions subject to intervention or liquidation, depending on either agency and subject to their hierarchical control.

In fact, within its regulatory powers SUDEBAN is empowered to decide and order -through an "administrative act"- not only the "intervention with or without precluding further financial intermediation" but must also set out the regime to which the bank or financial institution will be subject thereafter, as well as to whether the intervention will be carried out by means of a single auditor or an intervention board, and to appoint for such purposes either its own public servants or someone from outside the regulatory entity. As it has been decided by the Superior Sixth Court on Contentious Administrative Matters of the Capital District in ruling taken on July 9, 2012, the intervention of a bank or financial institution implies "from oversee the administration, developing, functioning and disposition of assets up to the assumption by itself of the activity in the name of the intervened entity. So, if the function is of SUDEBAN, that means that it can be accomplish directly by the organ or it can be accomplished through third persons outside the Agency. In case of doing it directly, as a legal person, it acts through its officials; and it can also hire persons outside the Agency in order to accomplish the functions".[174]

The same Court has added that without doubting on the public character of the functions exercised by those in charge of accomplishing the intervention of banks, it is necessary to differentiate if it is a public servant or a person outside to the civil service. Consequently:

---

174 See Decision of the Sixth Superior Court on Administrative Contentious matters of the Capital District dated July 9, 2010. File N° 09-2549 available at http://caracas.tsj.gov.ve/decisiones/2010/junio/2111-9-09-2549-.html. See also, decision of the Second Court on Administrative Contentious matters, N° 2011-0504, dated April 5, 2011 (Case *PERFOALCA y otros vs. SUDEBAN*) available at http://jca.tsj.gov.ve/decisiones/2011/abril/1478-5-AP42-N-2008-000287-2011-0504.html. (File N° AP42-N-2008-000287); 7); Decision of the Second Court on Administrative Contentious matters dated July 26, 2012. File N° AP42-R-2010-001201 (Case *Humberto Torres, Interventor v. SUDEBAN*, available at http://jca.tsj.gov.ve/deci-siones/2012/julio/1478-26-AP42-R-2010-001201-2012-1571.html; and Decision of the Fourth Superior Court on Civil and Administrative Contentious matters of the Capital region dated March 31, 2011. File N° 06296. Case: Ligia Carolina Jaimes Chaparro v. SUDEBAN available at http://caracas.tsj.gov.ve/decisiones/2011/marzo/2109-31-06296-.html

"Being that SUDEBAN can exercise by itself the functions [of intervention], it can accomplish it through the public servants of the Agency. The latter, when exercising the position of auditors, in addition of exercising the public functions inherent to the condition of auditor, continue to have the character of public servants due to the link of the public service that subjects them with the Administration. In such cases, they ought to be considered as public servants, due to the fact that the intervention is a function that is temporarily assigned to the public servant until SUDEBAN disposes otherwise.

On the other hand, if it is the case that the function has been assigned to an individual outside the cadre of the Administration, it cannot be considered as a public servant regarding the civil service effects, regardless that the law so states and that they are subject to provisions applicable to public servants as well as reached by certain degree of responsibility.

The manner in which the State decides to act, is subject to its will and interest. There is no doubt for this Court, that if [the intervention] is accomplished through a public servant of the same Administration, that he has complete and absolute knowledge of the norms, directions and guidelines that can be given by the authorities of the entity. If the function is accomplished by an individual, in the same way internal public servants will be needed in order to oversee not only the functioning of the intervened institution, but also to guarantee the accomplishment of the guidelines, which means greater efforts and costs".[175]

In either case those appointed to implement the intervention, with power to operate the intervened institution, according to article 245 of the Law, have "the broadest possible powers of administration, control and oversight, including all the powers the Law or the bylaws confer on the shareholders assembly, the board of directors, the president and to the other organs of the entity subject to official intervention." That is, the intervention appointees, as delegates from SUDEBAN from a banking and commercial point of view have the complete responsibility to operate the intervened bank or financial institution, subjected to SUDEBAN, which is the State's instrumentality in charge of the intervention. In cases of intervention, it is SUDEBAN the entity that exercises control over the intervened banks, not the appointed managers of managing boards, although such control is exercised through these organs as delegates and dependents of SUDEBAN.

175 See Decision of the Sixth Superior Court on Administrative Contentious matters of the Capital District dated July 9, 2010. File N° 09-2549 available at http://caracas.tsj.gov.ve/decisiones/2010/junio/2111-9-09-2549-.html. See also Decision of the Second Court on Administrative Contentious matters, N° 2011-0504, dated April 5, 2011 (Case *PERFOALCA y otros vs. SUDEBAN*) available at http://jca.tsj.gov.ve/decisio-nes/2011/abril/1478-5-AP42-N-2008-000287-2011-0504.html. (File N° AP42-N-2008-000287); Decision of the Second Court on Administrative Contentious matters dated July 26, 2012. File N° AP42-R-2010-001201 (Caso Humberto Torres, Interventor v. SUDEBAN) available at http://jca.tsj.gov.ve/decisiones/2012/julio/1478-26-AP42-R-2010-001201-2012-1571.html; and Decision of the Fourth Superior Court on Civil and Administrative Contentious matters of the Capital region dated March 31, 2011. File N° 06296. Case: Ligia Carolina Jaimes Chaparro v. SUDEBAN available at http://caracas.tsj.gov.ve/decisiones/2011/marzo/2109-31-06296-.html

Regarding the liquidation process of banks and financial institutions that have been intervened, article 264 of the Banking Sector Law assigns such procedure to FOGADE, or by decision of the *Órgano Superior del Sistema Financiero Nacional*, to another agency under the supervision of SUDEBAN. Nonetheless, the general rule in this matter is that it has been FOGADE the entity in charge of liquidation of banks that have been intervened and that have not deemed to be rehabilitated by SUDEBAN. Under Article 7 of the "Rules for the Liquidation of Institutions of the Banking Sector and Related Legal Persons" (*Normas para la Liquidación de Instituciones del Sector Bancario y Personas Jurídicas Vinculadas*) [176] ("Rules for the Liquidation"), the President of FOGADE is empowered to appoint liquidators of the financial institutions, named "Coordinators of the Process of Liquidation."

From the aforementioned it results that the processes of intervention and liquidation of banks and financial institutions can be carried out by an "auditor" "managing intervention board" or "Coordinators of the Process of Liquidation" respectively, as those in charge of the operation of the institution and of carrying out the required actions for the intervention and the liquidation to be accomplished; and as I mentioned, they can either be public servants working in SUDEBAN and in FOGADE, or persons appointed for such purposes, and that in any case perform public duties and functions.

4. The Peculiarities of the Intervention and Liquidation Processes of Banks and Financial Institutions, and its Implications

The intervention of banks and financial institution has been considered manifestation sign of police powers, or the control carried out by the State, through a decision of SUDEBAN that follows policies and guidelines given by the Central Administration (Ministry of Planning and Finance). Once the decision is taken by SUDEBAN, the process is materialized, for its implementation, in the appointment, through an administrative act of organization adopted by the same entity, of a particular person (auditor) or persons (managing intervention board) to carry out the acts in which the intervention materializes, that is, of the operation of the intervened institution. In these cases, the person or persons in charge of the process of intervention and the day-to-day operation of the intervened institution, develop an activity that has been personally assigned or delegated to them, that they carry out not in their personal interest, but in interest of others, that is, the State, the depositors and the public in general.[177]

As such, the intervention is the consequence of the exercise of an administrative power assigned to SUDEBAN, which implies the restriction of the activities of a bank that, because of such intervention submits to the complete control of SUDEBAN[178] that begins to operate it. As ruled by the Second Court on

176 See *Normas para la Liquidación de Instituciones del Sector Bancario y Personas Jurídicas Vinculadas*, in *Official Gazette* N° 39.602 de 26 de enero de 2011.

177 See Gonzalo Pérez Luciani, Gonzalo, "La intervención administrativa de los bancos o institutos de crédito", en *Revista de Derecho Público* N° 18, Editorial Jurídica Venezolana, Caracas 1984, pp. 39 ff.

178 See Aurilivi Linares Martínez, "Aproximación a la intervención administrativa de empresas a través de la legislación bancaria", *Desafíos del Derecho administrativo contemporáneo, Tomo II*, Paredes, 2009, pp. 895 ff.

Administrative Contentious matters, in a recent decision of 2011, "...a special relation is established between the financial institutions and the Administration, that will be empowered to intervene in the management and control of the banking action, being understood that the intervention is legally provided, and to it the financial institutions must be subject."[179]

For such purpose, the person or persons in charge of carrying out the intervention on behalf of SUDEBAN, that is those appointed by the Agency to assume the operation of the intervened institution, substitute the managing organs of the intervened institution, in what has been called the "*publicization*" of the management[180]: the operation and management of the intervened institution begins to be performed by persons executing public functions.

In general terms, the general legal doctrine in Venezuela concurs with this approach, considering that the intervention of banks and financial institutions is a decision taken by SUDEBAN, through an administrative act, exercising public police powers, whereas SUDEBAN is the public entity in charge and responsible for but implements it, from an organizational point of view, through the appointment of one or more persons for such purpose.[181]

The same can be said regarding the liquidation of banks and financial institutions once it is so decided by SUDEBAN: it is a process conducted by FOGADE, being its entire responsibility. In this case, also being FOGADE the public entity in charge and responsible for the liquidation of the intervened bank, such liquidation is implemented, from an organizational point of view, through the appointment of some Coordinators of the Liquidation Process.[182]

In all such cases, those persons appointed by either SUDEBAN or FOGADE have the task of assuming the material operations of the intervened bank or of its liquidation process, subject to decisions that are taken by the agencies responsible for such tasks, that is, SUDEBAN or FOGADE. The appointees are, as Gonzalo Pérez Luciani states, subjective figures that are part of the corresponding administrative organization of SUDEBAN and of FOGADE, and thus, execute a

---

179 The Court added in its ruling: that "To these ideas adder Muci Facchin y Martín-Ponte en Venezuela" (See. Morles Hernández, Alfredo. "Curso de Derecho Mercantil 'Las Sociedades Mercantiles'. Tomo II. Caracas 2007. p. 2839)." Decision of the Second Court on Administrative Contentious matters, Nº 2011-0504, dated April 5, 2011 (Case *PERFOALCA y otros vs. SUDEBAN*) available at http://jca.tsj.gov.ve/decisiones/2011/abril/1478-5-AP42-N-2008-000287-2011-0504.html. (File Nº AP42-N-2008-000287)

180 See Aurilivi Linares Martínez, "Los mecanismos de resolución bancaria en la nueva Ley de Instituciones del Sector Bancario", en *Análisis y comentarios de la Ley de Instituciones del Sector Bancario,* FUNEDA, Caracas, 2011, pp. 308 ff.; and "Algunos aspectos sobre el régimen jurídico administrativo de la intervención de instituciones del sector bancario", en *Libro homenaje al profesor Alfredo Morles Hernández,* Volumen III, Caracas, 2012, pp. 85 ff.

181 See Gustavo Muci Facchin, and Rafael Martín Ponte, *Regulación bancaria,* Universidad Católica Andrés Bello Caracas 2004, pp. 270 ff.; and Héctor Turuhpial, "El régimen administrativo de intervención de instituciones bancarias", *Libro Homenaje al Profesor Alfredo Morles Hernández,* Volumen III, *cit.*, pp. 205 ff.

182 See Alfredo Morles Hernández, *La Banca,* Universidad Católica Andrés Bello, Caracas 2011, pp. 262 ff.

commission assigned to them by those entities.[183] Consequently, those subjective figures or persons do not assume the direction and operation of the bank or institution subject to intervention or liquidation by means of decisions that they could adopt in an autonomous way. On the contrary, those subjective figures are essential part of the organization of SUDEBAN and of FOGADE, being these agencies, according to the Banking Sector Law, the ones in charge of directing and controlling all the decisions taken by the appointees to an intervention or liquidation process.

In fact, under article 251 of the Banking Sector Law, the special administrative regime established in it in cases of intervention of banks and financial institutions "...tend to maintain the banking institution under the management of a manager or of a managing board appointed by the State through SUDEBAN." The intervention, pursuant to the same provision of the Law, tends to "guarantee that the institution preserves its commercial operation with the purpose to adequate its activity to the instructions given by SUDEBAN in order to overcome the situation in which it is immerse." That is, the intervention must respond to the guidelines given by SUDEBAN, agency that must approve the report filed by the manager or managing board (article 251). According to the "Rules for Intervention"[184] SUDEBAN controls the actions of those in charge of it, being provided in article 8 of such Norms that "the manager or managing board cannot execute outstanding transactions without the authorization of SUDEBAN" that, as all administrative authorizations, are to be given prior to the action, reinforcing SUDEBAN's power of control as well as its responsibility in the process of intervention.

The aforementioned was ratified by Gonzalo Pérez Luciani when he stated that the intervention manager or managing board is not an organ with autonomy regarding SUDEBAN, being considered -on the contrary- as a subjective figure integrated in the organization of SUDEBAN, which is the agency in charge of the intervention of the bank, through the appointed intervention manager or managing board.[185]

That is the attributions the latter have under article 242 of the Law, in the sense of "the broadest possible powers of administration, control and oversight" of the institution subject to intervention, are not powers to be exercised regarding SUDEBAN, but only regarding the intervened institution, in itself, and third parties. This is why the Politico Administrative Chamber of the Supreme Tribunal of Justice in ruling dated October 7, 2004 (Case *María Coppola*) has qualified the intervention of banks as an act of the Public Power.[186] In the same sense has been decided by the Second Court on Administrative Contentious matters in a ruling dated April 5, 2011

183 See Gonzalo Pérez Luciani, Gonzalo, "La intervención administrativa de los bancos o institutos de crédito", en *Revista de Derecho Público* N° 18, Editorial Jurídica Venezolana, Caracas 1984, pp. 39 ff.

184 See for instance, *Normas para la Liquidación de Instituciones del Sector Bancario y Personas Jurídicas Vinculadas*, in *Official Gazette* N° 39.731 de 9 de agosto de 2011.

185 See Gonzalo Pérez Luciani, Gonzalo, "La intervención administrativa de los bancos o institutos de crédito", en *Revista de Derecho Público* N° 18, Editorial Jurídica Venezolana, Caracas 1984, pp. 39 ff.

186 See Politico Administrative Chamber of the Supreme Tribunal of Justice in ruling dated October 7, 2004 (Case *María Coppola*) available at http://www.tsj.gov.ve/decisiones/spa/Octubre/01727-071004-2002-0722.htm .

(Case *PERFOALCA y otros vs. SUDEBAN*), whereas it stated that the intervention "...implies an (extraordinary) interference in activities, implying that the owners or shareholders of an institution are temporarily deprived of its possession and administration".[187]

Therefore, from a legal point of view, the intervention of banks and financial institutions is imputable to the Administration, through SUDEBAN, and the manager or managing board in charge of it do not act on their own name or on their personal behalf. According to the Second Court on Administrative Contentious matters judicial doctrine, contained in a ruling dated August 9, 2010 "...the State in this scenario and by means of the banking control agency (SUDEBAN), decides the intervention of banking institutions in order to protect the interest of depositors and the public in general that could have any relation with the intervened institution" (Case *Banco Federal vs. SUDEBAN*)[188].

In the case of liquidation of banking institutions that have been subject to a process of intervention, the conclusion is more evident, due to the fact that FOGADE is the liquidation entity, even though is authorized in the Banking Law to appoint coordinators in order to implement the material operations of such process. That is, the liquidation can be take place in two ways: directly by FOGADE or by means of coordinators appointed by FOGADE, in which case the "coordinators" always act under FOGADE´s control. In such cases, pursuant to article 7 of the "Rules for the Intervention," the liquidation must be carried on "subject to the provisions of the Rules and within the terms established by the President of FOGADE." That is why the Second Court on Administrative Contentious matters in the already mentioned ruling dated August 9, 2010, stated that the liquidation is a measure imputable to the State, by means of the organ of the Administration that decides the intervention.[189]

---

187 See Decision of the First Court on Administrative Contentious pronounced on 2011 on File N° AW41-X-2011-000004. Case: *Nelson Mezerhane and Gilda Pabón v. SUDEBAN* (liquidation of Banco Federal) available at http://jca.tsj.gov.ve/decisiones/2011/mayo/1477-9-AW41-X-2011-000004-2011-0518.html; and Decision of the First Court on Administrative Contentious matters pronounced on 2011on File N° AW41-X-2011-000006. *Case: Nelson Mezerhane v. SUDEBAN* (liquidation of CANEY I, related company, Banco Federal) available at http://jca.tsj.gov.ve/decisiones/2011/junio/1477-9-AW41-X-2011-000006-2011-0675.html.

188 The Court has also say that in such cases, SUDEBAN "is the organ in charge of executing the intervention, passing provisory to exercise the control of the intervened entity". See Decision Nº 2010-1151 of the Second Court of Administrative Contentious matters dated August 9, 2010. Case: *Gilda Pabon, Nelson Mezerhane, Anibal Latuff, Rogelio Trujillo, Mashud Mezerhane and Enrique Urdaneta v. SUDEBAN*, available at http://jca.tsj.gov.ve/decisiones/2010/agosto/1478-9-AW42-X-2010-000008-2010-1151.html; Decision of the Second Court on Administrative Contentious matters pronounced on July 6, 2011 on File Nº AP42-N-2010-000626. Case: *Nelson Mezerhane v. SUDEBAN* (intervention of Seguros Federal, related company, Banco Federal) available at http://jca.tsj.gov.ve/decisiones/2011/julio/1478-6-AP42-N-2010-000626-2011-1032.html ; and Decision of the Second Court on Administrative Contentious matters, Nº 2011-0504, dated April 5, 2011 (Case *PERFOALCA y otros vs. SUDEBAN*) available at http://jca.tsj.gov.ve/decisiones/2011/abril/1478-5-AP42-N-2008-000287-2011-0504.html. (File Nº AP42-N-2008-000287).

189 See Decision Nº 2010-1151 of the Second Court of Administrative Contentious matters dated August 9, 2010. Case: *Gilda Pabon, Nelson Mezerhane, Anibal Latuff, Rogelio Trujillo,*

Therefore, following Gonzalo Pérez Luciani, the manager, the managing board and the coordinators are organs of the State in the sense that they are subjective figures that develop a specific administrative activity, that is, the material acts required to the intervention or the liquidation of a bank or financial institution. When such personnel is appointed from outside the personal of SUDEBAN, according to the Rules of Intervention, they develop their activities in a labor relation with SUDEBAN and FOGADE, that because of the nature of the activities they accomplish, has even been considered as not exclusively ruled by private labor law.[190] This means that when the manager or members of the managing board and coordinators have not "public servant" status within the Public Administration organization, although their appointment does not grant them such condition, they render public services to SUDEBAN or to FOGADE, which are the entities that direct their actions. In any case, it is considered that they always execute public functions, leading the courts to consider that there is no doubt about the "nature of public servants of the auditor, in the broad sense of the expression,"[191] i. e. persons that accomplish public functions on behalf of the State.

It follows that they have broad attributions regarding the intervened institution, but it does not mean that they can act in an autonomous way, being on the subject to SUDEBAN, FOGADE and the Central Bank of Venezuela.[192] As it has been decided by the Civil Cassation Chamber of the Supreme Tribunal of Justice: "The auditors are appointed temporarily, being their functions to protect and control the assets of the intervened institutions in order to reduce the cost that the State would have in case of cessation." [193]

Mashud Mezerhane and Enrique Urdaneta v. SUDEBAN, available at http://jca.tsj.gov.ve/decisiones/2010/agosto/1478-9-AW42-X-2010-000008-2010-1151.html.

190 In this regard, the Civil Cassation Chamber of the Supreme Tribunal of Justice, in decision of June 18, 2009 has ruled as follows: "Due to the legal nature of the figure of banking interventor, its normative regulation, as well as its attributions, it is not possible to establish the laber character of the rendering services relation, because the banking interventor regulated in the General Law on banks and other Financial Institutions, in force at the time, is provided as a subjective figure, in the terminology of Messineo in his *Contributo alla dottrina della Esecuzione Testamentaria* (Roma, 1923) o Giannini in his *Diritto Amministrativo,* as a legal operator that according to provisions of the same legal order, is in charge of take care of other people'assets, in a similar way to the judicial depository, of the trustee of a bankruptcy or other judicial "auxiliaries"'. See Decision R.C. N° AA60-S-2008-001166 of the Cassation Chamber of the Supreme Tribunal of Justice dated June 18, 2009.

191 The Superior Fourth Court on Civil and Administrative Contentious matters of the Capital Region in decision of March 31, 2011, has ruled as follows: "It is to highlight that the especial functions that by statute are attributed to the interventors, regarding their duties to oversee for the financial security of the country, shows the care that they are ask to have in favor of the general interest in charge of the State; from there that no doubt can exist on the nature of public servant ("*empleado público*") in the broad sense of the term, as it has been explain before, and that have the persons that accomplish such mission." See Decision of the Fourth Superior Court on Civil and Administrative Contentious matters of the Capital region dated March 31, 2011. File N° 06296. Case: *Ligia Carolina Jaimes Chaparro v. SUDEBAN* available at http://caracas.tsj.gov.ve/decisiones/2011/marzo/2109-31-06296-html .

192 See Decision R.C. N° AA60-S-2008-001166 of the Cassation Chamber of the Supreme Tribunal of Justice dated June 18, 2009

193 See Decision R.C. N° AA60-S-2008-001166 of the Cassation Chamber of the Supreme Tribunal of Justice dated June 18, 2009.

So despite the fact that when the manager or members of the managing boards of intervention are appointed from outside the organization of SUDEBAN, they formally do not have the condition of "public servants", the Second Court on Administrative Contentious matters in decision dated July 26, 2012 has recognized that they always exercise "administrative functions of the State," referring to the "public character of the function assigned to those having the condition of auditors" that because of such situation, are subject to the specific regulations referring to the protection of public assets and corruption cases in the public sector, as well as to criminal, civil and administrative liability.[194]

Consequently, the persons acting as managers or members of a managing board in cases of intervention of a bank or financial institution, are always considered auxiliaries of SUDEBAN through which such administrative agency assumes the control of the intervened institution, exercising its functions in the name and on behalf of SUDEBAN. As the Fourth Superior Court on Civil and Administrative Contentious matters of the Capital Region has ruled in decision dated March 31, 2012 "...to the person that has the position of auditor, a public function has been assigned, because such person acts exercising a public function that corresponds to the State, of such an importance that it exceeds any activity that could be of *derecho común*, due to the fact that in exercising its powers assumes in the name of SUDEBAN, the control, the management and even the disposition of assets owned by the financial institutions, public or private, which implies that he is subject to the provisions of the Corruption Law, as well as the person that accomplishes such functions is subject to the regime of criminal, civil and administrative liability that is applicable to the public function." [195]

In addition, the manager and members of managing boards in the case of intervention of banks or financial institutions, as well as the coordinators in cases of liquidation of such institutions have no real autonomy regarding SUDEBAN or FOGADE, due to the fact that they are part of the organization of such agencies and,

194 "There is no doubt on the public character of the function assigned to those with the condition of Interventor, because they act accomplishing a function assigned to the State." See Decision of the Second Court on Administrative Contentious matters dated July 26, 2012. File N° AP42-R-2010-001201 (Caso *Humberto Torres, Interventor v. SUDEBAN*) available at http://jca.tsj.gov.ve/decisiones/2012/julio/1478-26-AP42-R-2010-001201-2012-1571.html. See also Decision of the Sixth Superior Court on Administrative Contentious matters of the Capital District dated July 9, 2010. File N° 09-2549 available at http://caracas.tsj.gov.ve/decisiones/2010/junio/2111-9-09-2549-.html; See Decision of the Second Court on Administrative Contentious matters, N° 2011-0504, dated April 5, 2011 (Case *PERFOALCA y otros vs. SUDEBAN*) available at http://jca.tsj.gov.ve/decisio-nes/2011/abril/1478-5-AP42-N-2008-000287-2011-0504.html. (File N° AP42-N-2008-000287) 7); Decision of the Second Court on Administrative Contentious matters dated July 26, 2012. File N° AP42-R-2010-001201 (Case *Humberto Torres, Interventor v. SUDEBAN*) available at http://jca.tsj.gov.ve/deci-siones/2012/julio/1478-26-AP42-R-2010-001201-2012-1571.html; and Decision of the Fourth Superior Court on Civil and Administrative Contentious matters of the Capital region dated March 31, 2011. File N° 06296. Case: *Ligia Carolina Jaimes Chaparro v. SUDEBAN* available at http://caracas.tsj.gov.ve/decisiones/2011/mar-zo/2109-31-06296-.html.

195 See Decision of the Fourth Superior Court on Civil and Administrative Contentious matters of the Capital region dated March 31, 2011. File N° 06296. Case: *Ligia Carolina Jaimes Chaparro v. SUDEBAN* available at http://caracas.tsj.gov.ve/decisiones/2011/marzo/2109-31-06296-.html.

as expressed by Gonzalo Pérez Luciani, are subject to the general hierarchical principle applicable to Public Administration.[196]

On the other hand, the intervention and liquidation are administrative decisions adopted by SUDEBAN exercising powers directly established in the Banking Sector Law that consequently cannot be delegated to other organs of the Public Administration. Both intervention and liquidation come from powers given exclusively to SUDEBAN and FOGADE, and those agencies are the single ones that can exercise them,[197] either directly through its own public servants, or by hiring persons from outside the entity. For such purpose, as aforementioned, the Banking Law expressly authorizes SUDEBAN and FOGADE to accomplish its attributions of intervention or liquidation by means of appointing persons as manager, members of a managing board and coordinators, who are to follow SUDEBAN and FOGADE´s decisions. Thus, the appointees are to perform in the name of the agencies, authorized to accomplish all the material operations needed, but in no way it can it be understood as if they act on their own will. On the contrary, they only perform actions that have been assigned to them by the agencies, subject to their control.

In this sense the Second Court on Administrative Contentious matters in decision dated April 5, 2011 has pointed out that the intervention is a decision adopted and conducted by SUDEBAN that is the competent agency to rule on the matter, stating that if the function of intervention is of SUDEBAN "…it means that the agency can accomplish it directly, or by means of third persons outside the agency. If it accomplishes the function directly, as a legal person, it does so by means of natural persons working within it (as public servants); being also allowed to hire persons outside the agency in order to accomplish the intervention activities."[198]

Consequently, the appointment of persons as managers, or as part of a managing board or as coordinators to act in the intervention or liquidation, does not imply that such persons have any power to adopt by themselves the decisions derived from the process of intervention or liquidation. In fact, they act as organs of SUDEBAN or

---

196 See Gonzalo Pérez Luciani, Gonzalo, "La intervención administrativa de los bancos o institutos de crédito", en *Revista de Derecho Público* N° 18, Editorial Jurídica Venezolana, Caracas 1984, pp. 39 ff.

197 As decided by the Second Court of Administrative Contentious matters, resulting from the intervention "SUDEBAN, organ in charge of the intervention, take charge provisionaly of the control of the intervened institution, in order to avoid risks and perjudicial effects that are the consequence of the banking failure." See Decision N° 2010-1151 of the Second Court of Administrative Contentious matters dated August 9, 2010. Case: *Gilda Pabon, Nelson Mezerhane, Anibal Latuff, Rogelio Trujillo, Mashud Mezerhane and Enrique Urdaneta v. SUDEBAN*, available at http://jca.tsj.gov.ve/decisiones/2010/agos-to/1478-9-AW42-X-2010-000008-2010-1151.html; and Decision of the Second Court on Administrative Contentious matters pronounced on July 6, 2011 on File N° AP42-N-2010-000626. Case: *Nelson Mezerhane v. SUDEBAN* (intervention of Seguros Federal, related company, Banco Federal) available at http://jca.tsj.gov.ve/decisiones/2011/julio/1478-6-AP42-N-2010-000626-2011-1032.html

198 See Decision of the Second Court on Administrative Contentious matters, N° 2011-0504, dated April 5, 2011 (Case *PERFOALCA y otros vs. SUDEBAN*) available at http://jca.tsj.gov.ve/decisio-nes/2011/abril/1478-5-AP42-N-2008-000287-2011-0504.html. (File N° AP42-N-2008-000287); and Decision of the Second Court on Administrative Contentious matters dated July 26, 2012. File N° AP42-R-2010-001201 (Case *Humberto Torres, Interventor v. SUDEBAN*) available at http://jca.tsj.gov.ve/decisio-nes/2012/julio/1478-26-AP42-R-2010-001201-2012-1571.html.

FOGADE, so the intervention or liquidation is in fact conducted by such agencies of the Administration, which appoint them to accomplish a public function, which is precisely to conduct the intervention and liquidation process. These persons render services to the Public Administration, in this case, to SUDEBAN or FOGADE, and are subject to rules of subordination and dependency, as it is the rule regarding the accomplishment of any public service.

This explains why in general terms, the intervention and liquidation of banks and financial institutions are decisions adopted by the Administration, that is SUDEBAN and FOGADE, in exercise of the powers assigned to them in the Banking Sector Law.[199] The Administration, as is the general principle on matters of administrative activity, exercises its actions through natural persons that render services subject to the general rule of subordination and dependency. In the case of liquidation of banks and financial institutions, the liquidation activities are executed by public servants of FOGADE or through third persons specially hired for such purpose appointed as coordinators. In the case of the intervention of such institutions, the activities can also be done directly or by third persons appointed as managers or in a managing board, hired by SUDEBAN.

In all such cases, since the managers, the members of the managing boards or the coordinators, public servants or persons hired from outside the agencies, carry out public functions, they are always subject to the hierarchical principle, subject to SUDEBAN and FOGADE. In any of those cases, the natural persons designated to act in the intervention or liquidation of a bank or of a financial institution, do not act in their own capacity, following their own decisions autonomously adopted. On the contrary, they act as heads of administrative organs established to such effect, which are part of the organization of SUDEBAN and of FOGADE, being subject -when acting- to the hierarchical principle, which is the main principle of administrative organization. The persons acting in the intervention or liquidation have no autonomy whatsoever in the exercise of their function, due to the fact that they must follow the guidelines and decisions of SUDEBAN and of FOGADE as established in the Banking Law.

5. Final Comment on the Status of Sudeban and Fogade as "Autonomous Institutes" within the General Public Administration

SUDEBAN and FOGADE, as public entities or administrative agencies, from the organic point of view have certain similarities to the "Independent Administrations" existing worldwide in contemporary Public Administration,[200] as well as with the so-called "Public Corporations"[201] in comparative law, organized as "autonomous

199 See in addition, Decision N° 2010-1151 of the Second Court of Administrative Contentious matters dated August 9, 2010. Case: *Gilda Pabón, Nelson Mezerhane, Anibal Latuff, Rogelio Trujillo, Mashud Mezerhane and Enrique Urdaneta v. SUDEBAN*, available at http://jca.tsj.gov.ve/decisio-nes/2010/agosto/1478-9-AW42-X-2010-000008-2010-1151.html.

200 See Peter Strauss, Todd Rakoff, Roy Schotland and Cynthia Farina *Administrative Law*, Ninth Edition, Foundation Press Inc., NY 1995. pp. 34 ff.

201 See See Allan R. Brewer-Carías, *Les enterprises publiques en droit comparé*, Faculté internationald de droit comparé, Paris 1968, pp. 52-64 Available at http://www.allanbrewercarias.com/Con-tent/449725d9-f1cb-474b-8ab2-41efb849fea5/Content/II.1.8%20(1968).pdf

institutes" or decentralized institutions within the Public Administration.[202] According to the general administrative law principles, these entities are part of the General Public Administration, as decentralized entities, which in Venezuela have been established in article 142 of the Constitution, having their own "legal personality" separate from the Republic of Venezuela.

Pursuant to the Organic Law on Public Administration of 2014,[203] the activities of all public institutes are subject to the principles and bases established in the provisions regulating the administrative activity, in particular, the Organic Law on Administrative Procedure and the guidelines of the Centralized Planning (art. 99).

This means that the "autonomy and independence" of SUDEBAN and FOGADE as "autonomous institutes," is currently subject to the general regime of the "public institutes," and in particular, to the Central Planning system. That is, their "autonomy and independence" has been progressively limited, in the sense that they are subject to a stricter control by the Ministry of Planning and Finance to which they are attached, being such Ministry the organ that appoints their High officials (article 119 of the Organic Law on Public Administration). That is why the Law prescribes that the "autonomy" of SUDEBAN can only be exercised "according to the terms established in the legal order," (art. 153 of Law Banking Sector) which, as established in the Organic Law on Public Administration, is limited and subject to the control exercised by the Ministry of attachment and to the Central Planning System regime.

Regarding SUDEBAN, Article 153 of the 2014 Banking Sector Law, assigns to such public agency the mission of inspecting, supervising, overseeing, regulating, controlling and sanctioning banks and other financial institutions of the banking sector in order to protect the public, particularly, the users of the banking sector. As an "autonomous institute", the Law assigns SUDEBAN its own legal personality, and its own assets "separate and independent from the assets (*bienes*) of the Republic." Consequently, if it is true that from these provisions it can be said that SUDEBAN "controls its own assets subject to statutory guidelines," it is not correct to deduct that SUDEBAN manages itself autonomously, because it is subject to strict control by the Ministry of Planning and Finance. For such purpose, SUDEBAN receives policy guidance from the *Órgano Superior del Sistema Financiero Nacional* ("OSFIN") and administrative guidance from the *Ministerio de Poder Popular de Planificación y Finanzas* ("Ministry of Planning and Finance")"

Regarding FOGADE, it is also a public entity conceived in the Banking Law as an "autonomous institute" with its own legal capacity and owns assets, attached to the Ministry for Planning and Finance for the sole purpose of administrative supervision (*tutela administrative*). Its principal role is to guarantee deposits by the public at banking institutions and to liquidate banking institutions and their related

202 See Allan R. Brewer-Carías, *Derecho Administrativo*, Tomo II, Universidad Externado de Colombia, Bogotá 2005, pp. 127-140.

203 See *Ley Orgánica de la Administración Pública*, Decree Law 1.424 of November 2014, *Official Gazette*- Nº 6.47 Extra. of November 17, 2014. See Allan R. Brewer-Carías, "Introducción general al régimen jurídico de la Administración Pública", en Allan R. Brewer-Carías (Coordinador y Editor), Rafael Chavero Gazdik y Jesús María Alvarado Andrade, *Ley Orgánica de la Administración Pública, Decreto Ley Nº 4317 de 15-07-2008,* Colección Textos Legislativos, N° 24, 4ª edición actualizada, Editorial Jurídica Venezolana, Caracas 2009, pp. 68-70

corporations following the provisions of the Law (articles 103, 261). In the exercise of such attributions, the "autonomy" of FOGADE can only be exercised "according to the terms established in the legal order" (art. 104 of Law Banking Sector) which, as established in the Organic Law on Public Administration, is limited and subject to the supervision of SUDEBAN, to the control exercised by the Ministry of attachment and to the Central Planning System regime.

In addition, SUDEBAN and FOGADE are subject to the Central Commission of Planning, whose Secretary Executive is the same Ministry of Planning and Finance, acting subjected to the Organic Law on Public and Popular Planning Commission[204] is empowered to "control and coordinate Public Administration as a whole", that is, the ministries, the autonomous services, the autonomous institutes, enterprises, foundations, associations, civil societies of the State and other decentralized attached entities which will not have organizational autonomy nor autonomy for administrative financial planning. According to such Law, regarding National Public Administration, the ministries, the autonomous services, the autonomous institutes, enterprises, foundations, associations, civil societies of the State and other decentralized attached entities, are governed in their activities by the strategic guidelines, policies and plans approved according to the centralized planning.[205]

VII. SOME ASPECTS OF THE LEGAL REGIME OF CURRENCY EXCHANGE CONTROL (2014)

If it is true that in Venezuela, the general principle on matters of currency exchange, as it has been set forth in the Central Bank of Venezuela Organic Law[206]is that of the free currency convertibility (art. 121);[207] the same Law has authorized the Central Bank of Venezuela to regulate in terms agreed with the National Executive foreign currency negotiation and commerce, as well as the transfer of funds in national or foreign currency (art 122). The same Law has also assigned the Central Bank the competency to sign Currency Exchange Covenants (*Convenios Cambiarios*) with the National Executive in order to establish the general regime concerning the Venezuelan system of currency exchange, making it possible to

---

204 See Ley Orgánica de Planificación Pública y Popular, *Official Gazette* N° 6.148 Extra. of November 18, 2014. See on the antecedents of such Law: Allan R. Brewer-Carías, "Comentarios sobre la inconstitucional creación de la Comisión Central de Planificación, centralizada y obligatoria", in *Revista de Derecho Público*, N° 110, (abril-junio 2007), Editorial Jurídica Venezolana, Caracas 2007, pp. 79-89.

205 See Allan R. Brewer-Carías, "¿Reforma administrativa en Venezuela? O la transformación no siempre planificada de la Administración Pública, para la implementación de un Estado Socialista al margen de la Constitución, mediante la multiplicación, dispersión y centralización de sus órganos y entes," Paper submitted to the *Cuarto Congreso Iberoamericano y Quinto Mexicano de Derecho* Administrativo, Xalapa, México, octubre 2012. Available at http://www.allabrewercarias.com/Content/449725d9-f1cb-474b-8ab2-41efb849fea2/Content/I,%201,%201057.%20Reforma%20administrativa%20o%20trasformación%20no%20planificada%20de%20la%20Administración%20Pública.%20Venezuela%202001).pdf

206 See the reform of 2010, *Official Gazette* N° 39.419 of May 7, 2010.

207 See in general, Allan R. Brewer-Carías, "Aspectos del régimen jurídico de la moneda," in *Revista de Derecho Público*, N° 13, Editorial Jurídica Venezolana, Caracas, 1983, pp. 5-20.

establish limits or restrictions to the free convertibility of the national currency,[208] that is the Bolívar (BsF) (art. 124).

It was under these provisions of the Central Bank Law that on February 5, 2003, the Currency Exchange Covenant No. 1 was signed between the National Executive and the Central Bank,[209] establishing a general system of currency exchange control limiting free convertibility of foreign currency into local currency and vice versa. Consequently since 2003 currency exchange rate is not the product of market forces (purchase and sale requests) and does not fluctuate, but is set by the Central Bank of Venezuela. In February 2014, the official exchange rate was set in various scales, two regulated for specific purposes at BsF. 6,30 and BsF 12.00 per US$, and a third one according to the free market as it was stated in the Exchange Covenant s signed between the Ministry of Finances and the Central Bank of Venezuela.[210]

On this currency exchange control regime, foreign currency purchase or sale is regulated, via the Central Bank of Venezuela (BCV), through banks considered as exchange operators of the BCV, and in the fixed rates only when the controlling office authorizes such purchase or sale. The Agency in charge of monitoring the exchange control regime at the exchange rate of BsF 12.00 per US$ is the *Sistema Complementario de Administración de Divisas* (Sicad), which is empowered to establish regulation and requirements to purchase currency, to admit or deny currency purchase petitions, and to verify and control the use of currency, among others. The free-market exchange system is monitored by the *Sistema Marginal de Divisas (Simadi)*

Pursuant to the general regime of currency exchange control, any person or corporation wishing to purchase foreign currency from the BCV at the official exchange rate of BsF. 6,30 per US$, must obtain an authorization that can be granted only in cases specifically provided for. In any case, the petitioner must, first, register before an administrative agency and then, provided a qualifying situation for the purchase request is present, comply with the requirements to obtain the currency after filing the proper petition.

Once registration is achieved, then a petition to purchase currency can be filed, only in the case of specific provided for purposes authorized.

In addition to the exchange control regime established since in 2003, since 2007 the National Assembly passed a special statute on Exchange Control crimes,[211] defining some conducts as exchange crime. The Law applies to all persons and corporations that, acting for themselves or as representatives, officers, intermediaries or beneficiaries of currency exchange operations, contravene the

---

208 See in general, Allan R. Brewer-Carías, *Régimen Cambiario*, Vol. I, Editorial Jurídica Venezolana, Caracas, 1994.

209 See *Official Gazette*, N° 37.625 of February 5, 2003, re-published in *Official Gazette* N° 37.653 of March 19, 2003. In August 2015 the real "free market" exchange rate was almost BsF 1.000 per dolar.

210 See *Official Gazette* N° 6.171 Extra of February 11, 2014.

211 See *Ley contra los Ilícitos Cambiarios*, *Official Gazette* N° 5.975 (Extra) of May 17, 2010. In 2014 such Law was substittued by the Ley de Régimen Cambiario y sus Ilícitos, *Official Gacette* N. 6.150 of November 18, 2014. See on the previous Law, José Alfredo Giral Pimentel, *Ley contra los ilícitos cambiarios de 2012 y contratos en moneda extranjera*, Editorial Jurídica Venezolana, Caracas 2012.

Law, Exchange Covenants or any other applicable regulations (Article 3). In the case of corporations, officers and representatives are held responsible.

Pursuant to the Law, the following are qualified as exchange crimes sanctioned with penalty is either fine or imprisonment for up to 7 years: 1. Currency purchase, sale, offer, transfer, acceptance, export or import, either in one or several operations. The penalty varies according to the yearly amount of the operation. 2. To obtain currency through deceive, betrayal, mislead, by alleging a false cause or use any fraudulent mean. 3. To use legally obtained currency for purposes different from those that motivated the request and authorization. 4. To offer purchase or sale of goods and services in currency, either publicly or privately, in the country.

PART SIX

PRINCIPLES OF ADMINISTRATIVE LAW RELATED TO ENVIRONMENT PROTECTION AND TO THE MINING AND OIL INDUSTRIES

I. ADMINISTRATIVE LAW PRINCIPLES APPLICABLE TO THE ENVIRONMENTAL MANAGEMENT (ENVIRONMENTAL LAW) IN PARTICULAR REGARDING MINING ACTIVITIES

The 1999 Constitution includes a Chapter dedicated to environmental rights as part of the individual rights (and duties), whereas the State is to protect the environment, being its fundamental duty with the society's active participation to grant the people an environment free of contamination (Article 127).

The National State's police power in this matter also has being provided for in the Constitution: Article 129 requires for every activity that may have a negative impact in the ecosystem to be previously accompanied by an environmental and sociocultural impact study. It also provides for the mandatory inclusion of a provision stating the duty to preserve the ecological balance and to reinstate the environment to its natural state, if it was to be altered, in the terms provided for by the law, in State contracts or State granted permits that may have an effect on natural resources.

The National State is also constitutionally bound to develop land use policy, taking into account, among others, the ecological, geographic, social and financial realities towards a sustainable development; and to elaborate the principles and criteria to be followed in setting this land use policy through an Organic Law (Article 128).

Finally, the National State is the competent authority on environmental and land use planning matters, and thus, is empowered to legislate and regulate it, to the extent that the regime and management of Venezuela's natural resources, the national environmental policy, and the land use planning are matters assigned expressly to it in the Constitution (Articles 156, 16 and 23).

1. The general rules on land planning and land use for mining projects, in particular regarding the Areas with Special Administration Regime

In order to regulate the environmental and land use planning, the legal framework has been set forth, following the Constitution's provisions, in the Organic Law on the Environment (*Ley Orgánica del Ambiente*),[1] the Criminal Environmental Law (*Ley Penal del Ambiente*),[2] the Organic Law on Land Use Planning (*Ley Orgánica para la Ordenación del Territorio*)[3] and several Executive Decrees and Regulations related to specific environmental matters.

Regarding Land Use Planning, the Organic Law on Land Use Planning, following the Constitution, provides that it must be carried out by a set of plans that have to be observed and complied with, being mandatory for both the State and the individuals. The plans, in which a broad layout of activities is defined and the development strategy for the country is outlined, are the following: The National Plan of Land Use, the Regional Plans of Land Arrangement, the National Plans for the use of natural resources and other sector plans; the urban land use city-plans; the plans for the Areas Under Special Administration Regimes; and the other plans of land use that the process of integral development of the country may require (Article 5). In addition, the Organic Law on Land Use Planning specifically provides that all activities that could imply occupancy of the territories are subject to prior control by the *Ministry of the Environment*[4] through approvals or through authorizations. In the case of decisions to be adopted by entities or organs of the National Public Administration with important territorial incidence implying actions of occupancy of the territory as determined by the Regulations, they must be previously approved by the Ministry of Environment in order to verify its conformity with the lines and previsions of the National Plan of Land Use (Article 49). In such cases, the decision to approve or deny must be issued in a term of 60 days, with approval considered as granted when such term elapses without express decision (Article 49). In this case, the Organic Law has adopted the principle of positive administrative silence effects. In the case of activities to be developed by individuals and private entities implying occupancy of the territory, they must be previously authorized by the public entities in charge of the execution of the plans (like the Ministry of the Environment), in order to verify their conformity with the same (Article 53). Also, in these cases, the administrative decision must be issued within the term of 60 days, and if no decision has been adopted granting or denying the authorization, it must be considered as granted, and the public entity is then obliged to produce the corresponding certification of the authorization (Article 54).

As mining activities have an impact on and are capable of degrading the environment, and as they entail the occupation of territory and affect natural resources, they are subject to the environmental and land use laws, decrees and regulations, and thus are subject to the approvals and the authorizations established in the Organic Law as noted above.

---

1 Organic Law on the Environment, *Official Gazette* N° 5.833 of December 22, 2006.

2 Criminal Environmental Law, *Official Gazette* N° 4.358 Extra. of January 3, 1992.

3 Organic Law on Land Use Planning, *Official Gazette* N° 3.238 Extra. of August 11, 1983. See the general comments in Allan R. Brewer-Carías, *Ley Orgánica para la Ordenación del Territorio*, Editorial Jurídica Venezolana, Caracas 1983.

4 The "Ministry of Environment and Natural Resurces," created since 1976, was eliminated in 2014, assigning its compenecies and fonctions to anther Ministry of the National Executive: the *Ministry for Housing, Habitat and Ecosocialism*. See in *Official Gazette* No. N° 40.489 of September 3, 2014. Notwistanding, and spite of the change of name, in the text I will continue to use the expression: "Ministry of the Environment".

The Organic Law on Land Use Planning has also specifically provided for the establishment of Areas under Special Administrative Regimes on matters of environment protection and land use planning, comprising among others, National Parks, Protected Zones, Forestry Reserves, Special Areas for Security and Defense, Wildlife Reserves and Refuges, and Tourist Interest Areas (Article 15). In particular, Articles 6, 17 and 35 of the Organic Law on Land Use Planning empowers the President of the Republic to establish such Areas Under Special Administration Regimes, and also to approve the Land Use Plans and the Uses Regulations for such areas, setting the guidelines for the zoning uses and activities therein allowed (Article 35). These Areas Under Special Administration Regimes can be established wherein land use is determined by special plans conceived within the mentioned system of plans regulating and promoting the orderly occupation of the national territory.

"Forestry Reservations" are among those Areas Under Special Administration Regimes listed by Organic Law on Land Use Planning (Article 15), for which the existence of plans –to regulate and promote the orderly occupation of the territory– is anticipated within the mentioned system of plans[5]. Once created by the National Executive, the same authority must approve their use plan, which must contain guidelines, strategies and policies for their management, as well as the guidance for the allocation of uses and activities allowed within their scope of influence (Article 17 Organic Law on Land Use Planning). The Law also requires, in addition to the plan, a Special Regulation for the uses having degrading effects.

Mining activities, for instance can be performed within some of the Areas Under Special Administration Regimes, like a Forestry Reservation, as provided in the Plan regulating each area, which must expressly include the guidelines for such activities to be carried out. In the case of the *Imataca* Forestry Reservation in the Bolivar and Delta Amacuro States, both the first Master Plan and Use Regulation passed in 1997,[6] as well as the one currently in force, passed in 2004 (*Imataca* Plan and its Use Regulation), recognized mining as a preexisting activity in the area, further permitting it in the designated zones.[7]

In all these cases, the respective Plan for land use and territory occupation in Areas Under Special Administrative Regimes is the legal instrument governing the management and handling of the Area with respect to the permitted activities and uses, their allocation, the parameters to be followed when carrying them out, as well as their management. The Plans are the legal instruments that have to be observed when granting land occupation permits as, for instance, is provided in Articles 35 and 37 of the *Imataca* Forestry Reservation Plan.

The Plans require that a written request be filed before the Ministry of the Environment along with the requirements set forth in the environmental regulations to obtain a land occupation permit. As for the rest of the procedure for granting

---

5 "Forestry Reservations" were initially established in the Forestry, Water and Soil Law of 1966, to be created by the National Executive in wasteland and other territories mainly stately owned, when it was so required to assure the continuous provision of raw materials for the national industry. See *Official Gazette*, N° 1.004 Extra. of January 26, 1966. See the new Law on Forests and Forest Management, *Official Gazette* N° 38.946 dated June 5, 2008.

6 Decree N° 1.850 of May 14, 1997, *Official Gazette* N° 36.215 of May 28, 1997.

7 Decree N° 3.110 of Sept. 7, 2004, *Official Gazette* N° 38.028 of Sept. 22, 2004.

these permits, the Plans generally refer to Organic Law on Land Use Planning stating that once the requests have been filed, the Ministry of the Environment must decide on the matter within the period stated in the Organic Law on Land Use Planning, in compliance with the environmental regulations in place, including that the interested parties (in the case of private individuals) must fulfill their duty to file an Environmental and Socio-Cultural Impact Study (Article 39). The 1996 Rules on Environmental Evaluation of Activities that may degrade the Environment (Decree N° 1.257, 1996)[8] do not list any further particular requirements but only provide that land occupation permits are to be granted pursuant to Organic Law on Land Use Planning.

Indeed, as aforementioned under Organic Law on Land Use Planning, when a public entity is to adopt a decision that will have an effect on the space or imply occupation of territory, they have to be previously approved to ensure their conformity with the guidelines and provisions of the applicable Land Plan. This is what is provided, for instance, in Articles 43, 46 and 49 of the *Imataca* Reservation Plan. Thus, in this case, for instance, pursuant to Article 49 of Organic Law on Land Use Planning, a request for a land occupation approval, filed in accordance with the *Imataca* Plan and its Use Regulation must be either granted or rejected within sixty (60) days from the last request for information. In this case too, the Organic Law on Land Use Planning has expressly adopted the administrative procedure principle of giving positive effects to the absence of timely pronouncement by the Administration. Hence, if there is no formal pronouncement on a land occupation approval request made by a public entity, "the request is to be deemed granted." The Organic Law on Land Use Planning, as the Mines Law in the case of petitions for extensions of concessions, has also adopted the administrative procedure principle of positive silence, which results in an implied administrative act granting the requested land occupation.[9] Consequently in these cases if, for instance, the Ministry of Mines was the requesting public entity of the approval in order to grant mining concessions, the positive administrative silence effect of the absence of decision by the Ministry of the Environment, would mean that the petition of the Ministry of Mines was tacitly approved, with the result that the Ministry of Mines then would be able to grant the corresponding concession.

When the land occupation permit is granted, the Ministry of the Environment must set conditions to harmonize mining activities with those provided for the specific Area in the corresponding Plan, for instance in an Area like the *Imataca* Forestry Reservation, with those established in the Forestry Arrangement and Management Plans (Article 64 of the *Imataca* Plan and its Use Regulation). In such case, the approval must to be recorded in the special Registry that the *Imataca* Reserve Administration has to keep (Article 41 of the Plan).

---

8 See Decree N° 1.257 of April 25, 1996 (*Normas sobre Evaluación Ambiental de Actividades Susceptibles de Degradar el Ambiente*), *Official Gazette* N° 35.946 of April 25, 1996.

9 On positive administrative silence in the Organic Law on Land Use Planning, see Allan R. Brewer-Carías, *Ley Orgánica para la Ordenación del Territorio,* Editorial Jurídica Venezolana, Caracas 1983, pp. 66-67; Juan Domingo Alfonzo Paradisi, "Aplicabilidad del silencio administrativo positivo en la Ley Orgánica de Ordenación Urbanística," in Fernando Parra Aranguren (Ed.), *Temas de Derecho Administrativo. Libro Homenaje a Gonzalo Pérez Luciani,* Vol. I, Tribunal Supremo de Justicia, Caracas 2002.

2. General regime on the role of the Ministry of the Environment in granting authorizations and its various permitting and compliance requirements relating to mining activities

According to the Organic Law on the Environment and developing constitutional concepts, the State (through the Ministry of the Environment) is to exercise environmental control (both preceding and subsequently) over activities that are capable of degrading the environment and its effects (Article 77).

As the Political-Administrative Chamber of the Supreme Court of Justice in ruling N° 819 of July 13, 2004 has stated:

> "[P]reservation of the environment and sustainable development are principles developed widely by Chapter IX, Title III of the Constitution of 1999 (arts. 127 to 129) whereas it specifically provides for the duty of the State to unfold a land planning policy taking into account ecological, geographic, population, social, cultural, economic and political realities, in agreement with sustainable development premises, and also stipulates the express duty that all activities susceptible to have a negative impact on the ecosystems, must be previously accompanied by their corresponding environmental and socio-cultural impact study. Hence, after those constitutional dispositions went into force, the matter related to environmental impact declarations has been regulated by a systematized normative set that conveys what is to be a global policy on preservation and conservation of the atmosphere, which, fundamentally, must be carried out through the Ministry of the Environment and Natural Resources, the state and municipal authorities and other national authorities to whom such policy has been trusted, as it is the case, for instance, of the Ministry of Production and Commerce.
>
> In the opinion of the Chamber, this constitutional duty of prevention and environmental control does not belong exclusively to one specific local authority but, on the contrary, requires maximum levels of inter-institutional coordination (Article 26 of the Urban Land Planning Law) to promote the task of drawing and enforcing the National Land Use Plan that the State has to carry out, within which, of course, the Ministry of the Environment and Natural Resources, in fulfillment of the Constitution, carries out a crucial work of environmental control, and for that reason the Land Use Planning Law grants such Ministry the power to direct the enforcement of the National Land Arrangement Plan jointly with the state's Governors, acting as agents of the National Government, in accordance with the delegations that the former confer to the latter.
>
> Therefore, the Ministry of the Environment and Natural Resources, on the basis of the exercise of these faculties, can grant not only the corresponding authorizations, but also must impose administrative penalties in cases of violation of the National Land Arrangement Plan (Article 43 *ejusdem*)."[10]

10 See Ruling N° 00819 of the Political-Administrative Chamber of the Supreme Tribunal of Justice of July 13, 2004, available at http://www.tsj.gov.ve/decisiones/spa/julio/00819-140704-2003-0023.htm.

Mining activities encompasses fit the legal definition of activities capable of degrading the environment under Article 80 of the Organic Law on the Environment. Therefore, the Ministry of the Environment is to exercise environmental control over mining, both before the mining starts and after it has begun, and also over its effects.

A. Preceding environmental control

The State (the Ministry of the Environment) exercises its preceding police power through authorizations, approvals, permits, licenses, concessions, assignations, contracts and other (Article 82), instruments that are granted to those that require them in order to be allowed to perform those activities that are environmentally sensible but are, however, permissible.

Accordingly, those wishing to pursue mining activities have to obtain the State's consent to do so and, according to the regulations in place, even if they have already been granted the right to do so through a concession, they have to seek the National State's further approval prior to the start of those activities that are inherent to mining, if such activities may have an effect on the environment, since under the Organic Law on the Environment any activities that have the potential of degrading the environment, such as those inherent to mining, cannot be carried out unless the State has previously given its consent.

Consequently, a request for the corresponding entitling instrument must be filed. The Ministry of the Environment is then to evaluate the impact the activity may have in the environment in compliance with the provisions of the Organic Law on the Environment, the Organic Law on Land Use Planning and any other special laws and technical environmental regulations on the matter (Article 81), and must grant it, provided that the performance of such activity requested: (i) is permitted under land use regulation plans, (ii) produces effects that are tolerable, (iii) create socio-economic benefits, and (iv) the warranties, proceedings and provisions are complied with. Accordingly, it may impose conditions, limitations and restrictions when granting the petition (Article 83).

Both these requests and the evaluation process that follows have been further regulated by the Organic Law on Land Use Planning, the 1992 Rules Governing the Affecting of Natural Resources Associated with Mining (Decree N° 2.219, 1992),[11] and the 1996 Rules on Environmental Evaluation of Activities that may degrade the Environment (Decree N° 1.257, 1996).[12]

a. Land occupation permits

Under the Mines Law, the Organic Law on Land Use Planning and Decree N° 2.219, the first environmental consent to be obtained for mining activities is the approval or the authorization to occupy the territory, that is, a given piece of land for mining purposes that must be given by the Ministry of Environment. The purpose of this preliminary approval or authorization is to verify that the activities to be carried out are in those territories where the National State has planned them to be.

---

11 See Decree N° 2.219 of April 23, 1992 (*Normas para regular la afectación de los recursos naturales renovables asociados a la exploración y extracción de minerales*), *Official Gazette* N° 4.818 Extra. of April 27, 1992.

12 See Decree N° 1.257 of April 25, 1996 (*Normas sobre Evaluación Ambiental de Actividades Susceptibles de Degradar el Ambiente*), *Official Gazette* N° 35.946 of April 25, 1996.

The National State activities directed to protect the environment as well as to preserve it and/or to assure the rational use of natural resources, are an essential part of land planning policy. Therefore, any public decision involving land occupation and/or the use of a natural resource must integrate environmental policy. As Article 3 of the Organic Law on Land Use Planning provides, land planning includes "9. protection of the environment and conservation and rational use of water, soil, subsoil, forest resources and other renewable and nonrenewable natural resources based on land planning".

Decree N° 2.219, 1992, classified mining activities to be developed through concessions or contracts as "Type II" exploration and exploitations (Article 3). This implies that it is the Ministry of Mines that must file the request for the territory occupancy approval before the Ministry of Environment (and not the interested party requesting a concession), this administrative approval being a "condition" to be fulfilled prior to the granting –by the Ministry of Mines– of a given concession or mining contract within the area (Article 7). Consequently, in the case of mining activities to be developed through concessions or mining contracts it is the Ministry of Mines that is the administrative organ that must seek and obtain this environmental approval by the Ministry of the Environment prior to granting mining concessions or entering into contracts for mining. That was ratified by Decree N° 1.257 containing the Rules of Environmental Evaluation of Activities Susceptible of Degrading the Environment passed in 1996 (Article 15), which provided for those concessions and contracts already in place where neither operation had started nor a land occupation permit issued, the corresponding approval was to be sought as a prerequisite for the commencement of the activities (Article 15, Paragraph 2) by responding to an environmental questionnaire to be published by the Ministry of the Environment (Article 16).

Up to this point, by granting both the land occupation approval and the concession for mining purposes the State has exercised its police power twice: (i) first, by checking whether mining activities in a given area are in accordance with the applicable Plan for Land Use (for example, the *Imataca* Plan and its Use Regulation), that is to say, the appropriateness of the proposed activity, broadly speaking, and (ii) second, by selecting the concessionaire through the process established in the Mines Law, which refers to its suitability and that of the project or operation proposed.

b. Authorizations to affect natural resources

After a concession and the subsequent land occupation permit have been granted, a more specific, but still preliminary environmental control follows: before the concessionaire may initiate the exploratory phase of the mining operation he must get an authorization to affect natural resources for exploratory purposes and subsequently, before the commencement of the productive phase of the mining operation, an authorization to affect natural resources for productive purposes has also to be obtained.

c. Authorization to affect natural resources for exploratory purposes

Indeed, prior to the initiation of the exploratory phase of the mining operation, the concessionaire must file a petition to obtain from the Ministry of the Environment an authorization to affect natural resources for exploratory purposes (Article 17 of Decree N° 1.257, 1996). The Rules Governing the Affecting of Natural Resources

Associated with Mining lists the documents and requirements that must be filed along with the petition, and when exploratory drilling is foreseen, an Environmental Impact Study has to be prepared and submitted as well (Section IV, Chapter II of Decree N° 2.219, 1992 and Article 17 of Decree N° 1.257, 1996).

The purpose of these authorizations is to generally set the way in which the activities that will be performed are to be carried out, furthering the lesser impact on the natural resources that are to be affected, as well as to anticipate measures that can minimize such impacts. Thus, the measures and conditions that are included therein must directly relate to this end and cannot have a different or another goal. Basically, those measures and conditions are the terms under which the program or project is approved and can be accomplished. It follows that the conditions established in any such authorization are to be placed on the concessionaire, and not on the administration or third parties: it is the concessionaires who have to comply (through proper performance, either directly or not) with the measures and conditions that the Ministry *imposes on them* when granting the authorizations to affect.

Procedurally, when granting these petitions, the Ministry of the Environment is bound by the general principles of due process and administrative procedure set forth in the Organic Law on Administrative Procedures; otherwise, its acts are absolutely null and void (Article 91).

d. Authorization to affect natural resources for exploitation purposes

In addition to the authorization to affect natural resources for exploration purposes, the concessionaire ought to obtain an authorization to affect natural resources for exploitation purposes, prior to the beginning of the corresponding phase of the mining operation. For such purpose, the concessionaire must file a petition to the Ministry of the Environment together with an Environmental Impact Study in which the environmental concerns reflected in the Technical-Economic Feasibility Study and Mining Program are addressed (Article 20 of Decree N° 1.257, 1996) as well as other requirements set forth by the Rules Governing the Affecting of Natural Resources Associated with Mining (Decree N° 2.219, 1992).

The scope of this EIS is to be established by the Ministry of the Environment following a terms of reference proposal that has to be filed by the concessionaire, the contents of which are listed under Article 7 of the Rules on Environmental Evaluation of Activities (Articles 20 and 7 of Decree N° 1.257, 1996).

The authorization to affect natural resources for productive (exploitation) purposes, when granted, should follow the provisions set forth in the Environmental Impact Study, and should also include a short description of the program or project to be developed, the preventive, mitigating and corrective measures for the foreseen impact and the *conditions under which affecting of the environment will be permitted during the productive phase*. Under the Rules on Environmental Evaluation of Activities, the Ministry of the Environment is also expressly empowered to impose additional conditions as deemed necessary, in accordance with the law (Articles 21 and 18 of Decree N° 1.257, 1996).

The duration of these authorizations to affect for productive purposes should be coherent with that of the project to be accomplished. Corollary, under the Rules on Environmental Evaluation of Activities they are to be granted for up to the time estimated for the completion of the corresponding mining production program (Article 21).

B. Subsequent environmental control

The environmental authority, as we have stated previously, is also empowered to exercise its police power during the course of the authorized activities.

The State (through the Ministry of the Environment and other empowered bodies) exercises its subsequent environmental supervision and control, once an authorization to occupy or to affect (either for exploratory or productive purposes) has been granted, to confirm the compliance of rules and conditions set through those instruments, as well as to prevent environmental infringements. It does so through environmental safeguarding, auditing, supervision and police (Articles 92 and 93 of Organic Law on Environment).

Subsequent monitoring is achieved by pursuing the Environment Supervision Plan included in the Environmental Impact Study submitted by the concessionaire when applying for the authorization to affect. Accordingly, the designated environmental consultant (or designated responsible authority, if that is the case) must submit to the Ministry of the Environment a report assessing the status of the measures and conditions set in the ESP or in the authorization itself (Articles 28 to 30 of Decree N° 1.257, 1996).

After the Ministry of the Environment has thoroughly analyzed such reports, it may formulate recommendations or impose further conditions, if deemed necessary to minimize the environmental impact caused by the activities that are being carried out (Article 31 of Decree N° 1.257, 1996). The referenced reports have to be inserted in the program or project file, and are to be used by the Ministry of the Environment in further supervision and control (Article 32 of Decree N° 1.257, 1996). Indeed, the Ministry of the Environment is entitled to carry out inspections at any time in order to verify the accuracy of the reports and compliance with the measures as well as to enforce the legal framework (Article 33 of Decree N° 1.257, 1996).

On the other hand, mining concessionaires are entitled to request the Ministry of the Environment to issue certificates of compliance or environmental performance, where satisfaction of the general environmental framework as well as of the specific conditions imposed through the preceding control instruments, is assessed (Article 94 of Organic Law on Environment).

3. The Forestry Reserve of *Imataca* and the possibility of the development of mining activities in some of its areas (2004)

Many mining concessions are located within the area of the Forest Reserve of *Imataca* in the Bolivar and Delta Amacuro States of Venezuela, which was originally created by Resolution N° 47 of February 9, 1961 of the Public Works Ministry.[13] After the sanctioning of the Organic Law on Land Use Planning, the *Imataca* Forestry Reservation was considered according to Articles 6, 17 and 35 as an "Area Under Special Administration Regimes" (Article 15.3), regarding which Land Use Plan and the Uses Regulation was to be approved, setting the guidelines for the zoning uses and activities therein allowed (Article 35).

13 See *Official Gazette* N° 26.478 of February 9, 1961. The Reserve was extended by Resolution N° 15 of January 7, 1963. See *Official Gazette* N° 27.044 of January 8, 1963.

The first Master Plan and Regulation of Use of the *Imataca* Reservation was established through Decree N° 1.850 of May 14, 1997,[14] wherein the continuation of mining use and activities in the "Mixed Zone (ZMM)" and in all areas in which, before the publication of the said Plan, mining concessions and contracts were given, was recognized. This Plan, considered as an instrument for environment planning (Article 29 of OLE) was substituted by the currently in force *Plan de Ordenamiento y Reglamento de Uso de la Reserva Forestal Imataca, Estados Bolívar y Delta Amacuro*, in Decree N° 3.110 of September 7, 2004 (Imataca Plan and its Use Regulation).[15]

A. Zoning uses and mining activities

According to the *Imataca* Plan and its Use Regulation, ten (10) Zoning Uses (*Zonas de Ordenamiento*) were established in the Reservation: 1. *Zona de Manejo Forestal (ZMF); 2. Zona de Manejo Forestal con Limitaciones (ZMFL)*; 3. *Zona de Protección (ZP);* 4. *Zona de Reservorio de Genes (ZRG);* 5. *Zona de Recuperación (ZR);* 6. *Zona de Manejo Especial Forestal con Alta Presencia de Comunidades Indígenas (ZMEFAPCI)*; 7. *Zona de Manejo Especial Forestal - Minero (ZMEFM);* 8. *Zona de Manejo Especial Forestal - Minero con Alta Presencia de Comunidades Indígenas (ZMEFMAPCI);* 9. *Zona de Manejo Especial Agroforestal (ZMEA),* and 10. *Zona de Manejo Especial Agroforestal con Alta Presencia de Comunidades Indígenas (ZMEAAPCI)* (Article 7). In these zones, the uses allowed are the following: Forestry, Traditional, Eco-Tourism, Residential Rural, Mining, Services, Scientific and Security and Defense (Article 43).

B. Mining activities within the *Imataca* Reserve

Regarding the mining use and activities they are particularly allowed in the following two zones: 7) *Zona de Manejo Especial Forestal -Minero (ZMEFM),* located to the North of Cuyuní River, in Sifontes Municipality of Bolivar State and in the superimposition zone in the boundaries between the Municipalities Antonio Díaz of Delta Amacuro State and Sifontes of Bolívar State (Article 14) and 8) *Zona de Manejo Especial Forestal - Minero con Alta Presencia de Comunidades Indígenas (ZMEFMAPCI)*, located to the South of Cuyuní River in Sifontes Municipality of Bolivar State, in areas inhabited by the Pemón and Akawaio indigenous people (Article 15). Consequently, Article 61 of the Imataca Plan and its Use Regulation expressly sets forth that "The Mining Use will be made in the *Zona de Manejo Especial Forestal - Minero (ZMEFM)* and in the *Zona de Manejo Especial Forestal - Minero con Alta Presencia de Comunidades Indígenas (ZMEFMAPCI),* subject to the limitations and conditions established in this Decree and other applicable provisions." Corollary, Mining Uses and activities are expressly forbidden in Article 44, in the other Zones of the Reserve (Zone Nos. 1, 2, 3, 4, 5, 6, 9, and 10). The mining use is also forbidden in general in permanent and not permanent water beds (Article 44.5).

It must be noted that mining activities that were duly authorized and in place within the Imataca Reserve prior to the 2004 Imataca Plan and its Use Regulation defining the Zones allowing Mining Use, were allowed to continue subject to the

14 See *Official Gazette* N° 36.215 of May 28, 1997.

15 See *Official Gazette* N° 38.028 of September 22, 2004.

provisions of the Plan, the Mines Law, and the environmental normative framework (Third Transitory Provision of the Plan). Nonetheless, when deemed necessary, those activities were due to adjust their exploitation plans to the provisions of the Imataca Plan and its Use Regulation during the following year (2004-2005).

In any case, the mining activities permitted in the Zones 7 and 8 of the *Imataca* Reserve, according to Article 60 of the Imataca Plan and its Use Regulation, are those of prospection, exploration, exploitation, processing, transformation, storage, transport and commercialization of metallic and nonmetallic minerals, including associated installations to the mining projects, according to what is established in the Mines Law, and in the special mining statutes of the States Bolivar and Delta Amacuro regulating nonmetallic mines. According to the same provision of Article 60 of the *Imataca* Plan and its Use Regulation, the State has reserved its rights to the results of the searches with strategic or national security purposes.

In any event, pursuant to Article 62 of the *Imataca* Plan and its Use Regulation, mining activities in the *Imataca* Reserve must be carried out subject to the provisions contained in the technical regulations for controlling activities affecting the environment and all the other applicable environmental provisions, as well as those established in the Operative Plans indicated in the *Imataca* Plan and its Use Regulation (Article 62).

Moreover, under Article 27 of the *Imataca* Plan and its Use Regulation the Ministry of Mines, with the participation of the Ministry of the Environment and the Venezuelan Geographic Institute "Simón Bolívar" are in charge of the Evaluation Program of the Mining Activity in the Reserve (Article 18.9), which is to produce and maintain updated information, and to monitor and control the development of activities of land registry and mining exploration and exploitation. Within this program, the Sub-Program of Middle and Big Mining has the purpose of identifying the areas assigned to so-called middle and big mining; of establishing the integral development of infrastructure common to the projects; of establishing the socioeconomic aspects of the region for a better use of human resources; and of implementing the best techniques on matters of environment protection. The execution of such Program of Middle and Big Mining, according to Article 27.3, will be the responsibility of "the competent authorities, those proposing the infrastructure and those responsible for generating damage."

C. The authorizations for mining activities in the *Imataca* Reserve

According to Article 35 of the *Imataca* Plan and its Use Regulation, projects and activities to be carried out by individuals or corporations, either private or public, within the Imataca Forest Reserve, must be done in compliance with the Plan and the environment regulations in place. Consequently, the requests for authorizations of exploitation of natural resources must be made according to what is established in the Land Use and Forestry *manejo* Plan, subjected to what is established in the forestry legislation (formerly the Forestry, Soil and Water Law of 1965) and its Regulation, and in the Environment Organic Law.

Regarding the land occupation permits within the Imataca Reserve, pursuant to Article 36 of the Imataca Plan and its Use Regulation, they must be granted by the Ministry of the Environment following the environmental normative framework. Moreover, under Article 37 the request for such authorizations can only be granted in conformity with what is established in the Imataca Plan and its Use Regulation and the special statutes applicable. These requests are to be filed by the interested parties in writing before the Ministry of the Environment, with the attachments indicated in the environmental normative framework (Article 38). Once the petition for land occupation permit has been duly filed, the Ministry of the Environment must either grant it or deny it within the term set forth in the Organic Law on Land Use Planning. Providing that the request complies with the environmental normative framework and is granted, then the Ministry must inform the interested party of its obligation to file the Study of Environmental and Socio-cultural Impact (Article 39). The Ministry of the Environment must establish in the corresponding authorizations the conditions tending to harmonize the mining activities with those established in the Land Use and Forestry Manejo Plan (Article 64). These authorizations must be registered in the special Registry that must be kept by the Imataca Reserve Administration (Article 41). In any case, as I have already explained, for mining concessions and contracts classified in Decree N° 2.219, 1996 as Type II explorations and extractions (Article 3), it is the Ministry of Mines that must request from the Ministry of the Environment the corresponding territory occupancy permit as a condition to be fulfilled prior to granting concessions or contracts in a given area (Article 7), as was ratified by Decree N° 1.257, 1996.

Regarding authorizations for territory occupancy, according to the *Imataca* Plan and its Use Regulation, they terminate (*prescribe*), if within the term of three years after being issued, the interested party fails to initiate activities. This term can be extended by the Ministry of the Environment up to one more year, providing that a grounded request is made before the exhaustion of the initial term (Article 40).

Regarding the authorizations to Affect Natural Renewable Resources within the *Imataca* Reserve area, they must be filed by the interested parties before the State Environmental Directorate of the Ministry of the Environment with jurisdiction in the area. This request must be filed in writing, properly identifying the interested party with all the needed attachments established in the environmental legal framework (Article 42) as previously explained.

D. The challenge of the *Imataca* Reserve Decree on unconstitutional grounds before the Supreme Court

The Imataca Reserve Decree N° 1.850 of May 14, 1997 was challenged by a group of people before the former Supreme Court of Venezuela, which in a decision dated November 11, 1997, notwithstanding the opposition formulated by the Attorney General's Office (August 12, 1997), issued a preliminary or precautionary ruling "ordering the Ministry of Mines to refrain from, granting concessions, authorizations and any other act related to mining activity, exploration and infrastructure, projects for exploration and geological exploitation, based on Decree N° 1.850 dated May 14, 1997, until this Court issues a definitive ruling on the unconstitutionality and illegality of the normative provisions it contains". It must be highlighted that the order is given directly and exclusively to the Ministry of Mines, and not to the Ministry of the Environment, so the latter is not prevented by the Court's ruling to grant those authorizations, approvals and permits as required for the continuance of mining activities authorized by the Ministry of Mines prior to the Court's decision. The Political-Administrative Chamber also declared urgent the decision of the case, abbreviating terms. A motion to clarify the ruling was filed by one of the parties, Venezuelan Mining Chamber (CAMIVEN), but was rejected by the Court on December 9, 1997.

Other claims challenging the constitutionality of the same Decree were filed before the same Supreme Court and its Political-Administrative Chamber, so almost one year later, on August 11, 1998, the Court decided to accumulate all claims against the Decree in only one file.[16] Due to the lack of any procedural activity in the file by the parties, a motion to declare the claim perished was filed, but on February 2, 1999 the Court refused to rule on the matter and rather decided to postpone it and address it in a definitive ruling on the case.

After the new Constitution was sanctioned in December 1999, creating the Constitutional Chamber of the Supreme Tribunal of Justice, this Chamber, after receiving the files that where in process before the former Supreme Court of Justice, on September 24, 2003, almost three years after the new Constitution was sanctioned, decided it lacked jurisdiction in the case due to the fact that the challenged act was an Executive Decree and Regulation, given that the Political-Administrative Chamber of the Supreme Tribunal was the one to decide on its unconstitutionality.[17] On March 10, 2004, a representative of one of the parties in the process (*Minera Las Cristinas C.A.*) warned the Chamber that the Ministry of Mines had not respected the precautionary measure issued by the former Supreme Court.

One year after assuming jurisdiction in the case, through Decision N° 1.217 of September 2, 2004, the Political-Administrative Chamber of the Supreme Tribunal decided to accept jurisdiction in the case[18] and to reinstate the procedure, arguing that regarding the non-compliance by the Ministry of Mines on the precautionary measure, it was to decide promptly. No other decision has been adopted by the Political-Administrative Chamber in this process.

One aspect must be highlighted regarding this process originating with the challenging of Decree 1.850 of the *Imataca* Reserve: The Tribunal has not yet decided on the warning given to it by one of the parties, regarding the non-compliance by the Ministry of Mines with the precautionary measure ordering it to stop, beginning on November 13, 1997, granting concessions and authorizations for mining purposes in the *Imataca* Reserve Area.

In any case, the contentious administrative judicial process that was initiated with the challenging of the *Imataca* Reserve Decree N° 1.850 of May 14, 1997, ceased to have any valid object when the new *Imataca* Reserve Decree N° 3.110 of September 7, 2004 was issued that expressly abrogated the previous challenged Decree N° 1.850 of 1997. Having been abrogated, according to Supreme Tribunal doctrine, it cannot be annulled, because State acts that have ceased to have effects (due to being abrogated) cannot be annulled by means of judicial review actions.[19]

---

16 Record Nos. 0943, 0962, 0967 and 13.915.

17 Record N° 2000-1459.

18 Record N° 2003-1348.

19 See Decision N° 37 of the Constitutional Chamber of the Supreme Tribunal of Justice of January 27, 2004 (Case of *Cooperativa Mixta La Salvación, Responsabilidad Limitada*), in *Revista de Derecho Público*, N° 97-98, Editorial Jurídica Venezolana, Caracas 2004, pp. 402-403.

II. ADMINISTRATIVE LAW APPLICABLE TO MINING ACTIVITIES (MINING LAW)

1. Basic Legal Provisions Regarding Mining Activities: Administrative Procedure Principles and Mining Concessions

Both the Venezuelan 1999 Constitution (Article 12) and the 1999 Mines Law[20] (Article 2), following the general trend applicable in most of Latin American countries following the legal tradition initiated in Colonial times with the *Ordenanzas de Minería de Nueva España* (1783), declare mining deposits (*yacimientos mineros)* as State owned or public property or domain (*dominio público*).[21]

The general consequence of these constitutional and legal declarations is that the exploration and exploitation of such mining deposits is reserved to the National State, namely: The State has reserved for itself each and every mining right. This means that no individual or private corporation can claim, based on the economic freedom constitutionally secured (Article 112), to have "mining rights" for the exploration or exploitation of the subsoil, even if there happens to be mining deposits on his property. The only general exception on this matter provided for in the 1999 Mines Law refers to small-scale mining activities (*pequeña minería*), defined in the Law as "the activity performed by natural or juridical individuals of Venezuelan nationality, for the exploitation of gold and diamonds; during a period no longer than ten (10) years; in areas previously established by means of resolution by the Ministry of the Popular Power for Basic Industries and Mining (from now on, Ministry of Mines); and whose surface is not larger than ten (10) hectares, to be worked by a number of individually considered workers no greater than thirty (30)" (Article 64). In order to develop these small-scale mining activities, nonetheless, an Authorizations for Exploitation (Resolution) is required from the Ministry of Mines (Article 7.c of the Mines Law).

In all the other cases, in order to exercise mining rights, they must be granted by the National State, generally through concessions. Up to 1999, the general power on mining matters was attributed to the national level of government, being the National Executive the only competent authority to grant mining rights. In the 1999 Constitution, some power was granted to the States regarding the regime and use of non-metallic minerals (rocks) not reserved to the national level of government (Article 164.5). Consequently, in these cases only, concessions are granted by the States Governors.

20 Law of Mines, Decree-Law N° 295 of September 5, 1999, *Official Gazette* N° 5.382 Extra. of September 28, 1999.

21 See Elsa Amorer, *El régimen de la explotación minera en la legislación venezolana*, Editorial Jurídica Venezolana, Caracas 1991, pp. 9-10.

2. General framework of the mining exploration and exploitation regime under the 1945 Law

Before the 1999 Constitution and Mines Law were passed, the general regime related to mining activities was governed by the 1961 Constitution, the 1945 Mines Law[22] and several Executive Decrees and Resolutions passed thereafter.

Pursuant to such 1961 Constitution and the 1945 Mines Law, although it could be considered that the State owned the mining deposits, the mining activities were not reserved to it.

Exploring the territory and furthering the existence of such deposits was almost unrestricted, subject only to a simultaneous notice to be filed at the Ministry in charge of mining activities (*Ministerio de Fomento*) (and the main Municipal authority)[23] which was to issue an exploration permit[24] upon verification of compliance with the legally provided requirements[25]. Some scholars criticized this liberty to explore, stating that basic exploration had to be performed by the State, and that in upcoming statutory reforms an Article providing for exploration prior to mining (exploitation) should be included.[26] Exploitation, however, was subject to concessions[27] that were granted after notice (*denuncio*) of a mineral deposit finding was given and a thorough proceeding was completed. The person first giving the notice was entitled to be granted the exploitation title.[28]

This relatively general freedom changed in 1977 when, according to Article 11 of the 1945 Mines Law, the National Executive through Executive Decree N° 2039 of February 15, 1977, reserved to the State all exploration and exploitation activities of minerals not previously reserved to the State[29]. From that moment on, new notice (*denuncio*) regarding mineral deposits were not allowed, and the State generally reserved to itself all mining activities, and private entities could only attain them through concessions for exploration and exploitation granted by the Ministry of Mines[30]. Accordingly, for private individuals and corporations to further either

22 Law of Mines, *Official Gazette* N° 121 Extra. of January 18, 1945.

23 Arts. 119 ff. of the 1945 Mines Law.

24 Arts. 116, 129 and 130 of the 1945 Mines Law.

25 Pursuant to Articles 116 and 117 of the Law the Ministry was to grant such exploration permits (no more than 5 per petitioner) for no more than 2 years, after verifying that the legal tax had been paid and that: (i) the petitioner was legally capable to acquire concessions, (ii) the permit would not infringe vested rights previously granted; (iii) the areas subject to petition were not greater than 2000 hectares; and (iv) the borders, situation and extension of the area subject to permit and its duration were clearly established.

26 See Elsa Amorer, *El Régimen de la Explotación Minera en la Legislación Venezolana*, Editorial Jurídica Venezolana, Caracas 1991, p. 2.

27 Art. 13 of the 1945 Mines Law.

28 Arts. 2, 33 and 134 of the 1945 Mines Law.

29 Executive Decree N° 2.039 of February 15, 1977, *Official Gazette* N° 31.175 of the same date.

30 Article 11 and the procedure and requirements regarding a concession's petitions and granting was further regulated first through the "Rules on Granting of Prospection and Concession Permits and Mining Contracts" contained in Resolution N° 528 of the Ministry of Mines issued on December 17, 1986 (*Official Gazette* N° 33.729 of June 1, 1987) and later through the substitutive

mining exploration and subsequent exploitation or for exploitation, concessions were to be granted upon request, after taking into consideration several criteria set by such Executive Decree N° 2039[31] and pursuant to the procedure regulated in the Third Book of the 1945 Mines Law (Article 174 ff.).

When approved, concessions for exploration and subsequent exploitation granted the concessionaires, their heirs or executors, upon compliance with the relevant provisions,[32] the exclusive right to explore the area conceded for a period of two years and to obtain for its exploitation the lots chosen,[33] having then the exclusive right to exploit or dig out the minerals conceded, within the granted area, for forty (40) years.[34] For the purpose of exploitation, the concessionaire was to submit to the Ministry within the exploratory period, the general drawing of the zone or corresponding lots, in order to obtain a certificate of exploitation. This certificate of exploitation was to be granted after a drawings approbatory Resolution was granted by the Ministry and was final, since hearing to possible oppositions had to be granted, and it had to be registered in the Public Registry Office as a formal proof of the exclusive right to exploit minerals.[35]

All those concessions and contracts, as aforementioned, were granted pursuant to the provisions of the 1945 Mines Law. Such Law was amended in 1999, in and in view of the change of the new applicable legal framework that the amendment implied, the terms under which those concessions that were granted prior to September 28, 1999, were to be governed, as was established in Article 129 of the amended Mines Law, as follows: (i) the right to mine (exploit) previously granted was due to be preserved only regarding those minerals and genre for which the concession was originally granted; (ii) the concessionaires were compelled to pay the new legal taxes only after 1 year from the publication of the new Law in the *Official Gazette*; (iii) the duration of the concessions was the term established in the original title (or concession) to be counted from the date of the publication of the Mining Title; (iv) the concessionaires were immediately subjected to those environmental and other

---

"Rules on Granting of Concessions and Mining Contracts" contained in Resolution N° 115 of the Ministry of Mines issued on March 20, 1990 (*Official Gazette* N° 34.448 of April 16, 1990).

31 Article 2 of the Decree stated that the Ministry would take into account, for the discretionary granting of the concessions: (i) the technical and financial qualification of petitioner, (ii) the duty to manufacture or refine the mineral in the country, (iii) a tax regime to the satisfaction of the National Treasury, (iv) technology supply and transfer to local and national mining industry, (v) duty to revert to the State all goods at the end of the concession and (vi) whichever special advantage deemed convenient to national mining interests.

32 The Rules that further regulated the procedure for granting mining concessions issued several years after the Law was passed (1986 and 1990) provided as a special advantage that the petitioner could offer when requesting a concession, to have the 40-year legal duration reduced to a 20-year duration, with subsequent 10-year extensions, upon request made within 3 months prior to expiring. Most of the concession's petitioners under that regime did offer such a special advantage. Thus, there are many concessions granted at the time that do not have a 40-year duration, but were granted for 20 years, with subsequent 10-year extensions, to be requested within 3 months prior to the expiring date.

33 Art. 179 of the 1945 Mines Law.

34 Art. 188 of the 1945 Mines Law .

35 Arts. 180 and 182 of the 1945 Mines Law. In the 1945 Mines Law, this Certificate of Exploitation as also called Mining Title (Arts. 16, 24, and 26).

provisions on matters of superior national interest included in statutes and regulations in place; and (v) the concessionaires were compelled to maintain the special advantages originally offered to the Republic.

Regarding the constitutionality of Article 129 (as well as of Article 132) of the 1999 Mines Law, the Constitutional Chamber of the Supreme Tribunal, sustaining their constitutionality, stated in Decision N° 37 of January 27, 2004:

> "[T]he referred provision (Article 129) secures the continuance of the rights arising from mining concessions entered into prior to the passing of the new Law. It could not be otherwise, this Chamber believes, so as to guarantee the principle of legal safety and that of respect of preexisting legal situations. The 1999 legislator wanted to substitute mining contracts, giving their beneficiaries the opportunity to transform them in concessions but for such purpose he could not ignore, of course, that there were already in place concessions on different minerals, ways of presenting themselves and geographic areas.
>
> Thus, article 129, is a provision to guarantee the rights of those that previously acted through concessions. That is why, the first reaction on this challenge should be the surprise, since there is no way it violates the due process right of the concessionaires. [...]
>
> [T]he Mines Law in place accepts the division of the area and the distinction of concessionaires according to the ways the minerals are presented. What was fundamental to the legislator was to secure previous rights, of concessionaires as well as of contractors. In that way, what he did was to respect existing situations, which is not only constitutional but also correct. [...]
>
> This Chamber understands that the premise of Articles 129 and 132 is valid: to maintain concessions and allow for contracts conversion. With both decisions legal safety is kept and previously created situations are respected. It was not an election for the legislator but its duty."[36]

Therefore, regarding the right to mine, those concessions that were already in place when the 1999 Mining Law was passed, were to maintain such right only for the minerals and genre they had been originally granted in the corresponding Title (Article 129.a); and for example, if the concessions were granted originally to exploit alluvial gold, they were to continue being for alluvial gold only. The regime for those concessions' extinction was also established by Article 129, whereas it was provided that the duration of the concessions granted prior to the passing of the Law was to be the one established in the original Title, counted from the date of its publication in the *Official Gazette* (Article 129.c). Finally, it was provided that the special advantages offered in such concessions in favor of the Republic, were to be maintained, pursuant to Article 129.d.

In matters related to legal taxes Article 129.b set forth that mining concessions granted prior to the Law were compelled to pay the new legal taxes established in the new law, only after one (1) year from its publication. The same can be said for

---

36Decision N° 37 of the Constitutional Chamber of January 27, 2004 (Case of *Asociación Civil Mixta La Salvación SRL*), (Record N° 00-1496), available at http://www.tsj.gov.ve/decisiones/scon/Enero/37-270104-00-1496.htm.

the rest of the provisions of the 1999 Law, whereas Article 129.e provided that they would be fully applicable to mining concessions previously granted, after one year elapsed from the date of the publication of the Law in the *Official Gazette*. In addition, Article 130 of the Law, imposed upon the holders of mining rights, the obligation to conform their plans of exploitation within the term of one (1) year counted from the publication of the law, to the applicable environmental provisions, or otherwise be subject to sanctions.

As for pre-1999 existing contracts concluded with *Corporación Venezolana de Guayana* (C.V.G.), Article 132 of the Mines Law expressly provided for the right of the titleholders to have them converted into mining concessions, but also "only regarding the mineral and the presentation form established in the contract," and provided that the corresponding petition was made within three months after the publication of the Law. This transitory provision, allowed the titleholder of mining contracts with *CVG* to petition the Ministry of Mines to convert the contracts into mining concessions within the term established in the law. The Ministry of Mines had the general obligation to respond in a timely manner to such petitions according to both Article 51 of the Constitution and Article 5 of the Organic Law on Administrative Procedure. However, the Mines Law did not assign specific positive or negative effects to the administrative silence of the Administration in the case of these petitions, as it did in the cases of petitions for concessions (Article 41) or for extensions of concessions (Article 25). Consequently, in case of silence, although the petitioners could have filed a claim against the resulting tacit negative decision, according to article 4 of the Organic Law on Administrative Procedures, the decision to be adopted by the Ministry of Mines remained pending and to be issued, so the right of the titleholder of the CVG contract to have to the conversion also remained to be decided. That is, negative administrative silence never means that the petitioner lost his right.

Article 135 of the Mines Law added that "the conversion of contracts that could be petitioned on areas of the *Imataca* Forestry Reserve would be subject to the solution of the legal controversy affecting the zone," which prevented the Ministry from deciding on the petitions when the contracts were within the *Imataca* Forestry Reserve. However, such provision ceased to have any effect after Decree N° 1.850 dated May 14, 1997 of the *Imataca* Forestry Reserve (i.e., the one challenged before the Supreme Tribunal), was formally and expressly abrogated and substituted by Decree N° 3.110 dated September 7, 2004. That means that after September 2004, the Ministry of Mines had no legal impediment to convert the *CVG* contracts into concessions as requested in 1999, because the legal controversy affecting the zone of the *Imataca* Forestry reserve was resolved by abrogating the challenged provisions contained in Decree N° 1.850 of May 14, 1997.

3. General framework regarding mining exploration and exploitation regime under the 1999 Law

Pursuant to Article 302 of the Constitution and to the provisions of the 1999 Mines Law, in principle, all mining activities and mining rights regarding mining deposits, apart from small-scale mining activities, remained reserved to the State, which however does not imply the complete exclusion of private entities from carrying out mining activities. On the contrary, according to the Constitution and the

Law, the State can grant mining rights to private entities, again, through concessions. Moreover, Article 7 of the Mines Law lists the different means for exploration, exploitation and use of mining resources as follows[37]:

> "a) Directly by the National Executive; b) Through concessions for exploration and subsequent exploitation; c) Through authorizations for exploitation via small-scale mining activities; d) Through mining consortiums (*Mancomunidades Mineras*); and e) Through artisanal mining."

Notwithstanding these Mines Law provisions allowing private activities in the mining industry, the State is entitled to declare a complete and total reserve regarding mining activities when ordering the "exclusive exercise of mining activity by the National Executive," in which case, the National Executive is authorized, when deemed convenient for the public interest, to "reserve by means of Decree, certain mineral substances and areas containing them, in order to explore or exploit them directly by an entity of the Ministry of Mines, or by means of entities of the exclusive property of the Republic" (Article 23).

Additionally, pursuant to Article 86 of the Law, since the storing, possession, benefit, transportation, circulation and commercialization of minerals under the Law is subject to the scrutiny and inspection of the National Executive and to the regulations issued for the defense of the interests of the Republic and of mining activity, the National Executive, also when deemed convenient to the public interest, can reserve to itself by means of a decree, "any of said activities regarding certain minerals."

Thus, except for these cases of exclusive reserve, in all the other fields of mining activities generally reserved to the State, private entities are allowed to perform mining activities, through concessions.

4. General Regime of Mining rights granted through concessions of exploration and subsequent exploitation

Concessions are defined in Article 24 of the Mines Law as the administrative act of the National Executive through which rights are granted and obligations are imposed to individuals for the use of mineral resources existing in the national territory. A concession then grants its holder the exclusive right to explore and subsequently exploit the mineral substances found within the area granted. This ratifies the principle that private entities have no preexisting rights to develop mining activities, which can only be acquired through these administrative acts called concessions issued by the State.

According to the 1945 Mines Law, the holder of alluvial concessions had a preferred right regarding the request for hard rock concessions in the same area (Article 22). This principle was changed in the 1999 Mines Law, as can be read in the Official Document explaining its provisions where it was stated as one of the

---

37 See on private mining activities, Allan R. Brewer-Carías, "El régimen de participación del capital privado en las industrias petrolera y minera: Desnacionalización y regulación a partir de la Constitución de 1999," in Allan R. Brewer-Carías, *VII Jornadas Internacionales de Derecho Administrativo, El Principio de Legalidad y el Ordenamiento Jurídico-Administrativo de la Libertad Económica*, FUNEDA, Caracas November 2004, pp. 15-58.

features adopted was "the elimination of the distinction based on the presentation of minerals, in hard rock, mantle or alluvial; the concessionaire having the right to exploit the mineral no matter its presentation." As the Constitutional Chamber of the Supreme Tribunal of Justice has stated in its Decision N° 37 dated January 24, 2004 after analyzing this explanation, such feature of the "unity of the concession" was confirmed by the text of Article 24 (exclusive right to exploit mineral in a determined area), Article 26 (the volume derived from the existing terrain, within the superficial boundaries of the concession, established downward to the center of the Earth, descending in a pyramidal form) and Article 28 (the horizontal rectangular extension of the concession) of the 1999 Mines Law. Nonetheless, the Constitutional Chamber also pointed out that regarding the exploitation rights of concessions granted before the enactment of the new Law (1999), since the concessionaires have the right to maintain their rights regarding minerals "in the presentation form according to which the [original] Titles were granted", in cases of pre-1999 concessions and conversion of concessions according to article 132 of the Mines Law, "the division of areas and the distinction of the concessionaires according to the form of the presentation of minerals" was to be accepted.[38]

In the Mines Law concessions are exclusively conceived and issued "for exploration and subsequent exploitation," being these rights considered, in Article 29 of the Law, as "real immovable property" (*derecho real inmueble*). Similar provisions were established in the Mines Law of 1945, regarding the same concessions for exploration and subsequent exploitation (Article 105).

Mining concessions are to be granted, after the petitioner complies with all the requirements established by the Law and the procedure provided for is completed, by means of an express pronouncement (Resolution) by the Ministry of Mines, whereas a Mining Title for Exploration must be issued, which ought to be subsequently published on the *Official Gazette.*[39]

It is important to highlight that the Mines Law, in the administrative procedure regulations that it contains regarding the granting of concessions, has expressly given in several of its provisions, direct effects to the absence of response –or silence– of the Administration on specific requests filed by an interested party. For instance, in Articles 30 (on permits for transactions regarding mining rights) and 41 (petitions for mining concessions) the Law has adopted the administrative procedure principle of "negative" silence, in the sense that once the term established for a pronouncement to be adopted elapses, if no express resolution is adopted, according to the negative silence effects, it is considered that the absence of response is equivalent to a tacit administrative act of rejection of the request. Conversely, in Article 25 (petition for extension of concessions) the 1999 Mines Law has adopted the administrative procedure principle of "positive" silence, in the sense that once the term established

38 See Decision N° 37 of January 27, 2004 (Case of *Asociación Civil Mixta La Salvación SRL*), Record N° 00-1496, available at http://www.tsj.gov.ve/decisiones/scon/Enero/37-270104-00-1496.htm.

39 Since the 1999 Mines Law only provides for concessions *for exploration and subsequent exploitation*, when the concession is granted, the mining title is an Exploration Title. Once the exploratory phase is completed, and all requirements for further exploitation have been satisfied, the concessionaire must seek an exploitation certificate (Article 75 of the Law). Concessions granted prior to the 1999 Mines Law, may be different.

for a pronouncement to be adopted elapses, if no express resolution is adopted, according to the positive silence effects, it is considered that the absence of response is equivalent to a tacit administrative act of granting the request.

Pursuant to Article 48 of the 1999 Law, the concession of exploration and subsequent exploitation, grants the concessionaire, its heirs or executors, the exclusive right to *explore* the granted area, during the exploratory period, and to elect for the consequent exploitation (mining) the surface determined by the technical, financial and environmental feasibility study. Both periods, for exploration and exploitation could also be distinguished in the provisions of the 1945 Mines Law, where the so-called "certificate of exploitation" was in fact the Mining Title of the concession, generally published in the *Official Gazette* after being registered in the Public Registrar. In the 1999 Mines Law, the same two periods are distinguished in the concession of exploration and subsequent exploitation, establishing that the concessionaire during the period of exploration must obtain the "certificate of exploration" which is issued after being approved by the Ministry of Mines through Resolution (Article 56).

A. Exploration

Under Article 49 of the 1999 Mines Law and 20 of the General Regulation of the Mines Law,[40] the exploratory period must have a duration of no longer than three (3) years, depending on the nature of the mineral and other pertinent circumstances. Said exploratory period, however, can be extended, but only once and for a period of no longer than one (1) year.[41] According to Article 98 of the Law, the concession expires when the exploration is not carried out during the term previously foreseen.[42]

Since the Law provides that during the exploratory period the concessionaire has the right to *explore* the area of the granted concession, and to select the section or sections to be subsequently exploited (mined), according to the results of the technical, financial and environmental feasibility study that must be completed therein, it has been commonly accepted that in such period the concessionaire is to perform activities that further the finding of the mine bed or mineral deposits, and to ascertain whether mining is feasible and profitable through adequate means.[43] Conversely, no extraction or digging out of minerals can be carried out within the exploratory period, under penalty of the Law.[44]

---

40 General Regulations of the Mines Law, *Official Gazette* Nº 37.155 of March 9, 2001.

41 The petition for an extension of the exploratory period has to be filed no later than 180 days prior to the expiring date of such period, i.e., 6 months in advance of the expiration date. Article 23 of the General Regulation of the Mines Law.

42 As I have already stated, up to February 1977, when the Executive Decree reserving all exploratory and mining activities not previously reserved was passed, exploring the territory furthering the existence of mineral deposits was unrestricted (with the exceptions provided for in the 1945 Mines Law). Therefore, this is a change introduced by the 1999 Law.

43 See Elsa Amorer, *El Régimen de la Explotación Minera en la Legislación Venezolana.* Editorial Jurídica Venezolana, Caracas 1991, pp. 1-2.

44 Article 27 of the General Regulation of the Law expressly proscribes exploitation activities during the exploratory phase and subjects it to the administrative sanctions provided in Article 109 of the Law.

Exploration has to be done pursuant an *exploration program* that the concessionaire must file at the Ministry of Mines, along with a performance chronogram and an investment plan for such period, before the commencement of exploration activities (Article 21 of the General Regulation). The evolution of the activities performed within the exploratory period, following such exploration program, is to be acknowledged through periodic reports to be filed by the concessionaire within the first ten (10) days of each trimester.

The mining sections or parcels selected by the concessionaire as a result of the *exploration* are to be illustrated separately, in individual drawings one per each section, as well as collectively, in a general mining drawing (Article 50 of the Mines Law).

As already mentioned, within the exploratory period the concessionaire must also complete and file a technical, financial and environmental feasibility study of the concession, including any other information regarding the activities that are intended to be performed in order to make better use of the mineral.

Under Article 53 of the Mines Law, the concessionaire must file the drawings and the technical, financial and environmental feasibility study with the Ministry of Mines, along with a written request for its approval, as well as for the release of the "Exploitation Certificate" foreseen in Article 56. For the filing of these drawings and of the technical, financial and environmental feasibility study, the concessionaire may request an extension of up to one (1) year, before the period granted for exploratory purposes expires, which can be granted by the Ministry if it considers the request to be reasonable, except in case of force majeure in which case it would have to grant it (Article 55 of the Mines Law). According to Article 98 of the Law, failure to file either the technical, financial and environmental feasibility study or the drawings, within the time given, results in termination of the concession. Should the technical, financial and environmental feasibility study not be approved by the Ministry of Mines, the entity will inform the interested party by means of a duly reasoned pronouncement and the concessionaire would have up to ninety (90) continuous days to file a new study (Article 52 of the Mines Law).

Although not expressly provided for, the wording of Articles 30, 60 and 130 of the Law implies that in addition to the technical, financial and environmental feasibility study, drawings and written request, the concessionaire must also complete and file a development and mining (exploitation) program or plan[45].

Once the drawings and the technical, financial and environmental feasibility study are approved, pursuant to Article 56 of the Mines Law, the Ministry of Mines must state so by way of a Resolution, to be issued within a period of thirty (30) continuous days, in which it must provide for the issuance of the "Exploitation

45 When referring to negotiations pertaining to concessions, Article 30 of the Mines Law provides that no such negotiations are to be approved unless the negotiating concessionaire has accomplished all preliminary activities and investments required to present the development and mining (exploitation) program, which must be filed at least 30 days prior to the commencement of the mining (exploitation). Under Article 60, on the other hand, prior to starting mining, the concessionaire must secure fulfillment of said development and mining (exploitation) program through a performance bond. Thus, it follows that such program must also be filed by the concessionaire at this time. Article 130 requires holders of mining concessions granted prior to the passage of the Law to adapt their exploitation plans within 1 year's time.

Certificate" within a period of thirty (30) continuous days after the publication date of the said resolution. The "Exploitation Certificate" must show the parcel units selected by the concessionaire, who ought to file it before the Local Land Registry Office of the location of the concession's Circumscription within the subsequent thirty (30) days of its publication in the *Official Gazette*. Also, the concessionaire must obtain a certified copy of the general plan and of the plans of the chosen parcel units.

In the case of those concessions granted prior to 1999 that were granted for both exploration and exploitation and their respective mining titles so indicated; their Mining Titles (already published in *Official Gazette* pursuant to the requirements of Article 180 of the 1945 Mines Law) were the "Certificates of Exploitations," so the concessionaires were obviously exempted from requesting and obtaining the "Exploitation Certificates" provided in the 1999 Mines Law.

B. Exploitation (Mining)

The right to exploit (mine) that a concession grants is the right to extract or dig out, from the mines, those substances contained therein listed in the concession.

Prior to starting the exploitation phase the concession's holder must secure through filing of the appropriate bonds both environmental repair and performance of the exploitation and development program or plan (Articles 59 and 60 of the Mines Law).

Pursuant to Article 58 of the Mines Law, a concession is being exploited when the substances that are contained in it are being extracted or when all actions for that purpose are being taken, with the unequivocal intention of gaining economic profits from them in proportion to the nature of the substance and the magnitude of the deposit. When a concessionaire is in possession of a group of concessions, all of them are to be considered in exploitation when mining activity is being carried out on one of the facilities, in agreement with the aforementioned.

Exploitation, therefore, is being undertaken not only when the concessionaire is actually digging out minerals from the selected parcels, but also according to Article 58 of the 1999 Mines Law –as it was under the 1945 Mines Law regime (Article 24)– when the concessionaire is doing what is necessary in order to extract minerals, with the unequivocal intention of economically exploiting the concession and in proportion to the nature of the substance and the magnitude of the deposit (*yacimiento*).[46] Consequently, a concession can be considered as being in exploitation without minerals actually being extracted, in which case, although the concession is in exploitation, the concessionaire's obligation to pay exploitation taxes is not due under Article 90(2) and cannot be estimated.

Exploitation of a concession, understood in such way, must begin no later than 7 years after the publication of the "Exploitation Certificate," where applicable. Once exploitation has started, it cannot be interrupted, unless there is a justifying cause, in which case suspension cannot exceed one year, except in cases of acts of God or

---

46 See on exploitation, since the provision of the 1999 Mines Law is very similar to the previous one, the comments in Elsa Amorer, *El Régimen de la Explotación Minera en la Legislación Venezolana,* pp. 82, 85. The Ministry of Mines and the former Supreme Court of Justice constructed a restricted interpretation of Article 2 of the 1999 Mines Law. *Idem* pp. 86-92.

force majeure that must be reported to the Ministry of Mines for its assessment (Article 61 of the Mines Law).

As for the minerals to be extracted, pursuant to Article 62 of the Mines Law the holder of a concession granted for the exploitation of a specific mineral has a preferred right to extract other minerals.[47] Accordingly, if during the exploitation process the holder of a mining right finds minerals others than those specified in the Title, he is compelled to give notice about it to the Ministry of Mines, who – according to what is provided in Article 7.a and 7.b of the Law– can decide within 30 continuous days to exploit the mineral directly (Article 28 of the General Regulation). If the Ministry decides not to do to exploit directly, the concessionaire has a preferred right to such exploitation. In these cases, the exploitation is assigned to the concessionaire and no concession is required, it being enough to conclude an agreement between the concessionaire and the Ministry of Mines.

It must also be mentioned that due to the specific characteristic that each mine exploitation has, the process of extracting mineral in a given concession can normally need to be extended beyond the boundaries of the respective concession area, having layback over areas that may be subject to other concessions. That is why article 63 of the Mines Law establishes that when in a mining exploitation the concessionaire invades the area of another concession, the net value of the mineral extracted in the latter will be shared in half with the neighbor. Only when bad faith of the invader concessionaire is proven, he is then compelled to pay to the affected concession the double of the value of the extracted mineral. According to these provisions, the possibility of layback agreements between concessionaires is expected to be found in mining exploitations. In that regard, it is also relevant to note the following provisions of the Mines Law: Article 5.2 imposes the concessionaire the obligation to take all necessary measures not to waste mineral resources; and Article 11, in order to carry out mining activities, grant the concessionaire the possibility to request an easement, temporary occupation, and even the expropriation of property.

Finally, as in the case of exploration, both the absence of commencement of the exploitation within the indicated timeframe, as well as the suspension of it (*without a justifying cause*) for a longer period than the one permitted, result in termination of the concession (Articles 98.3 and 98.4 of the Mines Law).[48]

However, in the case of concessions granted prior to the passing of the 1999 Mines Law, since duration is to be governed by the original (ancient) title (Article 129.c of the Mines Law), termination of the concession for absence of commencement of exploitation is mitigated by a provision preventing it included in

---

47Under the 1945 Mines Law, the holder of a concession granted for the exploitation of a specific mineral also had a preferred right to extract other minerals, but was bound to seek another concession for such other minerals. Therefore, the pre-concession administrative procedure was to be followed, and the preferred right had to be exercised within the opposition period of the procedure (Article 199).

48As aforementioned, in the case of those concessions granted according to the 1945 Mines Law, the Certificate of Exploitation (Article 180) was the Mining Title approved by Resolution and published in the Official Gazette (as is the case of all of those associated to the Project), so the concessionaires were obviously exempted from requesting and obtaining a separate "Exploitation Certificate" provided in the 1999 Mines Law.

most of those titles. Under such provision, following Articles 24 and 55.2 of the previous 1945 Mines Law, and Article 9 of the Rules on Granting Concessions and Mining Contracts, late start of exploitation is permitted upon doubling the payment of the first special advantage up to the beginning of mining (exploitation).

5. The Ministry of Mines supervision and control regarding the compliance of the mining obligations of the concessionaires, and the "compliance certificates"

Pursuant to Article 88 of the Mines Law, the Ministry of Mines is the empowered authority to supervise and control the activities subjected to the said Law and its regulations, without prejudice of the supervision and control activities corresponding to the States, for instance on matters of non-metallic mines.

As a consequence of the permanent and continuous process of supervising mining activities, not only the concessionaries have the obligation to file monthly and annual reports before the Ministry about their activities, but at its turn, the Ministry must verify in a permanent way the compliance by the concessionaires of their duties and obligations, as prescribed in the Mines Law and its Regulations, as well as in the provisions of the Concessions, Mining Titles and mining contracts that could exist.

In order to accredit the compliance of such obligations of the concessionaires, the supervision and controlling officials of the Ministry of Mines, at the request of the concessionaries, issue "compliance certificates," which are declaratory administrative acts, that is, administrative acts through which the Administration certifies facts that are within its competency. In the case of mining activities, these "compliance certificates" are issued by the competent mining authorities, certifying the certainty of a determined fact, action or accomplishment. That is to say, after due verification and control, the Ministry certifies that the concessionaire has given due compliance to the different clauses of the Mining Titles, to the clauses of the mining contracts for instance signed with Corporación Venezolana de Guayana, and also to the provisions of the Mines Law and its Regulation, consequently being declared solvent.

All these "compliance certificates" are issued by officials of Ministry of Mines' Audit and Control of Mines Division, including the Technical Regional Inspectorates and the Fiscal Inspectorates. According to Article 88 of the Mines Law and Article 96.1 of the 2001 General Regulation of the Mines Law, the Audit and Control Division, and specifically the Technical Regional Inspectorate are in charge of verifying that the concessionaries and the titleholders of mining rights comply with all the obligations established in the Mines Law, its Regulations and other applicable provisions. The Fiscal Inspectorate takes direction from the Technical Regional Inspectorate, and assists the same in carrying out its duties (Article 96.7 and 97.8 of the 2001 General Regulations of the Mines Law). The Fiscal Inspectorate is charged with conducting necessary technical inspections to verify that mining activities are executed in accordance with the laws, regulations, decrees, resolutions and other applicable provisions of laws (Art. 97.7 of the 2001

Regulations).[49] In addition, inspectors may be given specific authority to conduct their functions by resolution of Ministry of Mines. In addition, it is possible to consider that these administrative acts have the force of a "public document" in the sense of their incontrovertible veracity and validity because being issued by the competent authorities to perform mining inspections. Also, these administrative acts of certification create legitimate confidence in the concessionaires regarding the verification by the public administration of the accomplishment of their mining duties and obligations according to the concessions or contracts.

6. The term of the concessions and its extension

In general terms, all concessions related to natural resources according to Article 113 of the Constitution must always be for a limited period of time. Under the Mines Law they cannot exceed twenty (20) years starting from the date public notice of the Mining Title of the concession is given, by promulgation in the *Official Gazette* (Article 25).

Nonetheless, according to Article 25 of the Law the term of mining concessions may be subject to extensions for successive periods of no more than ten (10) years if the Ministry of Mines deems it pertinent (*si lo considera pertinente)*, provided that the concessionaire requests such extension within three (3) years –but no later than six (6) months– prior to the expiration of the initial term. For the purpose of requesting the extension of a concession, according to the Single Paragraph of Article 25 of the Law, the concessionaire must have satisfied all his indebtedness to the Republic (*solvente con la República*) by the time of the extension request. All the extensions granted cannot exceed the length of time originally granted.

For the purpose of accrediting the compliance of all mining obligations, the concessionaires normally file with their extension requests, the "compliance certificates" issued by the Ministry of Mines.

Following the request for extension of concessions, therefore, the Administration must initiate an administrative procedure in which it must verify the compliance by the concessionaire with all its obligations with the Republic. For such purpose, without doubts, the "compliance" certificates (*solvencia*) that the same Ministry, through its mining organs and officials in charge of supervising and controlling mining activities, subsequently and systematically granted to the concessionaries, are the key formal elements in order to certify or accredit the day-to-day compliance by the concessionaire, as verified by the Ministry, of their obligations according to the terms of the concession. They are provided with "*fe pública*" in the sense that

49 A similar regime existed under the prior version of the Mining Law. Under the 1945 Mining Law and accompanying Regulations, the National Executive, through the Office of Mines (Dirección de Minas) of the Ministry of Public Works (Ministerio de Fomento), was empowered to verify and inspect mining activities. (1945 Mining Law, Art. 100; 1945 Mining Regulation, Art. 159-160). It was aided in this task by the Technical Service of Mining and Geology as well as by the General Technical Inspectorate and the Regional Fiscal Inspectorates. (1945 Mining Regulation, Art. 161), The General Technical Inspectorate was empowered to exercise control over mining companies to verify compliance with the Mining Law and Regulations (1945 Mining Regulations, Art. 163), and the Regional Inspectorate was authorized to exercise control over exploration and exploitation activities in its jurisdiction to verify compliance with the Mining Law and Regulations and to report on non-compliance (1945 Mining Law Regulations, Art. 164).

their content, as stated by the public official in charge of issuing them after verifying the accomplishment by the concessionaire of his mining duties, cannot be contradicted. In addition, as administrative acts of certifications they create for the concessionaire rights that make them irrevocable.

The provision of Article 25 of the Law regarding the duration of concessions, on the other hand, establishes the exclusive right of the concessionaire to request an extension of the concession he holds, but does not establish a right of the concessionaire to have such extension granted. This is a pronouncement that corresponds to the Ministry of Mines if it considers the extension to be pertinent, which is not a discretionary attribution, and in any case cannot be arbitrary. To deem a matter pertinent, that is pertaining to the issue at hand, is to decide according to the legal situation and the facts surrounding the case. On matters of extensions of mining concessions, the Ministry must consider all the facts surrounding the mining activities developed by the concessionaire that may justify its request for an extension, as well as the public policy conditioning the mining activities that lead to the granting of concessions. Consequently, the decision, for example, rejecting the petition of an extension of a given concession must be reasoned, namely, the Administration has to state its evaluation of the circumstances and how it ascertained an absence of pertinence, and cannot be arbitrary, but based on the general principles of administrative procedure of reasonability, rationality, proportionality, non-discrimination, bona fide and legitimate expectation.

In the case of petitions or requests for extensions of mining concessions, the Mines Law has established the obligation of the Ministry to respond within the same period of six (6) months in which the petition must be filed. The Law has also expressly adopted the administrative procedure principle of giving effects to the silence of Public Administration. In this case, however, contrary to other provisions of the Law regarding the same matter of administrative silence, the Mines Law has expressly established that if there is no formal notice of a pronouncement on the matter of the extension, "it is understood that the extension is granted." That is, the Mines Law in the cases of petitions for the extension of concessions has adopted the administrative procedure principle of positive silence, which produces a tacit administrative act granting the requested extension.

The basic condition from the side of the concessionaire, for the Ministry of Mines to grant the extension of a concession, is compliance by the concessionaire, by the time of his request, with all his obligations with the Republic (*solvente con la República*) according to the Mines Law, its regulations, and to the clauses of the concessions, the Mining Title and mining contracts. That is, administrative acts deciding to extend a mining concession are administrative acts that create rights in favor of the concessionaire, in general terms subjected to the principles and rules referred to the revocability of administrative acts as provided in the administrative procedure legislation. These principles apply, independently if the extension of the concession has been given through an express administrative act, or by means of a tacit administrative act resulting from the legal effects of the positive administrative silence aforementioned. Nonetheless, it must be noted that in the case of the Mines Law, administrative acts granting concessions or extending the term of concessions, as administrative acts creating rights in favor of the concessionaires, although being in principle irrevocable administrative acts, they can be declared as terminated (*caducidad*) and therefore, the mining rights contained in them extinguished, in the specific cases listed in Article 98 of the Mines Law, all related to compliance by the concessionaire of his legal and contractual obligations.

7. The extinction of mining rights

In fact, according to the Mines Law, the extinction of mining rights can occur in three different situations. First, mining rights can terminate if the concession is declared null and void (*nula de pleno derecho*), which according to Article 96 of the Mines Law, occurs when the concession is granted to high public officers (Articles 20 and 21), or to foreign governments (Article 22). In these cases of absolute nullity, the extinction of mining rights must be formally declared through an administrative act.

Second, pursuant to Article 97 of the Mines Law, mining rights extinguish due to the expiring of the term by which they were granted, without the need of any formal decision or administrative act.

Third, as I have already stated when referring to exploration and exploitation, concessions can also terminate (*caducar*) and the mining rights can be extinguished, in the following cases provided for by Article 98 of the Mines Law:

1. When the exploration is not carried out within the time period stated in Article 49 of the Law;

2. When the corresponding plans are not presented within the time period established in Article 50 or during the extension period that may have been granted according to the Law;

3. When exploitation is not started within the time period established in Article 61 of the Law[50];

4. When the exploitation is suspended for a time period longer than the one established in Article 61 of the Law;

5. When the taxes or fines established in the Law are not paid during one (1) year. In this case, however, where no express resolution has been issued, the Ministry of Mines can, upon request of the interested party, accept the payment of the unpaid taxes with applicable interest, and declare the termination of the extinction action;

6. When the technical, financial and environmental feasibility study is not filed within the time period established, according to the applicable norms;

7. When the concessionaire does not comply with any of the special advantages offered to the Republic;

8. When on three (3) occasions, in a period of six (6) months, legal infractions are committed that could have originated the application of the maximum financial sanctions established in the Law;

---

50 Except for those concessions granted under the previous Mines Law that contain a provision mitigating the extinction for lack of timely exploitation, upon double payment of the special advantage, provided that an extension of the concession has been timely requested.

9. Any other cause expressly foreseen in the respective mining title.

In all these cases, regarding concessions or extensions of concessions granted in an express way or tacitly via positive administrative silence, the Administration always can initiate an administrative procedure to review the compliance of the concessionaries' duties in order to decide upon the termination (*caducidad*) of the concession, which must be subject to the provisions of the Organic Law on Administrative Procedures,[51] guarantying the due process rights of the concessionaire. That procedure must end with an express administrative act declaring that there is no termination cause or otherwise, that termination must be issued, subject to all the formal and substantive conditions of validity of administrative acts provided in the Law. In particular, on these matters of termination of concessions, such administrative acts are governed by the principles of reasonability, proportionality, equity, impartiality, equality, bona fides and legitimate expectation, applicable to all administrative actions.

In fact, after the development of the corresponding administrative procedure, if the Administration, after analyzing the factual circumstances provided for in Article 98 of the Mines Law, arrives at the conclusion and demonstrates that a situation of non-compliance of the concessionaire's obligations exist, the procedure could result in the declaration of termination (*caducidad*) of the concession, and of the consequent extinction of the mining rights. In these cases, termination of concessions and extinction of mining rights ought to be formally declared by way of a motivated administrative act (resolution) of the Ministry of Mines, which must be published in the *Official Gazette*. The applicable appeals then can be filed against said resolution (Art. 108). In these cases, it is not that the concession or extension is revoked, but is declared "terminated," based on the particular set of circumstances of non-compliance of duties listed in said Article 98 of the Mines Law.

Of course, in these cases of termination (*caducidad*) of concessions, the standard for administrative action must be stricter, particularly because the matter of compliance by the concessionaire of his duties, is a day-to-day matter in the mining activities, and in the relations between concessionaires and the Administration, permanently subjected to verifications, supervisions and control by the mine's inspection authorities. In addition, in these constant relations between the concessionaries and the Administration, after verifying the compliance of obligations, the supervising authorities' issue "compliance certificates" that as aforementioned, are administrative acts of certification. Nonetheless, if after all the day-to-day supervision and control of mining activities, after the filing of subsequent (monthly and annual) reports as to the compliance of obligations, and after issuing successive "compliance certificates," all confirming, both implicitly and explicitly, compliance with the terms of a concession and the applicable legislation, the Administration realizes, contrary to earlier determinations, that in a particular situation listed in Article 98 of the Law, the concessionaire has not fulfilled its obligations and that there is non-compliance, in order to contradict the previous administrative actions, the Administration must be extremely cautious in order to terminate the concession. The administrative act terminating the concession must be issued in accordance with all the principles governing such acts that affect individual rights, and particularly, it has to be reasonable, rational, logic,

51 Organic Law on Administrative Procedures, *Official Gazette* N° 2.818 Extra. of July 1, 1981.

proportional, equalitarian and non-discriminative; and in this case, issued according to the principles of bona fide and respecting legitimate expectation (*confianza legítima*) created on the matter by the same Administration.

Finally, another way of extinction of mining rights according to Article 100 of the Law is by means of resignation that must be made by the applicant in a notarized writing before the Ministry of Mines. Once the aforementioned written waiver is received, it must be published through a resolution in the *Official Gazette*. This extinction of mining rights does not free its holder from the obligations owing at the time of the extinction (Article 101).

One of the consequences of the extinction of mining concessions is the reversion to the State of all assets affected to their object, which is the exploitation (extraction) of specific minerals, which is provided in Article 102 of the Mines Law, by establishing that the land, permanent works, including facilities, accessories and equipment that are an important part of them, as well as any other asset, either real estate or personal property, tangible or intangible, acquired for the purposes of mining activities granted by the concession, must be kept and maintained by the respective holder, in substantial working condition, according to applicable progress and technical principles, during the complete duration of the mining rights and of their possible extension. Under such Article, upon the extinction of mining rights, whatever the cause, said goods acquired or used by the concessionaire for the purpose of the concession, that is the exploration and exploitation 9extraction) of the minerals granted, become fully the property of the Republic, free of taxes and charges, without compensation of any kind.

III. THE PRINCIPLE OF REVERSION IN ADMINISTRATIVE CONCESSIONS, WITH PARTICULAR REFERENCE TO MINING CONCESSIONS

1. Activities reserved for the State, administrative concessions and the principle of reversion

A. Activities reserved for the State and Administrative Concessions

A concession is a public contract through which the State grants a private party or concessionaire, the right to perform certain activities have been legally reserved to the State, and that, consequently, cannot bc freely performed by individuals. Since the activity has been reserved to the State, the individuals have no economic right to perform it. The right is thus created by the concession, which has a constitutive nature and effect, in the sense that it is through such bilateral act that the State grants to an individual or concessionary the right to perform an activity that it previously did not have.[52]

---

52 See in general on administrative concessions in Venezuela: Alfredo Romero Mendoza (Coord.), *Régimen Legal de las Concesiones Públicas. Aspectos Jurídicos, Financieros y Técnicos,* Editorial Jurídica Venezolana, Caracas 2000; Víctor R. Heréndez Mendible, "La concesión de servicio público y la concesión de obra pública," in *Revista de la Facultad de Ciencias Jurídicas y Políticas,* Central University of Venezuela, N° 113, Caracas 1999, pp. 53-91; Rafael Badell, *Régimen de las concesiones de servicios públicos y construction projects públicas*

The concession differs from other administrative law institutions like the authorizations, which are unilateral administrative acts that allow individuals to perform certain activities that they have the right to perform, but that have been restricted by statutes, and require the State's intervention through such authorization. Contrary to a concession, an authorization has only declarative nature and effects, in the sense that it declares that the authorized person is allowed to perform activities that he previously had the right to perform, only subjected to the State intervention; a right that consequently is not created by the authorization.

It is the case, for instance, of the activities of exploration and exploration of the subsoil, which are mining activities that have been reserved by statute to the State, as it is ratified in the 1999 Constitution, when it declares the subsoil as of public domain (article 12). The consequence is that mining exploitation in the sense of extraction of mineral is an activities can only by performed by individuals or corporations by means of a concession granted by the State. This was the regime established in the 1945 Mines Law[53] (article 13), and it is also the one established in the 1999 Mines Law[54] (art. 24).

Therefore, as a general principle of Venezuelan law, only individuals who have been granted a concession from the State can perform mining activities of exploitation,[55] which are the ones that can be considered as the "primary activities" reserved to the State in the Mines Law, that can be distinguished from other activities that are not reserved to the State, that the concessionaire can also perform, considered as ancillary of related activities such as the processing or transformation of the extracted mineral, and its commercialization, which are not reserved to the State.

This distinction has been established in recent regulations of some recent nationalization processes, like for example, on matters of iron ore exploitation. Such exploitation was always considered as a primary activity reserved to the State, different to the steel industry, which was a related activity not reserved to the State. In 1974, "the industry of iron ore exploitation" that is, its extraction was nationalized through Decree Law No. 580 dated 26 November 1974,[56] being eliminated the possibility for private companies to obtain concessions of exploitation of iron ore. Nonetheless, such nationalization of the primary activity, did not affect the economic activities that individuals could carry, without a concession, for the industrial processing of such mineral, that is, for the performance of activities related to the steel industry. Nonetheless, a few years later, these auxiliary or related activities of the industry of transformation of iron ore in the Region of Guayana, where subsequently nationalized or reserved for the State, by

---

nacionales, at http://www.badell-grau.com/?pag=29&ct=189; Allan R. Brewer-Carías, "Notas sobre el régimen jurídico general de las concesiones administrativas en Venezuela," in *Libro Homenaje a la Ministra Margarita Beatriz Luna Ramos*, Universidad Nacional Autónoma de México, Mexico 2013, pp. 61-101; and in *Revista El derecho. Diario de Doctrina y Jurisprudencia. Administrativo,* Universidad Católica Argentina, Nº 13,290. Year LI, Buenos Aires 13 July 2013, pp. 1-8.

53 See in *Official Gazette* Extra. Nº 121 dated 18 January 1945.

54 See in *Official Gazette* Extra. Nº 5,382 dated 28 September 1999.

55 The only exception established in the 1999 Mines Law is for "small artisanal mining," that can be privately performed by means of authorizations (articles 6 and 68), which means that "small artisanal mining" has not been reserved to the State.

56 *Official Gazette* Nº 30,577, dated 16 December 1974.

means of the Organic Law regulating companies that performed activities in the iron and steel sector in the Region of Guayana, adopted through Decree Law No. 6,058 dated 30 April 2008[57] (Art 1).

Something similar occurred in the area related to gold mining activity. Being the extraction (exploitation) of gold ore reserved for the State, it was traditionally carried out, pursuant to provisions of the Mines Law, by means of concessions for exploration and exploitation. The reserve activity was the mining extractive one, which was different to the gold processing activities that were ancillary or related, but not reserved for the State. In 2011, however, an Organic Law was issued nationalizing the activities of gold exploration and exploitation, as well as all subsidiary and related activities,[58] and under which, not only "primary activities" of gold exploration, but activities subsidiary and related to development of gold can only be performed by the State." For such purpose Article 2 of the Law defined as primary activities: "the exploration and exploitation of gold mines and sites," and as subsidiary and related activities: "the storage, possession, benefit, circulation and national and foreign marketing of gold, provided that they contribute to the exercise of the primary activities."[59]

B. The Concept of Reversion related to Administrative Concessions

Since the activity granted to a concessionaire by means of a concession is an activity that has been previously reserved to the State by means of a statute, once the concession expires, the right created by the concession also expires. The State can then decide whether to continue itself performing the reserved activity, or to grant a new concession, and in order to allow for the continuity of the operations, the statutes, or in many cases the clauses of the concession, establish the figure of reversion, prescribing that once the concession expires, all assets acquired or used by the concessionaire for the purpose of performing the reserved activity object of the concession, must be compulsorily transferred to the State -in full ownership-, free of encumbrances or charges, and without compensation.

In this sense, reversion in administrative concessions is considered as one of the forms of termination of private property and of its acquisition by the State, as I summarized it in 1979, as follows:

> "it is a general principle of administrative concessions that the fact that once the concession ends, the concessionaire must transfer the assets subject to the concession to the State, without compensation, and the reason for this institution is that it is in the very nature of the concession: By this means, the State transfers to the particular concessionaire the privilege of performing an activity that the former generally has reserved for itself, and the compensation for

57 *Official Gazette* N° 38,928, dated 12 May 2008.

58 *Official Gazette* N° 39.759 dated 16 September 2011. See regarding this Law comments in: Allan R. Brewer-Carías, "Comentarios sobre la Ley Orgánica de Nacionalización de la minería del oro y de la comercialización del oro," in *Revista de Derecho Público,* N° 127, July-September 2011, Editorial Jurídica Venezolana, Caracas 2011 pp. 65-77.

59 The referenced Organic Law was reformed in 2014, by Decree law N° 1,395 dated 13 November 2014. See in *Official Gazette* Extra. N° 6,150 dated 18 November 2014.

having exercised this privilege based on a formal act of the State is that when the concession ends, all assets subject to the concession revert to it."[60]

Reversion, as a concept that applies to all types of concessions (such as public services, public works or exploitation of public assets or domain), has been defined as "the concessionaire's obligation to deliver to the Administration the construction project or service and all the necessary instruments: assets, actions and rights acquired or used for the purpose of the activity granted in the concession, in order to ensure the continuity of construction projects or service, after the concession is terminated."[61]

This figure, although traditionally considered as a general principle in administrative law, that was considered "implicit in the concession contract, when its termination occurs due to termination of the term, expiration or cancellation," more recently has been considered as a "legal doctrine that has been surpassed," [62] being currently only regulated in specific legal provisions, or in the clauses of the concession contract itself.[63] In this sense, for instance Juan Carlos Cassagne has argued that:

> "The origin of reversion that was connected with the development of the contractual concept of the public works concession, where it constituted a political clause intended to safeguard property of the crown, has currently been surpassed, and is now definitely considered to be nothing more than an economic clause.
>
> Strictly speaking, reversion of the concessionaire's assets cannot be considered an implicit clause of the concession contract or license, since the will to lose ownership is not presumed (as in general the waiver of rights) and any clause of waiver of the right of ownership is of strict interpretation."[64]

---

60 See Allan R. Brewer-Carías, "Adquisición de la propiedad privada por parte del Estado en el Derecho Venezolano," in Allan R. Brewer-Carías, *Jurisprudencia de la Corte Suprema 1930-74 y Estudios de Derecho Administrativo*, [Judicial Precedent of the Supreme Court, 1930-74, and Administrative Law Studies], Book VI. *Propiedad y expropiación,* Instituto de Derecho Público, Universidad Central de Venezuela, Caracas 1979, p. 26. The aforesaid work was also published in *Revista de Control Fiscal,* N° 94, Contraloría General de la República, Caracas 1979, pp. 61-84; and in: *Seminario Internacional sobre Derecho Urbano*, Asociación Colombiana de Ingeniería Ambiental, Cali 1994, pp. 191-245.

61 See Carlos García Soto, "Reversión de bienes en el contrato de concesión," in *Revista Derecho y Sociedad. Revista de los estudiantes de la Universidad Monteávila,* Caracas 2003, p. 95.

62 See Eduardo García de Enterría, *"El dogma de la reversión de las concesiones,"* in *Dos Estudios sobre la Usucapión en Derecho Administrativo*, Tecnos, Madrid, 1974, pp. 14-78. This author wrote that "In terminology of the principle of legal business the conclusion is that in Spanish law reversion is not an essential element, or even a natural element of the concession, but merely accidental. That is, it applies only in the case of express agreement (of course, without prejudice to the types of concession in which regulation establishes the rule of reversion, in specific scenarios)" pp. 73-74

63 See Carlos García Soto, "Reversión de bienes en el contrato de concesión," in *Revista Derecho y Sociedad. Revista de los estudiantes de la Universidad Monteávila,* Caracas, 2003, p. 95.

64 See Juan Carlos Cassagne, *Tratado de derecho administrativo*, Séptima Ed. actualizada, Lexis Nexis, Book II, Buenos Aires, p. 418. Available at: http://www.cubc.mx/biblio-

For this reason, for example, Roberto Dromi has said, regarding the concept of reversion in Argentine administrative law, that although "state assets must be restored to the conferring State, except for a provision to the contrary," on the other hand, "the particular assets of the concessionaire subject to providing the service, if the parties do not stipulate what will become of it when the contract is terminated, will continue to belong to the concessionaire," adding that, "however, generally it is stipulated that such assets, when the concession is terminated, will be owned by the conferring State with or without compensation to the concessionaire." Regarding this concept, however, Dromi cautions that "it is common for this "reversion" of things or assets from the contractor to the State to be specified. Thus, given that the referenced assets never belonged to the State, to say that they will revert to [the State] leads to confusion. For that reason, it is more appropriate to speak of transfer of the contracting party's assets to the State." [65]

C. Purpose and justification of the reversion

It has long been acknowledged in Venezuela that the essential basis of reversion is to ensure continuity of performance of the service, execution of the construction project or exploitation of the asset of public interest. This is stated in the Opinion of the Office of the Attorney General of the Republic issued in 1972, which indicated:

> "...the intended purpose of granting concessions is the performance of an activity that pertains to the Administration, due to which the service, role or task of the same may be directly carried out by agencies of the State. The idea is that the service be performed not only when the concession is in effect but for the entire time that Administration deems necessary, given the relevance of public interest in the service performed by the concessionaire. That is the reason for the

---

teca/libros/Cassagne,%20Juan%20C%20-%20Derecho%20Administrativo%20T%20II.pdf Also, see Miguel S. Marienhof, *Tratado de Derecho Administrativo,* Book III-B, Abeledo Perrot, Buenos Aires 1970, page 638.)

65 See Roberto Dromi *Tratado de Derecho Administrativo,* available at http://uai derechoadministrativo.wikispaces.com/file/view/TRATADO+DE+DER+ADMIN+DROMI.pdf/41 9922716/TRATADO+DE+DER+ADMIN+DROMI.pdf . Dromi himself, regarding the subject of "reversion" in cases of lapsing (abnormal termination) of concession contract, has said, "In principle, the property of the individual subject to performance of the contract continues to belong to him, except in those cases in which it had been agreed that the property allocation for performance would remain in the hands of the Government (as owner or with a precarious right of use until performance is concluded), in the hypothetical actions of invalidity of the contract, without any indemnification to the contract (CSJN, Awards, 141:212). There being no clause in the contract related to the property of the individual, if the Government takes possession of it, the contractor must be indemnified for its value, otherwise it would be an unlawful taking of property according to the provisions of Article 17 of the Constitution, which protects the right of ownership, not only of things subject to the performance of the public service, but also of works carried out by the contractor that are appropriated by the Government.// The CSJN has stated: "The declaration of invalidity does not in itself authorize occupation by the conferring authority of the concessionaire's property subject to the performance of the services that constitute the objective of the concession. The concession is one thing, the concessionaire's property is another, even though they are allocated as has been stated. The latter is protected by the inviolability of ownership which, in principle, only gives precedent to expropriation for causes of public interest formally declared and to indemnification (Art. 17, CN)" ("Compañía de Electricidad de Corrientes v. Provincia de Corrientes," Judgments, 201:432. Also "Bracamonte, Juan A., v. Provincia de Tucumán," Judgments, 204:626)." *Idem.*

concern that assets subject to concessions should pass to the State's ownership, because the service could not continue to be performed without them."[66]

More recently Carlos García Soto has observed the same in stating that what is pursued is that at the end of the concession term, the service or exploitation "that the concessionaire is performing should continue to be operative." For that, "it is necessary that certain assets subject to the concession should not be separated from it, but rather maintained at its service, such that the continuity of performance of the construction projects or service benefits the public interest without avoidable interruptions." It is what the author characterizes as assets "indispensable for performance to be viable," with which (the reverted assets)" the granting Administration can continue exploiting the concession directly or indirectly."[67]

Manuel Rachael has argued to the same effect, stating that:

> "Reversion has been conceived as a mechanism to ensure continuity of the service in the users' interest, such that the latter is not affected by termination of the contract term or by any form of termination of the latter. Therefore, assets that are necessary for performance of the concession could not be contractually excluded from the reversion."[68]

Therefore, precisely, "when the contract is performed in the foreseen term, the reversion must take place always in relation to the assets needed for continuous operation of the construction project or service."[69]

On the other hand, the term for which the concession is granted, as stated previously, in principle is calculated for the time necessary to amortize the investment made by the concessionaire, which is related to the principle of the reversion, which in principle does not cover the assets provided by the concessionaire that have not been amortized. Therefore, among the provisions of the Organic Law on Promotion of Private Investment under the Regime of Concessions of Venezuela of 1999,[70] is that which excludes the application of the principle of reversion of works and services of the assets allocated by the concessionaire to the construction project or service in question, when the same "could not be fully amortized" during the concession term (Art. 48). In such cases of assets subject to reversion that have not been fully amortized, for the transfer to occur and in view of the principle of economic equilibrium of the contract, the State

---

66 See Opinion Nº 324, A.E. dated 8 March 1972 in *20 Años de Doctrina de la Procuraduría General de la República 1962-1981,* Tomo III, Vol. I, Caracas 1984, pp. 142 et seq.

67 See Carlos García Soto, "Reversión de bienes en el contrato de concesión," in *Derecho y Sociedad. Revista de los estudiantes de la Universidad Monteávila,* Caracas 2003, pp. 96, 99.

68 See Manuel Rachadell, "Aspectos financieros de las concesiones" in Alfredo Romero Mendoza, (coordinator), *El régimen legal de las concesiones públicas. Aspectos jurídicos, financieros y técnicos*, EJV, Caracas 2000, p. 89.

69 *Idem.* In the same respect, Miguel Mónaco, in his article entitled "Destino de las Cláusulas de Reversión Incluidas en las Antiguas Concesiones para la Prestación de Servicios de Telecomunicación ante la Ley Orgánica de Telecomunicaciones," in the collective work *Libro Homenaje a Gonzalo Perez Luciani, Temas de Derecho Administrativo*, Vol. II, Colección Libros Homenajes, Tribunal Supremo de Justicia, Nº 7, Caracas 2002, pp. 127.

70 *Official Gazette Extra.* Nº 5,394 dated 25 October 1999

has to pay the concessionaire the amount equal to the amount needed for amortization.

D. The reversion in the judicial doctrine of the Supreme Court of Justice

The judicial doctrine of the former Supreme Court of Venezuela, has also elaborate on the figure of reversion, having referred to the basis of the reversion, considering in a ruling dated 12 December 1963 of the Political Administrative Division Court, that "being permanent the activity of the State," for such reason, the reversion of assets to the State at the end of the concession is what ensures "the administrative continuity of the exploitation entrusted temporarily to the concessionaire." This gives rise to the theory that reversion as "an expectation of right in favor of the Nation, that only materializes at the end of the concession, which includes only the permanent construction projects existing at that time in the concession areas, which, however, does not affect the right of the concessionaires during the effective term of the same to carry out in such areas all the constructions, modifications and demolitions that may be advisable in the interest of exploitation."[71]

Further, in another ruling of the Plenary Session of the former Supreme Court dated 3 December 1974, deciding on the petition for annulment brought against the Law of Assets Subject to Reversion in Hydrocarbons Concessions of 1971,[72] considered as unconstitutional, the Court stated that when the concession is terminated, "the assets of the concession will pass to the State without any compensation," indicating that:

> "In the performance of its activity, the beneficiary concessionaire of the concession obtains for its exclusive benefit through payment of a determined price, tax, bonuses and royalties, the benefits arising from the concession, and it is assumed that at the end of the term, it ceases activity. On the other hand, given that the State's activity is permanent, continuity of the administrative activity of exploitation that was temporarily entrusted to the concessionaire, which is also assumed and allowed, will pass directly to the State."[73]

The same Supreme Court, also argued that the "original purpose" of reversion is that the "assets used in the exploitation," which are those that were allocated to the concession, must be returned "without any reservation," for which reason "reversion has been accepted, and its original purpose is to avoid interruption of exploitation." The aforesaid ruling basically debated the claim of the complainants that only "real property assets" were subject to reversion, to which the Court stated that assets subject to reversion include "anything that was attributed to exploitation for a definite, permanent purpose and in order to make it possible"; therefore regarding the assets used for the performance of the activity granted through the concession, the lawmaker never intended to "divide the totality of assets ascribed to exploitation

---

71 See ruling of the Administrative Political Division Court of the former Supreme Court in *Official Gazette* N° 27,344 dated 15 January 1964, p. 203.336; and in *Official Gazette*, N° 42, Caracas 1963, pp. 469-473.

72 See *Official Gazette* N° 29,577 dated 6 August 1971.

73 Ruling published in Special *Official Gazette* Extra. N° 1718 dated 20 January 1975-

of the concession in order to distinguish between personal property and real property." The former Court spoke of this, in another part of the ruling. as follows:

> "when concessionaires accept the right of reversion without any compensation, they have agreed that in order for the State to continue meeting the collective needs that the concessionaire was meeting, they are also agreeing to the economic unity of the concession in view of which all the permanent instruments or public works, apparatuses and means of transportation that are used would be employed in the continuation of operations. Therefore, ab initio, the right to ownership has also been accepted, which the Nation reserves over the assets used in exploitation in order to continue with the same."

From the foregoing, the former Court concluded in analyzing the rules of the aforesaid Law of Assets subject to Reversion, that the same were:

> "limited to the original purpose when granting the concession, i.e., that at the end of the concessions, the land, facilities and equipment and other assets subject to exploitation will pass to the State without any compensation in order to ensure the life of the concession and enable the Nation to resume it under conditions that permit adequate performance of a public undertaking."

The Supreme Court also emphasized as an important part of the principles of reversion regulated in the challenged Law, the fact that the same recognized "the prerogatives conferred by the State to concessionaires, allowing them conflicting evidence with respect to assets subject to the concession, to the satisfaction of the Federal Executive Branch before carrying out acquisition of the asset or carrying out any of the acts [...] at the time of termination of the concessions"[74]. In other words, all assets that the co-concessionaire allocated to the concession are the ones that are subject to reversion. Therefore, in the case of any attempt by the State to revert assets that are not subject to the accomplishment of the purpose of the concession, the concessionaire always has the right to prove that those are not assets subject to the purpose of the concession and therefore are not reversionary assets.

From all of the foregoing, it may be said that reversion in administrative concessions is consistent with the following characteristic notes: *first,* that it is an institution linked to the regime of administrative concessions by means of which the State grants to an individual the right or privilege to perform an activity reserved to the State; *second,* that it takes effect when the term of the concession ends (even though it also takes effect when the concession ends for any reason, among them, in the event of early cancellation); *third,* that given that the concession right reverts to the State, the objective of the reversion is to ensure uninterrupted maintenance of the exploitation or of the concession service when the concession is terminated; *fourth,* that therefore, it refers exclusively to the assets subject to the concession, i.e., those essentially intended or necessary for the performance of the granted activity; *five,* it entails that the concessionaire must unavoidably transfer to the State the aforesaid assets subject to the purpose of the concession, i.e., intended for the exploitation or granted service; *six,* that such transfer must take place without the need for any compensation by the State to the concessionaire (except in the event, for example, of

74 *Idem,* pp. 19-23

early cancellation of the concession)[75]; and *seven*, that the transfer of assets subject to the concession due to reversion without payment of compensation, however, in principle does not take place with respect to assets that the concessionaire had not fully amortized during the term of the same.

2. The Distinction between Reversionary and Non-Reversionary Assets

A. The Scope of the Reversionary Assets

From the aforementioned, then, it can be said that reversion is a traditional concept of administrative law pertaining to the regime of administrative concessions, according to which, when the concession ends due to expiration of the agreed term (as well as for any other reason), are to be reverted to the State, on the one hand, the right granted or conferred to the concessionaire, and on the other hand, the assets that the latter has incorporated into the concession to exercise the granted right.

In the case of assets which, belonging to the public domain of the State, were allowed to be used by the concessionaire with the granted right, at the conclusion of the concession the State recovers them in full along with the concession right.[76] As was pointed out a few decades ago: "Assets subject to exploitation by the Administration that may be of public domain or property of the State, belongs to the Administration and do not revert, but cease to be used by the concessionaire, who must return it without being entitled to compensation."[77]

Aside from the public domain assets, the assets that must be transferred to the State as reversion at the end of the concession, as established by law or in the concession contract, are the assets acquired or constructed and used by the concessionaire in order to perform the activity granted by the concession; in order to ensure, as applicable, that the State Administration may continue directly or indirectly to carry out the conferred activity.[78]

---

75 Article 53 of the Organic Law on Promotion of Private Investment under the Concessions Regime of Venezuela of 1999 establishes that in cases of early cancellation of concessions for reasons of public convenience or interest "comprehensive compensation of the concession will take place, including retribution of loss of income for the time period remaining for termination of the concessions," and the bid documents of the concession conditions must establish "the elements or standards that will be used to set the amount of compensation to be paid to the concessionaire."

76 See for example the statement of Diego José Vera Jurado, "El regimen jurídico del patrimonio de destino en la concesión administrativa de servicio público", in *Revista de Administración Pública,* N° 109. Madrid, January-April 1986, pp. 18, et seq.

77 See Carretero Pérez, "La expropiación forzosa de concesiones" in *Revista de Derecho Administrativo y Fiscal,* N° 10, 1956, p. 83.

78 As indicated by Gladis Vásquez Franco, "reversion entails the concessionaire's obligation to hand over to the conferring Administration the property (works, facilities and other material elements) pertaining to the service, in the conditions provided in the concession clause, at no charge and in good condition and working order for continuity of the service. At the time of reversion, the Administration exercises the right of return and also of recovery in relation to the properties subject to the concession service, which return to the administrative sphere." *Idem,* p. 130. Regarding reversion to the Government of property subject to the public service concession, see also Marçal Justen Filho, *Teoria Geral das concessiões de serviço público,* Dialética, Sao Paulo, 2003, p. 569; and regarding property subject to the concession of public service property, see Rafael Fernández Acevedo, *Las concesiones administrativas de domino público,* Thomson

As summarized by Esteban Arimany Lamoglia, in this context the occurrence of reversion comes about when the concession is terminated, with two different connotations:

> "a) On one hand, the occurrence defines the idea of returning to the Administration the right to exercise the service held until then by the concessionaire [...]. It is definitively what we could call reversion of effective title to carry out the concession activity.
>
> b) On the other hand, the same concept of reversion alludes to the transfer from the concessionaire to the Administration of the rights held by the former during the concession period over the material elements subject to exploitation." [79]

In the same sense Ismael Mata, explains that the concept of reversion is used to refer to two different situations, says:

> "1° The return to the Administration of exploitation of the service, i.e., the return of its implementation, given that ownership always belonged to the Government.
>
> 2° In second place, by reversion is meant transfer to the State of assets subject to exploitation upon termination of title."[80]

This infers that for the concept of reversion to be valid as a consequence of termination of an administrative concession, the activity or objective of the concession must have been reserved for the State in the Constitution or by law, as is the case for example, of a public service declared as such in the Constitution or in the law,[81] or of exploitation of public works considered to be of public interest,[82] or

---

Civitas, Madrid 2007, pp. 419-420; and regarding reversion of property subject to exploration of public works in cases of public works concessions, see: Alberto Ruiz Ojeda, *La Concesión de Obra Pública*, Thompson Civitas, 2006, p. 719.

79 See Esteban Arimany Lamoglia, *La reversión de instalaciones en la concesión administrativa de servicio público*, Bosch Barcelona 1980, pp. 6-7.

80 See Ismael Mata, *Régimen de los bienes en la concesión de servicios públicos*, Universidad Austral, Seminario, Editorial Ciencias de la Administración, Buenos Aires, 1999, pp. 296. However, for the author, in the question of property contributed by the concessionaire, "...it does not make sense to say that it reverts to the State, because it never belonged to it; the proper statement is that its transfer or assignment to the State must take place." To the same effect, Miguel Marienhoff says in his *Tratado de Derecho Administrativo*, Tomo III-B, Abeledo-Perrot, Buenos Aires, 1970, pp. 632 et seq., for whom in spite of the fact that grammatically *reversion* is acceptable in order to refer also to things and property of the co-contracting party, that at the end of the concession it should pass to the ownership of the State, it is more proper to speak of *transfer*.

81 See for example in Venezuela, Allan R. Brewer-Carías, "Comentarios sobre la noción del servicio público como actividad prestacional del Estado y sus consecuencias," in *Revista de Derecho Público*, N° 6, Editorial Jurídica Venezolana, Caracas, April-June 1981, pp. 65-71; and "El régimen constitucional de los servicios públicos," en *VI Jornadas Internacionales de Derecho Administrativo Allan Randolph Brewer-Carías El nuevo servicio público. Actividades reservadas y regulación de actividades de interés general (electricidad, gas, telecomunicaciones y radiodifusión*, Fundación de Estudios de Derecho Administrativo, FUNEDA, Caracas 2003, pp. 19-49.

the exploitation of the subsoil or of water, declared to be of public domain or interest,[83] like the aforementioned example of mining exploitation.

Precisely because it is a matter of public assets of the State or activities reserved for the State, exploitation of the same is outside the sphere of economic freedom of citizens, who may only carry it out when the State expressly grants them such right, which occurs precisely by means of granting an administrative concession, whether to provide a public service or to use or exploit public assets. In all those cases, whatever the cause of termination, whether due to expiration of the term or early cancellation,[84] when the right granted by the State and granted to the concessionaire is terminated, the aforesaid right necessarily reverts to the State, and with it, the assets used for the exploitation of the concession activity also revert.

This means, for example, that at the end of the concession, in cases of concessions for exploitation of public assets, the State recovers or retakes possession of the same, and all the construction projects and facilities allocated by the concessionaire to perform the concession activity also pass to the State's ownership; and in the case of the concession to provide a public service, the reversion implies transfer to the State of all assets, construction projects and facilities that were incorporated by the concessionaire or allocated by the same for providing the public service or exploitation of the objective of the concession. Such assets are those that Fernando Garrido Falla considered to be assets that:

> "are subject to the concession such that they are a substantial part of it, and: 1) during the life of the concession such assets cannot be the object of enforcement of monetary judgment or seizure, because it endangers continuity of the service, and 2) at the end of the term for which the concession was granted, such assets revert to the "conferring Administration, precisely in order to ensure continuity of the service, either carried out by the Administration (by means of direct exploitation) or by a new concessionaire."[85]

The essential justification of reversion, as aforementioned, is to prevent a public service from being interrupted or that the lack of exploitation of an asset of the State may directly affect the interests of the community; and, as explained further on, is essential in the distinction between reversionary and non-recessionary assets.

Now, regarding the reversionary assets, incorporated by the concessionaire, it is deemed that when the reversion takes place, the concessionaire must have already recovered all of the investments that he had to make, which, if not the case, under

---

82 For example in Venezuela, Article 539 of the Civil Code on public railways and roads as property of public interest. Also Article 6 of the Law of Public Property, *Official Gazette* N° 39.952 dated 26 June 2012.

83 See in Venezuela, Articles 12 and 304 of the Constitution of 1999, on the official declaration of mining fields and waters as being of public interest.

84 See for example, Esteban Arimany Lamoglia, *La reversión de instalaciones en la concesión administrativa de servicio público*, Bosch Barcelona 1980, pp. 7-9.

85 See Fernando Garrido Falla, "Efectos económicos de la caducidad de las concesiones administrativas," in *Revista de Administración Pública*, N° 45, Madrid 1964, pp. -235 – 237. It is the same distinction made also by Gladis Vásquez Franco, *La Concesión administrativa de servicio público en el derecho español y colombiano*, Edit. Temis, Bogotá 1991, p. 235.

the principle of economic equilibrium of contracts of the State,[86] could bring about the concessionaire's right to request compensation for the amount needed to amortize the cost of such assets,[87] in keeping with the principle held in Venezuelan law.[88]

In conclusion, in all cases, when an administrative concession terminates as established in the law or in the contract's clauses, reversion takes place, and the objective is to allow the State, for which the Constitution and the law have reserved the concession activity, to continue directly or indirectly to provide the service or to carry out the concession activity or exploitation. That is why reversion as a concept of administrative law, with reference to assets that have been the concessionaire's property, is one of the traditional ways to terminate the property, which of course only takes effect in relation to assets subject to concession, i.e., by performance of the right that was granted,[89] in any case, provided that it was amortized by the concessionaire.

B. Principles related to the distinction between Reversionary and Non-Reversionary Assets

Granting an administrative concession to a concessionaire to perform an activity or exploitation reserved for the State, always entails the concessionaire's duty to

86 Regarding the principle, see Allan R. Brewer-Carías, "Algunas reflexiones sobre el equilibrio financiero en los contratos administrativos y la aplicabilidad en Venezuela de la concepción amplia de la Teoría del Hecho del Príncipe" in *Revista Control Fiscal y Tecnificación Administrativa,* XIII, Nº 65, Contraloría General de la Republica, Caracas 1972, pp. 86-93.

87 See the statement of Miguel Marienhoff in his *Tratado de Derecho Administrativo,* Tomo III-B, Abeledo-Perrot, Buenos Aires, 1970, pp. 634 ss.

88 In this regard, Manuel Rachadell has observed, in analyzing the financial aspects of concessions, that the matter of establishing the term of concessions is related to the matter of the time of amortization of investments made by the concessionaire, particularly in relation to property subject to the concession that is subject to reversion, such that when the latter takes effect at the end of the term of the same, the investment has been duly amortized. This principle, of which the aim is the concessionaire's benefit, observed Rachadell, "is set forth in the last paragraph of Transitory Provision Eighteen [of the Constitution of 1999] by providing that "The law establishes in public service concessions the concessionaire's profit and the financing of investments strictly connected with performance of the service, including improvements and expansions that the competent authority considers reasonable and approves in each case." This law, which is not a transitory provision, means *that the structure of prices or compensations received by concessionaires from users or from the granting entity must include the profit as well as the amounts necessary to amortize investments made by the former*, which must be strictly limited to those connected with performance of the service, including improvements and expansions of the services that may be advisable." Rachadell added in his commentary that "In short, the Transitory Provision sets forth in depth the same principle that appears in Article 38 of the Decree-Law of 1994, which was eliminated in the reform of 1999, according to which: "The economic-financial regime of the concession must allow the concessionaire to obtain sufficient revenue during the concession term to be able to cover costs and obtain fair and equitable compensation" See Manuel Rachadell, "Aspectos financieros de las concesiones" in Alfredo Romero Mendoza (Coord.), *Régimen Legal de las Concesiones Públicas. Aspectos Jurídicos, Financieros y Técnicos,* Editorial Jurídica Venezolana, Caracas 2000, pp. 71-72.

89 See for example in Venezuela, Allan R. Brewer-Carías, "Adquisición de la propiedad privada por parte del Estado en el derecho venezolano" in Allan R. Brewer-Carías, *Jurisprudencia de la Corte Suprema 1930-1974 y estudios de derecho administrativo*, Instituto de Derecho Público, Universidad Central de Venezuela, Vol. VI, Caracas 1979, pp. 17-45.

establish a company to perform the service or to carry out exploitation of the purpose of the concession. For such purpose, it must proceed to install, organize and put into operation the material and technical means necessary for exploitation of the granted service or activity. Consequently, the concessionaire undoubtedly has to use a group of assets that are essential to comply with the objective of the concession, i.e., to provide a public service, to exploit a public works or to exploit public assets, including mining sites, without which such purpose could not be achieved. Those are the assets subject to reversion in administrative concessions.

In addition to those assets, of course, the concessionaire may acquire and use other assets that are not allocated to the concession, for example, that are not allocate to exercising the concession right (such as exploitation of the mining site in the case of mining concessions), but that the concessionaire uses for another activity or connected activities that are not the purpose of the concession and therefore are not subject to reversion. Regarding this, Carlos García Soto indicated:

> "Reversion entails a gratuitous handover of unencumbered assets because, by such means, only assets that have been amortized and are essential for performance of the service will be handed over; they are the return assets. The existing assets of the concession that are not essential for performing the construction projects or service and therefore not subject to reversion cannot be passed to the Administration, and, that which is useful and subject to reversion, but not essential, must be paid for by means of compensation by the Administration."[90]

Consequently, different types of assets related to a concession could be distinguished depending on the character of being reversionary or non-reversionary assets, the latter being the ones that upon termination of the concession remain as the concessionaire's property.[91]

---

90 See Carlos García Soto, "Reversión de bienes en el contrato de concesión", in *Derecho y Sociedad. Revista de los estudiantes de la Universidad Monteávila,* Caracas 2003, p. 97

91 In particular, Esteban Arimany Lamoglia, in his referenced book: *La reversión de instalaciones en la concesión administrativa de servicio público* [, Bosch Barcelona 1980, pp. 52-53 refers to the following classifications of property prepared by the various authors: First, that prepared by Adolfo Carretero Pérez, in his book "La expropiación forzosa de concesiones," *cit.* distinguishing among the following properties: "1) property of the Administration, 2) property owned by the concessionaire incorporated into the concessions and divided in turn into a) necessary property, b) unnecessary but useful, c) neither necessary nor useful and 3) property owned by third parties," pp. 10-12. Second, García Trevijano, in his work: "Desintegración de la empresa y reversión de concesiones (Comentario a la Sentencia de 22 de diciembre de 1954)," RDM, Nº 57 (1955), p. 206, and in (...), *cit.,* p. 206 and in "Aspectos de la Administración (...)," *cit.,* p. 50, distinguishing as follows: "1) Property of the concession, 2) company or industrial property, 3) property owned by the concessionaire not included either in the company or in the concession." Third: Garrido Falla, in his work "Economic effects (...)," *cit.*, pages 235-37, distinguishes among the following types of property: "1) revertible property, 2) accessory property or indemnifiable reversion property, 3) property owned by the concessionaire." Four, Gasón Jèze, in his book, *Principios ()* [Principles, ( )], *cit.*, Tom. VI, pp. 341 et seq., distinguishes among the following types of property: "1) ownership of the concession, 2) private ownership of the concessionaire, 3) property not part of the exploitation but useful for the same. Similarly, J. Luis Guasch, *Concesiones en infraestructura. Cómo hacerlo bien,* Word Bank, Antoni Bosch editores, 2004, distinguishes between: "a). assets that are part of the concessionaire's net worth, and b) assets that are used to perform the service." p. 153.

To that effect, for example, Esteban Arimany Lamoglia has differentiated among the following assets generally involved in the concession:

> "First, a "series of elements needed to perform the concession activity that the Administration requires, and the individual agrees to provide. They are an integral part of the concession and are subject to the public service [or to the exploitation of the granted right that is the objective of the concession], following the exorbitant system characteristic of this type of assets."
>
> Second, assets that "the concessionaire usually voluntarily incorporates into the company that he organized, which are assets that are not necessary or useful for performance of the service (or exploitation of the concession right] [...] although they may be supplementary in some way. This type of factors is not an integral part of the concession and cannot be considered allocated to the same and therefore will always be of the common regimen. Similarly, they are never subject to reversion. If the Administration is interested in them, it can only acquire them with the owner's consent."
>
> Third, "a third group made up of several factors that are useful for the exploitation, which the concessionaire incorporates voluntarily to ensure the best performance of the service or [exploitation of the concession right] exceeding his contractual obligations. [...] It is doubtful that this type of assets should be considered subject to the concession with the privileged regime that such situation entails."[92]

From this classification, Arimany concludes by saying "that among the assets implicated in any way in the exploitation of a concession service, there is a group –without doubt the most important– that is of compulsory incorporation for the business and necessarily for the concession," which are those first indicated, "which are the only that are found to be subject to reversion."[93] These are the assets of the concession, i.e., directed to the performance of the public service, the exploitation of public works or exploitation of a mining site.

The distinction was established by André de Laubadère, distinguishing among the following properties regarding administrative concessions and the purpose of reversion: "1) *biens demeurant la propriété du concessionaire* [assets owned by the concessionaire], 2) *biens de retour* [reversionary assets] y 3) *biens de reprise* [compensable reversion assets].*"*[94] The same distention was made by Eduardo García de Enterría, distinguishing the "assets, due to being subject to the service, that must be handed over free of charge to the granting Administration (*biens de retour*), except when they have not been fully amortized, and others that, due to their usefulness for the service may revert to the Administration, subject to payment of their price to the concessionaire (*biens de reprise*)"[95].

---

92 See Esteban Arimany Lamoglia, *La reversión de instalaciones en la concesión administrativa de servicio público*, Bosch Barcelona 1980, pp. 53-54.

93 *Idem*, p. 55.

94 See André de Laubadère, *Traité des contrats administrattifs,* Librairie Général de Droit et de Jurisprudence, *Tomo*. III, Paris 1956, pp. 211-202

95 See Eduardo García de Enterría y Tomás Ramón Fernández, *Curso de Derecho Administrativo*, Tomo I, Fifteenth edition, Thompon Reuters-Civitas, Madrid 2011, p. 791.

It is also the distinction made by Fernando Garrido Falla, among 1) The concessionaire's assets; 2) Return or reversionary assets, and 3) recovered assets or compensable reversion assets, as follows:

> "1. Revertible assets (*biens de retour*), i.e., those that must become the property of the granting Administration after the expiration of the concession term. This group is made up, first, of public units (e.g., in the case of railroad concessions) that were made available to the granting Administration; works and facilities that are made available to the concessionaire by the granting Administration, as well as works and facilities that the concessionaire was required to build and the material allocated to the service.
>
> The characteristic of these assets is that they revert free of charge to the Administration, although in the case of assets that have not been fully amortized (e.g., due to having been acquired by the concessionaire during the last years of the concession), the right to compensation is recognized [...]
>
> 2. Accessory assets or assets for which reversion is indemnified (*biens de reprise*), that due to their usefulness for exploitation of the service are of discretionary reversion for the Administration, but for which their price must be paid to the concessionaire.
>
> The determination of such assets must be made according to the clauses of the concession, based on the principle that, for lack of other specifications, all facilities and material used by the concessionaire for the purpose of optimum exploitation of the service are revertible, although compensable to the extent they exceed the minimum required in the bid documents. ["].
>
> 3. Assets owned by the concessionaire: those that are not a part of the two foregoing groups. That is, for a positive characterization: a) assets acquired by the concessionaire that are not an integral part (by attribution or purpose) of exploitation of the service; b) those which, being revertible subject to compensation, the Administration does not deem advisable to acquire."[96]

This same distinction has also been developed in Venezuela by the Office of the Attorney General of the Republic, which, in preparing the content of the reversion, considered that "...it may be all or part of the group of properties (construction projects, facilities and other material elements) allocated to the service, or merely certain assets specified in the concession clauses" [97]; and for the determination "of its *material scope, it requires a careful distinction among the various properties*"[98] has followed, as a guideline to distinguish them coming from the French legal theory:

---

96 See Fernando Garrido Falla, "Efectos económicos de la caducidad de las concesiones administrativas", in *Revista de Administración Pública*, N° 45, Madrid 1964, pp. -235 – 237. The same distinction is also *made by* Gladis Vásquez Franco, *La Concesión administrativa de servicio público en el derecho español y colombiano*, Edit. Temis, Bogotá 1991, 143-144

97 See Opinion N° 325, DEJE dated 22 October 1981 in *20 Años de Doctrina de la Procuraduría General de la República 1962-1981,* Tomo III, Vol. I, Caracas 1984, pp. 164 ff.

98 *Idem.*

"1. Revertible assets (*biens de retour*), i.e., those that must pass to the ownership of the granting authority once the concession is terminated.

First, belonging to this group are the construction projects and facilities that the concessionaire was required to build, the assets contributed by the concessionaire or acquired in any way, under public law –expropriation– or under private law (purchase/sale), necessary or essential for performance of the public services of the concession.

Another group will be made up of those entities owned by the State that were put at the concessionaire's disposal, which are, rather than objectives of actual reversion, are assets over which the concessionaire's occupation ceases, due to being accessories, which therefore must revert to the granting authority.

2. Property for recovery of possession (*biens de reprise*): that which, in the case of a full reversion, in the opinion of the granting authority, is useful for exploitation of the service. The essential determining factor in this category is the idea of affecting public service.

As indicated by Villar Palasí (*ob. cit.* P. 758) in matters of reversion, as stated in the principle of the mining claim unit, according to which the construction projects and facilities of the reversion are restricted by their impact on the public service in question, as well as the reversion unity principle, according to which all such assets revert to the beneficiary, without any division.

3. Assets owned by the concessionaire (*biens propres*): assets that are not a part of the two preceding groups, i.e., the assets acquired by the concessionaire that are not an integral part – by allocation or intended purpose – of the exploitation of public service. Such assets may be acquired by the granting authority with compensation."[99].

The legal criteria adopted by the Office of the Attorney General of the Republic has been followed also by Rafael Badell, who also following the French legal theory, makes the distinction of the following assets regarding reversion:

"First are the *reversible assets* (*biens de retours*), i.e., those that must pass to the ownership of the granting authority after termination of the concession. These are the assets that are the indispensable and essential assets for providing the service. This category includes the construction projects and facilities that the concessionaire agreed to build, the assets and rights provided by the concessionaire or acquired by any means under public law (e.g. expropriation or governmental easement) or of private law (e.g. purchase/sale).

The reversible assets also include public facilities or assets that were put at the concessionaire's disposal for performance of the service. However, rather than being objects of reversion, they are merely assets that cease to be used by the concessionaire, due to their incidental nature and therefore must be referred to the granting authority.

99 *Idem*, pp. 164-165.

> Second are what are called the assets for recovery of possession (*biens de reprise*), which are those that, in a full reversion, in the opinion of the granting authority, are useful for exploitation of the service. In this category, the essential and defining element is the idea of impact on public service.
>
> Last are the *assets owned by the concessionaire* (*biens propres*), made up of assets that are not a part of the two previous groups; they are assets acquired by the concessionaire that are not a part of the exploitation of the public service. Such assets may be acquired by the grantor, subject to compensation."[100]

From the foregoing, the common representation of all the described classifications, as well as the described legal theory and case law, is that reversible assets in the administrative concessions are assets that, at the end of the concession term, are subject to the purpose of the same, i.e., the assets subject to the exercise of the right granted by the Administration to the concessionaire (which it previously did not have and acquired with the concession), the right to explore and exploit certain mining sites, the right to provide a certain public service, or to develop a certain public asset. Therefore, in no case may the reversion include assets that are not subject to the concession or that the concessionaire, for example, has acquired or constructed during the term of the concession but rather to be used, for example, for activities whose execution does not require any administrative concession.

3. The Regime of Reversion in Venezuelan Positive Law

A. The constitutional tradition

Unlike other legal systems, in the Venezuelan legal system, the concept of reversion has been regulated since the last century in connection with administrative concessions, which has even been incorporated although in a limited way in the Constitution itself.

To be specific, in relation to mining concessions in general, Article 70 of the Constitution of 1947 established the following:

> "Art. 70. Lands acquired by citizens or foreigners in Venezuelan territory and used for exploitation of mining concessions, including hydrocarbons concessions and concessions of other combustible minerals shall, pass in full ownership to the Nation, without compensation, upon termination of the respective concession for any cause."

Such law only referred to reversion on matters of mining concessions, including hydrocarbons concessions, which at the time were already regulated by the Mines Law (1945) as well as the Hydrocarbons Law (1943), and moreover only referred to reversion of lands acquired and used for exploitation of such mining and hydrocarbons concessions, without referring to any other asset, establishing that such lands were those that should be transferred to the Nation without any compensation at termination of the concession for any reason.

A similar provision was included in the Constitution of 1961 establishing as follows:

100 See Rafael Badell Madrid, *Régimen jurídico de las concesiones en Venezuela,* Caracas 2002, pp. 271.

"Art. 103. Lands used for exploration and exploitation of mining concessions, including hydrocarbons concessions, shall pass in full ownership to the Nation, without compensation, upon termination of the concession for any cause."

This provision completely disappeared from the Constitution of 1999, which established the general declaration that mining sites and hydrocarbons reservoirs of any kind in existence in national territory are public assets and are therefore inalienable and not subject to any prescription (Art. 12). Nonetheless, due to the 1975 nationalization of the oil industry, the concept of the hydrocarbons concession no longer existed.

B. Reversion in some special laws

a. Reversion in Hydrocarbons Concessions: Hydrocarbon Law, 1943

The principle of reversion, before its partial regulation in the Constitution of 1947, had begun to be regulated in special laws, particularly the Hydrocarbons Law of 1943[101], in which Article 80 set forth the principle that:

"Art. 80. The nation will reacquire the granted parcels without paying compensation and similarly will become the owner of all permanent construction projects that have been constructed on them."

The wording of this article was criticized by the Office of the Attorney General of the Republic, which considered as an *unfortunate* the expression the phrase to "granted parcels" used in the same, because "the objective of the concession is not the parcels" and therefore, regarding the scope and interpretation of the law, it sustained that:

"What reverts to the national wealth is the concession as a whole and not one of its parts, such as the parcel. In fact, paragraph 3 of Article 80 of the Hydrocarbons Law (which establishes the various alternatives of the Federal Executive Branch after a concession expires) provides that exploitation of the reacquired parcels may be carried out directly by the Federal Executive Branch. Thus, in order to be able to manage exploitability, theoretically it is necessary for the concession to have reverted under exploitable conditions, and that all its parts must be in full operation. Therefore, as a general rule it can be said that not only parcels (land) pass into the national wealth, but also the permanent facilities, which are all the assets that are part of the exploitation of the granted asset."[102]

Finally the scope of the law was developed in the mentioned Law of Assets Subject to Reversion in Hydrocarbons Concessions of 1971[103], which, in relation to the reversionary assets in hydrocarbons concessions, listed in Article 1 the

---

101 The last reform was that of 29 August 1967. See Special Edition *Official Gazette* N° 1149 dated 15 September 1967.

102 See Opinion N° 324, A.E. dated 8 March 1972 in *20 Años de Doctrina de la Procuraduría General de la República 1962-1981*, Tomo III, Vol. I, Caracas 1984, pp. 141.

103 See *Official Gazette* N° 29,577 dated 6 August 1971. See regarding this Law in general: Arístides Rengel-Romberg, "El derecho de reversión en la legislación de minas e hidrocarburos," in: *Estudios jurídicos: estudios procesales, escritos periodísticos, pareceres jurídicos,* Academia de Ciencia Políticas y Sociales, Caracas 2003, pp. 283 et seq.

following: “lands, permanent construction projects, including facilities, accessories and equipment that are an integral part of them; and other assets acquired for use or are subject to the work of exploration, exploitation, manufacture, refining or transportation in the hydrocarbons concessions,” also including, unless proved otherwise, “any other tangible or intangible assets acquired by the concessionaires.” The similar rule of the Hydrocarbons Law was also interpreted by the former Supreme Court in 1974, in its ruling issued after the challenging of the Law of Assets Subject to Reversion in Hydrocarbons Concessions of 1971, specifying that reversion only is valid regarding the lands and permanent construction projects built in the concession zone that are used for exploitation of the same, i.e., subject to or for the purpose of the concession.[104]

The essential information for classifying an asset as reversionary is that it should be an “integral part” of the concession and therefore “intended for the object of the work of the granted concession,” bearing in mind that the object of concessions in the Hydrocarbons Law, depends on the type of concessions, that can be: concessions of exploration and subsequent exploitation (Arts. 12 to 21); exploitation concessions (Arts. 22 to 27); manufacturing and refining concessions (Arts. 28 to 31) and hydrocarbons transportation concessions (Arts. 32 to 37). In a concession for manufacturing and refining of hydrocarbons, given that such activity was the object of the concession, the assets subject to such refining were to be included in the revertible assets according to the provisions of Article 1 of the Law of Assets Subject to Reversion

Such “special advantages” in case of mining concessions, being all concessions for exploitation, could provide for example, for manufacturing or industrialization of the extracted material, which is a completely different activity from exploitation. In this case, the assets used for such purpose are not to be considered as assets intended for the objective of the granted right.

b. Reversion in Railroad Concessions

Reversion had also been foreseen at the legislative level with respect to another series of concession contracts. For example, regarding railroad concessions, the repealed Railroad Law of 1956 [105] established the following:

> “Article 9. In the case of concessions terminated due to expiration of their term of duration, the Nation will reacquire without compensation all the granted rights and will become the owner of all construction projects, rolling stock, constructions and facilities realized during the concession.”

The provision referred to returning to the State all the granted rights, and the reversion of works, rolling stock, construction and facilities used during the concession for performance of the granted service. The same Law further established the principle of reversion in the event of invalidity due to breach of obligations by the contracting party, and Article 10 provided that the construction projects, rolling stock and constructions and facilities used for the object of the

---

104 The ruling was published in Special *Official Gazette* Extra. N° 1718 dated 20 January 1975.

105 *Official Gazette* N° 25,425 dated 7 August 1957. Regarding reversion clauses in public service concessions. See *Doctrina PGR 1981*, Caracas, 1982, pp. 33–39; *Doctrina PGR 1972*, Caracas, 1973, p. 327.

concession, in such event also was to become the property of the Nation, "without any compensation by the latter."

c. Reversion in Concessions for the use of Water Resources

In concessions for the use of water resources, reversion was also established expressly in the repealed Forestry Law of Soils and Waters of 1966,[106] which provided expressly in Article 92 that after the time period provided for the concession, "all works carried out by the concessionaire will be for the benefit of the Nation." The Regulation of the Law enacted in 1997 developed the legislative provision, reiterating it by establishing that the draft contract to be attached by the applicant of a concession for development of water resources must contain "the commitment that at the end of the term or termination of the contract, all construction projects executed by the contracting party will be for the benefit of the Nation, free of encumbrances" (Article 186.13).

d. Reversion in Municipal Concessions

The principle of reversion also was established in general with respect to concessions of municipal public services. The Organic Law of Municipal Regime of 1978, reformed in 1989,[107] provided in Article 41.10, among other minimum conditions, that municipal public service concessions, as well as concessions for exploration of the Municipality's assets, had to contain a clause providing the "transfer free of charge and encumbrances to the Municipality, of all assets, rights and actions under the concession upon termination of the latter for any cause."

In this manner, through constitutional principles and development by special laws that have regulated administrative concession contract, it can be said that the tendency of Venezuelan positive law has been for the provision of an obligatory clause in the matter of concessions related to reversion, establishing the obligation for the concessionaire to transfer to the State, free of encumbrances and without compensation, the assets subject to the concession once the latter terminates for any cause, [108] which does not include assets that may be acquired or constructed by the concessionaire and used for activities other than for the concession objective.

C. The Institution of Reversion in the General Law on Administrative Concessions of 1999

Beside sectorial statutes, the first of the general laws on administrative concessions issued in the country particularly regarding public construction projects and public services, was the Law of Construction, Exploitation and Maintenance of Roads and Transportation Construction Projects in the Concession Regime of 1983,[109] which expressly established in Article 76 the principle that "after expiration of the concession term, the concessionaire's assets allocated to performing the

106 *Official Gazette* N° 1,004 dated 25 January 1966

107 Special Official Gazette N° 4,107 dated 15 May 1989

108 See Allan R. Brewer-Carías, "Principios especiales y estipulaciones obligatorias en la contratación administrativa" in *El Derecho Administrativo en Latinoamérica*, Vol. II, Ediciones Rosaristas, Colegio Mayor Nuestra Señora del Rosario, Bogotá 1986, pp. 345-3789.

109 See *Official Gazette* Extra. N° 3,247 dated 26–8–83. On reversion clauses in public works concessions, see *Doctrina PGR 1972*, Caracas, 1973, pp. 312–325.

service will pass to the ownership of the Republic, without compensation and free of encumbrances and charges."

That rule was incorporated into Decree Law N° 318 dated 20 April 1994 regarding concessions of public construction projects and national public services,[110] reformed by Decree Law N° 138 dated 20 April 1999.[111] The principle of reversion was incorporated into this law, establishing that the same was applicable to "assets subject to the construction project or the service," and subsequently, in the Organic Law on Promotion of Private Investment under the Regime of Concessions of 1999,[112] which culminated the configuration of a general regime of concessions, particularly of those related to construction projects and public services.[113]

This Organic Law on Promotion of Private Investment under the Regime of Concessions of 1999, as explained in its Article 1, was issued to regulate the concessions for the "construction and exploitation of new construction projects, systems or infrastructure facilities for the maintenance, overhaul, modernization, expansion and exploitation of existing construction projects, systems or infrastructure facilities or merely for the modernization, improvement, expansion or exploitation of an established public service," also specifying in Article 2 that, for the effects of its rules, "concession contracts" are considered to be those entered into to "build, operate and maintain a construction project or asset intended for the service, public use or promotion of development or to manage, improve or organize a public service, including the performance of activities necessary for proper operation or performance of the construction project or service, on their own accord and at their own risk and under the supervision and oversight of the granting authority, in exchange for the right to exploit the construction project or service and to receive the product of tariffs, prices, tolls, rentals, valuation of real property, subsidies, profits shared with a public entity or other formula established in the pertinent contracts for a determined period of time, sufficient to recover the investment and exploitation expenses incurred and to obtain a reasonable rate of return for the investment."

Under this 1999 Organic Law, however, the regime of reversion was no longer based on a provision of positive law, and became an exclusively contractual regime[114], providing in Article 48 of the same that for effects of the "reversion of construction projects and services," the concession contract must establish the concession term, the investments that must be made by the concessionaire and also:

---

110 Special Edition *Official Gazette* N° 4719 dated 26 April 1994.

111 *Official Gazette* N° 36684 dated 29 April 1999.

112 *Official Gazette* Extra. N° 5,394 dated 25 October 1999.

113 The difference between assets subject to the concession and therefore subject to reversion, and non-reversible assets was demonstrated in Article 61 of Decree Law No. 318, which established that after termination of the concession, the concessionaire should hand over to the Republic the construction projects, facilities, machinery, equipment and accessories subject to the service, adding the obligation to sell to the Republic the other assets required by the latter, even though they were not a part of the concession.

114 However, Carlos García Soto deems that due to the legal provision, the reversion clause must be present in all concession contracts. See "Reversión de bienes en el contrato de concesión", in *Derecho y Sociedad. Revista de los estudiantes de la Universidad Monteávila,* Caracas 2003, p. 103.

"assets that, due to being subject to the construction project or the service in question, will revert to the granting entity, unless they have not been fully amortized during the aforementioned term.

Further, the contract will set forth the construction projects, facilities and assets to be carried out by the concessionaire not subject to reversion, which may be cause for reversion subject to payment of their price to the concessionaire."

Article 46 of the Organic Law also established the principle that upon termination of the concession, the construction projects or services may be again granted under a concession, which must be for the purpose of their preservation, repair, expansion or exploitation.

The consequence of the rule of Article 48 of the Organic Law, in any case, is the clear differentiation between reversionary and non-reversionary assets. First, regarding reversionary assets, they are defined as those that are "subject to the construction project or the service in question," regarding which, according to the same rule, during a prudent period prior to termination of the contract, "the granting entity must adopt provisions to ensure that delivery of the assets to be reverted is verified under the stipulated conditions."

In second place are the non-reversionary assets, which are the construction projects, facilities and assets used by the concessionaire that, due to not being subject to the objective of the concession are not subject to reversion, although regarding the same, the Administration always has the authority to acquire them for reasons of public convenience or necessity, "subject to payment of their price to the concessionaire," in which case obviously, it cannot be called "reversion", as the Law improperly does.[115]

It should also be pointed out that, in the regulation established in Article 60 of the Organic Law in the subject matter of "assets incorporated into the concession" the same differentiation is made between reversionary and non-reversionary assets by specifying that "as of execution of the concession contract, the concessionaire has the right to the use and enjoyment of public or private assets of the granting entity that are intended for execution and development of the construction projects or services under such contract," adding that "the assets or rights that the concessionaire acquires by any means *for use in the concession* will become a part of public property once they are incorporated into the construction projects, either by accession or by designation," "with the exception of construction projects, facilities or assets which, due to *not being allocated to the concession, will remain as property of the concessionaire* as established in the respective contract."

Regarding the application of such general legislation on administrative concessions, from the definitions of the aforementioned Articles 1 and 2 of the Organic Law, due to their scope, it could be understood that such sphere would include all concession contracts signed by the State, including concessions for exploitation of non-renewable natural resources such as mining concessions, which

---

115 For example, this is the opinion of Manuel Rachadell, "Aspectos financieros de las concesiones", in Alfredo Romero Mendoza, (coordinator), *El régimen legal de las concesiones públicas. Aspectos jurídicos, financieros y técnicos*, Editorial Jurídica Venezolana, Caracas 2000 p. 92.

are included within the purpose of "promotion of development." In this regard, for example, the Political Administrative Division Court of the Supreme Court has decided in various decisions that the provisions of such Organic Law on Promotion of Private Investment under the 1999 Regime of Concessions, in matters of early termination or early cancellation, are completely applicable to all types of concessions and particularly with respect to mining concessions.[116]

However, it should be mentioned that the lawmaker, in issuing such Organic Law, regarding its applicability to concessions in general, was specific and careful not to substitute the special specific regime established with respect to the same in special or sectorial laws that regulate them, as in the case of the regime provided in the Mines Law. Therefore, in spite of being an organic law, which, as provided by the Constitution, serves as a "legal framework for other laws" (Art. 203) and therefore could apply preferentially in the regulated subject matter, it ruled out the idea that its provisions could prevail *per se* over the specific rules of laws regulating the different concessions in the country. To the contrary, Article 4 of the Organic law provided that "the concession contracts whose execution, management or performance is regulated by special laws" –as is precisely the case of the mining concessions– "will be governed preferentially by such laws," and in such cases the provisions of the Organic Law on Promotion of Private Investment under the Concession Regime would be "additionally applicable."[117]

This means that the rules of the Organic Law on Promotion of Private Investment under the Concession Regime, being additionally applicable with respect to special laws regulating concessions, apply in all matters not expressly regulated in such special laws, such as for example the case of the legal regimen for early termination of concessions and determination of compensation in the case of such early cancellation, which is only regulated in Article 53 of such Organic Law.

D. The Institution of Reversion in the Mines Law of 1945

The institution of reversion in mining concessions was established in Article 61 of the Mines Law of 1945, which provided as follows:

---

116 See for example, decisions No. 1836 dated 7 August 2001 (Case: *David Montiel Guillén and Oscar Montiel Guillén*, at http://www.tsj.gov.ve/decisiones/spa/agosto/01836-080801-13619.htm), N° 1447 dated 8 August 2007 (Case: *Minera la Cerbatana C.A.*, at http://www.tsj.gov.ve/decisiones/spa/agosto/01447-8807-2007-2004-0779.html), N° 1929 dated 27 November 2007 (Case: *Canteras El Toco C.A.*, at http://www.tsj.gov.ve/decisiones/spa/noviembre/01929-281107-2007-2004-0676.html), N° 847 dated 16 July 2008 (Case: *Minas de San Miguel, C.A.*, at http://www.tsj.gov.ve/decisiones/spa/julio/00847-17708-2008-2005-5529.html), N° 395 dated 24 March 2009 (Case: *Unión Consolidada San Antonio C.A.*, at http://www.tsj.gov.ve/decisiones/spa/Marzo/00395-25309-2009-2005-5526.html) y N° 1468 dated 2 November 2011 (Case: *Agrominera Suárez C.A.*, at http://www.tsj.gov.ve/decisiones/spa/Noviembre/01468-31111-2011-2010-0945.html).

117 Carlos García Soto has observed regarding inclusion in the Organic Law of the concept of reversion, that in the future it would not be necessary to include in special laws rules on the same matter. See "Reversión de bienes en el contrato de concesión", in *Derecho y Sociedad. Revista de los estudiantes de la Universidad Monteávila,* Caracas 03, p. 104.

"Article 61: The concession returned to the State is returned free of encumbrances and with all the construction projects and any other permanent improvements it may have, as well as machinery, tools, equipment and materials that are abandoned within the concession zone.

Sole Paragraph. For effects of this Article and Article 53, abandonment of such articles will be considered permanent:

Due to not having been removed prior to having relinquished the concession;

2. Due to not having removed it prior to expiration of the term for which the concession was granted, and

3. Due to not having removed it prior to declaring expiration as referenced in Article 55."

This law embraced the principle of reversion which, as indicated, as an institution characteristic of administrative concessions in administrative law, in mining concessions only refers to the mining activities that can only be carried out in view of the granted right that brings about the concession itself, i.e., fundamentally the exploitation of the respective site.

According to this law, what should be returned to the State when the concession terminated was precisely the mining right granted through the "concession" (Mining license), and with it, "all the construction projects and any other permanent improvements." As concessions in the Law were only exploration and exploitation concessions that granted the "right of mining exploitation" (Art. 13), the reversion took effect with respect to the "concession" and in relation to the assets used for the performance of the mining activities inherent to the granted right (right of exploitation), which was the right granted to the concessionaire through the concession, which it previously did not have.

Those mining exploitation rights, once the concession ended for any cause, according to the Law returned to the ownership of the State, and therefore only the assets incorporated by the concessionaire during the effective term of the concession for realization of activities inherent to the same, i.e., mining exploitation, were those that became the property of the State, not being subject to reversion any assets used for activities other than the mining activities of the granted exploitation right, which were the objective and reason for the concession and which were those that the concessionaire should have removed from the concession zone. If not, it was assumed that they were abandoned assets.

In spite of the brevity of the law's text, this came from the characteristic legal expression used in the sense that when the times granted with the concession terminated (Arts. 53-61: invalidity, termination, abandonment and Art. 198), what returned "to the ownership of the State" was "the concession," which is the act of granting the right to exploit "with all the construction projects and other permanent improvement therein (in "the concession") (Art. 61). When that mining exploitation right terminated, the same returned to the State, including all the construction projects and other permanent improvements used for the concession, i.e., the granted and terminated exploitation rights which were none other than the "mining rights," i.e., those granted or conferred by the State to the concessionaire, which the latter did not have, but rather they derived from the concession, and were related to the exploitation of certain sites and minerals. These were the rights and works that with other permanent improvements used for the purpose of the exploitation of the concession, according to the Mines Law of 1945 were to "return to the State" with the same, when the rights are terminated.

All other assets acquired and used by the concessionaire for purposes other than the objective of the concession (mining exploitation) belong to the concessionaire, and therefore the 1945 Law, as a principle, provided that when the concession rights expired, and the latter return to the State, the aforesaid assets that were not reversible were to be removed by the concessionaire from the zone or area of the concession. In the event that the concessionaire does not remove such non-reversionary assets because not being subject to the granted activities upon termination of the concession, the Law established a presumption that they were to be considered as been abandoned, and therefore Article 61 provided that "any machinery, tools, equipment and materials that are abandoned within the concession zone" would all be transferred to the State, not due to being reversionary assets, but rather in such case due to abandonment by their owner. Thus, the transfer to the State of "abandoned assets" was not based on the application of the reversion principle, and therefore in no case could such assets be said to "revert" to the State, but rather it would acquire them due to abandonment by their owner.

For this, the Law established in the same rule of Article 61 of the 1945 Law a presumption of "abandonment" to the State of the aforesaid assets by the concessionaire, as *juris tantum* presumption. In particular, for cases of extinction of mining exploitation rights due to "termination of the term for which the concessions were granted" item number 2 of the Sole Paragraph of such law established that the "abandonment" of assets or items by the concessionaire in the concession zone was considered factual "due to not effecting their removal [of such assets not subject to the concession] before the referenced expiration.

Such legal distinction between assets subject to the mining activity inherent to the granted right, which the Law defines as "construction projects and other permanent improvements" of the concession, which are those that revert to the State with the concession, and assets intended for activities other than the actual activities of the concession that the concessionaire may carry out, and that the concessionaire as owner should have removed from the concession zone, was that which, according to the 1945 Mines Law, also allowed to distinguish in mining concessions, the mining activity inherent to the concession, i.e., the exploitation or extraction of mineral; from other related or ancillary activities that are not the object of the concession. From this rule of Article 61 of the 1945 Mines Law came the distinction among the concessionaire's activities that referred to the mining activities related to the objective of the concession (exploitation), and other activities that the concessionaire could carry out that were subsidiary or derived from the same, but that were not part of the concession objective.

When the concession terminated, the reversion – as a principle – only took effect with respect to works and other permanent improvements subject to the mining activities under the concession, i.e., the rights of exploitation, which should be transferred to the State with the concession. All the other assets used for activities other than the concession objective, when the same terminated, continued to be the property of the concessionaire and, as indicated, what the Law required was that the same should be removed by the concessionaire from the concession zone, establishing –however– the presumption that if they were not removed upon expiration of the concession, they were considered to have been left to the State.

Lastly, as the Law in this case established a *juris tantum* presumption of abandonment due to the lack of timely "removal" by the concessionaire of assets that it owned (machinery, tools, equipment and materials), which were not reversionary assets due to not being subject to the concession objective, and which however were inside the perimeter of the same at its expiration, such presumption could always be refuted by proof to the contrary as a result of the concessionaire's statement that he was not "abandoning" such assets, which would cover machinery, tools, equipment and materials, including for example those that may comprise a processing construction for processing the extracted mineral, or the extracted and processed mineral materials accumulated in the concession zone.

The foregoing was reinforced with the provisions of Decree No. 2039 dated 15 February 1977,[118] through which the Federal Executive Branch reserved in a general way in all the territory of the State and for all minerals, the mining activities of exploration and exploitation, establishing in general, the discretionary character of the act of granting for such purposes, in which cases, the Administration should take into account, among other aspects, the obligation to revert assets to the Nation upon termination of the concession for any cause (Articles 2 and 5). In other words, it established a guideline for the granting of exploration and exploitation concessions and the obligation of reversion to the State of construction projects and permanent improvements of the concession.

For the purpose of granting the concessions of exploration and exploitation of minerals, Resolution N° 115 dated 20 March 1990[119] was issued by the Ministry of Energy and Mines establishing the "Rules for Granting Mining Concessions and Contracts" which provided (in Article 19) that "assets of the concession" were those that were subject to reversion. For such purpose, article 19 of the Resolution provided as follows:

> "Article 19: In order to comply with the provisions of Article 2, paragraph 5 of Decree N° 2039 dated 15 February 1977, published in the *Official Gazette* of the Republic of Venezuela N° 31,175 dated the same date, the concessionaire agrees to the reversion of *the assets of the concession* to the Nation upon termination of the concession for any cause. Such reversion will take place in the terms provided in Article 61 of the Mines Law."

In the terms of this provision, such "assets of the concession" are obviously those that the Mines Law identifies as "construction projects and other permanent improvements" subject to the concession, set forth in the same (Art. 61), providing that "assets of the concession" are only those intended for its purpose, which was exploration and exploitation, regarding which the concessionaire agreed would be subject to reversion.

This acquires greater relevance considering that the approved regulations in effect prior to Resolution N° 115 of 1990, such as Resolution N° 528 dated 17 December

118 Decree N° 2039 of 15 February 1977, *Official Gazette* N° 31,175 of 15 February 1990.

119 *Official Gazette* N° 34,448 of 16 April 1990.

1986, for which the "Rules for Granting Permits for Mining Prospecting, Concessions and Contracts"[120] and Resolution N° 148 dated 21 March 1978, "Rules for Granting Mining Concessions,"[121] were established, were more specific and were more inclusive, embracing the reversion of lands, construction projects and other permanent improvements, machinery, utensils, tools and materials, including facilities, accessory equipment and other assets subject to the concession or used in subsidiary or related operations. However, in the referenced Resolution N° 115 of 1990 (Rules for Granting Mining Concessions and Contracts) such specificity and extensiveness were eliminated, limiting reversion as established in Article 61 of the Mines Law of 1945, with respect to construction projects and permanent improvements of the concession.

In relation to special advantages for the Nation, the 1945 Mines Law authorized the Federal Executive Branch to stipulate them in matters of taxes or in any other respect with reference to discretionally granted concessions (Article 91). They were later systematized, although cautiously, in Decree N° 2039 dated 15 February 1977,[122] and more specifically in the "Rules for Granting Mining Concessions" contained in the aforementioned Resolution N° 148 dated 21 March 1978, and later in the subsequent Resolutions that replaced the former. Among the special advantages are those related to payment of contributions, incorporation of national value added (metallurgy, mineralogy, industrialization), and transfer of technology as aspects other than those of the reserved right and objective of the concession that was the extraction of mineral from a site or mine.[123]

E. The Institution of Reversion in the Mines Law of 1999

a. The Mines Law of 1999 and its application to previously granted Concessions

The Mines Law of 1945 was repealed by the Mines Law of 1999 (Article 136), entering into effect since the date of its publication. The provisions of the new law, based on the principle of *lex posterior derogat priori,* had immediate efficacy and application, but establishing some exceptions.

One of such exception was related to the date for applicability of one of its provisions,[124] and other exceptions established in article 129, were related to the immediate applicability of the Law to the concessions granted according to the previous Law, by indicating that: (i) the right to exploit mines previously granted in concessions, was to be preserved as established those concessions, regarding the mineral granted for exploitation, as well as regarding its manner of presentation; (ii) the concessionaires would only be required to pay the taxes established in the new Law, only after one year following its publication in the *Official Gazette*; (iii) the

120 *Official Gazette* N° 33,129 of 1 June 1987.

121 Special Edition *Official Gazette* N° 2,210 of 6 April 1978.

122 *Official Gazette* N° 31,175 of 15 February 1990.

123 Article 16 of Resolution N° 148 of 1978 and 11 of Resolution N° 115 of 1990.

124 The Mines Law of 1999 provides in Article 136 that it repeals the 1945 Mines Law "with the exception of the provisions of Article 128," which provides that non-metallic minerals regulated in Articles 7 and 8 of the 1945 Mines Law will continue to be in subject to Articles 7, 8, 9 and 10 of the 1945 Law until the States [of the Venezuelan Federation] assume jurisdiction over such minerals in accordance with the Organic Law of Decentralization, Definition y Transference of Jurisdiction of the Power of the State issued in 1989.

duration of the concessions previously granted will remain in accordance with the term established in the original Title; and (iv) the concessionaires were required to maintain the special advantages initially offered to the Republic in the concession.[125] Under these provisions, therefore, in cases of concessions granted before the 1999 Law entered into effect, only in these four circumstances, the terms stipulated in the original Titles were to remain in effect, the provisions of the Mines Law of 1999 not being immediately applicable.

b. Treatment of Reversion in the Mines Law of 1999

Among the provisions of the Mines Law of 1999, which entered into effect as of its enactment and were applicable to all concessions granted before or thereafter, was the rule contained in Article 102 regulating the concept of reversion of assets acquired for use in the granted mining activities. Such rule establishes as follows:

> "Article 102. The lands, permanent construction projects, including facilities, accessories and equipment that are an integral part of them, as well as any other tangible and intangible movable or real property acquired for use in the mining activities, must be maintained and preserved by the respective owner, as well as verified as being in good operating condition in keeping with applicable technical advances and principles, for the entire duration of the mining rights and their possible extension, and shall become fully owned by the Republic, free of encumbrances and charges, without compensation, upon termination of such rights for any cause."

The referenced rule was supplemented with Article 103 of the same Law, providing as follows:

> "Article 103. The owner of mining rights shall submit to the Ministry of Energy and Mines a detailed inventory of all assets acquired for use in and subject to the mining activities, which may not be disposed of in any manner without prior written authorization of the Ministry of Energy and Mines."

Such rules of the Mines Law of 1999 repealed those provided in the 1945 Law, including derogation of any that could be regulated in regulatory rules of a sublegal nature,[126] and it is evident from their text that they contemplate the reversion only with respect to the assets acquired by the concessionaire "for use in the mining activities that it carries out" which are those that it may carry out under the concession, which constitute the objective of the same. All other assets acquired by the concessionaire and not intended for the mining activities of the granted mining rights (exploitation), including subsidiary activities or activities related to the same that are in any case not part of the concession objective, cannot be considered assets that may be "reversible."

In particular, it is noteworthy that the 1999 Law no longer established the provision on the "presumption of abandonment" that according to the 1945 Law was

---

125 The Constitutional Chamber of the Supreme Court of Justice expressly ruled in decision N° 37 dated 27 January 2004, on the constitutionality of the aforementioned Article 129 of the 1999 Mines Law. See Case: *Asociación Cooperativa Civil Mixta La Salvación SRL*, (Record N° 00-1496), available at *http://www.tsj.gov.ve/decisiones/scon/Enero/37-270104-00-1496.htm*

126 The 1999 Mines Law, repealing the provisions on reversion of the 1945 Mines Law, also implicitly repealed the provisions on reversion contained in Resolution N° 115 of 1990.

applied to cases of assets owned by the concessionaire that were not subject to the mining activities of the concession, but when not removed from the concession zone they passed to the ownership of the State, not by reversion but rather due to abandonment. The consequence of that repeal of the provision related to presumption of abandonment, is that, being the legal regime of presumption of public order, the provision contained in Article 61 of the 1945 Law on such presumption of abandonment cannot be applied to cases of termination of mining concessions after 1999, if they were granted before such date. That is to say that the regime of presumption of abandonment of non-revisionary assets in Article 61 of the repealed 1945 Mines Law is not applicable to cases of expiration of mining concessions that occurred as of the 1999 Law.

4. The Scope of Reversion Regarding Mining Concession

A. The law applicable to the Mining Concessions

Being mining concessions a sort of administrative contracts entered by Public Administration and a private corporation, for a public purpose, as all contracts, in addition to the specific statute applicable, like for instance the Mines Law regarding mining concessions, according to the Civil Code, their clauses "have force of Law between the parties" (Article 1.159 Civil Code) and they are compelled to comply with the duties set forth in the contract "precisely as they have been undertaken" (Article 1.264 Civil Code). Article 1.264 of the Civil Code further provides that "the debtor is responsible for damages, in case of breach." Additionally, under Article 1.160 of the Civil Code, contracts "shall be performed in good faith" and the parties are compelled to comply not only with what is expressly stated therein, "but also with all the consequences derived from such contracts, following equity, usage or the Law." The "law" in this provision of the Civil Code refers to the applicable law existing at the moment the contract was signed, which is the one integrated in it; except if a new statute establishes provisions of public order.

The consequence of the aforementioned is that as a matter of principle, the legal relationship between the parties to the contract, in addition to the provisions of public order established in the specific law referred to the matter, is basically regulated by the terms set forth in the clauses of the contract, being applicable to it, in a supplementary way, the articles of the Civil and Commercial Codes, and any other statutes in force at the moment of the signing of the contract that concern matters related to the content of its clauses. Consequently, also as a matter of principle, the Parties are entitled to establish the contents of the contract (although in practice, they are a sort of "adhesion contracts), which they can draft according to their own particular interests, within the limits set forth in a compulsory way by statutes, and except for clauses that must be incorporated in the contracts when a constitutional or legal mandate is provided

The compulsory application of certain provisions of specific statutes to contracts, which constitute a basic legal limitation to the parties' will, is established in Article 6 of the same Civil Code, when providing that the parties cannot, by agreement, alter statutes where "public order and good customs" (*orden público y buenas costumbres*) are involved. This concept of "public order" in the Venezuelan legal system refers to situations where the application of a statute concerns the general and indispensable legal order for the existence of the community that cannot be set aside by private agreement. Thus, a public order provision cannot be altered or ignored through covenant between the parties, and should that be the case, vested rights would not be recognized, nor can they be raised as per a legal regime that would oppose it and would have been abolished. [127]

Consequently, as aforementioned, being the contract the law between the parties (Article 1.159 Civil Code), they are always bound to the contractual provisions, which can only be modified by mutual agreement and not unilaterally; with the exception of "public order" provisions that are established in statutes, which even sanctioned after the signing of the contract, apply to all pre-existent contracts.

From what has been said it follows that although the law of the contract is the law in force at the moment of its signing, nonetheless, the public order provisions included in new statutes like the 1999 Mines Law are always immediately applicable to the concessions, even those signed before the enactment of the reform. It is the case, for instance, of all those provisions referred, for instance, to the protection of the environment, of those conferring the organs of Public Administration specific powers of control over the activities of the concessionaires, or of the provisions establishing the rules applicable to the reversion of assets.

Among such rules of public order is for example, Article 86 of the 1999 Mines Law that comprises Title V "Related or Subsidiary Mining Activities," which establishes the State's authority to monitor and inspect, not only the mining activities of a concession, but also activities that concessionaires may carry out other than the granted activities, such as related or subsidiary activities of mining (storage, possession, processing, transportation, circulation and commerce of minerals). The law in effect provides as follows:

> "Article 86. The storage, possession, processing, transportation, circulation and commerce of minerals governed by the Law will be subject to monitoring and inspection by the Federal Executive Branch and any regulation and other provisions that the same may issue to protect the interests of the Republic and of the mining activity. In accordance with public interest, the Federal Executive Branch may reserve for itself, by means of decree, any of such activities with respect to certain minerals."

This rule, by regulating the oversight authority of the State, is a rule of public order, which, when it came into effect with the effective date of the 1999 Mines Law, also became applicable to concessions granted before such date for instance under the effective term of the 1945 Mines Law. Therefore, although the same was not in the text of the Mines Law of 1945, it applies to concessions granted under such Law, being important to emphasize the differentiation that also derived from the Mines Law of 1945, among the activities that the concessionaires may carry out as a consequence of the concession objective (such as the mining activity of exploitation of a site, which is the " primary activity"), which are reserved for the State, of other related or subsidiary activities such as storage, possession, processing, transportation, circulation and commerce of extracted minerals, which

---

127 See regarding this concept of public order, Allan R. Brewer-Carías, *Administrative Law in Venezuela*, Editorial Jurídica Venezolana, Caracas 2013, p. 134, par. 343.

may be freely carried (because they are not reserved for the State) although under the "monitoring and inspection" by the State.

This provision of public order of Article 86 of the Mines Law of 1999 is, for example, important when establishing the differentiation between reversionary assets of the concession that are subject to the purpose of the concession (mineral exploitation), and non-reversionary assets, which are not intended for use in the concession objective and are, for example, intended for storage, possession, processing, transportation, circulation and commerce of the extracted minerals, and that remain under ownership of the concessionaire.

B. Reversionary and Non-Reversionary Assets in the Mining Concessions

In the case of mining concessions in general, the State, pursuant to the provisions of the Mines Law, as aforementioned, grants to a concessionaire mining rights for exploration and exploitation of certain minerals, that is to say, to the performance of mining activities previously reserved for the State.

In addition, through the Mining Titles of the concessions of exploitation, the State grants the concessionaire the exclusive right to extract a specific mineral, guarantying the exclusive right of the concessionaire to profit the extracted mineral, excluding any other third party from such activities. In such context, all the assets acquired and used by the concessionaire to perform the State's reserved and granted mining activity, that is, the exploitation or extraction of certain minerals, are the only one's subject to reversion in the terms provided in article 102 of the 1999 Mines Law.

Regarding such reversion, in addition to the referred provision of the Mines Law, it is common to find in the Title of the concession (mining titles), specific provisions referred to the reversion of assets, in which is considered as accepted by the parties that the construction projects and permanent improvements, in addition to machinery, utensils, tools and materials, including facilities, accessories and equipment, and any other assets used for the purpose of the object of the concession (extraction of mineral) and forming integral part of it, irrespective of the cause of acquisition, shall pass in full ownership to the State free of encumbrances or charges, without any compensation, upon the termination of the concession for any cause.

As a result, at the extinction of mining concessions, only the assets acquired or used by the concessionaire for the purpose of the mining exploitation activity (extraction of minerals) that is reserved to the State, which is the one granted through the concession, (different to the exclusive rights to profit from such mineral), are to be considered as reversionary assets. Conversely, any other assets acquired or used by the concessionaire for purposes other than the referred mining activity (exploitation of certain minerals), are to be considered as non-reversionary assets.

These assets acquired by the concessionaire for the purpose of activities different from those reserved to the State, and particularly related to the benefit or transformation of the extracted mineral, are of its own ownership and remain on his property after the extinction of the concession, not being subject to reversion. These different activities are considered in the Mines Law as "related or ancillary activities to mining activities" (article 86), and not as mining activities object of the concessions themselves, because they are not reserved to the State; being nonetheless expressly established that the National Executive by way of a Decree, could decide to reserve them to the State, regarding specific minerals (article 86).

Among these activities different from the object of the concession (exploitation of the mineral granted) are many activities generally offered to be accomplished by the concessionaire in the so called Special Advantages included in the Mining Titles, such as to incorporate, when considered possible or convenient, national value added for metallurgic, refining, manufacture or industrialization of the extracted minerals,; to establish the needed companies related to the transformation of the mineral object of the concession if it demonstrated to be beneficial; and to continue the development of industrial application activities of the minerals, by means of contributing with adequate technology, and to create industrial entities in areas still not existing in the country.

In such cases, none of those activities are in general reserved to the State, and could be freely performed as industrial activities by individuals, including the concessionaire in the mining concessions, without any additional concession required, and only subject to the general supervision power of the State, and in particular, to the administrative authorizations related to land use (*ordenación del territorio*) and to environment protection.

This situation of mining activities not subject to concessions, carried on by the concessionaire itself of by others for the purpose of industrial or manufacturing processes of the mineral extracted according to the concession existed, has been a common trend on the mining activities, as was the case, for instance, before the 2008 steel industry,[128] and cement industry nationalizations.[129] Those activities, not being subject to concessions because up to that date they were not reserved to the State, were then the ones reserved to the State or nationalized. In such cases, before the enactment of such statutes, only the corresponding exploitation mining activities for iron material extraction or rocks extraction were the ones subjected to concessions.

In the case of many mining concessions, in which in addition to the mining activities object of the concessions (exploitation of certain mineral), the concessionaire, even according to the so-called Special Advantage Clauses of the Mining Titles, may develop ancillary or related industrial activities for the processing of the extracted mineral and for the production, for instance, of some refined sub-product. For such purpose, the concessionaire can build a processing structure of its exclusive ownership outside or in the same site of the concession, which nonetheless is not part of the object of the concession (exploitation of certain mineral). Therefore, all the assets and machinery acquired and used for the purposes of such industrial activities that are not the object of the concession, are not to be considered as reversionary assets. That is, since this facilities, machinery, utensils and tools are not used for the mining activities that are the object of the concession (exploitation of certain mineral), and consequently, as non-reversionary assets, they are to remain of the exclusive property of the concessionaire.

In the same sense, for instance, all the stockpiled of processed and sub product minerals that are produced by the same industrial machinery prior to the extinction

128 Decree Law N° 6,058, *Official Gazette* N° 38.928, of 12 May 2008.

129 Decree Law N° 6091, *Official Gazette* Extra. N° 886 of 18 June 2008.

of the concessions, and that remained in the concession's site or in other deposits, are also of the exclusive property of the concessionaire, and to be considered as non-reversionary asset.

C. Differentiation between the Granted Mining Activities and Ancillary and Related Mining Activities

As stated previously, the differentiation in the mining concession between mining activities that the concessionaire must carry out in compliance with the objective of the concession such as exploitation of the mineral granted, and those that the concessionaire may carry out outside the objective of the concession, such as subsidiary or related activities, derived from Title V of the Mines Law of 1999 ("Related or subsidiary mining activities "), giving rise to the distinction between mining exploitation activity that could be considered as the "primary activity" in the concession, and the "matters that are subsidiary or related to mining" such as activities of "storage, possession, processing, transportation, circulation and commerce of minerals" which are those regulated in Article 86 of the Law.

A differentiation of this nature, as aforementioned, could be identified in hydrocarbons subject matter. According to the Organic Law of Nationalization of the Oil Industry of 1975,[130] and subsequently, according to the Organic Law of Hydrocarbons of 2001,[131] in addition to the participation of private companies in primary activities of petroleum exploitation that were reserved for the State, individuals and private companies could also participate and continued participating by means of operating agreements and joint venture agreements in unreserved activities of the industry and in the marketing of hydrocarbons, especially providing services or carrying out construction projects (related activities) by means of contracts signed with companies of the State.[132]

It was precisely those activities not reserved to the State, referred to ancillary of related matters of the oil industry that, in 2009, were reserved for the State by means of the Organic law that reserves for the State the assets and services related to primary activities of hydrocarbons.[133] This law in effect reserved for the State, due to its strategic nature, "the assets and services related to the primary activities provided in the Organic Law of Hydrocarbons" (Art. 1) that "previously were carried out directly by Petróleos de Venezuela, S.A., (PDVSA) and its affiliates and which were outsourced, due to being essential for the development of its activities" (Art. 2).

Derived from such Law also is the differentiation between primary activities and related or subsidiary activities; which is in general also clearly established in the mining concessions Titles, in which, on the one hand, as a "primary activity" is identified as the object of the concessions for "exploitation," that is, the exclusive right to extract certain minerals conferred to the concessionaire, thereby excluding

130 Organic Law reserving for the State the industry and commerce of hydrocarbons, Special Edition *Official Gazette* N° 1769 of 29 August 1975.

131 *Official Gazette* N° 37,323 of November 13 2001.

132 For such purpose the Law of Regularization of Private Participation in Primary Activities Provided in Decree N° 1,510 with Force of Organic Hydrocarbons Law, in *Official Gazette* N° 38,419 of 18 April 2006.

133 *Official Gazette* N° 39.173 of 7 May 2009

any other individual. That primary activity of exploitation is the one reserved for the State and granted to the concessionaire by means of the concession.

On the other hand, the concessionaire also has the by means of the concession the exclusive right to profit the extracted mineral, generally derived from the offered special advantages for the establishment of an industry connected with transformation of the extracted mineral, or the incorporation of national value added through metallurgy, refining, manufacture or industrialization of such extracted mineral, which are activities related or subsidiary to the primary mining one. Such industrial development activities, in general referred to in the special advantages offered by the concessionaire, are not the object of the concession (which is the exploitation of certain minerals) but rather a related or subsidiary activity like the activity of "processing" the extracted mineral referenced in Article 86 of the Mines Law of 1999. In this context, "processing" means the transformation of the extracted mineral of the concessions for conversion into another mineral, which is derived from the concessionaire's right not only to extract the mineral but to profit it exclusively. In the case of processing or transformation of the mineral extracted, once processed in the industrial construction installed in the concession zone, it produces a sub product that is of the exclusive property of the concessionaire.

The latter is also based on Article 546 of the Civil Code, which provides that "the product or value of legal work or industry...of any person, is their property and is governed by the laws related to property in general and special applicable laws." The product of work or industry developed by a concessionaire in the exercise of the mining extracting rights that were granted by the State are the property of the concessionaire. Moreover, in these cases, according to Article 552 of the Civil Code, the concessionaire also acquires ownership by accession of minerals produced in the exercise of the mining rights. Such rule provides that "the natural fruits" belong "by right of accession to the owner of the thing that produces them", defining as "the natural fruits" "those that come directly from the thing, with or without industry of man" such as "products from mines and quarries." Therefore, all minerals extracted from the exploitation of concessions, in the exercise of the mining rights, according to this rule, are assets that belong to the owner of the mining rights under the concession, which is the right in rem over real property that produces it, through which the holder acquires them by accession.

The mineral extracted by the concessionaire is owned by the concessionaire as well as the sub product produced in the industrial structure, when established by the concessionaire in compliance with one of the special advantages offered in the concession. At the extinction pf the concession, such assets will continue to be owned by the concessionaire as long as they are not assigned or abandoned. Such assets produced by the concessionaire therefore could not be "acquired" by the State except through expropriation, and never by "occupation" under Article 797 of the Civil Code. This law provides that "things *that are not the property of anyone,* but may become the property of someone, are acquired by occupation," listing among them "animals that are used for hunting or fishing, valuables and abandoned movable property." The extracted mineral in a concession as well as the sub products produced by the work of the concessionaire in processing and transforming the extracted mineral, could not be considered "not the property of anyone." On the contrary, they are the property of the concessionaire, given that they have been extracted and produced when the concession was in effect.

IV. SOME PRINCIPLES RELATED TO THE OIL INDUSTRY (HYDROCARBONS LAW)

1. The Nationalization of the Oil Industry and the modality for private companies to participate in the exploration and exploitation of Oil

In 1975, the oil industry and commerce in Venezuela were nationalized by means of the 1975 Organic Law Reserving to the State the Industry and Commerce of Hydrocarbons[134] (1975 Organic Nationalization Law), issued in application of Article 97 of the 1961 Constitution, equivalent to Article 302 of the 1999 Constitution. This nationalization of the Oil Industry was implemented by means of the same 1975 Organic Nationalization Law, which (i) reserved the activity to the State, (ii) terminated the then existing concessions for the exploration and exploitation of oil in the country that were assigned to foreign enterprises and granted according to the Hydrocarbon Law of 1943, and (iii) provided a procedure for the expropriation of private assets engaged in the activity, including the payment of compensation.

Article 5 of the 1975 Organic Nationalization Law, provided:

> "*Article 5*: The State shall exercise the activities indicated in article 1 of this Law [[135]] directly by the National Executive or through entities of its ownership, being able to enter into the operating agreements necessary for the better performance of its functions, but in no case shall these activities affect the very essence of the assigned activities.

In special cases and when it may be convenient to the public interest, the National Executive or the entities referred to may, in the exercise of any of the mentioned activities, enter into association agreements with private entities, with a participation such that guarantees control by the State, and with a determined duration. In order to enter into these agreements, the prior authorization by the [Congress] Chambers in joint session shall be required, within the conditions they establish, once they have been duly informed by the National Executive of all the pertinent circumstances."

Under Article 5 of the Organic Nationalization Law, the participation of private companies in oil industry activities in Venezuela was limited to two types of contractual relationship with the State or its public enterprises (PDVSA and its affiliates): (i) "Operating Agreements" for the performance of activities which were not to affect the essence of the reserved activities; and (ii), "Association

---

134 *Official Gazette Extraordinaria* N° 1.769 of August 29, 1975.

135 Article 1 reserved to the State all matters "related to the exploration of the national territory in search for petroleum, asphalt and any other hydrocarbons; to the exploitation of reservoirs thereof, the manufacturing or upgrading, transportation by special means and storage; internal and external trade of the exploited and upgraded substances, and the works required for their handling ..." (*Id.*, Article 1)

Agreements" designed to establish a partnership between PDVSA and private companies controlled by the State.[136]

Pursuant to the 1975 Organic Nationalization Law and the public policy called the Oil Opening (*Apertura Petrolera*) developed in Venezuela during the 1990's, private oil companies did in fact participate in primary hydrocarbon activities in Venezuela through Operating Agreements, Association Agreements for the Exploration at Shared-Risk-and-Profit (also referred to as Shared-Risk-and-Profit Exploration Agreements) and Association Agreements for the development of the Orinoco Oil Belt (*Faja Petrolífera del Orinoco*). These agreements were authorized and signed by subsidiaries of PDVSA and private oil companies during 1994-2001.

Article 126 of the 1961 Constitution provided that as a matter of principle "contracts of national interest" needed to be approved by both Chambers of Congress. Article 5 of the 1975 Organic Nationalization Law required that "Association Agreements" be submitted to prior legislative authorization by the Venezuelan Congress. Specifically, Article\provided that in order to sign the Association Agreements "the prior authorization by the [Congress] Chambers in joint session shall be required, within the conditions they establish, once they have been duly informed by the National Executive of all the pertinent circumstances." Accordingly, various "Association Agreements" (also known as "Strategic Associations") for the development of the Orinoco Oil Belt were authorized by the Venezuelan Congress between August 1993 and October 1997.[137] These *Acuerdos* of the former Venezuelan Congress (as well as the acts of the current National Assembly pursuant to Article 150 of the 1999 Constitution), whether of approval or of authorization of "contracts of national interest" signed by public entities are considered "parliamentary acts without the form of Statute" in the Venezuelan Constitutional law system.[138] Although they are not statutes, they have the same constitutional "rank of a law."[139] They are acts issued by the legislative body in direct execution of the Constitution. For that reason, they can be challenged for judicial review only before the court exercising "Constitutional Jurisdiction" (*Jurisdicción Constitucional*).[140] In the 1961 Constitution, the *Jurisdicción*

---

136 Regarding the interpretation of article 5 of LOREICH, and the participation of private companies in the oil industry activities, see: Isabel Boscán de Ruesta et al, *La Apertura Petrolera, I Jornadas de Derecho de Oriente*, Fundación Estudios de Derecho administrativo, Caracas 1997. See in general, Allan R. Brewer-Carías (Director) *Régimen Jurídico de las nacionalizaciones en Venezuela*, Vol. III, Archivo de Derecho Público y Ciencias de la Administración, Instituto de Derecho Público, Universidad Central de Venezuela, Caracas 1981.

137 See for instance, *Official Gazette* N° 36.224 of June 10, 1997; *Official Gazette* N° 36.313 of October 15, 1997.

138 See Allan Brewer-Carías, *Principios Fundamentales del Derecho Público*, Editorial Jurídica Venezolana, Caracas 2005, pp. 31, 101, 154.

139 *Id.* See also, Allan R. Brewer-Carías, "El régimen nacional de los hidrocarburos aplicable al proceso de la apertura petrolera en el marco de la reserva al Estado de la Industria Petrolera," in *La apertura petrolera, I Jornadas de Derecho de Oriente*, Fundación de Estudios de Derecho Administrativo FUNEDA, Caracas, 1997, pp. 2-3. See text in www.allanbrewercarias.com (Biblioteca Virtual, II.4 Artículos y Estudios, N° 360, 1997).

140 See Allan R. Brewer-Carías, *La Justicia Constitucional. Procesos y Procedimientos Constitucionales*, Instituto Mexicano de Derecho Procesal Constitucional, Ed. Porrúa, 2007, pp. 277-278, 303-305.

Constitucional was attributed to the Supreme Court of Justice in Whole Chamber (Article 215). Under the 1999 Constitution, this authority currently falls on the Constitutional Chamber of the Supreme Tribunal of Justice (Article 336.1).

It must be mentioned that in 1995 a group of individuals, including former members of Congress, initiated a popular action[141] before the Venezuelan Supreme Court of Justice challenging the constitutionality of the initial parliamentary act authorizing the Framework of Conditions for the "Association Agreements for the Exploration at Risk of New Areas and the Production of Hydrocarbons under the Shared-Profit Scheme" *("Convenios de Asociación para la exploración a riesgo de nuevas áreas y la producción de hidrocarburos bajo el esquema de ganancias compartidas")* (also known as Shared-Risk-and Profit Exploration Agreements) dated July 4, 1995.[142] That proceeding concluded with the Supreme Court decision of August 17, 1999 rejecting the action and upholding the constitutionality of the Congressional authorization issued according to the 1975 Organic Nationalization Law.[143] The court referred *inter alia* to the "administrative" character of those agreements,[144] based on the fact that they were intended to accomplish activities that were expressly reserved to the State. It also reasoned that by sanctioning Article 5 of the 1975 Organic Nationalization Law, Congress had sought "to optimize the use of those oil resources," making "more flexible the reserve regime" by empowering the State "for the better accomplishment of its functions" to exercise such activities "by means of entities owned by the State and also to enter into Association Agreements with private entities."[145]

The Supreme Court's decision in that case –which has *erga omnes* effects, in the sense that it is binding on all lower courts in Venezuela–[146] amounts to a ratification by the Supreme Court of the consistency of "Association Agreement" contracts with the legal framework for the regulation of the hydrocarbons industry in Venezuela. This 1999 Supreme Court decision put an end to the legal debate on the constitutionality of the "Shared-Risk and-Profit Exploration Agreements" with a reasoning that generally applies to other Association Agreements entered into under Article 5 of the 1975 Organic Nationalization Law.[147] In conclusion, the Operation

---

141 In Venezuela, statutes can be directly challenged before the Constitutional Chamber of the Supreme Tribunal of Justice on grounds of their unconstitutionality, by any individual without specific standing conditions. That is why it is called a "popular action" that anybody can file. See Allan R. Brewer-Carías, *La Justicia Constitucional. Procesos y Procedimientos Constitucionales*, Instituto Mexicano de Derecho Procesal Constitucional, Ed. Porrúa, 2007, pp. 279-80.

142 *Official Gazette* N° 35.754 of July 17, 1995.

143 The Court declared "*sin lugar*" (*i.e.* dismissed) the motion seeking the unconstitutionality of the parliamentary act (*Acuerdo*). See the text of the decision in Allan R. Brewer-Carías (Compilator), *Documentos del juicio de la Apertura Petrolera (1996-1999),* Caracas 2004, in www.allanbrewercarias.com (Biblioteca Virtual, I.2. Documentos, N° 22, 2004), pp. 280-328. I acted as counsel for PDVSA in this proceeding, defending the constitutionality of the *Acuerdo.*

144 *Id.,* pp. 312-315.

145 *Id.,* pp. 305, 309-310.

146 See Allan R. Brewer-Carías, *La Justicia Constitucional (Procesos y Procedimientos Constitucionales)*, Editorial Porrúa, Instituto Mexicano de Derecho Procesal Constitucional, México 2007, p. 339.

147 In 2001 the government applied the Oil Opening policy and made use of the provisions in Article 5 of the 1975 Organic Nationalization Law, when it sought legislative authorization for a

and Association Agreements entered into until 2001 between public enterprises of the Venezuelan oil industry and private companies to implement the Oil Opening public policy, were fully consistent with the legal framework governing the Venezuelan petroleum industry at the time they were signed. [148]

In 2001 a new Hydrocarbon Organic Law was sanctioned through Decree Law N° 1510 of November 2, 2001,[149] and entered in force on January 1, 2002. Ratifying the nationalization status of the Oil Industry, it established a different modality for the participation of private capital in primary activities of the Oil Industry, discarding the modality of Operation Agreements or of Strategic Agreements set forth in the 1975 Organic Nationalization Law, and substituting it, by allowing such participation of private capital as minority shareholders in mixed enterprises controlled by the State with its majority shareholding (article 22).[150]

This new 2001 Hydrocarbon Organic Law that substituted the previous 1943 Hydrocarbon Law (reformed in 1955 and 1967), was enacted as an "Organic Law" only because it expressly abrogated among other statutes, two previous "organic laws": the 1975 Nationalization Organic Law, and the 1998 Organic Law for the Opening of the Internal Market of Gasoline and other Hydrocarbon products for the

---

Strategic Association Agreement between Bitúmenes Orinoco (BITOR), a public enterprise subsidiary of PDVSA and the China National Oil and Gas Exploration and Development Corporation, a subsidiary of China National Petroleum Corporation (the BITOR Agreement). The object of the agreement was the production of bitumen and the design, construction and operation of a unit for production and emulsification of natural bitumen for the elaboration of *orimulsión*. The agreement was authorized by the National Assembly on December 17, 2001 (*Official Gazette* N° 37.347 of December 17, 2001), just days before the entry into force of the new 2001 Hydrocarbons Organic Law (January 1, 2002). (*Official Gazette* N° 37.323 November 13, 2001.) Notably, the 2001 Organic Hydrocarbons Law was enacted by Decree-Law N° 1510 of November 2, 2001, that is almost two months before the BITOR Agreement was authorized and signed. But the approval of the BITOR Agreement was possible because, when enacting the 2001 Organic Hydrocarbons Law, the National Executive included a provision postponing its entry into force until January 1, 2002, that is, after the BITOR agreement was already authorized and signed. See the comments in Allan R. Brewer-Carías, "La estatización de los convenios de asociación que permitían la participación del capital privado en las actividades primarias de hidrocarburos suscritos antes de 2002, mediante su terminación anticipada y unilateral y la confiscación de los bienes afectos a los mismos," in Víctor Hernández Mendible (Coordinador), *Nacionalización, Libertad de Empresa y Asociaciones Mixtas*, Editorial Jurídica Venezolana, Caracas 2008, pp. 123-188. Also in www.allanbrewercarias.com (Biblioteca Virtual, II.4 Artículos y Estudios, N° 559, 2008, pp. 17-18).

148 *Cf.* Allan R. Brewer-Carías, "El régimen nacional de los hidrocarburos aplicable al proceso de la apertura petrolera en el marco de la reserva al Estado de la Industria Petrolera," in *La apertura petrolera, I Jornadas de Derecho de Oriente*, Fundación de Estudios de Derecho Administrativo FUNEDA, Caracas, 1997, pp. 145-172. Also in www.allanbrewercarias.com (Biblioteca Virtual, II.4 Artículos y Estudios, N° 360, 1997)

149 *Official Gazette* N° 37.323 of November 13, 2001.

150 See Isabel Boscán de Ruesta, *La actividad petrolera y la nueva ley Orgánica de Hidrocarburos,* Funeda, Caracas 2002; Allan R. Brewer-Carías, "El régimen de participación del capital privado en las industrias petrolera y minera: Desnacionalización y regulación a partir de la Constitución de 1999", en *VII Jornadas Internacionales de Derecho Administrativo Allan R. Brewer-Carías, El Principio de Legalidad y el Ordenamiento Jurídico-Administrativo de la Libertad Económica,* Caracas noviembre 2004. Fundación de Estudios de Derecho Administrativo FUNEDA, Caracas 2004, pp. 15-58.

use of Automobiles.[151] According to article 218 of the Constitution, "Laws are abrogated by other laws," so any "organic law" can only be abrogated by other "organic law". Consequently, for abrogating the aforementioned 1975 Nationalization Organic Law and the 1998 Organic Law for the Opening of the Internal Market of Gasoline and other Hydrocarbon products for the use of Automobiles, the new Hydrocarbon Law needed to have the same "organic law" character and rank. No other significance or meaning in this case has the character of "organic law" given to the 2001 Hydrocarbon Organic Law. The concept of "organic law," has precise contours in the 1999 Constitution, where according to its article 203, four categories of "organic laws" can be distinguished, following two criteria: one, of a formal-technical character, referred to two categories: (i) the organic laws denominated as such in the Constitution or (ii) qualified as such by the National Assembly; and the other, of a substantive character, referred to (iii) the organization of the branches of government or to (iv) the development of constitutional rights.[152] In all these cases, except regarding the first category, the Constitutional Chamber of the Supreme Tribunal must decide in an *a priori* judicial review procedure on the constitutionality of the qualification of the "organic" character of the law (Article, 203). For such purpose the statutes must be sent to the Constitutional Chamber before their promulgation, and if the Chamber considers that the statute is not an organic law, it will lose this character.[153] This verification of the constitutionality of the "organic" character of a law also apply when the latter is sanctioned by means of Decree Law issued by the national Executive in case of legislative delegation (Enabling Laws). In the case of the 2001 Hydrocarbon Organic Law, it was submitted to the constitutional scrutiny by the Constitutional Chamber of the Supreme Tribunal, which by means of the decision No. 2264 of November 13, 2001[154] concluded declaring the constitutionality of the organic character of the Law, based among other arguments on the fact that it was "a frame law that constitutes the basis for the development of a specific legislation to be applied in each type of activity related to the hydrocarbon matter."

The legal consequence of the changing of the modality of participation of private capital in the primary hydrocarbon activities oil industry, reducing it to the constitution of mixed companies with a majority shareholding participation of the State in their capital, was that since January 1, 2002 no new Operating Agreements or Exploration at Risk and Profit Sharing Strategic Agreements (according to the repealed 1975 Nationalization Organic Law) could be subscribed, and the only possibility for private oil companies to participate in the future in primary hydrocarbon activities was through capital participation as minority shareholders in mixed companies controlled by the State as a majority shareholder. Therefore,

---

151 *Official Gazette* N° 36.537 of September 11, 1998.

152 Decision N° 537/2000 of the Constitutional Chamber, Supreme Tribunal of Justice.

153 The main formal special provisions regarding the organic laws is that also, except for the first category, in all the others cases the corresponding draft must be admitted for discussion, by the National Assembly, by a vote of the two third of the present members before beginning the debate of the draft statute; a majority that also apply in cases of reforms to organic laws (article 203). See Allan R. Brewer-Carías, *La Constitución de 1999. derecho Constitucional Venezolano*, Editorial Jurídica Venezolana, Caracas 2004, Vol. I, pp. 447 ff.

154 Expediente 01-2572.

regarding the Association Agreements, the main effect of the 2001 Hydrocarbon Organic Law, by abrogating the 1975 Nationalization Organic Law, was only to eliminate the possibility for any new Agreements to be entered into after January 1, 2002. That is why, for instance, between November and December 2001, the Government rush to obtain the legislative authorization and signing of the aforementioned Association Agreement between the public enterprise BITOR and the Chinese Oil enterprise for Bitumen and *Orimulsión* exploitation (December 17, 2001), after the sanctioning (November 2, 2001), and publishing (November 13, 2001) the new Law, but before it entered into effect which was postponed until January 1, 2002).

In any case, this main effect of the 2001 Hydrocarbon Organic Law was later expressly included in the 2006 Law Regulating Private Participation in Primary Activities regarding the Operative Agreements [155] by stating that:

> "[…] no future contract shall authorize any private, natural or legal person to participate in activities of exploration, production, storage or initial transportation of liquid hydrocarbons, or in the benefits derived from the production of such hydrocarbons, unless such person is a minority shareholder of a mixed company, incorporated pursuant the Organic Hydrocarbons Law where the State is assured shareholding and operational control of the company" (Art. 3).

By this provision, this 2006 statute ratified the principle already set forth in the 2001 Hydrocarbons Organic Law, when providing that private capital could only participate in primary activities by incorporating into mixed companies with the State regulated by the Law.

The 2001 Hydrocarbon Organic Law provided nothing regarding the situation of the previously established and in force modalities of participation of private enterprises in the Oil Industry, like the Association Agreements. Those were valid contracts subscribed according the applicable statutes existing at the time of their authorization, and in particular, according to the provisions of the 1975 Nationalization Organic Law. Those contracts, which were not modified by the provisions of the new 2001 Hydrocarbon Organic Law, continued to have their legal and contractual effects according to the applicable law. In this regard, the 2001 Hydrocarbon Organic Law, contrary for example to what was established the 1943 Hydrocarbon Law regarding the old concessions and the provisions for their possible and voluntary adaptation into the new concessions set forth in that Law; did not establish any kind of provisions seeking for the possible voluntary adaptation of the existing Association Agreements into the modality of the mixed enterprises with majority shareholding of the State. On the other hand, no compulsory adaptation was possible to be included because that would have meant to give retroactive effects to the Organic Law, which is prohibited in article 24 of the Constitution. Consequently, after the 2001 Organic Law on Hydrocarbons was published, in light of the general principle of Venezuelan law of the non-retroactive effects of laws (Article 24 of the 1999 Constitution), the provisions of the abrogated 1975 Nationalization Organic Law as the Applicable Law, remained in force regarding

155 *Official Gazette* Nº 38.419 of April 18, 2006.

the Agreements Association signed according to its provisions, as validly and in force contracts executed by the State.

2. The process for the adaptation of the private companies' participation to the 2001 Hydrocarbon Law regime

Starting in 2006, Venezuela initiated a process of "*statization*"[156] of the Oil Industry by eliminating or reducing private capital participation in the oil industry activities changing the regime conceived before the 2001 Organic Hydrocarbons Law was enacted. This process of eliminating or sharply reducing private capital's participation in the industry was achieved through three legislative instruments: Firstly, by the *Law Regulating Private Participation in Primary Activities,* of April 2006, that declared the extinction or rather the early and unilateral termination of the existing Operating Agreements. Secondly, by the *Decree-Law Nº 5200 Concerning the Migration of the Association Agreements of the Orinoco Belt and of the Exploration at Risk and Profit Sharing Agreements into Mixed Companies,* of February 2007, which initiated the process tending to the early and unilateral termination of the existing Association and Exploration at Risk and Profit Sharing Agreements entered into between 1993 and 2001, although providing, however, in the latter case, the possibility for such association agreements to be transformed into new mixed companies with minimum 50% State equity participation according to the 2001 Organic Hydrocarbon Law, Articles 22 and 27 to 32); and Thirdly, by the *Law on the Effects of the Migration Process to Mixed Companies of the Orinoco Belt Association Agreements and the Exploration at Risk and Profit-Sharing Exploration Agreements,* of October 2007, which formally extinguished the Agreement, in the sense of establishing date of their termination, "confiscating" the interests, shares, participation and rights of the private companies parties to such Agreements and Associations that did not reach the agreements for their participation in the new mixed companies

Pursuant to the first two laws, by the taking of the assets of the private parties to the existing public contracts, according to the Constitution, an expropriation process was to be initiated concerning the contractual rights corresponding to the private contracting companies, although carried out directly by a statute, as provided in the Expropriations Law (2001). This two Laws, however, pursuant to Article 115 of the Constitution, generated inalienable rights for the contracting companies to be fairly compensated for the damages (expropriation of assets and contractual rights) arising from the taking of their participation in the public contracts validly entered into by the State.

156 We use the word "statization" (*estatización*) in order to distinguish this process from the "nationalization" one, which in the Venezuelan constitutional system combines the decision to reserve to the State certain activities followed by the expropriation (by means of compensation) of the assets affected to the corresponding the activities. In the process developed in 2006-2007, the reserve to the State was already established in the 2001 Hydrocarbon Law, and the termination of the Agreements was made without compensation. See regarding the concept of nationalization in Venezuela, Allan R. Brewer-Carías, "Introducción al Régimen Jurídico de las Nacionalizaciones en Venezuela", in *Archivo de Derecho Público y Ciencias de la Administración*, Vol. III, 1972-1979, Tomo I, Instituto de Derecho Público, Facultad de Ciencias Jurídicas y Políticas, Universidad Central de Venezuela, Caracas 1981, pp. 23-44.

Nevertheless, according to the last of the above-mentioned laws, what formally terminated the Agreements and that could have initially been seen as the beginning of an expropriation process, became a "confiscation" of rights in the case of the companies that did not reach an agreement with the State to continue operating under the new imposed formula of mixed companies.

A. The extinction of the operating agreements

In fact, regarding the Operating Agreements executed pursuant to the former legislation between Petróleos de Venezuela S.A. (PDVSA) affiliates and private companies for the exploitation of primary hydrocarbons, the *Law Regulating Private Participation in Primary Activities*[157] passed on April 18, 2006 has as its specific purpose, to declare by Law their extinction, because their exercise as provided in article 1, had: "been denaturalized by the Operating Agreements that arose as a result of the so-called Oil Opening, to a point where it violated the higher interests of the State and the basic elements of sovereignty".

Hence, Article 2 of the Law declared that the content of the above-mentioned Operating Agreements that arose as a result of the Oil Opening process was "incompatible with the rules set forth in the oil nationalization regime," providing moreover "that they will be extinguished and the execution of their precepts will no longer be possible as of the publication of this Law in the *Official Gazette*" (Art. 2).

This means that on its April 18, 2006 publication date, a National Assembly statute terminated and extinguished all existing Operating Agreements, thus prematurely and unilaterally terminating validly executed public contracts. This was not the unilateral administrative rescission of a public contract by the contracting public Administration, in this case PDVSA affiliates, but an early and unilateral termination of such contracts by a decision of a State legislative body, through a new Law. In such cases, the State's liability for the damages caused by the unilateral and premature termination of the contracts and the co-contractors' right to compensation are unquestionable under the public contracts ("administrative contracts") régime, since the termination constitutes an expropriation of rights, even if the decision had been taken by means of a legislative act[158]. Moreover, the Law in question provided, in advance, that:

> "[...] no future contract shall authorize any private, natural or legal person to participate in activities of exploration, production, storage or initial transportation of liquid hydrocarbons, or in the benefits derived from the production of such hydrocarbons, unless such person is a minority shareholder of a mixed company, incorporated pursuant the Organic Hydrocarbons Law where the State is assured shareholding and operational control of the company" (Art. 3).

By this provision, the new statute legislatively ratified the principle set forth in the 2001 Hydrocarbons Organic Law, whereby private capital could only participate in

157 *Official Gazette* N° 38.419 of April 18, 2006.

158 See Allan R. Brewer-Carías, "Algunas reflexiones sobre el equilibrio financiero en los contratos administrativos y la aplicabilidad en Venezuela de la concepción amplia de la Teoría del Hecho del Príncipe", in *Revista Control Fiscal y Tecnificación Administrativa*, Año XIII, N° 65, Contraloría General de la República, Caracas 1972, pp. 86-93.

primary activities by incorporating into mixed companies with the State regulated by the Law, which was exactly what was proposed in the Constitutional Reform Draft that was rejected by referendum in 2007.[159]

The consequence of declaring the extinction of the existing Operating Agreements, apart from the State's obligation to indemnify the former contractors for the damages caused by the early and unilateral termination of the Agreements and the expropriation of their contractual rights, over which, however, the Law provided nothing in its text, was that, pursuant to Article 4 of the Law:

> "[...] the Republic, either directly or through its wholly-owned companies, will reassume the exercise of the oil activities performed by private parties, in order to guarantee the continuity of such activities and by reason of their public utility and social interest, without prejudice to the incorporation of mixed companies to such end, subject to approval by the National Assembly and prior favorable report by the National Executive through the Ministry of Energy and Petroleum and by the National Assembly's Permanent Energy and Mines."

To such end the National Assembly had already adopted in March 2006 the "Accord approving the Terms and Conditions for the creation and operation of Mixed Companies."[160]

B. The takeover by the state of the Operation of the Association Agreements and of the private parties' participation in those agreements

The "Enabling" Law (Legislative Delegation Law) of February 1, 2007[161] authorized the President of the Republic to dictate legislation that would allow the State to:

> "[...] either directly or through wholly-owned companies, assume control of the activities performed by the associations operating in the Orinoco Belt, including upgraders and exploration at-risk and profit-sharing assignments, to regulate and adjust their activities within the legal framework governing the national oil industry, through mixed companies or wholly-owned State-own enterprises."

This legislative delegation sought, firstly, the State's assuming "control of the activities performed by the associations operating in the Orinoco Belt, including upgraders and at-risk and profit-sharing exploration assignments;" a provision that was in fact unnecessary, since that control already existed through the decision-making methodology regulated by the Association Agreements, even when the State only had a minority participating interest in them. But apart from that, secondly, what was sought by the legislative delegation was what the Legislator failed to do with the 2001 Organic Hydrocarbons Law, that is to transform the Association Agreements into mixed companies, by providing the need to "regulate and adjust

---

159 See the comments in Allan R. Brewer-Carías, *La Reforma Constitucional de 2007 (Comentarios al Proyecto inconstitucionalmente sancionado por la Asamblea Nacional el 2 de Noviembre de 2007)*, Colección Textos Legislativos, N° 43, Editorial Jurídica Venezolana, Caracas 2007, pp. 129 ss.

160 *Official Gazette*, N° 38.410 of March, 31, 2006.

161 *Official Gazette* N° 38.617 of February 1, 2007.

their activities within the legal framework governing the national oil industry, through mixed companies or wholly-owned State-own enterprises."

In order to execute such legislative delegation, on February 26, 2007, the National Executive passed the Decree-Law N° 5200 Concerning the Migration of the Association Agreements of the Orinoco Belt and of the Exploration at Risk and Profit Sharing Agreements into Mixed Companies, thereby initiating the process for the unilateral and early termination of the association agreements executed between 1993 and 2001, which, for the contractors that did not agree to the terms unilaterally fixed by the State, implied the expropriation of their contractual rights and the consequent right to be fairly compensated for the damages caused by the execution of such Law. In fact, the Decree Law provided that:

> "[...] the associations between Petróleos de Venezuela S. A. affiliates and the private sector operating in the Orinoco Belt, and in the so-called Exploration at Risk and Profit-Sharing Agreements shall be adjusted to the legal framework governing the national oil industry by becoming mixed companies pursuant to the provisions set forth in the Organic Hydrocarbons Law." (Art. 1).

In addition, the same Decree Law also provided that:

> "[...] all activities performed by strategic associations in the Orinoco Belt, involving the companies Petrozuata, S.A., Sincrudos de Oriente, S.A., Sincor, S.A., Petrolera Cerro Negro S.A. and Petrolera Hamaca, C.A; the Exploration at Risk and Profit Sharing Agreements of Golfo de Paria Oeste, Golfo de Paria Este and la Ceiba, as well as the companies or consortia incorporated in their execution; Orifuels Sinovensa, S.A., as also the affiliates of such companies that conduct business activities in the Orinoco Belt, and throughout the production chain, *will be transferred* to the new mixed companies."

For such purpose, Decree-Law N° 5.200 established various steps to be followed, each of which were to occur at or by a specified date. Accordingly, the direct effects of Decree-Law N° 5.200 with respect to the aforementioned Association Agreements were as follows:

a. The takeover of the Operation of the Association Agreements

First, the *takeover of Operations*, for which, the decree Law provided for the need to ensure the State's immediate assumption of the actual industrial operation of each Association Agreement. To such end, the Law provided that the State shareholding company of the potential mixed companies was to be *Corporación Venezolana del Petróleo, S.A.* or the Petróleos de Venezuela, S.A. affiliate designated to such effect, had to form within 7 days following the publication of the Decree-Law, that is by March 5, 2007, "a Transition Commission for each association," also providing that such Commission had to include "the current board of directors of the respective association, in order to guarantee *the transfer to the state company* of control over all the activities performed by the associations," in a process that ended of April 30, 2007 (Art. 3).

To such end, the Law provided that the private sector companies that had formed part of the association agreements were to cooperate with *Corporación Venezolana de Petróleo, S.A.* in ensuring a safe and smooth changeover of the operator (Art. 3). And in regard to the situation of the workers on the contractor payroll of the associations to be transformed, the Law provided that as of its entry into force they were to enjoy job stability and would be covered by the Oil Industry Collective Bargaining Agreement in force for the workers of Petróleos de Venezuela, S.A. (Art. 10).

Article 2 of the Law, attributed to the Ministry of People's Power for Energy and Petroleum the power, in each case, to unilaterally determine: "the appraisal of the Mixed Company, the shareholding participation of the Petróleos de Venezuela, S.A. affiliated designated to such effect, and the appropriate economic and financial adjustments" (Art. 2).

So, it was for the State to unilaterally determine, through the respective Ministry, the value of the new mixed company to be set up to substitute each Association Agreement; the shareholding participation percentage corresponding to the PDVSA affiliate to be shareholder in each mixed company substituting each Agreement, which shareholding could in no case be less than 60% of total equity; and "the appropriate economic and financial adjustments."

Moreover, Article 7 of the Law expressly provided that the infrastructure, transportation services and improvements of the Orinoco Belt associations and of the so-called Exploration at Risk and Profit-Sharing Agreements, were to be "freely used according to the guidelines which, by means of a Resolution, are issued by the Ministry of People's Power for Energy and Petroleum," for which purpose, "the costs derived from the use of such services, will be determined by common agreement between the parties, failing which, the Ministry of People's Power for Energy and Petroleum will set the conditions for their rendering."

Consequently, and summarizing, regarding the takeover of the Operation, (i) Decree-Law 5.200 ordered a "change of operator" of the project. Article 3 provided that "the Corporación Venezolana del Petróleo, S.A. or the affiliate of Petróleos de Venezuela, S.A. designated to be the shareholder of the new Mixed Companies" was required to put together a "Transition Commission for each association," to be incorporated into the board of each of the affected associations, "in order to ensure the transfer to the State company of the control over all of the activities carried out by the associations;" and (ii), the Decree Law further ordered the private companies to "cooperate with the Corporación Venezolana del Petróleo, S.A., *to effect a safe and orderly change of operator*."[162] This process was to be completed by April 30, 2007.

b. The takeover of the Participation of the private parties in the Association Agreements

Decree Law 5.200, in addition of providing for the takeover of the Operation of the Association Agreements, also provided for the takeover of Participations of the private parties in them. In effect, although the Law provided that the transfer of the Association Agreements to the State be immediate, as well as the consequent assumption of the operation of the Agreements by the corresponding state company, Article 4 of the Decree Law gave the private sector companies that had been part of the extinguished Orinoco Belt Association Agreements and the so-called Exploration at Risk and Profit Sharing Agreements, a four (4) month term starting on the date the Law was published (February 26, 2007), that is, until June 26, 2007, to "agree on the terms and conditions of their *possible participation* in the new

162 Decree-Law N° 5.200, Article 3 (emphasis added.)

Mixed Companies," understood to be with the respective Ministry, also providing that in such case they would be conceded "two (2) extra months to submit the aforementioned terms and conditions to the National Assembly for the corresponding authorization, pursuant to the Organic Hydrocarbons Law."

Now, once the four-month term had elapsed, on June 26, 2007 "without having reached an agreement on the incorporation and operation of the Mixed Companies," then the Republic, through Petróleos de Venezuela, S.A. or any of its affiliates, was to *directly take over the activities* exercised by the associations to ensure their continuity, by reason of their character of public use and social interest (Art. 5).

The Law also provided that the acts, business and agreements conducted or executed to incorporate the Mixed Companies provided in the Law, as well as the assignment or transfer of assets and any other operations that generated enrichment or supposed the transfer, transmission or sale of assets destined to form part of the patrimony of such companies, would be exempt from the payment of taxes, rates, special contributions or any other tax liability created by the Authorities.

Nothing was mentioned in the Decree Law about the rights to be indemnified to the private companies that did not reach the agreement to continue as partners of the new mixed companies. However, as mentioned above, at this stage, the process initiated for the early and unilateral termination of the Association Agreements, implied the expropriation of the assets and contractual rights of the private parties under such Agreements, giving rise according to Article 115 of the Constitution, to the right to be fairly compensated for the damages caused.

Summarizing, regarding the takeover of the Participations, (i) Article 4 of Decree-Law N° 5.200 established a period of four months from the date of publication of the decree in *Official Gazette* (February 26, 2007) for the private parties to the association agreements to agree on the terms of their possible participation in the mixed companies. That term elapsed on June 26, 2007; (ii) Article 5 provided that if that term elapsed without an agreement, the Republic of Venezuela, through Petróleos de Venezuela, S.A. or any of its affiliates designated for such purpose, "shall directly assume the activities of the associations [...] in order to preserve their continuity [...]; and (iii) In the cases in which the private party to the Agreement did not reach an agreement by the end of the term established in Article 4, Decree-Law N° 5.200 resulted in the takeover of that party's participation in the "activities" of the Association. This takeover constituted an expropriation of the private party's interest in the Joint Venture and contractual rights pertaining to the activities of the joint venture as of June 27, 2007. Since the expropriation was not accompanied by payment of compensation as required by the Constitution (Article 115), it was technically a confiscation, in violation of Venezuelan law, including Articles 115 and 116 of the 1999 Constitution.

In producing these effects, Decree-Law N° 5.200 launched a process that was intended eventually to culminate in the replacement of the association agreements by new mixed enterprises. Such a replacement would have involved (as it in fact did) the termination of the association agreements. For that reason, it can be said that Decree-Law 5.200 initiated tending to the unilateral and early termination of the Association Agreements. Strictly speaking, however, Decree-Law 5.200 did not provide for the extinction of such agreements, so much so that the Venezuelan Government had to enact a separate law, the Law on Effects of the Migration Process, to provide for such formal extinction and to establish a date certain for it.

Consequently, not only decree Law initiated the process for the unilateral and premature termination of the contracts, but it was required that if the private investor partners in the Associations that were to be extinguished agreed to their transfer to new mixed companies, they could only opt to be shareholders of the mixed companies with up to a maximum participation of 40% in their equity, and having as State shareholder the *Corporación Venezolana de Petróleo, S.A.* or another affiliate of Petróleos de Venezuela, S.A. (PDVSA), with a minimum 60% share of the equity (Art. 2). If the investing partner of an Association Agreement agreed to become a minority shareholder of the new mixed company, Article 6 of the Law provided that:

> "[...] since this is a particular circumstance of public interest, and pursuant to the sole paragraph of Article 37 of the Organic Hydrocarbons Law, the choice of the minority partners in the migration process of the associations will be made directly."

The application of this exception to the general principle of selection by means of competitive bidding as required by the 2001 Organic Hydrocarbon Law could only happen, of course, if the private company that was part or partner of the Association Agreement decided to continue in the operation by forming part, as a minority shareholder, of the new mixed company. Otherwise, according to the Organic Hydrocarbons Law, if the company was not a party to one of the former Association Agreements, but rather a new private shareholder of the new mixed company that was to take on the operations of a former Association Agreement, it would have to have been selected by means of competitive procedures (Art. 37).

If the shareholding companies of the Association Agreements that were going to be unilaterally and prematurely terminated did not reach an agreement with the National Executive to form part, as shareholders, of the new mixed companies, the effect of the Law was to expropriate their contractual rights, whereupon they were entitled, pursuant to Article 115 of the Constitution, to be fairly compensated for the damages caused by the unilateral and early termination of the public contracts.

C. Rights of the new mixed companies

Article 8 of the Law provided that the National Executive had, by Decree, to transfer to the Mixed Companies resulting from the migration process "the right to conduct their primary activities, and to also adjudicate to them the ownership or other rights over movable or immovable property belonging privately to the Republic, that may be required for the efficient exercise of such activities." Such rights, however, can be revoked "if the operators fail to comply with their obligations, in such a way as to achieve the purpose for which such rights were transferred" (Art 8). Similarly, by Resolution, the Ministry of People's Power for Energy and Petroleum had to designate "the areas in which the Mixed Companies were to conduct their primary activities, which were to be divided into lots with a maximum area of one hundred square kilometers (100 km^2)" (Art. 9).

D. Applicable law and jurisdiction

Finally, Article 13 of the Migration Law provided that: "All facts and activities associated with this Decree-Law shall be governed by National Law, and the disputes deriving therefrom shall be submitted to Venezuelan jurisdiction, as provided in the Constitution of the Bolivarian Republic of Venezuela."

In regard to this provision, it should first be remembered that all the effects produced by any law passed in Venezuela, by virtue of the principle of territoriality are in principle governed by national legislation; thus, if nothing is expressly provided otherwise in the text of the law, all juridical situations deriving from any law are governed by "National Law."

Apart from this, the Law set forth, with faulty drafting, that disputes arising from its provisions are to be submitted to Venezuelan jurisdiction and, once again, such disputes could not be resolved in any other way, unless the legislator expressly renounced Venezuelan jurisdiction. Therefore, disputes arising in regard to the migration of the former Associations to the new mixed companies, or from the agreements reached by the former partners of Association Agreements upon incorporating their companies as minority partners of the new mixed companies, can only be resolved by national jurisdiction.

Moreover, for example, disputes arising from decisions in the Decree-Law and their application are, without doubt, in principle also subject to Venezuelan jurisdiction, for example, in regard to the possibility of challenging the regulations of the Migration Law before the Constitutional Jurisdiction, by reason of their unconstitutionality, or challenging before the Contentious-Administrative Jurisdiction the administrative actions dictated by the National Executive pursuant to the Migration Law.

But this provision of article 13 of the Law, in no way implies the annulment of the existing clauses of the Association Agreements whose early and unilateral termination was resolved by Law, providing the submission of controversies deriving from the execution, performance and breach of the Association Agreements, to arbitral jurisdiction, even in Venezuela, as authorized by Article 151 of the Constitution. In other words, according to such constitutional provision, the contractors are entitled to have the disputes deriving from the execution, performance, breach and early and unilateral termination of those Association Contracts, which are in fact public contracts ("administrative contracts"), in the event that they contain arbitration clauses or clauses concerning the application of a foreign legislation or jurisdiction, aired in the manner provided therein. The contrary would mean giving retroactive effect to the Migration Law, which is prohibited by Article 24 of the Constitution which disallows the attribution of retroactive effects to legislative provisions.

Therefore, Article 13 of the 2007 Law cannot be interpreted as a regulation that could signify the "annulment" of the previous contractual clauses themselves relative to the solution of disputes that were provided in the Association Agreements that are deemed terminated, derived precisely, for example, from the State's breach of the Agreements, such as would arise from its premature termination.

3. The "Extinction" of the Association Agreements and the "Confiscation" of Interests, Shares, Participations and Rights of Companies that did not Reach an Agreement with the State to be part of Mixed Companies

A. The definitive extinction of the former Agreements and Associations

According to the aforesaid, pursuant to the Decree Law N° 5200 of February 2000, the *activities* exercised by the former strategic associations of the Orinoco Belt, comprising the companies Petrozuata, S.A., Sincrudos de Oriente, S.A., Sincor,

S.A., Petrolera Cerro Negro S.A and Petrolera Hamaca, C.A; the Exploration at Risk and Profit Sharing Agreements of Golfo de Paria Oeste, Golfo de Paria Este and la Ceiba, as well as the companies or consortia incorporated in their execution; Orifuels Sinovensa, S.A., as also the affiliates of such companies that conducted business activities in the Orinoco Belt, and throughout the production chain, were ordered to be transferred to the new mixed companies; and from such order, it resulted that some of them were incorporated into mixed companies in which private capital participated.

The incomplete provisions established in Decree Law 5200 were supposedly completed with the Law on the Effects of the Migration Process to Mixed Companies of the Orinoco Belt Association Agreements and the Exploration at Risk and Profit Sharing Agreements of October 5, 2007 (Law on Effects of the Migration Process),[163] in which, after the State's takeover of the Operation of the Association Agreements and of the Participations in them of the Private parties to the Agreements, it provided for the extinction" of that Orinoco Belt Association Agreements and Exploration at Risk and Profit Sharing Agreements to Mixed Companies. Consequently, it was precisely because Decree-Law N° 5.200 had not "extinguished" the association agreements to which that decree applied, that the Law on Effects of the Migration Process was enacted to complete what I have elsewhere called the "*statization*" process of the oil industry, by establishing a *precise date* for the termination ("extinguishment") of those association agreements.[164]

Nonetheless, the Law on Effects of the Migration Process confirmed the expropriation effected by Decree-Law N° 5.200, still without providing for due compensation. Article 2 of the Law provided for the transfer to the new mixed companies "based on the principle of reversion" of the "interests, shares and participations" in the associations covered by Decree-Law N° 5.200 and in the "assets used to realize the activities of such associations, including property rights, contractual rights and [rights] of other nature," which by the terms of the law "belonged to the enterprises of the private sector with whom no agreement was reached to migrate" until the deadline established in Article 4 of Decree-Law N° 5.200 (June 26, 2007).

The Law on Effects of the Migration Process as aforementioned, also provided for the "extinguishment" (that is, the early termination) of the association agreements as of one of two dates: (i) the date of publication in *Official Gazette* of the decree transferring the right to exercise primary activities to the mixed companies —in

---

163 *Official Gazette* N° 38.785 of October 8, 2007.

164 See Allan R Brewer-Carías, "The 'Statization of the Pre 2001 Primary Hydrocarbons Joint Venture Exploitations: Their Unilateral termination and the Assets' Confiscation of Some of the Former Private parties" in *Oil, Gas & Energy Law Intelligence*, www.gasandoil.com/ogel/ ISSN: 1875-418X, Issue Vol 6, Issue 2, (OGEL/TDM Special Issue on Venezuela: The battle of Contract Sanctity vs. Resource Sovereignty, ed. By Elizabeth Eljuri), April 2008; and "La estatización de los convenios de asociación que permitían la participación del capital privado en las actividades primarias de hidrocarburos suscritos antes de 2002, mediante su terminación anticipada y unilateral y la confiscación de los bienes afectos a los mismos," in Víctor Hernández Mendible (Coordinador), *Nacionalización, Libertad de Empresa y Asociaciones Mixtas*, Editorial Jurídica Venezolana, Caracas 2008, pp. 123-188. See also in www.allanbrewercarias.com (Biblioteca Virtual, II.4 Artículos y Estudios, N° 559, 2008)

those cases when all or some of the private parties to the respective association agreement had reached an agreement for their participation in the corresponding mixed company; or (ii) the date of publication of the Law on Effects of the Migration Process (October 8, 2007)—in those cases when none of the private parties to the respective association agreement had reached an agreement for their participation in the respective mixed company (article 1).

As was said, the *Migration Law* (Decree Law N° 5.200) had made no mention of the rights to indemnity and compensation of the private companies that had not reached an agreement to continue as partners of the new mixed companies, by virtue of the early and unilateral termination of the Agreements and Associations, which they had according to the provisions of Article 115 of the Constitution. However, this was an expropriation initiated by a special law, by passing the provisions of the general Law of Expropriations, which implied, in accordance with the Constitution, the companies' right to be indemnified.

However, instead of proceeding to do this, the State chose to definitively "confiscate" such rights by purely and simply declaring the agreements extinguished as of the publication date of the *Law on the Effects of the Migration Process to Mixed Companies of the Orinoco Belt Association Agreements and the Exploration at Risk and Profit-Sharing Agreements* of October 5, 2007. And the consequence was that the public contracting parties could not perform their obligations according to the clauses of the contract, which were in effect prior to their extinguishment, giving rise to the right of the private contracting parties to claim for damages causes by such non-performance.

B. Confiscation of the rights of the private companies that participated in the Agreements and Associations by appealing to the principle of "reversion"

For purposes of executing the confiscation, Article 2 of the *Law on the Effects of the Migration Process* expressly provided that "the interests, shares and participations" in the associations referred to in Article 1 of the Migration Law in the companies incorporated to develop the corresponding projects, and in "the assets used to conduct the activities of such associations, including property rights, contractual and other rights," which, until June 26, 2007 (pursuant to the term established in Article 4 of the aforementioned Law), "belonged to the private sector companies with whom agreement was not reached for migrating to a mixed company, *are hereby transferred, based on the principle of reversion*, without the need for any additional action or instrument, to the new mixed companies incorporated as a result of the migration of the respective associations, except for the provisions of Article 2 herein." This provision, according to the Venezuelan constitutional régime constitutes a confiscation of such assets, which is prohibited in the Constitution (Art. 116).

In other words, the State, by Law, ordered the forced transfer of privately-owned assets to the newly incorporated mixed companies without compensation or process, in all the cases where *some* of the other private companies of the respective agreement or association will have agreed to form part of the mixed companies. Article 4 of the Law clarified that in such cases "the transfers of interests, shares, participations and rights" provided in the Law "shall not generate tax liabilities in the Bolivarian Republic of Venezuela for any person or entity."

But in the cases where "*none* of the companies making up the private part of the association agreements reached an agreement to migrate to a mixed company within the established term," pursuant to Article 3 of the *Law on the Effects of the Migration Process* "the interests, shares, participations and rights" of the same were ordered kept "*as property of the affiliate* of Petróleos de Venezuela, S.A. that took over the activities of the association in question, until the National Executive determines the affiliate that will definitively perform such activities."

This is, anyway, as was said, a forced transfer of privately-owned assets to the State, declared by the Legislator, without any compensation or process whatsoever, which constitutes a confiscation prohibited under Article 116 of the Constitution. On the other hand, in these cases, in no way the takeover can be justified by recurring to the "principle of reversion", a figure that is essentially associated with the figure of activities that are reserved for the State and that are granted to individuals by means of administrative "concessions" which do not exist in hydrocarbons matters, and that is applicable only when the corresponding contract arrives to its term, once the assets being duly amortized.

In fact, one of the classic principles of administrative law in relation to the concession of public services, to the construction and use of public works and the exploitation of public domain assets, has been the necessary reversion of the service or of the works constructed to the conceding Administration once such concession is extinguished according to the term of the contract. This was a principle that sought to ensure the continuation of the rendering of the service, of the use of a public work or of an exploitation of public assets, independently of the concessionary's participation, once the concession was extinguished at its term.

However, when it is a means of extinction of the private property of the concessionary over the assets used for the service or of the works constructed, property guarantees and legal reserves impose the need for the principle of reversion being set forth in an express legal text[165] or in the contract of concession. In matters of hydrocarbons concessions, for example, the principle was established in the 1961 Constitution itself (Art. 103) and in the old Hydrocarbons Law (Art. 80), pursuant to which was enacted the 1971 "Law on assets subject to reversion in the hydrocarbons concessions"[166]. In absence of an express legal text, therefore, the reversion can only proceed if it has been expressly regulated in the concession contract[167].

This was, moreover, the orientation followed by the Organic Law for the Promotion of Private Investment under the Concessions régime[168], when providing in Article 48 relative to the "reversion of works and services" which is the

165 Moreover, in this sense, it was the 1961 Constitution (Article 103) that established the principle of the concession in hydrocarbons matters, in regard to the land (immovable property) affected by such concessions.

166 See *Official Gazette* Nº 29577 of 06-08-1971

167 As has been said by Eduardo García de Enterría and Tomás R. Fernández, under this perspective, the reversion "loses its old character of being an essential element of every concession and comes to be regarded as an accidental element of the business, that is, it is admissible only in the case of an express accord, like one more piece, when conceived in this way, of the economic formula that all concessions consist in", in their *Curso de Derecho Administrativo. I.*, Thirteenth Edition, Thomson-Civitas, Madrid 2006, p. 763

168 *Official Gazette* Nº 5394 Extra. of 25-10-1999

respective *contract* that must establish, among other elements, "the assets which, since they are associated with the work or the service in question, *will revert to the conceding entity, unless it had not been possible to amortize them during the aforementioned term.*" To such end the regulation also provides that during a prudent period prior to the termination of the contract, the conceding entity shall adopt provisions such that upon delivery of the assets to be reverted, the *conditions accorded* in the contract are verified. The regulation also provides that the contract expresses "the works, facilities or assets *not subject* to reversion to be executed by the concessionary, which, if deemed to be of public usefulness or interest, may be subject to reversion after due payment of their price to the concessionary."

Therefore, if there is no legal provision that establishes the reversion of assets in concessions of public services, public works or the use or exploitation of assets of the public domain, or if such reversion is not provided in the concession contract, then upon termination of the concession, the concessionary is not obliged to revert any asset to the Administration that has been acquired or constructed or that has been associated with the concession, nor may the Administration pretend to appropriate or take possession of them. It would only be able to do so through expropriation, according to the Constitution and the Law.

In general terms, for instance, in relation to the Orinoco Belt Association Agreements and Exploration at Risk and Profit Sharing Agreements to Mixed Companies, after establishing a term of 35 years for their termination, expressly provided that at the Date of Termination, the foreign partners were to transfer to the State Own partner company, without compensation, their part on the Joint Venture, including the interest in any entity or association and the rights and interest in all the assets and contracts of common property of the Parties regarding the projects. This provision can be considered similar to the reversion institution of concessions, but in this case, the obligatory transfer of assets is only applicable when the Agreements arrives to their precise Date of Termination, that is, after the fixed 35 years of Duration have been elapsed, which means that it is not applicable in any other case of anticipated termination of the contracts not provided in the contracts. Otherwise, it would be a confiscation forbidden by the Constitution, such as has been decreed in the *Law on the Effects of the Migration Process.*[169]

C. Applicable legal regime to the new mixed corporations

In the cases in which the foreign companies affected with the extinction of the Association Agreements, decided to participate in the new mixed companies

---

169 This Law, moreover, does not refer to "hydrocarbons concessions," which disappeared from the legal order decades ago. In a December 3, 1974 decision of the former Supreme Court of Justice (Case: *Challenge to the Law of assets affected by reversion in the oil concessions*), when referring to the reversion established in Articles 103 of the 1961 Constitution and 80 of the old Hydrocarbons Law, the Court said that "both laws contemplate the transfer of assets to the State without compensation upon extinction of the concession, and it is evident also that both the confiscation by means of which determined assets are seized from a person without any indemnity whatsoever, and the expropriation, which supposes a special compensation procedure, are figures different to reversion, by virtue of which the assets belonging to the grantor, as well as those of the concessionary, that are for the concession, return to the hands of the grantor when for any reason the concession reaches its end". See *Official Gazette* Nº 1718 Extra., of January 20, 1975, pp. 22-23.

referred to in the Decree-Law N° 5.200 establishing the mandatory "migration" of the Association Agreements and in the Law on Effects of the Migration Process, the mixed company had to be established by decision of the President in Council of Minister approving the corresponding selection of the partners, and after the Ministry of Energy and Oil, pursuant to article 33 of the Hydrocarbons Organic Law, had requested the approval of National Assembly. In such cases, the result of this process of "*statization*" of the primary hydrocarbon activities in Venezuela was the radical transformation of the legal regime applicable to the companies operating in the oil industry. Under the 1975 Nationalization Law, corporations operating in the oil industry under Association Agreements, were subject to a private law regime, that is, the legal regime that applies to commercial companies, since the majority of the shares of the incorporated operating companies were owned by the private (national of foreign). In 2008, with the foreign and national private companies that had agreed with the State to continue operating in the oil industry, a completely new set of companies were incorporated, this time with a completely different legal status, as public mixed enterprises, with the majority of shares owned by the State, and thus, considered to be part of the Venezuelan National Public Administration.

Although such new mixed public corporation, with the State as majority shareholder, were incorporated pursuant to the provisions of the Commercial Code, and therefore, as a "private law" company, however, having a public owned corporation as a majority shareholder, they had to be considered a decentralized entity part of the National Public Administration as provided in the Public Administration Organic Law.[170] It that context, such companies are part of the National Public Administration, as a tier level entities, in general having the Corporación Venezolana del Petróleo S.A., a subsidiary of PDVSA, as majority shareholder. Nonetheless, and except for its relation with the other entities and organs of Public Administration, the legal regime that governs such company is basically the private commercial law regime applicable to all corporations.[171]

In fact, as it is established by article 107 of the Public Administration Organic Law, public companies are those incorporated following the rules of private law by the Republic, the States, the Metropolitan districts and the Municipalities, or by any of the decentralized entities regulated in the Law, having more that 50% of its shares. These public companies, however, pursuant to the same provision of the Organic Law, are subject to the common private law legislation. That is why the

---

170 See article 29 of the Organic Law on Public Administration (Decree-Law N° 6.217 of July 15, 2008, *Official Gazette* N° 5890 Extra. Of July 31, 2008. See on the distiction among State's legal persons, in Allan R. Brewer-Carías, "La distinción entre las personas jurídicas y las personas privadas y el sentido de la problemática actual de la clasificación de los sujetos de derecho" in *Revista Argentina de Derecho Administrativo*, N° 17, Buenos Aires 1977, pp. 15-29; and in *Revista de la Facultad de Derecho*, N° 57, Universidad Central de Venezuela, Caracas 1976, pp. 115-135; and "Sobre las personas jurídicas en la Constitución de 1999," in *Derecho Público Contemporáneo. Libro Homenaje a Jesús Leopoldo Sánchez*, Estudios del Instituto de Derecho Público, Universidad Central de Venezuela, enero-abril 2003, Volumen 1, pp. 48-54.

171 See on the legal nature of PDVSA and its affiliates or subsidiaries, as State's legaly persons of private law, in Allan R. Brewer-Carías, "El proceso jurídico-organizativo de la industria petrolera nacionalizada en Venezuela" en *Revista de la Facultad de Ciencias Jurídicas y Políticas*, N° 58, Universidad Central de Venezuela, Caracas 1976, pp. 53-88; "Consideraciones sobre el régimen jurídico-administrativo de Petróleos de Venezuela S.A." en *Revista de Hacienda*, N° 67, Año XV, Ministerio de Hacienda, Caracas 1977, pp. 79-99.

Constitutional Chamber of the Supreme Tribunal of Justice in decision No 464 rendered on March 18th, 2002 (Case: *Interpretation of the National Constituent Assembly Decree dated January 30th, 2000, through which negotiation of the Workers Collective Convention is suspended for 180 days*) regarding second and third level public enterprises of the Oil Industry, ruled that:

> "Petróleos de Venezuela S.A. and its subsidiaries have a legal regime that allow them to be clearly differentiated, not only from the centralized Public Administration and the public corporations (*institutos autónomos*), but also from other public companies. Therefore, this Chamber must conclude that the identification of the legal nature of such legal persons of the State with private law form, implies that the legal regime applicable to such entities is a mixed regime, altogether of public and private law, although preponderantly of private law, due to their form, but not exclusively, due to the fact that their intimate relation with the State, subjects them to mandatory provisions of public law enacted to rule their organization, functioning and control by Public Administration, by the organs established for such purpose."[172]

According to such precedent and pursuant to article 29 of the Organic Law on Public Administration, PDVSA and its subsidiaries, as is the case of the aforementioned new mixed corporations, are public enterprises incorporated according to the provisions of the Commercial Code, but are also part of National Public Administration, subject in many matters to some provisions of public law.

This is precisely the case of contracts that are governed by the general regime of the Civil Code, but are also subject to the provisions governing public contracts and, in particular, those provided in the Public Contracting Law of 2008.[173] This Law, in fact, applies to all contracts for the acquisition of goods, the rendering of services, and the execution of works (art. 1), entered not only by offices and entities of the Central and Decentralized National, State and Municipal levels of government (art. 3.1), but also by the commercial societies where the latter could have shares in a proportion of 50% or more (art. 3.4), as well as those other commercial companies where the latter also could have more than the 50% of their shares (art. 3.4). In the case of the aforementioned mixed public enterprise where Corporación Venezolana de Petróleo S.A. has more than 50% of its shares, the contracts entered by such enterprise are to be considered as public contracts in the terms of the Law on Public Contracts.

---

172 See *Revista de Derecho Público,* N° 89-92, Editorial Jurídica Venezolana, Caracas 2002, pp. 219-20

173 The Law was originally published in *Official Gazette* N° 5.877 of March 14, 2008. A reform of the Law was published in *Official Gazette* N° 39.165 of April 24, 2009. On this Law see Allan R. Brewer-Carías, "Los contratos del Estado y la Ley de Contrataciones Públicas. Ámbito de aplicación," in Allan R. Brewer-Carías *et al, Ley de Contrataciones Públicas*, Editorial Jurídica Venezolana, Colección Textos legislativos N° 44 (2ª Edición Actualizada y aumentada), Caracas 2009, pp. 9-47. See in addition, Allan R. Brewer-Carías, "Sobre los Contratos del Estado en Venezuela," en *Derecho Administrativo Iberoamericano (Contratos Administrativos, Servicios públicos, Acto administrativo y procedimiento administrativo, Derecho administrativo ambiental, Limitaciones a la libertad), IV Congreso Internacional de Derecho Administrativo*, Mendoza, Argentina, 2010, pp. 837-866.; and in *Revista Mexicana Statum Rei Romanae de Derecho Administrativo,* N° 6, Homenaje al Dr. José Luis Meilán Gil, Facultad de Derecho y Criminología de la Universidad Autónoma de Nuevo León, Monterrey, Enero-Junio 2011, pp. 207-252.

D. Applicable legal regime and jurisdiction

Just as provided in the *Migration Law* (Art. 13), Article 5 of the *Law on the Effects of the Migration Process* also provided that "all the facts and activities subject to its provisions, shall be governed by the laws of the Bolivarian Republic of Venezuela, and the controversies derived therefrom shall be submitted to its jurisdiction, as provided in the Constitution of the Bolivarian Republic of Venezuela." In regard to this provision, it must also be remembered that any effect produced by any law passed in Venezuela, by virtue of the principle of territoriality, is in principle governed by the national legislation; therefore, if nothing to the contrary is provided in the text of the law, all the legal situations deriving from any law are governed by the "National Law."

What is more, this Law also provides, with poor drafting, that the controversies deriving from its provisions will be submitted to Venezuelan jurisdiction and, again, this could not be any other way, unless the legislator were to expressly renounce Venezuelan jurisdiction. Therefore, the disputes arising on occasion of the migration of the former Associations to the new mixed companies, or the agreements that may have been reached by the former partners of the Association Agreements upon incorporation, pursuant to the Law's provisions, as minority partners, can only be resolved by national jurisdiction.

Moreover, for example, the controversies deriving from the decisions contained in the Law and its application are doubtless in principle subject to Venezuelan jurisdiction, for example, insofar as the possibility of challenging, by reason of unconstitutionality, the provisions of the Law on the Effects of the Migration Process before the Constitutional Jurisdiction, or of challenging the administrative acts which, pursuant to such Law, may be dictated by the National Executive, before the Contentious-Administrative Jurisdiction.

But this by no means implies the annulment of the clauses that may be contained in the Association Agreements whose early and unilateral termination led to ordering the forced transfer of privately-owned property to the State, for example, relative to the submission of disputes deriving from the execution, performance and breach of the Association Agreements, to arbitral jurisdiction, even outside Venezuela, as authorized by Article 151 of the Constitution. So, the contractors, in such cases, are entitled to seek the resolution of disputes deriving from the execution, performance and breach of such Association Agreements, being public contracts, in the event that they contain arbitration clauses either by application of the legislation or by a foreign jurisdiction, in the manner provided in them. If it were not so, it would mean giving retroactive effect to the *Law on the Effects of the Migration Process*, which is prohibited by Article 24 of the Constitution which prohibits giving retroactive effect to legislative provisions.

Therefore, Article 5 of the *Law on the Effects of the Migration Process* cannot signify the "annulment" of prior contractual dispute-resolution clauses set forth in the Association Agreements whose private rights are being confiscated, deriving precisely, for example, from the State's breach of the Agreements, which is what is occurring with this confiscation and its indirect consequence (political regionalization).

PART SEVEN

SOME PRINCIPLES OF ADMINISTRATIVE LAW ON THE PROMOTION AND PROTECTION OF INVESTMENTS

The regulations on Foreign Investments in Venezuela has a long tradition in the country, beginning with the statutes and regulations adopted after the incorporation of Venezuela in the Cartagena Agreement (later becoming the Andean Community of Nations from which Venezuela separated in 2006), following with the sanctioning of the 1999 Investments Promotion and Protection Law,[1] and ending with the sanctioning, in 2014, of the Law on Foreign Investments,[2] which abrogated the former

I. SOME ANTECEDENTS: LEGAL REGIME RELATED TO FOREIGN INVESTMENTS ACCORDING TO THE REGULATIONS OF THE FORMER ANDEAN PACT

Foreign Investments in commercial companies in Venezuela were first regulated by Decision N° 291 by the Commission of the Cartagena Agreement of Cartagena (Andean Pact) (March 21, 1992) that establishes the Common Regime for Treatment of Foreign Capital and on Trademarks, Licenses, and Royalties.[3]

1. Definition of direct foreign investment and the distinction between foreign and national enterprises

Article 2.1 of Decision N° 291 defines direct foreign investment as the contributions from overseas, made by foreign individuals or legal entities, to the capital of an enterprise, in freely convertible currency or in physical or tangible goods such as industrial plants, new or reconditioned machinery, new or reconditioned equipment, spare parts, new parts, raw materials, and finished products. It also considers as direct foreign investments those made in national currency with funds that can be remitted abroad, and reinvestments carried out under the Foreign Investment Regime.

Decree N° 2095 of February 13, 1992,[4] which contains the Regulations for the *Common Regime*, adds the following to the definition of direct foreign investment (Art. 2):

---

1 See Decree Law N° 356 of October 3, 1999 which was published in *Official Gazette* Extra. N° 5.390 of December 22, 1999.

2 *Official Gazette* N° 6.152 Extra. of November 18, 2014

3 *Official Gazette* Extra. of June 28, 1991

4 *Official Gazette* N° 34.930 of March 25, 1992

1. Investments and reinvestments carried out in accordance with the Regime, made in national currency belonging to persons of foreign nationality or foreign investors, drawn from earnings, capital gains, interest, amortization of loans or other rights, or any other resources which the foreign investors are entitled to transfer abroad.

2. Those drawn from Conversion of Foreign Debt to In-vestment (debt-equity swaps) belonging to foreign individuals or legal entities.

3. Those made in the form of intangible technological contributions such as trademarks, industrial models, technical assistance, and technical know-how, whether patented or not, which may take the form of physical goods, technical documents, and instructions.

In this context, one of the main aspects derived from the Andean pact regime on foreign investments, is the distinction between "foreign enterprises" and "national enterprises", which are concepts used to make emphasis on the status or nature of the legal persons (foreign or national) rather than on the nature of the investment in itself (international or Venezuelan). In effect, Decision 291 of the former Commission of the Cartagena Agreement of 21/22 March 1991, establishes the following distinction between "foreign" and "national" enterprises:

a) A "foreign enterprise" is defined as one incorporated or established in the recipient country (where the direct foreign investment is made) in which national investors *owns less* that the 51% of its capital, or when even owning more than that percentage, according to the decision of the national competent body (Superintendence of Foreign Investments), it is not reflected in the technical, financial, administrative or commercial direction of the enterprise (Article 1). Consequently, a "foreign enterprise" is one in which international investors own more than the 51% of its capital; or when owning less that such percentage of shares, the shares owned by the international investor are reflected in the technical, financial, administrative or commercial direction of the enterprise.

b) A "national enterprise" is the one incorporated in the country where the direct foreign investment is made, in which national investors own more than the 80% of its capital, provided that according to the decision of the national competent body (Superintendence of Foreign Investments), such percentage is reflected in the technical, financial, administrative or commercial direction of the enterprise (Article 1).

One of the main purposes of this distinction, according to Decree 2095 of February 13, 1992 containing the Regulation of the Common Régime on Foreign Investments established in Decision 291 of the Andean Pact, is the obligation for foreign enterprises to be registered before the competent national authority, and the establishment of some economic sectors as reserved for the exclusive exploitation by national enterprises.

2. Registration of Foreign Investments

Pursuant to article 3 of *Decision N° 291* all direct foreign investments must be registered with the "appropriate national agency in freely convertible currency," being such Agency, the Superintendence of Foreign Investments as established in

Decree N° 2095 of Feb 13, 1992, in which detailed requirements that must be fulfilled to register an investment are provided (Art. 13 and following). Nonetheless, regarding companies making foreign investments in the petrochemical, coal, and mining industries, as well as in hydrocarbons and related activities, the "appropriate national agency" for registration of investments is the Ministry of Energy and Mines, pursuant to *Decree N° 1103* of Sept. 6, 1990 (Article 3).[5]

Pursuant to article 26 of *Decree N° 2095*, the following areas of economic activity are the only ones reserved to national companies: a) Television and radio broadcasting, Spanish-language news-papers; and b) Professional services whose practice is regulated by national laws.

3. The Right to Re-export Investments and Profits

Pursuant to article 4 of *Decision N° 291*, the owners of a direct foreign investment are entitled to transfer the proven net earnings generated by their direct foreign investment abroad, in freely convertible currency (Art. 4). Moreover, article 5 of *Decision N° 291* entitles foreign investors to re-export the proceeds of any sale in the country of their shares, equity allotments, or rights, or the funds resulting from a reduction of capital or liquidation of the company, following payment of the taxes applicable thereto. *Decree N° 2095* regulates the distribution and remittance of profits in detail (Art. 35). Nonetheless, re-export of foreign investment has been limited by the exchange-control regulations established since 1994.

In any case, all the regulations referred to the Andean pact and the Andean Community of Nations since 2006 ceased to have enforcement in Venezuela, after the decision of the Government to withdraw from the Community.

II. THE 1999 LEGAL REGIME ON THE PROMOTION AND PROTECTION OF INVESTMENTS ABROGATED SINCE 2014

In 1999, an Investments Promotion and Protection Law[6] was enacted for the specific purpose to provide foreign, and also national investments and investors, with a stable and predictable legal framework, for them to work in a secure environment, by means of regulating the State actions regarding such investments and investors. In other terms, the main purpose of the Law was basically to regulate or to limit the State actions regarding investors and investments, assuring them a secure environment and a stable legal framework for their activities.

At the time of the enactment of this 1999 Investment Law, as aforementioned Venezuela was still a member State of the Andean Community of Nations, which resulted from the transformation of the original 1969 Andean Pact Integration Agreement.[7]

---

5 *Official Gazette* N° 34.548 of July 7, 1990

6 See Decree Law N° 356 of October 3, 1999 which was published in *Official Gazette* Extra. N° 5.390 of December 22, 1999.

7 The Andean Pact was later transformed into the Andean Community of Nations, from which Venezuela withdrew in 2006. The announcement was made by the President of the Republic of Venezuela in a meeting with the Presidents of Bolivia, Paraguay and Uruguay held in Asunción on

For that reason, at that time the Venezuelan legal order included Decision 291 of the Andean Community (Regime for the Common Treatment of Foreign Capital and Trademarks, Patents, Licensing Agreements and Royalties) of March 21, 1991, and the implementing Regulations, adopted by Decree N° 2.095 of March 25, 1992[8] (Andean Pact Regime).The Andean Pact Regime was the only legal regime concerning foreign investment that existed in Venezuela at the time the 1999 Investment Law was adopted.

As aforementioned, the Andean Pact Regime, although less restrictive than its predecessor regime under the Andean Pact, was still primarily concerned with the registration and strict regulation of foreign investment and did not contain provisions for the promotion or protection of such investments, other than a general principle of national treatment, subject to certain exceptions regarding economic sectors reserved to national enterprises.[9] In contrast, the 1999 Investment Law explicitly provides for the promotion and protection of investments (as its title indicates) and does so by establishing broad standards of protection, similar to those found in typical bilateral or multilateral treaties or agreements on investments. The aims of the 1999 Investment Law are clearly stated in its Article 1, which states:

> "This Decree-Law is intended to provide investments and investors, both domestic and foreign, with a stable and foreseeable legal framework in which they may operate in an environment of security, through the regulation of the State's action towards such investments and investors, with a view towards achieving the increase, diversification and harmonious integration of investments in favor of domestic development objectives."

While the primary focus of the Andean Pact Regime was to regulate foreign investment and the status of foreign enterprises in contrast to national enterprises, the primary focus of the 1999 Investment Law is to regulate the conduct of the State toward national and foreign investment and investors, in order to protect and promote investment. Indeed, even a superficial comparison between the two regimes shows that it was a fundamental objective of the 1999 Investment Law to complement the existing legal regime for the treatment of foreign investment and for foreign and national enterprises with a new regime better aimed at the promotion and protection of investments. Consequently, the Investment Law does not establish the distinction noir define the terms "foreign enterprise" or "national (Venezuelan) enterprise." In this Law, the distinction that is established refers to the nature of the investments, between Venezuelan or international investments, and not between the nature of the enterprise recipient of the investment, that is, independently of it them being foreign or national enterprise, in the sense of the Andean Pact regime. That is why, both regimes were complementary ones.

We will analyze the legal regime of the 1999 Investment Law due the important impact that it had in the Venezuelan regulations, *although the Law was repealed in*

April 20, 2006. See, *El Universal,* Caracas, April 21, 2006; *El Universal*, Caracas, April 24, 2006; *El Universal,* Caracas, April 20, 2006. The decision was formally notified by the Venezuelan Foreign Minister to the General Secretary of the Andean Community on April 22, 2006.

8 See *Official Gazette* N° 34.930 of March 25, 1992.

9 Decision 291, Article 2; Decree N° 2095, Articles 13, 26-28.

2014 and substituted by the Law on Foreign Investments,[10] which changed in a radical way the previous regime, eliminating any sort of promotion or protection of foreign investment, and providing basically for its control.

1. The notion of "Investment"

Article 3,1 of the 1999 Investment Law defined "investment" as "every asset destined to the production of income, under any of the entrepreneurial or contractual forms permitted by Venezuelan legislation." By way of illustration, the same provision indicated that "investment" includes:

> "personal and real property, tangible or intangible, over which property rights and other rights *in rem* are exercised; negotiable instruments; rights to any performance having an economic value; intellectual property rights, including know how, prestige and good will; and rights obtained in accordance with public law, including concessions for the exploration, extraction or exploitation of natural resources, and for the construction, exploitation, conservation and maintenance of national public works and for the provision of national public services, as well as any other right conferred by law or by administrative decision adopted in accordance with the law."

Under this definition, every asset destined to the production of income under any entrepreneurial or contractual form permitted by Venezuelan legislation was an "investment" for the purposes of the 1999 Investment Law. In contrast, the Andean Pact Regime did not contain any definition of "investment;" it defined particular types of investment, as discussed below.

2. The notion of "International Investment"

Article 3,2 of the 1999 Investment Law defined "international investment" as "the investment that is the property of or is effectively controlled by foreign natural or legal persons." It follows from this definition, together with the definition of "investment" in Article 3,1, that an "international investment" was "every asset destined to the production of income, under any of the entrepreneurial or contractual forms permitted by Venezuelan legislation," that is "the property of, or is effectively controlled by foreign natural or legal persons."

At the time the 1999 Investment Law was adopted, there were investments in Venezuela made under the Andean Pact Regime, which did not use the term "international investment." The Andean Pact Regime used an entirely different conceptual framework, based on the concepts of "foreign direct investment," "national investment," "sub regional investment," "neutral capital investment" (based on a definition of "neutral capital"), and "investment of a mixed enterprise" (based on a definition of "mixed enterprise").[11] Given this situation, it was necessary for the drafters of the 1999 Investment Law to determine how the conceptual structure of the preexisting Andean Pact Regime would fit within the new conceptual structure of the 1999 Investment Law.

---

10 *Official Gazette* N° 6.152 Extra. of November 18, 2014

11 Decree N° 2095, Article 2; and Decision 291, Article 1.

This was accomplished by establishing that the new concept of "international investment" included the various types of investment that, under the Andean Pact Regime, presupposed ownership or control by foreign natural or juridical persons. Article 3,2 of the 1999 Investment Law thus provided:

> "International investment embraces [*abarca*] foreign direct investment, sub regional investment, investment of neutral capital, and investment of an Andean Multinational Enterprise."

In turn, Article 3.3 clarified that "foreign direct investment," "sub regional investment," "investment of neutral capital" and "investment of an Andean Multinational Enterprise" were "those defined as such in the Decisions approved by the Andean Community of Nations, and in their regulations in Venezuela." Therefore, the concept of "international investment" in the 1999 Investment Law included those earlier concepts defined in the Andean Pact Regime, but was not limited to those concepts, because the concept of "international investment" as defined in the 1999 Investment Law, **was** more comprehensive, as discussed below, than those old concepts of the Andean Pact Regime put together.[12]

3. The notion of "International Investor"

Article 3,4 of the 1999 Investment Law defined "international investor" as "the owner of an international investment, or whoever effectively controls it." This definition was based on the definition of "international investment," which was in turn based on the definition of "investment." Notice that the definition of "international investor" did not require direct ownership or direct effective control of an international investment. The provision did not distinguish between different forms of ownership or effective control.

The Single Paragraph of Article 3 stated that "The Regulation of this Decree-Law shall set forth the conditions under which an investment shall be declared to be property of or effectively controlled by a Venezuelan or foreign natural or legal person." This provision was necessary because "international investment" and "Venezuelan investment" were defined in Article 3 in parallel terms, and in both cases the application of the concept depended on ownership or effective control by either a Venezuelan or foreign person. Since "international investment" and "Venezuelan investment" were mutually exclusive concepts, the legislator let to the regulator the task of avoiding conflicts by clarifying the operation of ownership and effective control.

The Regulation addressed ownership in Article 3 and effective control in Article 4. In both articles, the Regulation stated that "it is understood that an investment is" owned (or effectively controlled) by international investors when their participation in the enterprise receiving the investment was a certain percentage of the capital, patrimony or assets, depending on the legal form of the enterprise. The percentage

12 The concept of "international investment" in the 1999 Investment Law is more comprehensive than the aggregate of "foreign direct investment," "subregional investment," "investment of neutral capital" and "investment of an Andean Multinational Enterprise" because "international investment" is based on a broader concept of "investment" than that presupposed by the Andean Pact Regime.

of participation in the enterprise receiving the investment was 100% for ownership and at least 51% for effective control, although the Regulation provided for alternative criteria of effective control of the enterprise receiving the investment based on the investors' capacity to decide on the activities of the receiving enterprise, in the judgment of the *Superintendencia de Inversiones Extranjeras.*

The Regulation did not deal with ownership or effective control of the investment. The Regulation dealt only with ownership and effective control of the enterprise receiving the investment, but it did not require direct ownership or direct effective control of such enterprise. If the Regulation was interpreted as restricting the definition of "investment" in the statute by requiring ownership or effective control of an enterprise receiving the investment (a requirement that does not appear in the definition), the Regulation would be unconstitutional, because a norm of inferior rank (in this case, a regulation) cannot validly restrict the scope of a norm of superior rank (in this case, a decree having the rank and force of a statute). According to the Venezuelan constitutional system, regulations cannot introduce changes in the law or distort the spirit, purpose or reason of the law.

4. "International investment" and "direct investment"

For the reasons explained in the foregoing paragraphs, an "international investor" under the 1999 Investment Law, needs noted to be the 'owner' of the direct investments in Venezuela or to be the one who 'actually controlled' them," as might be the case according to the Andean Pact Regime concept of "foreign direct investment." There was nothing in the 1999 Investment Law suggesting that an "international investment" was limited, if made by foreign investors, to a "foreign direct investment" under the Andean Pact Regime or that an "international investor" was to be the owner of a "direct" investment, in the sense of an investment owned or controlled directly rather than through subsidiaries. The concept of "international investment" was defined as "every asset destined to the production of income, under any of the entrepreneurial or contractual forms permitted by Venezuelan legislation" that is "the property of, or is effectively controlled by foreign natural or legal persons." In contrast, the concept of "foreign direct investment" was defined merely in terms of contributions made by foreign natural or juridical persons to the capital of an enterprise.[13] In other words, the concept of "international investment" in the 1999 Investment Law was based on a much broader concept of "investment" than the "foreign direct investment" under the Andean Pact Regime. Furthermore, under the Andean Pact Regime, the contributions that constitute "foreign direct investment" were to be owned by the foreign investor,[14] while an "international investment" under the 1999 Investment Law might be either owned or effectively

---

13 Under the Andean Pact Regime, "Direct Foreign Investment" is defined as "contributions from abroad owned by foreign individuals or legal entities, to the capital of an enterprise, in freely convertible currency or in physical tangible assets, such as industrial plants, new and overhauled machinery, and new and overhauled equipment, spare parts, parts and pieces, raw materials and intermediate products. / Also considered as direct foreign investments are investments made in local currency from resources that are entitled to be remitted abroad and such reinvestments as may be made in accordance with this Regime. [...].) Decision 291, Article 1. See *also,* Decree N° 2.095, Article 2.

14 *Id.*

controlled by a foreign investor (Article 3,2). Therefore, an investor may hold an "international investment" for the purposes of the 1999 Investment Law, whether or not it held a "foreign direct investment" (or any other type of investment) under the Andean Pact Regime.

On the other hand, it was not necessary for an investor to hold an "international investment" directly, as opposed to holding it through subsidiaries. The 1999 Investment Law and the Regulation required only that an international investment be owned or effectively controlled by foreign natural or juridical persons; it did not require that the ownership (or more precisely the effective control) be direct, that is, without intermediate companies. As aforesaid, the definition of "foreign direct investment" in the Andean Pact Regime did not limit the scope of "international investment" in the 1999 Investment Law, not being relevant the fact that the 1999 legislator did not include the phrase "direct or indirect" as a qualification to ownership or effective control.[15]

In addition, the requirement that control be "effective" itself indicated that what mattered was not a particular legal form of control, but the way an investment was controlled in the reality of international business. In order to have "effective control" over an investment, the controlling person must in fact have the power to appoint those who manage the investment. Such power can be possessed either directly or indirectly, for instance, through ownership of a sufficient percentage of stock in a chain of companies established for the purpose of owning and controlling the investment in Venezuela.

Finally, for the purposes of applying the regime of the 1999 Investment Law, the status of an investment under the Andean Pact Regime did not matter. Article 4 of

---

15 For example, Article 5,24 of the former Organic Law of the Supreme Tribunal of Justice, provided for the competence of the Supreme Tribunal of Justice regarding claims filed against the Republic, the States, Municipalities, or any Autonomous Institute, public entity or enterprise, upon which the Republic "exercises *decisive and permanent control*, regarding their management or administration," without the direct or indirect qualification, being interpreted by the Supreme Tribunal as referring to "indirect" control. See Supreme Tribunal of Justice, Decision Nº 1.551 of September 18, 2007 (Case: *Administradora Onnis, C.A., v. Informática, Negocios and Tecnología S.A.*) (Exp. Nº 2007-0786). In this case, the Politico-Administrative Chamber acknowledged that the expression "decisive and permanent control" from Article 5,24 of the Organic Law of the Supreme Tribunal of Justice covers indirect control. The issue was whether the defendant Informática, Negocios y Tecnología S.A (INTESA) was an enterprise in which the Republic of Venezuela, a State or Municipality exercised "decisive and permanent control" to grant competence over the dispute to the administrative courts (*juzgado contencioso admnistrativo*). INTESA was a company incorporated in Venezuela, owned by SAIC Bermuda (60% shareholding) and PDV Informática y Telecomunicaciones, S.A. (PDV-IFT) (40% shareholding). PDV-IFT was in turn wholly owned by Petróleos de Venezuela, S.A. (PDVSA), and PDVSA is in turn wholly owned by the Republic of Venezuela. *Id.*, pp. 2, 4-5. The Politico-Administrative Chamber decided that "while the Republic through PDVSA is owner of only a 40% of the shares of [INTESA] [...] such percentage although it does not represent a majority shareholding, it does represent an important contribution by the Republic [...]" and concluded that "the Republic has a decisive participation in the defendant company [...]." *Id.*, p. 5 (emphasis added). Put differently, the Politico-Administrative Chamber recognized that **indirect** holding of shares of INTESA by the Republic of Venezuela was enough to satisty the "decisive and permanent control" requirement, needed to grant to the administrative courts competence over the case against INTESA. Given its quantum, the case was assigned to the relevant Regional Superior Administrative Court (*Juzgado Superior de lo Contencioso Administrativo Regional*). *Id.*, p. 6.

the 1999 Investment Law made it clear that, while investments made under the Andean Pact Regime continue to be subject to that regime, they "shall also enjoy the protection established in this Decree-Law, and shall be able to enjoy the benefits and incentives that this Decree-Law contemplates, within the limits that it establishes." The 1999 Investment Law thus protected all international investments, in accordance with its own terms, being improper to distort the meaning of the 1999 Investment Law by interpreting it in the light of the Andean Pact Regime.

III. INTERNATIONAL ARBITRATION AS ONE OF THE LEGAL MEANS FOR THE PROMOTION AND PROTECTION OF INVESTMENTS ESTABLISHED IN THE 1999 ABROGATED LAW

The 1999 Investments Promotion and Protection Law, was enacted when the 1999 Constitution was being discussed in the National Constituent Assembly, in which arbitration was expressly incorporated as an alternative means of adjudication and as a component of the judicial system (Article 253), requiring the State to promote it, in particular, through legislation (Article 258).[16] Specifically, Article 258 of the Constitution refers to "arbitration" as one of the formal means for achieving Justice, to the point that the Constitution establishes the State obligation to promote "arbitration, conciliation, mediation and any other alternate mean for the settlement of conflicts". Consequently, according to the values regarding Justice that were expressly inserted in the Constitution, beside the organization of the national judicial system, the obligation of the State to promote arbitration was established

One of the main elements to assure an institutional environment and a stable legal framework regarding investments is, precisely, to guarantee the settlement of disputes between the State and a foreign investor outside the national judicial system, through international arbitration, particularly the one established in the ICSID Convention. That is why, for instance, article 21 of the Law established the obligation for the State, when no treaty or agreement on investments was in effect, to eventually propose the settlement of disputes regarding the interpretation or application of the Law, to arbitration. That is why, in addition, the Investment Law, in order to develop and promote private investment, encouraged the adoption of alternative mechanisms for dispute resolution, such as arbitration. This was due, particularly, to the Government's official policy at that time, designed to offer the resolution of disputes by arbitration as a means of promoting investment and attract investments, surpassing the former past history of the country of reluctance on matters of arbitration.

In effect, it must be remembered that at the turn of the 20th Century, arbitration was generally rejected in Venezuela on matters of public law by

16 The promotion of arbitration is an obligation of all organs of the State. On the recognition of arbitration as an alternative means of adjudication by the 1999 Constitution, see generally Paolo Longo F., *Arbitraje y Sistema Constitucional de Justicia*, Editorial Frónesis S.A., Caracas, 2004; Supreme Tribunal of Justice, Constitutional Chamber, Decision Nº 186 of February 14, 2001 (Case: *Constitutional Challenge of Articles 17, 22 and 23 of the Investment Law*).

application of the "Calvo Clause,"[17] and as a result of events of 1902 that gave rise in Venezuela to the "Drago Doctrine."[18] On matters of private law, even though binding arbitration was authorized in the 19th Century in the civil procedure regulations as a means of alternative dispute resolution, although the 1916 Code of Civil Procedure established arbitration only as a non-binding method of dispute resolution, that is, without making the arbitration agreement mandatory (Articles 502-522).

That former attitude of suspicion or hostility to arbitration changed steadily from the middle of the 20th Century. After the 1961 Constitution adopted the principle of relative sovereign immunity (based on a similar provision contained in Article 108 of the 1947 Constitution), the insertion of binding arbitration clauses in public contracts became a generally accepted valid practice.[19] That is why, in August 1999, the Supreme Court of Justice dismissed a challenge to the constitutionality of the parliamentary act (*Acuerdo*) that authorized the Framework of Conditions for the "Association Agreements for the Exploration at Risk of New Areas and the Production of Hydrocarbons under the Shared-Profit Scheme" ("*Convenios de Asociación Para la Exploración a Riesgo de Nuevas Areas y la Producción de Hidrocarburos Bajo el Esquema de Ganancias Compartidas*"), dated July 4, 1995.[20] The Supreme Court of Justice held that the Congressional authorization and, in particular, the inclusion of

17 The Calvo Clause had its origin in the work of Carlos Calvo, who formulated the doctrine in his book *Tratado de Derecho Internacional*, initially published in 1868, after studying the Franco-British intervention in Rio de la Plata and the French intervention in Mexico. The Calvo Clause was first adopted in Venezuela in the 1893 Constitution as a response to diplomatic claims brought by European countries against Venezuela as a consequence of contracts signed by the country and foreign citizens. See Tatiana B. de Maekelt, "Inmunidad de Jurisdicción de los Estados" in *Libro Homenaje a José Melich Orsini*, Vol. 1, Caracas 1982, pp. 213 ff.; Allan R. Brewer-Carías, *Principios especiales y estipulaciones obligatorias en la contratación administrativa* in *El Derecho Administrativo en Latinoamérica*, Vol. II, Ediciones Rosaristas, Colegio Mayor Nuestra Señora del Rosario, Bogotá 1986, pp. 345-378; Allan R. Brewer-Carías, *"Algunos aspectos de la inmunidad jurisdiccional de los Estados y la cuestión de los actos de Estado (act of state) en la jurisprudencia norteamericana"* in *Revista de Derecho Público* N° 24, Editorial Jurídica Venezolana, Caracas October-December 1985, pp. 29-42.

18 The Drago Doctrine was conceived in 1902 by the then Argentinean Minister of Foreign Relations, Luis María Drago, who –in response to threats of military force made by Germany, Great Britain and Italy against Venezuela– formulated his thesis condemning the compulsory collection of public debts by the States. See generally Victorino Jiménez y Núñez, *La Doctrina Drago y la Política Internacional,* Madrid 1927.

19 See Alfredo Morles, "La inmunidad de Jurisdicción y las operaciones de Crédito Público" in *Estudios Sobre la Constitución, Libro Homenaje a Rafael Caldera*, Vol. III, Caracas, 1979, pp. 1.701 ff; Allan R. Brewer-Carías, *Contratos Administrativos*, Editorial Jurídica Venezolana, Caracas 1992, pp. 262-265. The same provision established in the 1961 Constitution was incorporated in the 1999 Constitution. See Beatrice Sansó de Ramírez, "La inmunidad de jurisdicción en el Artículo 151 de la Constitución de 1999" in *Libro Homenaje a Enrique Tejera París, Temas sobre la Constitución de 1999, Centro de Investigaciones Jurídicas* (CEIN), Caracas 2001, pp. 333-368.

20 *Official Gazette* N° 35.754 of July 17, 1995.

arbitration clauses in public law contracts, were valid under the 1961 Constitution in force at the time.[21]

In addition, Venezuela ratified the 1979 Inter-American Convention on Extraterritorial Validity of Foreign Judgments and Arbitral Awards,[22] the 1975 Inter-American Convention on International Commercial Arbitration,[23] and the 1958 United Nations Convention on the Recognition and Enforcement of Foreign Arbitral Awards (New York Convention).[24] In 1986, the Code of Civil Procedure was amended to allow parties to make a binding agreement to submit controversies to arbitral tribunals, and to exclude the jurisdiction of ordinary courts (Articles 608-629). In addition, special statutes allowed for arbitration in areas related to copyright, insurance, consumer protection, labor, and agrarian reform.[25] In 1995, Venezuela ratified the ICSID Convention[26] and, between 1993 and 1998, it signed many bilateral investment treaties providing for international arbitration.[27] In 1998, Venezuela adopted the Commercial Arbitration Law,[28] which is based on the Model Law on International Commercial Arbitration of UNCITRAL.[29]

---

21 The Supreme Court of Justice, in Temporary Plenary Session, Expediente N° 812-829, August 17, 1999. The Constitutional Chamber of the Supreme Tribunal of Justice recently confirmed the ruling made under the 1961 Constitution, holding that Article 151 of the 1999 Constitution allows the incorporation of arbitration provisions in contracts of "public interest" (*interés público*). See Decision N° 1.541, of October 17, 2008.

22 *Official Gazette* N° 33.144 of January 15, 1985.

23 *Official Gazette* N° 33.170 of February 22, 1985.

24 *Official Gazette* (Extra) N° 4832 of December 29, 1994. For an account of international instruments relevant to Venezuela's recognition of international arbitration, *see* Decision N° 1.541 of October 17, 2008, pp. 13-14.

25 See laws listed in Francisco Hung Vaillant, *Reflexiones Sobre el Arbitraje en el Sistema Venezolano*, Caracas, 2001, pp. 90-101; Paolo Longo F., *Arbitraje y Sistema Constitucional de Justicia*, Editorial Frónesis S.A., Caracas, 2004, pp. 53-77; and Decision N° 1.541, of October 17, 2008, pp. 12-13.

26 *Official Gazette* N° 35.685 of April 3, 1995.

27 See list of Venezuelan bilateral treaties on the promotion and protection of investments at Venezuelan Ministry of for Foreign Relations *available at* http://www.mre.gov.ve/metadot/index.pl?id=4617;isa=Category;op=show; ICSID Database of Bilateral Investment Treaties available at http://icsid.worldbank.org/ICSID/FrontServlet; UNCTAD, Investment Instruments On-line Database, Venezuela Country-List of BITs as of June 2008 available at http://www.unctad.org/Templa-tes/Page.asp?intItem-ID=2344&lang=1. See *also*, José Antonio Muci Borjas, *El Derecho Administrativo Global y Los Tratados Bilaterales de Inversión* (BITs), Caracas 2007, pp. 101-102; Tatiana B. de Maekelt, "Arbitraje Comercial Internacional en el sistema venezolano" in Allan R. Brewer-Carías (Editor), *Seminario Sobre la Ley de Arbitraje Comercial*, Academia de Ciencias Políticas y Sociales, Caracas 1999, pp. 282-283; Francisco Hung Vaillant, *Reflexiones Sobre el Arbitraje en el Sistema Venezolano*, Caracas 2001, pp. 104-105; and Decision N° 1.541, of October 17, 2008, pp. 13-14.

28 *Official Gazette* N° 36.430 of April 7, 1998.

29 See generally Arístides Rengel Romberg, "El arbitraje comercial en el Código de Procedimiento Civil y en la nueva Ley de Arbitraje Comercial (1998)" in Allan R. Brewer-Carías (Editor), *Seminario sobre la Ley de Arbitraje Comercial*, Academia de Ciencias Políticas y Sociales, Caracas 1999, pp. 47 ff.

In particular, regarding the ICSID Convention, that is, the *Convention on the Settlement of Investment Disputes between States and Nationals of Other States (ICSID),*[30] it was adopted by the Board of Directors of the International Bank for Reconstruction and Development (World Bank), in its annual meeting held in Kyoto, Japan, on September 10, 1964. The purpose of the Convention was to create the International Centre for Settlement of Investment Disputes (ICSID Center) in order to provide facilities for conciliation and arbitration of investment disputes between Contracting States and nationals of other Contracting States. In that meeting Venezuela, together with many others Latin American countries, rejected the Convention.

Nonetheless, the Executive Directors of the World Bank on March 18, 1965, submitted the Convention together with the "Report of the Executive Directors on the Convention on the Settlement of Investment Disputes Between States and Nationals of other States" dated March 18, 1965, to the member governments of the World Bank for their consideration with a view to its signature and ratification. The result was that the Convention was adopted and entered into force on October 14, 1966, when it had been ratified by 20 countries.

The Government of Venezuela signed the Convention on Aug 18, 1993, that is thirty years after its entering into force, being approved the following year, in 1994, by statute sanctioned by the Venezuelan Congress.[31] Such Law of approval entered into force on June 1, 1995, after the deposit of its ratification was made on May 2, 1995. As it was declared in the Preamble of the Convention, "no Contracting State shall by the mere fact of its ratification, acceptance or approval of this Convention and without its consent be deemed to be under any obligation to submit any particular dispute to conciliation or arbitration," so in addition to the ratification of the Convention, for a State to be subjected to ICSID arbitration Center, its written consent must be expressed. That is why, in Article 25.1 of the Convention, regarding ICSID jurisdiction, it is established that it "shall extend to any legal dispute arising directly out of an investment, between a Contracting State [...] and a national of another Contracting State, which the parties to the dispute consent in writing to submit to the Centre."

In 1999, consequently, it was possible to say that there was no prevailing culture of hostility to arbitration, and on the contrary, the 1999 Constitution, the legal system as a whole, and the international instruments to which Venezuela was a party embraced and promoted arbitration.[32]

Regarding ICSID International Arbitration system, according to article 25,1 of the Convention, the jurisdiction of the Center shall extend to any legal dispute arising directly out of an investment, which the parties to the dispute (a Contracting State and a national of another Contracting State) consent in writing to submit to the Center. The written consent by the Contracting State, as has been generally

30 Available at http://icsid.worldbank.org/ICSID/StaticFiles/basicdoc/ partA-preamble.htm

31 See the *Ley Aprobatoria del Convenio sobre Arreglo de Diferencias Relativas a Inversiones entre Estados y Nacionales de otros Estados*, in *Official Gazette* N° 4.832 Extra. of December 29, 1994.

32 ICSID arbitration continued to be incorporated in the bilateral treaties for promotion and protection of investments signed and ratified after 1999. See Venezuela-France Bilateral Investment Treaty in *Official Gazette* N° 37.896 of March 11, 2004).

admitted, can be given in three ways: First, in an agreement providing for ICSID arbitration, included in a specific clause of a public contract entered between a public entity of the Contracting State and an international investor; second, in an international multilateral or bilateral treaty or agreement in which the Contracting State and the international foreign investor's Contracting State of nationality, are Parties, providing for the disputes to be settled by reference to ICSID; and Third, in the national legislation enacted for the promotion of investments when containing a provision in which the State gives in advance its consent for the disputes on investments to be submitted to ICSID arbitration[33]. In this last case, the offering State and the foreign investor's State of nationality must be Contracting parties to the ICSID Convention, and the investor must accept the offer in writing.

These various forms of written consent for international arbitration by ICSID Contracting States, which include domestic legislation, were mentioned since the conception of ICSID in the *Report of the Executive Directors on the Convention on the Settlement of Investment Disputes Between States and Nationals of other States* dated March 18, 1965, in which was said that "a host state might in its investment promotion legislation offer to submit disputes arising out of certain classes of investments to the jurisdiction of the Centre, and the investor might give his consent by accepting the offer in writing."[34] Accordingly, since the drafting of the ICSID Convention, the way for the State to express consent by means of an open offers or unilateral promises to submit disputes arising out of international investments to the jurisdiction of the Center (*oferta abierta de arbitraje*), [35] as expressed in a national statute on promotion and protection of investment sanctioned by a Contracting State Party, has been considered as the written consent given in advance by the State for arbitration, that any investor can accept by giving its own consent by writing.[36] It was also considered as one of the most important instrument the States have for attracting foreign investors;[37] that is, "one of the ways States attract foreign investment is to make unilateral promise to submit disputes to ICSID arbitration."[38]

---

33 See, Christoph Schreuer, "The World bank/INCSID Dispute Settlement procedures", pp. 1-2, in http://www.oece.org/dataoecd/47/25/ 2758044.pdf; K.V.S.K Nathan, *ICSID Convention, The Law of International Centre for Settlement of Investment Disputes*, JurisPub, New York 2000, p. 117; Bernardo M. Cremades, "Arbitration in Investments Treaties: Public Offer of Arbitration in Investment-Protective Treaties", p. 10, in http://www.cremades.com/archivos/bernardo/arbitration%20investiment.pdf

34 See in 1 ICSID REPORTS 28, p. 24, in *History of the ICSID Convention* II-2 956 (1970).

35 See Bernardo Cremade and David J.A. Cairns, "La seguridad jurídica de las inversiones extranjeras: La protección contractual y de los Tratados, *Revista Internacional de Arbitraje*, N° 1, Universidad Sergio Arboleda, Bogotá, pp. 95 ss.

36 In the "Memorandum from the General Counsel and Draft Report of the Executive Directors accompany the Convention" dated January 19, 1965, on the matter of the written consent by the Contracting States, it was said that: "a host state might in its investment promotion legislation offer to submit disputes arising out of certain classes of investments to the jurisdiction of the Centre, and the investor might give his consent by accepting the offer in writing". See in *History of the ICSID Convention* II-2 956 (1970).

37 "States, desiring foreign investment, make unilateral promises in the hope of attracting foreign investors. The most common among them are not to expropriate foreign investment except on the payment of full compensation and to submit disputes to ICSID arbitration". See M. Sornarajah, *The Settlement of Foreign Investment Disputes*, Kluwer Law International, The Hague, 2000, p. 209. Referring to the "economic policy designated to attract foreign investments", and to

It was precisely in accordance with these possibilities and following the policy defined by the State in 1999 to promote and protect international investments[39] that Article 22 of the 1999 Investment Law expressed the consent of the Venezuelan State to submit to international arbitration controversies regarding international investment in the terms provided in the ICSID Convention. [40] That article provided as follows:

> Article 22. Disputes arising between an international investor whose country of origin has in effect a treaty or agreement for the promotion and protection of investments with Venezuela, or any disputes to which apply the provisions of the Convention Establishing the Multilateral Investment Guarantee Agency (MIGA) or the Convention on the Settlement of Investment Disputes between States and Nationals of other States (ICSID), shall be submitted to international arbitration under the terms provided for in the respective treaty or agreement, should it so provide, without prejudice to the possibility of using, when applicable, the systems of litigation provided for in the Venezuelan laws in force.

Regarding this provision, for instance, Gabriela Álvarez Ávila considered that the Venezuelan Law included ICSID as the proper jurisdiction for the settling of disputes by means of arbitration, stating the following:

> "A State can offer in its legislation on promotion of investments the option to resort to the ICSID Arbitration to settle disputes regarding certain type of investments, and the Investor can consent by writing accepting said offer (Note

---

the "incentives and guaranties" granted by the Egyptian Law N° 43, the ICSID Tribunal in the *SPP v. Egypt Case* indicated that "it is not surprising that these guarantees should include the promise of neutral or impartial dispute resolution, so as to dispel investors' concerns about Egypt's reputedly hostile attitude towards non domestic arbitration". See *Southern Pacific Properties (Middle East) v. Arab Republic of Egypt, Decision on Jurisdiction, 27 November 1985*, paragraph 107, *3 ICSID Reports*, Cambridge University Press, 1995. See the relevant parts in Doak Bishop, James Crawford and W. Michael Reisman, *Foreign Investment Disputes. Cases, Materials and Commentary*, Kluwer Law International, The Hague 2005, p. 384.

38 See A. Şule Akyüz, "The jurisdiction of ICSID: The Application of Article 25 of the Convention on the Settlement of Investment Disputes between States and National of Others States", p. 346, in http://aunf.ankara.edu.tr/anfd-arsiv/AUHF-2003-52-03/

39 Andrés A. Mezgravis has consider that article 22 of the Law must be interpreted favoring ICSID arbitration jurisdiction. See Andrés A. Mezgravis, "Las inversiones petroleras en Venezuela y el arbitraje ante el CIADI", in Irene Valera (Coordinadora), *Arbitraje Comercial Interno e Internacional. Reflexiones teóricas y experiencias prácticas*, Academia de Ciencias Políticas y Sociales, Comité Venezolano de Arbitraje, Caracas 2005, pp. 388-391.

40 Regarding the phrase contained in Article 8 of the Egyptian Law N° 43 ("within the framework of a treaty), similar to the one contained in Article 22 of the Venezuelan Law ("under the terms provided for in" the Convention), and its possible relation with the State consent in written in order for the disputes to be submitted to the Centre jurisdiction, the Center, in the *SPP v. Egypt* of 27 November 1985 Decision on Jurisdiction, ruled that it "does not import into a treaty additional requirements which the treaty does not contain. The Convention makes no mention of a separate *ad hoc* consent. It says only that there must be 'consent in writing'". *Southern Pacific Properties (Middle East) v. Arab Republic of Egypt, Decision on Jurisdiction, 27 November 1985*, paragraph 99, *3 ICSID Reports*, Cambridge University Press, 1995. See the relevant parts in Doak Bishop, James Crawford and W. Michael Reisman, *Foreign Investment Disputes. Cases, Materials and Commentary*, Kluwer Law International, The Hague 2005, p. 382.

22: *Informe de los Directores Ejecutivos acerca del Convenio sobre Arreglo de Diferencias Relativas a Inversiones entre Estados y Nacionales de Otros Estados*, ICSID, Doc. 2, note 4, p. 9.). In practice, around 30 States have followed this suggestion, by including ICSID in their legislation on promotion of investments, as the proper jurisdiction for the settling of disputes by means of arbitration (Note 23: This is the case of the Venezuelan Foreign Investments Promotion and Protection Law promulgated by means of Decree N° 356 of October 3, 1999)."[41]

This general consent given by the State, in any case, was coherent with the provisions of the Constitution and also with the general sense and purpose of the 1999 Investments Promotion Law, which as mentioned, was sanctioned precisely to promote and protect foreign investments and also for such purpose, to limit the State activities and powers. The submission of disputes regarding international investments to arbitration, and in particular to international arbitration, is precisely, one of the means directed to protect foreign investors and investments, assuring "the possibility of subjecting foreign investment disputes to an impartial dispute-settlement procedure of an international nature", as is the ICSID Center, which is considered as "truly delocalized and denationalized" and consequently, as "the natural forum for solving investor-State disputes."[42] That is why, that the *ratio legis* of the 1999 Investment Law, and in particular, of its article 22, justified its interpretation "in favor of arbitration."[43]

This was the same conclusion to which the Constitutional Chamber of the Supreme Tribunal of Justice arrived in its decision N° 186 of February 14, 2001, when ruling on a judicial review action precisely filed to challenge the constitutionality of article 22 of the Investment Law. In the ruling, the Tribunal rejected the petition to nullify the article because including an open offer for arbitration, arguing that:

> "The plaintiff incurred in an error considering that with the transcribed provisions (articles 22 and 23, Investment Law) it was intended to give an authorization in order to leave aside public law regulations in favor of arbitral institution, snatching away from the national courts their power to decide the disputes that could arise from the application of the Promotion and Protection Law. In effect, the Chamber considers that the latter statement is an error because it is the Constitution itself the one that incorporate within the Justice System the alternate means for justice, among which, obviously, the arbitration is placed ... The Chamber is attentive to the fact that the plaintiffs seeking the

41 See Gabriela Álvarez Ávila, "Las características del arbitraje del CIADI", en *Anuario Mexicano de Derecho Internacional*, Vol II 2002, Instituto de Investigaciones Jurídicas, Universidad Nacional Autónoma de México, UNAM, México 2002 (ISSN 1870-4654). http://juridicas.unam.mx/pu-blica/rev/derint/cont/2/cm/

42 See Bernardo M. Cremades, "Arbitration in Investments Treaties: Public Offer of Arbitration in Investment-Protective Treaties", p. 2, in http://www.cremades.com/archivos/ber-nardo/arbitra-tion%20investiment.pdf

43 See Andrés A. Mezgravis, "Las inversiones petroleras en Venezuela y el arbitraje ante el CIADI", in Irene Valera (Coordinadora), *Arbitraje Comercial Interno e Internacional. Reflexiones teóricas y experiencias prácticas*, Academia de Ciencias Políticas y Sociales, Comité Venezolano de Arbitraje, Caracas 2005, p 390.

nullity, have not noticed from the constitutional provision they claim as violated, that the alternate means of justice are also part of the Venezuelan system of justice and that the transcription they have made in their claim of the quoted Article 253, does not contain the last part of the provision"[44].

The Chamber continued in its ruling pointing out that Articles 253 and 258 of the Constitution are the ones that:

> "in an accurate and harmonic way recognize and include the alternate means of justice as part of the national Justice System, and in addition, establish a guideline to the legislative organs for the purpose for them to promote arbitration, conciliation, mediation and the other alternate means for settlement of disputes."[45]

Finally, the Constitutional Chamber in the same ruling, after transcribing, again, the final part or article 258 of the Constitution ("The law shall promote arbitration, conciliation, mediation and any other alternate means for the settlement of disputes"), concluded with the following assertion:

> "It is to point out that the Law, in this case a Decree Law, promoted and developed the aforementioned constitutional mandate by establishing arbitration as part of the means for the settlement of disputes arising between an international investor whose country of origin has in effect a treaty or agreement for the promotion and protection of investments with Venezuela; or any disputes to which the provision of the Constitutive Agreement of the Multilateral Investment Guarantee Agency (MIGA) or the Convention on Settlement of Investment Disputes between States and the Nationals of other States (ICSID) are applicable" ... "It is the opinion of this Chamber that with the provision for arbitration in the terms developed by the challenged articles, there have been no violation of the sovereign power of the national courts in order to administer justice, as it is affirmed by the plaintiff, but instead –it is reiterated- [the

44"A juicio de esta Sala Constitucional, los demandantes incurren en el error de considerar que en virtud de las normas impugnadas, precedentemente transcritas, se intenta hacer una autorización para dejar de lado normas de derecho público a favor de órganos arbitrales, arrebatando de tal forma a los tribunales nacionales, la potestad de decidir las eventuales controversias que pudieran surgir con ocasión de la aplicación del Decreto Ley de Promoción y Protección de Inversiones. En efecto, estima esta Sala que la anterior aseveración constituye un error por cuanto es la propia Carta Fundamental la que incorpora los medios alternativos de justicia, dentro de los cuales obviamente se ubica el arbitraje, al sistema de justicia"... "Llama la atención de esta Sala que los demandantes en nulidad no hayan advertido, de la norma constitucional que invocan como violentada, que los medios alternativos de justicia también forman parte del sistema de justicia venezolano y que la trascripción hecha en su escrito libelar del citado artículo 253 no contenga el último aparte de dicha norma." See in *Revista de Derecho Público,* N° 85-88, Editorial Jurídica Venezolana, Caracas 2001, pp. 167.

45"A la luz de las normas contenidas en los artículos 253 y 258 de la Carta Fundamental, debido a que son estas últimas las que de una manera acertada y armónica reconocen e incorporan los medios alternativos de conflictos, como parte integrante del sistema de justicia patrio y, aunado a ello, establece una directriz a los órganos legislativos a los fines de que éstos promuevan al arbitraje, conciliación, mediación y demás vías alternativas para solucionar las controversias". See in *Revista de Derecho Público,* N° 85-88, Editorial Jurídica Venezolana, Caracas 2001, pp. 167

challenged provisions] effectively develop the aforementioned programmatic norms contained in the Constitution of the Bolivarian Republic of Venezuela."[46]

The aforementioned article 22 of the Investment Law, in any case, was a compound provision that contained three parts: the first one, concerning bilateral or multilateral treaties or agreements on the promotion and protection of investments;[47] the second one, dealing with the MIGA Convention; and the last one, dealing with the ICSID Convention. Because the article addresses three different sets of treaties or agreements, it is hardly surprising that it did not follow any particular model or pattern of national legislation conceived to address only consent to ICSID jurisdiction. That is why it must be interpreted not by reference to any pattern or model, but in accordance with its own structure and terms, taking into account its compound nature.

This happened, for instance in a very well-known case decided by the ICSID Center, regarding the consent given by Egypt in a national statute for international arbitration. Following what the ICSID Center decided in such case, in relation to the acceptance of a written consent expressed by the Egyptian State in the Law N° 43 in order to submit disputes arising from investments to the Centre, and according to the quotation made by Christoph Schreuer regarding such Decision, when applying the same interpretation to article 22 of the Venezuelan Law, Andrés A. Mezgravis expressed that:

> "Around 30 States offer ICSID arbitration in their legislations on investments. Venezuela has been considered one of them (Note 95. Gabriela Álvarez Ávila, "Las características del arbitraje del CIADI", en *Anuario Mexicano de Derecho Internacional*, Vol. II 2002, Instituto de Investigaciones Jurídicas UNAM México 2002, p. 212. In note 23 the author and Legal Counsel to ICSID, precisely quotes the Venezuelan Investment Law as an example). Nonetheless, as Schreuer rightly points out, "some national investment laws unequivocally establish the solution of disputes by ICSID". "Other laws are not so clear, but nonetheless it can be deducted that they express the consent of the State on ICSID jurisdiction. In this regard, the national laws point out that the foreign investor "shall have the right to request" for the dispute to be definitively settled by means of some of the different methods, including the ICSID Convention; that any of the parties to the dispute 'may transfer the dispute' to one of the various institutions, including ICSID; or that the dispute 'shall be settled' (*será resuelta*) ("*sera réglé*") by one of those methods" (Note 96: Christoph M. Schreuer, *The ICSID Convention: A Commentary*, Cambridge University Press, 2001, pp 200, 201, specially paragraph 262). In our opinion, the Venezuelan Investment Law is in this last hypothesis"[48].

---

46 See in *Revista de Derecho Público,* N° 85-88, Editorial Jurídica Venezolana, Caracas 2001, pp. 168.

47 José Antonio Muci Borjas has affirmed that according to article 22 of the Venezuelan Law, "the Venezuelan State has given its consent for the disputes between a foreign investor protected by a BIT (bilateral investment treaty) by submitted to the Center". See in José Antonio Muci Borjas, *El derecho administrativo Global y los Tratados Bilaterales de Inversión (BITs)*, Editorial Jurídica venezolana, Caracas 2007, p. 215).

48 See Andrés A. Mezgravis, "Las inversiones petroleras en Venezuela y el arbitraje ante el CIADI", in Irene Valera (Coordinadora), *Arbitraje Comercial Interno e Internacional. Reflexiones*

This same expression, "shall be", used in Article 8 of the Egyptian Law N° 43 Concerning the Investment of Arab and Foreign Funds and the Free Zones, was precisely considered by the Centre in its Decision on Jurisdiction of 27 November 1985, in *South Pacific Properties (Middle East) Limited v. Arab Republic of Egypt*, Case N° ARB/84/3, as more correctly translated as "must be."[49] According to this approach, Article 22 of the Venezuelan Law was also considered as the written consent given by the Venezuelan State according to article 25,1 of the ICSID Convention, in order for the disputes on foreign investment to be submitted to international arbitration before the Center, as an obligation, once the open offer unilaterally made by the State was accepted by a foreign investor by expressing his written consent before the Center[50].

Consequently, as aforementioned, the Venezuelan Law was one of the categories of consent mentioned in the Report of the Executive Directors on the Convention on the Settlement of Disputes between States and Nationals of other States; as ruled by the INCSID Centre in the same *SPP v. Egypt* Decision when referring to the Report, expressing that the drafters of the ICSID Convention "anticipated that a State might unilaterally give advance consent in writing' to the Centre's jurisdiction through investment legislation"[51].

This was also the opinion I gave on the matter in a Paper written in 2005 for a Seminar organized by the Venezuelan Academy of Political and Social Sciences and the Venezuelan Arbitration Committee, in which regarding the interpretation of the Venezuelan Law and article 25,1 of the ICSID Convention, I expressed:

> "The main subject for discussion in this case, is to determine in which form the "written consent" can be given. In the Case: Southern Pacific Properties (Middle East) v. Arab Republic of Egypt, the Centre, in its Decision on Jurisdiction dated April 14 1988, as a source of the consent imposed by article

---

teóricas y experiencias prácticas, Academia de Ciencias Políticas y Sociales, Comité Venezolano de Arbitraje, Caracas 2005, p. 388.

49 *Southern Pacific Properties (Middle East) v. Arab Republic of Egypt, Decision on Jurisdiction, 27 November 1985*, paragraph 86, *3 ICSID Reports*, Cambridge University Press, 1995. See the relevant parts in Doak Bishop, James Crawford and W. Michael Reisman, *Foreign Investment Disputes. Cases, Materials and Commentary*, Kluwer Law International, The Hague 2005, p. 376

50 "The legislative provision containing consent to arbitration is merely an offer by the State to investors. In order to perfect an arbitration agreement that offer must be accepted by the investor. The investor may accept the offer simply by instituting arbitration". See Christoph Schreuer, "Consent Arbitration", 12 July 2005, in http://www.ila-hq.org/pdf/Foreign%20Investment/ILA%20paper%20Schreuer. "The State's offer to submit to ICSID jurisdiction in its national legislation is in itself insufficient to found jurisdiction under Article 25 of the ICSID Convention. The necessary agreement to arbitrate is perfected only when the investor also expresses its consent, in writing, which it may be in different ways", one of which is by virtue of the filing of the claim and request for ICSID arbitration. See Lucy Reed, Jan Peulsson, Niegel Blackaby, *Guide to ICSID Arbitration*, Kluwer Law International, The Hague 2004, p. 38

51 *Southern Pacific Properties (Middle East) v. Arab Republic of Egypt, Decision on Jurisdiction, 27 November 1985*, paragraph 98, *3 ICSID Reports*, Cambridge University Press, 1995. See the relevant parts in Doak Bishop, James Crawford and W. Michael Reisman, *Foreign Investment Disputes. Cases, Materials and Commentary*, Kluwer Law International, The Hague 2005, p. 382.

25,1 of the Convention, interpreted the value that internal law provisions have, when recognizing the jurisdiction of the Centre for the settling of disputes concerning foreign investments. The Center, in that case, interpreted as follows:" The Convention does not prescribe any particular form of the consent, not does require that consent be given on a case-by-case basis. To the contrary, the drafters of the Convention intended that consent could be given in advance through investment legislation. Accordingly, the Tribunal cannot accept the contention that the phrase "where it applies" in Article 8 of Law N° 43 requires a further or ad hoc manifestation of consent of the Centre's jurisdiction (Paragraph 101, 3 ICSID Reports, at 155-56).

Article 8 of the Egyptian N° 43 Law, established the following:

"Investment Disputes in respect of the implementation of the provisions of this Law shall be settled in a manner to be agreed upon with the investor, or within the framework of the agreements in force between the Arab Republic of Egypt and the investor's home country, or within the framework of the Convention for the Settlement of Investment Disputes between the State and the nationals of other countries to which Egypt has adhered by virtue of Law 90 of 1971, where such Convention applies".

In my opinion, this last expression of the Egyptian law is identical in its sense to the provision of article of the Venezuelan Law: "disputes to which the provision [of the ICSID Convention] are applicable."

This mean that according to the jurisprudence of the ICSID Center, when an internal law has a provision which refers to the Center jurisdiction the settling of disputes related to investments, the condition of article 25,1 of the ICSID Convention is fulfilled by that sole circumstance, and that for article 25,1 be applicable, it is only required that the dispute arose directly from an investment between Contracting State and a national of other Contracting State in the Convention, not being necessary *"a further or ad hoc manifestation of consent of the Center's jurisdiction."*[52]

The Decisions on Jurisdiction issued in the *Southern Pacific Properties (Middle East) v. Arab Republic of Egypt* ICSID Case were the first in which the Center based its jurisdiction on a unilateral offer made by a State in its national legislation on promotion of investments; a ruling which was contended by Egypt, alleging that the provision in its legislation contained only a promise for arbitration of ICSID, that it "was only an invitation" which could not be constructed as an offer. As was quoted in the 14 April 1988 ICSID Decision on Jurisdiction: "Egypt reiterated its objections to the Tribunal's jurisdiction arguing that article 8 of the Law N° 43 was intended only to inform potential investors that ICSID arbitration was one of a variety of dispute settlement mechanisms available and that, in the absence of a further certain and unequivocal written acceptance of ICSID jurisdiction, the Tribunal lacked

52 See Allan R. Brewer-Carías, "Algunos comentarios a la Ley de promoción y protección de Inversiones: contratos públicos y jurisdicción", in Irene Valera (Coordinadora), *Arbitraje Comercial Interno e Internacional. Reflexiones teóricas y experiencias prácticas*, Academia de Ciencias Políticas y Sociales, Comité Venezolano de Arbitraje, Caracas 2005, pp. 286-287.

jurisdiction over the dispute."[53] The Tribunal in its Decision on Jurisdiction of 27 November 1985 ruled as follows: "the Tribunal finds that Article 8 of Law N° 43 establishes a mandatory and hierarchic sequence of dispute settlement procedures, and constitutes an express 'consent in writing' to the Centre's jurisdiction within the meaning of Article 25 (1) of the Washington Convention in those cases where there is no other agreed-upon method of dispute settlement and no applicable bilateral treaty"[54]. In its subsequent Decision on Jurisdiction of 14 April 1988, the Tribunal held the following: "The ordinary grammatical meaning of the words in Article 8, taken together with other Laws and Decrees enacted in Egypt, showed that Article 8 *mandated the submission* of disputes to the various methods described therein, in hierarchical order, where such methods were applicable" and concluded that "Article 8 was legally sufficient manifestation of written consent to the jurisdiction of the Centre, and that no separate ad hoc written consent was required."[55]

As this was also the case of Venezuela, where the Investment Law expressed in its article 22 a unilateral written expression of consent of the State, in the form of an open offer given to international investors to submit investment disputes to international arbitration, including ICSID arbitration; according to such provision, in the first decade of the current XXI century many cases were filed before the ICSID Center against Venezuela,[56] and also many of them were decided by ICSID

53 See Southern *Pacific Properties (Middle East), Limited v. Arab Republic of Egypt, ICSID Case* N° ARB/84/3, decision on Jurisdiction of 20 May 1988, E. Lauterpacht and E. Rayfusse (Ed), *ICSID Reports,* Vol. 3. *Cambridge University Press,* 1995, p. 105. The Center ratified the matter on jurisdiction in its Decision of May 20, 1992 (ICSID Case N° ARB/84/3, *3 ICSID Review FILJ,* 1995, pp. 353-354, Paragraph 24. In the opinion of M. Sornarajah, in this case there was a "credible basis considering the civilian base of Egyptian law, for the view that Egypt had taken that a further agreement was necessary for there to be a binding arbitration agreement", in *The settlement of Foreign Investment Disputes*, 2000, p. 210.

54 *Southern Pacific Properties (Middle East) v. Arab Republic of Egypt, Decision on Jurisdiction, 27 November 1985,* paragraph 98, *3 ICSID Reports*, Cambridge University Press, 1995. Paragraph 116. See the relevant parts in Doak Bishop, James Crawford and W. Michael Reisman, *Foreign Investment Disputes. Cases, Materials and Commentary*, Kluwer Law International, The Hague 2005, p. 384.

55 E. Lauterpacht and E. Rayfusse (Ed), *ICSID Reports,* Vol. 3. *Cambridge University Press,* 1995, p. 106.

56 Up to June 2012, the following were the cases filed before ICSID Center against Venezuela: ICSID Case N° ARB/11/30, *Hortensia Margarita Shortt v. Bolivarian Republic of* Venezuela (Subject Matter: Maritime transport services); ICSID Case N° ARB/11/31 *Gambrinus, Corp. v. Bolviarian Republic of Venezuela* (Subject Matter: Fertilizer enterprise); ICSID Case N° ARB/00/5, *Autopista Concesionada de Venezuela, C.A. v. Bolivarian Republic of Venezuela* (Subject Matter: Contract for the construction of a highway system); ICSID Case N° ARB/06/4, *Vestey Group Ltd v. Bolivarian Republic of Venezuela* (Subject Matter: Farming enterprise); ICSID Case N° ARB/07/4, *Eni Dación B.V. v. Bolivarian Republic of Venezuela* (Subject Matter: Hydrocarbon rights); ICSID Case N° ARB/10/14, *Opic Karimun Corporation v. Bolivarian Republic of Venezuela* (Subject Matter: Oil exploration and production); ICSID Case N° ARB/11/1, *Highbury International AVV and Ramstein Trading Inc. v. Bolivarian Republic of Venezuela* (Subject Matter: Mining concession); ICSID Case N° ARB(AF)/11/1, *Nova Scotia Power Incorporated v. Bolivarian Republic of Venezuela* (Subject Matter: Coal supply agreement); ICSID Case N° ARB(AF)/11/2, *Crystallex International Corporation v. Bolivarian Republic of Venezuela* (Subject Matter: Mining company); ICSID Case N° ARB/11/10, *The Williams Companies, International Holdings B.V., WilPro Energy Services (El Furrial) Limited and WilPro Energy Services (Pigap II) Limited v. Bolivarian Republic of Venezuela* (Subject

Tribunals. In particular, among others, and specifically on matter of Jurisdiction of the ICSID Center based on article 22 of the 1999 Investment Law, the following three decisions were issued: ICSID Case N° ARB/07/27, *Mobil Corporation, Venezuela Holdings, B.V., Mobil Cerro Negro Holding, Ltd., Mobil Venezuela de Petróleos Holdings, Inc., Mobil Cerro Negro Ltd. and Mobil Venezolana de Petróleos, Inc. v. Bolivarian Republic of Venezuela*, decision on Jurisdiction dated June 10, 2010 (*Mobile* ICSID Case);[57] ICSID Case N° ARB/08/15, *Cemex Caracas Investments B.V. and Cemex Caracas II Investments B.V. v. Bolivarian Republic of Venezuela*, decisions on Jurisdiction dated December 30, 2010 (*Cemex* ICSID Case);[58] and ICSID Case N° Arb/08/3, *Brandes Investment Partners, LP v. The Bolivarian Republic of Venezuela,* decision dated August 2, 2011 (*Brandes* ICSID Case).[59] In all these three decisions, the ICSID Tribunals concluded that although article 22 of the 1999 Investment Law in effect contained an obligation imposed upon the State to go to international arbitration, which means that the State expressed in it its consent, being possible to grammatically interpret the condition in two valid ways, the intention of the State to submit disputes to international

Matter: Gas compression and injection enterprises); ICSID Case N° ARB/11/25, *OI European Group B.V. v. Bolivarian Republic of Venezuela* (Subject Matter: Industrial plants for production and distribution of glass containers); ICSID Case N° ARB/11/26, *Tenaris S.A. and Talta - Trading e Marketing Sociedade Unipessoal LDA v. Bolivarian Republic of Venezuela* (Subject Matter: Hot briquetted iron production plant); ICSID Case N° ARB/05/4, *I&I Beheer B.V. v. Bolivarian Republic of Venezuela* (Subject Matter: Debt instruments); ICSID Case N° ARB/07/27, *Mobil Corporation and others v. Bolivarian Republic of Venezuela* (Subject Matter: Oil and gas enterprise); ICSID Case N° ARB/09/3, *Holcim Limited, Holderfin B.V. and Caricement B.V. v. Bolivarian Republic of Venezuela* (Subject Matter: Cement production enterprise); ICSID Case N° ARB(AF)/09/1 , *Gold Reserve Inc. v. Bolivarian Republic of Venezuela* (Subject Matter: Mining company); ICSID Case N° ARB/10/19, *Flughafen Zürich A.G. and Gestión e Ingenería IDC S.A. v. Bolivarian Republic of Venezuela* (Subject Matter: Development, operation, and maintenance of an airport); ICSID Case N° ARB/11/5, *Longreef Investments A.V.V. v. Bolivarian Republic of Venezuela* (Subject Matter: Coffee production facilities); ICSID Case N° ARB/11/19, *Koch Minerals Sàrl and Koch Nitrogen International Sàrl v. Bolivarian Republic of Venezuela* (Subject Matter: Construction and operation of fertilizer plant); ICSID Case N° ARB/00/3, *GRAD Associates, P.A. v. Bolivarian Republic of Venezuela* (Subject Matter: Contract for the construction and modernization of penitentiaries); ICSID Case N° ARB(AF)/04/6, *Vannessa Ventures Ltd. v. Bolivarian Republic of Venezuela* (Subject Matter: Gold and copper mining project); ICSID Case N° ARB/07/30, *ConocoPhillips Company and others v. Bolivarian Republic of Venezuela* (Subject Matter: Oil and gas enterprise); ICSID Case N° ARB/08/3, *Brandes Investment Partners, LP v. Bolivarian Republic of Venezuela* (Subject Matter Telecommunication enterprise); ICSID Case N° ARB/08/15, *CEMEX Caracas Investments B.V. and CEMEX Caracas II Investments B.V. v. Bolivarian Republic of Venezuela* (Subject Matter: Cement production enterprise); ICSID Case N° ARB/10/5, *Tidewater Inc. and others v. Bolivarian Republic of Venezuela* (Subject Matter: Maritime-support services); ICSID Case N° ARB/10/9, *Universal Compression International Holdings, S.L.U. v. Bolivarian Republic of Venezuela* (Subject Matter: Oil and gas enterprise); ICSID Case N° ARB/96/3, *Fedax N.V. v. Republic of Venezuela* (Subject Matter: Debt instruments). Information available (on June 22, 2012, at http://icsid.worldbank.org/ICSID/FrontServlet?re-questType=SearchRH&actionVal=SearchSite&SearchItem=venezuela.

57 Available at http://icsid.worldbank.org/ICSID/FrontServlet?requestType=CasesRH &action Val= showDoc&docId=DC1510_En&caseId=C256.

58 Available at http://icsid.worldbank.org/ICSID/FrontServlet?requestType=CasesRH&action Val= showDoc&docId=DC1831_En&caseId=C420.

59 See at http://italaw.com/documents/BrandesAward.PDF.

arbitration, in the cases, lacked to be evidenced. In the end, due to lack of evidences, the ICSID Tribunal eventually declared that they had no Jurisdiction in those cases.

After these three cases were decided, in January 24, 2012 the Government of Venezuela officially withdraws in an irrevocable way from the *Convention on the Settlement of Investment Disputes between States and Nationals of other States*. After receiving the written notice of denunciation of the Convention, the World Bank as the depositary of the ICSID Convention, notified all ICSID signatory States of Venezuela's denunciation of the Convention. In accordance with Article 71 of the ICSID Convention, the denunciation took effect six months after the receipt of Venezuela's notice, that is on July 25, 2012.

The "Official Communiqué" of the Government justifying Venezuela's withdrawing from the ICSID Convention[60] mentioned that its ratification in 1993 was a decision adopted by "a week government without popular legitimacy pressed by traditional transnational economic sectors that participated in the dismantling of the national sovereignty of Venezuela." This statement referred to the government lead by President Ramón J. Velasquez (1993-1994), in which I served as Minister for Decentralization.

Contrary to such assertion, that Government lead by a President Velasquez was a very important transitional one, configured after its appointment by the Congress in June 1993, once the acting President Carlos Andrés Pérez was removed from office by decision of the same Congress, with the support of all the political parties, in order to complete the constitutional term of former President Pérez. That transitional Government had the important task of assuring the continuity of the democratic rule of the country and, in particular, the successful development of the general elections that took place on December 1993. That Government was able to continue conducting the State in the midst of a grave political and economic crisis, having for such purpose all the needed legitimacy derived from the Constitution. Important decisions were adopted in many fields,[61] and also on matters of promotion of investments. In that respect, the signing of the ICSID Convention, according to the general prevailing policy of attracting foreign investments to the country, was a very important one for such purpose.

The "Official Communiqué" of the Venezuelan Government of January 24, 2012, in order to justify the Venezuela's withdrawing from the Convention, in addition expressed that the text of article 151 of the 1999 Venezuelan Constitution[62] supposedly "invalidates, in its spirit and in its wording, the provisions of the ICSID Convention." This assertion only evidenced the most complete ignorance by the Government of President Hugo Chávez of the sense and meaning of such constitutional provision, in which, on the contrary, it is expressly established the

60 The text of the Official Communiqué is available at http://www.noticierodi-gital.com/2012/01ramirez-ratifica-salida-de-venezuela-del-ciadi/.

61 See the collective book: *Ramón J. Velásquez. Estudios sobre una trayectoria al servicio de Venezuela,* Universidad Metropolitana. Universidad de Los Andes-Táchira, Caracas 2003.

62 See the text of the Constitution in *Official Gazette* N° 5.908 Extra. Of February 2, 2009. See the general comments in Allan R. Brewer-Carías, *La Constitución de 1999 y la Enmienda Constitucional N° 1 de 2009*, Editorial Jurídica Venezolana, Caracas 2011; and in *Constitucional Law. Venezuela*, Supplement 97, International Encyclopaedia of Laws, Kluwer, Belguium 2012.

principle of relative jurisdictional sovereign immunity of the State[63] following previous constitutional provisions included in the Constitution since 1947, allowing international arbitration in public contracts except when considered inappropriate according to their nature. The restriction, on the other hand, only refers to matters of arbitration related to public contracts, and in principle is not directed to regulate arbitration resulting from the consent of the State express in a statute.

In effect, Article 151 of the 1999 Constitution establishes that

> "*Article 151*: In contracts of public interest, unless inappropriate according with their nature, a clause shall be deemed included even if not been expressed, according to which the doubts and controversies that may arise on such contracts and that could not be resolved amicably by the contracting parties, shall be decided by the competent courts of the Republic, in accordance with its laws and could not give rise by any motive or cause to foreign claims."

This provision is basically a reproduction of the content of article 127 of the 1961 Constitution, which was kept in the new 1999 Constitution due to my personal proposal made before the National Constituent Assembly,[64] in particular, in order to contradict the "bizarre" and "inappropriate" proposal contained in a document submitted by President of the Republic, Hugo Chávez before the Assembly[65] proposing some constitutional changes. Among those, Chávez first proposed to completely eliminate from the Constitution the "Calvo Clause,"[66] and second, he proposed to return to the principle of absolute jurisdictional sovereign immunity but exclusively regarding public contracts entered by the "Republic," eliminating all jurisdictional restriction regarding other public interest contracts signed by other public entities, that by the way, are the most common and important public contracts in the country, like for instance those signed in the oil and mining industry. That presidential proposal was without doubts, excessive permissive towards international arbitration on matters of pubic law.

63 See in general, Tatiana B. de Maekelt, "Inmunidad de Jurisdicción de los Estados, " in *Libro Homenaje a José Melich Orsini*, Vol. 1, Universidad Central de Venezuela, Caracas 1982, pp. 213 ff.

64 I was Elected Member of the 1999 Constituent Assembly. See my proposal regarding article 151 in Allan R. Brewer-Carías, "Propuesta sobre la cláusula de inmunidad relativa de jurisdicción y sobre la cláusula Calvo en los contratos de interés público," in *Debate Constituyente (Aportes a la Asamblea Nacional Constituyente)*, Vol. I (8-Agosto-8 Septiembre 1999), Fundación de Derecho Público/Editorial Jurídica Venezolana, Caracas 1999, pp. 209-233.

65 See Hugo Chávez Frías, *Ideas Fundamentales para la Constitución Bolivariana de la V República,* Caracas agosto 1999.

66 The *Calvo* Clause had its origin in the work of Carlos Calvo, who formulated the doctrine in his book *Tratado de Derecho Internacional*, initially published in 1868, after studying the Franco-British intervention in Rio de la Plata and the French intervention in Mexico. The *Calvo* Clause was first adopted in Venezuela in the 1893 Constitution as a response to diplomatic claims brought by European countries against Venezuela as a consequence of contracts signed by the State and foreign citizens. See Allan R. Brewer-Carías, *Historia Constitucional de Venezuela*, Vol. I, Editorial Alfa, Caracas 2008, pp. 411.

The two clauses contained in the text of article 151 of the Constitution have been in the text of all Venezuelan Constitutions since 1893.[67] The first clause is the one referred to the principle of jurisdictional sovereign immunity of the State regarding public contracts. Initially it was referred to public contracts entered by the Republic and the States (Venezuela has the federal form of Government), and was conceived as an "absolute" jurisdictional immunity clause. It was first changed in 1901, expanding its initial scope in order to include, not only the "national" and "states" public interest contracts, but also the "municipal" contracts and any other public contract entered by other organs ("public powers") of the State. And later, in 1947 it was also changed regarding the scope of the immunity, transforming it into a "relative" jurisdictional sovereign immunity clause, following the general trend prevailing in comparative constitutional law.[68]

The proposal of Mr. Chávez in 1999 regarding this constitutional clause was to reestablish the absolute sovereign jurisdictional immunity principle abandoned in 1947, but in a limited way only regarding some "national" public interest contracts, that is, only those entered by the Republic, eliminating any kind of restriction on jurisdictional matters regarding public interest contracts entered by the states, the municipalities and other public entities. This presidential proposal, as I argued, was excessive and inconveniently permissive, particularly due to the fact that commonly, the public interest contracts are entered precisely by other entities different to the Republic, and particularly by public corporations and public enterprises.[69]

In any case, leaving aside that failed proposal made by the President of the Republic in 1999, the way the clause has been in the Constitution since 1947, that is, following the "relative" jurisdictional sovereign immunity, cannot be considered as something extraordinary or unusual, particularly because it follows the general principle of relative immunity in contemporary world. According to this Clause, the State is authorized in the Constitution to submit to international arbitration matters of public interest contracts except if the "nature" of their object prevents it, which is referred to the matters generally known as of *ius imperii*. That is why the argument of the Government for withdrawing from ICSID Convention, as well as the suggestion given the by ICSID tribunals in the *Mobil* and *Cemex* cases, arguing that "Venezuela remained reluctant *vis-à-vis* contractual arbitration in the public sphere, as demonstrated by [...] Article 151 of the 1999 Constitution" (*Mobil* ICSID case, 131; 127, 128; *Cemex* ICSID case, 125), simply did not really understood the content of the provision of said article 151, from which no "reluctant" attitude towards arbitration can be deducted. On the contrary, the constitutional provision of article 151 is, precisely, the one that allows international arbitration involving the Venezuelan State according to the principle of relative sovereign jurisdictional

67 See the text of the 1893 Constitution as well as all the other Constitution in the history of the country in Allan R. Brewer-Carías, *Las Constituciones de Venezuela*, Academia de Ciencias Políticas y Sociales, Caracas 2008, 2 vols.

68 See in general the classical book of Ian Sinclair, *The Law of Sovereign Immunity. Recent Developments*, Académie International de Droit International, Recueil des Cours 1980, The Hague 1981.

69 See in Allan R. Brewer-Carías, "Propuesta sobre la cláusula de inmunidad relativa de jurisdicción y sobre la cláusula Calvo en los contratos de interés público," in *Debate Constituyente (Aportes a la Asamblea Nacional Constituyente)*, Vol. I (8-Agosto-8 Septiembre 1999), Fundación de Derecho Público/Editorial Jurídica Venezolana, Caracas 1999, pp. 209-233.

immunity that is the one generally accepted in contemporary world. Consequently, nothing in the Venezuela legal and constitutional order authorizes the Government to say that article 151 of the 1999 Venezuelan Constitution supposedly "invalidates, in its spirit and in its wording, the provisions of the ICSID Convention," which means to consider that an expression of consent for international arbitration as the one contained in article 22 of the Investment Law would be inconceivable in light of article 151 of the Constitution. On the contrary, it is the trend set forth in such article the one that authorizes for the State to go to international arbitration.

The second clause contained in article 151 of the Constitution, inserted in the constitutional text also in 1893, and that has remained without change, is the already mentioned "Calvo Clause," according to which in Venezuela is excluded and is inadmissible any diplomatic claims regarding public interest contracts signed between the different organs of the State and foreign entities or persons. The President of the Republic in his "bizarre" 1999 proposal before the Constituent Assembly, pretended to completely eliminated from the Constitution this centenary "clause," and consequently to allow the possibility that in public interest contracts, their execution could give rise to foreign diplomatic claims against the Republic.[70] From that proposal, it is impossible to deduct any restrictive approach of the President toward arbitration matters. On the contrary, his proposals were inadmissible, being contrary to the interest of the State.

Finally, it must be mentioned, that article 151 of the Constitution establishing the relative sovereign jurisdictional sovereign immunity clause and the *Calvo* Clause, is a provision referred to "public interest contracts," that is, basically, those entered by the three territorial divisions of the State (Republic, States, Municipalities). The clause allows the possibility for the State to give its consent to submit to international arbitration, for instance, disputes related to commercial matters derived from such public interest contracts.

In ICSID arbitration cases, based on jurisdiction through a State's consent given by a statute, as was the case of article 22 of the Investment Law, the ICSID Tribunals were not to deal with public interest contracts regulated in article 151 of the Constitution. The Tribunals in such cases only dealt with the consent given by the Venezuelan State in a statute (Article 22 of the 1999 Investment Law) to submit matters related to investment, generally of industrial, commercial or finance nature, to international arbitration.

In any case the decision of the government to "escape from ICSID,"[71] of course ignored the importance of the ICSID Convention for the purpose of attracting investment, which resulted evidenced by the fact that between 1993 and 1998, many bilateral treaties on investments (BITs) were signed, specifically providing for international arbitration, and in particular, for ICSID International Arbitration.[72] Its

---

70 *Idem.*

71 See James Otis Rodner, "Huyendo del CIADI,", in *El Universal*, Caracas February 7, 2012, available at http://www.eluniversal.com:80/opi-nion/120207/huyendo-del-ciadi

72 See lists of all those treaties at Venezuelan Ministry of for Foreign Relations at http://www.mre.gov.ve/metadot/index.pl?id=4617;isa=Category;op=show; ICSID Database of Bilateral Investment Treaties at http://icsid.worldbank.org/ICSID/FrontServlet; UNCTAD, Investment Instruments On-line Database, Venezuela Country-List of BITs as of June 2008 at http://www.unctad.org/Tem-plates/Page.asp?intItemID=2344 &lang=1. See also, in José Antonio

importance also resulted from the fact that in 2012 the Government that rejected international arbitration, was the same one that in 1999 sanctioned by means of a Decree Law N° 356 of October 3, the 1999 Investment Law containing express recognition of ICSID international arbitration. In it, the Government went farther an expressed, in Article 22 of the Law, the express written consent of the Republic of Venezuela to submit investments disputes to the ICSID arbitration Center, under Article 25.1 of the ICSID Convention. This is a historical fact that in spite of the decision to "escape from ICSID," cannot be denied.

Article 22 of the 1999 Investment Law was not a provision that was officially adopted by the Government without knowing its significance, or that "under the influence of globalization currents was filtered within the Venezuelan regime" as it was affirmed without foundations.[73] On the contrary, it was a conscious decision adopted by a Government that at the time was seeking to promote and encourage international investments in the country, giving investors legal security assurances, like for the disputes to be decided by arbitral tribunals.

For such purpose, in article 22 of the 1999 Investment Law, the State gave its consent to submit investments disputes to ICSID arbitration, expressed in the form of an open offer of arbitration (*oferta abierta de arbitraje*) subjected to acceptance by the investor-claimant to a relevant dispute, to go to international arbitration, or, at his will, to resort to national courts. Not only the signing of the ICSID Convention in 1993, but the text of Article 22 of the 1999 Investment Law, reflected the pro-arbitration trend existing in Venezuela at the time, developed over the past few decades, which crystallized not only in Article 258 of the 1999 Constitution, sanctioned in parallel to the 1999 Investment Law, compelling the State to promote arbitration. This same trend was reflected in an important number of other statutes sanctioned during the same year 1999.

In the ICSID *Mobil* and *Cemex* cases, the tribunals decided that in those particular cases, article 22 of the Investment Law did not provide a basis for their jurisdiction. In the ICSID *Brandes* case, the tribunal without any motivation also ruled that article 22 of the Investment Law did not provide basis for jurisdiction at all. Nonetheless, and contrary to those assertions, since 2005 I have had another opinion, considering that article 22 of the 1999 Investment Law contained the consent of the Venezuela State, as an open offer, to go to international arbitration. My intention in this chapter is to reaffirm the conviction I Have always had, stressing the erroneous motivation of the aforementioned three ICSID tribunals rulings, as well as of the erroneous content of Supreme Tribunal Decision N° 1.541 of 2008 issued by the Constitutional Chamber, at the request of the Government, interpreting Article 22 of the Investment Law in the sense asked by the Government.

Muci Borjas, *El derecho administrativo global y los tratados bilaterales de inversión (BITs)*, Caracas 2007; Tatiana B. de Maekel, "Arbitraje Comercial Internacional en el sistema venezolano," in Allan R. Brewer-Carías (Editor), *Seminario sobre la Ley de Arbitraje Comercial*, Academia de Ciencias Políticas y Sociales, Caracas 1999, pp. 282-283; Francisco Hung Vaillant, *Reflexiones sobre el arbitraje en el sistema venezolano*, Caracas 2001, pp. 104-105.

73 See Hildegard Rondón de Sansó, *Aspectos jurídicos fundamentales del arbitraje internacional de inversión*, Ed. Exlibris, Caracas 2010, p. 132.

IV. THE VENEZUELAN STATE'S EXPRESSION OF CONSENT TO ICSID ARBITRATION JURISDICTION IN ARTICLE 22 OF THE 1999 ABROGATED INVESTMENT LAW

As already mentioned, since 2005 I have considered that Article 22 of the 1999 Investment Law contained a unilateral written expression of consent, in the form of an open offer by the Republic of Venezuela, for international investors to submit investment disputes to international arbitration, including ICSID arbitration. I first expressed that opinion when analyzing in general terms the now abrogated 1999 Investment Law in a *Seminar* held in Caracas, organized by the *Academy of Political and Social Sciences* that was sponsored by the *Venezuelan Arbitration Committee*. That can be considered the first general academic approach made regarding the 1999 Investment Law made in Venezuela, in order to study its provisions, convening a numerous group of Scholars in order to study the different aspects of the Law, from the point of view of the different branches of law.

Previous to such occasion, nonetheless, it must be mentioned that perhaps the first specific analysis of the Venezuelan Law, particularly of its article 22, was made in 2000, immediately after its enactment, by two well-known Venezuelan lawyers, Fermín Toro Jiménez and Luis Brito García, when they filed a popular action challenging the constitutionality of article 22 of the Law before the Supreme Tribunal of Justice. They based their argument in the fact that such provision authorized investors to live aside the national courts and resort to international arbitration, which could only occur if the State in the same provision had already expressed its consent to arbitrate before international arbitration forum. The claimants argued that by leaving the decision to submit the disputes on investments with the State to international arbitration, on the exclusive hands of the international investors, it violated the Constitution. The Constitutional Chamber of the Supreme Tribunal dismissed the case upholding the constitutionality of article 22 in decision N° 186 of February 14, 2001.[74]

In 2005, a Conference on "*Arbitraje comercial interno e internacional. Reflexiones teóricas y experiencias prácticas*" was organized in the Academy of Social and Political Sciences, which was inaugurated by the then President of the Academy Alfredo Morles Hernández, who gave a general overview (*Presentación*) on arbitration. That Presentation altogether with all the papers submitted to the Seminar were all published in a book by the Academy.[75] That academic event followed a previous one, also organized by the same Academy in 1998, on the "*Ley de Arbitraje Comercial,*" in which it was my duty to make the "Presentation," as I was at that time the President of the Academy. All the papers submitted to that Seminar, were also published in the book.[76] In both Seminars, all the Papers

74 See the decision N° 186 of the Constitutional Chamber of the Supreme Tribunal of Justice of February 14, 2001, available at http://www.tsj.gov.ve/decisiones/scon/Febrero/186-140201-00-1438%20.htm.

75 See Irene Valera (Coord.), *Arbitraje comercial interno e internacional. Reflexiones teóricas y experiencias prácticas,* Academia de Ciencias Políticas y Sociales, Caracas 2005.

76 See Allan R. Brewer-Carías (Coord.), *Seminario sobre la Ley de Arbitraje Comercial*, Academia de Ciencias Políticas y Sociales, Caracas 1999.

submitted were academic papers given by Law Professors, with only academic purposes.

It was in the context of the 2005 Seminar on arbitration organized by the Academy in 2005, that I was asked by the Coordinator of the Seminar to submit comments on the 1999 Investment Law, from the exclusive point of view of public internal law, which I did, writing the aforementioned paper on "*Algunos comentarios a la ley de promoción y protección de Inversiones: Contratos Públicos y Jurisdicción*" ("Some Comments on the Law of promotion and Protection of Investments: Public Contracts and Jurisdiction").[77]

As the title of the paper announced, what I wrote, in fact, were "Some Comments" on the Law, making specific emphasis on the legal stabilization intention of the Law; the general legal guaranties given for the protection of investments; the figure of the public contracts for legal stabilization for investments; and the provisions established in the Law for the solution of disputes or controversies on matters of investments. All such comments were expressed in a brief paper written without footnotes, and only based in the analysis of text of the Law. The purpose was merely to divulgate comments on the institutions provided in the Law, which up to that moment, was one statute that have had very little attention in the legal academic world. Those "Some Comments," consequently, were just general comments made regarding the text of the Law from the internal public law point of view, without even quoting for such purpose any decisions of national courts on the matter. That is why no mention was made, for instance, to the Decision N° 186 of the Supreme Tribunal of February 14, 2001 dismissing the already mentioned popular action of unconstitutionality and upholding the constitutionality of article 22 of the Investment Law,[78] particularly because the discussion about the incorporation of arbitration in the 1999 Constitution as part of the judicial system was a matter I considered already without discussion.

Instead, in that occasion in 2005, in the Seminar organized by the Academy, when studying in particular article 22 of the Law and realizing that it contained a general expression of consent given by the Venezuelan State for international arbitration, researching for antecedents of such State's consent to arbitration given through a national statute, I only referred to an ICSID tribunal decision that was drown to my attention, issue in the case *Southern Pacific Properties (Middle East) Ltd. v. Arab Republic of Egypt* (ICSID Case N° ARB/84/3, Decision on Jurisdiction of April 14, 1988) (*SPP case*).[79]

---

77 See Allan R. Brewer-Carías, "Algunos comentarios a la Ley de promoción y protección de Inversiones: contratos públicos y jurisdicción", in Irene Valera (Coordinadora), *Arbitraje Comercial Interno e Internacional. Reflexiones teóricas y experiencias prácticas*, Academia de Ciencias Políticas y Sociales, Comité Venezolano de Arbitraje, Caracas 2005, pp. 279-288. This Paper was later included in my book *Estudios de Derecho Administrativo 2005-2007*, Editorial Jurídica Venezolana, Caracas 2007, pp. 453-462, and is also available at http://allanbrewercarias.com/Content/449725d9-f1cb-474b-8ab2-41efb849fea8/Content/II,%204,%20473.%20Protección%20de%20Inversiones.%20Contratos%20públicos%20y%20jurisdicción%20bis%2010-05.pdf, pp. 7-9.

78 Available at http://www.tsj.gov.ve/decisiones/scon/Febrero/186-140201-00-1438%20.htm

79 See *Southern Pacific Properties (Middle East) Ltd. v. Arab Republic of Egypt,* Case ARB/84/3, May 20, 1992. Decision Award on the Merits, in which mention is made to all the

The matter of the State's consent included in Article 22 of the Venezuelan Law and the solution given in the aforementioned *ICSID SPP* case decision, at that time was for me, from the internal public law point of view, one of the most interesting aspects of the Law, being in fact a novelty in Venezuelan law. It was the first time that I found in the text of a statute in Venezuela, that the State was unilaterally giving its consent for jurisdiction on matters of international arbitration. Never before I knew about any other Law in which the State assumed in a unilaterally way an obligation to submit controversies to international arbitration, that is, with international effects. This was the aspect that at that time called my attention, and doing some research for antecedents of such unilateral expressions of consent, I found the *ICSID SPP* case, which I mentioned in my "Some Comments,"[80] as aforementioned stressed.

As I mentioned, from the internal constitutional and administrative law point of view, the matter of the State expression of consent to ICSID arbitration through a *national statute* was, without doubts, a novelty matter in Venezuela. It was one of the instruments for the State to give consent to arbitration according to the ICSID Convention that authorized the States to give direct consent for international arbitration in an unilateral way through statutes, having as precedent, the case *ICSID SPP*, decided by an ICSID Tribunal by decision of April 14, 1988, precisely regarding matters of Jurisdiction. In it the Tribunal, determined that the aforementioned Article 8 of the Egyptian Law N° 43 constituted "an express 'consent in writing' to the Centre's jurisdiction within the meaning of Article 25.1 of the Washington Convention even in those cases where there is no other agreed-upon method of dispute settlement and no applicable bilateral treaty."[81]

I considered that Article 22 of the Investment Law had similarities to that provision of the Egyptian law, and that the *ICSID SPP* case provided support for the

previous decisions on Jurisdiction, available at http://icsid.worldbank.org/ICSID/FrontServlet?requestType=Cases RH&actionVal=showDoc&docId=DC671_En&caseId=C135

80 In the article, I quoted the 1985 ICSID Centre decision on Jurisdiction issued in the case *Southern Pacific Properties (Middle East) v. Arab Republic of Egypt,* referred to Article 8 of the Egyptian Law N° 43, considering as "an express 'consent in writing' to the Centre's jurisdiction within the meaning of Article 25.1 of the Washington Convention in those cases where there is no other agreed-upon method of dispute settlement and no applicable bilateral treaty." *Decision on Jurisdiction, 27 November 1985,* ¶ 98, *3 ICSID Reports*, Cambridge University Press, 1995. p. 116. At that time, I read the relevant parts of the decision in Doak Bishop, James Crawford and W. Michael Reisman, *Foreign Investment Disputes. Cases, Materials and Commentary*, Kluwer Law International, The Hague 2005, p. 384. In its subsequent Decision on Jurisdiction of 14 April 1988, the Tribunal held the following: "The ordinary grammatical meaning of the words in Article 8, taken together with other Laws and Decrees enacted in Egypt, showed that Article 8 *mandated the submission* of disputes to the various methods described therein, in hierarchical order, where such methods were applicable" and concluded that "Article 8 was legally sufficient manifestation of written consent to the jurisdiction of the Centre, and that no separate ad hoc written consent was required." Also at that time, I read the relevant parts of the decision in E. Lauterpacht and E. Rayfusse (Ed.), *ICSID Reports,* Vol. 3. *Cambridge University Press,* 1995, p. 106.

81 *Southern Pacific Properties (Middle East) Ltd. v. Arab Republic of Egypt,* ICSID Case N° ARB/84/3, Decision on Jurisdiction of April 14, 1988, ¶ 116.

idea that consent may be given through a statute as opposed to a BIT.[82] Article 22 of the 1999 Investment Law, in effect, stated:

> "*Article 22*. Controversies that may arise between an international investor, whose country of origin has in effect with Venezuela a treaty or agreement on the promotion and protection of investments, or controversies in respect of which the provisions of the Convention Establishing the Multilateral Investment Guarantee Agency (MIGA) or the Convention on the Settlement of Investment Disputes Between States and Nationals of Other States (ICSID) *are applicable, shall be submitted to international arbitration according to the terms of the respective treaty or agreement, if it so establishes, without prejudice to the possibility of using, as appropriate, the contentious means contemplated by the Venezuelan legislation in effect*."[83]

Both Articles in the Egyptian (E) and Venezuelan (V) Laws established the same expression of consent of the State to submit disputes on investments to international arbitration, by using the same wording, particularly in the following three expressions: "Shall be settled" (E) or "shall be submitted" (V) [by/to ICSID Center] "within the framework of the Convention"(E) or "under the terms provided for in the respective treaty or agreement"(V); "where such Convention applies"(E) or were such treaties or Convention "are applicable" (V).

In my opinion, the content and structure of both Articles were very similar, and the last expression of the Egyptian law "where such Convention applies," was identical in its meaning to the provision Article 22 of the Venezuelan Law concerning "disputes to which the provisions [of the ICSID Convention] are applicable." This means that, according to the jurisprudence of ICSID, when an internal law containing an expression of consent to submit disputes to international arbitration has a provision which referred to ICSID jurisdiction, the condition of Article 25.1 of the ICSID Convention was fulfilled. For such Article 25.1 to be applicable, it was only required that the dispute arose directly from an investment between the Contracting State and a national of another Contracting State in the

---

82 In its Decision on Jurisdiction of 14 April 1988, the Tribunal held that "[t]he ordinary grammatical meaning of the words in Article 8, taken together with other Laws and Decrees enacted in Egypt, showed that Article 8 *mandated the submission* of disputes to the various methods described therein, in hierarchical order, where such methods were applicable" and concluded that "Article 8 was legally sufficient manifestation of written consent to the jurisdiction of the Centre, and that no separate *ad hoc* written consent was required." *Southern Pacific Properties (Middle East) Ltd v. Arab Republic of Egypt*, ICSID Case N° ARB/84/3, Summary of Decision on Jurisdiction of April 14, 1988, 3 ICSID Reports, p. 106. See also in E. Lauterpacht and E. Rayfusse (Ed.), *ICSID Reports*, Vol. 3. *Cambridge University Press*, 1995, p. 106.

83 Spanish Text: *Artículo 22. Las controversias que surjan entre un inversionista internacional, cuyo país de origen tenga vigente con Venezuela un tratado o acuerdo sobre promoción y protección de inversiones, o las controversias respecto de las cuales sean aplicables las disposiciones del Convenio Constitutivo del Organismo Multilateral de Garantía de Inversiones (OMGI–MIGA) o del Convenio sobre Arreglo de Diferencias Relativas a Inversiones entre Estados y Nacionales de Otros Estados (CIADI), serán sometidas al arbitraje internacional en los términos del respectivo tratado o acuerdo, si así éste lo establece, sin perjuicio de la posibilidad de hacer uso, cuando proceda, de las vías contenciosas contempladas en la legislación venezolana vigente."* The term "*controversias*" has also been translated as "disputes" (instead of "controversies") and the expression "*si así éste lo establece*" has also been translated as "if it so provides" or "should it so provide" (instead of "if it so establishes").

Convention, so due to the mandatory provision to submit to arbitration, no "further or *ad hoc* manifestation of consent of the Center's jurisdiction" was necessary.[84]

While, in general, consent of the States to ICSID arbitration is less commonly given through statutes than through BITs, the *SPP* case provides an example of a statute providing such consent.[85] Based on such similarities, in 2005, I considered that Article 22 of the Venezuelan Investment Law was no different; conclusion that is shared by other commentators;[86] although others have a different point of view.[87]

On the other hand, the interpretation of article 22 of the Investment Law as an open offer of consent of the Venezuelan State for international arbitration was consistent with the policy defined by Congress and the National Executive of Venezuela in 1999 in order to promote and protect international investments. For such purpose, Article 22 of the Investment Law expressed the consent of the Venezuelan State to submit to international arbitration controversies regarding international investment.

Being a provision of a national law, the text of article 22 had to be interpreted according to the principles of interpretation established in Venezuelan law, particularly in article 4 of the Civil Code. Nonetheless, being a national law that gives consent to international arbitration it also has to be interpreted following

---

84 Allan R. Brewer-Carías, "Algunos comentarios a la Ley de promoción y protección de Inversiones: contratos públicos y jurisdicción," *loc. cit*., pp. 286-287.

85 It is therefore not surprising that similar legislations passed in other States have "received less attention from practitioners, academics and international organizations responsible for legal and policy issues related to foreign investments." See Ignacio Suarez Ansorena, "Consent to Arbitration in Foreign Investment Laws," in I. Laird and T. Weiler (Eds.), *Investment Treaty Arbitration and International Law*, Vol. 2, JurisNet LLC 2009, pp. 63, 79.. It is important to note that the constitutionality of the law was upheld in 2001 by the Constitutional Chamber of the Supreme Tribunal of Justice.

86 See, e.g., Andrés A. Mezgravis, "Las inversiones petroleras en Venezuela y el arbitraje ante el CIADI," in Irene Valera (Coordinadora), *Arbitraje Comercial Interno e Internacional. Reflexiones teóricas y experiencias prácticas*, Academia de Ciencias Políticas y Sociales, Comité Venezolano de Arbitraje, Caracas 2005, p. 392. Other commentators also have reached the same conclusion about the similarity between Article 8 of the Egyptian Nº 43 Law and Article 22 of the 1999 Venezuelan Investment Law. See, *e.g*., Victorino Tejera Pérez, "Do Municipal Investment Laws Always Constitute a Unilateral Offer to Arbitrate? The Venezuelan Investment Law: A Case Study," in Ian A. Laird and Todd J. Weiler (Ed.), *Investment Treaty Arbitration and International Law*, Vol 2, JurisNet LLC 2009, pp. 104-105; Victorino Tejera Pérez, *Arbitraje de Inversiones*, Magister Thesis, Universidad Central de Venezuela, Caracas 2010, p. 175. See also Gabriela Álvarez Ávila, "Las características del arbitraje del CIADI", en *Anuario Mexicano de Derecho Internacional*, Vol II 2002, Instituto de Investigaciones Jurídicas, Universidad Nacional Autónoma de México, UNAM, México 2002 (ISSN 1870-4654). http://juridicas.unam.mx/publica/rev/derint/cont/2/cm/; Guillaume Lemenez de Kerdelleau, "State Consent to ICSID Arbitration: Article 22 of the Venezuelan Investment Law" in *TDM*, Vol. 4, Issue 3, June 2007; M.D. Nolan and F.G. Sourgens, "The Interplay Between State Consent to ICSID Arbitration and denunciation of the ICSID Convention: The (Possible) Venezuela Case Study" in *TDM*, Provisional Issue, September 2007.

87 See for instance, Omar E. García-Bolívar, "El arbitraje en el marco de la ley de promoción y Protección de Inversiones: las posibles interpretaciones," in *Revista de Derecho*, Tribunal Supremo de Justicia, Nº 26, Caracas 2008, pp. 313 ff; and more recently, Hildegard Rondón de Sansó, *Aspectos jurídicos fundamentales del arbitraje internacional de inversión*, Ed. Exlibris, Caracas 2010, pp. 123 ff. Sansó, in particular, criticizes my opinion, pp. 146-148.

principles on international law. That is why the three ICSID Arbitral Tribunal decisions on Article 22 of the Venezuelan Investment already mentioned had considered relevant to give consideration of international law along with national law (See *Mobil* ICSID case, 85, 95) *Cemex* ICSID case, 79, 88), and *Brandes* ICSID case, 36). Consequently, it is possible to sustain that both Venezuelan law and international law were relevant in interpreting the Investment Law, bearing in mind that as such Tribunals concluded in the three cases, on matter of interpretation, Venezuelan law does not conflict with international law. That implied, among other principles, that the Tribunals, applying general principles of interpretation in a very similar way, considered that the text of the Article must be analyzed totality and not only in its separate parts.

Consistent with the conclusion that the wording of the law and the connection of the words used is central, and considering the general pro-arbitration content of the Venezuelan legislation issued at the same time by the Government, in my opinion, the only reasonable conclusion is that Article 22 was an expression of a general offer of consent given by the Venezuelan State to submit investment disputes to international arbitration when accepted by international investors; giving the international investor, at his will, the option to go to arbitration or to resort before the national courts.

In effect, the necessity of analyze the wording of article 22 in its context, is a principle of Venezuelan law established in Article 4 of the Civil Code,[88] resulting from it that the expression of consent to international arbitration contained in Article 22 of the Investment Law derived from the meaning of the words used in the provision, considered within the pro-arbitration policy of the Government at the time and within the general context of the whole text, and not from only one part of it. Notably, the language "shall be submitted to international arbitration" ("*serán sometidas al arbitraje internacional*") used in the provision, was an expression of command that conveyed the mandatory nature of Article 22. The phrase "if it so establishes" ("*si así éste lo establece*") mean that such command of Article 22 was subjected to a condition in the sense that it applied if the respective treaty or agreement (Article 22 referred to other treaties alongside the ICSID Convention) contained provisions establishing a framework for international arbitration, that is, "establishes arbitration."[89]

This condition was satisfied by the ICSID Convention, being the open offer of consent expressed in Article 22 confirmed in its last phrase which was a disclaimer: "without prejudice to the possibility of using, as appropriate, the contentious means contemplated by the Venezuelan legislation in effect" *("sin perjuicio de la posibilidad de hacer uso, cuando proceda, de las vías contenciosas contempladas en la legislación venezolana vigente")*. All of these factors in combination gave the

88 Spanish text: Civil Code, "Artículo 4: *A la Ley debe atribuírsele el sentido que aparece evidente del significado propio de las palabras, según la conexión de ellas entre sí y la intención del legislador. Cuando no hubiere disposición precisa de la Ley, se tendrán en consideración las disposiciones que regulan casos semejantes o materias análogas; y, si hubiere todavía dudas, se aplicarán los principios generales del derecho.*"

89 See Victorino Tejera Pérez, "Do Municipal Investment Laws Always Constitute a Unilateral Offer to Arbitrate? The Venezuelan Investment Law: A Case Study," *loc. cit.* pp. 95; Victorino Tejera Pérez, *Arbitraje de Inversiones*, Magister Thesis, Caracas 2010, cit.

international investor the possibility to unilaterally decide, at his will, to submit the particular dispute to international arbitration or to submit the dispute before the national courts. Given the command included in the first part of the Article, the option that the investor had can only exist and make sense if the State had already given its consent to international arbitration by virtue of the State's ratification of the ICSID Convention.

Article 22 of the Investment Law's expression of a unilateral consent by the State to submit disputes with international investors to the jurisdiction of ICSID arbitration on the other hand, was intentionally included by the Government (National Executive), acting as a Legislator, when it enacted the Decree Law N° 356 of October 3, 1999 sanctioning such Law. This intention of the National Executive was also consistent with the general policy defined by the Government at the time of its enactment for the purpose of attracting and promoting international investments in the country, which also lead, at the same time, to the drafting of the constitutional mandate of Article 258 of the 1999 Constitution. This Article 258 imposed on all organs of the State (not only the legislative organs but also the Judiciary)[90] the task to promote arbitration. Other pieces of legislation, from which the pro-arbitration principle was derived, also were issued at the time.[91]

What is absolutely clear from the aforementioned, regarding the content of Article 22 of the Investment Law, is that the reference it contained regarding ICSID international arbitration was not a mere declaration of principles, or a "mere reference in a national law to ICSID" as was suggested by the Supreme Tribunal of Justice in Decision N° 1541 of October 17, 2008, issued at the request of the Attorney general seeking an "official" interpretation of article 22 of the Investment Law.[92] Nor was Article 22 of the Investment Law intended to simply acknowledge the possibility of dispute resolution in ICSID Center. On the contrary, Article 22 of the Investment Law amounted to the binding consent given by the Venezuelan State to arbitral jurisdiction.

---

90 See Eugenio Hernández Bretón, "Arbitraje y Constitución. El arbitraje como derecho fundamental," in Irene Valera (Coordinadora), *Arbitraje Comercial Interno e Internacional. Reflexiones teóricas y experiencias prácticas*, Academia de Ciencias Políticas y Sociales, Comité Venezolano de Arbitraje, Caracas 2005, p. 27.

91 *Idem*, p. 31. See also Francisco Hung Vaillant, *Reflexiones sobre el arbitraje en el derecho venezolano*, Editorial Jurídica Venezolana, Caracas 2001, pp. 66-67.

92 See Decision N° 1.541 of October 17, 2008 of the Constitutional Chamber of the Supreme Tribunal of Justice, available at http://www.tsj.gov.ve/decisiones/scon/Octubre/1541-171008-08-0763.htm, pp. 10-14. It was also published in *Official Gazette* N° 39.055 of November 10, 2008. In this paper, when referring to the Decision No 1541 of 2008, I will quote the pages of the version published in the web site of the Tribunal. See the critical comment on this decision in Eugenio Hernández Bretón, "El arbitraje internacional con entes del Estado venezolano," in *Boletín de la Academia de Ciencias Políticas y Sociales*, N° 147, Caracas 2009, p. 156.

V. THE PRO-ARBITRATION TREND IN THE EVOLUTION OF THE VENEZUELAN LEGAL REGIME IN THE YEARS PREVIOUS TO THE ENACTMENT OF THE 1999 INVESTMENT LAW

At the moment at which the Investment Law was enacted, it can be said that the hostility or unfavorable attitude toward arbitration that existed in Venezuela since the last decade of the 19th century was already completely overcome. The 1999 Investment Law was therefore a piece of legislation completely reconcilable with its historical background, including the State's ratification between 1993 and 1998 of numerous treaties for the protection and promotion of investments (that also provided for international arbitration), as well as the other legal provisions regarding arbitration adopted at the time. Therefore, in 1999, and from a systematic and historical perspective, article 22 of the Investment Law by which the State offered unilateral consent to arbitration in order to promote investment, can be said that was an essential part of the *raison d'être* of the 1999 Investment Law, in complete accord with the political official trend in favor of international arbitration. Furthermore, using the teleological and sociological element of statutory interpretation, the economic and social situation prevailing at the time the 1999 Investment Law was enacted, explains that the former Congress and the National Executive, acting as legislators, intended to promote investments. Offering consent to international arbitration was a means to do so.

That economic policy and the whole legal order existing in 1999, in effect, tended to promote foreign investment and international arbitration,[93] being such policy clearly reflected in the 1999 Investment Law as a whole, primarily devoted to promoting and protecting foreign investment by regulating and limiting the actions of the State in the treatment of such investment. Submission of disputes to international arbitration is precisely one of the principals means of protecting foreign investors and investments. Even the 2008 Decision N° 1.541 of the Supreme Tribunal, recognized that one of the ways States have in order to attract foreign investment is to make a unilateral promise to submit disputes to arbitration. The Tribunal said: "It is not possible to ignore that States seeking to attract investments must in their sovereignty decide to grant certain guarantees to investors, in order for such relationship to take place. Within the variables used to achieve said investments, it is common to include an arbitration agreement, which in the investors' judgment provides them with security in relation to the –already mentioned– fear of a possible partiality of State tribunals in favor of [the tribunals'] own nationals" (p. 29).

1. The historical background of the matter of arbitration: from hostility towards acceptance

The historical background of the Investment Law was summarized in 2005 by the President of the Academy of Social and Political Sciences, Alfredo Morles

---

93 See Victorino Tejera Pérez, "Do Municipal Investment Laws Always Constitute a Unilateral Offer to Arbitrate? The Venezuelan Investment Law: A Case Study," *loc. cit.*, p. 113; Victorino Tejera Pérez, *Arbitraje de Inversiones*, Magister Thesis, Universidad Central de Venezuela, Caracas 2010, p. 154.

Hernández, in the already mentioned *Seminar* organized in 2005[94] in order to analyze and study the 1999 Investment Law. In his opening statement (*Presentación*), what Alfredo Morles said confirms that by 1999, the prevailing attitude towards arbitration in the Government was a favorable one, despite the voices that still existed that opposed to State arbitration as a principle. The statements of Morles also confirm his own favorable attitude towards arbitration. In the last part of the statement of Morles he said:

> "Now, all this hostile culture towards arbitration in general, and all the suspicious and prejudicial attitude of the legal community regarding the its use, has been giving way to a new situation, favored in the international field by the equalitarian treatment between Nations and because the action of international organizations like UNCITRAL in which a wide participation of the Nations of all Regions exists […]."[95]

After reviewing all the elements of that "new trend" favoring international arbitration, particularly the ratification during the past decades of all the most important international conventions on the matter, making particular emphasis on the ICSID Convention, which Morles considered as being "the object of a practically universal acceptance," he clarifies that if it was true that "during a length of time the Latin American counties showed reticence in adhering" "this tendency from some time on has reverted." [96] Morles ended his statement by pointing out that "lawyers and judges have to abandon, that is, forget the reticence towards arbitration; and learn the convenience of its use, for the simple reason that as well as the majority of citizens lack the resources to pay for expensive justice, they also don't have the patience to tolerate justice that is even more slow and suspicious." [97] From what Morles said in his Presentation, when read in totality, what is clear is that its "central theme" was not to consider the matter of traditional hostility towards arbitration, but on the contrary, to stress the "new situation" in favor of international arbitration that substituted the former "hostile culture," and to express the need for the legal community to overcome, that is to "abandon" and "forget" all "reticence towards arbitration" that he considered as an "ideal, rapid and transparent system of conflict resolution."[98] Morles position related to the possibility of the renunciation of jurisdictional immunity in public contracts entered by the Republic referring to external public debt (*empréstito público*) was very different. [99] Since 1970, Morles had criticized the legal opinion of the General Attorney's Office (expressed in 1977) that it was permissible to incorporate in external public debt contracts clauses

94 See Alfredo Morles Herández, "Presentación," in Irene Valera (Coord.), *Arbitraje comercial interno e internacional. Reflexiones teóricas y experiencias prácticas*, Academia de Ciencias Políticas y Sociales, Caracas 2005, pp. 7-14.

95 *Idem*, p. 12

96 *Idem*, pp. 12-13

97 *Idem*, pp. 13-14

98 *Idem*, p. 14

99 *Idem*, pp. 13-14

renouncing the State's jurisdictional immunity which at the time was extensively incorporated in public contracts.[100]

Therefore, it is an historical fact that, particularly after the sanctioning of the 1961 Constitution and well before 1999, the Republic had accepted in a very extensive way, specifically with respect to public contracts, its ability to renounce its jurisdictional immunity.

2. The constitutional evolution on jurisdictional immunity of the State and the healing of old diplomatic wounds

In any case, it is useful to recall the evolution of the constitutional provisions in Venezuela on matters of international arbitration and jurisdictional immunity. During the 19th century and the first two decades of the 20th century, international arbitration was the general rule that the Constitutions imposed to be established in a clause that had to be incorporated in all international treaties for the solution of all differences between the Contracting parties.[101] The clause was reestablished in 1947, although with a wider scope, referring to all international compromises (and not only treaties) and to the solution of controversies by pacific means (and not only arbitration) recognized in international law.

The Constitution has included, since 1893, an important Article with three specific clauses: first, the prohibition for public interest contracts (public interest contracts) to be transferred to foreign States; second, the absolute immunity for jurisdiction clause establishing the obligation of its inclusion in all public contracts; and third, the so called "*Calvo* clause" excluding any diplomatic claims regarding such public contracts. Following this provision, it was precisely, at the turn of the 20th Century, that arbitration was rejected in Venezuela on matters of public law by application of the "*Calvo* Clause," and as a result of events of 1902 that gave rise in Venezuela to the "*Drago* Doctrine."[102] In effect, ten years after the 1893 constitutional reform, a hostile action took place in 1902, with the military blockade of the Venezuelan ports by forces of Germany, Great Britain and Italy made seeking for the compulsory collection of public debts giving rise to the application in

100 See Alfredo Morles Hernández, "La inmunidad de jurisdicción y las operaciones de crédito público," in *Estudios sobre la Constitución, Libro Homenaje a Rafael Caldera*, Universidad Central de Venezuela, Caracas 1979, Vol. III, p. 1717.

101 In the 1864 (Article 112), 1874 (Article 112), 1881 (Article 109), 1891 (Article 109), 1893 (Article 141), 1901 (Article 133), 1904 (Article 120), 1909 (Article 138), 1914 (Article 120), and 1922 (Article 120) Constitutions, an Article was included establishing that in international treaties a clause was to be incorporated with the following text: "All the differences between the contracting parties must be decided, without recurring to war, by arbitration of friendly State or States." See in Allan R. Brewer-Carías, *Las Constituciones de Venezuela*, Academia de Ciencias Políticas y Sociales, Caracas 2008. See J. Eloy Anzola, "El fatigoso camino que transita el arbitraje," in Irene Valera (Coordinadora), *Arbitraje Comercial Interno e Internacional. Reflexiones teóricas y experiencias prácticas*, Academia de Ciencias Políticas y Sociales, Comité Venezolano de Arbitraje, Caracas 2005, p. 410.

102 The *Drago* Doctrine was conceived in 1902 by the then Argentinean Minister of Foreign Relations, Luis María Drago, who –in response to threats of military force made by Germany, Great Britain and Italy against Venezuela– formulated his thesis condemning the compulsory collection of public debts by the States. See generally Victorino Jiménez y Núñez, *La Doctrina Drago y la Política Internacional,* Madrid 1927.

Venezuela of the "*Drago* Doctrine."[103] In any case, all such clauses have remained up to date in the Constitution, although the second one was transformed in 1947 and since 1961, from an absolute jurisdictional sovereign immunity into a relative sovereign immunity for jurisdiction clause.

After all the experiences occurred at the turn of the 20th century, since 1961 and due to the reestablishment in the Constitution (Article 127) of the principle of relative sovereign immunity of jurisdiction, based on a similar provision contained in Article 108 of the 1947 Constitution, the insertion of binding arbitration clauses in public contracts became a generally accepted practice, recognized as valid.[104]

3. The general acceptance of arbitration on matters of private law

On the other hand, on matters of private law, after arbitration was initially established as a constitutional right in the 1830 Constitution (Art. 140),[105] and was authorized as binding in the 19th Century in the civil procedure regulations as a means of alternative dispute resolution, at the beginning of the 20th century, in the 1916 Civil Procedure Code, arbitration was established only as a non-binding method of dispute resolution, that is, without making the arbitration agreement mandatory (Articles 502-522). It was in 1986, with the amendments of the Civil Procedure Code, that the parties were allowed to make a binding agreement to submit controversies to arbitral tribunals, and to exclude the jurisdiction of ordinary courts (Articles 608-629).[106] In addition, special statutes allowed for arbitration in

103 See Allan R. Brewer-Carías, *Historia Constitucional de Venezuela*, Vol. I, Editorial Alfa, Caracas 2008, pp. 411.

104 See Allan R. Brewer-Carías, *Contratos Administrativos*, Colección Estudios Jurídicos N° 44, Editorial Jurídica Venezolana, Caracas 1992, pp. 262-265. The possibility for arbitration clauses to be incorporated in public contracts was first examined in Venezuela in 1960 even before the 1961 Constitution was enacted. See Antonio Moles Caubet, "El arbitraje en la contratación administrativa," in *Revista de la Facultad de Derecho*, N° 20, Universidad central de Venezuela, Caracas 1960, p. 22. See also Alberto Baumeister Toledo, "Algunas consideraciones sobre el procedimiento aplicable en los casos de arbitrajes regidos por la ley de Arbitraje Comercial," in Allan R. Brewer-Carías (Ed.), *Seminario sobre la Ley de Arbitraje Comercial*, Academia de Ciencias Políticas y Sociales, Caracas 1999, pp. 95-98; Allan R. Brewer-Carías, "El arbitraje y los contratos de interés públicos," in Allan R. Brewer-Carías (Coord.), *Seminario sobre la Ley de Arbitraje Comercial*, Academia de Ciencias Políticas y Sociales, Caracas 1999, pp 167-186; Francisco Hung Vaillant, *Reflexiones Sobre el Arbitraje en el Sistema Venezolano*, Editorial Jurídica Venezolana, Caracas 2001, pp. 125-130.

105 See J. Eloy Anzola. "Luces desde Venezuela: La administración de justicia no es monopolio exclusivo del Estado," in *Spanish Arbitration Review, Revista del Club Español de Arbitraje*, N° 4, 2009, p. 62.

106 On the importance and impact of the 1986 Civil Procedure Code reform on matters of arbitration, see Víctor Hugo Guerra Hernández. "Evolución del arbitraje commercial interno e internacional," in Irene Valera (Coordinadora), *Arbitraje Comercial Interno e Internacional. Reflexiones teóricas y experiencias prácticas*, Academia de Ciencias Políticas y Sociales, Comité Venezolano de Arbitraje, Caracas 2005, pp. 42-44; Arístides Rengel Romberg, "El arbitraje comercial en el Código de Procedimiento Civil y en la nueva Ley de Arbitraje Comercial (1998)," in Allan R. Brewer-Carías (Ed.), *Seminario sobre la Ley de Arbitraje Comercial*, Academia de Ciencias Políticas y Sociales, Caracas 1999; J. Eloy Anzola, "El fatigoso camino que transita el arbitraje," in Irene Valera (Coordinadora), *Arbitraje Comercial Interno e Internacional. Reflexiones teóricas y experiencias prácticas*, Academia de Ciencias Políticas y Sociales, Comité Venezolano de Arbitraje, Caracas 2005, p.408.

areas related to copyright, insurance, consumer protection, labor, and agrarian reform.[107]

In addition, Venezuela ratified the 1979 Inter-American Convention on Extraterritorial Validity of Foreign Judgments and Arbitral Awards,[108] the 1975 Inter-American Convention on International Commercial Arbitration,[109] and the 1958 United Nations Convention on the Recognition and Enforcement of Foreign Arbitral Awards (New York Convention).[110] This was followed in 1995, by the ratification of the ICSID Convention,[111] as well as by the signing of all the Bilateral Treaties on promotion and protection of investments (BITs) that were signed during the 90's providing for international arbitration. Finally, in 1998, Venezuela adopted the Commercial Arbitration Law,[112] which is based on the Model Law on International Commercial Arbitration of UNCITRAL.[113]

On the other hand, and specifically on matters of foreign investments, and according to the regime existing at the time, the Executive Decree 2.095 of February 13, 1992 containing the Regulation on the "Common Regime on the Treatment of Foreign Capitals and on Trademarks, patents, Licenses and Royalties, approved in Decisions Nos. 291 and 292 of the Commission of the Cartagena Agreement," established in a general way that "the solution of controversies or conflicts derived from direct foreign investments or sub-regional investors or from the transfer of foreign technology, the jurisdictional or conciliation and arbitration mechanisms established in the law can be used."[114] Consequently, it was a generalized practice to provide for arbitration for the possible solution of investments disputes.

4. The general acceptance of arbitration on matters of public contracts and the sense of the provisions of Article 4 of the Commercial Arbitration Law and of Article 151 of the Constitution

Specifically regarding the extensive use of the mechanisms of arbitration according to the relative jurisdictional immunity clause in public contracts, due to the constitutional provision in the 1961 Constitution that was highlighted by

107 See the laws listed, including the Copyright Law (1993), Insurance Companies Law (1994), Consumer Protection Law (1995), Organic Labor Law (1990), in Francisco Hung Vaillant, *Reflexiones Sobre el Arbitraje en el Sistema Venezolano*, *op. cit.*, pp. 90-101; Paolo Longo F., *Arbitraje y Sistema Constitucional de Justicia*, Editorial Frónesis S.A., Caracas, 2004, pp. 52-77; Víctor Hugo Guerra Hernández. "Evolución del arbitraje commercial interno e internacional," *loc. cit.*, pp. 44-46); and in 2008 Decision N° 1.541, pp. 12-13.

108 *Official Gazette* N° 33.144 of January 15, 1985.

109 *Official Gazette* N° 33.170 of February 22, 1985.

110 *Official Gazette* N° 4832 Extra of December 29, 1994. For an account of international instruments relevant to Venezuela's recognition of international arbitration, see Decision N° 1541 of 2008, pp. 13-14.

111 *Official Gazette* N° 35.685 of April 3, 1995.

112 *Official Gazette* N° 36.430 of April 7, 1998.

113 See generally Arístides Rengel Romberg, "El arbitraje comercial en el Código de Procedimiento Civil y en la nueva Ley de Arbitraje Comercial (1998)," *loc. cit.*, pp. 47 ff.

114 *Official Gazette* N° 34.930 of March 25, 1992.

Morles,[115] as pointed out by the ICSID tribunals in the *Mobil* and *Cemex* case, shows that in 1993 "the environment in Venezuela had become more favorable to international arbitration" (ICSID *Mobil* case, ¶ 130; ICSID *Cemex* case, ¶ 125) in the sense that "the traditional hostility towards international arbitration had receded in the 1990's in favor of a more positive attitude" (ICSID *Mobil* case, ¶ 131). Nonetheless, the ICSID Tribunal in the *Mobil* case added, in an incomprehensible way, that: "However, Venezuela remained reluctant *vis-à-vis* contractual arbitration in the public sphere, as demonstrated by [Article 4 of] the 1998 Arbitration Law and Article 151 of the 1999 Constitution" (Emphasis added) (ICSID *Mobil* case, ¶¶ 131; 127, 128). The same was asserted in the *Cemex* case (ICSID *Cemex* case, ¶ 125). These Tribunals have not really understood the content of both provisions from which no "reluctant" attitude towards arbitration can be drawn.

Article 4 of the Commercial Arbitration Law[116] is an elemental administrative procedural provision, providing the following:

> *Article 4*. When in an arbitral agreement one of the parties is a company in which the republic, the States, the Municipalities or the Public Corporations have a participation equal of higher that the 50% of the capital, or a company in which the legal persons aforementioned have a participation equal or higher that the 50% of the capital, for the validity of the contract the approval of the members of the Board of Directors of the company and the authorization of the Minister of control will be required. The arbitration agreement must specify the sort of arbitration and the number of arbiters, which in no case can be less than three.[117]

The provision imposes only that arbitration agreement can be entered into by decentralized entities in the public sector, according to their by-laws, and that for their validity the approval of the Board of Directors of the contracting entity must be given, as well as the authorization by the Ministry in charge of controlling the specific decentralized entity (*Ministro de tutela*).[118] This provision therefore only

115 See Alfredo Morles Hernández, "La inmunidad de jurisdicción y las operaciones de crédito público," *loc. cit*., p. 1717.

116 Se in *Official Gazette* N° 36.430 of April 7, 1998.

117 Spanish version: *Artículo 4. Cuando en un acuerdo de arbitraje al menos una de las partes sea una sociedad en la cual la República, los Estados, los Municipios y los Institutos Autónomos tengan participación igual o superior al cincuenta por ciento (50%) del capital social, o una sociedad en la cual las personas anteriormente citadas tengan participación igual o superior al cincuenta por ciento (50%) del capital social, se requerirá para su validez de la aprobación de todos los miembros de la Junta Directiva de dicha empresa y la autorización por escrito del ministro de tutela. El acuerdo de arbitraje especificará el tipo de arbitraje y el número de árbitros, el cual en ningún caso será menor de tres (3).*

118 The "*Ministerio de tutela*" expression used in article 4 of the Commercial Arbitration Law cannot be translated, as made by the ICSID Tribunal in the decision in the *Mobil* case, as "Ministry of Legal Protection (ICSID *Mobil* case, ¶ 128). In that Article of the Commercial Arbitration Law, the expression *Ministerio de tutela*, following the well established sense of the administrative law French expression "*contrôle de tutelle*" in order to differentiate it from the "hierarchical control," refers to the Ministry of the National Executive to which a decentralized entity is assigned or attached. In Venezuela, all public enterprises or public corporations must be assigned or attached to a Ministry, which is called *Ministerio de tutela* or *Ministerio de adscripción*. See for instance the expression as has been used in the Organic Law of Public Administration, Articles 78, 97.5, and 120-122. Decree Law N° 6217 of July 15, 2008, in *Official*

establishes administrative procedural requirements.[119] It is therefore incomprehensible to find from such provisions a "reluctant attitude" of Venezuela towards arbitration or that such provision establishes that the country "remained reluctant" towards contractual arbitration (ICSID *Mobil* case, ¶¶ 129, 131; ICSID *Cemex* case, ¶ 125).

More incomprehensible is the reference in the ICSID Mobil decision (ICSID *Mobil* case, ¶¶ 131; 127, 128) to Article 151 of the Constitution in order to prove the "reluctance" of Venezuela towards contractual arbitration. Such provision establishes, as it is generally admitted in international law, on the one hand, the principle of relative immunity for jurisdiction on matters of public contracts; and on the other hand, the principle that foreign States cannot initiate diplomatic claims against the Venezuelan State as a consequence of public contracts entered with foreign corporations ("*Calvo* clause").[120] Therefore, there is nothing extraordinary or unusual.

On the other hand, and as aforementioned explained, those two provisions (article 4, Commercial Arbitration Law; Article 151, Constitution) are precisely among those that are an essential and important manifestations of the pro-arbitration trend of the Venezuelan *legal system*. Consequently, and contrary to the erroneous comment contained in the ICSID Tribunal decisions in the *Mobile* and *Cemex* cases, from the general evolution in favor of arbitration, it is perfectly possible - using the same words of the decisions – (*Mobile ICSID* case, ¶ 138; *Cemex ICSID* case, ¶ 126) to draw "the conclusion that Venezuela, in adopting Article 22, intended to give in advance its consent to ICSID arbitration" particularly if the disclaimer included in the last part of the article giving the investor the right to unilateral chose to go to arbitration or to resort before the national courts, is not ignored. The inclusion of this last phrase of article 22 ("without prejudice to the possibility of using, as appropriate, the contentious means contemplated by the Venezuelan legislation in effect"), which the ISCID tribunals in the *Mobile* and *Cemex* cases did not consider at all, was the one that precisely confirmed the intention of Venezuela to give its advance consent to ICSID arbitration in general. That was the way chosen by the drafters of the 1999 Investment Law enacted by the National Executive to confirm that the first part of the article was an expression of consent as an open offer, by giving the investor the option to go to arbitration or to resort to the national courts.

The fact is that the inclusion of the disclaimer in the provision, only meant to ratify that the State's consent for international arbitration given in the first part of the Article, was given without excluding the possibility for the investor to resort to national courts, when not accepting the open offer made by the State. In other words, this disclaimer contained in the last part of the provision meant that despite the consent given by the Republic, as an open offer for international arbitration, the

---

Gazette N° 5890 Extra. of July 31, 2008. See the comments in Allan R. Brewer-Carías *et al.*, *Ley Orgánica de la Administración Pública*, Editorial Jurídica venezolana, Caracas 2008, pp. 77-79.

119 See on this Article, the comments in Allan R. Brewer-Carías, "El arbitraje y los contratos de interés nacional," *loc. cit.*, pp. 169-204.

120 See on this Article, our proposal before the National Constituent Assembly, in Allan R. Brewer-Carías, "Propuesta sobre la cláusula de inmunidad relativa de jurisdicción y sobre la cláusula Calvo en los contratos de interés público," in *Debate Constituyente (Aportes a la Asamblea Nacional Constituyente)*, Vol. I (8-Agosto-8 Septiembre 1999), Fundación de Derecho Público/Editorial Jurídica Venezolana, Caracas 1999, pp. 209-233.

investor had the option to unilaterally accept the offer to submit the dispute to international arbitration, or to use, as appropriate, the contentious means contemplated by the Venezuelan legislation. This option established in the last part of the article could only have sense and meaning if the first part of the article was interpreted as a unilateral expression of consent, that acted as an open offer given by the State. This meant that the open offer of consent, was given by the State "*sin perjuicio de la posibilidad de hacer uso*" (without prejudice to the possibility of using), as appropriate,[121] the contentious means contemplated by the Venezuelan legislation in effect," leaving to the investor, as a right, the election to submit disputes arising under the Investment Law to international arbitration or to Venezuelan courts.

The sense of the disclaimer of last part of article 22, was the direct consequence of the language used, in the sense that it disclaimed, explained or clarified that the investor had always the possibility to resort to national courts, meaning that after the State had expressed its consent to international arbitration, the investor had the option of accepting the offer given by the State or to submit the dispute to national courts. Otherwise, if one considers that no consent for arbitration was given by the State in the first part of the article, then the disclaimer would have no sense, because according to the Venezuelan Constitution the possibility to resort to national courts is always possible.

This provision of the disclaimer based on the expression "without prejudice," of course cannot be interpreted as having no meaning or purpose, for instance considering that it only applied when the investor had already proceeded to arbitration, or when international arbitration was already commenced. If it were for such purpose, the disclaimer of article 22 would have been superfluous, without any need to be expressed. On the contrary, the final part of article 22 had sense, only when considered as a provision giving the investor the right, as an absolute option, to unilaterally resort (or not) at his will, to international arbitration, once the State gave its consent in the first part of the article. That is, the right provided in the disclaimer could only possibly be granted, if the first part of the Article was a unilateral expression of consent that acted as an open offer, given by the State.

It is well known that the expression "*sin perjuicio de*" in the Spanish Grammar is known as a "*locución adverbial*" (adverbial expression or diction), mainly used in legal texts, equivalent to the expressions "*dejando a salvo,*" "*sin detrimento de*" or "*sin menoscabo de*" and used to specify that when a particular conduct is ordered in the specific legal provision, it does not mean that it excluded or affects other possible conduct. That is, that the inclusion of a conduct in the norm, does not affect other possible conducts allowed in the legal order, expressed in the provision. In order to have sense and meaning, therefore, a conduct must be regulated expressly in the provision in order to clarify that it does not affect other conducts that can be also accomplished. This is the sense of a norm providing for a particular conduct

121 The expression "as appropriate" was referred to the matters that in Venezuela could be submitted to arbitration, like the use of the power of taxation or the power of expropriation. See for instance, Allan R. Brewer-Carías, *Contratos Administrativos*, Caracas 1997, p. 265. These are the same State powers that cannot be subjected to transactions. See Allan R. Brewer-Carías, "Las transacciones fiscales y la indisponibilidad de la potestad y competencia tributarias," en *Revista de Derecho Tributario*, N° 18, Caracas, mayo-junio 1967, pp. 1-36.

"without prejudice to" the possibility of doing other thing, or not affecting the possibility of doing another thing.

It was precisely the sense of Article 22 of the 1999 Investment Law when providing for the State consent for international arbitration which was given without excluding the possibility for the investor to resort to national courts by not accepting the open offer made by the State. The adverbial expression allowing the investor to go to national courts had sense only if it had the choice to opt to go to international arbitration accepting the open offer expressed by the State in the provision, or to resort to national courts for the resolution of international investments disputes. In the case of article 22 of the Investment Law, if no open offer for arbitration was contained in the first part of the article, the disclaimer of the second part would have no sense, because national courts were and are always available for the resolution of disputes according to the Constitution, and there was no need to expressed it in the provision, except in order to emphasize that the consent given by the State for international arbitration do not prevented for the investor to opt to resort to national courts, at his will.

In any case, when interpreting a provision of a statute, the interpreter, including international arbitration tribunals, is obliged to analyze its whole text and its actual wording, and not only a part of the article; not being allowed to ignore another part of the article, and much less to arrive to an interpretative conclusion only based on the speculative point of view of the interpreter, including tribunals, on how it would have written the article if it would have been in the position of its drafter. And that exercise could not be admitted because it would be an invalid speculation due to the fact that in a "legal clinic or laboratory," in a *ex post facto* way, it would be impossible to reconstruct the political environment surrounding the drafting of a Law, and much less, the one existing in a new government seeking for international investments as was the case in 1999 regarding the Investment Law of that year. The judges' arguments and speculations on how would have been the better way to write or not to write an article of a law in 1999, in Venezuela, is not the correct way to resolve a dispute regarding the interpretation of a statute.

That is why, it is completely unacceptable for a tribunal to base its ruling by stating in a hypothetical way, as was the case of the ISCID tribunals in the *Mobile* and *Cemex* cases, on how "would have been easy for the drafters of Article 22 to express that intention clearly by using any of those well-known formula" (*Mobile ICSID* case, ¶ 139; *Cemex ICSID* case, ¶ 137). National courts and Arbitral tribunal decisions are not conceived as a means to give writing rules to the drafters of statutes on how to write or not to write them, but to interpret their provisions following the rules of interpretation, even if they are not written in the way the tribunal would have written them.

In any case, apart the writing lessons, the conclusions of the ICSID tribunals in the *Mobile* and *Cemex* cases, eventually were to say that from the wording of article 22 of the 1999 Investment Law the intention of the Government to express the State consent to submit investments disputes to international arbitration only subjected to the condition that a treaty or an agreement provide a framework or mechanisms for arbitration, "is not established" (*Mobile ICSID* case, ¶ 140; *Cemex ICSID* case, ¶ 138), and that they could not conclude specifically and only in such cases, "that Venezuela, in adopting the 1999 Investment Law, consented in advance [or "unilaterally"] to ICSID arbitration for all disputes covered by ICSID Convention" ruling therefore, that such article "does not provide basis for jurisdiction of the Tribunal in the present case" (*Mobile ICSID* case, ¶ 140; *Cemex ICSID* case, ¶ 138).

Nonetheless, as mentioned above, the ICSID Tribunal decision in the *Brandes* case, without any reasoning, arguments or motivation, proclaimed in a general and universal way, and not only for the "present case," that "it is obvious that Article 22 of the Law on Promotion and protection of Investments does not contain the consent of the Bolivarian Republic of Venezuela to ICSID jurisdiction" (*Brandes ICSID* case, ¶ 118).

The difference between this decision in the *Brandes* if compared with the decisions in the *Mobile* and *Cemex* cases, at least from the point of view of the general standard rules governing judicial decisions, as aforementioned, completely lacked of the reasons or motives on which it was based.

5. The legal doctrine of the Attorney General's Office on acceptance of arbitration on matters of public contracts

Since the 1970's, as was pointed out by Alfredo Morles,[122] in Venezuela, it was a generally accepted practice to include in public contracts the relative immunity clause.

Nonetheless, almost two decades later, the Office of the Attorney General of the Republic, as the constitutionally-appointed entity responsible for advising the National Executive on legal matters, intended to review the issue of jurisdictional sovereign immunity included in public external debt contracts (*contratos de empréstitos públicos*) entered into by the Republic.[123] In such regard, a formal Legal Opinion was given by the Attorney General's Office that same year, through Letter N° 4211 of December 19, 1996, directed to the Minister of Finance[124] reviewing the previous legal criteria expressed by the same Office in the 1970's regarding the "commercial" nature of the external public debt contracts, proposing that the Republic cease renouncing its entitlement to jurisdictional immunity in such contracts. This Opinion was unsuccessful in changing the legal principles that have been well-established since 1970's, and was, in any event, abandoned four months later, in April 1997. Nonetheless, the subject matter of the Opinion was only the

122 See Alfredo Morles Hernández, "La inmunidad de jurisdicción y las operaciones de crédito público," *loc. cit.*, p. 1717.

123 In that regard, Jesús Petit Da Costa, the Attorney General of the Republic at the time, published in September 1996 an Op-Ed in a mayor News paper of Caracas, containing its "personal opinion" regarding the possibility of subjecting the Republic, not to the jurisdiction of arbitral tribunals generally, but only to the jurisdiction of "foreign tribunals." In any case, the Article titled "*Blindar con la Constitución*" (*El Universal*, Caracas, September 14, 1996), had nothing to do with arbitration, and does not refer to international arbitration at all ("arbitration" is a word that is not even used in the Article), and only refers to "foreign tribunals" (*tribunal extranjero*) meaning courts of other foreign States.

124 Letter N° 4211 of December 19, 1996 directed to Luis Raúl Matos Azocar, Ministry of Finance.

matter of jurisdictional immunity in public debt contracts and not the availability or constitutionality of international arbitration.[125]

In effect, on April 21, 1997,[126] the Attorney General recognized the relevance of the relative jurisdictional sovereign immunity clause contained in Article 127 of the 1961 Constitution (equivalent to article 151 of the 1999 Constitution regarding to public contracts), and provided that the security of the Republic or its internal sovereignty is not compromised, admitting that 'the submission to a foreign jurisdiction cannot signify a violation of Article 127 of the Constitution."[127]

6. The inclusion of arbitration clauses in public contracts since the 1990's with the knowledge and consent of the Attorney General's Office

According to this legal doctrine, and even before the quickly defunct Opinion of 1996, the Attorney General's Office consistently gave its acceptance for the inclusion of arbitration clauses in many public statutes and public decisions.

First, in 1994, in the Decree Law N° 138 of April 20, 1994, which was another important statute on promotion of investments sanctioned by the Government, containing the Organic Law on Concessions of Public Works and National Public utilities,[128] issued by the President of the Republic with the legal consent of the General Attorney Office. This law includes an Article expressly establishing that "the National Executive and the concessionaire could agree that the doubts and controversies that may arise resulting from the interpretation and execution of the concession contract would be decided by an arbitral tribunal whose composition, competency, procedure and applicable law shall be determined by the parties" (Article 10).[129]

Second, in 1995, the Attorney General's Office also accepted an international arbitration clause that was included in the Congressional Resolution (*Acuerdo*) establishing the Framework of Conditions for the "Association Agreements for the

---

125 In addition, in the Opinion, the Attorney General, only ratified his personal assertion made in the Article published three months before, expressing the same concerns.

126 See excerpt of the Opinion in Margot Y. Huen Rivas, "El arbitraje internacional en los contratos administrativos," in *VIII Jornadas Internacionales de Derecho Administrativo "Allan Randolph Brewer-Carías," Los contratos administrativos. Contratos del Estado*, Fundación de Estudios de Derecho Administrativo, FUNEDA, Vol. I, Caracas 2005, pp. 434-435; and Juan Carlos Balzán, "El arbitraje en los contratos de interés a la luz de la cláusula de inmunidad de jurisdicción prevista en el artículo 151 de la Constitución," in *VIII Jornadas Internacionales de Derecho Administrativo "Allan Randolph Brewer-Carías," Los contratos administrativos. Contratos del Estado*, Fundación de Estudios de Derecho Administrativo, FUNEDA, Vol. II, Caracas 2006, pp. 345.

127 *Id.* This was later included even more expressly in the 2005 Law on the Financial Administration of the Public Sector, Article 104. See *Offical Gazette* N° 37.978 of July 13, 2004.

128 See *Official Gazette* N° 4719 Extra. of April 26, 1994.

129 See in Luis Fraga Pittaluga, "El arbitraje y la transacción como métodos alternativos de Resolución de conflictos administrativos," in *IV Jornadas Internacionales de Derecho Administrativo Allan Randolph Brewer Carías, La relación jurídico-administrativa y el procedimiento administrativo*, Fundación de Estudios de Derecho Administrativo, FUNEDA, Caracas 1998, p. 178. This means that Fraga considered in 1998 that "the admission of arbitration in administrative field is an irreversibly tendency," *Id.* p. 177.

Exploration at Risk of New Areas and the Production of Hydrocarbons under the Shared-Profit Scheme" ("*Convenios de Asociación Para la Exploración a Riesgo de Nuevas Areas y la Producción de Hidrocarburos Bajo el Esquema de Ganancias Compartidas*"), dated July 4, 1995.[130]

This provision was challenged on the grounds of its supposed unconstitutionality before the Supreme Courts of Justice through a popular action brought, among others, by Ali Rodríguez Araque then member of Congress, and appointed 1999 as Minister of Energy and Mines. Rodríguez Araque opposed, together with the other co-claimants, the inclusion of the arbitration clause in the Congressional Resolution and in the Association Agreements. Based on these antecedents, and knowing Mr. Rodríguez personally, I assume that in 1999, acting as the Minister of Energy and Mines, he must have opposed to the inclusion of Article 22 of the Investment Law because providing it provided the State's consent to arbitration.

In August 1999, the Supreme Court of Justice dismissed the action filed by Rodríguez Araque and others, upholding the constitutionality of the Congressional Resolution authorizing the Framework of Conditions for the "Association Agreements for the Exploration at Risk of New Areas and the Production of Hydrocarbons under the Shared-Profit Scheme," holding that such authorization and, in particular, the inclusion of arbitration clauses in public law contracts, were valid under Article 127 of the 1961 Constitution in force at the time (equivalent to Article 151 of the 1999 Constitution).[131] This decision of the Supreme Court of Justice, since then, has been considered as the leading judicial precedent on the matter of arbitration in public contracts and on the sense of the relative sovereign immunity of jurisdiction clause in the country.[132]

During the same time period, Article 4 was included in the Commercial Arbitration Law of 1998, expressly admitting, as previously mentioned, the inclusion of arbitral clauses in public contracts, upon approval by the competent

---

130 *Official Gazette* N° 35.754 of July 17, 1995.

131 See decision in Allan R. Brewer-Carías (Compilator), *Documentos del Juicio de la Apertura Petrolera (1996-1999)*, Caracas, 2004 *available at* http://allanbrewercarias.com/Content/449725d9 -f1cb-474b-8ab2-41efb849fea3/Content/I,%202,%2022.%20%20APERTURA%20PETROLERA.%20DOCU-MENTOS%20DEL%20JUICIO.pdf, pp. 280-328. I acted as counsel to PDVSA in that judicial proceeding, defending the constitutionality of that *Acuerdo*, and in particular, the constitutionality of the arbitration clause included in the Association Agreements. The Constitutional Chamber of the Supreme Tribunal of Justice has confirmed the ruling made under the 1961 Constitution, holding that Article 151 of the 1999 Constitution allows the incorporation of arbitration provisions in contracts of public interest. See 2008 Decision N° 1.541, pp. 23-24) and Decision N° 97 of February 11, 2009 (*Interpretation of Articles 1 and 151 of the Constitution. Fermín Toro Jiménez, Luis Brito García et al.*). See the comments on the August 1999 upholding the Congress Resolution approving the Framework of the Association Agreement I made when rejecting the constitucional proposal of President Chávez regarding Article 151 of the Constitution, in Allan R. Brewer-Carías, "Propuesta sobre la cláusula de inmunidad relativa de jurisdicción y sobre la cláusula Calvo en los contratos de interés público," in *Debate Constituyente (Aportes a la Asamblea Nacional Constituyente)*, Vol. I (8-Agosto-8 Septiembre 1999), Fundación de Derecho Público/Editorial Jurídica Venezolana, Caracas 1999, pp. 220-229.

132 See Juan Carlos Balzán, "El arbitraje en los contratos de interés a la luz de la cláusula de inmunidad de jurisdicción prevista en el artículo 151 de la Constitución," *loc. cit.*, pp. 349-357; Margot Y. Huen Rivas, "El arbitraje internacional en los contratos administrativos," *loc. cit.*, pp. 438-39.

organ according to the by-laws of the entity and written authorization by the Ministry in charge of controlling the activities of the specific decentralized entity. The provision is no more that the express ratification and express acceptance by Congress of the possibility to include arbitration clauses in public contracts.[133] It does not deal with the competence of public entities to include arbitration clauses in public contracts, which is accepted, being only an administrative procedural provision establishing one of the most elemental rules of management in Public Administration, which is control.

On the other hand, the availability of arbitration as a remedy was recognized in a number of subsequent judicial decisions, a number of which were issued before the 1999 Investment Law was enacted.[134] For example, in January 15, 1998, the Supreme Court of Justice in Politico Administrative Chamber issued another decision (*Industrias Metalúrgicas Van Dam, C.A. vs. República de Venezuela. Ministerio de la Defensa* case), in which an arbitration clause was recognized in public contracts, although because the military object of the contract in the specific case, in a restrictive way regarding the "technical aspects" of the contract excluding matters of matters of national security and defense.[135]

In any case, what is important to highlight is that the general situation during the decades (and not only years) prior to 1999, shows a clear tendency of surpassing the historic "reticence" that could have existed regarding arbitration clauses and State jurisdictional immunity in public law contracts before the 1961 Constitution was enacted and before the Civil Procedure Code was reformed in 1986. This reticence was supplanted by a general acceptance of the possibility for public entities to include in public contracts arbitral clauses, as was expressly ratified in the 1998 Commercial Arbitration Law. At that time, the official doctrine of the Attorney General's Office, the general constitutional, administrative and international law legal doctrine, and the jurisprudence of the Supreme Court of Justice were clearly in favor of these principles.

---

133 See Allan R. Brewer-Carías, "El arbitraje y los contratos de interés nacional," in *Seminario sobre la Ley de Arbitraje Comercial*, Biblioteca de la Academia de Ciencias Políticas y Sociales, Caracas 1999, pp. 169-204.

134 See the cases quoted in Juan Carlos Balzán, "El arbitraje en los contratos de interés a la luz de la cláusula de inmunidad de jurisdicción prevista en el artículo 151 de la Constitución," pp. 333-335, 349 and in José G. Villafranca, "Precisión jurisprudencial en torno a la inmunidad de jurisdicción en demandas por responsabilidad patrimonial (Comentario a la sentencia de la CSJ-SPA de fecha 30-07-1998)," in *Revista de Derecho Administrativo*, N° 4, Editorial Sherwood, Caracas 1998, p. 347-360.

135 See excerpt quoted in Juan Carlos Balzán, "El arbitraje en los contratos de interés a la luz de la cláusula de inmunidad de jurisdicción prevista en el artículo 151 de la Constitución," *loc. cit.*, pp. 349-350.

VI. PRINCIPLES OF INTERPRETATION OF ARTICLE 22 OF THE ABROGATED 1999 INVESTMENT LAW AS A STATE'S UNILATERAL OPEN OFFER OF CONSENT FOR INTERNATIONAL ARBITRATION

1. The inclusion of international and national arbitration provisions in the 1999 Investment law

As aforementioned, regarding the content of Article 22 of the 1999 Investment Law, the reference it contained regarding ICSID international arbitration was not a mere declaration of principles, or a mere reference in a national law to ICSID international arbitration Center as suggested by some commentators[136] and by the Supreme Tribunal of Justice Decision N° 1541 of 2008[137] (p. 49). Nor was Article 22 of the Investment Law intended just to acknowledge the possibility of dispute resolution by means of arbitration. On the contrary, Article 22 of the Investment Law amounted to the binding consent of Venezuela to arbitral jurisdiction. On the other hand, arbitration as a means for dispute resolution was included in many other statutes adopted by the Government at the same time, and there are other references to the availability of arbitration in the same 1999 Investment law.

In effect, beside Article 22, arbitration was also provided in Article 18.4 of the Law regarding the contracts for legal stabilization. Following the 1998 Commercial Arbitration Law regulations, the State and an international investor could establish arbitration, in a bilateral act –the contract for legal stabilization– as the means to resolve contractual controversies.[138]

Arbitration was also provided for in Article 21 of the Investment Law regarding the solution of controversies relating to the Investment Law that could arise between the Venezuelan State and the country of origin of the international investor.[139] In these cases, when the diplomatic means fail, the Law imposed the obligation on the State to seek for the submission of the dispute to an Arbitral Tribunal whose composition, mechanism of designation, procedure and cost regime had to be negotiated in a bilateral act with the other State. In these two first cases (Articles

---

136 See Hildegard Rondón de Sansó, *Aspectos jurídicos fundamentales del arbitraje internacional de inversión*, Ed. Exlibris, Caracas 2010, pp. 129, 139

137 Other commentators have expressed the same criticism of this decision. See, e.g., Eugenio Hernández Bretón, "El arbitraje internacional con entes del Estado venezolano," in *Boletín de la Academia de Ciencias Políticas y Sociales*, N° 147, Caracas 2009, p. 156.

138 Article 18.4 of the 1999 Investment Law provided that: "Any disputes that arise between the companies of investors which signed the legal stabilization contract and the Venezuelan State, concerning the interpretation and application of the respective contract may be submitted to institutional arbitration pursuant to the Law on Commercial Arbitration."

139 Article 21 of the 1999 Investment Law stated that: "Any dispute that arises between the Venezuelan State and the country of origin of the International investor with which no treaty or agreement on investments is in effect, concerning the interpretation and application of the provisions of this Decree Law shall be resolved through diplomatic channels. In no agreement is reached within twelve months following the date on which the dispute began, the Venezuelan State shall recommend that the dispute be placed before an Arbitral Tribunal, whose composition, mechanism for the appointment thereof, procedure and expense regime shall be agreed upon with the other State. The decisions of this Arbitral Tribunal shall be final and binding."

18.4 and 21), in order to proceed to arbitration, the Law was clear in providing for the need of a separate bilateral act to be negotiated between the parties.

On the contrary, in other two provisions of the same 1999 Investment Law which provided for arbitration, Articles 22 and 23, the State had given **in advance** its consent for arbitration, as an open offer in the same way as it is provided in almost all BITs, using similar wording that the dispute "shall be submitted" to international arbitration. Both the Investment Law and BITs provided that investors, at their will, could unilaterally choose to go to arbitration or to resort to the national courts.[140] In the case of Article 22, as aforementioned, the State expressed in advance, as an open offer, its consent to go to international arbitration subject to the only condition that the treaties or agreements provide mechanisms or a framework for international arbitration.

This interpretation of Article 22 of the Investment Law as containing a unilateral written expression of consent of the Republic of Venezuela to submit disputes with international investors to the jurisdiction of ICSID arbitration was shared by the majority of the Venezuelan legal commentators[141] as well as many foreign authors.[142] For example, one commentator stated in 2007 that the Investment Law leaves "no doubt at all on the viability of arbitration to resolve controversies between States and foreign investors .... [because it] establishes in a very clear way that the investor, in case of controversy, has the possibility to opt between resort to the ordinary judicial mean or to ICSID, provided that (i) Venezuela and the country from which the investors is a national have signed a treaty on promotion and protection of investments, or (ii) the provisions of the Constitutive Convention of MIGA or of ICSID Convention are applicable, in which case –in our opinion– the

140 See in this regard, Tatiana B. de Maekelt, "Tratados Bilaterales de Protección de Inversiones. Análisis de las cláusulas arbitrales y su aplicación," in Irene Valera (Coord.), *Arbitraje Comercial Interno e Internacional. Reflexiones teóricas y experiencias prácticas*, Academia de Ciencias Políticas y Sociales, Comité Venezolano de Arbitraje, Caracas 2005, pp. 340-341.

141 See for instance Andrés A. Mezgravis, "Las inversiones petroleras en Venezuela y el arbitraje ante el CIADI", in Irene Valera (Coordinadora), *Arbitraje Comercial Interno e Internacional. Reflexiones teóricas y experiencias prácticas*, Academia de Ciencias Políticas y Sociales, Comité Venezolano de Arbitraje, Caracas 2005, p. 388; Eugenio Hernández Bretón, "Protección de inversiones en Venezuela" in *Revista DeCITA, Derecho del Comercio Internacional, Temas de Actualidad, (Inversiones Extranjeras)*, N° 3, Zavalía, 2005, pp. 283-284; José Antonio Muci Borjas, *El Derecho Administrativo Global y los Tratados Bilaterales de Inversión (BITs)*, Caracas 2007, pp. 214-215; José Gregorio Torrealba R, *Promoción y Protección de las Inversiones Extranjeras en Venezuela*, Funeda, Caracas 2008. pp. 56-58, 125-127; Victorino Tejera Pérez, "Do Municipal Investment Laws Always Constitute a Unilateral Offer to Arbitrate? The Venezuelan Investment Law: A Case Study," pp. 90, 101, 109; Victorino Tejera Pérez, *Arbitraje de Inversiones*, Magister Thesis, Caracas 2010, *cit.*, pp. 162, 171, 173, 177, 193.

142 See for instance Gabriela Álvarez Ávila, "Las características del arbitraje del CIADI", en *Anuario Mexicano de Derecho Internacional*, Vol. II 2002, Instituto de Investigaciones Jurídicas, Universidad Nacional Autónoma de México, UNAM, México 2002; Guillaume Lemenez de Kerdelleau, "State Consent to ICSID Arbitration: Article 22 of the Venezuelan Investment Law" in *TDM*, Vol. 4, Issue 3, June 2007.

country of nationality of the investor must also have signed and ratified at least one of such Conventions."[143]

The contrary opinion in the sense that Article 22 of the Investment Law did not constitute a standing, general consent of the Republic to arbitrate all investments disputes before ICSID" was shared only by a few authors,[144] which considered in general, that since the ICSID Convention supposedly did not provide for a consent to ICSID arbitration, a separate instrument of consent was required as a condition in Article 22. This was of course a misrepresentation of the wording of Article 22, because the condition established in it only referred to the need for mechanisms of arbitration to be provided in the treaties or agreements, not for a separate consent as was required for instance in Article 21 of the same 1999 Investment Law. To adopt this interpretation would amount to accepting, in an inadmissible tautological way, that the right given to the investor to opt between going to arbitration or before the national court, did not actually allow the investor to choose between those options, which would make the disclaimer of the last phrase of Article 22 completely meaningless.[145]

These opinions failed to analyze the content of Article 22 as a whole, in the general context of the 1999 Law, particularly the last part of the provision, which as aforementioned was generally ignored, and not even mentioned or analyzed in the referred ICSID *Mobil, Cemex* and *Brandes* cases. They fail to acknowledge that the provision gave the investor the right, as an absolute option, to unilaterally resort (or not) at his will, to international arbitration. This was a right that could only possibly be granted if the first part of the Article is a unilateral expression of consent that acted as an open offer, given by the State. This means that when the words of Article 22 (including those used in the last phrase of Article 22: "without prejudice to the possibility of using, as appropriate, the contentious means contemplated by the Venezuelan legislation in effect") are contrasted with those of Article 23 of the same Law,[146] the wording of Article 22 is stronger than Article 23, which contained a unilateral consent to arbitration on the part of the Republic. Article 22 and also Article 23, both gave investors the option to submit disputes arising under the Investment Law to arbitration. In the case of Article 22, to international arbitration

143 See Juan C. Bracho Ghersi, "Algunos Aspectos fundamentales del Arbitraje Internacional," in *Cuestiones actuales del Derecho de la empresa en Venezuela,* Grau, García, Hernández, Mónaco, Caracas 2007, pp. 18.

144 See for instance, Omar E. García-Bolívar, El arbitraje en el marco de la ley de promoción y Protección de Inversiones: las posibles interpretaciones," in *Revista de Derecho*, Tribunal Supremo de Justicia, Nº 26, Caracas 2008, pp. 313 ff. Moer recently, see Hildegard Rondón de Sansó, *Aspectos jurídicos fundamentales del arbitraje internacional de inversión*, Ed. Exlibris, Caracas 2010, pp. 123 ff.

145 See Victorino Tejera Pérez, *Arbitraje de Inversiones*, Magister Thesis, Caracas 2010, *cit*., p. 190; Victorino Tejera Pérez, "Do Municipal Investment Laws Always Constitute a Unilateral Offer to Arbitrate? The Venezuelan Investment Law: A Case Study," *loc. cit*., pp. 107. See also Eugenio Hernández Bretón, "El arbitraje internacional con entes del Estado venezolano," *loc. cit*., pp. 141-168.

146 Article 23 of the Investment Law states: "Any dispute arising in connection with the application of this decree Law, once the administrative remedies have been exhausted, may be submitted by the investor to the National Courts or Arbitral Tribunals of Venezuela, at the election of the investor."

or to Venezuelan courts; and in the case of Article 23, to Venezuelan courts or Venezuelan arbitral tribunals. In both cases, the decision was made *at the election of the investors*.

That is, Article 23 contained an arbitration clause or a unilateral consent to arbitration on the part of the Republic by giving investors the option to submit disputes under the investment Law to Venezuelan courts or Venezuelan arbitral tribunals; and also, Article 22 provided the same option, but between international arbitration and national courts, not being correct to ignore the choice offered in that provision. In a similar way, regarding clauses for arbitration in BIT's executed by Venezuela, which define the scope of the dispute to be resolved, giving the foreign investor the option to initiate arbitration before ICSID or in another forum, leaving no doubt that Venezuela is consenting to arbitration of that dispute before ICSID; also Article 22 of the Investment Law was an express consent to arbitration given by the State, leaving also to the international investor the option to initiate arbitration before ICSID or in Venezuelan courts, leaving no doubt that Venezuela was consenting to arbitration of that dispute before ICSID.

This is what was precisely decided in the *Mobil* and *Cemex* cases, in which the Tribunals determined without doubt, that Article 22 contained a unilateral declaration of the State establishing an obligation to go to arbitration, although subjected to a condition. Consequently, Article 22 of the Investment Law was considered in both ICSID tribunals' decisions as a unilateral expression of consent given by the Venezuelan State to submit disputes to international arbitration, although subjected to a condition. This also is true of the *Brandes* decision. The reason why these Tribunals nevertheless determined that this did not provide consent for the international investor to resort to ICSID arbitration was only based in the lack of evidence regarding the intent of the State when enacting the Law and assuming the obligation, but not in the fact that the obligation to go to arbitration (although conditional) was not established in article 22.

The sanctioning of the Investment Law by the Government in 1999 had the clear intention to serve as an instrument for the development and promotion of private (foreign and domestic) investment in Venezuela, in accordance with the mandate included in parallel in article 258 of the 1999 Constitution to promote alternative mechanisms for dispute resolution. For such purpose, Article 22 of the Investment Law offered assurance that the resolution of investment disputes by arbitration was a means for their promotion, leaving the option for the investor to go to international arbitration or to resort to the national courts. That is why the National Council for the Promotion of Investment (CONAPRI), a mixed public-private association for the promotion of private investment in the country, incorporated by the Attorney General of the Republic in 1990,[147] in its March 2000 *Report* on the "Legal Regime of the Foreign Investments in Venezuela" devoted an entire Chapter to examine the various types of arbitration established in the legal system, that were offered to investors for the resolution of investment disputes, repeating the same terms and words used in the Law.[148]

---

147 Decree N° 1102 published in *Official Gazette* N° 34.549 of 1990.

148 See Consejo Nacional de Promoción de Inversiones (CONAPRI), *Régimen Legal para la Inversión Extranjera en Venezuela*, Caracas marzo 2000, pp. 29-36.

In this context, the *Mobil* and *Cemex* ICSID Tribunals, after accepting that article 22 of the 1999 Investment Law contained a conditional obligation for the State to go to arbitration, ruled on whether the article provided consent *in particular regarding those cases*, based on matters of evidence regarding the intention of the State when issuing the statute, but not as a universal ruling applicable to all circumstances. Consequently, it is not accurate to say that the ICSID Tribunal decisions in the cases *Mobil* and *Cemex* supposedly had found, in general, that Article 22 of the Investment Law does *not* provide a basis for ICSID jurisdiction. This is simply not true because the conclusion of the Tribunals was that Article 22 "does not provide basis for jurisdiction of the Tribunal *in the present case*".

That is, in these two ICSID cases, the Tribunals did not find, in general, that Article 22 did ***not*** provide a basis for ICSID jurisdiction; but only that Article 22 "does not provide basis for jurisdiction of the Tribunal *in the present case.*"

Nonetheless, as mentioned, the ICSID tribunal decision in the *Brandes* case, without any reasoning, arguments or motivation, and without explaining any "findings in the paragraphs" of its decision, it not only copied and ratified the aforementioned conclusion of the ICSID tribunals in the *Mobil* and *Cemex* cases, but went further, proclaiming in a general and universal way, and not only for the "present case," that "it is obvious that Article 22 of the Law on Promotion and Protection of Investments does not contain the consent of the Bolivarian Republic of Venezuela to ICSID jurisdiction" (ICSID *Brandes* case, ¶ 118).

In summary, after having studied the matter in detail and from the stand point of Venezuelan public law, and after having read the ICSID tribunals' decisions interpreting Article 22 of the Investment Law (*i.e.,* the *Mobil*, *Cemex*, *Brandes* cases) as a provision establishing an obligation for the State (although conditional) to go to arbitration, I remain convinced and ratify my prior opinion that from the stand point of national Venezuelan law, Article 22 of the Investment Law contained an expression of consent of the State given as an open offer to submit investment disputes to international arbitration, and in particular to ICSID arbitration, leaving in the hands of the international investor the right to unilaterally decide to go to arbitration or to resort to the national **courts**.

2. Article 22 of the 1999 Investment Law was a Unilateral Declaration of the State according to the Principles of Statutory Interpretation in Venezuelan Law

In effect, Article 22 of the 1999 Investment Law, as was evident from its wording, and as was admitted by the ICSID tribunal in the *Mobil* case (ICSID *Mobil* case, ¶ 103), was a "compound" provision that contained a number of parts: the first one, concerning bilateral or multilateral treaties or agreements on the promotion and protection of investments; the second one, dealing with the MIGA Convention; and the third one, dealing with the ICSID Convention.[149] Because Article 22 addressed *three different* sets of treaties or agreements, providing for all of them at the same

149 See on the various alternatives of application of Article 22 of the Investment Law, Victorino Tejera Pérez, "Do Municipal Investment Laws Always Constitute a Unilateral Offer to Arbitrate? The Venezuelan Investment Law: A Case Study," pp. 92-94; Victorino Tejera Pérez, *Arbitraje de Inversiones*, Magister Thesis, Caracas 2010, *cit.*, pp. 166-170.

time, it needed to be interpreted in the same way as other legal provisions, being consequently hardly surprising, that it did not followed any particular model or pattern of other national legislations that address only consent to ICSID jurisdiction.

On the other hand, it makes no sense to draw inferences from a comparison between Article 22 and expressions of consent to arbitration in bilateral investment treaties executed by Venezuela or even in contracts. Article 22 of the 1999 Investment Law was not a bilateral treaty nor was it the product of a negotiation with another State. Bilateral contracts, constructed by two parties, are the product of an interchange of proposals that are negotiated between them.

No doubt we have to suppose that the public officials of the Republic knew how to draft an obligatory consent to international arbitration when that was their intention, but there is also no doubt that for such purpose they chose to use the language contained in the Investment Law different to any model. That choice does not mean there was no consent. Article 22 of the Investment Law was a piece of national legislation, unique because it was the first time in Venezuelan recent legislative history that the State, in an internal law, discussed unilateral consent to international arbitration. Definitively, in that perspective, the Republic had no previous experience in drafting this type of statute.

That is why Article 22 of the 1999 Investment Law, as a principle, could be interpreted by just comparing its content with any sort of bilateral established and negotiated clauses for arbitration included in BITs or in "model clauses" that were to be negotiated by two Contracting States as "consent clauses." Article 22 needed to be interpreted not by reference to any pattern or model, but in accordance with its own structure and terms, taking into account its compound nature. Nonetheless, because the aims expressed in Article 1 of the Investment Law as affirmed in the *ICSID Mobile* and *Cemex* cases were "in general comparable to those of the treaties on promotion and reciprocal protection of investments and are reflected in the text of the law itself" which contains provisions "which are comparable to those incorporated in BITs" (as expressed in the ICSID *Mobil* case, ¶¶ 121, 122; and in the ICSID *Cemex* case, ¶ 119), the unilateral open offer of consent by the State to arbitration contained in both BITs and the Investment Law were of paramount importance. Although the *Mobil* case failed to mention this feature of the Investment Law, Article 22 unquestionably represented such an expression which leaved to the international investors the option to accept or reject the State's offer.[150]

3. The rules of interpretation of statutes under Venezuelan Law

The interpretation of Article 22 of the 1999 Investment Law as an instrument of national law that purported to express consent to international arbitration by reference to international treaties and agreements, including ICSID Convention, due to its international effects could be considered as properly governed by

150 As it is pointed out by Tatiana B. de Maekelt, "Tratados Bilaterales de Protección de Inversiones. Análisis de las cláusulas arbitrales y su aplicación," pp. 340-344; Andrés A. Mezgravis, "Las inversiones petroleras en Venezuela y el arbitraje ante el CIADI", *loc. cit.*, p. 357; José Gregorio Torrealba, *Promoción y protección de las inversiones extranjeras en Venezuela*, *op. cit.*, pp. 128-129.

principles of international law, although the provision could also be interpreted from the standpoint of Venezuelan Law, which is also relevant due to the fact that it was a national statute. In this regard, the Tribunal in the *ICSID Mobil* case interpreted Article 22 on the basis of the "rules of international law governing the interpretation of unilateral acts formulated within the framework and on the basis of a treaty" (ICSID *Mobil* case, ¶ 95), although considering that the national law should not "be completely ignored" being called to "play a useful role" regarding "the intention of the State having formulated such acts" (ICSID *Mobil* case, ¶ 96).[151]

In Venezuela, the main rules on statutory interpretation are set forth in Article 4 of the Civil Code. This article, as aforementioned provides that the interpreter must attribute to the law "the sense that appears evident from the *proper meaning of the words*, according to *their connection* among themselves and the *intention of the Legislator*." The article goes on to state that, "when there is no precise provision of the Law, the provisions regulating similar cases or analogous matters shall be taken into account; and should doubts persist, general principles of law shall be applied."

In Decision N° 895 of July 30, 2008, the Politico-Administrative Chamber of the Supreme Tribunal of Justice referred to four relevant elements to be taken into account in the interpretation of legal provisions.[152] The first element is the *literal, grammatical or philological* one, which must always be the starting point of any interpretation. The second element of interpretation is the *logical, rational or reasonable* one, which aims at determining the *raison d'être* of the provision within the legal order. The third element is the *historical* one, through which a legal provision is to be analyzed in the context of the factual and legal situation at the time it was adopted or amended and in light of its historical evolution. The fourth element is the *systematic* one, which requires the interpreter to analyze the provision as an integral part of the relevant system.

The Politico-Administrative Chamber noted that interpretation of statutes is not a matter of choosing among the four elements, but of applying them together, even if not all of the elements are of equal importance. Nonetheless although the ICSID tribunal in the *Brandes* case said to having interpreted Article 22 of the Investment Law "according to the parameters set by the Republic's legal system" (ICSID *Brandes* case, ¶ 36), in fact followed a different approach, applying what it referred to as an "initial analysis" of the elements mentioned in Article 4 of the Civil Code: first the "purely grammatical analysis" and "if this initial analysis fails to define clearly the meaning of the provision, it then becomes necessary to examine the contents..." (ICSID *Brandes* case, ¶ 35). This approach is not in accordance with the principles of statutory interpretation that must be always applied together. In this sense, the Constitutional Chamber of the Supreme Tribunal in a recent decision N° 1067 of November 3, 2010 (Case *Astivenca Astilleros de Venezuela C.A*,), has ruled regarding the elements for interpretation derived from Article 4 of the Civil Code, that "the normative elements must be harmonized as a

151 See also ICSID *Cemex* case (ICSID Mobil case, ¶¶ 88, 89) and ICSID *Brandes* case (ICSID, *Brandes* case, ¶ 36.

152 See in *Revista de Derecho Público*, N° 115, Editorial Jurídica Venezolana, Caracas 2008, pp. 468 ff.

whole, in the sense that it one must not ignore the other, but all must be kept in mind in order to make a correct valuation of the content of the legal text.[153]"

In addition, it must be mentioned that the Supreme Tribunal of Justice in Decision N° 895 of 2008, has identified two other elements of interpretation: the teleological one – that is, the need to identify and understand the social goals or aims that led to the law being adopted – and the sociological one, which helps to understand the provision within the context of the social, economic, political and cultural reality where the text is going to be applied.[154]

From the standpoint of Venezuelan law, only the principles that govern the *interpretation of statutes* may have some bearing on the interpretation of Article 22, not being proper to interpret the provision following the rules established for contractual clauses (*cláusula compromisoria*) providing arbitration but seeking to exclude in an absolute way the possibility to resort to national courts.[155] There is a basic conceptual distinction between Venezuelan principles of statutory interpretation and alleged specific requirements for the efficacy of a contractual agreement to arbitrate under the domestic legal order. The latter had no application in a case of article 22 of the Investment Law, where the matter at stake was whether the State's expression of consent embodied in a statute met the requirements of an international treaty (the ICSID Convention) to set in motion the jurisdiction of international tribunals operating under that treaty.[156]

---

153 See in http://www.tsj.gov.ve/decisiones/scon/Noviembre/1067-31110-2010-09-0573.html, pp. 39 of 60.

154 See in *Revista de Derecho Público*, N° 115, Editorial Jurídica Venezolana, Caracas 2008, pp. 468 ff.

155 This refers, specifically, to the Politico- Administrative Chamber of the Supreme Tribunal of Justice, decisions imposing the need for arbitral clauses that pretend to exclude completely the possible resort to national courts, to be clear and unequivocal. See Decision N° 1209 of June 20, 2001 (Case: *Hoteles Doral C.A. v. Corporación L. Hoteles C.A*) at http://www.tsj.gov.ve/decisiones/spa/Junio/01209-200601-0775.htm; Decision N° 00098 of January 29, 2002 (Case: *Banco Venezolano de Crédito, S.A.C.A. v. Venezolana de Relojería, S.A. (Venrelosa) y Henrique Pfeffer C.A*) at http://www.tsj.gov.ve/decisiones/spa/Enero/00098-290102-1255.htm; Decision N° 00476 of March 25, 2003 (Case: *Consorcio Barr, S.A v. Four Seasons Caracas, C.A.*) at http://www.tsj.gov.ve/decisiones/spa/Marzo/00476-250303-2003-0044.htm; Decision N° 00038 of January 28, 2004 (Case: *Banco Venezolano de Crédito, S.A. Banco Universal*) at http://www.tsj.gov.ve/decisiones/spa/Enero/00038-280103-2003-1296.htm.

156 As Hung Vaillant states that, according to the pro-arbitration principle in Article 258 of the Constitution, "[...] *se debe tratar de sostener la validez en to- dos aquellos casos de duda, siempre que tal admission no conduzca a una violación de normas de orden público ni atente contra las buenas costumbres. En resumen, en caso de duda, se deberá pronunciar a favor de la existencia del Arbitraje.* [...]" ("[...] one should try to sustain its validity [of Arbitration] in all those cases of doubt, as long as such admission does not lead to a violation of norms of public order or impairs good customs. In sum, in case of doubt, one should pronounce in favor of the existence of Arbitration. [...]"). Francisco Hung Vaillant, *Reflexiones sobre el Arbitraje en el Sistema Venezolano*, Caracas 2001, p. 66. Vaillant makes this statement in the context of discussing the general principles that govern arbitration under Venezuelan Law., pp. 63-69. In that section, Vaillant addresses those principles that should serve to "*establecer la solución adecuada cada vez que existe una antinomia o una laguna legal; así como también en aquellos casos en los cuales es necesario interpretar un texto oscuro de una cláusula o de un pacto arbitral.*" ("to provide for an adequate solution each time that there is an antinomy or a legal gap; as well as in those cases in

In the *Cemex* case, the ICSID Tribunal noted that in all of the BITs concluded by Venezuela before 1999, a "compulsory arbitration clause" was always incorporated (ICSID *Cemex* case, ¶ 120), but failed to compare such solution with the one included in Article 22 of the 1999 Investment Law. More importantly, both the Investment Law and BITs also provided for the right of the international investor to unilaterally accept the arbitration offer or to resort to the national courts in order to resolve investments disputes. This is valid in the terms of Article 4 of the Civil Code. Even if analogy is not applied between BITs and the Investment Law, contrary to was asserted in the *Mobil* and *Cemex* ICSID case, it is perfectly possible –using the same words of such decisions (ICSID *Mobil* case, ¶ 123; ICSID *Cemex* case, ¶ 120)– to draw from the law as a whole the conclusion that Article 22 had to be interpreted as establishing consent by Venezuela to submit ICSID disputes to arbitration particularly if the disclaimer of the last part of Article 22 ("without prejudice to the possibility of using, as appropriate, the contentious means contemplated by the Venezuelan legislation in effect") was not ignored. Both decisions of the ICSID Tribunals, in an incomprehensible way ignored it, and therefore considered the disclaimer as meaningless. The fact that the *Mobil* and *Cemex* decisions did not consider this when interpreting Article 22, giving the last part of the provision a meaningful interpretation, rendered its text "meaningless," which cannot be accepted under Venezuelan law.

On the other hand, the fact that another State or States in the world have written national laws containing the expression of consent in a way that was different to the way chosen by Venezuela in 1999, cannot demonstrate that the State in article 22 did not manifest its clear and unequivocal consent to arbitrate in the provision. The wording used in the Law in 1999 was in its text, and this cannot be replaced; so, there was no need to compare the way the State enacted its laws with the way used for instance in Albania, in the Central African Republic or in Côte d'Ivoire. The way legislation is made in other States cannot demonstrate anything regarding Venezuela's drafting of its own statutes. Nonetheless, in order to interpret correctly a compound provision such as Article 22 of the 1999 Investment Law, what have to be used are the rules and tools established in the legal order of the relevant State – here, Venezuela. And even if a comparison could be made between the 1999 Investment Law and the laws of other States, however, it was useful to do this with one law that was similar to the 1999 Investment Law, which was the Egyptian law, which was the object of an ICSID decision that found that Egyptian law as a national law in which consent to international arbitration exist.

Consequently, according to Venezuelan law, Article 22 had to be interpreted not by reference to any international pattern or model, but in accordance with its own structure and terms, taking into account its compound nature, and the purpose for its enactment. It needed also, as all statutes, to be interpreted in harmony or in conformity with the Constitution[157] and with the pro-arbitration trend existing in

---

which it is necessary to interpret an obscure text of an arbitration clause or of an arbitration agreement"). *Idem*. p. 63.

157 This is a general principle accepted in Venezuelan judicial review system. See José Peña Solís, "La interpretación conforme a la Constitución," *Libro Homenaje a Fernando Parra Aranguren*, Tomo II, Universidad Central de Venezuela, Caracas 2001. On the application of this principle regarding arbitration matters, see Eugenio Hernández Bretón, "Arbitraje y Constitución.

Venezuela in 1999, when it was enacted, which was extensively developed and promoted by the then new Government. Nonetheless, being an instrument of national law that expressed consent of the State to international arbitration, as mentioned, it needed also to be interpreted according to the applicable international conventions and to the rules of international law governing unilateral declarations of the State.

Consequently, if it is from the stand point of being a national law Article 22 of the Investment Law had to be interpreted following the rules of statutory interpretation and construction in Venezuelan Law, that is, according to Article 4 of the Civil Code, meaning that it had to be read in all its content, taking into account its context, purpose and intent.[158]

It was in that sense that it can be said that when interpreting article 22 of the Investment Law, the ICSID Tribunals in the *Mobil* and *Cemex* cases, concluded that such provision established or contained an obligation for the State to go to arbitration (although subjected to a condition), or in their own words, a "conditional obligation to go to arbitration" (ICSID *Mobil* case, ¶ 102),[159] which is equivalent to say that the provision is an expression of consent given by the State subjected to a condition. This obligation or consent was established in an unequivocal way in the sense that the provision clearly contained such obligation or consent.

The ICSID tribunals, nonetheless, considered that it was the condition established in the article, the one that was equivocal because supposedly allowed for two possible grammatical interpretations (ICSID Mobil case, ¶¶ 109, 111). Those were that the condition could be for the State to go to international arbitration if the treaties or agreements "provide for international arbitration" or that such treaties or agreements were to "provide for the submission to international arbitration." This assertion, in any case, was a wrong grammatical proposition because the second interpretation would result in a tautology, equivalent to say that "I will go to international arbitration if the treaty obliged me to go to arbitration." This option would render the provision meaningless. The correct and only valid interpretation of the condition, was the first option, equivalent to say "I will go to arbitration if the treaty provides a framework for international arbitration."

In any case, the consequence of the assertion made by the ICSID tribunals considering that the condition set forth in Article 22 allowed for two possible interpretations, lead the tribunals to try to established the "intent" of the State when sanctioning the Law (1999), concluding in those cases, and only in them, that *because of lack of evidence* it could not be deducted from article 22 the expression of consent to go to ICSID international arbitration.

El arbitraje como derecho fundamental," *loc. cit.*, pp. 31; Andrés A. Mezgravis, "Las inversiones petroleras en Venezuela y el arbitraje ante el CIADI," *loc. cit.*, p. 390.

158 The Tribunal in the *ICSID Mobil* considered that the interpretation of Article 22 according to the national statutory rules of interpretation "play a useful role" regarding "the intention of the State having formulated such acts" (ICSID *Mobil* case, ¶ 96).

159 What is clear from the aforementioned is that the provision related to ICSID arbitration in Article 22, is not at all a mere reference in a law to ICSID, not a part of a list of options without any effect.

4. The Principle that Consent for Arbitration has to be Expressed in Writing

Another matter that must be clarified regarding consent for arbitration in Venezuelan law is the matter of the "form" or condition that is required in order for the Republic to express consent for arbitration. In Venezuela, in this matter, the only applicable "dogma," as explained by the Supreme Tribunal of Justice in its decision N° 1541 of 2008 is that the expression of consent must be in writing (pp. 31-34). No provision in any law requires that the writing consent must also be "clear," "express" or "unequivocal" as suggested in other parts of the same decision (pp. 31-48).

In this sense, Venezuelan law is perfectly consistent with international principles, in the sense that an expression of consent for arbitration need only to be expressed in writing in order to comply with the Commercial Arbitration Law. This is what was definitively decided by the Constitutional Chamber of the Supreme Tribunal in a decision issued on November 3, 2010 (Case *Astivenca Astilleros de Venezuela C.A.*), affirming that in any judicial decision regarding the verification of "the validity, efficacy and applicability of the arbitral clause it must be limited to verify the written character of the arbitration agreement."[160]

On the other hand, as aforementioned, Article 4 of the Civil Code, which establishes the rules for the interpretation of statutes, provides that in the absence of a precise provision of the Law, the provisions regulating similar cases or analogous matters shall be taken into account. Consequently, regarding the way consent for arbitration must be given, in the absence of a general and precise provision, the Venezuelan 1998 Commercial Arbitration Law, which is inspired by the UNCITRAL Model Law, must be applied. Like the ICSID Convention, that Law requires only that the consent or agreement to arbitration be evidenced "in writing."[161]

---

160 The Constitutional Chamber has established an obligatory interpretation in the sense of ruling that the judicial "verification of arbitral clauses must be limited to verify the written character of the arbitration agreement, excluding any analysis related to the consent devices that could derived from the written clause." See decision N° 1067 of November 3, 2010 (Case *Astivenca Astilleros de Venezuela C.A.*), at http://www.tsj.gov.ve/decisio-nes/scon/ Noviembre /1067-31110-2010-09-0573.html, pp. 35 of 60 and 38 of 60.

161 Article 6 of the Commercial Arbitration Law: "The arbitration agreement must be evidenced *in writing* in any document or group of documents placing on record the will of the parties to submit them to arbitration. A reference in a contract to a document containing an arbitration clause shall constitute an arbitration agreement, provided that said contract is evidenced in writing and the reference implies that said clause is a part of the contract. In adhesion contracts and standard-form contracts, the manifestation of the will to submit the contract to arbitration must be made in an express and independent manner." In this regard, and according to this Law, as Alberto Baumeister has pointed out when analyzing the "form of the arbitral clause" that it is only required to be in writing in the contract or in any document assuring that the parties have agreed to submit disputes to arbitration. See Alberto Baumeister, "Algunos tópicos sobre el procedimiento en la Ley de Arbitraje Comercial,", in Irene Valera (Coord), *Arbitraje comercial interno e internacional. Reflexiones teóricas y experiencias prácticas*, Academia de Ciencias Políticas y Sociales, Caracas 2005, pp. 140-141. For additional support for the contention that the arbitration clause need only be in writing, see Francisco Hung Vaillant, *Reflexiones Sobre el Arbitraje en el Sistema Venezolano*, *op. cit.*, pp. 203-204; Alfredo De Jesús O., "Validez y eficacia del acuerdo de

As mentioned, in Venezuelan law there no legal principle is established in the sense that in addition to being in writing, consent for arbitration must be clear and unequivocal. That is, there is no legal provision in Venezuelan law requiring the consent for arbitration to be clear and unequivocal. Even in cases of commercial arbitration establishing arbitration clauses, following the pro-arbitration trend of the Venezuelan legal system, in case of doubt, one must find in favor of arbitration.[162] For example, as Francisco Hung, has argued that "in all those cases in which doubts can rise regarding the interpretation of the will to submit to arbitration in an arbitral clauses or agreements, those called to decide must prefer the application of the '*favor arbitri*' principle, and declare the arbitral [tribunal] competent," that is "in cases of doubt, the decision must be in favor of arbitration."[163] This is based on the *intention* of the parties, taking into account the *good faith* intention.[164]

It must be mentioned, that the matter of consent for arbitration was considered in a few decisions of the Politico Administrative Chamber of the Supreme Tribunal, not regarding the merits on the "conditions" of consent for arbitration, but only the way in which it is expressed in order to decide conflicts of jurisdiction between national courts and arbitral tribunals. In particular, those decisions are: Decision N° 1.209 of June 20, 2001 (Case: *Hoteles Doral C.A. v. Corporación L. Hoteles C.A.*) (Exp. N° 2000-0775); Decision N° 00098 of January 29, 2002 (Case: *Banco Venezolano de Crédito, S.A.C.A. v. Venezolana de Relojería, S.A. (Venrelosa) y Henrique Pfeffer C.A., Abraham Ricardo Pfeffer Almeida, Marianela de la Coromoto Núñez de Pfeffer et al.g*) (Exp. N° 2000-1255); Decision N° 00476 of March 25, 2003 (Case:

---

arbitraje en el derecho venezolano," in Irene Valera (Coordinadora), *Arbitraje Comercial Interno e Internacional. Reflexiones teóricas y experiencias prácticas*, Academia de Ciencias Políticas y Sociales, Comité Venezolano de Arbitraje, Caracas 2005, pp. 73, 94-97, 130; Andrés A. Mezgravis, "La promoción del arbitraje: un deber constitucional reconocido y vulnerado por la jurisprudencia," in *Revista de Derecho Constitucional*, N° 5, Editorial Sherwood, Caracas 2001, p. 133.

162 The "pro-arbitration" principle of interpretation regarding arbitration in the Venezuelan legal system has been established as an obligatory doctrine of interpretation by the Constitutional Chamber of the Supreme Tribunal in decision in decision N° 1067 of November 3, 2010 (Case *Astivenca Astilleros de Venezuela C.A,*) *cit.*, pp. 34 of 60 and 40 of 60.

163 See Francisco Hung Vaillant, "Apostillas a cinco sentencias en materia arbitra dictadas por el Tribunal Supremo de Justicia," in *Derecho privado y procesal en Venezuela. Homenaje a Gustavo Planchart Manrique*, Tomo II, UCAB, Escritorio Tinoco, Caracas 2003, pp. 654. See the comments on the pro-arbitration trend of the Venezuelan legal system in Andrés A. Mezgravis, "La promoción del arbitraje: un deber constitucional reconocido y vulnerado por la jurisprudencia," in *Revista de Derecho Constitucional*, N° 5, Editorial Sherwood, Caracas 2001, p. 133; Andrés Mezgravis, "El principio pro arbitraje en el ordenamiento jurídico venezolano", in *Ámbito Jurídico* Año IV, N° 55, abril 2002; Carlos Alberto Urdaneta Sandoval, "Aspectos del arbitraje en la contratación administrativa," in *VIII Jornadas Internacionales de Derecho Administrativo "Allan Randolph Brewer-Carías," Los contratos administrativos. Contratos del Estado*, Fundación de Estudios de Derecho Administrativo, FUNEDA, Vol. I, Caracas 2005, p. 359; Eugenio Hernández Bretón, "Arbitraje y Constitución. El arbitraje como derecho fundamental," *loc. cit.*, p. 30. As mentioned this has been the obligatory principle established by the Constitutional Chamber of the Supreme Tribunal in decision N° 1067 of November 3, 2010 (Case *Astivenca Astilleros de Venezuela C.A,*), cit. pp. 34 of 60 and 40 of 60.

164 See Andrés A. Mezgravis, "La promoción del arbitraje: un deber constitucional reconocido y vulnerado por la jurisprudencia," *loc. cit.*, p. 133; Francisco Hung Vaillant, *Reflexiones Sobre el Arbitraje en el Sistema Venezolano*, Editorial Jurídica Venezolana, Caracas 2001, pp. 63-69, 341.

Consorcio Barr, S.A. v. Four Seasons Caracas, C.A.) (Exp. Nº 2003-0044); and Decision Nº 00038 of January 28, 2004 (Case: *Banco Venezolano de Crédito, S.A. Banco Universa v. Armando Días Guía y Marisela Riera de Guía*) (Exp. Nº 2003-1296). From these decisions issued in resolving conflicts of jurisdiction and not resolving the merits of matter of arbitration, deductions have been made in the sense that in the country exits a requirement that *consent for arbitration* has to be "clear and unequivocal,"[165] which is incorrect.

In fact, this assertion has no basis. First, in Venezuela, the decisions of the Supreme Tribunal of Justice in Politico Administrative Chamber in these matters of arbitration do not refer to the substance of arbitration or to the consent for arbitration, being the Chamber only called upon to decide conflict of jurisdiction between courts or between arbitral tribunals and the courts. Second, in Venezuela the decisions of the Politico Administrative Chamber of the Supreme Tribunal, notwithstanding their importance, cannot be qualified as "precedents" because they do not have an obligatory character. Only the Constitutional Chamber of the Supreme Tribunal, acting as Constitutional Court when exercising its competencies on judicial review, can issue obligatory decisions on constitutional matters (*decisions vinculantes*) when interpreting the Constitution (Article 335 of the Constitution).[166] Third, the decisions of the Politico Administrative Chamber are issued for the purpose of granting jurisdiction or to national courts or to arbitration courts, based on the interpretation of the valid consent clauses for arbitration in the sense of determining if they exclude or not in an absolute, clear and unequivocal way the possibility to resort to national courts. Fourth, in a Constitution like the Venezuelan one that establishes arbitration as integral part of the judicial system (Article 253) and that imposes an obligation on the State to promote arbitration (Article 258), arbitration cannot be considered as an exception to a supposed constitutional mandate of jurisdiction in national courts.[167] And fifth, there are not

165 See the critical comments on these decisions, in Alfredo de Jesús O., "Validez y eficacia del acuerdo de arbitraje en el derecho venezolano," *loc. cit.*, pp. 73-75, 78; Andrés Mezgravis, "El principio pro arbitraje en el ordenamiento jurídico venezolano", in *Ámbito Jurídico* Año IV, No 55, abril 2002, p. 16; Andrés A. Mezgravis, "La promoción del arbitraje: un deber constitucional reconocido y vulnerado por la jurisprudencia," *loc. cit.*, pp. 133-134; Francisco Hung Vaillant, "Apostillas a cinco sentencias en materia arbitra dictadas por el Tribunal Supremo de Justicia," in *Derecho privado y procesal en Venezuela. Homenaje a Gustavo Planchart Manrique*, Tomo II, UCAB, Escritorio Tinoco, Caracas 2003, pp. 654 ff; J. Eloy Anzola, "El fatigoso camino que transita el arbitraje," in Irene Valera (Coordinadora), *Arbitraje Comercial Interno e Internacional. Reflexiones teóricas y experiencias prácticas*, Academia de Ciencias Políticas y Sociales, Comité Venezolano de Arbitraje, Caracas 2005, pp. 425-426.

166 See on this obligatory decisions (*decisiones vinculantes*) Allan R. Brewer-Carías, "La potestad de la Jurisdicción Constitucional de interpretar la Constitución con efectos vinculantes," in Jhonny Tupayachi Sotomayor, (Coord.), *El precedente constitucional vinculante en el Perú (Análisis, comentarios y doctrina comparada)*, Editorial Adrus, Arequipa 2009, pp. 791-817.

167 On the contrary, in Venezuela arbitration is considered an integral part of the "system of justice" (Article 253). The Constitutional Chamber of the Supreme Tribunal, in its decision Nº 1067 of November 3, 2010 (Case *Astivenca Astilleros de Venezuela C.A,*) has ruled establishing an obligatory doctrine excluding the consideration of arbitration as an exception regarding ordinary jurisdiction, considering that arbitration is an integral part of the judicial system (pp. 19 of 60 to 26 of 60; 29 of 60).

Venezuelan judicial "precedents" that have developed on matters of commercial arbitration that the consent for arbitration must be "clear, express and unequivocal."

In effect, in the 2001 *Hoteles Doral C.A. v. Corporación de L'Hoteles C.A* case,[168] the Supreme Tribunal does not explain that, as arbitration supposedly constitutes an exception to the constitutional jurisdiction of national courts, it is required that there be 'manifest, express and indisputable' consent to arbitration." In such case, as can be read in the full Spanish text of the decision (not in the cuttings made for translation), the lower court "declared its lack of jurisdiction to decide the case, by considering the existence of an arbitral clause (*cláusula compromisoria de arbitraje*) capable of subtracting the decision of the dispute of the ordinary jurisdiction" (pp. 3-4). The Politico Administrative Chamber in order to determine the competent jurisdiction, proceeded to determine the "validity of the arbitral clause" just in order to determine "the efficacy or not of the arbitral clause in the sense that it could exclude or not the Judicial Power from its constitutional rank competence to decide cases (p. 4), and to determine "from the contractual clauses if it exist or not, a manifest, express and unquestionable will to exclude any judicial decision on the disputes" and instead to submitted to arbitration (p. 5). That is, the Supreme Tribunal only elaborated on the unequivocal and express manifestation of will of the parties to completely exclude the competence of the courts (not on the consent for arbitration), concluding, in the case, that it did not "exist a manifest and unequivocal will to submit to the jurisdiction of private arbiters, that is, it does not exist an undoubted disposition to renounce to the free access to the judicial organs of the ordinary jurisdiction" (p. 5); and then interpreting that because in the specific arbitral clause in the case, "the possibility to resort to the judicial means remained opened" in the sense that in such clause "the submission to arbitration was an option for the parties" (p. 19), concluded that in the case "there was no pact renouncing in an absolute way to the possibility or alternate option to access to the ordinary organs of the Judiciary, which does not exclude their competence to decide on the *litis*" (pp. 19-20). Consequently, the decision adopted by the Supreme Tribunal in the *Hoteles Doral C.A. v. Corporación de L'Hoteles C.A* case, was a completely different matter and of course in it, the Tribunal did not require the consent to arbitration to be 'manifest, express and indisputable.'"

In 2002 *Banco Venezolano de Crédito, S.A.C.A. v. Venezolana de Relojeria, S.A. (Venrelosa)* y *Henrique Pfeffer C.A, Abraham Ricardo Pfeffer Almeida, Marianela de la Coromoto Núñez de Pfiffer et al.*[169] cases, the Supreme Tribunal did not upheld the principle of "consent to arbitration" be "manifest, express and indisputable" and did not stated that arbitration 'requires the compliance and verification of the manifestation of an unequivocal and express will of the parties involved." In such case, as can also be read in the full Spanish text of the decision (not in the cuttings made for translation), what the Supreme Tribunal quoting what the Tribunal had decided in the already mentioned *Hoteles Doral C.A. v. Corporación de L'Hoteles C.A* case (pp. 8-9), was that in the specific commercial contract, the arbitral clause

168 See Decision N° 1209 of June 20, 2001, Case: *Hoteles Doral C.A. v. Corporación L. Hoteles C.A,* at http://www.tsj.gov.ve/decisio-nes/spa/Junio/01209-200601-0775.htm.

169 See Decision N° 00098 of January 29, 2002, Case: *Banco Venezolano de Crédito, S.A.C.A. v. Venezolana de Relojería, S.A. (Venrelosa) y Henrique Pfeffer C.A.*, at http://www.tsj.gov.ve/decisiones/spa/Enero/00098-290102-1255.htm

leaved opened the option for one of the parties to resort to the courts, arguing that it such clause "it doesn't exists a manifest and unequivocal will to submit to the jurisdiction of private arbiters, that is, it does not exist an undoubted disposition to renounce to the free access to the judicial organs of the ordinary jurisdiction" (p. 16). The Supreme Tribunal determined that the specific arbitral clause in the case was conceived as an "optional arbitration" in the sense of "submission to arbitration in an optional and partial way, that is, always leaving open the possibility that either parties could opt to resort to the judicial mean" (p. 16), interpreting that because in the specific arbitral clause in the case, "the submission to arbitration –contained in it– is an option in order for the parties to select it as an alternate mechanism for controversies solutions (p. 17), concluded that in the case "there was no pact renouncing in an absolute way to the possibility or alternate option to access to the ordinary organs of the Judiciary, which does not exclude their competence to decide on the *litis*." (pp. 17). Consequently, the decision adopted by the Supreme Tribunal in the *Banco Venezolano de Crédito, S.A.C.*A. v. Venezolana de Relojeria, S.A. *(Venrelosa)* case y *Henrique Pfeffer C.A, Abraham Ricardo Pfeffer Almeida, Marianela de la Coromoto Núñez de Pfiffer et al.*, case, was also a completely different matter and of course, in it, the Tribunal did not require the compliance and verification of the manifestation of an unequivocal and express will of the parties involved.

In 2003 *Consorcio Barr, S.A v. Four Seasons Caracas, C.A.* case[170] the Tribunal did not hold that in order to find a valid arbitration agreement, there must exist an unequivocal and express consent. In such case, as can also be read in the full Spanish text of the decision (not in the cuttings made for translation), the lower court declared its jurisdiction to decide the case, by considering "that the arbitral clause (*Cláusula compromisoria*) in the case, was not in accordance with article 5 of the Commercial Arbitration Law, because its wording does not express the excluding and undoubted character of the election of manifestation of will to subtract the solution of controversies or disputes originated in relation to the contract from the judicial jurisdiction, due to the fact that in the same contract, in the jurisdictional clause, the parties declared to be subjected to the nonexclusive jurisdiction of the courts of the Bolivarian Republic of Venezuela" (p. 12). What the Supreme Tribunal considered that needed to be determined in this case was if the arbitral clause had "the derogatory force regarding the Venezuelan jurisdiction" (p. 16), concluding that from its wording "the exclusion of the ordinary jurisdiction is not demonstrated because it result confusing that in it the same it is agreed to resort to the judicial mean" (p. 18), being in such content and for the exclusive purpose of "derogating the jurisdiction that correspond to the Venezuelan courts to decide the case [that] the lacks of the legal efficacy needed for such purposes. So is declared" (p. 18). And it was for such purpose of determining if in the case it existed an absolute exclusion of the jurisdiction of the Venezuelan courts that the Supreme Tribunal considered that for such purpose, for "the validity of the arbitral clause in must exist a unequivocal and express manifestation of will of the involved parties to subtract the decision of the case from the ordinary courts" (p. 18). Consequently, the decision adopted by the Supreme Tribunal in the *Consorcio Barr, S.A v. Four*

---

170 See Decision N° 00476 of March 25, 2003, Case: *Consorcio Barr, S.A v. Four Seasons Caracas, C.A.*, at http://www.tsj.gov.ve/decisio-nes/spa/Marzo/00476-250303-2003-0044.htm

Seasons Caracas, C.A. case was also a completely different matter, and of course, in it, the Tribunal did not hold that in order to find a valid arbitration agreement, there must exist an unequivocal and express consent.

In 2004 *Banco Venezolano de Crédito, S.A. Banco Universal v. Armando Díaz Egu y Marisela Riera de Díaz* case[171] the Supreme Tribunal did not hold that arbitration was not mandatory because there was no manifest and unequivocal' submission to arbitration. In this case, the decision of the Supreme Tribunal originated because a lower court decided in the case to declare its jurisdiction to decide the case, because observing that in the existing arbitral clause the parties did not "expressly renounced to the ordinary jurisdiction in order to resolve the conflicts" observing that the arbitral clause was only to be applied only when in enforcement actions (*ejecución de garantías*) and only where there is "opposition from the defendants" (p. 3). In the case, the Supreme Tribunal, quoting again what it had decided in the already mentioned *Hoteles Doral C.A. v. Corporación de L'Hoteles C.A* case (pp. 3-4), refused to remove the case to arbitration because in such "cases of enforcements actions established in the contract, it doesn't exists a manifest and unequivocal attitude of a submission to arbiters, due to the fact that it is only to be applied in case of opposition by the defendants," (pp. 5), confirming the lower court decision. Consequently, the decision adopted by the Supreme Tribunal en the *Banco Venezolano de Crédito, S.A. Banco Universal v. Armando Díaz Egu y Marisela Riera de Díaz* case was also a completely different matter, and of course, in it, the Tribunal did not hold that arbitration was not mandatory because there was no 'manifest and unequivocal' submission to arbitration.

On the other hand, the so-called fundamental requirement of 'clear, express and unequivocal' consent to arbitrate is not a general opinion in the legal Venezuelan doctrine. Precisely, Francisco Hung Vaillant, has stated that, according to the pro-arbitration principle in Article 258 of the Constitution, "one should try to sustain its validity [of Arbitration] in all those cases of doubt, as long as such admission does not lead to a violation of norms of public order or impairs good customs. In sum, in case of doubt, one should pronounce in favor of the existence of Arbitration;[172] addressing those principles that should serve "to provide for an adequate solution each time that there is an antinomy or a legal gap; as well as in those cases in which it is necessary to interpret an obscure text of an arbitration clause or of an arbitration agreement."[173]

In conclusion, none of the aforementioned four decisions of the Politico-Administrative Chamber of the Supreme Tribunal of Justice sustain such assertions; and nothing can be deducted from them by picking isolated phrases out of context.

---

171 See Decision N° 00038 of January 28, 2004, Case: *Banco Venezolano de Crédito, S.A. Banco Universal,* at http://www.tsj.gov.ve/decisiones/spa/Enero/00038-280103-2003-1296.htm

172 See Francisco Hung Vaillant, *Reflexiones sobre el Arbitraje en el Sistema Venezolano*, Caracas 2001, p. 66.

173 *Idem.* p. 63. Ivor D. Mogollón-Rojas, assertion based on the need for a "written" and "documented" agreements to arbitrate than must be included in contracts as a proof "express and unequivocal consent to submit to arbitration," is made only and basically in order to stress the core of his statement which is that no "tacit acceptance for arbitration" is acceptable. See Ivor D. Mogollón, *El arbitraje comercial venezolano*, Vadell Hermanos Editores, Caracas 2004, pp. 61-62.

All these decisions, as mentioned, do not deal in the internal legal order with the substantive requirements for the validity of arbitration, for consent to arbitration, or for the validity of bilateral expressions of consent to arbitration (*cláusula compromisoria*). The decisions deal, only and exclusively with the issue of the parties' ability to exclude *in a total an absolute way* the possibility for one of the parties to resort to national courts, The fact that the Politico Administrative Chamber of the Supreme Tribunal when deciding jurisdictional conflicts, used to impose a rule that there must be "clear, express and unequivocal" expression in excluding the availability of an option is a completely different matter than an expression that provides for the consent to arbitration.

But in any case, regarding such "doctrine" and in the context that the Politico Administrative Chamber of the Supreme Tribunal used to apply it, the Constitutional Chamber of the Supreme Tribunal in its decision N° 1067 of November 3, 2010 (Case *Astivenca Astilleros de Venezuela C.A*,) has formally decided, in an obligatory way for all courts that from the moment of the publication of the decision, that is November 3, 2010,

> "the jurisprudence criteria sustained on these matters by the Politico Administrative Chamber of the Supreme Tribunal up to this date, are not applicable" (Vid. Among others, the decisions Numbers 1209 and 832, of June 20, 2001 and June 12, 2002, Cases: *"Hoteles Doral, C.A"*. and *"Inversiones San Ciprian, C.A."*)" (pp. 43 of 60).[174]

From what has been previously said, and as a conclusion, is possible to affirm that in Venezuela there is not at a requirement for the consent for arbitration to be "clear and unequivocal," and the only thing that has happened is that a confusion has been generated on the matter based on the aforementioned jurisprudence of the Politico Administrative Chamber of the Supreme Tribunal of Justice, ruling exclusively acting in the resolution of conflict of jurisdiction between national courts and national arbitral tribunals, giving always jurisdiction to the national courts when the clause providing for arbitration was not clear and unequivocal, excluding any sort of jurisdiction of national courts. That is, when the arbitral clause in a contract (without any consideration regarding its validity or the efficacy of the expression of consent) excluding the jurisdiction of national courts was considered not to be clear or unequivocal, then in cases of conflict of jurisdiction, the Chamber used to give always jurisdiction to the national courts. Also, when the arbitral clause provided the possibility for the parties to resort to the national courts, not having a clear and unequivocal expression of absolute rejection of the jurisdiction of national courts, the Supreme Tribunal used to give always jurisdiction to the national courts.

This was the jurisprudence of the Politico Administrative Chamber of the Supreme Court, which does not refer at all, to the requirements for the validity of consent of arbitration clauses, which was changed by means of the aforementioned decision adopted by the Constitutional Chamber of the Supreme Tribunal Decision N° 1067 of the November 3, 2010 (Case: *Astivenca Astilleros de Venezuela C.A)*[175]. It is enough to read completely the text of such decision in order to understand the

---

174 See at http://www.tsj.gov.ve/decisiones/scon/Noviembre/1067-31110-2010-09-0573.html, pp. 43 of 60

175 See at http://www.tsj.gov.ve/decisiones/scon/Noviembre/1067-31110-2010-09-0573.html

sense of the obligatory interpretation (*interpetación vinculante*) it contains for all courts established according to article 335 of the Constitution, expressed by the Chamber, in which it has established the rule that the judicial "verification of arbitral clauses must be limited to verify the written character of the arbitration agreement, excluding any analysis related to the consent devices that could derived from the written clause;" adding, regarding the already mentioned "doctrine" applied by the Politico Administrative Chamber of the Supreme Tribunal in order to resolve conflicts of jurisdiction, that "the jurisprudence criteria sustained on these matters by the Politico Administrative Chamber of the Supreme Tribunal up to this date, are not applicable" (Vid. Among others, the decisions Numbers 1209 and 832, of June 20, 2001 and June 12, 2002, Cases: "*Hoteles Doral, C.A*". and "*Inversiones San Ciprian, C.A.*")," reaffirming that in any judicial decision regarding the verification of "the validity, efficacy and applicability of the arbitral clause it must be limited to verify the written character of the arbitration agreement." The *Hoteles Doral C.A.* case was precisely the leading case of the "doctrine" overruled by the Constitutional Chamber, in which is based the supposed "doctrine" of "clear and unequivocal" consent, which resulted from a completely different concept of arbitration that the Chamber overruled.

As it has been argued, and is useful to remember, the Political Administrative Chamber in order to establish the aforementioned "doctrine," considered arbitration as an "exception" regarding the constitutional attributions of ordinary courts in order to resolve controversies submitted by citizens to their decision (the Constitutional Camber made reference among others to the decision N° 1.209/01 of the Politico Administrative Chamber). On the contrary, in the decision of the Constitutional Chamber adopted in the 2010 *Astivenca* Case, issued in a procedure for constitutional revision of a decision of the Politico Administrative Chamber of the Supreme Tribunal (N° 687 of May 21, 2009) precisely deciding on a conflict of jurisdiction, it argued that arbitration was a "fundamental right," considered as an entirely "part of the judicial system" and of "jurisdiction," and as an effective mean for obtaining justice (*tutela judicial efectiva*). Consequently, the Constitutional Chamber considered arbitration as an effective institution for jurisdictional protection that cannot be considered as an "exceptional" institution regarding the jurisdiction exercised by the Judicial Power. The Chamber ruled, based on the considerations it made "on the principle competence-competence and in the coordination and subsidiary relations of the Judicial Power organs regarding the arbitral system," that "the organs of the Judicial Power can only make a formal, preliminary or summary 'prima facie' exam or verification of the conditions of validity, efficacy and applicability of the arbitral clause, which must be limited to verify the written character of the arbitral agreement, and exclude any other analysis related to the vices of consent that derives from the written clause." In other words, the Chamber ruled that due to the fact that article 258 of the Constitution imposes the promotion of arbitration (as decided by the same Chamber quoting decision N° 1.541/08), "any legal provision or judicial interpretation that could contradict it, must be considered contrary to the fundamental text, and thus, unconstitutional;" and consequently, "the organs of the Judicial Power when they have not noticed a manifest nullity, inefficacy or inapplicability, must sent the disputes submitted to their consideration to arbitration."

The result of this new doctrine is that the courts must rule in principle in favor of arbitration, considered part of the judicial system and of jurisdiction, from which result that arbitration cannot be considered any more by the courts as an exemption to jurisdiction. That is why, the rule imposed by the Constitutional Chamber to the courts when analyzing prima facie arbitral clauses, is to verify just the written character of the arbitral clause without any other consideration regarding the validity or efficacy in order to reject arbitration. The result of this new doctrine has been the pro arbitration trend adopted even by the Politico Administrative Chamber, which precisely can be appreciate in many of the decisions it has adopted after the *Astivenca* Case ruling, in which, in many cases, the Chamber ruled to maintain the cases in the arbitral jurisdiction. In those cases, the argument of the Politico Administrative Chamber was not that in order to submit disputes resolution to arbitral tribunals, the consent for arbitration was supposedly to be "clear and unequivocal." On the contrary, in many of the cases, the decision of the Chamber was only to consider that there were not enough "inaccurate or incomplete" statements or "unambiguous" intent to remove the decisions from the arbitral tribunals, leaving the matter for their decision.

In addition, the procedural settings of international arbitration cases are entirely different. In such cases, the parties are not in a Venezuelan court debating whether a national court must be deprived of jurisdiction by a contractual arbitration clause. On the contrary, Article 22 does not have the effect of preventing investors from resorting to litigation remedies that may be available under Venezuelan law. Article 22 expressly permits recourse to local courts as an option for the investors when expressing in its last phrase: "[...] without prejudice to the possibility of using, whenever it should be appropriate, the contentious means contemplated by the Venezuelan legislation in effect." As the language of Article 22 contains no option for the Republic of Venezuela to resort to the national court, the premise of those decisions – that no longer can be applied by the courts – is not present in international arbitration proceeding. Article 22 does not preclude resort to "the contentious means contemplated by the Venezuelan legislation in effect," being that, on the contrary, an option only for the international investor, because the Republic of Venezuela has already expressed its unilateral consent to arbitration. The very purpose of arbitration provisions is to give the investor the option to resort to arbitration instead of being required to litigate the dispute in the courts of the host-State. In fact, one might argue that if the Republic wanted for there to be the option for an international investor to have recourse **only** to national courts (if there was no applicable treaty) it would need to be expressed in a "clear, express and unequivocal" way. As explained above, this has since been overruled. What is clear, express and unequivocal is that in Article 22 of the Investment Law, it is expressly, unequivocally and clearly provided that, because it contains the consent of the State for international arbitration, it is possible for the international investor to opt between going to international arbitration of to resort to national courts.

In addition, and despite its inapplicability since November 3, 2010, the cases decided by the Politico Administrative Chamber of the Supreme Tribunal, were not and are not binding. The other Venezuelan judges could and may depart from such decisions. According to Article 321 of the Code of Civil Procedure, Judges shall try to follow the "*cassation* doctrine established in analogous cases, in order to defend the integrity of the legislation and the uniformity of the jurisprudence," but even in this case, it is not established as a mandate. Therefore, such judicial decisions could not and cannot be considered to have established a general rule of the Venezuelan Law on matters of resolving conflicts of jurisdiction, and much less on matters of consent for arbitration which was not their purpose.[176] In any case, as already mentioned, the Constitutional Chamber of the Supreme Tribunal has ruled in an obligatory way that such doctrine could no longer be applied by the courts, establishing on the contrary that the only condition of validity of arbitral clauses is to be in writing.

But in any case, a reading of the full text of these four cases reveals that all that they decided was that in the specific commercial contracts on which the cases were based, the arbitral clauses included an option for one of the parties to resort to the courts. The court concluded that such a clause "doesn't present a manifest and unequivocal will to submit to the jurisdiction of private arbiters, that is, it does not exist an undoubted disposition to renounce to the free access to the judicial organs of the ordinary jurisdiction" (See, e.g., p. 16). The Politico Administrative Chamber of the Supreme Tribunal determined that the specific arbitral clause in the cases was conceived as an "optional arbitration" in the sense of "submission to arbitration in an optional and partial way that is, always leaving open the possibility that either parties could opt to resort to the judicial mean" (p. 16). But the fact was that on the contrary, the validity of the consent for arbitration was not in question in those cases; what was in question was that the consent for arbitration did not completely and absolutely exclude the option to resort to the national courts.

Contrary to the so-called and no longer applicable requirement of "clear, express and unequivocal" consent to arbitrate" that has been deducted from those decisions, the general opinion in Venezuelan legal doctrine is to the contrary, as has been definitively established by the Constitutional Chamber of the Supreme Tribunal of Justice in its Decision N° 1067 of November 3, 2010 (Case *Astivenca Astilleros de Venezuela C.A*,). For example, in this regard Francisco Hung Vaillant, has stated that, according to the pro-arbitration principle in Article 258 of the Constitution, now adopted in an obligatory way by the Constitutional Chamber, "one should try to sustain [the] validity [of arbitration clauses] in all those cases of doubt, as long as such admission does not lead to a violation of norms of public order or impairs good customs. In sum, in case of doubt, one should pronounce in favor of the existence of arbitration. ... [which should] provide for an adequate solution each time that there is an antinomy or a legal gap; as well as in those cases in which it is necessary to interpret an obscure text of an arbitration clause or of an arbitration agreement."[177]

176 The decisions have also been criticized because the Commercial Arbitration Law (Article 6) only requires that the consent be in writing. See Andres Mezgravis "La Promoción del Arbitraje: un deber constitucional reconocido y vulnerado por la jurisprudencia", in *Revista de Derecho Constitucional* N° 5, Diciembre 2001, Editorial Sherwood, Caracas 2001, pp. 133-135; Francisco Hung Vaillant, "Apostillas a cinco sentencias en materia arbitra dictadas por el Tribunal Supremo de Justicia," in *Derecho privado y procesal en Venezuela. Homenaje a Gustavo Planchart Manrique*, Tomo II, UCAB, Escritorio Tinoco, Caracas 2003, pp. 654.

177 See Francisco Hung Vaillant, *Reflexiones sobre el Arbitraje en el Sistema Venezolano*, Caracas 2001, p. 63, 66. Other authors refered to the matter: José Luis Bonnemaison only copied one of the decisions of the Politico Administrative Chamber of the Supreme Tribunal, but does not give his personal opinion. See José Luis Bonnemaison, *Aspectos fundamentales del arbitraje comercial, Tribunal Supremo de Justicia*, Caracas 2006, p. 24. Ivor D Mogollón-Rojas, bases his

VII. THE CORRECT INTERPRETATION OF ARTICLE 22 OF THE ABROGATED 1999 INVESTMENT LAW

1. The correct interpretation of the words of Article 22 of the Investment Law

As discussed below, when the text of Article 22 is interpreted according to the rules of interpretation set forth in Article 4 of the Civil Code, the sense that evidently appears from the proper meaning of the words used, in accordance with their connection and with the *intention of the legislator*, the conclusion is that it *stated the unilateral consent of the Republic of Venezuela to the submission of disputes to ICSID arbitration, leaving to qualified investors the right to decide whether to give their own consent or to resort to the Venezuelan courts*.

In the Spanish phrase "*serán sometidas an arbitraje internacional*" (shall be submitted to international arbitration), the tense of the verb indicates that it is an expression of command. The phrase conveyed the fact that international arbitration of disputes was a mandatory system, in the sense that, once properly invoked by the other party to a dispute, the Republic of Venezuela had a duty or obligation to comply with the applicable procedural rules and to abide by the decision of the arbitral tribunal. In this regard, the English translation "shall be submitted" for "*serán sometidas*," which is common ground between the parties, showed that the translators correctly understood the Spanish original as conveying this mandatory obligation.[178] Consequently, the text of this provision ("*shall be submitted to international arbitration*") was a unilateral express statement of consent to ICSID arbitration freely given in advance by the Republic of Venezuela;[179] or in the words of the ICSID Tribunal in the *Mobil* case, Article 22 "creates a conditional

---

assertion on the need for a "written" and "documented" agreements to arbitrate that must be included in contracts as a proof that an "express and unequivocal consent to submit to arbitration" has been made, basically in order to stress the core of his statement which is that no "tacit [or implicit] acceptance for arbitration" is acceptable. See Ivor D. Mogollón, *El arbitraje comercial venezolano*, Vadell Hermanos Editores, Caracas 2004, pp. 61-62. Carlos J. Sarmiento Sosa, also refers to the written consent for arbitration only to stress that there cannot be a "presumed or implicit arbitral agreement." Carlos J. Sarmiento Sosa, *Ley de arbitraje comercial*, Livrosca, Caracas 1999, p. 12.

178 "Shall can express (A) the subject's *intention to perform a certain action* or cause it to be performed, and (B) *a command*." The use of shall to express *a command* "is chiefly used in regulations or legal documents. In less formal English must or are to would be used instead of shall in the above sentences." See A. J. Thomson and A. V. Martinet, *A Practical English Grammar*, Fourth Edition, Oxford University Press 2001, pp. 208, 246.

179 In the same sense, see e.g., Gabriela Álvarez Ávila, "Las características del arbitraje del CIADI," in *Anuario Mexicano de Derecho Internacional*, Vol. II, Instituto de Investigaciones Jurídicas, Universidad Nacional Autónoma de México, UNAM, México 2002, pp. 4-5, 17 footnote 23, available at http://juridicas.unam.mx/publica/rev/derint/cont/2/cm/; Eugenio Hernández Bretón, "Protección de inversiones en Venezuela," in *Revista DeCITA, Derecho del Comercio Internacional, Temas de Actualidad, (Inversiones Extranjeras)*, N° 3, Zavalía, 2005, pp. 283-284; José Antonio Muci Borjas, *El Derecho Administrativo Global y los Tratados Bilaterales de Inversión (BITs)*, Caracas 2007, pp. 214-215; José Gregorio Torrealba R, *Promoción y Protección de las Inversiones Extranjeras en Venezuela*, Funeda, Caracas 2008. pp. 56-58, 125-127.

obligation" to go to arbitration (ICSID Mobil case, ¶ 102). None of the other aspects of the text or the other elements of interpretation led to a different conclusion.

The mandate to submit disputes to ICSID arbitration referred to "disputes to which" the ICSID Convention applied. As an initial observation, the term "disputes" appears for a second time in Article 22, in parallel to the first reference to "disputes" between an international investor whose country of origin had in effect a treaty or agreement for the promotion and protection of investments and the Republic of Venezuela. Grammatically, this duplicate and parallel reference indicated that the second category of "disputes" related to the ICSID Convention was not necessarily subsumed within the first category of "disputes" related to investment treaties or agreements. Therefore, when Article 22 referred to the "disputes" related to the ICSID Convention no reference was made to "international investor," as this term was defined in the Investment Law.

The second category of "disputes" comprises those in respect of which the provisions of the ICSID Convention were applicable. According to Article 25,1 of the ICSID Convention, ICSID jurisdiction "shall extend to any legal dispute arising directly out of an investment, between a Contracting State [...] and a national of another Contracting State, which the parties to the dispute consent in writing to submit to the Centre." As the ICSID Convention does not itself supply consent, it was unreasonable to interpret Article 22, which expressly provided that disputes shall be submitted to arbitration, as looking to the ICSID Convention to supply the consent that Article 22 itself purported to supply. Consequently, the only way to give effect to the mandate in Article 22 that disputes "shall be submitted" to ICSID arbitration was to interpret the phrase "disputes to which apply the provisions of the [ICSID Convention]" as referring to any disputes that met all the requirements for ICSID jurisdiction other than consent, which was supplied by Article 22 itself. Any other interpretation would have rendered this portion of Article 22 circular and would have deprive it of any effect, in violation of the principle of effective interpretation or *effect utile*.

The portion of Article 22 referring to the ICSID Convention ended with the phrase "if it so establishes" ("*si así éste lo establece*") also translated as "if it so provides". This phrase, interpreted according to the sense that evidently appears from the proper meaning of the words used, in accordance with their connection with the entirety of that section and consistent with the intention of the Legislator, refer to the need for the "respective treaty or agreement" to contain provisions establishing international arbitration[180] in order for the preceding express command (shall be submitted) to be capable of being executed; and for the last part of the Article that leaved the option to the international investor to decide whether or not to resort to international arbitration, to be effective. As the ICSID Convention paradigmatically establishes a framework or system of international arbitration for the settlement of investment disputes, the condition "if it so establishes" was clearly satisfied in the

180 In this sense, Victorino Tejera Pérez considers that the expression "if it so establishes" means "if it [respective treaty or agreement] establishes arbitration." See Victorino Tejera Pérez, "Do Municipal Investment Laws Always Constitute a Unilateral Offer to Arbitrate? The Venezuelan Investment Law: A Case Study," *loc. cit.*, p. 95; Victorino Tejera Pérez, *Arbitraje de Inversiones*, Magister Thesis, Caracas 2010, *cit.*, p. 170.

case of the portion of Article 22 that refers to the ICSID Convention. On the other hand, the phrase "should it so provide" referred primarily to the possibility that treaties or agreements for the promotion and protection of investments might not provide for international arbitration of disputes to which they apply.

As already mentioned, Article 22 was a compound provision that combined three rules concerning three different kinds of international instruments: first, treaties or agreements on the promotion and protection of investments; second, the MIGA Convention; and third, the ICSID Convention. Although the phrase "should it so provide" applied to each of the three rules, the condition that it embodied (that the treaty or agreement established international arbitration) was satisfied in the case of the ICSID and MIGA Conventions,[181] which clearly provided for arbitration, and was also satisfied in the case of those treaties or agreements for the promotion and protection of investments that did provide for international arbitration.[182] On the contrary, the condition was not satisfied in the case of treaties or agreements for the promotion and protection of investments that did not provide for international arbitration of disputes between the host State and foreign investors. Accordingly, "should it so provide" (if it so establishes) reflected a contingency only in the case of treaties or agreements for the promotion and protection of investments, which may or may not provide for international arbitration of such disputes.

Consequently, it was an error to suppose that the phrase "should it so provide" referred to the State's **consent** to arbitration. First, there was nothing in the text of Article 22 suggesting or supporting such an interpretation. The antecedent sentence ("shall be submitted to international arbitration under the terms of the respective treaty or agreement") made no reference to consent; it referred to international arbitration. The "so" in "should it so provide" referred to

181 The MIGA Convention contemplates two kinds of disputes: (a) disputes between the Agency and a Member country (Article 57), which shall be settled in accordance with the procedures set out in Annex II to the Convention and (b) disputes involving MIGA and a holder of a guarantee or reinsurance (Article 58), which shall be submitted to arbitration in accordance with such rules as shall be provided for or referred to in the contract of guarantee or reinsurance. Article 22 of the Investment Law can refer only to disputes of the first kind (those that could arise between MIGA and a Member State), because disputes of the second type do not involve the Venezuelan State or any other Venezuelan instrumentality. In the case of disputes that could arise between MIGA and a Member State, Annex II of the Convention provides a procedure for settlement that calls for negotiation followed by arbitration, with conciliation as a permissible alternative. According to Article 57(b)(ii) of the MIGA Convention, this procedure may be superseded by an agreement between the State and MIGA concerning an alternative method for the settlement of such disputes, but such an agreement must be based on Annex II, which means that it must also contain resort to arbitration. As the MIGA Convention provides for international arbitration in either situation, the condition "should it so provides" is satisfied and Article 22 requires submission of such disputes to international arbitration according to the terms of the MIGA Convention.

182 The Spanish text, which uses the subjunctive mood, makes clear that it refers not only to treaties or agreements of this kind to which the Republic of Venezuela was a party at the time the Investment Law was adopted, but also treaties or agreements to which it may become a party at any time in the future. Historically, while most agreements of this kind concluded by States around the world provide for international arbitration of investor-State disputes, some agreements do not. The Republic of Venezuela may become a party to treaties or agreements of this kind that do not provide for the resolution of controversies through arbitration.

"international arbitration" and cannot refer to a concept ("consent") that was not included in the antecedent sentence. Thus, the interpretation that the "so" referred to the act of consent, was unfounded.

Second, it should be remembered that the "it" in "should it so provide" referred to the ICSID Convention. Therefore, interpreting "should it so provide" as though it meant "should the ICSID Convention provide consent to arbitration" would turn this phrase into an impossible condition (one that cannot be fulfilled), because the ICSID Convention does not itself provide for a Contracting State's consent to ICSID arbitration. It was precisely because the ICSID Convention required consent by a separate written instrument, such as a piece of national legislation like Article 22 of the 1999 Investment Law,[183] that it cannot be presumed that the drafters of Article 22 intended the absurdity of subjecting the mandate relating to ICSID arbitration to a condition that was not and could not be fulfilled.

Under Venezuelan law, any interpretation of a statute that leads to absurdity or that would deprive a statutory provision of any effect must be rejected.[184] The principle of effective interpretation (*effet utile*) has been recognized to be a critical canon for the interpretation of statutes. For example, the Civil Cassation Chamber of the Supreme Tribunal of Justice has declared that "it would be absurd to suppose that the Legislator does not try to use the most precise and adequate terms in order to express the purpose and scope of its provisions, or deliberately omits elements that are essential for their complete understanding."[185]

On the other hand, the final part of Article 22 ("without prejudice to the possibility of using, when applicable the systems of litigation provided for in the Venezuelan laws in force") further confirmed that Article 22 was an expression of consent to arbitration. That statement indicated that Article 22 did not have the effect of preventing the investor from using domestic litigation remedies. If Article 22 was to be considered as a mere declaration of the State's willingness to agree to arbitration in a separate document as opposed to a firm expression of consent to arbitration by the State, there would have been no need to disclaim that Article 22 did not prevent the investor from resorting to domestic remedies.

The interpretation of Article 22 as containing an open offer by the State to submit investment disputes to ICSID arbitration not only resulted from the literal or grammatical element of statutory interpretation, but also from applying the logical, rational or reasonable element of interpretation derived from the fact that the State's offering of unilateral consent to arbitration in order to promote investment was part of the *raison d'être* of the Investment Law.

183 It is settled that under Article 25.1 of the ICSID Convention an ICSID Contracting State may express its written consent to submit to the jurisdiction of the Centre by way of the Contracting State's legislation for the promotion of investments.

184 See Supreme Tribunal of Justice, Constitutional Chamber, Decision N° 1.173 of June 15, 2004 (Case: Interpretación del Artículo 72 de la Constitución de la República Bolivariana de Venezuela) (Exp. 02- 3.215), in *Revista de Derecho Público* N° 97-98, Editorial Jurídica Venezolana, Caracas 2004, pp. 429 ff.

185 See Supreme Tribunal of Justice, Civil Cassation Chamber, Decision N° 4 of November 15, 2001 (Case: *Carmen Cecilia López Lugo v. Miguel Angel Capriles Ayala et al.*), ar http://www.tsj.gov.ve/decisiones/scc/Noviembre/RECL-0004-151101-99003-99360.htm, p. 7.

The Constitutional Chamber of the Supreme Tribunal of Justice in Decision N° 1.173 of June 15, 2004 held that the determination of the intention of the Legislator must "start from the will of the creator of the provision, as it results from the debates prior to its promulgation."[186] Being the Investment Law enacted through a Decree Law and not as the result of a parliamentary debate, the "creator" of such Law was not the National Assembly, but the President acting in Council of Ministers, that is, with all the Cabinet (Article 236.8 of the Constitution). Such intention "of the Legislator," therefore, resulted from the debates prior to the promulgation of the Law that were sustained in the Council of Ministers itself, in the Economic Cabinet, and from the proposals made by the drafter of the Law, who in this case, was Ambassador Werner Corrales-Leal. At that time Corrales was Head of the Permanent Representation of Venezuela before the WTO and the UN entities headquartered in Geneva, and was charged by the Government to prepare a draft of the Investment Law.[187] This is particularly important, in the absence of an *Exposición de Motivos* of the Law formally explaining its motives and content. All those elements contributed to establish the intention of the National Executive as the "creator" of the Law.

In effect, the intention of the National Executive when enacting the Investment Law, in a consistent way with the general policy defined by the Government at the time of its enactment for the purpose of attracting and promoting international investments in the country, was the same reflected in all the other pieces of legislation enacted by the Executive at the same time, all according to the pro-arbitration principle that prevailed in 1999. If according to Article 4 of the Civil Code, the interpretation of a statute results from "the sense that appears evident from the proper meaning of the words, according to their connection among themselves and the *intention of the Legislator*;" the latter is one of the key elements in the interpretation to be taken into consideration.

Being the Investment Law the product of a bureaucratic drafting process and not of a parliamentary process with recorded debates in a legislative body, the intention of the drafters is a valid source to determine the intention of the "legislator," or of the "creator" of the statute. In this case of the 1999 Investment Law, as mentioned, it was not the product of a diffuse "creator" (Parliament, Congress, Legislative Assembly) composed by representatives, parliamentary commissions, legislative assistance, interacting in close or open debates that are normally involve in the sanctioning of a statute; but was the product of an executive bureaucratic process, that in that case allowed to identify a "drafter" of the law. Consequently, in that sense it was possible to understand that "the will of the creator of the provision" eventually was the will of the drafter of the provision.

---

186 See Supreme Tribunal of Justice, Constitutional Chamber, Decision N° 1.173 of June 15, 2004 (Case: Interpretación del Artículo 72 de la Constitución de la República Bolivariana de Venezuela) (Exp. 02-3.215), in *Revista de Derecho Público*, N° 97-98, Editorial Jurídica Venezolana, Caracas 2004, pp. 429 ff.

187 See in Eduardo Camel A., "Ley de promoción de Inversiones viola acuerdos suscritos por Venezuela", *El Nacional*, Caracas September 15, 1999. The character of Corrales as drafter was officially recognized, for instance, in a press released of the Ministry of Foreign Affairs, *Oficina de Comunicaciones y Relaciones Institutionales*, "Resúmen de Medios nacionales e Internacionales", April 29, 2009, p. 23. See also, in Alberto Cova, "Venezuela incumple Ley de Promoción de Inversiones,' in *El Nacional*, April 24, 2009.

That is to say, whenever a statute, even when approved by a Congress, can be identify with its drafter (and that is why so many statutes and laws have or takes the name of its drafters), it is compulsory for the interpreter to seek for the intention of the "drafter" in order to establish the intention of the legislator. In such cases, there is no other "creator" of the Law different to its drafter. And this is the case, in general, regarding decree laws or executive regulations, which normally are approved without a "debate" like the parliamentary ones. Commonly, it is the respective Minister of the Executive in charge of drafting and proposing of the text, the one that can eventually express the will or the intention of the body approving the text.

But it can also be a public official, specialized in the subject or matter of the text, by assignment or delegation by the President, the one in charge of drafting a proposal of a statute or regulation. And this was the case of the 1999 Investment Law, in which the Ambassador before the specialized United Nations Agencies on Commerce in Geneva, Mr. Corrales was charged by the Executive of drafting the Law. In these cases, the opinion or the intention of the drafter is essential to identify the intention of the legislator. Consequently, the intention of the drafter is absolutely relevant to determine the intention of the legislator, not being at all inappropriate to look to the intention of the drafter. In each case, and according to each circumstance, in order to determine the intention of the legislator, the interpreter has the obligation to precise and identity the sometimes diffuse "creator" of the text. And that was what must had to be done in a case like the one of the 1999 Decree Law on the Investment Law, in the absence of any "Statements of Purposes" or other official document explaining the motives of the statute as for instance the Minute (*Acta*) of the Council of Minister (different to the deliberations, which are the only reserved part of its actions).

According to the public information available, being Mr. Werner Corrales and Mr. Gonzalo Capriles the drafters of the Law, acting by delegation of the President of the Republic, the only way to determine the will of the legislator or of the Council of Ministers as "creator" of the law, was to determine the intention the drafters. Consequently, in the case of the 1999 Investment Law, this intention of the legislator, being the National Executive who enacted the Law, was not other that the intention expressed by the drafters of such law; and in particular regarding its Article 22, in the sense that it had the intention to express a unilateral consent by the State to submit disputes with international investors to the jurisdiction of ICSID arbitration, as a main tool in order to attract and promote international investments in the country.

This intention, on the other hand and as aforementioned, was completely consistent with the pro arbitration trend that characterized all the legislation enacted by the Congress and the Executive at the same time of the Investment law, particularly by means of decree laws, in execution of the Enabling Organic Law of April of 1999 authorizing the President of the Republic to "enact provisions in order to promote the protection and promotion of national and foreign investments with the purpose of establishing a legal framework for investments and to give them greater legal security," as well as in the 2000 Enabling Law with similar purposes.

It was the case of the *1999 Law on Gassed Hydrocarbons*, recognizing the possibility to submit to arbitration disputes on matters relating to licenses given by the State for the exploration or exploitation of non-gas hydrocarbons;[188] of the *1999 Law on the Promotion of Private Investments through the Regime of Concessions*, in which it was provided that the parties, in public concessions contracts, could agree to submit their differences to the decision of an Arbitral Tribunal; [189] of the *2001 Organic Taxation Code* that included a general admission of arbitration as a means for the solution of disputes between taxpayers and the State; the *2001 Organic Hydrocarbons Law* in which the possibility to submit to arbitration the solution of disputes resulting from activities in the hydrocarbon sector when mixed companies are constituted with private investors is expressly recognized. [190]

In all these laws, referred all of them to key sectors of the economy, there was a clear legislative tendency admitting arbitration. The pro arbitration trend that characterized the legislation enacted between 1999 and 2001, derived not from its provision as compulsory (this was only the case of Article 22 of the 1999 Investment Law), but of its consistent regulation in all those laws as a means for conflict resolution

Consequently, considering Article 22 systematically and in a historical perspective, expressing consent to international arbitration was in accord with the trend in favor of international arbitration described above, including the State's ratification between 1993 and 1998 of treaties for the protection and promotion of investments that accepted international arbitration, as well as the other legal provisions regarding arbitration adopted at the time.

Furthermore, using the teleological and sociological element of statutory interpretation, the economic and social situation prevailing at the time the Investment Law was enacted (1999) explains the legislator's intent to promote investments and the offering of consent to international arbitration as a means to do so. The economic policy and the whole legal order existing in 1999 tended to promote foreign investment and international arbitration. This general intent was clearly reflected in the Investment Law as a whole, which was primarily devoted to promoting and protecting foreign investment by regulating the actions of the State in the treatment of such investment. Submission of disputes to international arbitration was and is precisely one of the principal means of protecting foreign investors and investments.[191]

---

188 Decree Law Nº 310 of September 12, 1999, *Official Gazette* Nº 36.793 of September 23, 1999.

189 Ley Orgánica sobre promoción de la inversión privada bajo el régimen de concesiones, *Official Gazette* Nº 5.394 Extra. of October 25, 1999. See *in general* on this Law, Alfredo Romero Mendoza "Concesiones y otros mecanismos no tradicionales para el financiamiento de obras públicas", in Alfredo Romero Mendoza (Coord.), *Régimen Legal de las Concesiones Públicas. Aspectos Jurídicos, Financieros y Técnicos*, Editorial Jurídica Venezolana, Caracas 2000, pp. 28-29.

190 *Ley Orgánica de Hidrocarburos, Official Gazette* Nº 37.323 of November 13, 2001. See Diego Moya-Ocampos Pancera and Maria del Sol Moya-Ocampos Pancera, "Comentarios relativos a la procedencia de las cláusulas arbitrales en los contratos de interés público nacional, en particular: especial las concesiones mineras," en *Revista de Derecho Administrativo*, Nº 19, Editorial Sherwood, Caracas 2006, p. 174.

191 Even the Decision Nº 1541 of 2008 p. 28 recognizes that one of the ways States attract foreign investment is to make a unilateral promise to submit disputes to arbitration ("It is impossible to be unaware that States which attempt to attract investment must, on a national

2. The efforts made since 2000 in order to change the meaning of Article 22 of the Investment Law by means of Judicial Interpretation without reforming the Statute

Since the 1999 Investment Law was adopted, and particularly after it began to be effective once that claims began to be brought before the ICSID Center, some commentators thought that article 1999 needed to be revised, in order to "get rid of all the problems it shall create."[192] But the fact was that the government never reviewed the Law.

Conversely, various attempts were made by individual opponents of the pro-arbitration policy of the Government and to the principle of relative jurisdictional immunity, in order to obtain a different interpretation from the Venezuelan courts.[193] Eventually, after various failed efforts, the Venezuelan Government itself filed before the Constitutional Chamber of the Supreme Tribunal of Justice a petition for the interpretation of the provision, and obtained, in record time, the Decision N° 1.541 of October 17, 2008 on the supposed interpretation of Article 258 of the Constitution and effectively on the interpretation of Article 22, in the sense that those opposing to international arbitration were seeking for years. Nonetheless, prior to that decision, other previous decisions concerning Article 22 of the 1999 Investment Law were issued in various proceeding seeking judicial interpretation of the Constitution, which must be also analyzed in order to understand how the interested legal community reacted to the content of Article 22 of the Investment Law.

Only a few months after the approval of the 1999 Law, judicial review actions began to be filed before the Supreme Tribunal seeking the annulment of the article 22 of the Investment Law or seeking for its new interpretation. For such purpose, and following a long tradition, the Venezuelan mixed system of judicial review contained all the necessary judicial tools, combining the classical diffuse method of judicial review (American model) established in Article 334 of the Constitution,[194] with the concentrated method of control of constitutionality of statutes (European model), established in Articles 335 and 336 of the Constitution. According to these constitutional provisions the Supreme Tribunal is the "highest and final interpreter" of the Constitution, having within its role to assure its "uniform interpretation and application" and to guarantee the "supremacy and effectiveness of constitutional norms and principles." For such purpose, the Constitution created the Constitutional Chamber within the Supreme Tribunal, whose role is to exercise "Constitutional

---

sovereignty level, decide to grant certain guarantees to investors, in order to ensure that the relationship materializes and, within the variables used to encourage these investments, it is common to include an arbitration agreement which, in the opinion of the investors, provides them with security to mitigate the fear of possible partiality by State courts in favor of nationals of their own country...").

192 See for instante Hildegard Rondón de Sansó, "La muerte definitiva del 22," *Quinto Día*, August 26, 2012, p. 13.

193 See on these decisions Hildegard Rondón de Sansó, *Aspectos jurídicos fundamentales del arbitraje internacional de inversión*, Ed. Exlibris, Caracas 2010, pp. 152 ff.

194 1999 Constitution, Article 334 [...] In the event of an incompatibility between this Constitution and a law or any other legal norm, the Constitutional provisions shall be applied, corresponding to the courts in any case, even *ex officio* (*sua sponte*), to decide what is needed.

Jurisdiction." (Articles 266,1 and 262), having the exclusive power to declare the nullity of statutes and other State acts issued in direct and immediate execution of the Constitution, or having the force of law (statute) (Article 334).[195]

In effect, following a long tradition,[196] the Venezuelan system of judicial review has been conceived as a mixed system,[197] which combines the classical diffuse method of judicial review (American model) established in Article 334 of the Constitution,[198] with the concentrated method of control of constitutionality of statutes (European model), established in Articles 335 and 336 of the Constitution. According to Articles 335 and 336, in the Venezuelan legal order, the Supreme Tribunal is the "highest and final interpreter" of the Constitution. Its role is to assure a "uniform interpretation and application" of the Constitution and "the supremacy and effectiveness of constitutional norms and principles." For such purpose, the Constitution created a Constitutional Chamber within the Supreme Tribunal, whose role is to exercise "constitutional jurisdiction" (Articles 266.1 and 262). That Chamber has the exclusive power to declare the nullity of statutes and other State acts issued in direct and immediate execution of the Constitution or having the force of law (statute) (Article 334).[199]

To implement the concentrated method of judicial review, the Constitution provides for different means of recourse to the courts, including the action for unconstitutionality of statutes (*acción de inconstitucionalidad*), which any citizen can file directly before the Constitutional Chamber.

In addition to the means of judicial review established in the Constitution, the Constitutional Chamber of the Supreme Tribunal of Justice has created a petition (*recurso*) for abstract interpretation of the Constitution (petition for constitutional interpretation), which has been extensively used.[200] The petition

---

195 These include "acts of government," internal acts of the National Assembly, and executive decrees having the rank of statutes.

196 See generally Allan R. Brewer-Carías, *Instituciones Políticas y Constitucionales*, Vol. VI, La Justicia Constitucional, Universidad Católica del Táchira, Editorial Jurídica Venezolana, San Cristóbal-Caracas, 1998; Allan R. Brewer-Carías, *Estado de Derecho y Control Judicial*, Instituto de Administración Pública, Madrid 1985; Allan R. Brewer-Carías, *Justicia Constitucional. Procesos y Procedimientos Constitucionales*, Ed. Porrúa, México 2006.

197 See Allan R. Brewer-Carías, *Judicial Review in Comparative Law,* Cambridge University Press, Cambridge 1989, pp. 275-277; Allan R. Brewer-Carías, *El Sistema Mixto o Integral de Control de Constitucionalidad en Colombia y Venezuela,* Bogotá 1995.

198 1999 Constitution, Article 334. "[...] In the event of an incompatibility between this Constitution and a law or any other legal norm, the Constitutional provisions shall be applied, corresponding to the courts in any case, even *sua sponte*, to decide what is needed. [...]").

199 These include "acts of government," internal acts of the National Assembly, and executive decrees having the rank of statutes.

200 See Supreme Tribunal of Justice, Constitutional Chamber, Decision N° 1077 of September 22, 2000 (Case: *Servio Tulio León Briceño*) in *Revista de Derecho Público* N° 83, Caracas, 2000, pp. 247 ff. See Allan R. Brewer-Carías, "Quis Custodiet Ipsos Custodes: De la interpretación constitucional a la inconstitucionalidad de la interpretación," in *VIII Congreso Nacional de Derecho Constitucional, Peru*, Fondo Editorial 2005, Colegio de Abogados de Arequipa. Arequipa, September 2005, pp. 463-489; Allan R. Brewer-Carías, "Le recours d'interprétation abstrait de la Constitution au Vénézuéla," in *Renouveau du droit constitutionnel, Mélanges en L'honneur de Louis Favoreu*, Dalloz, Paris, 2007, pp. 61-70.

for constitutional interpretation was created by the Constitutional Chamber without any constitutional or legal support. The Constitutional Chamber attributed to itself the sole power to decide it.[201]

In cases dealing with interpretations of the Constitution, the Constitutional Chamber is empowered to give binding effect to its decisions (Article 335). According to Decision N° 1.309 of June 19, 2001 (Case: *Hermann Escarrá*),[202] the decisions of the Constitutional Chamber on petitions of abstract interpretation of the Constitution have effects *erga omnes*, that is to say, they are binding on all courts of the Republic of Venezuela, but they apply only prospectively (*pro futuro, ex nunc*), that is, they do not have retroactive effects.

There is a second type of petition of interpretation in Venezuela: the petition (*recurso*) of interpretation of statutes. Unlike the prior one, this type is provided for in the Constitution (Article 266.6) and in the 2004 Organic Law of the Supreme Tribunal of Justice (Article 5, paragraph 1.52). The competence to decide these petitions corresponds to the Chamber of the Supreme Tribunal (Politico-Administrative, Civil, Criminal, Social or Electoral Chamber) that has competence over the subject-matter of the statute.[203] When a petition for interpretation results in the interpretation of a statute, such interpretation applies only prospectively.

A petition (*recurso*) of interpretation has the purpose of obtaining from the Supreme Tribunal a declarative ruling to clarify the content of legal or constitutional provisions. To have standing to file a petition of interpretation, a petitioner must invoke an actual, legitimate and juridical interest in the interpretation based on a particular and specific situation in which he stands, which requires interpretation of the legal or constitutional provision in question. The Constitutional Chamber has held that in a petition for constitutional interpretation, the petitioner must always point to "the obscurity, the ambiguity or contradiction between constitutional provisions."[204] In Decision N° 2.651 of October 2, 2003, the Constitutional Chamber ruled that the proceeding did not

---

201 No provision of the 2004 Organic Law of the Supreme Tribunal of Justice attributes this power to the Constitutional Chamber of the Supreme Tribunal of Justice. See Allan R. Brewer-Carías, *Ley Orgánica del Tribunal Supremo de Justicia. Procesos y Procedimientos Constitucionales y Contencioso-Administrativos*, Editorial Jurídica Venezolana, Caracas 2004, pp. 103-109.

202 Ratified in Supreme Tribunal of Justice, Constitutional Chamber, Decision N° 1.684 of November 4, 2008 (Case: *Carlos Eduardo Giménez Colmenárez*) (Exp. N° 08-1016), available at http://www.tsj.gov.ve/deci-siones/scon/Noviembre/1684-41108-2008-08-1016.html, pp. 9-10.

203 Before 2000, the only petition (*recurso*) of interpretation existing in the Venezuelan legal order was the petition of interpretation of statutes in cases expressly provided by them. It was established in Article 42,24 of the 1976 Organic Law of the Supreme Court of Justice, and exclusively attributed to the Politico-Administrative Chamber of that court. This changed in the 1999 Constitution.

204 Allan R. Brewer-Carías, "*Quis Custodiet Ipsos Custodes*: De la interpretación constitucional a la inconstitucionalidad de la interpretación," in *VIII Congreso Nacional de Derecho Constitucional, Peru*, Fondo Editorial 2005, Colegio de Abogados de Arequipa. Arequipa, September 2005. pp. 463-489,

have an adversarial nature and left it to the court's discretion whether to call to the proceeding those that could have something to say on the matter.[205]

As a matter of principle, when deciding a petition of statutory interpretation, the Chambers of the Supreme Tribunal (other than the Constitutional Chamber) are not empowered to establish a binding interpretation of constitutional provisions. Conversely, when the Constitutional Chamber decides a petition of interpretation of the Constitution, it is not empowered to establish binding interpretations of statutory provisions except when it is as a consequence of the interpretation of the Constitution. Accordingly, a petition of statutory interpretation, for instance, of an Article of the 1999 Investment Law could only be filed before the Politico-Administrative Chamber of the Supreme Tribunal. Consistent with this, the Constitutional Chamber declined to assume jurisdiction to precisely to decide a petition of interpretation of Article 22 of the 1999 Investment Law filed by three Venezuelan lawyers in 2007.[206] It was within this judicial review system that various attempts were made in order to obtain a judicial interpretation of Article 22 of the Investment Law different to the one expressed in that Article and to the sense of what was intended by be expressed by the Government when the Law was sanctioned. These intents were the following:

A. The first attempt, in 2000, to change the meaning of Article 22 of the 1999 Investment Law through a popular action challenging its constitutionality and seeking its annulment

The first case filed before the Supreme Tribunal in connection with Article 22 of the 1999 Investment Law, was an action of unconstitutionality brought before the Constitutional Chamber by two lawyers, Fermín Toro Jiménez and Luis Brito García, challenging Articles 17, 22 and 23 of the 1999 Investment Law.

The Constitutional Chamber in Decision N° 186 of February 14, 2001,[207] eventually upheld the constitutionality of the challenged provisions, from which it can be concluded that in doing so, the Tribunal eventually accepted the

---

205 Supreme Tribunal of Justice, Constitutional Chamber, Decision N° 2.651 of October 2, 2003 (Case: *Ricardo Delgado,* Interpretation of Article 174 of the Constitution), available at http://www.tsj.gov.ve/deci-siones/scon/Octubre/2651-021003-01-0241.htm, pp. 30-32.

206 Supreme Tribunal of Justice, Constitutional Chamber, Decision N° 609 of April 9, 2007 (Case: *Interpretation of Article 22 of the 1999 Investment Law*), available at http://www.tsj.gov.ve/deci-siones/scon/Abril/609-090407-07-0187.htm.

207 See Supreme Tribunal of Justice, Constitutional Chamber, Decision N° 186 of February 14, 2001 (Case: *Challenging the constitutionality Articles 17, 22 and 23 of the 1999 Investment Law, Fermín Toro Jiménez, Luis Brito García*), available at http://www.tsj.gov.ve/decisiones/scon/Fe-brero/186-140201-00-1438%20.htm. Also in *Revista de Derecho Público*, N° 85-88, Editorial Jurídica Venezolana, Caracas 2001, pp. 166-169. See the comments on this decision in José Gregorio Torrealba, *Promoción y protección de las inversions extranjeras en Venezuela*, *op. cit*., pp. 123-124; in Eloy Anzola, "El fatigoso camino que transita el arbitraje," in Irene Valera (Coordinadora), *Arbitraje Comercial Interno e Internacional. Reflexiones teóricas y experiencias prácticas*, Academia de Ciencias Políticas y Sociales, Comité Venezolano de Arbitraje, Caracas 2005, p. 413.; Diego Moya-Ocampos Pancera and Maria del Sol Moya-Ocampos Pancera, "Comentarios relativos a la procedencia de las cláusulas arbitrales en los contratos de interés público nacional, en particular: especial las concesiones mineras," en *Revista de Derecho Administrativo*, N° 19, Editorial Sherwood, Caracas 2006, p. 173.

constitutionality of the open offer of consent that the State gave in Article 22 for international arbitration.

In effect, when the Constitutional Chamber rejected the allegations of Fermín Toro and Luis Brito considering unconstitutional the provision of article 22 of the Investment Law, based in the allegation that it gave the investors the right to reject the submission of disputes to national courts (leaving aside national courts) resorting to arbitration, that implied con consider that the provision contained an order or command compelling the State to be submitted to international arbitration at the will of the investors. The rejection of this argument logically meant the acceptance by the Supreme Tribunal of the text of the Article 22 as it was written, with all its consequences, that is, the open offer given by the State for international arbitration, and the disclaimer contained in its last part, giving the investor the option to accept or not offer the open offer, and to resort at its will to national courts.

The claimants in the popular action, acting by themselves, as aforementioned, were Fermín Toro Jiménez and Luis Brito García. The former wad a Professor of International Law for many years, both having very close ties with the then new Government. At the time of the drafting of the Investment Law Toro was Head of the Diplomatic Academy of the Ministry of Foreign Affairs, and years after he was the Venezuelan Ambassador before the United Nations in New York. He had a very well-known opinion regarding the interpretation of article 127 of the Constitution of 1961 (equivalent to article 151 of the 1999 Constitution) in the sense of considering that in it, "public interest contracts" were equivalent to "international treaties"[208] He also considered that in Venezuela, even with the text of such constitutional article establishing the principle of relative jurisdictional immunity of the State (depending of the nature of the contract), on the contrary and according with the tradition initiated in 1893, the State had "absolute jurisdictional immunity regarding public interest contracts entered with natural or juridical persons of foreign nationality" independently of the "nature" of the contract.[209] Toro Jiménez also said that the opinion of Luis Brito García appears to coincide with his, although expressed with "vacillations."[210]

Nonetheless, the opinion of Luis Brito García, also a well-known lawyer and writer in Venezuela, expressed since 1968 was in the same direction. He expressed his concerns about the subjection of disputes arising from public interest contracts to foreign courts and to be decided according to laws different to the Venezuelan law, a situation that he considered as "unacceptable,"[211] arguing in addition that the exception established in article 127 of the Constitution (equivalent to article 151 of the 1999 Constitution) could only be applicable if one considers that contracts of public interest are equivalent to international treaties.[212] Brito finished his argument, in particular regarding arbitration clauses in public interest contract expressing his

---

208 See Fermín Toro Jiménez, *Manual de Derecho Internacional Público*, Vol. 1, Universidad Central de Venezuela, Caracas 1982, pp. 324, 437, 438, 441, 443, 444.

209 *Id.* pp. 444, 446, 451, 500, 501.

210 *Id.* pp. 441, 445.

211 Luis Brito García, "Régimen constitucional de los contratos de interés público," in *Revista de Control Fiscal y Tecnificación Administrativa*, N° 50, Contraloría General de la República, Caracas 1968, pp. 124.

212 *Id.* p, 124

criterion that "it is not possible to include in contracts of public interest clauses in which is established that the controversies arising from such contracts would be submitted to arbitration."[213]

These personal opinions of Toro Jiménez and Brito García, explain why they personally filed an action of unconstitutionality (*action popularis*) against the provisions of a statute such the Investment Law (particularly articles 22 and 23), that contrary to their thoughts and believes, not only established arbitration as a mean to resolve controversies on investments between the State and a private investor; but in both cases contained the consent given in advance by the State, as an open offer, to submit disputes to arbitration leaving in the hands of the investors to decide to go to arbitration and not to resort to the national courts, allowing them to decide unilaterally to withdraw the case from the possible jurisdiction of national courts. Nonetheless, they did not file the judicial review action against the possibility in itself of the State being subject to arbitration, as it is also provided in other articles of the Law (articles 18.4 and 21), but only regarding the provisions expressing the consent of the State to go to arbitration, which were the ones they considered unconstitutional.

Because they have for a longtime opposed in their wittings to the State subjected to international or national arbitration, therefore, these two Venezuelan authors and lawyers were the first to formally acknowledge the existence of the unilateral consent given by the State to go to ICSID arbitration in the challenged articles of the Investment Law, giving international investors, and exclusively to them, the right to opt in an unilateral way, in cases of investments disputes, between resorting to arbitration or before the national court. The constitutional review suit filed by them in their personal character, as citizens, on April 27, 2000, before the Supreme Tribunal, was their personal written reaction to the decision adopted by the Government just five months after the Law was published. The popular action challenging the constitutionality of articles 22 and 23 of the Decree Law, was intended to seek for the annulment of such provisions by the Supreme Tribunal of Justice, and consequently, to change the meaning of the law without seeking to be formally reformed.

Based on the summary and quotations of the text of the popular action included in the Decision of the Supreme Tribunal N° 186 of February 14, 2001 rejecting the petitioners request, the petitioners based their request on the argument that Article 22 being a provision of "obligatory application," was contrary to Articles 157 and 253 of the Constitution, because it:

> "attempts to authorize private parties [*los particulares*] to put aside the application of Venezuelan public law provisions, in favor of arbitral organs, which as it is known, freely apply equity criteria without necessarily following positive law provisions." (pp. 3, 4, 5, 21).

The petition also was based on the fact that Article 23 of the Investment Law also was an "obligatory application," which:

> "also is unconstitutional because it attempts to authorize to put aside the administration of justice, which is obligated to the precise application of public

---

213 *Id.* pp. 125-126.

order provisions, in favor of resort to 'Arbitral Tribunals,' which in its condition as arbitrators would put aside non-negotiable and sovereign order public provisions [...]" (pp. 3, 4, 5, 21).

From these statements, it is evident that the petitioners understood, both, that Article 22 and Article 23 of the Law, as open offers of consent made unilaterally by the State to submit controversies on investments to arbitration (international arbitration in the case of Article 22, and national arbitration in the case of Article 23), gave the investors the right –in the words of the petitioners– "to put aside the application of Venezuelan public law provisions in favor of arbitral organs" or "Arbitral Tribunals." The only way to understand the petitioners complain of the unconstitutionality of Articles 22 and 23 was based on the fact that they made possible for "private parties" to decide by themselves to leave aside the application of Venezuelan public law provisions in favor of arbitral organs, which is only possible if the State in such provisions gave already its consent to submit disputes to arbitration.

On the contrary, if the State would not have expressed its consent to go for arbitration in such provisions of "obligatory application" –as qualified by the petitioners–, if would have been impossible to say that the provisions (unilaterally) authorizes private parties to go to arbitration, that is "to put aside the application of Venezuelan public law provisions in favor of arbitral organs" or "Arbitral Tribunals."

The Constitutional Chamber, of course, denied the petition, finding that these provisions were consistent with the Constitutional right to arbitration as an "alternative means of justice." (p. 22-23). In rejecting the petition of annulment as it concerned Article 22, the Constitutional Chamber reasoned that:

> "the plaintiffs incur in the mistake of considering that by virtue of the challenged provisions previously quoted [Articles 22 and 23 of the 1999 Investment Law], there is an attempt to give an authorization to leave aside public law provisions in favor of arbitral organs, taking away from national courts their power to decide the potential disputes that may arise in connection with the application of the Decree Law on the Promotion and Protection of Investments. In fact, this Chamber considers that the prior statement is an error because it is the Constitution itself which incorporates within the system of justice the alternative means of justice, among which, the arbitration is obviously placed." (p. 22).

That is, the Constitutional Chamber accepted that it was the Constitution, that in article 253 incorporated the alternative means of justice, among which, arbitration, so the authorization given in the Law "to leave aside public law provisions in favor of arbitral organs, taking away from national courts their power to decide the potential disputes that may arise in connection with the application" of the Investment Law, as happened in the challenged provisions, was in conformity to the Constitution, warning the petitioners that "from the constitutional provision they claim as violated [article 253], the alternative means of justice are also part of the Venezuelan system of justice" (p. 23). The Constitutional Chamber decision, in addition, referred to article 151 of the Constitution as the founding provision for admitting the possibility for the State to be subjected to arbitration (p. 25).

The Constitutional Chamber noted that the Constitution incorporated alternative means of adjudication, including arbitration, within the Venezuelan system of justice. It highlighted that arbitration – national and international – had a constitutional basis in Article 258 of the 1999 Constitution, and specifically concluded that "the arbitral settlement of disputes, provided for in the impugned articles 22 and 23, does not conflict in any manner with the Fundamental Text." (p. 25).

The Constitutional Chamber it its decision referred to the mandate to promote arbitration in Article 258 of the Constitution ("The law shall promote arbitration, conciliation, mediation and any other alternative means of dispute resolution") and explained that:

> "[...] the law, in this case an act with rank and force of such, promoted and developed the referred constitutional mandate, by establishing arbitration as an integral part of the mechanisms for settlement of controversies that arises between an international investor, whose country of origin has in effect with Venezuela a treaty or agreement on the promotion and protection of investments, or controversies with respect to which the provisions of the Convention Establishing the Multilateral Investment Guarantee Agency (OMGI-MIGA) or the Convention on the Settlement of Investment Disputes between States and Nationals of Other States (ICSID) are applicable" (p. 24).

It must be noticed that the Constitutional Chamber, when referring to article 22 of the Investment Law and confirming that arbitration was "an integral part of the mechanisms" for settlement of investments disputes, it referred simply to "controversies with respect to which the provisions of the ICSID Convention "are applicable"(p. 24), without copying, using or referring to any other phrases of the article, assuming, with that assertion, that the ICISD Convention applied by virtue of the same provision and because of the consent the State gave in it, which was the justification to the clarification immediately made, in the sense that being a provision that gave the State consent for arbitration, this did not prevent the investor to resort to the national courts, by saying:

> "It must be made clear that in accordance with the challenged norm itself, the possibility of using the contentious means established under the Venezuelan legislation in effect remains **open**, when the potential dispute arises and these avenues are appropriate" (p. 24).[214]

The only meaning of this clarification is to consider that it was made by the Constitutional Chamber because in the decision it was accepted that the State in the challenged provision had given its general consent for arbitration, as an open offer, which did not prevent for the investor, at his will, to decide to use the contentious means established in the legislation. This allowed the Chamber to conclude in its decision "that the provision for arbitration under the terms developed in the challenged norm, as it is affirmed by the claimants, does not violate the sovereign power of national courts to administer justice, but in fact – it is reiterated - the

214 See the comments in this same sense in Victorino Tejera Pérez, "Do Municipal Investment Laws Always Constitute a Unilateral Offer to Arbitrate? The Venezuelan Investment Law: A Case Study," *loc. cit.*, p. 94; Victorino Tejera Pérez, *Arbitraje de Inversiones*, Magister Thesis, Caracas 2010, *cit.*, p. 168-169.

programmatic provisions outlined above contained in the Constitution of the Bolivarian Republic of Venezuela, are effectively implemented" (p. 24).

In this context, the Constitutional Chamber by upholding the constitutionality of Article 22 in effect did address the "meaning and scope of the provision" in the sense of accepting the consent expressed in it by the Republic, leaving in the hands of the investors to decide to go to international arbitration or to resort to the national courts.

Consequently, in this first attempt to change the meaning of articles 22 and 23 of the Investment Law containing open offers of the State' consent to go to arbitration for the resolution of investments disputes, the Constitutional Chamber rejected the popular action of unconstitutionality filed by Toro Jiménez and Brito García, accepting, in particular, that Article 22 contains the express consent of the State to submit to international arbitration controversies regarding investment. The quoted reasoning of the Supreme Tribunal would make no sense unless the Constitutional Chamber understood Article 22 as expressing the State's consent to international arbitration, in the same sense that article 23 does it.

In this context, consequently, the Constitutional Chamber by upholding the constitutionality of Article 22 addressed the "meaning and scope of the provision,"[215] as was reported in the Venezuelan Public Law Journal (*Revista de Derecho Público)* that same year 2001,[216] highlighting the pertinent excerpt considered important in the matter after the sanctioning of the 1999 Constitution, that is: "International Arbitration is admitted in the Constitution as part of the system of justice, and thus, the solution of controversies established in articles 22 and 23 of the Decree law of Promotion and Protection of Investments is not contrary in any way to the Fundamental Text."[217]

B. The second attempt, in 2007, to obtain a different interpretation of Article 22 of the Investment Law

On February 6, 2007, as aforementioned, a group of lawyers (Omar Enrique Valentier, Omar Enrique García and Emilio Enrique García Bolívar) filed a petition or recourse for statutory interpretation of Article 22 of the 1999 Investment Law before the Constitutional Chamber of the Supreme Tribunal, which was rejected by Decision N° 609 of April 9, 2007 because the Chamber lacked competence to decide

---

215 The opinion on the meaning of article 22 given by the claimants (Fermín Toro and Luis Brito) in the etxt of their popular action, remained in the files of the Supreme Tribunal after such upholding of the constitutionality of the challenged provisions of the Law. Toro and Brito did not publish in a separate way their comments on the Law after challenging it, and their written arguments were not commonly known.

216 In the *Journal*, after analyzing the Constitutional Chamber Decision N° 186 (not the arguments filed by Toro and Brito), when reporting on the decision, the most important and interesting parts of it, from the stand point of internal public law, references were made, on the one hand, to the challenging of the provision establishing "public contacts for legal stabilization" (art. 17); and on the other hand, to the provision referred to the "admission of international arbitration" (art. 22). See the Section of *Jurisprudencia Administrativa y Constitutional* (Constitutional and Administrative Jurisprudence), by Maria Ramos Fernández, in the *Revista de Derecho Público,* N° 85-86/87-88, Caracas 2001, pp. 220-225 and pp. 166-169.

217 See in *Revista de Derecho Público*, N° 85-88, Caracas 2001, p. 166.

on the matter.[218] The stated purpose of the petition was precisely to obtain an interpretation of Article 22 "to determine whether [Article 22] established or not the consent necessary to allow foreign investors to initiate international arbitrations against the Venezuelan State" (p. 2).

The petitioners expressed that they were not asking for the Constitutional Chamber to declare Article 22 unconstitutional, a matter that they said, had been resolved in Decision N° 186 of February 14, 2001. Instead they argued that "one thing is that the Article at issue is constitutional and another very different is that such Article establish a general and universal consent to allow any foreign investor to request that its disputes with the Venezuelan State be resolved by means of international arbitration, a matter with respect to which the wording of the Article is not clear" (p. 2). Accordingly, the petitioners formulated before the Court the following specific questions:

> "Does Article 22 of the Law on the Promotion and Protection of Investments contain the arbitral consent by the Venezuelan State in order for all the disputes that may arise with foreign investors to be submitted to arbitration before ICSID?
>
> In case of a negative [answer] (sic), what is the purpose and use of Article 22 of the Law on the Promotion and Protection of Investments?" (p. 2).

In Decision N° 609 of April 9, 2007, the Constitutional Chamber ruled that it had *no* competence to decide on the interpretation of Article 22 of the Investment Law, which corresponded to the attributions of the Politico Administrative Chamber of the Tribunal (p. 12-13). This was a ratification of the Constitutional Chamber's position that it had no competence to decide petitions of interpretation of statutes in an isolated way; its competence being limited to petitions of interpretation of the Constitution and of instruments within the "block of constitutionality," and of statutes but as a consequence of interpreting constitutional provisions.

In the case, the Constitutional Chamber concluded that the matter referred to in the Investment Law was "a matter of public law, on the relations (in this case, the solution of controversies) derived from foreign investments in the Venezuelan State, which means that competence, according to the subject-matter, corresponds to the Politico-Administrative Chamber of this Supreme Tribunal, on the basis of number 6 of article 266 of the Constitution and number 52 of article 5 of the Organic Law of the Supreme Tribunal of Justice."

Accordingly, the Constitutional Chamber ordered that the file be transferred to the Politico-Administrative Chamber of the same Supreme Tribunal of Justice.

C. The third attempt, in 2007, to obtain a different interpretation of Article 22 of the Investment Law

The case on the interpretation of Article 22 of the 1999 Investment Law, rejected by the Constitutional Chamber of the Supreme Tribunal of Justice, was sent to the Politico Administrative Chamber of such Tribunal was decided through Decision N°

218 Available at available at http://www.tsj.gov.ve/decisio-nes/scon/Abril/609-090407-07-0187.htm.

927 of June 5, 2007,[219] but the Tribunal failed to decide on the matter by declaring the request inadmissible because the petitioners lacked standing.

The Politico-Administrative Chamber reasoned that the petitioners failed to demonstrate the existence of a particular juridical situation affecting them in a personal and direct way that could justify a judicial decision on the scope and application of Article 22 (p. 14). The Politico-Administrative Chamber noted that the petitioners had based their interest only on their activities as lawyers, and had not referred expressly to any personal and direct interest in the requested interpretation. The Chamber also emphasized that a petition of interpretation must not be used for mere academic purposes (p. 15).

D. The fourth and final attempt, in 2008, to obtain a different interpretation of Article 22 of the Investment Law

After the aforementioned failed attempts by various individuals to obtain judicial decisions interpreting Article 22 of the 1999 Investment Law, in a different way to the its text, it was the Republic itself, which through the Attorney general filed an action obtaining a "custom made" judicial decision issued by the Constitutional Chamber of the Supreme Tribunal of Justice.

This was the decision N° 1.541 of October 17, 2008, issued in response to a petition of interpretation of Article 258 of the Constitution filed on June 12, 2008 by representatives of the Attorney General of the Republic (Hildegard Rondón de Sansó, Alvaro Silva Calderón, Beatrice Sansó de Ramírez *et al),*[220] prompted by the ICSID cases against the Republic of Venezuela pending at the time the petition was filed (p. 10). Although labeled as a request for "constitutional interpretation" of Article 258 of the Constitution, the Constitutional Chamber, contradicted its previous ruling, and having no matters to interpret on the text of such article (which states: "The law shall promote arbitration, conciliation, mediation and any other alternative means of dispute resolution"), went on to issue a "statutory interpretation" of Article 22 of the 1999 Investment Law. As already discussed, this was a matter that the Constitutional Chamber itself had acknowledged to be within the exclusive competence of the Politico-Administrative Chamber.

The Constitutional Chamber's 2008 "custom made" decision, which was highly criticized, [221] was issued containing an "obligatory interpretation" (*interpretación*

219 Available at http://www.tsj.gov.ve/decisiones/spa/Junio/00927-6607-2007-2007-0446.html.

220 Available at http://www.tsj.gov.ve/decisiones/scon/Octubre/1541-171008-08-0763.htm. It was also published in *Official Gazette* N° 39.055 of November 10, 2008. In this paper, when referring to the Decision N° 1541 of 2008, I will quote the pages of the version published in the web site of the Supreme Tribunal.

221 See for example Tatiana B. de Maekelt; Román Duque Corredor; Eugenio Hernández-Bretón, "Comentarios a la sentencia de la Sala Constitucional del Tribunal Supremo de Justicia, de fecha 17 de octubre de 2008, que fija la interpretación vinculante del único aparte del art. 258 de la Constitución de la República," in *Boletín de la Academia de Ciencias Políticas y Sociales*, N° 147, Caracas 2009, pp. 347-368; Eugenio Hernández Bretón, "El arbitraje internacional con entes del Estado venezolano," in *Boletín de la Academia de Ciencias Políticas y Sociales*, N° 147, Caracas 2009, pp. 148-161; Victorino Tejera Pérez, "Do Municipal Investment Laws Always Constitute a Unilateral Offer to Arbitrate? The Venezuelan Investment Law: A Case Study," pp. 92-109; Victorino Tejera Pérez, *Arbitraje de Inversiones*, Magister Thesis, Caracas 2010, *cit.*, pp. 180-193.

vinculante) of Article 258 of the Constitution, although ostensibly it was an interpretation of Article 22 of the Investment Law.

The Constitutional Chamber did not confirm that Article 22, by itself, does not constitute a general offer to submit disputes to international arbitration before ICSID, and basically changed the sense of the provision, depriving it of its content in a certain way pretending to "revoke" the unilateral expression of consent of the State to go to international arbitration it contained, without a formal reform of the statute – which of course has no legal effect.[222] By doing this, it left without meaning the last part of the provision, the one that allows the investors to opt to go to arbitration or to resort to the national courts.

In effect, in the 2008 Decision N° 1.541[223] the Supreme Tribunal admitted that it is possible for a State to express its consent to submit the resolution of disputes to international arbitration in a statute (pp 34-38), issuing it in a judicial process developed without input from any parties other than the Government, accepting the Government's opinion that Article 22 does not have that effect.

The Constitutional Chamber decided the matter in a very unusual abbreviated proceeding within only 120 days (including 30 days of judicial vacation) and without any adversarial hearings. The petition was filed on June 12, 2008 and it was notified to the Constitutional Chamber on June 17, 2008. Only one month later, on July 18, 2008, the Chamber issued a Decision admitting the petition, after omitting the oral hearing on the ground that it was a "merely legal" matter. The Constitutional Chamber set a maximum term of 30 days to decide the case, which would begin to count five days after a newspaper notice giving interested parties five days to file their arguments.[224] The newspaper notice was published on July 29, 2008. On September 16, 2008, three individuals filed arguments as third parties (*escrito de coadyuvancia*), but their participation was denied by the Constitutional Chamber on grounds of lack of standing.[225] The final decision in the case was issued one month later, on October 17, 2008.

In the Venezuelan judicial review system, the recourse of constitutional interpretation was accepted by the jurisprudence of the same Constitutional Chamber for the sole purpose of interpreting *obscure, ambiguous or inoperative* constitutional provisions. As aforementioned, Article 258 required no such interpretation, as it can be confirmed from its own text ("*The law shall promote arbitration, conciliation, mediation and any other alternative means of dispute resolution*") in which there is nothing obscure, ambiguous or inoperative. As was pointed out by J. Eloy Anzola, in his comments on the decision, it was obvious that

222 See the comments on the inefficacy of such revocation without reforming the Law regarding international arbitration, in Andrés A. Mezgravis, "El estándar de interpretación aplicable al consentimiento y a su revocatoria en el arbitraje de inversiones," in Carlos Alberto Soto Coaguila (Director), *Tratado de Derecho Arbitral*, Universidad Pontificia Javeriana, Instituto peruano de Arbitraje, Bogotá 2011, Vol. II, pp. 858-859.

223 See in general, the comments on this Decision in Tatiana B. de Maekelt; Román Duque Corredor; Eugenio Hernández-Bretón, "Comentarios a la sentencia de la Sala Constitucional del Tribunal Supremo de Justicia, de fecha 17 de octubre de 2008, que fija la interpretación vinculante del único aparte del art. 258 de la Constitución de la República," pp. 347-368.

224 *Id.*, p. 8.

225 Decision N° 1541 of 2008, pp. 5-7.

the representatives of the Republic when filing its request for interpretation, "did not hide the real intention of the recourse" that was to obtain "the interpretation of legal norm instead of a constitutional one,"[226] in the sense "that Article 22 of the Investment Law does not contain such consent. It is there where the decision is heading." (pp. 73-74).

Therefore, as there was nothing obscure, ambiguous or inoperative in this provision, it is obvious that the real purpose of the petition of constitutional interpretation filed by the representatives of the Republic of Venezuela was not to obtain a clarifying interpretation of Article 258, but to use their petition as a vehicle for obtaining an interpretation of Article 22 of the Investment Law in the sense that it did not contain the State's unilateral consent to arbitration. In particular, the Republic of Venezuela requested a declaration that "article 22 of the 'Investment Law' may not be interpreted in the sense that it constitutes the consent of the State to be subjected to international arbitration" and

> "that Article 22 of the Investment Law does not contain a unilateral arbitration offer, in other words, it does not overrule the absence of an express declaration made in writing by the Venezuelan authorities to submit to international arbitration, nor has this declaration been made in any bilateral agreement expressly containing such a provision [...]."[227]

The Constitutional Chamber noted that the 1999 Constitution allows the Republic of Venezuela to give its unilateral consent to have disputes, particularly disputes regarding foreign investments, resolved by international arbitration,[228] and subsequently went on to interpret Article 22 of the Investment Law and concluded, as the Representatives of the Republic of Venezuela had requested, that this provision did not constitute such an expression of unilateral consent.[229]

There have been numerous critics of this decision in the sense that the petition did not referred to Article 258 of the Constitution but was an improper request to interpret Article 22 of the Law.[230] In addition, Magistrate Pedro Rafael Rondón Haaz, who dissented from the Constitutional Chamber decision to admit the petition, also dissented from 2008 Decision N° 1.541, stressing that the Constitutional Chamber acted *ultra-vires* when engaging in the interpretation of a statutory provision (Article 22) (pp. 56-59). He reiterated his earlier dissent and stated that:

---

226 See J. Eloy Anzola, "Luces desde Venezuela: La Administración de la Justicia no es monopolio exclusivo del Estrado," in *Spain Arbitration Review, Revista del Club Español de Arbitraje*, N° 4, 2009, pp. 64, 64.

227 Decision N° 1541 of 2008, p. 9.

228 Decision N° 1541 of 2008, pp. 32, 40.

229 Decision N° 1541 of 2008, pp. 48-53. The flaws in the Constitutional Chamber's reasoning are addressed elsewhere in this Opinion.

230 See the critics mentioned in Eugenio Hernández Bretón, "El arbitraje internacional con entes del Estado venezolano," in *Boletín de la Academia de Ciencias Políticas y Sociales*, N° 147, Caracas 2009, pp. 148-161; Victorino Tejera Pérez, "Do Municipal Investment Laws Always Constitute a Unilateral Offer to Arbitrate? The Venezuelan Investment Law: A Case Study," pp. 92-109; Victorino Tejera Pérez, *Arbitraje de Inversiones*, Magister Thesis, Caracas 2010, *cit.*, pp. 180-193.

-*Article 258* does not raise any reasonable doubt. It does not require a clarifying interpretation because it only contains a request directed to the Legislator in order to promote arbitration.

-The petition of interpretation at issue had the purpose of obtaining from the Constitutional Chamber a "legal opinion" by means of an a priori judicial review process that does not exists in Venezuela. It sought the exercise of a legislative function by the Constitutional Chamber.

-The decision of the majority does not interpret or clarify Article 258 of the Constitution because this clear provision does not give rise to any doubts.

-The Constitutional Chamber exceeded its competence when it engaged in the interpretation of Article 22 of the 1999 Investment Law. The interpretation of statutory provisions is of the exclusive competence of the Politico-Administrative Chamber of the Supreme Tribunal of Justice.

-The Constitutional Chamber contradicted its own jurisprudence and exceeded its powers of constitutional interpretation, as well as its powers of judicial review concerning international treaties.

The dissenting Magistrate correctly noted that the Constitutional Chamber in interpreting Article 22 exercised a "legislative function" by providing, through an *a priori* judicial review procedure, rules that the Legislature must follow in the future in order to express the State's consent to international arbitration through a statute (pp. 56-59). Of course, those effects are limited to the Venezuelan courts, that is, the effects of 2008 Decision N° 1.541 under Venezuelan law do not affect the powers of an ICSID tribunal to interpret Article 22 independently in ruling on its own jurisdiction.

The political purpose of 2008 Decision N° 1.541 perhaps is the only factor that can explain its arbitrariness and lack of coherence and logical legal analysis. By its own admission, the Constitutional Chamber was operating on the understanding that it was bound to further the interests of the State. (p. 41) ("national sovereignty and self-determination ...oblige the organs of the Government to establish the most favorable conditions for the achievement of the interests and purposes of the State"). The Court betrayed its prejudice against the impartiality of arbitral jurisdiction, noting that "settlement of disputes will be made by arbitrators who [,] in [a] considerable [number of] cases[,] are related to and tend to favor the interests of multinational corporations, thus becoming an additional instrument of domination and control of national economies [...]" and adding that "it is somewhat unrealistic simply to make an argument of the impartiality of arbitral justice." (p. 24). Given these statements, the decision was neither objectively reasonable or neutral nor was it in any way reliable.

The following year, the Supreme Tribunal of Justice officially "responding" to criticisms formulated by Luis Brito García[231] against the Constitutional Chamber of the Supreme Tribunal decision N° 97 of February 11, 2009 in which the Tribunal

231 See Carlos Díaz, interview to Luis Britto García, "Perdimos el derecho a ser juzgados según nuestras leyes, nunca las juntas arbitrales foráneas han favorecido a nuestro país," *La Razón*, Caracas 14-06-2009, published on June 20, 2009 by Luis Britto García in http://luisbrittogarcia.blogspot.com/2009/06/tsj-lesiono-soberania.html

dismissed a recourse for the interpretation of Articles 1 and 151 of the Constitution filed by Fermín Toro Jiménez and the same Luis Brito García, published a "Press Communiqué (*Boletín de Prensa*) on its web site on June 15, 2009 ("*Author*: Prensa TSJ").[232] In this Press Communiqué the Supreme Tribunal decided to express some conclusions on the scope of previous decisions adopted by the Constitutional Chamber, without any sort of request made by anybody, without any constitutional process and without any parties or contradictory procedure. It was then a "decision" issued by means of a "Press Communiqué,"[233] in which the Supreme Tribunal referred, among other issues, precisely referred to Article 22 of the Investment Law "declared" that:

> "The [Supreme Tribunal] decisions eliminate the risk that signified to interpret Article 22 of the Investment Law as an open offer or invitation of Venezuela to be submitted to the jurisdiction of other countries, as it has been tried to argue in the International Forum, by subjects with interest's contrary to the Bolivarian Republic of Venezuela, as is the case of the big energy transnational."

This "Press Communiqué" is not a proper judicial decision and does not have force of law.[234] In addition, it confuses submission to an international tribunal with submitting a dispute to "the jurisdiction of other countries."

The "custom-made" Decision N° 1.541 can only be fully understood by taking into account that unfortunately the Judicial Branch in Venezuela and in particular, the Constitutional Chamber of the Supreme Tribunal, are subject to political interference in all politically sensitive cases. Since 1999, the independence of the Venezuelan Judiciary has been progressively and systematically dismantled, resulting from the tight Executive control over the Judiciary, and especially of the Constitutional Chamber of the Supreme Tribunal of Justice.[235] Since 2000, the

---

232 See in http://www.tsj.gov.ve/informacion/notasdeprensa/notasde-prensa.asp?codigo=6941.

233 See Luis Britto García, "¡Venezuela será condenada y embargada por jueces y árbitros extranjeros!," in http://www.aporrea.org/actuali-dad/a80479.html. Publication date: June 21, 2009.

234 See, e.g., Víctor Raúl Díaz Chirino, "El mecanismo de arbitraje en la contratación pública," in Allan R. Brewer-Carías (Coord.), *Ley de Contrataciones Públicas*, 2d. ed. Editorial Jurídica Venezolana, Caracas 2011, pp. 356-357.

235 Since 2004, and from the academic point of view, I have systematically studied this situation. See for instance, "La progresiva y sistemática demolición de la autonomía e independencia del Poder Judicial en Venezuela (1999-2004)" in *XXX Jornadas J.M Domínguez Escovar, Estado de Derecho, Administración de Justicia y Derechos Humanos*, Instituto de Estudios Jurídicos del Estado Lara, Barquisimeto 2005, pp. 33-174; "La justicia sometida al poder. La ausencia de independencia y autonomía de los jueces en Venezuela por la interminable emergencia del Poder Judicial (1999-2006)" in *Cuestiones Internacionales. Anuario Jurídico Villanueva 2007,* Centro Universitario Villanueva, Marcial Pons, Madrid 2007, pp. 25-57, *available at* www.allanbrewercarias.com, (Biblioteca Virtual, II.4. Artículos y Estudios N° 550, 2007) pp. 1-37; Allan R. Brewer-Carías, *Dismantling Democracy. The Chávez Authoritarian Experiment*, Cambridge University Press, 2010, pp. 226-244; "Sobre la ausencia de independencia y autonomía judicial en Venezuela, a los doce años de vigencia de la constitución de 1999 (O sobre la interminable transitoriedad que en fraude continuado a la voluntad popular y a las normas de la Constitución, ha impedido la vigencia de la garantía de la estabilidad de los jueces y el funcionamiento efectivo de una "jurisdicción disciplinaria judicial")", in *Independencia Judicial*, Colección Estado de Derecho, Tomo I, Academia de Ciencias Políticas y Sociales, Acceso a la Justicia, Fundación de Estudios de Derecho Administrativo (Funeda), Universidad Metropolitana

appointment of Magistrates to the Supreme Court of Justice have been conducted in an unconstitutional manner and in a way that violates the citizens' right to political participation,[236] to a point that the President himself admitted his own influence on the Supreme Tribunal, when he publicly complained that the Supreme Tribunal had issued an important ruling in which it "modified" a Law in 2007, without previously consulting the "leader of the Revolution," and warning courts against decisions that would be "treason to the People" and "the Revolution."[237] One important expression of this executive control on the Supreme Tribunal of Justice occurred in 2010, after an illegitimate "reform" of Organic Law of the Supreme Tribunal of Justice by means of its "reprinting" due to a supposed printing error,[238] allowing the appointment of new Magistrates of the Tribunal without the input of the Nominating Committee established in the Constitution, before the new National Assembly elected in September 2010 convene in January 2011.[239] With this legal "reform", the National Assembly proceeded to fill the Supreme Tribunal of Magistrates with

---

(Unimet), Caracas 2012; and "The Government of Judges and Democracy. The Tragic Situation of the Venezuelan Judiciary," en *Venezuela. Some Current Legal Issues 2014, Venezuelan National Reports to the 19th International Congress of Comparative Law, International Academy of Comparative Law, Vienna, 20-26 July 2014*, Academia de Ciencias Políticas y Sociales, Caracas 2014, pp. 13-42.

236 See for instance, what was publicly expressed by the Representative head of the Nomination Committee of magistrates in *El Nacional*, Caracas December 13, 2004. The Inter-American Commission on Human Rights suggested in its Report to the General Assembly of the OAS for 2004 that "These provisions of the Organic Law of the Supreme Court of Justice also appear to have helped the Executive manipulate the election of judges during 2004." See Inter-American Commission on Human Rights, *2004 Report on Venezuela*, par. 180, available at http://www.cidh.oas.org/annualrep/2004sp/cap.5d.htm. See Allan R. Brewer-Carías, "La participación ciudadana en la designación de los titulares de los órganos no electos de los Poderes Públicos en Venezuela y sus vicisitudes políticas" in *Revista Iberoamericana de Derecho Público y Administrativo*, Year 5, N° 5-2005, San Jose, Costa Rica 2005, pp. 76-95, *available at* www.allanbrewercarias.com, (Biblioteca Virtual, II.4. Artículos y Estudios N° 469, 2005) pp. 1-48

237 See the President's speech identifying the alleged "treason" of judicial decisions taken "behind the back of the Leader of the Revolution" in *Discurso en el Primer Encuentro con Propulsores del Partido Socialista Unido de Venezuela desde el teatro Teresa Carreño* (Speech in the First Event with Supporters of the Venezuela United Socialist Party at the Teresa Carreno Theatre), March 24, 2007, *available at* http://www.minci.gob.ve/alocuciones/4/13788/primer_encuentro_con.html, p. 45. The decision to which he is referring specifically is the Supreme Tribunal of Justice, Constitutional Chamber, Decision N° 301 of February 27, 2007 (Case: *Adriana Vigilanza y Carlos A. Vecchio*) (Exp. N° 01-2862) (*Official Gazette* N° 38.635 of March 1, 2007) in *Revista de Derecho Público,* N° 101, Editorial Jurídica Venezolana, Caracas 2007, pp. 170-177.

238 See the comments of Víctor Hernández Mendible, "Sobre la nueva reimpresión por "supuestos errores" materiales de la Ley Orgánica del Tribunal Supremo, octubre de 2010," y Antonio Silva Aranguren, "Tras el rastro del engaño, en la web de la Asamblea Nacional," in *Revista de Derecho Público*, N° 124, Editorial Jurídica Venezolana, Caracas 2010, pp. 110-113.

239 Hildegard Rondón de Sansó, who was Magistrate of the former Supreme Court of Justice, regarding such reform, has said that "the Nomination Judicial Committee was unconstitutionally converted into an appendix of the Legislative Power." See Hildegard Rondón de Sansó, "*Obiter Dicta*. En torno a una elección," in *La Voce d'Italia*, Caracas, December 14, 2010.

individuals who did not comply with the constitutional conditions to be Magistrate.[240]

Unfortunately, the political control over the Supreme Tribunal of Justice has permeated to all the judiciary, due mainly to the fact that in Venezuela, it is the Supreme Tribunal that is in charge of the government and administration of the Judiciary. This has affected gravely the autonomy and independence of judges at all levels of the Judiciary, which has been aggravated by the fact that during the past decade the Venezuelan Judiciary has been composed primarily of temporary and provisional judges, without career or stability, appointed without the public competition process of selection established in the Constitution, and dismissed without due process of law, for political reasons.[241] The fact is that, in Venezuela, no judge can adopt any decision that could affect the government policies, or the President's wishes, the state's interest, or public servants' will, without previous authorization from the same government,[242] That is why the Inter-American Commission on Human Rights in its *2009 Annual Report*: "The lack of judicial independence and autonomy vis-à-vis political power is, in the Commission's opinion, one of the weakest points in Venezuelan democracy."[243] It is within the aforementioned context that the Government's 2008 request to the Constitutional Chamber of the Supreme Tribunal must be viewed.

Without doubt, the 2008 Decision N° 1.541 was the product of a politically influenced judiciary that was called upon by the Republic of Venezuela to try to bolster its position in pending ICSID cases. The Constitutional Chamber acted *ultra vires* when it undertook to interpret Article 22 of the 1999 Investment Law at the request of the Government of the Republic,[244] because the Politico-Administrative Chamber has exclusive competence (*competencia*) to interpret statutes by means of a recourse of interpretation of statutes; and to interpret such article with the excuse of interpreting Article 258 of the Constitution that needs no interpretation at all.

3. The incorrect interpretation adopted by the Supreme Tribunal of Justice in 2008 at the request of the Government

The consequence of the Government's request was that the Supreme Tribunal of Justice through its Constitutional Chamber in Decision 1541 of October 17, 2008, ruled that Article 22 of the 1999 Investment Law only recognizes international arbitration where the treaty or agreement itself contains an obligatory submission to

240 See Hildegard Rondón de Sansó, "*Obiter Dicta*. En torno a una elección," in *La Voce d'Italia*, 14-12-2010.

241 See Inter-American Commission on Human Rights, *Report on the Situation of Human Rights in Venezuela*, OEA/Ser.L/V/II.118, doc. 4 rev. 2, December 29, 2003, par. 174, *available at* http://www.cidh.oas.org/countryrep/Venezuela2003eng/toc.htm.

242 See Antonio Canova González, *La realidad del contencioso administrativo venezolano (Un llamado de atención frente a las desoladoras estadísticas de la Sala Político Administrativa en 2007 y primer semestre de 2008)*, Funeda, Caracas 2008, p. 14.

243 See in ICHR, *Annual Report 2009*, paragraph 483, available at http://www.cidh.oas.org/annualrep/ 2009eng/Chap.IV.f.eng.htm .

244 See Allan R. Brewer-Carías, "La Sala Constitucional vs. La competencia judicial en materia de interpretación de las leyes," in *Revista de Derecho Público*, N° 123, Editorial Jurídica Venezolana, Caracas 2010, pp. 187-196.

arbitration arguing that while the ICSID Convention provides a mechanism for international arbitration, it did not itself provide for the arbitration of any dispute without the separate instrument of consent (pp. 45-48). This is contrary to the wording of the Article, the connection of the words used in it, considering the whole of its text, and the intention of the National Executive when enacting the Law.

In particular, to interpret the expression "if so provides" in Article 22, in the sense if the respective treaty or agreement provides according to its terms, that the dispute shall be submitted to international arbitration, meant to ignore the final provision of the Article in which a right was given to the international investor to unilaterally opt for international arbitration or to resort before the national courts. The disclaimer of the last phrase of the Article, which the Constitutional Chamber did not even consider, with its interpretation resulted without any meaning, when considering that the condition set forth in the provision was referred to the need for a consent to be necessarily established in the respective treaty or agreement. This is particularly so because interpreting "if it so establishes" as an equivalent of "if the ICSID Convention establishes consent" turned this phrase into an impossible condition (a condition that cannot be fulfilled), depriving Article 22 of any meaningful effect.

In addition, the interpretation of the condition included in Article 22 of the Investment Law adopted by the Supreme Tribunal of Justice was fundamentally flawed. It was incorrect to interpret "if it so establishes" as a requirement that the State's consent that was already given in the Law needed to be incorporated in the ICSID Convention, because "so" cannot refer to a term ("consent") that was not used in the preceding sentence containing the command ("shall be submitted to international arbitration according to the terms of the respective treaty or agreement"). It was unreasonable to interpret Article 22, as looking to the ICSID Convention to supply the consent that Article 22 itself purports to supply.

The final part of Article 22 ("without prejudice to the possibility of using, as appropriate, the contentious means contemplated by the Venezuelan legislation in effect") was a confirmation that Article 22 was an expression of consent to arbitration, in the sense that it indicated that the unilateral expression of consent of Article 22 did not have the effect of preventing the investor from using domestic litigation remedies. On the contrary, it confirmed the unilateral consent given by the State as an open offer that could be accepted or not, at his will, by the investor. If Article 22 was a mere declaration of the State's willingness to agree to arbitration in a separate document as opposed to a firm expression of consent to arbitration by the State, there would have been no need to disclaim that Article 22 did not prevent the investor from resorting to domestic remedies.

Consequently, the Supreme Tribunal of Justice decision regarding the reading of Article 22 ignored the condition included by the Legislator, and most important, the very right given to the international investor to make a choice which was a result clearly impermissible under either Venezuelan or international legal principles.

On the other hand, the Decision N° 1541 of 2008 (p. 48) attempted to show that interpreting Article 22 as expressing the State's consent to international arbitration would have been "unacceptable" in any legal order. Those attempts missed the mark, and showed an internal contradiction in the decision. While on the one hand the Constitutional Chamber conceded that a State could express its consent unilaterally and generically in investment legislation (p. 44) a method of consent that is clearly allowed in the ICSID Convention and is firmly established in international practice, on the other hand, the Chamber offered arguments that amount to denying that very same point. In particular, the Decision N° 1541 of 2008 argued that, if Article 22 was interpreted as a general offer of consent and that offer was accepted by an investor, a wide range of matters within the scope of the statute would automatically (*de pleno derecho*) be submitted to arbitration, without the State being able to assess the benefits or disadvantages of arbitration in each case, in violation of an alleged principle of "informed" consent (p. 41). Yet this is precisely what happens, as the intended consequence, whenever a State chooses to consent to arbitration, generically, by means of a national statute or a treaty.

In the same vein, the Decision N° 1541 of 2008 argued that to interpret Article 22 as containing "a general offer to submit disputes to the Convention on Settlement of Investment Disputes between States and Nationals of Other States in matters related to foreign investment would absurdly imply that the State cannot select a forum or jurisdiction which is more convenient or favorable to its interests (Forum Shopping)." (p. 49). This is not an absurdity at all; it is the normal effect of a generic expression of consent, which is uniformly accepted under the ICSID Convention. A State that gives generic consent to arbitration in treaties or in statutes gave up the right to assess the benefits or disadvantages of international arbitration on a case-by-case basis, in exchange for the investment promotion benefits derived from a generic offer of international arbitration to foreign investors.

The Decision N° 1541 of 2008 also argued that interpreting Article 22 as a generic offer of consent would have in effect abrogated bilateral and multilateral investment treaties that provided for different dispute resolution methods, because investors protected by those treaties could have invoke the most-favored-nation clause (MFN) contained in them to take advantage of ICSID arbitration, thereby avoiding the dispute resolution mechanisms provided for in the treaty (p. 49). This argument had no basis. Assuming that an investment treaty to which Venezuela was a party had an MFN clause that covered dispute settlement, and assuming that ICSID arbitration was more favorable than the dispute-settlement method contemplated in such treaty, an investor claiming under that treaty would already had the right to invoke ICSID arbitration, because the MFN clause of that treaty would have incorporated by reference the dispute-settlement provisions of other investment treaties to which Venezuela was a party, which provide for ICSID arbitration. Under the logic of the Decision N° 1541 of 2008, the treaty of the example would have been "abrogated" by the other treaties, independently of how Article 22 was interpreted, a conclusion that showed that the argument proved nothing. Besides, the argument in the Decision N° 1541 of 2008 amounted to assert that a State cannot consent to ICSID jurisdiction by statute if it had entered into investment treaties that provided for different methods of dispute resolution, a conclusion that had no basis.

In any case, the lack of a coherent and logical legal analysis of the Decision N° 1541 of 2008 contrasted with various of its statements that made it evident that this ruling was the product of a political agenda that the Constitutional Chamber was called upon to defend. By its own admission, the Constitutional Chamber was operating on the understanding that it was bound to further the interests of the State. Most notably, the Chamber stated:

> "Although the Republic and the government, in accordance with the Constitution and current law, are limited in the scope of their authority before other international law provisions based on jurisprudential principles, such as the limitations set forth in Article 13 of the Constitution of the Bolivarian Republic of Venezuela "[…] territory may not be assigned, transferred, leased or in any way conveyed, even temporarily or partially, to foreign governments or other parties subject to international law […]," also that *national sovereignty and self-determination allow and obligate the Federal Government to establish conditions which are most favorable to the interests and purposes of the State* as set forth in the Constitution."[245]

The protection of national sovereignty and self-determination were a constant theme informing various statements in the 2008 Decision N° 1.541. For example, when holding that the interpretation of all laws must be made in accordance with the Constitution, the Tribunal went on to explain that this meant "to protect the Constitution itself from any deviation of principles and from any separation from the political project that it embodies by the will of the people" adding that "part of the protection and guarantee of the Constitution of the Bolivarian Republic of Venezuela is rooted, then, in a political perspective *in fieri, disinclined toward ideological linkages to theories that may limit, under the pretext of universal validity, the national sovereignty and self-determination*, as required by article 1° *eiusdem* (…)." (p. 40). Earlier, 2008 Decision N° 1.541 expressed some skepticism about a generalized perception of impartiality of arbitral jurisdiction, noting that "the displacement of the jurisdiction from State tribunals to those of arbitration frequently occurs because the settlement of disputes will be made by arbitrators who[,] in [a] considerable [number of] cases[,] are related to and *tend to favor the interests of multinational corporations, thus becoming an additional instrument of domination and control of national economies* […]" and adding that "it is somewhat unrealistic simply to make an argument of the impartiality of arbitral justice in detriment of the justice provided by the judicial authorities of the Judiciary, to justify the applicability of the jurisdiction of contracts of general interest." (p. 24).

245 Decision N° 1541 of 2008, 40-41 (emphasis added). The protection of national sovereignty and self- determination were a constant theme informing various statements in this decision. For example, when holding that the interpretation of all laws must be made in accordance with the Constitution, the Court went on to explain that this meant "*safeguarding the Constitution from all deviations in principles and separation from the political plan which is the will of the people incarnate*" adding that *"part of the protection and guarantee of the Constitution of the Bolivarian Republic of Venezuela therefore rests on an* in fieri, *political perspective resistant to the ideological connections with theories which could restrict it, under the pretext of universal truths, sovereignty and national self determination, as required by Article 1° eiusdem* (...)." *Id.*, p. 40 (emphasis added). Earlier, the Decision N° 1541 of 2008 had expressed some skepticism about a generalized perception of impartiality of arbitral jurisdiction, noting that "moving the jurisdiction of the state courts to arbitration courts, in many situations, is due to the fact that dispute resolution is conducted by arbiters which, in a number of cases, are connected to and tend to favor the interests of transnational corporations, and thus become an additional instrument of domination and control of national economies" and adding that "it is not very realistic to simply use the argument of the impartiality of arbitral justice to the detriment of justice administered by the jurisdictional branches of the Judiciary to justify the admissibility of the jurisdiction of general interest contracts." *Id.*, p. 24 (emphasis added).

The following year, the Supreme Tribunal of Justice officially "responding" to critics formulated by Luis Brito García[246] against the Constitutional Chamber of the Supreme Tribunal decision N° 97 of February 11, 2009 dismissing a recourse for the interpretation of articles 1 and 151 of the Constitution filed by Fermín Toro Jiménez and himself (Luis Brito García), in the aforementioned "Press Communiqué (*Boletín de Prensa*),[247] affirmed in a way contrary to the possibility in Venezuela on any sort of international arbitration, that "any decision or arbitral ruling can be the object of judicial review if it pretend to be executed in Venezuela, as the Constitutional Chamber ruled in decisions N° 1.939/08, in the case: "*Corte Interamericana de Derechos Humanos vs. Jueces de la Corte Primera de lo Contencioso Administrativo*", and in the decision N° 1.541/08, which at its turn was ratified in the decision N° 1.942/03."[248]

4. The insufficient interpretation of Article 22 of the 1999 Investment Law made by the ICSID Tribunals in the Mobil and Cemex Cases

The matter of the interpretation of Article 22 of the 1999 Investment Law was also considered by the ICSID Tribunals in the *Mobil* and *Cemex* cases, in which the tribunals did not decide that Article 22 did not constitute a standing, general consent of the Republic to arbitrate all investments dispute before ICSID.

On the contrary, in the *Mobil* case, the ICSID Tribunal decided that Article 22 effectively "creates an obligation to go to arbitration," although it refers to it as "a conditional obligation" (ICSID *Mobil* case, ¶ 102). This condition to which the obligation is subjected according to the decisions, results from the phrase "if it so provides" or "establishes." The ICSID Tribunals in these two cases completely ignored the existence of the disclaimer included in the last phrase of Article 22, holding that it can be interpreted in two ways, in the sense that the treaty, agreement or convention can (i) provide "for international arbitration," or (ii) "for mandatory submission of disputes to international arbitration" (ICSID *Mobil* case, ¶ 109) ("creates an obligation for the State to submit disputes to international obligation," ICSID *Cemex* case, ¶ 101).

---

246 See Carlos Díaz, interview to Luis Britto García, "Perdimos el derecho a ser juzgados según nuestras leyes, nunca las juntas arbitrales foráneas han favorecido a nuestro país," *La razón*, Caracas 14-06-2009, published on June 20, 2009 by Luis Britto García in http://luisbrittogarcia.blogspot.com/2009/06/tsj-lesiono-soberania.html

247 See "The inmunity of Venezuela regarding foreign courts is consolidated" (*Se consolida la inmunidad de Venezuela frente a tribunales extranjeros*), 15 de junio de 2009, in http://www.tsj.gov.ve/informacion/notasdeprensa/notasdeprensa.asp?codigo=6941. See on such sort of judicial "decision," Allan R. Brewer-Carías, "Comentarios sobre el 'Caso: Consolidación de la inmunidad de jurisdicción del Estado frente a tribunales extranjeros,' o de cómo el Tribunal Supremo adopta decisiones interpretativas de sus sentencias, de oficio, sin proceso ni partes, mediante 'Boletines de Prensa,'" in *Revista de Derecho Público*, N° 118, Editorial Jurídica Venezolana, Caracas 2009, pp. 319-330. See on what is called an "unfortunate Press Communiqué," Víctor Raúl Díaz Chirino, "El mecanismo de arbitraje en la contratación pública," in Allan R. Brewer-Carías (Coord.), *Ley de Contrataciones Públicas*, 2d. ed. Editorial Jurídica Venezolana, Caracas 2011, pp. 356-357

248 See in http://www.tsj.gov.ve/informacion/notasdeprensa/notasdeprensa.asp?codigo=6941.

The ICSID Tribunals then concluded, exclusively regarding the condition established in the provision, that "both interpretations are grammatically possible" (ICSID *Mobil* case, ¶ 110; ICSID *Cemex* case, ¶ 102). This assertion, as aforementioned is incorrect because the second option is a denial in itself not only of the premise that the Article effectively contained a "conditional obligation," but of the disclaimer included in the last phrase of the provision that gave the investor the right to go to arbitration or to resort to the national courts. That is, if it is true that in the first option, the existence in Article 22 of a "conditional obligation" to go to arbitration remained subject only to the condition that the treaties or agreements provided for international arbitration, the second option denied the "conditional obligation" given its requirement of "mandatory submission". This second interpretation resulted in a tautology which is grammatically incorrect.

As aforementioned, the ICSID Tribunals also failed in their grammatical analysis to consider and analyze the last part of the Article. By ignoring it, they erased the part of the Article that precisely confirmed the existence in the Article of the "conditional obligation" to go to arbitration. This was improper under Venezuelan law because it leaved the last part of the provision to be interpreted as "meaningless."[249]

As it has also been decided by the Venezuelan Supreme Tribunal, "it would be absurd to assume that the legislator would not try to use the most precise and adequate terms to express the purpose and scope of its provisions, or deliberately omit elements that are essential for their complete understanding."[250] This means, from the stand point of the interpreter and according to a well-established principles of interpretation of statutes, that one must assume that the legislator did not deliberately draft the provision in an ambiguous way or omit elements that are essential for the complete understanding of the provision. However, one cannot ignore the words, phrases or elements that the legislator used in the provision.

On the other hand, it also is a well-established principle of statutory interpretation that the interpreter, when interpreting a statute, must reject and avoid all absurd interpretations.[251] As mentioned, each and every part of Article 22 had a meaning and purpose, and when interpreting it, no part could be just ignored, as occurred in the ICSID Tribunal decisions which ignored the last part of Article 22. Given the failure of the *Mobil* and *Cemex* tribunals to consider and to give any meaning to a crucial part of Article 22 that was essential for its interpretation, without interpreting the provision "in a manner compatible with the effect sought" by the State making the Law (ICSID *Mobil* case, ¶ 118), these decisions failed to properly interpret the provision in accordance with Venezuelan or international law. In the end, the tribunals' conclusions were issued for the purpose *of those cases* (and only those cases).

---

249 The same is true, of course, for the ***Brandes*** decision, which also did not ascribe meaning to the disclaimer.

250 Decision N° 4 of November 15, 2001 (*Carmen Cecilia López Lugo v. Miguel Ángel Carpiles Ayala et al.* case), available at http://www.tsj.gov.ve/decisiones/scc/Noviembre/RECL-0004-151101-99003-99360.htm.

251 See Supreme Tribunal of Justice, Constitutional Chamber, Decision N° 1.173 of June 15, 2004 (Case: *Interpretación del Artículo 72 de la Constitución de la República Bolivariana de Venezuela*) (Exp. 02-3.215), in *Revista de Derecho Público* N° 97-98, Editorial Jurídica Venezolana, Caracas 2004, pp. 429 ff.

5. The absence of interpretation of Article 22 of the 1999 Investment Law in the ICSID tribunal Brandes Case

In another case, the ICSID tribunal *Brandes* case, in an astonishing way and in contrast with the *Mobil* and *Cemex* cases, reached the same conclusion, but without making any effort to interpret Article 22 of the 1999 Investment Law.

Instead, the ICSID tribunal limited itself only to refer to the tools and principles for interpretation of the Article, without applying them in the case. The ICSID tribunal pointed out in its decision: (i) that Article 22 was to be interpreted beginning with the principles of the Venezuelan legal system "starting with the Political Constitution" (ICSID *Brandes* case, ¶ 36, 81) but also in accordance with the principles of international law (ICSID *Brandes* case, ¶¶ 36, 81); (ii) that nonetheless, when applying the principles of Venezuelan law the elements of Article 4 of the Civil Code, were not to be applied together as imposed by the Venezuelan Article 4 of the Civil Code, but in a lineal way, beginning with the grammatical analysis (ICSID *Brandes* case, ¶ 35); (iii) that Article 22 of the Investment Law was required to be interpreted taking into account its relationship with "other legal norms of the Republic" (ICSID *Brandes* case, ¶ 30, 35, 97); and (iv) that it was essential for the Tribunal to analyze other Articles of the Investment Law constituting the immediate context for Article 22 (ICSID *Brandes* case, ¶ 88).

After announcing all these tools and principles of interpretation, but without applying any one of them to the case, the Tribunal issued its decision without analyzing the text of the Article, the words it contains, and the relationship of the words used in it to each other. In addition, the Tribunal did not establish the relationship between the words used in the Article within the content of its entire text, including the last phrase of the disclaimer. That is, the Tribunal, without making any effort to even take the first step announced in the decision, defined as the "purely grammatical analysis" (ICSID *Brandes* case, ¶ 35), and without any reasoning and motivation, just concluded that "the wording of Article 22 of the LPPI is confusing and imprecise, and that it is not possible to affirm, based on a grammatical interpretation, whether or not it contains the consent of the Bolivarian Republic of Venezuela to ICSID jurisdiction" (ICSID *Brandes* case, ¶ 86).

The astonishing aspect of this conclusion is that the same Tribunal concluded that it was "unnecessary to summarize" the "laborious and thorough efforts of the parties to scrutinize the meaning of Article 22" (ICSID *Brandes* case, ¶ 85).

Within the parameters of any judicial decision in the Venezuelan legal system, this decision could be considered as an unmotivated judicial one, susceptible to being annulled. It is not possible to reach a conclusion like the one expressed by the tribunal under Venezuelan law without explaining which part of the provision is "confusing," which other part is "imprecise," and as any tribunal of justice must do when deciding cases of justice, to make its best effort to try to explain what is imprecise in a provision, and to explain what is confusing in it. This is precisely the role that any tribunal has, not being allowed just to issue a decision without stating the reasons on which it is based.

The only minor and indirect interpretative effort the *Brandes* Tribunal made regarding Article 22 of the Investment Law referred to its "context" (ICSID *Brandes* case, ¶ 87), pointing out that the Investment Law had similarities in its structure and contents with many BITs (ICSID *Brandes* case, ¶ 89). The tribunal failed to refer to the most important similarity for the purpose of interpreting Article 22 of the Investment Law, which was the open offer as expression of consent made by the State in all BIT's to date leaving in the hands of the international investor the right to go to arbitration or to resort to national courts. Instead, it asked only why the consent formula of the BITs was not used (ICSID *Brandes* case, ¶ 90).

A law containing an unilateral offer as expression of consent to go to arbitration, is not a bilateral treaty on investments, and despite the similarities in the structure or content of the Law with the BITs, the Law must be examined and interpreted as a unilateral effort by a Government seeking to attract investments without negotiating anything with another State (ICSID *Brandes* case, ¶ 94). In this way it differs from BITs that are negotiated between two parties. It is this distinction that the ICSID tribunal in the *Brandes* case failed to consider. It is only because it ignored the essential part of Article 22 that gave the investor the choice to resort to arbitration or to a Venezuelan court that the ICSID tribunal in the *Brandes* case then arrived to the conclusion that "Despite the similarities between the content of the LPPI and that of a BIT, the Tribunal does not find in the Article that it has analyzed (*sic*) nor in any other Article of the LPPI (*sic*), any provision that would allow it to assert that it provides for Venezuela's consent to ICSID jurisdiction" (ICSID *Brandes* case, ¶ 92). Of course, the Tribunal could not find the consent of the State if it ignored the right given to the investor to make a choice. The only way to understand this unfounded conclusion is then to recognize that the Tribunal, in its decision, did not actually "analyzed" in any way Article 22, or other relevant Articles of the Investment Law (such as Articles 21 and 23).

The *Brandes* tribunal also decided that it was "unnecessary, for the purpose of resolving this dispute, to establish the actual role played by Mr. Corrales in the drafting of the LPPI, his knowledge of the issue under discussion and the relevance of his publications about this issue" because "Mr. Corrales' opinion cannot provide the basis for finding that Article 22 of the LPPI contains the consent of the Bolivarian Republic of Venezuela to submit to ICSID arbitration" (ICSID *Brandes* case, ¶ 103). Again, it is astonishing how the tribunal could simply and abruptly arrive at these "conclusions," without any reasoning, analysis, and worst of all, without expressing any reason to disqualify in a general and universal way one of the two key people involved in the drafting of the Investment Law, who was put in charge of that task at the request and direction of the Government.

In the end, after extensively copying and enumerating –without analyzing them– the "valid arguments" of the parties, the ICSID Tribunal in the *Brandes* case just concluded without addressing at all the "fundamental" issue, that it "has not found anything that may lead it to depart from the conclusions arrived at by those tribunals [in the *Cemex* and *Mobil* cases] with respect to the specific matter at issue here" (ICSID *Brandes* case, ¶ 114). In the following Paragraph the Tribunal copied the final ruling in those cases (ICSID *Brandes* case, ¶ 115), in which those Tribunals had concluded that Article 22 did "not provide a basis for the jurisdiction of the Tribunal *in the present case*" (ICSID *Mobil* case, ¶ 140; ICSID *Cemex* case, ¶ 138), without pretending to preclude or prejudice other cases. Nonetheless, the ICSID Tribunal in the *Brandes* case, without any reasoning, arguments, and without explaining any "findings in the paragraphs" of its decision, went further, proclaiming in a general and universal way, and not only for the "present case," that "it is obvious that Article 22 of the Law on Promotion and protection of Investments does not contain the consent of the Bolivarian Republic of Venezuela to ICSID jurisdiction" (ICSID *Brandes* case, ¶ 118). This decision, at least from the point of view of the general standard rules governing judicial decisions in internal law, failed to state the reason on which it was based, that is, it lacked foundation.

The ICSID tribunals in the three decisions, concluded that in cases of unilateral obligations like the one included in article 22 of the Investment Law, derived from the supposed existence of an ambiguity regarding the condition established that could have two possible grammatical interpretation, it was compulsory, after analyzing the principle of effect utile (ICSID *Mobil* case, ¶ 112 ff; ICSID *Cemex* case, ¶ 104), to seek for the "effect sought by the State" when enacting the Law "), which could only be determined establishing the "intention of the State when adopting article 22" (ICSID *Mobil* case, ¶ 118, 119; ICSID *Cemex* case, ¶ 111, 112). Examining the evidences filed in those cases regarding the intention of the State, and bearing in mind the "general evolution in favor of BITs regarding arbitration in the country," the tribunals concluded that they could not draw "the conclusion that Venezuela, in adopting Article 22, intended to give in advance its consent to ICSID arbitration in the absence of such BITs" (ICSID *Mobil* case, ¶ 131; ICSID *Cemex* case, ¶ 126); and "that the legislative history of Article 22 did not establish that, in adopting the Investment Law, Venezuela intended to consent in general and in advance to ICSID arbitration" (ICSID *Mobil* case, ¶ 138; ICSID *Cemex* case, ¶ 135). The *thema decidendum* eventually was referred to evidences in order to establish the intention.

Our purpose in the following parts is precisely to analyze this matter of the intention of the State when the Government included its consent for international arbitration in article 22 of the Investment Law, within the general trend prevailing at the time in favor of arbitration.

VIII. THE PRO-ARBITRATION PUBLIC POLICY DEFINED BY THE GOVERNMENT IN 1999, REFLECTED IN THE 1999 CONSTITUTION

1. The pro-arbitration trend of all the legislation enacted in 1999

The enactment of the 1999 Investment Law was the result of a defined economic policy of the new government that began in February that year. It was intended to attract investments, and particularly, foreign investments.

For such purpose, regarding the origin and intent of the 1999 Investment Law, President Hugo Chávez, who was first elected in December 1998 and took office on February 2, 1999, requested the Congress to sanction an Organic Law enabling him (the President of the Republic) to enact a group of statutes on matters related to Public Administration, Finance, Taxation and the Economy, and regarding the latter, in order to promote, protect and encourage investment in the country.

Consequently, following the draft submitted by same National Executive, a few weeks later, on April 1999, the Congress sanctioned the enabling Organic Law of

April of that year 1999.[252] This law authorized the President of the Republic not only to "enact provisions in order to promote the protection and promotion of national and foreign investments with the purpose of establishing a legal framework for investments and to give them greater legal security" (Article 1.4.f); but also to "reform the decree-Law on Public Works and National Public Utilities Concessions to stimulate private investments" for both existing and prospective projects (Art. 1.4.h) and to issue the necessary measures for the exploitation of gas, modernizing the legislation on the matter (Art. 1.4.i).

It was the National Executive that defined the economic policy of the country focused on the promotion and protection of investments in general, and on matters of public works and public utilities, hydrocarbons, gas and mines, for which purpose it received a very wide and comprehensive legal authorization to enact statutes by means of delegate legislation. It was precisely within this legislative authorization that the Executive Power issued the Decree Law containing the 1999 Investment Law, as well as many other Decree Laws all of which were issued by the President of the Republic, not "exercising the power vested in him by the new Political Constitution", as erroneously asserted in the *Brandes* case decision (ICSID *Brandes* case, ¶ 25), but based on a "legislative delegation" granted according to the 1961 Constitution. The new 1999 Constitution was sanctioned after the April 1999 Enabling Law and after the Investment Law was approved.

A month after the August 1999 Supreme Court of Justice decision rejecting the challenge to the Legislative Conditions defined for the Hydrocarbons Association Agreements was published,[253] the President of the Republic proceeded to enact four important Decree Laws executing the provisions of the Enabling Law already mentioned, containing statutes on matters of investments (Articles 1.4.f,; 1.4.h; 1.4.i; and 1.4.j), and in all of them, providing for arbitration as a means for the solution of disputes between the State and private persons.[254] Of these four authorizations, three Decree Laws –those regarding Gassed Hydrocarbons, Promotion and Protection of Investments through Concessions and the Investment Law– were of particular importance.

In the Law on Gassed Hydrocarbons,[255] Article 127 of the 1961 Constitution that provided that in all the licenses given to private persons in order to execute activities of exploration and exploitation of gassed hydrocarbons, a clause shall be deemed to

---

252 See *Ley Orgánica que autoriza al Presidente de la República para dictar medidas extraordinarias en materia económica y financiera requeridas por el interés iúblico* (Organic Law Authorizing the President of the Republic to Issue Extraordinary Measures in Economic and Financial Matters Required by the Public Interest), in *Official Gazette* N° 36.687 of April 26, 1999.

253 See in Allan R. Brewer-Carías (Compilator), *Documentos del Juicio de la Apertura Petrolera (1996-1999),* Caracas, 2004 *available at* http://allanbrewercarias.com/Content/449725d9-f1cb-474b-8ab2-efb849fea3/Content/I,%202,%2022.%20%20APERTURA%20PETROLERA.%20DOCUMENTOS%20DEL%20JUICIO.pdf, p. 25

254 See *Official Gazette* N° 5.382 Extra of September 28, 1999 (controversies concerning mining titles may be arbitrated). The other three laws are the laws concerning Gassed Hydrocarbons, the Promotion and Protection of Investments through Concessions and the Investment Law.

255 Decree Law N° 310 of September 12, 1999, *Official Gazette* N° 36.793 of September 23, 1999.

be included (even if not expressed in writing), establishing that "the doubts and controversies of any kind that may arise resulting from the license, and that could not be resolved amicably by the parties, *including by arbitration*, shall be decided by the competent courts of the Republic, in accordance with its laws, not being able to give rise by any motive or cause to foreign claims" (Article 25.6.b). This Law expressly recognized the possibility to submit to arbitration disputes on matters relating to licenses given by the State for the exploration or exploitation of non-gas hydrocarbons.[256]

In the Law on the Promotion of Private Investments through the Regime of Concessions,[257] the President provided that the parties, in public concessions contracts:

> "can agree in the respective contract to submit their differences to the decision of an Arbitral Tribunal, whose composition, competence, procedure and applicable law shall be determined by mutual agreement, in conformity with the provisions applicable on the matter."

This pro-arbitration disposition of the government in the sensitive area of public contracts of concessions for public works and public utilities was subsequently re-affirmed by a number of Venezuelan court decisions.[258]

The third statute establishing arbitration enacted by the President of the Republic using the delegated legislation powers was precisely the Decree-Law N° 356 of October 13, 1999 on the Law on the Promotion and Protection of Investments. As aforementioned, this law contained consent to arbitration in a number of places in the text: first, Article 21 (state-to-state arbitration); second, in Article 22 (international arbitration or national litigation with an international investor); and third, Article 23 (national litigation or arbitration with a national or international investor). In these last two cases, the consent of the State to submit disputes to arbitration was expressed in the Law, and it was for the investor –as its right– to decide to go to arbitration or to the national courts.

---

256 Other commentators have agreed with this interpretation of the Law. See, *e.g.*, J. Eloy Anzola, "El fatigoso camino que transita el arbitraje," in Irene Valera (Coordinadora), *Arbitraje Comercial Interno e Internacional. Reflexiones teóricas y experiencias prácticas*, Academia de Ciencias Políticas y Sociales, Comité Venezolano de Arbitraje, Caracas 2005, p.419) ("We must presume that it was made with the clear intention of admitting arbitration as a mean of solution of conflicts in the exploration and exploitation contracts according to the constitutional text ....in order to incentivize private participation that without doubt will be more comfortable seeking justice before an arbitral tribunal without the need to resort to local tribunals.").

257 Ley Orgánica sobre promoción de la inversión privada bajo el régimen de concesiones, *Official Gazette* N° 5.394 Extra. of October 25, 1999. See Diego Moya-Ocampos Pancera and Maria del Sol Moya-Ocampos Pancera, "Comentarios relativos a la procedencia de las cláusulas arbitrales en los contratos de interés público nacional, en particular: especial las concesiones mineras," en *Revista de Derecho Administrativo*, N° 19, Editorial Sherwood, Caracas 2006, p. 174. See *in general* on this Law, Alfredo Romero Mendoza "Concesiones y otros mecanismos no tradicionales para el financiamiento de obras públicas", in Alfredo Romero Mendoza (Coord.), *Régimen Legal de las Concesiones Públicas. Aspectos Jurídicos, Financieros y Técnicos*, Editorial Jurídica Venezolana, Caracas 2000, pp. 28-29.

258 See for example the summary in Alfredo Romero Mendoza (Coord.), *Régimen Legal de las Concesiones Públicas. Aspectos Jurídicos, Financieros y Técnicos*, pp. 12, 28, 29, 155.

As demonstrated in the aforementioned legislation, without doubts, the prevailing attitude of the Government in 1999 regarding the solution of disputes on matter of investments was, a pro-arbitration one; which was confirmed not only by the parallel discussion during August-November 1999 on the matter of the State's obligation to promote arbitration contained in the new Constitution, but also by the text submitted by the President of the Republic himself to be included in the new Constitution. [259]

2. The pro-arbitration trend of the 1999 Constitution and the bizarre proposal submitted to the Constituent Assembly by President Chávez in 1999

The 1999 Constitution incorporated arbitration as an alternative means of adjudication and as a component of the judicial system (Article 253), requiring the State in article 258, to promote it, in particular through legislation ("The law shall promote arbitration, conciliation, mediation and any other alternative means of dispute resolution");[260] and guarantying arbitration as a fundamental right.[261] The text of the Constitution itself imposes upon all the organs of the State the duty to promote arbitration, establishing as a constitutional (fundamental) right of the citizens the ability to submit disputes to arbitration. All of this confirms that, at the time, there was no prevailing "culture of hostility" to arbitration. On the contrary, the 1999 Constitution, the laws sanctioned by the new Government in 1999, the legal system as a whole, and the international instruments to which Venezuela was a party, embraced and promoted arbitration.[262]

The project submitted by President Chávez to the National Constituent Assembly in August 1999 proposing the text of an Article to replace Article 127 (current Article 151 of the 1999 Constitution), contrary to any assumed "restrictive" character regarding arbitration, was excessively permissive towards international

---

259 I was a Member of the National Constituent Assembly that was responsible for drafting many aspects of the new Constitution in 1999. In that capacity, I contributed to the drafting of the 1999 Constitution, and in particular, the drafting of Article 151 which establishes the possibility for arbitration in public contracts, rejecting the project proposed by the President of the Republic. See on the discussion of my contributions to the National Constituent Assembly's drafting of the 1999 Constitution in Allan R. Brewer-Carías, *Debate Constituyente (Aportes a la Asamblea Nacional Constituyente),* 3 Vols., Fundación de Derecho Público/Editorial Jurídica Venezolana, Caracas 1999. Available at http://allanbrewercarias.com/

260 On the recognition of arbitration as an alternative means of adjudication in the 1999 Constitution, and the promotion of arbitration as a constitutional obligation of all organs of the State, see Eugenio Hernández Bretón, "Arbitraje y Constitución. El arbitraje como derecho fundamental," *loc cit.*, p. 27; 2008 N° 1.541 Decision, (p. 11); Supreme Tribunal of Justice, Constitutional Chamber, Decision N° 186 of February 14, 2001 (Case: Constitutional Challenge of Articles 17, 22 and 23 of the 1999 Investment Law, Fermín Toro Jiménez and Luis Brito García).

261 On arbitration as a fundamental right, see Eugenio Hernández Bretón, "Arbitraje y Constitución. El arbitraje como derecho fundamental," *loc. cit.*, pp. 25, 27-28 (noting the 1830 Constitution provides that arbitration is a citizens' fundamental right). In the same sense, J. Eloy Anzola, "El fatigoso camino que transita el arbitraje," in Irene Valera (Coord.), *Arbitraje Comercial Interno e Internacional. Reflexiones teóricas y experiencias prácticas*, Academia de Ciencias Políticas y Sociales, Comité Venezolano de Arbitraje, Caracas 2005, p. 409-410.

262 ICSID arbitration continued to be incorporated in the bilateral treaties for promotion and protection of investments signed and ratified after 1999. See for instance Venezuela-France Bilateral Investment Treaty in *Official Gazette* N° 37.896 of March 11, 2004.

arbitration.[263] That was precisely the reason for this author, as member of the National Constituent Assembly, to oppose firmly such proposal, and instead to propose to include in the new Constitution the same text of Article 127 of the 1961 Constitution.[264] Fortunately my proposal prevailed in the current Article 151 of the 1999 Constitution, which in any case was not really debated.

Because it was coherent with the pro-arbitration trend of the various Decree Laws issued by President Chávez in September 1999, including the Investment Law provisions of Articles 21, 22 and 23, President Chávez was at the same time proposing to reduce the jurisdictional immunity principle only to be applied in contracts entered by the "Republic." (and not by the States, Municipalities and decentralized public entities). Such contracts are almost inexistent (almost all public contracts are entered by decentralized public entities), except on matters of public external debt. It was only regarding those contracts that the Republic, and only the Republic (not the states, the municipalities, the public corporations or the public enterprises), as proposed by Chávez, would never agree to submit to foreign jurisdictions in a contract of public interest. Nonetheless, regarding public contracts entered by other entities of the State (that are the overwhelming majority of public contracts) and regarding international treaties or agreements and national laws providing for international arbitration, President Chávez significantly proposed to eliminate all limits to arbitration, allowing arbitration without even the consideration of the "nature" of the contract or the matter involved. From this, the proposal of President Chávez makes clear that Venezuela had all the intention to make an open and unlimited offer to arbitrate disputes in an international forum; that is, the Government at the time effectively intended to provide a general, open-ended consent to submit to arbitration in all investment's disputes.

In order to realize these assertions, it is important to really understand the consequences that President Chávez's proposal would have had, by comparing the text of Article 127 of the 1961 Constitution (maintained as Article 151 of the 1999 Constitution), with the proposal of Chávez:

> *Article 127.1961 Constitution*: "In contracts of public interest, unless inappropriate according with their nature, a clause shall be deemed included even if not been expressed, according to which the doubts and controversies that may arise on such contracts and that could not be resolved amicably by the contracting parties, shall be decided by the competent courts of the Republic, in accordance with its laws and could not give rise by any motive or cause to foreign claims."

---

263 See Hugo Chávez Frías, *Ideas Fundamentales para la Constitución Bolivariana de la V República,* Caracas agosto 1999. See also the quotations of the proposal of President Chávez in Hildegard Rondón de Sansó, *Aspectos jurídicos fundamentales del arbitraje internacional de inversión*, Ed. Exlibris, Caracas 2010, pp. 150. Sansó finds that from such proposal is not possible to deduct that the intention was to open the doors to international arbitration, p. 151.

264 The notion of "contracts of public interest" was fixed in the same Constitution (Article 126) as comprising "contracts of national, states and municipal public interest." That is, contracts of public interest not only entered by the Republic, but also by the States and by the Municipalities, as well as by public national, states and municipal entities (public corporations and public enterprises). See Allan R. Brewer-Carías, *Contratos Administrativos*, Editorial Jurídica Venezolana, Caracas 1997, pp. 28 ff.

> *Article proposed by President Chávez*: "In contracts entered into by the Republic that are of public interest, a clause shall be deemed included even if not expressed, according to which the doubts and controversies that may arise on such contracts, shall be decided by the competent courts of the Republic in accordance with the laws."[265]

The proposal submitted by President Chávez was extremely bizarre and inappropriate regarding the principle of immunity jurisdiction of the State. The proposal meant that in contracts entered by all other public entities or juridical persons (as distinct from the Republic), such as the states, the municipalities, the autonomous institutions and other juridical persons of public law as well as by any public enterprises, no limit would exist regarding any matter related to the principle of immunity jurisdiction. President Chávez proposed provision was more liberal than the provision in the 1961 Constitution, only including those contracts entered by the "Republic" itself, and not by decentralized public entities.

Second, the proposal of President Chávez implied the complete elimination from the Constitution of the more than a century old "Calvo clause," admitting in consequence the possibility that public interest contracts could gave rise to foreign diplomatic claims against the Republic. From his proposals one cannot conclude that President Chávez was "opposed" to international arbitration. On the contrary, with such proposal, as I argued in the debate in the National Constituent Assembly in September 1999,[266] he attempted to eliminate from the Constitution the restrictions on the matters of relative jurisdictional immunity.

Far from being inconceivable, the constitutional proposal of President Chávez was completely coherent with the intention to provide a general, open-ended consent to submit to arbitration in all investment's disputes. By making his constitutional proposal at the same time that he enacted the Investment Law, President Chávez without doubt had the intention to make an open and unlimited offer to arbitrate disputes in an international forum.

3. The ratification of the pro-arbitration trend in the legislation enacted by President Chávez in 1999

The extremely favorable trend regarding arbitration resulting from all the aforementioned Decree Laws issued by President Chávez in 1999 on matters of investments, in general, and in particular, regarding investments in administrative concessions and licenses for public works and public utilities, and in the field of gassed hydrocarbons and mines, was ratified two years later, in 2001, in a new set of Legislation that included the general admission of arbitration as a means for the solution of disputes. For example, the Organic Taxation Code of October of 2001,

265 See Hugo Chávez Frías, *Ideas Fundamentales para la Constitución Bolivariana de Venezuela*, August 5, 1999.

266 See Allan R. Brewer-Carías, "Propuesta sobre la cláusula de inmunidad relativa de jurisdicción y sobre la cláusula Calvo en los contratos de interés público," in *Debate Constituyente (Aportes a la Asamblea Nacional Constituyente)*, Vol. I (8-Agosto-8 Septiembre 1999), Fundación de Derecho Público/Editorial Jurídica Venezolana, Caracas 1999, pp. 209 233.

included a general admission of arbitration as a means for the solution of disputes between taxpayers and the State.[267]

Subsequently, also in 2001, arbitration was generally admitted by establishing it as a means for the solution of disputes between the State and private parties in the very important nationalized oil public sector, in cases related to the incorporation of mixed companies for the exploitation of primary hydrocarbons activities. President Chávez, through the Decree Law N° 1.510 of November 2, 2001, issued the Organic Hydrocarbons Law[268] in execution of a new Organic Enabling Law approved by the newly elected National Assembly in November 2000,[269] in which the provision of Article 151 of the 1999 Constitution was ratified. This Law provided that contracts establishing mixed companies for the exploitation of hydrocarbons, "shall be deemed [to] include, even if not ... expressed," a clause establishing that "the doubts and controversies of any kind that may arise resulting from the execution of activities and that could not be resolved amicably by the parties, *including arbitration* ...." will be resolved by the courts (Article 34.3.b). This provision expressly recognized in the Law the possibility to submit to arbitration the solution of disputes resulting from activities in the hydrocarbon sector when mixed companies were constituted with private investors.[270]

All of these Decree Laws and acts of the National Assembly between 1999 and up to 2001, confirmed that in Venezuela, "without doubt, a clear legislative tendency existed in order to admit arbitration in contract related to the commercial activity of Public Administration."[271]

4. The elemental administrative procedural provisions assuring the correct legal opinion to be issued on matters of arbitral clauses in public contracts

It was within this pro-arbitration trend of the Government on matters of investments, that President Chavez approved Instruction N° 4 of March 12, 2001, establishing elemental rules for the "internal review" of public contracts drafts containing arbitration clauses.[272] Far from being any sign of the intention of the government against arbitration clauses for the State,[273] this Presidential instruction was no more that the correct administrative response to the extension of arbitration

267 Articles 312-326. Organic Code on Taxation, *Official Gazette* N° 37.305 of October 17, 2001.

268 *Ley Orgánica de Hidrocarburos, Official Gazette* N° 37.323 of November 13, 2001

269 *Ley Orgánica Habilitante* of November 2000, *Official Gazette* N° 37.076 of November 13, 2000.

270 The same occurred with the reform of the Organic Statute of the Development of Guayana, also sanctioned by means of Decree Law N° 1531 of November 7, 2001, *Official Gazette* N° 5561 Extra. of November 28, 2001 and the Organic Law on Drinking Water Services and Sanitation enacted by the National Assembly in December 2001. See *Ley Orgánica para le prestación de los servicios de agua potable y de saneamiento, Official Gazette*, N° 5.568 Extra. of December 31, 2001.

271 See Juan Carlos Balzán, "El arbitraje en los contratos de interés a la luz de la cláusula de inmunidad de jurisdicción prevista en el artículo 151 de la Constitución," *loc. cit.*,p. 299.

272 *Official Gazette* N° 37.158 of March 14, 2001.

273 As pointed out by Hildegard Rondón de Sansó, *Aspectos jurídicos fundamentales del arbitraje internacional de inversión*, Ed. Exlibris, Caracas 2010, pp. 151-152..

clauses included in public contracts entered into only by the "Republic," encouraged as a general policy defined by the same Government. On the other hand, further provisions enacted by the President regarding rules of management in public administration, assigning to the Attorney General's office the function of reviewing any contracts containing submission to arbitration on public interests, were perfectly and completely reconcilable with the attitude reflected in laws, decrees and statements made both before and after the 1999 Investment Law with the notion that Article 22 of the Investment Law intended to constitute a standing, general consent of the Republic to arbitrate all investments disputes before ICSID.

Regarding public debt contracts which were a matter of discussion in the previous years, in an Opinion given on March 14, 2003, the same Attorney General's Office reiterated the opinion of the relative character of the clause of jurisdictional immunity in lending agreements, and suggested that:

> "in future contracts in which the Republic is a party, in lieu of the ordinary jurisdictional means, arbitral clauses should be incorporated, due to the fact that currently the arbitral means constitute an expedited, efficient and economic form for the resolution of conflicts that could arise from contractual relationships."[274]

This attitude and opinion of the Attorney General's Office was far from "reticent" regarding arbitration in public contracts, and was completely coherent with the general pro-arbitration policy of the Government, particularly since 1999, when the Investment Law was enacted.

IX. THE INTENTION OF THE GOVERNMENT IN 1999 TO EXPRESS THE STATE CONSENT FOR INTERNATIONAL ARBITRATION IN ARTICLE 22 OF THE ABROGATED 1999 INVESTMENT LAW

And that was precisely the intention of the drafters of the Investment Law and of the National Executive when considering it and approving it in September 1999: to express in Article 22 the consent of the Republic to submit disputes to international arbitration, particularly before the ICSID. This offer was an open offer, subject only to the condition that the respective treaties or agreements, like the ICSID Convention, established a framework or mechanism for international arbitration. It created a right for the investors to go at their will to international arbitration or to resort to the national courts.

1. The absence of a formal "Statement of Purposes" and the motives of the Investment Law as exposed by its drafters

Contrary to the practice observed in almost all other Decree Laws issued by the President of the Republic at the time, the 1999 Decree Law on the Investment Law did not have "Statement of Purposes" (*Exposición de Motivos*). This did not mean that the Law itself had no "motives" or purposes, or that the National Executive had

---

274 Quoted in Margot Y. Huen Rivas, "El arbitraje internacional en los contratos administrativos," *loc. cit.*, pp. 435-436; and in Juan Carlos Balzán, "El arbitraje en los contratos de interés a la luz de la cláusula de inmunidad de jurisdicción prevista en el artículo 151 de la Constitución," *loc. cit.*, p. 346-347.

no specific intention by issuing the Decree law. The Investment Law had precise motives, not only to promote and protect investments but to promote arbitration, to guarantee arbitral resolution of disputes, thus, limiting the scope of the national courts on the matter. The intention of the Investment Law was in this sense expressed in its first Article, in which was clear that its provisions were "directed to regulate the action of the State regarding investments and investors, whether nationals or foreign," that is, the Law:

> "comes to fix the extension of the competencies of the State in a way such as to assure such investments and investors the stable legal cadre that guarantees the enough security, devoted to achieve the harmonic increase, the diversification and complementation of investments in favor of the objectives of national development" (Article 1).[275]

And this was what the Law precisely worked out in Article 22: to limit –not to exclude– the jurisdiction of the national courts on matters of investments by providing for international arbitration; but always leaving in the hands of the investors the choice of venue.

In this regard, in the absence of a published "Statement of Purposes" for the Decree Law on the Investment Law, and being the product of a bureaucratic drafting process and not of a parliamentary process with recorded debates in a legislative body, the intention of the drafters are a valid source to determine the intention of the "legislator." [276] This is particularly so of the "preparatory work" of the text of the Decree.[277] In this sense, it was a matter of public knowledge that the 1999 Investment Law was drafted under the direction of the then Ambassador Werner Corrales-Leal, Head of the Permanent Representation of Venezuela before the WTO and the UN entities headquartered in Geneva.[278] Ambassador Corrales, who since 1998 had an important role in the formulation of Venezuelan policy toward investments, including the negotiations of a failed bilateral investment treaty with the U.S.[279] was entrusted with the task of drafting the Investment law[280] being

275 See Eugenio Hernández Bretón, "Protección de Inversiones en Venezuela," in *Boletín de la Academia de Ciencias Políticas y Sociales*, N° 142, Caracas 2004 pp. 221-222.

276 The Constitutional Chamber of the Supreme Tribunal of Justice has held that the determination of the intention of the Legislator must "start from the will of the creator of the provision, as it results from the debates prior to its promulgation." See Supreme Tribunal of Justice, Constitutional Chamber, Decision N° 1.173 of June 15, 2004 (Case: *Interpretación del Artículo 72 de la Constitución de la República Bolivariana de Venezuela*) (Exp. 02-3.215), in *Revista de Derecho Público* N° 97-98, Editorial Jurídica Venezolana, Caracas 2004, pp. 429 ff.

277 It is what in the Vienna Convention on the law of treaties of 1969 is called as "supplementary means of interpretation" which includes referring to treaties, its "preparatory work" and the "circumstances of its conclusion" (Article 32).

278 See in Eduardo Camel A., "Ley de promoción de Inversiones viola acuerdos suscritos por Venezuela", *El Nacional*, Caracas September 15, 1999. The character of Corrales as drafter was officially recognized, for instance, in a press released of the Ministry of Foreign Affairs, *Oficina de Comunicaciones y Relaciones Institutionales*, "Resúmen de Medios nacionales e Internacionales", April 29, 2009, p. 23. See also, in Alberto Cova, "Venezuela incumple Ley de Promoción de Inversiones,' in *El Nacional*, April 24, 2009.

ratified in such task by the then new Chávez administration.[281] As Head of that Permanent Representation, Ambassador Corrales prepared reports and opinions for the Government.

One of those reports, dated April 1999 and written by Ambassador Corrales with Marta Rivera Colomina, an official at the Permanent Representation, contains ideas for the design of the legal regime of promotion and protection of investments in Venezuela.[282] The document explains that "a regime applicable to foreign investments, must leave open the possibility to resort to international arbitration, which today is accepted almost everywhere in the world, either by means of the mechanism provided for in the Convention on the Settlement of Investment Disputes between States and Nationals of Other States (ICSID) or by means of the submission of the dispute to an international arbitrator or an *ad hoc* arbitral tribunal like the one proposed by UNCITRAL."[283]

This view was made even more explicit in an essay written by the same authors explaining "Some ideas on the New regime on the promotion and protection of Investments in Venezuela" ("*Algunas ideas sobre el Nuevo régimen de promoción y protección de inversiones en Venezuela*") published shortly after the 1999 Investment Law came into effect. The authors and co-drafters of the Investment Law in that essay, stated that "a regime applicable to foreign investments, must leave open the possibility to *unilaterally* resort to international arbitration, which today is accepted almost everywhere in the world, either by means of the mechanism provided for in the Convention on the Settlement of Investment Disputes between States and Nationals of Other States (ICSID) or by means of the submission of the dispute to an international arbitrator or an *ad hoc* arbitral tribunal like the one proposed by UNCITRAL."[284] The reference to *unilateral* resort to international

279 For instance see Gioconda Soto, "Cancillería llama a consultas a Corrales y Echeverría,"in *El Nacional*, June 10, 1998; Fabiola Zerpa, "Venezuela rechaza presiones para firmar Acuerdo con EEUU," *El Nacional*, Caracas June 12, 1998; Alfredo Carquez Saavedra, "Tratado de inversiones con EE.UU. divide a negociadores venezolanos," in *El Nacional*, Caracas June 16, 1998.

280 In January 1999 Ambassador Corrales as head of the Permanent Representation of Venezuela before the WTO and the UN entities headquartered in Geneva, filed before the Government a document titled *"Formulación de un Anteproyecto de ley de promoción y Protección de Inversiones (Términos de referencia), enero 1999"*. This document is cited in Werner Corrales Leal and Marta Rivera Colomina, "Algunas ideas sobre el Nuevo régimen de promoción y protección de inversiones en Venezuela," in Luis Tineo and Julia Barragán (Comp.), *La OMC como espacio normativo. Un reto para Venezuela,* Asociación Venezolana de Derecho y Economía, Caracas, p. 195; also in Victorino Tejera Pérez, "Do Municipal Investment Laws Always Constitute a Unilateral Offer to Arbitrate? The Venezuelan Investment Law: A Case Study," *loc. cit.*, p. 116; Victorino Tejera Pérez, *Arbitraje de Inversiones*, pp. 155-156.

281 As mentioned in the ICSID *Mobil* case, the Republic has "doubt[ed]" the character of Corrales as the drafter of the Law (ICSID *Mobil* case, ¶ 133).

282 See Werner Corrales-Leal and Martha Rivera Colomina, "Algunas ideas relativas al diseño de un régimen legal de promoción y protección de inversiones en Venezuela," April 30, 1999. Document prepared at the request of the Minister of CORDIPLAN.

283 *Id*., pp. 10-11.

284 See Werner Corrales-Leal and Marta Rivera Colomina, "Algunas ideas sobre el nuevo régimen de promoción y protección de inversiones en Venezuela" p. 185. In the absence of "legislative history" of the decree Law, Victorino Tejera Pérez considers that this article of Corrales and Rivera "could even be assimilated to a supplementary means of interpretation, as

arbitration makes it clear, without doubt, that the persons entrusted with drafting the 1999 Investment Law intended Article 22 to express the State's consent to ICSID arbitration, which is the only way for the investor to have the option to unilaterally resort to such international arbitration, or to decide to go before the national courts. Given that the State through the Government (the Executive) was the one giving the instructions to the drafters and also was involved (through the Executive Cabinet) in approving the Investment Law once it was drafted, this was therefore an expression of intent on behalf of the State. Put differently, providing for unilateral resort to arbitration in connection with the 1999 Investment Law presupposed that said law provided the State's consent that was necessary for the investor to have the right to unilaterally resort to international arbitration.

The ICSID tribunal in its Decisions in the *Mobil* and *Cemex* cases, referring to these contemporaneous works of Corrales when the Law was being drafted, said that Corrales "did not say that the drafters or Article 22 intended to provide for consent in ICSID arbitration in the absence of any BITs" (ICSID *Mobil* case, ¶ 136; ICSID *Cemex* case, ¶ 132), which is an erroneous way to read those essays. Corrales and his colleague wrote in their own words, and with the authorization of the Republic for them to conceive of an Investment Law, that they considered necessary, in the benefit of the investors, to "leave open the possibility to *unilaterally* resort to international arbitration," this being possible only if the State had provided in the same text of Article 22 of the Investment Law for consent to ICSID arbitration in the absence of any BITs.

As was correctly noted by the ICSID tribunal in the *Cemex* case the "the word 'unilaterally' did not appear in the first article of 30 April, 1999. It was added to the second article in 2000" (ICSID *Cemex* case, ¶ 131, Footnote 118), precisely because the second article was published after the Investment Law was approved and published (while the first article was published before the Investment Law was approved by the Republic). With the adding of that word, the authors and co-drafters of the Law, emphasized the inclusion of this word, in order to stress that the only way for the investor to have that possibility to "unilaterally resort to arbitration," was if he had the right, as an option, to go to arbitration or to resort to national courts. This, in its turn, could only occur when the State had expressed its consent to go to arbitration, also unilaterally, and as an open offer in the same text of Article 22. Consequently, the only way to understand the reason for the erroneous assertion of the ICSID tribunals in the *Mobil* and *Cemex* cases, is to realize that when reading Article 22, the tribunals simply ignored the disclaimer included in the last phrase of the provision, which was not even considered in the whole text of the decisions, as discussed in detail above.

---

established in Article 32 of the Vienna Convention on Treaty Law." See Victorino Tejera Pérez, *Arbitraje de Inversiones*, p. 187; Victorino Tejera Pérez, "Do Municipal Investment Laws Always Constitute a Unilateral Offer to Arbitrate? The Venezuelan Investment Law: A Case Study," p. 115.

2. The discussion of the Draft of the Investment Law in the Council of Ministers in 1999

The Draft of the 1999 Investment Law was coordinated in Venezuela by the Central Office of Coordination and Planning, and not by a pàrticular Ministry. It was considered in meetings of the Economic Cabinet of the Council of Ministers, particularly in the meeting held on August 24, 1999 with the assistance of Ambassador Werner Corrales presenting the text.[285] The specific matter of Article 22 as expression of the State consent for arbitration was discussed. Specifically, in that meeting, as was reported to the press by the General Director of Central Office of Coordination and Planning (Cordiplan) that "the possibility for arbitration is maintained."[286]

In the press it was reported that:

> "The Director General of Cordiplan Fernando Hernández, as the spokesman of the economic group of President Chávez, assured that this legal draft 'will offer national and foreign investors legal and fiscal security, in order to create confidence'. One of the aspects regarding this law regarding which Hernández was asked is the one related to the resolution of controversies. Specifically, he was asked about the judicial body before which investors entering into contracts with the Republic would have to go. 'International arbitration is maintained,' Hernández said without giving details."[287]

The Ministry of Production and Commerce replaced the previous Ministry of Industry and Commerce in August 1999. Juan de Jesús Montilla, who was appointed as Minister [288] in substitution of the former Minister of Industry and Commerce (Gustavo Márquez), commented a few months later in mid-2000 on the provisions of the 1999 Law Investment Law without mentioning the unilateral offer expressed by the Republic for arbitration. No conclusion can be legitimately drawn from the Minister's silence, particularly since the drafters of the Law have expressed the contrary. Nonetheless, as mentioned, Minister Montilla was not a member of the National Executive or Council of Ministers during the months in 1999 when the Law was drafted (before September 1999). Therefore, although he signed the Decree Law on October 3, 1999, as the new Minister of Production and Commerce, he did not participate in the conception of the Investment Law and was not involved in its Drafting, and not even his Office was involved (given it succeeded the previous Ministry of Industry and Commerce).[289] Consequently, the fact that this Minister

---

285 In the press it was reported as a consequence of this Meeting and in relation to the discussions of the Draft, that "In the Draft, international arbitration is provided as an option for the resolution of conflicts." See "El proyecto prevé el arbitraje internacional como opción para resolver conflictos. Evalúan Ley de Inversiones," in *El Universal*, August 25, 1999.

286 See Andrés Rojas Ramírez, "Decreto para la protección de Inversions contradice Constitución de Chávez", *El Nacional*, Caracas August 25, 1999.

287 *Id.*

288 See Decree N° 288 published in *Official Gazette* N° 36.779 of September 3, 1999

289 See in Victorino Tejera Pérez, *Arbitraje de Inversiones*, Magister Thesis, Caracas 2010, *cit*., p. 158. As is mentioned by Tejera Pérez, even the predecessor of Montilla, the Minister of Industry and Commerce, Gustavo Marquez, who attended the meetings where the Decree Law was

Montilla over six months after the approval of the Investment Law did not mention that the Investment Law included unilateral offer by the Republic permitting foreign investors to resort to arbitration could not lead to the conclusion that it did not contain consent to arbitration.[290] Nonetheless, in an incomprehensibly way, the ICSID Tribunal in the *Cemex* case, considered that when the Minister said what he said (that "the solution in the case of controversies or disputes where it is set forth that these shall be resolved in national courts or within a framework of acknowledgment of the commitments that have been undertaken in international agreements"), this supposedly is a statement that is "contrary" to say that "Article 22 intended to provide for consent to ICSID arbitration in the absence of any BIT" (ICSID *Cemex* case, ¶¶ 132, 133). A conclusion that had no basis at all.

In the meetings of the Economic Cabinet of the Council of Ministers in which the draft of the Investment Law was considered, one of the High Officials who attended was Alvaro Silva Calderón, then Vice Minister of Energy and Mines.[291] In that meeting, I presumed that Vice Minister Calderón opposed the inclusion in Article 22 of the open offer of expression of consent by the State to go to international arbitration, bearing in mind his well-known personal opinion opposing the idea of the State subjection to international investment arbitration.[292] Nonetheless, and despite his possible opposition in the meeting, Vice Minister Calderón's personal opinion and opposition did not prevail, and instead, the proposal made by Werner Corrales and his legal adviser Gonzalo Capriles in favor of the State expressing consent in Article 22 for international arbitration, was the one accepted by the Cabinet[293] According to the Organic Law on Central Administration of 1995,[294] in force when the Investment Law was discussed in the Economic Cabinet, the documents considered and the opinions expressed in the meetings of the Economic Cabinet (acting as a Sector Cabinet with respect to the Investment Law) were not secret. Only "the deliberations of the Council of Ministers" themselves were secret.[295]

---

considered, declined to comment on the drafting of the Law, explaining that his *Ministry was not involved in the drafting of it*. *Id*., p. 158 Footnote 557.

290 On this particular point, the *Cemex* tribunal is simply incorrect.

291 As it is referred to in Victorino Tejera Pérez, *Arbitraje de Inversiones*, Magister Thesis, Caracas 2010, *cit*., p. 158.

292 See for instance, Alvaro Silva Calderón, "Apreciaciones sobre el arbitraje jurídico en Venezuela," available at http://www.pdvsa.com/inter-face.sp/database/fichero/free/5000/639.PDF, pp. 14-16. Alvaro Silva Calderón was one of the representatives of the Republic in the recourse of interpretation on Article 22 of the 1999 Investment Law ending with the Supreme Tribunal 2008 Decision N° 1.541. He also participated in 1995 challenge of the constitutionality of the arbitration clause of the Association Agreements of the *Apertura petrolera*. See in Allan R. Brewer-Carías (Compilator), *Documentos del Juicio de la Apertura Petrolera (1996-1999)*, Caracas, 2004, p. 125.

293 See the information in Victorino Tejera Pérez, *Arbitraje de Inversiones*, Magister Thesis, Caracas 2010, *cit*., pp. 155-158, who personally interviewed Corrales and Capriles (Footnote 558).

294 See *Official Gazette* N° 5.025 Extra of December 20, 1995.

295 The 1999 Organic Law of Central Administration established the same principles regarding the Sector Cabinets, as bodies different from the Council of Ministers. In the 2008 Organic Law on Public Administration, the Sector Cabinets were transformed into Sector Boards

Ambassador Corrales was also publicly reported to have been the one who made the presentation of the Draft of the Investment Law in another meeting of the Economic Cabinet of the Government, held on September 14, 1999.[296] The Law eventually was approved by President Chavez in the Council of Ministers session held on October 3, 1999,[297] with the assistance of the acting Minister of Energy and Mines, Alí Rodríguez. Based on Minister Rodríguez's prior strong and public objections to international investment arbitration, I assume that he issued a dissenting vote and opposition to the inclusion in Article 22 of the express consent of the State of an open offer to investors to go to international arbitration. His personal and political opinion opposing the idea of the *Apertura Petrolera* in general, and in particular of the State subjection to international investment arbitration, was well known and expressed in 1996 when he was a Member of the Congress[298] and opposed the inclusion of arbitration clauses in the Congress resolution on the General Conditions regarding the Association Agreements of the *Apertura Petrolera.*[299] At the same time, he also was the leading person who filed the popular action brought before the Supreme Court challenging the constitutionality of the arbitration clause authorized by the former Congress to be included in such Association Agreements for oil exploitation.

In effect, in that popular action, Alí Rodríguez and other co-claimants requested the Supreme Court to declare:

> "the nullity of Clause Seventeen of Article 2 of the Congress Resolution (*Acuerdo*) because it provides ...'The way to resolve controversies on matters others that those attributed to the Control Committee and that could not be resolved by the parties' agreement, shall be arbitration, which will be achieved according to the procedural rules of the International Chamber of Commerce, in force at the moment of the signing of the Agreement.' Such provision is a flagrant contravention to article 127 of the Constitution [equivalent to article 151 of the 1999 Constitution] that does not authorize the submission to legal provisions other than the Venezuelan; so, we respectfully ask."[300]

---

with the same functions, but with power of only advisory bodies for the study of matters to be consider in the Council of Ministers (Articles 67, 68).

296 See Eduardo Camel Anderson, "Ley de promoción de inversiones viola acuerdos suscritos por Venezuela," in *El Nacional*, Caracas September 15, 1999.

297 This is the date of the decree Law. Nonetheless, on September 29, 1999, the Vice Minister of Production and Commerce, Eduardo Ortíz Bucarán, informed the press that the Law had been approved in Council of Ministers ten days earlier. See in Maribel Osorio, "Ley de Inversiones otorga al Presidente facultad para otorgar incentivos," in *El Nacional*, September 29, 1999.

298 See the Dissenting Vote in the Congress approval of the Conditions for Association Agreements of the *Apertura Petrolera*, in the Bi-cameral Report of the Energy and Mines Commissions (Senate and Chamber of Representatives) of June 19, 1996, in http://www.minci.gob.ve/doc/convasocia-cion19061996.pdf

299 See in *Official Gazette* N° 35.754 of July 17, 1995.

300 See in Allan R. Brewer-Carías (Compilator), *Documentos del Juicio de la Apertura Petrolera (1996-1999),* Caracas, 2004 *available at* http://allanbrewercarias.com/Content/449725d9-f1cb-474b-8ab2-efb849fea3/Content/I,%202,%2022.%20%20APERTURA%20PETROLERA.%20DOCUMENTOS%20DEL%20JUICIO.pdf, p. 25.

In the Final Arguments expressed in the process before the Supreme Court in such case, which took place on January 22, 1998, Alí Rodríguez himself submitted a written argument in which he insisted in asking for the annulment of the Clause, in which, he denounced, that by providing "that always, the doubts and controversies shall be submitted to arbitration according to the rules of the International Chamber of Commerce of Paris," it has allowed that "some Association Agreements have established [for the State] the unconditional renunciation to allege the jurisdictional immunity, arbitrarily declaring that such contractual forms are of mere contractual nature establishing that always such arbitration will take place abroad." He added that "article 127 of the Constitution does not leave the most far doubt by establishing in a niter way that, in public interest contracts, the doubts and controversies shall be decided by the competent tribunals of the republic, in conformity with the laws." With the challenged clause, Alí Rodríguez argued that "the sovereign abdicates its condition as such, and leaves in the private hands the solution of the doubts and controversies on matters of contracts that are indissolubly *public*, as it were a simple lawsuit between private parties a purely commercial matter." [301]

In that regard, if Rodríguez opposed the Investment Law (as I assume, he must have done, given his position on international arbitration), President Chavez overruled any such opposition and signed into law the Investment Law containing consent to international arbitration. It is perhaps due to potential disagreements in the Council of Ministers, presumably manifested by Alí Rodríguez as Acting Minister of Energy and Mines, that the Decree Law N° 356 of October 3, 1999 was only published twenty days later in the *Official Gazette* of October 22, 1999[302] without its corresponding "*Exposición de Motivos*" (Statement of Purposes), although a Draft of such Statement of Purpose was reportedly written.[303] Finally, it must be mentioned that Ambassador Corrales continued his official activities related to the promotion of investments from his position in Geneva until 2002.[304]

From all the elements aforementioned, it can be said, contrary to what was concluded in the ICSID tribunals in the *Mobil* and *Cemex* cases, that "the legislative history of Article 22 in this respect" effectively provides very important "information on the intention of the drafters in the Investment Law," and that, in those cases, as in this case, the Tribunal had, indeed, "direct information" on the preparation of the Law as it was discussed in the Executive Council of Ministers. The intention of Ambassador Corrales, who was operating at the specific instance and direction of the Republic as a co-drafter of the Investment Law regarding the unilateral expression of consent for Arbitration given by the Venezuelan State contained in Article 22 of the Law, was clarified in a speech he gave on March 28,

---

301 *Id.* pp. 104-105

302 *Official Gazette* N° 5.390 Extra. of October 22, 1999.

303 A Draft of the "Statement of Purpose" of the Investment Law was prepared by Gonzalo Capriles, Legal Expert hired by Cordiplán to work with Ambassador Corrales, with the title: "*Borrador de Exposición de Motivos de la Ley de promoción y protección de Inversiones,*" 1999. See the reference in Victorino Tejera Pérez, *Arbitraje de Inversiones en Venezuela,* Master Thesis, *cit.* Caracas 2010, p. 154, Footnote 154.

304 See for instance Adriana Cortes, "Venezuela oficializó restricciones a la importación de productos agrícolas," in *El Nacional*, Caracas March 13, 2000.

2009 at a Conference organized in Caracas by the *Centro Empresarial de Conciliación y Arbitraje (CEDCA)* on "Investment Arbitration in Comparative Law." At that conference, he explained the following:

> "Today this forum is discussing whether Article 22 of the official version of the Investments law really includes a unilateral or open offer of arbitration. ....
>
> In my scope of competence at least, I can state the intention of offering the possibility of open unilateral arbitration and this can be verified in several articles on the matter which we published in international journals and which we also took to international congresses. Referring to the protection of investors, after dealing with contributions to development, in the first article of 1998, it states more or less something like "the possibility to arbitration must be opened", and in the second article it states "the unilateral possibility of arbitration must be opened to foreign investors".
>
> With this, I hope to leave sufficiently clear that my purpose as co-drafter was to offer in the broadest and most transparent manner the possibility of the investors resorting to international arbitration as a unilateral offer made by the Venezuelan state. And I add that whoever participates in public policies – including those who participate in the drafting or administration of a law or any legal policy instrument– must act with very clear objectives and be always respectful of the principles therein created. At that time we thought –as I continue to believe– that it was absolutely necessary for a public policy closely linked to promoting development such as the case of an investment policy, must aid in the investments acting in pro of development and we thought – as I think today that it is absolutely indispensable for legal instruments to protect the investments from the possibility that the justice system of the country receiving the investment not be independent, as is unfortunately the case we are seeing in Venezuela today."[305]

This statement of Corrales, contrary to what the ICSID tribunals said in the *Mobil* and *Cemex* cases, is fully supported "by the contemporaneous written documents" already discussed, as well as by the "contemporaneous" references published in the press regarding the discussions of the draft in the Council of Ministers. As revealed in these documents, Corrales and Capriles, acting with the express permission of the Republic, intended to include an open, unilateral offer to arbitration in the Investment Law. That is why, there is no other way than to express astonishment, to read what the ICSID Tribunal decided in the *Brandes* case, without any sort of reasoning or motivation, to consider "to be unnecessary, for the purpose of resolving this dispute, to establish the actual role played by Mr. Corrales in the drafting of the LPPI, his knowledge of the issue under discussion and the relevance of his publications about this issue" (¶ 103), affirming that "What is apparent to the Tribunal is that Mr. Corrales' opinion cannot provide the basis for finding that Article 22 of the LPPI contains the consent of the Bolivarian Republic of Venezuela to submit to ICSID arbitration (¶ 103).

305 See in CEDCA, BUSINESS MAGAZINE (June 2009), *Legal Report*, Caracas 2009, pp. 77-82.

X. THE WITHDRAWAL OF VENEZUELA OF THE ICSID CONVENTION IN 2012

In any case, after a series of decisions were issued by ICSID Arbitral Tribunals against Venezuela, in January 24, 2012 the Government officially withdraws in an irrevocable way from the *Convention on the settlement of Investment Disputes between States and Nationals of other States*. After receiving the written notice of denunciation of the Convention, the World Bank as the depositary of the ICSID Convention, notified all ICSID signatory States of Venezuela's denunciation of the Convention. In accordance with Article 71 of the ICSID Convention, the denunciation took effect six months after the receipt of Venezuela's notice, that is on July 25, 2012.

The "Official Communiqué" of the Government justifying Venezuela's withdrawing from the ICSID Convention[306] expressed that its ratification in 1993 was a decision adopted by "a week government without popular legitimacy pressed by traditional transnational economic sectors that participated in the dismantling of the national sovereignty of Venezuela." This statement referred to the government lead by President Ramón J. Velasquez (1993-1994), in which I served as Minister for Decentralization.

Contrary to such assertion, that Government lead by a President Velasquez was a very important transitional one, configured after his appointment by Congress in June 1993, once the acting President Carlos Andrés Pérez was removed from office by decision of the same Congress, with the support of all the political parties, in order to complete the constitutional term of former President Pérez. That transitional Government had the important task of assuring the continuity of the democratic rule of the country and, in particular, the successful development of the general elections that took place on December 1993. That Government was able to continue conducting the State in the midst of a grave political and economic crisis, having for such purpose all the needed legitimacy derived from the Constitution. Important decisions were adopted in many fields,[307] and also on matters of promotion of investments. In that respect, the signing of the ICSID Convention, according to the general prevailing policy of attracting foreign investments to the country, was a very important one for such purpose.

The "Official Communiqué" of the Venezuelan Government of January 24, 2012, in order to justify the Venezuela's withdrawing from the Convention, in addition expressed that the text of article 151 of the 1999 Venezuelan Constitution[308] supposedly "invalidates, in its spirit and in its wording, the provisions of the ICSID Convention." This assertion only evidenced the most complete ignorance by the Government of President Hugo Chávez of the sense and meaning of such

---

306 The text of the Official Communiqué is available at http://www.noticierodigital.com/2012/01/ramirez-ratifica-salida-de-venezuela-del-ciadi/

307 See the collective book: *Ramón J. Velásquez. Estudios sobre una trayectoria al servicio de Venezuela,* Universidad Metropolitana. Universidad de Los Andes-Táchira, Caracas 2003.

308 See the text of the Constitution in *Official Gazette* No. 5.908 Extra. Of February 2, 2009. See the general comments in Allan R. Brewer-Carías, *La Constitución de 1999 y la Enmienda Constiucional No. 1 de 2009*, Editorial Jurídica Venezolana, Caracas 2011; and in *Constitucional Law. Venezuela*, Supplement 97, International Encyclopaedia of Laws, Kluwer, Belguium 2012.

constitutional provision, in which, on the contrary, it is expressly established the principle of relative jurisdictional sovereign immunity of the State[309] following previous constitutional provisions included in the Constitution since 1947, allowing international arbitration in public contracts except when considered inappropriate according to their nature. The restriction, on the other hand, only refers to matters of arbitration related to public contracts, and in principle is not directed to regulate arbitration resulting from the consent of the State express in a statute.

In effect, as has already been explained, Article 151 of the 1999 Constitution establishes that:

> "Article 151: In contracts of public interest, unless inappropriate according with their nature, a clause shall be deemed included even if not been expressed, according to which the doubts and controversies that may arise on such contracts and that could not be resolved amicably by the contracting parties, shall be decided by the competent courts of the Republic, in accordance with its laws and could not give rise by any motive or cause to foreign claims."

This provision is basically a reproduction of the content of article 127 of the 1961 Constitution, which was kept in the new 1999 Constitution due to my personal proposal made before the National Constituent Assembly,[310] in particular, in order to contradict the "bizarre" and "inappropriate" proposal contained in a document submitted by President of the Republic, Hugo Chávez before the Assembly[311] suggesting some constitutional changes. Among those, Chávez first proposed to completely eliminate from the Constitution the "Calvo Clause,"[312] and second, he proposed to return to the principle of absolute jurisdictional sovereign immunity but exclusively regarding public contracts entered by the "Republic," eliminating all jurisdictional restriction regarding other public interest contracts signed by other public entities, that by the way, are the most common and important public contracts in the country, like for instance those signed in the oil and mining industry. That presidential proposal was without doubts, excessive permissive towards international arbitration on matters of public law.

---

309 See in general, Tatiana B. de Maekelt, "Inmunidad de Jurisdicción de los Estados," in *Libro Homenaje a José Melich Orsini*, Vol. 1, Universidad Central de Venezuela, Caracas 1982, pp. 213 ff.

310 I was Elected Member of the 1999 Constituent Assembly. See my proposal regarding article 151 in Allan R. Brewer-Carías, "Propuesta sobre la cláusula de inmunidad relativa de jurisdicción y sobre la cláusula Calvo en los contratos de interés público," in *Debate Constituyente (Aportes a la Asamblea Nacional Constituyente)*, Vol. I (8-Agosto-8 Septiembre 1999), Fundación de Derecho Público/Editorial Jurídica Venezolana, Caracas 1999, pp. 209-233.

311 See Hugo Chávez Frías, *Ideas Fundamentales para la Constitución Bolivariana de la V República,* Caracas agosto 1999.

312 The *Calvo* Clause had its origin in the work of Carlos Calvo, who formulated the doctrine in his book *Tratado de Derecho Internacional*, initially published in 1868, after studying the Franco-British intervention in Rio de la Plata and the French intervention in Mexico. The *Calvo* Clause was first adopted in Venezuela in the 1893 Constitution as a response to diplomatic claims brought by European countries against Venezuela as a consequence of contracts signed by the State and foreign citizens. See Allan R. Brewer-Carías, *Historia Constitucional de Venezuela*, Vol I, Editorial Alfa, Caracas 2008, pp. 411.

The two clauses contained in the text of article 151 of the Constitution have been in the text of all Venezuelan Constitutions since 1893.[313] The first clause is the one referred to the principle of jurisdictional sovereign immunity of the State regarding public contracts. Initially it was referred to public contracts entered by the Republic and the States (Venezuela has the federal form of Government), and was conceived as an "absolute" jurisdictional immunity clause. It was first changed in 1901, expanding its initial scope in order to include, not only the "national" and "states" public interest contracts, but also the "municipal" contracts and any other public contract entered by other organs ("public powers") of the State. And later, in 1947 it was also changed regarding the scope of the immunity, transforming it into a "relative" jurisdictional sovereign immunity clause, following the general trend prevailing in comparative constitutional law.[314]

The proposal of Mr. Chávez in 1999 regarding this constitutional clause was to reestablish the absolute sovereign jurisdictional immunity principle abandoned in 1947, but in a limited way only regarding some "national" public interest contracts, that is, only those entered by the Republic, eliminating any kind of restriction on jurisdictional matters regarding public interest contracts entered by the states, the municipalities and other public entities. This presidential proposal, as I argued, was excessive and inconveniently permissive, particularly due to the fact that commonly, the public interest contracts are entered precisely by other entities different to the Republic, and particularly by public corporations and public enterprises.[315]

In any case, leaving aside that failed proposal made by the President of the Republic in 1999, the way the clause has been in the Constitution since 1947, that is, following the "relative" jurisdictional sovereign immunity, cannot be considered as something extraordinary or unusual, particularly because it follow the general principle of relative immunity in contemporary world. According to this Clause, the State is authorized in the Constitution to submit to international arbitration matters of public interest contracts except if the "nature" of their object prevents it, which is referred to the matters generally known as of *ius imperii*. That is why the argument of the Government for withdrawing from ICSID Convention, as well as the suggestion given the by ICSID tribunals in the *Mobil* and *Cemex* cases, arguing that "Venezuela remained reluctant *vis-à-vis* contractual arbitration in the public sphere, as demonstrated by [...] Article 151 of the 1999 Constitution" (*Mobil* ICSID case, ¶¶ 131; 127, 128; *Cemex* ICSID case, ¶ 125), simply did not really understood the content of the provision of said article 151, from which no "reluctant" attitude towards arbitration can be deducted. On the contrary, the constitutional provision of article 151 is, precisely, the one that allows international arbitration involving the

313 See the text of the 1893 Constitution as well as all the other Constitution in the history of the country in Allan R. Brewer-Carías, *Las Constituciones de Venezuela*, Academia de Ciencias Políticas y Sociales, Caracas 2008, 2 vols.

314 See in general the classical book of Ian Sinclair, *The Law of Sovereign Immunity. Recent Developments*, Académie International de Droit International, Recueil des Cours 1980, The Hague 1981.

315 See in Allan R. Brewer-Carías, "Propuesta sobre la cláusula de inmunidad relativa de jurisdicción y sobre la cláusula Calvo en los contratos de interés público," in *Debate Constituyente (Aportes a la Asamblea Nacional Constituyente)*, Vol. I (8-Agosto-8 Septiembre 1999), Fundación de Derecho Público/Editorial Jurídica Venezolana, Caracas 1999, pp. 209-233.

Venezuelan State according to the principle of relative sovereign jurisdictional immunity that is the one generally accepted in contemporary world.

Consequently, nothing in the Venezuela legal and constitutional order authorizes the Government to say that article 151 of the 1999 Venezuelan Constitution supposedly "invalidates, in its spirit and in its wording, the provisions of the ICSID Convention," which means to consider that an expression of consent for international arbitration as the one contained in article 22 of the Investment Law would be inconceivable in light of article 151 of the Constitution. On the contrary, it is the trend set forth in such article the one that authorizes for the State to go to international arbitration.

The second clause contained in article 151 of the Constitution, inserted in the constitutional text also in 1893, and that has remained without change, is the already mentioned "Calvo Clause," according to which in Venezuela is excluded and is inadmissible any diplomatic claims regarding public interest contracts signed between the different organs of the State and foreign entities or persons. The President of the Republic in his "bizarre" 1999 proposal before the Constituent Assembly, pretended to completely eliminated from the Constitution this centenary "clause," and consequently to allow the possibility that in public interest contracts, their execution could gave rise to foreign diplomatic claims against the Republic.[316] From that proposal, it is impossible to deduct any restrictive approach of the President toward arbitration matters. On the contrary, his proposals being excessively permissible were inadmissible, being contrary to the interest of the State.

Finally, it must be mentioned that article 151 of the Constitution establishing the relative sovereign jurisdictional sovereign immunity clause and the *Calvo* Clause, is a provision referred to "public interest contracts," that is, basically, those entered by the three territorial divisions of the State (Republic, States, Municipalities). The clause allows the possibility for the State to give its consent to submit to international arbitration, for instance, disputes related to commercial matters derived from such public interest contracts.

In ICSID arbitration cases, based on jurisdiction through a State's consent given by a statute, as was the case of article 22 of the Investment Law, the ICSID Tribunals were not to deal with public interest contracts regulated in article 151 of the Constitution. The Tribunals in such cases only dealt with the consent given by the Venezuelan State in a statute (Article 22 of the 1999 Investment Law) to submit matters related to investment, generally of industrial, commercial or finance nature, to international arbitration.

In any case the decision of the government to "escape from ICSID,"[317] of course ignored the importance of the ICSID Convention for the purpose of attracting investment, which resulted evidenced by the fact that between 1993 and 1998, many bilateral treaties on investments (BITs) were signed, specifically providing for

316 *Idem.*

317 See James Otis Rodner, "Huyendo del CIADI,", in *El Universal*, Caracas February 7, 2012, available at http://www.eluniversal.com:80/opinion/120207/huyendo-del-ciadi

international arbitration, and in particular, for ICSID International Arbitration.[318] Its importance also results from the fact that it was the same Government that in 2012 rejected international arbitration, the one that in 1999 sanctioned by means of a Decree Law N° 356 of October 3, the 1999 Investment Law containing express recognition of ICSID international arbitration. In it, the current Government went farther an expressed, in Article 22 of the Law, the express written consent of the Republic of Venezuela to submit investments disputes to the ICSID arbitration Center, under Article 25.1 of the ICSID Convention. This is a historical fact that in spite of the decision to "escape from ICSID," cannot be denied.

Article 22 of the 1999 Investment Law was not a provision that was officially adopted by the Government without knowing its significance, or that "under the influence of globalization currents was filtered within the Venezuelan regime" as it has been affirmed without foundations.[319] On the contrary, it was a conscious decision adopted by a Government that at the time was seeking to promote and encourage international investments in the country, giving investors legal security assurances, like for the disputes to be decided by arbitral tribunals.

For such purpose, in article 22 of the 1999 Investment Law, the State gave its consent to submit investments disputes to ICSID arbitration, expressed in the form of an open offer of arbitration (*oferta abierta de arbitraje*) subject to acceptance by the investor-claimant to a relevant dispute, to go to international arbitration, or, at his will, to resort to national courts. Not only the signing of the ICSID Convention in 1993, but the text of Article 22 of the 1999 Investment Law, reflected the pro-arbitration trend existing in Venezuela at the time, developed over the past few decades, which crystallized not only in Article 258 of the 1999 Constitution, sanctioned in parallel to the 1999 Investment Law, compelling the State to promote arbitration. This same trend was reflected in an important number of other statutes sanctioned during the same year 1999. All was ended with the withdrawal of Venezuela from the ICSID Convention in 2012, and two years later, with the repeal of the 1999 Investment Law.

XI. THE EPILOGUE: THE REPEALING AND SUBSTITUTION OF THE 1999 INVESTMENT LAW BY THE FOREIGN INVESTMENT LAW OF 2014

The epilogue of the whole process leads by the Government of retracting from what was established in the 1999 Investment Law, after the withdrawal of

318 See lists of all those treaties at Venezuelan Ministry of for Foreign Relations at http://www.mre.gov.ve/metadot/index.pl?id=4617;isa=Category;op=show; ICSID Database of Bilateral Investment Treaties at http://icsid.worldbank.org/ICSID/FrontServlet; UNCTAD, Investment Instruments On-line Database, Venezuela Country-List of BITs as of June 2008 at http://www.unctad.org/Templates/Page.asp?intItemID=2344&lang=1. See also, in José Antonio Muci Borjas, *El derecho administrativo global y los tratados bilaterales de inversión (BITs)*, Caracas 2007; Tatiana B. de Maekel, "Arbitraje Comercial Internacional en el sistema venezolano," in Allan R. Brewer-Carías (Editor), *Seminario sobre la Ley de Arbitraje Comercial*, Academia de Ciencias Políticas y Sociales, Caracas 1999, pp. 282-283; Francisco Hung Vaillant, *Reflexiones sobre el arbitraje en el sistema venezolano*, Caracas 2001, pp. 104-105.

319 See Hildegard Rondón de Sansó, *Aspectos jurídicos fundamentales del arbitraje internacional de inversión*, Ed. Exlibris, Caracas 2010, p. 132.

Venezuela from the ICSID Convention, was the repeal of the 1999 Investment Law, and its substitution in 2014, by the Law on Foreign Investments of November 2014,[320] in which international arbitration was just eliminated, as well as the general regulations for the purpose of promoting investments. The general principle in the new statute is that foreign investments are subjected to the jurisdiction of national courts, being the State authorized to participate and use the means of solution of controversies established within the integration process of Latin America and the Caribbean (article 5).

The new Law, can be considered as a classical statute issued for the purpose of regulating, restricting and controlling foreign investments in order to "attain the harmonic and sustainable development of the Nation." All foreign investments made of equipment, or tangible goods assets" (article 23); must be registered before the Administration, in an amount of at least one million US$ or equivalent in foreign currency (article 24), and must remain in the country for at least five years (article 25). The Ministry of Commerce and the National Center for External Commerce (*Centro Nacional de Comercio Exterior (CENCOEX*), are the administrative bodies in charge of enforcing the Law.

On the other hand, according to the Law, all strategic sectors are reserved to the State (article 21) which means that also the Venezuelan investors are excluded for inestment.

320 See in Official Gazette N° 6.152 Extra of. November 19, 2014.

PART EIGHT

SOME PRINCIPLES OF ADMINISTRATIVE LAW REGARDING THE STATUS OF INDIVIDUALS AND CITIZENS

Venezuelan Constitutions, as all contemporary ones, establish a basic distinction regarding the status of persons, between national or citizens and aliens. As persons or human beings, they all have the same rights without discrimination of any kind, except for political rights that are reserved to nationals or to citizens.

I. CONSTITUTIONAL AND LEGAL STATUS OF PERSONS REGARDING NATIONALITY OR CITIZENSHIP

The Venezuelan Constitution, as mentioned, establishes a basic distinction regarding persons between citizens (national) and aliens.

1. Venezuelan citizenship

Citizens are the Venezuelan nationals; citizenship being the political bond existing between a person and the State that allows a person to participate in the political system. That is why article 39 of the Constitution, declares that only Venezuelan "exercise the citizenship and, therefore, are entitled to political rights and duties as per this Constitution."

This provision has been repeated in Article 50 of the 2004 Nationality and Citizenship Statute[1] specifying that "citizens are those Venezuelans not subject to political impediment or to civil interdiction and fulfill the age requirements foreseen in the Constitution and in the statutes." These age conditions differ regarding the corresponding political right to be exercised. For example, to vote, it is enough to be older than 18 years old (Art. 64), but to be elected Governor of a State of the federation it is necessary to be older than 25 years old (Art. 160); to be Congressmen to the National Assembly and to a State Legislative Council, it is necessary to be older than 21 years old (Arts. 188 and 162); to be Mayor of any Municipality, 25 years old (Art. 174); to be President and Vice President of the Republic, older than 30 (Arts. 227 and 238); as well as to be People's Defender (Art.

---

1 See *Official Gazette*, N° 37971 of July 1, 2004. See the text in Allan R. Brewer-Carías, *Régimen Legal de la Nacionalidad, Ciudadanía y Extranjería. Ley de Nacionalidad y Ciudadanía, Ley de Extranjería y Migración, Ley Orgánica sobre Refugiados y Asilados*, Colección Texto Legislativos N° 31, 1ª edición, Editorial Jurídica Venezolana, Caracas 2005, pp. 87 ff.

280) and General Controller of the Republic (Art. 288); and to be Minister, older than 25 (Art. 244).

Furthermore, as regards the Justices to the Supreme Tribunal of Justice (Art. 263), the Attorney General (Art. 249) and the General Prosecutor of the Republic (Art. 284), the Constitution requires to be at least 35 years old, which is set forth in the conditions to exercise such positions.

2. Migrants and non-migrants' aliens

All other persons in Venezuela not being Venezuelans are considered aliens. In this sense, article 3 of the 2004 Aliens and Migration Statute,[2] provides that all those who are not considered to be Venezuelans are legally considered to be foreigners or aliens.

Aliens, according to the same Statute, and regarding their access and permanency in the territory of the Republic, can be admitted in two categories: as non-migrants or as migrants.

As to the non-migrant aliens, these are the people who enter the territory of the Republic to remain in it for a limited time of 90 days, without having the intention to establish his or his family's permanent residence in it. These non-migrant aliens cannot perform activities that involve remuneration or profit.

As to the migrants, they are those aliens who enter the territory of the Republic to reside in it temporal or permanently,[3] being then classified in two categories: temporary migrants and permanent migrants (Art. 6). The temporary migrants, are those entering the territory of the Republic with the intention of residing in it temporarily while the activities that origin their admission last; and the permanent migrants, those who have authorization to remain indefinitely in the territory of the Republic.

These migrants are basically the "migrant workers", defined in the International Conventions on Migrant Workers as the "person who is to be engaged, is engaged or has been engaged in a remunerated activity in a State of which he or she is not a national."[4]

---

2 See in *Official Gazette* N° 37.944 of May 24, 2004. See the text in Allan R. Brewer-Carías, *Régimen Legal De La Nacionalidad, Ciudadanía y Extranjería. Ley de Nacionalidad y Ciudadanía, Ley de Extranjería y Migración, Ley Orgánica sobre Refugiados y Asilados*, Colección Texto Legislativos N° 31, 1ª edición, Editorial Jurídica Venezolana, Caracas 2005, pp. 101 ff.

3 As established in article 3 of the Statute governing aliens and migration of 2004 (*Official Gazette* N° 37.944 of 05-24-2004). This Statute derogated the Aliens Statute of 1937 (*Official Gazette* N° 19.329 dated August 3, 1937), the Statute about Alien activities in the Venezuelan territory of 1942 (*Official Gazette* N° 20.835 dated June 29, 1942) and the Immigration and Colonization Statute of 1966 (Extraordinary *Official Gazette* N° 1.032 dated July 18, 1966), as well as all other dispositions that violate it.

4 See for instance article 2,1 of the *International Convention on the Protection of the Rights of all Migrant Workers and Members of their Families*, Adopted by the General Assembly at its 45th session on 18 December 1990 (A/RES/45/158).The same definition is contained in the IOL *Covenant on Migrant Workers* (1949), in effect in Venezuela since 1983, in which in addition is clarified that the Covenant is not applicable to "border workers", the entry for a short period of time of artists or persons exercising liberal professional activities, and people of see (Article 11,2).

3. Aliens with status of refuge and asylum

But in addition to the status of migrants and non-migrants' aliens, article 69 of the Constitution set forth in the section related to political rights, "that the Bolivarian Republic of Venezuela acknowledges and guarantees the right of asylum and refuge." Therefore, in addition to the non-migrants and migrants aliens, two other categories of aliens can be identified in Venezuela internal law, the refugees and asylees aliens, following the provisions of the 2001 Organic Statute on Refugees and Asylees[5].

A. Asylum

Pursuant to article 38 of this Statute, the asylum status is granted to aliens the State considers to be persecuted due to their believes, opinions, or political affinities, or due to acts that might be considered as political crimes, or to common crimes committed with political purposes.

The Venezuelan State, exercising its sovereignty and as per the international treaties, conventions and agreements ratified by the Republic, shall grant asylum within its territory to a person persecuted for political reasons or crimes (art. 38), once the nature of such is qualified (art.39) (territorial asylum).

The State shall also grant asylum to a person seeking it before diplomatic missions, Venezuelan war ships, or military aircrafts, as per international treaties and conventions on the matter of which Venezuela is part (article 40 of the Organic Law) (Diplomatic asylum).

On the other hand, asylum cannot be granted, to a person accused, processed or convicted before ordinary competent Courts due to common crimes, or having committed crimes against peace, war crimes, or crimes against mankind, as defined in international treaties (article 41 of the Organic Law).

All these provisions related to the asylum, according to article 24 of the Organic Law, shall be construed pursuant the 1948 Universal Declaration of Human Rights, and the 1954 Caracas Convention on Territorial Asylum and other provisions of international treaties on human rights, duly executed and ratified by the Government of Venezuela.

B. Refugees

The same Organic Statute on Refugees and Asylees also establishes, regarding the refugee status, that the Venezuelan State shall grant refugee status "to every person recognized as such by the competent authority, in virtue of having entered in the national territory due to persecution because of his or her race, gender, religion, nationality, membership in a social group or political opinion, and is outside his or her home country and shall not or does not want to be protected by that country, or that, having no nationality, shall not or does not want to return the country where he or she has his residence." (article 5).

---

5 See in *Official Gazette* N° 37.296 of October 3, 2001. See the text in Allan R. Brewer-Carías, *Régimen Legal de la Nacionalidad, Ciudadanía y Extranjería. Ley de Nacionalidad y Ciudadanía, Ley de Extranjería y Migración, Ley Orgánica sobre Refugiados y Asilados*, Colección Texto Legislativos N° 31, Editorial Jurídica Venezolana, Caracas 2005, pp. 117 ff

The main legal trend regarding the refugee status is that according to the Law, no person asking refugee protection shall be punished due to illegal entrance or stay in the national territory, provided that he or she appears without delay before the national authorities, and plea just cause (Art. 6). Additionally, a person making a refugee protection claim shall not be denied admission or subject to a measure forcing him or her to return to the country where his or her life, physical integrity or personal freedom is jeopardizing (due to the reasons set forth in article 5 of the Law). However, these benefits shall not be granted to an alien considered, due to well-founded reasons, a danger for the Republic's security or that having been convicted for a serious crime, he or she represents a community threaten (Art. 7).

Moreover, according to the Statute, every alien claiming Venezuelan State protection as refugee, shall be admitted in the national territory and shall be authorized to stay in it until his or her claim be decided, including a reconsideration period. However, an alien considered, due to well-founded reasons, a danger for the Republic's safety or that having been convicted for a serious crime, is a threaten to the community, cannot claim these benefits (art. 2).

On the other hand, the refugee protection, as per article 9 of OLRA, shall not be granted to aliens in the following cases: 1. When the alien committed a crime against peace, war crimes or crimes against mankind, as defined in international treaties; 2. When the alien committed common crimes outside the country granting refugee protection that are not compatible with the refugee status; and 3. When the alien committed acts against the principles of the United Nations Organization.

All these internal provisions related to the refugee status, according to article 4 of the Organic Law, shall be construed pursuant the 1948 Universal Declaration of Human Rights, 1967 Protocol on the Status of Refugees, the 1969 American Convention on Human Rights, and other provisions of international treaties on human rights, duly executed and ratified by the Government of Venezuela.

C. Common regime

Pursuant article 2 of the Organic Law, Venezuela acknowledges and guarantees the right of asylum and refugee, according to the following principles:

1. Every person is able to file a refugee protection claim in the Bolivarian Republic of Venezuela, due to well-founded fear to be persecuted by the reasons and the conditions set forth in the 1967 Protocol on the Refugee Status.

2. Every person is able to make a refugee protection claim in the Bolivarian Republic of Venezuela as well as in its diplomatic missions, war ships and military aircrafts abroad, when persecuted for political reasons or crimes in the conditions set forth in that Law.

3. No person claiming asylum or refugee protection shall be neglected or subjected to any measure that force him or her to be repatriated to the territory where his or her life, physical integrity or freedom is jeopardize due to the reasons set forth in that Law.

4. Authorities shall impose no punishment due to the irregular entrance or stay in the territory of the Republic on persons that claim refugee protection or asylum, pursuant the terms set forth in the Constitution.

5. Discriminations based on race, gender, religion, political opinions, social condition, country of origin or those that in general lessen or annulled the acknowledge, enjoy or exercise in equal situation of the refugee or asylee condition of every person shall not be permitted.

6. The unity of a refugee's or asylee family shall be guaranteed, and specially, the protection of children refugees and teenagers without company or separated from the family, in the terms set forth in the Law.

All the procedures set forth in the Law to grant refugee and asylum protection are subject to the principles of accessibility, orality, swiftness and freeness (art. 3).

Regarding refugees, according to article 22 of the Organic Law, they hold in the territory of the Republic the same rights foreigners have with the limitations set forth in the Constitution and laws. A refugee, moreover, is entitled to request assistance before the Office of the High Commissioner of the United Nations for Refugees or before any other entity, public or private, national or international. (art. 23).

On the other hand, refugees shall receive all sort of help to process his or her Venezuelan citizenship (art. 26). The Executive Regulation to the Organic Law turns this provision into a right when pointing out that "Every alien staying in the country with a refugee status is entitled to petition for the Venezuelan nationality by naturalization in the terms set forth in the Constitution of the Bolivarian Republic of Venezuela and the laws ruling the matter" (art. 18)[6].

On the other hand, regarding duties, the asylee admitted in the national territory shall comply the Republic's Constitution and laws, and cannot participate in political matters or in any other matter compromising national security or the Venezuelan State interests (art. 44). Regarding refugees, article 24 of the Organic Law set forth also that those with refugee status in the Republic shall obey the Constitution and laws and not intervene in political or any other matters compromising the national security and internal or external Venezuelan interests. Additionally, refugees are forced to notify the National Commission for Refugees of every change of residence within the national territory (art. 25). Moreover, as per article 17 of the By Law, a refugee cannot leave the country without written authorization issued by the National Commission for Refugees, which shall have an up dated file with every authorization granted.

II. GENERAL LEGAL REGIME REGARDING MIGRANT ALIENS

Venezuela, particularly during the twentieth Century, has been a country of immigrants. First after World War II when a huge flow of peoples arriving from Italy, Spain and Portugal was incorporated in the activities of the country, contributing in a very important way to its social and economic development, producing a completely integrated and mixed population. Second, since the seventies', with the arrival in the country of an important flow of citizens from other Latin American countries, like Colombia, seeking employment and other economic better conditions. An important contingent of these latter migrants has been illegal immigrants.

6 Decree N° 2491, *Official Gazette* N° 37.740 of July, 28, 2003

1. General Legal regime

Notwithstanding the special provisions referred to refugees and asylees aliens, the general regime regarding all aliens is established in the 2004 Aliens and Migration Statute[7], which applies to all foreigners located within the territory of the Republic notwithstanding their migratory condition (art. 2).

The only exception to this general rule is "diplomatic and consular representatives, members of diplomatic missions and consular offices, representatives, delegates and other members of international bodies and specialized organizations of which the Republic and their families are part of, accredited before the National Government" (art. 4); to which such regime does not apply.

This general regime established in the Law provides for everything related to the admission, entry, stay, registry, control and information, departure and reentry of foreigners in the Republic's territory, as well as their rights and duties. Consequently, the 2004 Law repealed the 1937 Aliens Law, the 1942 Law on Aliens' Activity in Venezuelan Territory and the 1966 Immigration and Colonization Law, as well as every other provision contravening it.

On the other hand, regarding Indigenous people sharing the boundaries with Colombia and with Brazil, article 60 of the Statute, aiming at facilitating their cultural integration as well as their right to practice their values, uses and customs, impose the country with the need to enter into agreements with those countries in order to promote the cultural unity and the preservation of their life style.

2. Admission system for migrant aliens

A. Necessary documents for admission

The basic condition for a migrant alien to be admitted, to entry, re-entry and to remain in the territory of the Republic, is to have a valid passport, with the respective visa or other document authorizing the entry or permanence in the territory of the Republic, according to the applicable statutes and international treaties signed and ratified by the Republic of Venezuela (art. 7).

For such purpose, aliens must present themselves at the entry Terminal "with their passport with a valid visa or a document authorizing their entry or permanence in the territory to the Republic" (article 10 of the Statute).

In the case of an alien representative of any religion or cult who enters the territory of the Republic to perform religious activities or any other activity related to it, he must obtain the respective authorization, accrediting his condition, from the National Executive through the competent authority (art. 11).

B. Entry control of aliens

It is up to the competent authorities in matters of aliens and migration located in ports, airports and border zones, to impede the entrance to the territory of the

7 See Allan R. Brewer-Carías, "*Legal Situation of Migrants in Venezuela* (*La situación jurídica de los migrantes*), National Report for the XVII International Congress of Comparative Law, International Academy of Comparative Law, Utrecht, 16-22 de julio de 2006. See in www.allanbrewercarías.com (Section I,1, 2006).

Republic, of those aliens who do not comply with the requirements established by the Statute for their legal entry into the country (art. 12). Exception is made in cases set forth in international agreements signed by the Republic exonerating aliens from complying with any of the requirements for their entry, established by the Statute. This is the case of persons seeking refuge that could not be rejected or be subjected to any measure implying his return to the territory where his life, physical integrity and personal freedom be at risk due to the factors enunciated in article 5 of the Refugee and Asylum Statute (article 7 of the same Statute).

C. Entry and departure places for aliens

The entry and departure of aliens from the territory of the Republic can only be made through Terminals legally authorized for said effects.

In case of emergency or proved need, said legally authorized places can be temporarily closed for traffic of people and, in this case, in accordance to article 9 of the Statute, the act containing this measure must be issued following the provisions regarding estates of exception situations.

This act must be dully motivated in the facts as well as in the law on which it is based. In consequence, in order to have the "closing of borders", the respective Act must occur in the frame of the state of exception regulated by articles 337 of the Constitution and the State of Exception Organic Statute[8].

D. The negative towards the admission of aliens

Aliens, who are compromised in the following cases listed in article 8 of the Statute, cannot be admitted into the territory of the Republic:

1. When his presence can cause alteration of the domestic public order or compromises the international relations of the Republic, because being requested by foreign police or judicial authorities, for common criminal causes or for being connected to national or international criminal organizations.

2. When they have been deported from the territory of the Republic and the prohibition of entrance into the country is still in effect.

3. When they have committed a felony qualified and punished by Venezuelan laws, in cases when they have not served their sentence, or the action or penalty has not prescribed.

4. When they had committed violations of Human Rights, Humanitarian International Law or of the dispositions content in international instruments of which the Republic is part of.

5. When they are involved in the traffic of drugs or psychotropic substances or performing similar activities.

6. When they suffer from infect-contagious diseases or others that might risk public health.

8 Organic Statute of Exception Status (Statute N 32), O.G. N° 37.261 de 08-15-2001.

3. The labor authorization system

A. Prohibition for Non-Migrant Aliens to perform a Remunerated Activity.

As previously said, the non-migrant alien category corresponds to those who enter the country with the purpose of staying for a 90-day limited time, without having the intention of setting permanent residence for him or his family in it. The Statute establishes, in general, that they cannot perform activities that involve remuneration or profit.

However, the Statute establishes exceptions by regulating labor authorizations, and establishing in its article 17, that non-migrant aliens in the following cases do not require labor authorizations for the exercise and activities that motivate their granting:

1. Scientifics, professionals, technicians, experts and specialized personnel who come to counsel, provide training or perform temporal labor, for a period of no more than ninety (90) days.

2. Technicians and professional invited by public or private entities to perform academic, scientific or research activities, as long as these activities do not exceed the ninety (90) day period.

3. Those that enter the territory of the Republic to develop activities protected by cooperation and technical assistance agreements.

4. Workers of foreign media dully accredited for the exercise of informative activities.

5. Members of international scientific missions performing research works in the territory of the Republic authorized by the Venezuelan government.

B. Labor Authorization in cases of Migrant Workers

Article 16 of the Statute set forth that every person who enter the territory of the Republic under a work contract, must obtain the labor authorization from the Ministry of Labor. The procedure to obtain the corresponding authorization must be performed by the alien, through his contracting party, in the territory of the Republic.

In case of working aliens who want to be contracted by a public enterprise (that belong to the Republic, the States and Municipalities), they must also obtain the corresponding labor authorization (Art. 19).

The visa authorizing the permanence of the aliens in the territory of the Republic must have the same length of duration as the labor authorization and must be renovated when the circumstances that determined its issuance, persists (Art. 20).

In the cases of the employment of alien's workers for agriculture, fishery and cattle rising, in specific areas and for a specific period of time, corresponds to the Ministries of Lands, of Labor and Production and Commerce, to issue the respective procedures, through joint resolution (Art. 18).

4. Control of Migrant Aliens

A. Competent administrative entity

The Government authority with attributions in the area of governing aliens and migration, according to Decree N° 5.246 dated March 20, 2007 about Organization and Functioning of the Central Public Administration[9], is the Ministry of the Interior and Justice. This Ministry is therefore, the national migratory authority in charge of the admission, entrance, permanence, registry, departure and reentry of aliens. However, the Ministries with competence in the areas of Foreign Affairs, and Defense and Labor, must help in the execution of the objectives of the Statute.

Another regulated body in the Statute is the National Migration Commission which, according to article 28, has the object of advising the National Executive to comply with the functions established in the Statute.

This National Migration Commission is integrated by the Minister of the Interior and Justice, who presides it and by a representative of the Ministries with competence in Foreign Affairs, Defense, Education, Fishery, Agriculture, Cattle rising, Production, Commerce and Labor.

B. The National Registry of Aliens

Article 21 of the Statute created the "National Registry of Aliens" (both male and female) in the Ministry of the Interior and Justice. The Ministry of the Interior and Justice, in exercise of its control functions, must continuously update the statistics about both female and male aliens in the territory of the Republic, independently of their migratory category (Art. 27).

C. The Obligations to Inform

-The duty of hotel, boarding houses and lodging places.

Owners or administrators of hotels, boarding houses or lodging places must keep a registry of their alien users, specifically about their nationality; and this information must be sent every 8 days to the National Registry of Aliens (art. 25).

-The duty of the owners or administrators of transport businesses

Owners or administrators of the passenger transportation and national and international tourism companies must keep a registry of their alien users; this information must also be sent every 8 days to the National Registry of Aliens (art. 26).

-The duties of the employers of alien people

Every employer of an alien person must demand from him/her to furnish identification documents and must inform the National Registry of Aliens, in writing, the terms and conditions of the labor relation, as well as its termination within a 30-day period following the respective event (article 24).

Additionally, every employer or contractor of aliens workers must agree before the competent authority in the matter of aliens and migration, to pay for the return ticket of the alien and his/her family, if that was the case, back to his/her country of

---

9 *Official Gazette* Nº 38.654, March 28, 2008.

origin or of last residence, within the following month of the termination of his contract.

- *The duty of the civil registry authorities*

The civil authority before which a change of the civil status of an alien is performed, must inform the National Registry of Aliens of it, within an 8-day period after the event (art. 22).

- *The duty of prisons institutions*

The directors of the prisons must send every 3 months an updated list of the alien persons imprisoned for having been found guilty by final judgment (art. 23).

5. Expedite procedure for the Legalization of Illegal immigrants (2004)

In 2004, months before a recall referendum regarding the President of the Republic took place, and before the new laws on Nationality and Citizenship and Foreigners and Migration enter into force, an Executive Regulation was issued by means of Decree N° 2823 of February 3, 2004[10] in order "to legalize the admission and permanence of illegal immigrants in the territory of the Republic, and also to grant the opportunity to apply for the Venezuelan citizenship for those foreigners fulfilling the requirements set forth" (art. 1). Although such Decree was repeal by the new Laws on Nationality and Citizenship and Foreigners and Migration Laws, it has been subsequently been applied.

The basic motivation of the Decree was "the duty of the State to defend and guarantee human rights, dignity, fair and equal treatment, freeness, prompt and appropriate answer, honesty, transparency, impartiality and good faith, in order to introduce an effective procedure to attend requests made by aliens located in the territory of the Bolivarian Republic of Venezuela" (article 3).

For such purpose, the Executive assigned the Ministry of Interior and Justice jurisdiction to apply the Regulation through the National Office of Identification and Immigration (arts. 3 and 4), granting to such office the attribution to ease or suppress administrative paperwork in the process of legalizing the admission and permanence of illegal foreigners (or in irregular condition) and in the citizenship process, pursuant to the principles and rules set forth in the Law ruling this matter (art. 5), which at the time was the now repealed Law on Aliens of 1937 and the Naturalization Law of 1955.

For such purpose, the Decree established for illegal immigrants in order for them to regularize their legal situation, to register themselves in the Foreigners Registry (article 7), and to file before the National Office of Identification and Aliens the following documents for their legalization: Passport or any other identification document; evidence of the activity or occupation in the country; residence letter issued by a competent authority, and three pictures carnet size (article 8).

Pursuant to article 9 of the Decree, the situation of those foreigners that fulfilled those requirements shall be legalized by granting them "condition of resident" of the territory of the Republic. Consequently, the National Office of Identification and

10 See in *Official Gazette* N° 37.871 of February 3, 2004. Reformed by Decree N° 3042 of August 3, 2004, *Official Gazette* N° 38.002 of August 17, 2004.

Aliens must issue a triple legalization certificate, one of which shall be given to the foreigner, another shall be filed in the Office of Foreigners Control, and the third one shall be filed in the office issuing the certificate. Said legalization certificate, which shall have foreigner's identification data, is valid for 30 days counted from the date it was issued (article 10).

III. GENERAL REGIME REGARDING CIVIL RIGHTS AND DUTIES OF MIGRANT ALIENS

1. The civil and political rights' system

According to Article 13 of the Statute, aliens who are living in the territory of the Republic, have the same rights as nationals (Venezuelan citizens), with no more limitations than those stated in the Constitution and the laws, which in the 1961 Constitution was expressly set forth in article 45, as follows: "Aliens have the same rights and duties as Venezuelans, with the limitations or exceptions established by this Constitution and the laws".[11]

Even though this rule disappeared from the constitutional text of 1999, the same principle applies derived from the fundamental right to equal protection (art. 21). That mean that aliens in Venezuela have the same rights to Venezuelan, except political rights which are reserved to Venezuelan citizens (article 40).

Nonetheless, this principle has an express exception regarding the political right to vote in regional or local (municipal, parish and states) elections, which article 64 of the Constitution also recognize to aliens having reached the age of 18, when not subjected to civil disability or political impediment and having more than 10 years of residence in the country. In this same sense, article 51 of the Law repeats that "except for the cases provided for in the Constitution, and the laws, the exercise of political rights is solely for Venezuelans."

These other political rights enumerated in the Constitution reserved only to nationals, are the following: right to political participation (articles 62 and 70); right to vote, except for parish, county and states elections (article 63); right to participate in referenda (approbatory, abrogatory or recall referenda) (article 71 and ss.); right to hold public posts (article 65); right to request rendering accounts to those elected (article 66); right to be associate for political purposes (article 67) and right to public demonstration (article 68).

2. Particular reference to the right to the effective protection by court

On the other hand, and in an express way, article 15 of the Aliens and Migrants Statute guarantees aliens the right to be judicially and effectively protected regarding all the acts related to them or in which they are involved, in regards to their alien condition.

---

11 A complete and important Declaration of Rights of Migrants has been incorporated in the International Convention on the Protection of the Rights of all Migrant Workers and Members Of Their Families, Adopted by the General Assembly at its 45th session on 18 December 1990 (A/RES/45/158).

The rule adds that in all administrative procedures established in matters regarding aliens, the guarantees foreseen in the Constitution and the Statutes on administrative procedure must be observed in any case, especially regarding the publicity of the acts, the contradictory principle, the hearing of the interested party and the motivation of the resolutions. The application of the administrative acts related to alien condition or situation must be performed as established by the Organic Statute of Administrative Procedures when applicable. Additionally, acts and administrative resolutions adopted in relation to aliens are, as in general administrative acts, essentially reviewable, in conformity to the Statute regulating administrative procedures when applicable.

3. The duties system

According to article 14 of the Statute, aliens who remain in the territory of the Republic, without prejudice of the duties and obligations imposed by the Constitution and the Statutes, must comply with the following duties:

1. To comply with the requirements and conditions of identification, permanence and address in Venezuela, as established in the legal system.

2. To show, before the authorities, the documents that identify them, any time they are asked to do so. Said documents may not be retained by the authorities.

3. To register in the National Registry of Aliens in the ministry with competence in the matter, within the following 30 days of their arrival, when entering the territory of the Republic as temporary migrant or acquiring the category of permanent migrant.

4. To file, before the civil authority corresponding to his/her place of domicile, the certifications relative to the marital status duly legalized or with the respective *apostille*, his/hers as well as the family information, and particularly of any change of domicile or residence when the matter is about aliens located in the categories of temporal and permanent migrants.

5. To keep the visas or any other document, authorizing his permanence in the territory of the Republic, in force.

6. To appear before the competent authority in the time lapse fixed for the citation.

IV. THE DISCIPLINARY ADMINISTRATIVE REGIME

1. Administrative Sanctions

Any failure by aliens to comply with the obligations foreseen in the Foreigners and Migrants Statute, as stated in article 35, can be sanctioned by the Ministry of the Interior, applying the following sanctions: admonishment, fines or the deportation from the territory of the Republic. For such purpose, a 72 hour long pleading hearing must be opened in every case, in order to determine the type of sanction applicable according to the seriousness or recurrence of the infringement.

The person sanctioned by any of these measures has a period of 5 working days to file recourses, exceptions and defenses according to the Organic Statute of Administrative Procedures.

A. The fines

The fines that can be imposed upon aliens, as listed in article 36, are the following:

> 1. To aliens who fails to fulfill the duty of registering in the National Registry of Aliens and of making the respective participations to authorities in the terms contained in article 14 of the Statute, a fine of ten tributary units (10 U.T.).
>
> 2. To natural persons or corporations referred to in articles 24, 25 and 26 of the Statute, who infringe the obligations to inform about aliens there foreseen, a fine of fifty tributary units (50 U.T.).
>
> 3. To any employer who hires illegal aliens for the rendering of a determined service, a fine of two hundred tributary units (200 U.T.).

Once the respective fines are imposed, the offender must make its payment within the 8 following days of the notification of the decision. After said period has expired, in case of it's failing to comply, the procedure foreseen in the Organic Tax Code must be applied (art. 37).

B. Deportation and expulsion of aliens

Among the sanctions that can be imposed upon aliens, the Statute distinguishes between the deportation and the expulsion of aliens.

The deportation from the territory of the Republic can be imposed according to article 38 of the stature, to aliens who incur in any of the following offenses:

1. Those who enter and remain in the territory of the Republic without the correspondent visa.

2. Those who have entered the territory of the Republic to perform activities submitted to the labor authorization and fail to comply with said requirement.

3. Those who fail to comply with the obligation of renovating the visa within the lapse established by the Regulations of this Statute.

4. Alien workers (female and male) who perform activities different from those they were hired for and in a different jurisdiction from the one they were authorized for.

5. Those who have been fined twice or more times by the competent authority in matters of aliens and migration, and refuse to pay for it.

Regarding expulsion from the territory of the Republic, according to article 39 of the Statute, this sanction can be imposed upon aliens in following cases:

1. Those who have obtained or renovated the visa authorizing their entrance or permanence in the territory of the Republic in defraudation to the law.

2. Those dedicated to the production, distribution or possession of drugs and psychotropic substances or other related activities.

3. Those who, while legally in the territory of the Republic, propitiate the legal or illegal entrance of other aliens under false promises of work contracts, visas or work authorizations.

4. Those who compromises the security and defense of the Nation, alters the public order or is incurred in crimes against Human rights, Humanitarian International Law or against the dispositions content in international instruments of which the Republic is part of.

According to article 40 of the Statute any authority that has knowledge of an alien incurring in any of the deportation or expulsion situations, have the duty of notifying the Ministry of the Interior and Justice, without delays, in order to begin the corresponding administrative procedure.

2. The procedure

A. The opening of the administrative procedure

For the imposition of the sanctions of deportation or expulsion, the Ministry of the Interior and Justice can proceed *ex officio* or at the denunciation of anybody (article 41).

Once the competent authority within the Ministry of the Interior and Justice has the knowledge of an alien incurring in any of the situations for deportation or expulsion, it must formally order the opening of the corresponding administrative procedure, which must be informed to the interested alien within 48 hours following the opening of the said procedure, following the notification rules established in the Organic Statute of Administrative Procedures.

According to article 42, said notifications must clearly indicate the facts motivating these proceedings, as well as the alien's right to have access to the administrative file and of having the time he considers necessary to examine it, for what he can be assisted by a lawyer of his trust.

B. The precautionary measures

The competent authority of the Ministry, in the order to guaranty the eventual execution of the measure of deportation or expulsion, when opening the respective administrative procedure, can impose the alien subjected to the procedure of deportation or expulsion, the following precautionary measures established in article 46 of the Statute:

1. Periodical presentations before the competent authority in matters of aliens and migration.

2. Prohibition of leaving the location in which he resides without the corresponding authorization.

3. Presentation of an adequate monetary bail; for this, the economic status of the alien must be taken into consideration.

4. Move to a determined location while the administrative procedure lasts.

5. Any other measure that seems pertinent in order to guarantee the fulfillment of the decision of the competent authority, as long as said measure does not involve depravation or restriction of the right for personal freedom.

The imposition of these precautionary measures cannot exceed 30 days, starting from the date of the decision.

C. The oral hearing before the competent authority

In the same opening order of the aforementioned administrative procedure, the competent authority must order the notification of the interested alien, who must appear before it on the third working day following his notification, in order to participate in the oral hearing and file his plea for his defense, for which he would dispose of all the evidence means he considers necessary (article 43). This oral hearing can be postponed for up to three working days when requested by the interested alien in duly motivated petition.

In the oral hearing, the interested alien may be assisted by a lawyer of his trust; and an interpreter will be assigned to him/her in case he/she does not speak Spanish or cannot communicate verbally.

If in the public hearing the interested alien request to be recognized in a refugee condition, the matter must handle according to the procedure established by the Organic Statute of Refugees.

D. The Administrative Decision

After the aforementioned oral hearing has been terminated and within the following 72 hours of its celebration, the competent authority must decide on the matter, in writing and through a duly motivated administrative act, issued according to the provisions of the Organic Statute of Administrative Procedures (article 44), in which the term for its compliance must be indicated (article 50).

The decision for deportation or expulsion ought to be notified to the interested alien within the following 24 hours; it must contain the complete text of the administrative act indicating the recourses that can be filed against it, the lapse to file it and the entities or courts before which they must be introduced.

The interested alien can file a hierarchic recourse before the Ministry of the Interior and Justice within the following 5 working days of the decision; the Ministry must decide through motivated administrative action during the following 2 working days of its mediation (article 45 of the Statute).

The administrative decision ordering the deportation or expulsion of aliens, must determine a term for its fulfillment or execution, which can only begin once all the administrative or judicial recourses have been exhausted. After such exhaustion, the deportation or expulsion measure can be considered final (article 44).

In case of failure in the fulfillment of the term fixed in the deportation or expulsion administrative measure (art. 50) to abandon the territory of the Republic, the alien must be taken to the departure Terminal enabled for this purpose where the competent authority must make the expulsion effective (art. 50).

3. The administrative consequence of the deportation or expulsion measure

The main legal effect of the order of deportation and expulsion of aliens issued by the Ministry of the Interior and Justice is that through motivated Resolution, it must revoke their visa or document of entry or permanence in the territory of the Republic (article 48).

4. Rights of aliens in deportation or expulsion cases

A. The right to move acquired possessions

Aliens subjected to deportation or expulsion measures who possess legally acquired goods, have a one-year time period –starting from the date the measure is final– to move and place them safe. Said transportation can be made by themselves or through a representative or attorney duly authorized by authenticated document (article 47).

B. The right to receive labor benefits

According to article 49 of the Statute, alien workers subjected to deportation or expulsion measures have the right to perceive the salaries, social services and all the benefits established in the Statute regulating the Labor Relations, collective trade unions instruments and other social laws applicable about the labor relation.

V. THE CRIMINAL OFFENCES AND RESPONSIBILITY SYSTEMS

1. The offences

The following offences have been regulated in the Statute governing aliens and migration:

First, the offence of facilitating the illegal entry, established in article 52, according to which every person who facilitates or allows the illegal entry of aliens (female and male) into the territory of the Republic can be punished with a prison sentence of 4 to 8 years.

Second, the offence of facilitating the illegal entry in the case of public officials, in which case, article 59 of the Statute states that the public official or police or military authority who, for any reason, favors or induces, by action or omission, the entrance or departure of people from the territory of the Republic either clandestine or by fraud of the migratory control established in our legal system, will be penalized with a prison sentence of 4 to 8 years, and will not be able to perform any function in the Public Administration for 10 years.

Third, the offence of alien labor exploitation, established in article 53 of the Statute, according to which a prison sentence of 4 to 8 years can be given to "those who hire aliens (female and male) whose permanence in the territory of the Republic is illegal, in order to exploit them as workforce in conditions that might harm, suppress or limit the labor rights recognized by legal dispositions, collective agreements or individual contracts". The same punishment must be given to the individual who by simulating a contract or collocation, or by a similar deception, determines or favors the migration of a person to another country.

Forth, the offence of illicit immigration, established in article 55 of the Statute, which states that everyone who promotes or favors by any mean the illicit immigration of aliens into the territory of the Republic will be punished with a prison sentence of 4 to 8 years.

Fifth, the offence of illegal traffic of people, established in article 56 of the Statute, according to which a punishment of a 4 to 8 year long prison sentence will be given to the natural person and the representatives of the corporation who, by action or omission, promote or mediate in the illegal traffic of people in transit or with destination in the territory of the Republic. Article 57 of the Statute establishes, as aggravating circumstance, when those who perform these conducts obtain profit from it or using violence, intimidation, deceit or by taking advantage of the need situation of the victim, his/her gender or vulnerable groups, will be punished with a prison sentence of 8 to 10 years.

Likewise, for all the offences aforementioned (articles 52, 53, 54, 55, 56), article 58 of the Statute states that the corresponding sentences will be augmented in their halves superior, when in the perpetration of the events, the life, health or integrity of the persons or victim is placed in jeopardy.

2. Criminal responsibility of corporations

According to article 54 of the Statute, when the events foreseen in articles 52 (offence of facilitating of illegal entry) and 53 (offence of alien labor exploitation) of the Statute were imputed to corporations, the sentence must be imposed to the administrators or people in charge of the service who had been responsible of them and who in knowledge and been able to solve it, did nothing to do so.

PART NINE

JUDICIAL REVIEW OF ADMINISTRATIVE ACTION AND THE PROBLEM OF THE LACK OF INDEPENDENCE OF THE JUDICIARY

I. CONSTITUTIONAL JURISDICTION AND CONTENTIOUS ADMINISTRATIVE JURISDICTION

The formal consolidation in the Constitution of the principles of the rule of law (*Estado de Derecho*), following the general trends of modern constitutionalism, has led to the reinforcement in the Constitution not only of the aforementioned principle of its supremacy, considered as the foundation of the juridical order (Article 7), but also of various judicial means in order to guarantee such supremacy. In this regard, the 1999 Constitution follows a long tradition on the matter and the general trends already set forth in the previous 1961 Constitution,[1] by establishing a system of judicial review of the constitutionality of legislation and State acts issued in direct execution of the Constitution attributed to the Supreme Tribunal of Justice (Constitutional Jurisdiction); a specific means for the judicial protection of human rights, known as the *amparo* action or recourse; and a system of judicial review of administrative action, attributed to the Contentious Administrative Jurisdiction.

Regarding judicial review of constitutionality, Article 334 of the Constitution provides for the diffuse method of judicial review allowing any court to apply the Constitution in any case of incompatibility between its provisions and a statute.

In addition to the diffuse method, in Venezuela there also exists the concentrated method of judicial review being attributed to the Supreme Tribunal of Justice, as Constitutional Jurisdiction, exercised by its Constitutional Chamber, which has the exclusive powers to declare the nullity of statutes and other State acts issued in direct and immediate execution of the Constitution, or that have the force of law (Article 334)., like the decree laws, the acts of government, and the Parliamentary acts without the form of statute.

---

1. See *Allan R. Brewer-Carías, Instituciones Políticas y Constitucionales, vol VI: La Justicia Constitucional* (San Cristóbal-Caracas: Universidad Católica del Táchira, Editorial Jurídica Venezolana, 1998); *Estado de Derecho y Control Judicial* (Madrid: Instituto de Administración Pública, 1985); *Judicial Review in Comparative Law* (Cambridge: Cambridge University Press, 1989); *El Sistema de Justicia Constitucional en la Constitución de 1999: Comentarios sobre su desarrollo jurisprudencial y su explicación a veces errada, en la Exposición de Motivos* (Caracas: Editorial Jurídica Venezolana, 2000); *Justicia Constitucional. Procesos y Procedimienos constitucionales* (México: Ed. Porrúa, 2007).

Administrative acts, are subjected to judicial review through the Contentious Administrative Jurisdiction, and the court decisions (sentencias) are subjected to judicial review through the ordinary appeals and extraordinary recourses like the cassation recourse.

II. PRINCIPLES REGARDING THE ADMINISTRATIVE CONTENTIOUS JURISDICTION

The most important consequence of the rule of law and of the principle of legality applied to Public Administration is the possibility to for the citizens and any interested party to control de activity of Public Administration and to subject to judicial review administrative acts.

For such purpose, the 1999 Constitution has established the Administrative Contentious Jurisdiction *(Jurisdicción contenciosa administrativa*) (Article 259) in order to assure the judicial review of administrative action, attributed to various courts integrated in the general organization of the Judiciary.

With this constitutional provision the Constitution adopted the judicial system regarding the Judicial review of Administrative Action (Contentious Administrative) Jurisdiction, departing from the French model and reaffirming the traditional tendency in the national legislation to assign to the Judicial Branch the power to control the legality of administrative acts. [2]

The difference between the "Constitutional Jurisdiction" attributed to the Constitutional Chamber of the Supreme Court of Justice, and the "Administrative Contentious Jurisdiction" attributed to the Politico Administrative and Electoral Chambers of the Supreme Tribunal and to other special courts for judicial review of administrative actions, resides on the State's acts subjected to control: The

---

2. *See* Luis Torrealba Narváez, "Consideraciones acerca de la Jurisdicción Contencioso Administrativa, su Procedimiento y Algunas Relaciones de éste con el de la Jurisdicción Judicial Civil", in *Anales de la Facultad de Derecho,* Universidad Central de Venezuela, Caracas, 1951; Hildegard Rondón de Sansó, *El Sistema Contencioso administrativo de la Carrera Administrativa. Instituciones, Procedimiento y Jurisprudencia,* Ediciones Magón, Caracas, 1974; José Araujo Juárez, José, *Derecho Procesal Administrativo,* Vadell Hermanos editores, Caracas, 1996; Allan R. Brewer–Carías, *Instituciones Fundamentales del Derecho Administrativo y la Jurisprudencia Venezolana*, Universidad Cenbtral de Venezuela, Caracas 1964, pp. 451 ff.; *Estado de derecho y Control Judicial,* Madrid, 1985, pp. 281 ff., and *Contencioso Administrativo,* Vol. VII of *Instituciones Políticas y Constitucionales,* Editorial Jurídica Venezolana, Caracas-San Cristóbal, 1997; Antonio Canova González, *Reflexiones para la reforma del sistema contencioso administrativo venezolano,* Editorial Sherwood, Caracas, 1998. See also, *El Control Jurisdiccional de los Poderes Públicos en Venezuela,* Instituto de Derecho Público, Facultad de Ciencias Jurídicas y Políticas, Universidad Central de Venezuela, Caracas, 1979; *Contencioso Administrativo en Venezuela,* Editorial Jurídica Venezolana, tercera edición, Caracas, 1993; *Derecho Procesal Administrativo,* Vadell Hermanos editores, Caracas, 1997; *8ª Jornadas "J.M. Domínguez Escovar" (Enero 1983), Tendencias de la jurisprudencia venezolana en materia contencioso administrativa,* Facultad de Ciencias Jurídicas y Políticas, U.C.V., Corte Suprema de Justicia; Instituto de Estudios Jurídicos del Estado Lara, Tip. Pregón, Caracas, 1983; *Contencioso Administrativo, I Jornadas de Derecho Administrativo Allan Randolph Brewer-Carías,* Funeda, Caracas, 1995; *XVIII Jornadas "J.M. Domínguez Escovar, Avances jurisprudenciales del contencioso– administrativo en Venezuela,* 2 Tomos, Instituto de Estudios Jurídicos del Estado Lara, Diario de Tribunales Editores, S.R.L. Barquisimeto, 1993.

Constitutional Jurisdiction is in charge of annulling unconstitutional statutes and other acts of similar rank or issued in direct and immediate execution of the Constitution; and the Administrative Contentious Jurisdiction is in charge of annulling unconstitutional or illegal administrative acts or regulations, with general *erga omnes* effects.

The courts of this Jurisdiction have the power to annul general and individual administrative acts when contrary to the legal order, including those issued with abuse of public power (*desviación de poder*). They are also competent to order the State to pay sums of money, and to repair injuries or damages caused by the Administration, to hear claims concerning the rendering of public services, and to rule as necessary to re-establish subjective legal rights affected by administrative acts (Article 259).

Regarding the standing to challenge administrative acts on the grounds of unconstitutionality and illegality, when referring to normative administrative acts or regulations, anybody can bring an action before the court by means of the popular action of nullity. Consequently, a simple interest in the legality or constitutionality is enough for any citizen to be sufficiently entitled to raise the nullity action for unconstitutionality or illegality against regulations and other normative administrative acts. This simple interest has been defined, as "the general right granted by law upon every citizen to access the competent courts to raise the nullity of an unconstitutional or illegal administrative general act."[3]

As to the administrative acts of particular effects, the standing to challenge such acts before the Administrative Jurisdiction courts corresponds solely to those who have a personal, legitimate and direct interest in the annulment of the act (Article 5, Law). This has been the general rule on the matter even though some decisions have been issued by the Politico-Administrative Chamber of the Supreme Tribunal, giving standing to any person with only a legitimate interest.[4]

Additionally, in the case of the Administrative Jurisdiction, even before the new Constitution took effect in 1999, the possibility of protecting collective interests was also made available. In particular, it is now widely accepted that a collective or diffuse right exists against city-planning acts.

Nonetheless, despite very impressive advances regarding judicial review of administrative actions experienced in the past decades, due to the political control of the Judiciary during the past seven years, the role of the Administrative Jurisdiction in controlling Public Administration has dramatically diminished in Venezuela, affecting the rule of law.[5]

---

3. See decision of the First Administrative Court dated Mar. 22, 2000, case: *Banco de Venezolano de Crédito v. Superintendencia de Bancos, Revista de Derecho Público*, N° 81, Editorial Jurídica Venezolana, Caracas 2000, pp. 452-53.

4. See decision of the Supreme Court of Justice in Political-Administrative Chamber of April 13, 2000, case: *Banco Fivenez vs. Junta de Emergencia Financiera, Revista de Derecho Público*, N° 82, Editorial Jurídica Venezolana, Caracas, 2000, pp. 582-83.

5. See Allan R. Brewer-Carías, "La progresiva y sistemática demolición institucional de la autonomía e independencia del Poder Judicial en Venezuela 1999-2004", in *XXX Jornadas J.M Dominguez Escovar, Estado de derecho, Administración de justicia y derechos humanos*, Instituto de Estudios Jurídicos del Estado Lara, Barquisimeto, 2005, pp. 33-174.

The procedure and organization of the Administrative Contentious Jurisdiction, since 1976 up to 2010, was transitorily regulated in the statute referred to the Supreme Tribunal: first, by the 1976 Organic Law of the Supreme Court of Justice in 1976,[6] and after the sanctioning of the 1999 Constitution by the 2004 Organic Law of the Supreme Tribunal of Justice. In the latter, regarding the organization of the Jurisdiction, it was attributed to the Politico Administrative Chamber of the Supreme Tribunal, to the First and Second Administrative Contentious Courts and to eight Superior Courts on Administrative Contentious. In addition, other special statutes attributed to other courts with special aspects of the Administrative Contentious Jurisdiction, as had happened with the Taxation Superior Courts for the taxation contentious recourses; and with the Agrarian Superior Courts, with the agrarian contentious actions.

In any case, the transitory regime was substituted in 2010 by the Organic Law on the Administrative Contentious Jurisdiction[7] in which the judicial competence on the matter was distributed among the Politico-Administrative Chamber of the Supreme Tribunal, and the National Tribunals, the States Tribunals and the Municipal Tribunals of Administrative Contentious Jurisdiction.

The Constitution assigns to the Politico Administrative Chamber of the Supreme Tribunal exclusive jurisdiction to totally or partially annul Executive regulations and other general or individual administrative acts issued by the National Executive; to decide administrative controversies between the Republic, a State, a Municipality and other public entities, when the other party involved is one of them, except controversies between Municipalities that can be attributed to other courts; and to decide recourses of interpretation of statutes (Article 266,5). Consequently, competencies to decide actions challenging administrative acts of the states and of the municipalities and any other public corporations of entity are assigned to the other courts of the Jurisdiction.

According to the provision of Article 259 of the Constitution, the Administrative Contentious Jurisdiction in Venezuela is governed by the following general principles: [8]

First, the universal character of the judicial control of constitutionality and illegality exercised over any regulations and administrative acts, which means that it is made without exception regarding the challenged act and no matter the motive of the challenging action. The Constitution allows the challenging of those acts when "contrary to the law."

Second, the multiplicity of recourses or means of actions to be filed against administrative acts seeking to nullify unconstitutional or illegal executive regulations and administrative acts, to which it must be added those recourses of

6 Organic Law Supeme Court of Justice, *Official Gazette* N° 1.893, Extra, of July 30, 1976. See Allan R. Brewer-Carías and Josefina Calcaño de Temeltas, *Ley Orgánica de la Corte Suprema de Justicia*, Editorial Jurídica Venezolana, Caracas 1994.

7. See *in Gaceta Oficial* N° 39.451 of 22 Jun. 2010. See Allan R. Brewer-Carías y Víctor Hernández Mendible, *Ley Orgánica de la Jurisdicción Contencioso Administrativa* (Caracas: Editorial Jurídica Venezolana, 2010).

8 See Allan R. Brewer-Carías, *Nuevas Tendencias en el Contencioso Administrativo en Venezuela*, Editorial Jurídica Venezolana, Caracas, 1993.

amparo seeking to obtain constitutional protection of human rights violated by the challenged administrative act; the actions against administrative omissions particularly regarding responses to administrative petitions; the recourse of interpretation of statutes; the various actions that can be filed against Public Administration seeking liability and compensation for damages caused by its functioning; the recourse for the solution of administrative conflicts between public entities; the recourses for the solution of conflicts regarding public contracts, whether between the parties to the contracts or in cases of actions filed by any interested person seeking the annulment of public contracts; and the actions filed because of the malfunctioning of public services.

Third, the broad and extended power of control assigned to the administrative contentious judges of extended powers of control, not only to annul administrative acts, but to decide on the various subjective rights or interests that the individuals could have regarding Public Administration.

Consequently, the administrative contentious system in Venezuela has not only been conceived as an objective process against administrative acts, but also as a subjective process for the protection of personal subjective rights and interest of persons regarding Public Administration, including the protection of fundamental rights. That is why administrative contentious judges not only have power to annul administrative acts, but to restore subjective individual situations harmed by administrative authorities.

Nonetheless, and unfortunately, the authoritarian regime installed in the country since 1999, in practice, due to the political control of the courts, has neutralized the possibility of judicial control of administrative action, to the point that only a very small percentage of cases have been decided condemning the State or annulling illegal administrative acts. [9]

III. PRINCIPLES REGARDING THE "AMPARO" PROCEEDING FOR THE PROTECTION OF FUNDAMENTAL RIGHTS AGAINST ADMINISTRATIVE ACTION

The amparo proceeding is an extraordinary judicial remedy specifically conceived for the protection of constitutional rights against harms or threats inflicted by authorities or individuals. It is a Latin American procedural mean for constitutional litigation that normally concludes with a judicial order or writ of protection (*amparo, protección* or *tutela*), that has been indistinctly called as action, recourse or suit of amparo.[10]

---

9 See Antonio Canova González, *La realidad del contencioso administrativo venezolano (Un llamado de atención frente a las desoladoras estadísticas de la Sala Político Administrativa en 2007 y primer semestre de 2008)*, (Caracas, Funeda, 2008).

10 See Héctor Fix-Zamudio and Eduardo Ferrer Mac-Gregor (Coord.), *El derecho de amparo en el mundo*, Edit. Porrúa, México, 2006; Allan R. Brewer-Carías, *El amparo a los derechos y libertades constitucionales. Una aproximación comparativa*, Cuadernos de la Cátedra de Derecho Público, N° 1, Universidad Católica del Táchira, San Cristóbal, 1993, 138 pp.; also published by the Inter-American Institute on Human Rights, (Interdisciplinary Course), San José, 1993 (mimeo), 120 pp. and in *La protección jurídica del ciudadano. Estudios en Homenaje al Profesor Jesús González Pérez*, Tomo 3, Editorial Civitas, Madrid, 1993, pp. 2.695–2.740; and Allan R.

This constitutional litigation mean was introduced in the American Continent during the nineteenth century, and although similar remedies were established in the twentieth century in some European countries, like Austria, Germany, Spain and Switzerland, and also in Canada, it has been adopted by all Latin American countries, except in Cuba, being considered as one of the most distinguishable features of Latin American constitutional law.[11] As such, it has influenced the introduction of a similar remedy in the Philippines, the writ of amparo, which was created by the Supreme Court in 2007.[12]

This specific remedy provided for the protection of fundamental rights contrasts with the constitutional system of the United States, where the effective protection of human rights is effectively assured, following the British procedural law tradition, through the general judicial actions and equitable remedies, particularly the injunctions, which are also used to protect any other kind of personal or property rights or interests.

The amparo proceeding was first introduced in Mexico in 1857 as the *juicio de amparo*, evolving in that country into a unique and very complex institution exclusively found in Mexico, not only designed to guaranty judicial protection of constitutional guarantees against the State acts or actions, but to perform multipurpose judicial roles, including actions and procedures that in all other countries are separated processes, like judicial review, cassation review and judicial review of administrative actions.

In the rest of Latin America the amparo gave rise to a very different specific judicial remedy established with the *exclusive* purpose of protecting human rights and freedoms, becoming in many cases more protective than the original Mexican institution; being named in various ways, always meaning the same, as follows: *Amparo* (Guatemala); *Acción de amparo* (Argentina, Ecuador, Honduras, Paraguay, Uruguay, Dominican Republic, Venezuela); *Acción de tutela* (Colombia); *Proceso de amparo* (El Salvador, Peru); *Recurso de amparo* (Bolivia, Costa Rica, Nicaragua, Panama); *Recurso de protección* (Chile) or *Mandado de segurança* and *mandado de injunçao* (Brazil).[13] In all of the Latin American countries, the provisions for the action are embodied in the constitutions; and in all of them, except Chile, the actions

---

Brewer-Carías, *Mecanismos nacionales de protección de los derechos humanos (Garantías judiciales de los derechos humanos en el derecho constitucional comparado latinoamericano)*, Instituto Interamericano de Derechos Humanos, San José, 2005. See also "The Amparo Proceeding In Venezuela: Constitutional Litigation and Procedural Protection of Constitutional Rights and Guarantees, in *Duquesne Law Review*, Volume 49, Spring 2011, Pittsburgh, pp. 161-241.

11 See in general, Allan R. Brewer-Carías, *Constitutional Protection of Human Rights in Latin America. A Comparative Study of the Amparo Proceedings*, Cambridge University Press, New York 2009.

12 See, in general, Allan R. Brewer-Carías, "The Latin American Amparo Proceeding and the Writ of Amparo in The Philippines," en *City University of Hong Kong Law Review,* Volume 1:1 October 2009, pp 73–90.

13 See, in general, Allan R. Brewer-Carías, *El amparo a los derechos y garantías constitucionales (una aproximación comparativa)*, Caracas, 1993; Eduardo Ferrer Mac-Gregor, "Breves notas sobre el amparo latinoamericano (desde el derecho procesal constitucional comparado)," in Héctor Fix-Zamudio and Eduardo Ferrer Mac-Gregor, *El derecho de amparo en el mundo*, Edit. Porrúa, México, 2006, pp. 3–39.

of amparo have been expressly regulated by statutes; particularly in special statutes related to constitutional litigations, with the exception of Panama and Paraguay where the amparo action is regulated in the general procedural codes (*Código Judicial, Código Procesal Civil)*).

1. Right to Amparo in Venezuela

Since 1961, the Venezuelan Constitution establishes a "constitutional right for amparo" or to be protected by the courts,[14] that everybody have for the protection of all the rights, freedoms and guarantees enshrined in the constitution and in international treaties, or which, even if not listed in the text, are inherent to the human person. The constitution does not set forth a separate action of habeas corpus for the protection of personal freedom and liberty (habeas corpus); instead it establishes that the action for amparo is also set forth for the protection of personal freedom or safety that can be exercised by any person in which cases "the detainee shall be immediately transferred to the court, without delay."

Additionally, the Venezuelan Constitution has also set forth the habeas data recourse, in order to guarantee the right to have access to the information and data concerning the claimant, contained in official or private registries, as well as to know about the use that has been made of such information and about its purpose, and to petition the competent court for the updating, rectification or destruction of erroneous records and those that unlawfully affect the petitioner's right (Article 28).

The amparo proceeding, has been regulated in the Organic Law on Amparo for the protection of constitutional rights and guaranties that was sanctioned in 1988 (*Ley Orgánica de Amparo sobre derechos y garantías constitucionales*).[15] According to its provisions, the right to amparo can be exercised through an "autonomous action for amparo"[16] that in general is filed before the first instance courts[17] (Article 7 Amparo

14 Article 49 of the 1961 Constitution, and Article 27 of the 1999 Constitution. See on the action of amparo in Venezuela, in general, see Gustavo Briceño V., *Comentarios a la Ley de Amparo*, Editorial Kinesis, Caracas, 1991; Rafael J. Chavero Gazdik, *El nuevo régimen del amparo constitucional en Venezuela*, Editorial Sherwood, Caracas, 2001; Gustavo José Linares Benzo, *El Proceso de Amparo*, Universidad Central de Venezuela, Facultad de Ciencias Jurídicas y Políticas, Caracas, 1999; Hildegard Rondón De Sansó, *Amparo Constitucional*, Caracas, 1988; Hildegard Rondón De Sansó, *La acción de amparo contra los poderes públicos*, Editorial Arte, Caracas, 1994; Carlos M. Ayala Corao and Rafael J. Chavero Gazidk, "El amparo constitucional en Venezuela," in Héctor Fix-Zamudio and Eduardo Ferrer Mac-Gregor (Coord.), *El derecho de amparo en el mundo*, Universidad Nacional Autónoma de México, Editorial Porrúa, México, 2006, pp. 649–692.

15 See *Official Gazette* N° 33.891 of January 22, 1988. See Allan R. Brewer-Carías, Carlos M. Ayala Corao and Rafael Chavero G., *Ley Orgánica de Amparo sobre Derechos y Garantías Constitucionales*, Caracas, 2007. See also Allan R. Brewer-Carías, *Instituciones Políticas y Constitucionales, Tomo V, El derecho y la acción de amparo*, Editorial Jurídica Venezolana, Caracas, 1998, pp. 163 ff.; Hildegard Rondón de Sansó, *Amparo constitucional*, Caracas, 1988; Gustavo J. Linares Benzo, *El proceso de amparo*, Universidad Central de Venezuela, Caracas, 1999; Rafael J. Chavero Gazdik, *El Nuevo regimen del amparo constitucional en Venezuela*, Editorial Sherwood, Caracas, 2001; Carlos Ayala Corao and Rafael Chavero G., "El amparo constitucional en Venezuela," in Héctor Fix-Zamudio and Eduardo Ferrer Mac-Gregor, *Idem,* Edit. Porrúa, México, 2006, pp. 649–692.

16 See Allan R. Brewer-Carías, "El derecho de amparo y la acción de amparo," in *Revista de Derecho Público*, n° 22, Editorial Jurídica Venezolana, Caracas, 1985, pp. 51 ff.

Law), whit a re-establishing nature, in general regarding flagrant, vulgar, direct and immediate constitutional harm upon the plaintiff's rights. The constitutional protection can also be claimed by means of other preexisting ordinary or extraordinary legal actions or recourses already established in the legal system to which an amparo petition is joined. This can be, the popular action of unconstitutionality of statutes; the judicial review of administrative actions' recourses; and the any other "ordinary judicial procedures" or "preexisting judicial means," through which the "violation or threat of violation of a constitutional right or guaranty may be alleged." In these cases, in which the competent judge is empowered to immediately reestablish the infringed legal situation, it is not that the ordinary means substitute the constitutional right of protection (or diminish it), but that they can serve as the judicial mean for constitutional litigation because the judge is empowered to protect fundamental rights and immediately reestablish the infringed legal situation.[18]

From these regulations it results that the Venezuelan right for amparo, has certain peculiarities that distinguish it from the other similar institutions for the protection of the constitutional rights and guaranties established in Latin America.[19] Besides the adjective consequences of the amparo being a constitutional right, in Venezuela it can be characterized by the following trends:

First, the right of amparo can be exercised for the protection of all constitutional rights, not only of civil individual rights. Consequently, the social, economic, cultural, environmental and political rights declared in the constitution and in international treaties are also protected by means of amparo. The habeas corpus is an aspect of the right to constitutional protection, or one of the expressions of the amparo.

Second, the right to amparo seeks to assure protection of constitutional rights and guaranties against any disturbance in their enjoyment and exercise, whether originated by public authorities or by private individuals without distinction. In addition, in the case of disturbance by public authorities, the amparo is admissible

---

17According to Article 7 of the Organic Law on Amparo, the competent courts to decide amparo actions are the courts of First Instance with competent on matters related to the constitutional rights or guaranties violated, in the place where the facts, acts or omission have occurred. Regarding amparo of personal freedom and security, the competent courts should be the criminal first instance courts (Article 40). Nonetheless, when the facts, acts or omissions harming or threatening to harm the constitutional right or guaranty occurs in a place where no First Instance court exists, the amparo action may be brought before and any judge of the site, which must decide according to the law, and in a twenty-four hour delay it must send the files for consultation to the competent First Instance court (Article 9). Only in cases in which facts, acts or omissions of the President of the Republic, his Cabinet members, the National Electoral Council, the Prosecutor General, the Attorney General and the General Comptroller of the Republic are involved does the power to decide the amparo actions correspond to the Constitutional Chamber of the Supreme Tribunal of Justice (Article 8).

18 Allan R. Brewer-Carías, "La reciente evolución jurisprudencial en relación a la admisibilidad del recurso de amparo," in *Revista de derecho público*, N° 19, Caracas, 1984, pp. 207–218.

19 See, in general, H. Fix-Zamudio, *La protección procesal de los derechos humanos ante las jurisdicciones nacionales*, Madrid, 1982, p. 366.

against statutes; against legislative, administrative and judicial acts; and against material or factual courses of action of Public Administration or public officials.

Third, the decision of the judge, as a consequence of the exercise of this right to amparo, whether through the preexisting actions or recourses or by means of the autonomous action for amparo, is not limited to be of a precautionary or preliminary nature, but to reestablish the infringed legal situation by deciding on the merits, that is, the constitutionality of the alleged disturbance of the constitutional right.

Fourth, because the Venezuelan system of judicial review is a mixed one, judicial review of legislation can also be exercised by the courts when deciding action for amparo when, for instance, the alleged violation of the right is based on a statute deemed unconstitutional. In such cases, if the protection requested is granted by the courts, it must previously declare the statute inapplicable on the grounds of it being unconstitutional. Therefore, in such cases, judicial review of the constitutionality of legislation can also be exercised when an action for amparo of fundamental rights is filed.

Finally, in the Venezuelan systems of judicial review and of amparo, according to the 1999 Constitution, an extraordinary review recourse can be filed before the Constitutional Chamber of the Supreme Court against judicial final decisions issued in amparo proceedings, and also by any court when applying the diffuse method of judicial review resolving the inapplicability of statutes because they are considered unconstitutional (Article 336,10).

Following these main general trends, I will analyze the amparo proceeding in Venezuela, specifically when is used for the protection of constitutional rights against administrative actions, studying the rules regarding the injured party; the justiciable rights; the conditions of the injury; the reparable character of harms and the restorative character of amparo; the imminent character of threats and preventive character of the amparo; the injuring party; the conditions of the injuring public actions and omissions; the admissibility condition and the extraordinary condition of the action; the rules of procedure; the preliminary protective measures; and the final decision. In each case where it proceeds, I have made the corresponding comparisons with the civil right injunctions in the United States.

2. The injured party in the amparo proceeding

One of the most distinguishable principles regarding the amparo proceeding as an extraordinary judicial mean for the protection of constitutional rights is the principle of bilateralism, which implies the need for the existence of a controversy between two or more parties. The main consequence of this principle is that the amparo proceeding can only be initiated at a party's request, which excludes any case of *ex officio* amparo proceeding.

Consequently, in order to initiate this proceeding, an action must be brought before a court by a plaintiff as the injured party, against the injurer party or parties, who as defendants, must be called to the procedure as having caused the harm or the violation to the constitutional rights of the former.

The injured party, in principle is the person having the constitutional right that has been violated; a situation that gives him a particular interest in bringing the case before a court. That is why the amparo action has been considered as an action *in personam* (*personalísima*) through which, seeking for the protection of constitutional rights, the plaintiff must be precisely the injured or aggrieved person.

Because the action has a personal character (*acción personalísima*), the plaintiff, as the person whose constitutional rights have been injured or threatened of being harmed,[20] being the titleholder of the harmed or violated right,[21] is the injured party with justiciable interest in the subject matter of the litigation, which can be a natural person (citizens or foreigner), or an artificial person (associations, foundations, corporations or companies). For such purpose it can act directly *in personam* or through his representative.[22] Thus, nobody can file an action for amparo alleging in his own name a right belonging to another,[23] being the general exception the cases of actions of habeas corpus, in which case, because generally the injured person is physically prevented from acting personally because of detention or restrained freedom, the Amparo Law authorizes anybody to file the action on his behalf.[24]

On the other hand, as not all constitutional rights are individual, and on the contrary, some are collective by nature, in the sense that they correspond to a more or less defined group of persons, their violations affect not only the personal rights

---

20 See decisions of the former Venezuelan Supreme Court of Justice, Politico Administrative Chamber of June 18, 1992, in Revista *de Derecho Público* N° 50, Editorial Jurídica Venezolana, Caracas, 1992, p. 135; and of August 13, 1992, in Revista *de Derecho Público*, n° 51, Editorial Jurídica Venezolana, Caracas, 1992, p. 160.

21 Regarding injunctions in the U.S. it was ruled in *Parkview Hospital v. Com.*, Dept. of Public Welfare, 56 Pa. Commw. 218, 424 A. 2d 599 (1981) that to bring an action "requires an aggrieved party to show a substantial, direct, and immediate interest is the subject matter of the litigation." See the reference in Kevin Schroder *et al*, "Injunction," *Corpus Juris Secundum*, Thomson West, Volume 43A, 2004, p. 331, note 4. Or as ruled in *Warth v. Seldin*, 422 U.S. 4909, 498-500 (1975): the plaintiff must "allege such a personal stake in the outcome of the controversy" as to justify the exercise of the court's remedial powers on his behalf, because he himself has suffered "some threatened or actual injury resulting from the putatively illegal action." See M. Glenn Abernathy and Barbara A. Perry, *Civil Liberties Under the Constitution*, University of South Carolina Press, 1993, p. 4. That is why standing to seek injunctive relief in the United States is only attributed to the person affected. See *Alabama Power Co. v. Allabama Elec. Co-op., Inc.*, 394 F.2d 672 (5th Cir. 1968), in John Bourdeau *et al.*, "Injunctions," in Kevin Schroder, John Glenn and Maureen Placilla (Ed.), *Corpus Juris Secundum*, Vol. 43A, West 2004, p. 229.

22 As it was ruled by the former Supreme Court of Justice of Venezuela regarding the personal character of the amparo suit that imposes for its admissibility: "A qualified interest of who is asking for the restitution or reestablishment of the harmed right or guaranty, that is, that the harm be directed to him and that, eventually, its effects affect directly and indisputably upon him, harming his scope of subjective rights guaranteed in the Constitution. It is only the person that is specially and directly injured in his subjective fundamental rights by a specific act, fact or omission the one that can bring an action before the competent courts by mean of a brief and speedy proceeding, in order that the judge decides immediately the reestablishment of the infringed subjective legal situation." See decision of August 27, 1993 (*Kenet E. Leal* case), in *Revista de Derecho Público*, N° 55-56, Editorial Jurídica Venezolana, Caracas, 1993, p. 322; and decision of the Venezuelan First Court on Judicial review of administrative actions, November 18, 1993, in *Revista de Derecho Público*, N° 55–56, Editorial Jurídica Venezolana, Caracas, 1993, pp. 325–327.

23 See decision of the former Venezuelan Supreme Court of Justice, Politico Administrative Chamber, of February 14, 1990, in *Revista de Derecho Público*, N° 41, Editorial Jurídica Venezolana, Caracas, 1990, p. 101.

24 Venezuela (Article 39: anybody acting on his behalf.

of each of the individuals who enjoy them, but also, the whole group of persons or collectivity to which the individuals belongs. In these cases, the amparo action can also be filed by the group or the association of persons representing their associates, even if they do not have the formal character of an artificial person. For such purpose, the Venezuelan constitution expressly sets forth as part of the constitutional right of everybody to have access to justice, to seek for the enforcement not only of personal rights but also of "collective" and "diffuse" rights (Article 26).[25] This has been the case, for instance, of amparo actions filed for the protection of electoral rights, in which case, any citizen, invoking the general voters' rights, can file the action.[26] In other words, the Constitutional Chamber has admitted that: "Any capable person that tends to impede harm to the population or sectors of it to which he appertains, can file actions in defense of diffuse or collective interest," extending the "standing to the associations, societies, foundations, chambers, trade unions and other collective entities devoted to defend society, provided that they act within the limits of their societal goals referring to the protection of the interests of their members."[27]

In these cases, the Constitutional Chamber has determined the general conditions that the action filed must be based "not only on the personal right or interest of the claimant, but also on a common or collective right or interest."[28] Consequently, in these cases, a bond or relation must exist, "even if it is not a legal one, between

25 The Constitutional Chamber has referred to the diffuse and collective interests or rights as concepts established for the protection of a number of individuals that can be considered as representing the entire or an important part of a society, which are affected on their constitutional rights and guaranties destined to protect the public welfare by an attack to their quality of life. See decision of the Constitutional Chamber N° 656 of May 6, 2001, *Defensor del Pueblo vs. Comisión Legislativa Nacional* case, as referred in decision N° 379 of February 26, 2003, *Mireya Ripanti et vs. Presidente de Petróleos de Venezuela S.A. (PDVSA)* case, in *Revista de Derecho Público*, N° 93–96, Editorial Jurídica Venezolana, Caracas, 2003, pp. 152 ff.

26 In these cases, the Chamber has even granted precautionary measures with *erga omnes* effects "to both individuals and corporations who have brought to suit the constitutional protection, and to all voters as a group." See decision of the Constitutional Chamber N° 483 of May 29, 2000, *"Queremos Elegir" y otros* case, in *Revista de Derecho Público*, N° 82, 2000, Editorial Jurídica Venezolana, pp. 489–491. In the same sense, see the decision of the same Chamber N° 714 of July 13, 2000, *APRUM* case, in *Revista de Derecho Público*, N° 83, Editorial Jurídica Venezolana, Caracas, 2000, pp. 319 ff.

27 The Chamber added that: "Those who file actions regarding the defense of diffuse interest do not need to have any previously established relation with the offender, but has to act as a member of society, or of its general categories (consumers, users, etc.) and has to invoke his right or interest shared with the population's, because he participates with all regarding the harmed factual situation due to the noncompliance of the diminution of fundamental rights of everybody, which gives birth to a communal subjective right, that although indivisible, is actionable by any one place within the infringed situation." Decision of the Constitutional Chamber of June 30, 2000, *Defensoría del Pueblo* case. See also the reference and comments in Rafael Chavero, *El nuevo régimen del amparo constitucional en Venezuela*, Caracas, 2001, pp. 110–114.

28 That is, the reason of the claim or the action for amparo must be "the general damage to the quality of life of all the inhabitants of the country or parts of it, since the legal situation of all the members of the society or its groups have been damaged when their common quality of life was worsened"; thus the damage "concerns an indivisible right or interest that involves the entire population of the country or a group of it." See decision N° 1948 of February 17, 2000, *William O. Ojeda O. vs. Consejo Nacional Electoral* case.

whoever demands in the general interest of the society or a part of it (social common interest), and the damage or danger caused to the collectivity."[29]

These collective actions have some similarities with the civil rights class actions developed in the United States,[30] where they have been very effective for the protection of civil rights in cases of discrimination.[31]

---

29 See decision N° 1948 of February 17, 2000, *William O. Ojeda O. vs. Consejo Nacional Electoral* case. But in spite of all the aforementioned progressive decisions regarding the protection of collective and diffuse rights, like the political ones, in a recent decision dated November 21, 2005, the Venezuelan Constitutional Chamber has reverted its ruling, and in a case originated by a claim filed by the director of a political association named "Un Solo Pueblo" against the threat of violations of the political rights of the aforesaid political party and of all the other supporters of the calling of a recall referendum regarding the President of the Republic, the Chamber ruled that: "The action of amparo was filed for the protection of constitutional rights of an undetermined number of persons, whose identity was not indicated in the filing document, in which they are not included as claimants. It is the criteria of this Chamber, those that could result directly affected in their constitutional rights and guaranties by the alleged threat attributed to the Ministry of Defense and the General Commanders of the Army and the National Guard are, precisely, the persons that are members or supporters of "Un solo Pueblo," or those who prove they are part of one of the groups that promoted the recall referendum; in which case they would have standing to bring before the constitutional judge, by themselves or through representatives, seeking the reestablishment of the infringed juridical situation or impeding the realization of the threat, because the *legitimatio ad causam* exists in each one of them, not precisely as constitutionally harmed or aggrieved. Due to the foregoing, the Chamber considers that Mr. William Ojeda, who said he acted as Director of the political association called "Un Sólo Pueblo," a quality that he furthermore has not demonstrated, lacks the necessary standing to seek for constitutional amparo of the constitutional rights set forth in Articles 19, 21 and 68 of the constitution regarding the members, supporters and participants of the mentioned political association as well as the political coalition that proposed the recall referendum of the President of the Republic, and consequently, this Chamber declares the inadmissibility of the amparo action filed. See *Willian Ojeda vs. Ministro de la Defensa y los Comandantes Generales del Ejército y de la Guardia Nacional* Case, in *Revista de Derecho Público*, N° 104, Editorial Jurídica Venezolana, Caracas, 2005.

30 Regulated in the Rule 23 of the Federal Rules of Civil Procedure filed for the protection of civil rights, according to which, in cases of a class of persons whom have questions of law or fact common to the class, but have so many members that joining all of them would be an impracticable task, then the action can be filed by one or more of its members as representative plaintiff parties on behalf of all, provided that the claims of the representative parties are typical of the claims of the class and that such representative parties will fairly and adequately protect the interests of the class (Rule 23, Class Actions, a).

31 It was the case decided by the Supreme Court in *Zablocki, Milwaukee County Clerk v. Redhail* of January 18, 1978, 434 U.S. 374; 98 S. Ct. 673, 54 L. Ed. 2d 618, as a result of a class action brought before a federal court under 42 U.S.C.S. § 1983, by Wisconsin residents holding that the marriage prohibition set forth in Wisconsin State § 245.10 (1973) violated the equal protection clause, U.S. Constitution, fourteenth amendment. According to that statute, Wisconsin residents were prevented from marrying if they were behind in their child support obligations or if the children to whom they were obligated were likely to become public charges. The Court found that the statute violated equal protection in that it directly and substantially interfered with the fundamental right to marry without being closely tailored to effectuate the state's interests. Another Supreme Court decision, *Lau et al., v. Nichols et al.*, dated January 21, 1974, 414 U.S. 563; 94 S. Ct. 786; 39 L. Ed. 2d 1; 1974 also decided in favor of a class on discrimination violations. In the case, non-English-speaking students of Chinese ancestry brought a class suit in a federal court of California against officials of the San Francisco Unified School District, seeking relief against alleged unequal educational opportunities resulting from the officials' failure to

Although being of a personal character, even in cases of actions for the protection of collective and diffuse rights, the People's Defender created in Venezuela as an independent and autonomous separate branch of government for the protection of human rights,[32] have enough standing to file amparo actions on behalf of the community or of groups of persons,[33] for instance, in cases of the protection of indigenous people's rights, the right to the environment and the citizens' right to political participation.[34]

---

establish a program to rectify the students' language problem. The Supreme Court eventually held that the school district, which received federal financial assistance, violated dispositions that ban discrimination based on race, color, or national origin in any program or activity receiving federal financial assistance, and furthermore violated the implementing regulations of the Department of Health, Education, and Welfare by failing to establish a program to deal with the complaining students' language problem.

32 The 1999 Venezuelan Constitution, in this regard, establishes a penta separation of powers, distinguishing five branches of government, separating the Legislative, Executive, Judicial, Electoral and Citizens branches; creating the People's Defender within the Citizens Power, in addition to the Public Prosecutor Office and the General Comptroller Office (Article 134). The People's Defender was created for the promotion, defense and supervision of the rights and guaranties set forth in the Constitution and in the international treaties on human rights, as well as for the citizens' legitimate, collective and diffuse interests (Article 281). In particular, according to Article 281 of the constitution, it also has among its functions to watch for the functioning of public services power and to promote and protect the peoples' legitimate, collective and diffuse rights and interests against arbitrariness or deviation of power in the rendering of such services, being authorized to file the necessary actions to ask for the compensation of the damages caused from the malfunctioning of public services. It also has among its functions, the possibility of filing actions of amparo and habeas corpus.

33 As has been decided by the Constitutional Chamber of the Supreme Tribunal of Venezuela: "As a matter of law, the Defender has standing to bring to suit actions aimed at enforcing the diffuse and collective rights or interests; not being necessary the requirement of the acquiescence of the society it acts on behalf of for the exercise of the action. The Defender of the People is given legitimate interest to act in a process defending a right granted to it by the Constitution itself, consisting in protecting the society or groups in it, in the cases of Article 281."

34 The Constitutional Chamber of the Supreme Tribunal of Venezuela admitted the standing of the Defender of the People to file actions for amparo on behalf of the citizens as a whole, as was the case of the action filed against the Legislative body pretension to appoint the Electoral National Council members without fulfilling the constitutional requirements. In the case, decided on June 6, 2001, the Constitutional Chamber, when analyzing Article 280 of the constitution, pointed out that "the protection of diffuse and collective rights and interests may be raised by the Defender of the People, through the action of amparo," adding the following: "As for the general provision of Article 280 *eiusdem*, regarding the general defense and protection of diffuse and collective interests, this Chamber considers that the Defender of the People is entitled to act to protect those rights and interests, when they correspond in general to the consumers and users (6, Article 281), or to protect the rights of Indian peoples (paragraph 8 of the same Article), since the defense and protection of such categories is one of the faculties granted to said entity by Article 281 of the Constitution in force. It is about a general protection and not a protection of individualities. Within this frame of action, and since the political rights are included in the human rights and guaranties of Title III of the Constitution in force, which have a general projection, among which the ones provided in Article 62 of the Constitution can be found, it must be concluded that the Defender of the People on behalf of the society, legitimated by law, is entitled to bring to suit an action of amparo tending to control the Electoral Power, to the citizen's benefit, in order to enforce Articles 62 and 70 of the Constitution, which were denounced to be breached by the National Legislative Assembly…(right to citizen participation). Due to the difference between diffuse and collective interests, both the Defender of the People, within its attributions,

3. The justiciable constitutional rights and guarantees through the amparo proceeding

As a matter of principle, in Venezuela, all rights and guarantees enshrined in the Constitution or those that have acquired constitutional rank and value are justiciable rights[35] by means of the amparo action; that is, they have to be, in spite of being regulated in statutes, out of reach from the Legislator in the sense that they cannot be eliminated, or diminished through statutes.

The consequence of this principle is that the purpose of the amparo actions is to protect individuals against violations of the "constitutional" provision regarding their right; not being possible to file an action for amparo just based in the violation of the "statutory" provisions that regulate the constitutional right. For instance, as it happens with the right to property, regarding which an amparo action for its protection can be admitted when, for instance, arbitrary administrative acts prevent or impede in absolute terms the use of property; but on the contrary, it is not admitted for the protection of property, for instance, against trespassing, being in these cases, the ordinary civil judicial expedite actions (*interdictos*) the ones that should be filed.[36]

---

and every individual residing in the country, except for the legal exceptions, are entitled to bring to suit the action (be it of amparo or an specific one) for the protection of the former ones; while the action of the collective interests is given to the Defender of the People and to any member of the group or sector identified as a component of that specific collectivity, and acting defending the collectivity. Both individuals and corporations whose object be the protection of such interests may raise the action, and the standing in all these actions varies according to the nature of the same, that is why law can limit the action in specific individuals or entities. However, in our Constitution, in the provisions of Article 281 the Defender of the People is objectively granted the procedural interest and the capacity to sue." See decision of the Constitutional Chamber N° 656 of May 6, 2001, *Defensor del Pueblo vs. Comisión Legislativa Nacional* case, as referred in Decision N° 379 of February 26, 2003, *Mireya Ripanti et vs. Presidente de Petróleos de Venezuela S.A. (PDVSA)* case, in *Revista de Derecho Público*, N° 93–96, Editorial Jurídica Venezolana, Caracas, 2003, pp. 152 ff.

35 "Their quality of being suitable to be protected by courts." See Brian A. Garner (Editor in Chief), *Black's Law Dictionary*, West Group, St. Paul, Minn. 2001, p. 391.

36 Property rights are not only established in the constitutions but are also extensively regulated in the Civil Code. The latter not only contains substantive regulations regarding the exercise of such rights but they provide for adjective ordinary remedies in case those rights are affected. In particular, the Civil Code and the Civil Procedure Codes establishes some sort of civil injunctions to guaranty immediate protection in cases of trespasses (*interdictos*) for instance of possession rights, which are effective judicial remedies for the protection of land owners or occupant rights. Thus, in cases of property trespass, the *interdicto de amparo* or of new construction are effective judicial means for protection of property rights, not being possible to file an amparo action in such cases. In this regard, the Constitutional Chamber of the Supreme Tribunal of Justice of Venezuela, in a case decided in 2000, argued as follows: "The amparo action protects one aspect of the legal situations of persons referred to their fundamental rights, corresponding the defense of subjective rights –different to fundamental rights and public liberties– to the ordinary administrative and judicial recourses and actions. For instance, it is not the same to deny a citizen the condition to have property rights, than to discuss property rights between parties, the protection of which corresponds to a specific ordinary judicial action of recovery (reivindicación). This means that in the amparo proceedings the court judges the actions of public entities or individuals that can harm fundamental rights; but in no case can it review, for instance, the applicability or interpretation or statutes by Public Administration or the courts, unless from

In general terms, this implies the extraordinary character of the amparo action, in the sense that it can only be filed when no other appropriate and effective ordinary judicial means for protection are legally provided or when if provided, they are ineffective.

This condition of admissibility of the amparo actions is very similar to the so-called "inadequacy" condition established in the United States regarding the equitable injunction remedies, in the sense that they are only admissible when there are no adequate remedies in law to assure the protection; or when the law cannot provide an adequate remedy because of the nature of the right involved, as was the case regarding school segregation.[37]

Now, regarding the rights protected through the amparo action they are the "constitutional rights," expression that comprises, first, the rights expressly declared in the constitution; second, those rights that even not enumerated in the constitution are inherent to human beings; and third, those rights enumerated in the international instruments on human rights ratified by the State, that in Venezuela have constitutional rank being applied with preference in all cases in which they provide more favorable conditions for the enjoyment of the right (article 23, Constitution). Consequently, all the rights listed in Title III of the constitution, which refers to Human Rights, Guaranties and Duties, are protected though the amparo action. Those rights are the following: citizenship rights, civil (individual) rights, political rights, social and family rights, cultural and educational rights, economic rights, environmental rights and the indigenous people's rights enumerated in Articles 19 to 129. Additionally, all other constitutional rights and guaranties derived from other constitutional provisions can also be protected even if not included in Title III, like for instance, the constitutional guaranty of the independence of the Judiciary, or the constitutional guaranty of the legality of taxation (that taxes can only by set forth by

---

them a direct violation of the Constitution can be deduced. The amparo is not a new judicial instance, nor the substitution of ordinary judicial means for the protection of rights and interest; it is an instrument to reaffirm constitutional values, by mean of which the court, hearing an amparo, can decide regarding the contents or the application of constitutional provisions regulating fundamental rights; can review the interpretation made by Public Administration or judicial bodies, or determine if the facts from which constitutional violations are deduced constitute a direct violation of the Constitution." Decision N° 828 of July 27, 2000, *Seguros Corporativos (SEGUCORP), C.A. et al. vs. Superintendencia de Seguros* Case, in *Revista de Derecho Público*, N° 83, Editorial Jurídica Venezolana, Caracas, 2000, pp. 290 ff.

37 See Owen M. Fiss and Doug Rendleman, *Injunctions,* 2d Ed, The Foundation Press, Mineola, 1984, p. 59. This inadequacy condition, of course, normally results from the factual situations regarding the case or from the nature of the right which in some cases impedes or allows the granting of the protection. In this sense, for instance it was resolved since the well-known case of *Wheelock v. Nooman* (NY 1888); in which case the defendant, having left on the plaintiff's property great boulders beyond the authorization he had, the injunction was granted in order to require such defendant to remove them. The plaintiff in the case could not easily remove the boulders and sued the cost of removal of the trespassing rocks because of their size and weight. On the contrary, in another case, the remedy at law was considered adequate because the litter the defendant left on the property could be removed by the plaintiff paying for someone to remove the trash, in which case he could just sue the defendant for the cost incurred, as was decided in *Connor v. Grosso* (Cal. 1953).

statute).[38] Also, regarding the protected rights, through the open clause of constitutional rights, the constitution admits the amparo action for the protection of those other constitutional rights and guaranties not expressly listed in the constitution, but that can be considered inherent to human beings (article 22, Constitution).

The most important question regarding the justiciability of constitutional rights, refers to the scope of the protection particularly regarding social rights, and particularly, for example, regarding the right of the people for their health to be protected by the State (Article 83), and consequently the obligation of the State in terms of providing public health services. In this regard, the Constitutional Chamber of the Supreme Tribunal of Justice of Venezuela in decision N° 487 of April 6, 2001, (*Glenda López y otros vs. Instituto Venezolano de los Seguros Sociales* case) pointed out that the right to health or to the protection of health is "an integral part of the right to life, set forth in the Constitution as a fundamental social right (and not simply as an assignment of State purposes) whose satisfaction mainly belongs to the State and its institutions, through activities intended to progressively raise the quality of life of citizens and the collective welfare." This implies, according to the Court's decision that "the right to health is not to be exhausted with the simple physical care of a person, but must be extended to the appropriate treatment in order to safeguard the mental, social, environmental integrity of persons, including the community."

4. The injury in the amparo proceeding

The injuries violating constitutional rights, against which the amparo action is established, can consist of harms or threats affecting those rights. Harms are always damages affecting or destroying the object of the right; and threats are injuries that, without destroying such object, put the enjoyment of the right in a situation of danger or of suffering a decrease.

These injuries –harms or threats– caused to constitutional rights, in order to be protected by means of the amparo proceeding, must be evident, actual and real, that is, they must affect personally and directly the rights of the plaintiff, in a manifestly arbitrary, illegal and illegitimate way, which the plaintiff must not have consented.

Yet in addition to these general conditions, specifically regarding harms, they must have a reparable character; and regarding threats, they must affect the rights in an imminent way. That is why the type of injuries inflicted on constitutional rights, conditions the purpose of the amparo proceeding: if harms, being reparable, the amparo has a restorative effect; and if threats, being imminent, the amparo has a preventive effect.

Regarding the general conditions that the injuries to constitutional rights must comply in order for an amparo actions to be admitted, the following are the ones established in the Amparo Law: first, it must have a personal and direct character, in the sense that it must personally affect the plaintiff; second, it must be actual and real; third, it must be manifestly or ostensibly arbitrary, illegal and illegitimate; fourth, it must be evidenced in the case; and fifth, it must not be consented to by the plaintiff.

---

38 See Allan R. Brewer-Carías, *Instituciones Políticas y Constitucionales*, Vol. V, *Derecho y Acción de Amparo,* Caracas, 1998, pp. 209 ff. See decision of the First Court on Judicial Review of Administrative Action, *Fecadove* case, in Rafael Chavero G., *El nuevo régimen del amparo constitucional en Venezuela*, Ed. Sherwood, Caracas, 2001, p. 157.

The first condition of the injury inflicted to the plaintiff's constitutional rights, in order for an amparo action to be admitted, is that the plaintiff must have suffered a "direct, personal and present harm or threat in his constitutional rights,"[39] that is, the plaintiff must be personally affected. Consequently, the amparo action cannot be file when the affected rights belong to another person different to the claimant or only affects the plaintiff in an indirect way.

If the harm does not affect the constitutional rights of the plaintiff, in a personal and direct way, the action must be considered inadmissible; being also inadmissible when the harm or threat is not attributed to the person identified as the injuring party, that is, when the injury is not personally caused by the defendant.[40]

However, in addition to directly affecting the constitutional rights of the plaintiff, the injury must be "actual," in the sense that by the moment of the filing of the action, the harm or threat must be presently occurring and must not have ceased or concluded.

This same rule is also applied in the United States regarding injunctions, in the sense that for a person to be entitled to injunctive relief, it must establish an actual, substantial and serious injury, or an affirmative prospect of such an injury. Consequently, a petitioner is not entitled to an injunction where no injury to the petitioner is shown from the action sought to be prevented.[41]

In other words, the injury must be real, in the sense that it must have effectively occurred; a fact that must be clearly demonstrated by the plaintiff in his petition. That is why, as has been ruled by the courts in Venezuela:

---

39 As for example, it has been ruled by the courts in Venezuela: "It is necessary, though, that the denounced actions directly affect the subjective sphere of the claimant, consequently excluding the generic conducts, even if they can affect in a tangential way on the matter." See decision of the First Court on Judicial Review of Administrative Actions of December 2, 1993, in *Revista de Derecho Público*, N° 55-56, Editorial Jurídica Venezolana, Caracas, 1993, pp. 302–303.

40 In this sense, for instance, it was decided by the former Venezuelan Supreme Court of Justice in 1999, in an amparo filed against the President of the Republic, denouncing as the injuring acts, possible measures to be adopted by the National Constituent Assembly that the President had convened, once installed. The Court rejected the action considering that "the reasons alleged by the plaintiff were of eventual and hypothetical nature, which contradicts the need of an objective and real harm or threat to constitutional rights or guaranties" in order for the amparo to be admissible. Regarding the alleged defendant in the case, the Court ruled as follow: "This court must say that the action for constitutional amparo serves to give protection against situations that in a direct way could produce harm regarding the plaintiff's constitutional rights or guaranties, seeking the restoration of its infringed juridical situation. In this case, the person identified as plaintiff (President of the Republic) could not be by himself the one to produce the eventual harm which would condition the voting rights of the plaintiff, and the fear that the organization of the constituted branches of government could be modified, would be attributed to the members of those that could be elected to the National Constituent Assembly not yet elected. Thus in the case there does not exist the immediate relation between the plaintiff and the defendants needed in the amparo suit." See decision of April 23, 1999 (*A. Albornoz* case). See the reference in Rafael Chavero, *El nuevo régimen del amparo constitucional en Venezuela*, Ed. Sherwood, Caracas, 2001, p. 240.

41 See *U.S. Boyle v. Landry*, 401 U.S. 77, 91 S. Ct.758, 27 L. Ed. 2d 696 (1971), in John Bourdeau *et al.*, "Injunctions," in Kevin Schroder, John Glenn and Maureen Placilla (Ed.), *Corpus Juris Secundum*, Vol. 43A, Thomson West, 2004, p. 66.

"The amparo action can only be directed against a perfectly and determined act or omission, and not against a generic conduct; against an objective and real activity and not against a supposition regarding the intention of the presumed injurer, and against the direct and immediate consequences of the activities of the public body or officer."[42]

This actual and real character of the injury regarding the amparo suit implies that it cannot be of a past character, or of a probable future one. In this sense, for instance, the Venezuelan courts have argued that the injury "must be alive, must be present in all its intensity," in the sense of being "referring to the present, not to the past; it does not refer to facts that already had happened, which appertain to the past, but to present situations, which can be prolonged during an indefinite length of time."[43]

Based precisely on this condition, the former Supreme Court of Justice of Venezuela rejected the possibility of filing amparo actions against statutes, in cases in which they are not directly applicable, needing additional acts for their execution.[44]

On the other hand, this same condition for the harm or threat to be actual, implies that it must not have ceased or concluded, as could happen, for instance, when during the course of the procedure the challenged act is repealed.[45] Consequently, in order to grant the amparo protection, the Venezuelan courts have ruled that the harm must not have ceased before the judge's decision is adopted; on the contrary, if the

---

42 See decision of the Venezuelan former Supreme Court of Justice, Politico Administrative Chamber, of December 2, 1993, in which the Court added, "that is why the amparo action is not a popular action for denouncing the illegitimacy of the public entities of control over convenience or opportunity, but a protector remedy of the claimant sphere when it is demonstrated that it has been directly affected," in *Revista de Derecho Público*, N° 55–56, Editorial Jurídica Venezolana, Caracas, 1993, pp. 302–303. In another decision, the same former Supreme Court of Justice ruled about the need that: "The violation of the constitutional rights and guaranties be a direct and immediate consequence of the act, fact or omission, not being possible to attribute or assign to the injurer agent different results to those produced or to be produced. The right's violation must be the product of the harming act." See decision of August, 14 1992, in *Revista de Derecho Público*, N° 51, Editorial Jurídica Venezolana, Caracas, 1992, p. 145.

43 See decision of the First Court on Judicial Review of Administrative Actions, May, 7 1987, *Desarrollo 77 C.A.* case, in FUNEDA *15 años de Jurisprudencia de la Corte Primera de lo Contencioso Adminsitrativo 1977–1992,* Caracas, 1994, p. 78. In this sense, Article 6,1 of the Amparo Law of Venezuela establishes for the admissibility of the amparo action, that the violation "must be actual, recent, alive."

44 The Court ruled: "When an amparo action is filed against a norm, –that is, when the object of the action is the norm in itself–, the concretion of the possible alleged harm would not be "immediate," due to the fact that it would always be necessary for the competent authority to proceed to the execution or application of the norm, in order to harm the plaintiff. One must conclude that the probable harm caused by a norm will always be mediate and indirect, needing to be applied to the concrete case. Thus, the injury will be caused through and by means of an act applying the disposition that is contrary to the rule of law." See decision of the former Supreme Court of Justice, Politico Administrative Chamber, May 24, 1993, in *Revista de Derecho Público*, N° 55–56, Editorial Jurídica Venezolana, Caracas, 1993, pp. 289–290.

45 In this regard, the First Court on Judicial Review of Administrative Actions of Venezuela resolved the inadmissibility of an action for amparo because, during the proceedings, the challenged act was repealed. Decision of August 14, 1992, in *Revista de Derecho Público,* N° 51, Editorial Jurídica Venezolana, Caracas, 1992, p. 154.

harm has ceased, the judge *in limine litis* must declare the inadmissibility of the action.[46] For instance, in the case of amparo actions against judicial omissions, if before the filing of the action or during the preceding the court has issued its decision, the harm can be considered as having ceased[47] and the amparo action must be declared inadmissible. The same principle applies in the United States regarding the actual character of the harm for granting the injunctive protection because the rule in federal cases is that an actual controversy must exist, not only at the time of the filing of the action, but at all stages of the procedure, even at appellate or certiorari review stages.[48]

Nonetheless, this principle of the actual character of the injury has some exceptions, for instance in Venezuela, regarding the effects already produced by a challenged act. Because additional suits are necessary in order to establish civil liabilities and compensation, even if the effects of the challenged act have ceased, the amparo protection can be granted in order for the responsible person to be judicially determined, allowing the subsequent filing of an action just seeking compensation.

Yet in order for an amparo action to be admitted, in addition for the injury to be a direct, real and actual one, the harm or threat to the constitutional right must be manifestly arbitrary, illegal or illegitimate. Regarding public authorities' acts, this general condition of admissibility of the amparo action derives from the general public law principle of the presumption of validity that benefit the State acts, which implies that in order to overcome such presumption, the plaintiff must demonstrate that the injury caused is manifestly illegal and arbitrary. The same principle applies in the United States precisely imposing on the plaintiff, in civil right injunctions

---

46 Decision of December 15, 1992, in *Revista de Derecho Público* N° 52, Editorial Jurídica Venezolana, Caracas, 1992, p. 164, See First Court on Judicial Review of Administrative action, decision of December 12, 1992, Allan R. Brewer-Carías case, in *Revista de Derecho Público*, N° 49, Editorial Jurídica Venezolana, Caracas, 1992, pp. 131–132; and decision of the former Supreme Court, Politico Administrative Chamber of May 27, 1993, in *Revista de Derecho Público*, N° 53–54, Editorial Jurídica Venezolana, Caracas, 1993, p. 264.

47 See Rafael Chavero G., *El nuevo régimen del amparo constitucional en Venezuela*, Editorial Sherwood, Caracas, 2001, pp. 237–238.

48 Nonetheless, in the important case *Roe v. Wade*, 410 U.S. 113 (1973), the Supreme Court expanded women's right to privacy, striking down states' laws banning abortion. The Court recognized that even if this right of privacy was not explicitly mentioned in the constitution, it was guaranteed as a constitutional right for protecting "a woman's decision whether or not to terminate her pregnancy," even though admitting that the states' legislation could regulate the factors governing the abortion decision at some point in pregnancy based on "safeguarding health, maintaining medical standards and in protecting potential life." But the point in the case was that, pending the procedure, the pregnancy period of the claimant came to term, so the injury claimed lost its present character. Nonetheless, the Supreme Court ruled in the case that "[When], as here, pregnancy is a significant fact in the litigation, the normal 266-day human generation period is so short that pregnancy will come to term before the usual appellate process is complete. If that termination makes a case moot, pregnancy litigation seldom will survive much beyond the trial stage, and appellate review will be effectively denied. Our law should not be that rigid. Pregnancy comes more than once to the same woman, and in the general population, if man is to survive, it will always be with us. Pregnancy provides a classic justification for a conclusion of non mootness. It truly could be capable of repetition, yet evading review." See M. Glenn Abernathy and Barbara A. Perry, *Civil Liberties under the Constitution*, University of South Carolina Press, 1993, pp. 4–5.

against administrative officials, the burden to prove the alleged violations in order to destroy the presumption of validity of official acts.[49]

The consequence of this condition is that the challenged act or omission must be manifestly contrary to the legal order, that is, to the rules of law contained in the constitution, the statutes and the executive regulations; must be manifestly illegitimate because lacking of any legal support; and must be manifestly arbitrary, because resulting from an unreasonable or unjust act is an act contrary to justice or to reason.

The condition of the injury –harm or threats–, to be manifestly arbitrary, illegal and illegitimate and to affect in a direct and immediate way the plaintiff rights, implies that for the filing of the amparo action, it has to be evident, thus, directly imposing the plaintiff the burden to prove his assertions. That is, the plaintiff has the burden to destroy the presumption of validity, having to build his arguments upon reasonable basis by proving the unreasonable character of the public officer's challenged act or omission, and that it has personally and directly harmed his rights. Also, in this matter, the rule in the amparo proceeding is similar to the rules on matters of injunctions, as they have been resolved by the United States' courts, according to which, "the party seeking an injunction, whether permanent or temporary, must establish some demonstrable injury."[50]

Consequently, in the amparo proceeding, it is for the plaintiff to prove the harm or the threats caused to his rights, and as being caused precisely by the defendant. This implies that when the proof of the harms or threats can be established by means of written evidence (documents, for instance), the Amparo Law expressly impose on the claimant the duty to always attach them to the complaint.

Finally, the injury to constitutional rights allowing the filing of the amparo action must not only be actual, possible, real and imminent, but must also be an injury that has not been consented by the plaintiff, who, in addition, must not have provoked it. That is, the plaintiff must not have expressly or tacitly consent the challenged act or the harm caused to his right. On the contrary, the amparo action would be considered inadmissible. The Amparo Law in this matter distinguishes two sorts of possible ways of consenting conducts: the express consent and the tacit consent; also, with some exceptions.

Regarding the express consent, as established in the Venezuelan Amparo Law, it exists when there are "unequivocal signs of acceptance" (Article 6,4) by the

---

49 As M. Glenn Abernathy and Perry have commented: "The courts do not automatically presume that all restraints on free choice are improper. The burden is thrown on the person attacking acts to prove that they are improper. This is most readily seen in cases involving the claim that an act of the legislature is unconstitutional...Judges also argue that acts of administrative officials should be accorded some presumption of validity. Thus a health officer who destroys food alleged by him to be unfit for consumption is presumed to have good reason for his action. The person whose property is so destroyed must bear the burden of proving bad faith on part of the official, if an action is brought as a consequence." See M. Glenn Abernathy and Barbara A. Perry, *Civil Liberties under the Constitution*, University of South Carolina Press, 1993, p. 5.

50 See *Mt. Emmons Min. Co. V. Town of Crested Butte*, 690 P.2d 231 (Colo. 1984), in John Bourdeau *et al.*, "Injunctions," in Kevin Schroder, John Glenn and Maureen Placilla (Editors), *Corpus Juris Secundum*, Vol. 43A, Thomson West, 2004, p. 54.

plaintiff, of the acts, facts or omissions causing the injury, in which case the amparo action is inadmissible. In certain aspects, this inadmissibility clause for the amparo proceeding when an express consent of the plaintiff exists, also has some equivalence in the United States injunctions procedure with the equitable defense called "*estoppel*," referring to actions of the plaintiff prior to the filing of the suit, when being inconsistent with the rights he is asserting in his claim.[51]

Apart from the cases of express consent, the other clause of inadmissibility in the amparo proceeding also occurs in cases of tacit consent by the plaintiff regarding the act, fact or omission causing the injury to his rights. This situation is considered as happening when the precise term, legally established to file the complaint, has elapsed without the action being brought before the courts. This clause for the inadmissibility of the amparo suit is also equivalent to what in the United States procedure for injunction is called "laches," which seeks to prevent a plaintiff from obtaining equitable relief when he has not acted promptly in bringing the action, which is summarized in the phrase, that "equity aids the vigilant, not those who slumber in their rights."[52] The difference between the doctrine of "laches" regarding injunctions and the Venezuelan Law concept of tacit consent, basically lies in the fact that the term to file the amparo action is expressly established in the Amparo Law (six months, Article 6,4), so the exhaustion of the term without the filing of the action is what it is considered to produce the tacit consent regarding the act, the fact or the omission causing the injury.

The sense of this clause of inadmissibility of the amparo action was summarized by the former Supreme Court of Justice of Venezuela when ruling as follows:

> "Since the amparo action is a special, brief, summary and effective judicial remedy for the protection of constitutional rights…it is logical for the Legislator to prescribe a precise length of time between the moment in which the harm is produced and the moment the aggrieved party has to file the action. To let more than 6 months pass from the moment in which the injuring act is issued for the exercise of the action is the demonstration of the acceptance of the harm from the side of the injured party. His indolence must be sanctioned, impeding the use of the judicial remedy that has its justification in the urgent need to reestablish a legal situation."[53]

---

51 The classic example of estopell, as referred to by Tabb and Shoben, "is that a plaintiff cannot ask equity for an order to remove a neighbor's fence built over the lot line if the plaintiff stood by and watched the fence construction in full knowledge of the location of the lot line. The plaintiff silence with knowledge of the facts is an action inconsistent with the right asserted in court." See William M. Tabb and Elaine W. Shoben, *Remedies*, Thomson West, 2005, pp. 50–51.

52 *Idem,* p. 48. As argued in Lake Development Enterprises, *Inc. v. Kojetinsky*, 410 S.W. 2d 361, 367–68 (Mo. App. 1966): "Laches" is the neglect, for an unreasonable and unexplained length of time under circumstances permitting diligence, to do what in law, should have been done. There is no fixed period within which a person must assert his claim or be barred by laches. The length of time depends upon the circumstances of the particular case. Mere delay in asserting a right does not of itself constitute laches; the delay involved must work to the disadvantage and prejudice of the defendant. Laches is a question of fact to be determined from all the evidence and circumstances adduced at trial." See the reference Owen M. Fiss and Doug Rendelman, *Injunctions*, The Foundation Press, Mineola New York, 1984, pp. 102–103.

53 See decision of October 24, 1990, in *Revista de Derecho Público*, Nº 44, Editorial Jurídica Venezolana, Caracas, 1990, p. 144.

However, regarding this tacit consent effect, an exception has been established in the Venezuelan Amparo Law in cases of violations affecting "public order" provisions[54] (Article 6,4), which refers to situations where the application of a statute may concern the general and indispensable legal order for the existence of the community.[55]

This notion of "public order" is important because even when the term to sue has elapsed without the action being filed, the courts can admit the action because of reasons of "public order," not considering applicable in the case the rule of the tacit consent. As was decided by the Venezuelan First Court of Administrative Judicial Review:

> "The extinction of the amparo action due to the elapse of the term to sue... is produced in all cases, except when the way through which the harm has been produced is of such gravity that it constitutes an injury to the juridical conscience. It would be the case, for instance, of flagrant violations to individual rights that cannot be denounced by the affected party; deprivation of freedom; submission to physical or psychological torture; maltreatment; harms to human dignity and other extreme cases.[56]

Consequently, in such cases where no tacit consent can be considered as having been produced, the amparo judicial is admitted even though the term to file the action would have been exhausted.

Another general exception to the rule of tacit consent refers to situations where the harms inflicted to the rights are of a continuous nature, that is, when they are continuously occurring. In the same sense, in the United States, it is considered that

---

54 As ruled by the cassation Chamber of the Supreme Court in Venezuela in a decision of April 3, 1985, "the concept of public order allows the general interest of the Society and of the State to prevail over the individual particular interest, in order to assure the enforcement and purpose of some institutions." See the reference in decisions of the former Supreme Court of Justice, Politico Administrative Chamber, of February 1, 1990, *Tuna Atlántica C.A.,* case and of June 30, 1992, in *Revista de Derecho Público*, N° 60, Editorial Jurídica Venezolana, Caracas, 1992, p. 157. In many cases, it is the Legislator itself that has expressly declared in a particular statute that its provisions are of "public order" character, in the sense that its norms cannot be modified through contracts." See decision of former Supreme Court of Justice, Politico Administrative Chamber, March 22, 1988, in *Revista de Derecho Público*, N° 34, Editorial Jurídica Venezolana, Caracas, 1988, p. 114.

55 The exception, of course, cannot be applied in cases only concerning the parties in a contractual or private controversy. That is the case for instance, of the Venezuelan 2004 Consumers and Users Protection Law where Article 2 sets forth that its provisions are of public order and may not be renounced by the parties. *Official Gazette*, N° 37.930, May 4, 2004.

56 See the decisions of First Court on Judicial Review of Administrative Action of October 13, 1988, in *Revista de Derecho Público*, N° 36, Editorial Jurídica Venezolana, Caracas, 1988, p. 95; of the former Supreme Court of Justice, Politico Administrative Chamber, of November 1, 1989, in *Revista de Derecho Público*, N° 40, Editorial Jurídica Venezolana, Caracas, 1989, p. 111; and of the cassation Chamber of the same Supreme Court of Justice, of June 28, 1995, (Exp. N° 94–172). See the reference in Rafael Chavero G., *El nuevo régimen del amparo constitucional en Venezuela*, Editorial Sherwood, Caracas, 2001, p. 188, note 178. See another judicial decision on the matter in pp. 214 and 246.

"laches" cannot be alleged as a defense to challenge a suit for injunction to enjoin a wrong that is continuing in its nature.[57]

For instance, the Venezuelan courts have ruled regarding a defense argument on the inadmissibility of an amparo action because the term of six months to file the action was elapsed, that in the particular case:

> "In spite that the facts show that the challenged actions occurred more than six months ago, they have been described revealing a supposed chain of events that, due to their constancy and re-incidence, allows presuming that the plaintiff is presently threatened by those repeated facts. This character of the threat is what the amparo intends to stop. According to what the plaintiff points out, no tacit consent can be produced from his part … Consequently, there are no grounds for the application to any of the inadmissibility clauses set forth in the Amparo Law."[58]

In Venezuela, the Amparo Law also provides a few exceptions regarding the tacit consent rule, when the amparo action is filed conjointly with another nullity action, in which case the general six-month term established for the filing of the action does not apply. This is the rule in cases of harms or threats that have originated in statutes or regulations, and in administrative acts or public administration omissions, when the amparo action is filed jointly with the popular action for judicial review of unconstitutionality of statutes,[59] or with the judicial review action against administrative actions or omissions.[60]

5. The reparable character of the harms and the restorative character of the amparo proceeding

As mentioned, the injury inflicted upon constitutional rights in order to the filing of an amparo action, can be the result of harms or threats, which must fulfill the general conditions aforementioned. In addition, two other conditions must fulfill the injury, depending on being harms or threats. If it is a harm inflicted on the persons' rights, it has to be a reparable one, the amparo proceeding seeking to restore the enjoyment of the right, having a restorative character; but if the injury is a threat

57 *Pacific Greyhound Lines v. Sun Valley Bus Lines*, 70 Ariz. 65, 216 P. 2d 404, 1950; Goldstein v. Beal, 317 Mass. 750, 59 N.E. 2d 712, 1945. See in Jhon Bourdeau *et al.*, "Injunctions," in Kevin Schroder, John Glenn and Maureen Placilla (Ed.), *Corpus Juris Secundum*, Vol. 43A, Thomson West, 2004, p. 329.

58 See decision of October 22, 1990, *María Cambra de Pulgar* case, in *Revista de Derecho Público*, N° 44, Editorial Jurídica Venezolana, Caracas, 1990, pp. 143–144.

59 Regarding the judicial review popular action against statutes, it is conceived in the Organic Law of the Supreme Tribunal as an action that can be filed at any time, so if a petition for amparo is filed together with the popular action, no delay is applicable (Article 21,21). See Allan R. Brewer-Carías, *Ley Orgánica del Tribunal Supremo de Justicia*, Editorial Jurídica Venezolana, Caracas, 2006, p. 255. This is why no tacit consent can be understood when the harm is provoked by a statute.

60 Similarly, the tacit consent rule does not apply either in cases of administrative acts or omissions, when the amparo action is filed together with the judicial review action against administrative acts or omissions, in which case, due to the constitutional complaint, the latter can be filed at any moment, as is expressly provided in the Amparo Law (Article 5).

caused upon the right, it must be imminent, the amparo tending to prevent or impede the violation to occur, having a preventive character.

In effect, in case of harms, the amparo proceeding seeks to restore the enjoyment of the plaintiff's injured right, reestablishing the situation existing when the right was harmed, by eliminating or suspending, if necessary, the detrimental act or fact. In this regard, the amparo action also has similarities with the reparative injunctions in the United States, which seeks to eliminate the effects of a past wrong or to compel the defendant to engage in a course of action that seeks to correct those effects.[61]

However, in some cases, due to the factual nature of the harm that has been inflicted, these restorative effects cannot be obtained, in which cases the amparo decision must tend to place the plaintiff right "in the situation closest or more similar to the one that existed before the injury was caused."[62]

Because of the restorative character of the amparo, the main specific condition the harms must fulfill for an amparo petition to be granted is that they must have a reparable character. Consequently, as for instance is established in the Venezuelan Amparo Law, the amparo actions are inadmissible, "when the violation of the constitutional rights and guaranties turns out to be an evident irreparable situation, and is impossible to restore." In these cases, the Law defines the irreparable harms as those that by means of the amparo action cannot revert to the status existing before the violation had occurred (Article 6,3).

The main consequence of this reparable character of the harm, and of the restorative effect of the amparo proceeding, is that through the amparo action, it is

---

61 As has been explained by Owen M. Fiss: "To see how it works, let us assume that a wrong has occurred (such as an act of discrimination). Then the missions of an injunction –classically conceived as a preventive instrument– would be to prevent the recurrence of the wrongful conduct in the future (stop discriminating and do not discriminate again). But in *United States v. Louisiana* (380 U.S. 145, (1965)), a voting discrimination case, Justice Black identified still another mission for the injunction: the elimination of the effects of the past wrong (the past discrimination). The reparative injunction –long thought by the nineteenth-century textbook writers, such as High (A *Treatise on the Law of Injunction* 3, 1873) to be an analytical impossibility– was thereby legitimated. And in the same vein, election officials have been ordered not only to stop discriminating in the future elections, but also to set aside a past election and to run a new election as a means of removing the taint of discrimination that infected the first one (*Bell v. Southwell*, 376 F.2de 659 (5TH Cir. 1976)). Similarly, public housing officials have been ordered to both cease discriminating on the basis of race in their future choices of sites and to build units in the white areas as a means of eliminating the effects of the past segregative policy (placing public housing projects only in the black areas of the city) (*Hills v. Gautreaux*, 425 U.S. 284 (1976)). Seen Owen M. Fiss, *The Civil Rights Injunction*, Indiana University Press, 1978, pp. 7–10.

62 In this sense, it has been decided by the former Venezuelan Supremo Court of Justice ruling that "one of the principal characteristics of the amparo action is to be a restorative (restablecedor) judicial means, the mission of which is to restore the infringed situation or, what is the same, to put the claimant again in the enjoyment of his infringed constitutional rights." See decision of February 6, 1996, *Asamblea legislativa del Estado Bolívar* case. See in Rafael Chavero, *El nuevo régimen del amparo constitucional en Venezuela*, Ed. Sherwood, Caracas, 2001, pp. 185, 242–243.

not possible to create new juridical situations for the plaintiff, nor is it possible to modify the existing legal situations.[63]

In this sense, for instance, the Venezuelan Constitutional Chamber of the Supreme Tribunal of Justice denied a request formulated by means of an amparo action for the plaintiff to obtain asylum because what it was seeking was to obtain the Venezuelan citizenship without accomplishing the established administrative conditions and procedures. The Court ruled in the case, that "this amparo action has been filed in order to seek a decision from this court, consisting in the legalization of the situation of the claimant, which would consist in the creation of a civil and juridical status that the petitioner did not have before filing the complaint for amparo." Thus, in the case, the petition was considered "contrary to the restorative nature of the amparo."[64]

Consequently, regarding harms, the restorative effects of the amparo proceedings, impose the need for the harm to be of a reparable character so the courts can restore things to the status or situation they had at the moment of the injury, disappearing the challenged infringing fact or act. On the contrary, when the violation to a constitutional right turns out to be of an irreparable character, the amparo actions is inadmissible.

This is congruent with the main objective of the amparo proceeding as it is for instance provided in Article 27 of the Venezuelan Constitution and Article 1 of Amparo Law, in the sense that it seeks to "immediately restore the infringed situation or to place the claimant in the situation more similar to it."[65] This is also a general condition for the admissibility of the injunctions in the United States where

---

63 See decisions of the Politico Administrative Chamber of the former Supreme Court of Justice, of October 27, 1993, *Ana Drossos* case, and of November 4, 1993, *Partido Convergencia* case, in *Revista de Derecho Público*, Nº 55–56, Editorial Jurídica Venezolana, Caracas, 1993, p. 340.

64 See decision dated January 20, 2000, *Domingo Ramírez Monja* case, in Rafael Chavero, *El nuevo régimen del amparo constitucional en Venezuela*, Ed. Sherwood, Caracas, 2001, p. 244. In another decision issued on April 21, 1999, *J. C. Marín* case, the former Supreme Court in a similar sense, declared inadmissible an amparo action in a case in which the claimant was asking to be appointed as judge in a specific court or to be put in a juridical situation that he did not have before the challenged act was issued. The Court decided that in the case, it was impossible for such purpose to file an amparo action, declaring it inadmissible, thus ruling as follows: "This Court must highlight that one of the essential characteristics of the amparo action is its reestablishing effects, that is, literally, to put one thing in the situation it had beforehand, which for the claimant means to be put in the situation he had before the production of the claimed violation. The foregoing means that the plaintiff's claim must be directed to seek 'the reestablishment of the infringed juridical situation'; since the amparo actions are inadmissible when the reestablishment of the infringed situation is not possible; when through them the claimant seeks a compensation of damages, because the latter cannot be a substitution of the harmed right; nor when the plaintiff pretends to the court to create a right or a situation that did not exist before the challenged act, fact or omission. All this is the exclusion for the possibility for the amparo to have constitutive effects." *Idem*, pp. 244–245.

65 See First Court on Judicial Review of Administrative Action, decision of January 14, 1992, in *Revista de Derecho Público*, Nº 49, Editorial Jurídica Venezolana, Caracas, 1992, p. 130; and decision of the former Supreme Court of Justice, Politico Administrative Chamber, of March 4, 1993, in *Revista de Derecho Público*, Nº 53-54, Editorial Jurídica Venezolana, Caracas, 1993, p. 260

the courts have established that because the purpose of an injunction is to restrain actions that have not yet been taken, an injunction cannot be filed to restrain an already completed action at the time the action is brought before the courts since the injury has already been caused.[66]

In this same sense, for instance, the former Venezuelan Supreme Court declared inadmissible an amparo action against an illegitimate tax collecting act after the tax was paid, considering that in such case it is not possible to restore the infringed situation.[67] Also regarding women's pregnancy rights, Venezuelan courts have declared inadmissible an amparo action seeking the protection of maternity leave rights when filed after childbirth, ruling that:

> "It is impossible for the plaintiff to be restored in her presumed violated rights to enjoy a maternity leave during six month before and after the childbirth, because we are now facing an irremediable situation that cannot be restored, due to the fact that it is impossible to date back the elapsed time."[68]

In other cases, the same former Venezuelan Supreme Court of Justice has considered inadmissible amparo actions when the only way to restore the infringed juridical situation is by declaring the nullity of an administrative act, which the amparo judge cannot do in his decision.[69]

From these regulations it can be sustained, in conclusion, that the amparo proceeding regarding violations are restorative in nature, imposing the need for the illegitimate harm to be possibly stopped or amended, in order for the plaintiff's situation to be restored by a judicial order; or if having continuous effects, for its suspension when not being initiated. Regarding those effects already accomplished, it implies the possibility to set back things to the stage they had before the harm was initiated. Consequently, what the amparo judge cannot do is to create situations that

---

66"There is no cause for the issuance of an injunction unless the alleged wrong is actually occurring or is actually threatened or apprehended with reasonable probability and a court cannot enjoin an act after it has been completed. An act that has been completed, such that it no longer presents a justiciable controversy, does not give grounds for the issuance of an injunction." See *County of Chesterfield v. Windy Hill, Ltd.*, 263 Va. 197, 559 S.E. 2d 627 (2002); *Kay v. David Douglas School Dist.* n° 40, 303 Or. 574, 738 P 2d 1389, 40 Ed. Law Rep. 1027 (1987); *Exparte Connors*, 855 So. 2d 486 (Ala. 2003); *Patterson v. Council on Probate Judicial Conduct*, 215 Conn. 553, 577 A. 2d 701 (1990), in John Bourdeau *et al*, "Injunctions," in Kevin Schroder, John Glenn, Maureen Placilla (Editors), *Corpus Juris Secundum*, Vol. 43A, Thomson West, 2004, p. 73.

67 See decision of the former Supreme Court of Justice, Politico Administrative Chamber, of March 21, 1988, in *Revista de Derecho Público*, N° 34, Editorial Jurídica Venezolana, Caracas, 1988, p. 114.

68 See decision of the First Court on Judicial Review of Administrative Actions of September 17, 1989, in *Revista de Derecho Público*, N° 40, Editorial Jurídica Venezolana, Caracas, 1989, p. 111.

69 See decision of the former Supreme Court of Justice, Politico Administrative Chamber of November 1, 1990, in *Revista de Derecho Publico*, N° 44, Editorial Jurídica Venezolana, Caracas, 1990, pp. 152–153; *Cfr.* First Court on Judicial Review of Administrative Action, decision of September 10, 1992, in *Revista de Derecho Público*, N° 51, Editorial Jurídica Venezolana, Caracas, 1992, p. 155.

were inexistent at the moment of the action's filing; or to correct the harms infringed on rights when it is too late to do so.[70]

In this regard, for instance, referring to the right to the protection of health, the former Venezuelan Supreme Court of Justice ruled as follows:

> "The Court considers that the infringed situation is reparable by means of amparo, due to the fact that the plaintiff can be satisfied in his claims through such judicial mean. From the judicial procedure point of view, for the protection of health it is possible for the judge to order the competent authority to assume precise conduct for the medical treatment of the claimant's conduct. The petitioner's claim is to have a particular and adequate health care, which can be obtained via the amparo action, seeking the reestablishment of a harmed right. In this case, the claimant is not seeking her health to be restored to the stage it had before, but to have a particular health care, which is perfectly valid."[71]

6. The imminent character of the threats and the preventive character of the amparo against threats

However, the amparo proceeding is not only a judicial mean seeking to restore harmed constitutional rights, it is also a judicial mean established for the protection of such rights against illegitimate threats that violate those rights. It is in these cases that the amparo proceeding has a preventive character in the sense of avoiding harm, similar to the United States preventive civil rights injunctions seeking "to prohibit some act or series of acts from occurring in the future,"[72] and designed "to avoid future harm to a party by prohibiting or mandating certain behavior by another party."[73]

It would be absurd for the affected party, when having complete knowledge of the near occurrence of harm, to patiently wait for the harming act to be issued with all

---

70 As decided by the First Court on Judicial Review of Administrative Action of Venezuela, regarding a municipal order for the demolition of a building, in the sense that if the demolition was already executed, the amparo judge cannot decide the matter because of the irreparable character of the harm. See the January 1, 1999, decision, *B. Gómez* case, in Rafael Chavero, *El nuevo régimen del amparo constitucional en Venezuela*, Ed. Sherwood, Caracas, 2001, p 242. The First Court also ruled in a case decided in February 4, 1999, *C. Negrín* case, regarding a public university position contest that, "the pretended aggrieved party is seeking to be allowed to be registered himself in the public contest for the Chair of Pharmacology in the School of Medicine José María Vargas, but at the present time, the registration was impossible due to the fact that the delay had elapsed the previous year, and consequently the harm produced must be considered as irreparable, declaring inadmissible the action for amparo." *Idem*, p. 243.

71 See decision of March 3, 1990, in *Revista de Derecho Público*, Nº 42, Editorial Jurídica Venezolana, Caracas, 1990, p. 107.

72 See Owen M. Fiss, *The Civil Rights Injunction*, Indiana University Press, 1978, p. 7.

73 See William M. Tabb and Elaine W. Shoben, *Remedies*, Thompson West, 2005, p. 22. In Spanish the word "preventive" is used in procedural law (medidas preventivas o cautelares) to refer to the "temporary" or "preliminary" orders or restraints that in the United States the judge can issue during the proceeding. So the preventive character of the amparo and of the injunctions cannot be confused with the "medidas preventivas" or temporary or preliminary measures that the courts can issue during the trial for the immediate protection of rights, facing the prospect of an irremediable harm that can be caused.

its consequences in order to file the amparo action. On the contrary, it has the right to file the action to obtain a judicial order prohibiting the action to be accomplished, thus avoiding the harm to occur.

The main condition for this possibility of filing amparo actions against threats (*amenaza*) to constitutional rights, as it is expressly provided in the Amparo Law (Articles 2; 6.2), is that they must be real, certain, immediate, imminent, possible and realizable.

On the other hand, there are some constitutional rights that essentially and precisely need to be protected against threats, like the right to life in cases of imminent death threats, because on the contrary, they could lose all sense. In this case, the only way to guaranty the right to life is to avoid the threats to be materialized, for instance, by providing the person with effective police protection.

If the specific main condition for the admissibility of the amparo action against harms to constitutional rights is their reparable character; regarding threats, the specific main condition is that they must be of an imminent character.

This condition is also expressly established in the Amparo Law (Articles 2; 6,2), which provides that in order to file an amparo action against threats, they must not only be real, certain, possible and realizable, but additionally, they must have an immediate and imminent character, provoking fear to persons, or making persons feel in danger regarding their rights. On the contrary, harm refers to situations in which a fact has already been accomplished, so no threat is possible.

Consequently, in order to file an amparo action against a threat, it must consist in a potential harm or violation that must be imminent in the sense that it may occur soon; being this same rule of the imminent character of the threat applied in the United States, as an essential condition for granting preventive injunctions. This means that the courts will order injunctions only when the threat is imminent, prohibiting future conduct; and not when the threat is considered remote, potential or speculative.[74]

74 In *Reserve Mining Co. v. Environmental Protection Agency* 513 F.2d, 492 (8th Cir 1975), the Circuit Court did not grant the requested injunction ordering Reserve Mining Company to cease discharging wastes from its iron ore processing plant in Silver Bay, Minnesota into the ambient air of Silver Bay and the waters of Lake Superior because even though the plaintiff has established that the discharges give rise to a "potential threat to the public health…no harm to the public health has been shown to have occurred to this date and the danger to health is not imminent. The evidence calls for preventive and precautionary steps. No reason exists which requires that Reserve to terminate its operations at once." See the comments in Owen M. Fiss and Doug Rendelman, *Injunctions*, The Foundation Press, Mineola, New York, 1984, pp. 116 ff. In another classically cited case, *Fletcher v. Bealey*, 28 Ch. 688 (1885), which referred to waste deposits in the plaintiff's land by the defendant, the judge ruled that since the action is brought to prevent continuing damages, for a quia-timet action, two ingredients are necessary: "There must, if no actual damage is proved, be proof of imminent danger, and there must also be proof that the apprehended damage will, if it comes, be very substantial. I should almost say it must be proved that it will be irreparable, because, if the danger is not proved to be so imminent that no one can doubt that if the remedy is delayed, the damage will be suffered, I think it must be shown that, if the damage does occur at any time, it will come in such a way and under such circumstances that it will be impossible for the Plaintiff to protect himself against it if relief is denied to him in a *quia timet* action." See the reference in *Idem*, pp. 110–111.

In the same sense as the amparo, the injunctions in the United States cannot be granted "merely to allay the fears and apprehensions or to soothe the anxieties of individuals, since such fears and apprehensions may exist without substantial reasons and be absolutely groundless or speculative."[75] The injunctions, as the amparo, are extraordinary remedies "designed to prevent serious harm, and are not to be used to protect a person from mere inconvenience or speculative and insubstantial injury."[76]

This condition is also generally established in Venezuela, in the sense that threats that can be protected by the amparo suits must be imminent (Article 2), so the action for amparo is inadmissible when the threat or violation of a constitutional right has ceased or ended (Article 8,1) or when the threat against a constitutional right or guaranty is not "immediate, possible and feasible (Article 6,2).[77]

In the same sense, the former Supreme Court of Justice of Venezuela ruled in 1989 that:

> "The opening of a disciplinary administrative inquiry is not enough to justify the protection of a party by means of the judicial remedy of amparo, moreover when the said proceeding, in which all needed defenses can be exercised, may conclude in a decision discarding the incriminations against the party with the definitive closing of the disciplinary process, without any sanction to the party."[78]

The criteria of the imminent character of the threat to constitutional rights for the admission of the amparo action has also led the former Supreme Court of Justice of Venezuela to reject the amparo proceeding against statutes, arguing that a statute or a legal norm, in itself, cannot originate a possible, imminent and feasible threat.[79]

---

75 See *Callis, Papa, Jackstadt & Halloran, P.C. v. Norkolk and Western Ry. Co.*, 195 Ill. 2d 356, 254 Ill. Dec. 707, 748 N. E.2d 153 (2001); *Frey v. DeCordova Bend Estates Owners Ass'n*, 647 S.W2d 246 (Tex. 1983); *Ormco Corp. v. Johns*, 19 I.E.R. Cas. (BNA), 1714, 148 Lab. Cas. (CCH), 59741, 2003 WL 2007816 (Ala. 2003), in John Bordeau *et al.*, "Injunctions," in Kevin Schroder, John Glenn and Maureen Placilla (Editors), *Corpus Juris Secundum*, Vol. 43A, Thomson West, 2004, p. 57.

76 See *Kucera v. State, Dept. of Transp.*, 140 Wash. 2d 200, 955 O.2d 63 (200)), *Idem*, pp. 57–58.

77 See decisions of the former Supreme Court of Justice, Politico Administrative Chamber of June 9, 1988, in *Revista de Derecho Público*, N° 35, Editorial Jurídica Venezolana, Caracas, 1988, p. 114, and of August 14, 1992, in *Revista de Derecho Público*, N° 51, Editorial Jurídica Venezolana, Caracas, 1992, pp. 158–159. See also decision of the First Court on Judicial Review of Administrative Action, decision of June 30, 1988, in *Revista de Derecho Público*, N° 35, Editorial Jurídica Venezolana, Caracas, 1988, p. 115. These general conditions have been considered as being concurrent ones when referring to the constitutional protection against harms that someone will soon be inflicting on the rights of other. See decisions of the former Supreme Court of Justice, Politico Administrative Chamber, of June 24, 1993, in *Revista de Derecho Público*, N° 55–56, Editorial Jurídica Venezolana, Caracas, 1993, p. 289; and of March 22, 1995, *La Reintegradora* case, in Rafael Chavero, *El nuevo régimen del amparo constitucional en Venezuela,* Ed. Sherwood, Caracas, 2001, p. 239.

78 See Decision of the Politico Administrative Chamber of October 26, 1989, *Gisela Parra Mejía* case, in Rafael Chavero, *El nuevo régimen del amparo constitucional en Venezuela*, Ed. Sherwood, Caracas, 2001, pp. 191, 241.

79 In a decision of May 24, 1993, the Politico Administrative Chamber of the former Supreme Court ruled: "The same occurs with the third condition set forth in the Law; the threat, that is, the

Nonetheless, the Court has considered that the plaintiff can always file the amparo action against the public officer that must apply the statute, seeking a court prohibition directed to the said public officer, compelling him not to apply the challenged norm."[80]

7. The injuring party in the amparo proceeding

Because the amparo procedure is governed by the principle of bilateralism, the party that initiates it, that is the plaintiff, whose constitutional rights and guaranties have been injured or threatened, must always file the action against an injuring party, whose actions or omissions are those that have caused the harm or threats. This means that the action must always be filed against a person or a public entity that must also be individuated as defendant.[81] That is why in the amparo proceeding, as well as the injunctions in the United States, the final result has to be a judicial order "addressed to some clearly identified individual, not just the general citizenry."[82]

Thus, since the beginning of the proceeding when the action is filed, or during the procedure, the bilateral character of the amparo suit implies the need to have a

---

probable and imminent harm, will never be feasible –that is, concreted– by the defendant. If it could be sustained that the amparo could be filed against a disposition the constitutionality of which is challenged, then it would be necessary to accept as defendant the legislative body or the public officer that had sanctioned it, being the latter the one that would act in court defending the act. It can be observed that in case the possible harm would effectively arrive to be materialized, it would not be the legislative body or the state organ which issued it, the one that will execute it, but the public official for whom the application of the norm will be imposing in all the cases in which an individual would be in the factual situation established in the norm. If it is understood that the norm can be the object or an amparo action, the conclusion would be that the defendant (the public entity sanctioning the norm the unconstitutionality of which is alleged) could not be the one entity conducting the threat; but that the harm would be in the end concretized or provoked by a different entity (the one applying to the specific and concrete case the unconstitutional provision)." See in *Revista de Derecho Público*, N° 55-56, Editorial Jurídica Venezolana, Caracas, 1993, pp. 289–290.

80 In the same decision, the Court ruled as follows: "Nonetheless, this High Court considers necessary to point out that the previous conclusion does not signify the impossibility to prevent the concretion of the harm –objection that could be drawn from the thesis that the amparo can only proceed if the unconstitutional norm is applied–, due to the fact that the imminently aggrieved person must not necessarily wait for the effective execution of the illegal norm, because since he faces the threat having the conditions established in the Law, he could seek for amparo for his constitutional rights. In such case, though, the amparo would not be directed against the norm, but against the public officer that has to apply it. In effect, being imminent the application to an individual of a normative disposition contrary to any of the constitutional rights or guaranties, the potentially affected person could seek from the court a prohibition directed to the said public officer plaintiff, compelling not to apply the challenged norm, once evaluated by the court as being unconstitutional." *Idem*, p. 290.

81 The only exception to the principle of bilateralism is the case of Chile, where the offender is not considered a defendant party but only a person whose activity is limited to inform the court and give it the documents it has. That is why in the Regulation set forth by the Supreme Court (*Auto Acordado*) it is said that the affected state organ, person or public officer "can" just appear as party in the process (4). See Juan Manuel Errazuriz G. and Jorge Miguel Otero A., *Aspectos procesales del recurso de protección*, Editorial Jurídica de Chile 1989, p. 27.

82 See Owen M. Fiss, *The Civil Rights Injunction*, Indiana University Press, 1978, p. 12.

procedural relation that must be established between the injured party and the injuring one who must also participate in the process.[83]

This need for the individuation of the defendant also derives from the subjective or personal character of the amparo in the sense that in the complaint, as provided in article 18,3 of the Amparo Law, in the sense that the plaintiff must clearly identify the authority, public officer, person or entity against whom the action is filed. In the case of amparo actions filed against artificial persons, public entities or corporations, the petition must also identify them with precision and if possible, also identify their representatives.

In these cases of harms caused by entities or corporations, the action can be filed directly against the natural person acting on his behalf as representative of the entity or corporation, for instance, the public official; or directly against the entity in itself.[84] In this latter case, according to the expression used in civil right injunctions in the United States, the action is filed against "the office rather than [to] the person."[85]

Consequently, in cases of amparo actions filed against entities or corporations, the natural person representing them can be changed, as it commonly happens regarding public entities, [86] a circumstance that does not affect the bilateral relation between aggrieved and aggrieving parties.

83 In this regard, the former Supreme Court of Justice of Venezuela in a decision of December 15, 1992, pointed out that: "The amparo action set forth in the Constitution, and regulated in the Organic Amparo law, has among its fundamental characteristic its basic personal or subjective character, which implies that a direct, specific and undutiful relation must exist between the person claiming for the protection of his rights, and the person purported to have originated the disturbance, who is to be the one with standing to act as defendant or the person against whom the action is filed. In other words, it is necessary, for granting an amparo, that the person signaled as the injurer be in the end, the one originating the harm." See Supreme Court of Justice, Politico Administrative Chamber, decision dated December 16, 1992, *Haydée Casanova* Caso, in *Revista de Derecho Público*, N° 52, Editorial Jurídica Venezolana, Caracas, 1992, p. 139.

84 This implies that in the filing of the action of amparo in cases of Public Administration activities, "the person acting on behalf of (or representing) the entity who caused the harm or threat to the rights or guaranties must be identified, which is, the signaled person who has the exact and direct knowledge of the facts." See decision of the First Court on Judicial Review of Administrative Actions, dated June 16, 1988, in *Revista de Derecho Público*, N° 35, Editorial Jurídica Venezolana, Caracas, 1988, p. 138.

85 See Owen M. Fiss, *The Civil Rights Injunction*, Indiana University Press, 1978, p. 15

86 As it has been decided by the Venezuelan First Court on Judicial Review of Administrative Action in a decision of September 28, 1993, regarding an amparo action filed against the dean of a Law Faculty, in which case the person in charge as Dean was changed: "The heading of the position does not change its organic unity. If the dean of the Faculty changes, it will always be a subjective figure that substitutes the previous one. That is why in a decision of September 11, 1990, this Court ruled that the circumstance of the head of an organ mentioned as aggrieving being changed does not alter the procedural relation originated with the amparo action. In addition, it must be added that it would have no sense to rule for the procedural relation be continued with the person that doesn't occupy anymore the position, because in case the constitutional amparo is granted, then the ex public official would not be in a position to reestablish the factual infringed situation. As much, the former public officer could be liable for the damages caused, but as it is known, the amparo action has the only purpose of reestablishing the harmed legal situation, and that can only be assured by the current public official." See the First Court on Judicial Review of

As aforementioned, the action can also be personally filed against the representative of the entity or corporation himself, for instance the public officer or the director or manager of the entity, particularly when the harm or threat has been personally provoked by him, independently of the artificial person or entity for which he is acting.[87]

In these cases, when for instance the public official responsible for the harm can be identified with precision as the injuring party, it is only him, personally, who must act as defendant in the procedure, in which case no notice is needed to be sent to his superior or to the Attorney General.[88] In such cases, it is the individuated natural person or public officer that must personally act as injuring party.[89]

On the contrary, if the action is filed, for instance, against a Ministerial entity as a Public Administration organ, in this case the Attorney General, as representative of the State, is the entity that must act in the process as its judicial representative.[90] In other cases, when the amparo action is exercised against a perfectly identified and individuated organ of a Public Administration and not against the State, the Attorney General, as its judicial representative, does not necessarily have a procedural role to play,[91] and cannot act on its behalf.[92]

One of the most important aspects in the Venezuelan amparo proceeding regarding the injuring party is that the action for amparo can be filed not only

---

Administrative Action in a decision of September, 28, 1993, in *Revista de Derecho Público*, N° 55-56, Editorial Jurídica Venezolana, Caracas, 1993, p. 330.

87 In such cases, when the action is filled against public officers, as it is established in Article 27 of the Venezuelan Amparo Law, the court deciding on the merits must notify its decision to the competent authority "in order for it to decide the disciplinary sanctions against the public official responsible for the violation or the threat against a constitutional right or guaranty."

88 Venezuelan First Court on Judicial Review of Administrative Action, decision of May 12, 1988, in Revista *de Derecho Público*, N° 34, Editorial Jurídica Venezolana, Caracas, 1988, p. 113; Venezuelan Supreme Court of Justice, Politico Administrative Chamber, decision of March 16, 1989, in *Revista de Derecho Público*, N° 38, Editorial Jurídica Venezolana, Caracas, 1989, p. 110; Venezuelan First Court on Judicial Review of Administrative Action, decision of September 7, 1989, in *Revista de Derecho Público*, N° 40, Editorial Jurídica Venezolana, Caracas, 1989, p. 107.

89 Former Venezuelan Supreme Court of Justice, Politico Administrative Chamber, March 8, 1990, in *Revista de Derecho Público*, N° 42, Editorial Jurídica Venezolana, Caracas, 1990, p. 114; Venezuelan First Court on Judicial Review of Administrative Action, decision of November 21, 1990, in *Revista de Derecho Público*, N° 44, Editorial Jurídica Venezolana, Caracas, 1990, p. 148.

90 Venezuelan First Court on Judicial Review of Administrative Action, decision of September 7, 1989, in Revista *de Derecho Público*, N° 40, Editorial Jurídica Venezolana, Caracas, 1989, p. 107.

91 Venezuelan First Court on Judicial Review of Administrative Action, decision of November 21, 1990, in Revista *de Derecho Público*, N° 44, Editorial Jurídica Venezolana, Caracas, 1990, p. 148.

92 Venezuelan First Court on Judicial Review of Administrative Action, decision of October 10, 1990, in Revista *de Derecho Público*, N° 44, Editorial Jurídica Venezolana, Caracas, 1990, p. 142; Former Supreme Court of Justice, Politico Administrative Chamber, decision of August 1, 1991, in Revista *de Derecho Público*, N° 47, Editorial Jurídica Venezolana, Caracas, 1991, p. 120; Venezuelan First Court on Judicial review of Administrative Action, decision of July 30, 1992, in Revista *de Derecho Público*, N° 51, Editorial Jurídica Venezolana, Caracas, 1992, p. 164; Former Venezuelan Supreme Court of Justice, Politico Administrative Chamber, December 15, 1992, in Revista *de Derecho Público*, N° 52, Editorial Jurídica Venezolana, Caracas, 1992, p. 13.

against public authorities but also against individuals. In other words, this specific judicial mean is conceived for the protection of constitutional rights and guaranties against harms or threats regardless of the author, which can be public entities, authorities, individuals or private corporations.

The amparo proceeding was originally created to protect individuals against the State; and that is why some countries like Mexico remain with that traditional trend; but that initial trend has not prevented the possibility for the admission of the amparo proceeding for the protection of constitutional rights against other individual's actions. The current situation is that in the majority of Latin American countries the admission of the amparo action against individuals is accepted, as is the case in Argentina, Bolivia, Chile, the Dominican Republic, Paraguay, Peru, Venezuela and Uruguay, as well as, although in a more restrictive way, in Colombia, Costa Rica, Ecuador, Guatemala and Honduras. In this sense the writ of amparo is also regulated in the Philippines, which can be filed against acts or omission "of a public official or employee, or of a private individual or entity" (Sec. 1). Only a minority of Latin American countries the amparo action remains exclusively as a protective mean against authorities, as happens in Brazil, El Salvador, Panama, Mexico and Nicaragua. This is also the case in the United States where the civil rights injunctions, in matters of constitutional or civil rights or guaranties,[93] can only be admitted against public entities.[94]

In Venezuela, the amparo action is admitted against acts of individuals. The 1988 Organic Law of Amparo[95] provides that the amparo action "shall be admitted against any fact, act or omission from citizens, legal entities, private groups or organizations that have violated, violates or threaten to violate any of the constitutional guaranties or rights" (Article 2).

---

93 In other matters the injunctions can be filed against any person as "higher public officials or private persons." See M. Glenn Abernathy and Barbara A. Perry, *Civil Liberties under the Constitution*, Sixth Edition, University of South Carolina Press, 1993, p. 8.

94 As explained by M. Glenn Abernathy and Barbara A. Perry: "Limited remedies for private interference with free choice. Another problem in the citizen's search for freedom from restriction lies in that many types of interference stemming from private persons do not constitute actionable wrongs under the law. Private prejudice and private discrimination do not, in the absence of specific statutory provisions, offer grounds for judicial intervention on behalf of the sufferer. If one is denied admission to membership in a social club, for example, solely on the basis of his race or religion or political affiliation, he may understandably smart under the rejection, but the courts cannot help him (again assuming no statutory provision barring such distinctions). There are, then, many types of restraints on individual freedom of choice which are beyond the authority of courts to remove or ameliorate. It should be noted that the guaranties of rights in the U.S. Constitution only protect against governmental action and do not apply to purely private encroachments, except for the Thirteenth Amendment's prohibition of slavery. Remedies for private invasion must be found in statutes, the common law, or administrative agency regulations and adjudications." *Idem*, p. 6.

95 See Allan R. Brewer-Carías, *Instituciones Políticas y Constitucionales*, Vol V, *Derecho y Acción de Amparo*, Editorial Jurídica Venezolana, Caracas, 1998, pp. 96, 128; Rafael Chavero, *El nuevo régimen del amparo constitucional en Venezuela*, Editorial Sherwood, Caracas, 2001.

8. The injuring public actions and omissions

Being the amparo action originally established to defend constitutional rights from State and authorities' violations, the most common and important injuring parties in the amparo proceeding are, of course, the public authorities or public officials when their acts or omissions, whether of legislative, executive or judicial nature, cause the harm or threats.

The general principle in this matter in Venezuela, with some exceptions, is that any authority –and not only administrative authorities– can be questioned through amparo actions, and that any act, fact or omission of any public authority or entity or public officials causing an injury to constitutional rights can be challenged by means of such actions. This is the wording used in the Amparo Law of Venezuela, providing that the action can be filed against "any fact, act or omission of any of the National, State, or Municipal branches of government" (*Poderes Públicos*) (Article 2); which mean that the constitutional protection can be filed against any public action, that is, any formal state act, any substantive or any factual activity (*vía de hecho*) (Article 5); as well as against any omission from public entities. That is also why the courts in Venezuela have decided that "there is no State act that can be excluded from revision by means of amparo, the purpose of which is not to annul State acts but to protect public freedoms and restore its enjoyment when violated or harmed," thereby admitting that the constitutional amparo action can be filed even against legislative acts excluded from judicial review, when a harm or violation of constitutional rights or guaranties has been alleged.[96]

---

96 See the former Supreme Court of Justice decision dated January 31, 1991, *Anselmo Natale* case, in *Revista de Derecho Público*, N° 45, Editorial Jurídica Venezolana, Caracas, 1991, p. 118. See also the decision of the First Court on Judicial Review of Administrative Action of June 18, 1992, in *Revista de Derecho Público*, N° 46, Editorial Jurídica Venezolana, Caracas, 1991, p. 125. This universality character of the amparo regarding public authorities acts or omissions, according to the Venezuelan courts, implies that: "From what Article 2 of the Amparo law sets forth, it results that no type of conduct, regardless of its nature or character or their authors, can per se be excluded from the amparo judge revision in order to determine if it harms or doesn't harm constitutional rights or guaranties." See decision of the First Court on Judicial Review of Administrative Action of November 11, 1993, *Aura Loreto Rangel* case, in *Revista de Derecho Público*, N° 55–56, Editorial Jurídica Venezolana, Caracas, 1993, p. 284. The same criterion was adopted by the Political Administrative Chamber of the former Supreme Court of Justice in a decision of May 24, 1993, as follows: "The terms on which the amparo action is regulated in Article 49 of the Constitution (now Article 27) are very extensive. If the extended scope of the rights and guaranties that can be protected and restored through this judicial mean is undoubted; the harm cannot be limited to those produced only by some acts. So, in equal terms it must be permitted that any harming act –whether an act, a fact or an omission– with respect to any constitutional right and guaranty, can be challenged by means of this action, due to the fact that the amparo action is the protection of any norm regulating the so-called subjective rights of constitutional rank, it cannot be sustained that such protection is only available in cases in which the injuring act has some precise characteristics, whether from a material or organic point of view. The jurisprudencia of this Court has been constant regarding both principles. In a decision N° 22, dated January 31, 1991, *Anselmo Natale* case, it was decided that 'there is no State act that could not be reviewed by amparo, the latter understood not as a mean for judicial review of constitutionality of State acts in order to annul them, but as a protective remedy regarding public freedoms whose purpose is to reestablish its enjoyment and exercise, when a natural or artificial person, or group or private organization, threatens to harm them or effectively harm them. See,

Consequently, in Venezuela, amparo actions can be filed against legislative actions or omissions, although regarding statutes the jurisprudence of the Supreme Tribunal imposes the need to file the action only against the State acts issued to apply the statutes and not directly against them,[97] considering that a statute cannot be a threat to constitutional rights, because for an amparo to be filed, a threat must be "imminent, possible and realizable," considering that in the case of statutes such conditions are not fulfilled.[98] Regarding judicial decisions, and contrary to what

---

regarding the extended scope of the protected rights, decision of December 4, 1990, *Mariela Morales de Jimenez* case, N° 661, in *Revista de Derecho Público*, N° 55-56, Editorial Jurídica Venezolana, Caracas, 1993, pp. 284–285. In another decision dated February 13, 1992, the First Court ruled: "This Court observes that the essential characteristic of the amparo regime, in its constitutional regulation as well as in its statutory development, is its universality.., so the protection it assures is extended to all subjects (physical or artificial persons), as well as regarding all constitutionally guaranteed rights, including those that without being expressly regulated in the Constitution are inherent to human beings. This is the departing point in order to understand the scope of the constitutional amparo. Regarding Public Administration, the amparo against it is so extended that it can be filed against all acts, omissions and factual actions, without any kind of exclusion regarding some matters that are always related to the public order and social interest." See in *Revista de Derecho Público*, N° 49, Editorial Jurídica Venezolana, Caracas, 1992, pp. 120–121.

97 In a decision dated May 24, 1993, the Politico Administrative Chamber of the former Supreme Court issued a decision that has been the leading case on the matter, ruling that: "thus, it seem that there is no doubt that Article 3 of the Amparo law does not set forth the possibility of filing an amparo action directly against a normative act, but against the act, fact or omission that has its origin in a normative provision which is considered by the claimant as contrary to the Constitution and for which, due to the presumption of legitimacy and constitutionality of the former, the court must previously resolve its inapplicability to the concrete case argued. It is obvious, thus, that such article of the Amparo law does not allow the possibility of filing this action for constitutional protection against a statute or other normative act, but against the act which applies or executes it, which is definitively the one that in the concrete case can cause a particular harm to the constitutional rights and guaranties of a precise person." See in *Revista de Derecho Público*, N° 55-56, Editorial Jurídica Venezolana, Caracas, 1993, pp. 287–288.

98 The Court, in the same decision, rejected the possibility of a threat caused by a statute, with the following argument: "In case of an amparo action against a norm, the concretion of the possible harm would not be 'immediate', because it will always be the need for a competent authority to execute or apply it in order for the statute to effectively harm the claimant. It must be concluded that the probable harm produced by the norm will always be a mediate and indirect one, due to the need for the statute to be applied to the particular case. So that the harm will be caused by mean of the act applying the illegal norm. The same occurs with the third condition, in the sense that the probable and imminent threat will never be made by the possible defendant. If it would be possible to sustain that the amparo could be admissible against a statute whose constitutionality is challenged, it would be necessary to accept as aggrieved party the legislative body issuing it, being the party to participate in the process as defendant. But it must be highlighted that in the case in which the possible harm could be realized, it would not be the legislative body the one called to execute it, but rather the public officer that must apply the norm in all the cases in which an individual is located in the situation it regulates. If it is understood that the object of the amparo action is the statute, then the conclusion would be that the possible defendant (the public entity enacting the norm whose unconstitutionality is alleged) could not be the one that could make the threat. The concrete harm would be definitively made by a different entity or person (the one applying the unconstitutional norm to a specific and concrete case). See in *Revista de Derecho Público*, N° 55-56, Editorial Jurídica Venezolana, Caracas, 1993, pp. 288 a 290. From the abovementioned, the Venezuelan Supreme Court concluded rejecting the amparo action against statutes and normative acts, not only because it considered that the Amparo Laws do

happens in the majority of Latin American countries, in Venezuela, the amparo action is admitted against judicial acts, except decisions of the Supreme Tribunal of Justice (Article 6,6). Article 4 of the Amparo Law provides that in the cases of judicial decisions "the action for amparo shall also be admitted when a court, acting outside its competence, issues a resolution or decision, or orders an action that impairs a constitutional right."

But specifically, regarding executive authorities, the general principle is that the action is admitted against acts, facts or omissions from public entities or bodies conforming to the Public Administration at all its levels (national, state, municipal), including decentralized, autonomous, independent bodies and including acts issued by the Head of the Executive, that is, the President of the Republic. This last aspect, for instance, is contrary to the rule regarding injunctions in the United States where the principle is that such coercive remedy cannot be directed against the President.[99]

Regarding administrative acts, as mentioned, the Law admits the filing of amparo actions against them, providing for possibility of exercising the amparo action in two ways: in an autonomous way or conjunctly with nullity recourse for judicial review of the administrative act (Article 5).[100] The main distinction between both means[101] lies, first, in the character of the allegation: in the first case, the alleged and

not set forth such possibility –bypassing its text–, but because even being possible to bring the extraordinary action against a normative act, it would not comply with the imminent, possible and realizable conditions of the threats set forth in Article 6,2 of the Amparo Law.

99 See *Sloan v. Nixon*, 60 F.R.D. 228 (S.D.N.Y. 1973), aff'd, 93 F.2d 1398 (2d Cir. 1974), judgment aff'd, 419 U.S. 958, 95 S. Ct. 218, 42 L. Ed. 2d 174 (1974), in John Bourdeau *et al.*, "Injunctions," in Kevin Schroder, John Glenn and Maureen Placilla, *Corpus Juris Secundum*, Volume 43A, Thompson West, 2004, p. 229.

100 Regarding the latter, the former Supreme Court of Justice in the decision of July 10, 1991 (*Tarjetas Banvenez* case), clarified that in such case, the action is not a principal one, but subordinated and ancillary regarding the principal recourse to which it has been attached, and subjected to the final nullifying decision that has to be issued in it. See the text in *Revista de Derecho Público*, N° 47, Editorial Jurídica Venezolana, Caracas, 1991, pp. 169–174, and comments in *Revista de Derecho Público*, N° 50, Editorial Jurídica Venezolana, Caracas, 1992, pp. 183–184. That is why, in such cases, the amparo pretension that must be founded in a grave presumption of the violation of the constitutional right, has a preventive and temporal character, pending the final decision of the nullity suit, consisting in the suspension of the effects of the challenged administrative act. This provisional character of the amparo protection pending the suit is thus subjected to the final decision to be issued in the nullity judicial review procedure against the challenged administrative act. See in *Revista de Derecho Público*, N° 47, Editorial Jurídica Venezolana, Caracas, 1991, pp. 170–171.

101 The main difference between both procedures according to the Supreme Court doctrine is that: in the first case of the autonomous amparo action against administrative acts, the plaintiff must allege a direct, immediate and flagrant violation to the constitutional right, which in its own demonstrates the need for the amparo order as a definitive means to restore the harmed juridical situation. In the second case, given the suspensive nature of the amparo order which only tends to provisionally stop the effects of the injuring act until the judicial review of administrative action confirming or nullifying it is decided, the alleged unconstitutional violations of constitutional provisions can be formulated together with violations of legal or statutory provisions developing the constitutional ones, because it is a judicial review action against administrative acts, seeking their nullity, they can also be founded on legal texts. What the court cannot do in these cases of filing together the actions, in order to suspend the effects of the challenged administrative act, is to found its decision only in the legal violations alleged, because that would mean to anticipate the final decision on the principal nullity judicial review recourse. *Idem*, pp. 171–172.

proved constitutional right violation must be a direct, immediate and flagrant one; in the second case, what has to be proved is the existence of a grave presumption of the constitutional right violation. And second, in the general purpose of the proceeding: in the first case, the judicial decision issued is a definitive constitutional protection one, of restorative character; in the second case, it has only preliminary character of suspension of the effects of the challenged act pending the decision of the principal judicial review process.[102]

Beside the legislative, executive and judicial branches of government, the amparo action can also be filed against the acts of other independent organs or branches of government that accomplish administrative actions like for instance, the Electoral bodies in charge of governing the electoral processes, the People's Defendant Office, the Public Prosecutor Office, of the General Comptroller Office, including the Judiciary organs in charge of the government and administration of courts and tribunals. Because those entities are State organs, in principle their acts, facts and omissions can also be challenged by means of amparo actions when violating constitutional rights.

Apart from the positive acts or actions from public officers, authorities or from individuals, that amparo action can also be filed against the omissions of authorities when the corresponding entities or public officials fail to comply with their general obligations, thereby causing harm of threat to constitutional rights. In the cases of public officers' omissions, the amparo action is generally filed in order to obtain from the court an order directed against the public officer compelling him to act in a matter with respect to which he has the authority or jurisdiction. In these cases, the effects of the amparo decision regarding omissions is similar to the United States mandamus or mandatory injunction,[103] which consists in "a writ commanding a public officer to perform some duty which the laws require him to do but he refuses or neglects to perform."[104]

102 *Idem*, p. 172. See also regarding the nullity of Article 22 of the Organic Amparo Law the former Supreme Court decision dated May 21, 1996, in Allan R. Brewer-Carías, *Instituciones Políticas y Constitucionales,* Vol. V, *Derecho y Acción de Amparo*, Editorial Jurídica Venezolana, Caracas, 1996, pp. 392 ff.

103 In the United States, it has been considered that while as a general rule courts will not compel by injunction the performance by public officers of their official duties (*Bellamy v. Gates*, 214 Va. 314, 200 S.E. 2d 533, (1973)), a court may compel public officers or boards to act in a matter with respect to which they have jurisdiction or authority (*Erie v. State By and Through State Highway Commission*, 154 Mont. 150, 461 P 2d 207 (1969)). See in John Bourdeau *et al.*, "Injunctions," in Kevin Schroder, John Glenn and Maureen Placilla, *Corpus Juris Secundum*, Volume 43A, Thompson West, 2004, pp. 221, 222, 244.

104 The consequence of this rule is that mandamus cannot be used if the public officer has any discretion in the matter; "but if the law is clear in requiring the performance of some ministerial (nondiscretionary) function, then mandamus may properly be sought to nudge the reluctant or negligent official along in the performance of his or her duties." As it was decided by the Supreme Court in *Wilbur v. United States*, 281 U.S. 206, 218 (1930): "Where the duty in a particular situation is so plainly prescribed as to be free from doubt and equivalent to a positive command, it is regarded as being so far ministerial that its performance may be compelled by mandamus, unless there be provision or implication to the contrary, but where the duty is not thus plainly prescribed but depends upon a statute, the construction or application of which is not free from doubt, it is regarded as involving the character of judgment or discretion which cannot be

In any case, for an omission to be the object of an amparo action, it must also inflict a direct harm to the constitutional right of the plaintiff, so if the violation is only referring to a right of legal rank, the amparo action is inadmissible and the affected party is obliged to use the ordinary judicial remedies, like the judicial review of administrative omission action to be filed before the special courts of the matter (*contencioso-administrativo*).[105] In order to determine when it is possible to file an amparo action against public officers' omissions, the key element established by the Venezuelan courts refers to the nature of the public officers' duties because the amparo action is only admissible when the matters refer to a generic constitutional duty and not to specific legal ones.[106]

Because the judicial order of mandamus in the amparo decision regarding public authorities' omissions is a command directed to the public officer to perform the duty the constitution requires him to do, which he has refused or neglected to perform,[107] the general rule is that the court order cannot substitute the public

---

controlled by mandamus." See the references in M. Glenn Abernathy and Barbara A. Perry, *Civil Liberties under the Constitution*, Sixth Edition, University of South Carolina Press, 1993, p. 8.

105 According to the judicial doctrine established by the former Supreme Court of Justice of Venezuela, the amparo action against omissive conducts of Public Administration, must comply with the following two conditions: "a) That the alleged omissive conduct be absolute, which means that Public Administration has not accomplished in any moment the due function; and b) that the omission be regarding a generic duty, that is, the duty a public officer has to act in compliance with the powers attributed to him, which is different to the specific duty that is the condition for the judicial review of administrative omissive action. Thus, only when it is a matter of a generic duty, of procedure, of providing in a matter which is inherent to the public officer position, he incurs in the omissive conduct regarding which the amparo action is admissible." See the decisions of the former Supreme Court of Justice, Politico Administrative Chamber, dated November 5, 1992, *Jorge E. Alvarado* case, in *Revista de Derecho Público*, N° 52, Editorial Jurídica Venezolana, Caracas, 1992, p. 187; and November 18, 1993, in *Revista de Derecho Público*, N° 55-56, Editorial Jurídica Venezolana, Caracas, 1993, p. 295.

106 As defined by the same Supreme Court in a decision dated February 11, 1992: "In cases of Public Administration abstentions or omissions, a distinction can be observed regarding the constitutional provisions violated when they provide for generic or specific duties. In the first case, when a public entity does not comply with its generic obligation to answer [a petition] filed by an individual, it violates the constitutional right to obtain prompt answer [to his petition] as set forth in Article 67 of the Constitution; whereas when the inactivity is produced regarding a specific duty imposed by a statute in a concrete and ineludible way, no direct constitutional violation occurs, in which case the Court has imposed the filing of the judicial review of administrative omissions recourse..." The Court continued: "From the aforementioned reasons the Court deems conclusive that the inactivity of Public Administration to accomplish a specific legal duty precisely infringes in a direct and immediate way the legal (statutory) text regulating the matter, in which case the Constitution is only violated in a mediate and indirect way. For the amparo judge, in order to detect if an abstention of the aggrieved entity effectively harms a constitutional right or guaranty, it must first, rely himself on the supposedly unaccomplished statute in order to verify if the abstention is regarding a specific obligation; in which case it must deny the amparo action, having the plaintiff the possibility to file another remedy, like the judicial review action against Public Administration omissions." See in *Revista de Derecho Público*, N° 53-54, Editorial Jurídica Venezolana, Caracas, 1993, pp. 272–273.

107 For instance, to promptly issue the corresponding decision accordingly to the formal petition filed before the authority (Article 51, Constitution). See the former Venezuelan Supreme Court decision dated August 26, 1993, *Klanki* case, in *Revista de Derecho Público*, N° 55-56, Editorial Jurídica Venezolana, Caracas, 1993, p. 294.

officer's power to decide. Only in cases when a specific statute provides what it is called a "positive silence" (the presumption that after the exhaustion of a particular term, it is considered that Public Administration has tacitly decided accordingly to what has been asked in the particular petition) the judicial order is considered as implicitly giving positive effects to the official abstention or omission.[108]

9. The admissibility conditions of the amparo action based on its extraordinary character

Being a judicial means specifically established for the protection of constitutional rights, the amparo action is conceived in Venezuela as an extraordinary judicial instrument that, consequently, does not substitute for all the other ordinary judicial remedies established for the protection of personal rights and interest. This implies that the amparo action, as a matter of principle, only can be filed when no other adequate judicial mean exists and is available in order to obtain the immediate protection of the violated constitutional rights. This has implied the provisions of rules referred to the admissibility of the action, established in order to determine the existence or inexistence of other adequate judicial mean for the immediate protection of the rights, which justifies or not the use of the extraordinary action.

This question of the adjective rules of the admissibility of the amparo action derives from the relation that exists between the amparo action as an extraordinary judicial mean, and the other ordinary judicial means. In this context, the general rule of admissibility refers to two aspects: first, that the amparo action can only be admissible when there are no other judicial means for granting the constitutional protection; and second, that when the legal order provides for these other judicial means for protection of the right, they are inadequate in order to obtain the immediate protection of the harmed or threatened constitutional rights. In a contrary sense, the amparo action is inadmissible for the protection of a constitutional right if the legal order provides for other actions or proceedings that are adequate for such purpose, guarantying immediate protection to the right.

This rule of admissibility of the amparo action is similar to the general rule existing in the United States regarding the injunctions and all other equitable remedies, like the mandamus and prohibitions, all reserved for extraordinary cases,[109] in the sense that they are available only "after the applicant shows that the

---

108 See the Venezuelan former Supreme Court decision dated December 20, 1991, *BHO, C.A.* case, in *Revista de Derecho Público*, N° 48, Editorial Jurídica Venezolana, Caracas, 1991, pp. 141–143.

109 *Ex-parte Collet*, 337 U.S. 55, 69 S. Ct 944, 93 L. Ed. 1207, 10 A.L.R. 2D 921 (1949). See in John Bourdeau *et al.*, "Injunctions," in Kevin Schroder, John Glenn and Maureen Placilla, *Corpus Juris Secundum*, Volume 43A, Thomson West, 2004, p. 20. This main characteristic of the injunction as an extraordinary remedy has been established since the nineteenth century in *In re Debs* 158 U.S. 564, 15 S.Ct 900, 39 L. Ed. 1092 (1895), in which case, in the words of Justice Brewer, who delivered the opinion of the court, it was decided that: "As a rule, injunctions are denied to those who have adequate remedy at law. Where the choice is between the ordinary and the extraordinary processes of law, and the former are sufficient, the rule will not permit the use of the latter." See in Owen M. Fiss and Doug Rendleman, *Injunctions*, The Foundation Press, Mineola, 1984, p. 8.

legal remedies are inadequate."[110] Is the traditional and fundamental principle for granting an injunction referred to the inadequacy of the existing legal remedies (*Beacon Theatres, Inc. v. Westover*, 359 U.S. 500, 79 S.Ct. 948, 3L.Ed. 2d 988, 2 Fed. R. Serv. 2d 650 (1959)).[111] This condition of the "availability" or of the "sufficiency"[112] has also been referred to as the rule of the "irreparable injury," meaning that the injunction is only admissible when the harm "cannot be adequately repaired by the remedies available in the common law courts." That is, if the threatened rights are rectified by a legal remedy, then the judge will refuse to grant the injunction.[113]

This rule always imposes the need for the plaintiff and for the court to determine in each case, not only the existence and availability of ordinary judicial means for obtaining the constitutional protection, but also the adequacy of such existing and available recourses for granting the immediate constitutional protection to the constitutional right. In this sense, in Venezuela without an express provision in the Amparo Law, the Supreme Court has ruled that "the amparo is admissible even in cases where, although ordinary means exist for the protection of the infringed juridical situation, they would not be suitable, adequate or effective for the immediate restoration of the said situation."[114] Also, the question of the adjective

110 *Idem*, p. 59.

111 See in John Bourdeau *et al.*, "Injunctions," in Kevin Schroder, John Glenn and Maureen Placilla, *Corpus Juris Secundum*, Volume 43A, Thomson West, 2004, p. 89. The judicial doctrine on the matter has been summarized as follows: "An injunction, like any other equitable remedy, will only be issued where there is no adequate remedy at law. Accordingly, except where the rule is changed by statute, an injunction ordinarily will not be granted where there is an adequate remedy at law for the injury complained of, which is full and complete. Conversely, a court of equitable jurisdiction may grant an injunction where an adequate and complete remedy cannot be had in the courts of law, despite the petitioner's efforts. Moreover, a court will not deny access to injunctive relief when procedures cannot effectively, conveniently and directly determine whether the petitioner is entitled to the relief claimed." See in *Idem*, pp. 89–90; 119 ff.; 224 ff.

112 *Idem*, pp. 119 ff.

113 See Owen M. Fiss and Doug Rendleman, *Injunctions*, The Foundation Press, Mineola New York, 1984, p. 59. This situation, as pointed out by Owen M. Fiss "makes the issuance of an injunction conditional upon a showing that the plaintiff has no alternative remedy that will adequately repair the injury. Operationally this means that as general proposition the plaintiff is remitted to some remedy other than an injunction unless he can show that his noninjunctive remedies are inadequate." See Owen Fiss, *The Civil Rights Injunction*, Indiana University Press, 1978, p. 38. This term "inadequacy," according to Tabb and Shoben, "has a specific meaning in the law of equity because it is a shorthand expression for the policy that equitable remedies are subordinate to legal ones. They are subordinate in the sense that the damage remedy is preferred in any individual case if it is adequate." See William M. Tabb and Elaine W. Shoben, *Remedies*, Thomson West, 2005, p. 15. But in particular, regarding constitutional claims involving constitutional rights such as those for school desegregation, it has been considered that their protection precisely requires the extraordinary remedy that can be obtained by equitable intervention, as was decided by the Supreme Court regarding school desegregation in its second opinion in *Brown v. Board of Education* (S. Ct. 1955) and regarding the unconstitutional cruel and unusual punishment in the prison system in *Hutto v. Finney* (S.Ct. 1978). *Idem*, pp. 25–26.

114 See decision of the former Supreme Court of Justice of Venezuela of March 8, 1990, in *Revista de Derecho Público*, N° 42, Editorial Jurídica Venezolana, Caracas, 1990, pp. 107–108. In a similar sense, the Supreme Court in a decision dated December 11, 1990, ruled that: "The criteria of this High Court as well as the authors' opinions has been reiterative in the sense that the amparo action is an extraordinary or special judicial remedy that is only admissible when the other

consequences resulting from the plaintiff's previous election of other remedies for the claimed protection filed before the amparo action must also be analyzed.

Of course, this question of the availability and of the adequacy of the existing judicial means for the admissibility or inadmissibility of the amparo action eventually is a matter of judicial interpretation and adjudication, which must always be decided in the particular case decision, when evaluating the adequacy question.[115]

In Venezuela, particularly regarding the amparo action against administrative acts, the prevalent doctrine on the matter for many years, established by the former Supreme Court of Justice, was to admit the amparo action in spite of the existence of the specific recourse before the Judicial Review of Administrative Action Jurisdiction. Yet this wide protective doctrine has been unfortunately abandoned in recent years by the Supreme Tribunal of Justice, applying a restrictive interpretation regarding the adequacy of the judicial review action for the annulment of administrative acts, and rejecting the amparo action when filed directly against them.[116]

---

procedural means that could repair the harm are exhausted, do not exist or would be inoperative. Additionally, Article 5 of the Amparo Law provides that the amparo action is only admissible when no brief, summary and effective procedural means exist in accordance with the constitutional protection." This objective procedural condition for the admissibility of the action turns the amparo into a judicial mean that can only be admissible by the court once it has verified that the other ordinary means are not effective or adequate in order to restore the infringed juridical situation. If other means exist, the court must not admit the proposed amparo action." See in *Revista de Derecho Público*, Nº 45, Editorial Jurídica Venezolana, Caracas, 1991, p. 112. The Supreme Court in another decision dated June 12, 1990, decided that the amparo action is admissible: "when there are no other means for the adequate and effective reestablishment of the infringed juridical situation. Consequently, one of the conditions for the admissibility of the amparo action is the nonexistence of other more effective means for the reestablishment of the harmed rights. If such means are adequate to resolve the situation, there is no need to file the special amparo action. But even if such means exists, if they are inadequate for the immediate reestablishment of the constitutional guaranty, it is also justifiable to use the constitutional protection mean of amparo." See the decision of the Politico Administrative Chamber of the Supreme Court of Justice of June 12, 1990, in *Revista de Derecho Público* Nº 43, Editorial Jurídica Venezolana, Caracas, 1990, p. 78. See also in *Revista de Derecho Público*, Nº 55-56, Editorial Jurídica Venezolana, Caracas, 1993, pp. 311–313.

115 For instance, in a decision of the First Court on administrative jurisdiction dated May 20, 1994 (*Federación Venezolana de Deportes Equestres* case), it was ruled that the judicial review of administrative acts actions were not adequate for the protection requested in the case, seeking the participation of the Venezuelan Federation of Equestrian Sports in an international competition, being the opinion of the courts "that when the action was brought before it, the only mean that the claimant had in order to obtain the reestablishment of the infringed juridical situation was the amparo action, due to the fact that by means of the judicial review of administrative acts recourse seeking its nullity, they could never be able to obtain the said reestablishment of the infringed juridical situation that was to assist to the 1990 international contest." See the reference in Rafael Chavero G. *El nuevo amparo constitucional en Venezuela*, Ed. Sherwood, Caracas, 2001, p. 354.

116 This can be realized from the decision taken in a recent and polemic case referring to the expropriation of some premises of a corn agro-industry complex, which developed as follows: In August 2005, officers from the Ministry of Agriculture and Land and military officers and soldiers from the Army and the National Guard surrounded the installation of the company *Refinadora de Maíz Venezolana, C.A. (Remavenca)*, and announcements were publicly made regarding the appointment of an Administrator Commission that would be taking over the industry. These actions were challenged by the company as a *de facto* action alleging the violation of the

The other question related to the admissibility of the amparo action is related to the question of the existence of a pending action or recourse already filed or brought before a court for the same purpose of protecting a constitutional right. This question regarding the admissibility of the amparo action has also some similarities with what in the United States' injunctions procedure regarding defenses is called the "doctrine of the election of remedies," which is applied when an injured party having two available but inconsistent remedies to redress a harm, chooses one, such act being considered as constituting a binding election that forecloses the other.[117] In a similar sense this is the general rule in Venezuela, which is nonetheless only applied when the plaintiff has filed other judicial mean for protection; not being applied if only administrative recourses have been filed before the Public Administration organs.[118]

This condition of inadmissibility of the amparo action when the plaintiff has chosen to file another action has been also regulated, in particular regarding the case of the previous filing of another amparo action that is pending to be decided.[119] In

---

company's rights to equality, due process and defense, economic freedom, property rights and to the nonconfiscation guaranty of property. A few days later, the Governor of the State of Barinas, where the industry was located, issued a Decree ordering the expropriation of the premises, and consequently the Supreme Tribunal declared the inadmissibility of the amparo action that was filed, basing its ruling on the following arguments: "The criteria established up to now by this Tribunal, by which it has concluded on the inadmissibility of the autonomous amparo action against administrative acts has been that the judicial review of administrative act actions –among which the recourse for nullity, the actions against the administrative abstentions and recourse filed by public servants– are the adequate means, that is, the brief, prompt and efficient means in order to obtain the reestablishment of the infringed juridical situation, in addition to the wide powers that are attributed to the administrative jurisdiction courts in Article 29 of the Constitution. Accordingly, the recourse for nullity or the expropriation suit are the adequate means to resolve the claims referring to supposed controversies in the expropriation procedure; those are the preexisting judicial means in order to judicially decide conflicts in which previous legality studies are required, and which the constitutional judge cannot consider. Thus, the Chamber considers that the claimants, if they think that the alleged claim persists, can obtain the reestablishment of their allegedly infringed juridical situation, by means of the ordinary actions and to obtain satisfaction to their claims. So because of the existing adequate means for the resolution of the controversy argued by the plaintiff, it is compulsory for the Chamber to declare the inadmissibility of the amparo action, according to what is set forth in Article 6,5 of the Organic Law." See decision of the Constitutional Chamber of the Supreme Tribunal of Justice N° 3375 of November 4, 2005, *Refinadora de Maíz Venezolana, C.A. (Remavenca), y Procesadora Venezolana de Cereales, S.A. (Provencesa) vs. Ministro de Agricultura y Tierras y efectivos de los componentes Ejército y Guardia Nacional de la Fuerza Armada Nacional* Case. See in *Revista de Derecho Público*, n° 104, Editorial Jurídica Venezolana, Caracas, 2005, pp. 239 ff.

117 See William M. Tabb and Elaine W. Shoben, *Remedies,* Thomson West, 2005, p. 56.

118 In this case, the inadmissible clause is not applied, because the administrative recourses are not judicial ordinary means that can prevent the filing of the amparo action. See the decision of the First Court on administrative jurisdiction, which decided on a decision dated March 8, 1993, *Federico Domingo* case, in *Revista de Derecho Público*, N° 53-54, Editorial Jurídica Venezolana, Caracas, 1994, p. 261. See also the decision dated May 6, 1994, *Universidad Occidental Lisandro Alvarado* case, in *Revista de Derecho Público*, N° 57-58, Editorial Jurídica Venezolana, Caracas, 1994. See Rafael Chavero G. *El nuevo amparo constitucional en Venezuela*, Ed. Sherwood, Caracas, 2001, pp. 250 ff.

119 Article 6,8 of the Amparo Law provides the inadmissibility of the action for amparo when a decision regarding another amparo suit has been brought before the courts regarding the same

these cases, it is necessary that a previous amparo action had been filed regarding the same violation, the same action and the same persons.

10. The main principles of the procedure in the amparo proceeding

The extraordinary character of the amparo proceeding also conditions the general rules governing the procedure, which in general terms are related to its bilateral character; to the brief and preferred character of the procedure; to the role of the courts directing the procedure and to the need for the substantial law to prevail regarding formalities.

In effect, as aforementioned, one of the fundamental principles regarding the amparo proceeding is that although being of an extraordinary nature, the bilateral character of the proceeding must always be guaranteed. This implies, as previously said, that the amparo proceeding must always be initiated by a party or parties (the injured or offended party), so no *ex officio* amparo proceeding is admissible.[120] Consequently, the amparo proceeding must always be initiated by means of an action or a recourse brought before the competent court by a party against another party (the injurer or offender party) whose actions or omissions have violated or have caused harm to his constitutional rights. This party, as defendant, must always be brought to the procedure in order to guaranty his rights to defense and due process.

From the amparo proceeding, its final outcome is always a judicial order, as also happens in the United States with the writs of injunction, mandamus or error, which are directed to the injuring party ordering to do or to abstain from doing something, or to suspend the effects, or in some cases, to annul the damaging act.[121] In Venezuela, as already mentioned, the amparo statutes not only refer to the amparo as a remedy or as the final court written order (writ) commanding the defendant to do or refrain from doing some specific act, but in addition, it is regulated as a complete proceeding that is specifically designed to protect constitutional rights following an adversary procedure according to the "cases or controversy" condition. All the phases or stages of the procedure are regulated; the procedure ending with a judicial decision or judicial order directed to protect the constitutional rights of the injured party.

---

facts and is pending decision. See for instance the decision of the Politico Administrative Chamber of the Supreme Court of Justice of October 13, 1993, in *Revista de Derecho Público*, Nº 55-56, Editorial Jurídica Venezolana, Caracas, 1993, pp. 348–349.

120 Only in cases of habeas corpus actions do some Amparo Laws provide for the power of the courts to initiate the proceeding *ex officio*: Guatemala (Article 86), Honduras (Article 20).

121 The amparo suit has similarities with the civil suit for an injunction that an injured party can bring before a court to seek for the enforcement or restoration of his violated rights or for the prevention of its violation. It also can be identified with a "suit for mandamus" brought by an injured party before a court against a public officer whose omission has caused harm to the plaintiff, in order to seek for a writ ordering the former to perform a duty that the law requires him to do but he refuses or neglects to perform. Also, the suit for amparo has similarities with a "suit for writ of error" brought before the competent superior court by an injured party whose constitutional rights have been violated by a judicial decision, seeking the annulment or the correction of the judicial wrong or error.

Consequently, the general rule in the amparo proceeding is that although being brief and speedy, the procedural adversary principle or the aforementioned principle of bilateralism, must be preserved, assuring the presence of both parties and the respect of the due process constitutional guaranties, particularly the rights to defense.[122] That is why no definitive amparo adjudication can be issued without the participation of the defendant or at least without his knowledge about the filing of the action. The exception to this rule being very rare, as is the case of Colombia, where the *Tutela* Law admits the possibility for the court to grant the constitutional protection (tutela) *in limene litis*, that is, "without any formal consideration and without previous enquiry, if the decision is founded in an evidence that shows the grave and imminent violation of harm to the right" (Article 18).

This Colombian provision undoubtedly was inspired by the 1988 Venezuelan Amparo Law that also provided for the possibility for the amparo judge "to immediately restore the infringed juridical situation, without considerations of mere form and without any kind of brief enquiry," requiring in such cases, that "the amparo protection be founded in an evidence constituting a grave presumption of the violation of harm of violation" (Article 22). Nonetheless, in Venezuela this article was annulled by the former Supreme Court, which refused to interpret it in harmony with the Constitution, as only providing for preliminary decisions and as not intending to establish the possibility of a definitive amparo decision that could be issued *inaudita parte* because it would be unconstitutional. In particular, a popular action was filed in 1988 before the former Supreme Court of Justice based on the alleged unconstitutionality of such provision, requesting the Supreme Court to interpret it according to the constitution (*secundum constitucione*), in the sense that what was intended was to establish a legal authorization for the courts to just adopt in an immediate way preliminary protective measures, pending the resolution of the case, but not definitive amparo decisions. Nonetheless, the Supreme Court rejected this interpretation, and in decision dated May 21, 1996, eventually annulled Article 22 of the Amparo Law considering that it violated in a flagrant way the constitutional right to defense.[123] The adjective consequence was that failing to interpret the norm according to the constitution, no legal support could be identified in the special Amparo Law empowering the courts to adopt provisional or

122 Thus, a judicial guaranty of constitutional rights as is the amparo suit can in no way transform itself in a proceeding violating the other constitutional guaranties like the right to defense. Except regarding preliminary judicial orders, the principle of *audi alteram partem* (hear the other party or listen to both sides) must then always be respected.

123 This Article, as mentioned, allowed the courts to adopt final decisions on amparo matters in cases of grave violations of constitutional rights, reestablishing the constitutional harmed right without any formal or summary inquiry and without hearing the plaintiff or potential injurer. Even if the article could have been constitutionally interpreted as only directed to allow the adoption of *inaudita partem* preliminary decisions or injunctions in the proceeding, the Supreme Court considered its contents as a vulgar and flagrant violation of the constitutional right to self-defense, and annulled it. See Decision of the Supreme Court of Justice of May 21, 1996, in *Official Gazette Extra*. N° 5071 of May 29, 1996. See the comments in Allan R. Brewer-Carías, *Instituciones Políticas y Constitucio-nales*, Vol V, *Derecho y Acción de Amparo,* Universidad Católica del Táchira, Editorial Jurídica Venezolana, Caracas, 1998, pp. 388-396 ff.; and in Rafael Chavero, *El Nuevo Régimen del Amparo Constitucional en Venezuela*, Caracas, 2001, pp. 212, 266 ff. and 410 ff.

preliminary relief,[124] which were then adopted applying the general provisions of the Procedural Civil Code.

Because the amparo suit is an extraordinary remedy for the immediate protection of constitutional rights, its main feature is the brief and prompt character of the procedure, which is justified because the purpose of the action is to immediately protect persons in cases of irreparable injuries or threats to constitutional rights. This irreparable character of the harm or threat and the immediate need for protection have been the key elements that have molded the procedural rules not only of the amparo proceeding, but also of the injunctions in the United States, where the judicial doctrine on the matter is also that "an injunction is granted only when required to avoid immediate and irreparable damage to legally recognized rights, such as property rights, constitutional rights or contractual rights." [125]

The same principles also apply to the amparo proceeding, originating the configuration of a brief and preferred procedure, precisely justified because of the protective purpose of the action and the immediate protection required because of the violations of constitutional rights. For these purposes, Article 27 of the Venezuelan Constitution expressly provides that the procedure of the constitutional amparo action must be oral, public, brief, free and not subject to formality.[126]

---

124 See the comments in Allan R. Brewer-Carías, *Instituciones Políticas y Constitucionales*, Vol V, *Derecho y Acción de Amparo*, Universidad Católica del Táchira, Editorial Jurídica Venezolana, Caracas, 1998, pp. 398.

125 Consequently, "There must be some vital necessity for the injunction so that one of the parties will not be damaged and left without adequate remedy," *Treadwell v. Investment Franchises, Inc*., 273 Ga. 517,543 S.E.2d 729 (2001). In other words, "to warrant an injunction it ordinarily must be clearly shown that some act has been done, or is threatened, which will produce irreparable injury to the party asking for the injunction," *U.S. v. American Friends Service Committee*, 419 U.S. 7, 95 S.Ct. 13, 42 L. Ed. 2d 7 (1974). In the same sense it has been established that: "The very function of an injunction is to furnish preventive relief against irreparable mischief or injury, and the remedy will not be awarded where it appears to the satisfaction of the court that the injury complained of is not of such a character," *State Com'n on Human Relations v. Talbot County Detention Center*, 370 Md. 115, 803 A.2d 527 (2002). More specifically, a permanent, mandatory injunction, a preliminary, interlocutory or temporary injunction, a preliminary mandatory injunction, or a preliminary, interlocutory or temporary restraining order, "will not, as a general rule, be granted where it is not shown that an irreparable injury is immediately impending and will be inflicted on the petitioner before the case can be brought to a final hearing, no matter how likely it may be that the moving party will prevail on the merits," *Packaging Industries Group, Inc. v. Cheney*, 380 Mass. 609, 405 N.E.2d. 106 (1980). See the reference to the corresponding cases in John Bourdeau *et al.*, "Injunctions," in Kevin Schroder, John Glenn and Maureen Placilla, *Corpus Juris Secundum*, Volume 43A, Thomson West, 2004, pp. 76–78.

126 Regarding some of these principles, the Venezuelan First Court on Judicial Review of Administrative Actions, even before the sanctioning of the Amparo Law in 1988, ruled that because of the brief character of the procedure, it must be understood as having "the condition of being urgent, thus it must be followed promptly and decided in the shortest possible time"; and additionally it must be summary, in the sense that "the procedure must be simple, uncomplicated, without incidences and complex formalities." In this sense, the procedure must not be converted in a complex and confused procedural situation." See decision of January 17, 1985, in *Revista de Derecho Público*, N° 21, Editorial Jurídica Venezolana, Caracas, 1985, p. 140. According to these principles, the 1988 Venezuelan Amparo Law provided for the brief, prompt and summary procedure that governed the amparo proceeding up to the enactment of the 1999 Constitution, when the Constitutional Chamber of the Supreme Tribunal of Justice interpreted the provisions of

One of the consequences of the brief and prompt character of the procedure in the amparo proceeding is its preferred character that imposes, as it is provided in the Venezuelan Constitution, that "any time will be workable time, and the courts will give preference to the amparo regarding any other matter" (Article 27). This preferred character of the procedure also implies that the procedure must be followed with preference, so when an amparo action is filed, the courts must postpone all other matters of different nature (Article 13, Amparo Law).

In the amparo procedure, as a general rule, due to its brief character, the procedural terms cannot be extended, nor suspended, nor interrupted, except in cases expressly set forth in the statute; any delay in the procedure being the responsibility of the courts. In addition, Article 11 of the Amparo Law restricts motion to recuse judges, establishing specific and prompt procedural rules regarding the cases of impeding situations of the competent judges to resolve the case

Another principle governing the procedural rules in matters of amparo, in order to guaranty the brief and prompt character of the procedure, is the principle of the prevalence of substantive law over formal provisions, which for instance is referred in the Venezuelan Constitution as a general principle applicable to all proceedings (Articles 26, 257), regarding the prevalence of "substantive justice" over "formal justice."

Another aspect to be analyzed regarding the procedure in the amparo proceeding refers to the specific configuration of the main phases or steps of the procedure, in particular, those related to the filing of the petition, the court decision on the admissibility of the action, the evidence activity, the defendant pleading, and the hearing of the case.

The first specific trend to be highlighted regarding the judicial procedure of the amparo proceeding refers to the formalities of the petitions that are to be brought before the courts, being the general principle, as is also the case regarding the injunctions in the United States,[127] that the petition must be filed in writing. Nonetheless, the Amparo Law allows the oral presentation of the amparo in cases of urgency (Articles 16, 18), cases in which the petitions must be subsequently ratified in writing.

In any case, in the written text of the action, the petitioner must always express in a clear and precise manner all the necessary elements regarding the alleged right to be protected and the arguments for the admissibility of the action. That is why the Amparo Law establishes, in general terms, the minimal content of the petition or

---

the Law, according to the new Constitution, in some way re-writing its regulations through constitutional interpretation. See the decision of the Constitutional Chamber of the Supreme Tribunal of Justice N° 7 dated February 1, 2000 (Case *José Amando Mejía*), in *Revista de Derecho Público*, N° 81, Editorial Jurídica Venezolana, Caracas, 2000, pp. 245 ff. See the comments in Allan R. Brewer-Carías, *El sistema de justicia constitucional en la Constitución de 1999. Comentarios sobre su desarrollo jurisprudencial y su explicación, a veces errada, en la Exposición de Motivos*, Editorial Jurídica Venezolana, Caracas, 2000; and in Rafael Chavero Gazdik, *El nuevo régimen del amparo constitucional en Venezuela*, Edit. Sherwood, Caracas, 2001, pp. 203 ff.

127 See *Vasquez v. Bannworths, Inc.*, 707 S.W.2d 886 (Tex. 1986); *Hall v. Hanford*, 64 So. 2d 303 (Fla. 1953), in John Bourdeau *et al.*, "Injunctions," in Kevin Schroder, John Glenn and Maureen Placilla, *Corpus Juris Secundum*, Volume 43A, Thomson West, 2004, pp. 346 ff.

complaint, which in particular must refer to the following aspects (Article 18): First, the complete identification and information regarding the plaintiff, and if someone is acting on behalf of the plaintiff, his identification is also required. If the plaintiff is an artificial person, the references regarding its registration as well as the representative's complete identification is also required. Second, the petition must establish the individuation of the injurer party. Third, the detailed narration of the circumstances in which the harm or the threat has been caused, and the act, action, omission or fact causing the harm or threat must be identified. Fourth, the written text of the petition must indicate the constitutional right or guaranty that has been violated, harmed or threatened, with precise reference to the articles of the constitution or the international treaties containing the rights or guaranties denounced as violated or harmed. Fifth, the plaintiff must specify the particular protective request asked from the court as well as the judicial order to be issued in protection of his rights that is requested from the court. And, finally, the plaintiff must argue about the fulfillment of the conditions for the admissibility of the action, in particular, regarding the inadequacy of other possible judicial remedies and the irreparable injury the plaintiff will suffer without the amparo suit protection.[128]

In order to soften the consequences of not mentioning correctly all the above-mentioned requirements that have to be contained within the written text of the petition, the Amparo Law, in protection of the injured party's right to sue, provide that the courts are obliged to return to the plaintiff the petition that does not conform with those requirements in order for the plaintiff to make the necessary corrections. Consequently, in these cases, the petition will not be considered inadmissible because of formal inadequacies regarding the noncompliance with the petition's requirements set forth in the statutes, and in order to have them corrected or mended the court must return it to the petitioner for him to correct it in a brief amount of time. Only if the petitioner does not make the corrections will the complaint be rejected (Article 19).

The second important phase of the procedure in the amparo proceeding is the power of the competent courts at the beginning of the procedure to decide upon the admission of the petition when all the admissibility conditions set forth in the Amparo Law are satisfied. Consequently, the courts are empowered to decide *in limine litis* about the inadmissibility of the action when the petition does not accomplish in a manifest way the conditions determined in the statute; for instance, when the term to file the action is evidently exhausted; when the challenged act is one of those excluded from the amparo protection; when there are ordinary means for the protection of the rights that must be previously filed or that gives adequate protection; or when ordinary judicial means that can adequately guaranty the claimed rights have already been filed.

The main effect of the admission decision of the action is for the court to notify the interested parties of the initiation of the process; to request from the defendant a report on the violations; and to adopt, if necessary, preliminary amparo decisions for

---

128 In a similar way as in the injunction petition in the United States." See *International Westminster Bank Ltd. V. Federal Deposit Ins. Corp.*, 509 F2d 641 (9th Cir. 1975); *Thomas v. Morton*, 408 F. Supp. 1361 (D. Ariz. 1976), judgment aff'd, 552 F. 2d 871 (9th Cir. 1977), in John Bourdeau *et al.*, "Injunctions," in Kevin Schroder, John Glenn and Maureen Placilla, *Corpus Juris Secundum*, Volume 43A, Thomson West, 2004, pp. 346, 352.

the immediate protection of the harmed or threatened constitutional rights, pending the development of the process.

The third phase in the procedure of the amparo proceeding refers to the evidence activity and the burden of proof. As has been mentioned, the amparo suit is a specific judicial mean regulated in order to obtain the immediate protection of constitutional rights and guaranties when the aggrieved or injured parties have no other adequate judicial means for such purpose. That is why this situation must be alleged and proven by the claimant. This implies that in order to file an amparo action and to obtain the immediate judicial protection, the violation of the constitutional right must be a flagrant, vulgar, direct and immediate one, caused by a perfectly determined act or omission. Regarding the harm or injury caused to the constitutional rights, it must be manifestly arbitrary, illegal or illegitimate, a consequence of a violation of the constitution. All these aspects for obtaining the immediate judicial protection must be clear and ostensible, the plaintiff being obliged to argue them in his petition and support it with the needed evidence.

Consequently, as it is also established in the United States regarding the injunctions,[129] in the amparo proceeding, the plaintiff has the burden to prove the existence of the right, the alleged violations of threat, and the illegitimate character of the action causing it, with clear and convincing evidence. The consequence of the aforementioned is that in matters of amparo, due to the brief and prompt character of the procedure, the immediate protection of constitutional rights that can be granted needs to be based on existing sufficient evidence.

Accordingly, the courts have rejected amparo actions in complex cases where a major debate is needed, and in cases in which proof is difficult to provide, which is considered incompatible with the brief and prompt character of the amparo suit that requires that the alleged violation be "manifestly" illegitimate and harming. Even without clear provisions on the matter, this principle has been applied by the courts in Venezuela.[130]

In this matter of constitutional protection, the courts among their *ex officio* powers have the competence to obtain evidence, provided that it does not cause an irreparable prejudice to the parties (Article 17).

On the other hand, the general principle in the amparo procedure is that all kind of evidence is admitted, so the court can base its decision to grant or not the required protection in any evidence.

The fifth important phase of the amparo proceeding is the need for the court to notify the aggrieving party in order to request from it a formal written answer or report regarding the alleged violations of constitutional rights of the plaintiff, to which, in addition, the defendant can put forward his counter evidence, before the

129 See *U.S. School Dist. 151 of Cook County*, Ill., 404 F. 2d 1125 (7th Cir. 1968); *Dickey v. Williams*, 1940 OK 28, 186 Okla. 376, 98 P. 2d 604 (1940), in John Bourdeau *et al.*., in "Injunctions," in Kevin Schroder, John Glenn and Maureen Placilla (Editors), *Corpus Juris Secundum*, Vol. 43A, Thomson West, 2004, p 54.

130 See Rafael Chavero G., *El nuevo amparo constitucional en Venezuela*, Ed. Sherwood, Caracas, 2001, p. 340.

hearing on it.[131] Due to the bilateral and adversary character of the procedure, as also happens in the injunctive relief procedure in the United States, an amparo ruling must not be issued until the defendant has been asked to file its plea.[132]

This defendant's answer or plea regarding the harm or threat alleged by the plaintiff must be sent to the court within a very brief term of forty-eight hours (Article 23). The omission of the defendant to send his report or plea in answer to the court, implies that the plaintiff's alleged facts must be considered as accepted by the defendant (Article 23).

Finally, one of the most important phases in the procedure is the hearing that the court must convene, also in a very prompt period of time, seeking the participation of the parties before adopting its decision on the case (Article 26). This hearing which must be oral, public and contradictory, in principle must always take place and must not be suspended.

The absence of the defendant's participation in the hearing, in general terms, does not produce its suspension, in which case, the evidence presented by the plaintiff will be accepted and the court must then proceed to decide. Regarding the plaintiff, his absence from the hearing is understood as his abandonment of the action.

The final decision of the amparo proceeding must be adopted after the hearing has taken place, although the Constitutional Chamber of the Supreme Tribunal has established that the in matters of amparo the court must make its decision in the same hearing or trial.[133]

11. The preliminary protective measures on matter of amparo

The purpose of the amparo proceeding eventually is for the plaintiff to obtain a judicial adjudication from the competent court, providing for the immediate protection of his harmed or threatened constitutional rights, for instance, through a

---

131 This is what was established in the Venezuelan Amparo Law (Article 24); which nonetheless has been eliminated by the Constitutional Chamber in its decision Nº 7 of February 1, 2000, *José A. Mejía et al.* issue interpreting the Amparo Law according to the new 1999 Constitution, and reshaping the amparo suit procedure. See in *Revista de Derecho Público*, Nº 81, Editorial Jurídica Venezolana, Caracas, 2000, pp. 349 ff. See Rafael Chavero G., *El nuevo amparo constitucional en Venezuela*, Ed. Sherwood, Caracas, 2001, pp. 264 ff.; and Allan R. Brewer-Carías, "El juez constitucional como legislador positivo y la inconstitucional reforma de la Ley Orgánica de Amparo mediante sentencias interpretativas," in Eduardo Ferrer Mac-Gregor y Arturo Zaldívar Lelo de Larrea (Coordinators), *La ciencia del derecho procesal constitucional. Estudios en homenaje a Héctor Fix-Zamudio en sus cincuenta años como investigador del derecho*, Instituto de Investigaciones Jurídicas, Universidad Nacional Autónoma de México, México 2008, Tomo V, pp. 63-80.

132 See *Conseco Finance Servicing Corp. v. Missouri Dept. of Revenue*, 98 S.W. 3d 540 (Mo. 2003), in John Bourdeau *et al.*, "Injunctions," in Kevin Schroder, John Glenn and Maureen Placilla, *Corpus Juris Secundum,* Volume 43A, Thomson West, 2004, pp. 357 ff.

133 In Venezuela, the Amparo Law established that the decision ought to be issued in the following days (Article 24) after the hearing. Nonetheless, the Constitutional Chamber in decision Nº 7 of February 1, 2000 (*José A. Mejía et al.* case), has modified this provision, providing that the decision must be issued at the end of the hearing. See in *Revista de Derecho Público*, Nº 81, Editorial Jurídica Venezolana, Caracas, 2000, pp. 349 ff.

judicial decision restraining some actions, preserving the status quo, or commanding or prohibiting actions.[134]

Amparo and injunctions are both extraordinary remedies having the same purpose, the main difference between them being the rights to be protected. In the United States, injunctions are equity remedies that can be used for the protection of any kind of personal or property rights, but in Latin America, the amparo proceeding is conceived only for the protection of constitutional rights, which explains its regulations in the constitutions, and not for the protection of rights established in statutes.[135]

---

134 In a very similar way to the injunctive decisions that the United States' courts can adopt for the immediate protection of rights, which can consist of restrain action or interference of some kind (*Putnam v. Fortenberry*, 256 Neb. 266, 589 N.W.2d 838, 1999; *Anderson v. Granite School Dist.*, 17 Utah 2d 405, 413 P2d 597, 1996); to furnish preventive relief against irreparable mischief or injury; or to preserve the *status quo* (*Jenkins v. Pedersen*, 212 N.W.2d 415 Iowa 1973; *Snyer v. Sullivan*, 705 P.2d 510, Colo 1985). It is a remedy designed to prevent irreparable injury by prohibiting or commanding certain acts (*National Comprsed Steel Cor. V. Unified Government of Wyandotte County/Kansas City*, 272 Kan. 1239, 38 P.3d 723, 2002). The function of injunctive relief is to restrain motion and to enforce inaction (*State ex rel. Great Lakes College, Inc. v Medical Bd.*, 29 Ohio St. 2d 198, 58 Ohio Op. 2d 406, 280 N.E 2dd 900, 1972). An injunction is designed to prevent harm, not redress harm; it is not compensatory (*Klinicki v. Lundgren*, 298 Or. 662, 695 P.2d 906, 1985; *Simenstad v. Hagen*, 22 Wis. 2d 653, 126 N.W.2d 529, 1964). The remedy grants prospective, as opposed to retrospective, relief (*Jefferson v. Big Horn County*, 2000 MT 163, 300 Mont. 284, 4 P3d 26, 2000); it is preventive, protective or restorative (*Hunsaker v. Kersh*, 1999 UT, 106, 991 P2d 67, Utah 1999; *Colendrea v. Wilde Lake Community Ass'n, Inc.*, 361, Md. 371, 761 A.2d 899, 2003; *Stoetzel & Sons, Inc. v. City of Hatings*, 265 Neb. 637, 658 N.W.2d 636, 2003; *U.S. v. White County Bridge Commission*, 275 F.2d 529, 7th Cir. 1960), but not addressed to past wrongs (*Snyder v. Sullivan*, 705 P.2d 510, Colo. 1985). See in John Bourdeau *et al.*, "Injunctions," in Kevin Schroder, John Glenn and Maureen Placilla, *Corpus Juris Secundum*, Volume 43A, Thomson West, 2004, p. 20.

135 In this sense, in Venezuela the courts have ruled that the harm caused must always be the result of a violation of a constitutional right that must be "flagrant, vulgar, direct and immediate, which does not mean that the right or guaranty is not due to be regulated in statutes, but it is not necessary for the court to base its decision in the latter to determine if the violation of the constitutional right has effectively occurred." See Supreme Court of Justice, *Tarjetas Banvenez* case, July 10, 1991, in *Revista de Derecho Público*, N° 47, Editorial Jurídica Venezolana, Caracas, 1991, pp. 169–170. See also decision of May 20, 1994, First Court on Judicial Review of Administrative Actions, *Federación Venezolana de Deportes Ecuestres* Case, in *Revista de Derecho Público*, N° 57-58, Editorial Jurídica Venezolana, Caracas, 1994. In other words, only direct and evident constitutional violations can be protected by means of amparo; thus, for instance, as ruled in 1991 by the Venezuelan courts, the internal electoral regime of political partics or of professional associations could not be the object of an amparo action founded in the right to vote set forth in the constitution, "which only applies to the national electoral process [not being applied] to the internal electoral process of the political parties," concluding that the amparo only protects constitutional rights and guaranties and not legal (statutory) ones, and much less the ones contained in association's by laws." See decision of August 8, 1991, in *Revista de Derecho Público*, n° 47, Editorial Jurídica Venezolana, Caracas, 1991, p. 129. In other decisions, the courts declared inadmissible amparo actions for the protection of rights when the allegations were only founded "in legal (statutory) considerations," as the right to work commonly conditioned by statutes regarding dismissals. Thus, the amparo is not the judicial mean for the protection of such right if the violation is only referring to the labor law provisions. See decision of October 8, 1990, in *Revista de Derecho Público*, N° 44, Editorial Jurídica Venezolana, Caracas, 1990, pp. 139–140. In a similar sense, the violation of the right to self-defense because a party's right to cross-examine a witness was denied according to Article 349 of the Civil Procedural Code cannot be founded in

In this matter of the amparo proceeding, as well as in matters of injunctions, two general sorts of judicial adjudications can be issued by the courts for the protection of constitutional rights: preliminary measures that can be ordered from the beginning of the procedure, with effects subject to the final court ruling; and definitive decisions preventing the violation or restoring the enjoyment of the threatened or harmed rights.

In Venezuela, as in all Latin American countries, according to the general regulations established in the Civil Procedure Codes, all courts are empowered to adopt, during the course of a procedure, what are called "*medidas preventivas*" or "*medidas cautelares*," that is, interlocutory and temporal judicial measures that are also applied to the amparo proceeding. The expression refers to interlocutory or preliminary measures; so in this sense, a "*medida preventiva*" is not equivalent to the English expression "preventive measure," which is used in the sense of to prevent or to avoid harm, which can be decided both in a definitive or a preliminary injunction.[136] That is, both the definitive and preliminary judicial amparo decisions can have "preventive" effects in the sense of preventing harms or preserving the status quo, the preliminary ones having only a temporary basis, pending the termination of the procedure.[137] Consequently, in order to avoid confusion, I am using the expression "preliminary" measures to identify what in the Latin American procedural law are called "*medidas preventivas* or *medidas cautelares*," as interlocutory, preliminary and temporal judicial protective measures that can be issued pending the procedure, similar to the United States "preliminary injunctions" also issued as interlocutory and temporal relief pending the trial.[138]

Based on this distinction between preliminary measures (*cautelares*) and definitive adjudications or decisions, the amparo proceedings in Venezuela is not

---

Article 68 of the Constitution because it implies the need to analyze norms of legal rank and not of constitutional rank. In this regard it was decided by the former Supreme Court of Justice, Politico Administrative Chamber, decision of November 8, 1990, in *Revista de Derecho Público*, N° 44, Editorial Jurídica Venezolana, Caracas, 1990, pp. 140–141.

136 In other words, as explained by Tabb and Shoben: "The classic form of injunctions in private litigation is the preventive injunction. By definition, a preventive injunction is a court order designed to avoid future harm to a party by prohibiting or mandating certain behavior by another party. The injunction is "preventive" in the sense of avoiding harm. The wording may be either prohibitory ("Do not trespass") or mandatory ("Remove the obstruction")." See William M. Tabb and Elaine W. Shoben, *Remedies*, Thomson West, 2005, p. 22.

137 As the same authors Tabb and Shoben have said: "Upon a compelling showing by the plaintiff, the court may issue a coercive order even before full trial on the merits. A preliminary injunction gives the plaintiff temporary relief pending trial on the merit. A temporary restraining order affords immediate relief pending the hearing on the preliminary injunction. Both of these types of interlocutory relief are designed to preserve the status quo to prevent irreparable harm before a court can decide the substantive merits of the dispute. Such orders are available only upon a strong showing of the necessity for such relief and may be conditioned upon the claimant posting a bond or sufficient security to protect the interests of the defendant in the event that the injunction is later determined to have been wrongfully issued." *Idem*, p. 4.

138 In both cases, the preliminary measures are different to the final judicial protective (permanent injunction) decisions which can have preventive or restorative effects. See *Bayer v. Associated Underwriters, Inc.*, 402 S.W.2d 11 (Mo. Ct. App. 1966), in John Bourdeau *et al.*, "Injunctions," in Kevin Schroder, John Glenn and Maureen Placilla, *Corpus Juris Secundum*, Volume 43A, Thomson West, 2004, pp. 24 ff.

just of a "*cautelar*" or preliminary nature, and on the contrary, it seeks to protect in a definitive way the constitutional right alleged as harmed or threatened. The precision is important because in some countries a distinction has been made in procedural law between "*cautelar*" measures and "*cautelar*" actions, causing some terminological confusion when giving to the amparo the character of a "*cautelar*" action. In such cases, the expression is used, not in the sense of just having a "preliminary" nature, but in the sense of being confined just to decide the immediate protection of a constitutional right without resolving any other matters or merits of the controversy.[139]

However, putting aside these terminological differences, in the amparo procedure, preliminary measures can be adopted by the courts pending the final adjudication and with effects during the development of the procedure, in order to preserve the status quo, avoiding harms or restoring the plaintiff's situation to the original one it had before the harm was inflicted. These preliminary measures are regulated in Amparo Law and the Civil Procedure Code in two ways:

First, by establishing a precise and identified measure, called a *medidas cautelares nominada*, as is the case of the suspension of the effects of the challenged act object of the amparo action. This is the most common preliminary judicial measure expressly established in the Amparo Law, when the action is filed against State acts, particularly administrative acts, is the power given to the courts to suspend their effects, at the request of the affected party, during the course of the procedure and pending the final decision of the proceeding (Article 5). Also, in addition to the provision establishing the courts' possible decision to suspend the effects of the challenged acts, in the case of the filing of the amparo petition conjunctly with other actions seeking judicial review of statutes or administrative acts, the amparo essentially has suspensive effects.[140]

---

139 In this sense, in Ecuador and Chile, the amparo proceeding has been considered to have "*cautelar*" nature, but in a sense not equivalent to a "preliminary" nature. The Constitutional Court of Ecuador, for instance, has decided as followed: "That the amparo action set forth in Article 95 of the Constitution is in essence *cautelar* regarding the constitutional rights, not allowing [the court] to decide on the merits or to substitute the proceedings set forth in the legal order for the resolution of a controversy, but only to suspend the effects of an authority act which harms those rights; and the decisions issued in the amparo suit do not produce *res judicata*, so the authority, once having corrected the incurred defects, may go back to the matter and issue a new act, providing it is adjusted to the constitutional and legal provisions." See the text and comments in Hernán Salgado Pesantes, *Manual de Justicia Constitucional Ecuatoriana,* Corporación Editora Nacional, Quito, 2004, p. 78. In a similar way, in Chile the action for protection has been considered to have a "*cautelar*" nature, not in the sense of "preliminary" measures, but as tending to obtain a definitive protective adjudication regarding constitutional rights. See Eduardo Soto Kloss, *El recurso de protección. Orígenes, doctrina y jurisprudencia*, Editorial Jurídica de Chile, Santiago, 1982, p. 248; Juan Manuel Errazuriz and Jorge Miguel Otero A., *Aspectos procesales del recurso de protección*, Editorial Jurídica de Chile, Santiago, 1989, pp. 34–38.

140 When the amparo action is filed jointly with the judicial review popular action for nullity against statutes or with the judicial review of administrative actions recourse, the amparo petition has always this preliminary (*cautelar*) character, in the sense that the decision granting the amparo pending the principal nullity suit is always of a preliminary character of suspension of the effects of the challenged act. Thus, in case of statutes, the Constitutional Chamber the competent court decides to suspend its effects, in such cases, even with *erga omnes* effects. See Rafael Chavero G. *El nuevo amparo constitucional en Venezuela,* Ed. Sherwood, Caracas, 2001, pp. 468 ff. 327 ff.; Allan R. Brewer-Carías, *Instituciones Políticas y Constitucionales*, Vol V, *Derecho y Acción de*

Second, without any particular enumeration, other measures that can be adopted by the courts in order to protect the injured right are the *medidas cautelares innominadas* according to the provisions of the Civil Procedure Code.

In order to adopt all these preliminary measures, a few conditions must be met as has been established by the jurisprudence of the courts, in the sense that the courts must consider, first, "the appearance of the existence of a good right" (*fumus boni juris*), that is, the need for the petitioner to prove the existence of his constitutional right or guaranty as being violated or threatened; second, the "danger because of the delay" (*periculum in mora*), that is, the need to prove that the delay in granting the preliminary protection will make the harm irreparable; third, the "danger of the harm" (*periculum in dammi*"), that is the need to prove the imminence of the harm that can be caused; and fourth, the balance between the collective and particular interest involved in the case.[141] As was ruled by the Politico Administrative Chamber of the Supreme Tribunal of Justice of Venezuela, in a Decision N° 488 dated March 3, 2000:

> "In order for an anticipated protective measure to be granted, due to its preliminary content it is necessary to examine the existence of three essential elements, always balancing the collective or individual interest; such conditions are:
>
> 1. *Fumus Boni Iuris*, that is, the reasonable appearance of the existence of a "good right" in the hands of the petitioner alleging its violation, an appearance that must derive from the written evidences (documents) attached to the petition.
>
> 2. *Periculum in mora*, that is, the danger that the definitive ruling could be illusory, due to the delay in resolving the incident of the suspension.
>
> 3. *Periculum in Damni*, that is, the imminence of the harm caused by the presumptive violation of the fundamental rights of the petitioner and its irreparability. These elements are those that basically allow one to seek the necessary anticipatory protection of the constitutional rights and guaranties."[142]

All these general conditions for the issuance of the preliminary protective measures are very similar to those prerequisites needed to be tested by the United States' courts when issuing the preliminary injunctions, which are: 1) a probability of prevailing on the merits; 2) an irreparable injury if the relief is delayed; 3) a balance of hardship favoring the plaintiff; 4) and a showing that the injunction

---

Amparo, Editorial Jurídica Venezolana, Caracas, 1998, pp. 277 ff.; and regarding administrative acts, the courts of the Administrative Jurisdiction are the ones that can decide the matter of the suspension of the effects of the administrative challenged act, pending the judicial review proceeding final decision. *Idem*, pp. 281 ff.

141 As for instance has been decided by the Venezuelan First Court on Administrative Jurisdiction, *Video & Juegos Costa Verde, C.A. vs. Prefecto del Municipio Maracaibo del Estado Zulia* case, in *Revista de Derecho Público*, N° 85-98, Editorial Jurídica Venezolana, Caracas, 2001, p. 291.

142 See the Politico Administrative Chamber decision in the *Constructora Pedeca, C.A. vs. Gobernación del Estado Anzoátegui* case, in *Revista de Derecho Público*, N° 81, Editorial Jurídica Venezolana, Caracas, 2000, p. 459.

would not be adverse to the public interest; all of which must be proven by the plaintiff.[143]

Due to the extraordinary character of the amparo action, the preliminary protective measures requested by the plaintiff, if the above-mentioned conditions are fulfilled, can be decided and issued by the court in an immediate way, even without a previous hearing of the potential defendants, that is, *inadi alteram parte* or *inaudita pars*, as it is expressly provided in the Civil Procedure Code. In a similar sense, the courts in the United States, in cases of great urgency and when an immediate threat of irreparable injury exists, can issue preliminary injunctions or restraining orders without giving reasonable notice to the plaintiff, but always balancing the harm sought to be preserved with the rights of notice and hearing.[144]

Finally, regarding the effects of the preliminary measures, the general rule is that in the amparo proceeding, as it is also the rule regarding the injunctions in the United States,[145] are essentially modifiable or revocable by the court, particularly at the request of the defendant or of third parties.

On the other hand, as mentioned, the preliminary measures have effects during the course of the procedure, finishing with the definitive decision granting or rejecting the amparo. Nonetheless, if the final decision grants the amparo, the effects of the preliminary measures will be kept and be converted if definitive.

12. The definitive judicial adjudication on matter of amparo

Regarding the definitive judicial decisions in the amparo proceedings, their purpose for the injured party (the plaintiff) is to obtain the requested judicial protection (*amparo*) of his constitutional rights when illegitimately harmed or threatened by an injuring party (the defendant).

Consequently, the final result of the process, characterized by its bilateral nature that imposes the need for the defendants to have the right to participate and to be heard,[146] is a formal judicial decision or order issued by the court for the protection of the threatened rights or to restore the enjoyment of the harmed one, which can consist, for instance, in a decision commanding or preventing an action, or commanding someone to do, not to do or to undo some action.[147] This is to say, the

---

143 See William M. Tabb and Elaine W. Shoben, *Remedies*, Thomson West, 2005, p. 63.

144 See for instance *Carroll v. President and Com'rs of Princess Anne*, 393 U.S. 175, 89 S. Ct. 347, 21 L. Ed.2d 325, 1968; *Board of Ed. of Community Unit School Dist. Nº 101 v. Parlor*, 85 Ill. 2d 397, 54 Ill. Dec 249, 424 N.E 2d 1152, 1981; in John Bourdeau *et al.*, "Injunctions," in Kevin Schroder, John Glenn and Maureen Placilla, *Corpus Juris Secundum*, Volume 43A, Thomson West, 2004, pp. 339 ff.

145 See for instance *García-Marroquin v. Nueces County Bail Bond Bd.*, 1 S.W.3d 366 (Tex. App. Corpus Christi 1999), in John Bourdeau *et al.*, "Injunctions," in Kevin Schroder, John Glenn and Maureen Placilla, *Corpus Juris Secundum*, Volume 43A, Thomson West, 2004, pp. 421.

146 Similarly, regarding definitive injunctions, they only can be granted if process issues and service is made on the defendant. See for instance *U.S. v. Crusco*, 464 F.2d 1060, #d Cir. 1972; *Murphy v. Washington American League Baseball Club, Inc.*, 324 F2d. 394, D.C. Cir. 1963, in John Bourdeau *et al.*, "Injunctions," in Kevin Schroder, John Glenn and Maureen Placilla, *Corpus Juris Secundum*, Volume 43A, Thomson West, 2004, p. 339.

147 In the United States' injunction, the order can be commanding or preventing virtually any type of action (*Dawkins v. Walker*, 794 So. 2d 333, Ala. 2001; *Levin v. Barish*, 505 Pa. 514, 481

amparo, as the injunction,[148] is a writ framed according to the circumstances of the case commanding an act that the court regards as essential in justice, or restraining an act that it deems contrary to equity and good conscience.

Consequently, the function of the amparo court's decision is, on the one hand, to prevent the defendant from inflicting further injury on the plaintiff, that can be of a prohibitory or mandatory character; or on the other hand, to correct the present by undoing the effects of a past wrong.[149]

That is why the amparo judicial order in Venezuela, as in all Latin American countries, even without the distinction between equitable remedies and extraordinary law remedies, is very similar in its purposes and effects not only to the United States' injunction, but also to the other equitable and non-equitable extraordinary remedies, like the mandamus, prohibition and declaratory legal remedies. Accordingly, for instance, the amparo order can be first, of a prohibitory character, similar to the prohibitory injunctions, issued to restrain an action, to forbid certain acts or to command a person to refrain from doing specific acts. Second, it can also be of a mandatory character, that is, like the mandatory injunction requiring the undoing of an act, or the restoring of the status quo; and like the writ of mandamus, issued to compel an action or the execution of some act, or to command a person to do a specific act. Third, the amparo order can also be similar to the writ of prohibition or to the writ of error when the order is directed to a court,[150] which normally happens in the cases of amparo actions filed against judicial decisions. And fourth, it can also be similar to the declaratory legal remedy through which courts are called to declare the constitutional right of the plaintiff regarding the other parties.

Consequently, in the amparo proceeding, the courts have very extensive powers to provide for remedies in order to effectively protect constitutional rights, issuing final adjudication, orders to do, to refrain from doing, to undo or to prohibit,[151] or as the Amparo Law establishes in Article 32,b the decision must "determine the conduct to be accomplished."[152]

A.2d 1183, 1984), or commanding someone to undo some wrong or injury (*State Game and Fish Com'n v. Sledge*, 344 Ark. 505, 42 S.W.3d 427, 2001). It is a judicial order requiring a person to do or refrain from doing certain acts (*Skolnick v. Altheimer & Gray*, 191 Ill 2d 214, 246 Ill. Dec. 324, 730 N.E.2d 4, 2000), for any period of time, no matter its purpose (*Sheridan County Elec. Co-op v. Ferguson*, 124 Mont. 543, 227 P.2d 597, 1951). *Idem,* p. 19.

148 See *Nussbaum v. Hetzer*, 1, N.J. 171, 62 A. 2d 399 (1948). *Idem,* p. 19.

149 Similar to the "preventive injunction" and to the "restorative or reparative injunction," in the United States. See William M. Tabb and Elaine W. Shoben, *Remedies*, Thomson West, 2005, pp. 86–89; John Bourdeau *et al.*, "Injunctions," in Kevin Schroder, John Glenn and Maureen Placilla, *Corpus Juris Secundum*, Volume 43A, Thomson West, 2004, pp. 28 ff.

150 See William M. Tabb and Elaine W. Shoben, *Remedies*, Thomson West, 2005, pp. 86 ff. 246 ff.; and in John Bourdeau *et al.*, "Injunctions," in Kevin Schroder, John Glenn and Maureen Placilla, *Corpus Juris Secundum*, Volume 43A, Thompson West, 2004, pp. 21 ff.; 28 ff.

151 See Allan R. Brewer-Carías, *Instituciones Políticas y Constitucionales,* Vol V, *Derecho y Acción de Amparo,* Editorial Jurídica Venezolana, Caracas, 1998, pp. 143 ff.

152 Rafael Chavero G. *El nuevo amparo constitucional en Venezuela,* Ed. Sherwood, Caracas, 2001, p. 185 ff., 327 ff.; Allan R. Brewer-Carías, *Instituciones Políticas y Constitucionales,* Vol V, *Derecho y Acción de Amparo,* Editorial Jurídica Venezolana, Caracas, 1998, pp. 399 ff.

The judicial amparo order can be of a restorative or of a preventive nature. In the first case, it may consist in an order seeking for the reestablishment of the juridical situation of the plaintiff to the stage it had before the violation or to the most similar one; and in the second case, when of a preventive nature, it can consist in compelling the defendant to do or to refrain from doing certain acts in order to maintain the enjoyment of the plaintiff's rights. Nonetheless, in the case of being of a restorative character, in general terms, when the amparo action is filed against acts, particularly authorities' acts causing the harms or threats to constitutional rights, the immediate effect of the decision is to suspend the effects of the challenged act regarding the plaintiff, the amparo proceeding not having the purposes of annulling those State acts. In principle, it is for the Constitutional Jurisdiction and for the Administrative Jurisdictions' courts and not for the amparo judges to adopt decisions annulling statutes or administrative acts.

In particular, regarding statutes and specifically self-executing ones, when an amparo action is filed directly against them,[153] the amparo judge when granting the amparo has no power to annul them, and in order to protect the harmed or threatened right what he can do is to declare their inapplicability to the plaintiff in the particular case. The competence to annul statutes is exclusively granted to the Constitutional Chamber of the Supreme Tribunal of Justice (Article 336, Constitution).

Regarding administrative acts, the general rule is also that the amparo decision cannot annul the challenged administrative act, being the amparo judge only empowered to suspend its effects and application to the plaintiff. The power to annul administrative acts is also exclusively a power attributed to the Administrative Jurisdiction courts (Article 259l, Constitution).[154]

Conversely, regarding the amparo actions filed against judicial decisions the effects of the ruling granting the amparo protection consists in the annulment of the challenged judicial act or decision.[155]

Another aspect that must be mentioned regarding amparo decisions in Venezuela is that it has not compensatory character[156] because it is the function of the courts in these proceedings only to protect the plaintiff's rights and not to condemn the defendant to pay the plaintiff any sort of compensation for damages caused by the

---

153 Rafael Chavero G. *El nuevo amparo constitucional en Venezuela,* Ed. Sherwood, Caracas, 2001, pp. 468 ff.; Allan R. Brewer-Carías, *Instituciones Políticas y Constitucionales,* Vol V, *Derecho y Acción de Amparo,* Editorial Jurídica Venezolana, Caracas, 1998, pp. 399 ff.

154 See Rafael Chavero G. *El nuevo amparo constitucional en Venezuela,* Ed. Sherwood, Caracas, 2001, pp. 358 ff.; Allan R. Brewer-Carías, *Instituciones Políticas y Constitucionales,* Vol. V, *Derecho y Acción de Amparo,* Editorial Jurídica Venezolana, Caracas, 1998, pp. 144; 400.

155 See Rafael Chavero G. *El nuevo amparo constitucional en Venezuela,* Ed. Sherwood, Caracas, 2001, p. 511; Allan R. Brewer-Carías, "Derecho y Acción de Amparo, Vol. V, *Instituciones Políticas y Constitucionales* Editorial Jurídica Venezolana, Caracas, 1998, p. 297; Allan R. Brewer-Carías, "El problema del amparo contra sentencias o de cómo la Sala de Casación Civil remedia arbitrariedades judiciales," in *Revista de Derecho Público*, N° 34, Editorial Jurídica Venezolana, Caracas, abril-junio 1988, pp. 157–171.

156 In a similar way to the United States injunctions. See *Simenstad v. Hagen*, 22 Wis. 2d 653, 126 N.W.2d 529, 1964, in John Bourdeau *et al.*, "Injunctions," in Kevin Schroder, John Glenn and Maureen Placilla, *Corpus Juris Secundum*, Volume 43A, Thomson West, 2004, p. 20.

injury.[157] That is, the amparo proceeding is, in general terms, a preventive and restorative process, but not a compensatory one,[158] the courts being empowered to prevent harms or to restore the enjoyment of a right, for instance by suspending the effects of the injuring act, but not to condemn the defendant to the payment of a compensation. The judicial actions tending to seek for compensation from the defendant, because of its liability as a consequence of the injury inflicted to the constitutional right of the plaintiff, must be filed by means of a separate ordinary judicial remedy established for such purpose before the civil or administrative judicial jurisdiction.[159]

Finally, regarding the economic consequences of the amparo suit, in Venezuela the order to pay the costs is established in a very restrictive way, only in cases of amparo actions filed against individuals and not against public authorities (Article 33).

Another important aspect of the amparo definitive decisions is related to their effects. The general rule regarding the amparo judicial decisions is that they only have *inter partes* effects, that is, between the parties that have been involved in the suit (the plaintiff, the defendant and the third parties) and those that have participated in the process. So in a similar way to the injunctive decisions in the United States,[160] the amparo decisions only have binding effects regarding the parties to the suit, and only regarding the controversy; this being the most important consequence of the personal character of the amparo, as an action mainly devoted for the protection of personal constitutional rights or guaranties.[161] The only exception to this principle in the United States refers to the effects of the ruling when constitutional questions are decided by the Supreme Court, in which cases, due to the doctrine of precedent (*stare decisis*), all courts are obliged to apply the same constitutional rule in cases with similar controversies.[162] The same rule exists

157 For instance in the case of an illegitimate administrative order issued by a municipal authority demolishing a building, if executed, even if it violates the constitutional right to property, the amparo action has not the purpose to compensate, being in this case inadmissible, particularly due to the irreparable character of the harm.

158 See Rafael Chavero G. *El nuevo amparo constitucional en Venezuela,* Ed. Sherwood, Caracas, 2001, pp. 185, 242, 262, 326, 328; Allan R. Brewer-Carías, *Instituciones Políticas y Constitucionales,* Vol. V, *Derecho y Acción de Amparo,* Editorial Jurídica Venezolana, Caracas, 1998, p. 143.

159 Article 27 of the Venezuelan Amparo Law also expressly provides that in cases of granting an amparo, the court must send copy of the decision to the competent authority where the public officer causing the harm works, in order to impose the corresponding disciplinary measures.

160 See for instance *ESP Fidelity Corp. v. Department of Housing & Urban Development*, 512 F.2d 887, (9th Cir. 1975), in John Bourdeau *et al.*, "Injunctions," in Kevin Schroder, John Glenn and Maureen Placilla, *Corpus Juris Secundum*, Volume 43A, Thomson West, 2004, pp. 414.

161 The Venezuelan regulations can be highlighted in this regard. In principle, the court decisions have been constant in granting the action of *amparo* a personal character where the standing belongs firstly to "the individual directly affected by the infringement of constitutional rights and guaranties." See for example, decision of the Constitutional Chamber of March 15, 2000, in *Revista de Derecho Público*, N° 81, Editorial Jurídica Venezolana, 2000, pp. 322–323.

162 See M. Glenn Abernathy and Barbara A. Perry, *Civil Liberties under the Constitution*, University of South Carolina Press, 1993, p. 5.

in Venezuela regarding the Constitutional Chamber rulings (Article 336 of the Constitution) that can be issued with binding general character and effects.

Nonetheless, the general principle of the *inter partes* effects also has its exceptions due to the progressive development of the collective nature of some constitutional rights, as for instance, is the case of violation of environmental rights, indigenous People's rights and other diffuse rights,[163] in which cases,[164] the definitive ruling can benefit other persons different to those that have actively participated in the procedure as plaintiff. In these cases, due to the constitutional provision regarding the protection of diffuse or collective interests, the Constitutional Chamber of the Supreme Tribunal has admitted action for amparo seeking for the protection and enforcement of those collective interests, including for instance, voting rights. In such cases, the Chamber has even granted *erga omnes* effects to the precautionary measures adopted "for both the individuals and entities that have filed the action for constitutional protection and to all the voters as a group.[165] In addition, the Office of the People's Defendant has the authority to promote, defend, and guard constitutional rights and guaranties "as well as the legitimate, collective or diffuse interests of the citizens" (Articles 280 and 281,2 of the Constitution); being consequently his standing admitted to file actions for amparo on behalf of the citizens as a whole.[166] In all these cases, consequently, the judicial ruling benefits all the persons enjoying the collective rights or interest involved.

On the other hand, as all definitive judicial decisions, the amparo decisions also have *res judicata* effects, providing stability to the ruling. That means that the courts' decisions are binding not only for the parties in the process or its beneficiaries, but also regarding the court itself, which cannot modify its ruling

---

163 See Rafael Chavero G. *El nuevo amparo constitucional en Venezuela,* Ed. Sherwood, Caracas, 2001, pp. 333 ff.

164 As also happens regarding the Class Actions in the United States. See M. Glenn Abernathy and Barbara A. Perry, *Civil Liberties under the Constitution*, University of South Carolina Press, 1993, p. 6.

165 See decision of the Constitutional Chamber N° 483 of May 29, 2000, *"Queremos Elegir" y otros* case, in *Revista de Derecho Público*, N° 82, Editorial Jurídica Venezolana, 2000, pp. 489–491. In the same sense, decision of the same Chamber N° 714 of July 13, 2000, *APRUM* Case, in *Revista de Derecho Público*, N° 83, 2000, Editorial Jurídica Venezolana, pp. 319 ff. The Constitutional Chamber has decided that "any individual is entitled to bring suit based on diffuse or collective interests" and has extended "standing to companies, corporations, foundations, chambers, unions and other collective entities, whose object is the defense of society, as long as they act within the boundaries of their corporate objects, aimed at protecting the interests of their members regarding those objects. See decision of the Constitutional Chamber N° 656 of May 6, 2001, *Defensor del Pueblo vs. Comisión Legislativa Nacional* Case, as referred in decision N° 379 of February 26, 2003, *Mireya Ripanti et vs. Presidente de Petróleos de Venezuela S.A. (PDVSA)* case, in *Revista de Derecho Público*, N° 93-96, Editorial Jurídica Venezolana, Caracas, 2003, pp. 152 ff.

166 In one case the Defender of the People acted against a threat by the 2000 National Legislative Commission to appoint the Electoral National Council members without fulfilling constitutional requirements. In that case, the Constitutional Chamber decided that "the Defender has standing to bring actions aimed at enforcing diffuse and collective rights or interests" without requiring the acquiescence of the society on whose behalf he acts, but this provision does not exclude or prevent citizens' access to the judicial system in defense of diffuse and collective rights and interests (Article 26). Decision of the Constitutional Chamber N° 656 of May 6, 2001, *Defensor del Pueblo vs. Comisión Legislativa Nacional* case, *Idem.*

(immutability). *Res judicata* implies then, the impossibility for a new suit to take place regarding the same matter already adopted, or that a decision is issued in a different sense than the one already decided in a previous process.[167] Nonetheless, on this matter, of the *res judicata* effects, the scope of those effects are different when referring to the so-called "substantive" (*material*) or to the "formal" *res judicata* effects. In general terms, the concept of "formal *res judicata*" effects apply to judicial decisions that even when enforced do not impede the development of a new process between the same parties, provided that the matter has not been decided in the amparo proceeding on the merits of the case and its defense. On the other hand, the concept of "substantive *res judicata*" effects apply when the judicial decision has decided on the merits, not allowing for other processes to develop regarding the same matter.

The matter decided in the amparo proceeding, that is the merits of the case, is related to the manifest illegitimate and arbitrary harm or threat caused by an identified injuring party to the constitutional right or guaranties of the plaintiff; a matter that is to be resolved in a brief and prompt procedure. Thus, the merits on the matters in the amparo proceeding are reduced to determining the existence of such illegitimate and manifest violation of the right, regardless of the other possible matters that can or may be resolved by the parties in other processes. In this regard, Article 36 of the Venezuelan Amparo Law, giving a different approach regarding the substantive or formal *res judicata* effects[168] provides that "The definitive amparo decision will produce legal effects regarding the right or guaranty that has been the object of the process, without prejudice of the actions or recourses that legally correspond to the parties."

According to this provision, the *res judicata* in the amparo proceeding only refers to what has been argued and decided in the case regarding the violation or injury inflicted to a constitutional right or guaranty,[169] Thus, in general terms, the amparo decision does not resolve all the other possible matters that could be raised, but only

---

167 In contrast, these *res judicata* effects, as a general rule, are not applicable to the injunction orders in the United States which can be modified by the court. As it has been summarized regarding the judicial doctrine on the matter: "Injunctions are different from other judgments in the context of *res judicata* because the parties are often subject to the court's continuing jurisdiction, and the court must strike a balance between the policies of *res judicata* and the right of the court to apply modified measures to changed circumstances." See *Town of Durham v. Cutter*, 121 N.H. 243, 428 A. 2d 904 (1981), in John Bourdeau *et al.*, "Injunctions," in Kevin Schroder, John Glenn and Maureen Placilla, *Corpus Juris Secundum*, Volume 43A, Thomson West, 2004, p. 416. See also Owen M. Fiss and Doug Rendleman, *Injunctions*, The Foundation Press, 1984, pp. 497–498, 526.

168 In this regard, the First Court on Administrative Jurisdiction, in a decision dated October 16, 1986, *Pedro J. Montilva* case, decided that if in a case "the action of amparo is filed with the same object, denouncing the same violations, based on the same motives and with identical object as the previous one and directed against the same person, then it is evident that in such case, the res judicata force applies in order to avoid the rearguing of the case, due to the fact that the controversy to be resolved has the same subjective and objective identity than the one already decided." See Rafael Chavero G. *El nuevo amparo constitucional en Venezuela,* Ed. Sherwood, Caracas, 2001, pp. 338 ff.; Gustavo Linares Benzo, *El proceso de amparo en Venezuela*, Caracas, 1999, p. 121 f.

169 See in *Revista de Derecho Público,* N° 28, Editorial Jurídica Venezolana, Caracas, 1986, p. 106.

the aspect of the violation or injury to the constitutional rights or guaranties, this being the only aspect regarding which the decision can produce *res judicata* effects. For example, if an amparo decision is issued regarding an administrative act because it causes harm to constitutional rights, it only has restorative or reestablishing effects suspending the application of the challenged act, but it does not have annulling effects.[170] Consequently, the amparo decision in such cases does not have *res judicata* effects regarding the judicial review action that can be filed against the administrative act before the Administrative Jurisdiction courts in order to have its nullity declared.[171]

In these cases, after the amparo decision has been issued, other legal questions can remain pending to be resolved in other processes, and that is why the amparo decision in these cases is issued "without prejudice of the actions or recourses that could legally correspond to the parties."

One last aspect that must be highlighted regarding the effects of the amparo decision refers to its obligatory character. As all judicial decisions, the amparo ruling is obligatory not only for the parties to the process but regarding all other persons or public officers that must apply them. The defendant, for instance, is compelled to immediately obey it, as it is expressly set forth in the Amparo Law (Articles 29, 30).

In order to execute the decision, the courts, *ex officio* or at the party's request, can adopt all the measures directed to its accomplishment. Yet the amparo judges in Venezuela do not have direct power to punish by imposing criminal sanctions for disobedience of their rulings. In other words, they do not have criminal contempt power, which in contrast is one of the most important features of the injunctive relief system in the United States.[172] These contempt powers are precisely what gave the

---

170 Due to this fact, by means of the amparo suit, as it has been ruled by the Supreme Court of Venezuela, "none of the three types of judicial declarative, constitutive or to condemn decision can be obtained, nor, of course, the interpretative decision." See decision of the Politico Administrative Chamber of July 15, 1992, in *Revista de Derecho Público,* Nº 51, Editorial Jurídica Venezolana, Caracas, 1992, p. 171.

171 See Allan R. Brewer-Carías, *Instituciones Políticas y Constitucionales,* Vol. V, *Derecho y Acción de Amparo,* Editorial Jurídica Venezolana, Caracas, 1998, pp. 346 ff.

172 This is particularly important regarding criminal contempt, which was established since the *In Re Debs* case (158 U.S. 564, 15 S.Ct. 900, 39 L.Ed. 1092 (1895)), where according to Justice Brewer who delivered the court's opinion, it was ruled: "But the power of a court to make an order carries with it the equal power to punish for a disobedience of that order, and the inquiry as to the question of disobedience has been, from time immemorial, the special function of the court. And this is no technical rule. In order that a court may compel obedience to its order it must have the right to inquire whether there has been any disobedience thereof. To submit the question of disobedience to another tribunal, be it a jury or another court, would operate to deprive the proceedings of half its efficiency." In *Watson v. Williams,* 36 Miss. 331, 341, it was said: "The power to fine and imprison for contempt, from the earliest history of jurisprudence, has been regarded as the necessary incident and attribute of a court, without which it could no more exist than without a judge. It is a power inherent in all courts of record and coexisting with them by the wise provisions of the common law. A court without the power effectually to protect itself against the assaults of the lawless, or to enforce its orders, judgments, or decrees against the recusant parties before it, would be a disgrace to the legislation, and a stigma upon the age which invented it." See Owen M. Fiss and Doug Rendleman, *Injunctions*, The Foundation Press, 1984, p. 13. See also William M. Tabb and Elaine W. Shoben, *Remedies*, Thomson West, 2005, pp. 72 ff.

injunction in the United States its effectiveness regarding any disobedience, being the same court empowered to vindicate its own power by imposing criminal or economic sanctions by means of imprisonment and fines. In Venezuela, in contrast, the amparo courts do not have such powers, and regarding the application of criminal sanctions to the disobedient party, the amparo courts or the interested party must seek for the initiation of a judicial criminal procedure against the disobedient to be brought before the competent criminal courts (Article 31).

Due to the general by-instance procedural principle, the amparo decisions can be appealed before the superior courts according to the general rules established in the procedural codes. This general principle, of course, does not apply when the decision is adopted by the Supreme Tribunal. Consequently, the amparo decisions can only be adopted by the Supreme Tribunal, when having original jurisdiction, when deciding on appellate jurisdiction or when an extraordinary mean for revision is filed, similar to the writ for certiorari in the United States. In effect, particularly when constitutional issues are involved, the United States Supreme Court, when considering a petition for a writ of certiorari, is authorized to review all the decisions of the federal courts of appeals, and of the specialized federal courts, and all the decisions of the supreme courts of the states involving issues of federal law, but on a discretionary basis. In all such cases where there is no right of appeal and no mandatory appellate jurisdiction of the Supreme Court established, the cases can reach the Supreme Court as petitions for certiorari, when a litigant who has lost in a lower court petitions a review in the Supreme Court, setting out the reasons why review should be granted.[173] This method of seeking review by the Supreme Court is expressly established in the cases set forth in the 28 U. S. Code, and according to Rule No. 10 of the Rules of the Supreme Court adopted in 2005, where it is established as not being "a matter of right, but of judicial discretion," granted only "for compelling reasons," that is, when there are special and important reasons.

According to this rule, consequently, in order to promote uniformity and consistency in federal law, the following factors might prompt the Supreme Court to grant certiorari: 1. Important questions of federal law on which the court has not previously ruled; 2. Conflicting interpretations of federal law by lower courts; 3. Lower courts' decisions that conflict with previous Supreme Court decisions; and 4. Lower courts' departures from the accepted and usual course of judicial proceedings.[174]

Of course, review may be granted on the basis of other factors or denied even if one or more of the above-mentioned factors is present. The discretion of the Supreme Court is not limited, and it is the importance of the issue and the public interest considered by the Court in a particular case that leads the Court to grant certiorari and to review some cases.

In countries with a mixed system of judicial review, as is the case in Venezuela, the appellate jurisdiction of the Constitutional Chamber of the Supreme Court as Constitutional Jurisdictions in order to review lower courts' decisions on

173 See L. Baum, *The Supreme Court*, Washington, 1981, p. 81.

174 See regarding the previous Rule N° 17,1: R. A. Rossum and G. A. Tarr, *American Constitutional Law*, New York, 1983, p. 28.

constitutional matters, is also established in a discretionary basis,[175] and by means of an extraordinary recourse for review, regarding lower courts decisions applying the diffuse method and also the decisions issued on amparo proceedings (Article 336,10).

In this matter, in Venezuela, in addition, the Constitutional Chamber of the Supreme Court, as Constitutional Jurisdiction, developed *ex officio* powers for reviewing lower courts' decisions on constitutional matters, without any constitutional or statutory support. Based in the aforementioned power of the Constitutional Chamber to review in a discretionary way, judicial lower courts' decisions on constitutional matters because their constitutional importance, the Constitutional Chamber distorting its review powers, extended it far beyond the precise cases of decisions adopted on judicial review and on amparo proceedings established in the constitution. Through obligatory judicial doctrine, the Chamber extended its review power regarding any other judicial decision issued in any matters when it considers it contrary to the constitution, a power that the Chamber considered authorized to exercise although without any constitutional provision, even *ex officio*. These review powers have also been developed in cases of particular judicial decision when considered contrary to a Constitutional Chamber interpretation of the constitution, or when considered that is affected by a grotesque error regarding constitutional interpretation.[176]

On the other hand, since 2004, the Organic Law of the Supreme Tribunal, following such doctrine established by the same Tribunal, gave general powers to all the Chambers of the Tribunal, to take away cases (*avocamiento*) from the jurisdiction of lower courts, also *ex officio* or through a party petition, when considered convenient, and to decide them.[177] This power, which has been highly criticized because breaches the due process rights, and particularly, the right to trial in a by-instance basis by the courts, has allowed the Constitutional Chamber to intervene in any kind of processes, including cases being trialed by the other Chambers of the Supreme Tribunal, with very negative effects. For instance, the Constitutional Chamber power was used in order to annul a decision issued by the Electoral Chamber of the Supreme Tribunal[178] seeking to protect the citizens' right

---

175 In a similar way to the writ of certiorari in the United States. See Jesús María Casal, *Constitución y Justicia Constitucional,* Caracas, 2002, p. 92.

176 See decision N° 93 of February 6, 2001, *Olimpia Tours and Travel vs. Corporación de Turismo de Venezuela* Case, in *Revista de Derecho Público*, N° 85-88, Editorial Jurídica Venezolana, Caracas, 2001, pp. 414–415. See Allan R. Brewer-Carías, "*Quis Custodiet ipsos Custodes*: De la interpretación constitucional a la inconstitucionalidad de la interpretación," in *VIII Congreso Nacional de Derecho Constitucional, Perú, September 2005*, Fondo Editorial, Colegio de Abogados de Arequipa, Arequipa, 2005, pp. 463–489.

177 See article 25.16 of the *Ley Orgánica del Tribunal Supremo de Justicia*, *Official Gazette* N° 5991 Extra. of July 29, 2010. See Allan R. Brewer-Carías, *Crónica de la "In"justicia constitucional. La Sala Constitucional y el autoritarismo en Venezuela*, Editorial Jurídica Venezolana, Caracas 2007, p. 91 ff.

178 See Decisions N° 24 of March 15, 2004, (Exp. AA70-E 2004-000021; Exp. x-04-00006); and N° 27 of March 29, (*Julio Borges, César Pérez Vivas, Henry Ramos Allup, Jorge Sucre Castillo, Ramón José Medina y Gerardo Blyde vs. Consejo Nacional Electoral* case (Exp. AA70-E-2004-000021- AA70-V-2004-000006). See in *Revista de Derecho Público,* N° 97-98, Editorial Jurídica Venezolana, Caracas, 2004, pp. 373 ff.

to political participation, in which the latter suspended the effects of a decision of the National Electoral Council (Resolution N° 040302-131 of March 2, 2004), objecting the presidential repeal referendum petition of 2004. The Constitutional Chamber, in this way, by means of a decision N° 566 of April 12, 2004, interrupted the process that was normally developing before the Electoral Chamber of the Supreme Tribunal, took away the case from such Chamber, and annulling its decision, decided in contrary sense, according to what was the will of the Executive, restricting the people's right to participate through petitioning referendums.[179]

13. Some conclusions

The two centuries tradition of Venezuelan constitutions of inserting very extensive declarations on human rights, has proven that in order for human rights to be effectively protected, independently of such formal declarations, the most important and necessary tool is to have not only effective judicial remedies for the immediate protections of rights but an independent and autonomous Judiciary.

Due to the traditional inefficacy of the ordinary and extraordinary judicial remedies that in other countries have proven to be effective for the protection of rights, in Venezuela, since 1961, the Constitution have incorporated express provision regarding the judicial guaranty of constitutional rights, establishing a specific judicial remedy for its protection, called the amparo action or proceeding, having different procedural rules when compared with the general judicial remedies the legal systems provides for the protection of personal or property rights. As it has been analyzed, this constitutional feature is one of the most important of Latin America constitutional law, particularly when contrasted with the constitutional system of the United States or of the United Kingdom, where the protection of human rights is effectively carried on through the general judicial actions and equitable remedies, that are also used to protect any kind of personal or property rights or interests.

This amparo remedy has been a very effective mean for the protection of constitutional rights, particularly in democratic regimes where the Judiciary has been preserved as an independent branch of government. Consequently, even providing in the constitution for this specific remedy of amparo to assure the immediate protection of constitutional rights, the very essence of its effectiveness is the existence of an independent and autonomous Judiciary that could effectively protect human rights. Unfortunately, in the Latin American countries, the judiciary has not always accomplished its fundamental duty, so that in spite of the constitutional declarations and provisions for amparo, many countries have faced, and others are still facing, a rather dismal situation regarding the effectiveness of the Judiciary as a whole, as an efficient and just protector of fundamental rights.

That is why, in spite of the extensive constitutional declarations of rights, in order to achieve the aims of the State of Justice, the most elemental institutional condition needed in any country, is the existence of a really autonomous and independent

---

179 See in Allan R. Brewer-Carías, *La Sala Constitucional versus el Estado Democrático de Derecho. El secuestro del poder electoral y de la Sala Electoral del Tribunal Supremo y la confiscación del derecho a la participación política*, Los Libros de El Nacional, Colección Ares, Caracas, 2004.

Judiciary, out of the reach and control from the other branches of government, empowered to interpret and apply the law in an impartial way and protect citizens, particularly when referring to the enforcement of rights against the State. Such Judiciary has to be built upon the principle of separation of powers. If this principle is not implemented and the Government controls the courts and judges, no effective guaranty can exist regarding constitutional rights, particularly when the offending party is a governmental agency. In this case, and in spite of all constitutional declarations, it is impossible to speak of rule of law, as happens in many Latin American countries.

This is important, precisely on matters of amparo, particularly when the petition is filed against a government or authority act, in which case, no judicial protection can be given if the government controls the Judiciary. Just one example can highlight this situation, in a case developed in Venezuela in 2003, where as a consequence of an amparo decision; the Judicial Review of Administrative Action Jurisdiction (*Jurisdicción contencioso-administrativa*) was intervened by the government, after being for three decades a very important autonomous and independent jurisdiction in order to control the legality of Public Administration activities.

In effect, based on the democratic tradition the country had since 1958 in matters of control and review of Public Administration actions, on July 17, 2003, the Venezuelan National Federation of Doctors brought before the aforementioned Judicial Review of Administrative Actions highest Court in Caracas (First Court), a nullity claim against the Mayor of Caracas and the Ministry of Health and the Caracas Metropolitan Board of Doctors (*Colegio de Médicos*) acts deciding to hire Cuban doctors for an important popular governmental health program in the Caracas slums, but without complying with the legal conditions established for foreign doctors to practice the medical profession in the country. The National Federation of Doctors considered that the program was discriminatory and against the rights of Venezuelan doctors to exercise their medical profession, allowing foreign doctors to exercise it without complying with the Medical Profession Statute regulations. The consequence was the filing an amparo petition against both public authorities, seeking the collective protection of the Venezuelan doctors' constitutional rights.[180]

One month later, in August 21, 2003, the First Court issued a preliminary protective amparo measure, considering that there were sufficient elements to deem that the equality before the law constitutional guaranty was violated in the case. The Court ordered in a preliminary way the suspension of the Cuban doctors' hiring program and ordered the Metropolitan Board of doctors to substitute the Cuban doctors already hired, by Venezuelan ones or foreign Doctors who had fulfilled the legal regulations in order to exercise the medical profession in the country.[181]

Nonetheless, in response to that preliminary judicial amparo decision, instead of enforcing it, the Minister of Health, the Mayor of Caracas, and even the President of the Republic made public statements to the effect that the decision

180 See Claudia Nikken, "El caso "Barrio Adentro": La Corte Primera de lo Contencioso Administrativo ante la Sala Constitucional del Tribunal Supremo de Justicia o el avocamiento como medio de amparo de derechos e intereses colectivos y difusos," in *Revista de Derecho Público*, N° 93-96, Editorial Jurídica Venezolana, Caracas, 2003, pp. 5 ff.

181 See Decision of August, 21 2003, in *Idem*, pp. 445 ff.

was not going to be respected or enforced.[182] Following these statements, the government-controlled Constitutional Chamber of the Supreme Tribunal of Justice adopted a decision, without any appeal being filed, assuming jurisdiction over the case and annulling the preliminary amparo ordered by the First Court; a group of Secret Service police officials seized the First Court's premises; and the President of the Republic, among other expressions he used, publicly called the President of the First Court a "bandit."[183] A few weeks later, in response to the First Court's decision in an unrelated case challenging a local registrar's refusal to record a land sale, a Special Commission for the Intervention of the Judiciary, which in spite of being unconstitutional continued to exist, dismissed all five judges of the First Court.[184] In spite of the protests of all the Bar Associations of the country and also of the International Commission of Jurists;[185] the First Court remained suspended without judges, and its premises remained closed for about nine months,[186] period during which simply no judicial review of administrative action could be sought in the country.[187]

The dismissed judges of the First Court brought a complaint to the Inter-American Commission of Human Rights for the government's unlawful removal of them and for violation of their constitutional rights. The Commission in turn brought the case, captioned *Apitz Barbera et al.* (*Corte Primera de lo Contencioso Administrativo vs. Venezuela*) before the Inter-American Court of Human Rights. On August 5, 2008, the Inter-American Court ruled that the Republic of Venezuela had violated the rights of the dismissed judges established in the American Convention of Human Rights, and ordered the State to pay them due compensation, to reinstate them to a similar position in the Judiciary, and to publish part of the

---

182 The President of the Republic said: "*Váyanse con su decisión no sé para donde, la cumplirán ustedes en su casa si quieren ...*" (You can go with your decision, I don't know where; you will enforce it in your house if you want ..."). See *El Universal,* Caracas, August 25, 2003 and *El Universal*, Caracas, August 28, 2003.

183 See Inter-American Court of Human Rights, *Apitz Barbera et al. (Corte Primera de lo Contencioso Administrativo) v. Venezuela* (Judgment of August 5, 2008), *available at* www.corteidh.or.cr. See *also, El Universal,* Caracas, October 16, 2003; and *El Universal*, Caracas, September 22, 2003.

184 See *El Nacional*, Caracas, November 5, 2003, p. A2. The dismissed President of the First Court said: "*La justicia venezolana vive un momento tenebroso, pues el tribunal que constituye un último resquicio de esperanza ha sido clausurado.*" ("The Venezuelan judiciary lives a dark moment, because the court that was a last glimmer of hope has been shut down.") *Id.* The Commission for the Intervention of the Judiciary had also massively dismissed almost all judges of the country without due disciplinary process, and had replaced them with provisionally appointed judges beholden to the ruling power.

185 See in *El Nacional*, Caracas, October 10, 2003, p. A-6; *El Nacional*, Caracas, October 15, 2003, p. A-2; *El Nacional*, Caracas, September 24, 2003, p. A-4; and *El Nacional*, Caracas, February 14, 2004, p. A-7.

186 See *El Nacional*, Caracas, October 24, 2003, p. A-2; and *El Nacional*, Caracas, July 16, 2004, p. A-6.

187 See *generally* Allan R. Brewer-Carías, *La justicia sometida al poder (La ausencia de independencia y autonomía de los jueces en Venezuela por la interminable emergencia del Poder Judicial (1999-2006))* in Cuestiones Internacionales. Anuario Jurídico Villanueva 2007, Centro Universitario Villanueva, Marcial Pons, Madrid 2007, pp. 25–57, *available at* www.allanbrewercarias.com, (Biblioteca Virtual, II.4. Artículos y Estudios N° 550, 2007).

decision in Venezuelan newspapers.[188] Nonetheless, on December 12, 2008, the Constitutional Chamber of the Supreme Tribunal issued Decision N° 1.939, declaring that the August 5, 2008 decision of the Inter-American Court of Human Rights was non-enforceable (*inejecutable*) in Venezuela. The Constitutional Chamber also accused the Inter-American Court of having usurped powers of the Supreme Tribunal of Justice, and asked the Executive Branch to denounce the American Convention of Human Rights.[189]

In general terms, this was the global governmental response to an amparo judicial preliminary decision that affected a very sensitive governmental social program; a response that was expressed and executed through the government-controlled judiciary.[190] The result was that the subsequent newly appointed judges replacing those dismissed, began to "understand" how they needed to behave in the future. That same Commission for the Intervention of the Judiciary, as mentioned, was the one that massively dismissed without due disciplinary process almost all judges of the country, substituting them with provisionally appointed judges, thus dependent on the ruling power, who in 2006 were granted permanent status without complying with the constitutional provisions.[191]

This emblematic case, contrast with the very progressive text of the constitution in force in Venezuela (1999), which contains one of the most extensive declaration of constitutional rights in all Latin America, including the provision for the amparo action, even considering it as a constitutional right; shows that the judicial guaranty of constitutional rights always requires an independent and autonomous Judiciary, conducted out of the reach of the government. On the contrary, with a Judiciary controlled by the Executive, as the aforementioned Venezuelan case illustrates, the declaration of constitutional rights is a death letter, and the provision of the action for amparo is no more than an illusion. This has been the tragic institutional result of the deliberated process of dismantling democracy to which Venezuela has been

---

188 Inter-American Court of Human Rights, *Apitz Barbera et al. (Corte Primera de lo Contencioso Administrativo) v. Venezuela* (Judgment of August 5, 2008), *available at* www.corteidh.or.cr.

189 Supreme Tribunal of Justice, Constitutional Chamber, Decision N° 1.939 of December 18, 2008 (Case: *Abogados Gustavo Álvarez Arias et al.*) (Exp. N° 08-1572).

190 See Allan R. Brewer-Carías, "La progresiva y sistemática demolición institucional de la autonomía e independencia del Poder Judicial en Venezuela 1999–2004," in *XXX Jornadas J.M Domínguez Escovar, Estado de derecho, Administración de justicia y derechos humanos,* Instituto de Estudios Jurídicos del Estado Lara, Barquisimeto, 2005, pp. 33–174.

191 In this regard, the Venezuelan 1999 Constitution established, in general terms, the regime for entering the judicial career and promotion only "through public competition that assures suitability and excellence," guarantying "citizen's participation in the procedure of selection and appointment of the judges." The consequence is that they may not be removed or suspended from their positions except through a legal proceeding before a disciplinary jurisdiction (Article 255). This, again, unfortunately is just a theoretical aim, because all contests for judge's appointment have been suspended since 2002. Almost all judges are being provisionally appointed without citizen participation, and there is no disciplinary jurisdiction for their dismissal. Furthermore, the suspension and dismissal of all judges corresponds to a Commission for the intervention of the Judiciary that is not regulated in the constitution. See Inter-American Commission on Human Rights, *Informe sobre la Situación de los Derechos Humanos en Venezuela*, OEA/Ser.L/V/II.118, d.C. 4 rev. 2, December 29, 2003, Paragraph 11, p. 3.

subjected during the past decade, through the imposition of an authoritarian government, defrauding the constitution and democracy itself.[192].

III. THE TRAGIC INSTITUTIONAL SITUATION OF THE JUDICIARY

1. Democracy and Separation of Powers

The essential components of democracy are much more than the sole popular or circumstantial election of government officials, as it has been formally declared in the Inter American Democratic Charter *(Carta Democrática Interamericana)* adopted by the Organization of American States in 2001, [193] after so many antidemocratic, militarist and authoritarian regimes disguised as democratic because of their electoral origin that Latin American countries have suffered.

The Charter, in effect, enumerates among the *essential elements of the representative democracy,* in addition to having periodical, fair and free elections based on the universal and secret vote as expression of the will of the people; the following: respect for human rights and fundamental liberties; access to power and its exercise with subjection to the Rule of law; plural regime of the political parties and organizations; and what is the most important of all, "*separation and independence of public powers*" (Article 3), that is, the possibility to control the different branches of government. The *Inter-American Charter* in addition, also defined the following *fundamental components of the democracy*: transparency of governmental activities; integrity, responsibility of governments in the public management; respect of social rights and freedom of speech and press; constitutional subordination of all institutions of the State to the legally constituted civil authority, and respect to the Rule of law of all the entities and sectors of society.

The principle of separation and independence of powers is so important, as one of the "essential elements of democracy ", that it is the one that can allow all the other "fundamental components of democracy" to be politically possible. To be precise, democracy, as a political regime, can only function in a constitutional Rule of law system where the control of power exists; that is, check and balance based on the separation of powers with their independence and autonomy guaranteed, so that power can be stopped by power itself. Consequently, without separation of powers and the possibility of control of power, any of the other essential factors of democracy cannot be guaranteed, because only by controlling Power, can free and fair elections and political pluralism exist; only by controlling Power, can effective democratic participation be possible, and effective transparency in the exercise of government be assured; only by controlling Power can there be a government submitted to the Constitution and the laws, that is, the Rule of law; only by controlling Power can there be an effective access to justice functioning with

192 See generally Allan R. Brewer-Carías, *Dismantling Democracy. The Chávez Authoritarian Experiment,* Cambridge University Press, New York 2010.

193 See on the Inter-American Democratic Charter, in Allan R. Brewer-Carías, 2002. *La crisis de la democracia venezolana. La Carta Democrática Interamericana y los sucesos de abril de 2002*, Caracas: Ediciones El Nacional, pp. 137 ff.; Asdrúbal Aguiar, 2008. *El Derecho a la Democracia*, Caracas: Editorial Jurídica Venezolana.

autonomy and independence; and only by controlling Power can there be a true and effective guaranty for the respect of human rights.[194]

The consequence of the aforementioned, is that democratic regimes cannot exist without separation of powers, and in particular, without the possibility of an independent and autonomous Judicial Power with the capacity of controlling all the other powers of the State. That is why the most important principle governing the functioning of the Judiciary in democratic regimes, is the independence and autonomy of judges, so they can apply the rule of law without interference from other State's Powers, from institutions, corporation or even from citizens; and only subjected to the rule of the Constitution and of law.

2. The Provisions of the Constitution regarding the Judicial System and its Governance

For such purpose, in contemporary world, Constitutions have included express provisions in such respect, being no exception the Venezuelan Constitution of 1999.[195] In effect, according to article 253 of the Constitution, the power to render or administer justice emanates from the citizenry and is imparted "in the name of the Republic and by the authority of the law." For such purposes, Article 26 of the Constitution provides that the State must guaranty a "cost-free, accessible, impartial, adequate, transparent, autonomous, independent, accountable, equitable, and expeditious justice, without undue or dilatory delay, formalism, or unnecessary replication of procedures."[196] Consequently, the Constitution denies the Judiciary the power to establish court costs or fees, or to require payment for services (Article 254).

The system of justice, according to the same Article 253 of the Constitution, is composed not only by the organs of the Judicial Branch (Supreme Tribunal of Justice and all the other courts established by law), but by the offices of the Prosecutor General, the Peoples' Defender, the criminal investigatory organs, the penitentiary system, the alternative means of justice, the citizens who participate in the administration of justice as provided in the law, and the attorneys authorized to practice law.[197]

The principle of the independence of the Judicial Power is set forth expressly in Article 254 of the Constitution, which, in addition, establishes its financial

194 See Allan R. Brewer-Carías, 2007. Democracia: sus elementos y componentes esenciales y el control del poder. Nuria González Martín (Comp.), 2007. *Grandes temas para un observatorio electoral ciudadano, Vol. I, Democracia: retos y fundamentos,* México. Instituto Electoral del Distrito Federal, pp. 171-220.

195 See on the Venezuelan 1999 Constitucion, Allan R. Brewer-Carías, 2004. *La Constitución de 1999. Derecho Constitucional Venezolano*, 2 Vol. Caracas: Editorial Jurídica Venezolana.

196 See Gustavo Urdaneta Troconis, 2001. El Poder Judicial en la Constitución de 1999. *Estudios de Derecho Administrativo: Libro Homenaje a la Universidad Central de Venezuela,* Vol. I. Caracas: Imprenta Nacional, pp. 521-564.

197 See the Law on the Judicial System, (2009). *Official Gazette* N° 39.276 of October 1, 2009, Caracas: Imprenta Nacional. See Román J. Duque Corredor 2008. El sistema de Justicia, in Jesús María Casal, Alfredo Arismendi y Carlos Luis Carrillo Artiles (Coord.), 2008, *Tendencias Actuales del Derecho Constitucional. Homenaje a Jesús María Casal Montbrun,* Vol. II, Caracas: Universidad Central de Venezuela/Universidad Católica Andrés Bello, pp. 87-112.

autonomy,[198] and assigns "functional, financial, and administrative autonomy" to the Supreme Tribunal. For such purpose the Constitution provides that within the National general annual budget, an appropriation of at least two percent (2%) of the ordinary national budget is established for the judiciary, a percentage amount that cannot be changed without prior approval by the National Assembly.

With the purpose of guaranteeing the impartiality and independence of judges in the exercise of their duties, Article 256 of the Constitution requires that magistrates, judges and prosecutors of the Public Prosecutor and the Public Defenders' offices may not, from the time of entering their respective jobs until they step down, engage in partisan political activity other than voting. This includes political party activism, union, guild and similar activities. Magistrates, judges and prosecutors are also prohibited from engaging in private or business activities that are incompatible with their judicial functions, on their own behalf or on the behalf of others, and they may not undertake any other public functions other than educational activities. In addition, Judges are prohibited from associating with one another (Article 256), which is a limit regarding the constitutional right of association set forth in Article 52 of the Constitution.

According to Article 257 of the Constitution, the fundamental instrument for the realization of justice is the judicial process; regarding which the procedural laws must establish simplified, uniform and effective procedures, and adopt brief, public, and oral proceedings, through which in no case justice should be sacrificed based on the omission of non-essential formalities. These provisions are complemented by Article 26 of the Constitution that set forth that the State must guarantee expeditious justice without undue delay, formalisms, or useless procedural repositions. In addition, being the alternative means of justice part of the judicial system (Article 253), Article 258 of the Constitution imposes on the Legislator the duty to promote arbitration, conciliation, mediation, and other alternative means for conflicts resolution.

Finally, Article 255 of the Constitution, judges are personally responsible for unjustified errors, delays, or omissions, for substantial failures to observe procedural requirements, for abuse of or refusal to apply the law (*denegación*), for bias, for the crime of graft (*cohecho*) and for criminally negligent or intentional injustice (*prevaricación*) effectuated in the course of performing their judicial functions.

One of the innovations of the 1999 Constitution was to confer to the Supreme Tribunal of Justice "the Governance and Administration of the Judicial Branch," while eliminating the former Council of the Judiciary (*Consejo de la Judicatura*) which exercised these functions under Article 217 of the Constitution of 1961, as one of the organ with functional autonomy separate and independent from all the branches of government, including the former Supreme Court of Justice.

Consequently, since 2000, as provided in Article 267 of the Constitution, the Supreme Tribunal of Justice is charged with the direction, governance and administration of the Judicial Branch, including inspection and oversight of the

198 See Juan Rafael Perdomo, 2003. Independencia y competencia del Poder Judicial, *Revista de derecho del Tribunal Supremo de Justicia,* N° 8, Caracas, pp. 483 a 518.

other courts of the Republic as well as the offices of the Public Defenders.[199] For such purposes the Supreme Tribunal is in charge of drafting and putting into effect its own budget and the budget of the Judicial Branch in general, according to principles set out in Article 254.

In order to perform these functions, the plenary Supreme Tribunal of Justice has created an Executive Directorate of the Judiciary (*Dirección Ejecutiva de la Magistratura*) with regional offices. Judicial Circuits are to be established and organized by statute, as are the creation of jurisdictions of tribunals and regional courts in order to promote administrative and jurisdictional decentralization of the Judicial Power (Article 269).

As mentioned, jurisdiction for judicial discipline is to be carried out by disciplinary tribunals as determined by law (Article 267), which nonetheless was only formally established in 2010-2011 after the sanctioning of the Code of Ethics of the Venezuelan Judge, providing that disciplinary proceedings must be public, oral, and brief, in conformity with due process of law.

3. The Constitutional regulations regarding the Stability and Independence of Judges

The basic constitutional provision in order to guaranty the independence and autonomy of courts and judges is established in Article 255, which provides for a specific mechanism to assure the independent appointment of judges, and to guaranty their stability.

In this regard, the judicial tenure is considered as a judicial career, in which the admission as well as the promotion of judges within it must be the result of a public competition or examinations to assure the excellence and adequacy of qualifications of the participants, who are to be chosen by panels from the judicial circuits (Article 255). The naming and swearing-in of judges is to be done by the Supreme Tribunal of Justice, and the citizens' participation in the selection procedure and designation of judges are to be guaranteed by law. Unfortunately, up to 2011, all these provisions have not been applicable because of a lack of legislation implementing them.

The Constitution also creates a Judicial Nominations Committee (Article 270) as an organ for the assistance of the Judicial Branch in selecting not only the Magistrates for the Supreme Tribunal of Justice (Article 264), but also to assist judicial colleges in selecting judges for the courts including those of the jurisdiction in Judicial Discipline. This Judicial Nominations Committee is to be composed of

199 See the Organic Law of the Supreme Tribunal of Justice 2010. *Official Gazette* Nº 39.522 of October 1, 2010. See Allan R. Brewer-Carías and Víctor Hernández Mendible, 2010. *Ley Orgánica del Tribunal Supremo de Justicia 2010, Caracas:* Editorial Jurídica Venezolana; Laura Louza, 2002. El Tribunal Supremo de Justicia en la Constitución de la República Bolivariana de Venezuela, *Revista del Tribunal Supremo de Justicia,* Nº 4. Caracas, pp. 379-437; Nélida Peña Colmenares, 2002. El Tribunal Supremo de Justicia como órgano de dirección, gobierno, administración, inspección y vigilancia del Poder Judicial venezolano", *Revista de derecho del Tribunal Supremo de Justicia,* Nº 8, Caracas, pp. 391 a 434; and Olga Dos Santos, 2002. Comisión Judicial del Tribunal Supremo de Justicia, in *Revista de derecho del Tribunal Supremo de Justicia,* Nº 6, Caracas, pp. 373 a 378.

representatives from different sectors of society, as determined by law. The law is required to promote the professional development of judges, to which end universities are to collaborate with the judiciary by developing training in judicial specialization in law school curricula. Nonetheless, none of these provisions have been implemented, and on the contrary, since 1999, the Venezuelan Judiciary has been almost completely composed by temporal and provisional judges,[200] lacking stability and being subjected to political manipulation, altering the people's right to an adequate administration of justice.

On the other hand, in order to guaranty the stability of judges according to the express provision of the Constitution, they can only be removed or suspended from office through judicial procedures or trails expressly established by statutes, led by Judicial Disciplinary Judges (Article 255). Nonetheless, up to 2011, because of the lack of implementing the Disciplinary Jurisdiction, judges were removed without due process guaranties by a "transitory" Reorganization Commission of the Judicial Power in charge of the disciplinary procedures, only eliminated in June 2011, which has been substituted by courts but whose judges are appointed by the political organ of the State, the National Assembly, instead of by the Supreme Tribunal of Justice.

4. The Catastrophic Dependence of the Judiciary in the Venezuelan Authoritarian Government

Now, despite all the provisions included in the text of the 1999 Constitution, since 1999, Venezuela has experienced a process of progressive concentration of powers, implemented by controlling the nomination of the head of the State's organs. In effect, one of the mechanism established in the 1999 Constitution in order to assure their independence of powers was the provision of a system to assure that their appointment by the National Assembly was to be limited by the necessary participation of special collective bodies called Nominating Committees that must be integrated with representatives of the different sectors of society (arts. 264, 279, 295). Those Nominating Committees were to be in charge of selecting and nominating the candidates, guaranteeing the political participation of the Citizens in the process.

Consequently, the appointment of the Justices of the Supreme Tribunal, and of all other head of the other State's powers can only be made among the candidates proposed by the corresponding "Nominating Committees," which are the ones in charge of selecting and nominating the candidates before the Assembly. These constitutional previsions, were designed in order to limit the discretional power the political legislative organ traditionally had to appoint those high officials through

200 The Inter-American Commission on Human Rights said: "The Commission has been informed that only 250 judges have been appointed by opposition concurrence according to the constitutional text. From a total of 1.772 positions of judges in Venezuela, the Supreme Court of Justice reports that only 183 are holders, 1331 are provisional and 258 are temporary", 2003. *Informe sobre la Situación de los Derechos Humanos en Venezuela*; OAS/Ser.L/V/II.118. d.C. 4rev. 2; December 29, 2003, paragraph 11. The same Commission also said that "an aspect linked to the autonomy and independence of the Judicial Power is that of the provisional character of the judges in the judicial system of Venezuela. Today, the information provided by the different sources indicates that more than 80% of Venezuelan judges are "provisional". *Idem*, Paragraph 161.

political party agreements, by assuring political Citizenship participation. [201] Unfortunately, these exceptional constitutional provisions have not been applied, due to the fact that the National Assembly during the past years, defrauding the Constitution, has deliberately "transformed" the said Committees into simple "parliamentary Commissions" reducing the civil society's right to political participation. The Assembly in all the statutes sanctioned regarding such Committees and the appointment process, has established the composition of all the Nominating Committees with a majority of parliamentary representatives (whom by definition cannot be representatives of the "civil society"), although providing, in addition, for the incorporation of some other members chosen by the National Assembly itself from strategically selected "non-governmental Organizations."[202] The result has been the complete political control of the Nominating Committees, and the persistence of the discretional political and partisan way of appointing the official heads of the non-elected branches of government, which the provisions of the 1999 Constitution intended to limit, by a National Assembly that since 2000 has been completely controlled by the Executive.

That is why, that in this context, it was hardly surprising to hear former President Chávez, when referring to the delegate legislation enacted by him, to say in August 2008, simply: "*I am the Law.... I am the State* !!;[203] repeating the same phrases he used in 2001, also referring to other series of decree-laws he enacted at that time as delegate legislation.[204] Such phrases, as we all know, were attributed in the seventeen century to Louis XIV, in France, as a sign of the meaning of an Absolute Monarchy –although in fact he never expressed them–;[205] but to hear in our times a Head of State saying them, is enough to understand the tragic institutional situation that Venezuela is currently facing, characterized by a complete absence of separation of powers and, consequently, of a democratic and rule of law

---

201 See Allan R. Brewer-Carías, 2005. La participación ciudadana en la designación de los titulares de los órganos no electos de los Poderes Públicos en Venezuela y sus vicisitudes políticas, *Revista Iberoamericana de Derecho Publico y Administrativo,* Año 5, N° 5-2005, San Jose, Costa Rica, pp. 76-95.

202 See regarding the distortion of the "Judicial Nominating Committee" in Allan R. Brewer-Carías, 2004. *Ley Orgánica del Tribunal Supremo de Justicia*, Caracas: Editorial Jurídica Venezolana; the distortion on the "Citizen Power Nominating Committee" in Allan R. Brewer-Carías *et al.*, 2005. *Ley Orgánica del Poder Ciudadano*, Caracas: Editorial Jurídica Venezolana; and in Sobre el nombramiento irregular por la Asamblea Nacional de los titulares de los órganos del poder ciudadano en 2007, 2008. *Revista de Derecho Público*, N° 113, Caracas: Editorial Jurídica Venezolana, pp. 85-88; and the distortion on the Electoral Nominating Committee in Allan R. Brewer-Carías, 2007. *Crónica sobre la "in" justicia constitucional. La Sala Constitucional y el autoritarismo en Venezuela*, Colección Instituto de Derecho Público, Caracas: Universidad Central de Venezuela, N° 2, pp 197-230.

203 Hugo Chávez Frías, August 28, 2008. See in Gustavo Coronel, 2008. Las Armas de Coronel, October 15, 2008, available at http://lasarmasdecoronel.blogspot.com/2008/10/yo-soy-la-leyyo-soy-el-estado.html

204 See in *El Universal,* Caracas, December 4, 2001, pp. 1,1 and 2,1. This explains what was said by the Head of State in 2009 considering "representative democracy, separation of Powers and alternate government" as doctrines that "poisons the masses mind." See Hugo Chávez, 2009. Hugo Chávez seeks to catch them young, *The Economist*, August 22-28, 2009, p. 33.

205 See Yves Guchet, 1990. *Histoire Constitutionnelle Française (1789–1958)*, Paris : Ed. Erasme, p.8.

government.[206] Consequently, since 1999, a tragic setback has occurred in Venezuela regarding democratic standards, by means of a continuous, persistent, and deliberate process of demolishing the rule of law institutions[207] and of destroying democracy in a way never before experienced in all the constitutional history of the country.[208]

This has led to the complete control of the Judiciary, which after being initially intervened by the Constituent National Assembly in 1999, [209] with the consent and complicity of the former Supreme Court of Justice, which endorsed the creation of a Commission of Judicial Emergency[210] that continued to function, although with

---

206 See the summary of this situation in Teodoro Petkoff, 2008. Election and Political Power. Challenges for the Opposition", *ReVista. Harvard Review of Latin America*, David Rockefeller Center for Latin American Studies, Harvard University, pp. 12. See also Allan R. Brewer-Carías, 2005. Los problemas de la gobernabilidad democrática en Venezuela: el autoritarismo constitucional y la concentración y centralización del poder," in Diego Valadés (Coord.), 2005. *Gobernabilidad y constitucionalismo en América Latina*, Mexico: Universidad Nacional Autónoma de México, pp. 73-96.

207 See in *general*, Allan R. Brewer-Carías, 2005. La progresiva y sistemática demolición de la autonomía e independencia del Poder Judicial en Venezuela (1999-2004), *XXX Jornadas J.M Dominguez Escovar, Estado de Derecho, Administración de Justicia y Derechos Humanos*, Barquisimeto, Instituto de Estudios Jurídicos del Estado Lara, pp. 33-174; Allan R. Brewer-Carías, 2007. El constitucionalismo y la emergencia en Venezuela: entre la emergencia formal y la emergencia anormal del Poder Judicial, Allan R. Brewer-Carías, 2007. *Estudios Sobre el Estado Constitucional (2005-2006)*, Caracas: Editorial Jurídica Venezolana, pp. 245-269; and Allan R. Brewer-Carías 2007. La justicia sometida al poder. La ausencia de independencia y autonomía de los jueces en Venezuela por la interminable emergencia del Poder Judicial (1999-2006), *Cuestiones Internacionales. Anuario Jurídico Villanueva 2007,* Centro Universitario Villanueva, Madrid: Marcial Pons, pp. 25-57, available at www.allanbrewercarias.com, (Biblioteca Virtual, II.4. Artículos y Estudios N° 550, 2007) pp. 1-37. See also Allan R. Brewer-Carías, 2008. *Historia Constitucional de Venezuela*, Vol II. Caracas, Editorial Alfa, pp. 402-454.

208 See, in general, Allan R. Brewer-Carías, 2007. El autoritarismo establecido en fraude a la Constitución y a la democracia y su formalización en "Venezuela mediante la reforma constitucional. (De cómo en un país democrático se ha utilizado el sistema eleccionario para minar la democracia y establecer un régimen autoritario de supuesta "dictadura de la democracia" que se pretende regularizar mediante la reforma constitucional), *Temas constitucionales. Planteamientos ante una Reforma,* Fundación de Estudios de Derecho Administrativo, Caracas FUNEDA, pp. 13-74; and Allan R. Brewer-Carías, 2009. La demolición del Estado de Derecho en Venezuela Reforma Constitucional y fraude a la Constitución (1999-2009), *El Cronista del Estado Social y Democrático de Derecho*, N° 6, Madrid, Editorial Iustel, pp. 52-61.

209 See on the national Constituent Assembly of 1999: Allan R. Brewer-Carías, 2008. Constitution Making in Defraudation of the Constitution and Authoritarian Government in Defraudation of Democracy. The Recent Venezuelan Experience", *Lateinamerika Analysen*, 19, 1/2008, GIGA, German Institute of Global and Area Studies, Hamburg: Institute of Latin American Studies, pp. 119-142. On August 19, 1999, the National Constituent Assembly decided to declare "the Judicial Power in emergency." *Official Gazette* N° 36.772 of August 25, 1999 reprinted in *Official Gazette* N° 36.782 of September 8, 1999. See in Allan R. Brewer–Carías, 1999. *Debate Constituyente,* vol. I, Fundación de Derecho Público, Caracas: Editorial Jurídica Venezolana, pp. 57-73; and in *Gaceta Constituyente (Diario de Debates), Agosto–Septiembre de 1999,* Session of August 18, 1999, N° 10, pp. 17-22. See the text of the decree in *Official Gazette* N° 36.782 of September 08, 1999

210 "Resolution" of the Supreme Court of Justice of August 23, 1999. See the comments regarding this Resolution in Allan R. Brewer–Carías, 1999. *Debate Constituyente,* vol. I, Fundación de Derecho Público, Caracas: Editorial Jurídica Venezolana, pp. 141 ff. See also the

another name, in violation of the new Constitution, until 2011.[211] In this matter, in the past fifteen years the country has witnessed a permanent and systematic demolition process of the autonomy and independence of the judicial power, aggravated by the fact that according to the 1999 Constitution, as aforementioned, the Supreme Tribunal that is completely controlled by the Executive is in charge of administering all the Venezuelan judicial system, particularly, by appointing and dismissing judges.[212]

The process began by the National Constituent Assembly, after eliminating the Supreme Court itself, and dismissing its Magistrates, with the appointment, in 1999, of new Magistrates of the new Supreme Tribunal of Justice, without complying with the constitutional conditions, by means of a Constitutional Transitory regime sanctioned after the Constitution was approved by referendum.[213]. That Supreme Tribunal, completely packed with the government supporters, has been precisely the one that during the past fifteen years has been the most ominous instrument for consolidating authoritarianism in the country. From there on, the intervention process of the Judiciary continued up to the point that the President of the Republic has politically controlled the Supreme Tribunal of Justice and, through it, the complete Venezuelan judicial system.

For that purpose, the constitutional conditions needed to be elected Magistrate of the Supreme Tribunal and the procedures for their nomination with the participation of representatives of the different sectors of civil society, were violated since the beginning. First, as aforementioned, in 1999 by the National Constituent Assembly itself once it dismissed the previous Justices, appointing new ones without receiving any nominations from any Nominating Committee, and many of them without compliance with the conditions set forth in the Constitution to be Magistrate. Second, in 2000, by the newly elected National Assembly, by sanctioning a Special Law in order to appoint the Magistrates in a transitory way without complying with the Constitution.[214] This reform, as the Inter-American Commission on Human

---

comments of Lolymar Hernández Camargo, 2000. *La Teoría del Poder Constituyente,* San Cristóbal: Universidad Católica del Táchira, pp. 75 ff..

211 See Allan R. Brewer–Carías, 2002. *Golpe de Estado y proceso constituyente en Venezuela,* México: Universidad Nacional Autónoma de México, p. 160.

212 See Rafael J. Chavero Gazdik, 2011. *La Justicia Revolucionaria. Una década de reestructuración (o involución) Judicial en Venezuela,* Caracas: Editorial Aequitas; Laura Louza Scognamiglio, 2011. *La revolución judicial en Venezuela,* Caracas: FUNEDA; Allan R. Brewer-Carías, 2005. La progresiva y sistemática demolición de la autonomía e independencia del Poder Judicial en Venezuela (1999-2004), *XXX Jornadas J.M. Dominguez Escovar, Estado de derecho, Administración de justicia y derechos humanos,* Barquisimeto: Instituto de Estudios Jurídicos del Estado Lara, pgs. 33-174; and Allan R. Brewer-Carías, 2007. La justicia sometida al poder (La ausencia de independencia y autonomía de los jueces en Venezuela por la interminable emergencia del Poder Judicial (1999-2006), *Cuestiones Internacionales. Anuario Jurídico Villanueva 2007,* Centro Universitario Villanueva, Madrid: Marcial Pons, pp. 25-57.

213 See in *Gaceta Constituyente (Diario de Debates), Noviembre 1999–Enero 2000,* Session of December 22, 1999, N° 51, pp. 2 ff. See *Official Gazette* N° 36.859 of December 29, 1999; and *Official Gazette* N° 36.860 of December 30, 1999.

214 For this reason, in its 2003 *Report on Venezuela,* the Inter-American Commission on Human Rights, observed that the appointment of Judges of the Supreme Court of Justice did not apply to the Constitution, so that "the constitutional reforms introduced in the form of the election of these authorities established as guaranties of independence and impartiality were not used in

Rights emphasized in its *2004 Annual Report*, "lack the safeguards necessary to prevent other branches of government from undermining the Supreme Tribunal's independence and to keep narrow or temporary majorities from determining its composition." [215] Third, in 2004, again by the National Assembly by sanctioning the Organic Law of the Supreme Tribunal of Justice, increasing the number of Justices from 20 to 32, and distorting the constitutional conditions for their appointment and dismissal, allowing the government to assume an absolute control of the Supreme Tribunal, and in particular, of its Constitutional Chamber.[216] And fourth, in 2010, once more, the National Assembly reformed the Organic Law of the Supreme Tribunal of Justice, firs in a regular way,[217] and subsequently in an irregular manner,[218] in order to pack the Tribunal with new government controlled members.

After this 2004 reform, the process of selection of new Justices has been subjected to the President of the Republic will, as was publicly admitted by the President of the parliamentary Commission in charge of selecting the candidates for Magistrates of the Supreme Tribunal Court of Justice, who later was appointed Minister of the Interior and Justice. On December 2004, he said the following:

> "Although we, the representatives, have the authority for this selection, the President of the Republic was consulted and his opinion was very much taken into consideration." He added: "Let's be clear, we are not going to score auto-goals. In the list, there were people from the opposition who comply with all the requirements. The opposition could have used them in order to reach an agreement during the last sessions, but they did not want to. We are not going to do it for them. There is no one in the group of postulates that could act against us..."[219]

---

this case. See Inter-American Commission of Human Rights, 2003 *Report on Venezuela*; paragraph 186.

215 See IACHR, *2004 Annual Report* (Follow-Up Report on Compliance by the State of Venezuela with the Recommendations made by the IACHR in its Report on the Situation of Human Rights in Venezuela [2003]), para. 174. Available at http://www.cidh.oas.org/annual rep/2004eng/chap.5b.htm

216 *Official Gazette* N° 37.942 of May 20, 2004. See the comments in Allan R. Brewer-Carías, 2004. *Ley Orgánica del Tribunal Supremo de Justicia*, Caracas: Editorial Jurídica Venezolana.

217 *Official Gazette* N° 39.483 of August 9, 2010 and N° 39.522 of October 1, 2010. See the comments in Allan R. Brewer-Carías and Víctor Hernández Mendible, 2010. *Ley Orgánica del Tribunal Supremo de Justicia*, Caracas: Editorial Jurídica Venezolana.

218 See the comments Víctor Hernández Mendible, 2010.Sobre la nueva reimpresión por 'supuestos errores' materiales de la Ley Orgánica del Tribunal Supremo, octubre 2010, *Revista de Derecho Público*, N° 124, Caracas Editorial Jurídica Venezolana, pp-110-123; and Antonio Silva Aranguren, 2010. Tras el rastro del engaño, en la web de la Asamblea Nacional," *Revista de Derecho Público*, N° 124, Caracas: Editorial Jurídica Venezolana, pp-112-113.

219 See in *El Nacional*, Caracas 12-13-2004. That is why the Inter-American Commission on Human Rights suggested in its Report to the General Assembly of the OAS corresponding to 2004 that "these regulations of the Organic Law of the Supreme Court of Justice would have made possible the manipulation, by the Executive Power, of the election process of judges that took place during 2004". See Inter-American Commission on Human Rights, 2004 *Report on Venezuela*; paragraph 180.

This configuration of the Supreme Tribunal, as highly politicized and subjected to the will of the President of the Republic has been reinforced in 2010,[220] eliminating all autonomy of the Judicial Power and even the basic principle of the separation of power, as the corner stone of the Rule of Law and the base of all democratic institutions.

On the other hand, as aforementioned, according to Article 265 of the 1999 Constitution, the Magistrates can be dismissed by the vote of a qualified majority of the National Assembly, when grave faults are committed, following a prior qualification by the Citizen Power. This qualified two-thirds majority was established to avoid leaving the existence of the heads of the judiciary in the hands of a simple majority of legislators. Unfortunately, this provision was also distorted by the 2004 Organic Law of the Supreme Tribunal of Justice, in which it was established in an unconstitutional way that the Magistrates could be dismissed by simple majority when the "administrative act of their appointment" is revoked (Article 23,4). This distortion, contrary to the independence of the Judiciary, although eliminated in the reform of the Law in 2010, also pretended to be constitutionalized with the rejected 2007 Constitutional reform, which proposed to establish that the Magistrates of the Supreme Tribunal could be dismissed in case of grave faults, but just by the vote of the majority of the members of the National Assembly.

The consequence of this political subjection is that all the principles tending to assure the independence of judges at any level of the Judiciary have been postponed. In particular, the Constitution establishes that all judges must be selected by public competition for the tenure; and that the dismissal of judges can only be made through disciplinary trials carried out by disciplinary judges (Articles 254 and 267). Unfortunately, none of these provisions have been implemented, and on the contrary, since 1999, the Venezuelan Judiciary has been composed by temporal and provisional judges,[221] lacking stability and being subjected to the political manipulation, altering the people's right to an adequate administration of justice. And regarding the disciplinary jurisdiction of the judges, it was only in 2010[222] when it was established. Until then, with the authorization of the Supreme Tribunal,

---

220 See Hildegard Rondón de Sansó, 2010. *Obiter Dicta*. En torno a una elección, *La Voce d'Italia*, Caracas December 14, 2010.

221 The Inter-American Commission on Human Rights said: "The Commission has been informed that only 250 judges have been appointed by opposition concurrence according to the constitutional text. From a total of 1772 positions of judges in Venezuela, the Supreme Court of Justice reports that only 183 are holders, 1331 are provisional and 258 are temporary", *Informe sobre la Situación de los Derechos Humanos en Venezuela*; OAS/Ser.L/V/II.118. d.C. 4rev. 2; December 29, 2003; paragraph 11. The same Commission also said that "an aspect linked to the autonomy and independence of the Judicial Power is that of the provisional character of the judges in the judicial system of Venezuela. Today, the information provided by the different sources indicates that more than 80% of Venezuelan judges are "provisional". Idem, Paragraph 161.

222 The Law on the Etics Code of the venezuelan Judges *Official Gazette* N° 39.494 of August, 24, 2010, created the expected Disciplinary Judicial Jurisdiction. In 2011 the corresponding tribunal was appointed.

a "transitory" Reorganization Commission of the Judicial Power created since 1999, continued to function, removing judges without due process.[223]

The worst of this irregular situation is that since 2006 the problem of the provisional status of judges has been "regularized" through a "Special Program for the Regularization of Tenures", addressed to accidental, temporary or provisional judges, bypassing the entrance system constitutionally established by means of public competitive exams (Article 255), by consolidating the effects of the provisional appointments and their consequent power dependency.

5. The Judiciary packed by Temporal and Provisional Judges and the use of the Judiciary for Political Persecution

Through the Supreme Tribunal, which is in charge of governing and administering the Judiciary, the political control over all judges has been also assured, reinforced by means of the survival until 2011, of the 1999 "provisional" Commission on the Functioning and Restructuring of the Judicial System, which was legitimized by the same Tribunal, making completely inapplicable the 1999 constitutional provisions seeking to guarantee the independence and autonomy of judges. [224]

In effect, as aforementioned, according to the text of the 1999 Constitution, judges can only enter the judicial career by means of public competition that must be organized with citizens' participation. Nonetheless, this provision has not yet been implemented, being the judiciary almost exclusively made up of temporary and provisional judges, without any stability. Regarding this situation, for instance, since 2003 the Inter-American Commission on Human Rights has repeatedly express concern about the fact that provisional judges are susceptible to political manipulation, which alters the people's right to access to justice, reporting cases of dismissals and substitutions of judges in retaliation for decisions contrary to the government's position.[225] In its *2008 Annual Report*, the Commission again verified the provisional character of the judiciary as an "endemic problem" because the

---

223 See Allan R. Brewer-Carías, 2007. La justicia sometida al poder y la interminable emergencia del poder judicial (1999-2006)", *Derecho y democracia. Cuadernos Universitarios*, Órgano de Divulgación Académica, Vicerrectorado Académico, Año II, N° 11, Caracas: Universidad Metropolitana, pp. 122-138.

224 See in general, Allan R. Brewer-Carías, 2005. La progresiva y sistemática demolición de la autonomía e independencia del Poder Judicial en Venezuela (1999-2004)," *XXX Jornadas J.M Dominguez Escovar, Estado de Derecho, Administración de Justicia y Derechos Humanos*, Barquisimeto: Instituto de Estudios Jurídicos del Estado Lara, pp. 33-174; Allan R. Brewer-Carías, 2007. El constitucionalismo y la emergencia en Venezuela: entre la emergencia formal y la emergencia anormal del Poder Judicial, in Allan R. Brewer-Carías, *Estudios Sobre el Estado Constitucional (2005-2006)*, 2007. Caracas: Editorial Jurídica Venezolana, pp. 245-269; and Allan R. Brewer-Carías 2007. La justicia sometida al poder. La ausencia de independencia y autonomía de los jueces en Venezuela por la interminable emergencia del Poder Judicial (1999-2006),"*Cuestiones Internacionales. Anuario Jurídico Villanueva 2007,* Centro Universitario Villanueva, Madrid: Marcial Pons, pp. 25-57, available at www.allanbrewercarias.com, (Biblioteca Virtual, II.4. Artículos y Estudios N° 550, 2007) pp. 1-37. See also Allan R. Brewer-Carías, 2008. *Historia Constitucional de Venezuela*, vol II. Caracas: Editorial Alfa, pp. 402-454.

225 See *Informe sobre la Situación de Derechos Humanos en Venezuela*; OAS/Ser.L/V/II.118. doc.4rev.2; December 29, 2003, Paragraphs 161, 174, available at http://www.cidh.oas.org/countryrep/Venezuela2003eng/toc.htm.

appointment of judges was made without applying constitutional provisions on the matter –thus exposing judges to discretionary dismissal– which highlights the "permanent state of urgency" in which those appointments have been made. [226]

Contrary to these facts, according to the words of the Constitution in order to guarantee the independence of the Judiciary, judges can be dismissed from their tenure only through disciplinary processes, conducted by disciplinary courts and judges of a Disciplinary Judicial Jurisdiction. Nonetheless, as aforementioned, that jurisdiction was only created in 2011, corresponding to that year the disciplinary judicial functions to the already mentioned transitory Commission, [227] which, as reported by the same Inter-American Commission in its *2009 Annual Report*, "in addition to being a special, temporary entity, does not afford due guarantees for ensuring the independence of its decisions,[228] since its members may also be appointed or removed at the sole discretion of the Constitutional Chamber of the Supreme Tribunal of Justice, without previously establishing either the grounds or the procedure for such formalities."[229]

The Commission had then "cleansed" the Judiciary of judges not in line with the authoritarian regime, removing judges in a discretionary way when they have issued decisions not within the complacency of the government.[230] This lead the Inter-American Commission on Human Rights, to observe in its *2009 Annual Report,* that "in Venezuela, judges and prosecutors do not enjoy the guaranteed tenure necessary to ensure their independence." [231]

One of the leading cases showing this situation, which we have previously analyzed, took place in 2003, when a High Contentious Administrative Court ruled against the government in a politically charged case regarding the hiring of Cuban physicians for medical social programs. In response to a provisional judicial measure suspending the hiring procedures, due to discrimination allegations made by the Council of Physicians of Caracas, [232] the government after declaring that the

226 See *Annual Report 2008* (OEA/Ser.L/V/II.134. Doc. 5 rev. 1. 25 febrero 2009), paragraph 39.

227 The Politico Administrative Chamber of the Supreme Tribunal has decided that the dismiss of temporal judges is a discretionary power of the Commission on the Functioning and Reorganization of the Judiciary, which adopts its decision without following any administrative procedure rules or due process rules. See Decision N° 00463-2007 of March 20, 2007; Decision N° 00673-2008 of April 24, 2008 (cited in Decision N° 1.939 of December 18, 2008, p. 42). The Chamber has adopted the same position in Decision N° 2414 of December 20, 2007 and Decision N° 280 of February 23, 2007.

228 See Decisión N° 1.939 of December 18, 2008 (Caso: *Gustavo Álvarez Arias et al.*)

229 Véase *Annual Report 2009*, Par. 481, en http://www.cidh.org/annualrep/2009eng/Chap.IV.f.eng.htm.

230 Decision N° 1.939 (Dec. 18, 2008) (Case: *Abogados Gustavo Álvarez Arias y otros*), in which the Constitutonal Chamber declared the non-enforceability of the decision of the Inter American Court of Human Rights of August 5, 2008, Case: *Apitz Barbera y otros ("Corte Primera de lo Contencioso Administrativo") vs. Venezuela* Serie C, N° 182.

231 See *Informe Anual de 2009*, paragraph 480, available at http://www.cidh.oas.org/annualrep/2009eng/Chap.IV.f.eng.htm

232 See Decision of August, 21 2003, in *Revista de Derecho Público*, N° 93-96, Caracas: Editorial Jurídica Venezolana, pp. 445 ff. See the comments in Claudia Nikken, 2003. El caso "Barrio Adentro": La Corte Primera de lo Contencioso Administrativo ante la Sala Constitucional

decision was not going to be accepted [233] seized the Court using secret police officers, and dismissed its judges after being offended by the President of the Republic.[234] The case was brought before the Inter-American Court of Human Rights and after it ruled in 2008 that the dismissal effectively violated the American Convention on Human Rights,[235] the Constitutional Chamber of the Supreme Tribunal response to the Inter-American Court ruling, at the request of the government, was that the decision of the Inter-American Court could not be enforced in Venezuela.[236] As simple as that, showing the subordination of the Venezuelan judiciary to the policies, wishes, and dictates of the President.

In December 2009, another astonishing case was the detention of a criminal judge (María Lourdes Afiuni Mora) for having ordered, based on a previous recommendation of the UN Working Group on Arbitrary Detention, the release of an individual in order for him to face criminal trial while in freedom, as guaranteed in the Constitution. The same day of the decision, the president publicly asked for the judge to be incarcerated asking to apply her a 30–year prison term, which is the maximum punishment in Venezuelan law for horrendous or grave crimes. The fact is that judge has remained to this day in detention without trial. The UN Working Group described these facts as "a blow by President Hugo Chávez to the independence of judges and lawyers in the country," demanding "the immediate release of the judge," concluding that "reprisals for exercising their constitutionally guaranteed functions and creating a climate of fear among the judiciary and lawyers' profession, serve no purpose except to undermine the rule of law and obstruct justice."[237]

The fact is that in Venezuela, no judge can adopt any decision that could affect the government policies, or the President's wishes, the state's interest, or public

---

del Tribunal Supremo de Justicia o el avocamiento como medio de amparo de derechos e intereses colectivos y difusos," *Revista de Derecho Público*, Nº 93-96, Caracas: Editorial Jurídica Venezolana, pp. 5 ff.

233 The President of the Republic said: "*Váyanse con su decisión no sé para donde, la cumplirán ustedes en su casa si quieren* ..." (You can go with your decision, I don't know where; you will enforce it in your house if you want ..."). See *El Universal,* Caracas, August 25, 2003 and *El Universal*, Caracas, August 28, 2003.

234 See in *El Nacional*, Caracas November 5, 2004, p. A2.

235 See Inter-American Court of Human Rights, case: *Apitz Barbera et al. (Corte Primera de lo Contencioso Administrativo) v. Venezuela,* Decision of August 5, 2008, available at www.corteidh.or.cr. See *also*, *El Universal,* Caracas, October 16, 2003; and *El Universal*, Caracas, September 22, 2003.

236 Supreme Tribunal of Justice, Constitutional Chamber, Decision Nº 1.939 of December 18, 2008 (Case: *Abogados Gustavo Álvarez Arias et al.*) (Exp. Nº 08-1572), available at http://www.tsj.gov.ve/decisiones/scon/Diciembre/1939-181208-2008-08-1572.html

237 See the text of the UN Working Group in http://www.unog.ch/unog/website/news_media.nsf/%28httpNewsByYear_en%29/93687E8429BD53A1C125768E00529DB6?OpenDocument&cntxt=B35C3&cookielang=fr. In October 14, 2010, the same Working Group asked the venezuelan Government to subject the Judge to a trail ruled by the due process guaranties and in freedom." See *in El Universal*, October 14, 2010, available at http://www.eluniversal.com/2010/10/14/pol_ava_instancia-de-la-onu_14A4608051.shtml

servants' will, without previous authorization from the same government. [238] That is why the Inter-American Commission on Human Rights, after describing in its *2009 Annual Report* "how large numbers of judges have been removed, or their appointments voided, without the applicable administrative proceedings," noted "with concern that in some cases, judges were removed almost immediately after adopting judicial decisions in cases with a major political impact," concluding that "The lack of judicial independence and autonomy vis-à-vis political power is, in the Commission's opinion, one of the weakest points in Venezuelan democracy." [239]

In this context of political subjection, the Constitutional Chamber, since 2000, far from acting as the guardian of the Constitution, has been the main tool of the authoritarian government for the illegitimate mutation of the Constitution, by means of unconstitutional constitutional interpretations, [240] not only regarding its own powers of judicial review, which have been enlarged, but also regarding substantive matters. The Supreme Tribunal has distorted the Constitution through illegitimate and fraudulent "constitutional mutations" in the sense of changing the meaning of its provisions without changing its wording. And all this, of course, without any possibility of being controlled, [241] so the eternal question arising from the uncontrolled power, – *Quis custodiet ipsos custodes* –, in Venezuela also remains unanswered.

On the other hand, regarding some fundamental rights essentials for a democracy to function, like the freedom of expression, contrary to the principle of progressiveness established in the Constitution, it has been the Supreme Tribunal of Justice the State organ in charge of limiting its scope. First, in 2000, it was the Political-Administrative Chamber of the Supreme Tribunal that ordered the media not to transmit certain information, eventually admitting limits to be imposed to the media, regardless of the general prohibition of censorship established in the Constitution.

The following year, in 2001, it was the Constitutional Chamber of the Supreme Tribunal, the one that distorted the Constitution when dismissing an *amparo* action filed against the President of the Republic by a citizen and a nongovernmental organization asking for the exercise of their right to response against the attacks made by the President in his weekly TV program. The Constitutional Chamber reduced the scope of freedom of information, eliminating the right to response and rectification regarding opinions in the media when they are expressed by the president in a regular televised program. In addition, the tribunal excluded

---

238 See Antonio Canova González, 2008. *La realidad del contencioso administrativo venezolano (Un llamado de atención frente a las desoladoras estadísticas de la Sala Político Administrativa en 2007 y primer semestre de 2008)*, Caracas: FUNEDA, p. 14.

239 See in ICHR, *Annual Report 2009*, paragraph 483, available at http://www.cidh.oas.org/-annualrep/2009eng/Chap.IV.f.eng.htm .

240 See Allan R. Brewer-Carías, 2008. *Crónica sobre la "In" Justicia Constitucional. La Sala Constitucional y el autoritarismo en Venezuela*, Caracas: Editorial Jurídica Venezolana.

241 See Allan R. Brewer-Carías, 2005. *Quis Custodiet ipsos Custodes*: De la interpretación constitucional a la inconstitucionalidad de la interpretación, *VIII Congreso Nacional de Derecho Constitucional*, Arequipa: Fondo Editorial and Colegio de Abogados de Arequipa, 463-89; and Allan R. Brewer-Carías, 2007. *Crónica de la "In" Justicia constitucional: La Sala constitucional y el autoritarismo en Venezuela*, Caracas: Editorial Jurídica Venezolana, pp. 11-44 and 47-79.

journalists and all those persons that have a regular program in the radio or a newspaper column, from the right to rectification and response. [242]

In addition, in 2003, the Constitutional Chamber dismissed an action of unconstitutionality filed against a few articles of the Criminal Code that limit the right to formulate criticism against public officials, considering that such provisions could not be deemed as limiting the freedom of expression, contradicting a well-established doctrine in the contrary ruled by the Inter-American Courts on Human Rights. The Constitutional Chamber also decided in contradiction with the constitutional prohibition of censorship, that through a statute it was possible to prevent the diffusion of information when it could be considered contrary to other provisions of the Constitution. [243]

Regarding other cases in which the Judiciary has been used for political persecution, they are referred to the exercise of freedom of expression, concluding in the shutdown of TV stations that had a line of political opposition regarding the government and the persecution of their main shareholders. One leading case was the *Radio Caracas Televisión* case, referred to a TV station that, in 2007, was the most important television station of the country, critical of the administration of President Hugo Chavez. In that case, it was the Supreme Tribunal in 2007, the State organ that materialized the State intervention in order to terminate authorizations and licenses of the TV station, whose assets were confiscated and its equipment assigned to a state-owned enterprise through an illegitimate Supreme Tribunal decision. [244] The case is the most vivid example of the illegitimate collusion or confabulation between a politically controlled Judiciary and an authoritarian government in order to reduce freedom of expression, and to confiscate private property. For such purpose, it was the Constitutional Chamber of the Supreme Tribunal of Justice and the Political Administrative Chamber of the same Tribunal that in May 2007, instead of protecting the citizens' right of freedom of expression, conspired as docile instruments controlled by the Executive, in order to kidnap and violate them. In this case, it was the highest level of the Judiciary that covered the governmental arbitrariness with a judicial veil, executing the shout down of the TV Station, reducing the freedom of expression in the country, and with total impunity, proceeded to confiscate private property in a way that neither the Executive nor the

---

242 See Allan R. Brewer-Carías, 2001. La libertad de expresión del pensamiento y el derecho a la información y su violación por la Sala Constitucional del Tribunal Supremo de Justicia, in Allan R. Brewer-Carías et al., 2001. *La libertad de expresión amenazada (Sentencia 1013),* Caracas/San José: Edición Conjunta Instituto Interamericano de Derechos Humanos y Editorial Jurídica Venezolana, pp. 17-57; and Jesús A. Davila Ortega, 2002. El derecho de la información y la libertad de expresión en Venezuela (Un estudio de la sentencia 1.013/2001 de la Sala Constitucional del Tribunal Supremo de Justicia), *Revista de Derecho Constitucional* 5, Caracas: Editorial Sherwood, pp. 305-25.

243 See *Revista de Derecho Público,* 93–94, 2003. Caracas: Editorial Jurídica Venezolana, 136ff. and 164ff. See comments in Alberto Arteaga Sánchez et al., 2004. *Sentencia 1942 vs. Libertad de expresión*, Caracas.

244 See the Constitutional Chamber Decision N° 957 (May 25, 2007), in *Revista de Derecho Público* 110, Editorial Jurídica Venezolana, Caracas 2007, 117ff. See the comments in Allan R. Brewer-Carías, 2007. El juez constitucional en Venezuela como instrumento para aniquilar la libertad de expresión plural y para confiscar la propiedad privada: El caso RCTV, *Revista de Derecho Público*", N° 110, (abril-junio 2007), Caracas: Editorial Jurídica Venezolana, pp. 7-32.

Legislator, could have done, because being forbidden in the Constitution (art. 115). In the case, it was the Supreme Tribunal, which violated the Constitution, with the aggravating circumstance that the conspirators knew that their actions could not be controlled. This case has also been recently submitted before the Inter American Court of Human Rights.

Other cases of political persecution, also related to freedom of expression are the cases against Guillermo Zuloaga and Nelson Mezerhane; two very distinguish businessman that were the principal shareholders of Globovisión, the other independent TV station that after the takeover of Radio Caracas Television, remained with a critic line of opinion regarding the government. They both were harassed by the Public Prosecutor Office and by the Judiciary; accused of different common crimes that they did not commit; they were detained without any serious base; their enterprises were occupied and their property confiscated. They both had to leave the country, without any possibility of obtaining Justice. Their cases have also been submitted before the Inter American Commission of Human Rights.

The Judiciary, particularly on criminal matters, has also been used as the government instrument to pervert Justice, distorting the facts in specific cases of political interest, converting innocent people into criminals, and liberating criminals of all suspicion. It was the unfortunate case of the mass killings committed by government agents and supporters as a consequence of the enforcement of the so-called Plan Avila, a military order that encouraged the shooting of peoples participating in the biggest mass demonstration in Venezuelan history which on April 11, 2002, was asking for the resignation of President Chávez. The soothing provoked a general military disobedience by the high commanders, in a way witnessed by all the country in TV, which ended with the military removal of the President, although just for a few hours, until the same military reinstated him in office. Nonetheless, in order to change history, the shooting and mass killing were re-written, and those responsible that everybody saw in live in TV, because being government supporters were gratified as heroes, and the Police Officials trying to assure order in the demonstration, like the Officers Simonovic and Forero, were blamed of crimes that they did not commit, and condemned of murder with the highest term of 30 years of prison. The former Chief Justice of the Criminal Chamber of the Supreme Tribunal of Justice, general Eladio Aponte, confessed last year 2012 in a TV Program (SolTV) in Miami, when answering about if there were "political persons in prison in Venezuela, saying "Yes, there are people regarding which there is an order not to let them free," referring particularly to "the Police Officers," mentioning Officer Simonovic. The same former Justice, answering a question about "*Who gives the order,*" simply said: "The order comes from the President's Office downwards," adding that "we must have no doubts, in Venezuela there are no sewing point if it is not approved by the President." He finally said, answering a question if he "*received the order not to let free Simonovis*" he explained that: "the position of the Criminal Chamber" was "To validate all that arrived already done; that is, in a few words, to accept that these gentlemen could not be freed."[245]

245 See the text of the statement on, in *El Universal*, Caracas 18-4-2012, available at: http://www.eluniversal.com/nacional-y-politica/120418/historias-secretas-de-un-juez-en-venezuela

To hear this answers given by one who until recently was the highest Justice in the Venezuelan Criminal System, produce no other than indignation, because it was him, as Chief Criminal Justice, the one in charge of manipulating justice, in the way he confessed; condemning the Police Officers to 30 years in prison, just because obeying orders from the Executive.

6. The use of the Judiciary to facilitate the Concentration of Power and the Dismantling of Democracy

On different matters, regarding the organization of the State, the same illegitimate constitutional mutation has occurred regarding the federal system of distribution of competencies among territorial entities of the State, which in Venezuela is constitutionally organized as a "decentralized federal State;" a distribution that cannot be changed except by means of a constitutional reform. Specifically, for instance, the Constitution provides that the conservation, administration, and use of roads and national highways, as well as of national ports and airports of commercial use, are of the exclusive powers of the states, which they must exercise in "coordination" with the Federal government.

One of the purposes of the rejected 2007 constitutional reform was precisely to change this competency of the States. But in spite of the popular rejection of the reform, nonetheless, it was the Constitutional Chamber, through a decision adopted four months after the referendum (April 15, 2008), the State organ in charge of implementing the reform. The Chamber, in effect, when deciding an autonomous recourse for the abstract interpretation of the Constitution filed by the Attorney General, modified the content of that constitutional provision, considering that the exclusive attribution it contained, was not "exclusive," but a "concurrent" one, to be exercised together with the federal government, which even could reassume the attribution or decree its intervention..[246]

With this interpretation, again, the Chamber illegitimately modified the Constitution usurping popular sovereignty, compelling the National Assembly to enact legislation contrary to the Constitution, which it did in March 2009, by reforming of the Organic Law for Decentralization. [247]

In other cases, the Constitutional Chamber has been the instrument of the government in order to assume direct control of other branches of government, as happened in 2002 with the take-over of the Electoral Power, which since then has been completely controlled by the Executive. This began in 2002 after the Organic Law of the Electoral Power[248] was sanctioned and the National Assembly was due to

---

246 See Allan R. Brewer-Carías, 2008. La Sala Constitucional como poder constituyente: la modificación de la forma federal del estado y del sistema constitucional de división territorial del poder público, *Revista de Derecho Público*, N° 114, (abril-junio 2008), Caracas: Editorial Jurídica Venezolana, pp. 247-262; and Allan R. Brewer-Carías, 2009. La ilegitima mutación de la Constitución y la legitimidad de la jurisdicción constitucional: la "reforma" de la forma federal del Estado en Venezuela mediante interpretación constitucional," *Memoria del X Congreso Iberoamericano de Derecho Constitucional,* Lima: Instituto Iberoamericano de Derecho Constitucional, Asociación Peruana de Derecho Constitucional, Instituto de Investigaciones Jurídicas-UNAM y Maestría en Derecho Constitucional-PUCP, IDEMSA, tomo 1, pp. 29-51

247 See *Official Gazette* N° 39 140 of March 17, 2009

248 See *Official Gazette* N° 37.573 of November 19, 2002

appoint the new members of the National Electoral Council. Because the representatives supporting the government did not have the qualified majority to approve such appointments by themselves and did not reached agreements on the matter with the opposition, when the National Assembly failed to appoint the members of the National Electoral Council, that task was assumed, without any constitutional power, by the Constitutional Chamber itself. Deciding an action that was filed against the unconstitutional legislative omission, the Chamber instead of urging the Assembly to comply with its constitutional duty, directly appointed the members of the Electoral Council, usurping the Legislator's functions, but without complying with the conditions established in the Constitution for such appointments.[249] With this decision, the Chamber assured the government's complete control of the Council, kidnapping the citizen's rights to political participation, and allowing the official governmental party to manipulate the electoral results.

Consequently, the elections held in Venezuela during the past decade have been organized by a politically dependent branch of government, without any guarantee of independence or impartiality. This is the only explanation, for instance, of the complete lack of official information on the final voting results of the December 2007 referendum rejecting the constitutional reform drafted and proposed by the President. The country, nowadays, still ignored the majority number of votes that effectively rejected the constitutional reform draft tending to consolidate in the Constitution the basis for a socialist, centralized, militaristic, and police state, as proposed by President Chávez.

The Constitutional Chamber of the Supreme Tribunal has also been the instrument in order to attack the democratic principle, limiting the right to be elected, imposing non-elected officials as Head of State, or revoking the popular mandate of elected officials without having competency or jurisdiction.

Between January and March 2013, the Constitutional Chamber of the Supreme Tribunal, openly violated the democratic principle by imposing a non-elected official as head of State, during the illness of former President Chávez and after his death, in two decisions adopted, in addition, without proving anything. The decisions were issued after deciding interpretations recourses of the Constitution: The first decision, N° 2 of January 9, 2013, was issued to resolve the legal situation of the nonattendance by the President elected to his Inauguration for the presidential term 2013-2019, refusing the Constitutional Chamber to consider that the situation was one of absolute absence of the elected President, and instead constructing, without proving anything on the heath condition of the elected and ill President, a supposed "administrative continuity" of Chávez, affirming that even been absent of the country (he was said to be in an Hospital in La Habana), he was supposedly effectively in charge of the Presidency, so his nonelected Vice President (N.

249 See Decision N° 2073 of August 4, 2003, Case: *Hermánn Escarrá Malaver y oros*), and Decision N° 2341 of August 25, 2003, Case: *Hemann Escarrá y otros*. See in Allan R. Brewer-Carías, 2003/2004. El secuestro del poder electoral y la conficación del derecho a la participación política mediante el referendo revocatorio presidencial: Venezuela 2000-2004, *Stvdi Vrbinati, Rivista tgrimestrale di Scienze Giuridiche, Politiche ed Economiche*, Año LXXI – 2003/04 Nuova Serie A – N. 55,3, Urbino: Università degli Studi di Urbino, pp.379-436

Maduro) was to be in charge of the Presidency. [250] The second decision, N° 141, of March 8, 2013, was issued after the announcement of the death of President Chávez, but without proving such fact or when it did effectively occurred, in order to assure that the Vice President (N. Maduro), already imposed as President in charge by the same Supreme Tribunal, was to continue in charge of the Presidency; and additionally allowing him, contrary to the text of the Constitution, to be candidate to the same position in the subsequent election, without leaving the post.[251]

In other decisions, also contrary to the democratic principle, the Constitutional Chamber of the Supreme Tribunal revoked the popular mandate of two mayors, a decision that according to the Constitution only can be adopted by the people that elected the officials by means of a referendum (art. 74). The Supreme Tribunal, ignoring such principle and provision, without having constitutional competency and usurping the jurisdiction of the criminal courts that are the only competent to impose criminal sanctions to officials for not obeying judicial decisions, issued decision N° 138 of March 17, 2014,[252] condemning the Mayors by considering that they had committed a crime (not to obey a preliminary injunction), and imprisoning them, without guarantying a due process of law. The common trend in this case was that both Mayors were from the opposition to the government

In another case, the Constitutional Chamber of the Supreme Tribunal also revoked the popular mandate of a representative to the National Assembly, which also can only be revoked by the people through a referendum, issuing decision N° 207 of March 31, 2014, [253] in a case that the Tribunal had already concluded because the action was declared inadmissible, proceeding the Tribunal to act ex officio, and interpret an article of the Constitution (Article 93), that prevent representatives to accept another public positions without losing their elected one. The initial petition that was declared inadmissible was a requested for the Tribunal to condemn the *the facto* actions of the President of the National Assembly to strip out the elected condition of one representative; being the result of the case, once declared the petition inadmissible, for the Tribunal, to *ex officio* decide to revoke the popular mandate to the representative that was supposed to be protected by the Tribunal. The reason for such decision was that the representative (María Corina Machado), had talked as such representative, before the Permanent Council of the Organization of American States, in a session devoted to analyze the political situation of Venezuela, from the site of the representative of Panama that had invited her to do so.

Finally, in another decision, the Supreme Tribunal, also in violation of the democratic principle, accepted that the right of a citizen to be elected, which is a constitutional right, could be limited by an administrative body as the General Audit Office, when issuing decisions imposing public officials the sanction of disqualifying them to run for elected positions. In decision N° 1265 of August 5,

250 See the text of the decision in http://www.tsj.gov.ve/decisiones/scon/Enero/02-9113-2013-12-1358.html

251 See the text of the decision in http://www.tsj.gov.ve.decisioes/scon/Marzo/141-9313-2013-13-0196.html

252 See the text of the decision in http://www.tsj.gov.ve/decisiones/scon/marzo/162025-138-17314-2014-14-0205.HTML

253 See the text of the decision in http://www.tsj.gov.ve/decisiones/scon/marzo/162546-207-31314-2014-14-0286.HTML. Also in *Official Gazette* N° 40385 April 2, 2014

2008, [254] the Supreme Tribunal refused to declare that such disqualification for the exercise of a political right was contrary to the American Convention of Human Rights, that in Venezuela had constitutional hierarchy (Article 23). The lack of justice in Venezuela, lead the interested person, a former Mayor, to filed a petition before the Inter American Court of Human Right, seeking the protection of his political right, the result being a decision of such Court of September 1st, 2011 (case *López Mendoza vs. Venezuela*), condemning the Venezuelan State for the violation of the Convention. Nonetheless, the response of the State was to file before the Supreme Tribunal of Justice, at the initiative of the Attorney General, an action for "judicial review" of the Inter American Court decision, which was astonishingly admitted by the Constitutional Chamber, which through decision No. 1547 of October 17, 2011, [255] declared the Inter American Court of Human Rights as "non enforceable" in Venezuela, recommending the Government to denounce the Convention, This eventually happened in 2012.

7. Some Conclusions

The result of all these facts is that at the beginning of the twenty-first century, Latin America has witnessed in Venezuela the birth of a new model of authoritarian government that did not immediately originate itself in a military coup, as had happened in many other occasions during the long decades of last century, but in a constituent coup d'état and as result of popular elections, which despite its final goal of destroying the rule of law and democracy, have provided it the convenient camouflage of "constitutional" and "elective" marks, although of course, lacking the essential components of democracy, which are much more than the sole popular or circumstantial election of governments.

In particular, among all the essential elements and components of democracy, the one regarding the separation and independence of public powers is maybe the most fundamental pillar of the rule of law, because it is the only one that can allow the other factors of democracy to become political reality. To be precise, democracy, as a rule of law political regime, can function only in a constitutional system where control of power exists, so without effective check and balance, no free and fair elections can take place; no plural political system can be developed; no effective democratic participation can be ensured; no effective transparency in the exercise of government can be assured; no real government accountability can be secure; and no effective access to justice can be guaranteed in order to protect human rights.

All these factors are lacking at the present time in Venezuela, where a new form of constitutional authoritarianism has been developed, based on the concentration and centralization of state powers, which prevent any possibility of effective democratic participation, and any possible check and balance between the branches of government. Today, all the State organs are subjected to the National Assembly, and through it, to the President. That is why the legislative elections are so important, particularly bearing in mind that according to the Constitution, the presidential

254 See the text of the decision in http://www.tsj.gov.ve:80/decisiones/scon/Agosto/1265-050808-05-1853.htm

255 See the text of the decision in http://www.tsj.gov.ve/decisiones/scon/Octubre/1547-171011-2011-11-1130.htmll

system of government was conceived to function only if the government has complete control over the Assembly. A government that does not have such control will find difficult to govern, being that the reason, for example, for the then President of the Republic, to declare just before the 2010 parliamentary election, that if the opposition was to win the control of the Assembly, "that would signify war."

The fact is that after a fifteen years of demolishing the rule of law and the democratic institutions, by controlling, at the government will, all the branches of government, it will be very difficult for the government and its official party to admit the democratic need they have to share power in the Assembly.[256] They are not used to democracy, that is to say, they are not used to any sort of compromise and consensus, but only to impose their decisions; and that is why they, when in 2010 they lost the 2/3majority they used to have in the Assembly, they announced that they were not going to participate in any sort of dialogue. That is why, even before the new elected representative took their sits in the Assembly in January 2011, the old Assembly approved an unconstitutional legislation in order to enforce what the people had rejected in a referendum of December 2007, the so called "Communal State" which is based on the centralized framework of the so-called "Popular Power" to be exercised by "Communes" and by the government controlled "Communal Councils."[257]

One further example of the perversion of the Constitution and of the will of the people expressed in the September 2010 Legislative election, was the move made regarding the appointment of the new Magistrates of the Supreme Tribunal. What just a weeks before was only a treat of the government, once it lost the 2/3 control of the National Assembly which prevented the government representatives to appoint by themselves in 2011, such magistrates; they immediately proceed to appoint the new magistrates of the Supreme before the inauguration of the new elected members of the National Assembly in January 2011, avoiding the participation in the nominating process of the opposition members of the Assembly. Nonetheless, in order to make such appointments, which required a previous reform the Organic Law of the Supreme Tribunal, for which they had no time to approve it; they proceed to make such "reform," not through the ordinary procedure, but through a completely irregular mechanism of "reprinting" the text of the statute in the *Official Gazette* based in a supposed "material error" in the copying of the text of the statute.[258]

Article 70 of the Organic Law of the Supreme Tribunal, in effect, established that the term in order to propose candidates to be nominated Magistrate of the Supreme Tribunal before the Nominating Judicial Committee "must not be *less* than thirty continuous days;" wording that has been change through a "notice" published by the Secretary of the Assembly in the Official Gazette stating that establishing that

---

256 See Allan R. Brewer-Carías, 2009. *Dismantling Democracy. The Chávez's Authoritarian Experiment*, New York: Cambridge University Press; Allan R. Brewer-Carías, 2014. *Authoritarian Government v. The Rule of Law*, Caracas: Editorial Jurídica Venezolana.

257 See the Organic Laws on the Popular Power, in *Official Gazette* N° 6.011 Extra. December 21, 2010. See on these Laws, Allan R. Brewer-Carías *et al.*, 2011. *Leyes Orgánicas del Poder Popular*, Caracas: Editorial Jurídica Venezolana.

258 See *Official Gazette* N° 39.522 of October 1, 2010

instead of the word "*less*" the correct word to be used in the antonym word "*more*" in the sense of the term "must not be more than thirty continuous days." That means that the "reform" of the statute by changing a word (less to more), transformed a minimum term was transformed into a maximum term in order to reduce the term to nominate candidates and allow the current national Assembly to proceed to make the election before the new National Assembly initiates its activities in January 2010.[259] This is the "procedure" currently used in order to reform statutes, by means of the reprinting of the text in the *Official Gazette*, without any possible judicial review

With this legal "reform," the National Assembly, composed by representatives that by December 2010, after the Legislative elections, can be said that they did not represented the majority of the people, proceeded to fill the Supreme Tribunal of Magistrates members of the Official political party, and even with members of the same Assembly that were finishing their tenure and that did not comply with the constitutional conditions to be Magistrate. As the former magistrate of the Supreme Court of Justice, Hildegard Rondón de Sansó, wrote:

> "The biggest risk for the State of the improper actions of the Nation al Assembly in the recent nomination of the magistrates of the Supreme Tribunal of Justice, lies not only in the lacking, in the majority of the appointed of the constitutional conditions, but having taken into the apex of the Judicial Power the decisive influence of one sector of the legislative Power, due to the fact that for different Chambers, five legislators were elected."[260]

The same former Magistrate Sansó affirmed that "a whole fundamental sector of the power of the State is going to be in the hands of a small group of persons that are not jurist, but politician by profession, to whom will correspond, among other functions, the control of normative acts," adding that "the most grave I that those appointing, even for a single moment realized that they were designating the highest judges of the Venezuelan legal system that, as such, had to be the most competent, and of recognized prestige as the Constitution imposes."[261] She concluded, as aforementioned, recognizing within the "grave errors" accompanying the nomination, the fact of:

> "The configuration of the Nominating Judicial Committee, that the Constitution created as a neutral organ, representing the 'different sectors of society' (Article 271), but the Organic Law of the Supreme Tribunal converted it in an unconstitutional way, into an appendix of the Legislative Power. The consequence of this grave error was unavoidable: those electing elected their own colleagues, considering that acting in such a way was the most natural thing

---

259 See the comments in Víctor Hernández Mendible, 2010. Sobre la nueva reimpresión por "supuestos errores" materiales de la LOTSJ en la *Official Gazette* N° 39.522, de 1 de octubre de 2010, Addendum to Allan R. Brewer-Carías and Víctor Hernández Mendible, 2010. *Ley Orgánica del Tribunal Supremo de Justicia de 2010,* Caracas: Editorial Jurídica Venezolana; and Antonio Silva Aranguren, 2010. Tras el rastro del engaño, en la web de la Asamblea Nacional, Addendum to Allan R. Brewer-Carías and Víctor Hernández Mendible, 2010. *Ley Orgánica del Tribunal Supremo de Justicia de 2010,* Caracas: Editorial Jurídica Venezolana.

260 See Hildegard Rondón de Sansó, 2010. *Obiter Dicta*. En torno a una elección, *La Voce d'Italia*, 14-12-2010.

261 *Id.*

in this world, and, as example of that, were the shameful applauses with which each appointment was greeted."[262]

Unfortunately, the political control over the Supreme Tribunal of Justice has permeated to all the judiciary, due mainly to the already mentioned fact that in Venezuela, it is the Supreme Tribunal the one in charge of the government and administration of the Judiciary. This has affected gravely the autonomy and independence of judges at all levels of the Judiciary, which has been aggravated by the fact that during the past fifteen years the Venezuelan Judiciary has been composed primarily of temporary and provisional judges, without career or stability, appointed without the public competition process of selection established in the Constitution, and dismissed without due process of law, for political reasons.[263] This reality amounts to political control of the Judiciary, as demonstrated by the dismissal of judges who have adopted decisions contrary to the policies of the governing political authorities.

262 *Id.*

263 See Inter-American Commission on Human Rights, *Report on the Situation of Human Rights in Venezuela*, OEA/Ser.L/V/II.118, doc. 4 rev. 2, December 29, 2003, par. 174, *available at* http://www.cidh.oas.org/countryrep/Venezuela2003eng/toc.htm.

www.ingramcontent.com/pod-product-compliance
Lightning Source LLC
Chambersburg PA
CBHW021022210326
41598CB00016B/882

* 9 7 8 9 8 0 3 6 5 1 9 9 2 *